★

THE DESTINY CHILDREN

★ ★ ★ ★ ★

UNLIMITED STYLED ARTISTS

★

CONTENTS

New York City Graffiti

The Destiny Children

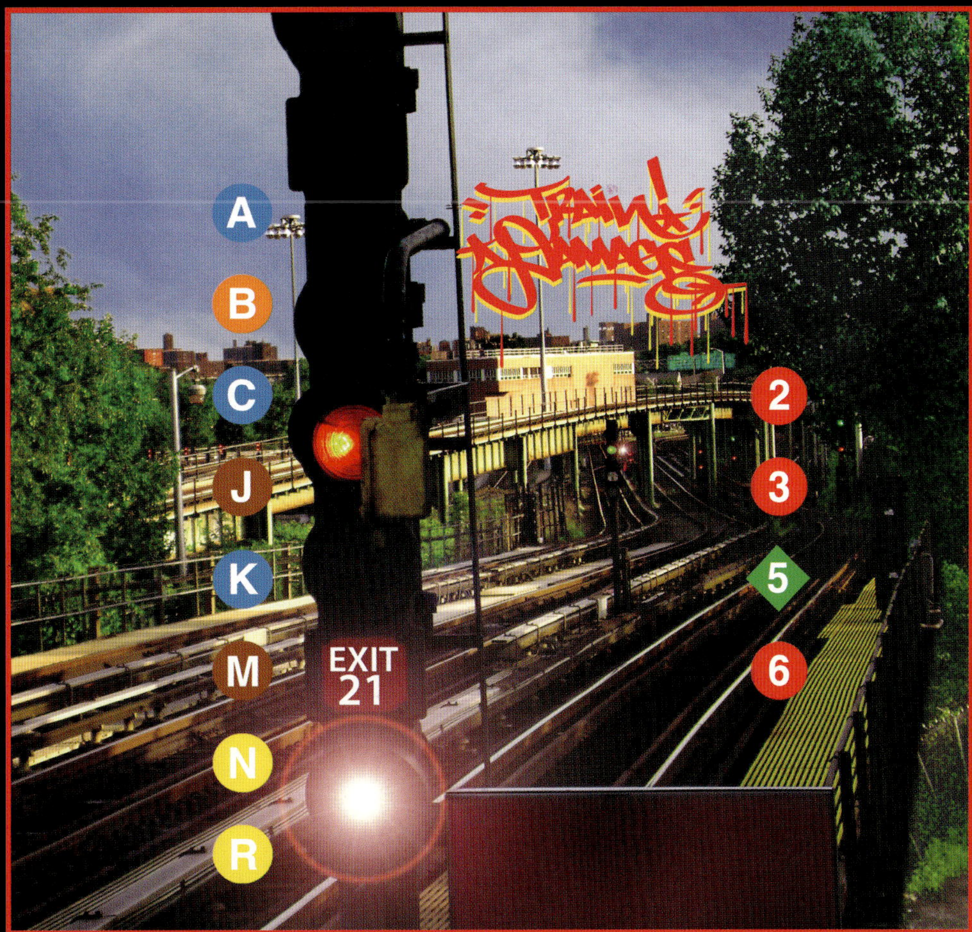

Schiffer Publishing Ltd

4880 Lower Valley Road • Atglen, PA 19310

CHAPTER 1

Introduction to the Original TDC Crew Members. Very Early Rare Artwork and the First Trains We Painted.

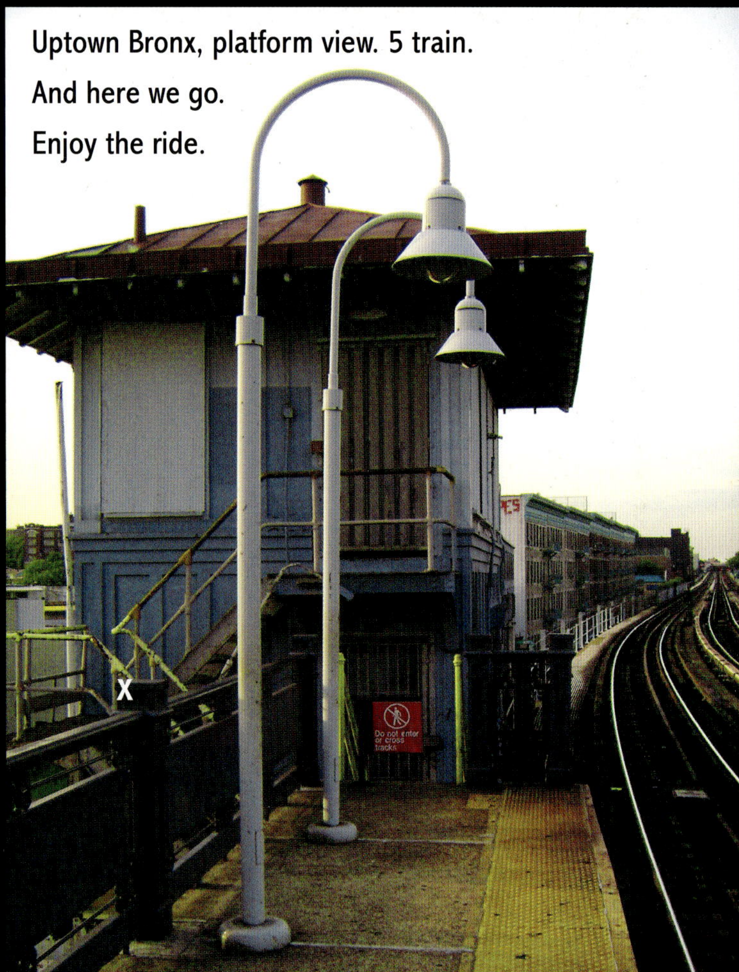

Uptown Bronx, platform view. 5 train.

And here we go.

Enjoy the ride.

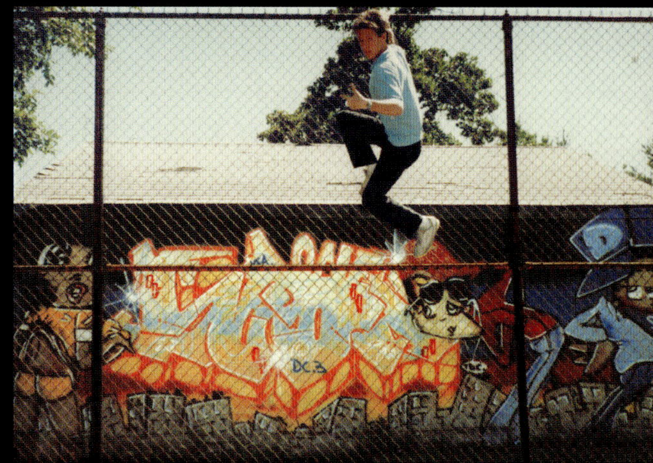

Soon One, DC3 alias.

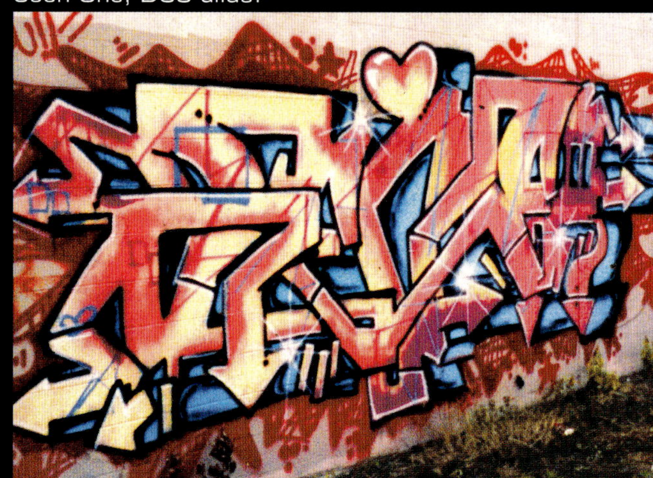

DECE3

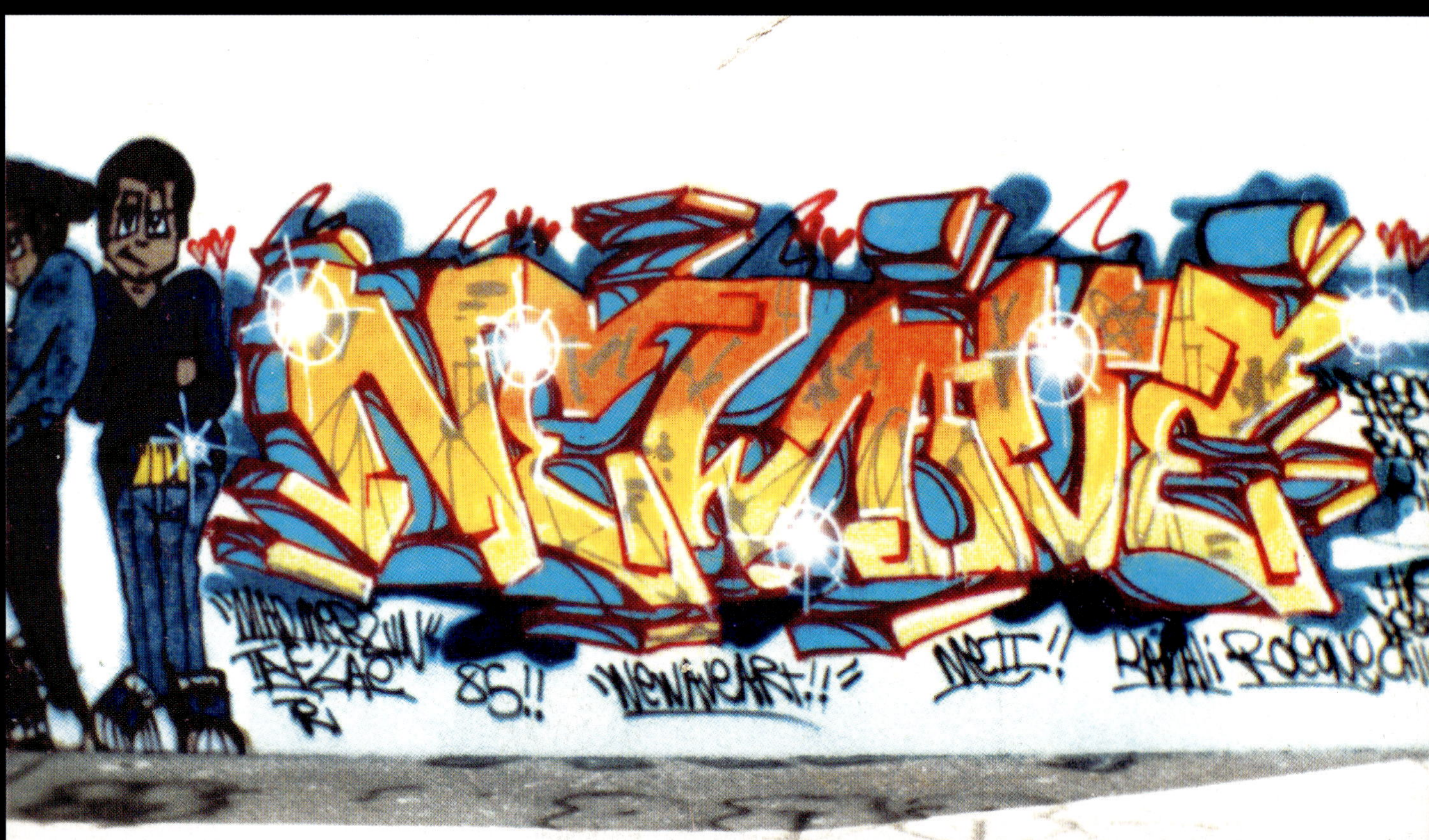

"New Wave Art," by DC3, Oct. 1985.

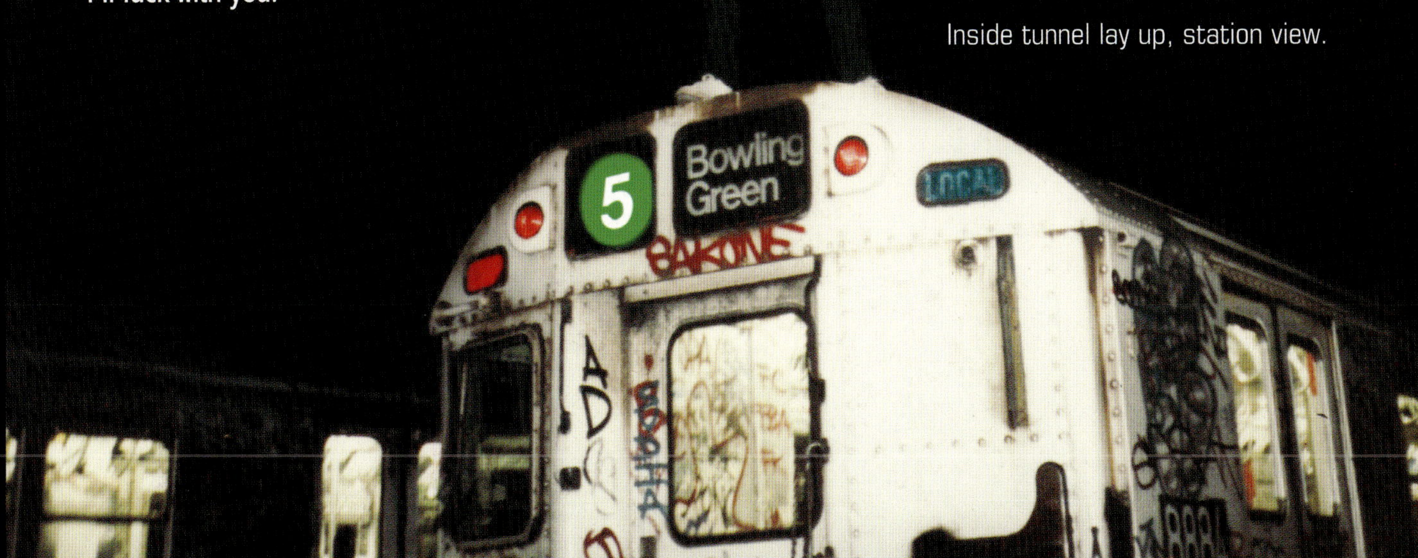

SHO fearing nobody in Esplanade, Sep. 1986.
Man, I see so many graffiti books worldwide it's sick.
A message to all Graff enthusiasts, lets be clear:
In the Graffiti world, the only thing that ever
mattered was having more trains than
you could count. You got transit,
I'll fuck with you.

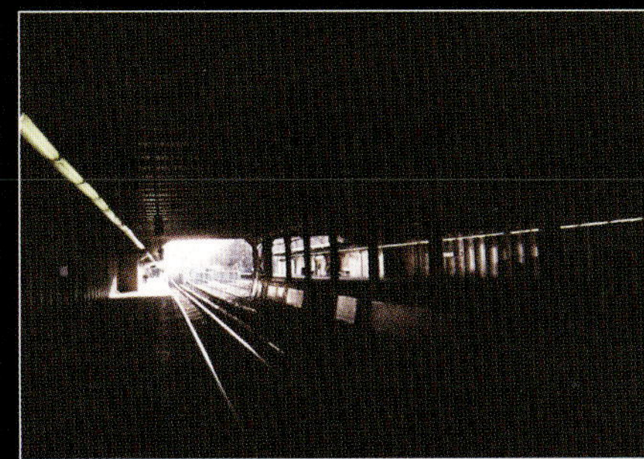

Inside tunnel lay up, station view.

The whole lay up stayed bombed.

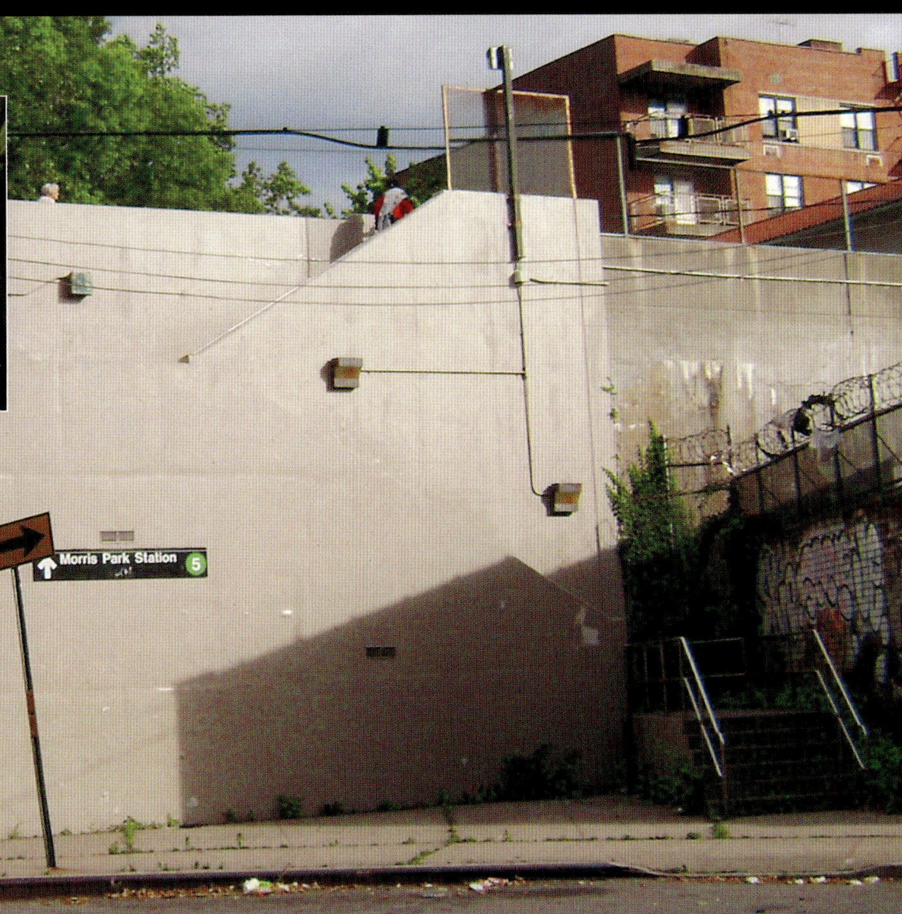

Morris Park Station, down below street level.

KENT3 and BASH, Bronx City Writers, 5 Train, Oct. 1985.

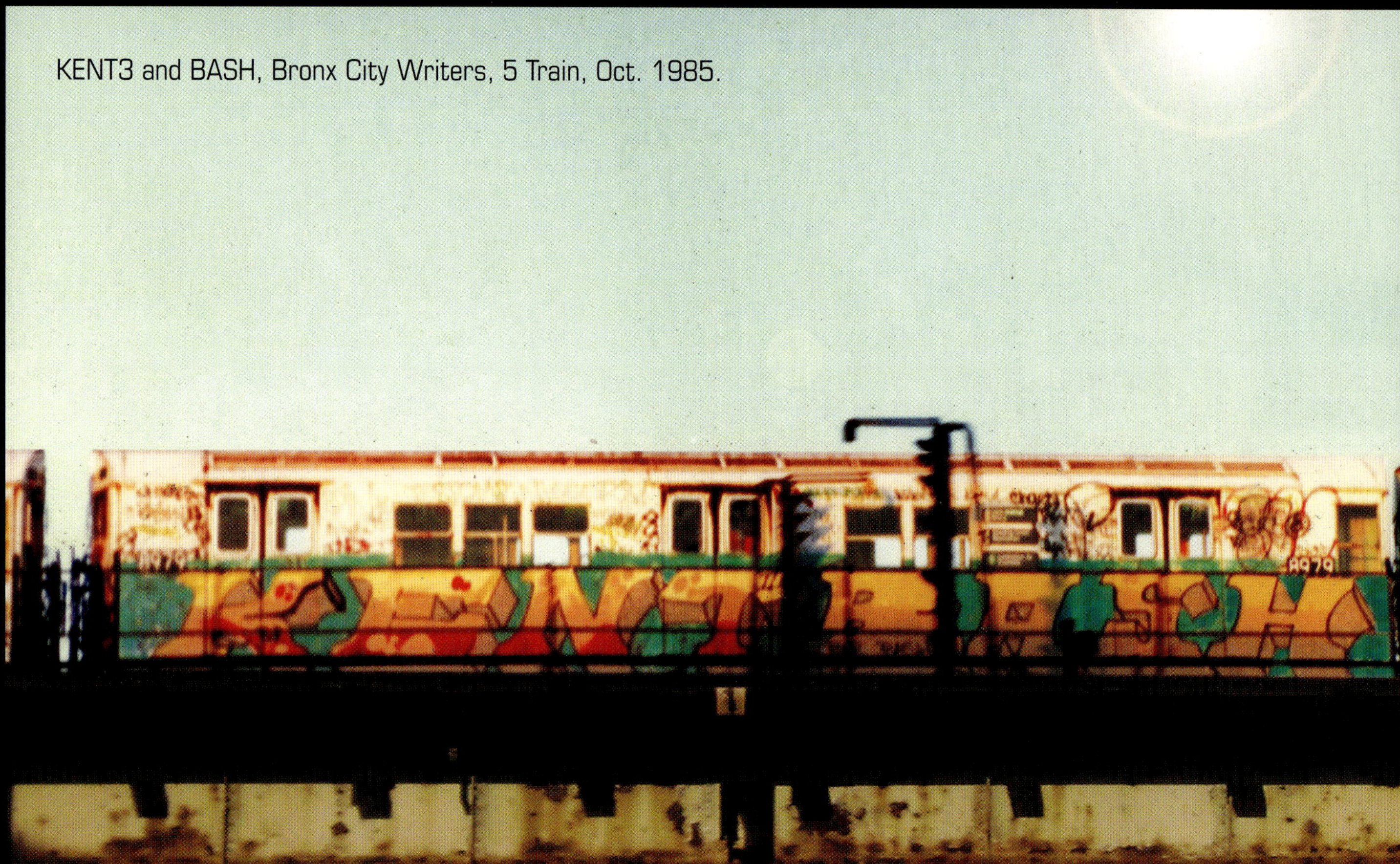

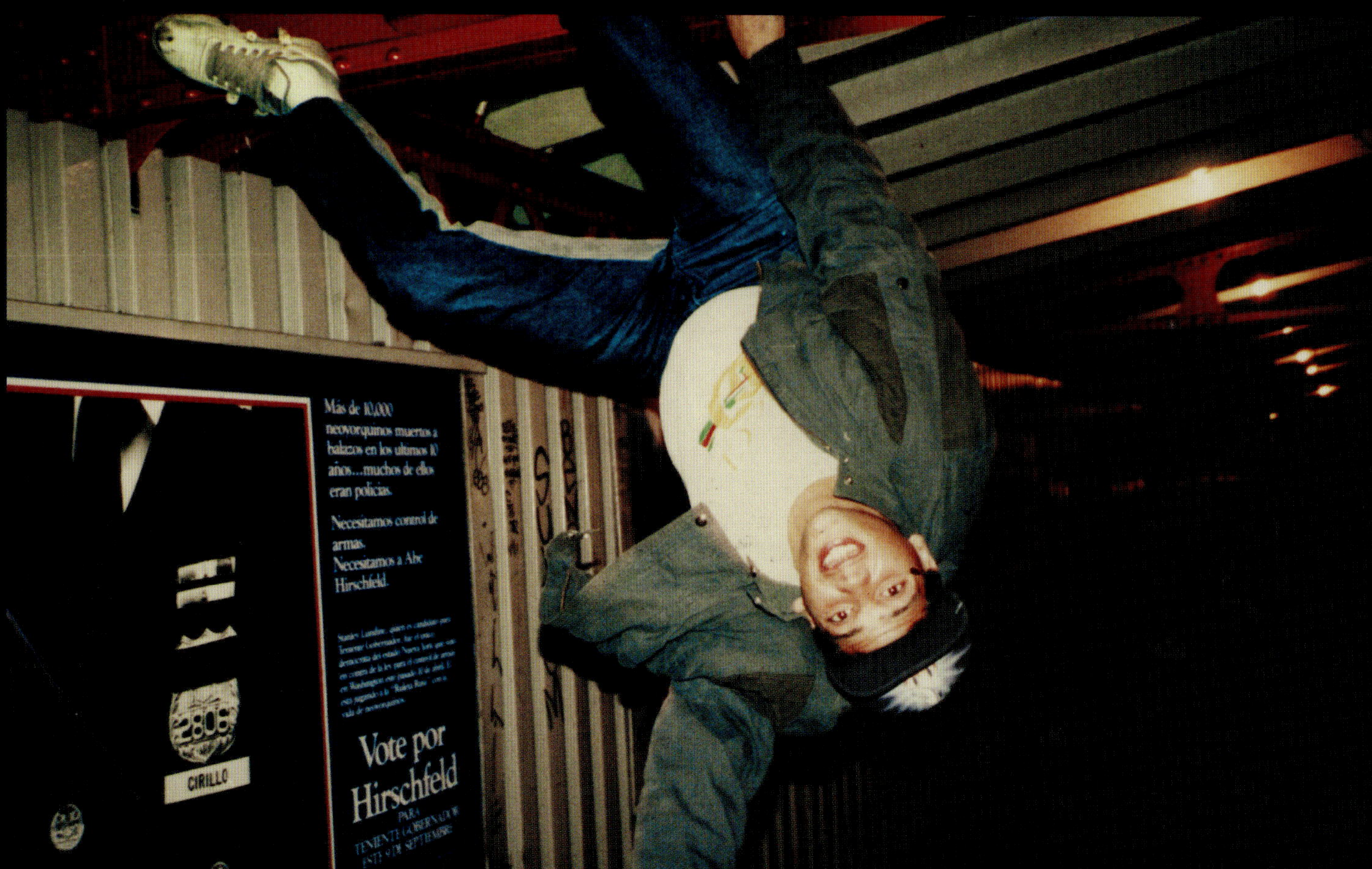

Dome waiting for a 2 Train; before we had a car.

Dome on Kent Bash, The First Hits.

★

Enter my Dome. Primarily I write DOME, but I also use ZOO to get up with. It all started out for me in 1975 at my aunt's house up in the Bronx at a family get together with my brother Luis and my cousin Freddy, who wrote MEAN and my brother wrote LUCHO. My cousin Freddy (MEAN) introduced us to the lifestyle of writing on trains, he was from East Harlem, NYC, Carver Projects, which is 106th Street between Madison Avenue and Park Avenue (sound familiar?). Well we were in my aunt's building hallway watching the 4 Train and my cousin Mean knew all the names on the train passing by, and I couldn't understand how he knew that. But when the doors closed on the train and I saw a painted Yosemite Sam character, it changed my life for ever. Keep in mind, I was not a writer yet! It would be ten years later before I did my first piece of art on the trains. So I did a lot of benching before I actually became a real writer! So, there's a difference from when you watched writers on trains and from when you actually started writing on trains. Fast forward to 1985. I was attending Laguardia Community College and met up with writers from all over the city. That's where I met this Bronx writer called Kent 3 from Jackson Avenue. One day he came in with pictures of the 2 & 5s with all these bad ass burners from TAT, and then Kent 3 showed me a picture of his burner on the train with his partner Bash. I was like, "Yo! Where did you do this train?" He said, "Esplanade," so I told him I'm down to go, he said OK, no questions asked. We went in the spring of 1985 on a Saturday night, and when we arrived to Esplanade, the pull outs were not in but the tunnels were. Kent 3 didn't trust them, they were hot. So we ended up doing pieces in the Jackson Avenue projects. Several weeks later the lay ups were in and we went in for the kill. We did a KENT, ZOO window-down car. Months later I met DC3 & SHO, I saw they were good writers, so I asked them if they wanna go do a train up in the Bronx? They didn't even hesitate, they had boxes of paint and were ready to go. It was KENT 3, BASH, DOME, DC3, SHO. This time we had a car, it changed our whole game. We prepped like soldiers and went to Esplanade. KENT3 was busy with work and school that September so it just became DOME, SHO, DC3. We started going every week and got more comfortable with doing burners collectively on the trains—each time we got better. Keep in mind none of the other writers that were active at the time, like Dero, Wane, Sent, knew who we were, and we started pulling out whole cars top-to-bottom end-to-end. So we knew other writers were like, "OH SHIT!" Then the other crews started doing whole cars after that. So within a year, the 2 & 5s had whole-car burners on almost every other car from TDC and C.O.D. Before that it was all throw ups and Dero had burners running. TDC & C.O.D. were part of the very last era of great writers on trains we will always be grateful for that and for gracing the same tunnels and trains of all the legendary writers that came before us. We were glad to walk in the same foot steps.

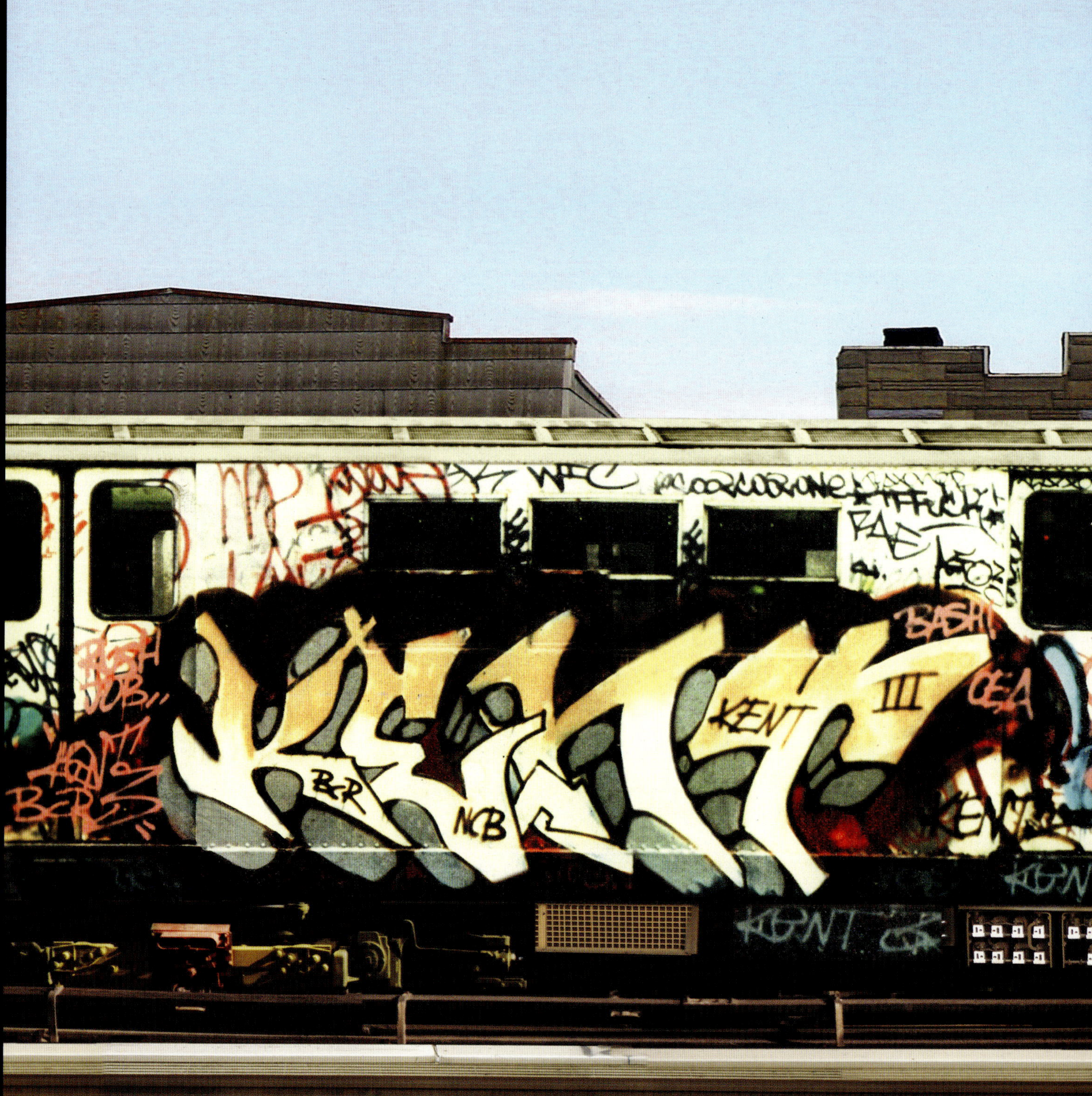

The first KENT3 BCR, NCB, and ZOO TDC 5 Train, Sep. 1985.

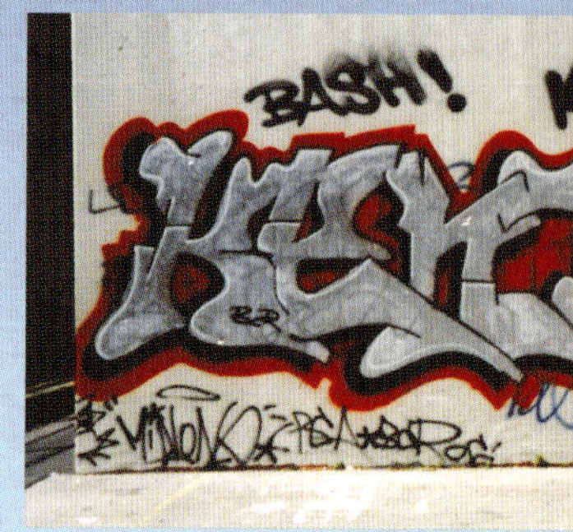

KENT3 and BASH handball court, South Bronx, NY, 1985.

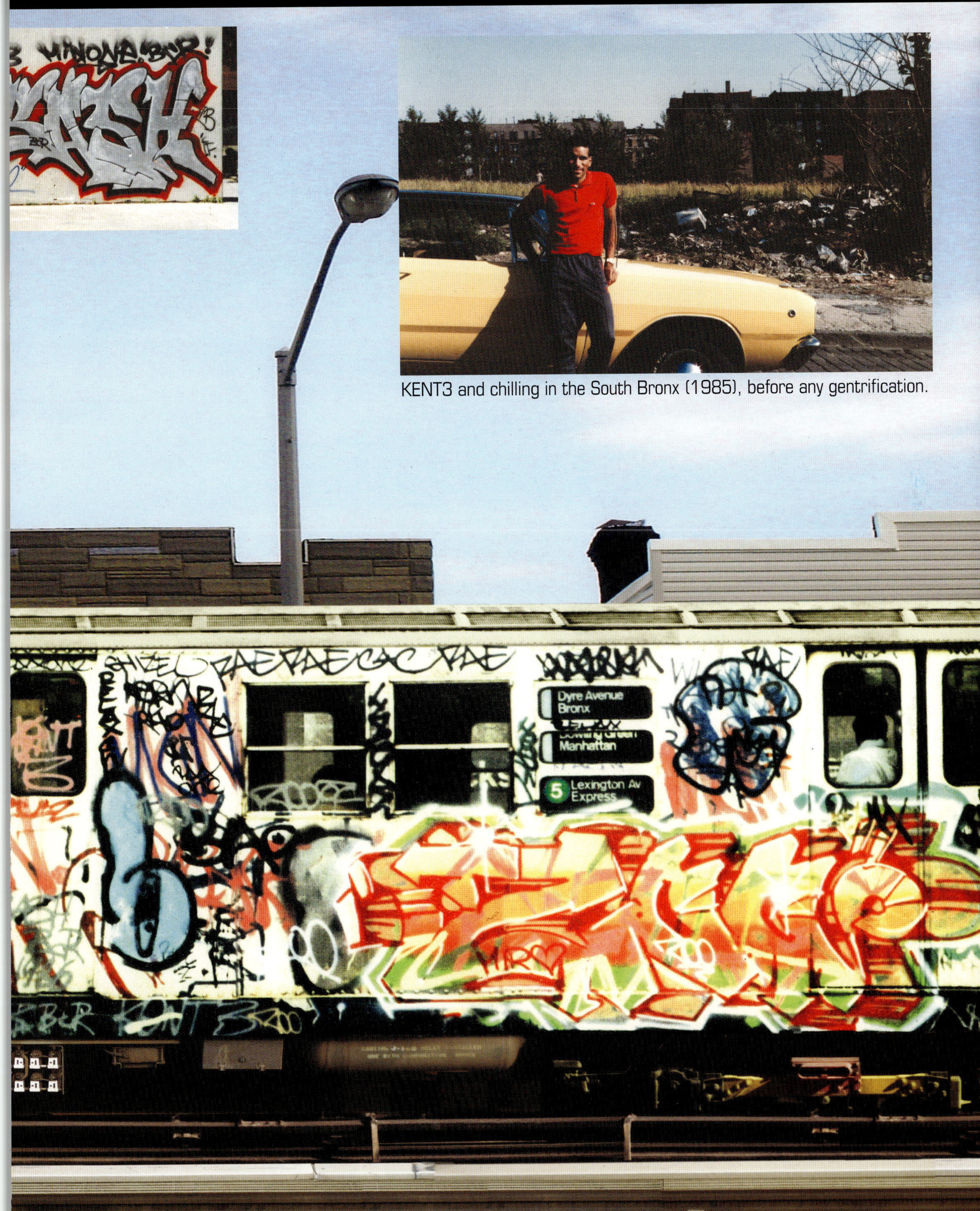

KENT3 and chilling in the South Bronx (1985), before any gentrification.

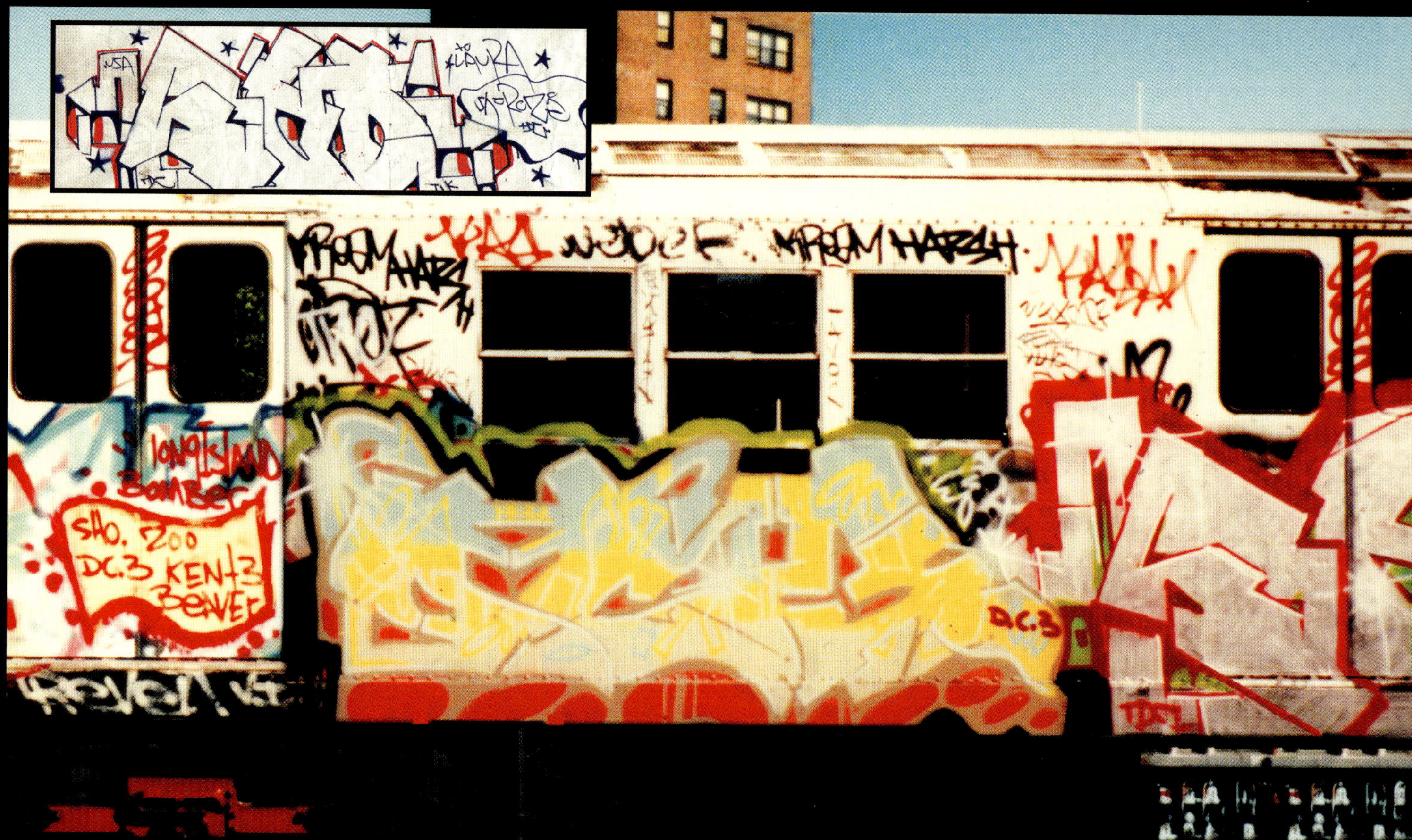

DC3, SHO TDC, and ZOO, 5 Train.

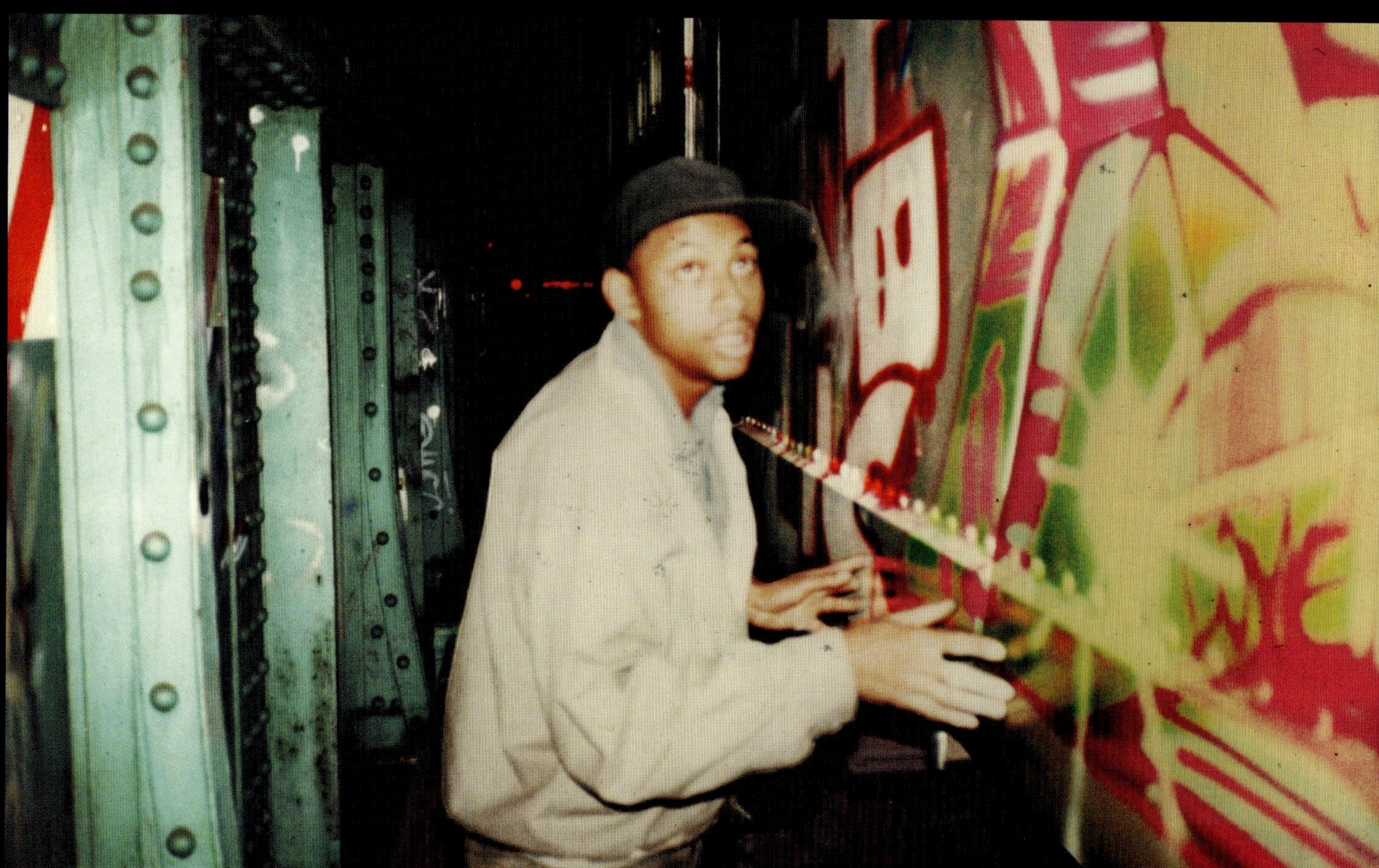

DC3 bout to break out.

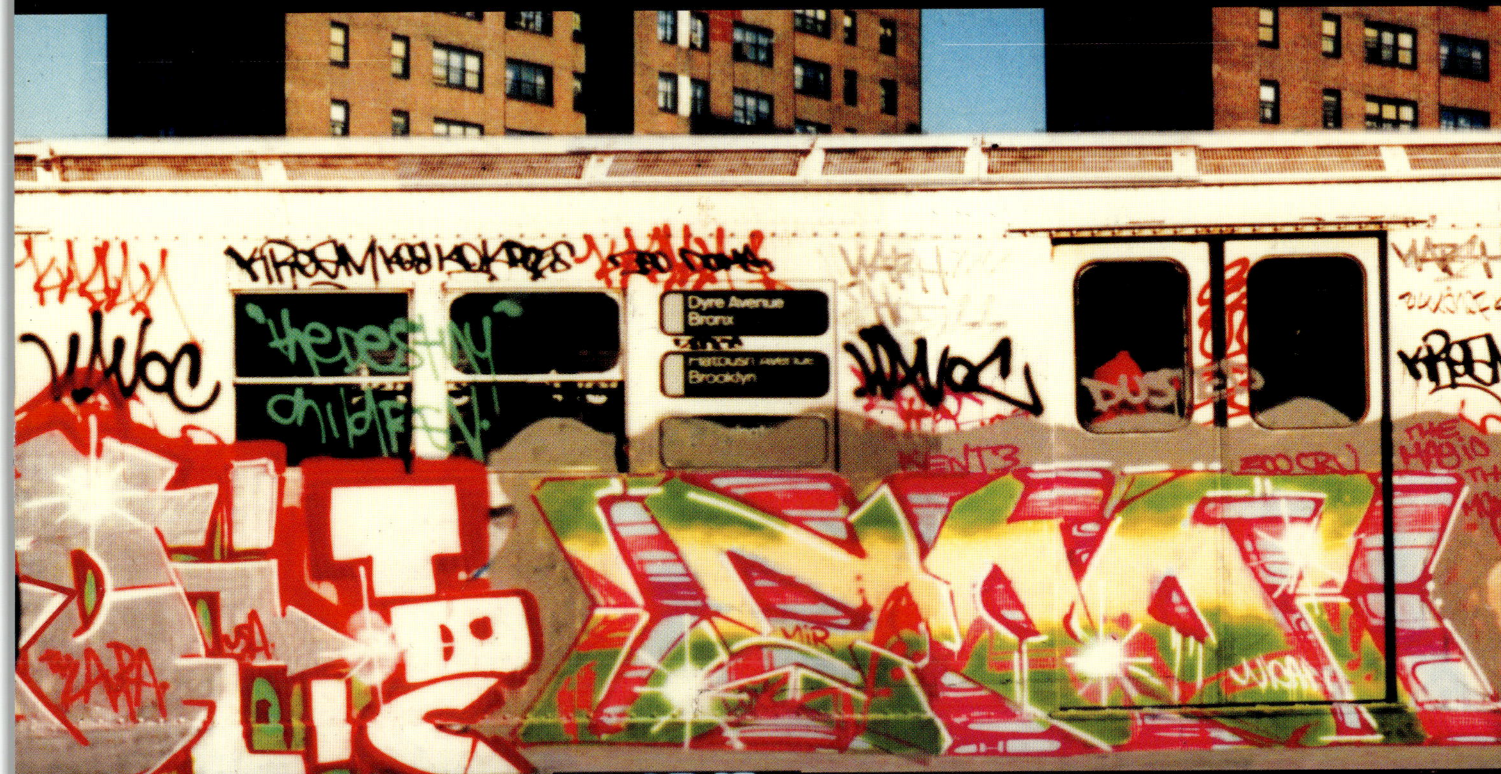

First SHO outline done on a 5 Train in
Esplanade pull outs, Bronx, NY, September 12, 1986.

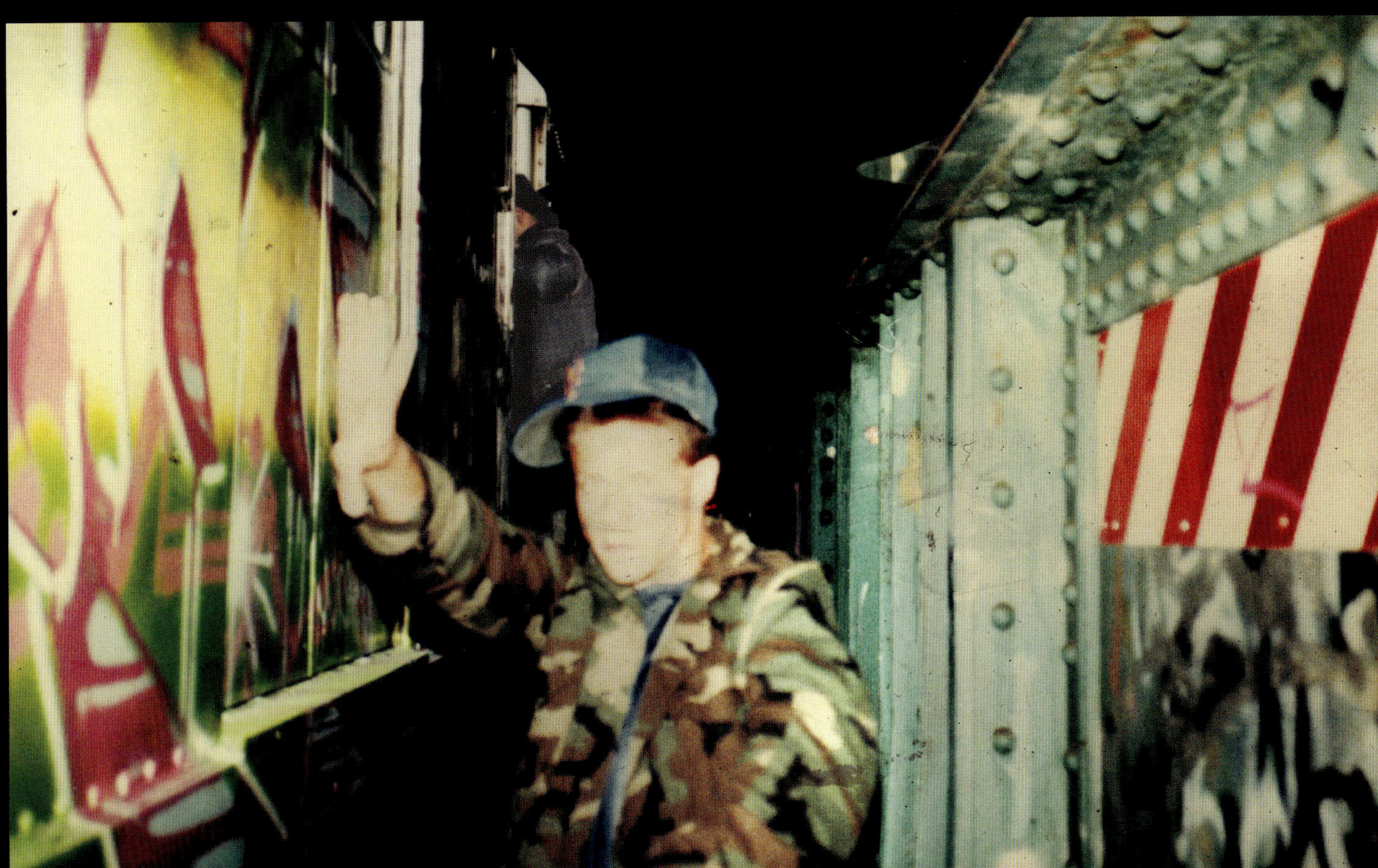

SHO and ZOO first time hitting the 5 Train. At the beginning of a long journey.

My mother left my father when I was two years old, she moved backed to Seattle, Washington, where she was from. My parents had a very emotional relationship and sometimes arguments ended in violence. Shit got so bad that once my father pulled a gun on my mother, and said he would kill her if she tried to leave him and take the kids. Fast forward, to the early eighties, a woman close to the family got in contact with my mother, and we all began to speak to her on the phone. One by one, she sent plane tickets for all the kids to come see her and come back. My two older sisters went first, and they never came back. I was the last one to go, being that I was the youngest at the time. When I first arrived in Seattle, I was about 15 years old; it was wet, dark, and dismal but the city was exciting. My mother enrolled me in high school. There, in my art class, I met this Asian artist name Mr. Clean.

Seattle was a very diverse place, a lot of different races living together: Black, white, Vietnamese, Cambodian, Japanese, Chinese, Samoan, Filipino, etc. One day I was watching TV and I saw that a movie called *Style Wars* was coming on TV, so I was glued to the set. That movie taught me everything I needed to know to start my graffiti career. So I grabbed my markers and started doing my first piece. Then I went out the next day and I racked my first cans to do my first wall. It was the beginning of an adventure for me. The movie *Style Wars* changed my life forever. I went out and bombed everything in downtown Seattle, I went to different high schools and snuck inside and bombed them, I bombed buses, walls, freight trains, etc. New York was still learning about graffiti, Seattle, Washington, didn't know what hit them. I became very popular in Seattle, my name made the news several times, but only a few people knew who I was. I became so popular out there, my art class got permission from J.C Penney to do a mural on their wall in downtown Seattle. Mr. clean and I did the mural in the middle of the day on the weekend, it made the news and we had a huge crowd.

By this time I thought I was invincible, so I was doing a piece in broad daylight and someone called the cops on me. The cops chased me in a car and I was on foot all the way to my mothers house. I ran in the house out of breath and my moms (who is a pastor of a church with her husband) asked me what had happened. I said, "nothing" then the cops banged on the door! The cops asked my mother if I was there and she told me to come to the door. I was in the bathroom trying to wash the paint off my hands. The cops told my moms that I was wanted for destroying property all over Seattle, I denied it, so the cops said "let me see your hands" I showed them my hands, then they arrested me right there on the spot. My mom and her husband came down to the precinct and bailed me out. The cops told her I was responsible for a $100,000 or more in property damage. My mother had no idea what I was doing on my spare time, she cried and we argued. So my mother and her husband told me I had to leave, they bought me a one-way bus ticket back to New York and that was the end of my Seattle run, it only lasted about eight months. It took four days for me to get back to New York, so I had a lot of time to think and all I was thinking about was graffiti and what I was going to do when I get home, finally I was back in the graffiti mecca. It's incredible that the movie *Style Wars* had taught me how to do graffiti thousands of miles away from home.

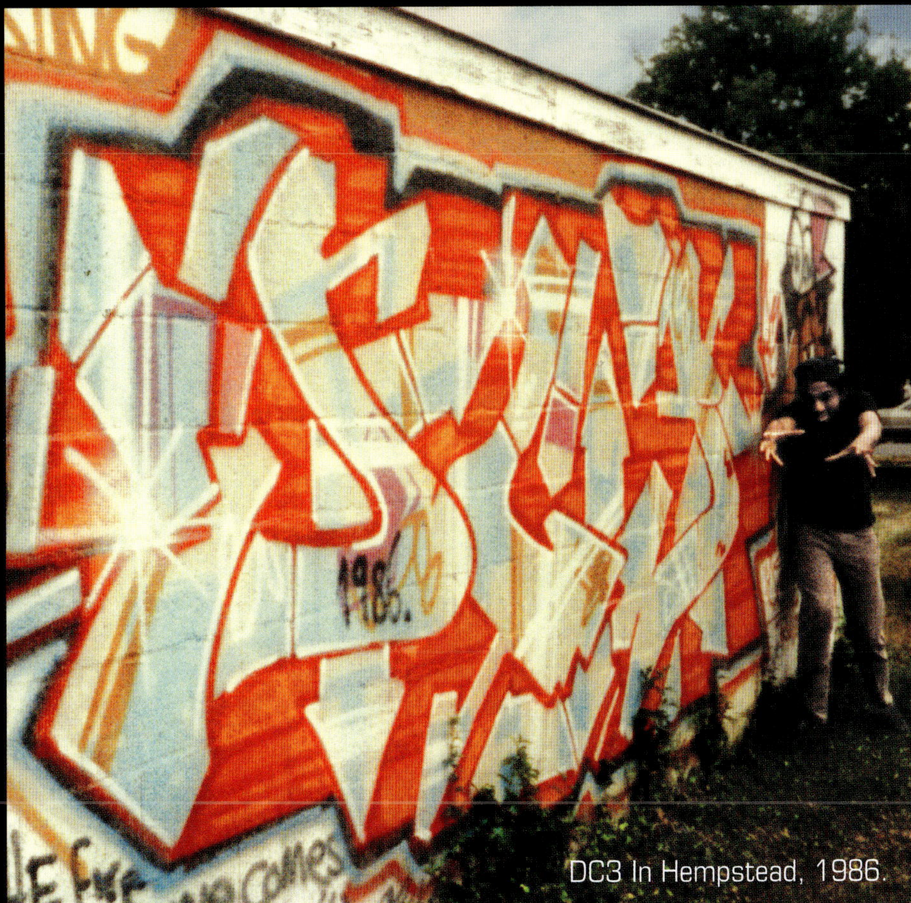
DC3 In Hempstead, 1986.

When I had first started piecing with DC3 was right after he did the Fly Girls wall. This kid was doing major pieces by himself all the time. He was living in Hempstead and was crazy, up killing the whole village. He was hitting up most of the parks' handball courts with me and bombing streets all by himself including the buses. DC3 also wrote Soon, which he threw in to confuse other writers.

-SHO

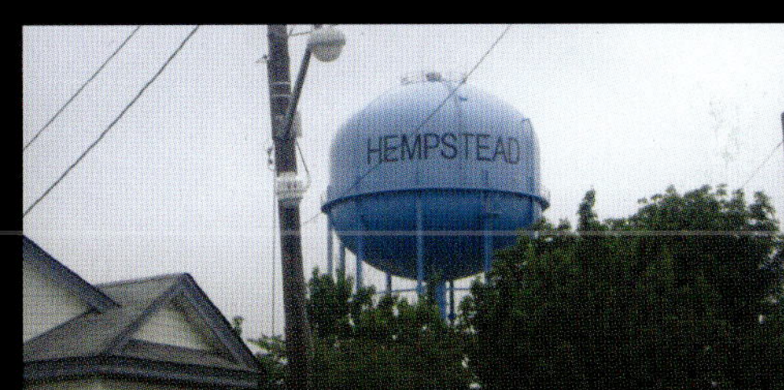

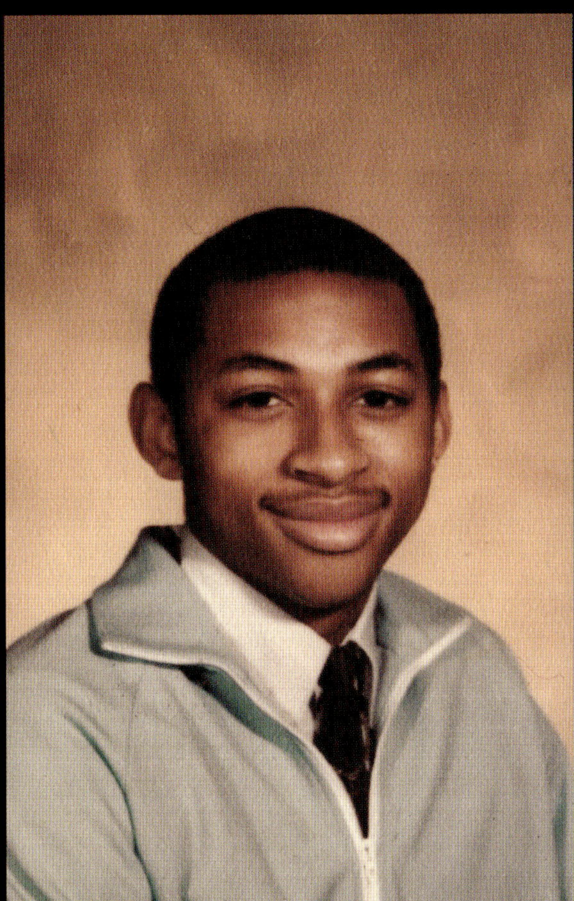
DC3 chilling in Seattle, Washington, 1982.

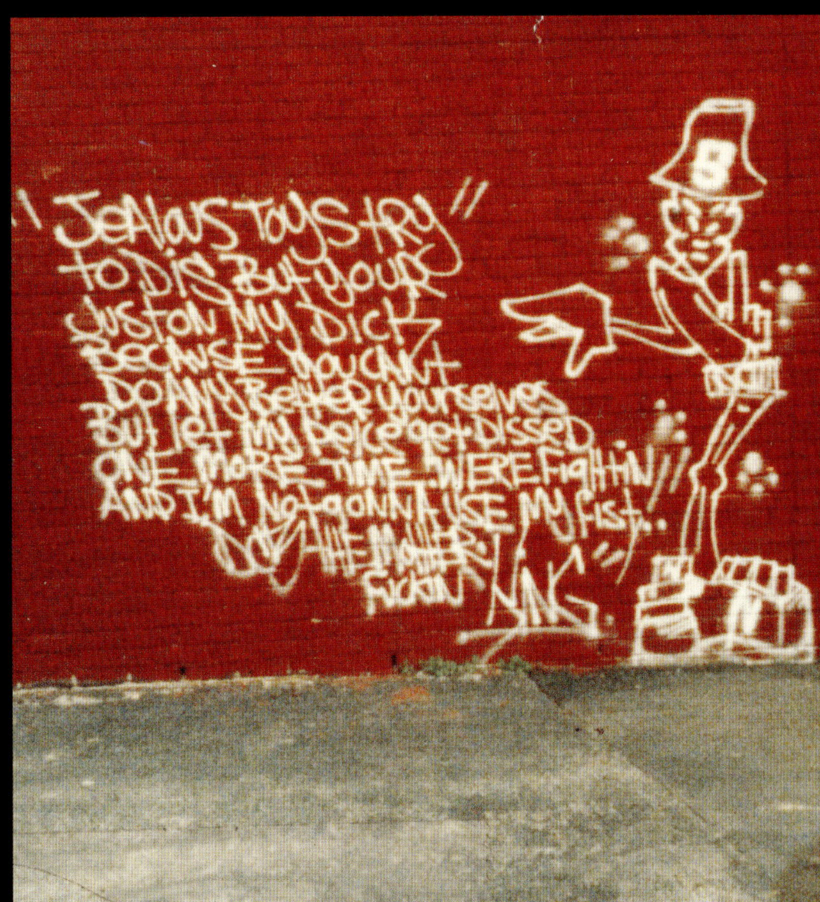

A message to all the haters.

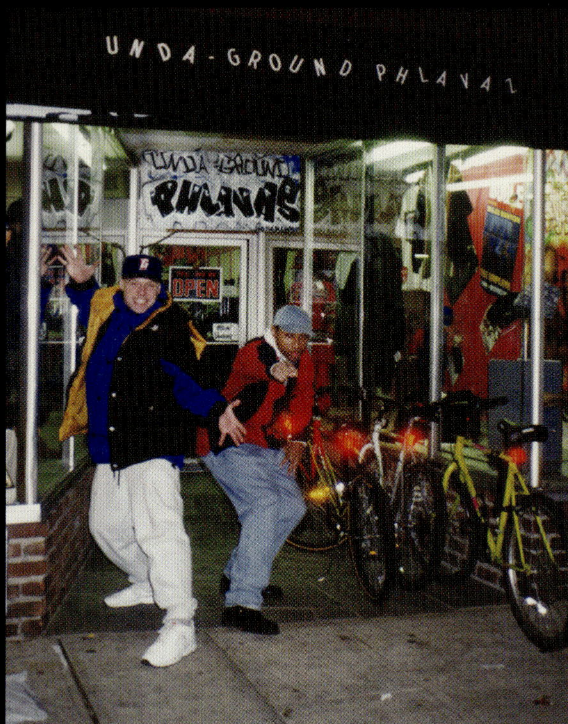

When I returned to Freeport, my father had plans of moving down south, so the day before I got back, he and my two younger brothers and my step mother had left, leaving my two older brothers in the house. So I stayed at the house for about a month until my father came back for me. So I took the bus and subway to 34th Penn Station to see the trains. I asked a stranger which way was the Bronx because I wanted to go to the Writers Bench. I jumped on the 2 Train and took it to the Writers Bench. When I first got there, some writers were there, I showed them my black book and they asked me what I write and where I was from. I told them Long Island and they were in shock that I came so far to show my artwork. I started bombing in Freeport and kept hearing about this kid named Beaver, so I went up to the high school to see who he was. They said he was the best graffiti writer in Freeport. So I was getting my name out there and then we met, he was a tall skinny Dominican kid; at first there was tension then we became cool later. He told me about this white boy named Merlin, aka Shoroz. He had painted this hat that was amazing for that time, and the whole school was talking about it. Beaver wanted me to help him jump SHO because he didn't like him and wanted his hat. I told them I wasn't with it, so they jumped him anyway. SHO and me finally met, I always thought he did the hat and had the talent. So SHO and me began a lifelong friendship that has lasted 26 years.

A month had passed and my father returned and took me to Alabama to live. I hated the South it was too slow and graffiti was running threw my blood. My father couldn't register me in high school in Alabama cause it took to long for my Seattle records to get transferred down there. So I had to stay home and clean the house and help my grandmother feed the cows. She would wake me up at 6 A.M. everyday to clean the barn and feed the cows. On my free time I was drawing, working on my style. My father told me I could work with him cleaning churches to make some extra money. So every dime I got I saved it, so I could buy me a bus ticket back to New York. It took about two or three months to save up the money. I think it was 60 to 100 dollars for a one-way ticket. I told my father I was leaving and going back to New York, he told me if I leave that I could never come back and he wouldn't help me. I was on the

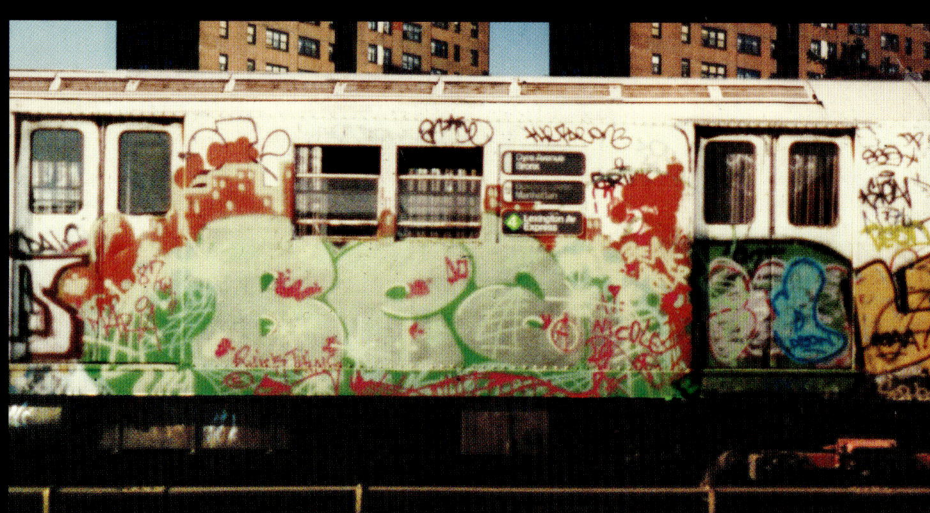

BEA, by Beaver One, Feb. 1987.

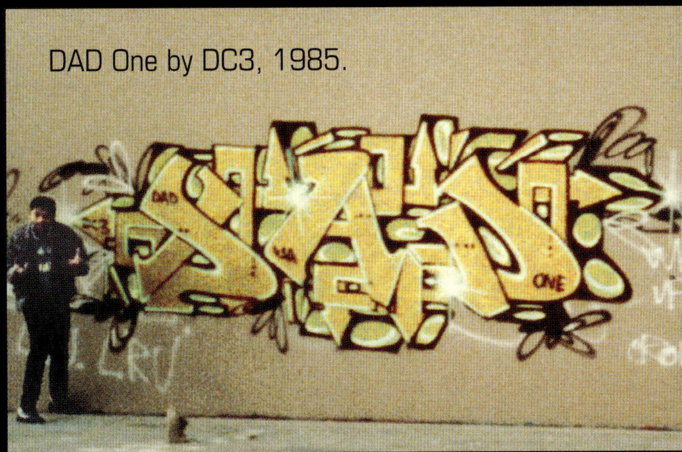

next bus, my grandmother drove me to the bus stop. I was back in Freeport and I went to my old house, my two older brothers were still living there, they wouldn't let me in and they told me I couldn't stay there, so I had to move in with the next door neighbor. I started going hard with the graffiti; I was determined to be the best. I did jackets, jeans, and black books for extra money. I started doing big murals by myself. My name DC3 was on fire, (my man DOOJ wrote me while I was in Seattle and said I should call myself DC3 and it's been my name for life). One night me and Beaver went to a Patty Astor's art gallery on Chambers Street in Manhattan and we met a who's who of the graffiti world: DOZE, FAB FIVE FREDDY, FUTURA 2000, DONDI, etc. I was invited by Patty Astor because I took her my portfolio and she liked my work, so she invited me to the party. I met all the artist I liked and they tagged my book. So now I knew I was going in the right direction. I was in the Bronx every-day just walking around looking at murals, studying and learning everything about graffiti and hip hop. I went to Fashion Moda in the Bronx with Sho, where I met DAZE, and he told me I was good and keep practicing.

I had to get a job, so I got a job at a record distributor where I met my man Roc and I told Roc I do graffiti, he said he knew this Puerto Rican kid that was ill with graffiti. I went by Roc's house in Hempstead and he took me to meet Dome, aka Zoo. Dome said he had seen my work and wanted to know who I was. Dome was ill with the colors and had style that I thought was up there with mine. So, I told him I knew this other kid name SHO who was ill with graffiti. So we linked up and The Destiny Children (TDC) was born. One black, one Spanish, and one white came together for the love of the art. We started bombing the walls and tractor trailers hard. Me and Dome did a lot a pieces together cause I moved to Hempstead after I had to leave my neighbors' house and become a man. So me and Dome was chilling all the time at my crib drawing in black books. Then Dome came to me one day and said he had a friend from the Bronx that would take him to the train yard. I couldn't believe I would get to do a train. So Dome and me took the bus and subway to the Bronx, met up with his friend and he took us to the yard. I was nervous, but once I started painting I was cool, then when we were halfway done, the train pulled out on us while we was painting. We started running cause we didn't know what was going on. I got the fuck out of their. I lost Dome and his friend Kent. So I went to Penn Station the next day to see my piece on the train and I waited there for about four hours, then I finally seen it running live. That's when I knew I was gonna do this again and again. The love was too strong and there is absolutely nothing like the first time you see your shit running packed wall to wall with people.

-DC3 TDCUSA.

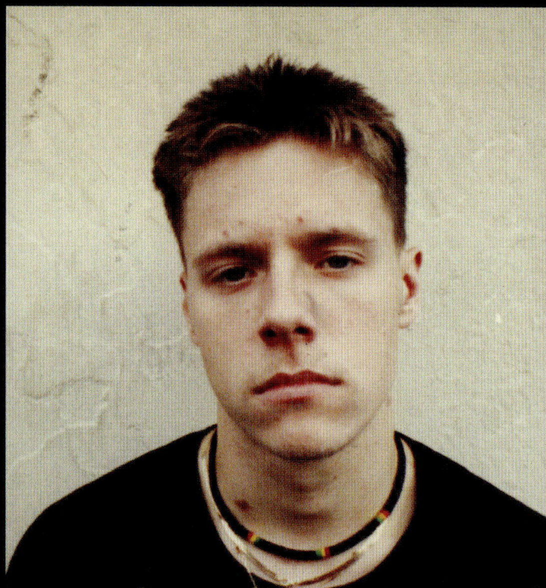

Now my story begins...I started writing graffiti in February 1983 officially. That means when I rocked my first piece on a wall. I had become interested big time after seeing street bombing in Queens and Brooklyn, where I had relatives living. One of the best parts of going to visit them was the car ride. I was, unbeknownst to my parents, secretly taking notes on anybody I had seen up. While at my uncle Franks house in Cypress Hills, Brooklyn, I watched *Dreams Don't Die,* a made-for-TV movie about a writer named Danny who wrote King 65 and his rise to Graff fame. This was a major influence to start my own art career. Another was the movie *The Warriors* about a Coney Island-based gang and a subsequent gang war that occurs after Cyrus, a leader trying to broker peace in NYC, gets killed. Both Major classics. I had begun practicing and started my career writing the name Merlin originally. I was a quick self starter and also wrote 2Kool. Merlin just came to me and 2Kool was kind of a homage to 2Nice, who I had seen up in Rosedale and Laurelton Queens with dope pieces.

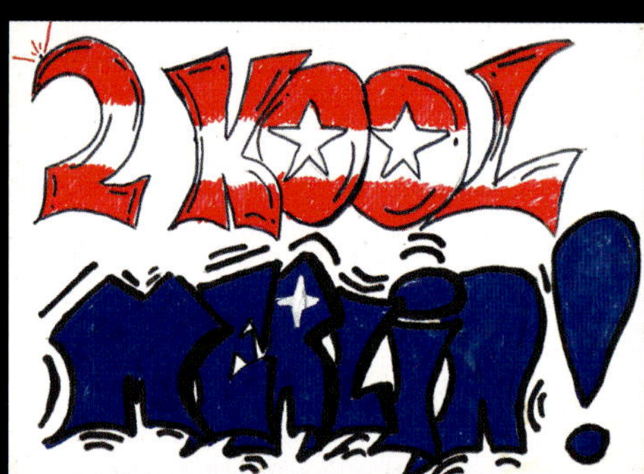

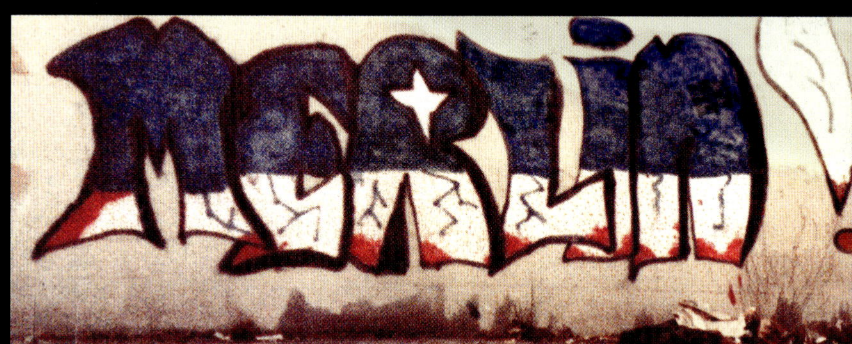

Merlin One, 1983.

I was working with my brother at Grand Beverages in Baldwin stocking beers and soda as well as unloading the trucks at the age of 13 years old. I also had to clean up the parking lot. In the storeroom next to the bathroom, for what ever reason, were roughly 30 cans of paint. So I took 'em and said that I had thrown them out cause they didn't work or whatever. These were the ammunition I needed to get started and did my first Merlin piece on a Keyfood supermarket back where they parked the trucks. I hit those too, it was always at night and it was a great addictive feeling to see your work the next day. At night you couldn't even sleep while waiting for it to turn daytime so you could run and go get pictures. Now I know that people are going to say it might not be that good but like my man Dero TFA once said, "everyone starts out as a toy more or less and tries to get better and for you 2 fly cats who say no to that they are just lying. Next up I used the better Krylon colors for my second piece on a garage at the Brooklyn Waterworks. This was a building that was abandoned after a large fire and was located next to the Freeport and Baldwin woods which were huge.

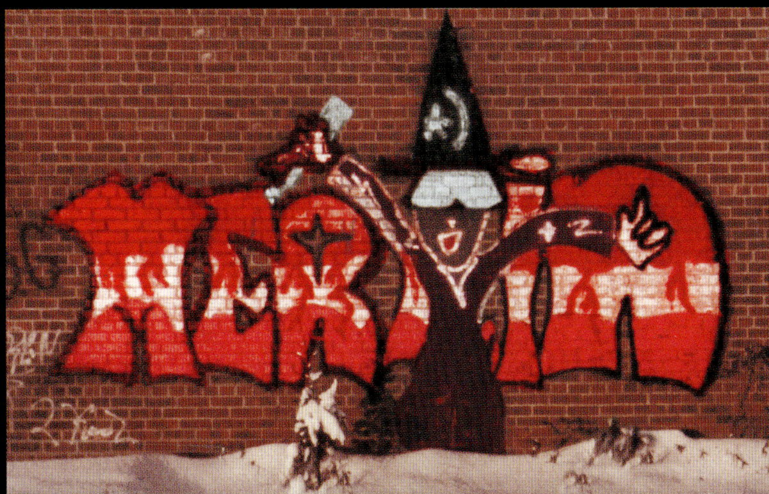

Merlin at Castle Grey Skull.

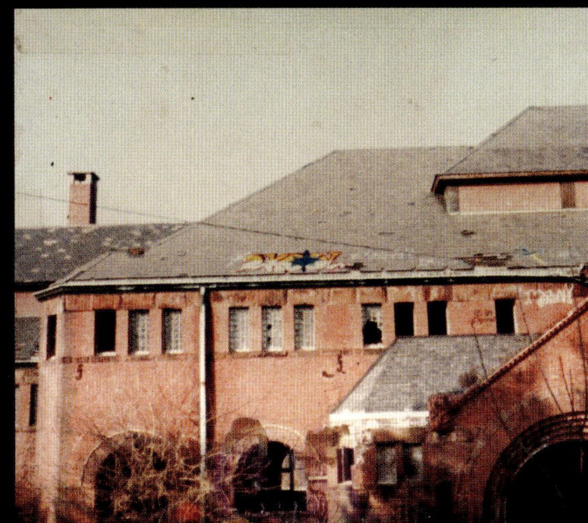

2Kool rooftop, 1984.

We were always cutting out of school regularly and hanging out here and in the main buildings. Blue Oyster Cult had filmed a video here and we knew the area like the back of our hand and would be here at night. I did the above Merlin while I had my friends David, Darrin, and Steven looking out. It was done February 2, 1983, and it snowed the very next morning. It was an incredible feeling. We also were very daring to say the least. Our parents would have been shocked to know that we were doing pieces on the highly slanted slate roof at night, 75 feet up in the air. I rocked the 2Kool piece here after having done another one at the park hand ball court earlier in the week and didn't even get a picture because it got painted over the next day. This could be clearly seen from Freeport High School, Sunrise Highway, and the Long Island Railroad. It was key for us to take ever increasing risks to get the maximum exposure. Since graffiti was brand new, most of it would stay up a long time and that made it worth taking the chance, plus it was a real rush and adventure that did take planning. My friend Steven was the most reckless and daring of us all and scaled the roof and tower roofs to their peaks. Any mistake or misstep could have been fatal. When you're young you take stupid unnecessary chances without thinking. No one knew who I was other than my friends, so it was kool to hear people talk about your shit and be curious, who did it and why. I also did a "Fresh" piece and a Dagger burner but don't have those pictures. I did two other Merlin pieces here and decided to change my name up. I started to write SHO after that and had become known as Shoroz at school. It was a cool sounding name that my oldest friend to this day, Darrin, and I had created and wrote also. I was just on a mission and really took off with it and made it mine. I was painting now every weekend on my own and was getting fame at school. At school there now were lots of people that were break dancing, MCing, wearing graffiti painted jackets, and also writing. So I made this huge statement and came in with this dope graffiti painted hat. It was incredible for the time and some people were hating on me for being the only white kid doing graff and that I was up. I still have this hat saved from 1984, crazy.

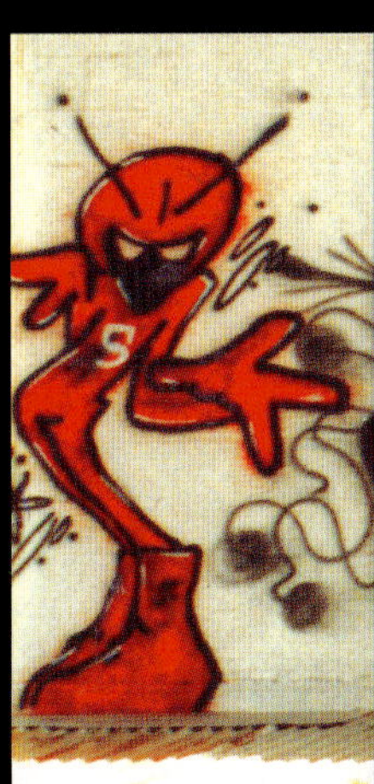

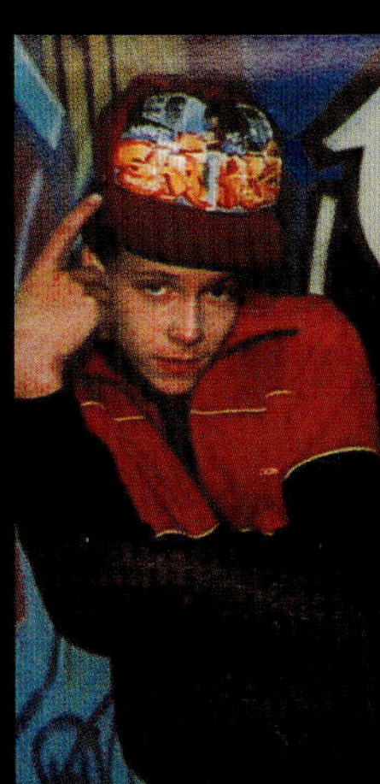

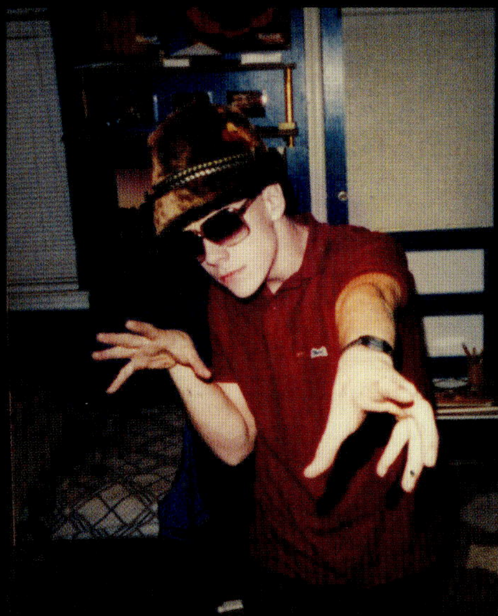

To really get down with graffiti, which was the streets, you had to put in work. No suckers allowed, and it took a commitment that had a lot of risks. I was walking thru the school lobby at dismissal and found mad writers were there. These kids rolled up and Beaver said, "Yo homeboy, let me run that hat" and snatched that shit as I was walking past. So I fought and grabbed that shit back and got into a fight with several of them right in front of the school by all the buses, mad people were there. Shit lasted just a couple of minutes and we all broke out before security came, at which point we would all have gotten suspended. Man they asked me about that shit the following Monday and I was like fuck that I don't know what you're talking about. Soon thereafter I was back rocking that shit. I had met DC3 at night school and he brought us all together and after that we was all kool. Right after that we did a lot of crew production together like "Oh Shit Boys" and several whole court in Memory of walls. Beaver even rocked a couple of 5 Trains with DC3 in the Bronx and it wasn't even until I did this book that I knew that. He and DC3 were the first ones to go to the writers' bench and rep for Long Island.

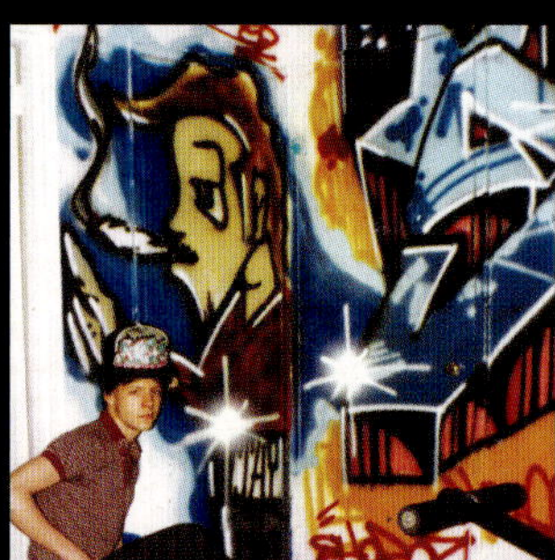

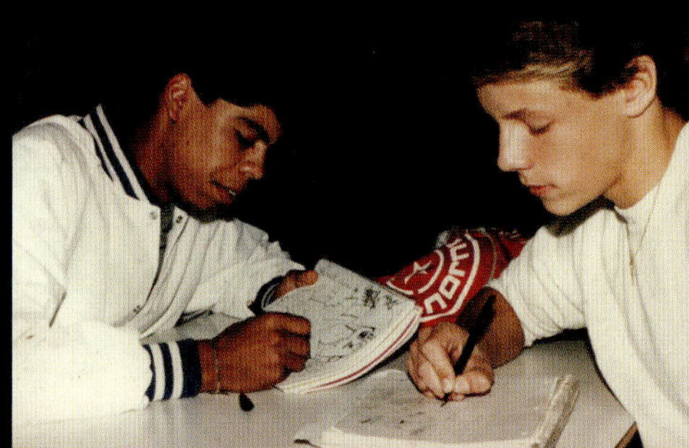

Rocking outlines at lunch.

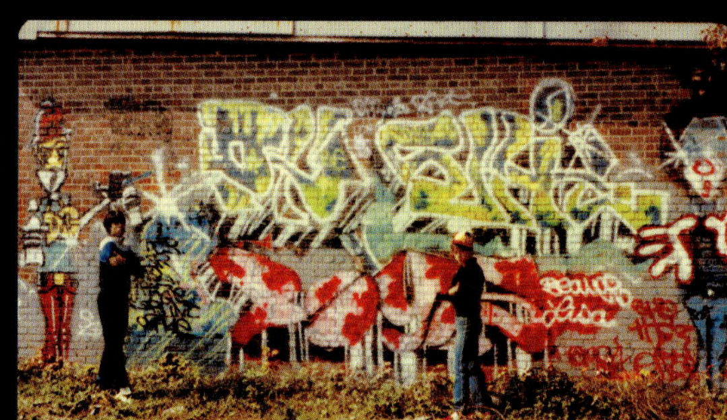

SHO and Beaver One.

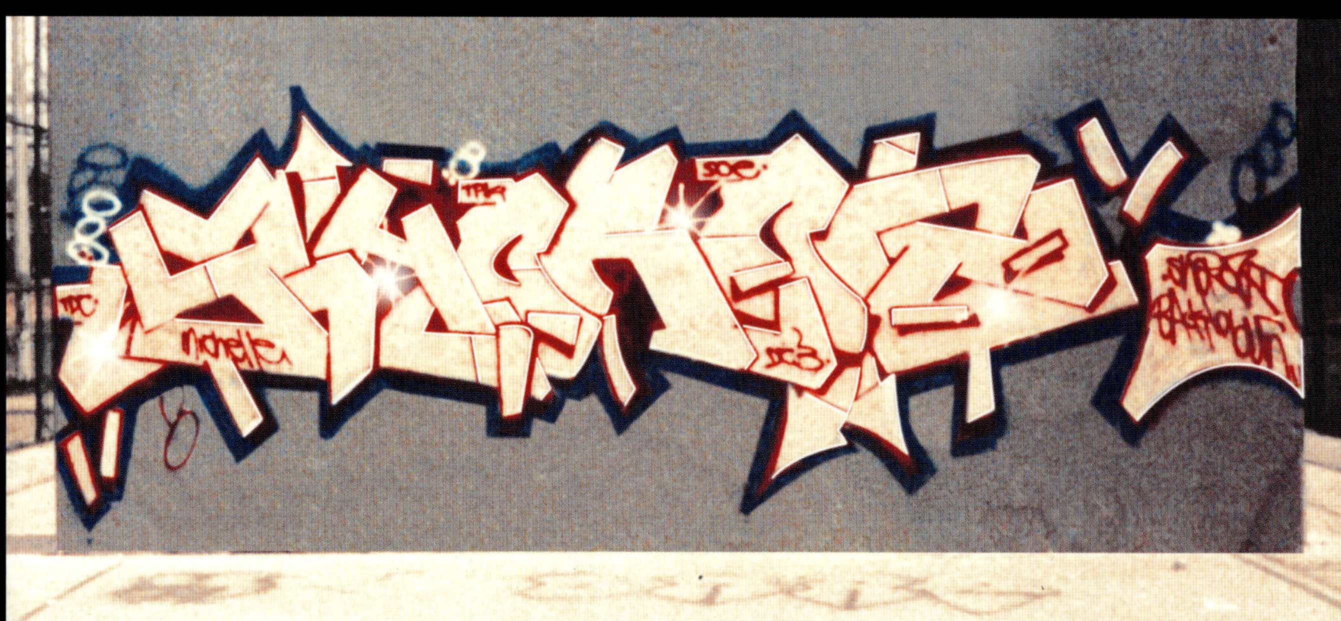

SHOROZ, Northwest Park, Freeport, "Back to Burn," Sep. 1985.

ONE2, Stevens St., Freeport, Jul. 3, 1986, by ONE2, SHO, and DC3.

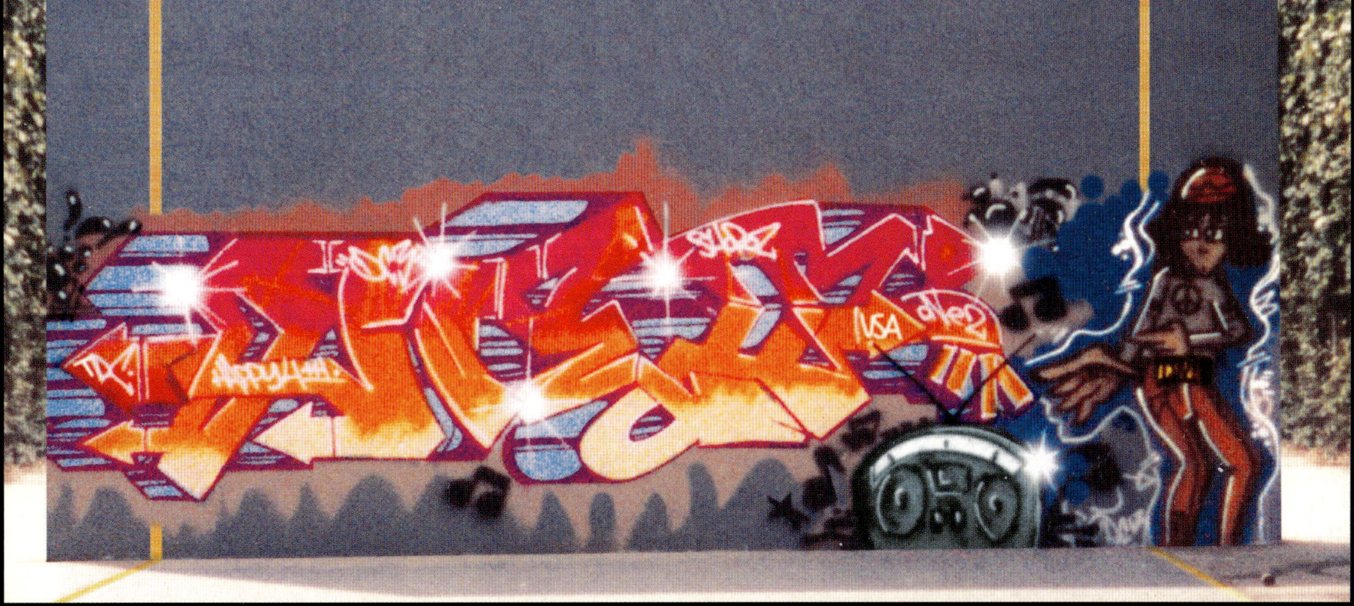

One of my best friends and original graffiti partners at Freeport High School was Jayson, who wrote ONE2. We went thru a lot and always had each others back and still stay in contact to this day. Jay and I would take two long bus rides each way to Pearl Art and Tops art stores in East Meadow and rack stupid spray paint from them. These were the best stores on L.I. because they had all the flavors to die for. Dope colors made a burner the shit. ONE2 mostly bombed tags and we worked on the productions together, I also rocked 5 Trains for him.

-SHO

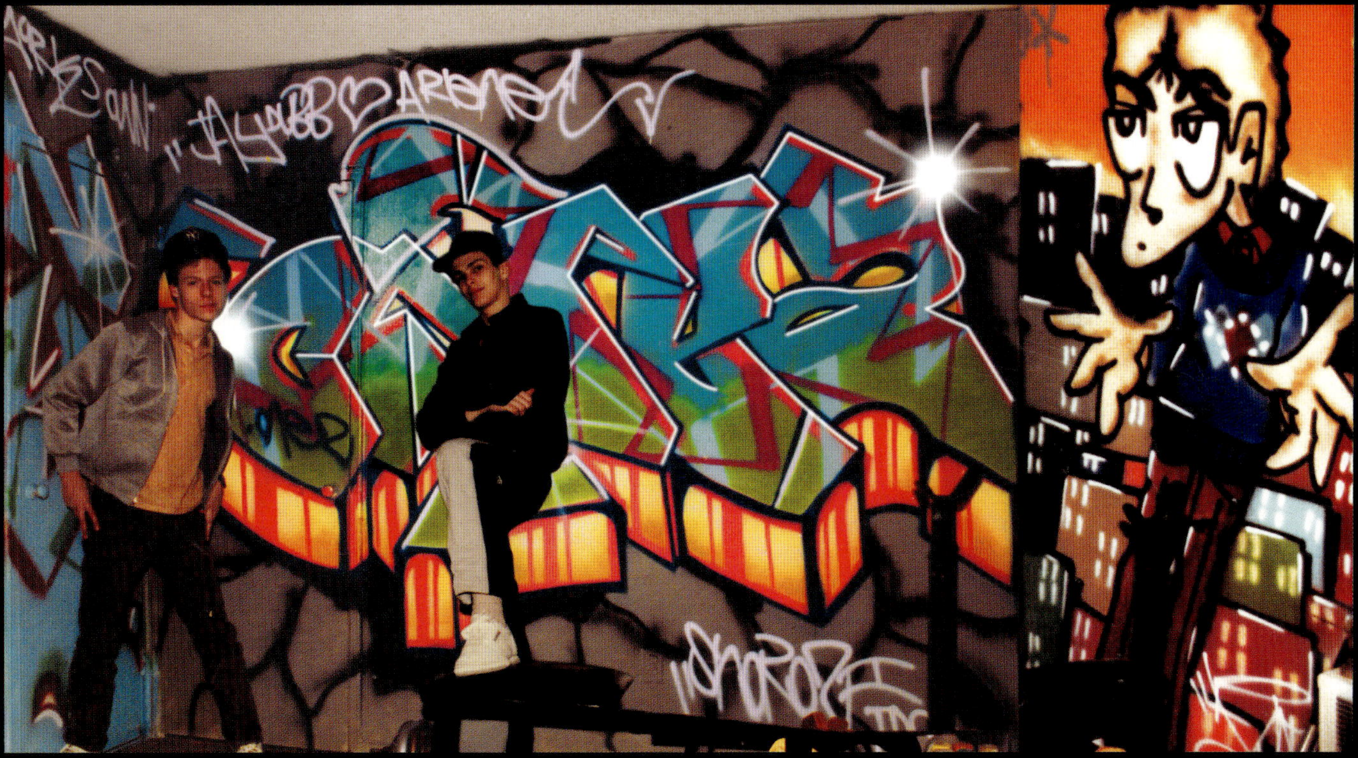

SHO and ONE2, aka Jay Dubb NYO.

DC3, Dome, and Sho, done on a 5 Train in Esplanade pull outs Bronx, NY, October 28, 1986. This represented the third train we had done as a crew together. Zoo was the one who started it all off for us. He had been up in the Bronx chilling with writers like Kent, Bash, Rave, and Seak, all of whom were pushing NCB "No Comp Boys" and BCR "Bronx City Writers." Zoo hit the 5 Train first with them, Kent and Bash were up for the time, and after successful missions, Zoo put DC3 on. We was all from Long Island and put Freeport, Hempstead, and Roosevelt on the map. I remember DC3, who was my original partner, telling me how he had met ZooRoc

DC3, DOME, SHO, "NOW IS THE TIME TO ROCK SHIT," 5 Train, Oct. 1986.

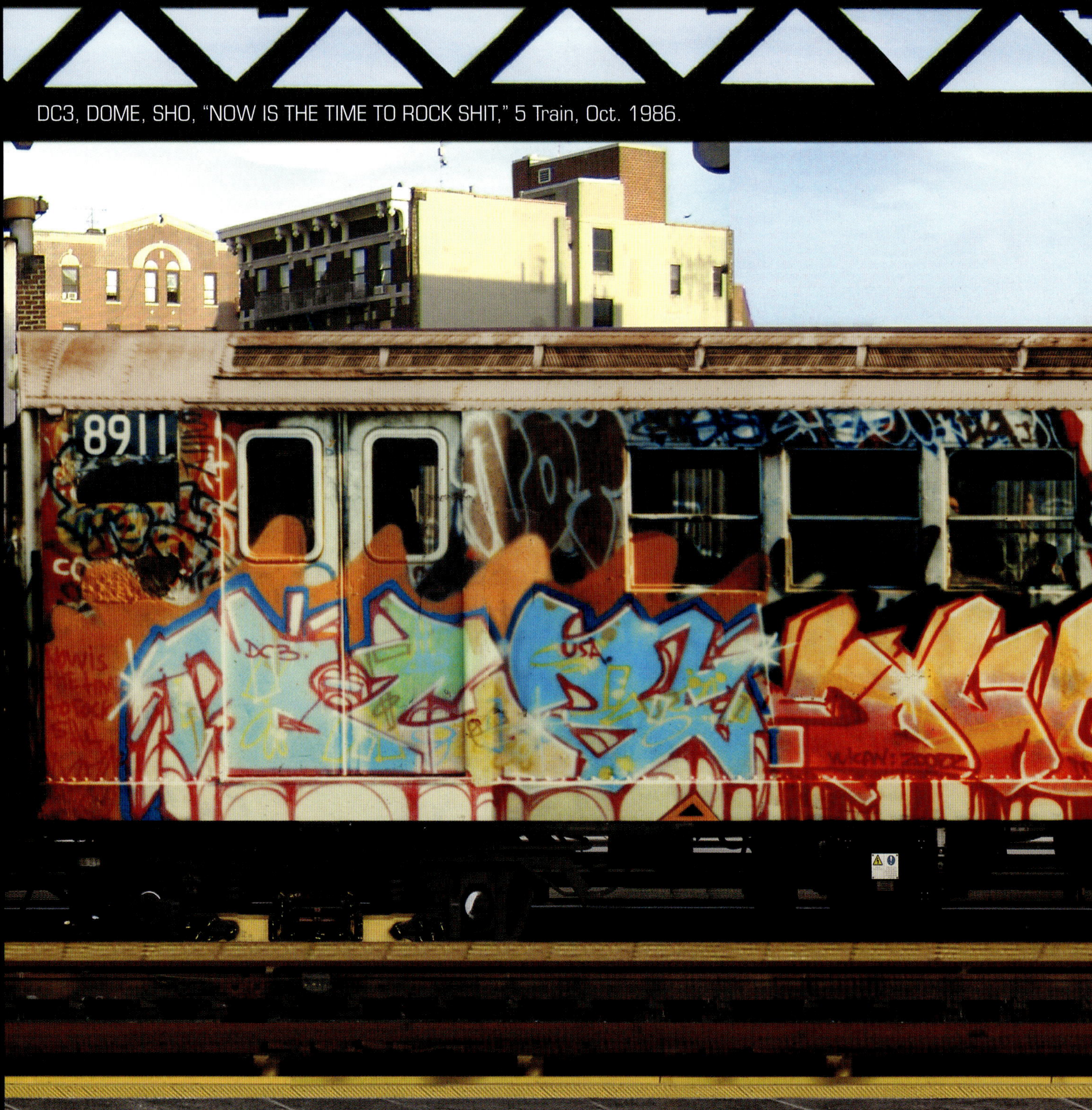

thru a mutual friend from Hempstead. So one day he tells me Zoo wants to meet me, so we all hook up at North West park in Freeport. There he shows me the Kent Zoo flicks and DC3 shows me a window-down that he had already done a couple of nights ago. From there shit moved fast and we wasted no time getting busy hitting trains. At the time I didn't even have a car and we was on the super troop mission taking the bus to the train.

"LI" Long Island Stand The Fuck Up!!!!!!

-SHO

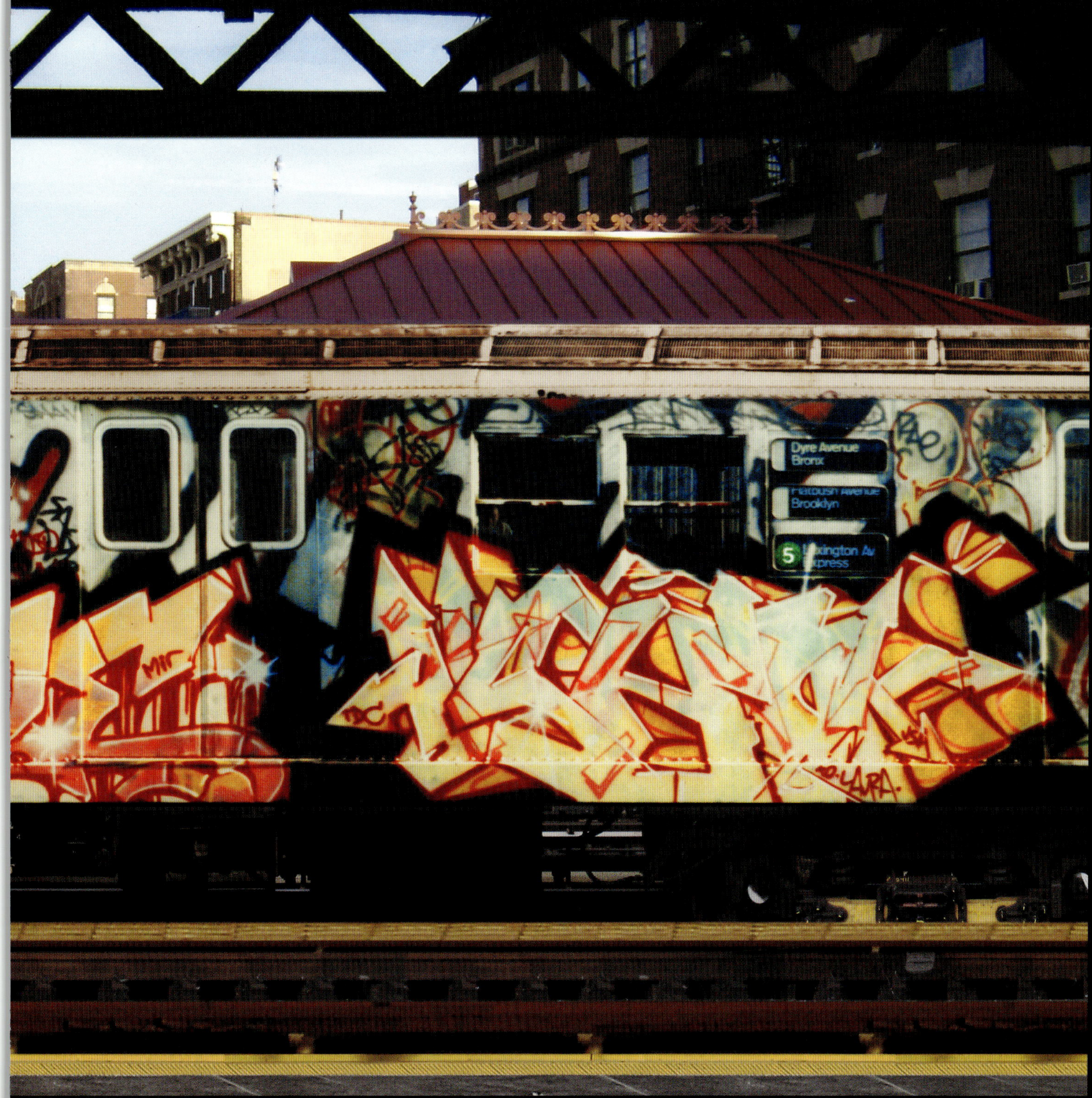

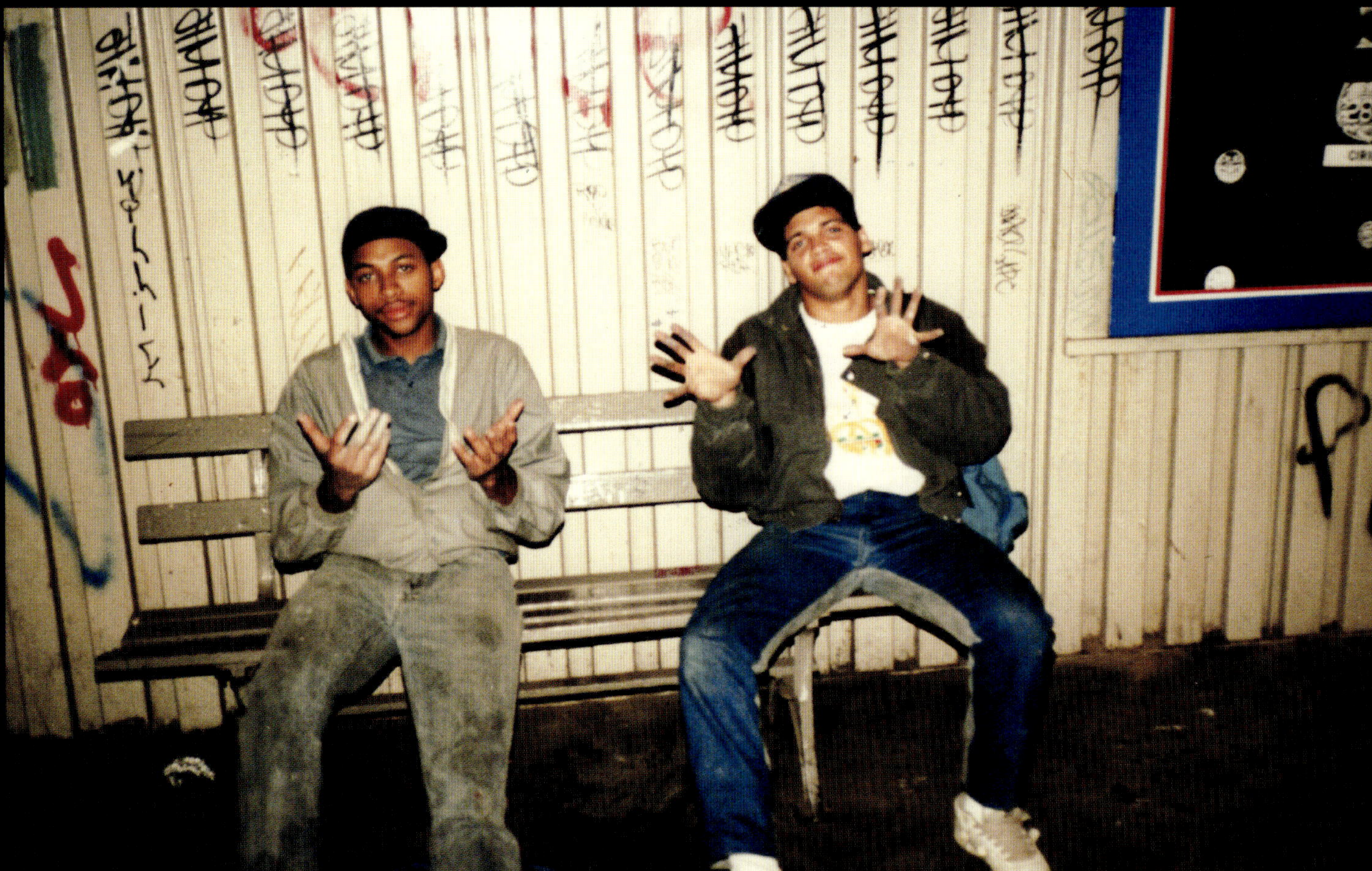

DC3 and ZOO after their second successful 5 Train hit.

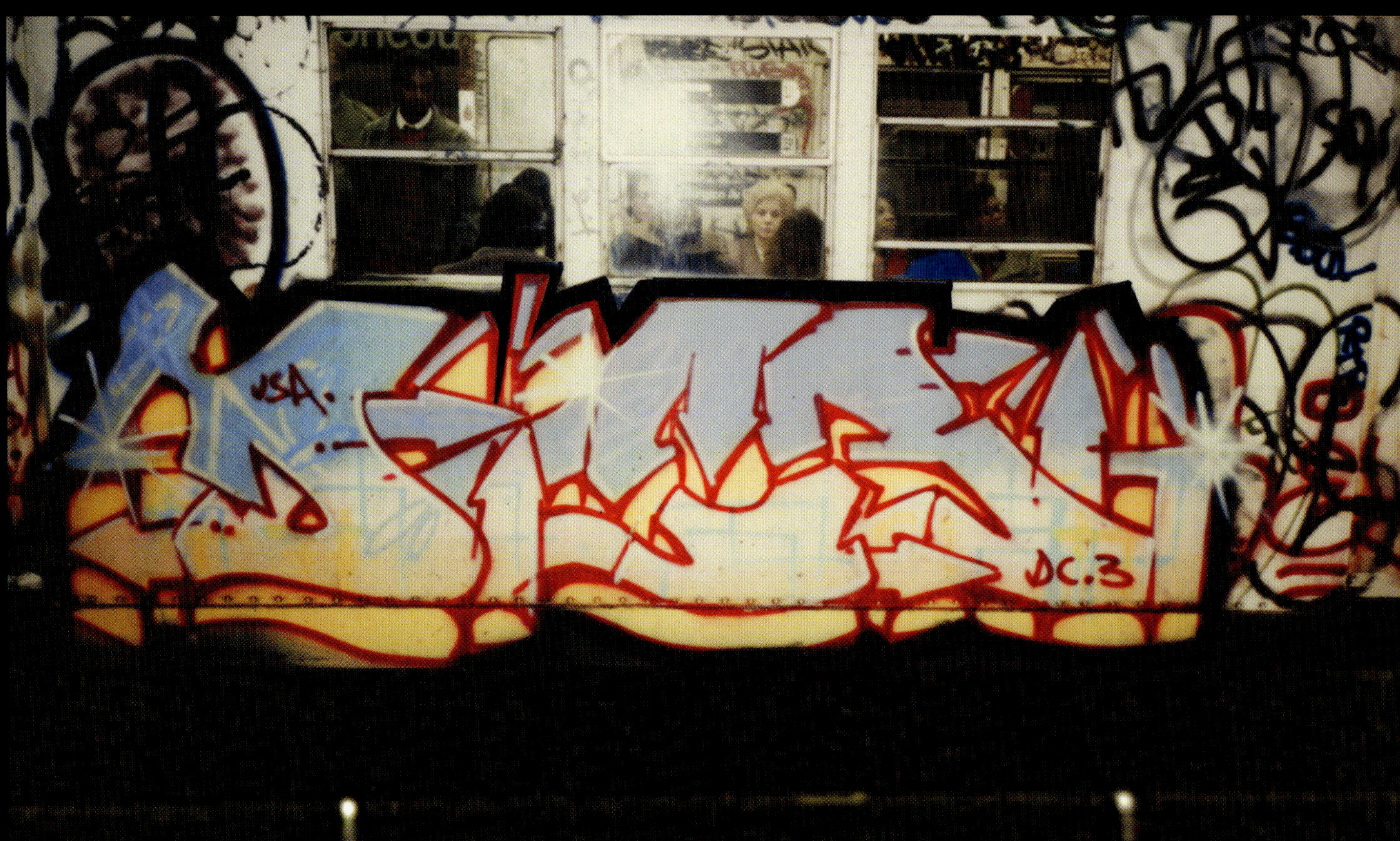

First DC3 and DOME 5 Train, Aug. 1986. It pulled out while we were doing it. Dirty work bums!!!

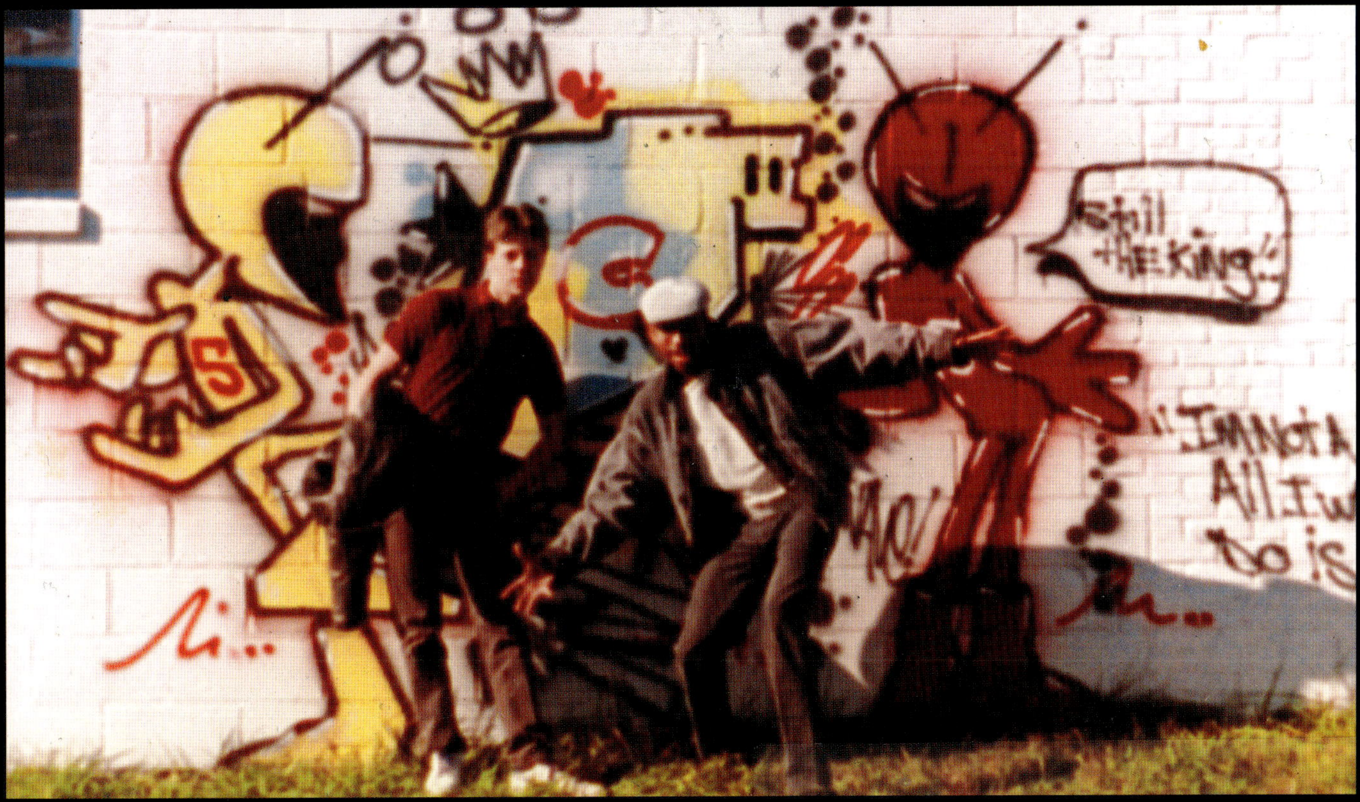

Above is SHO and DC3 at Nunleys Amusement Park on Sunrise Highway, where everyone from school would chill out. Before we ever hit trains we went to Fashion Moda in the South Bronx and said that we was up next, writers there laughed and said it takes balls of steel to get over. Below is DC3 chilling out front. We promptly killed shit. Who's laughing now??????

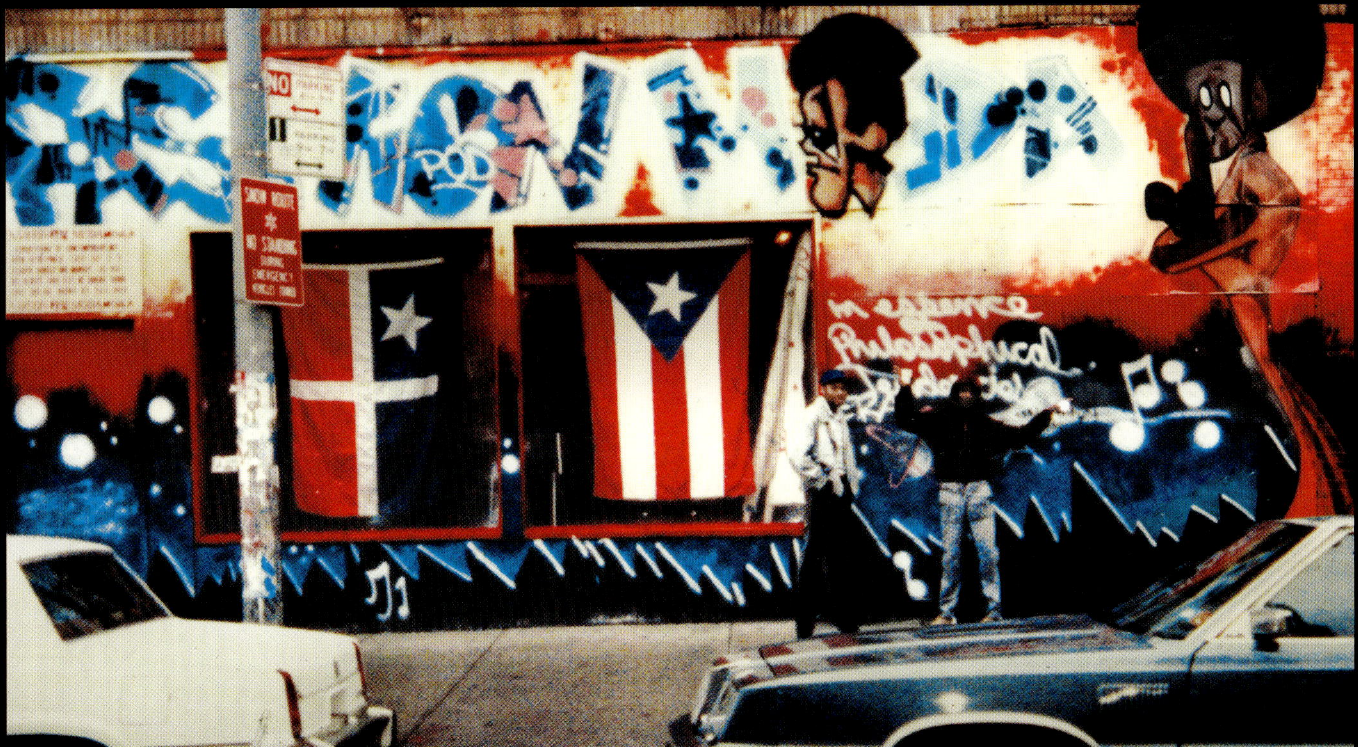

Fashion Moda, c. 1986. True inspiration.

Happy Mothers Day, by DC3, Freeport. NY, May, 1985.

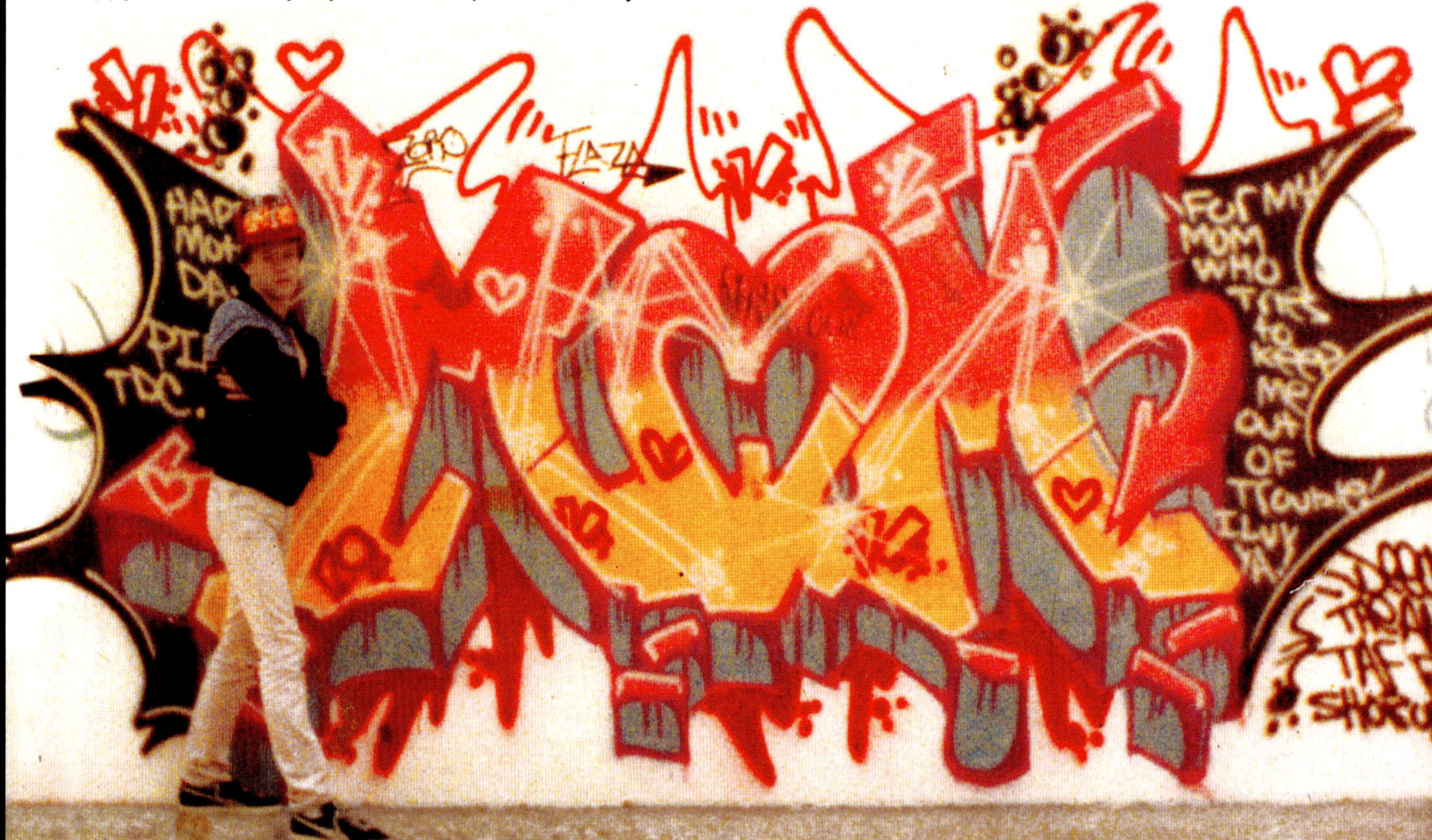

PIA crew, Partners in Art.

When I fell In Love.

By DC3 TDCrew Unlimited Style Artists...Early 1980s.

Growing up in Freeport was rough and cool at the same time. I grew up in a small two-bedroom house with seven kids, five boys and two girls. My father made the attic out of two small rooms, one for me and my two older brothers to share. The other room was for my sisters, my two little brothers had there room downstairs. My father and my step-mother had the biggest room in the house, which was still small. We were a close knit family at first, but as we got older things fell apart. All the boys in the house used to take turns helping my father work on Sunday. My father was a messenger, he used his own pick up truck to deliver packages all over New York City. One Sunday, it was my first time to work, I must have been about 11 years old at the time. He had to make a delivery to A&P supermarket in the Bronx. I was sitting in the truck while he made is delivery, I heard the subway pass, but I didn't pay attention to it. I was sitting there drawing in a sketch pad I had taken with me, when I just so happened to look up as the subway passed me by. I said, "What the hell is that on the train?" I couldn't believe what I had just seen, beautiful art painted on a train. I didn't know what it was called or how they did it. All I knew was that I wanted to do it. That day changed my life forever.

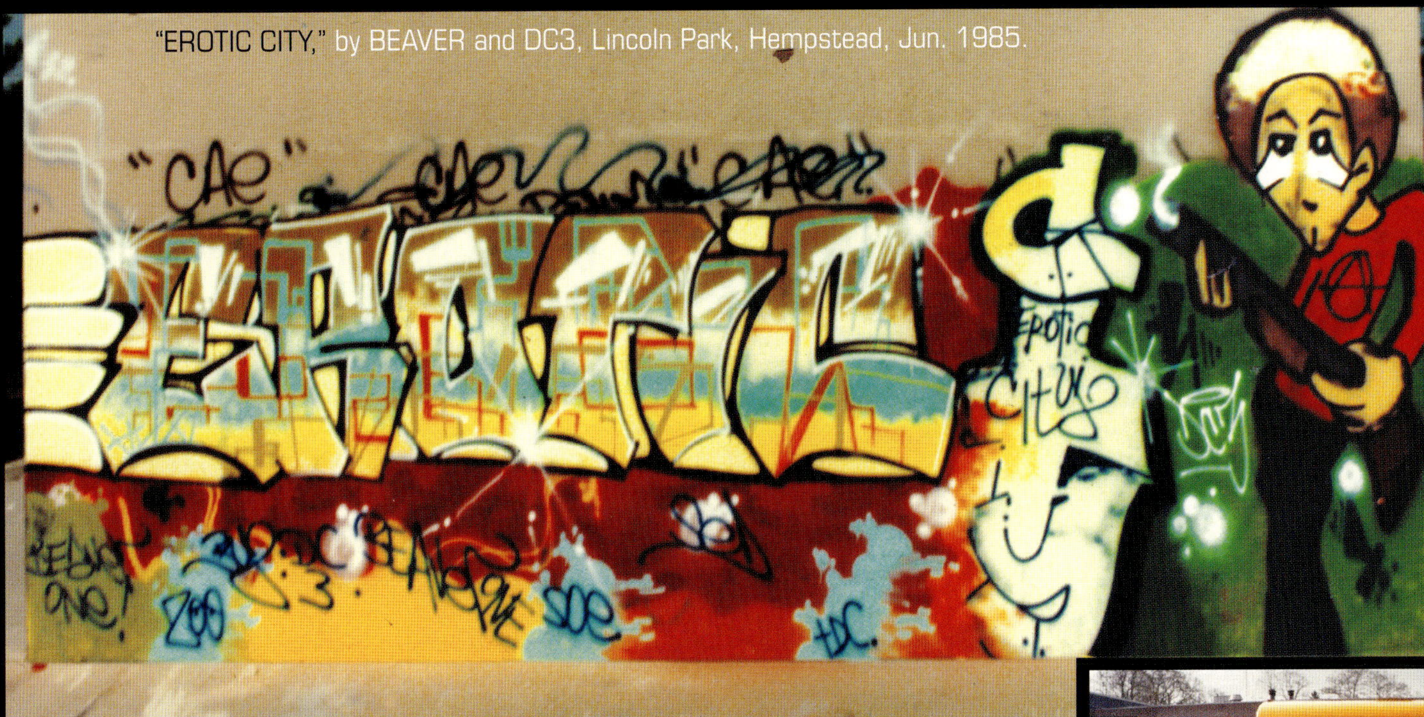

"EROTIC CITY," by BEAVER and DC3, Lincoln Park, Hempstead, Jun. 1985.

DC3, BEAVER, and Fashion.

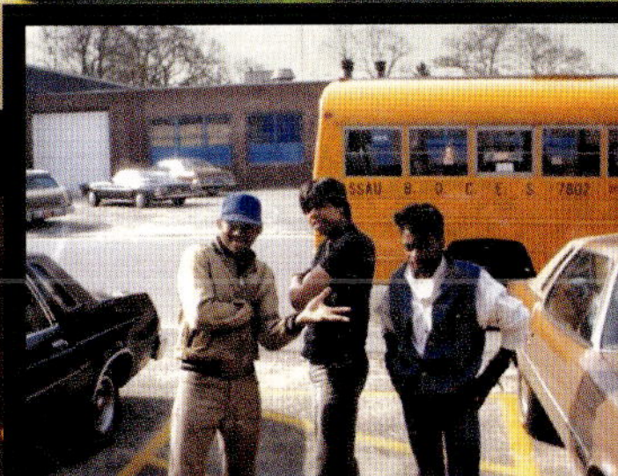

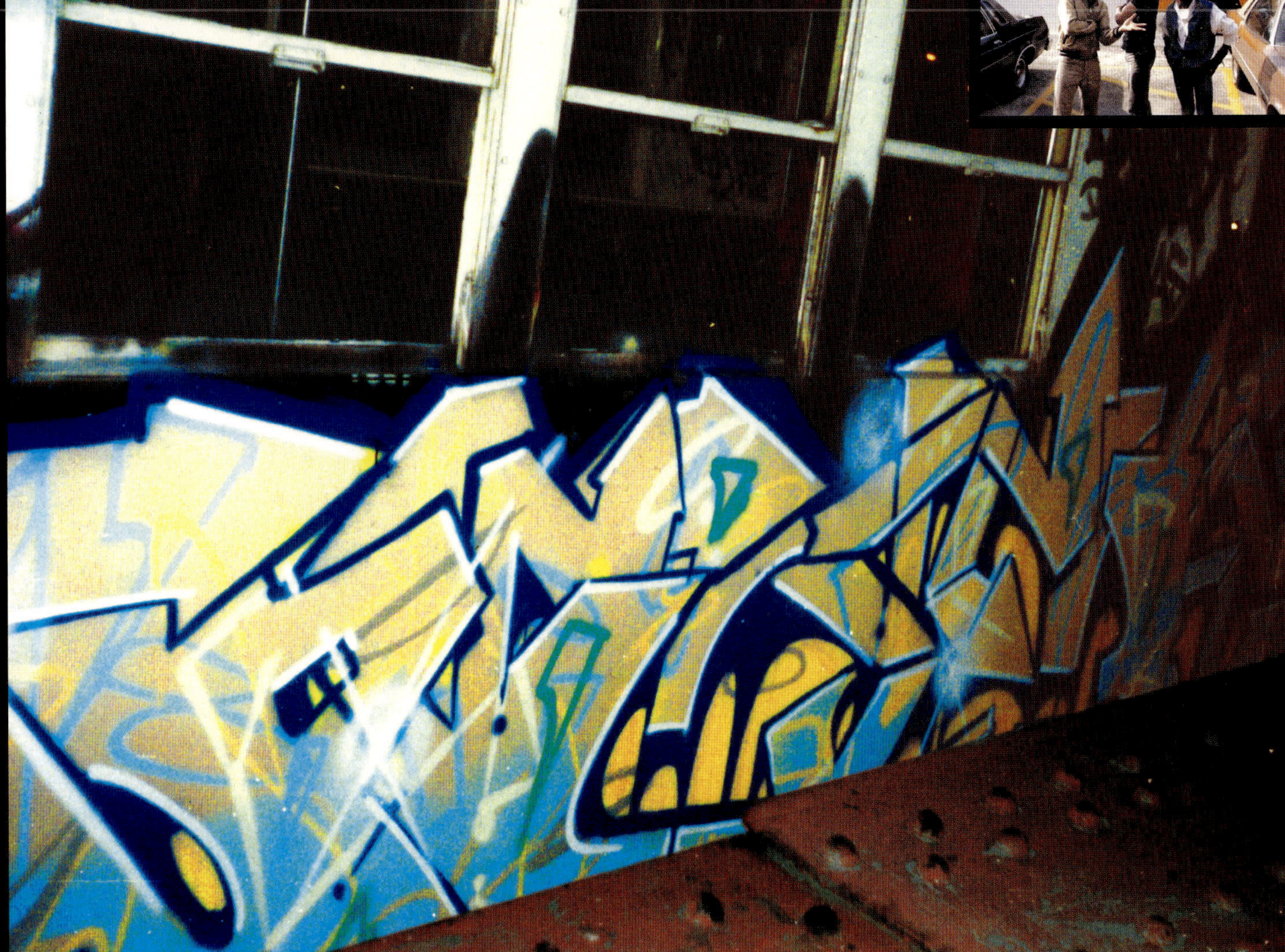

DC3 in the yard...

That was TDC's first window-down whole car in 1986.

★

The Mets won the World Series and we were in the Esplanade lay ups while the game was in progress. When the Mets won, we heard people from the apartment complex across the way screaming, "the Mets won," and the streets were buzzin' while we were quietly painting our train. And then all of a sudden we see a train coming our way real slow (Oh Shit!) we thought we were getting raided, so we packed up real quick, hid some bags of paint and hid before they saw us. As the train came to a halt, it was just work bum's there to sweep the inside of the trains, so we just chilled and waited them out. We went back to finish our train and get the paint we had hidden—the work bum's fucking stole it. Dome's plan for a red outline was curtains so he ended up using a pink outline and we all fudged the background with black, which was not the original plan—we were gonna do gray 'round bricks. In the end, we accomplished what we came for: a window-down whole car. Every time after that we only did whole cars to let other crews know the bar was set higher. At that time the crew's that were writing were only doing window-downs, if you saw a whole car, which would be once every five months, it wold be an older crew that didn't get up anymore just letting you know they're alive. TDC did whole cars and top-to-bottoms every week.

The Hall of Fame Don't Play

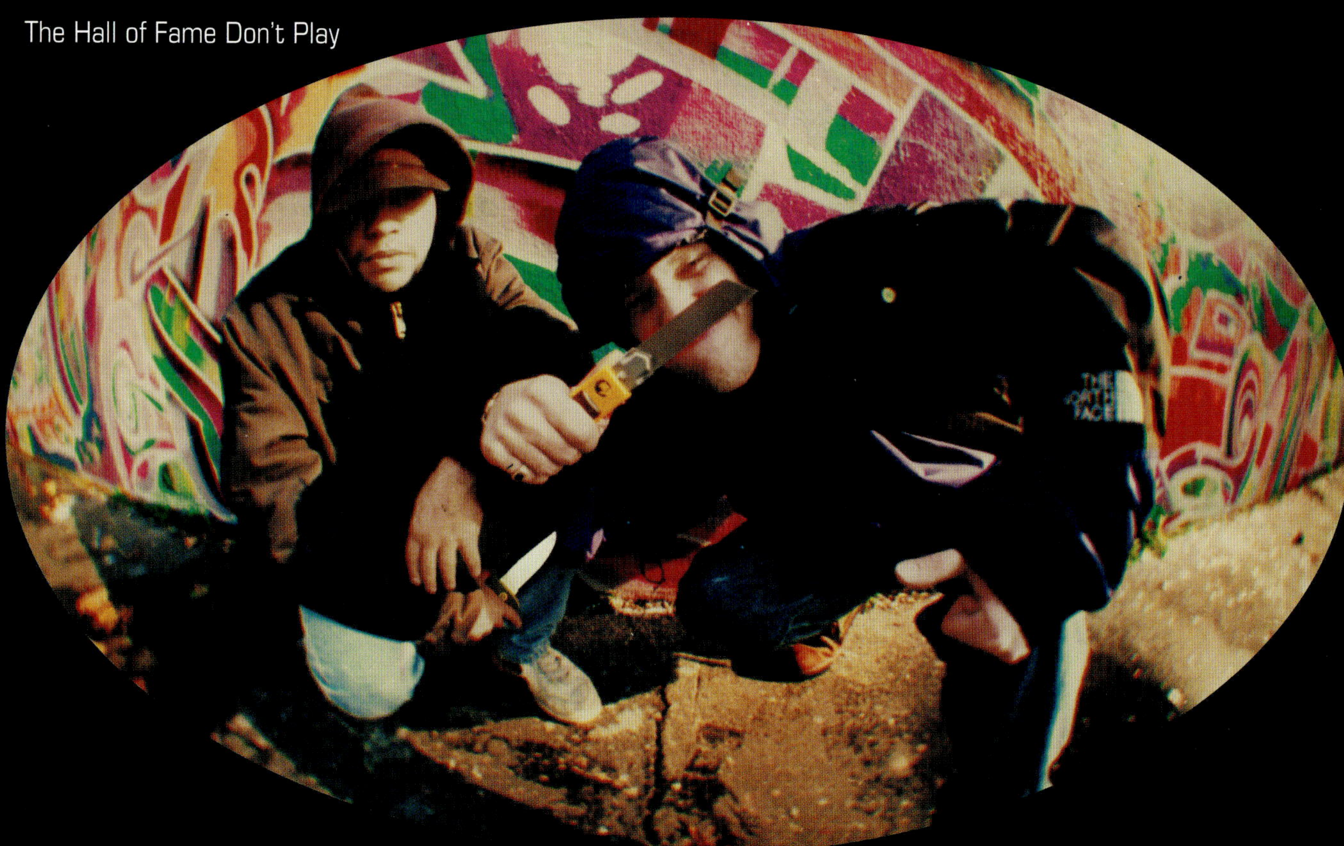

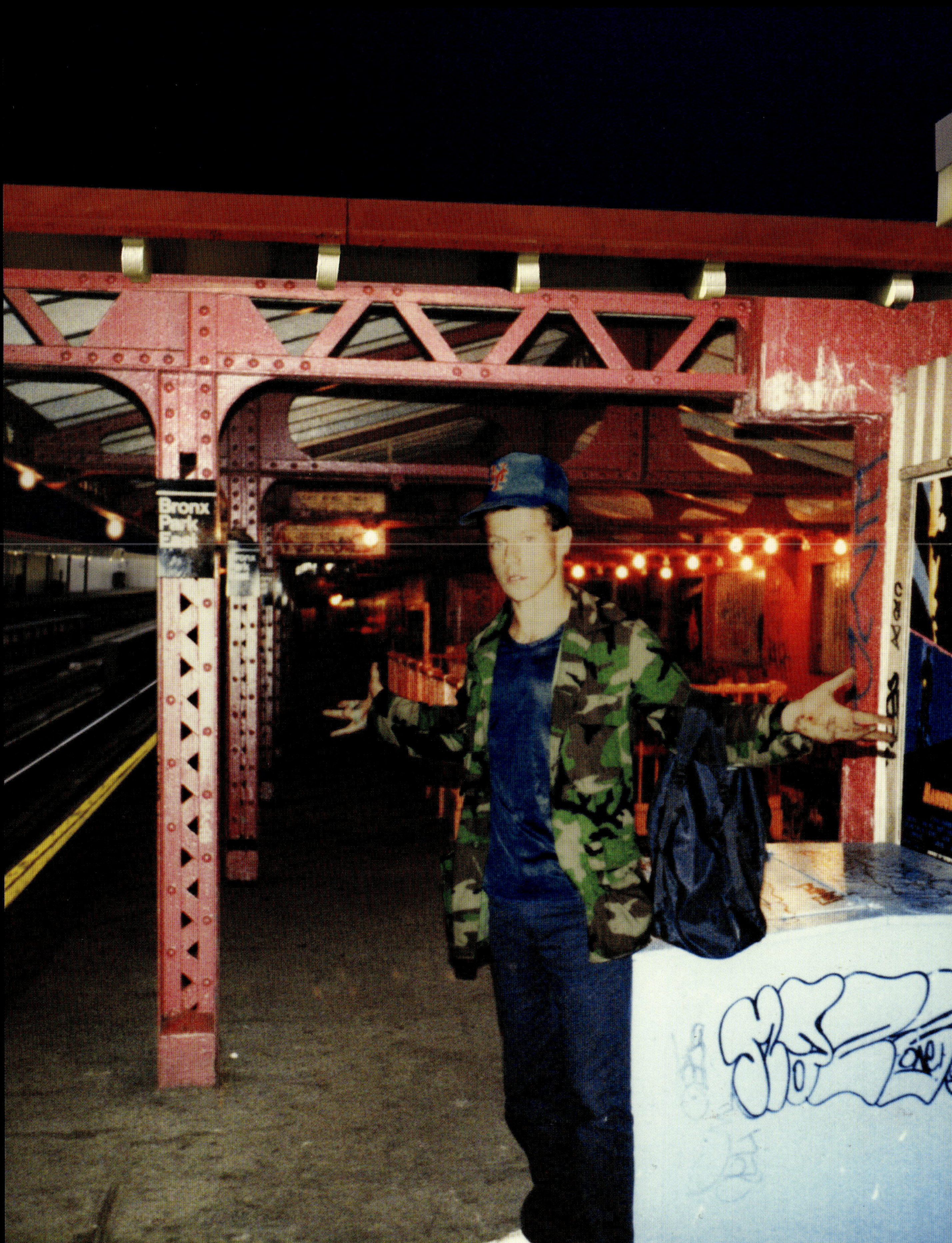

SHO at Bronx Park East after doing first 5 Train.

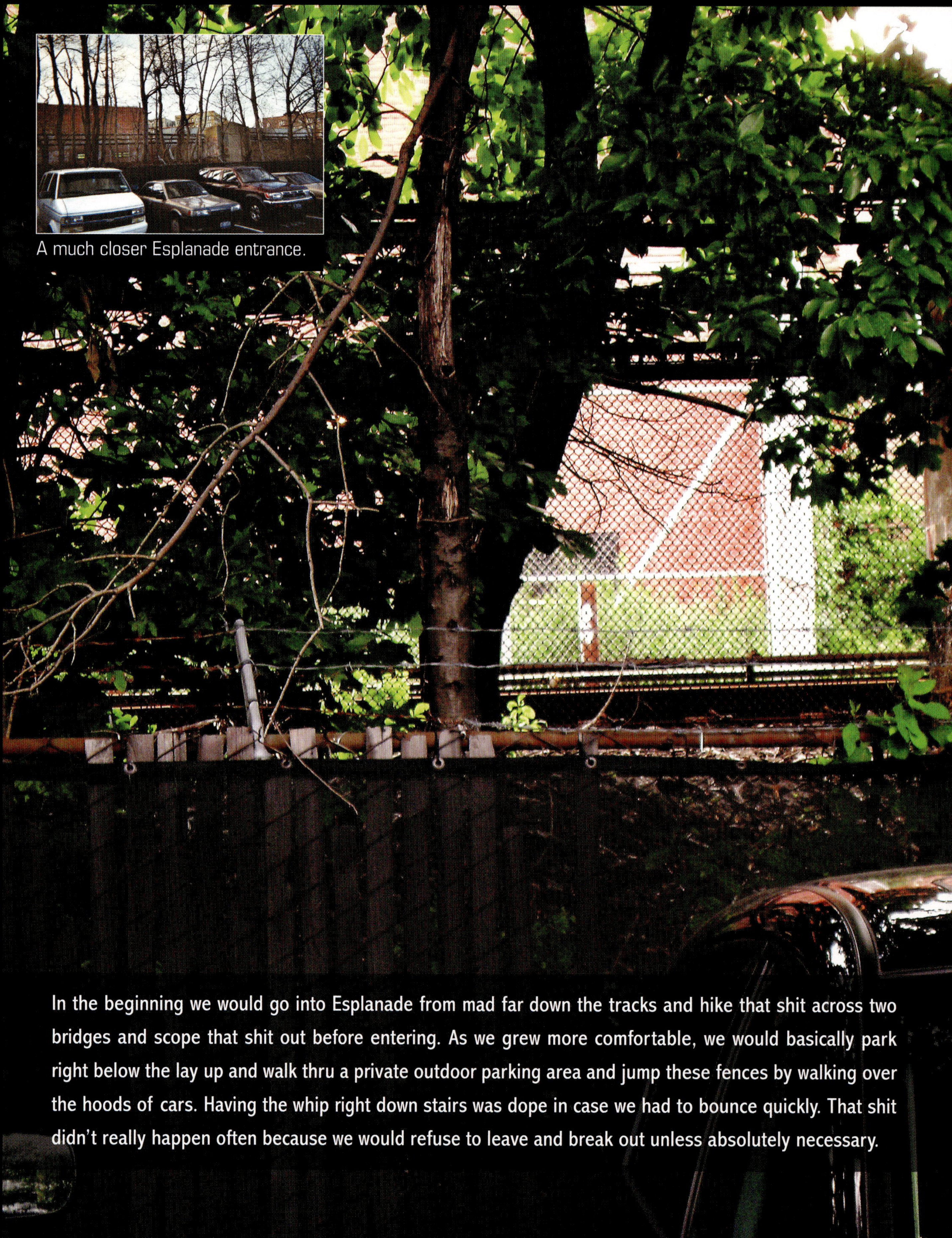

A much closer Esplanade entrance.

In the beginning we would go into Esplanade from mad far down the tracks and hike that shit across two bridges and scope that shit out before entering. As we grew more comfortable, we would basically park right below the lay up and walk thru a private outdoor parking area and jump these fences by walking over the hoods of cars. Having the whip right down stairs was dope in case we had to bounce quickly. That shit didn't really happen often because we would refuse to leave and break out unless absolutely necessary.

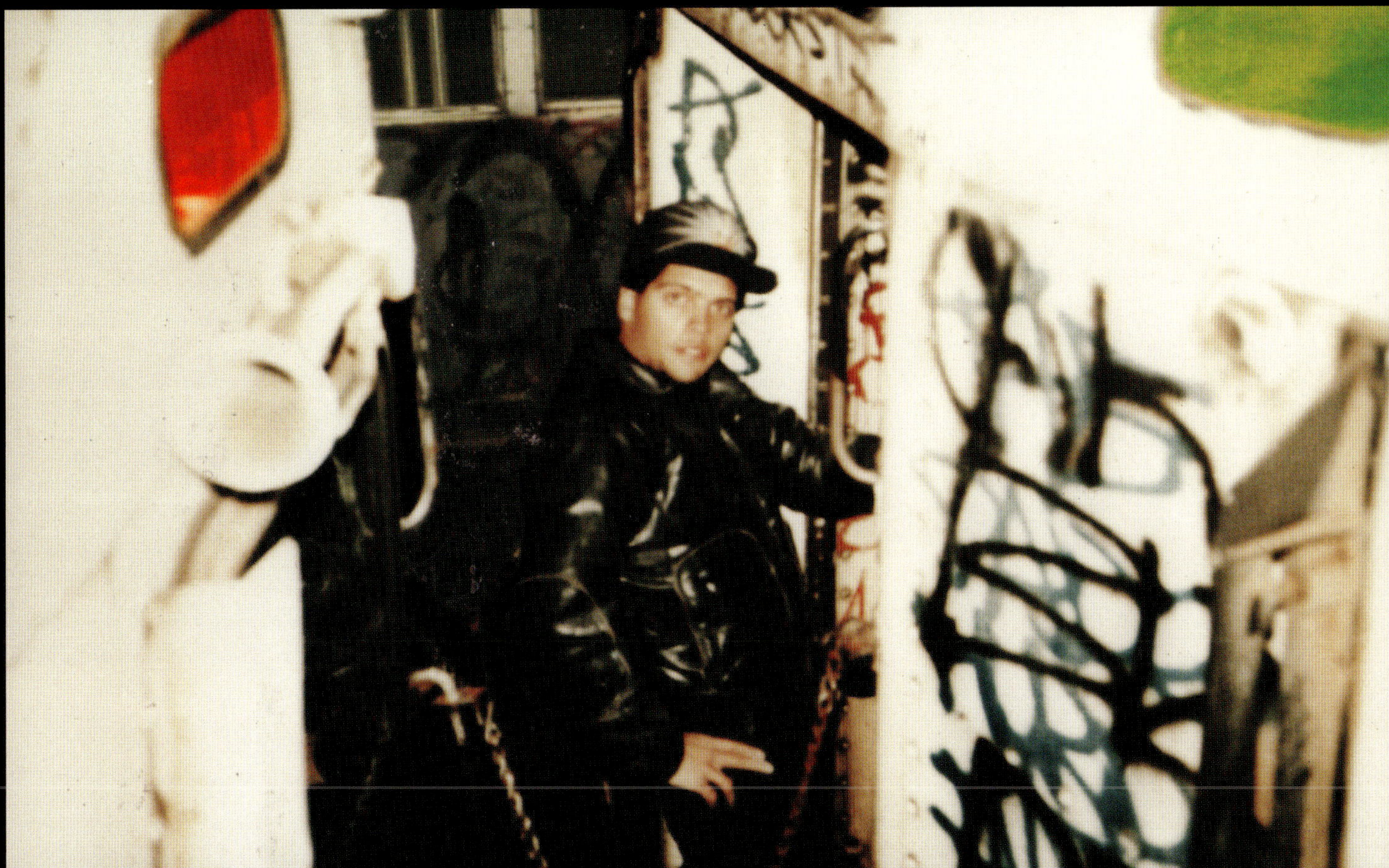

La De Da Deee...

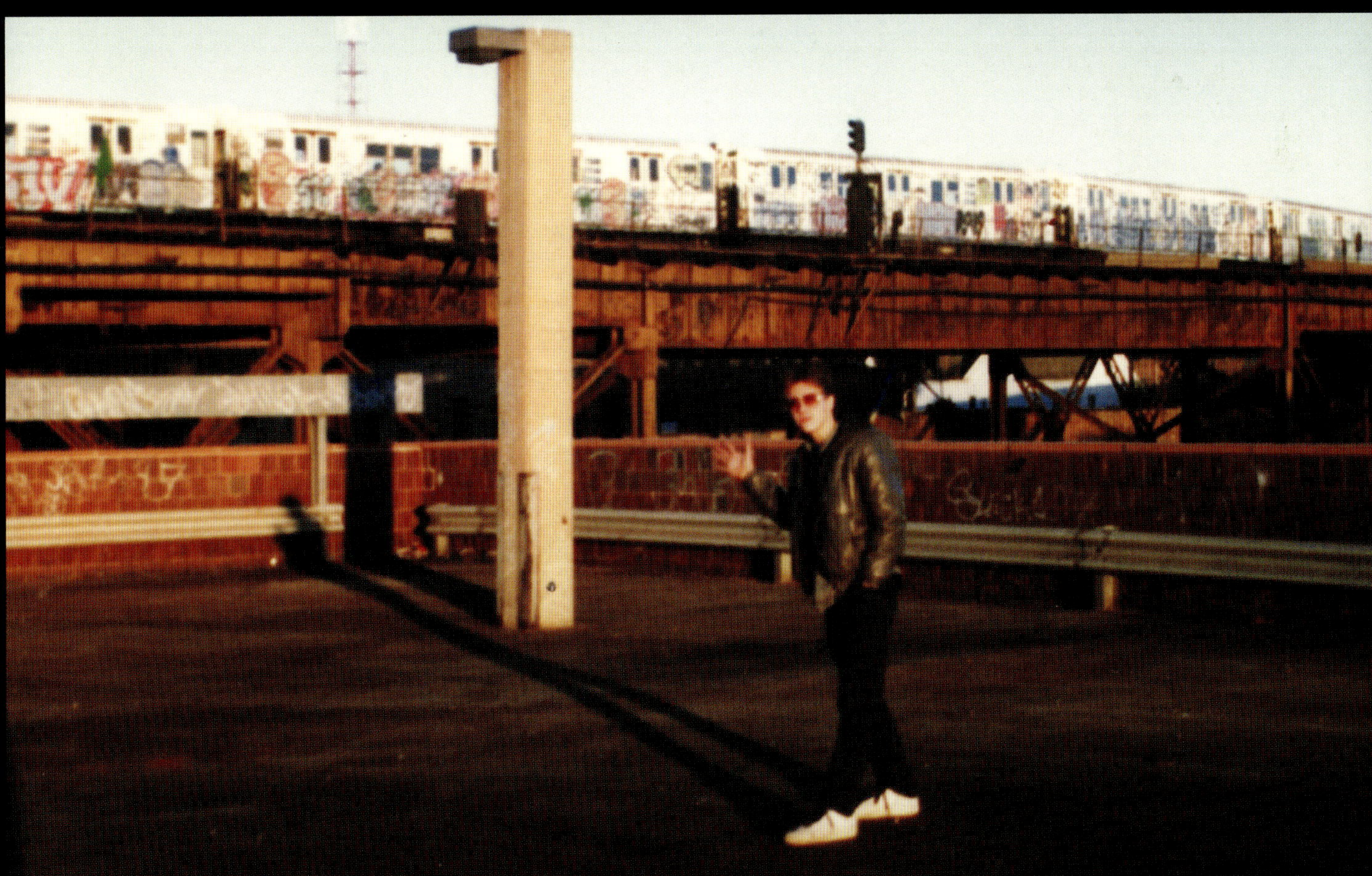

SHO chilling on the Supermercado roof in E. Tremont.

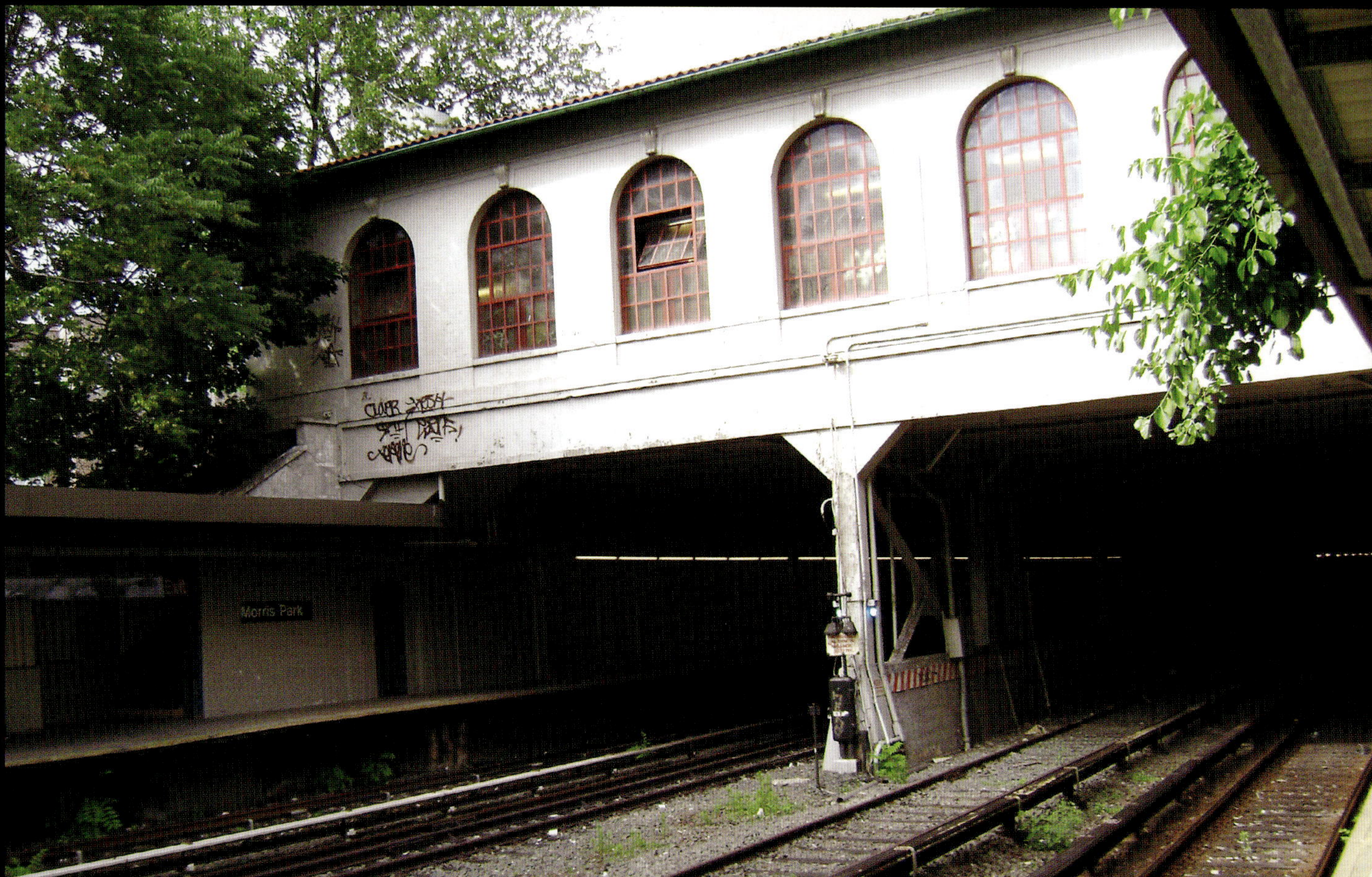

Esplanade station and 2-track tunnel lay up extending to Pelham Parkway Station.

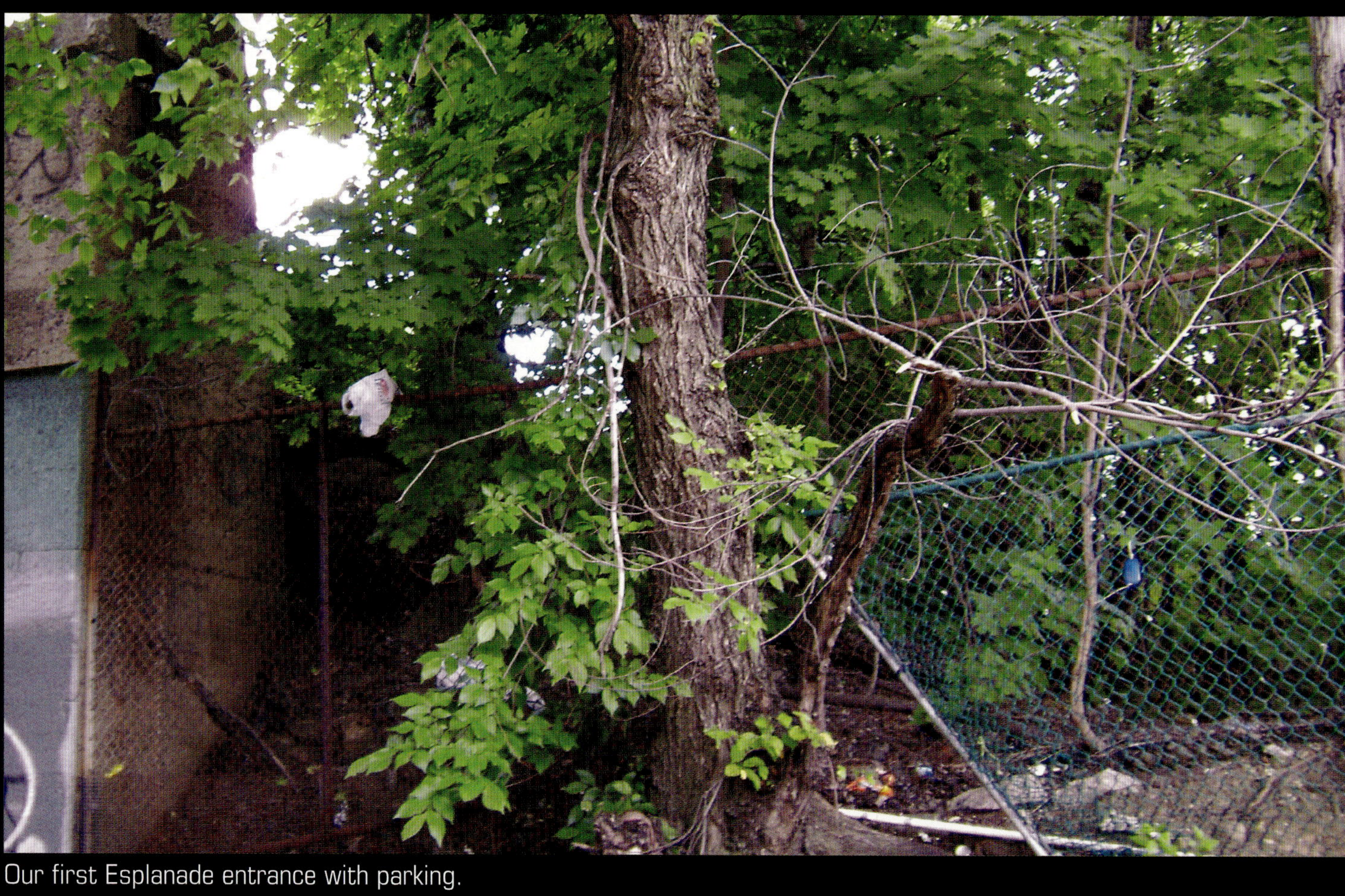
Our first Esplanade entrance with parking.

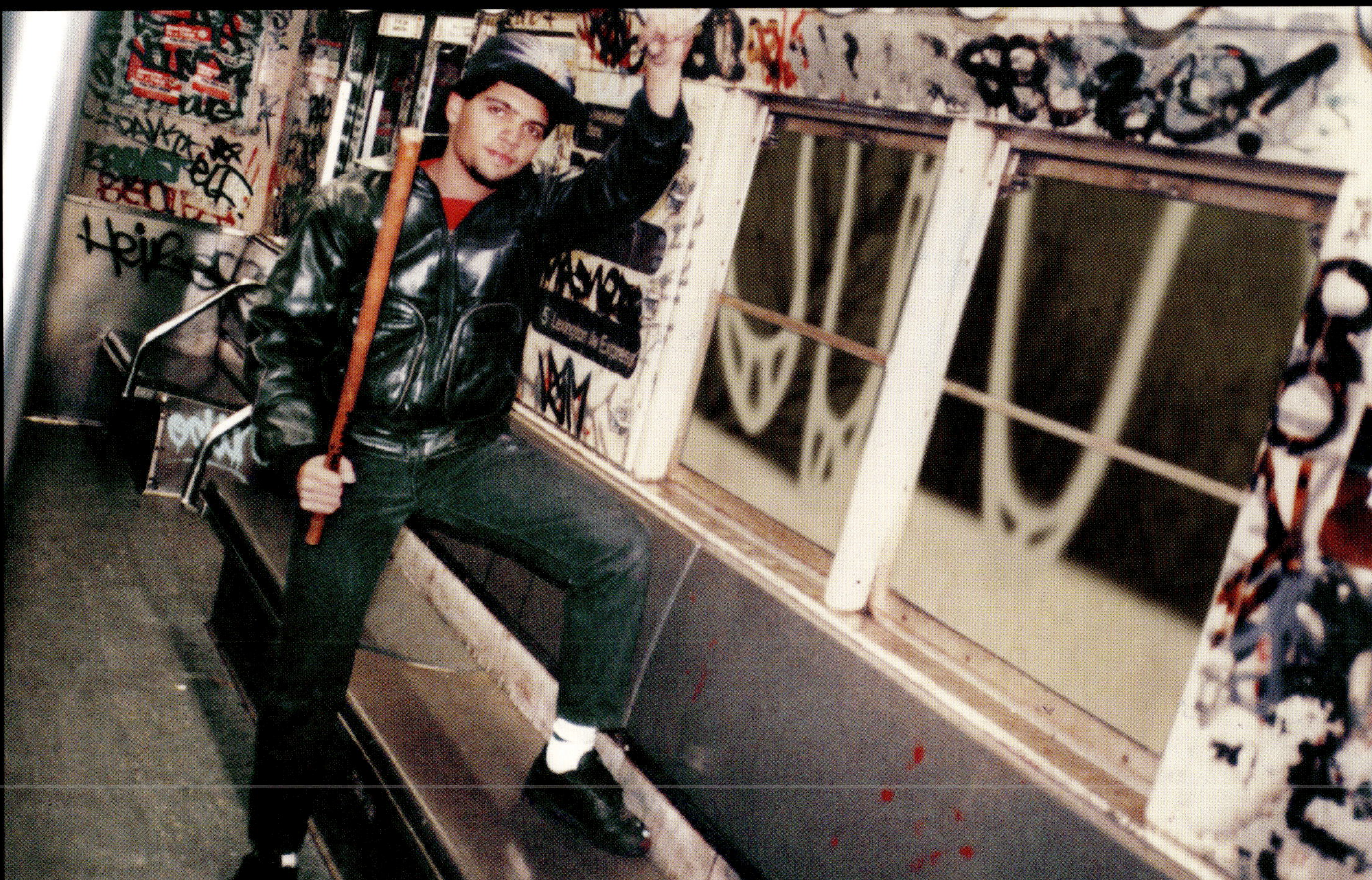
5 Lexington Av Express

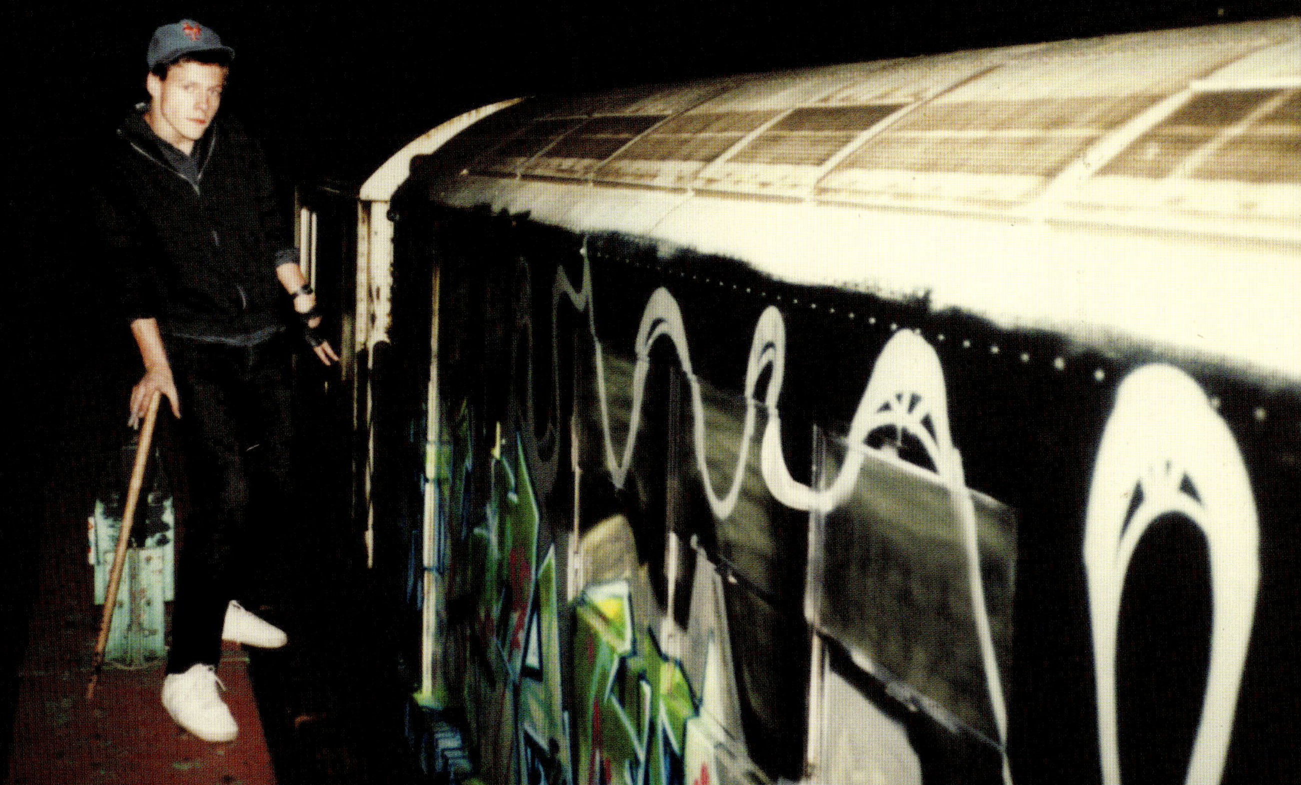

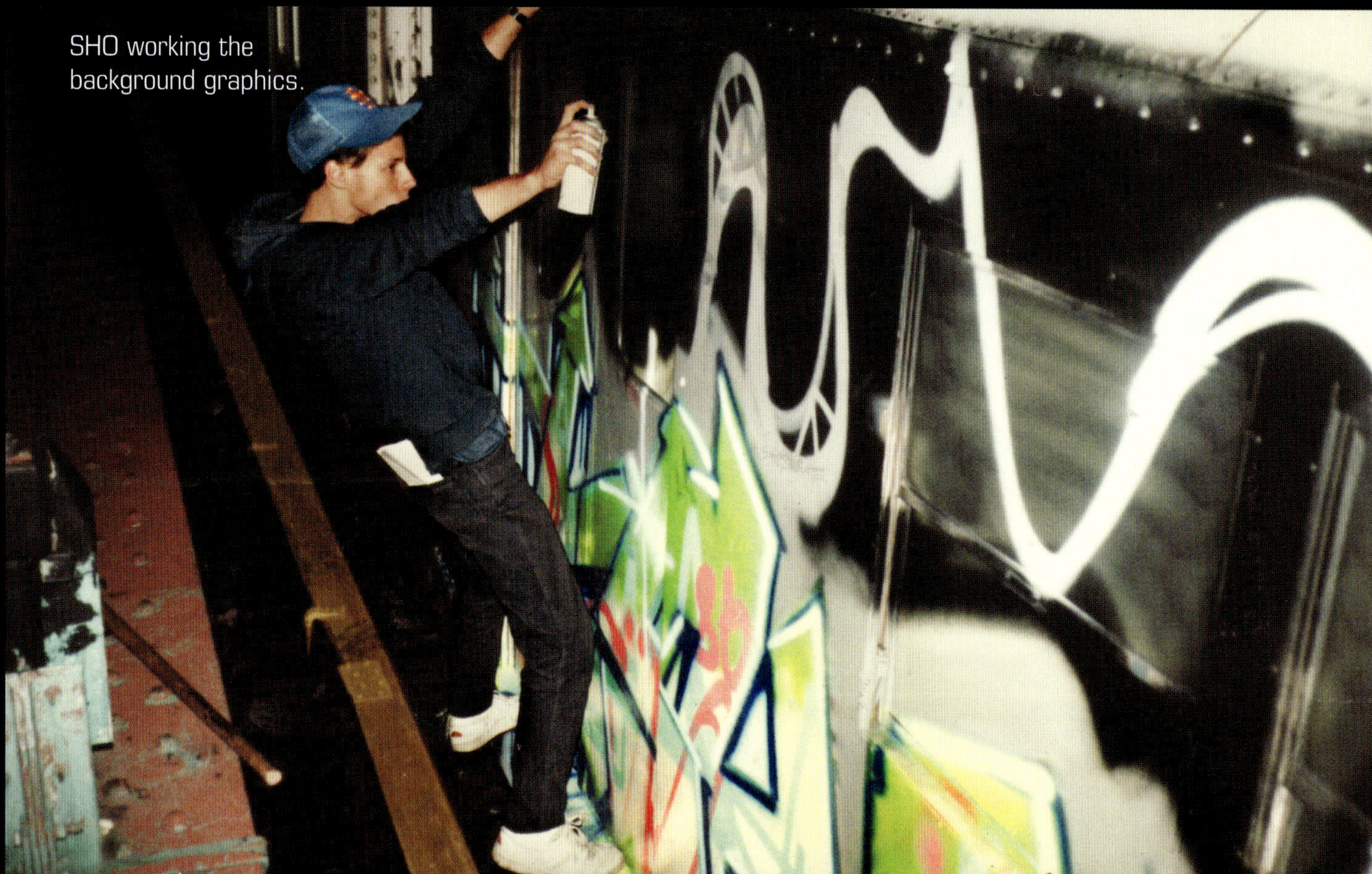

SHO working the background graphics.

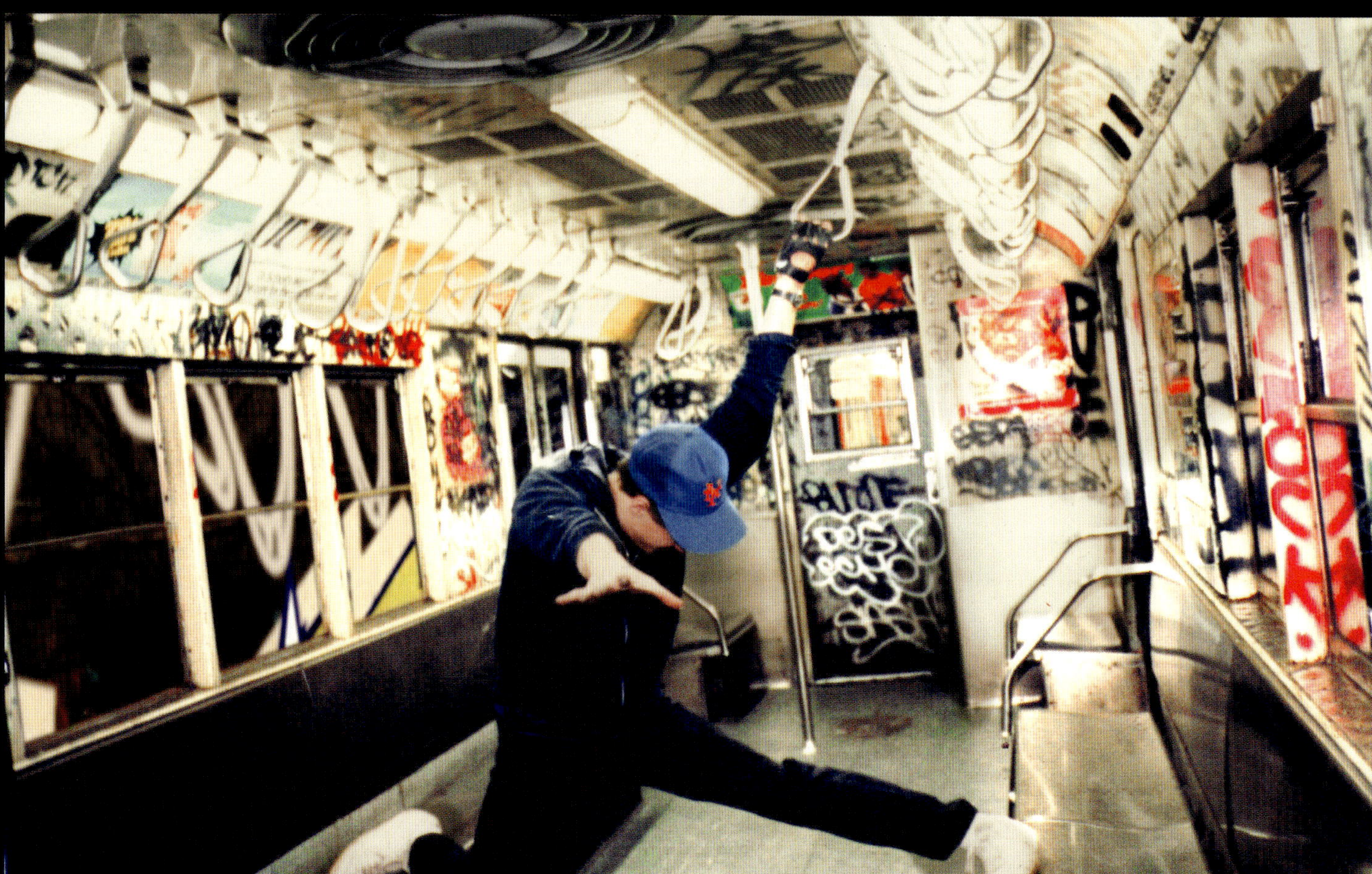

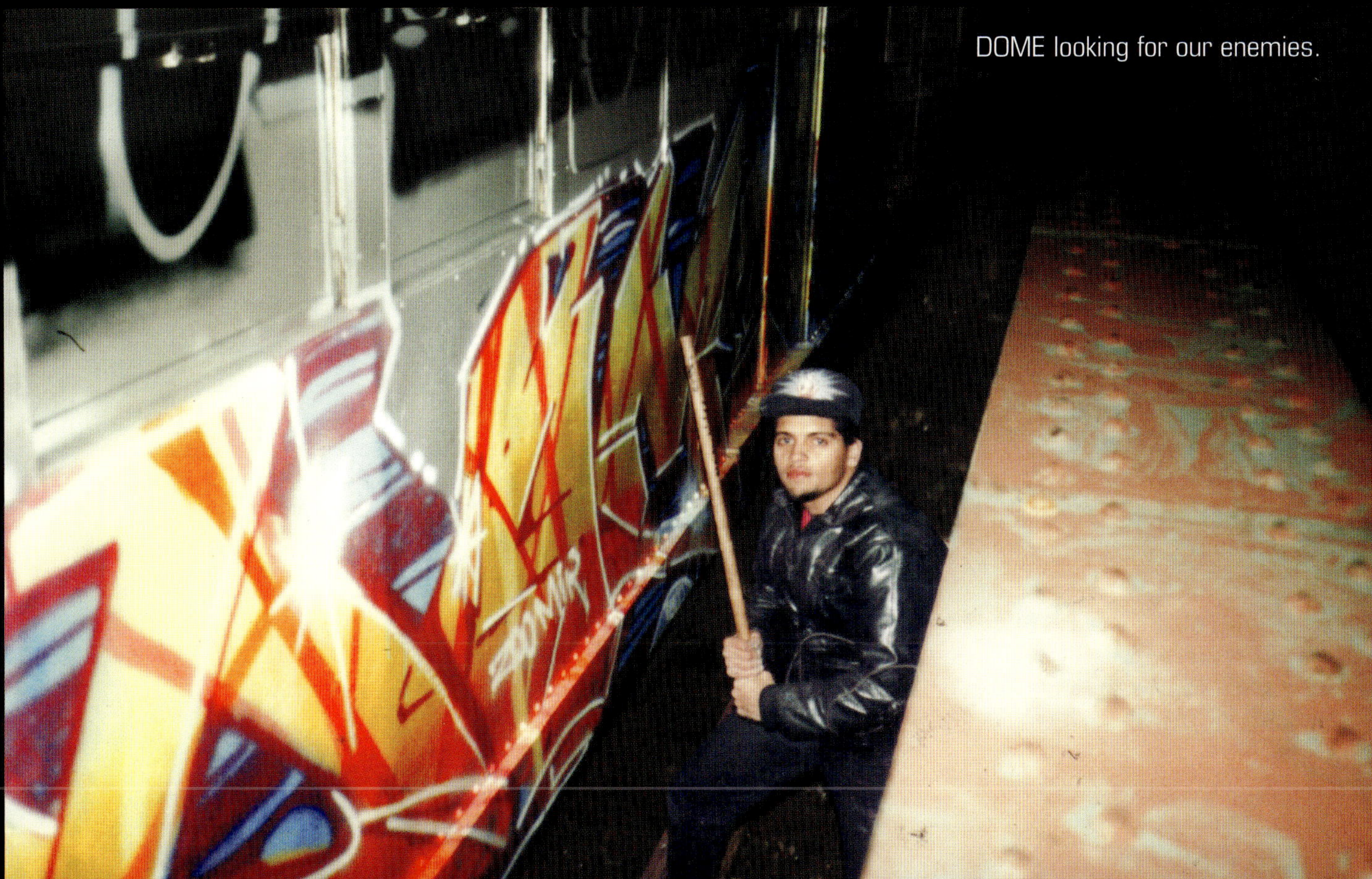

DOME looking for our enemies.

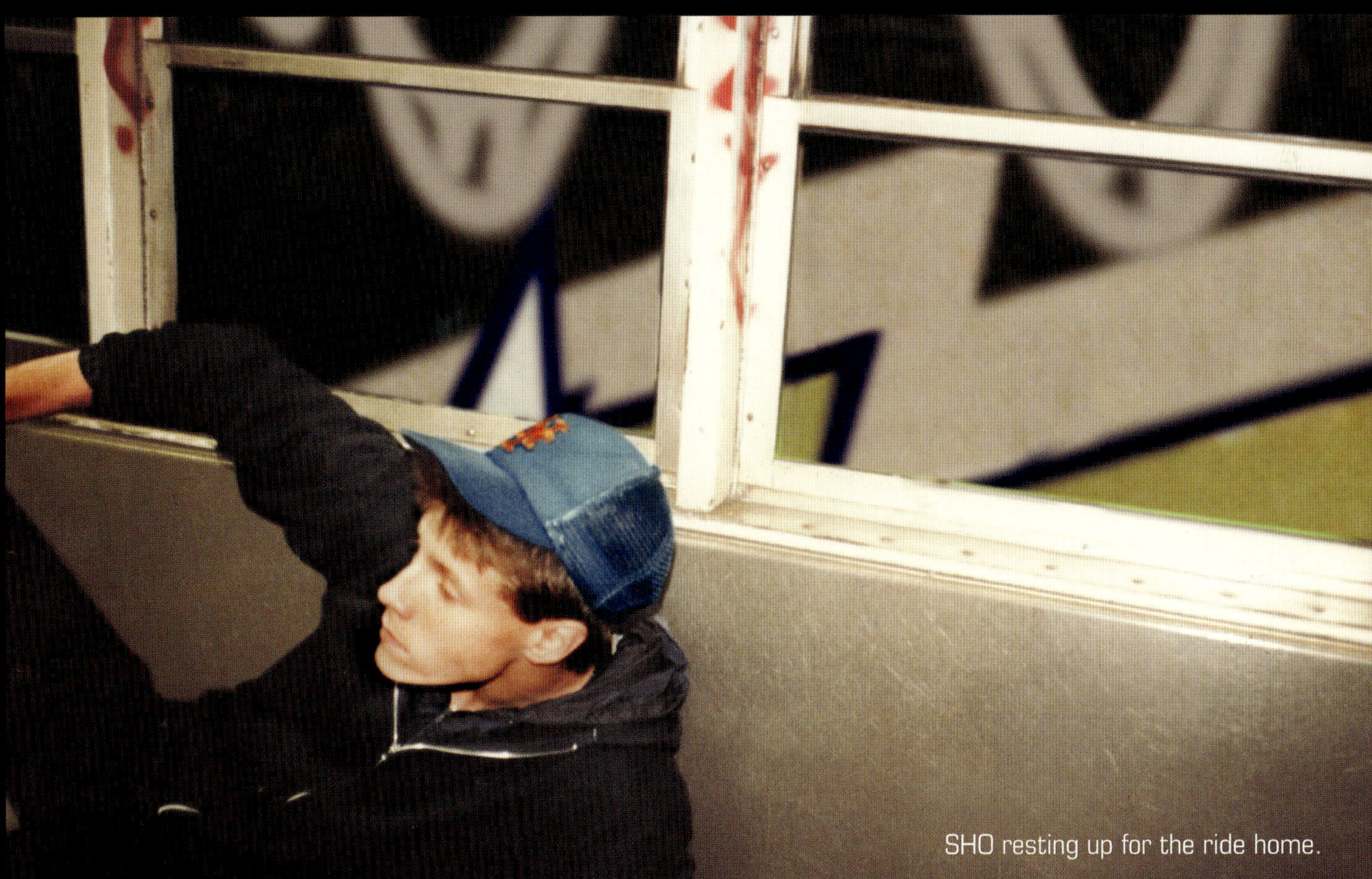

SHO resting up for the ride home.

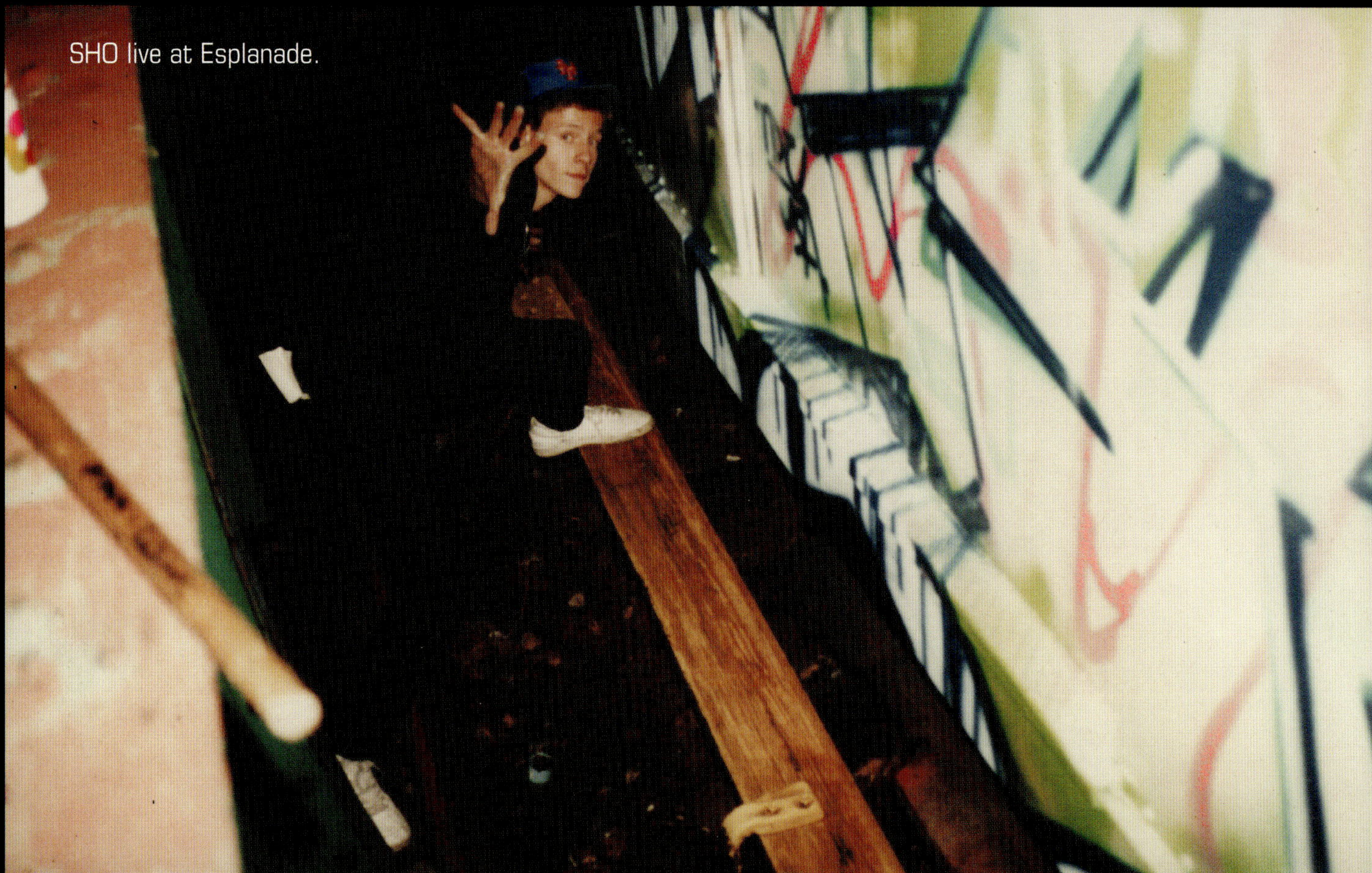
SHO live at Esplanade.

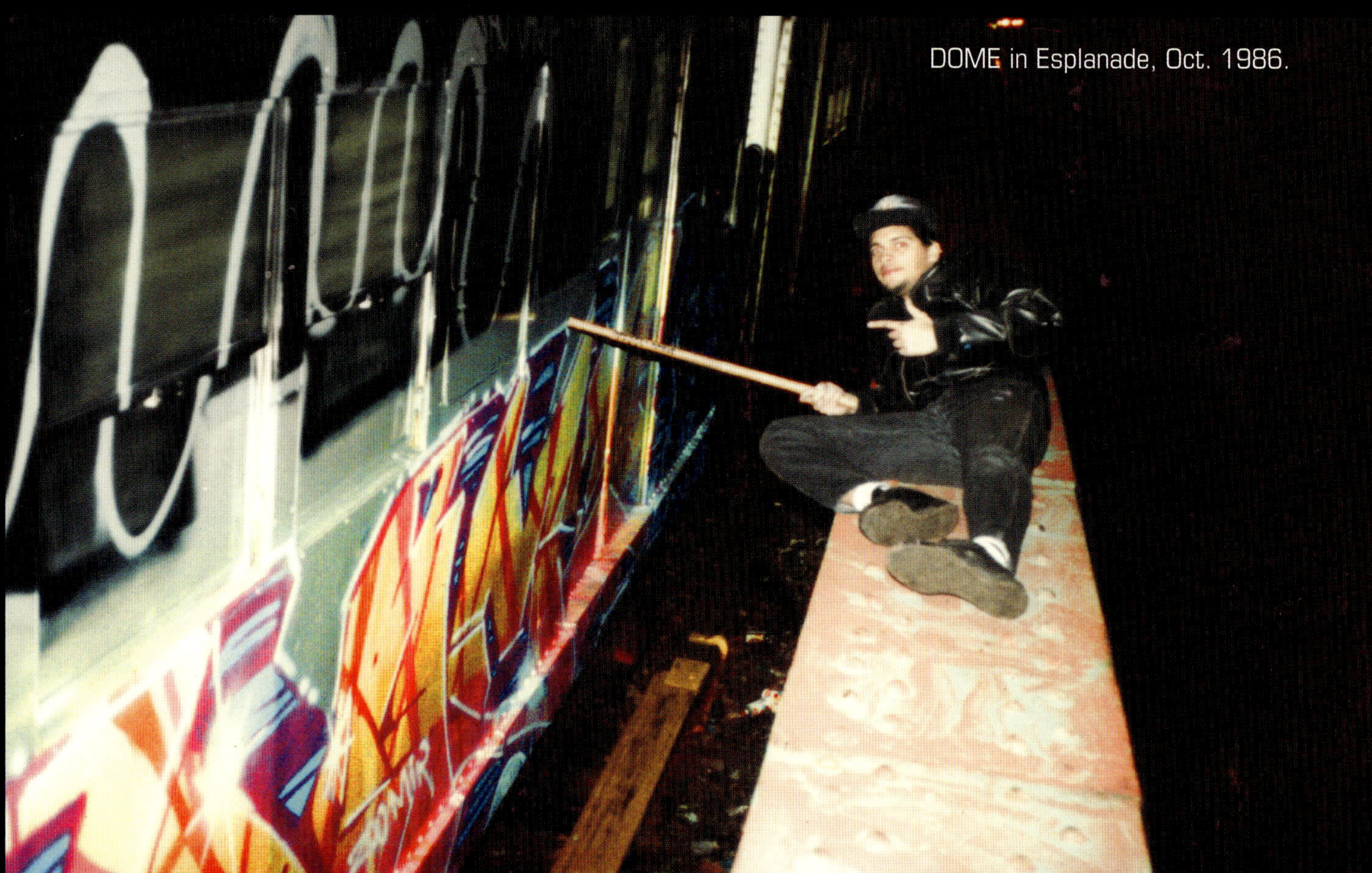
DOME in Esplanade, Oct. 1986.

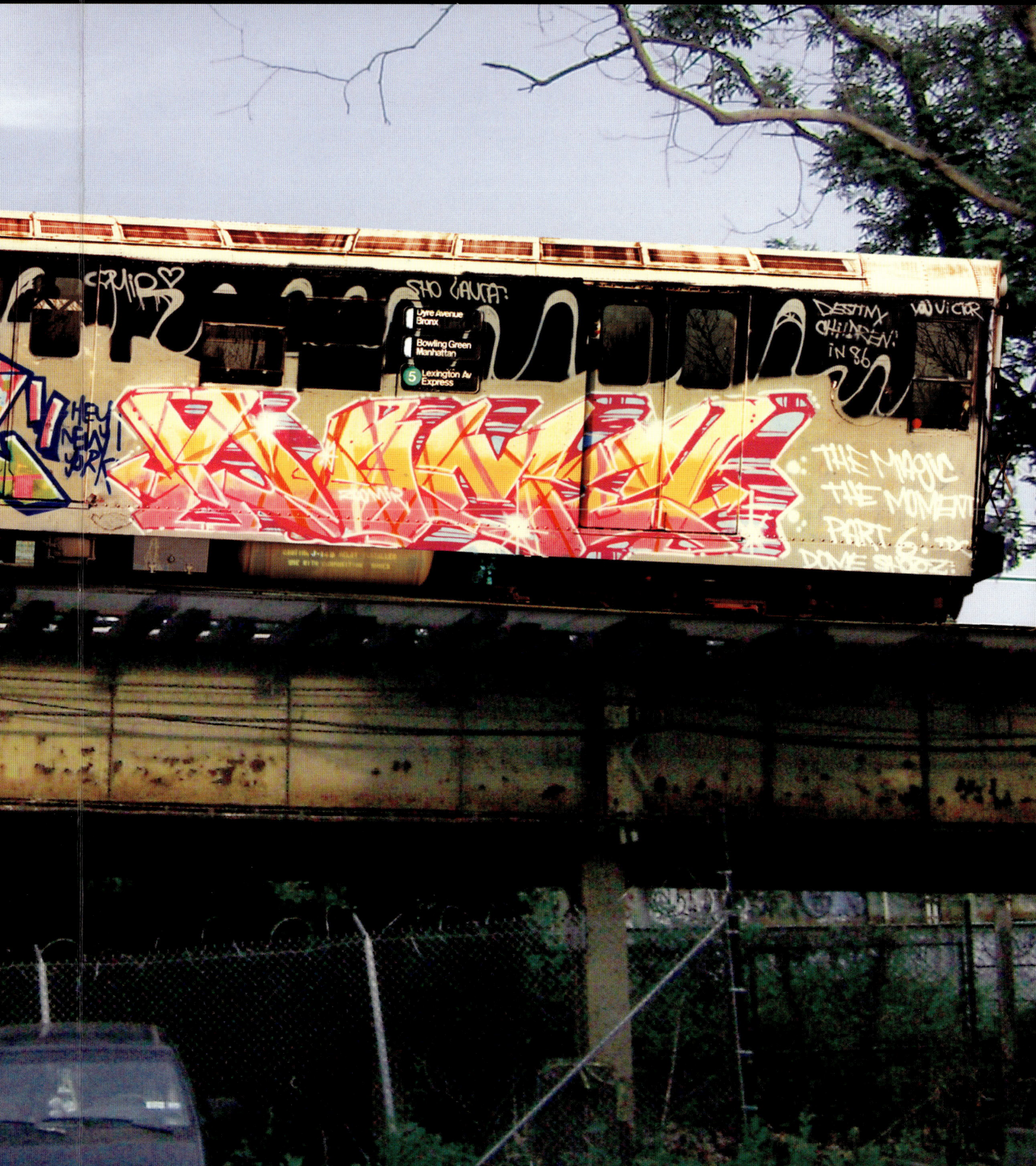

Dyre Avenue
Bronx
Bowling Green
Manhattan
5
Lexington Av
Express
HEY NEW YORK!
THE MAGIC
THE MOMENT
PART 6

"AIDS IS A CHEMICAL WARFARE," 5 Train by ZOO, DC3, and SHO, Aug. 1987…"AND THEN WE CAME!!"

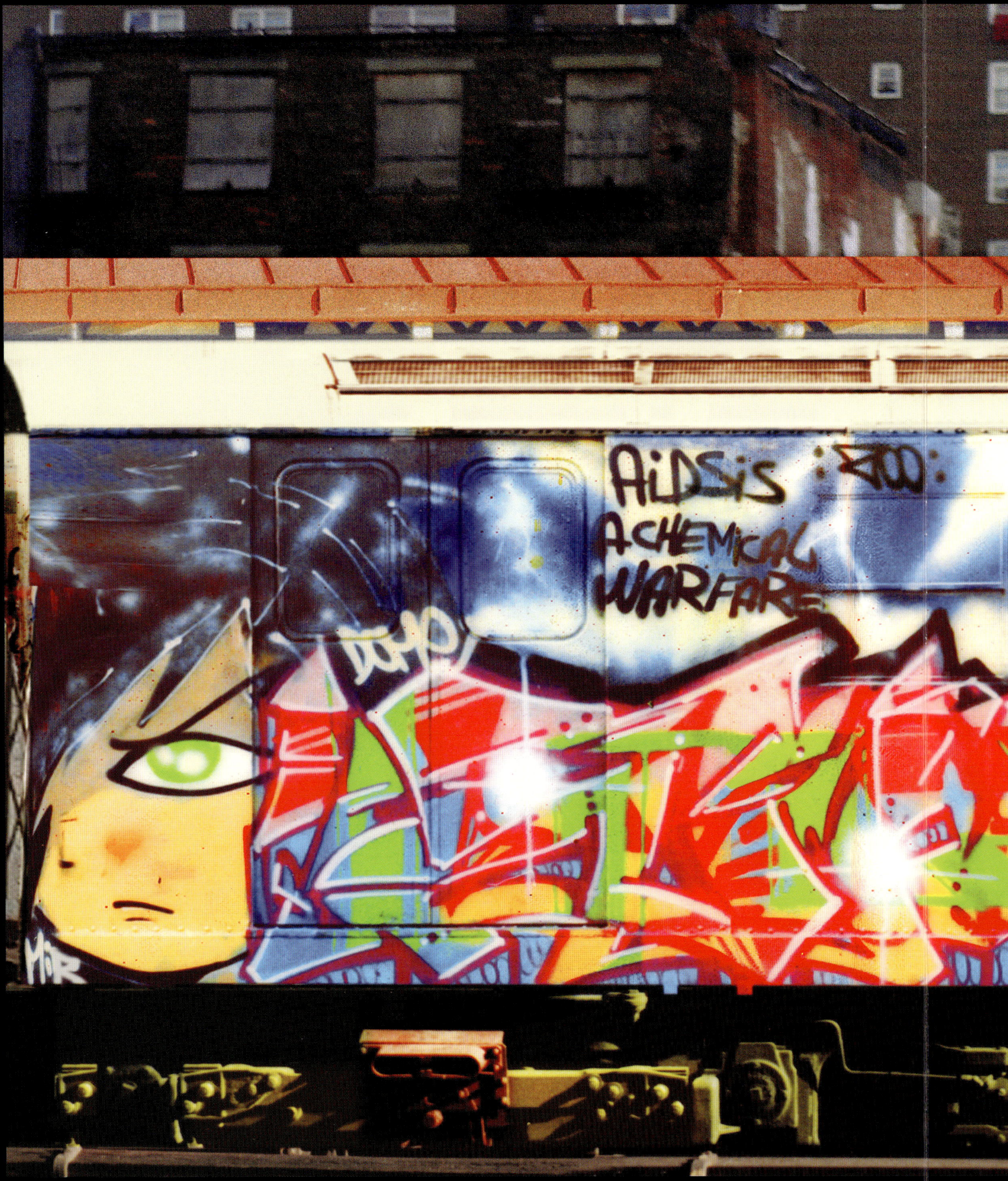

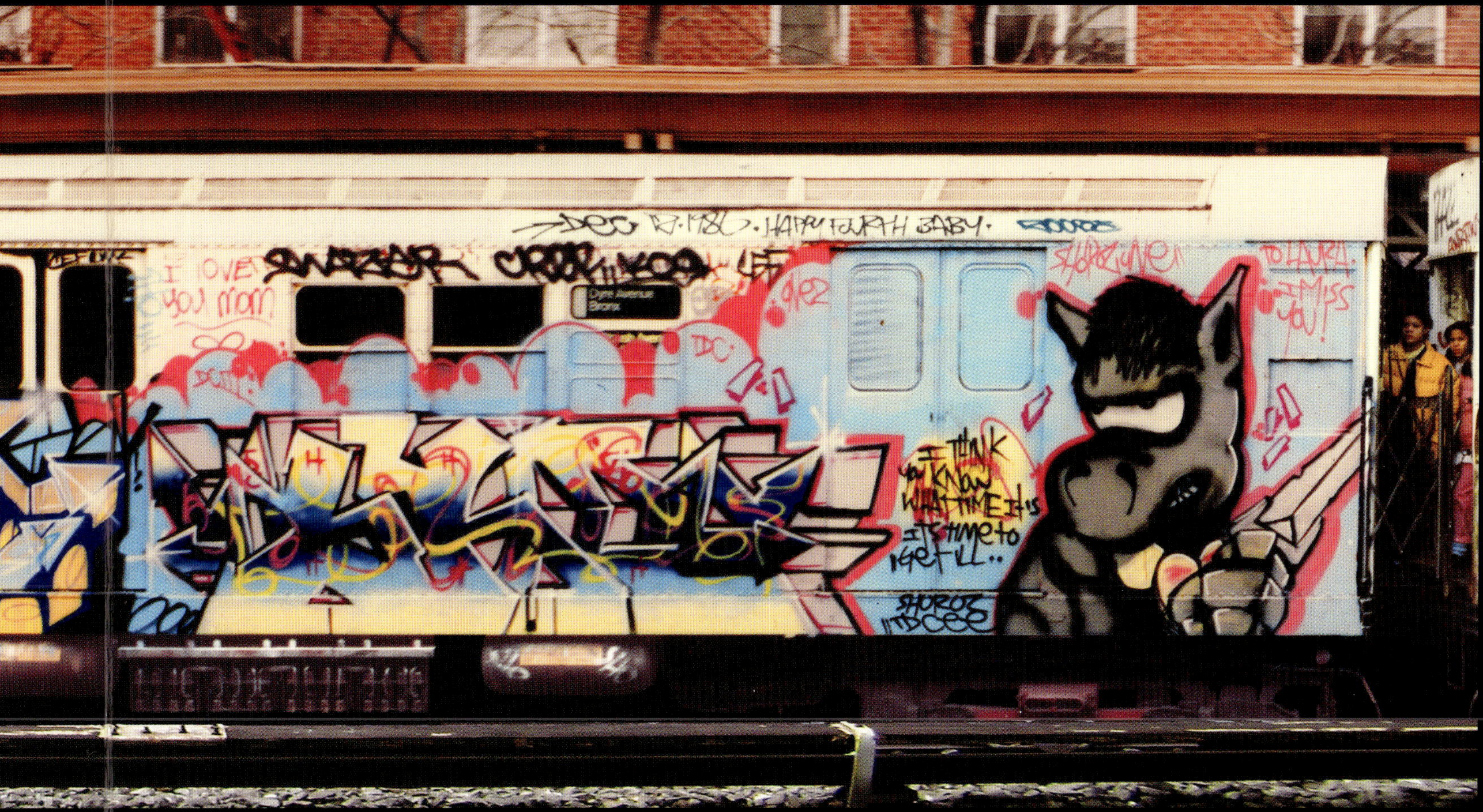

SHOROZ TDCEE, "I THINK YOU KNOW WHAT TIME IT IS, IT'S TIME TO GET ILL."

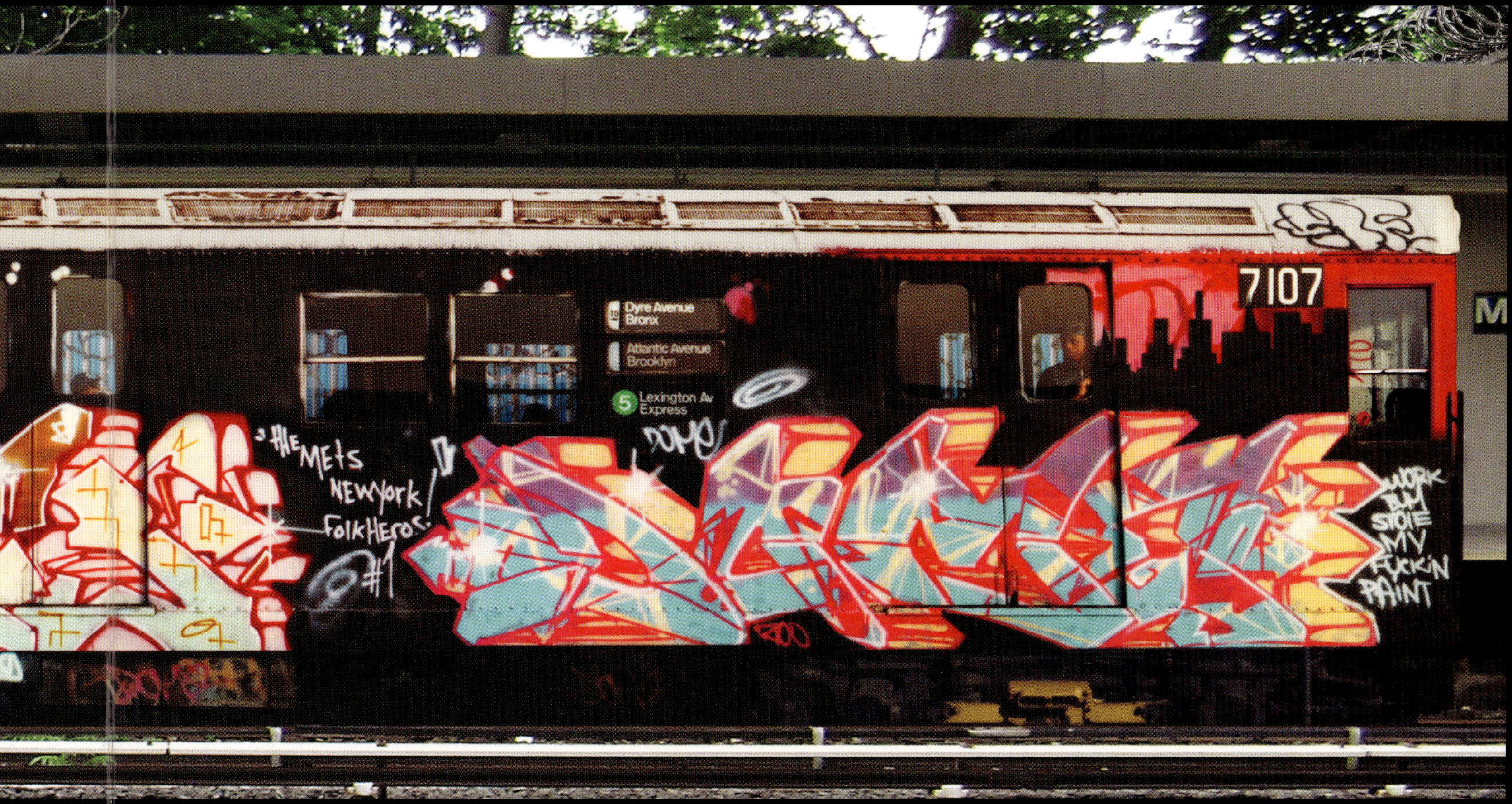

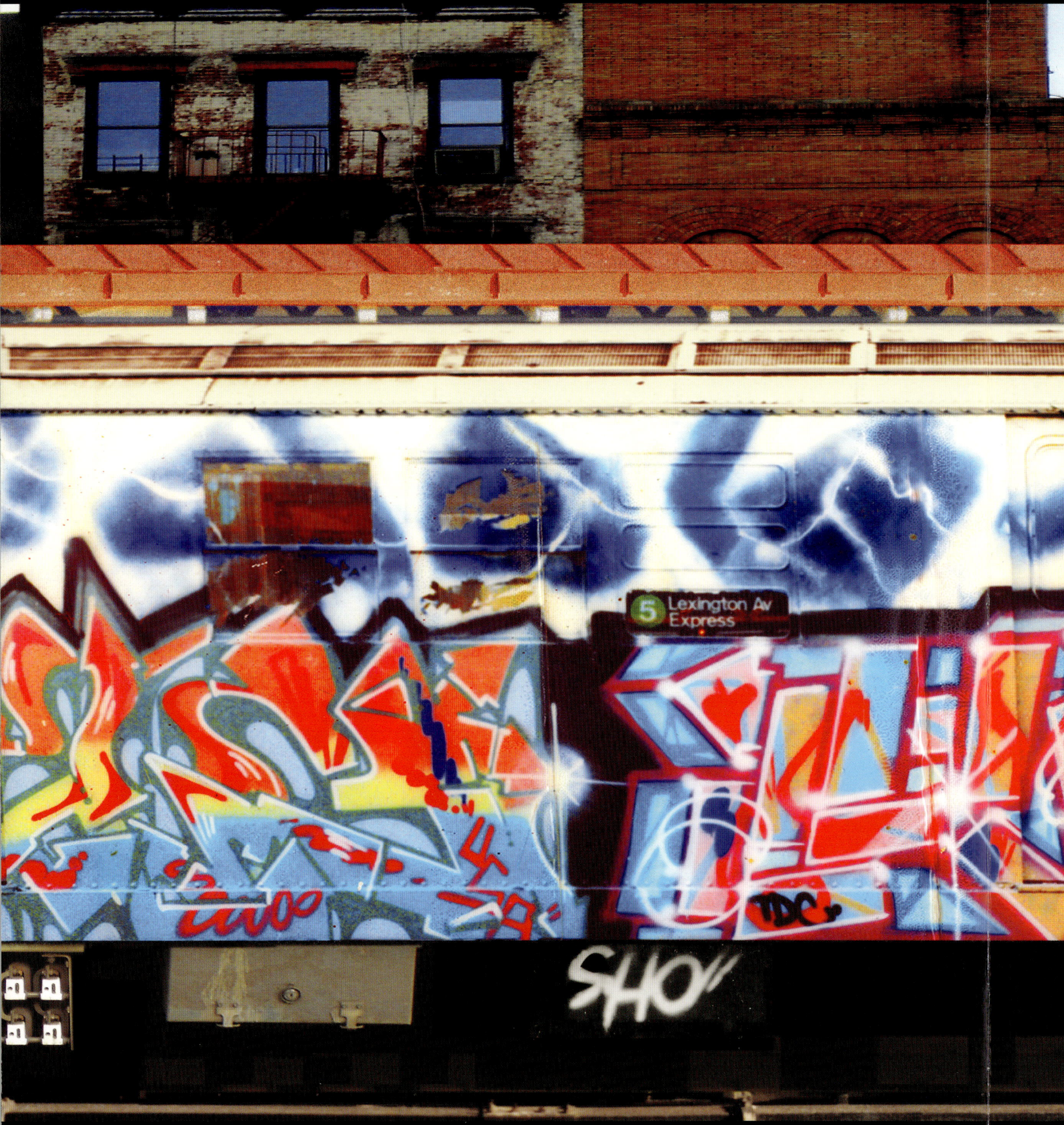

The fu

CHAPTER 2

Early Experiences in Esplanade.

DC and ME2.

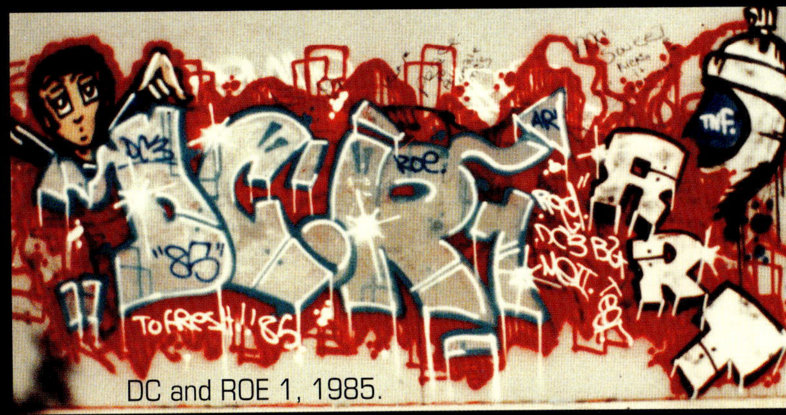

DC and ROE 1, 1985.

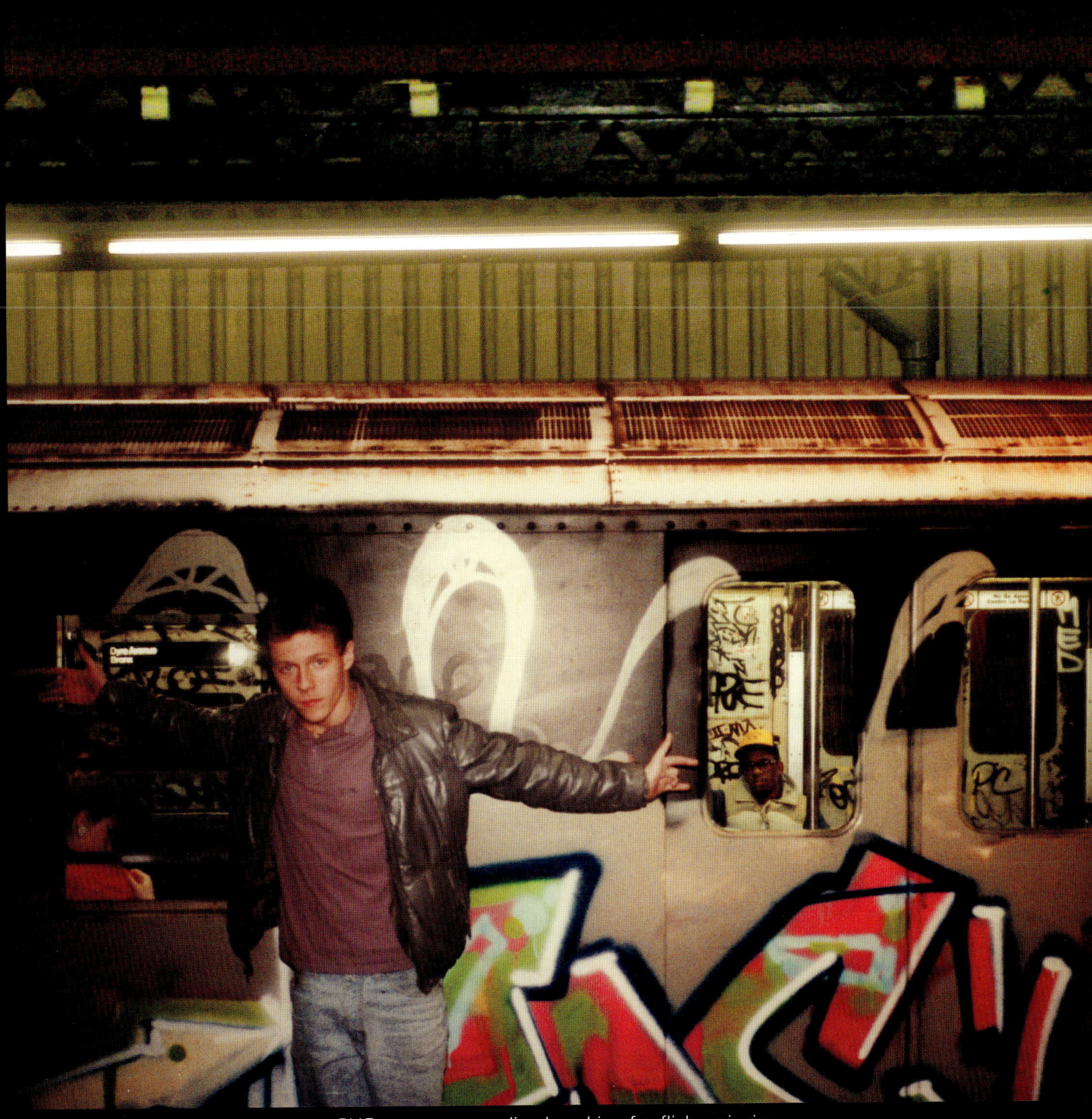

SHO on a never-ending benching for flicks mission.

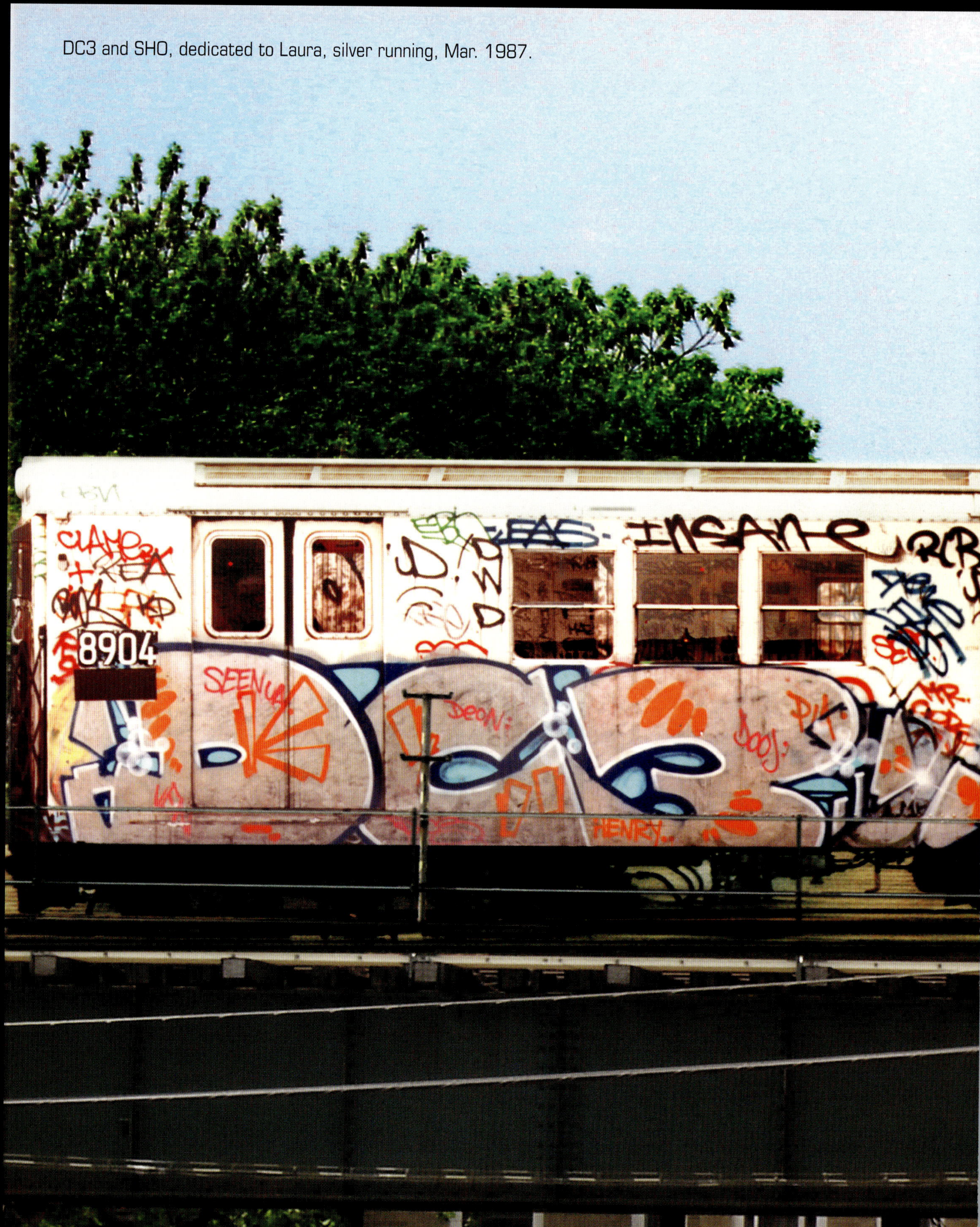

DC3 and SHO, dedicated to Laura, silver running, Mar. 1987.

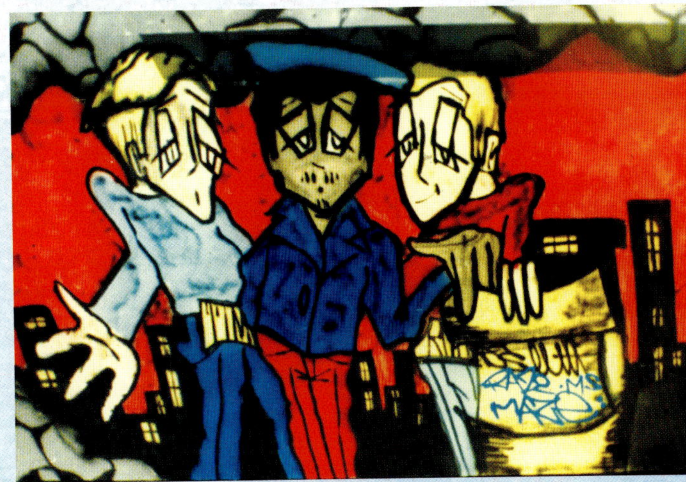

DCEE3, RAZE, and MAZE, The 3 Amigos Bracos, Freeport, NY, 1985.

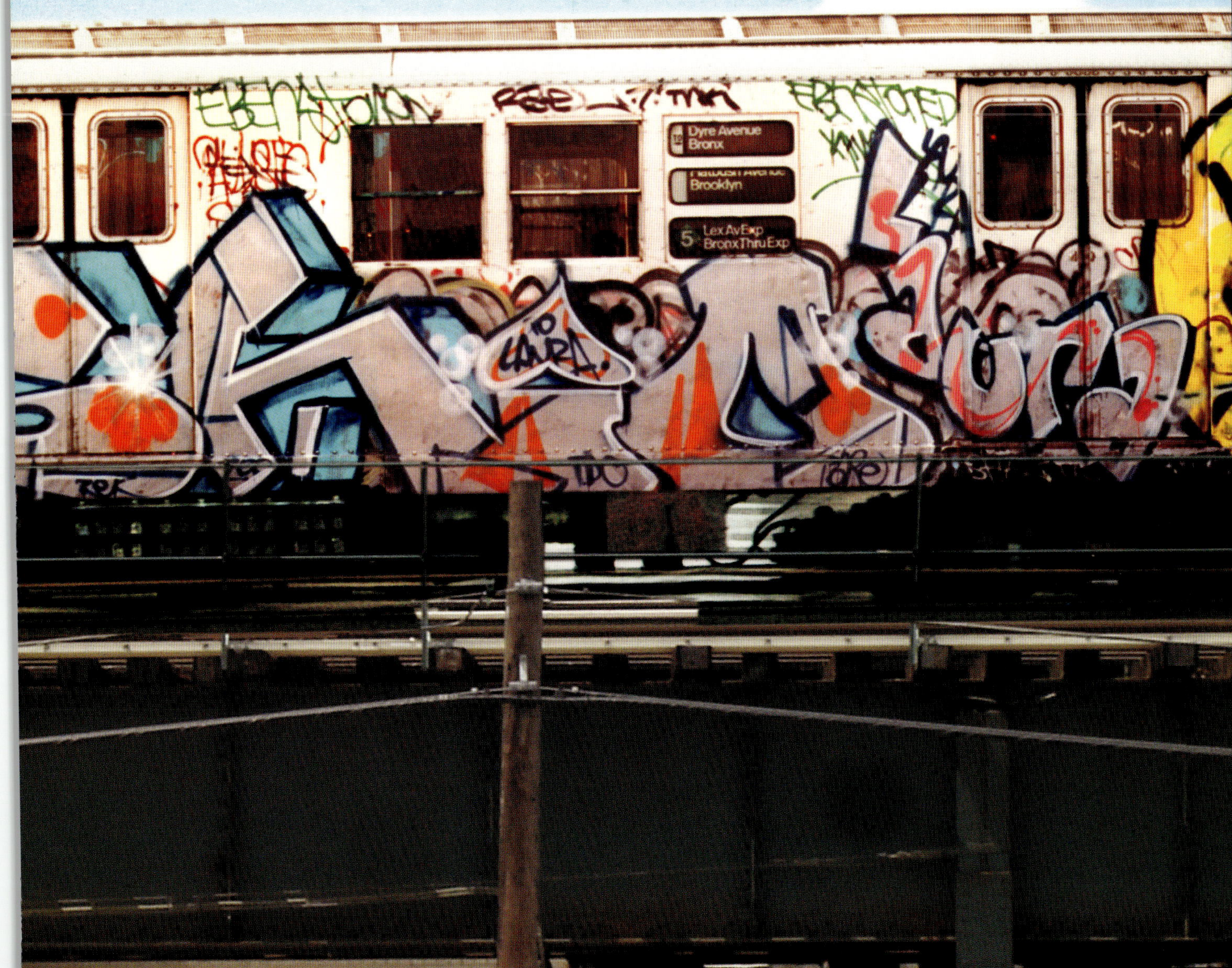

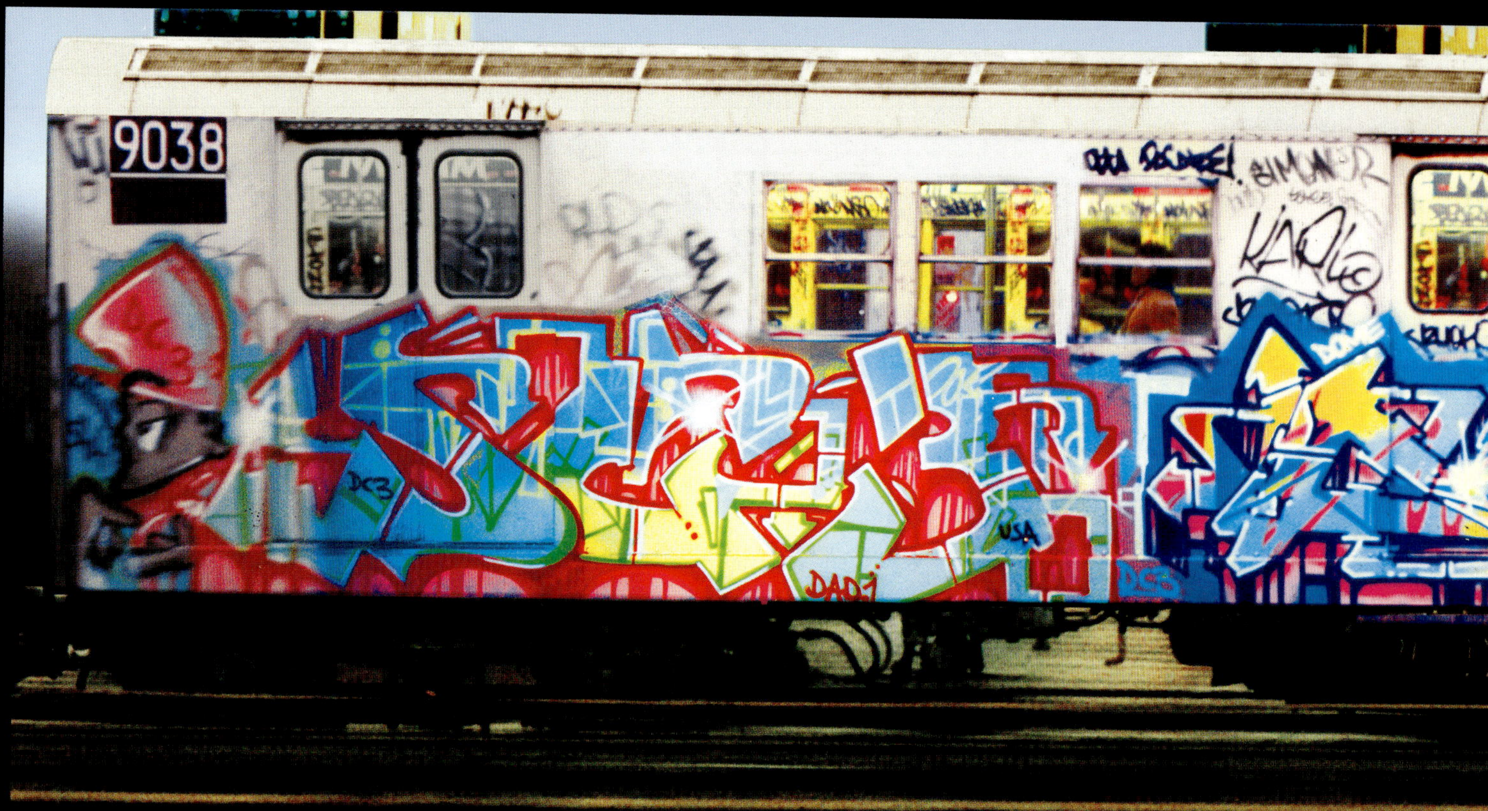

DC3 USA, DOME, and SHO TDC, 5 Train, Jan. 1987.

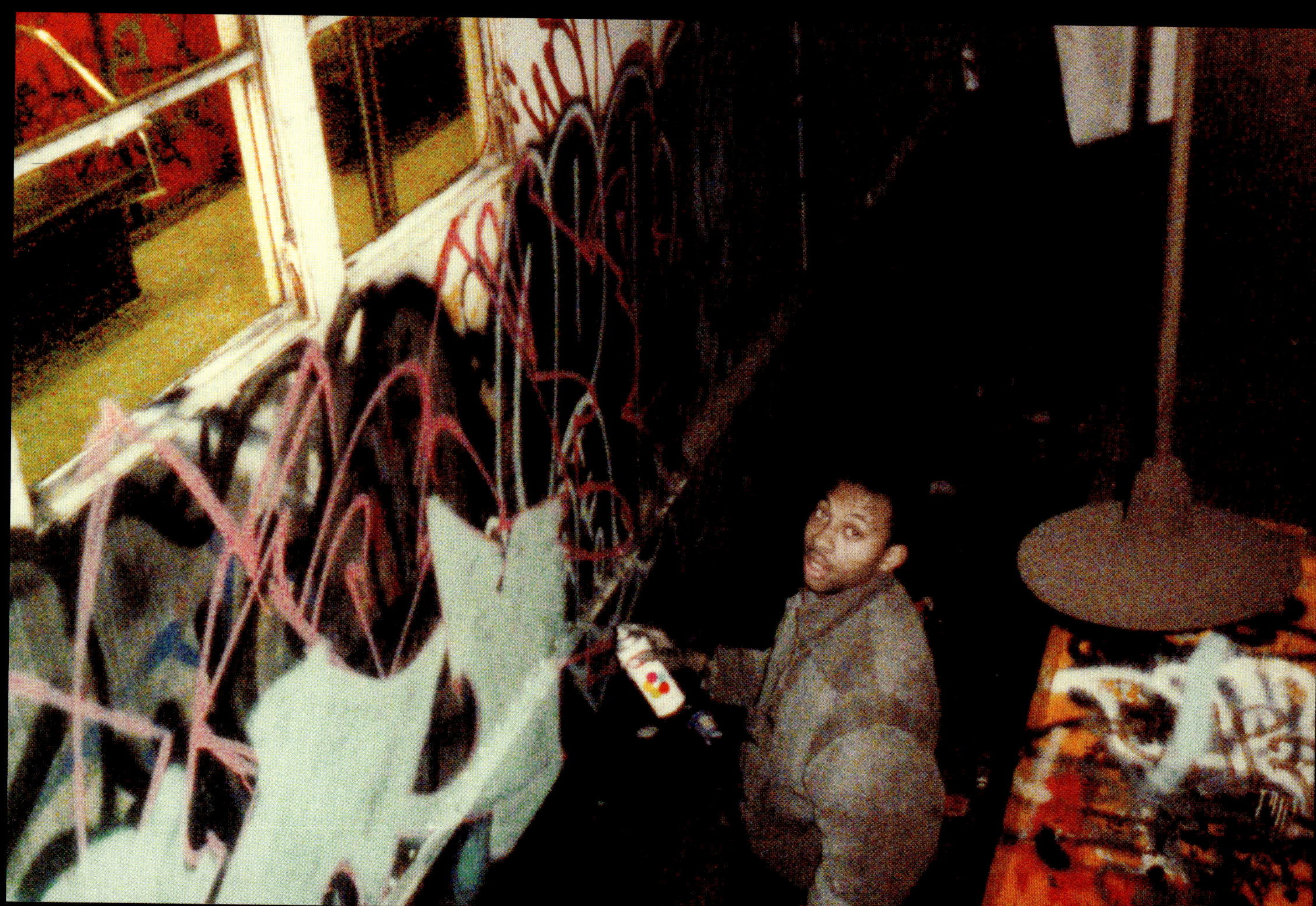

DC3 on his third piece of the night.

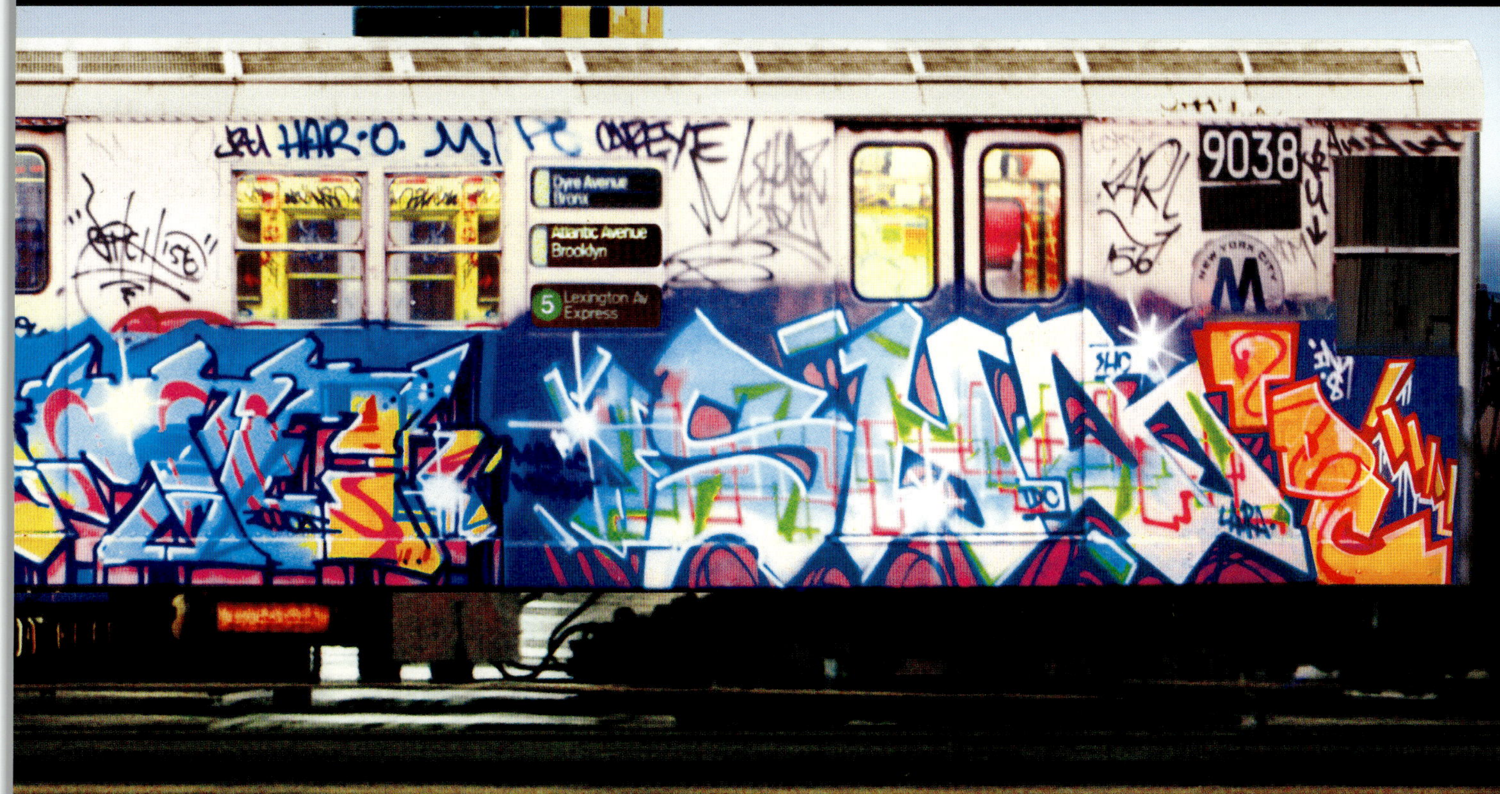

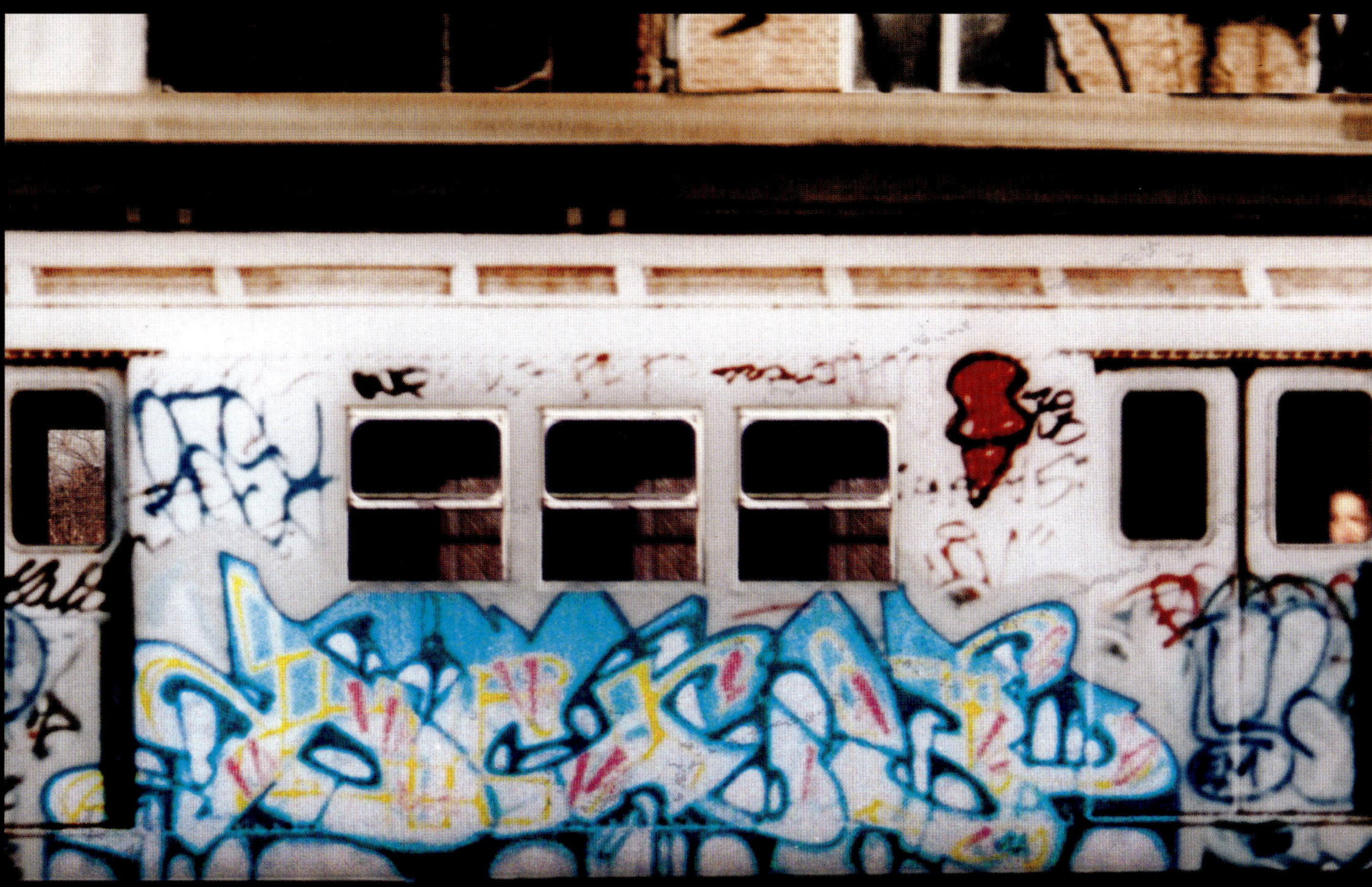

DC3 piece running.

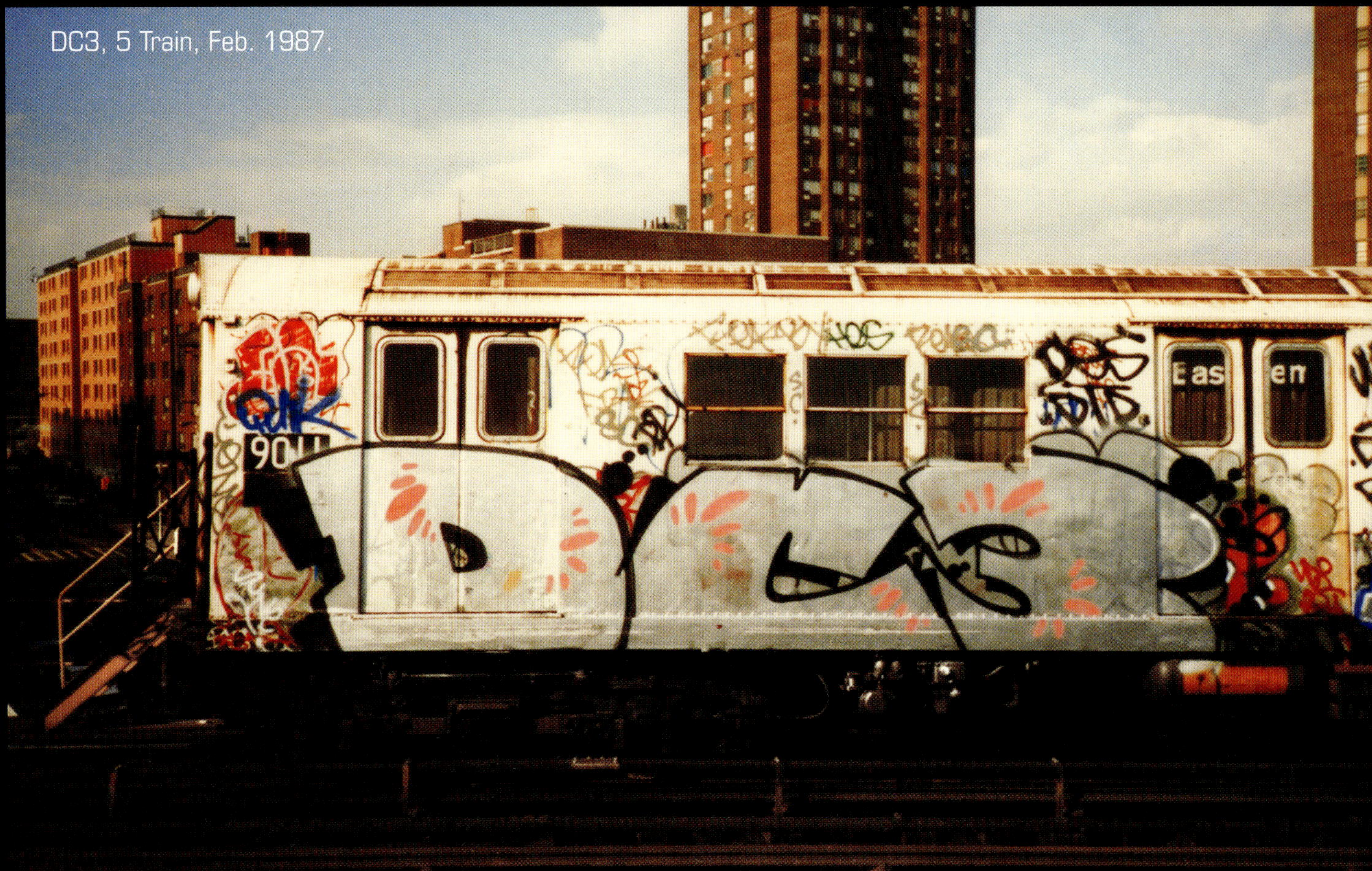
DC3, 5 Train, Feb. 1987.

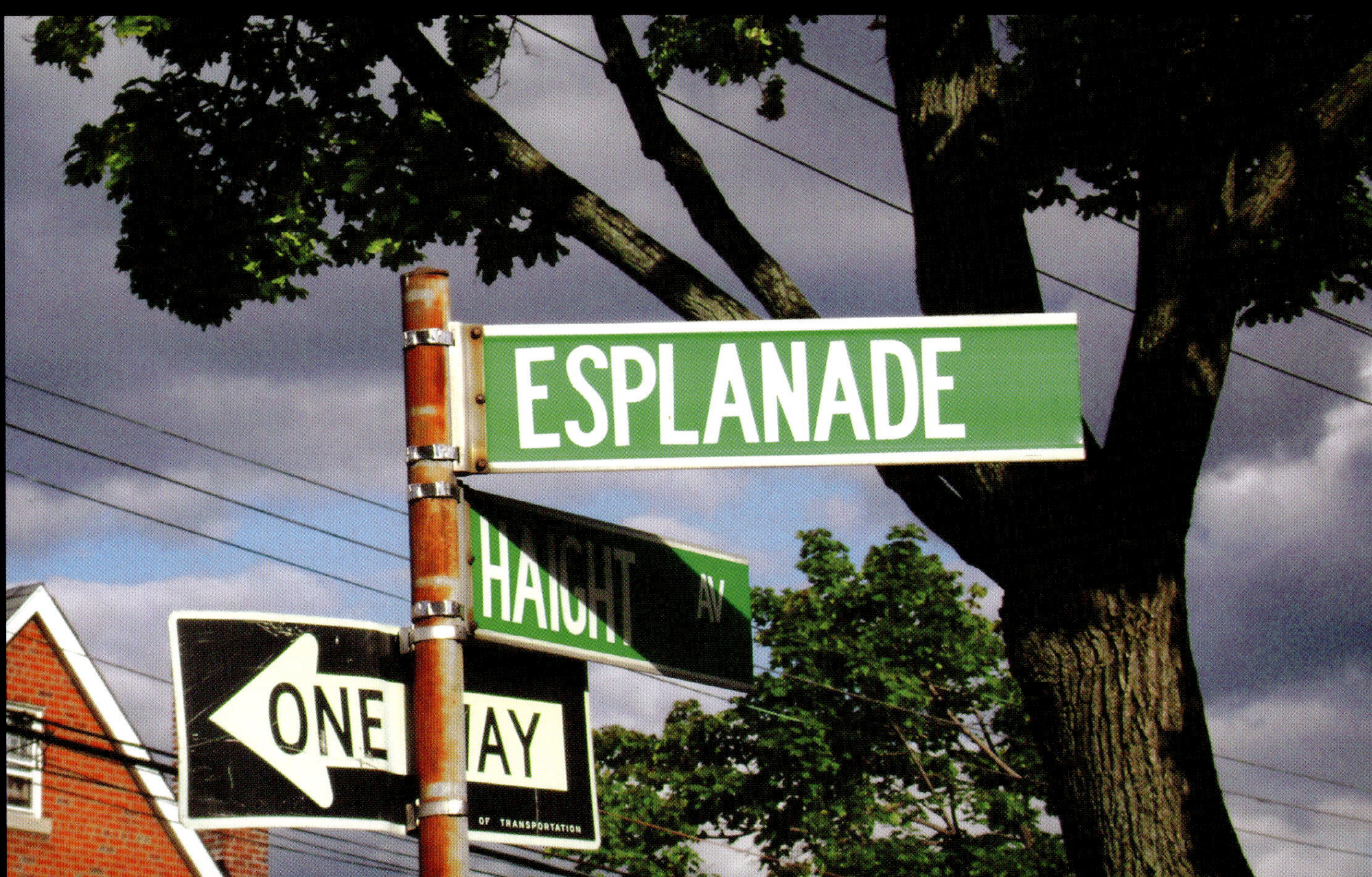

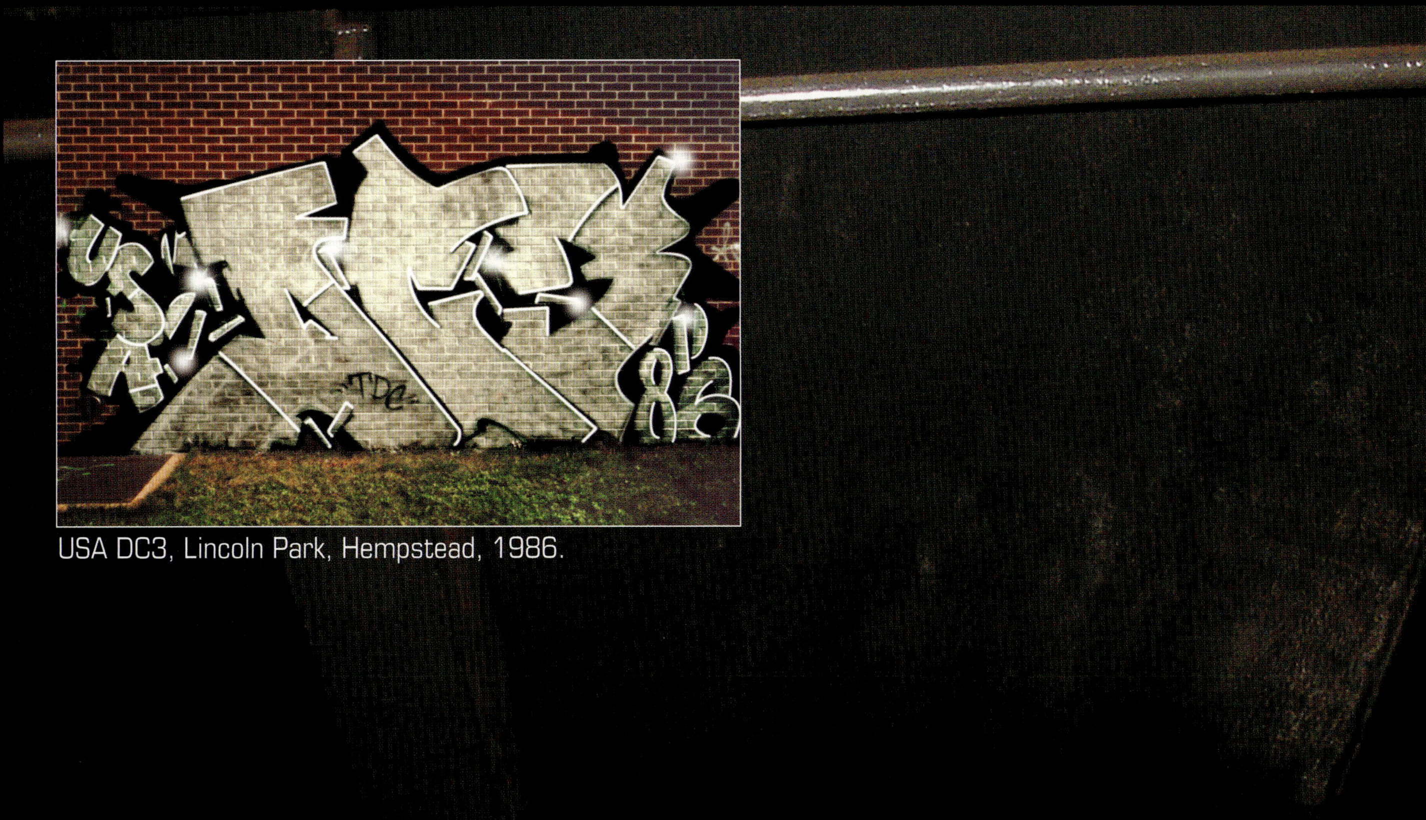

USA DC3, Lincoln Park, Hempstead, 1986.

ZOOROC catching Uni tags.

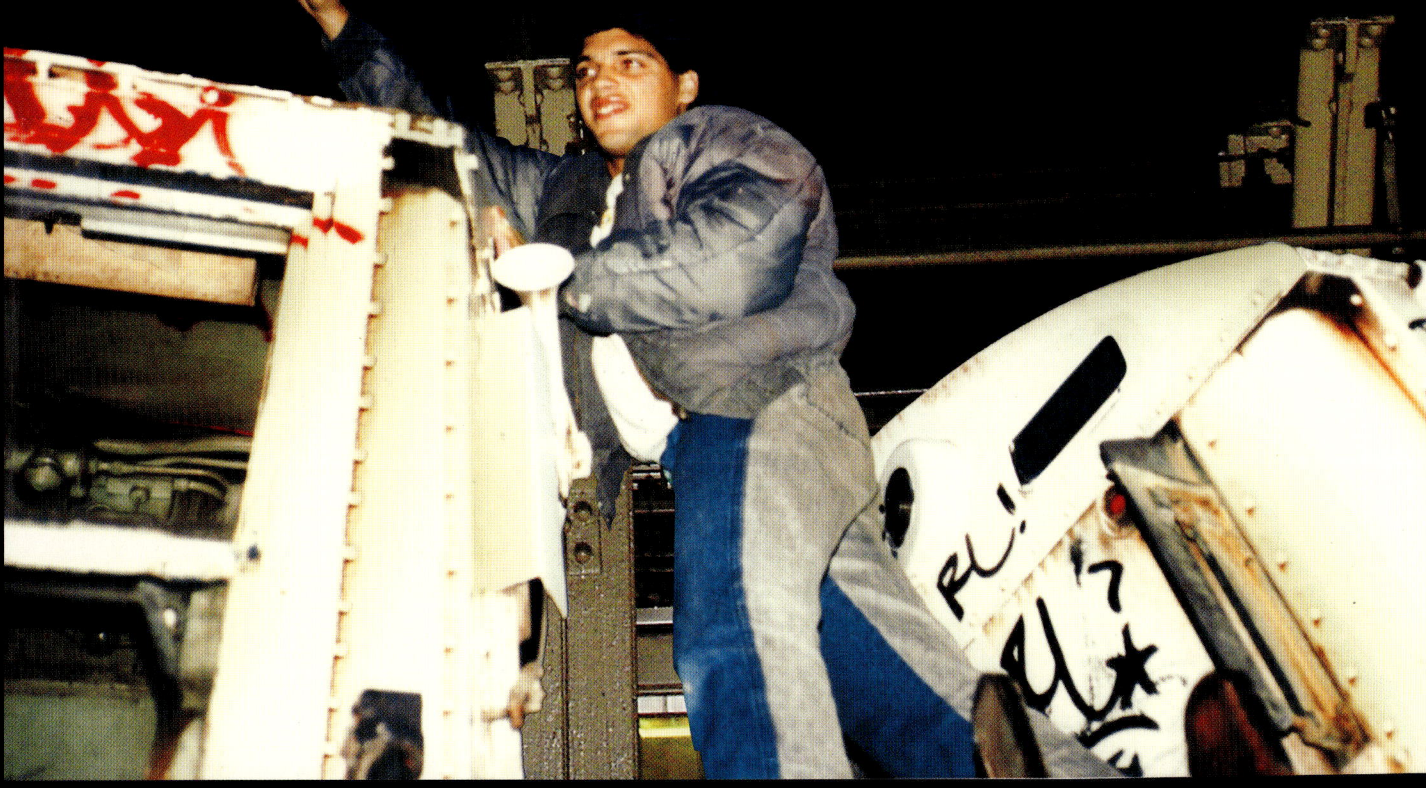

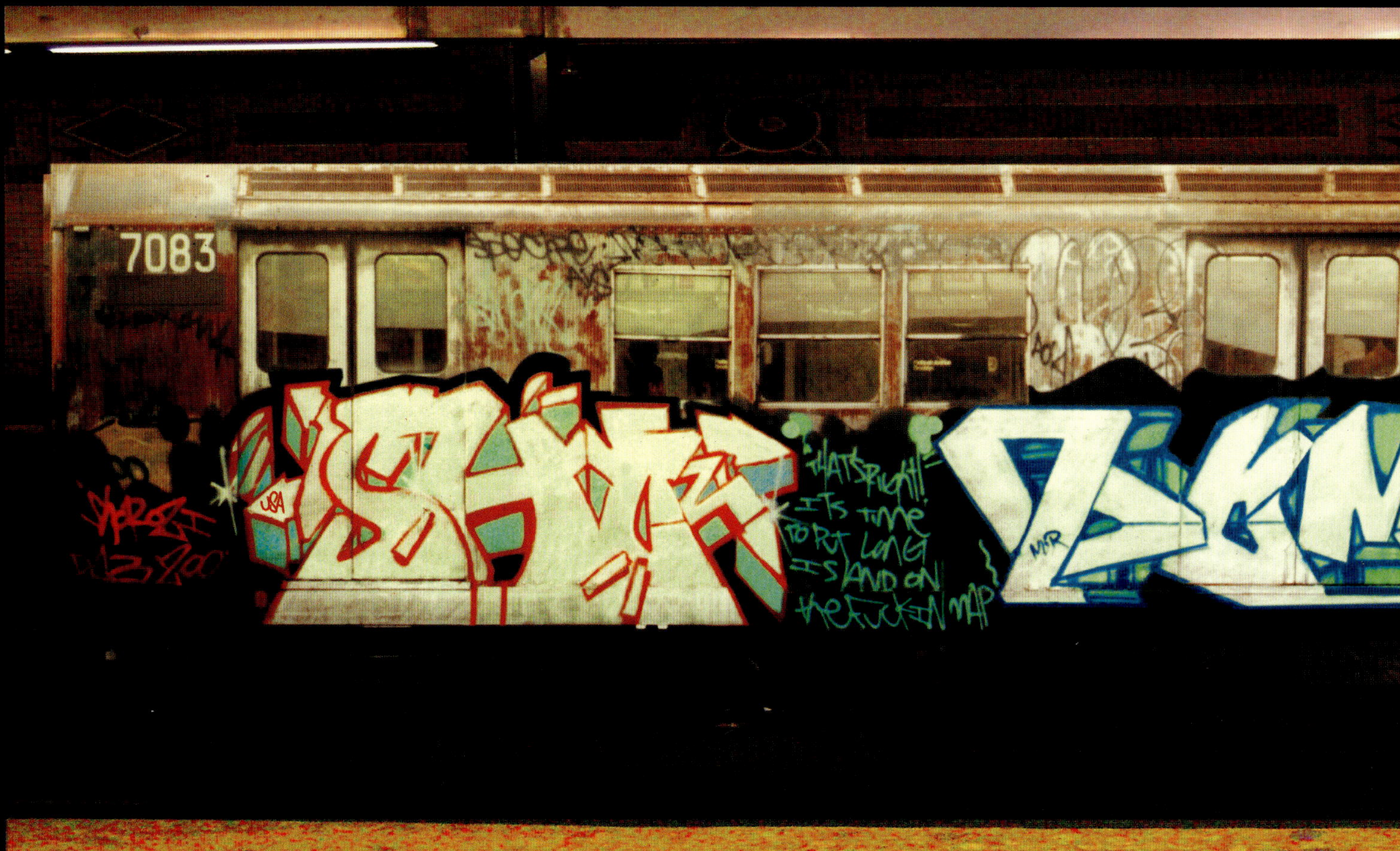

SHO, DOME, and DC3 at Grand Concourse, 5 Train, Nov. 1986.

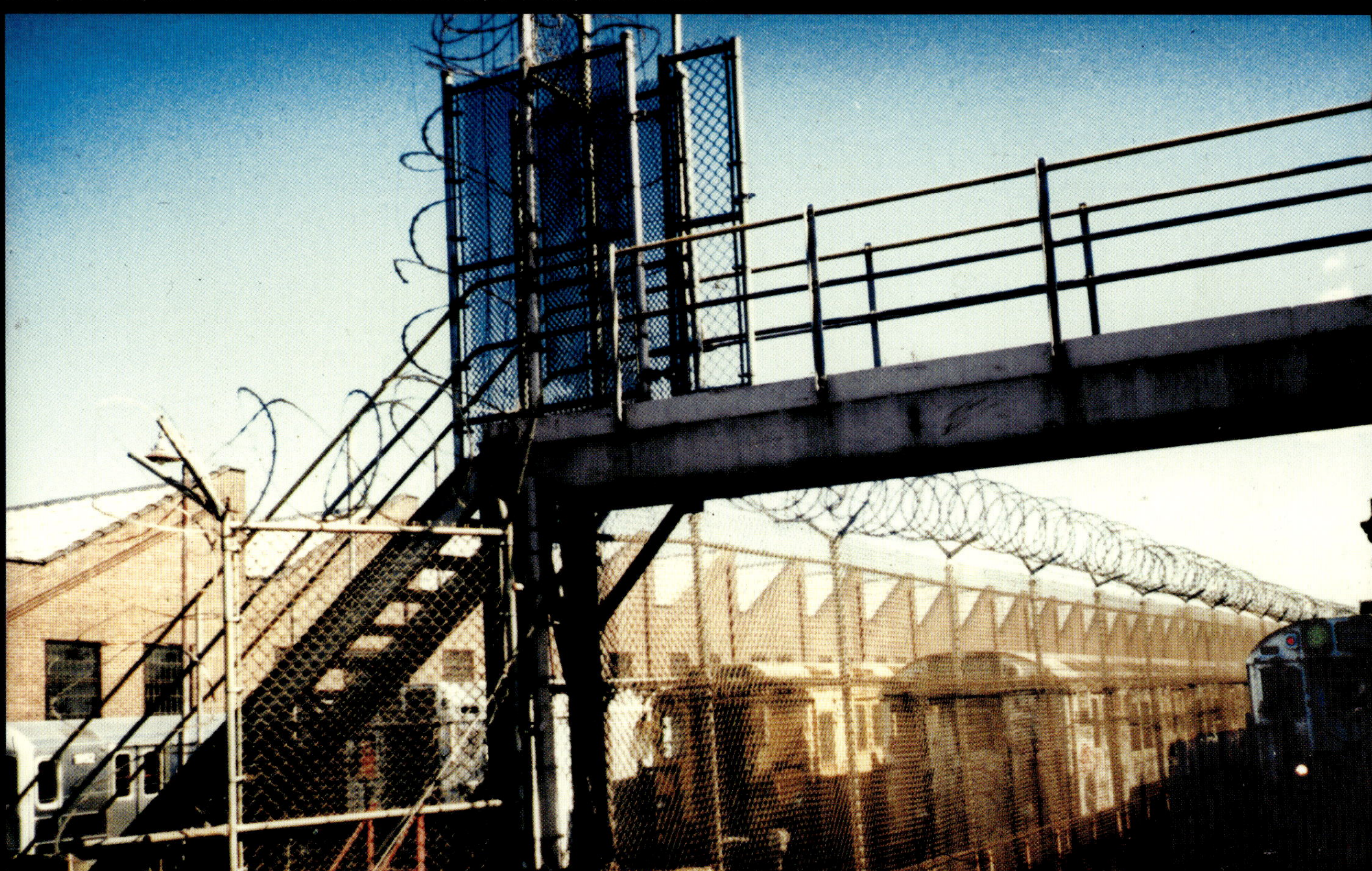

180th St. Yard and Station.

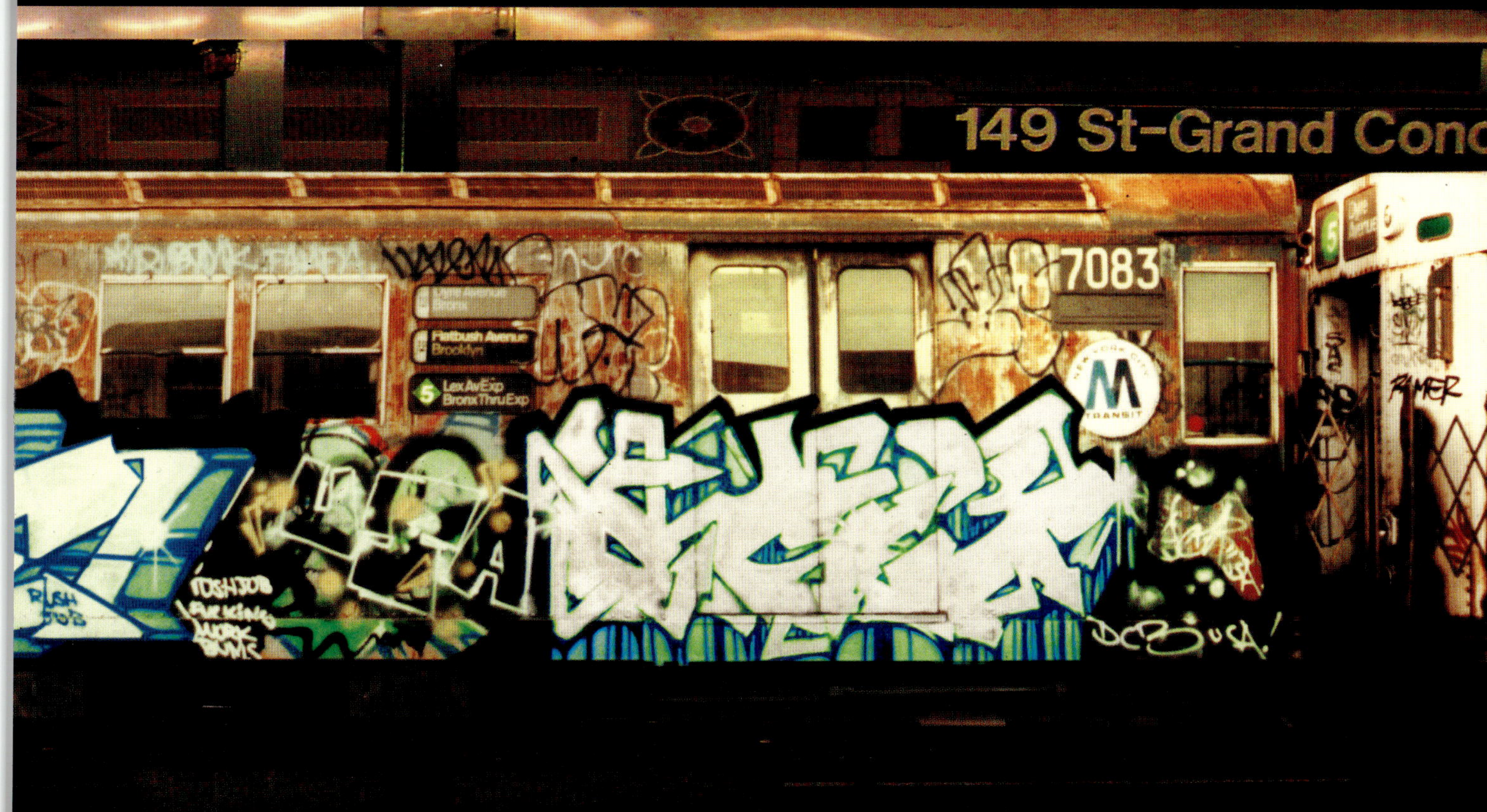

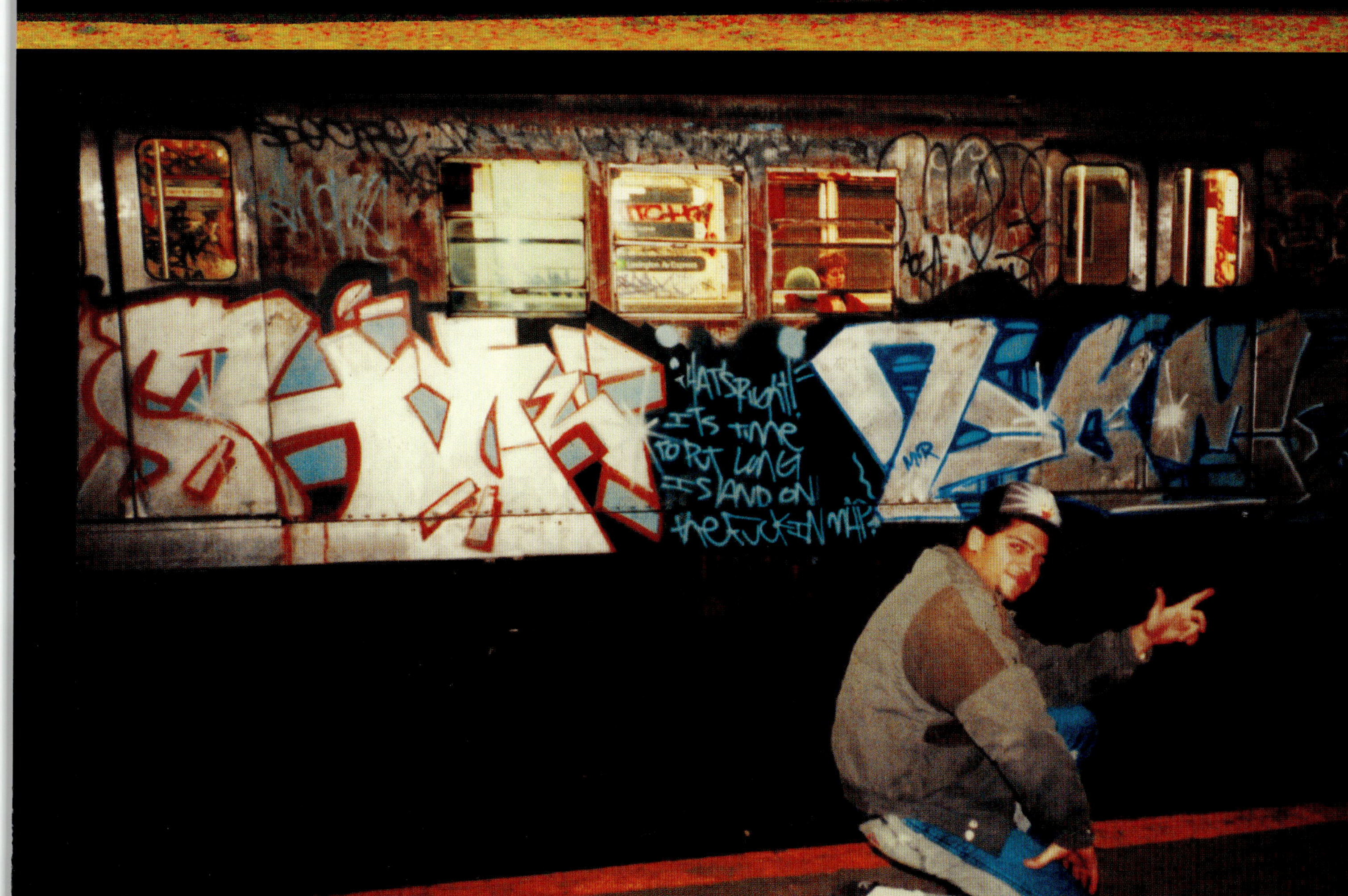

DOME chilling at the Writers Bench, 1986.

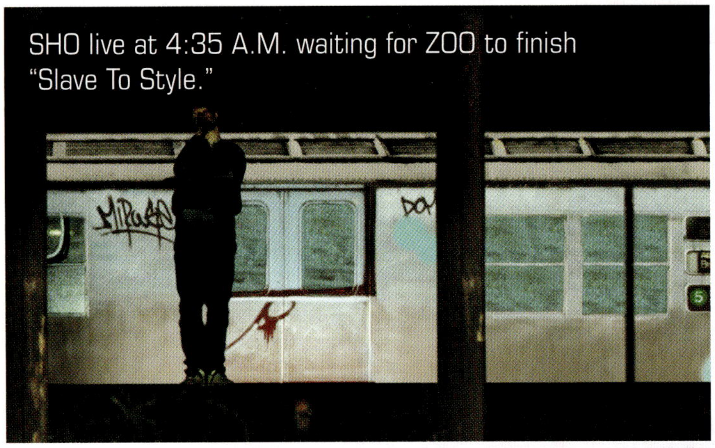

SHO live at 4:35 A.M. waiting for ZOO to finish "Slave To Style."

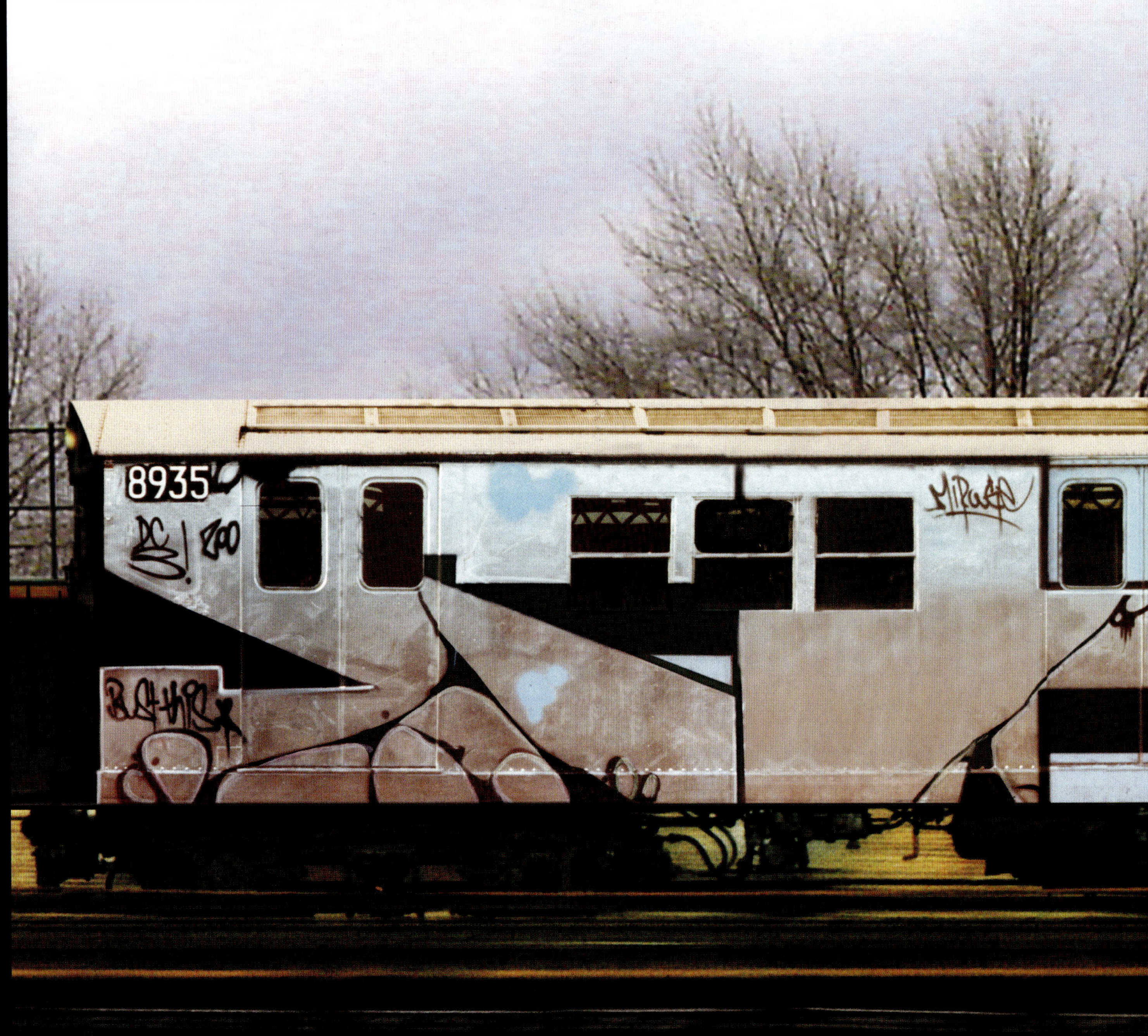

SHO, top-to-bottom silver 5 Train, April 21, 1987. Rocked in Esplanade Tunnels.

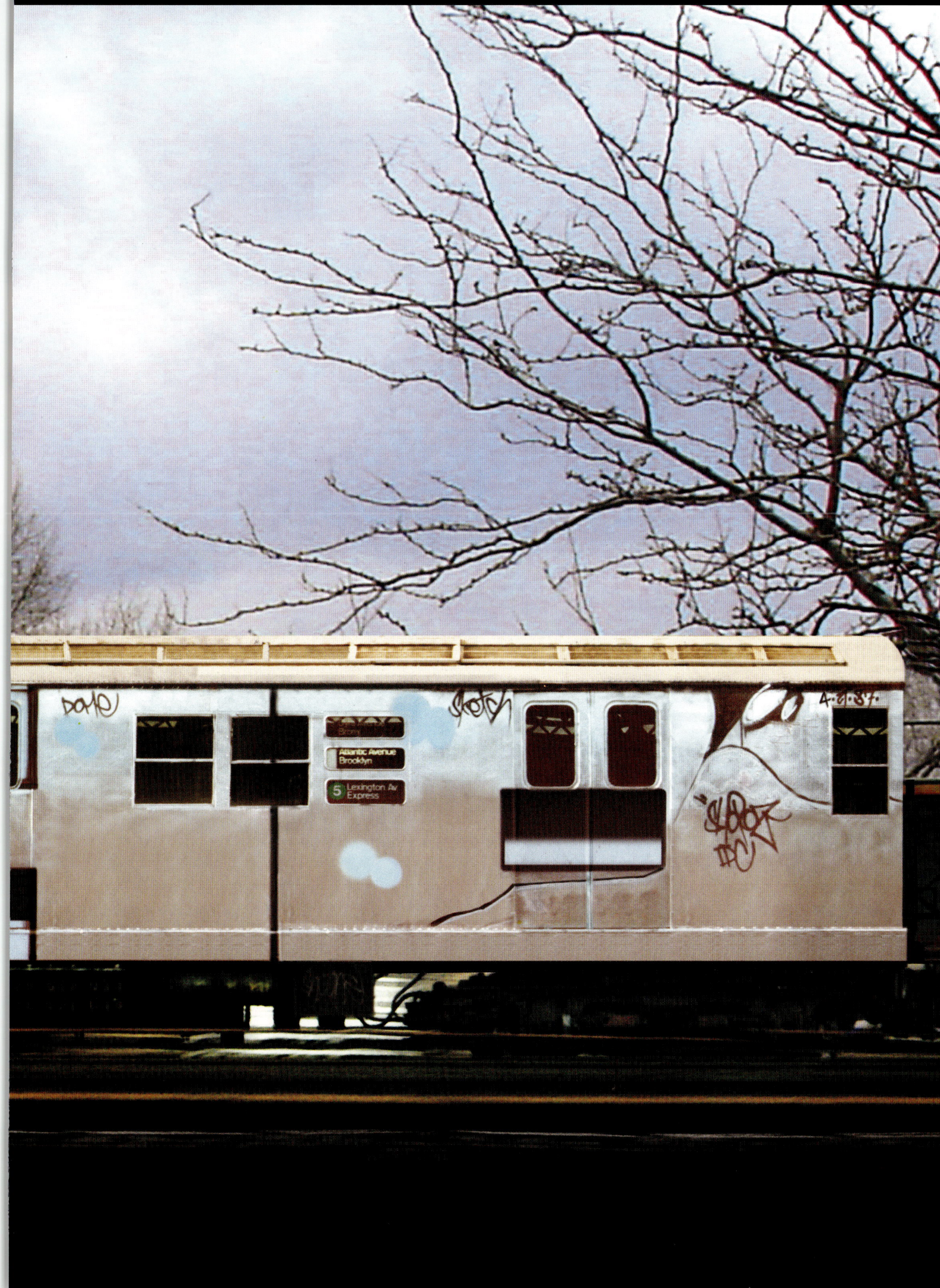
Atlantic Avenue
Brooklyn
5
Lexington Av
Express

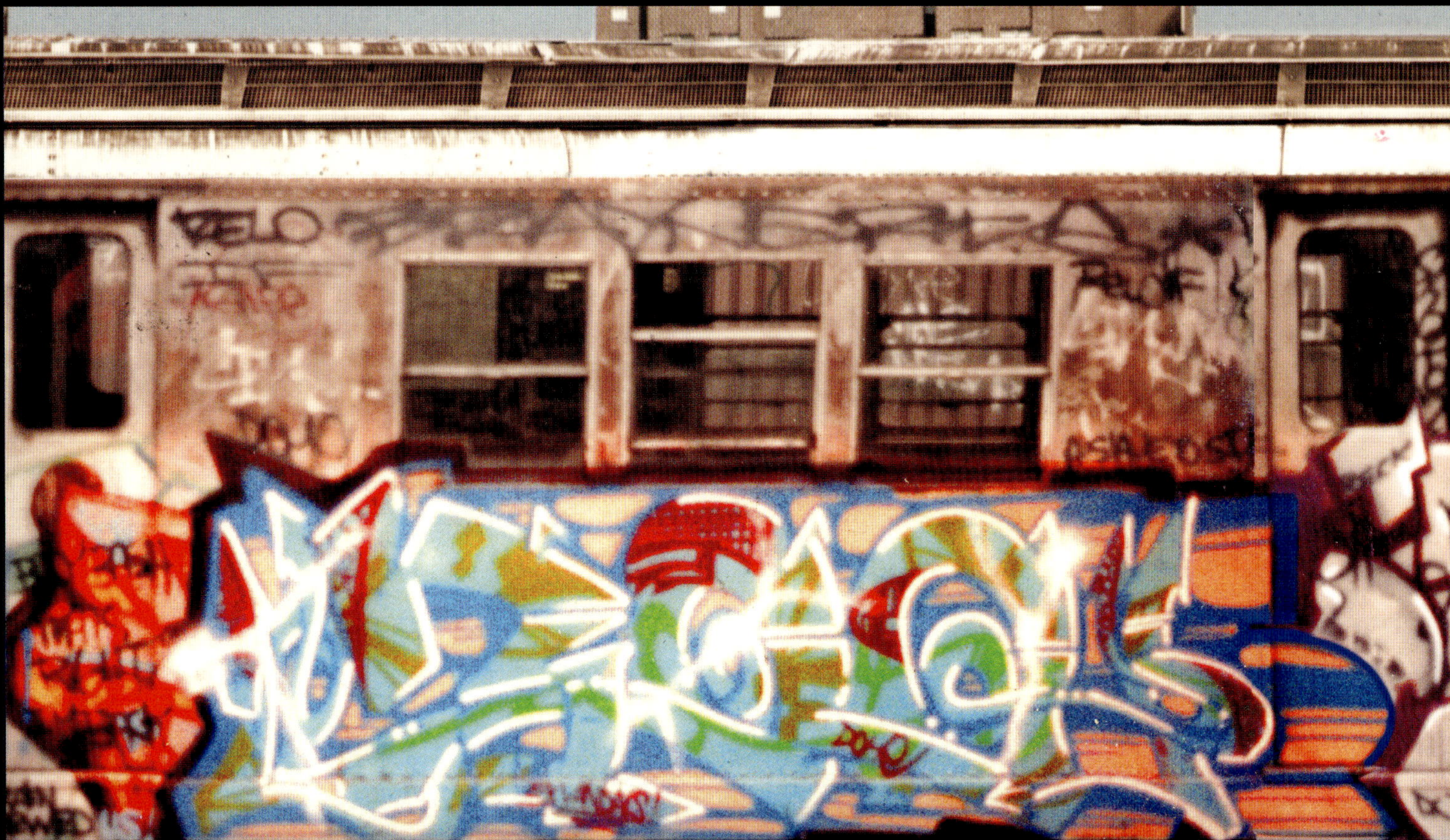

ZOO TDC SHO window-down rocked in broad daylight, Utica Tunnels, Brooklyn, NY, Apr. 1987.

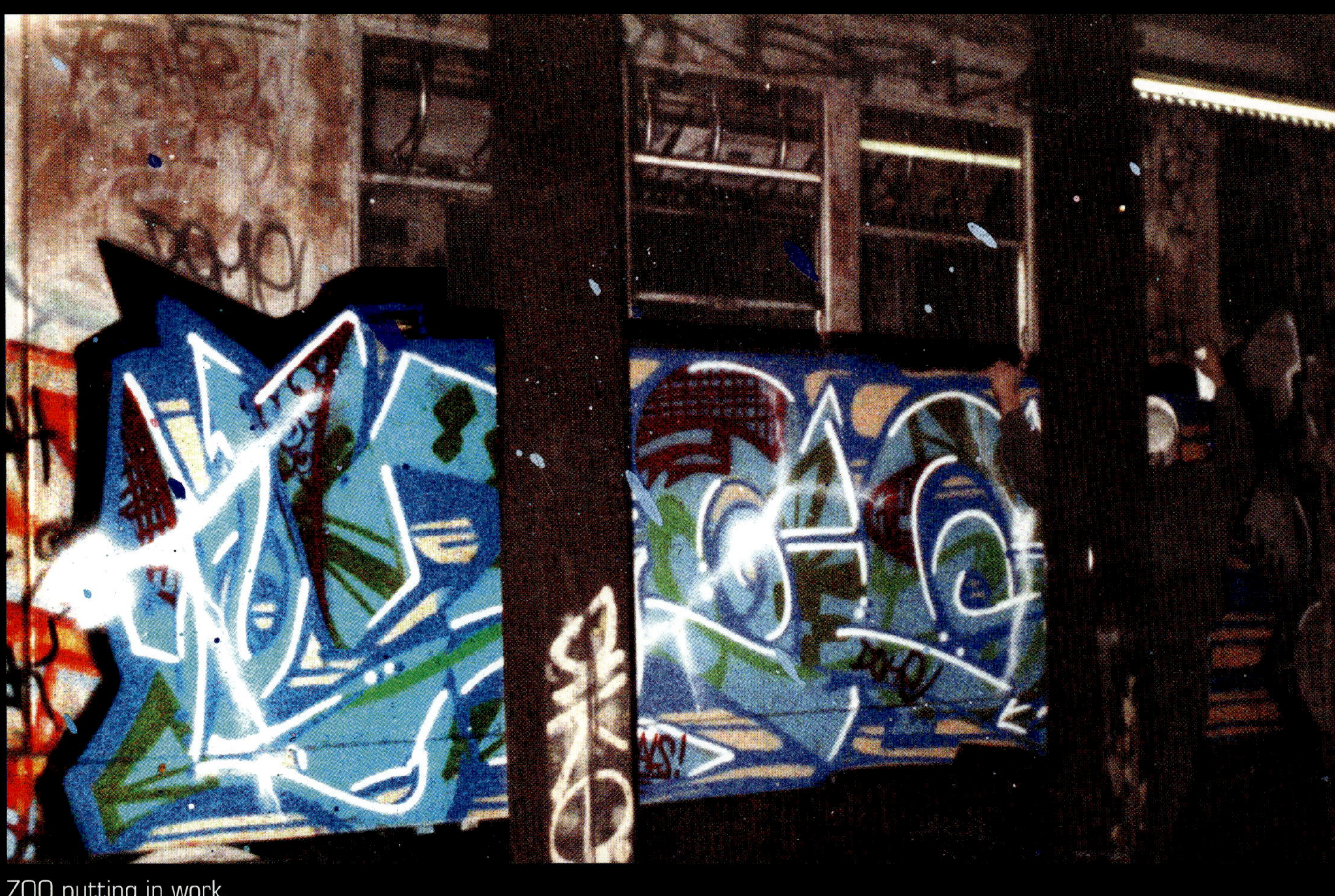

ZOO putting in work.

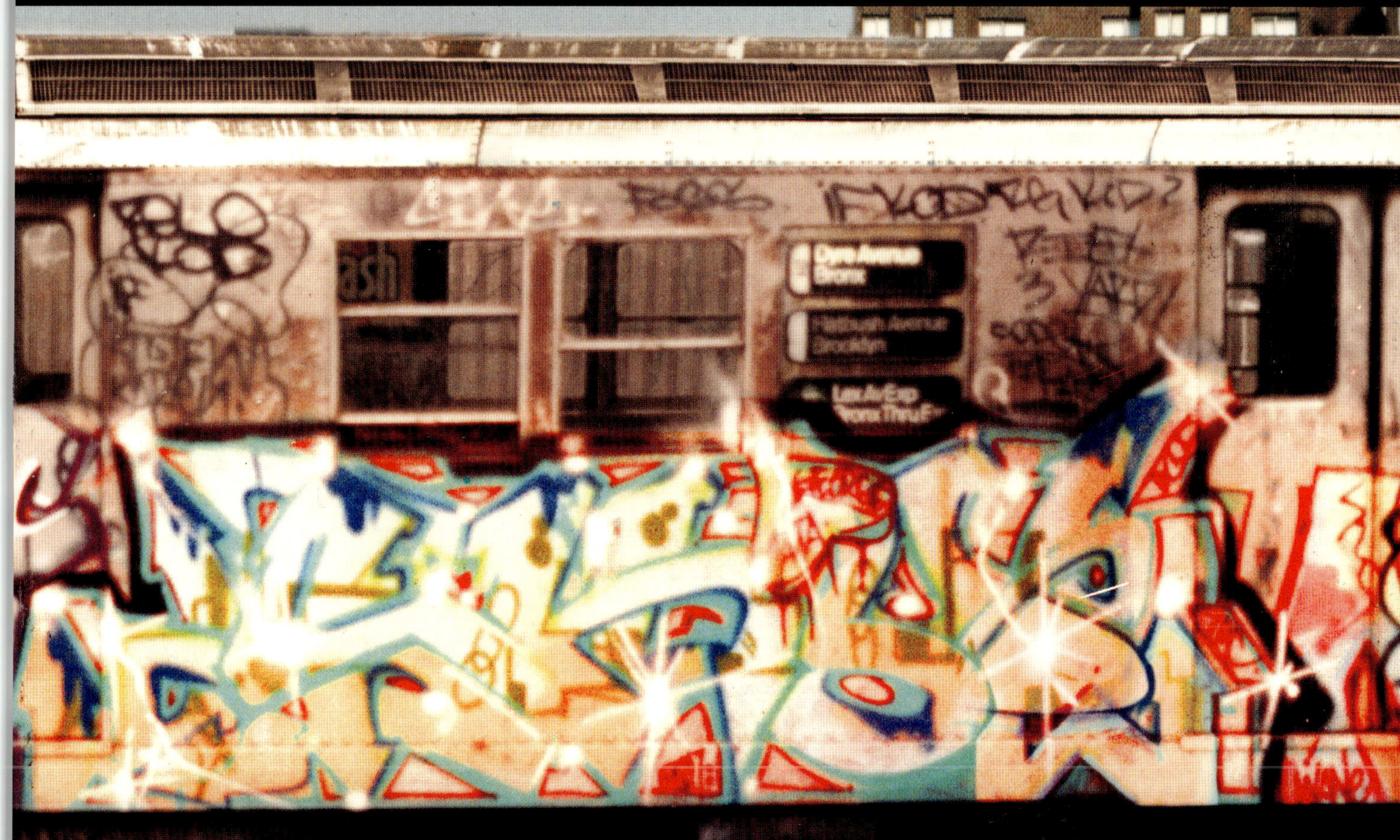

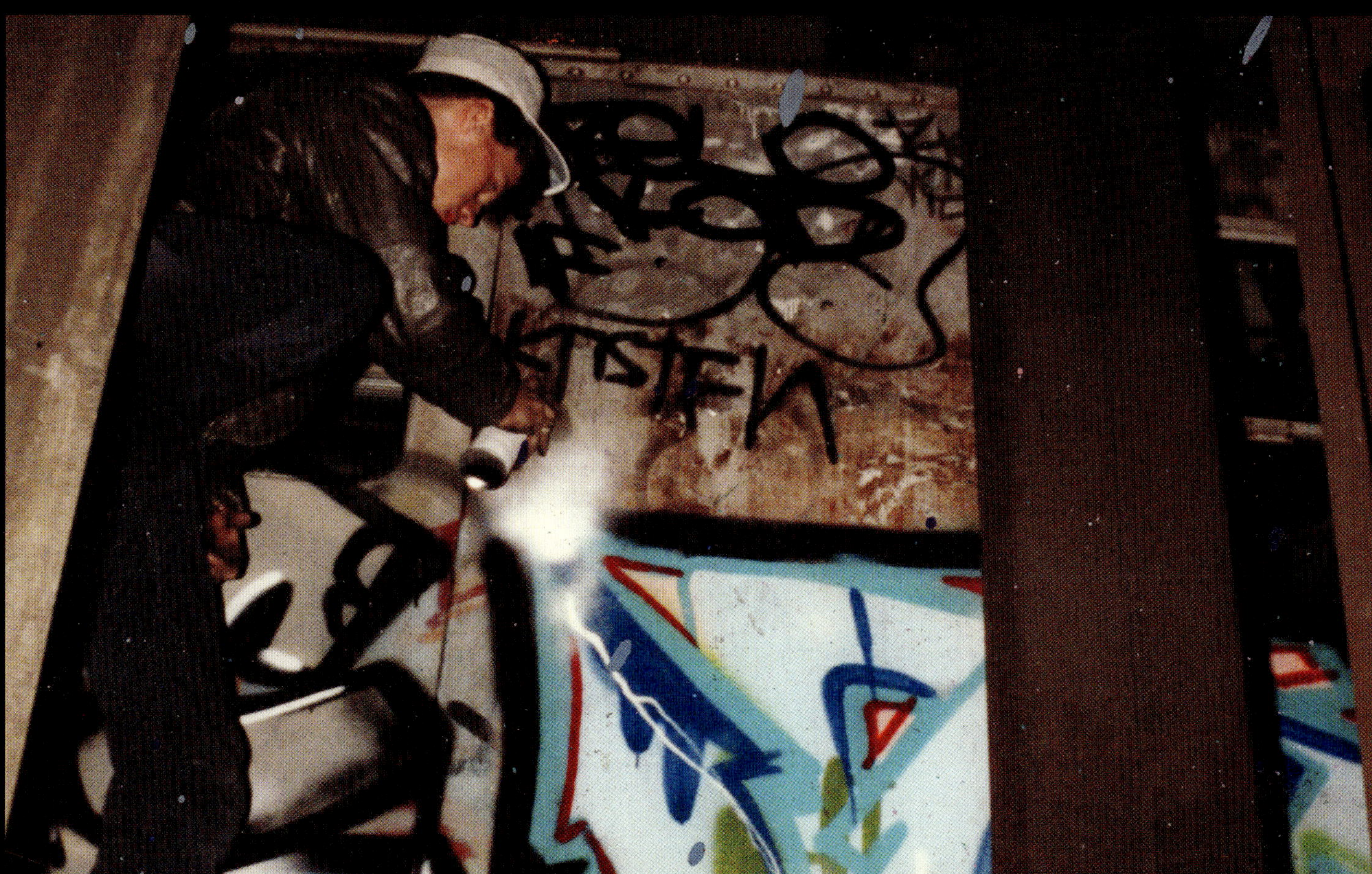

SHO calisthenics.

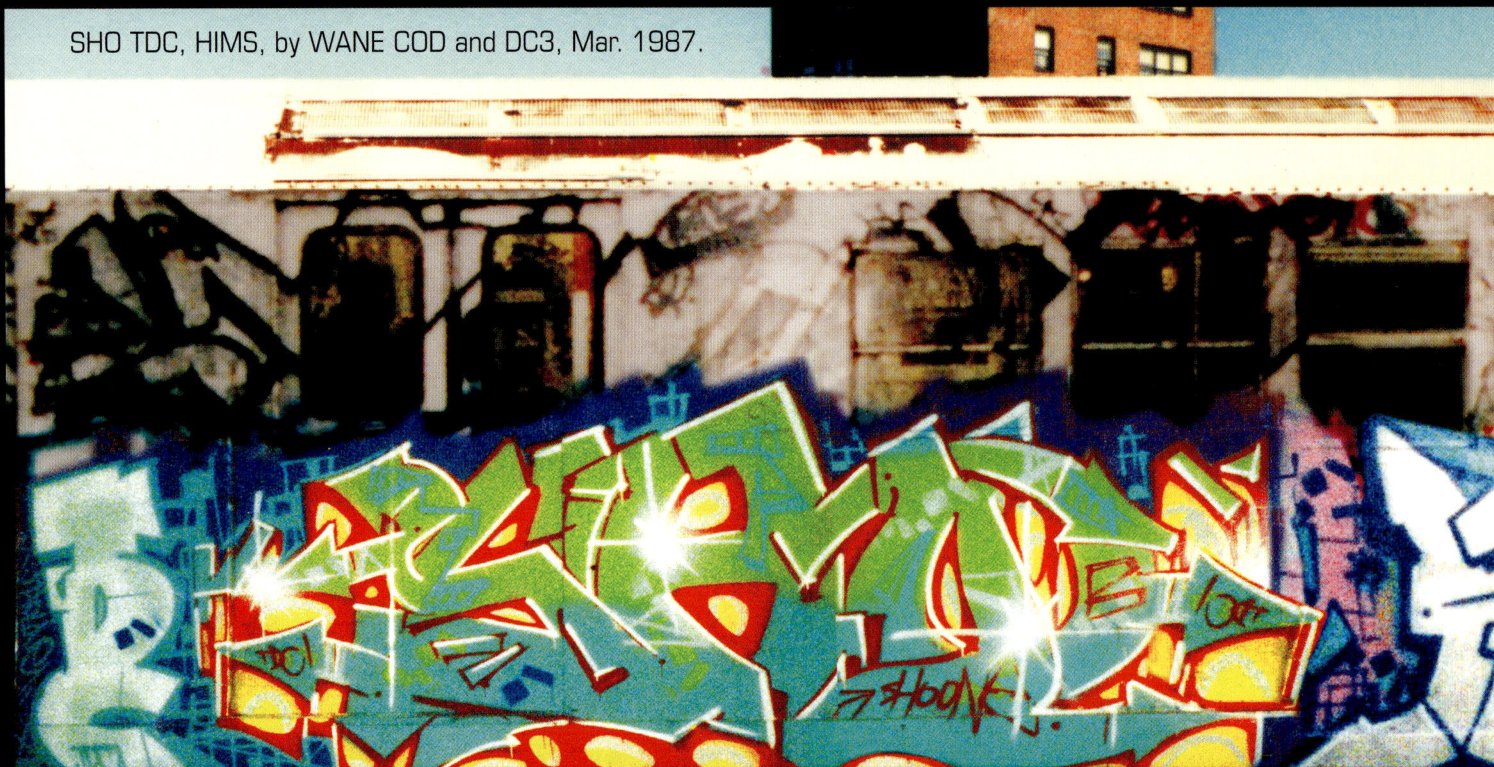

SHO TDC, HIMS, by WANE COD and DC3, Mar. 1987.

DC3, "Connect, eject, and collect respect checkout this art because I come correct."

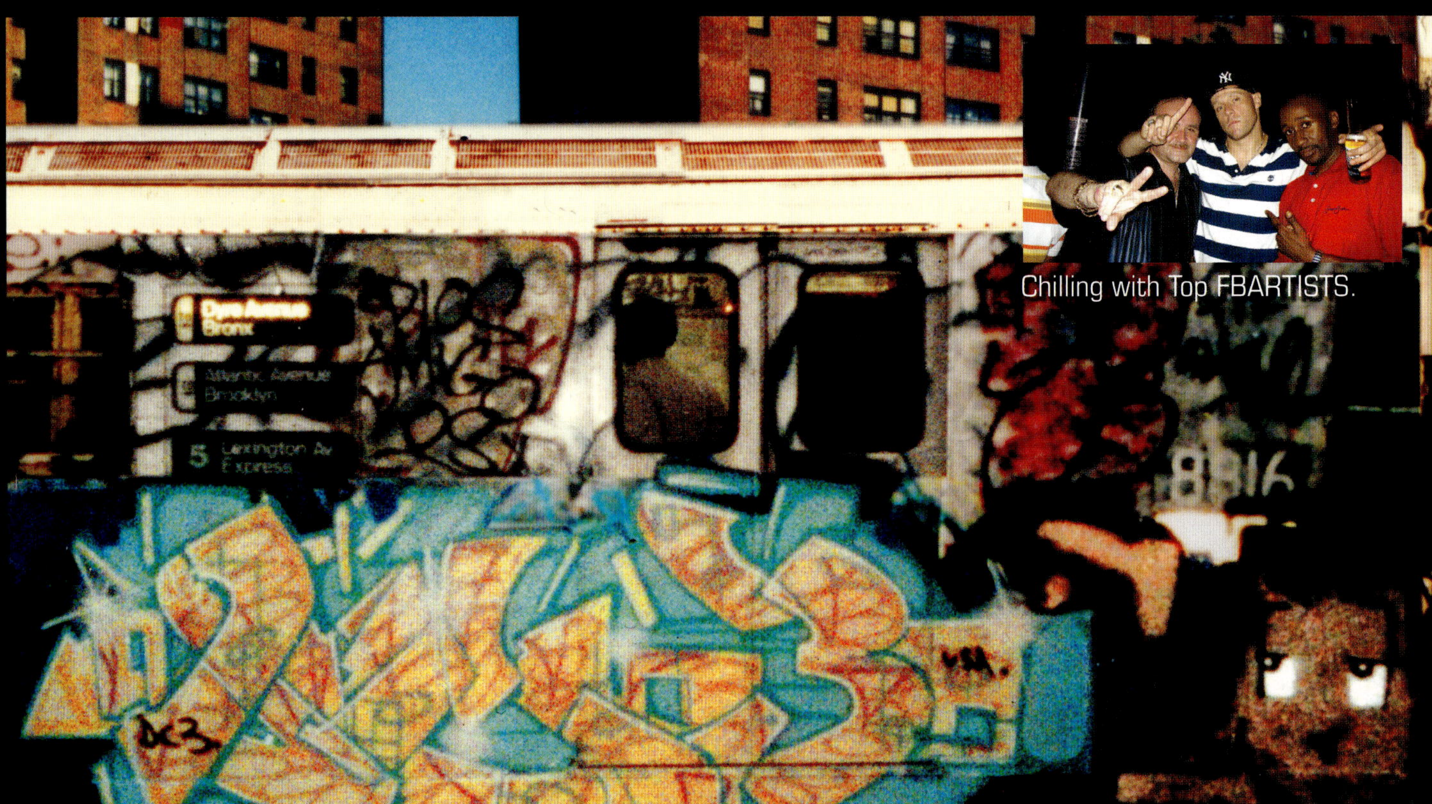

Chilling with Top FBARTISTS.

This is the first burner we rocked with COD.

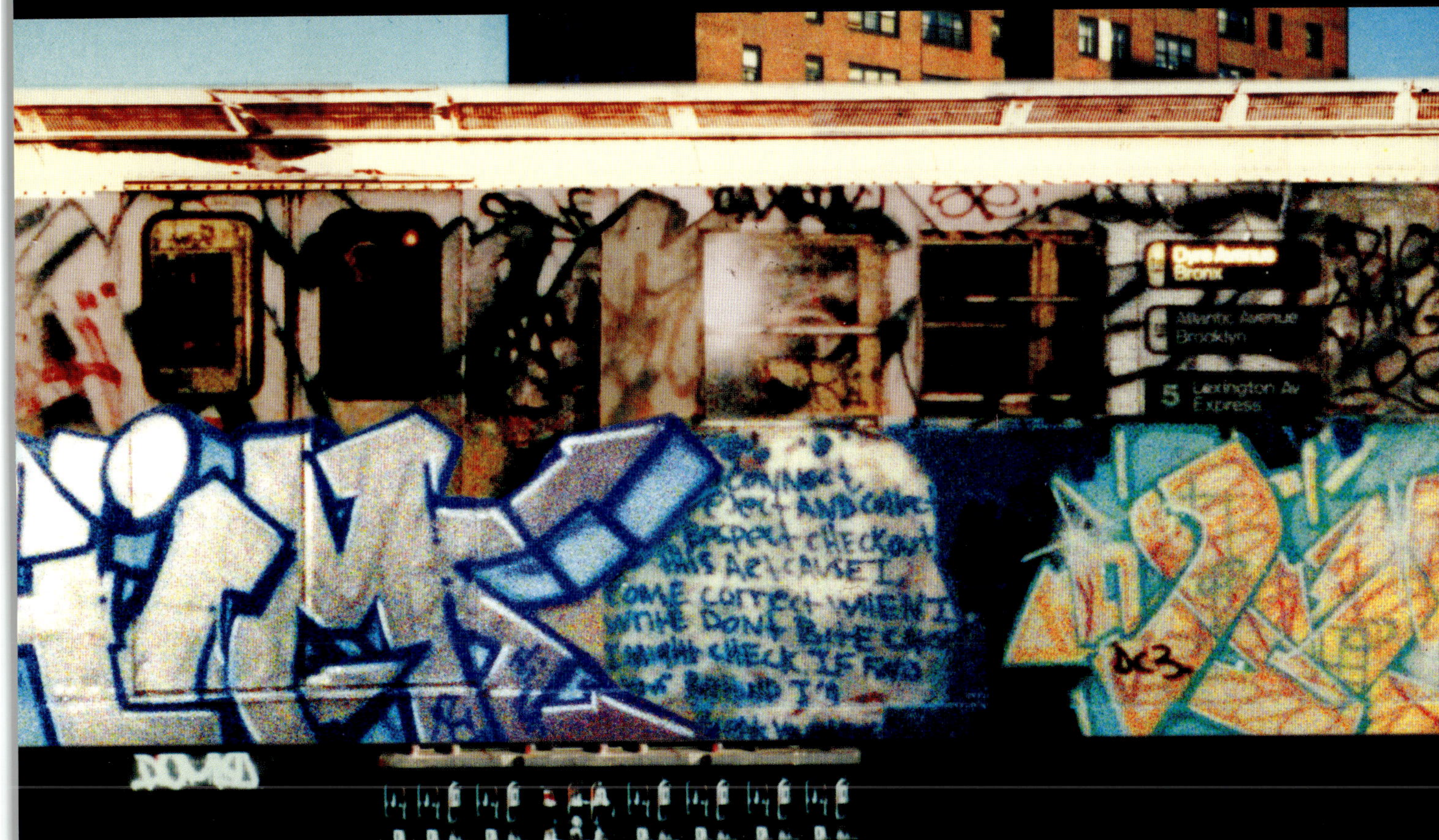

"WHEN I WRITE, DON'T BITE CAUSE I WILL CHECK AND IF I FIND YOU'RE BEHIND, I'LL BREAK YOUR NECK!"

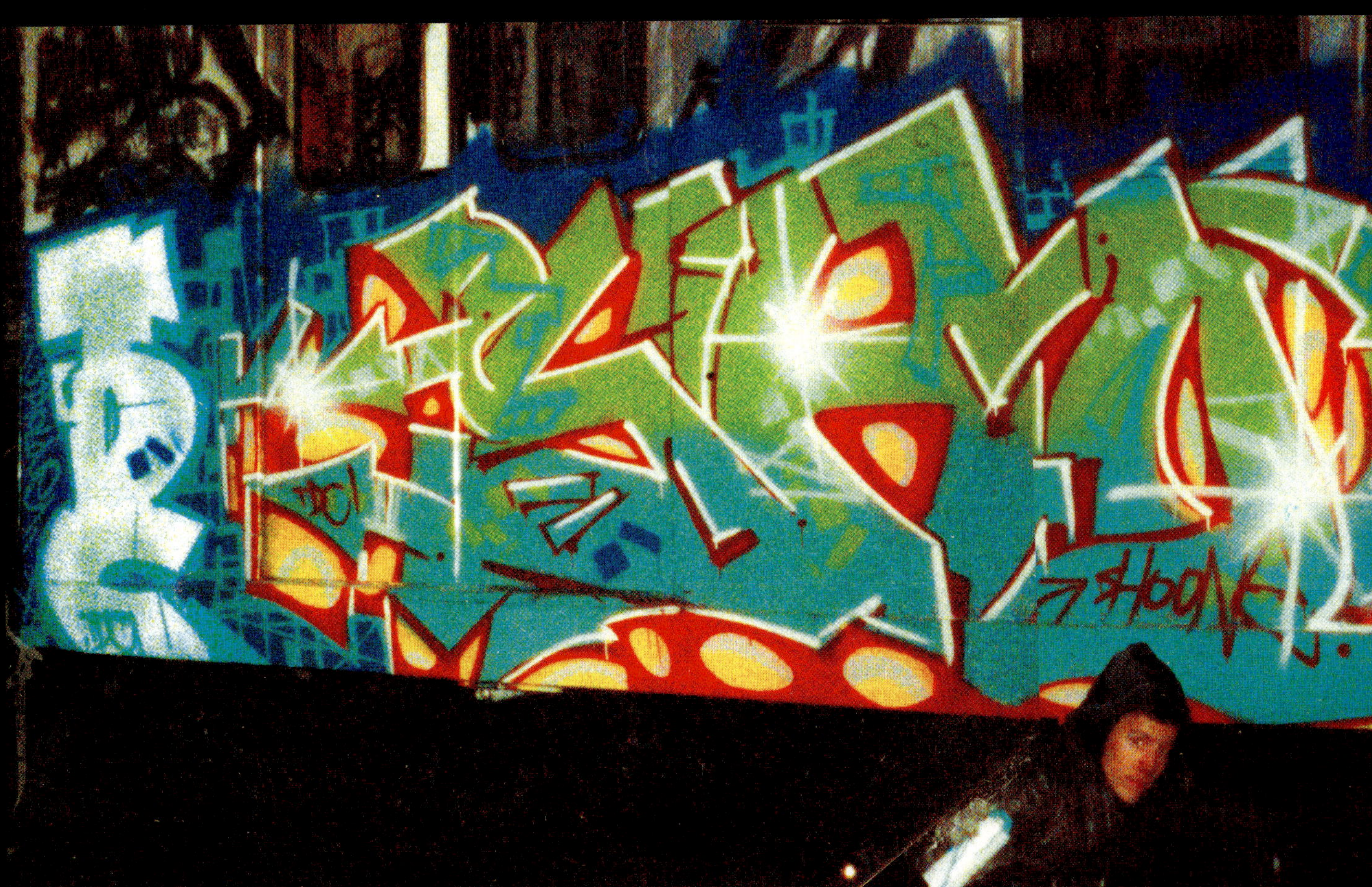

SHO live at Allerton Ave. Station above-ground lay up.

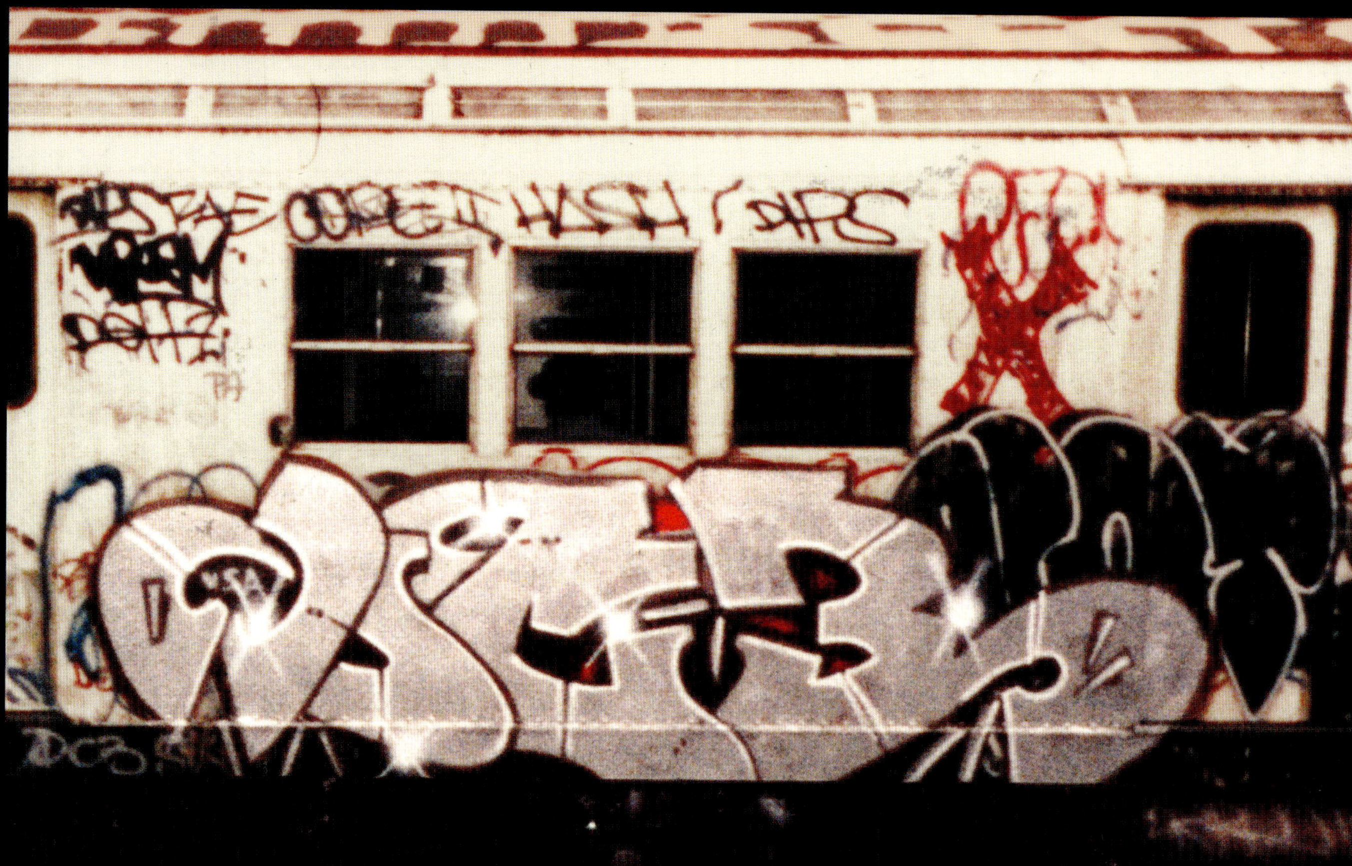

Quickie DC3, silver 5 Train, Jan. 1988.

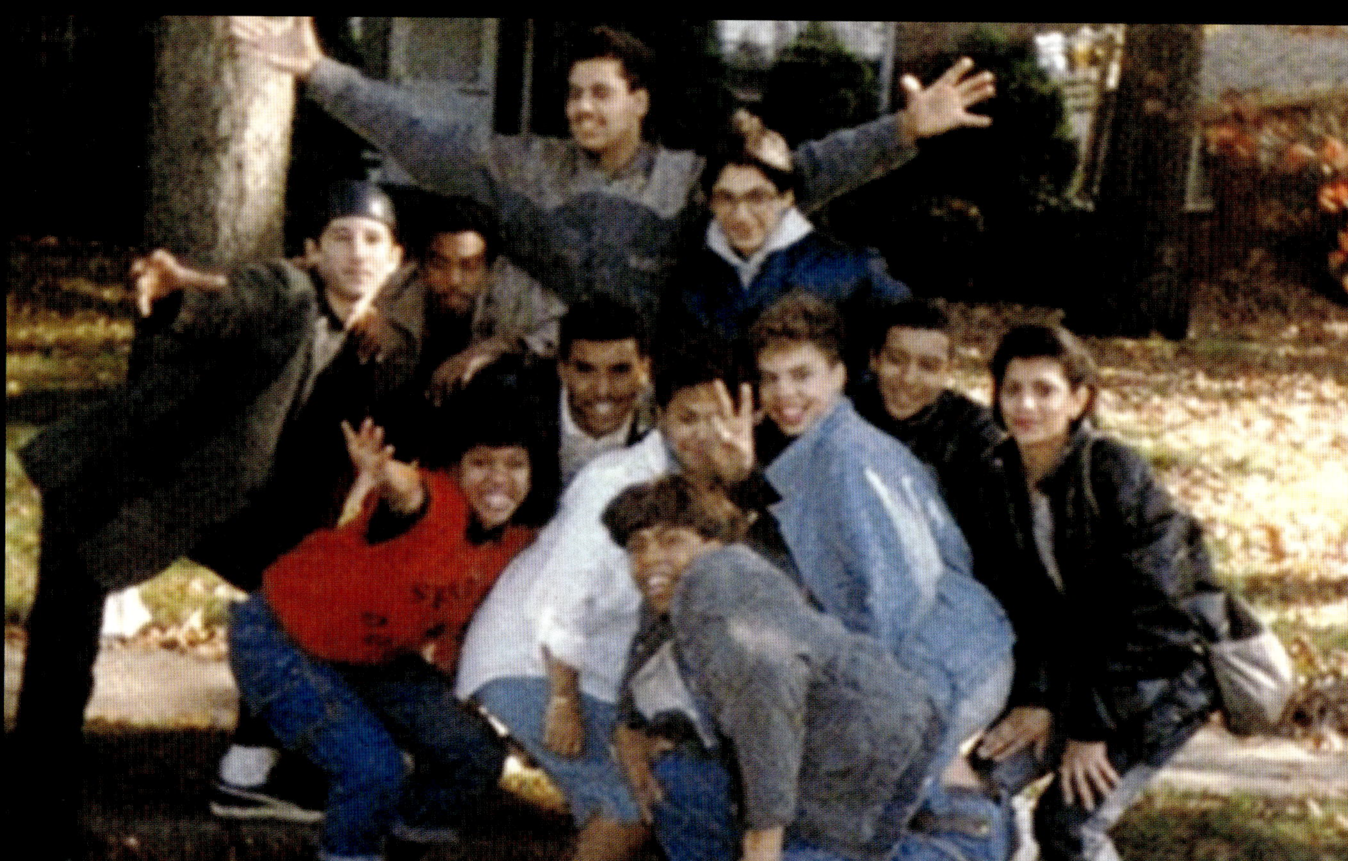

Beaver One, Billy Doctor, and Freeport Crew, 1986.

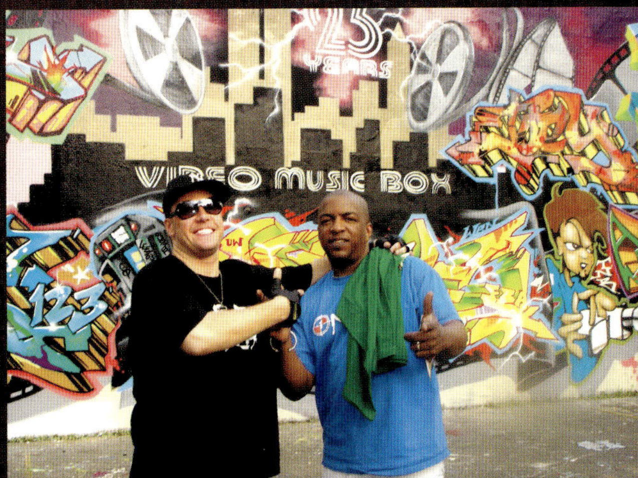

Chilling with Uncle Ralph McDaniels in the Hall of Fame...a true hip hop pioneer.

The story behind why ZOO did the "Slave To Style" Train? As a young writer, watching the kings of that time doing top-to-bottom whole cars with their name or a phrase inspired me to dream that one day I would rock a train like that. So as I got better as a writer and started painting for real and got up on the trains, it was always in the back of my mind to paint one. I had a black book that I let other writers do pieces in and the writer VULCAN from TAT cru and Ex Vandals did a tag on the bottom of the page that said "Slave To Style" and I thought that was a great phrase, so my dream turned to determination, and then that night a mission, and then in the Esplanade Tunnels for six hours it became a reality. The reason we dared pull off major productions in the tunnels was because it was freezing cold in the middle of winter and there was like ten inches of snow on the ground. Mission accomplished! I did a "SLAVE TO STYLE" top-to-bottom whole car. That car got a lot of respect it ran to the very end of the bombed cars era, I even saw it years later in the scrap yard untouched! Even my rivals had to respect it. Meanwhile SHO did a top-to-bottom silver block letter, and DC3 and Karl TCM did a wicked top-to-bottom car with characters. Also DEON and FENT rocked window-down pieces that night. Just think of it, we did four trains in a row, two top-to-bottom whole cars, one top-to-bottom block buster, and a window-down end-to-end. When that shit pulled out with windows what a sight to see. That's pure ecstasy because you knew that shit made major noise. We was surprised to get over because the platform must of smelled like mad paint fumes. It was all about hurting Niggas feelings. Ha Ha.

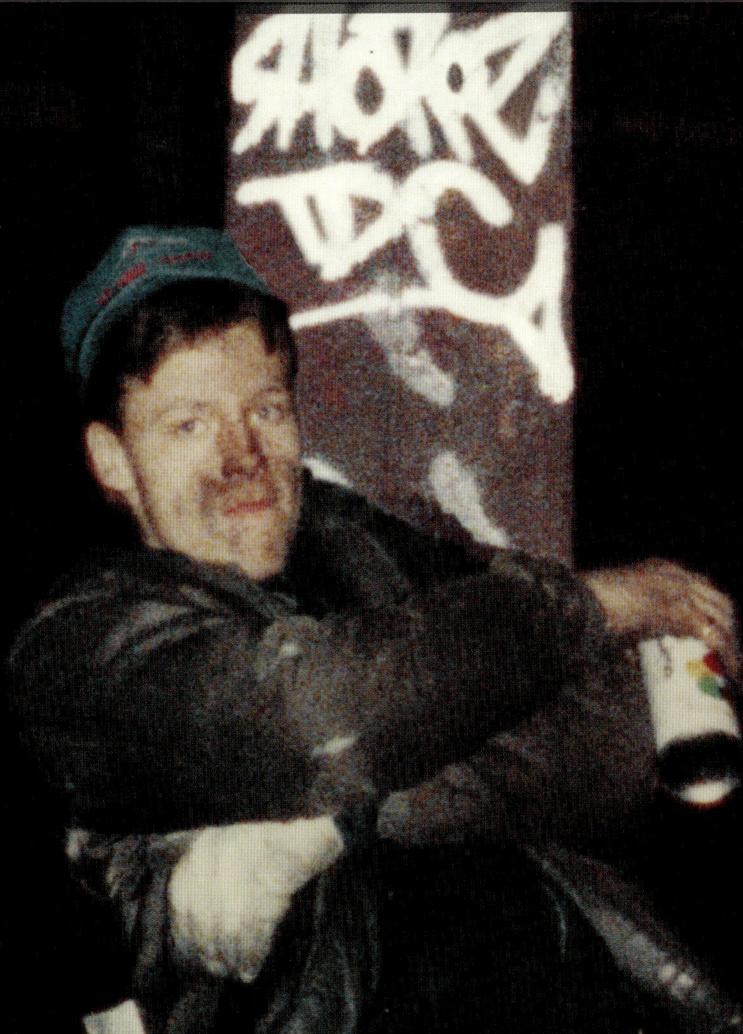

SHOROZ TDC bombing the tunnels before breaking out. 7:10 A.M.—pushing our luck!!!

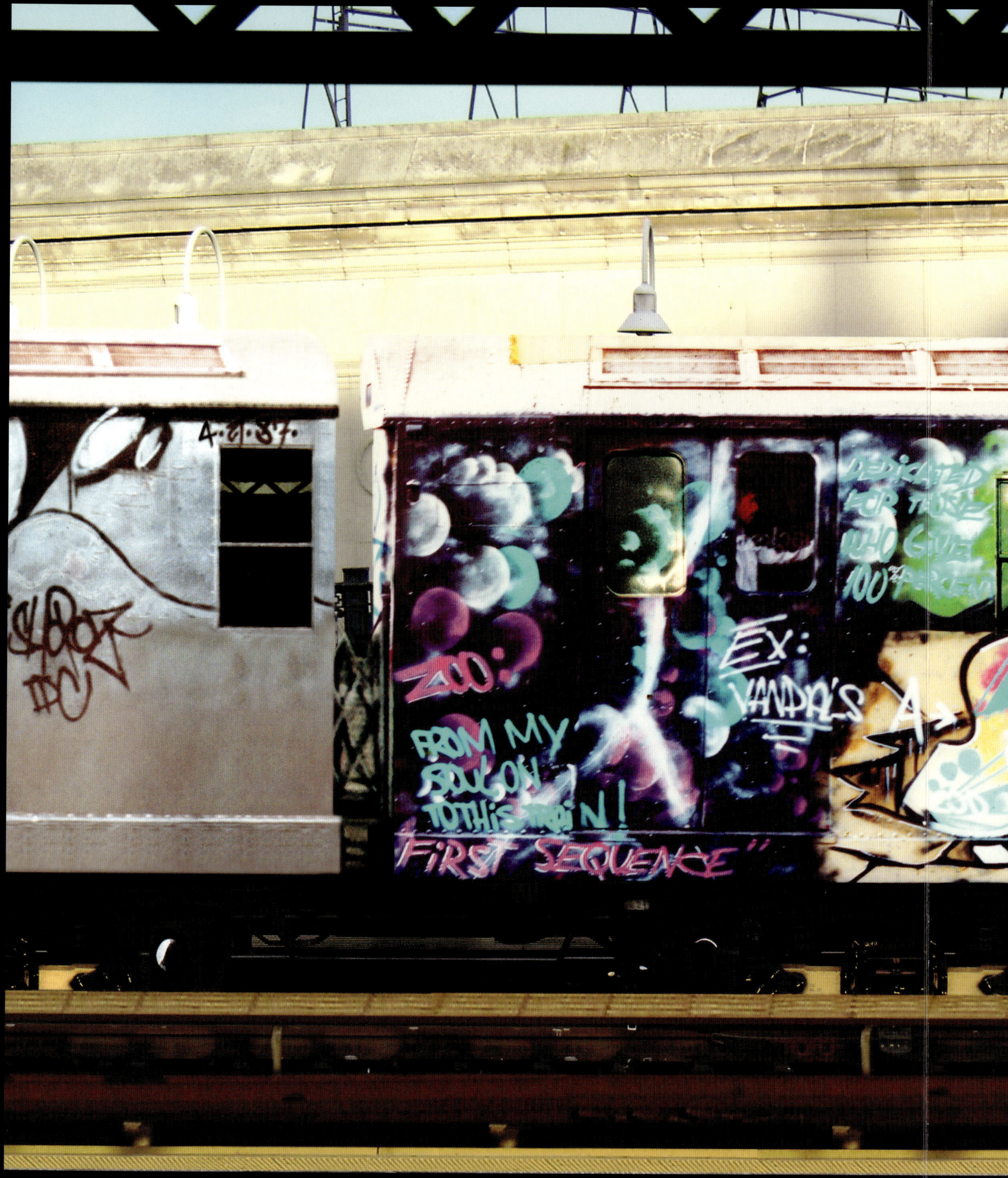

"A SLAVE TO STYLE," 5 Train, August 21, 1987, by ZOOROC, "FROM MY SOUL ON TO THIS TRAIN / FIRST SEQUENCE / DEDICATED TO A

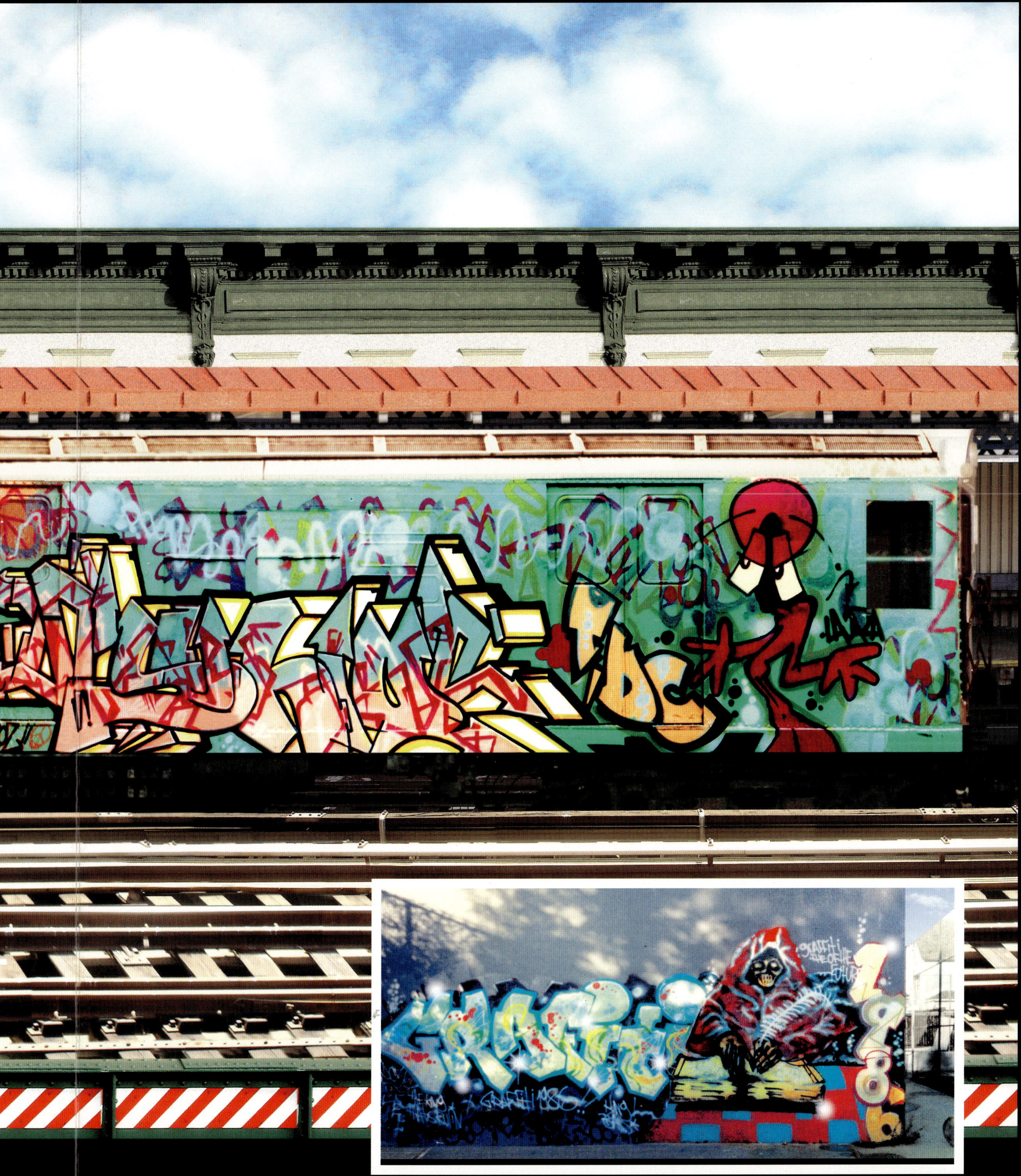

"GRAFFITI OF THE FUTURE," wall by DC3, Stevens St. Park, 1986.

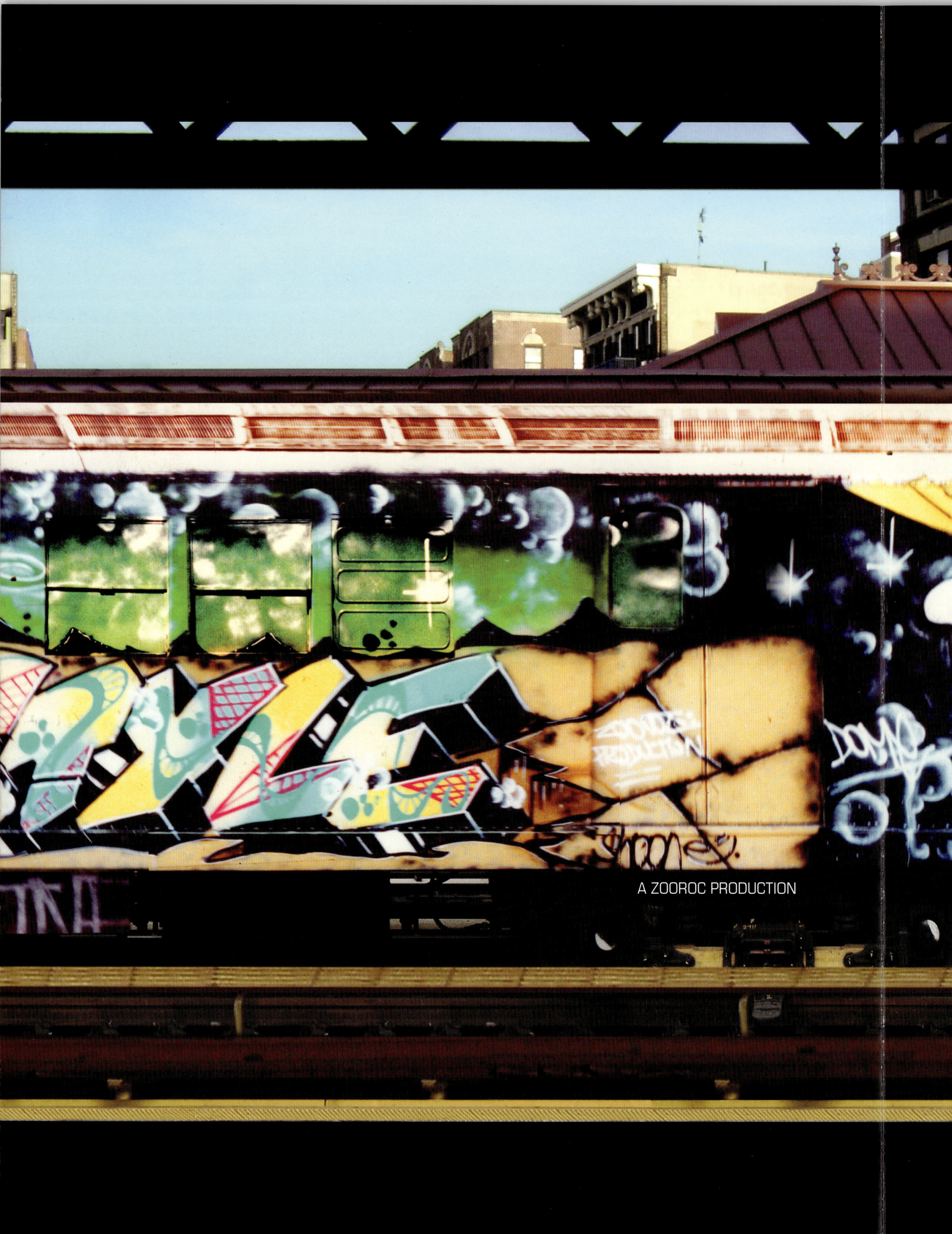

A ZOOROC PRODUCTION

CHAPTER 3

Burning Trains in Baychester Bronx and Utica in Brooklyn.

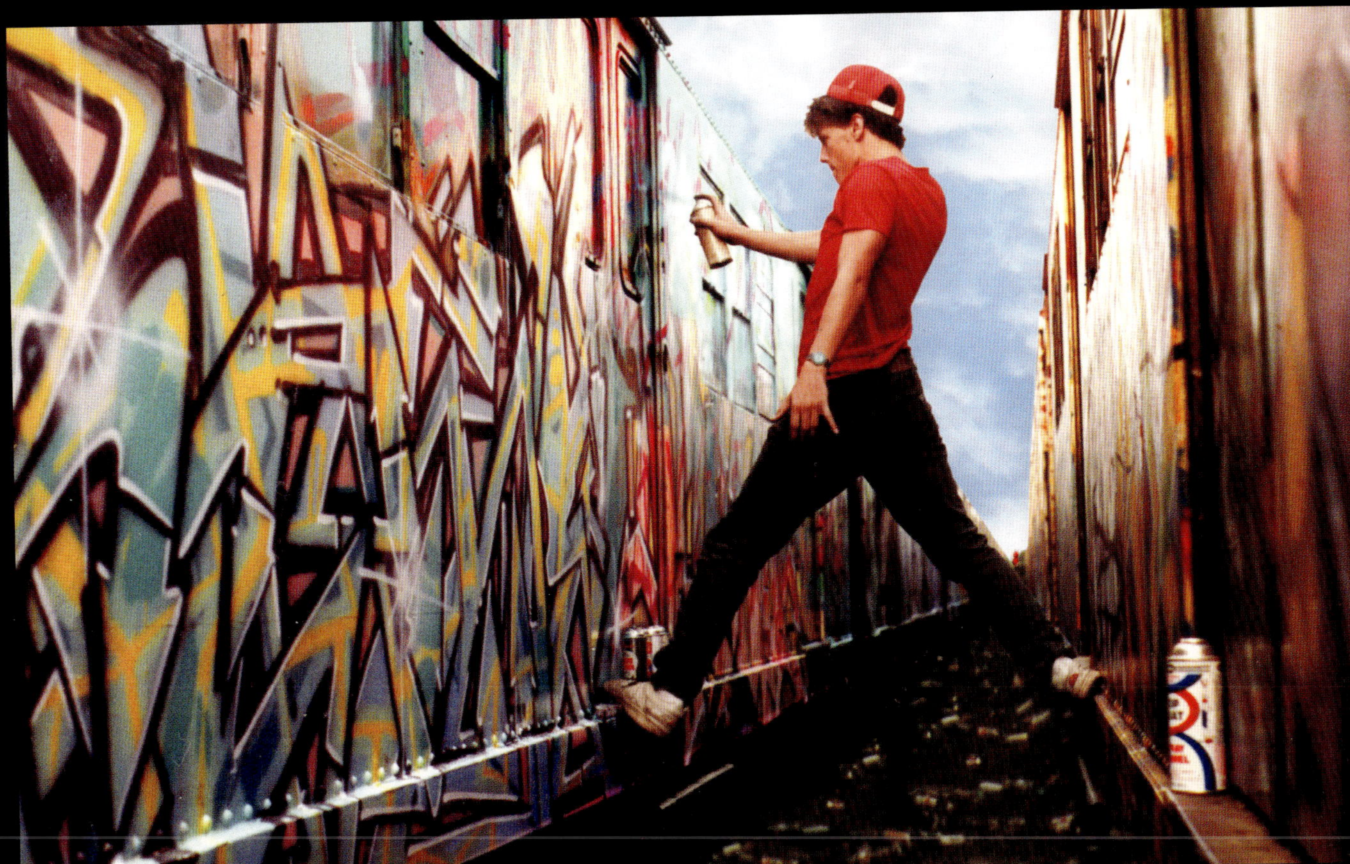

SHO live In Baychester, May 1988.

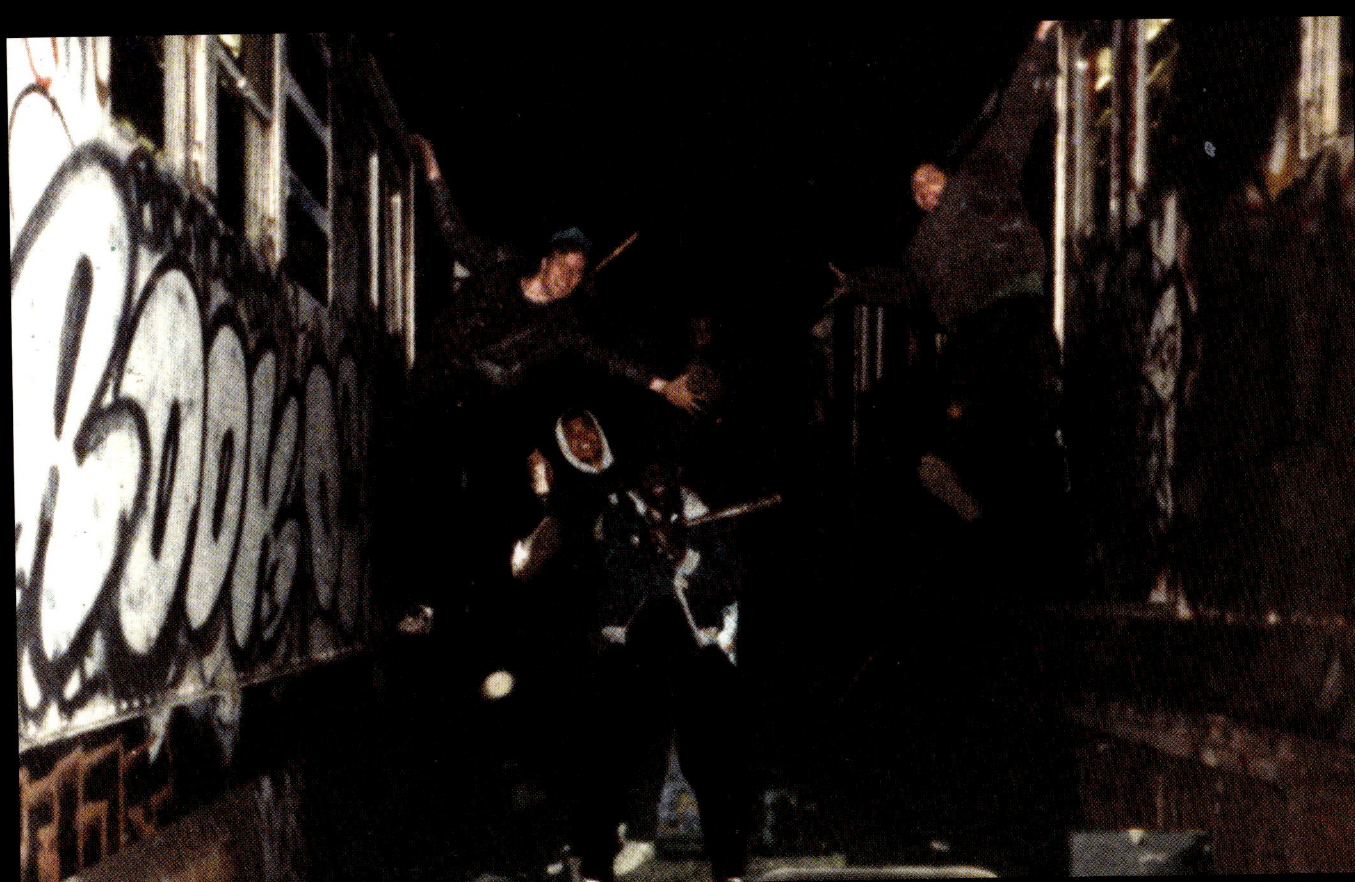

The Destiny Children holding it down...1987.

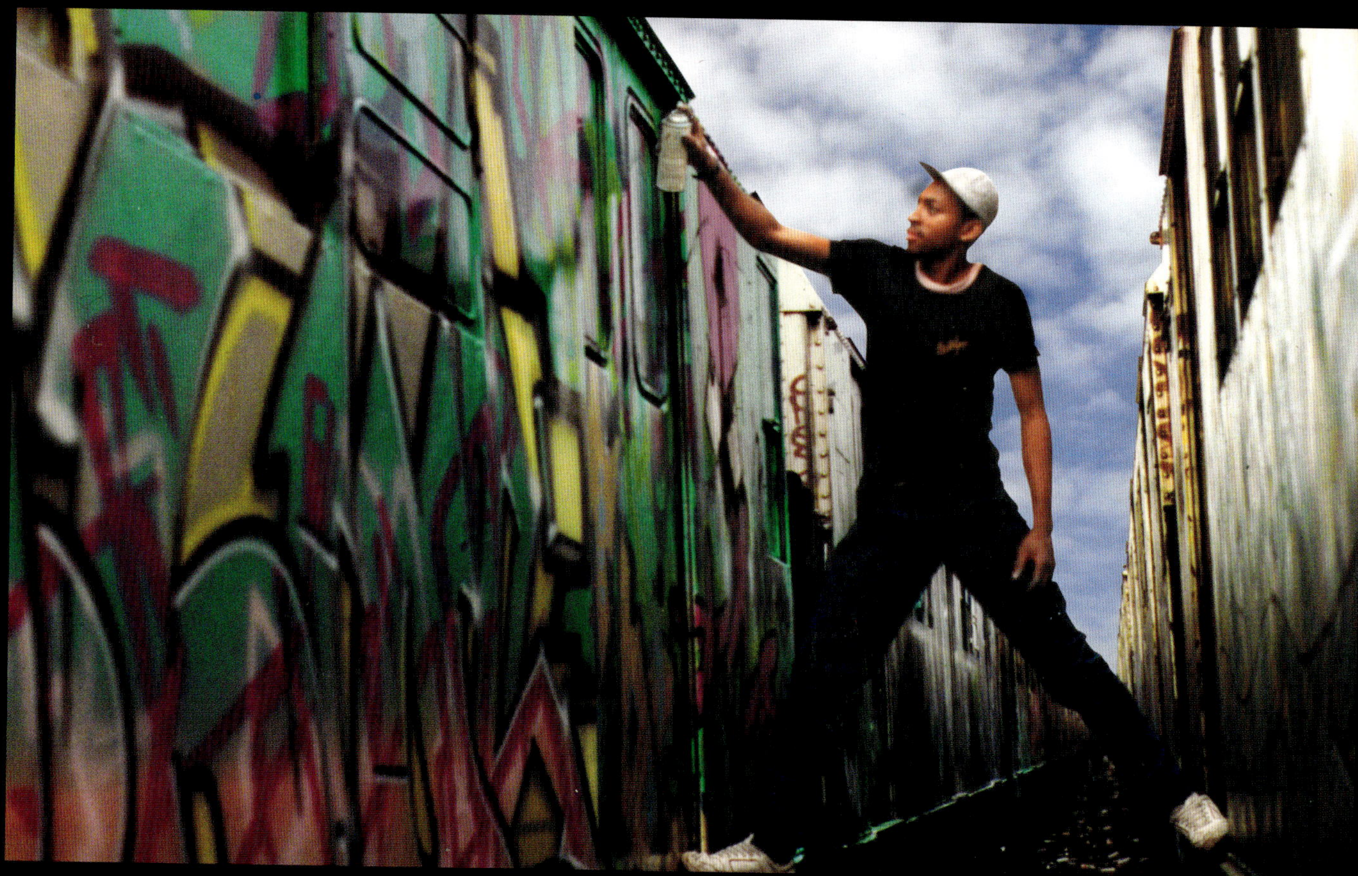

DC3 finishing background graphics and characters.

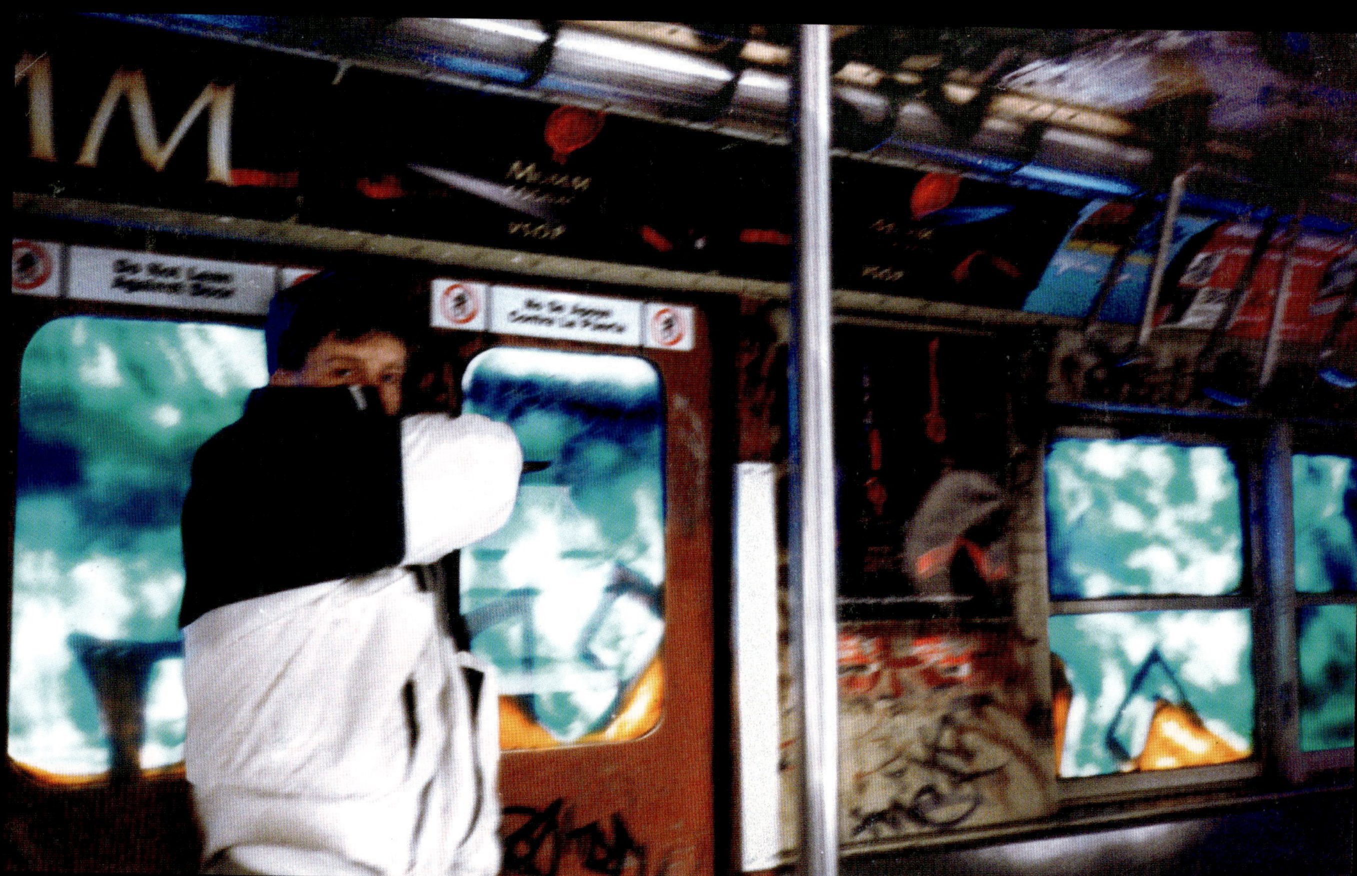

I always loved to be inside any train we did that still had the windows painted. A very satisfying feeling.

SHO and DC3 USA, 5 Train, Feb. 1988.

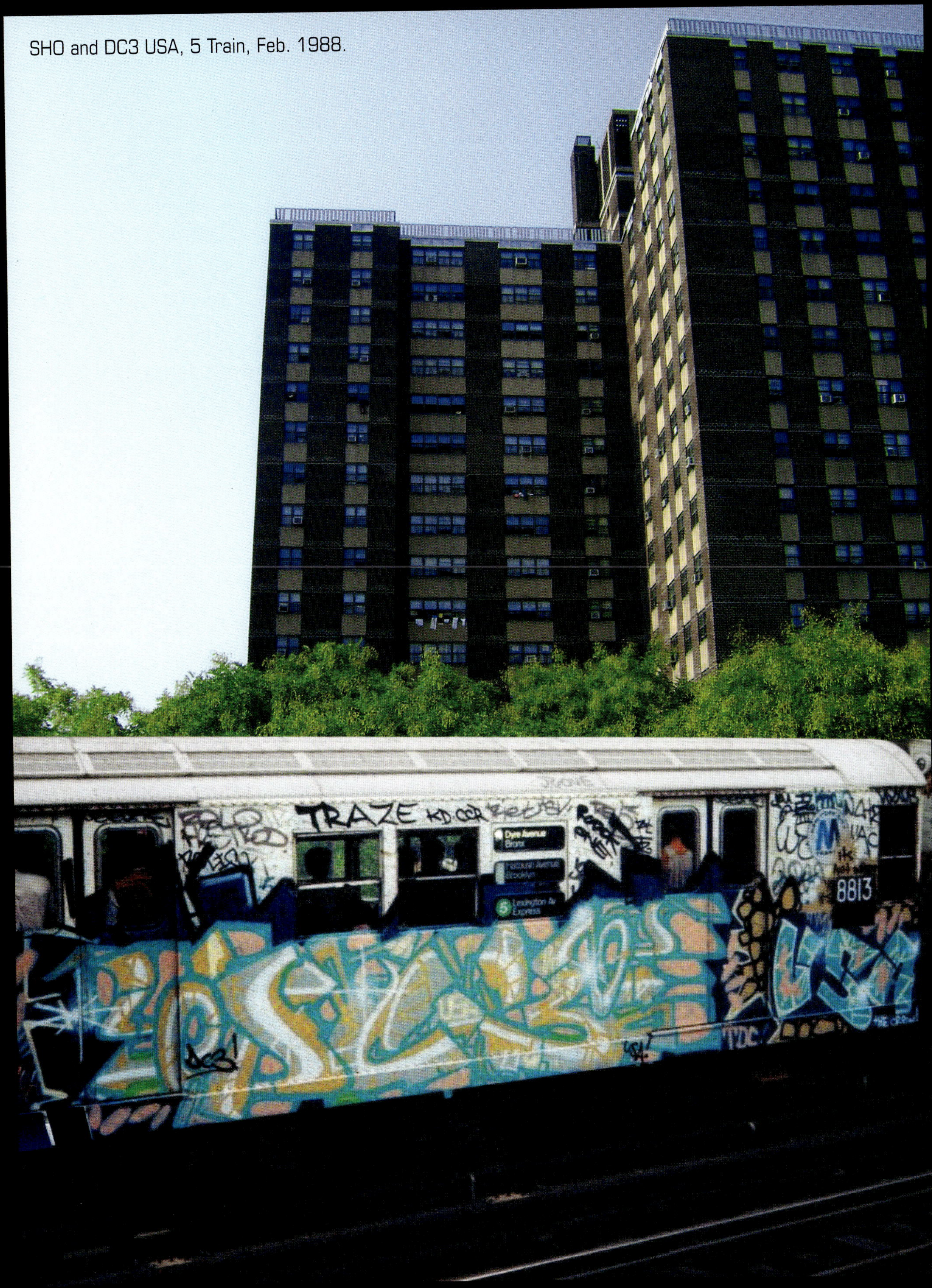

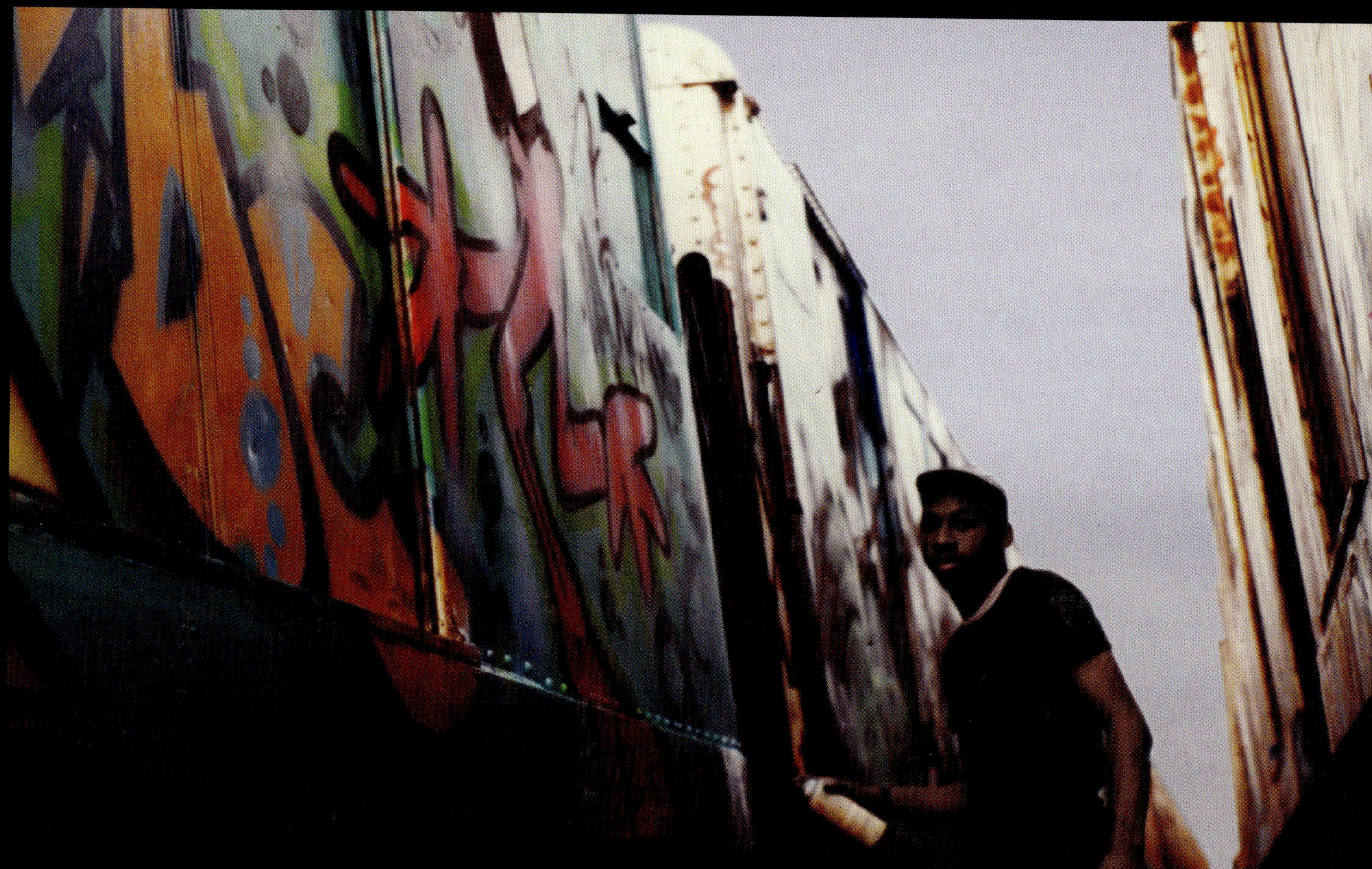

DC3 live In Baychester, 5:35 A.M., May 1988.

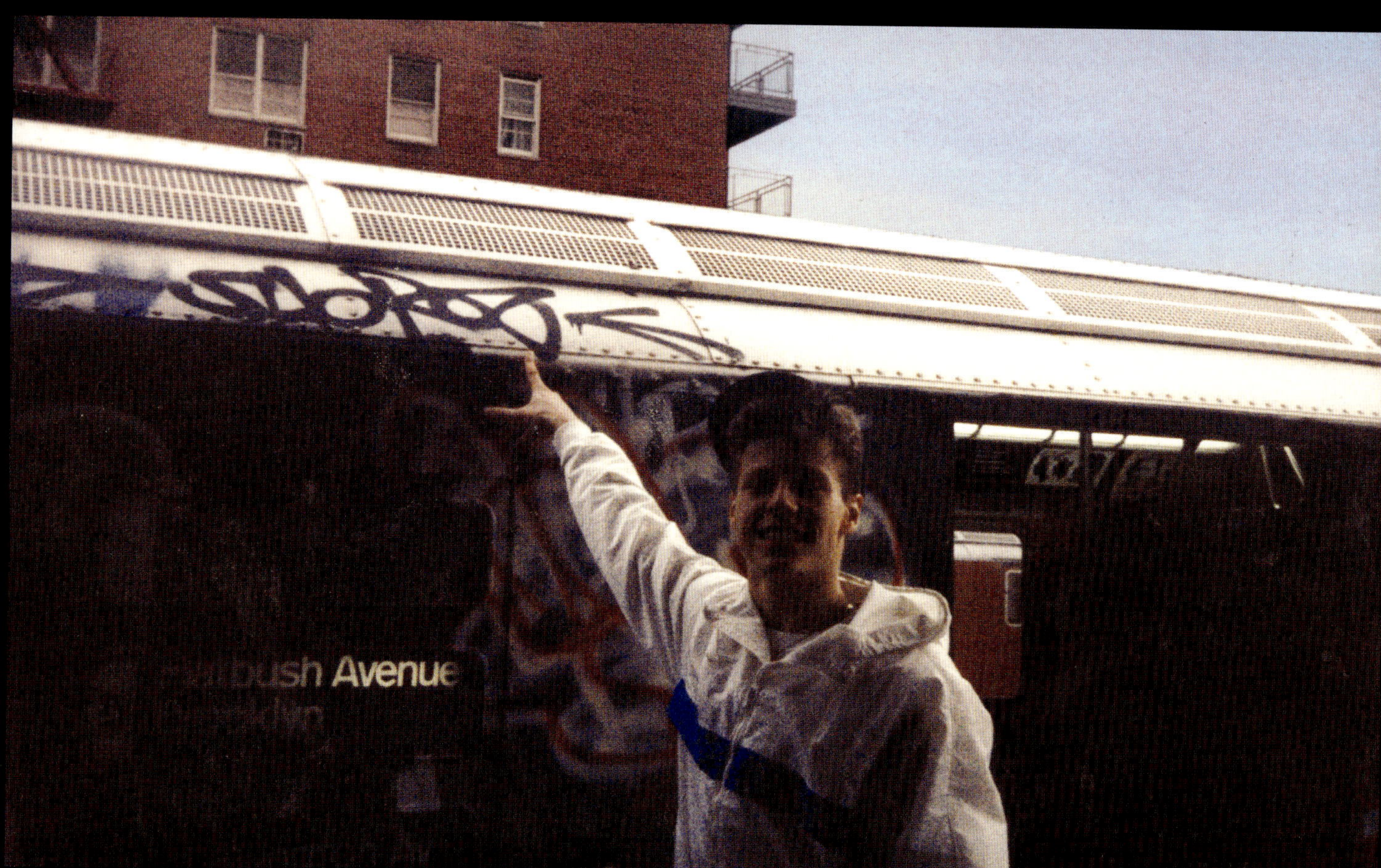

Even tags count...

We was doing so many burners that I found time to do pieces for my boys even though they wasn't even there, I did this SHIM top-to-bottom 1/2-car piece in broad daylight in the Kingston Tunnels in BK and happened to catch the flick while in Baychester looking for our trains. Niggas broke into my Honda Prelude in broad day light while we was looking for our shit not giving a fuck during a Sunday late afternoon...Bye Bye Benzi radio and back window, that shit must have slipped out from the seat when we moved the whip. The fucked up shit was I had both of mines stolen, the first one was when we was chilling at the Paladium for free and some how on some random shit, niggas broke into the trunk despite the face we hid that shit like a mile away and I put that shit under the tire underneath the floor board. We was mad tight and Dome snuffed some shady homeless nigga just to make some one pay... Ha Ha!!!!! That day we also flicked the Goldie Dome unfinished due to the 116 Tunnel raid where all of us almost got caught and miraculously all of us escaped.

-Sho TDC

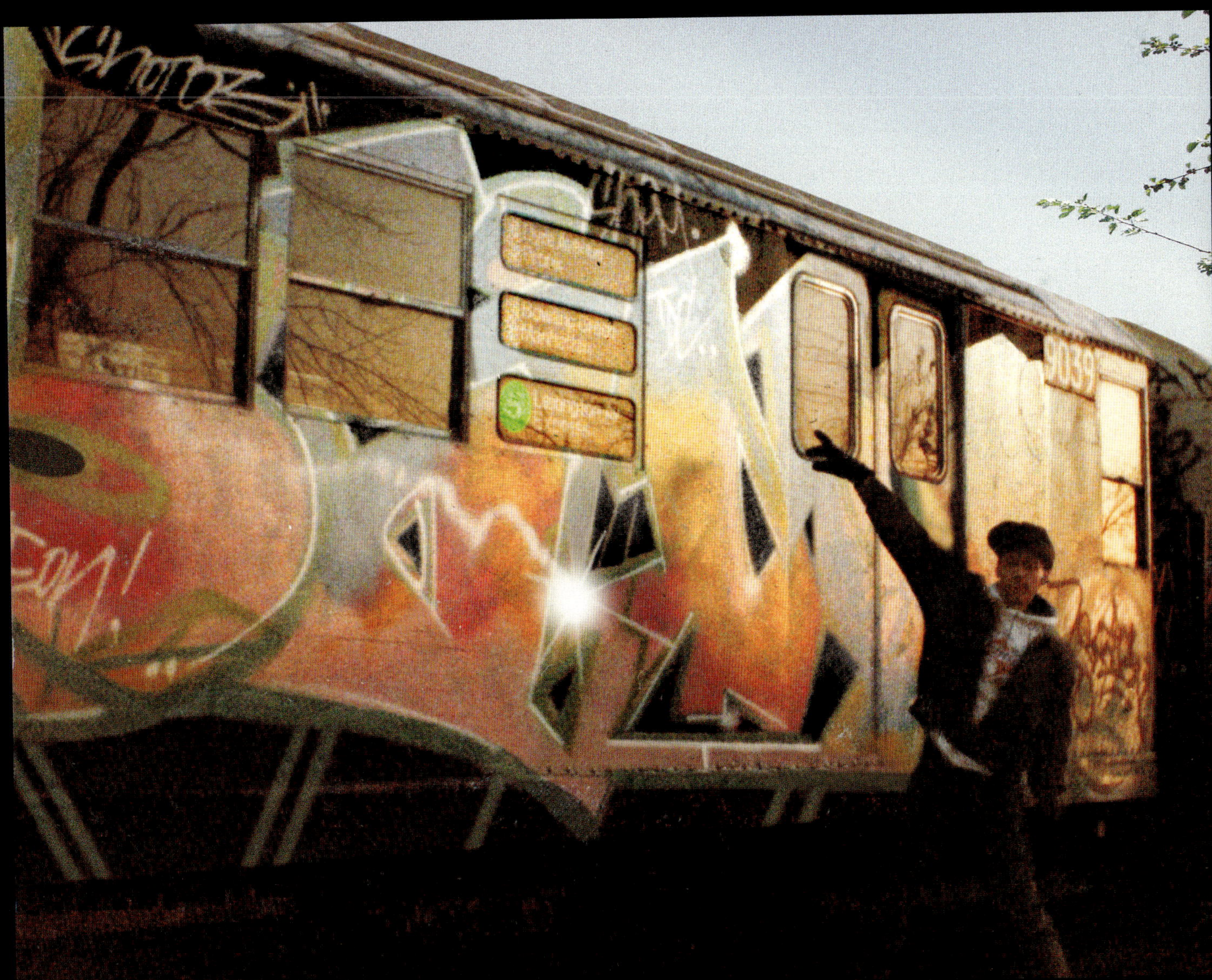

SHIM top-to-bottom caught in Baychester, Bronx, NY, 4 P.M., May 1987.

"The Jungle is Wild at Night," Kingdom.

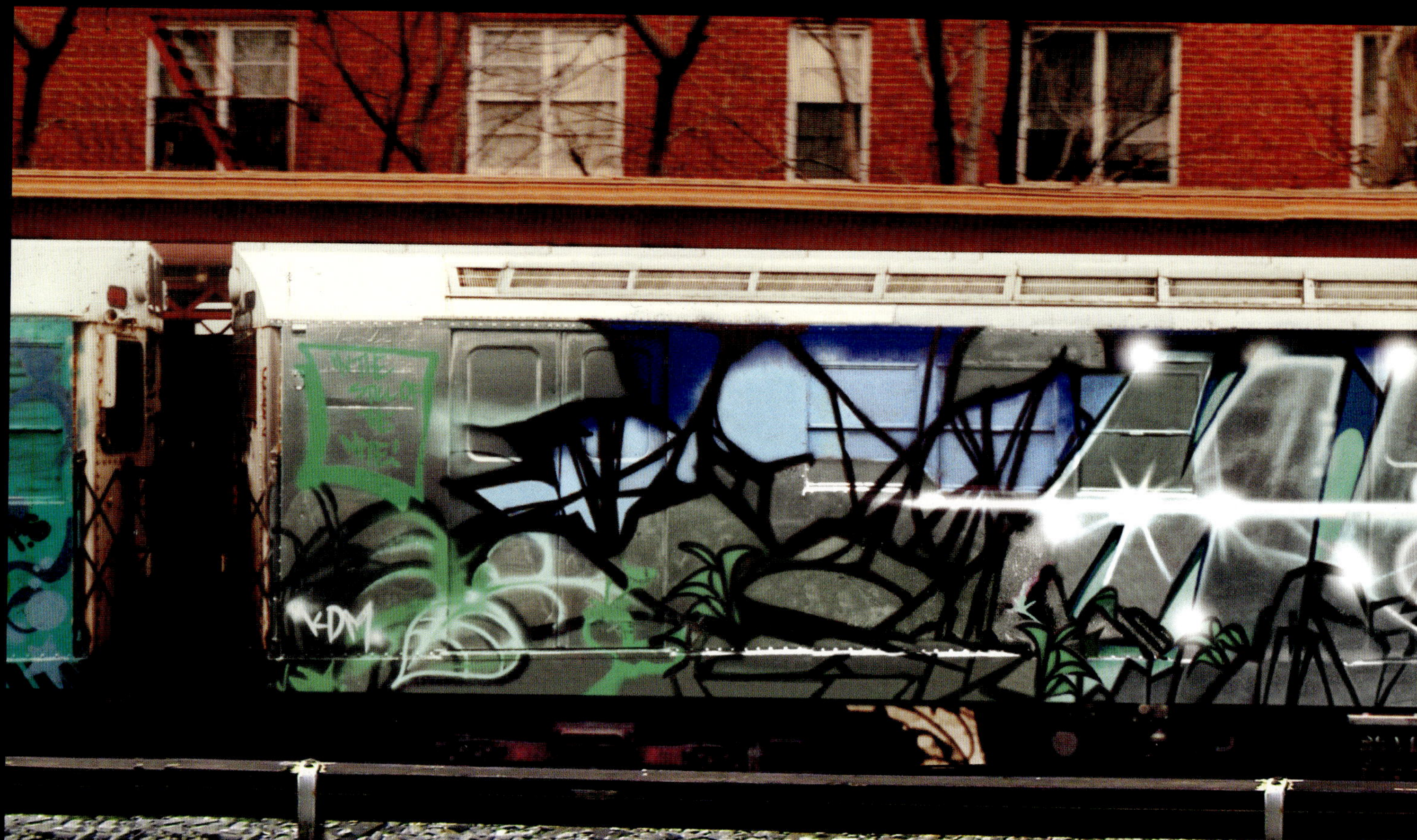

This MAC 5 Train was next to the DC3 SHO "Martians Train." We finished these trains at like 5:50 A.M. It was already fucking daylight and we was getting nervous. Painting top-to-bottoms in Baychester was hard because you had to straddle in between two sets of trains,

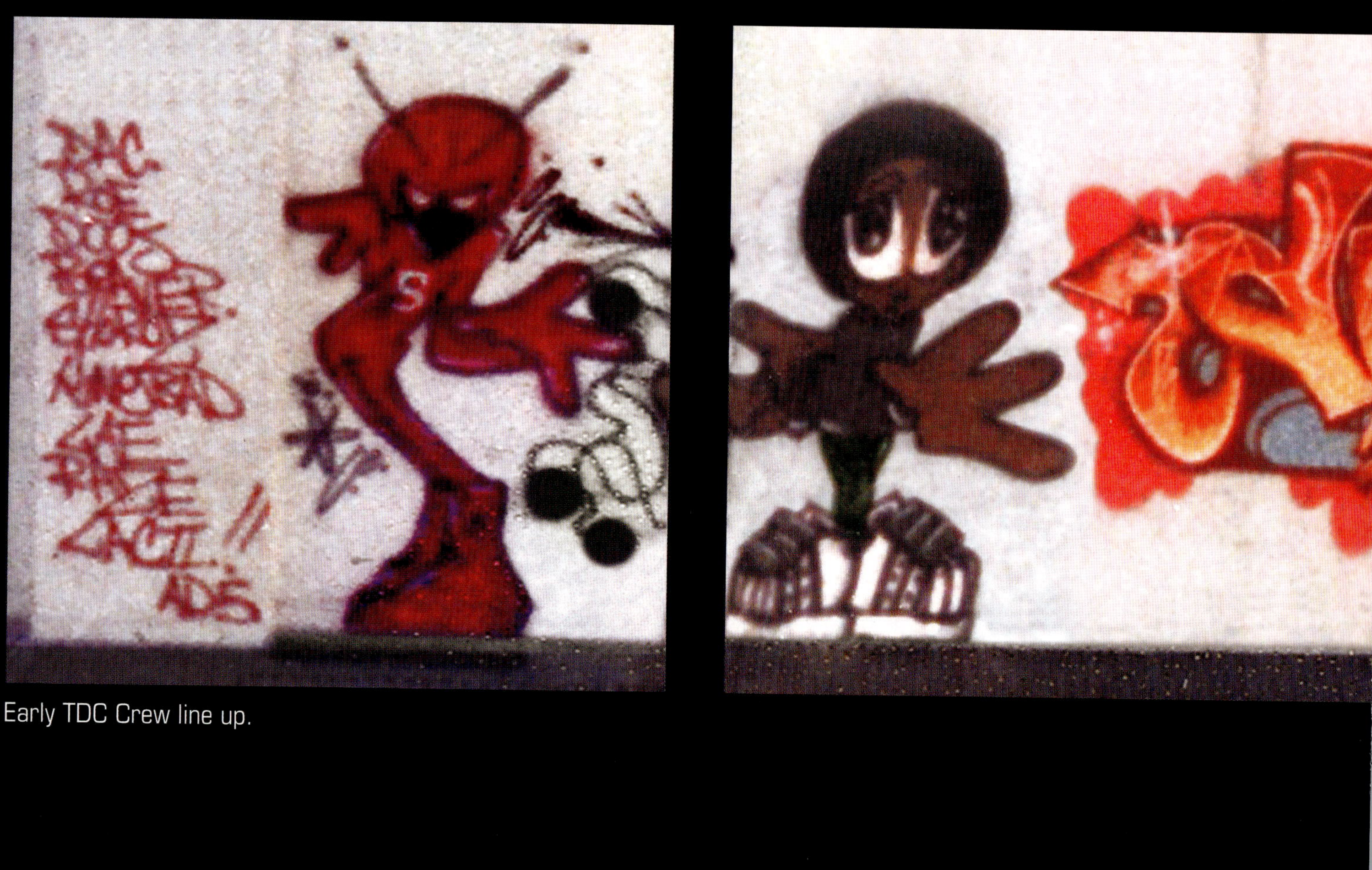

Early TDC Crew line up.

MAC, "The CONCRET JUNGLE" top-to-bottom by Mirage rocked in Baychester, May 1988.

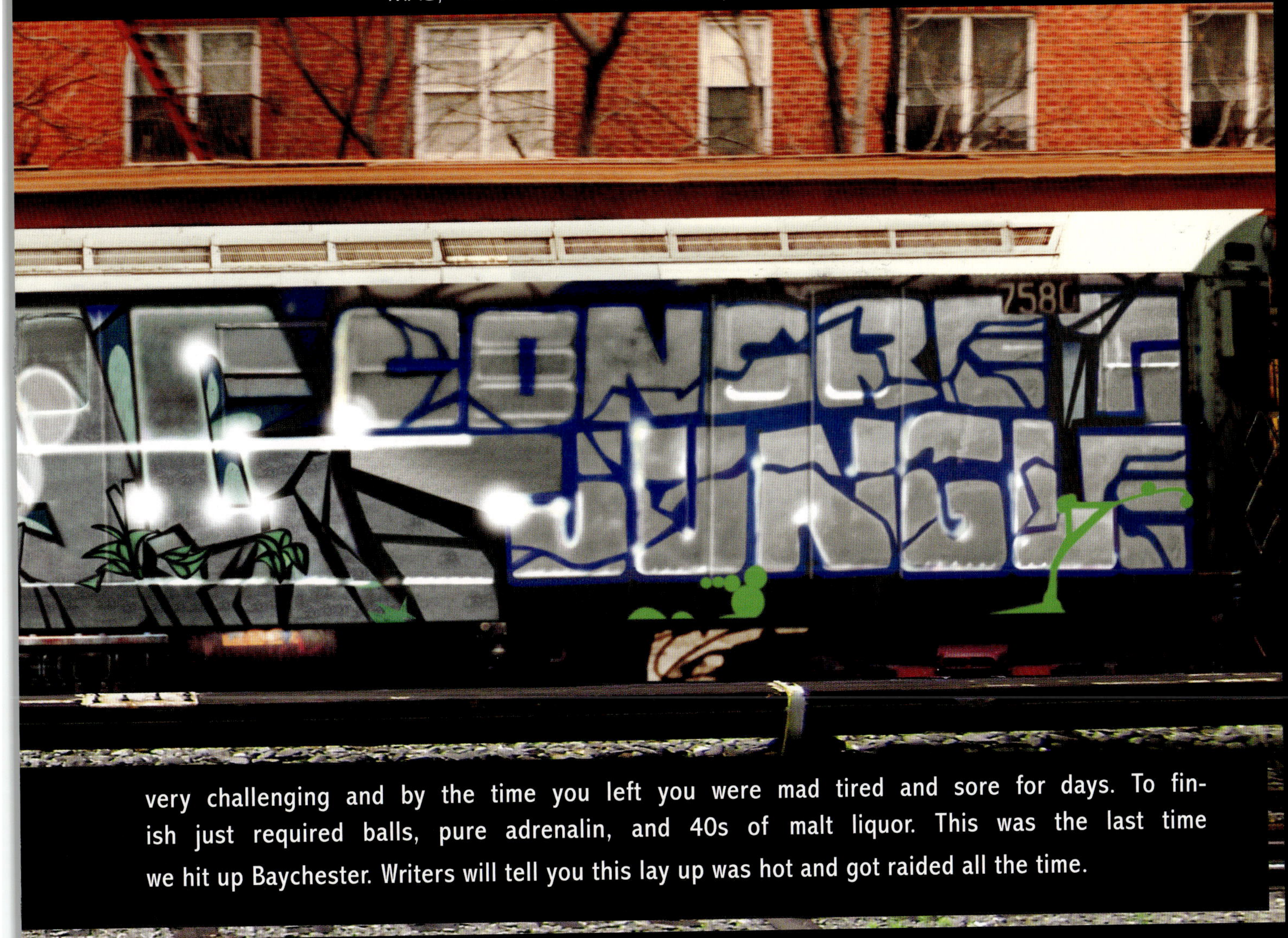

very challenging and by the time you left you were mad tired and sore for days. To finish just required balls, pure adrenalin, and 40s of malt liquor. This was the last time we hit up Baychester. Writers will tell you this lay up was hot and got raided all the time.

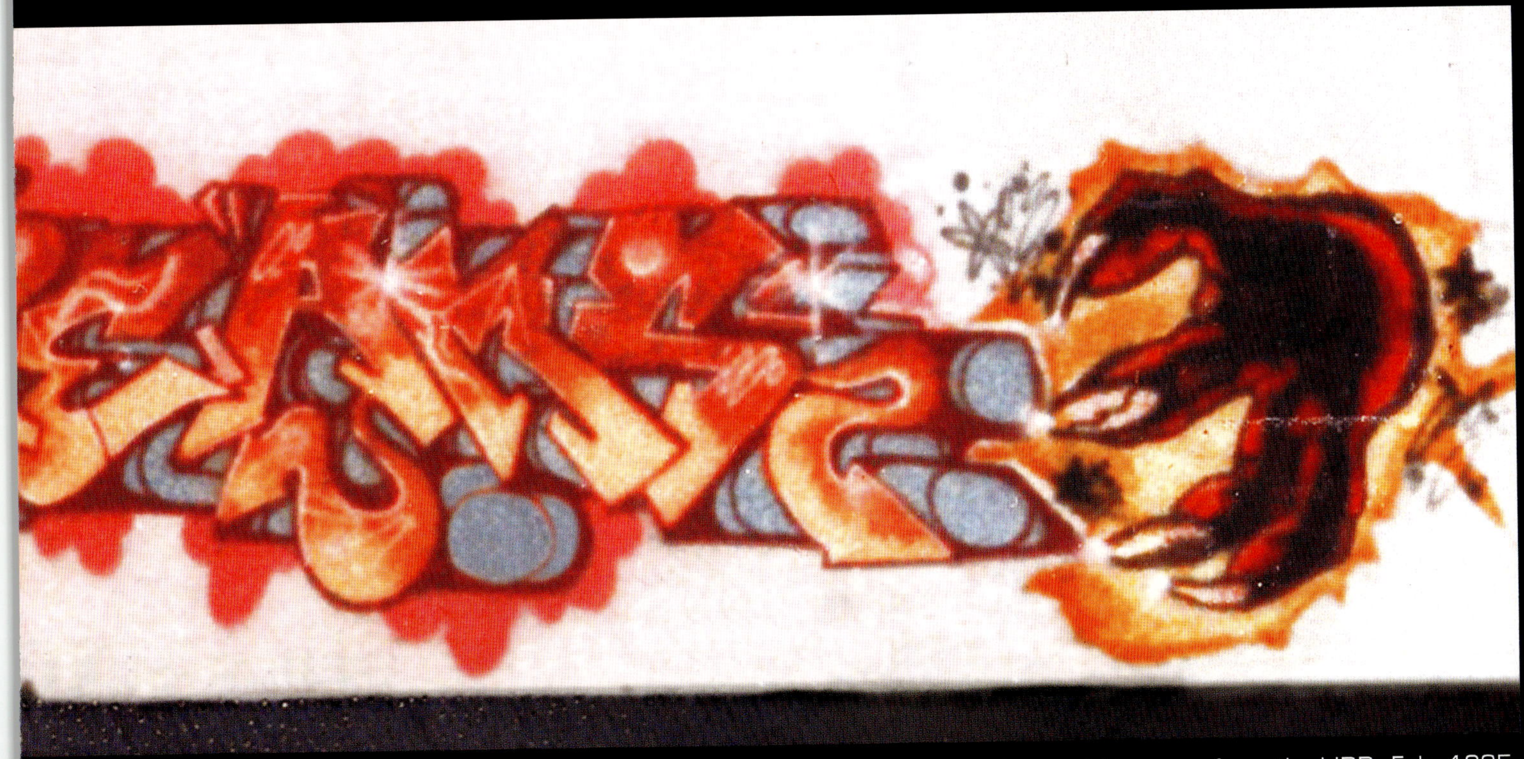

"DREAMS," by DC3, one of the first TDC rooftops that could be seen from the LIRR, Feb. 1985.

This DC3 was done on a 6 Train in the middle of the winter. The 6 Trains were gorgeous trains to paint on because they were one of the cleanest trains to hit at the time. We only knew of a couple of outdoor hitable train station lay ups. These were Zerega Avenue and Middleton and we wasn't fucking with the 6 Yard. DC3 was the only one of us to do burners on them and he had known Seen, so I he wanted to rep the crew on a different line. We liked that.

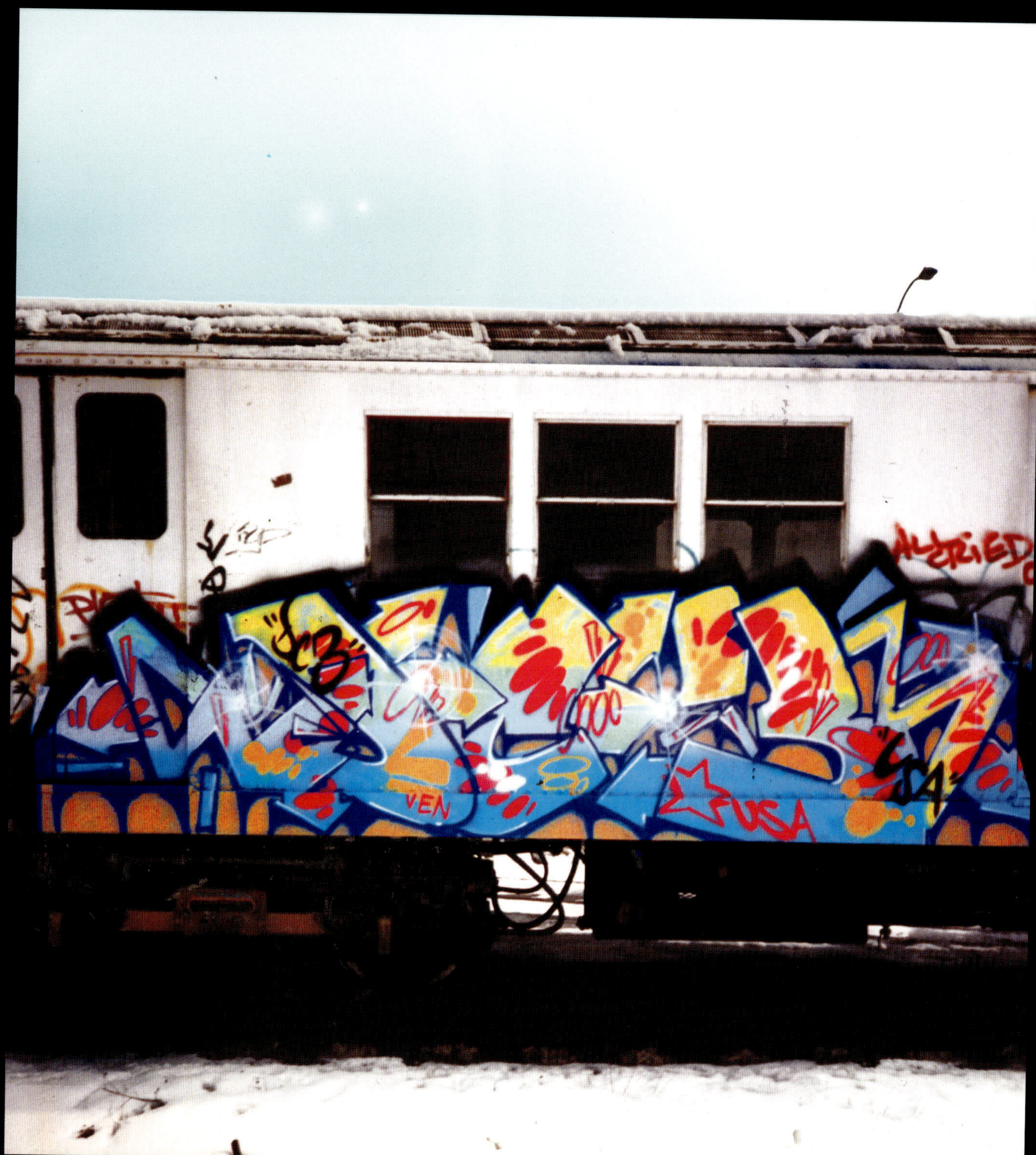

DC3 window-down burner on a 6 Train, Jul. 1987.

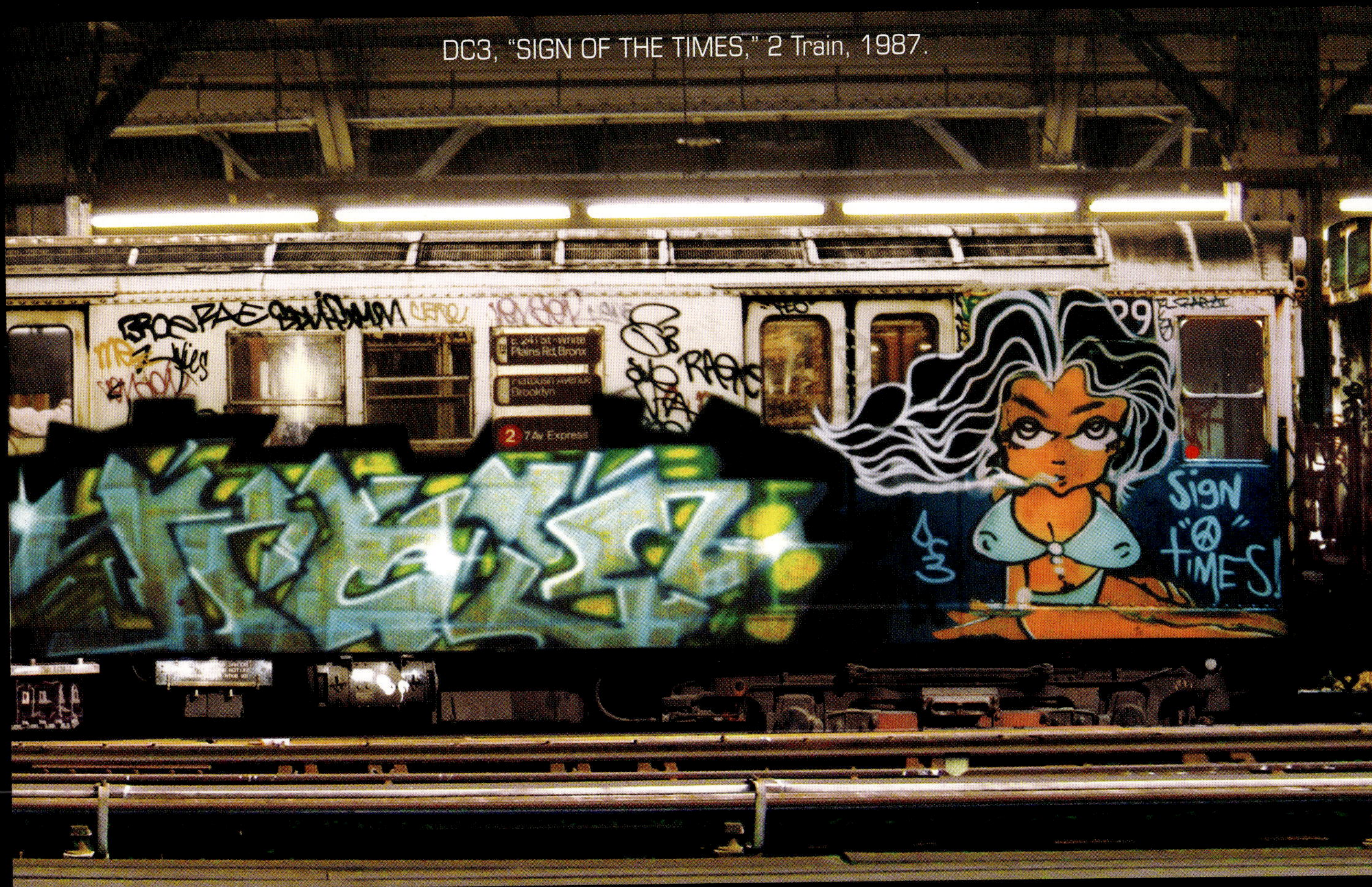

DC3, "SIGN OF THE TIMES," 2 Train, 1987.

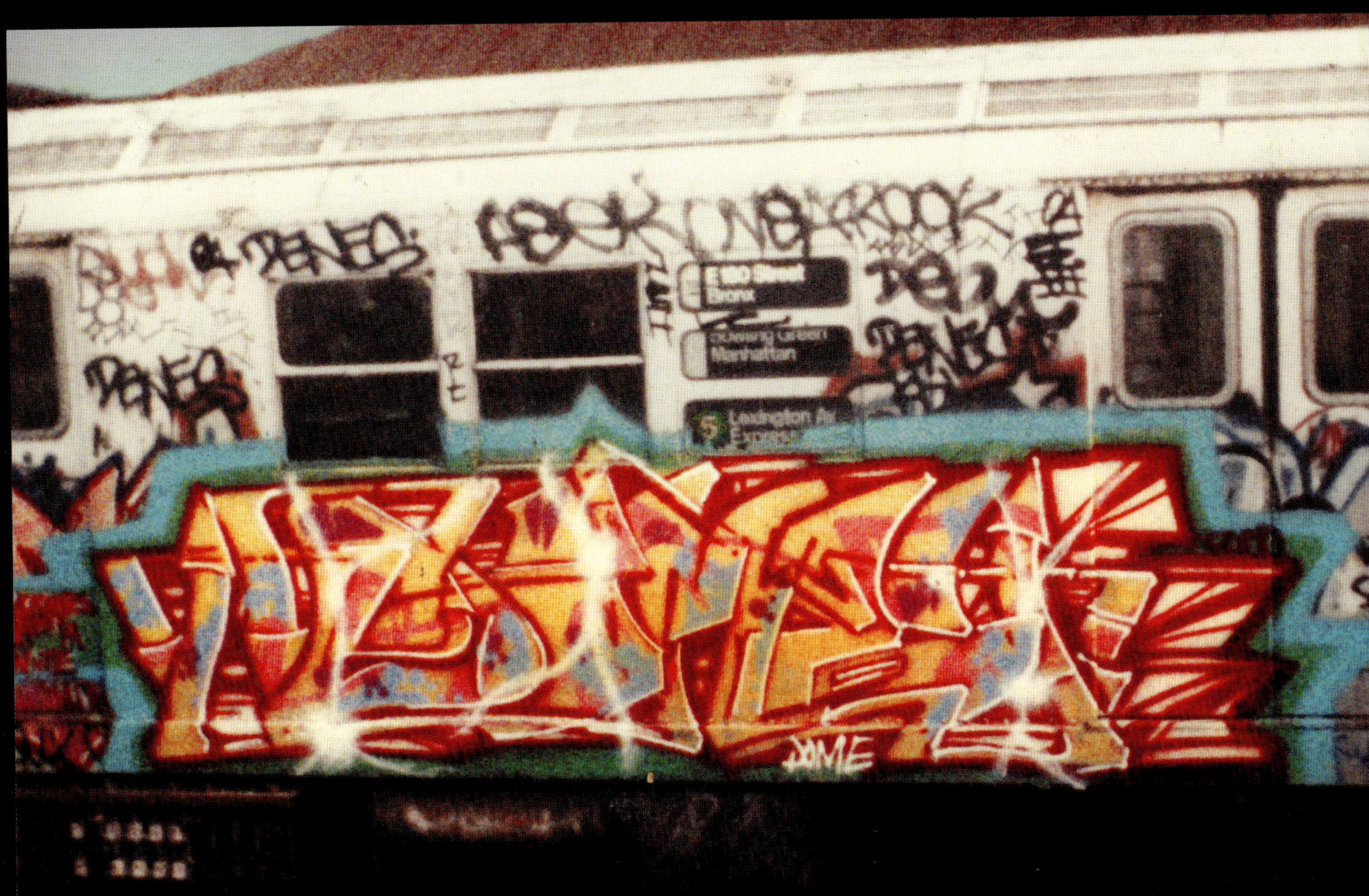

DOME, 5 Train, Feb. 1988.

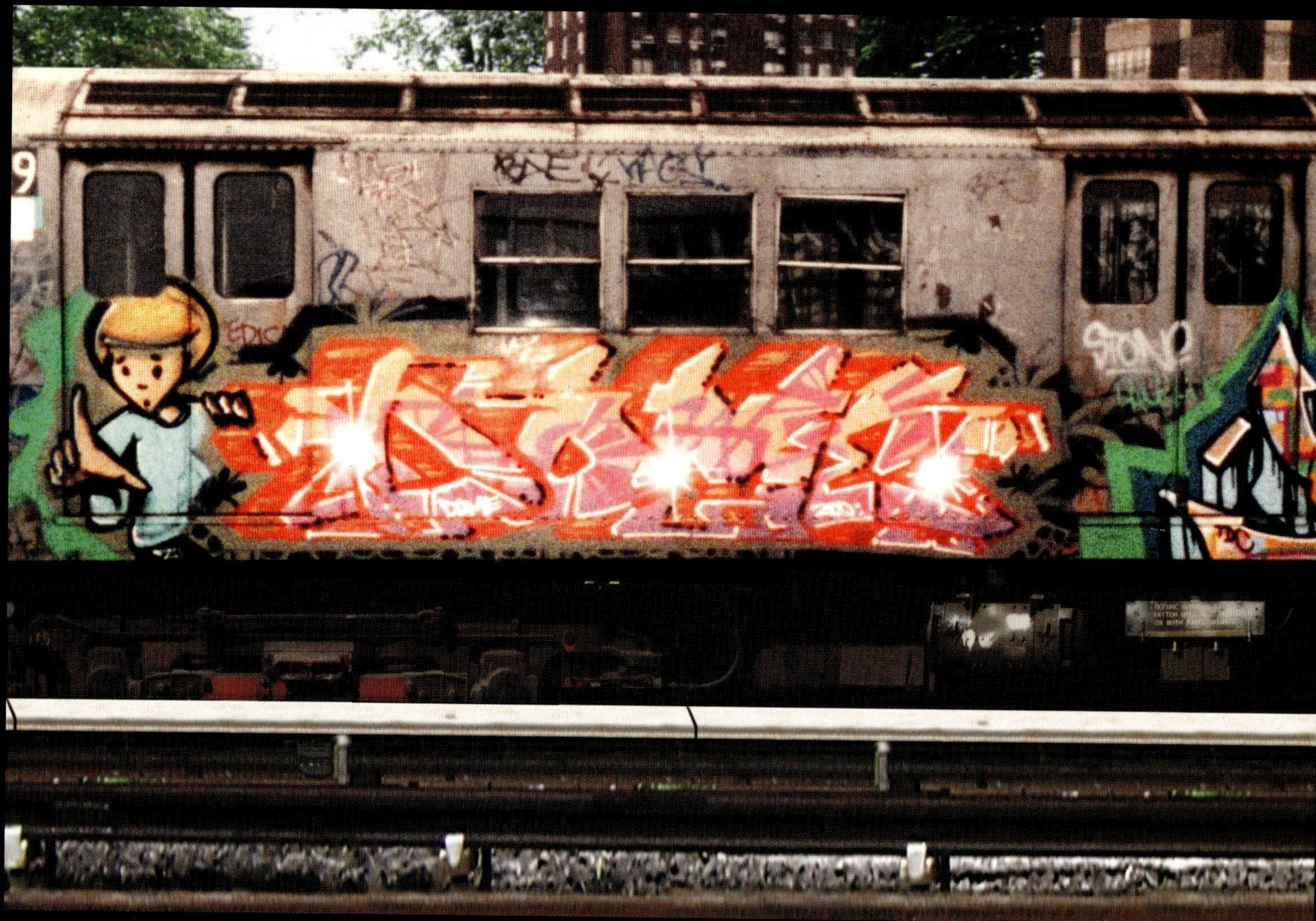

DOME and SHO window-down on an old rusted 5 Train.

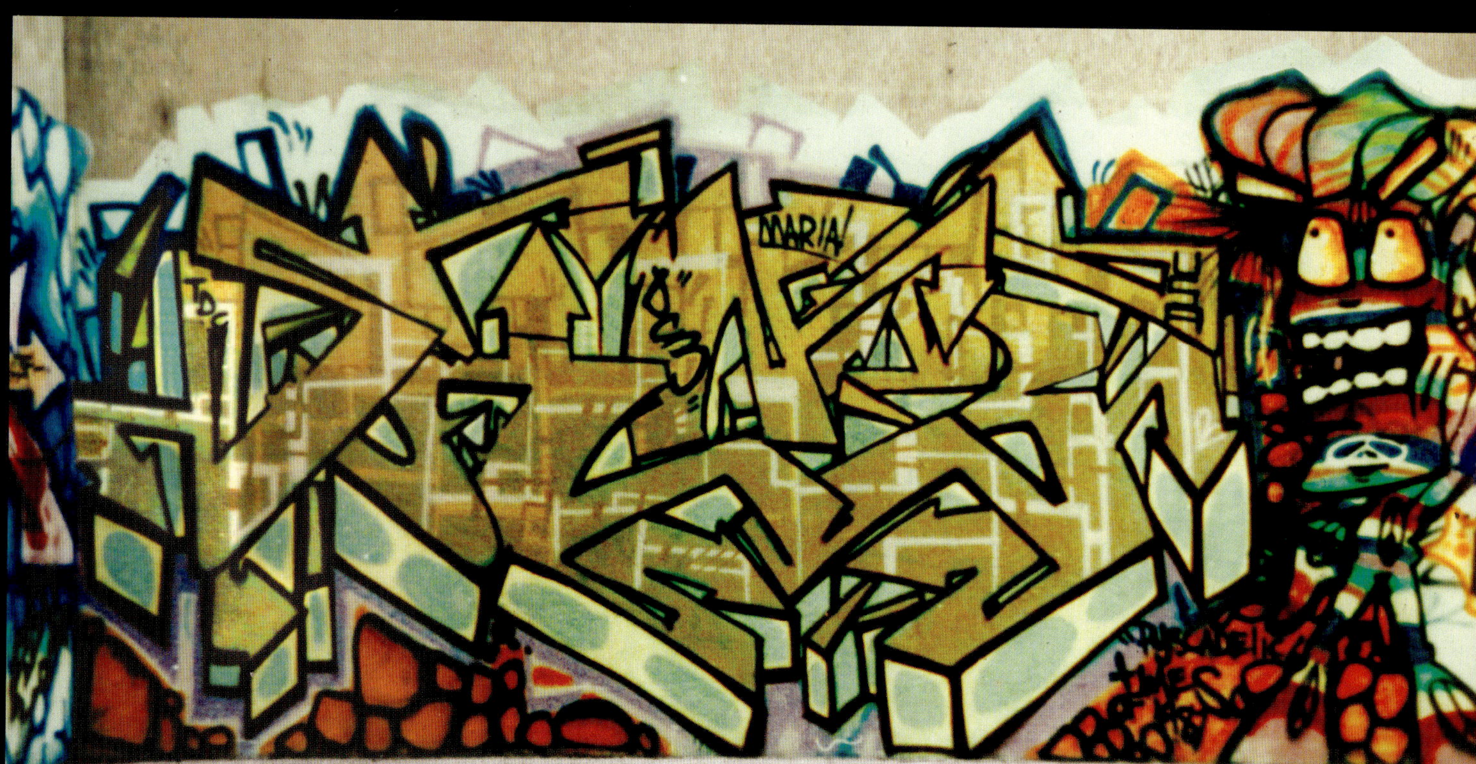

DC3, "PYSEDELIC TIMES," Hempstead, Long Island, 1986.

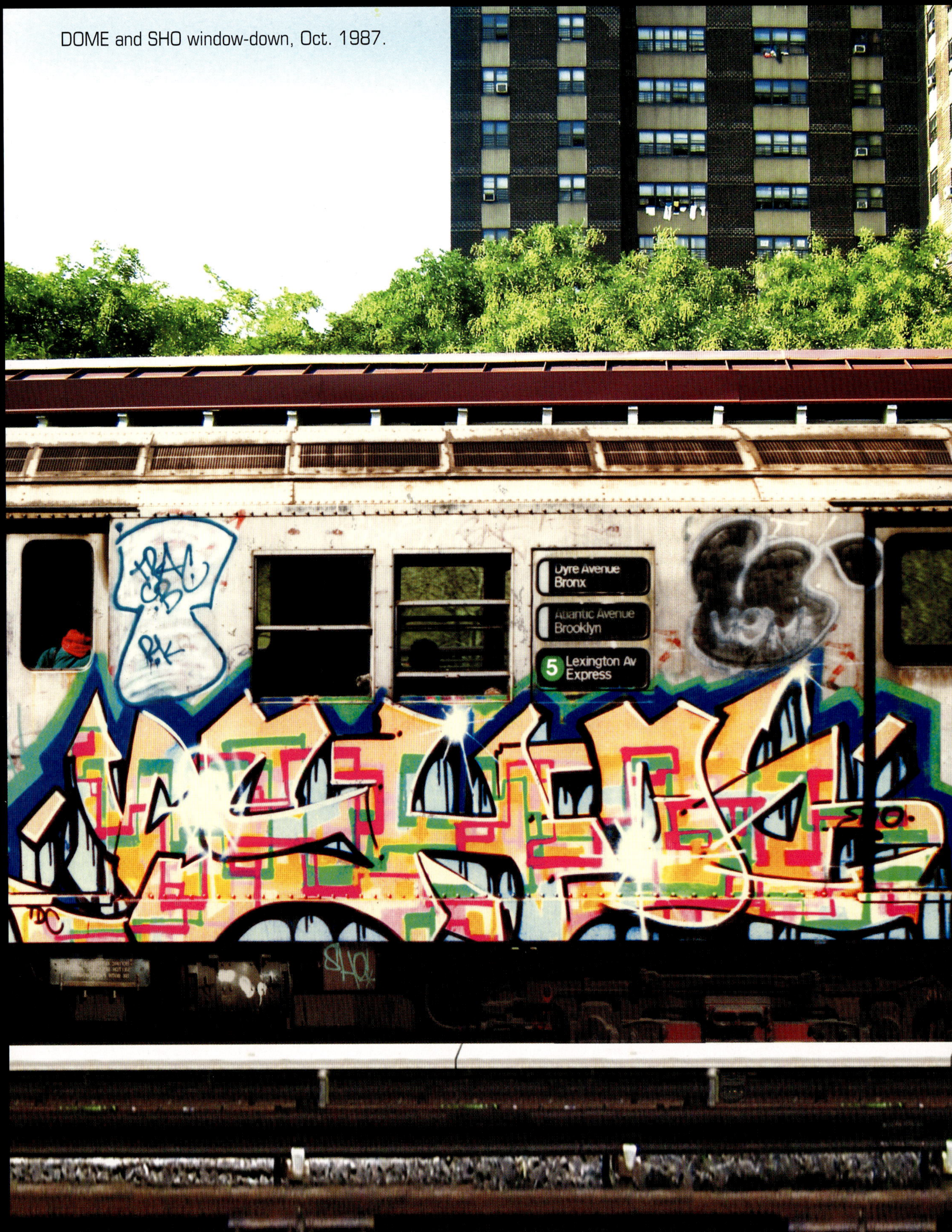

DOME and SHO window-down, Oct. 1987.

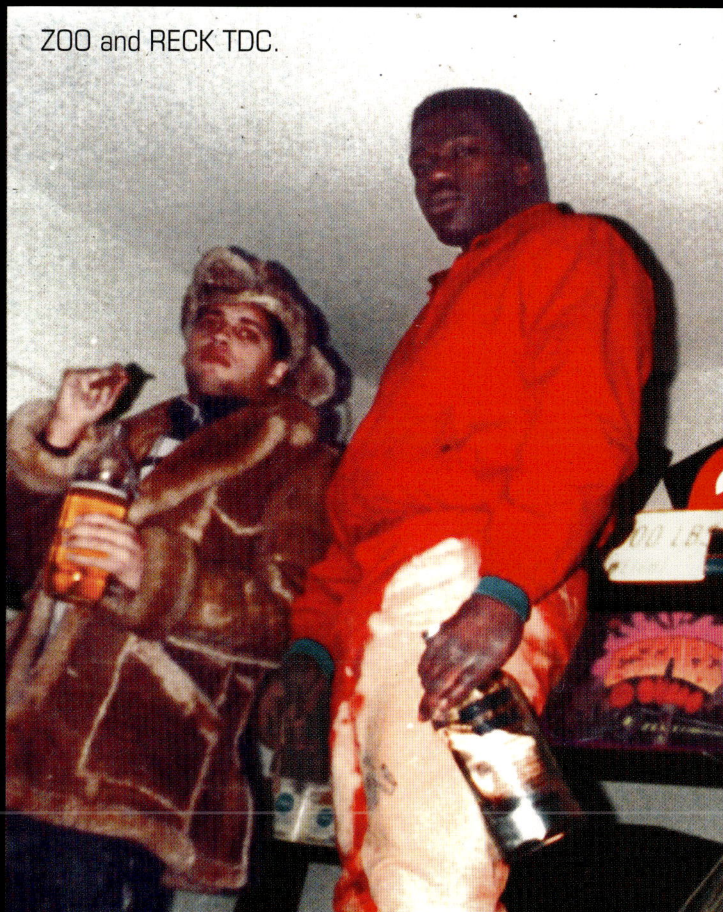

ZOO and RECK TDC.

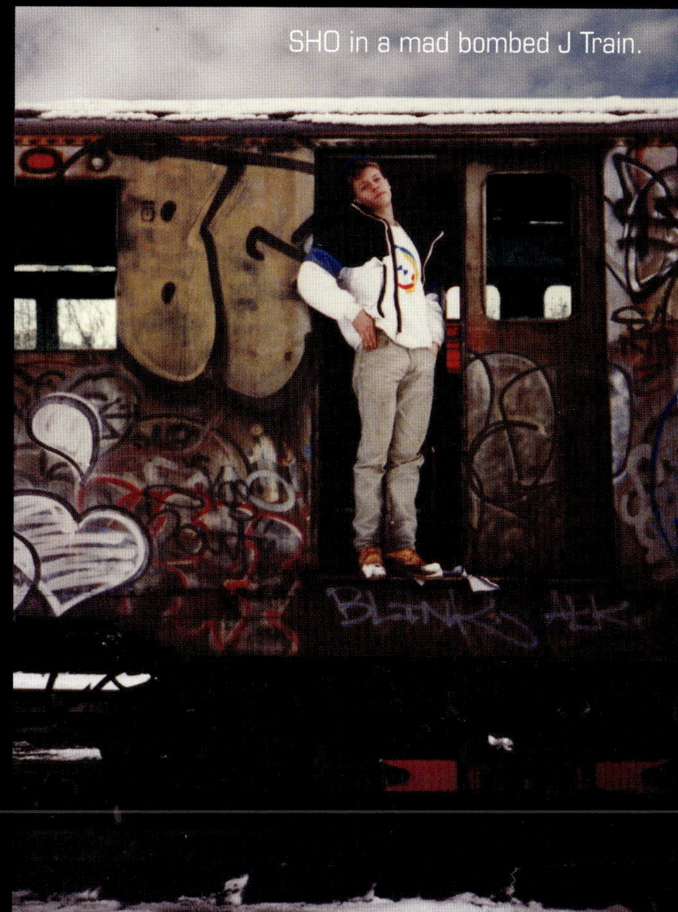

SHO in a mad bombed J Train.

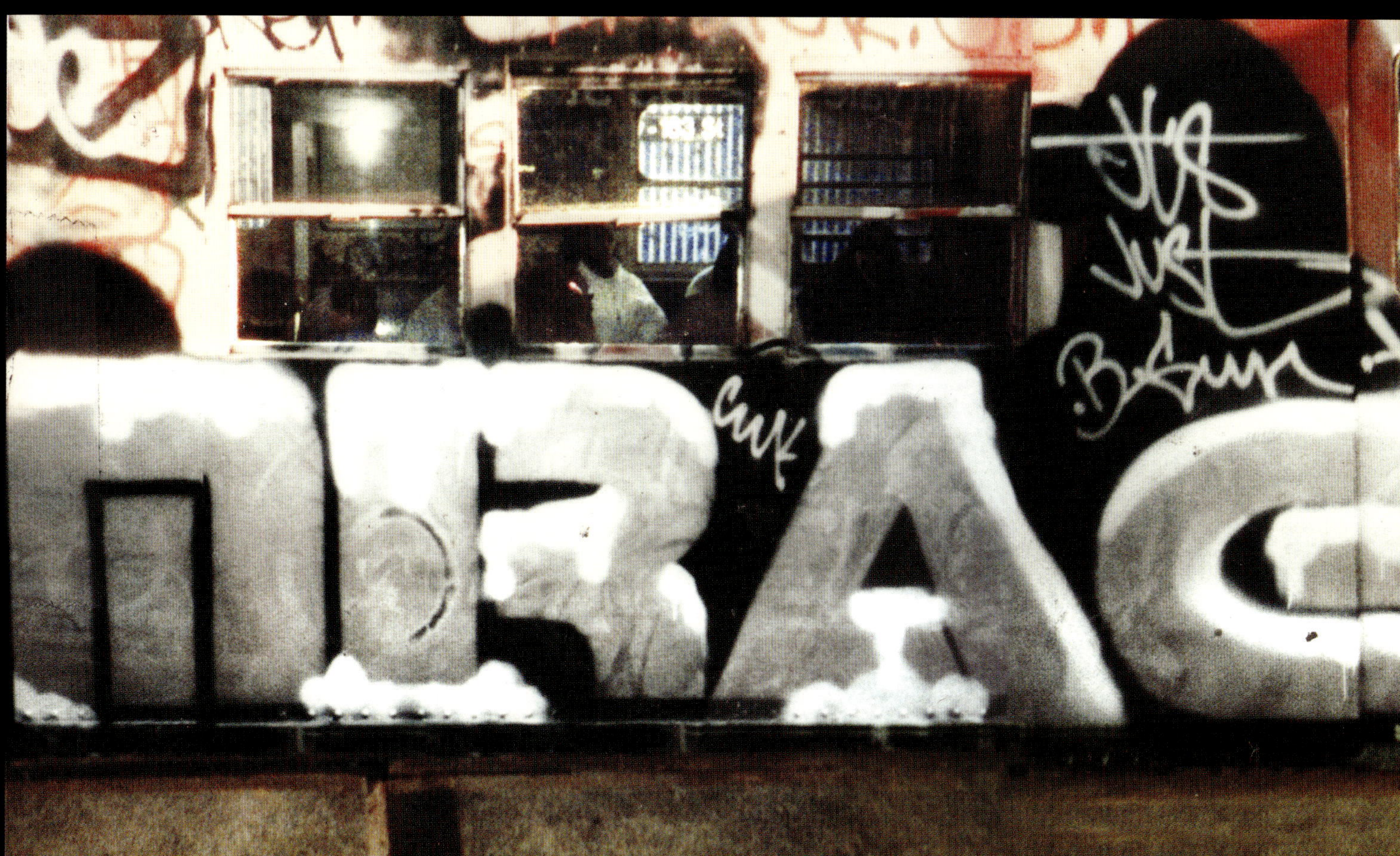

"MRAGE," by MIRAGE. "JUS JUST BUGGING," CWK, Apr. 1987.

SHO gets busy on a J Train, June, 1987.

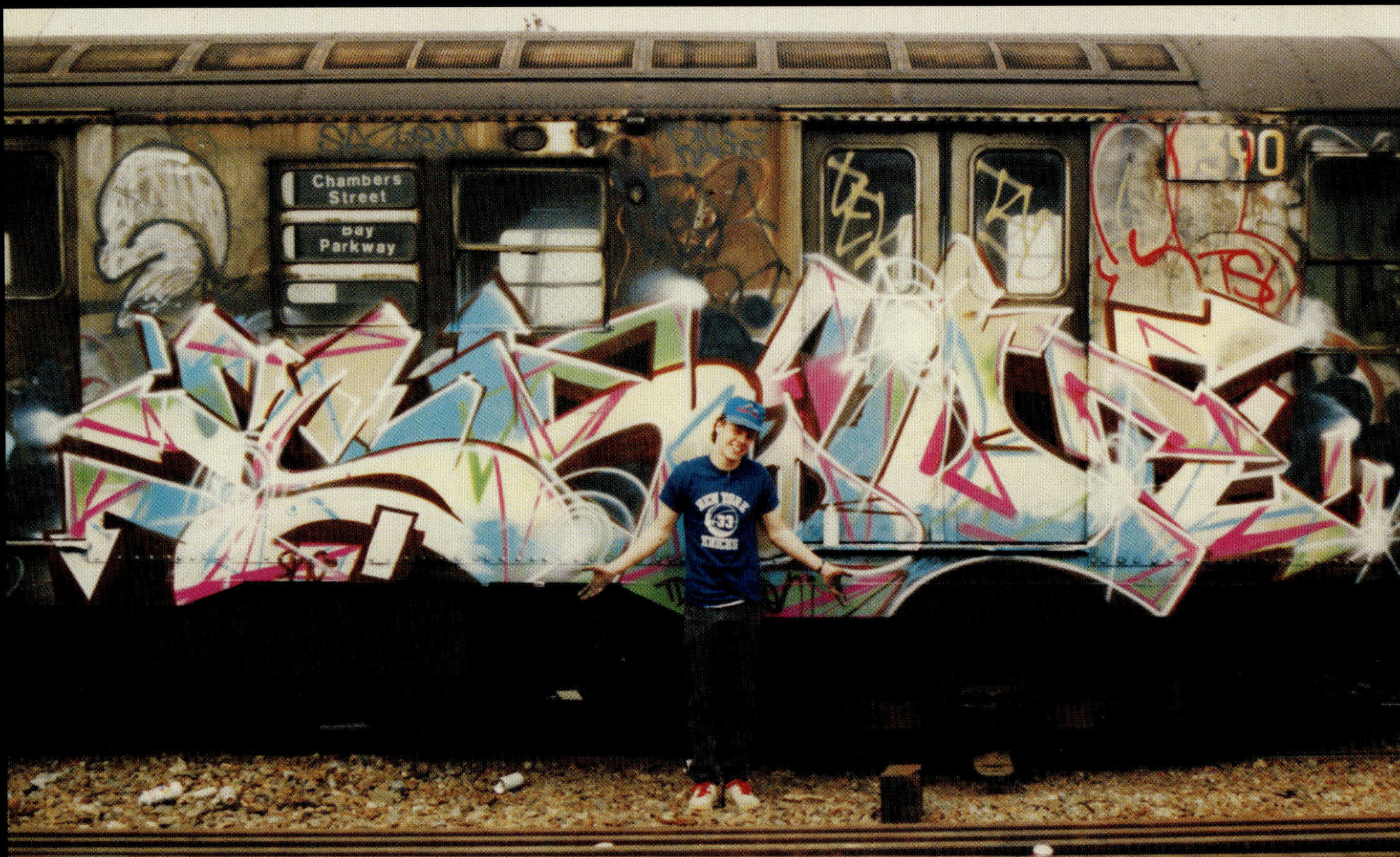

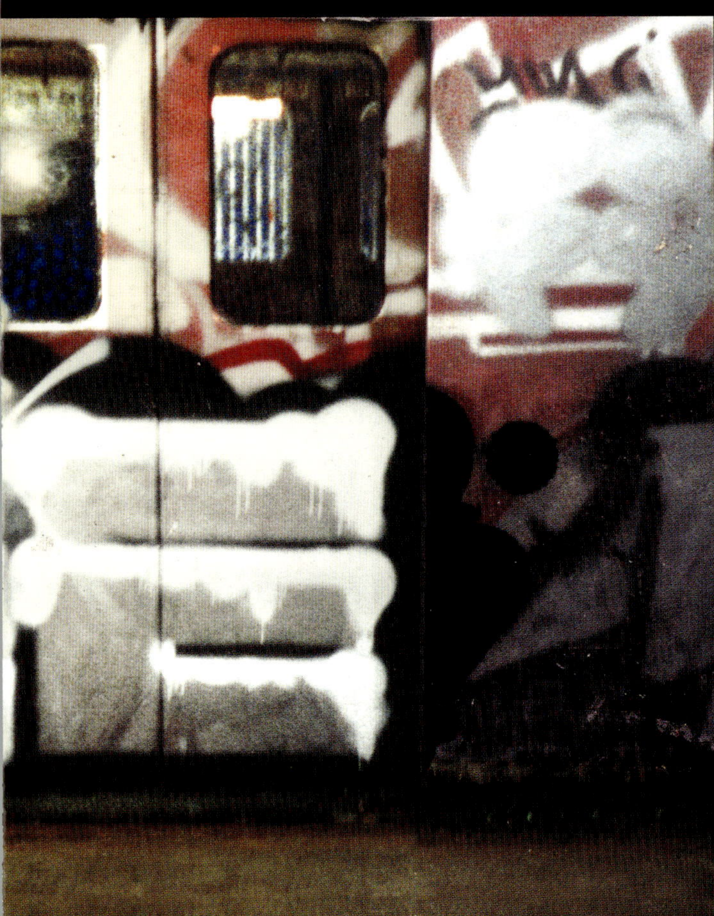

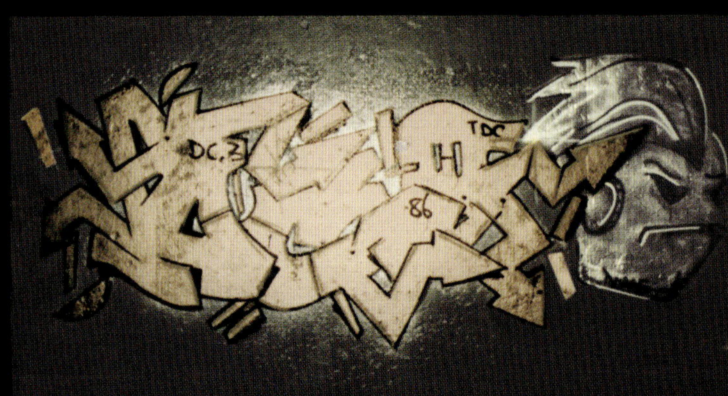

DC3 with a Dome character, Roosevelt, LI, 1986.

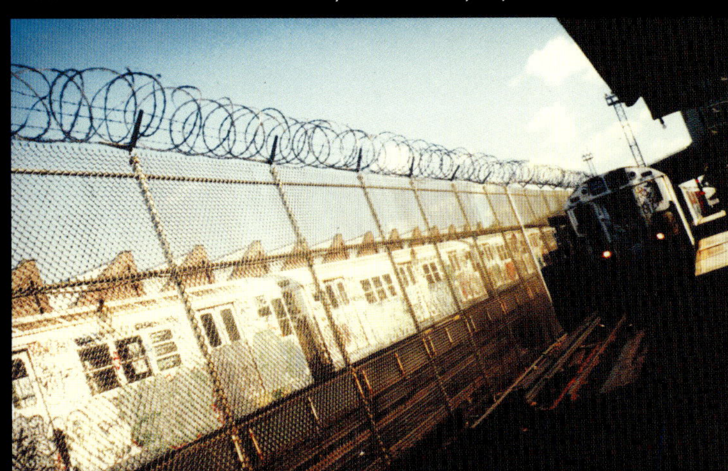

180th St. Station at rush hour.

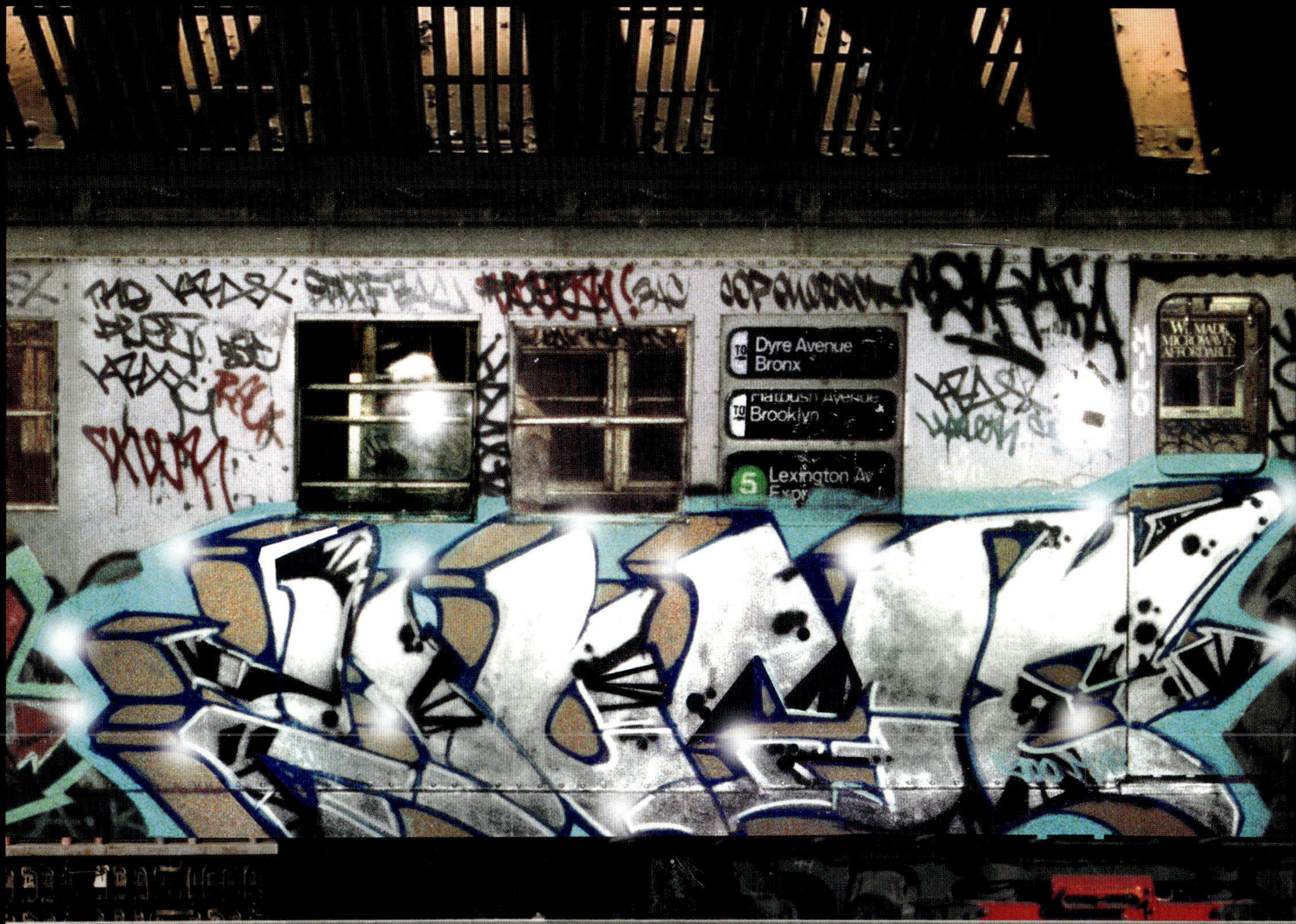

UBI, by DERO and DOME, Jan. 1988.

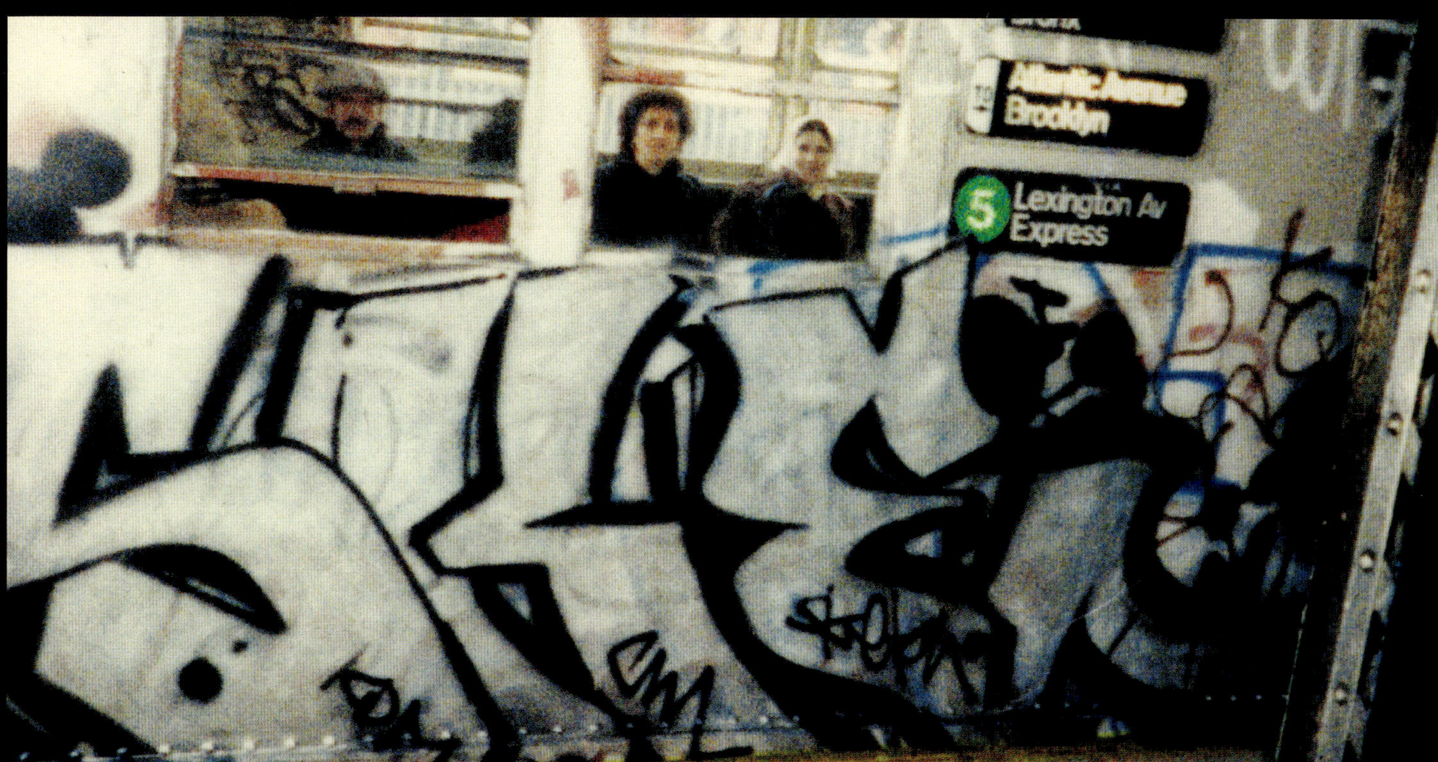

MIRAGE and SKETCH silvers.

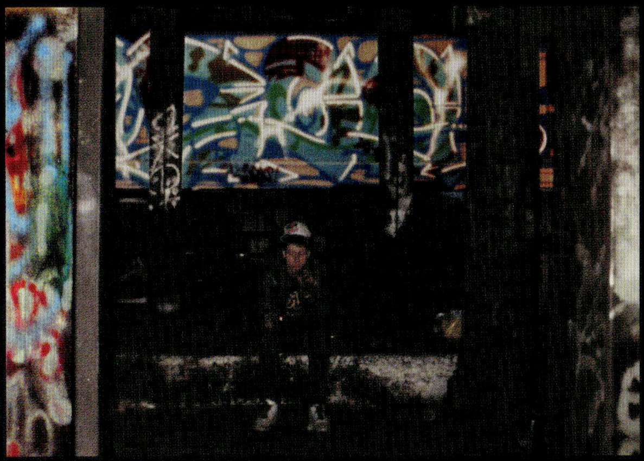

SHO smoking some trees in front of a Zoo car deep in the back of the Utica Ave. daytime lay up.

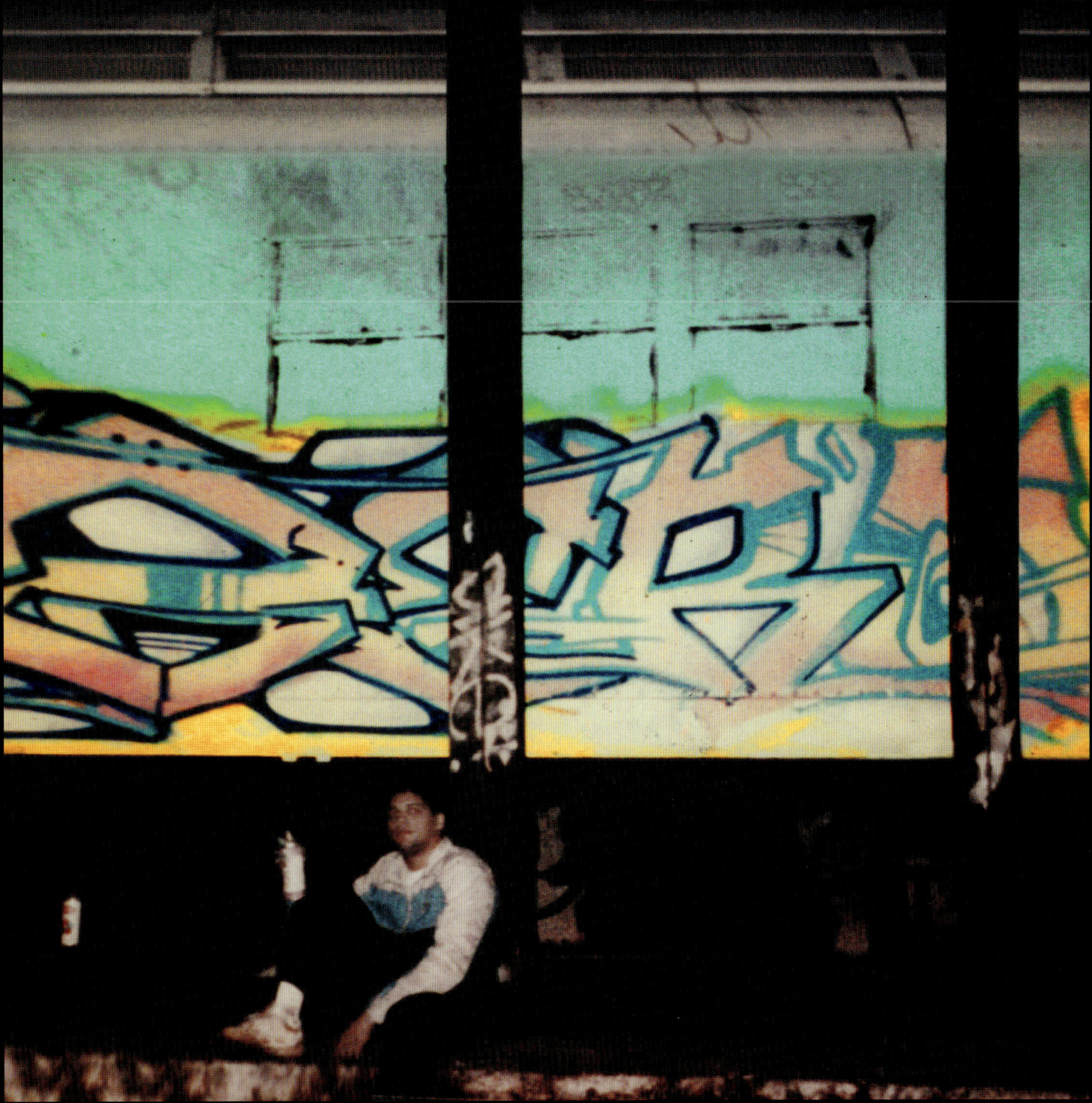

ZERO, aka DOME, taking a break before finishing his outline.

This ZERO SHO train was a real good example of how arrogant and ballsy TDC had become in 1987.Zero was one of Zoos alias names to piece underand I believe it was the only time he burned under this tag. Right around now it was August 1987 and we was getting sick and tired of all the marker mop tags on the 5 Train, forget about the bombing with paint because you could easily paint over it with most colors.

In the event we used flower paint, we would coat the fill-in with white paint let it dry and paint over that shit with the floral paint. As everyone knows, anybody who was anybody racked 100% of everything. We racked paint, markers, black books, cameras, film, and even the processing. Even the Triboro Bridge toll got beaten on a regular basis. We had it made out in Long Island as far as rack spots went, for the floral colors we would hit different spots niggas wouldn't think of, like landscaping and floral supply stores.

This train was a stand out because we did the shit in broad daylight starting at 10:30 A.M. in the after morning rush hour daytime lay up in the Utica Tunnels in Brooklyn, New York. We would literally walk off a packed double-sided, 4-track platform into the tunnels not giving a fuck if anybody saw us. Our motto was, "Don't act petro," and people would just assume you were work bums going to work. The main thing was to hide from workers and the conductors. Dome and I did this train in 2.5 hours, which was a super fast result because they started pulling them out for the afternoon rush at 2 P.M. The train was beyond bombed, but that shit didn't matter because I brought a gallon of baby blue house paint and literally rolled the whole train in 20 minutes.

Man, I'm telling you, I was covered in paint when we left out and walked right back up onto the platform and out the station to the car upstairs. That also was the only time I ever rolled a train, but it worked well. We laughed all the way home after getting beers and blunts.

-SHO TDC

ZERO and SHO 5 Train, "MY TRAINS ARE HUNGRY BECAUSE THEY HAVEN'T BEEN FED," TDCRU, Aug. 1987.

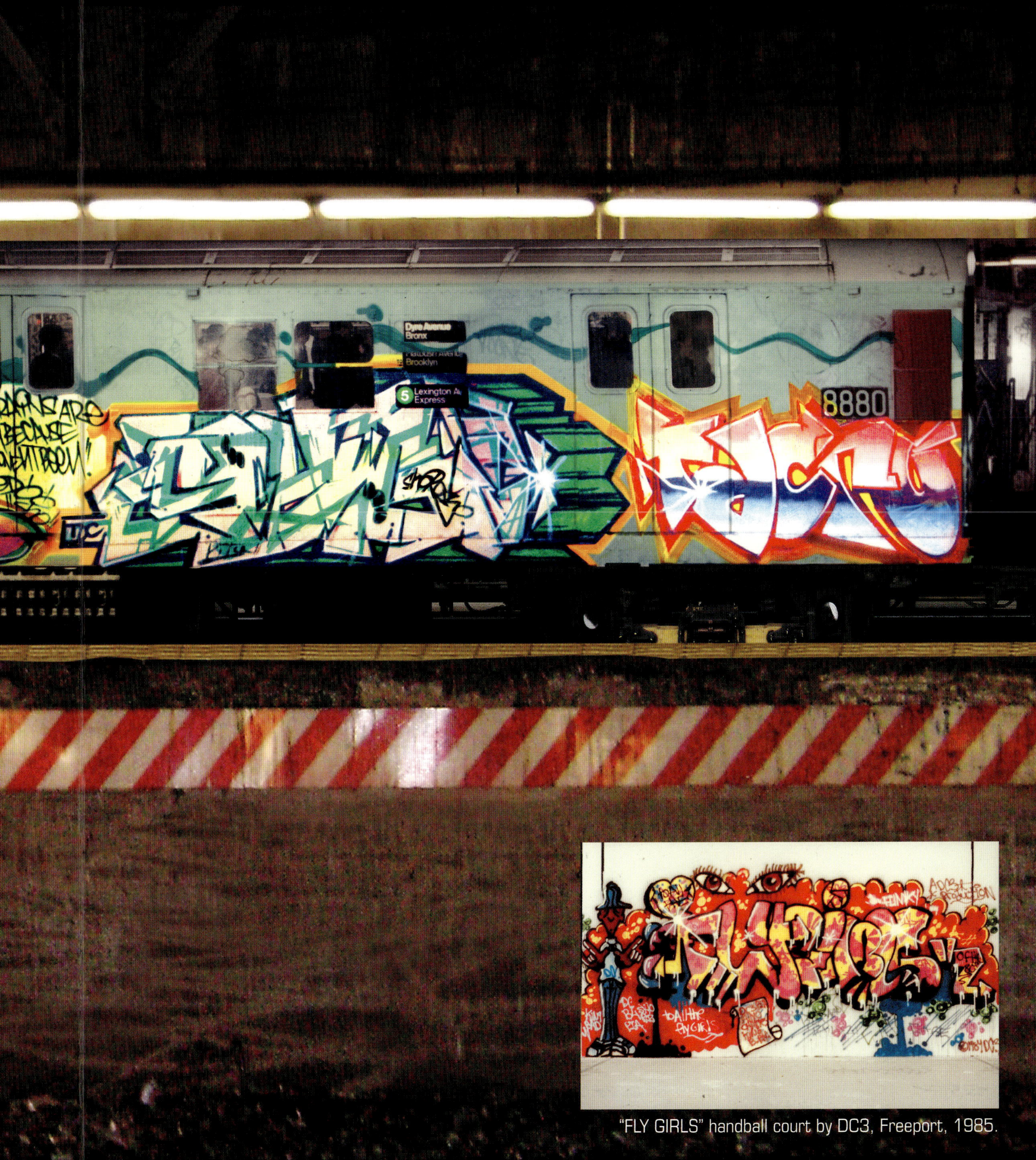

"FLY GIRLS" handball court by DC3, Freeport, 1985.

"The JUGGERNAUT SHO" train rocked during a blizzard at the Harlem (103rd-125th St.) Lexington Ave. Tunnels.

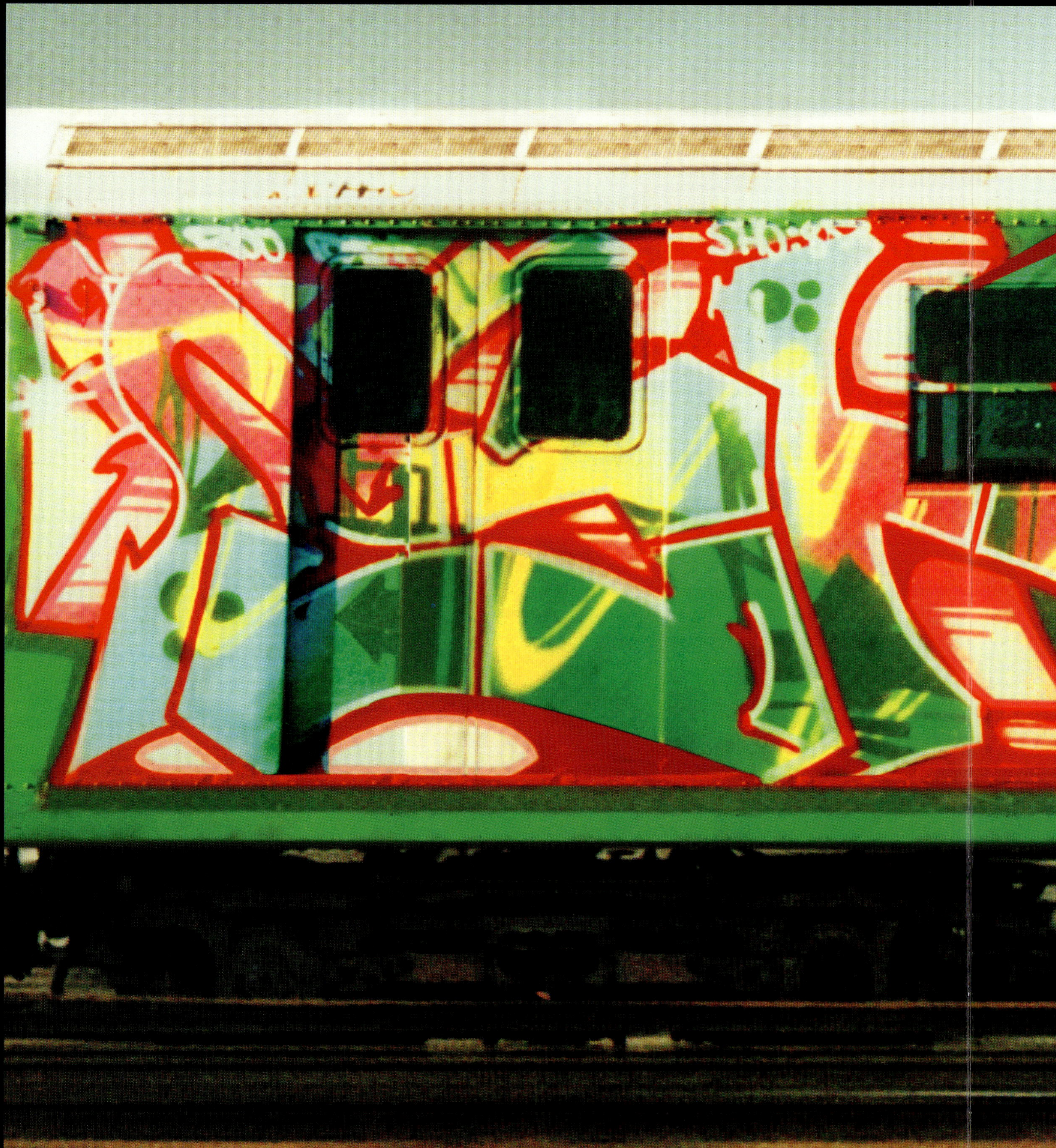

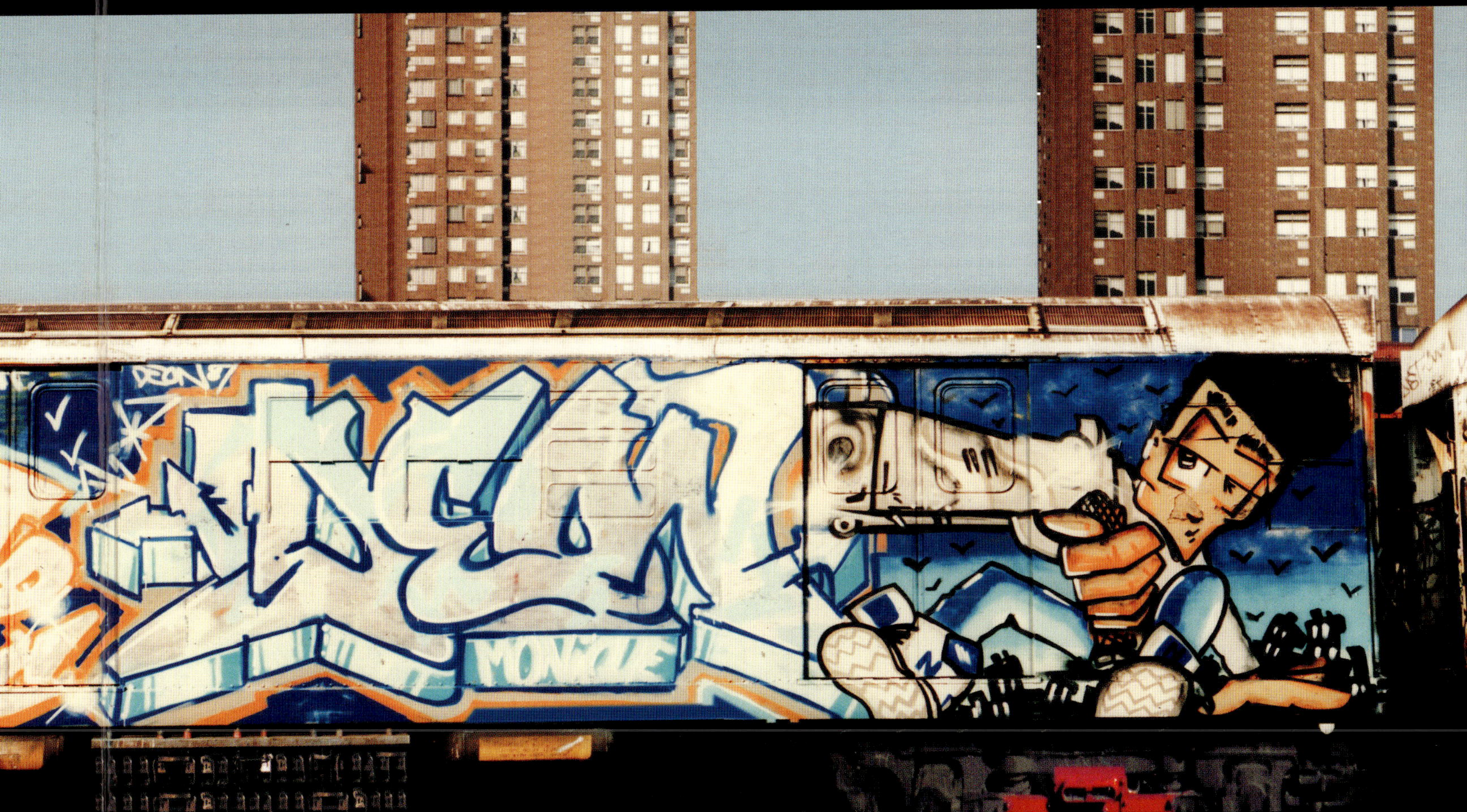

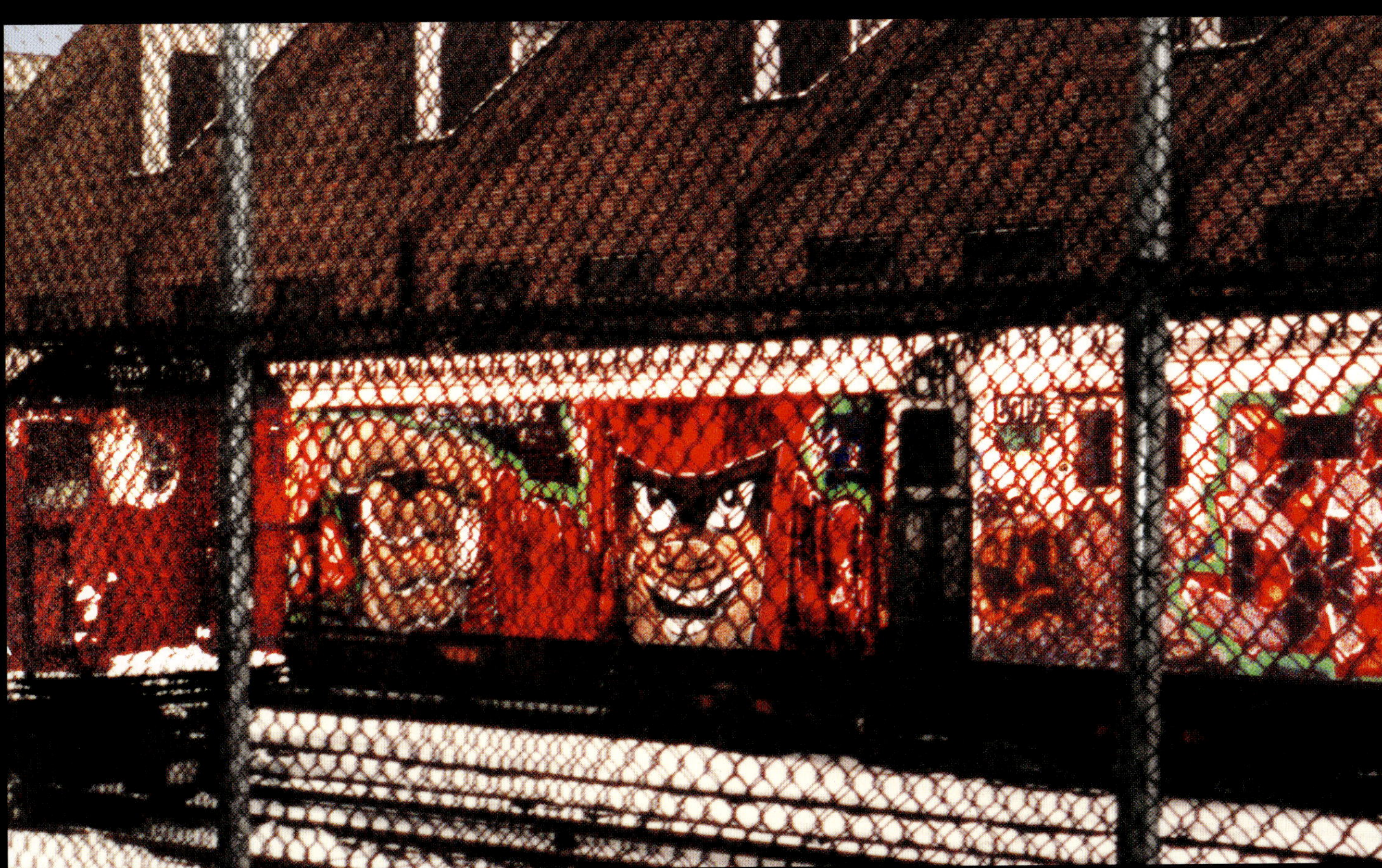

The "Juggernaut" train parked in the 180th St. Yard.

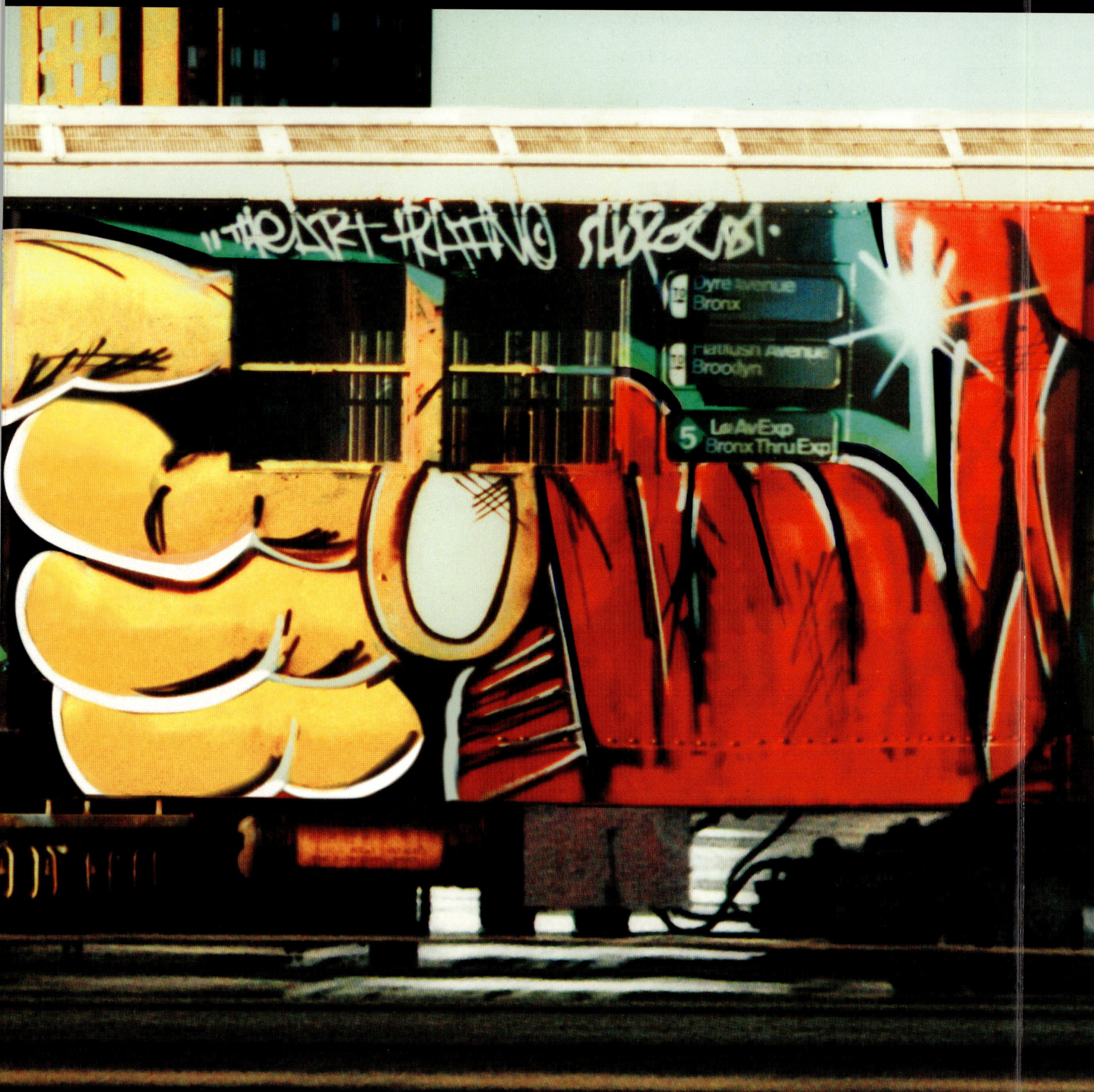

The entire

CHAPTER 4

Winter Bombing and the Night of the Illest Raid.

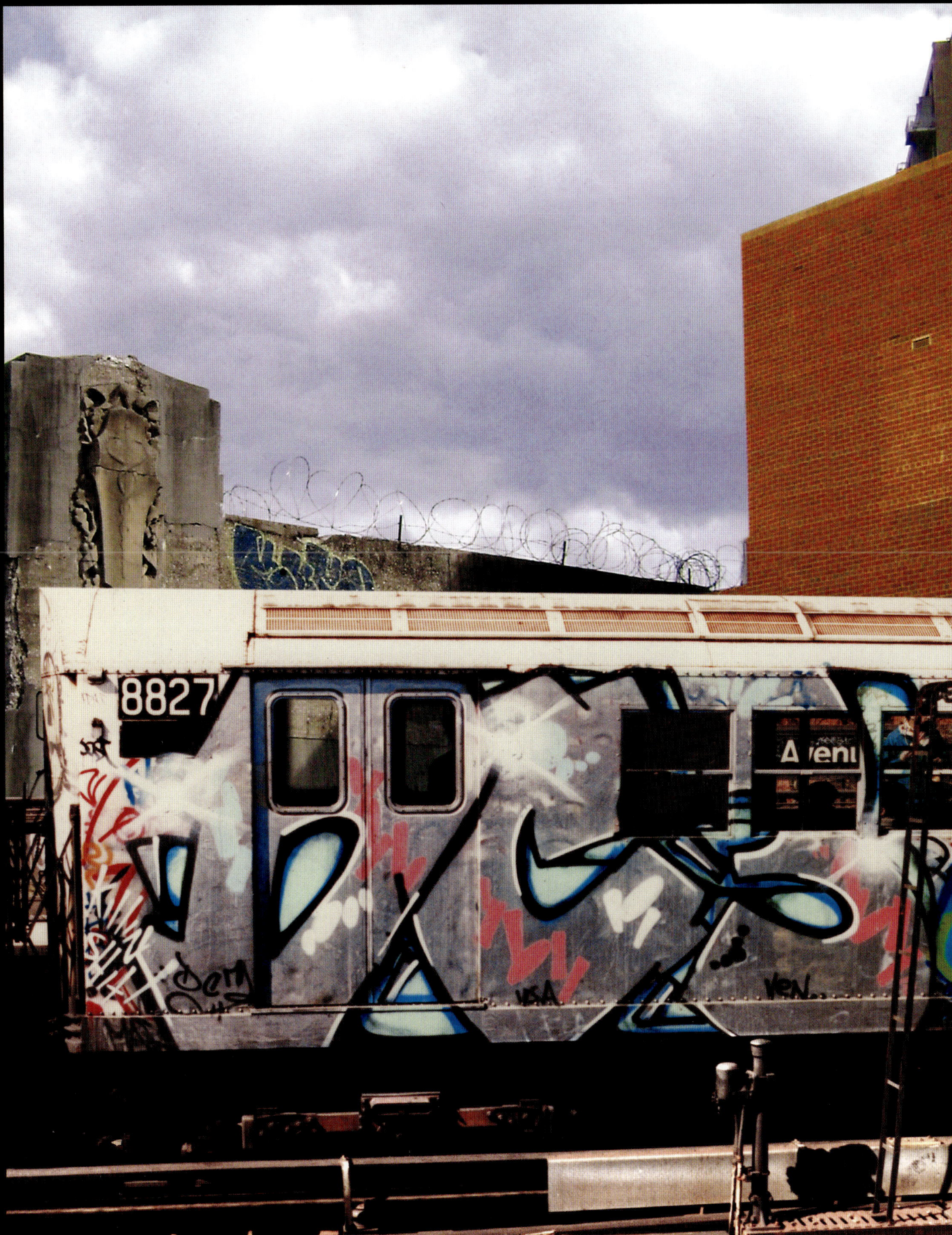

DC3, "KILLING SHIT," top-to-bottom with FENT and DEON, Mar. 1988.

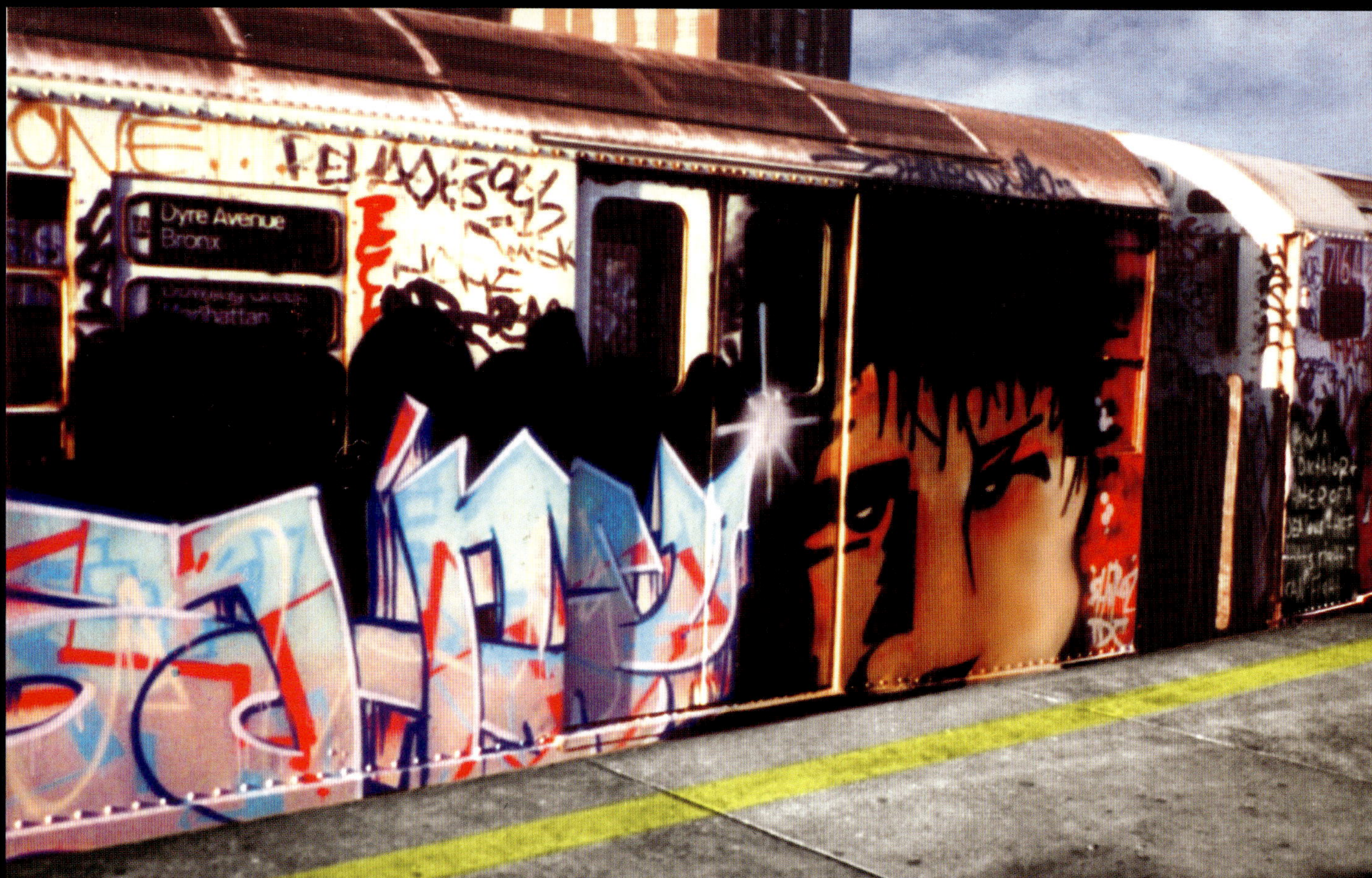

SHO, "Self Portrait" platform shot running at East Tremont.

The "H" extension on the Dome SHO Self portrait train wrapping around the back is fucking classic! I remember it was the fall of 1986, earlier in that day we did a nice rack session (stealing paint) and we had a plan for a window-down—this could have been the first time we did characters on trains. I remember in the middle of our painting this car, work bums walked thru and they recognized us from a couple of days ago and we gave them some beer and just talked to them about us not painting on the windows and they was cool with it. That's how often we were going painting—we were running into the same work bums on the weekday nights. We went on weekdays a lot cause we felt it was less hot, no toys making noise and being careless. The weekends were also sweet cause you had less overall train traffic. One time we were painting and some toys walked thru slamming doors talking loud and they broke into the conductors booth and they turned on the intercom and started rhyming thru the speakers real loud. I don't now how we didn't get raided that night, but as much as I was pissed, I thought that shit was funny as hell!!!! Every night was a new animal and you had to expect the unexpected. Lots of great bombing memories.

-DOME TDC

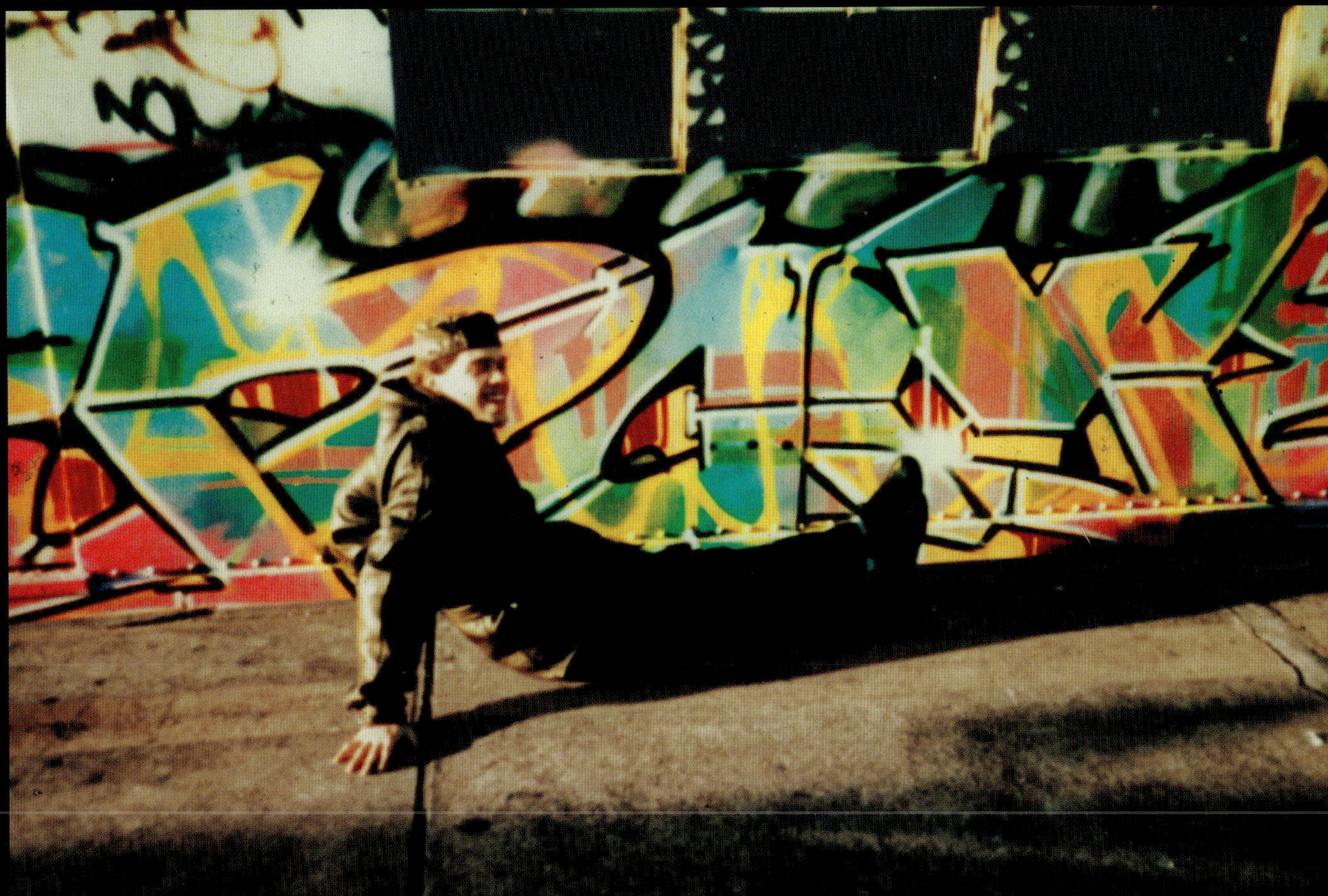

DOME enjoying himself while benching his trains at East Tremont.

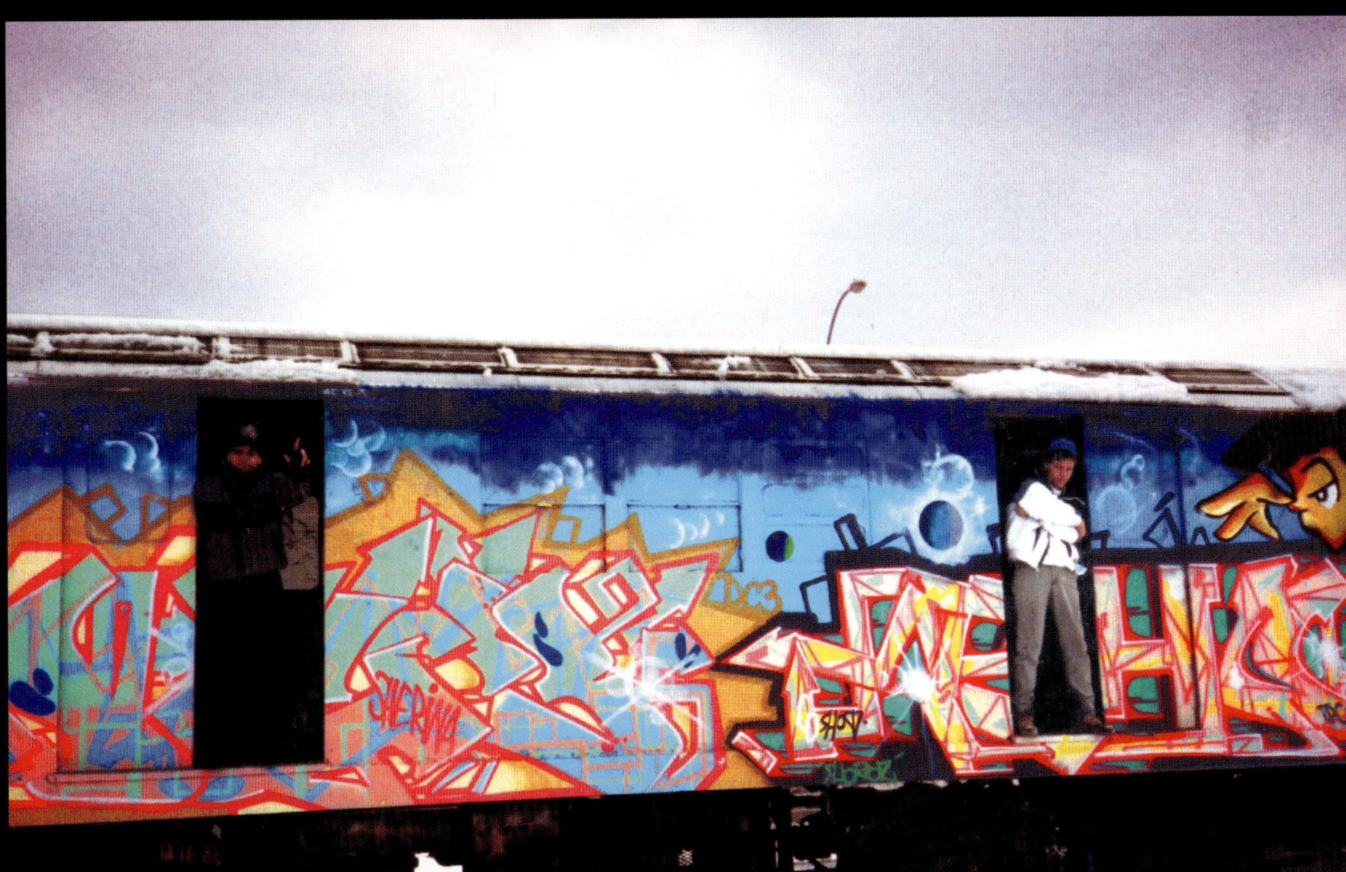

ZOO and SHO getting pictures that writers only dream of...

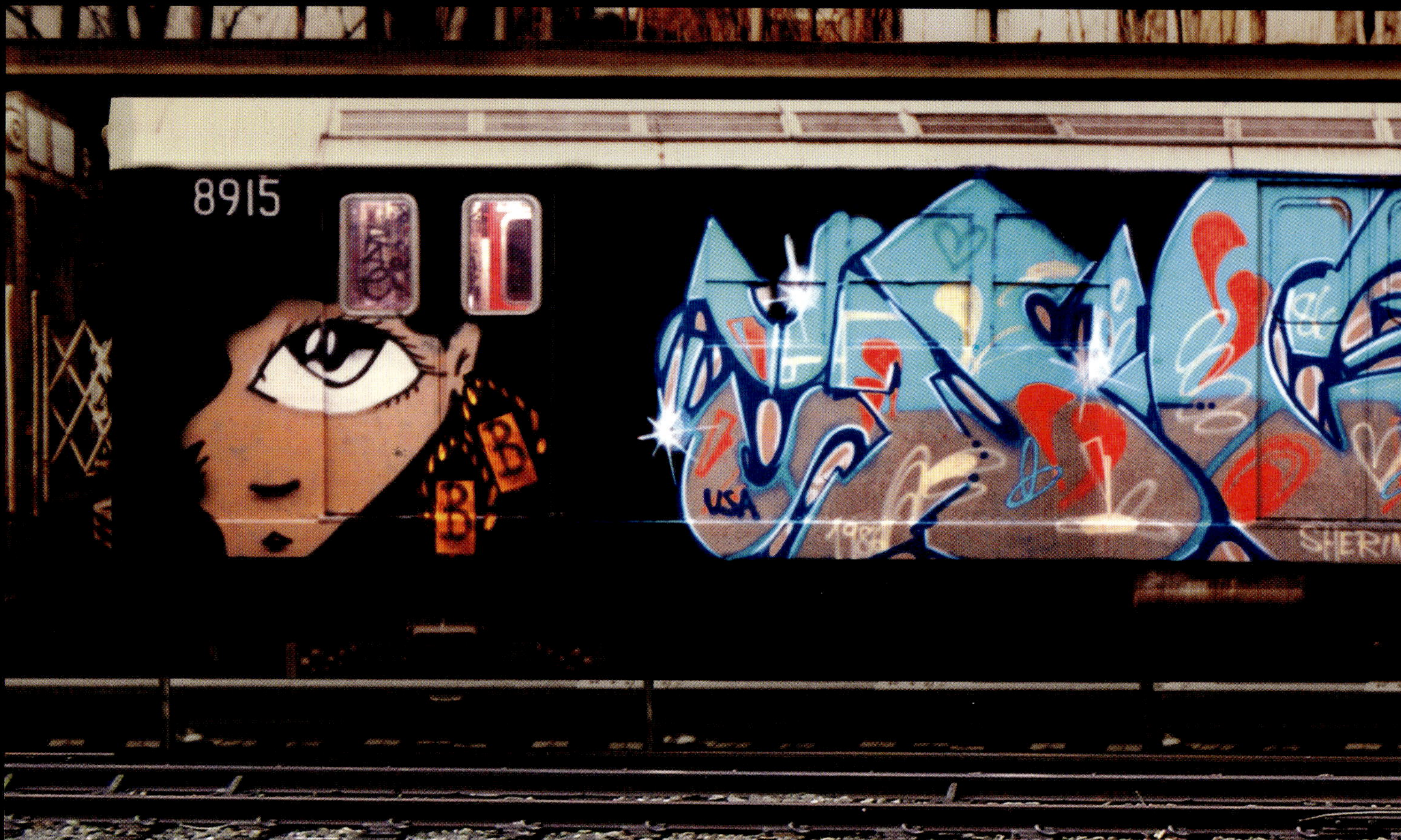

DC3 top-to-bottom with Bally Girl characters, Oct. 1987.

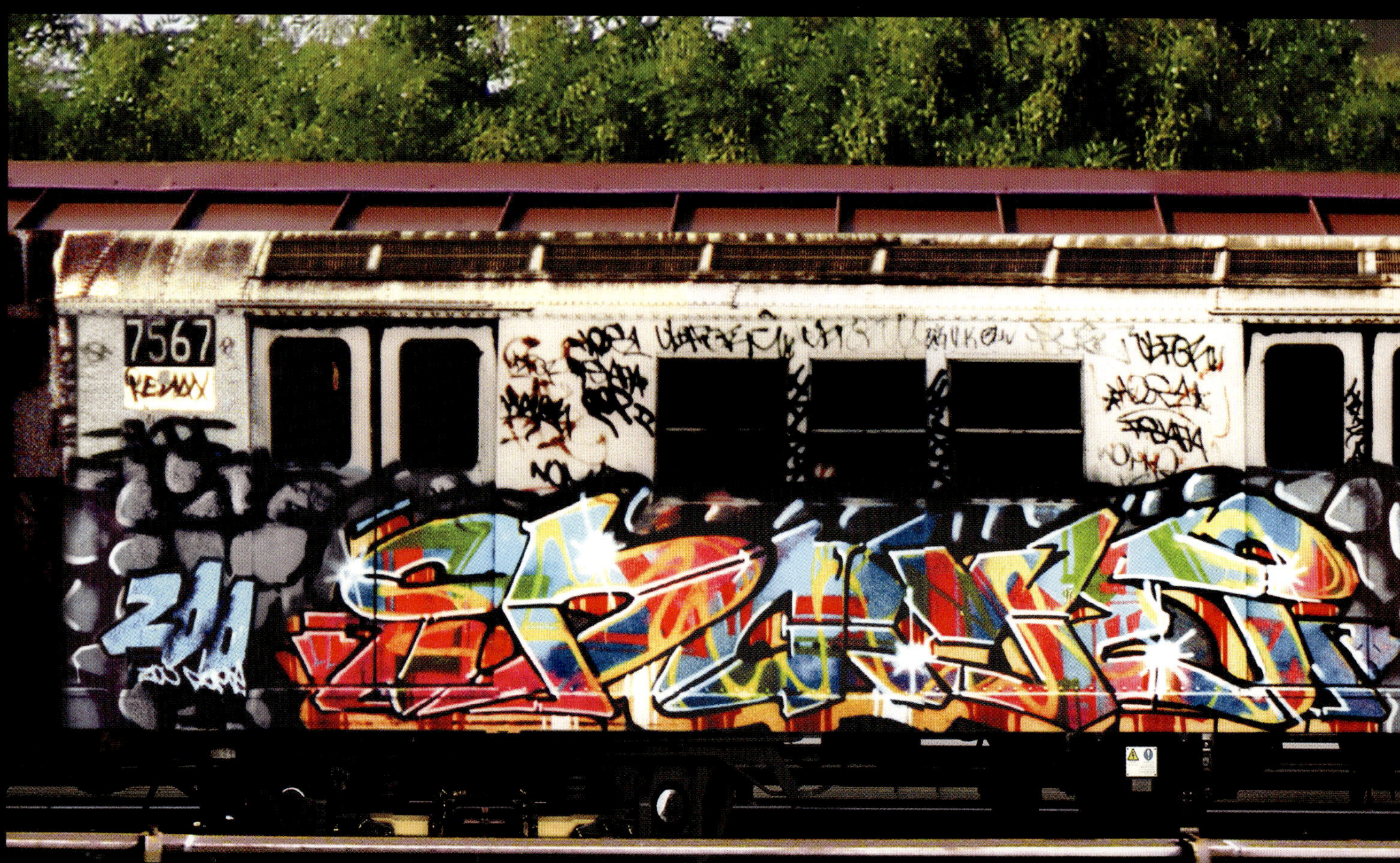

ZOO, aka DOME, and SHO, "Self Portrait," 5 Train, Nov. 1986.

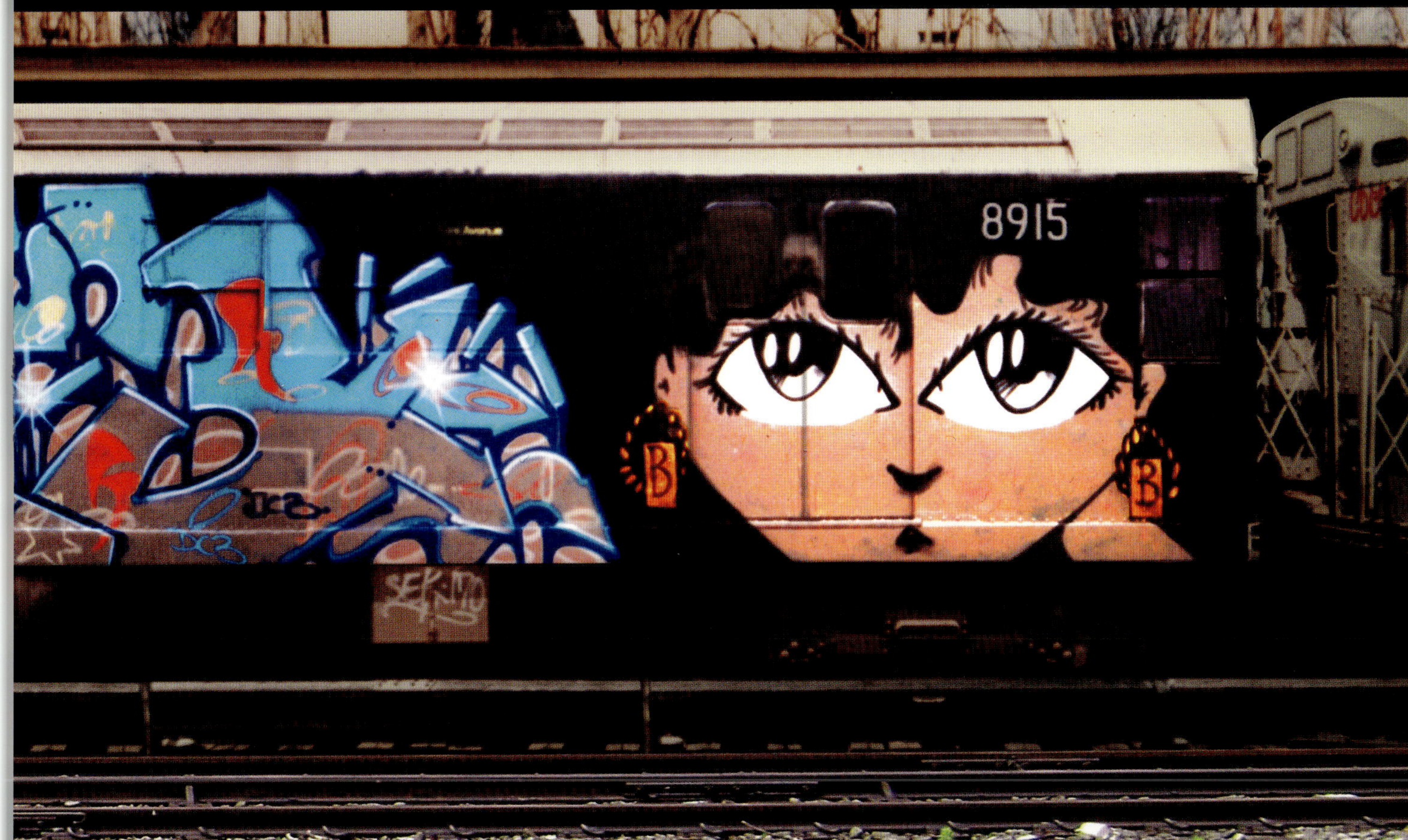
8915

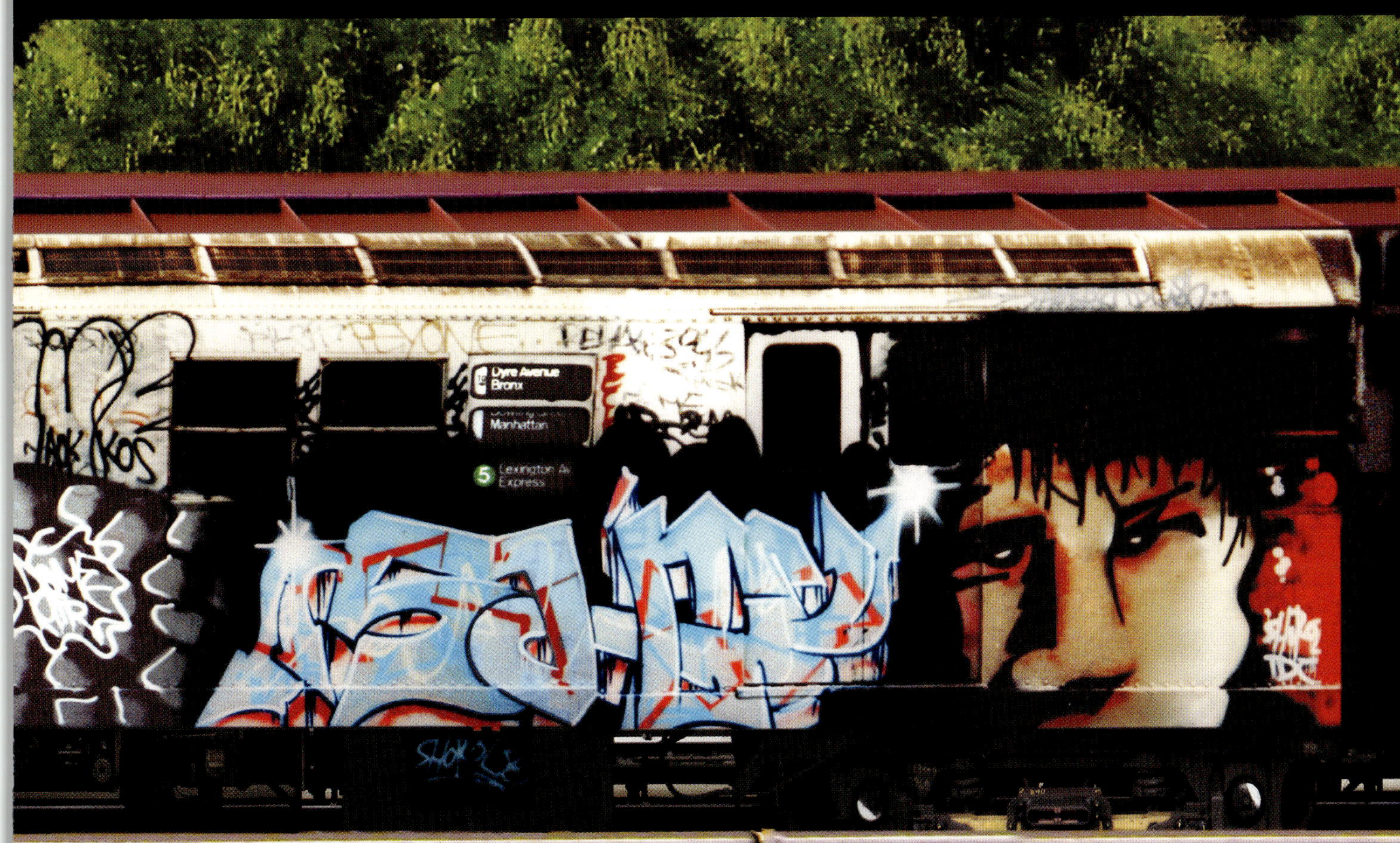
Dyre Avenue
Bronx
Manhattan

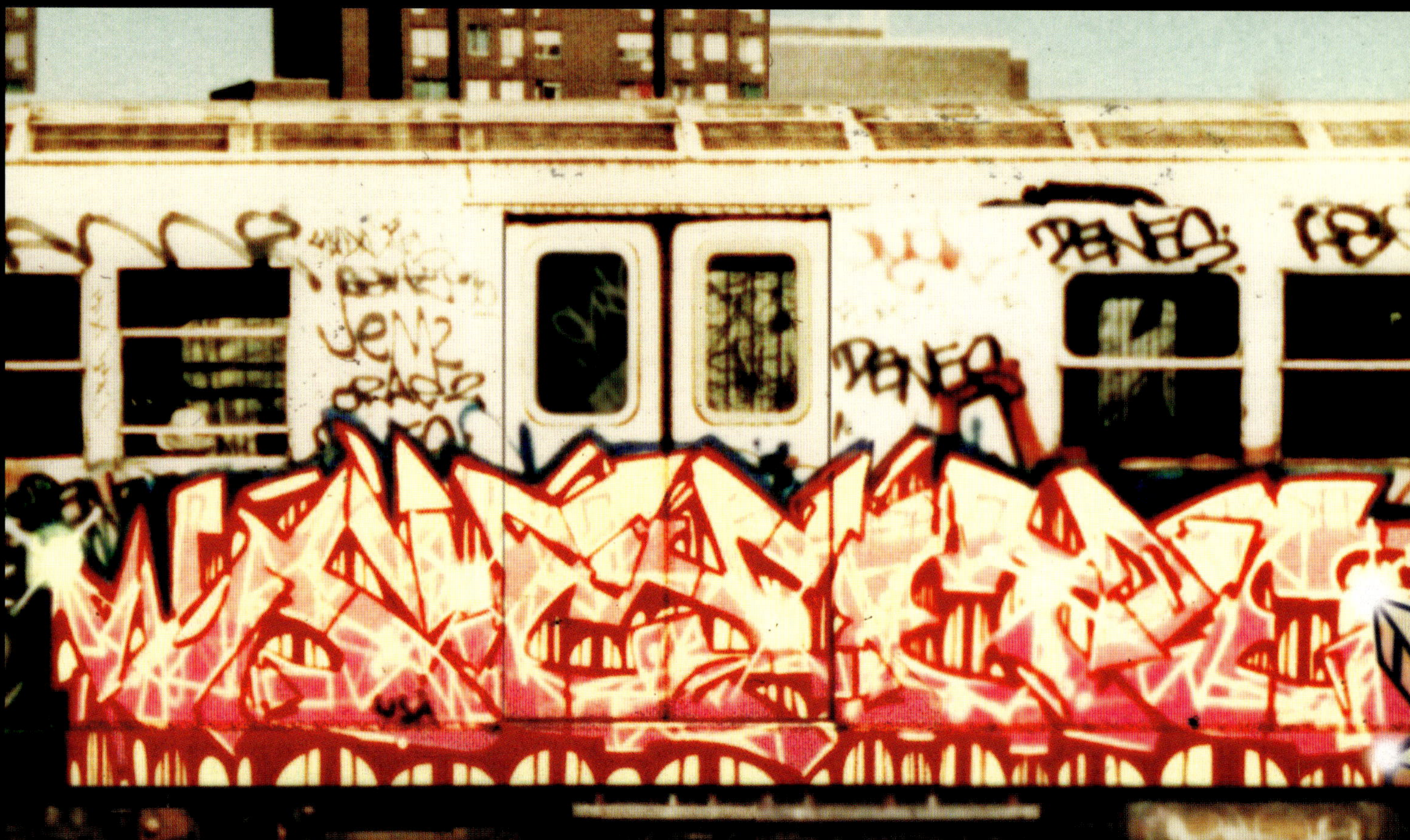

DCEE3 and SHO, 5 Train, Dec. 1986.

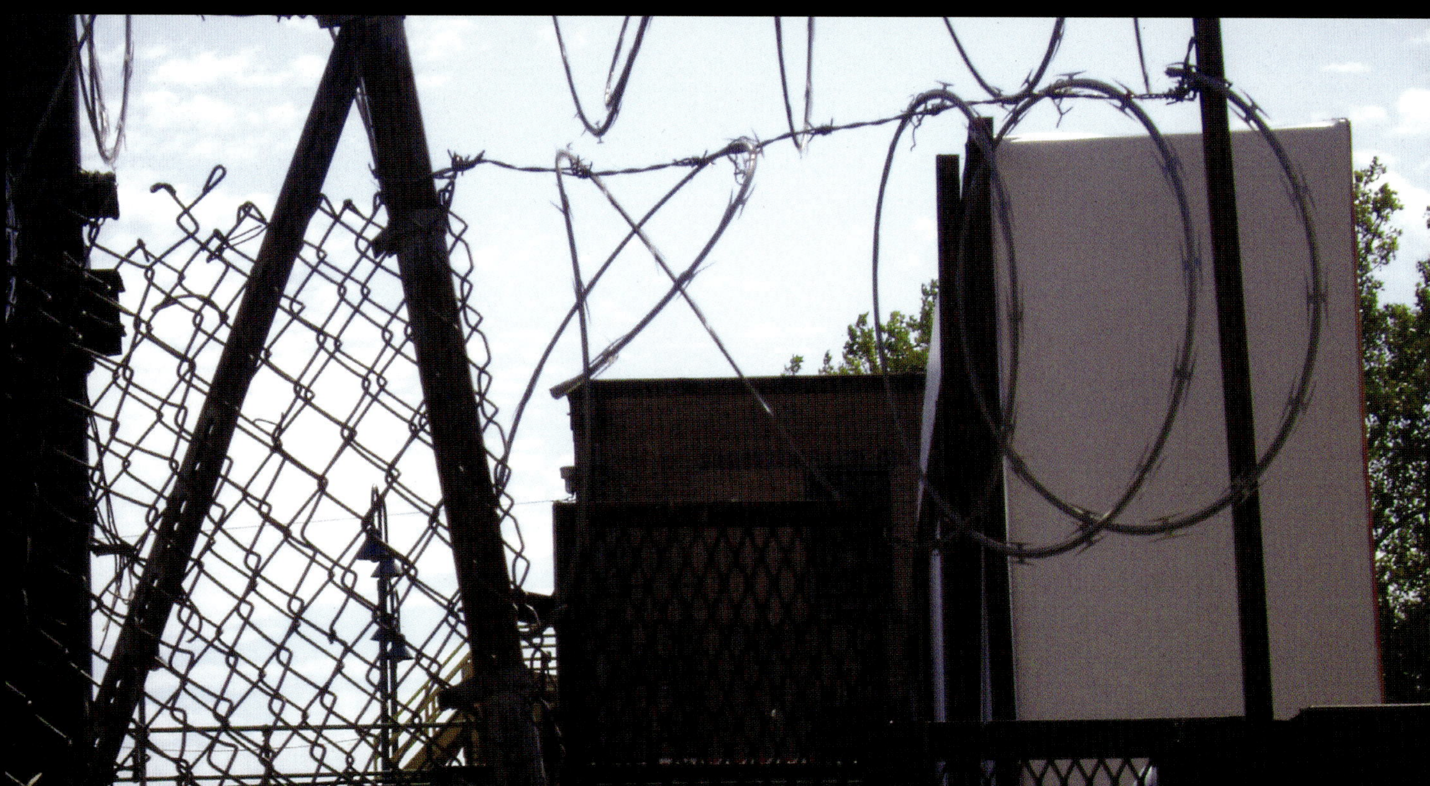

Even the stations had razor ribbon...

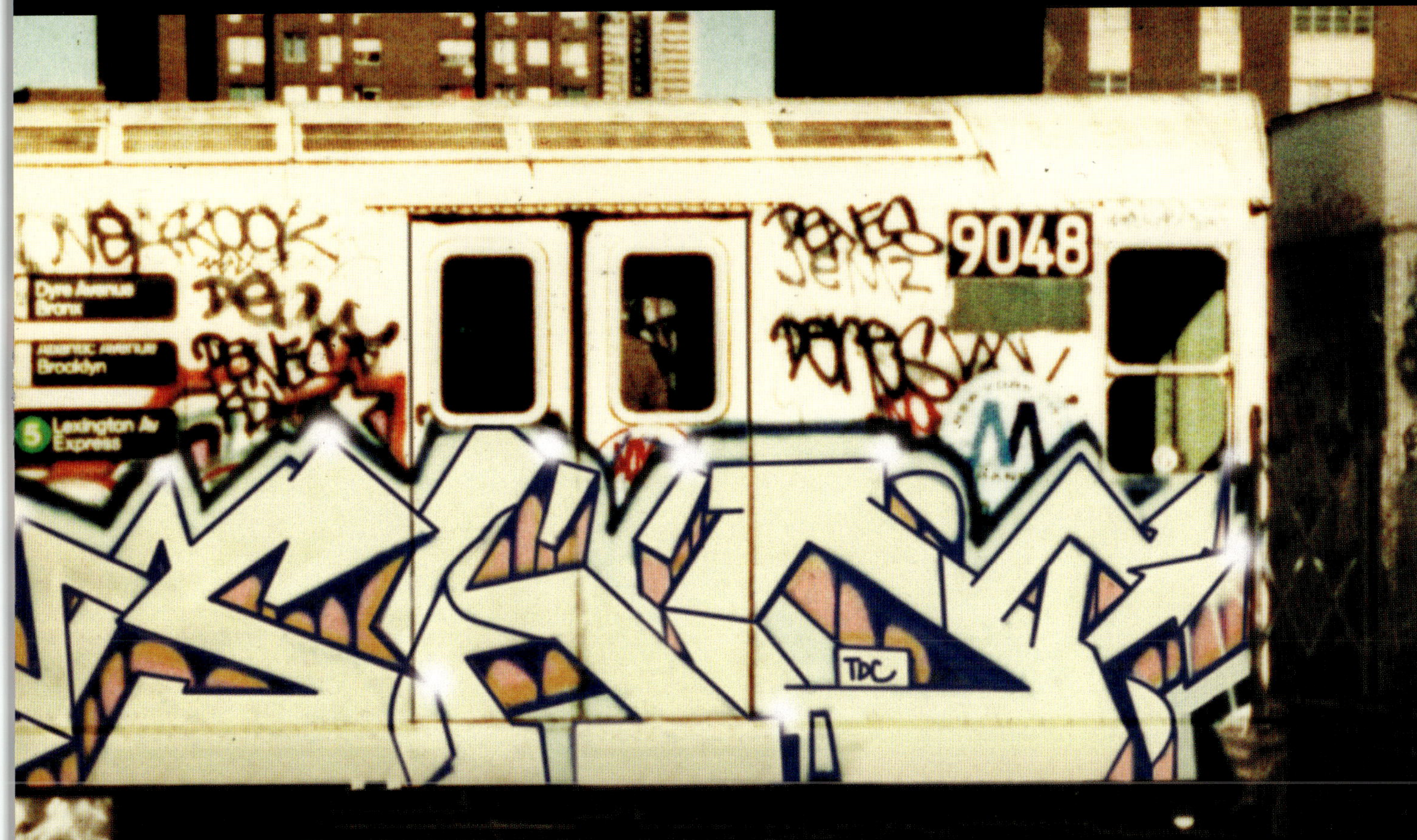

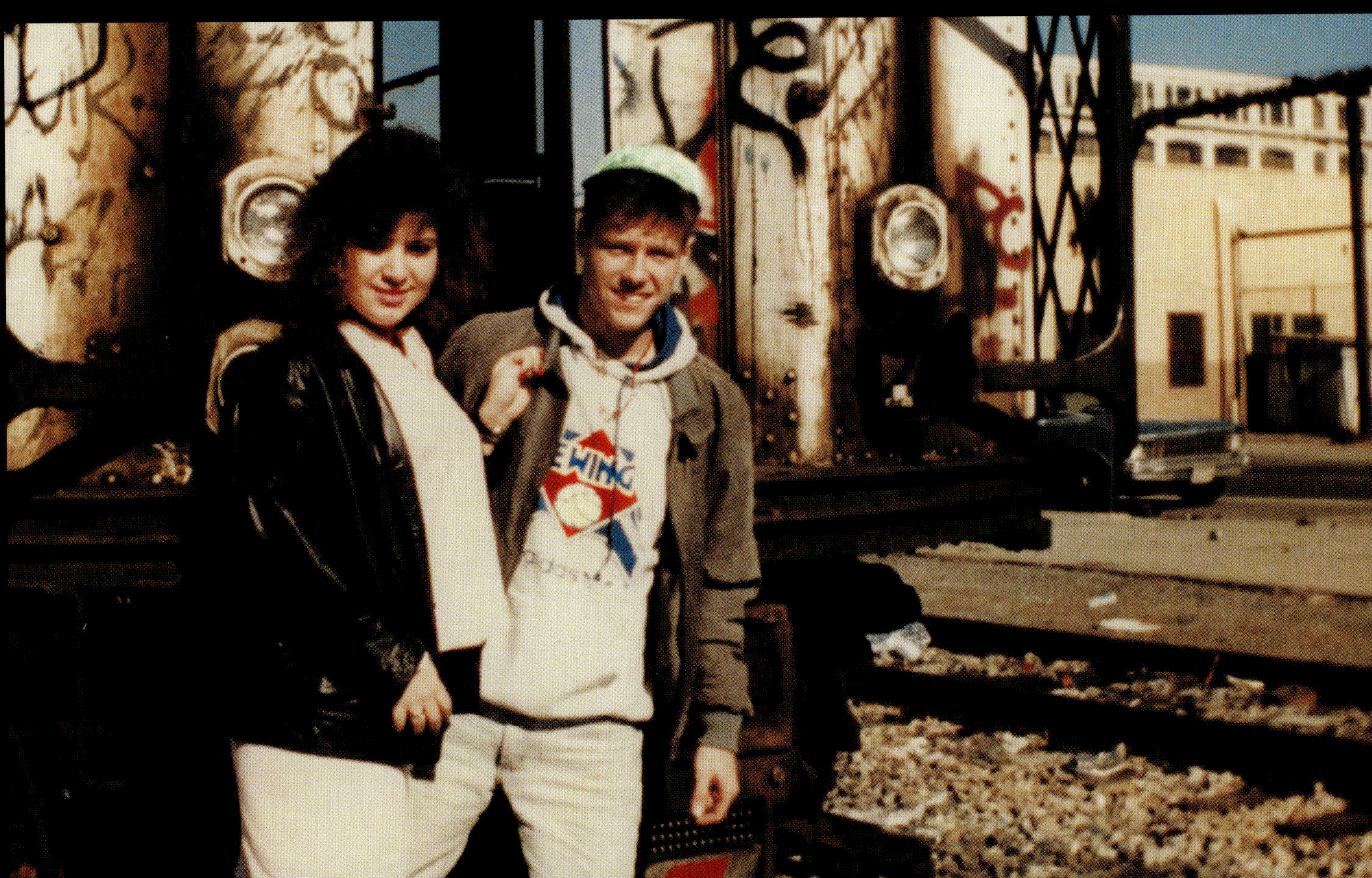

George and Laura enjoying their afternoon.

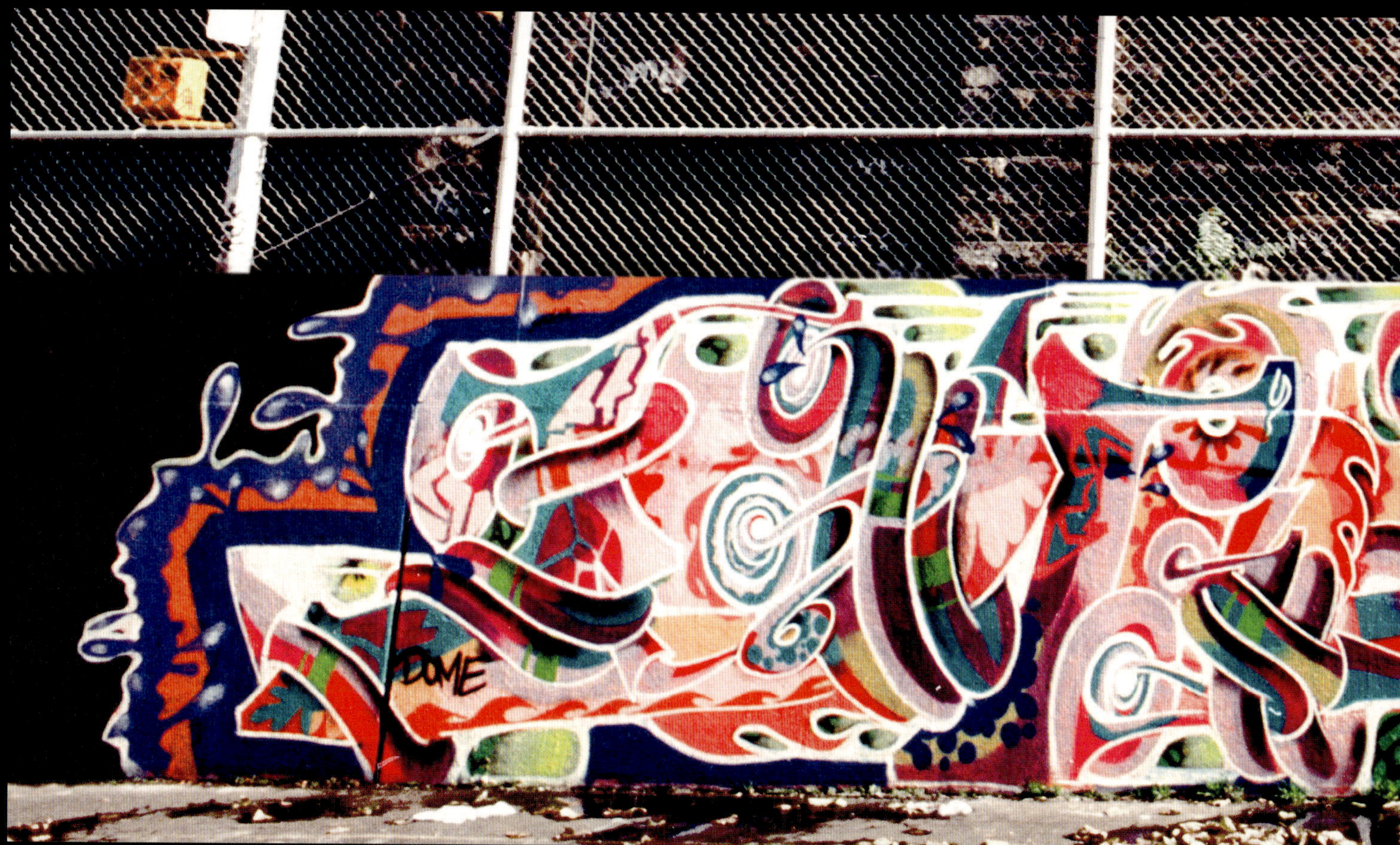

DOME, "Hall of Fame," 1993.

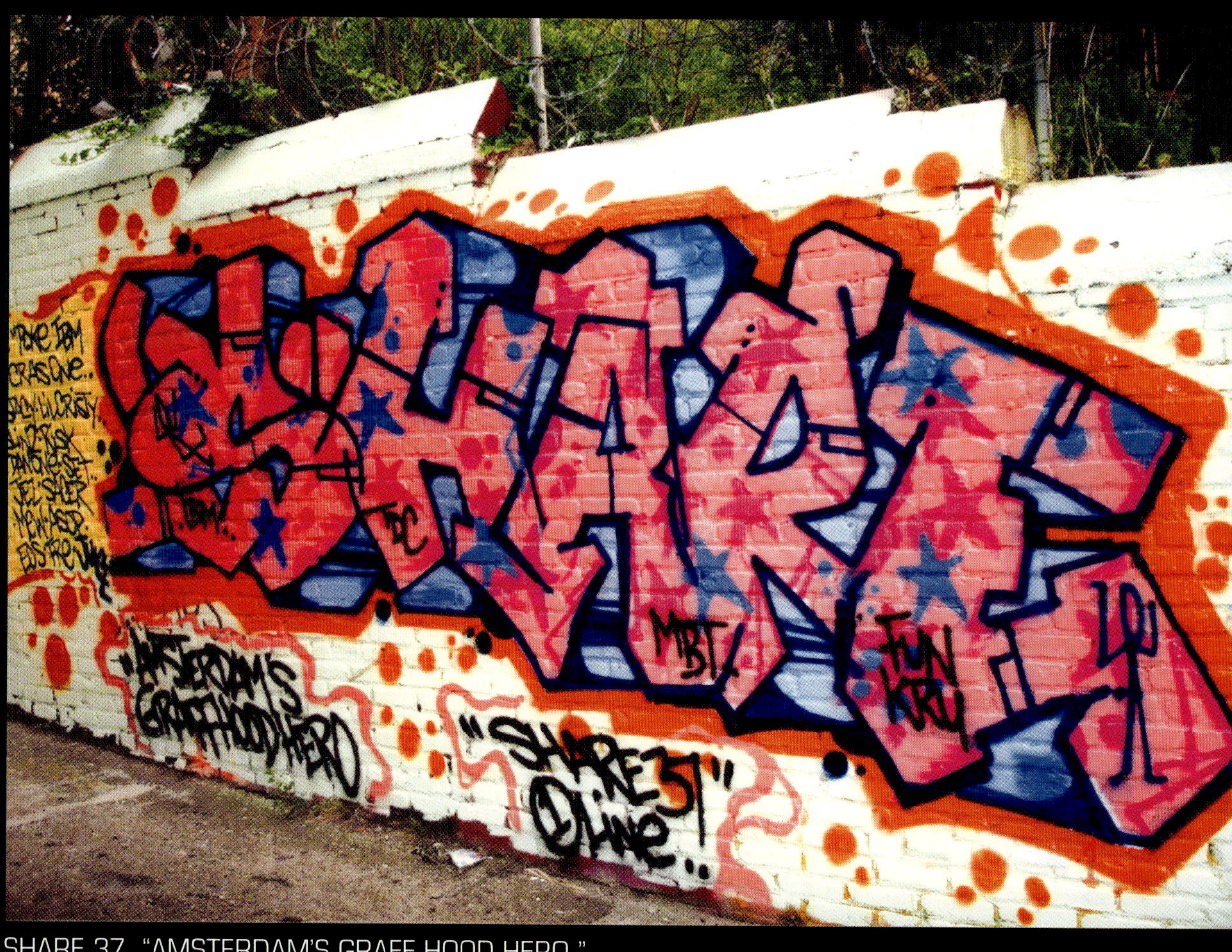

SHARE 37, "AMSTERDAM'S GRAFF HOOD HERO."

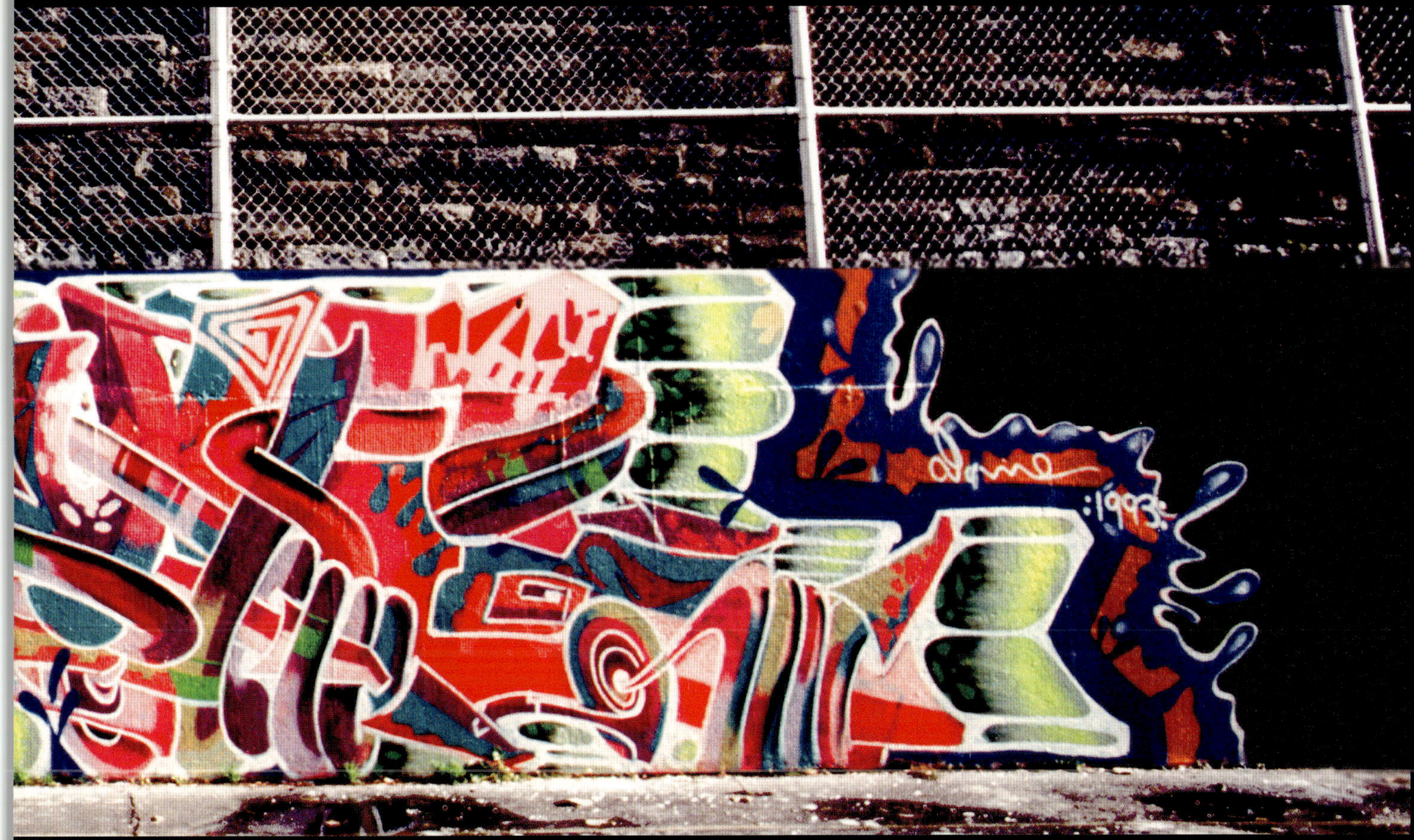

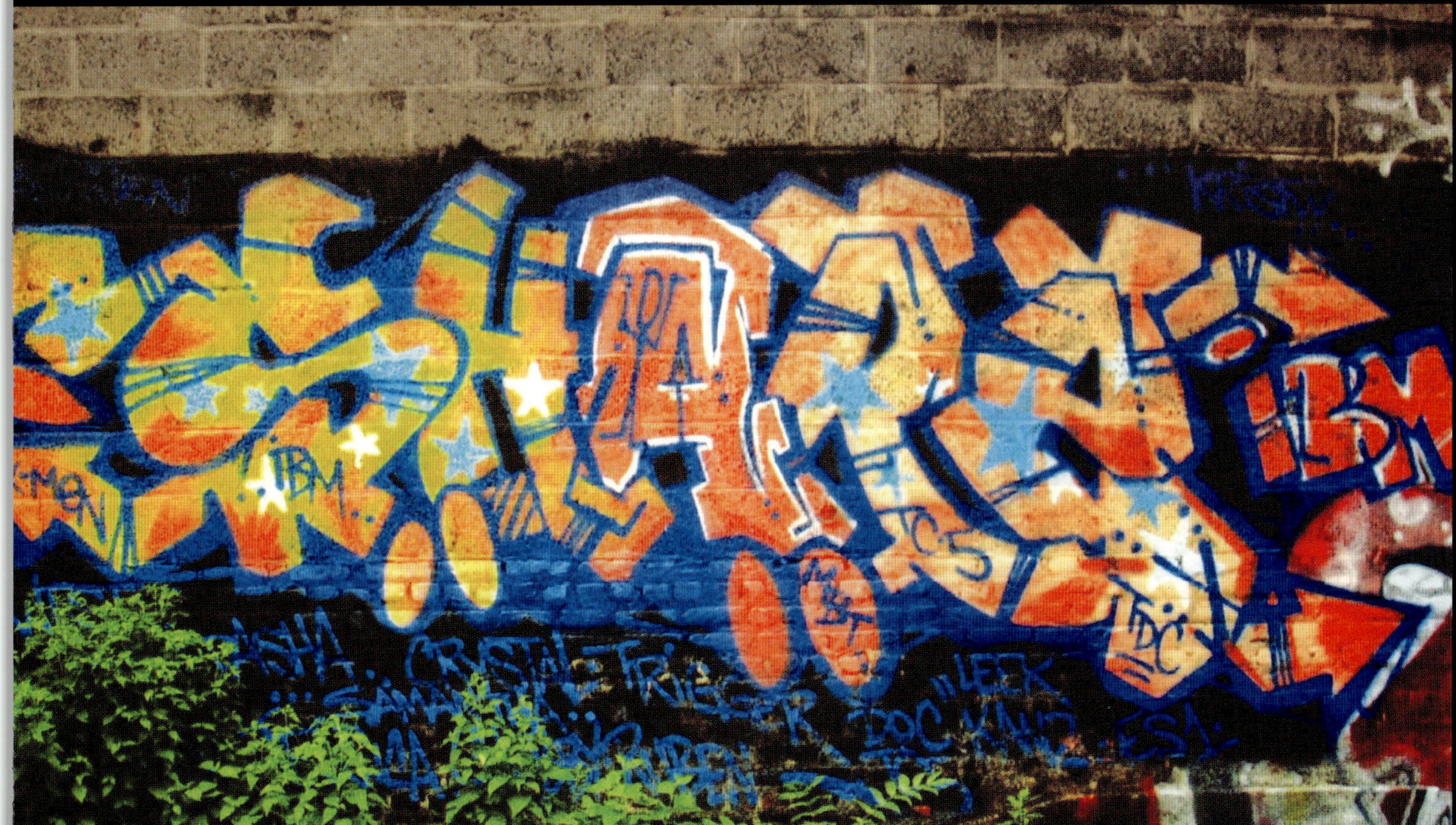

SHARE 37, TDC, IBM, X-MEN, MBT, and TC5, rocked in Manhattan 2000.

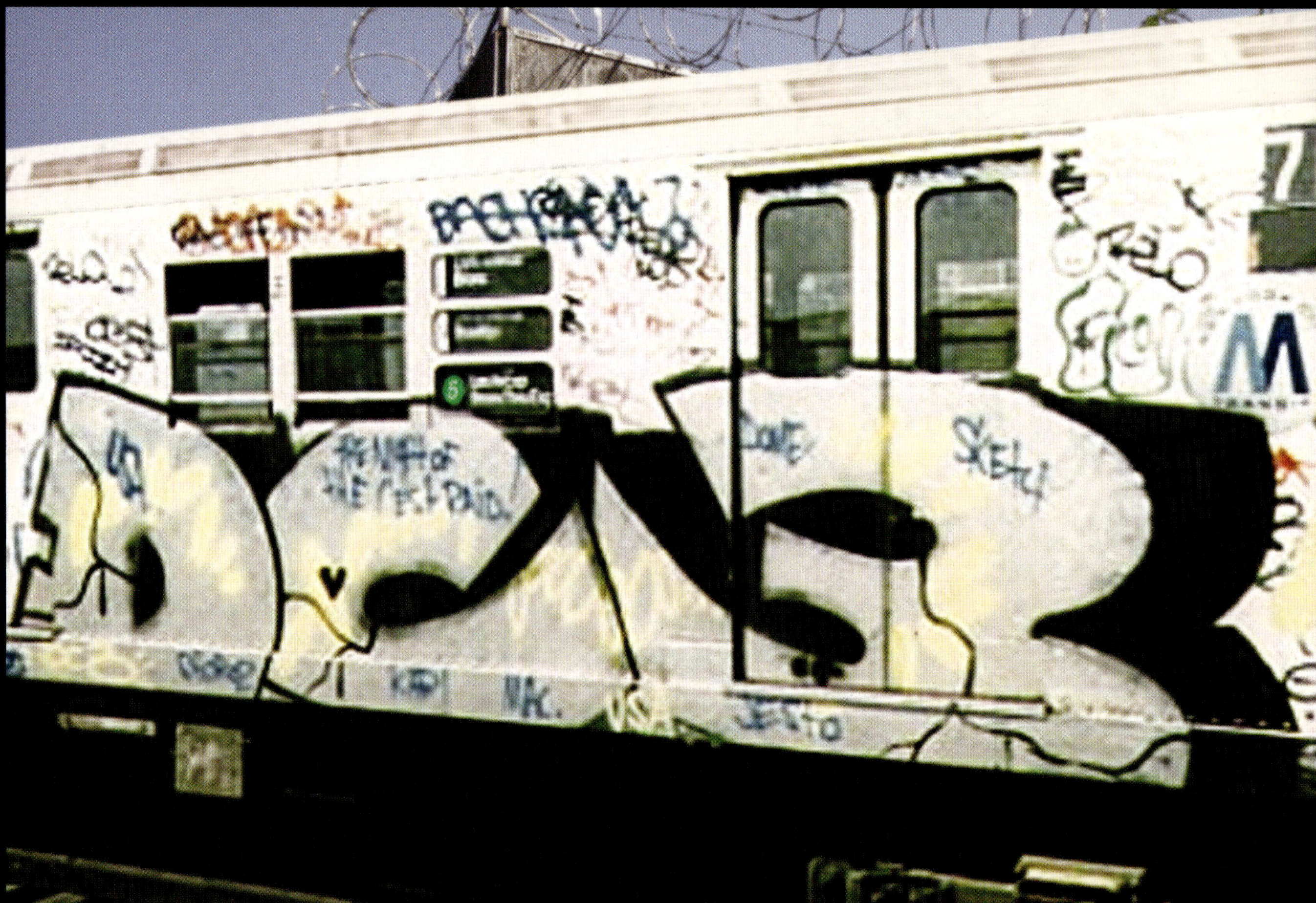

DC3, 5 Train, Jan.1987.

The Night of the Illest Raid, 1987

I had been thru numerous Esplanade work bum and subway conductor raids or what we though was the transit police. When you in a train yard or lay up at night you have to always assume if you hear radios that it is the transit cops or vandal squad. We would be in between the lanes, sometimes it was sweet with lights out and not too dark outside because you could still see what you was doing. Other times, which was far more risky, but was way sweeter was when all the interior lights was on inside the train sets. You never wanted to hear people walking thru the train because they could be right up on you and open up all the doors on one side or on both if they wanted and jump down onto to the tracks or pull guns in an attempt to apprehend you.

This night, DC3 and I were attempting to do the Six Line, which was still hittable and the white trains were also not too bombed. We met up with this kid who DC3 knew who wrote Beamer in my Grand Prix by the Six Yard and we caught some tags on the 6 at Zerega Avenue elevated lay up. We thought it was kinda hot and didn't think we had that kind of time to do burners, so we broke out and went to see how Esplanade looked, as it wasn't even pulled in when we first went. Shit was crazy because when we got there there was at least ten other writers up in there, some we knew from TCM and some of their boys. The best thing was most of the time we burned we never bumped into anybody.

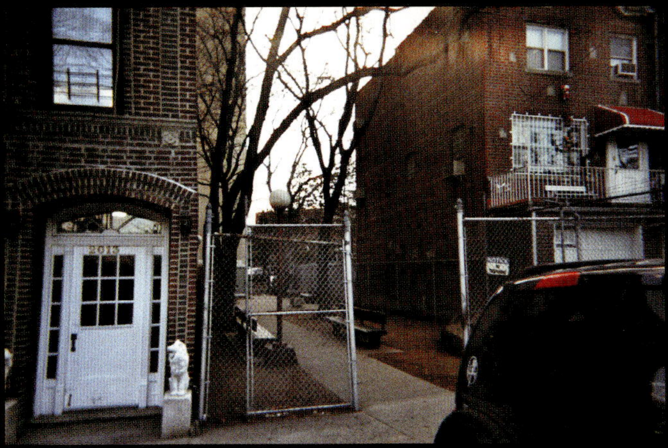

So we roll up in between the sets and here comes a Dyre Avenue bound 5. Toys are dangerous because they're stupid and will get you busted. This one idiot almost got fucking hit by the train and the conductor hit the horn. So we waited but the train stayed at the station. Now everyone was anxious and we was checking both side of the tracks and this guy jumps off the downtown platform alone and is walking towards us. This kid Beamer pulls out the toast, and to my amazement the whole pack of writers is talking about robbing and fucking this nigga up while walking directly towards him. They got three cars closer and then see he's transit police with his gun out.

Holy shit you've never seen fifteen plus niggas about-face and jet the fuck outta there. So, now everybody leaves over this one fence into a private parking lot, I'm talking about people was running over sets of cars to get to the street. Meanwhile Mirage, Sketch, and Jesto was in the small park getting their paint ready. I ran by Mirage like, "Whoa!!!" In five minutes there was no less than ten blue and white police cars. We was running thru back yards. Shit was so nuts and we was under such pressure I was hiding on an upper level of a house and had to bounce when spotted with flashlights. So me and Jesto actually ran back up onto Esplanade past police cars with all the doors open to get away and were promptly chased by cops up there again, we damn near ran to the 180th Street Yard and had to hide out for hours underneath a train trestle. You could hear the police above searching for us and they couldn't find us because where we was it was really remote, dark, and filthy. All the Morris Park birds lived here.

Sunrise came and we jumped fifteen feet down to the street and took the long way back to the car. Low and behold, here comes Mirage and DC3 with some other writers. No one got busted even though mad of us lost our paint all except, some how, Mirage!!!! God bless him, this sick fuck and DC3 even went back and did this silver train window-down block letter piece.

-SHO TDCUSA

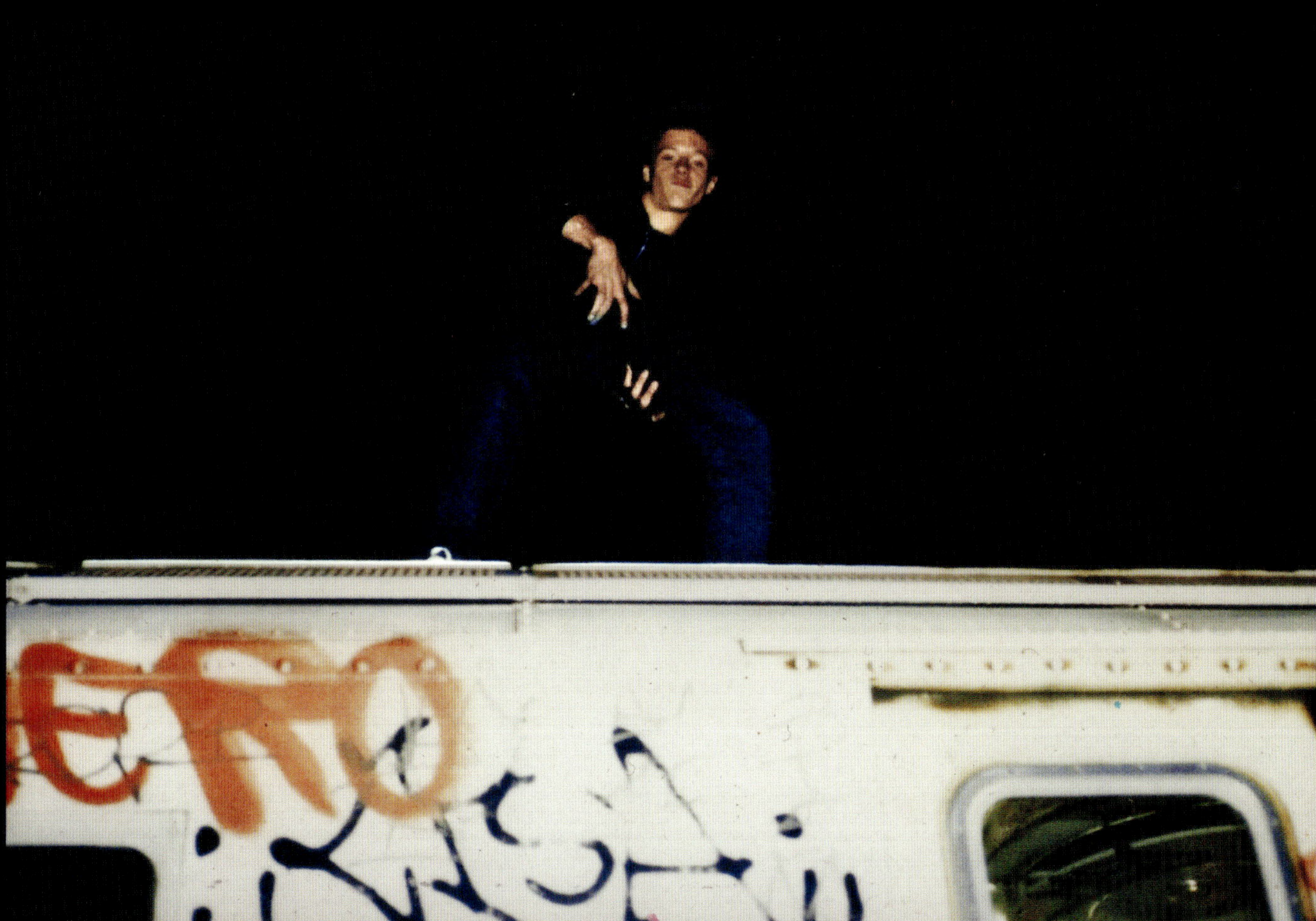

SHO making a statement.

It was ZOOROC's, aka DOME, who's motto was,
"I AIN'T GETTING CAUGHT YO!!!!!!!"
That influenced me the most because we was always
holding mad shit up in the Bronx every single night out. Period.
I defy anybody or writer to ever say they robbed us, please!!!!
No one ever tested us in Esplanade!!!!!! Our house, you heard?!!
Check my man Mirage out to the right.
Always props to my man. RIP, MARC from SHO TDC.
From day one Mirage CWK was no joke!!!!! His work stands for
itself, as well as Sketch CWK and Rush KDMingdom.
Mirage fit in with us real well because we did fuck people
up that deserved it up. Always respect and beware of
those who held that aluminum bat in the tunnels
and yards, you just knew they meant that shit for real
from the look in their eyes, yo!!!!

I spit this in memory of Mirage CWK KDM TDC in his behalf, we will meet again my brother!!
We love you and will never forget you.
-SHO TDC

Dome introduced me to Marc early in 1986, he was also from Long Island.
I knew him and Sketch was doing it up as far as burners went, they had a lot. Mirage also wrote Mac and him and Sketch, plus a couple of other writers, had been doing some nice pieces and parkway bombing. When we started on the trains I heard lots of writers went to Esplanade and a lot got busted right before we came on the line. Niggas told us, "Good luck!!" There was just numerous major vandal squad raids four weeks in a row!!!! We was never shook, remember from day one it was an addiction! I never thought about that shit because it was an acceptable risk that you had to take to get up. Our best time was when we painted in the first eleven months straight, when very few writers knew who we was. It was all worth doing
since our shit was running hard. Graffiti isn't worth doing unless you have the rush and excitement of doing it illegally. Pure damage, B!!!!!

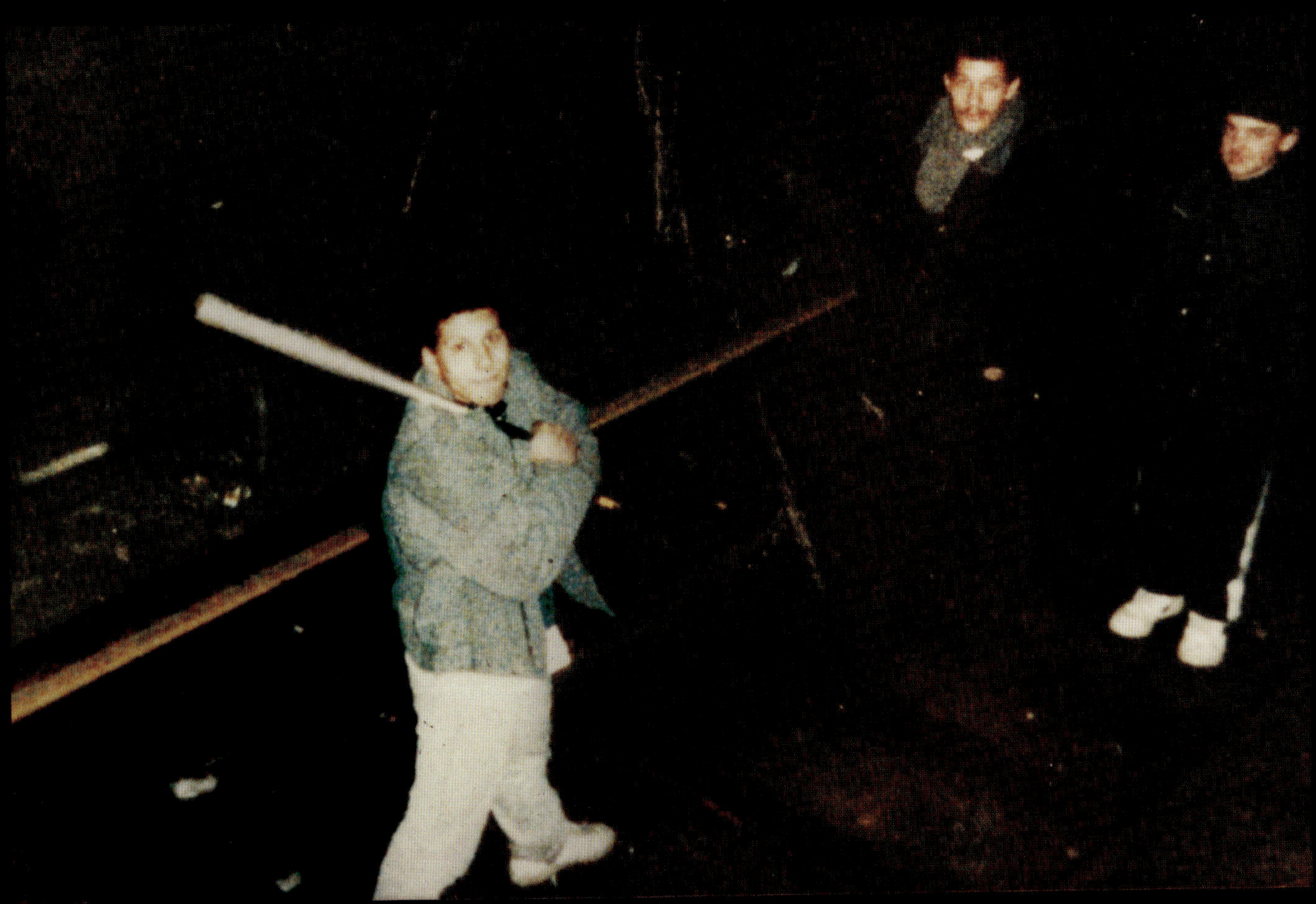

Mirage with Tyke and Rea in Esplanade Tunnels, Jan. 1988.

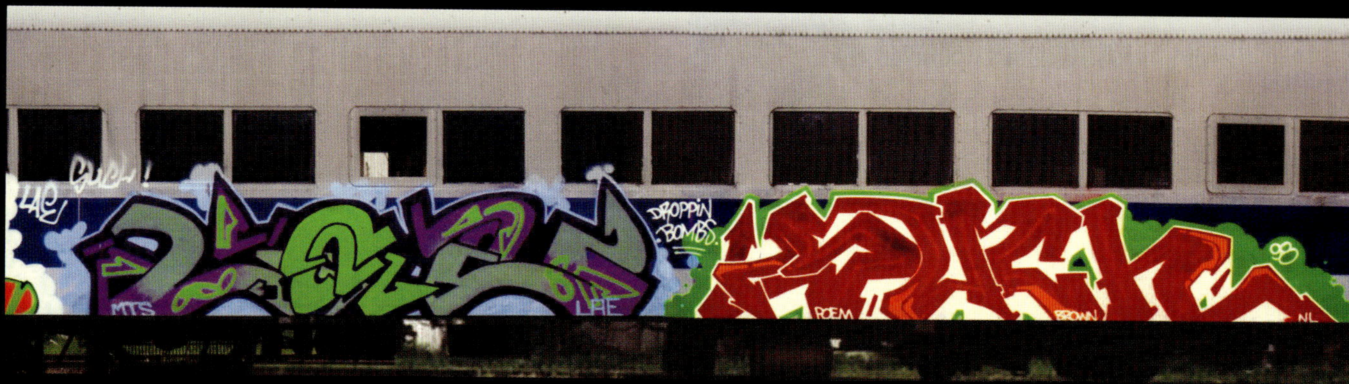

LAE TDC and SUCH TDC MTS, LIRR, 1998.

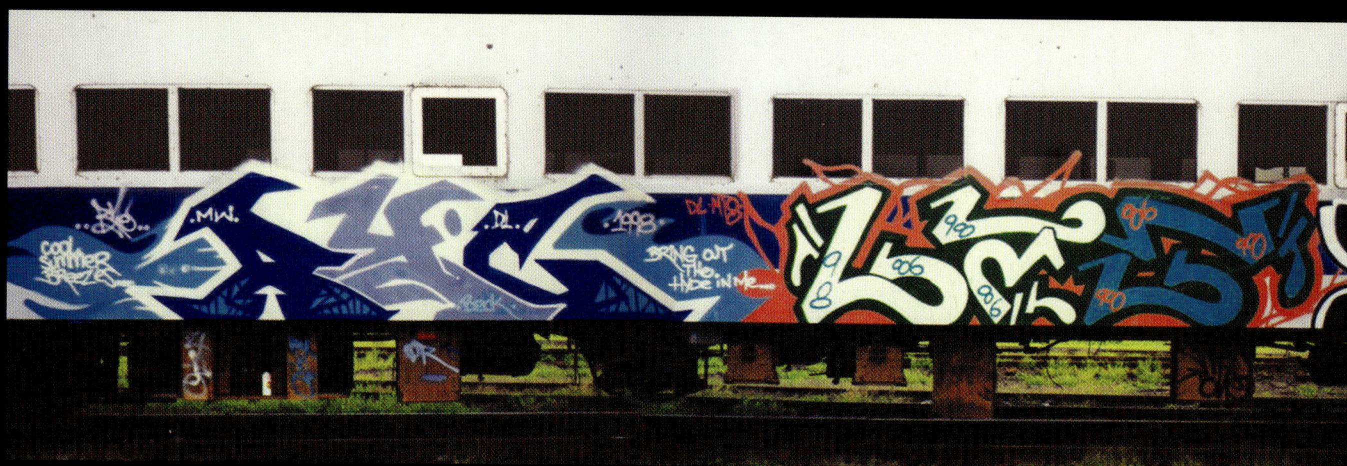

RYE MW and LAE TDC, LIRR, 1998.

TDC was created in 1985 by DC3, SHO, and BEAVER. We was deep and had many members early on. The only way you got down was to street bomb with the crew. We hit up mad walls and streets but we wanted more. SHO and DC3 one night even bombed all the way from Freeport thru Rosedale by walking and riding the N4 bus. They continued all the way to the Jamaica bus terminal, bombing all the way, and then killed the terminal. This was a long night and the effort lasted like five hours but produced crazy ups. LAE lived in Rockville Center and was Beaver's people. They put together a bus yard mission for the crew and we formed like Voltron that night. BEAVER, DC3, RAZE, MAZE, LAE, SHOROZ, TRI, NEVER, and CRAZE swarmed the yard at like 12 A.M. BEAVER and LAE were the ink and mop masters. They made them the old school way with chalk board erasers, Flomaster ink, and shoe polish containers. LAE had told people no spray paint cause it makes noise but SHO and RAZE rocked it anyway. The crew smashed like 25 buses outsides and even some insides which was risky but we didn't care. I guess they heard the spray paint cause after twenty minutes we got raided by the police. Everyone somehow got away and the buses ran for like two weeks bombed.

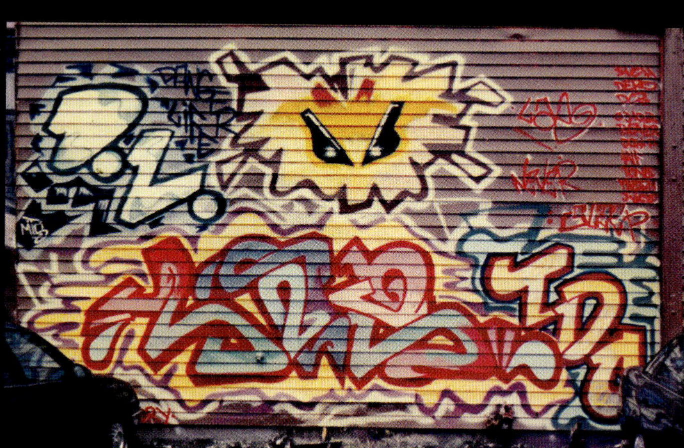

-LAE TDC

Well, it was probably the fall of 1987. TDC was doing a lot of window-down whole cars every week and the time came for me to challenge myself by planning out this top-to-bottom, end-to-end, ZOO whole car with a character. I was planning this on paper, but also during our countless rack session, so I was stealing a lot of jungle greens, baby blues, and turquoise, which were the major fill-in colors. Up until that moment TDC was only used to doing window-down whole cars and made our names fit the whole car by eye and respecting each others space. I did not have the experience of doing a one-man, top-to-bottom, end-to-end, whole car yet, but I was young and I didn't give a shit and I knew I was gonna pull this one off...SHO and DC3 drove up to the crib as planned with bags of paint, I had to slip my bags of paint thru my back window so mom and pop dukes wouldn't worry about me getting caught, so the night had finally come and I sprung a surprise on SHO and DC3 inside the car and said, I'm gonna do a one-man, top-to-bottom, end-to-end, whole car...DC3's reaction was, "OH SHIT!" and shook his head. SHO just laughed and asked if I had enough paint, then requested to see the sketch. We all didn't really know what was going to happen that night but we drove up to the Bronx jerked the toll booth once again, pulled up to Esplanade lay ups, jumped over the fence and headed towards the pull outs. We found our trains to paint on, they were parallel to each other, which made us face back to back to keep an eye out for cops. We proceeded to paint our pieces, we all came with our "A" game that night. SHO and DC3 did some serious window-down burner's with a Cerebus character.

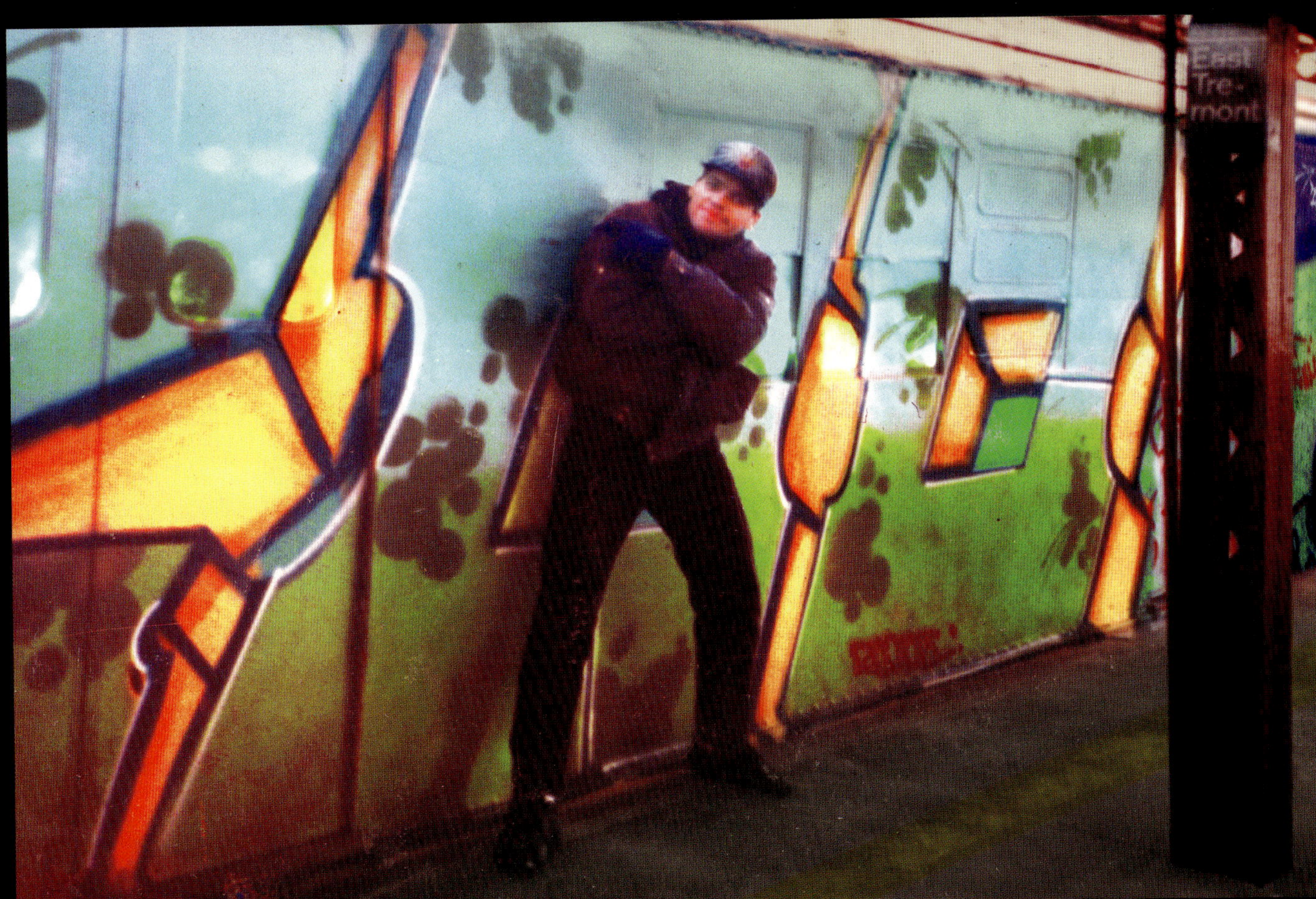

ZOO's first top-to-bottom 5 Train, Sept 1987 at 7:30 A.M.

They were done pretty fast, so when they finished they started helping me fill in my whole car—only the letters "ZOO" and robot character were done so far. I didn't know at the time to measure out my letters by feet so It wasn't proportioned right, but you live and learn. SHO and DC3 filled in the rest as I finished the outline with details, the rest is history. It pays to have a good team! We waited until day break and went to East Tremont train station to catch the photos of our trains. This is the moment you dream of as a writer painting a one-man, top-to-bottom, end-to-end, it puts you on a different level of your writing career. We caught both trains with windows that morning, I even posed for a picture in front of the finished train. It looked like a giant billboard running thru the city with my name "ZOO" in block letters on it. It's a great felling! It separates you from just being a writer. It makes you a KING for ever...

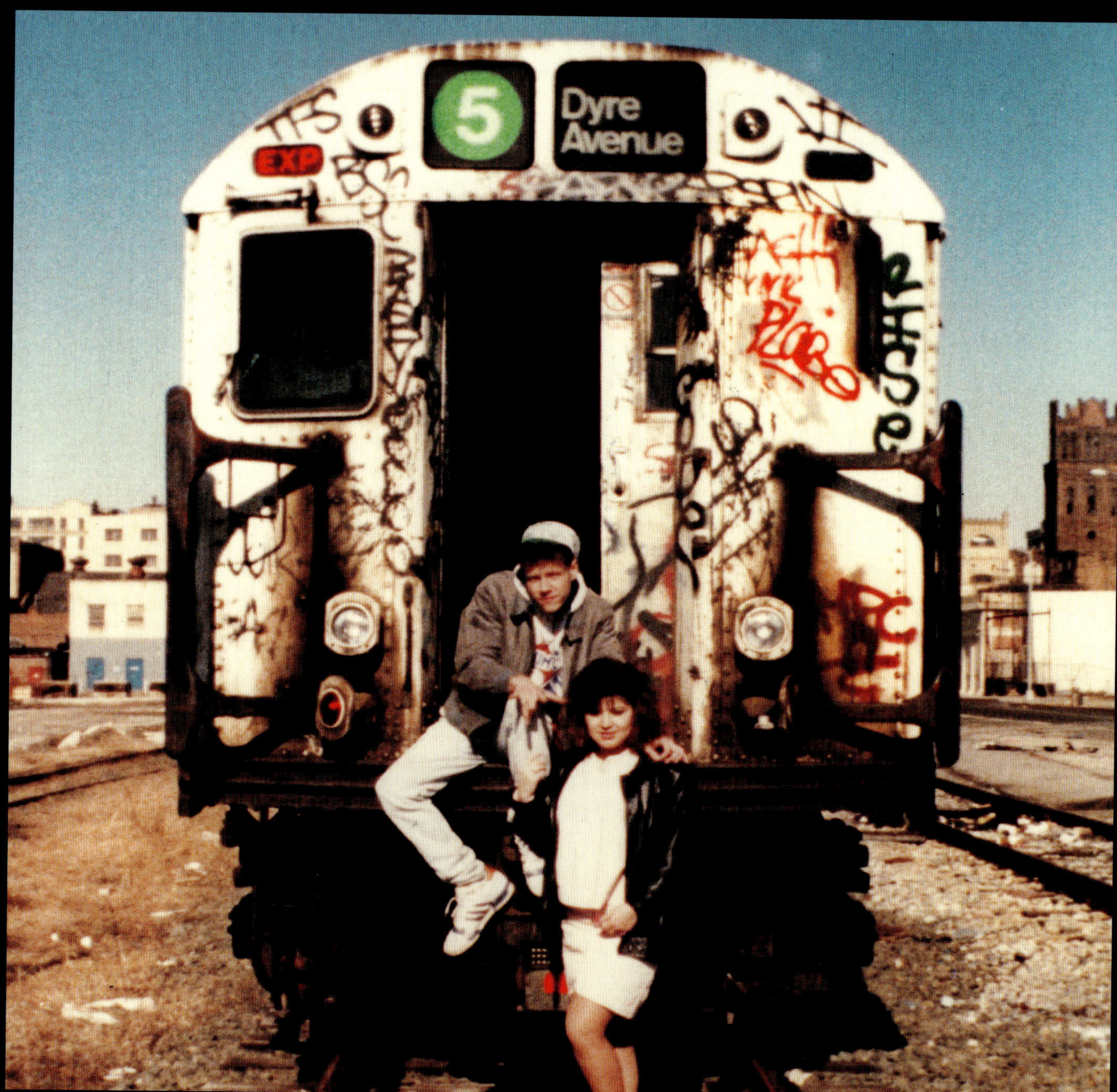

SHO and Laura, 1988.

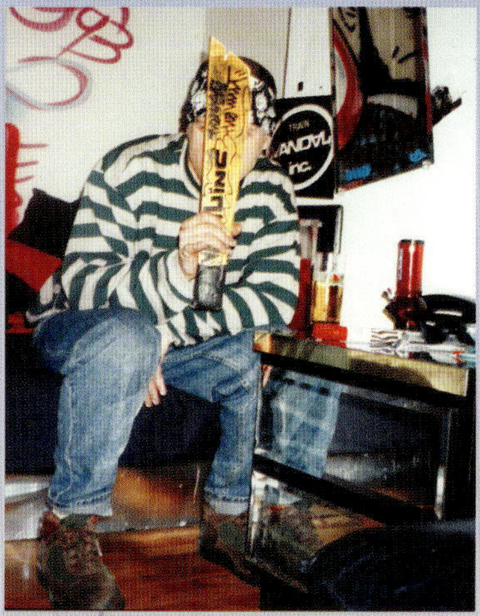

A chiseled work bum's paddle.

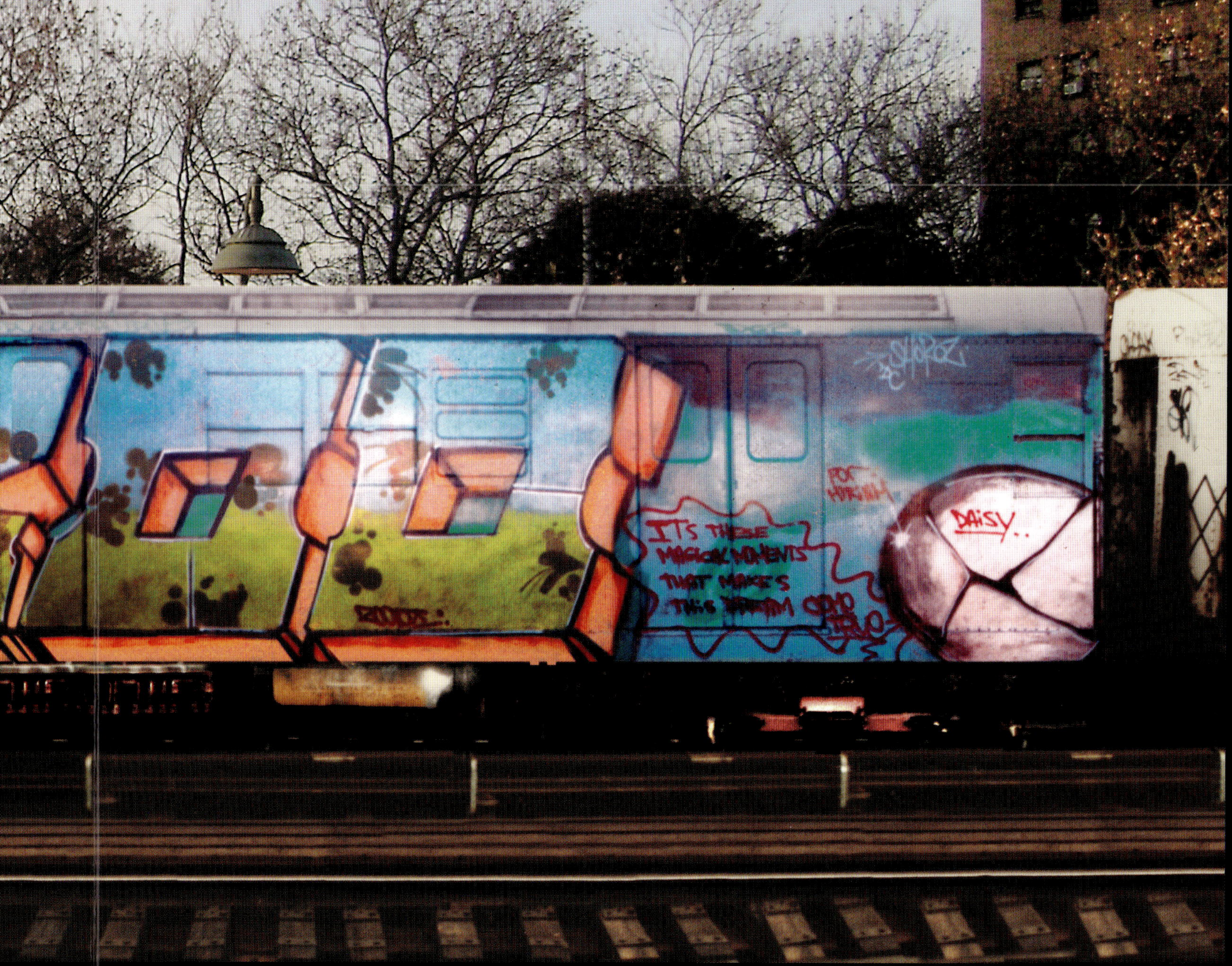

ZOO top-to-bottom, "It's these magical moments that makes this dream come true," 5 Train, Sep. 1987.

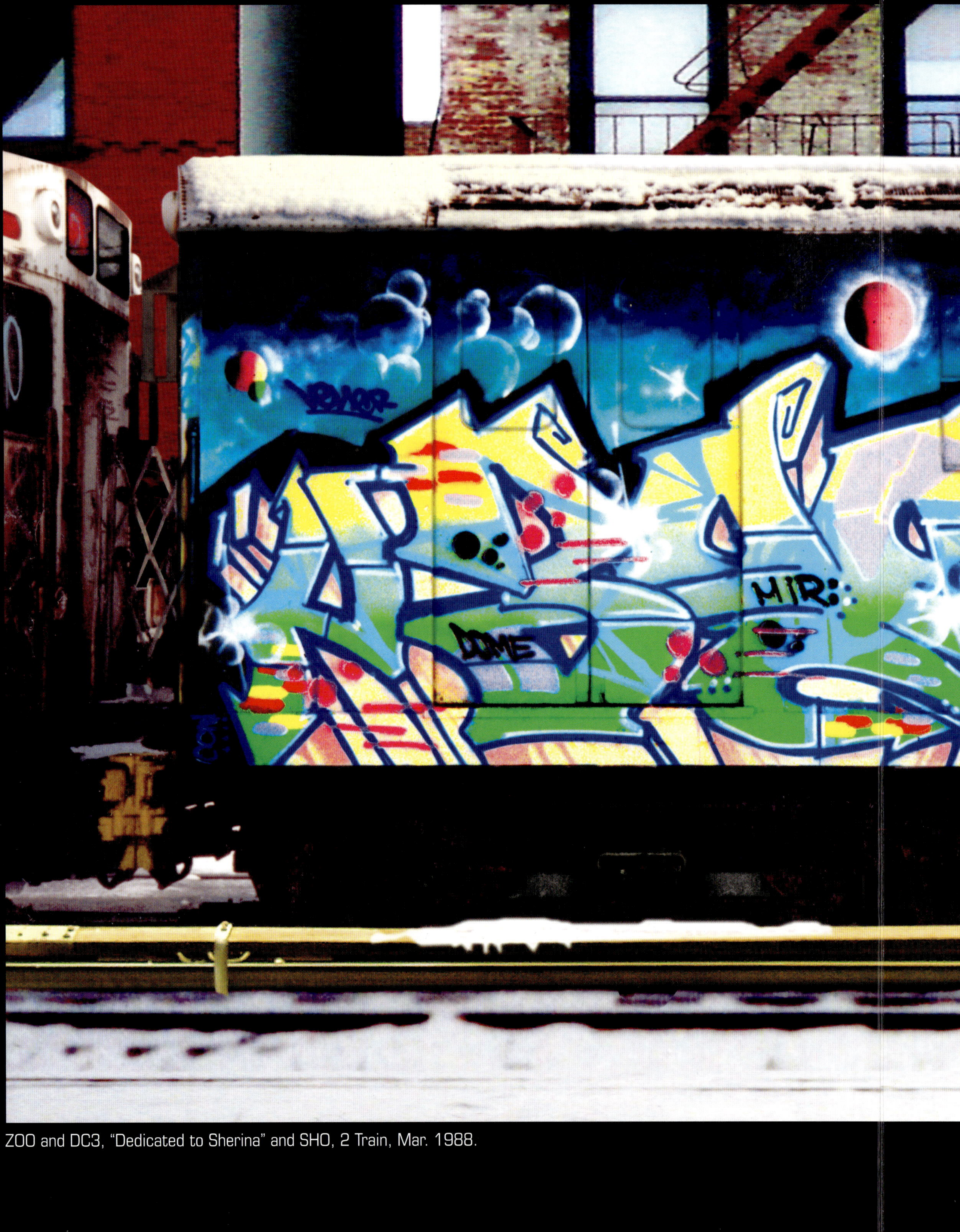

ZOO and DC3, "Dedicated to Sherina" and SHO, 2 Train, Mar. 1988.

In Memory of Mirage, CWK, KDM, TDC

★

DOME, SHO, and VULCAN painted this wall in memory of Mirage, a tribute to our partner who died tragically in a car accident on Long Island. We repped this production in the Hall of Fame in Harlem on 106th street and Park Avenue on November 3, 1992. I had to research when we did this and was able to get the exact date because I remember that the NYC Marathon was being run that day as we were painting it. TDC crew had painted the Hall of Fame many times, all without any permission because back in the days it wasn't really like it is today, a corporate-sponsored neighborhood event. I would say that all of the previous times we painted here were large scale productions that started after dark, sometimes very late so that you wouldn't get busted by the housing police and would finish painting in the early morning hours. This production was notable because it was a long time overdue and because we did the entire wall in broad daylight on some not giving a fuck shit. I recall the cops even saw us and we told them we had permission from the school. I don't think they believed us but were too busy to bust us as they were part of Central Park crowd control that day. Looks like we won that race. Ha Ha.

"A lesson in wild from slaves to style," VULCAN TAT crew and PHASE2.

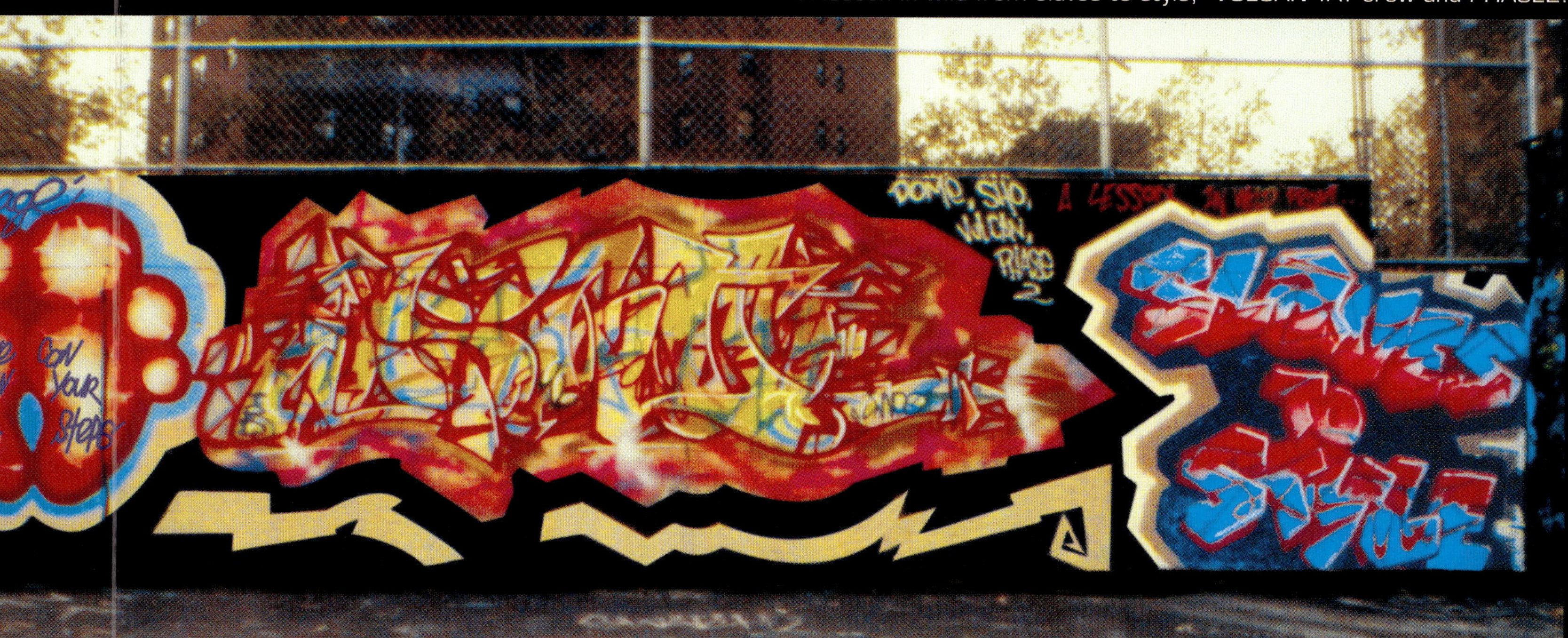

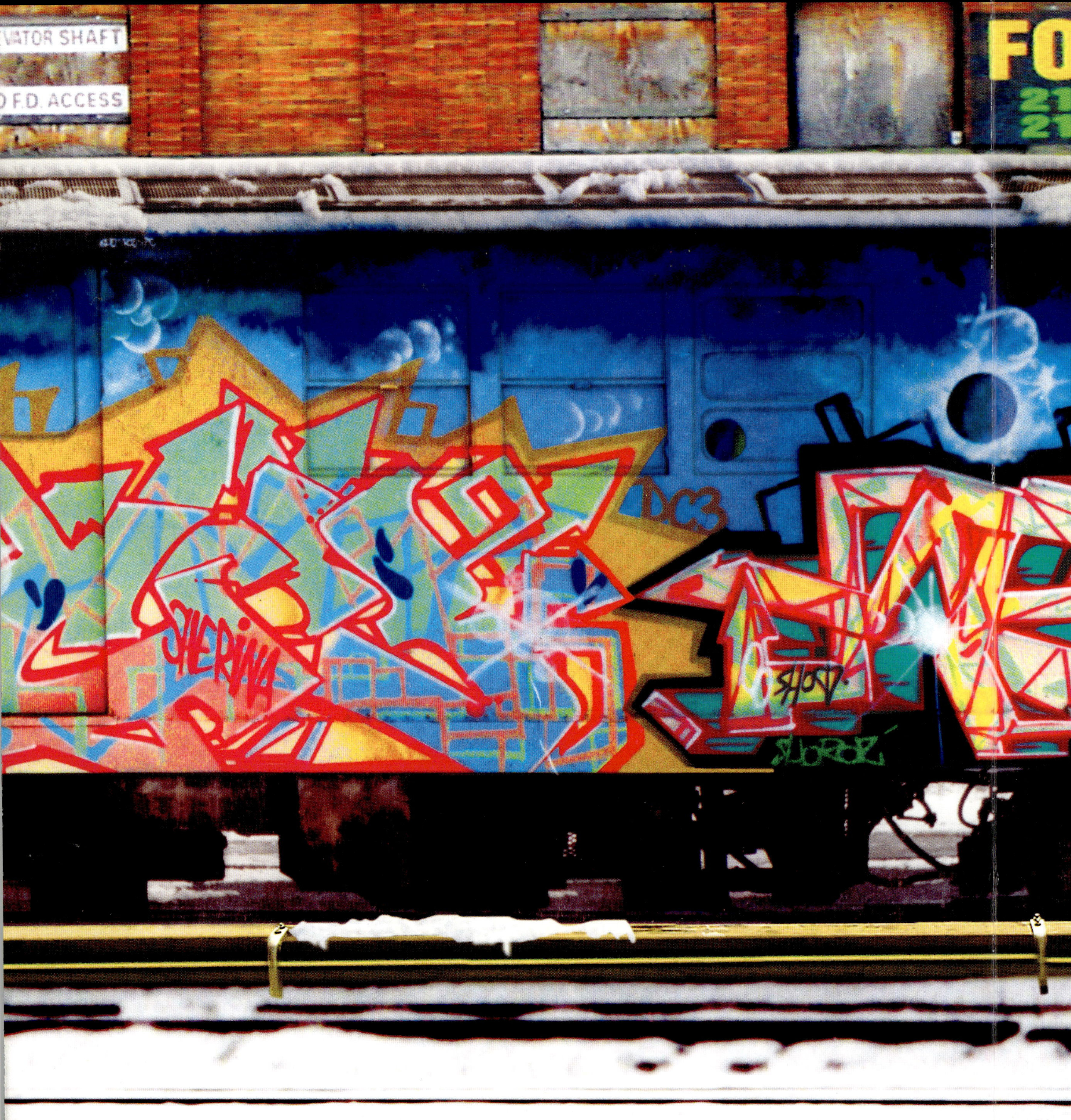
F.D. ACCESS

CHAPTER 5

Hitting the 3 Line

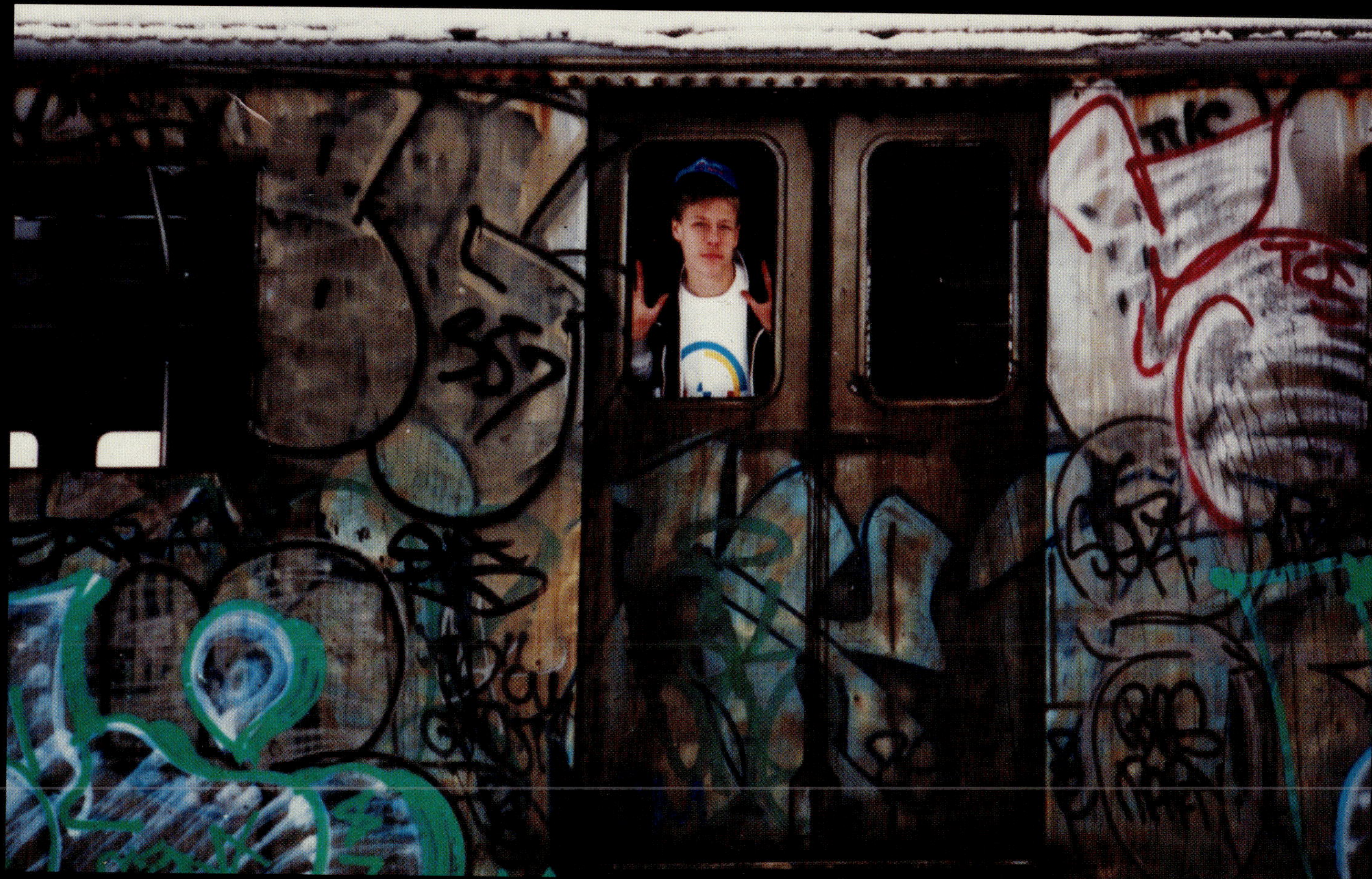

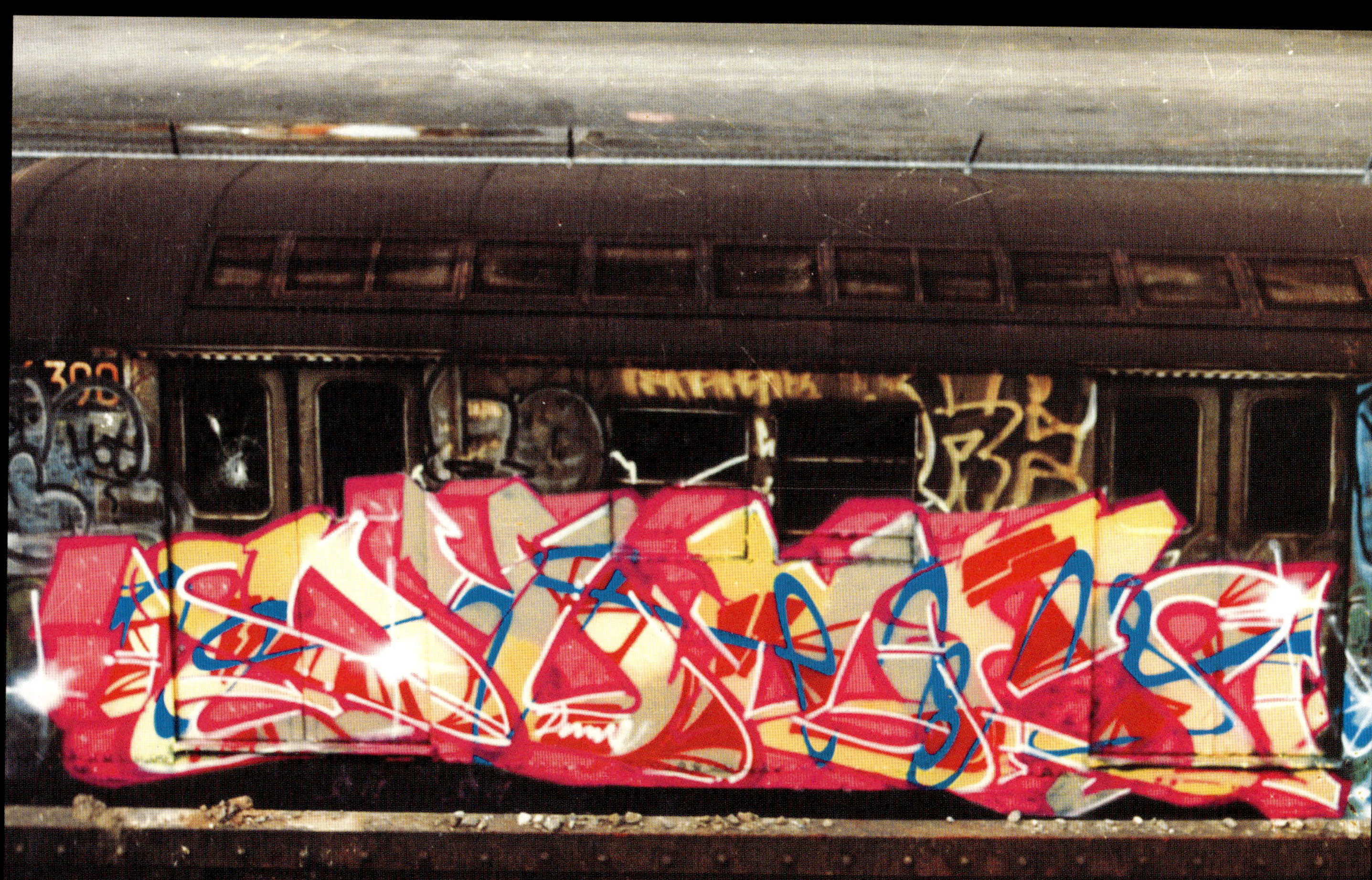

DOME, J Train, Jun. 1988.

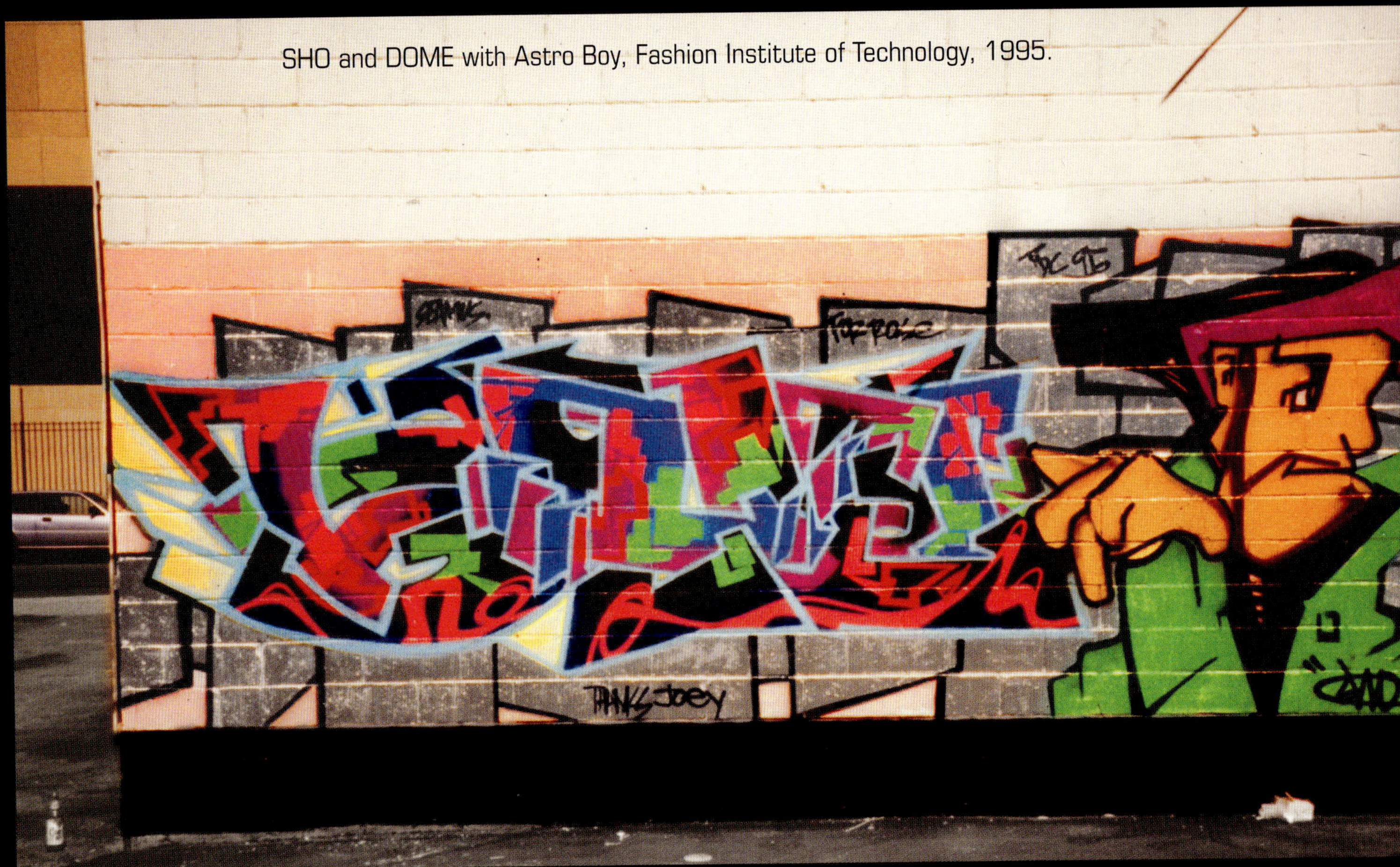
SHO and DOME with Astro Boy, Fashion Institute of Technology, 1995.

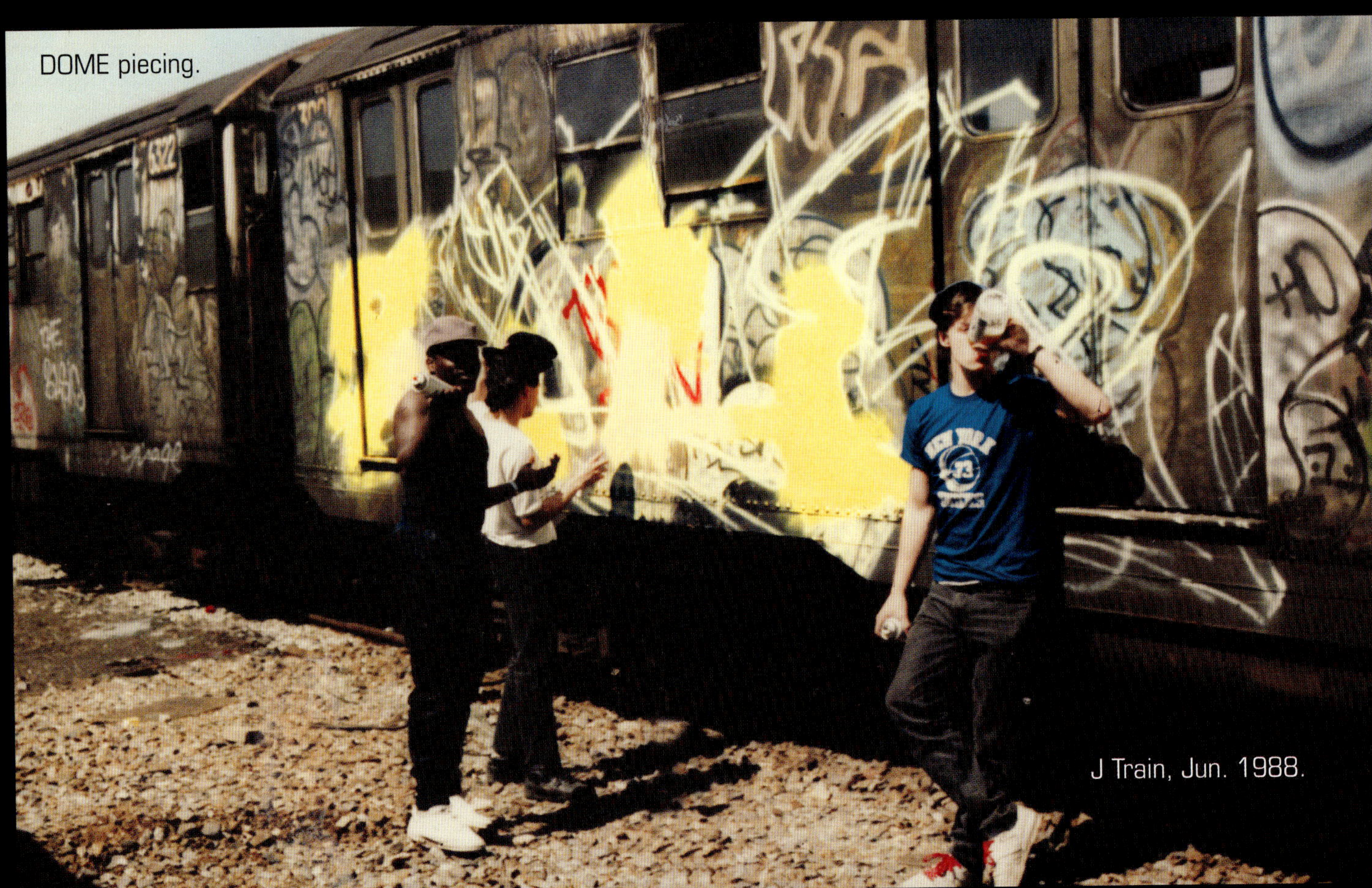
DOME piecing.

J Train, Jun. 1988.

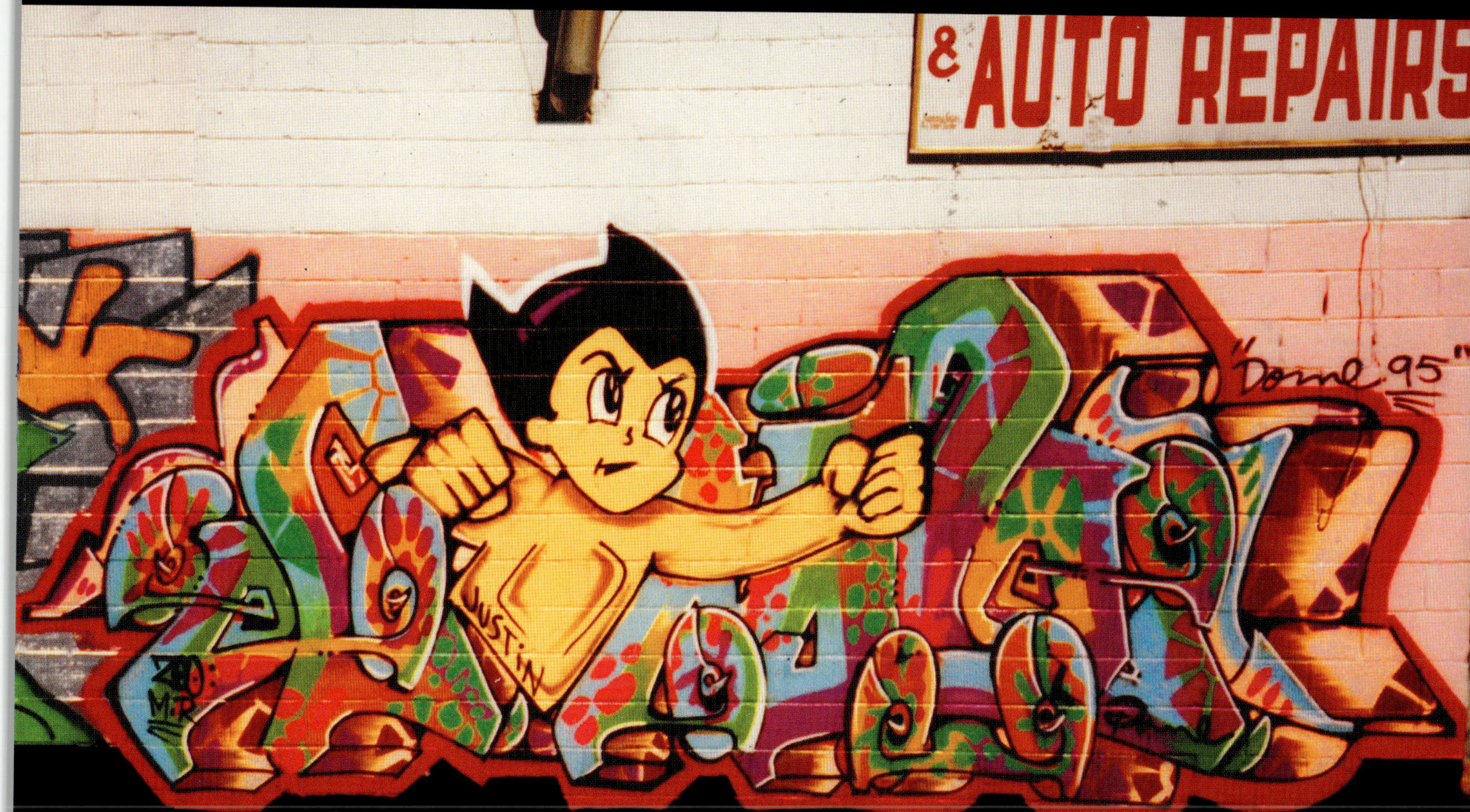

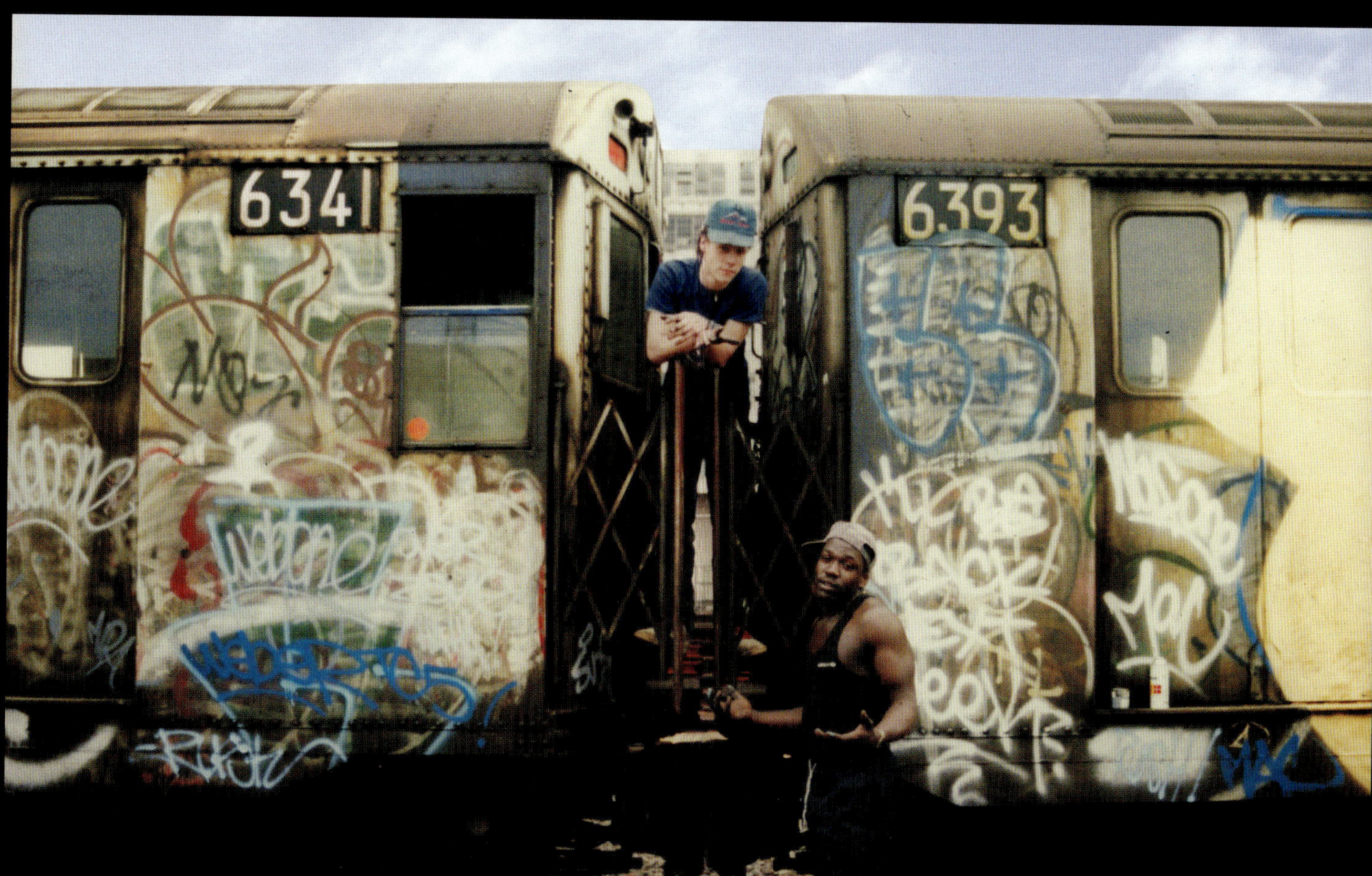

SHO and RECK "Mr. Rudd" chilling out.

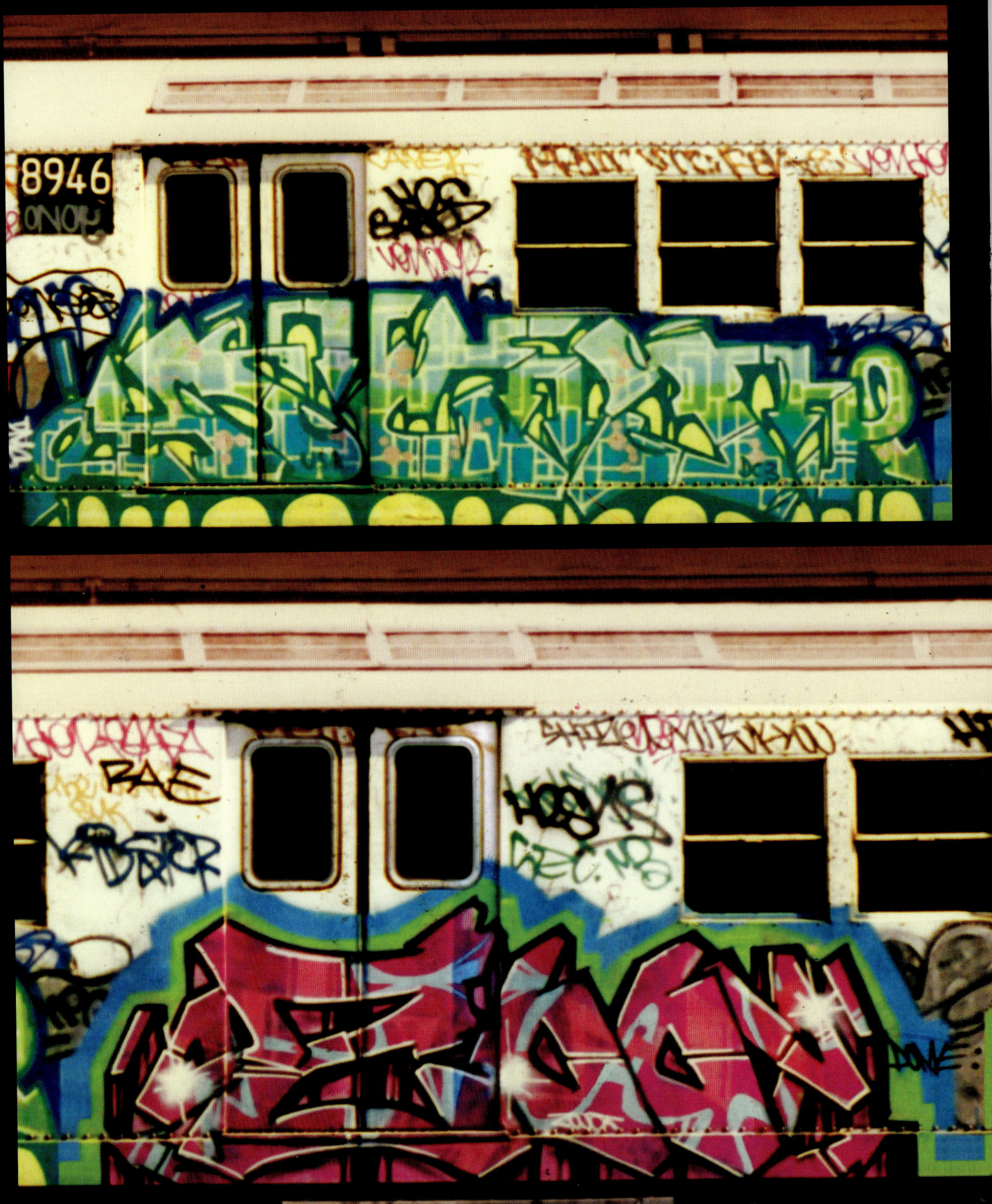

DC3, ZOO, and SHO. Rocked in Esplanade stick-outs, Dec. 1986.

Ahh, Number #8946

★

Here's a little-known fact—we always wrote down the train's number and which side we painted that shit on cause this way it made it a lot easier to bench trains you hadn't got pictures of yet. We did this for two reasons

1. On the 5ives, in the beginning, your trains would run for a long time. So as long as you were out there benching and you knew what side, uptown or downtown you had a good shot of getting your pictures.

2. No matter what, the MTA always replaced the train's number, so even if other writers painted over it because of beef or because it was crossed out and niggas painted pieces over it like a top-to-bottom, you would know what happened to it and you could stop looking for it.

This DC3, ZOO, and SHO was the fifth train we pulled out in Esplanade and it ran untouched for five months.

-SHO TDC

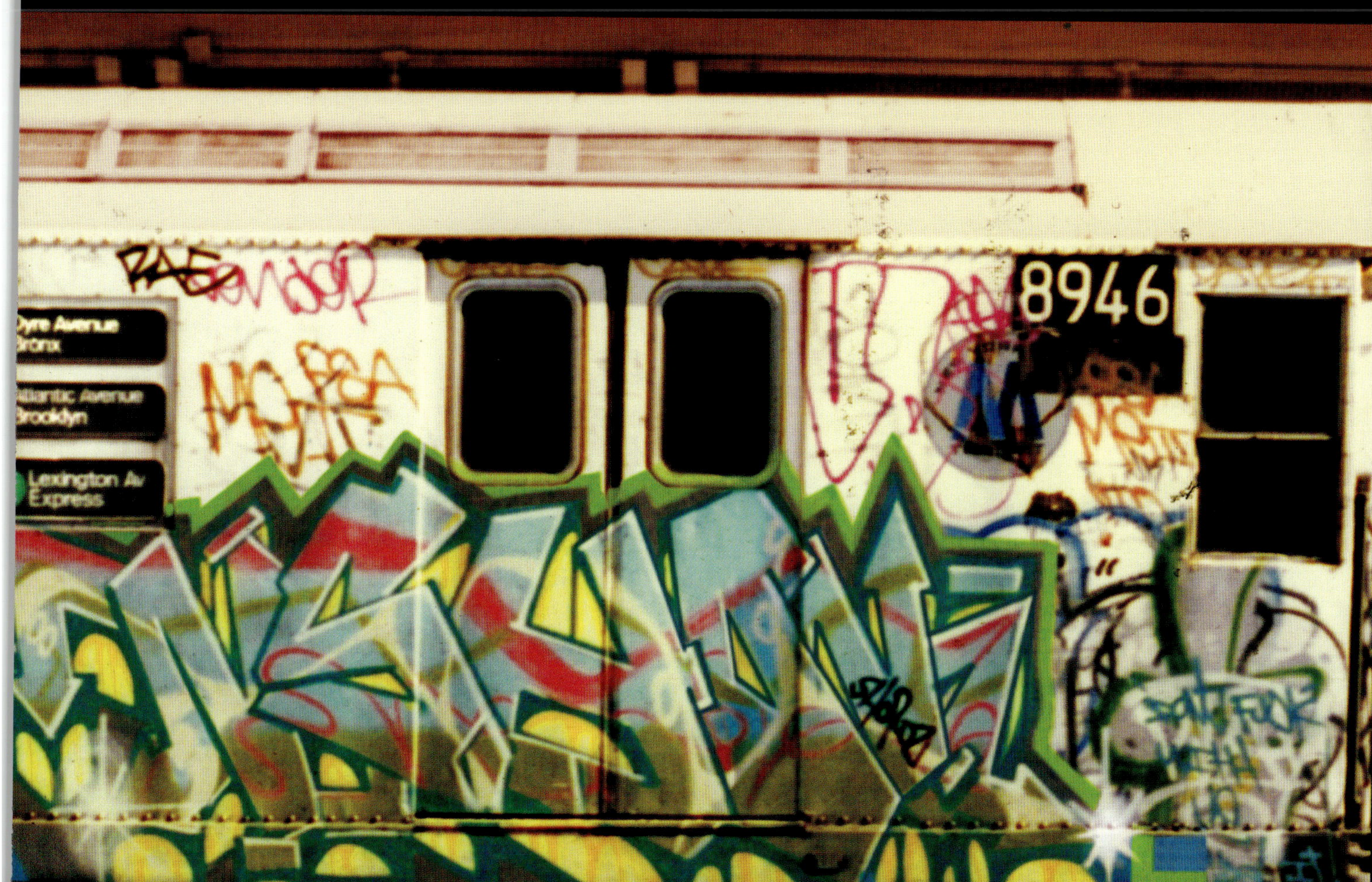

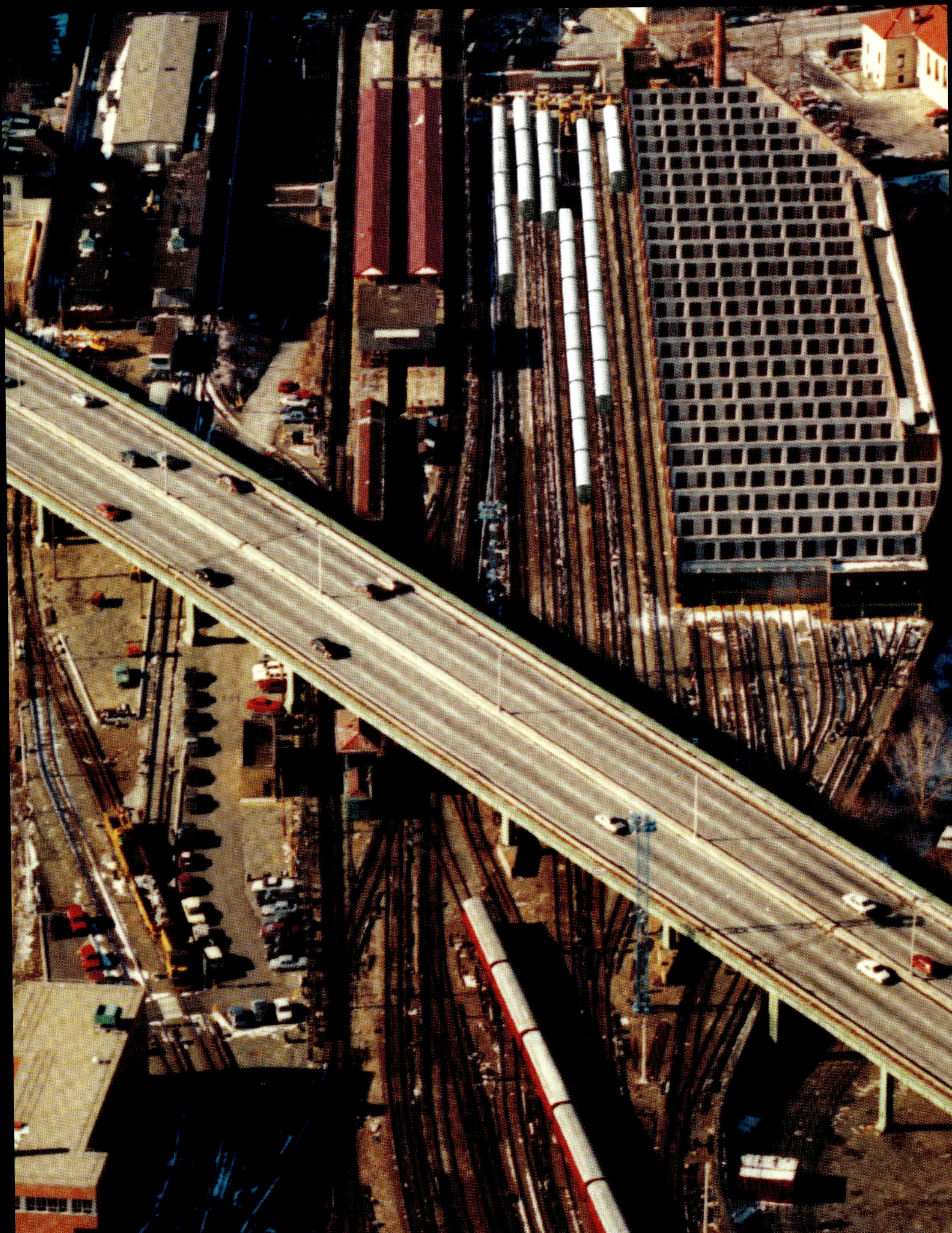

Aerial view from an MTA helicopter of the 180th St. Yard, Station, and Maintenance House.

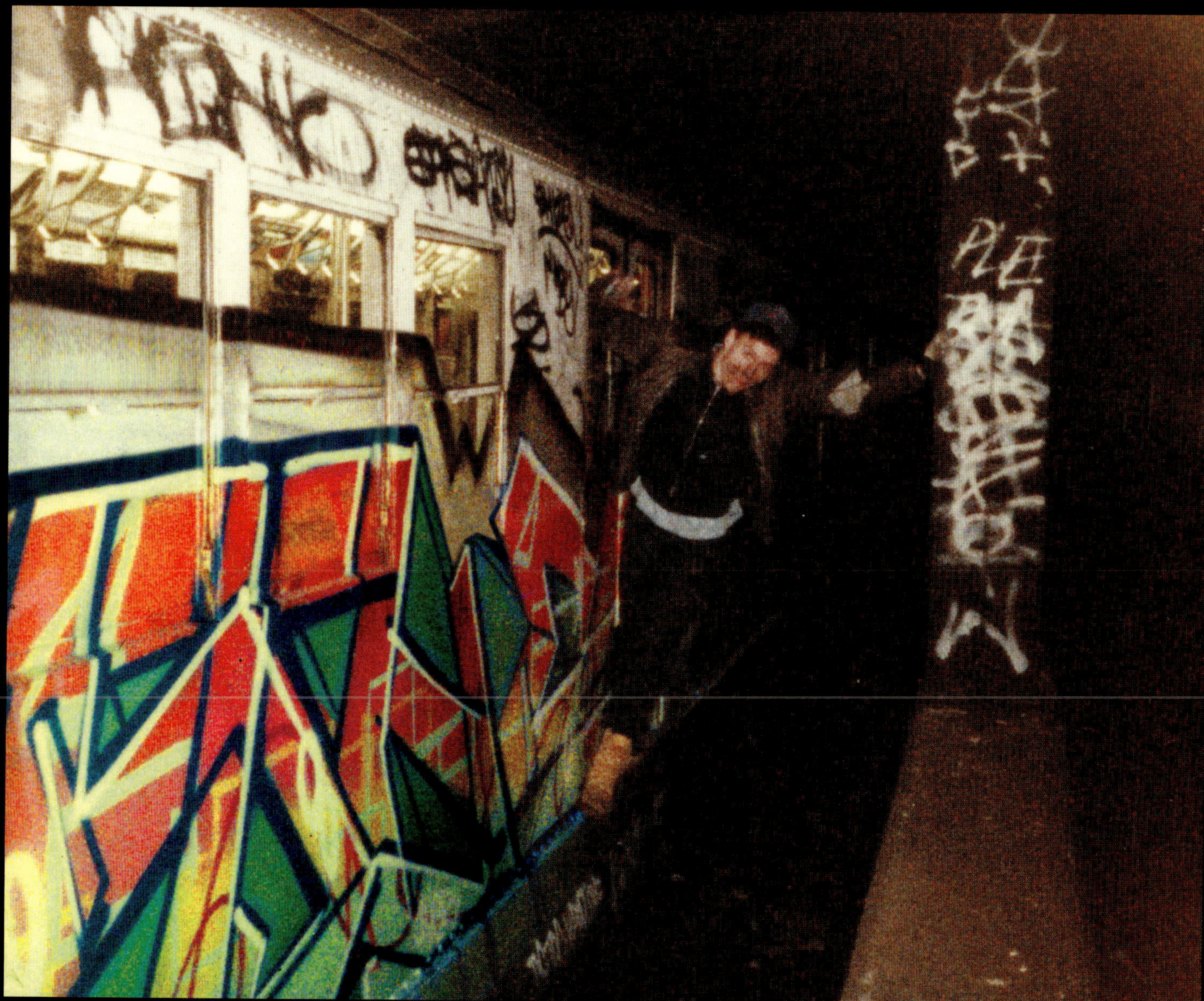

SHOROZ live in Esplanade Tunnels, 5:50 A.M.

Aerial view of the 180th Street Yard.
This photo was taken at the end of 1989. This was when all of the 5 trains were being phased out for the new Red Birds and marked the end of graffiti as we knew it on subway IRTs. We at TDCUSA had largely stopped hitting the 5ives in the fall of 1989 because they was too bombed with marker mop ink and throw ups. But we had a great 3-year run on the line and had switched off to hit other lines as there now were just too many toys hitting the line with throwies and as the number of bombed trains decreased, it became harder to hit them cause the MTA sure as hell wasn't gonna park the Red Birds in the same spots. Those did get hit but just not in 180th Yard, that was just fucking suicidal.

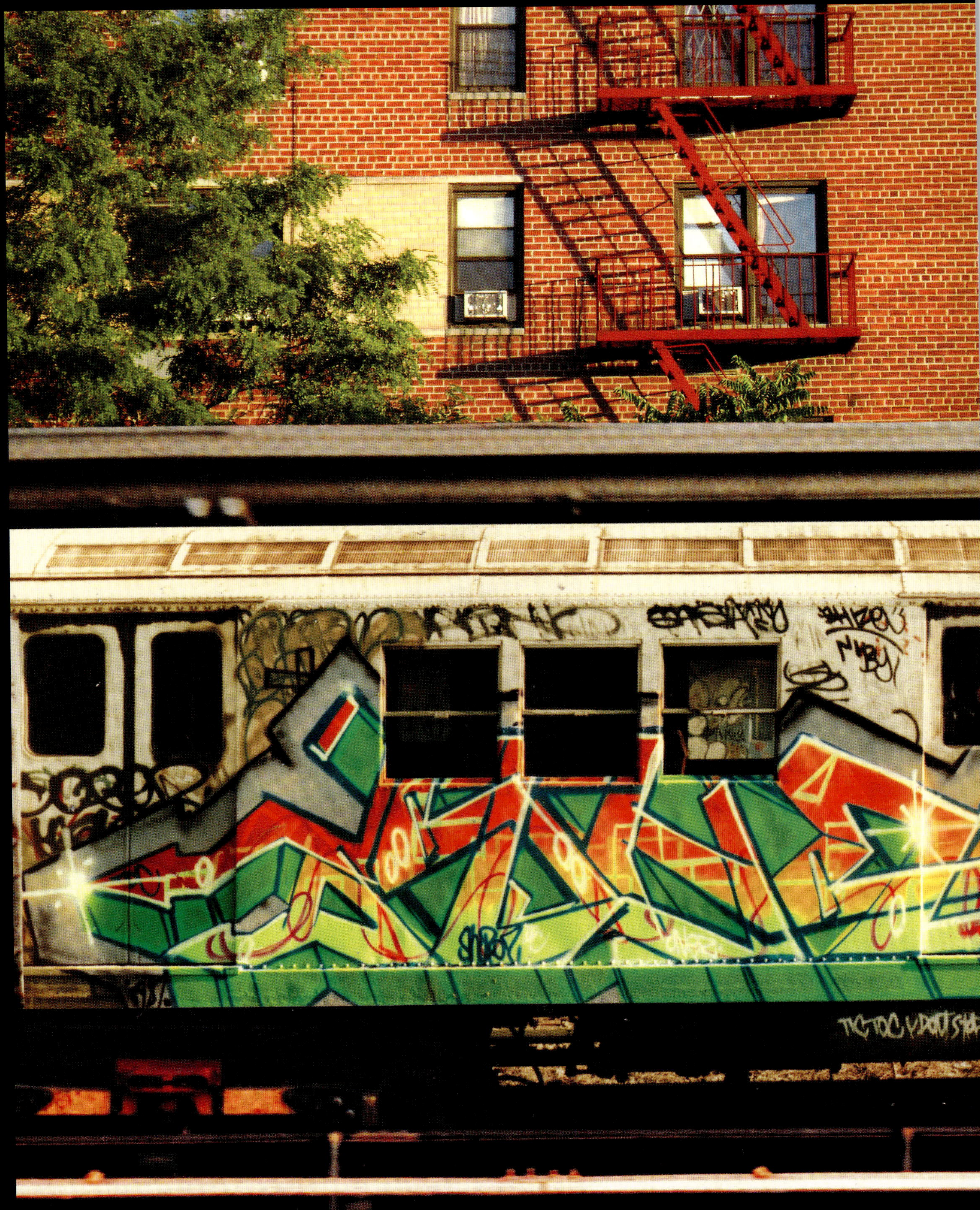

SHOROZ 3/4 car, window-down burner, "TIC TOC U DON'T STOP," Dec. 1987.

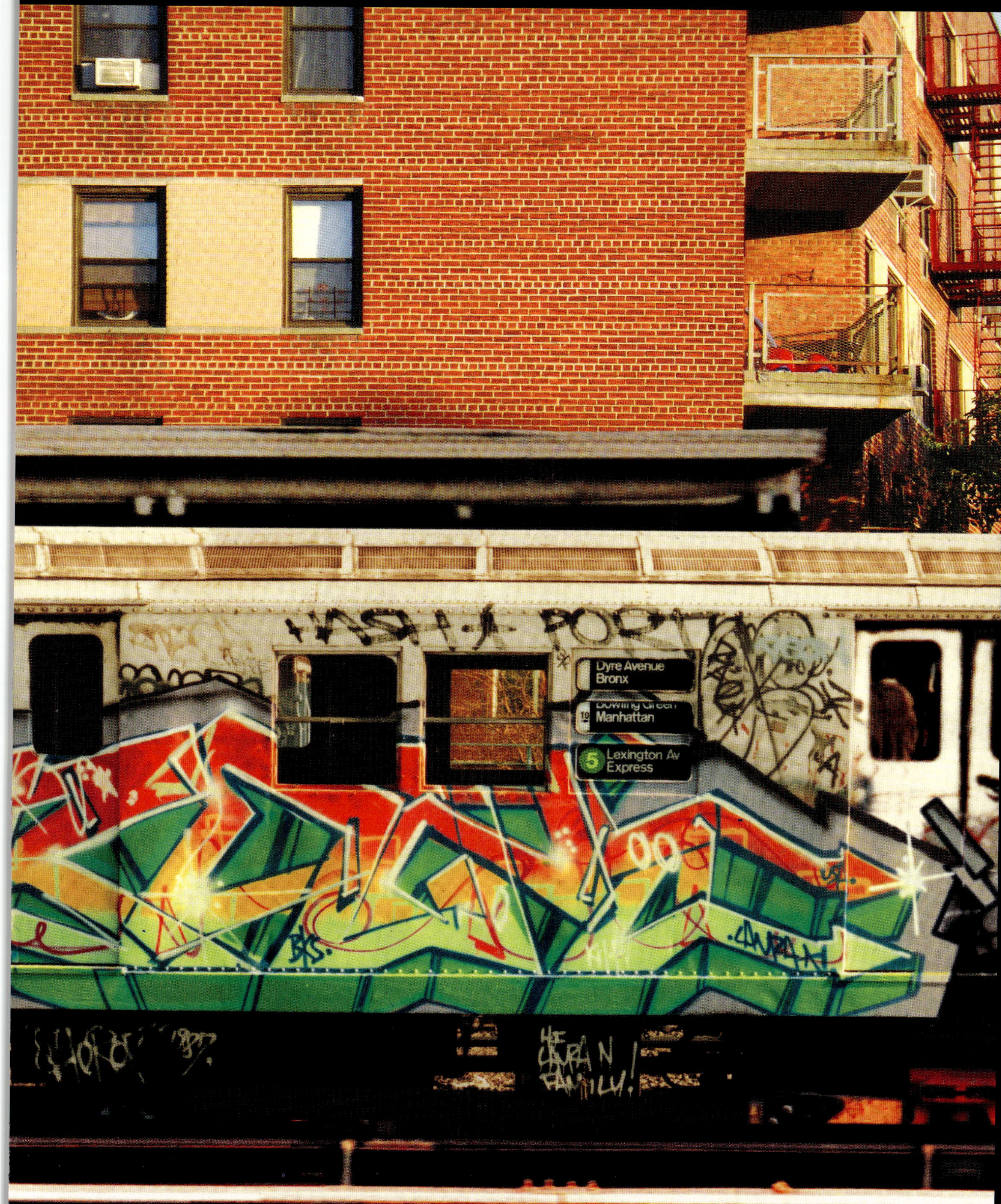
Dyre Avenue
Bronx
Manhattan
5
Lexington Av
Express

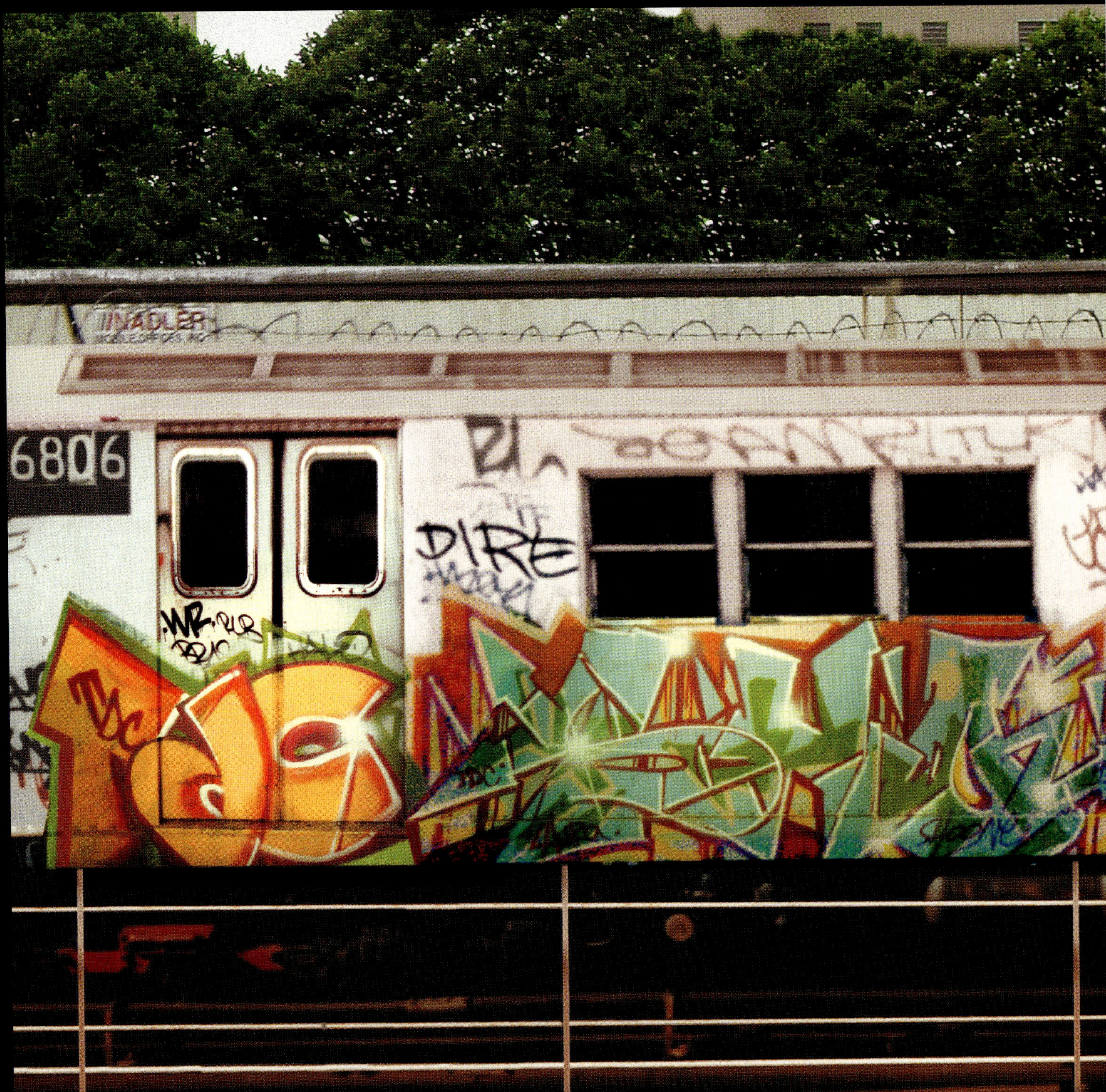

TDC SHO and DC3, "THE THREES YALL," done in the 148th St. and Lenox Terminal Yard, Oct. 1987.

This was a good night, yo!!!! The other side was done by Zoo and Mirage CWK.

As much as we was killing the 5 Train at the moment, we still wanted more. We painted mad train lines a little something, something. We was really all about the white IRT train lines though. Hitting the 3s and having cars running meant a lot to us because it was, in my opinion, much harder to smash them, but the increased risk and effort was definitely worth it because they would run untouched for months sometimes. Plus they ran on the most premier IRT line, the 1, 2, and 3 line which ran from the top of the Bronx, much

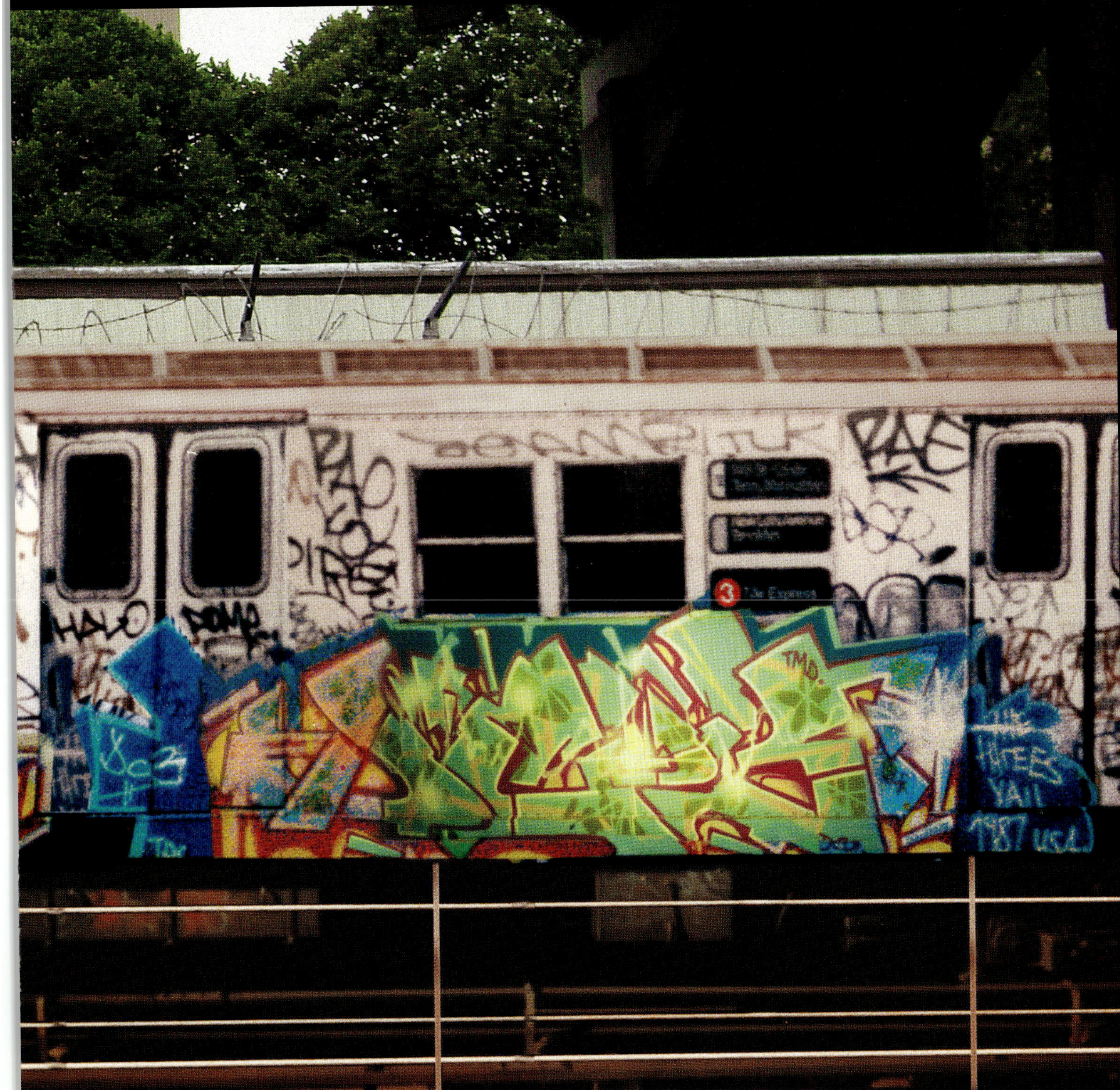

like the 4, 5, and 6s, but ran straight thru Times Square and Penn Station. These stations were where I first benched trains in my life, originally, other than the As and Js in 1983. Painting on white trains was the shit because you could rock all colors, even pastels. We rocked this train in the 3 Yard in October, 1987, after trying unsuccessfully to piece here once before. The first time we had to cut thru several fences and walk thru razor ribbon only for the train to be pulled out while we was painting that shit. It wasn't the first time and it wasn't the last. Painting burners here was a dream come true.

-SHO TDC

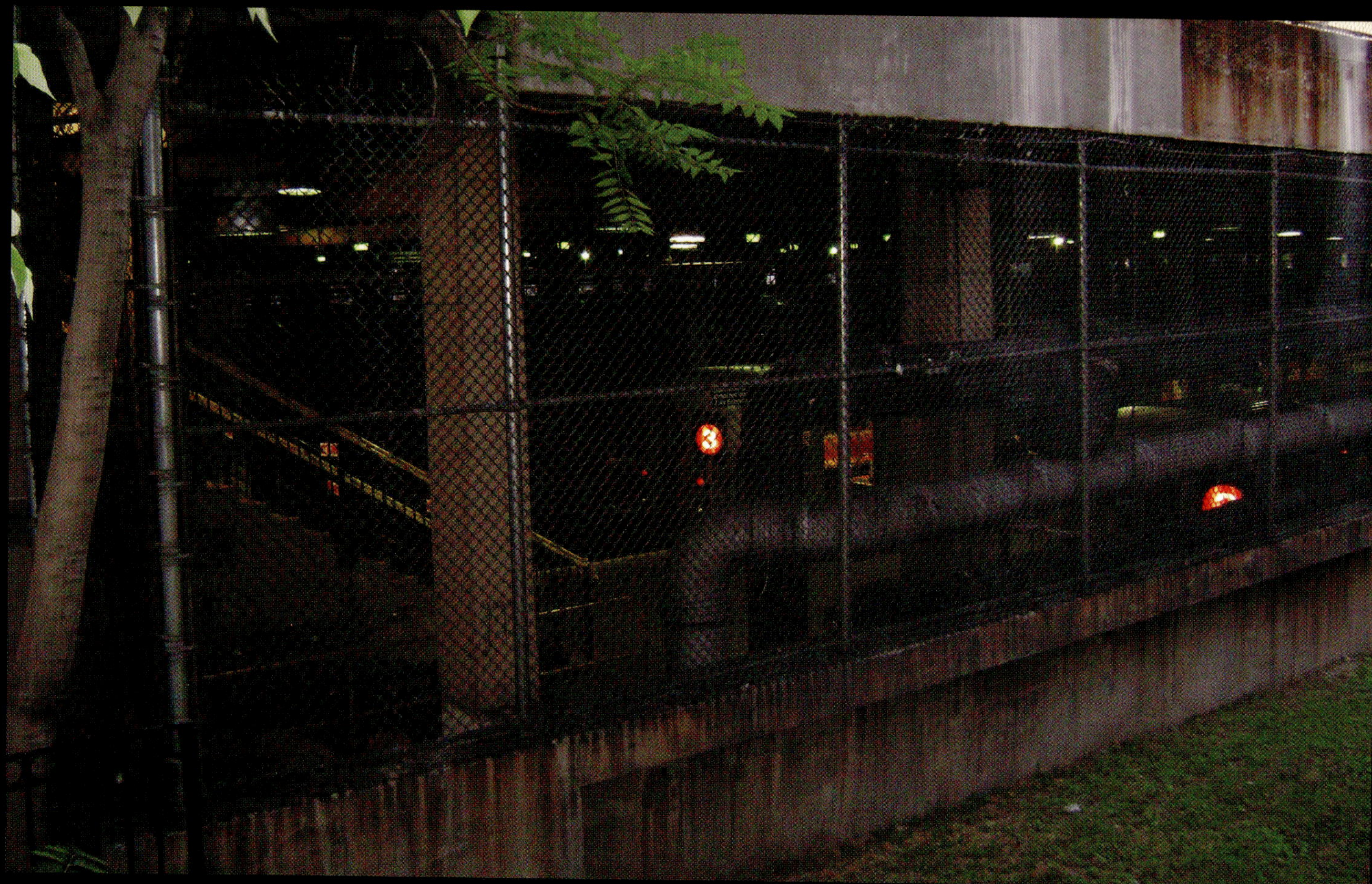

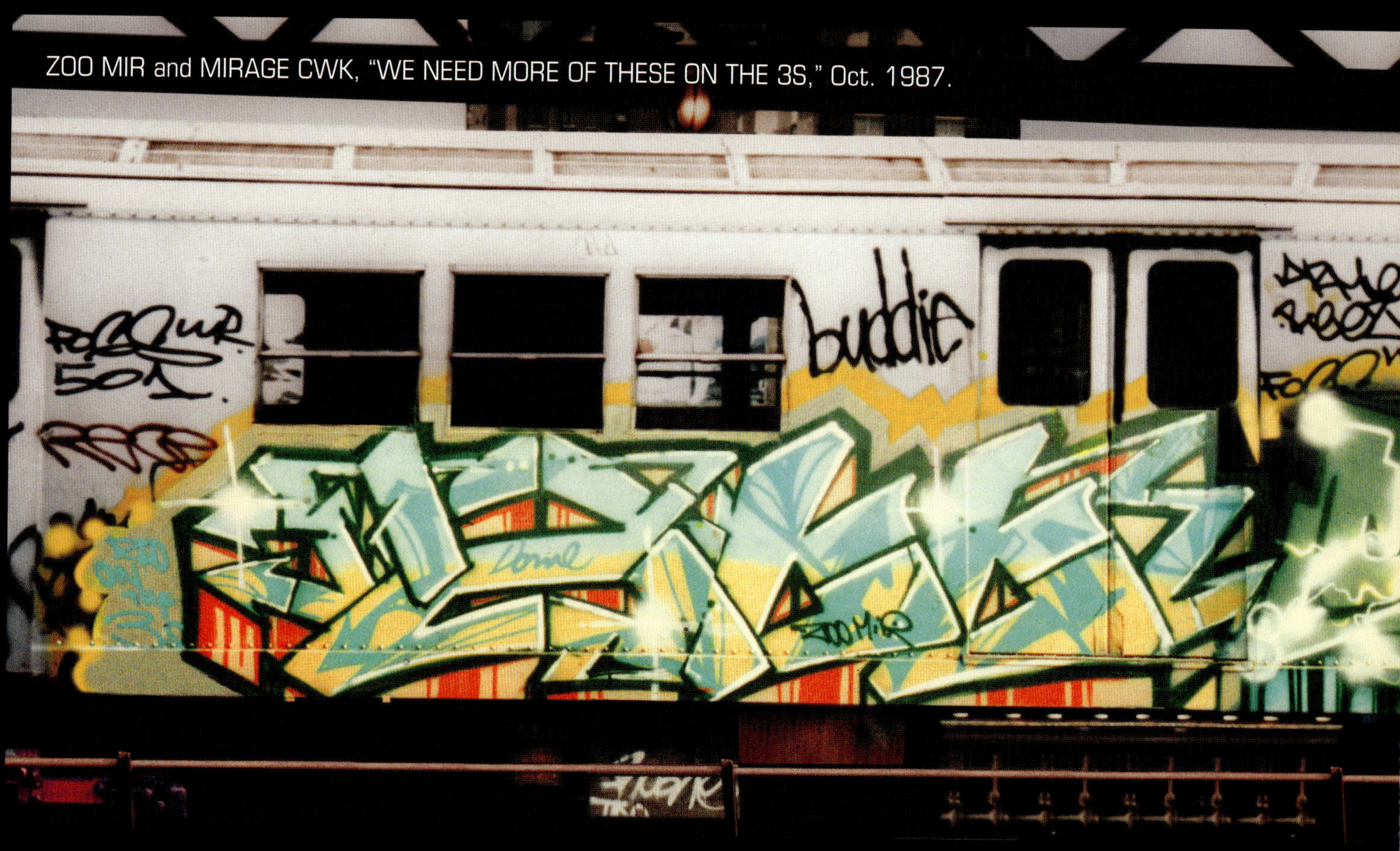

ZOO MIR and MIRAGE CWK, "WE NEED MORE OF THESE ON THE 3S," Oct. 1987.

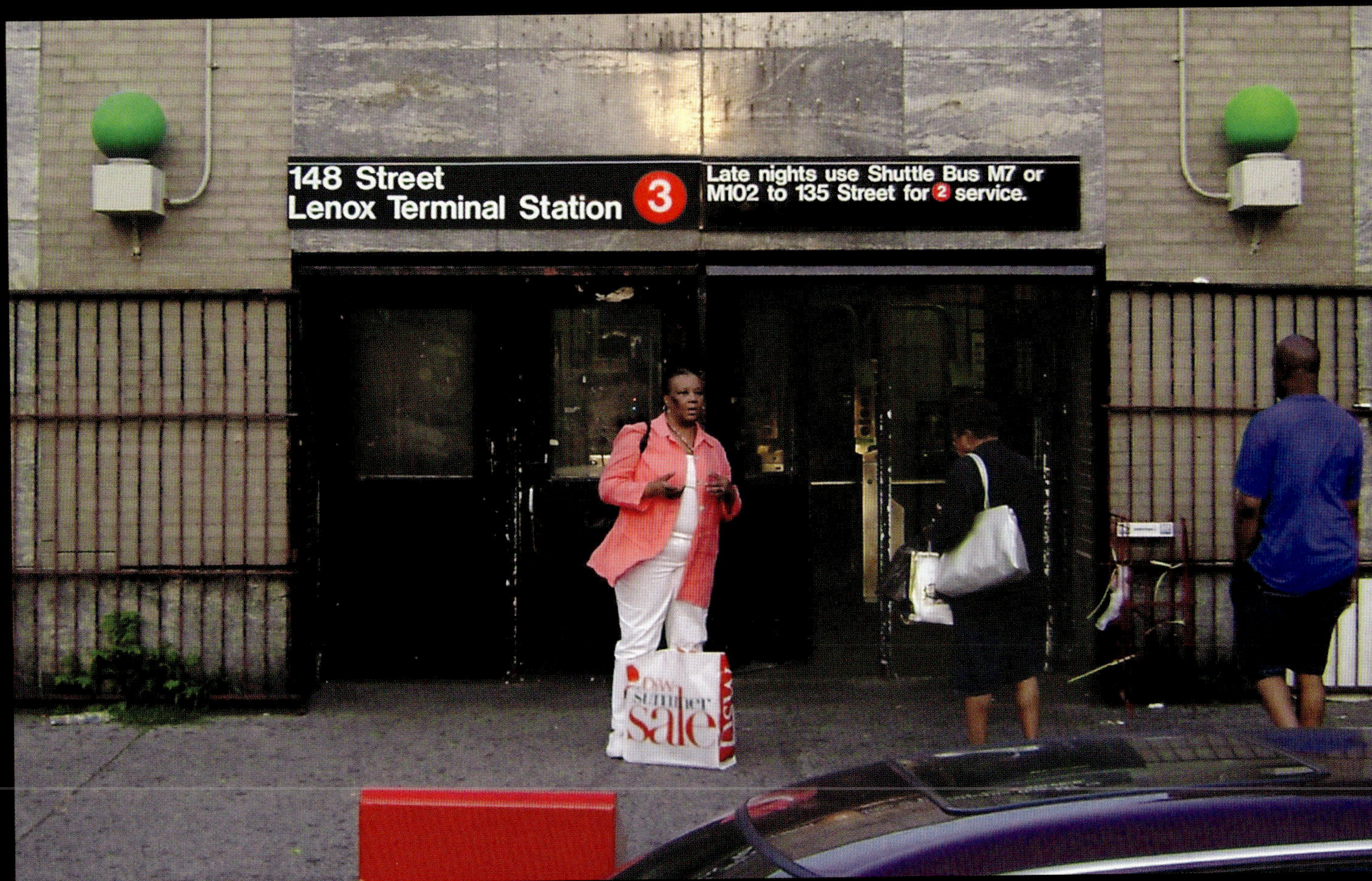

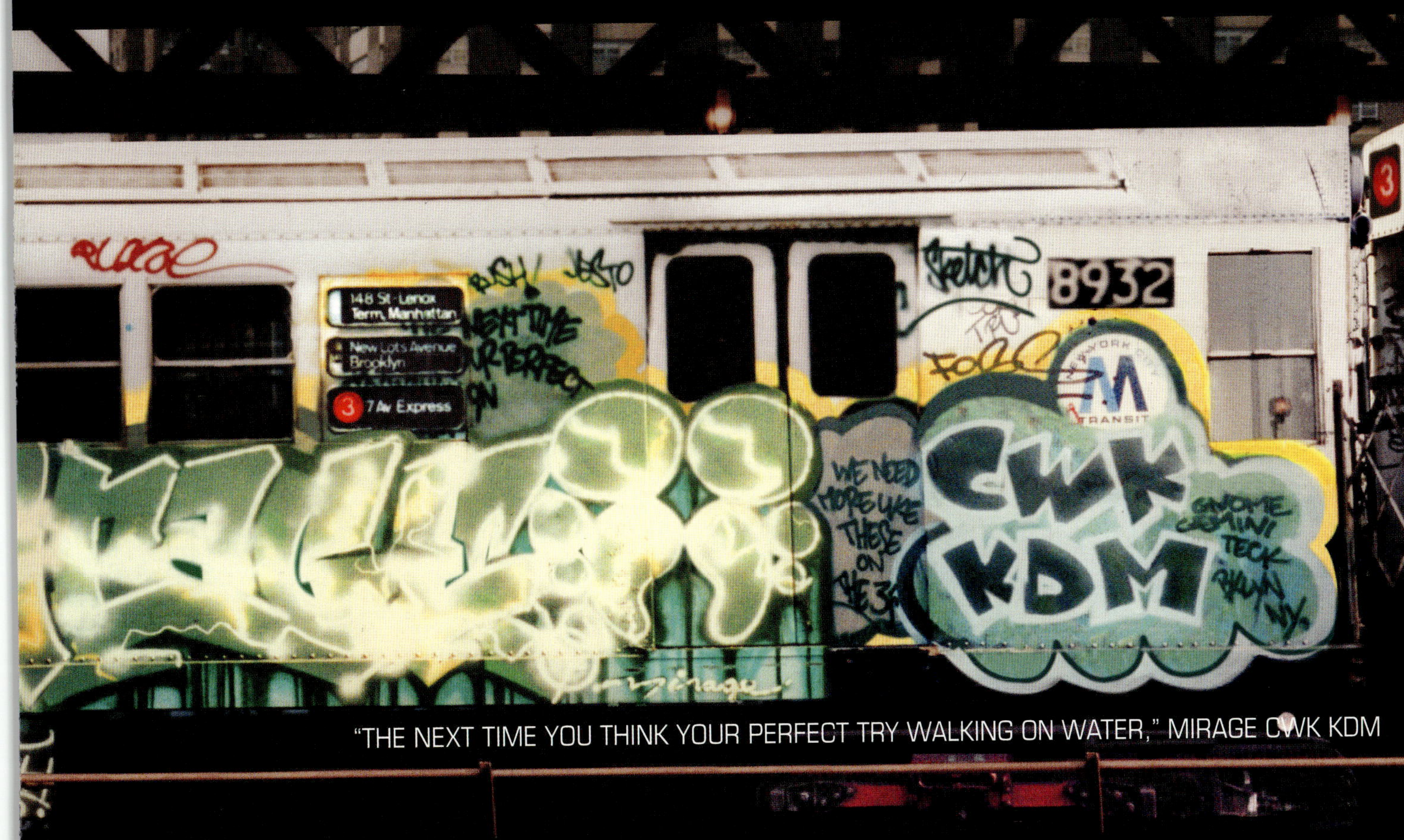

"THE NEXT TIME YOU THINK YOUR PERFECT TRY WALKING ON WATER," MIRAGE CWK KDM

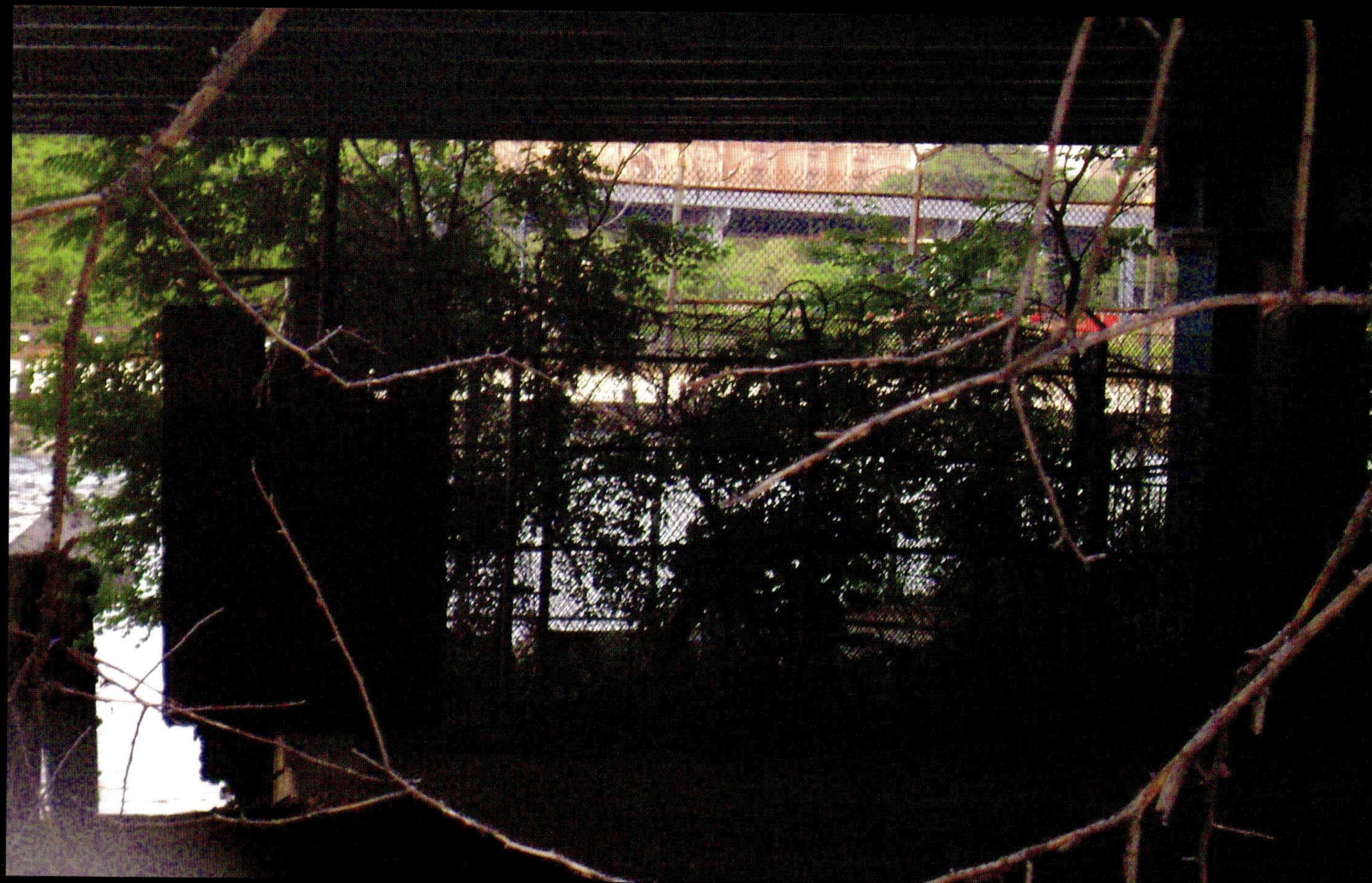

A risky second option to try and get into the 3 Yard. No mistakes allowed here.

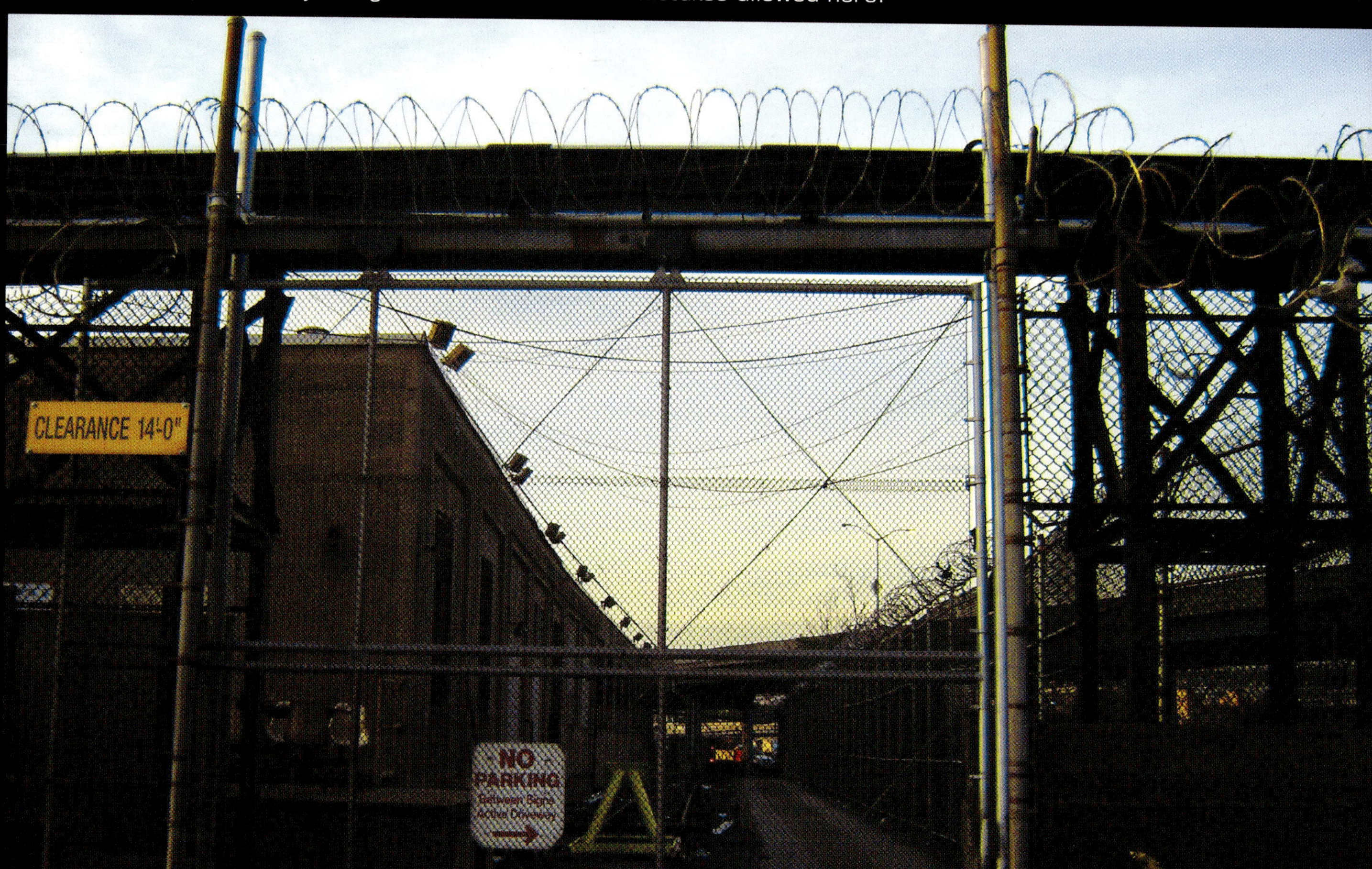

Another 3 Yard entrance.

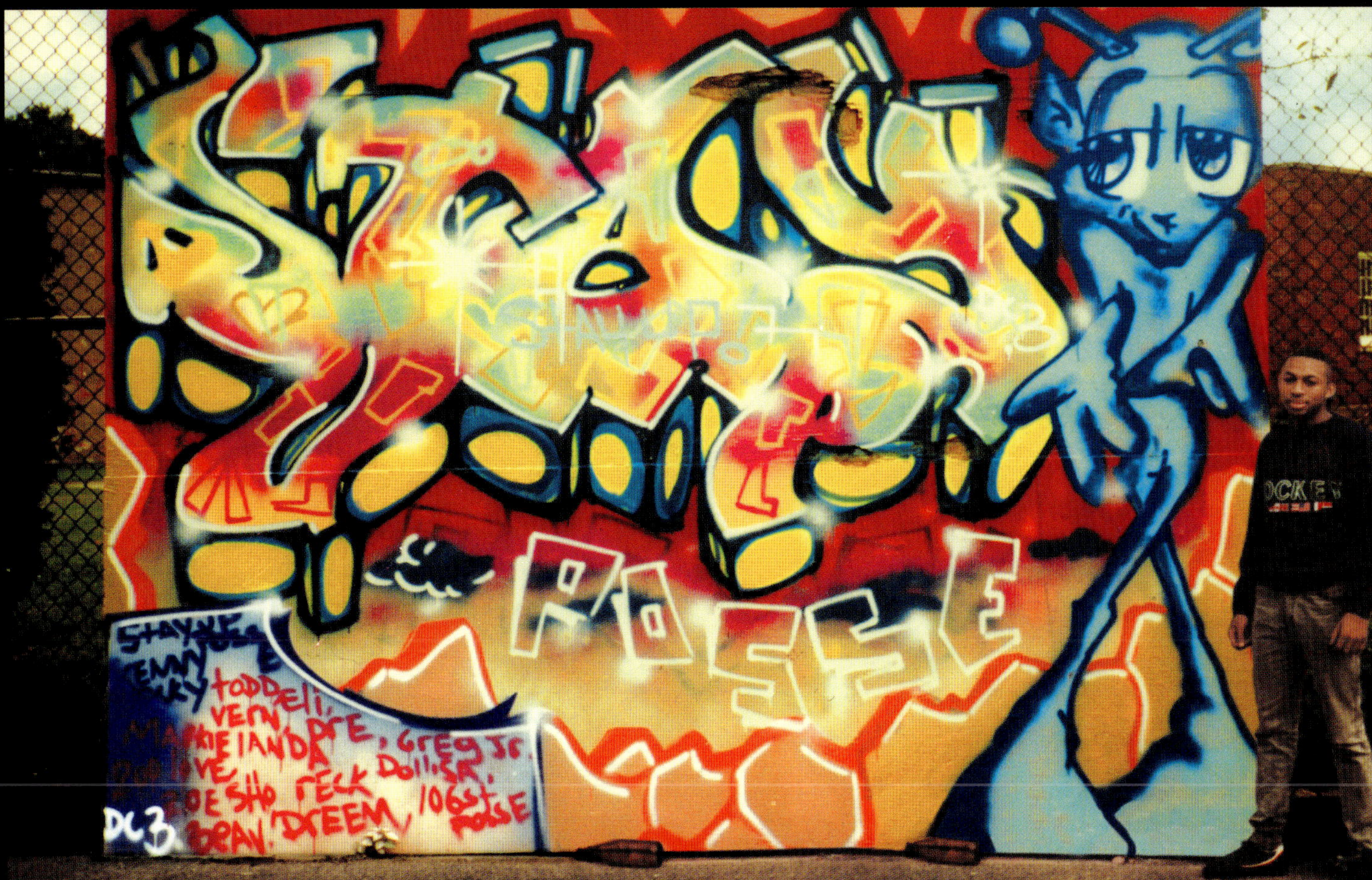

DC3 live at the Stay Up Posse wall, Sep. 1985.

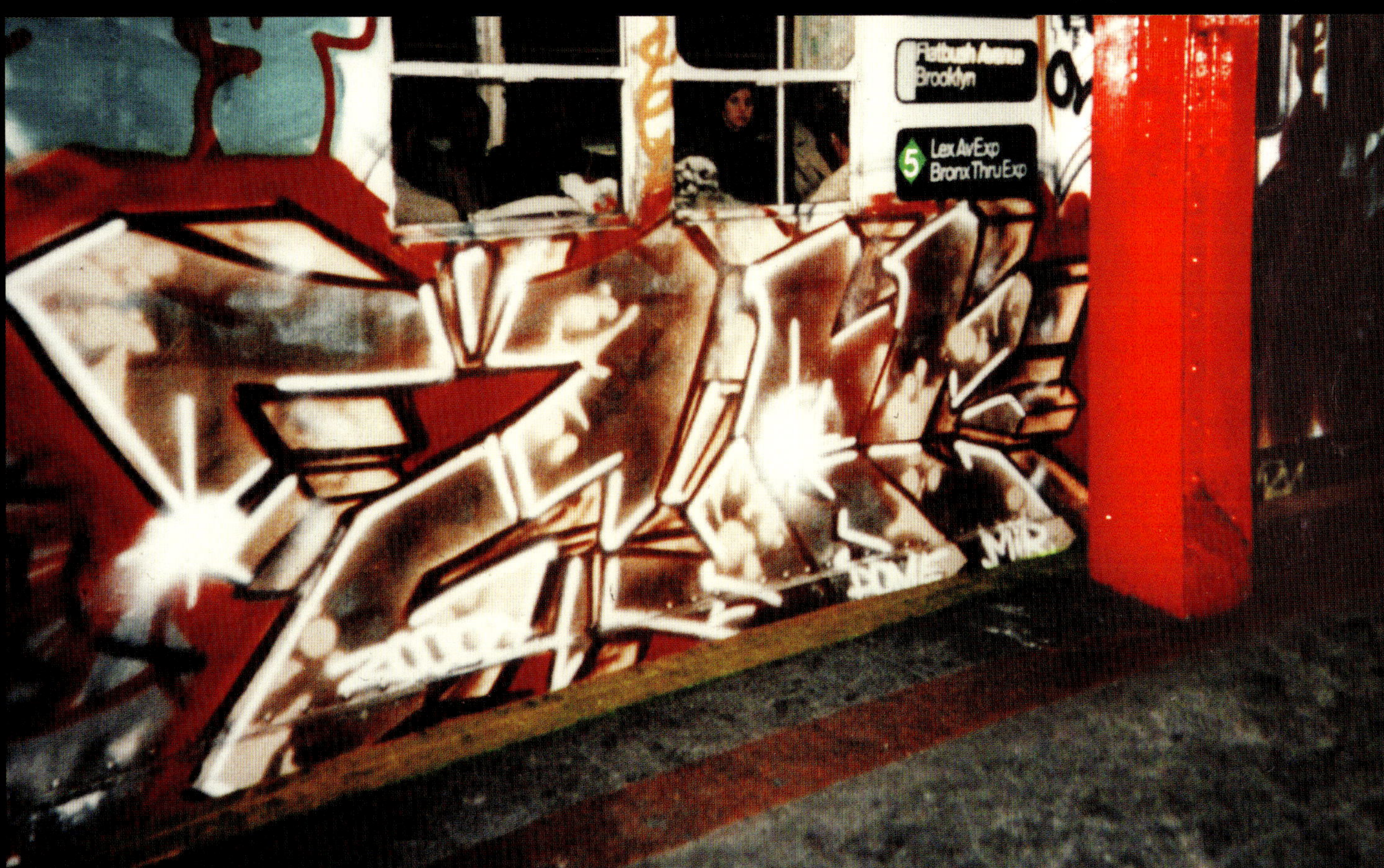

ZOO and SHO's gold pieces running, 5 Train, Nov. 1987.

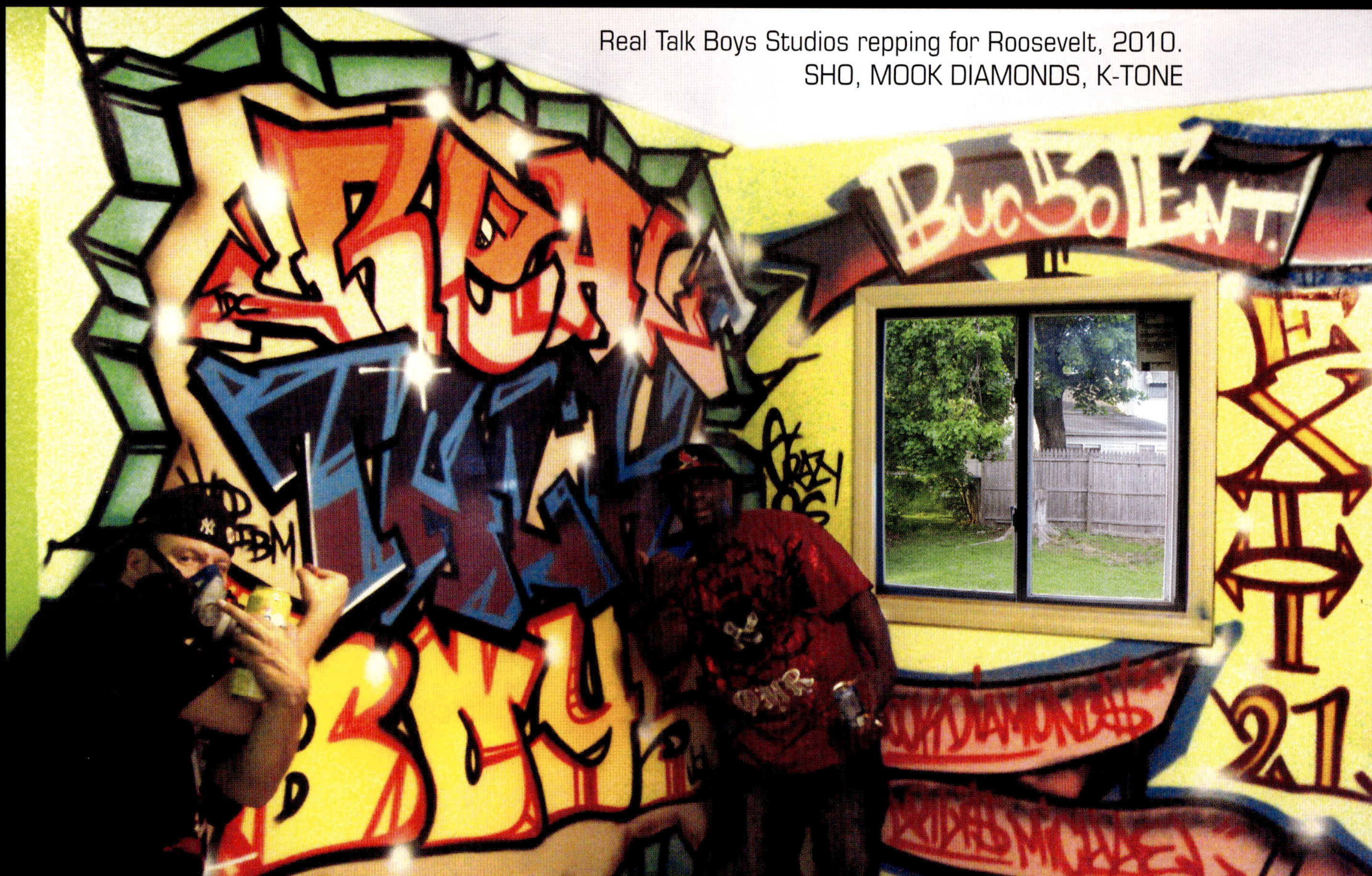

Real Talk Boys Studios repping for Roosevelt, 2010.
SHO, MOOK DIAMONDS, K-TONE

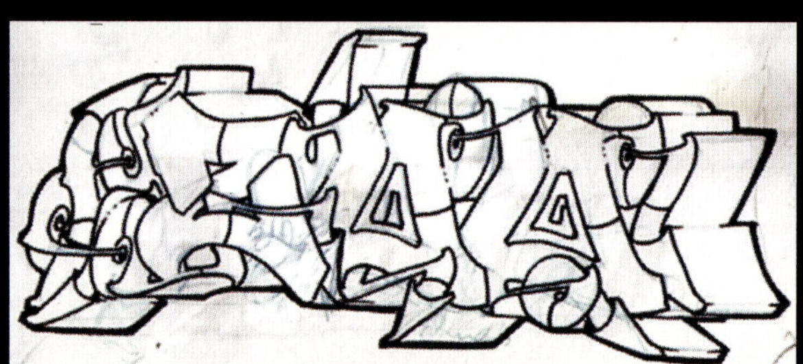

ZOO's outlines in Domes' black book were the basis for the completed piece in Brooklyn, NY, 1992.

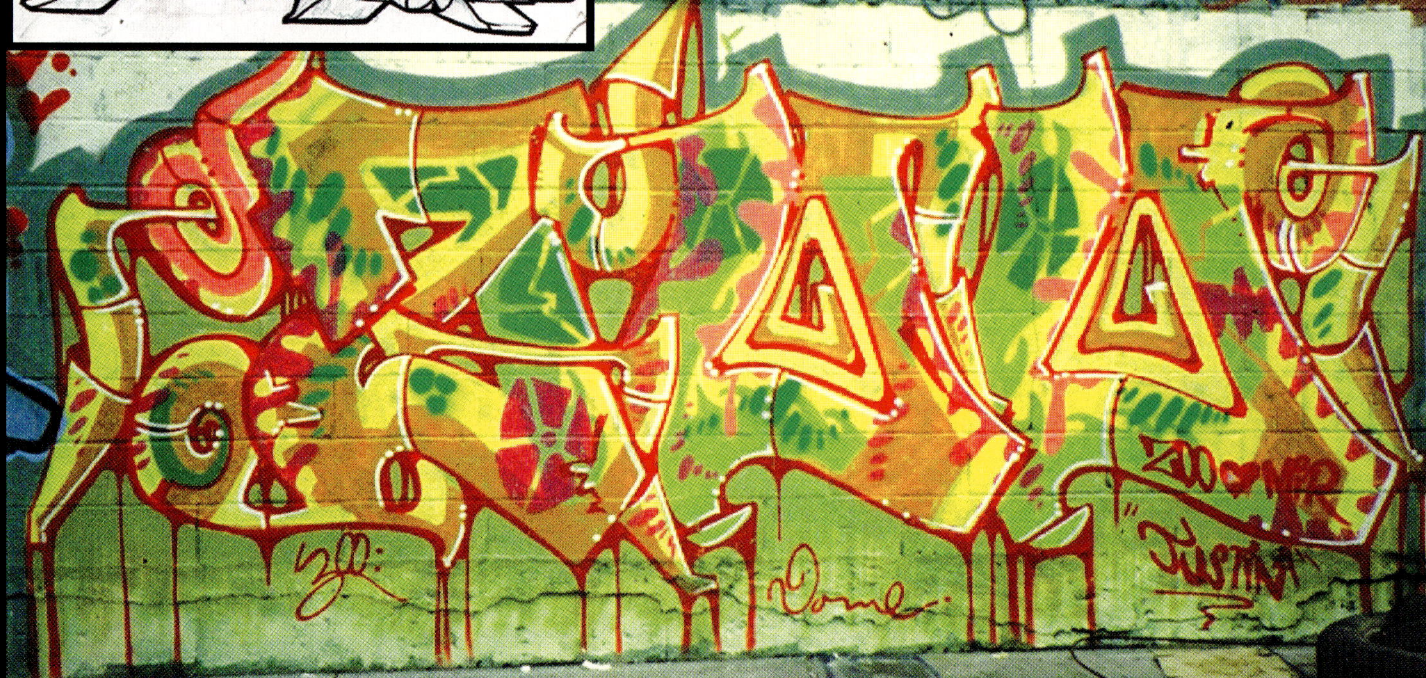

ZOO Loves Miriam wall, Franklin K. Lane, Feb. 1992.

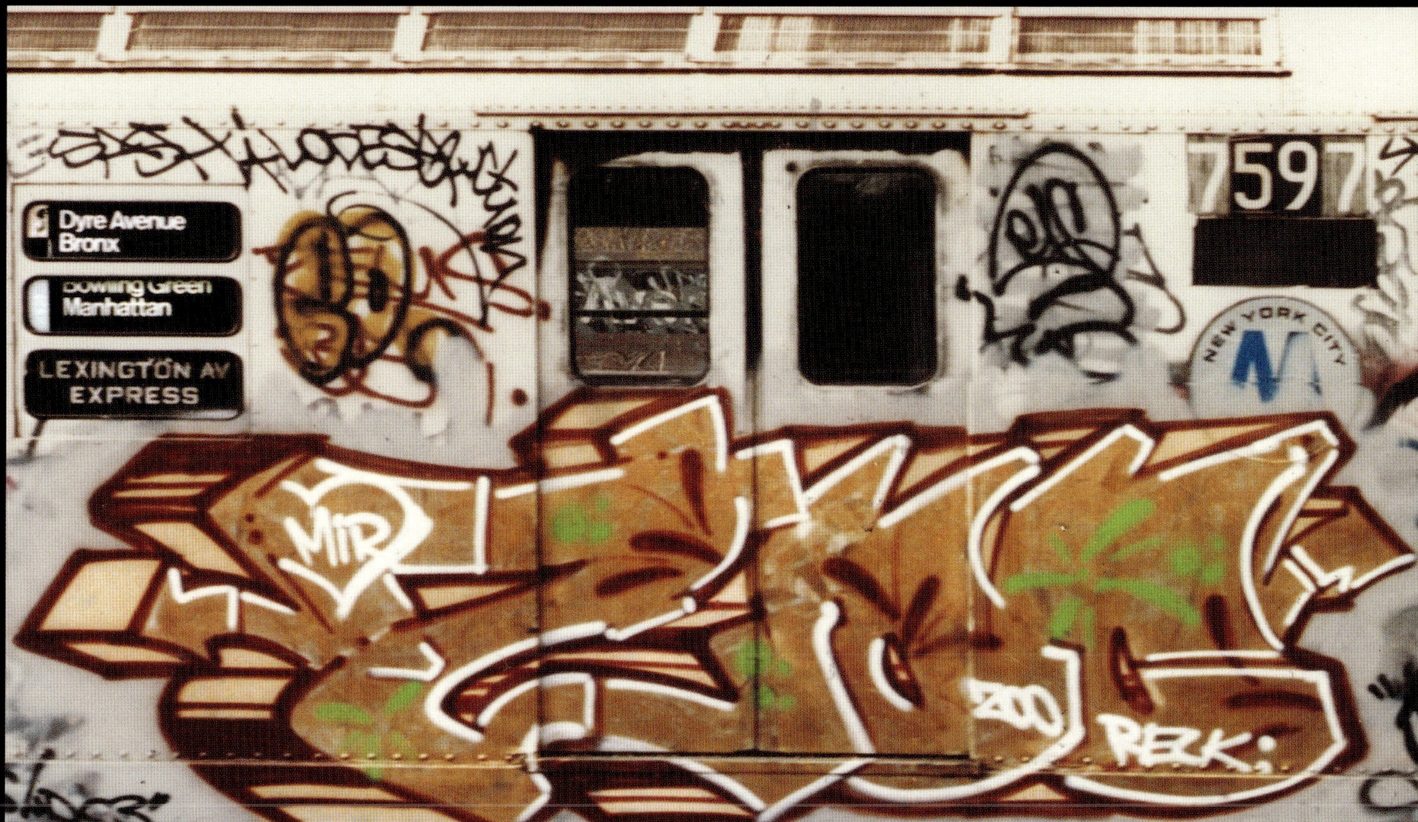

ZOO, 5 Train, December 1986.

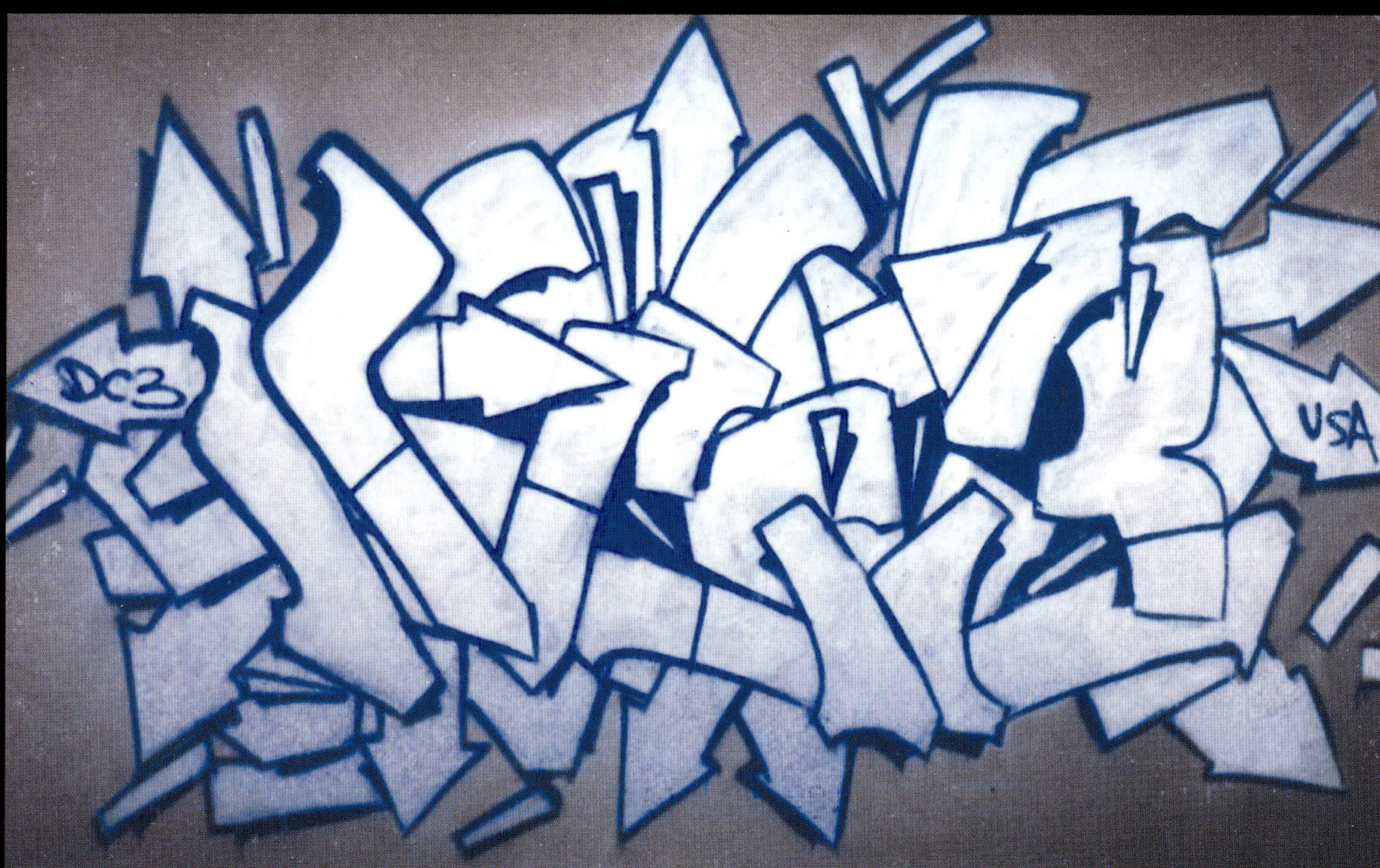

DC3 USA, silver piece, Roosevelt, LI, 1985.

KARL, aka SERT, TCMOB burning with ZOO EX-Vandals, Dec. 1987.

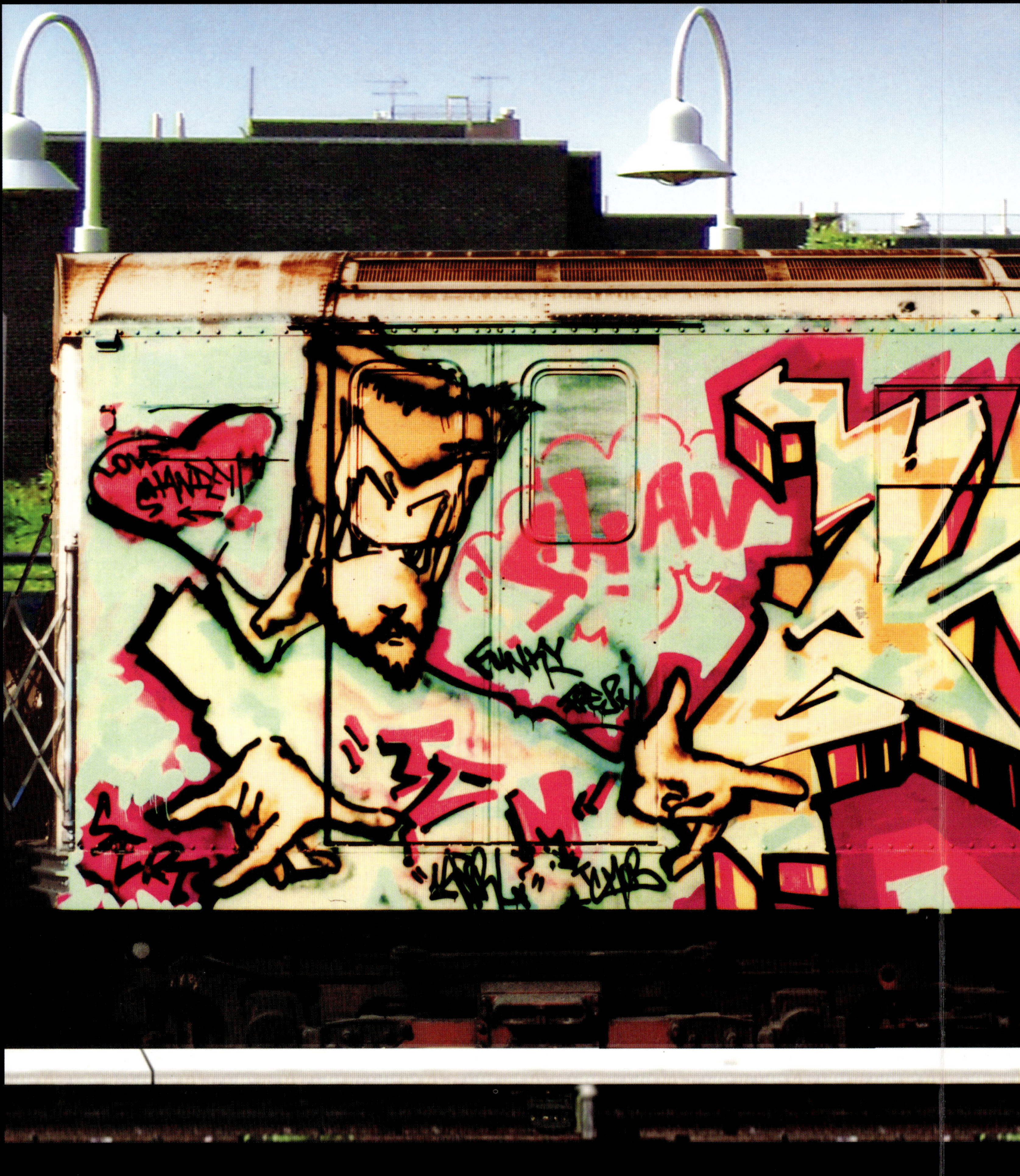

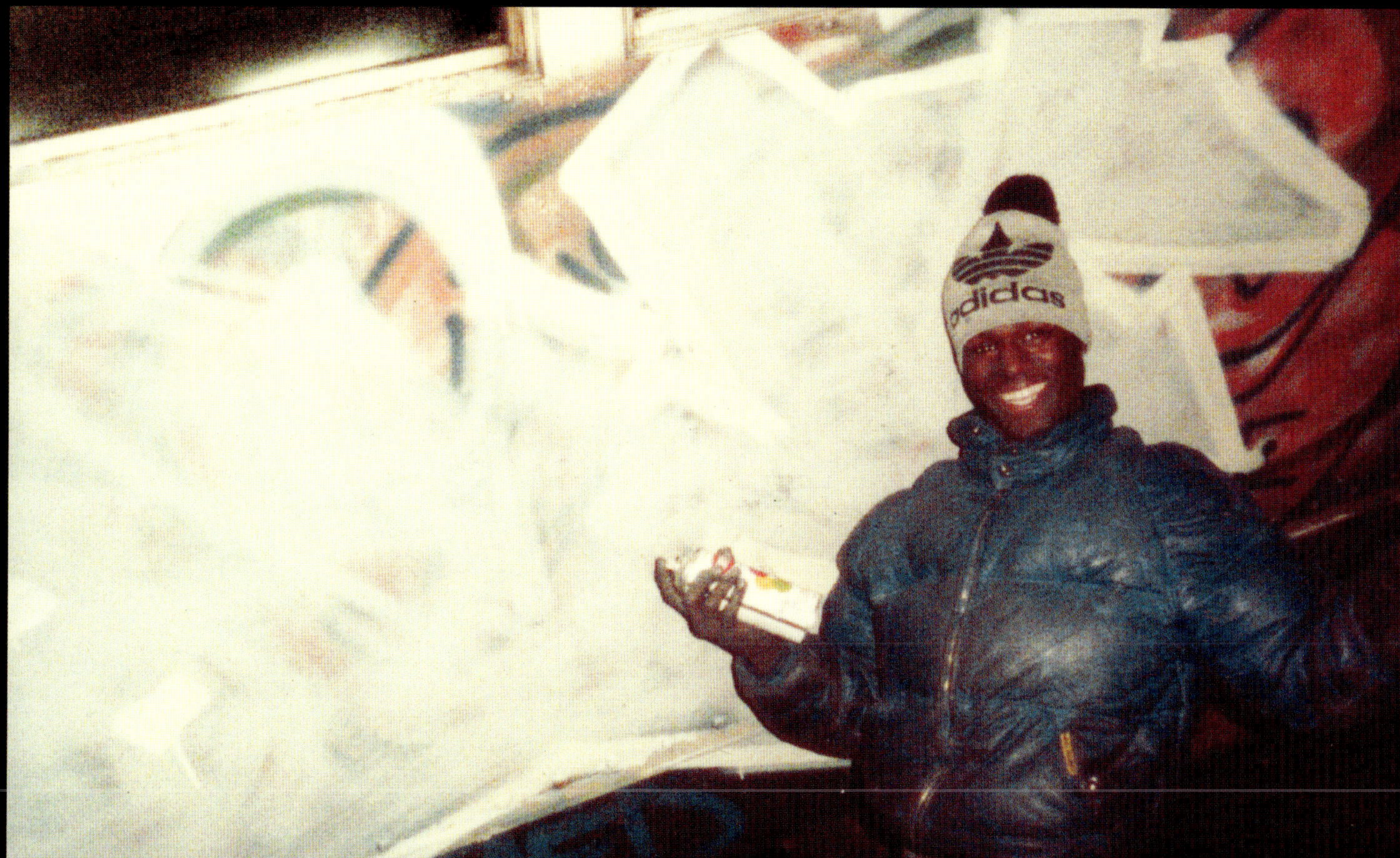

DEON TCM getting busy.

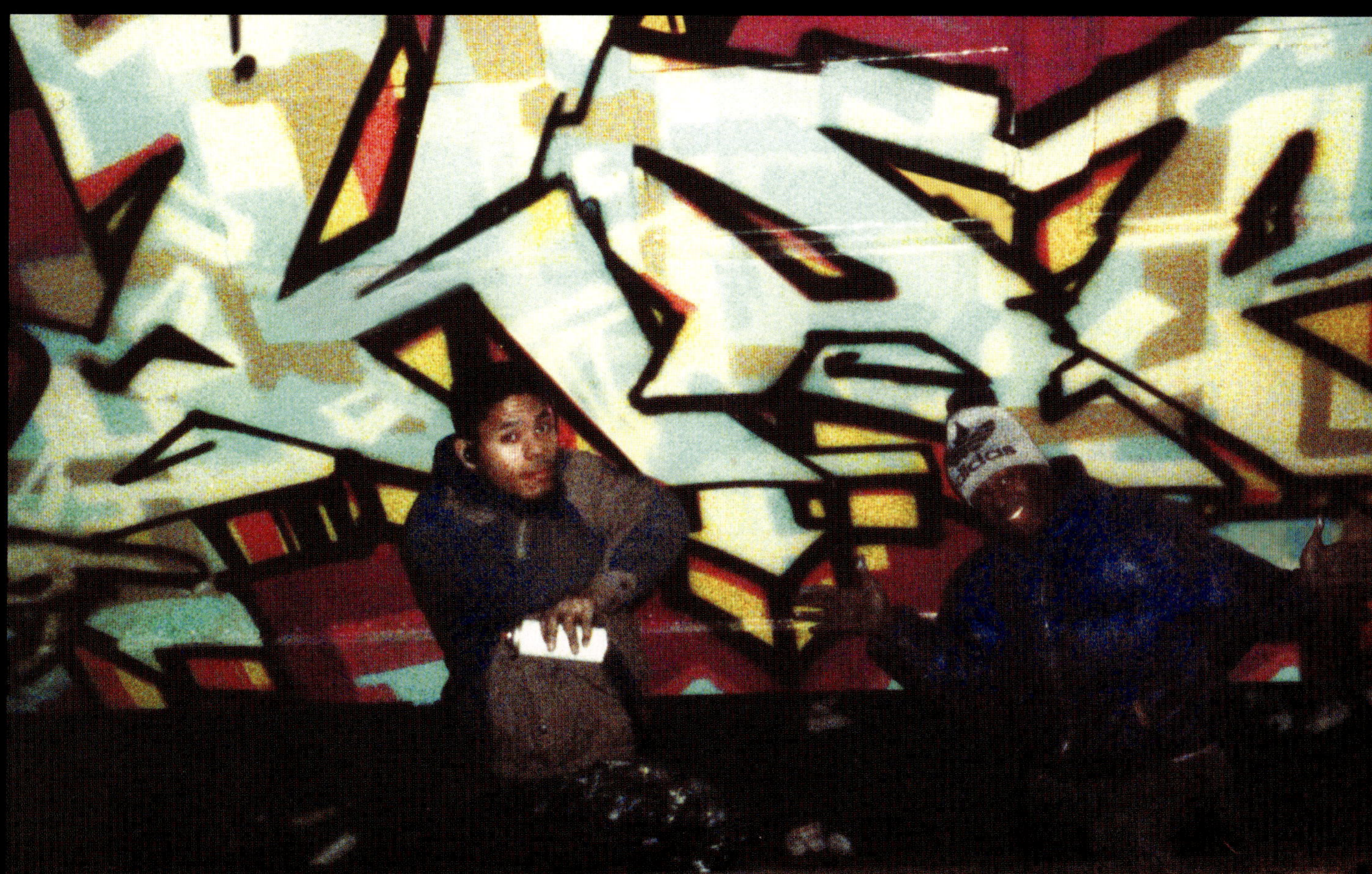

KARL TCM and DEON wrecking shit in Esplanade Tunnels.

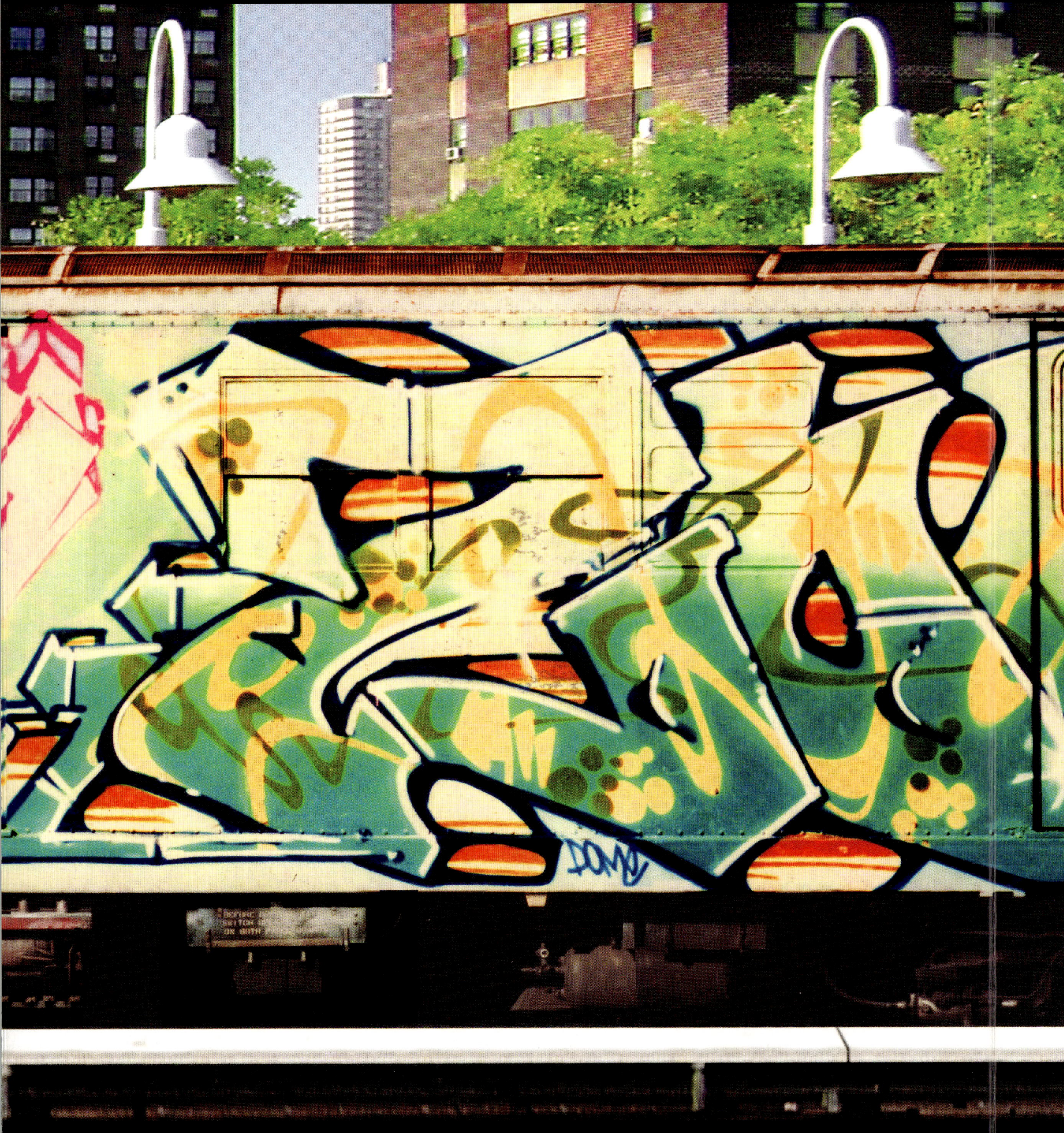

CHAPTER 6

New Lots Yard

ROZ FUN CLUB Biography

The TDC Silver and Gold "SHO DC3 ZOO" Train

★

We rocked this car at The 3 Yard in September 1987. Once again we was hunting for new ways to get in, back in the days there was a way you could go thru these sets of doors at the beginning of the platform back by the token booth and walk right the fuck in, but not anymore. So we seen the holes we cut underneath the stairs was back on lock down so we went round back thru a small park towards the river and piers. Yo this shit was a mission, you had to basically walk along a small ledge while holding on to the fence while you were above the river, and if you fell in you were definitely fucked. Picture that shit, the waters probably freezing at night and there would be no way out of the water plus your clothes would make you sink, soaking wet. I got in to trouble trying to go around a long hanging circle of razor ribbon and got my clothes caught up and then my bag with the paint. I almost fell in and had to abandon the bag on the razor ribbon but Dome helped me, shit was ill that night.

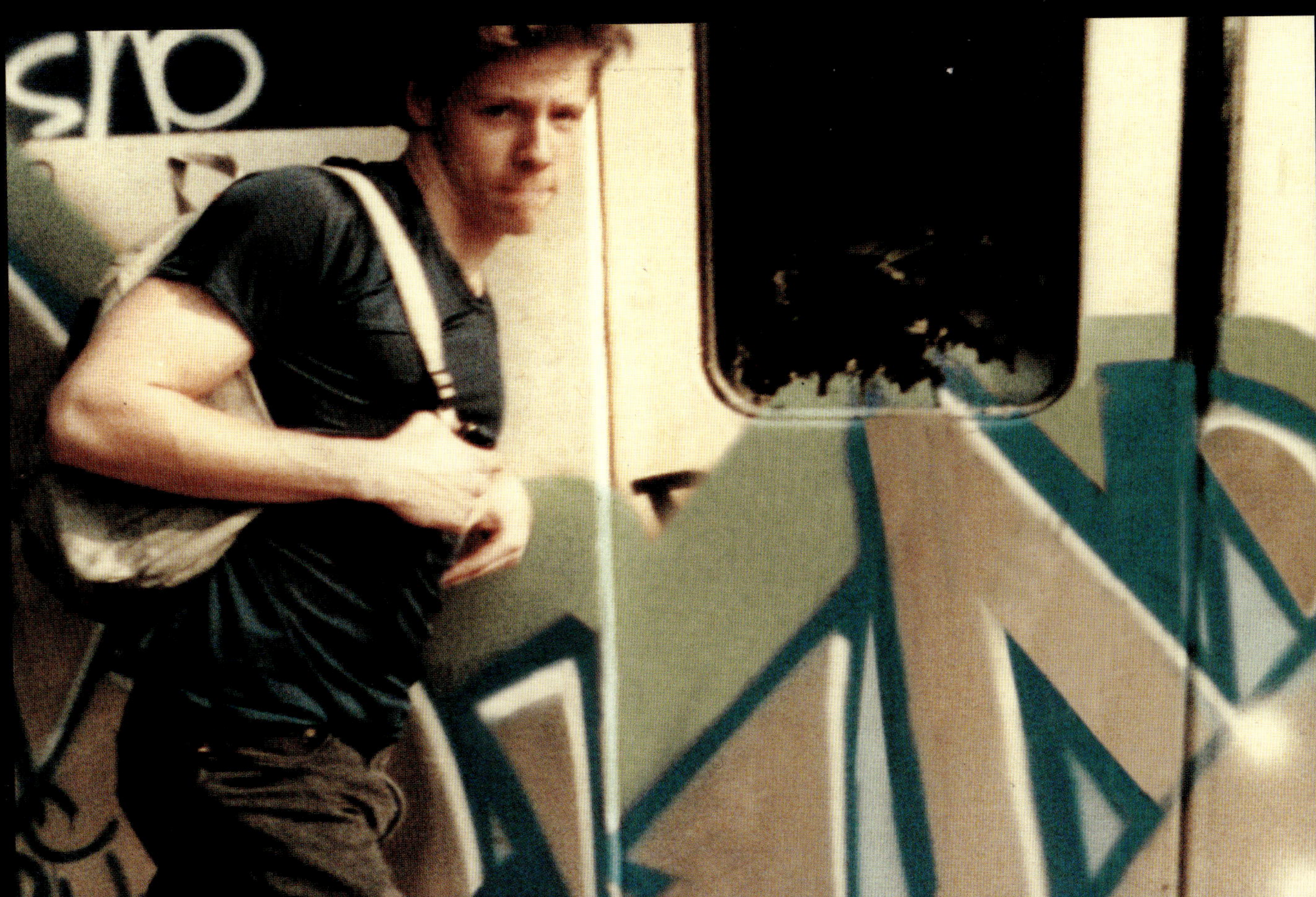

SHO on the go!!! Benching my shit in Brooklyn all day.

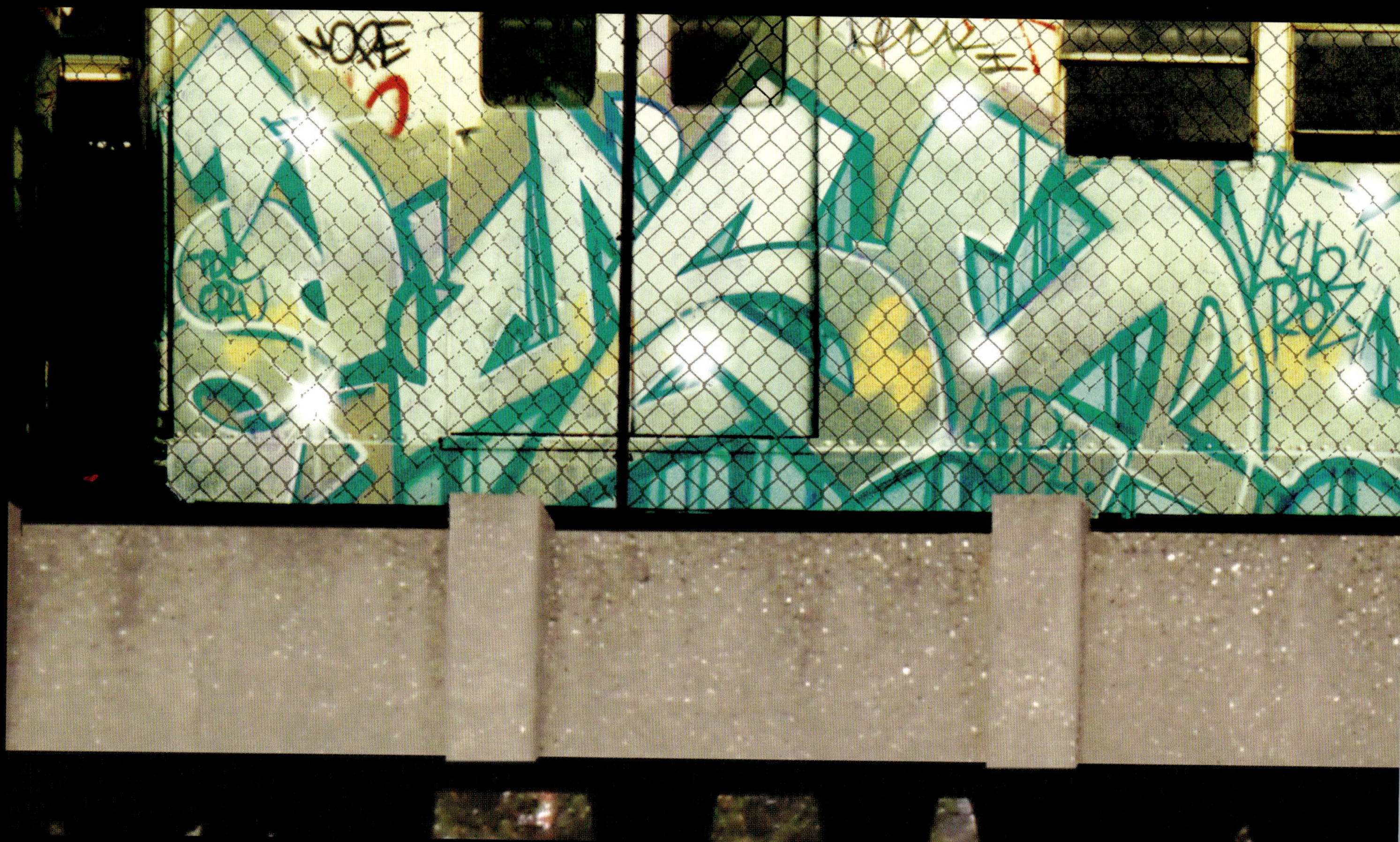

Silver TDC SHO, DC3 pushing NCB and 357 crews with ZOO gold window-downs, Sep. 1987.

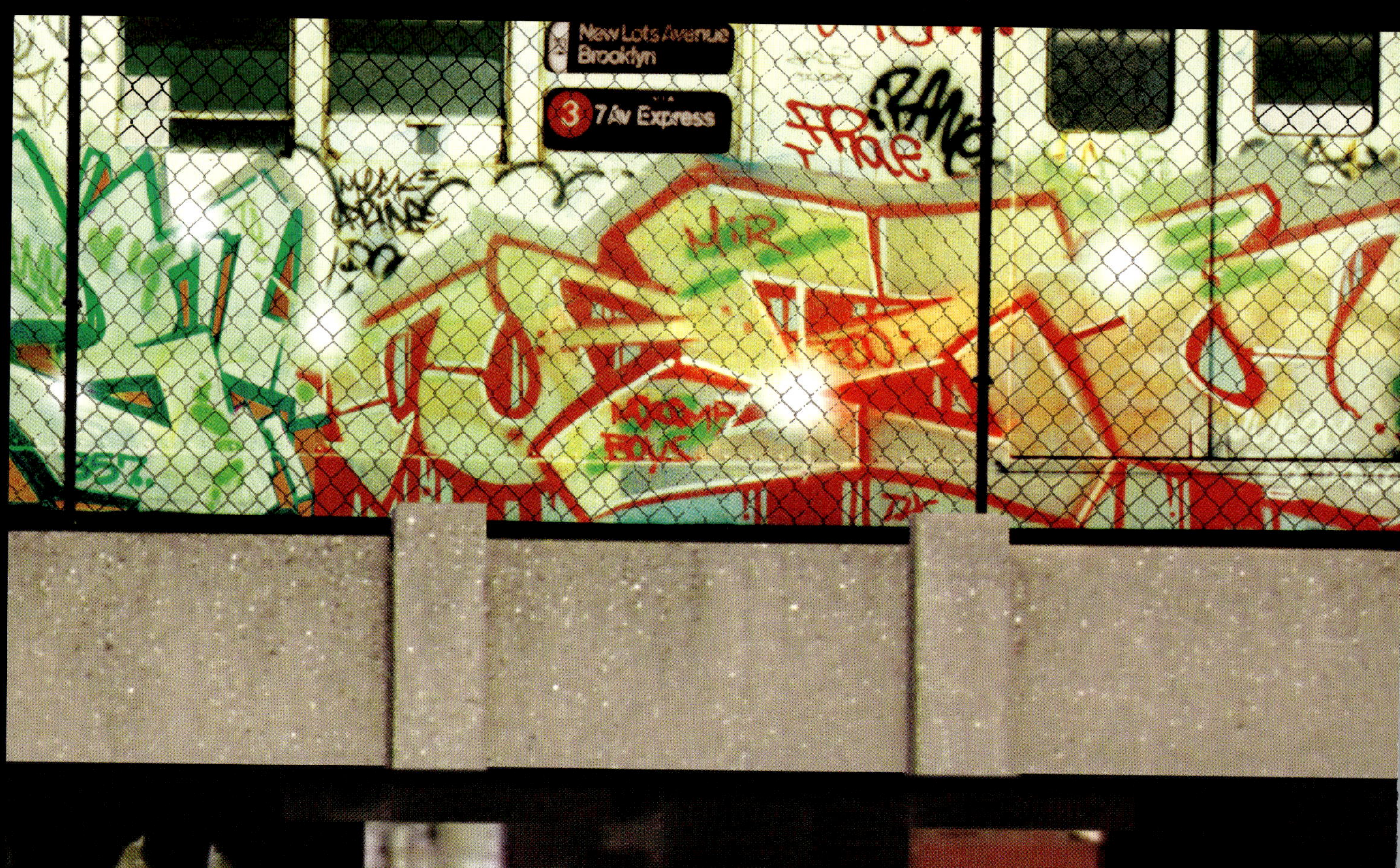

We also hit the 3s parked in tunnels off of 110th St. between 116th St. We only saw them here once.

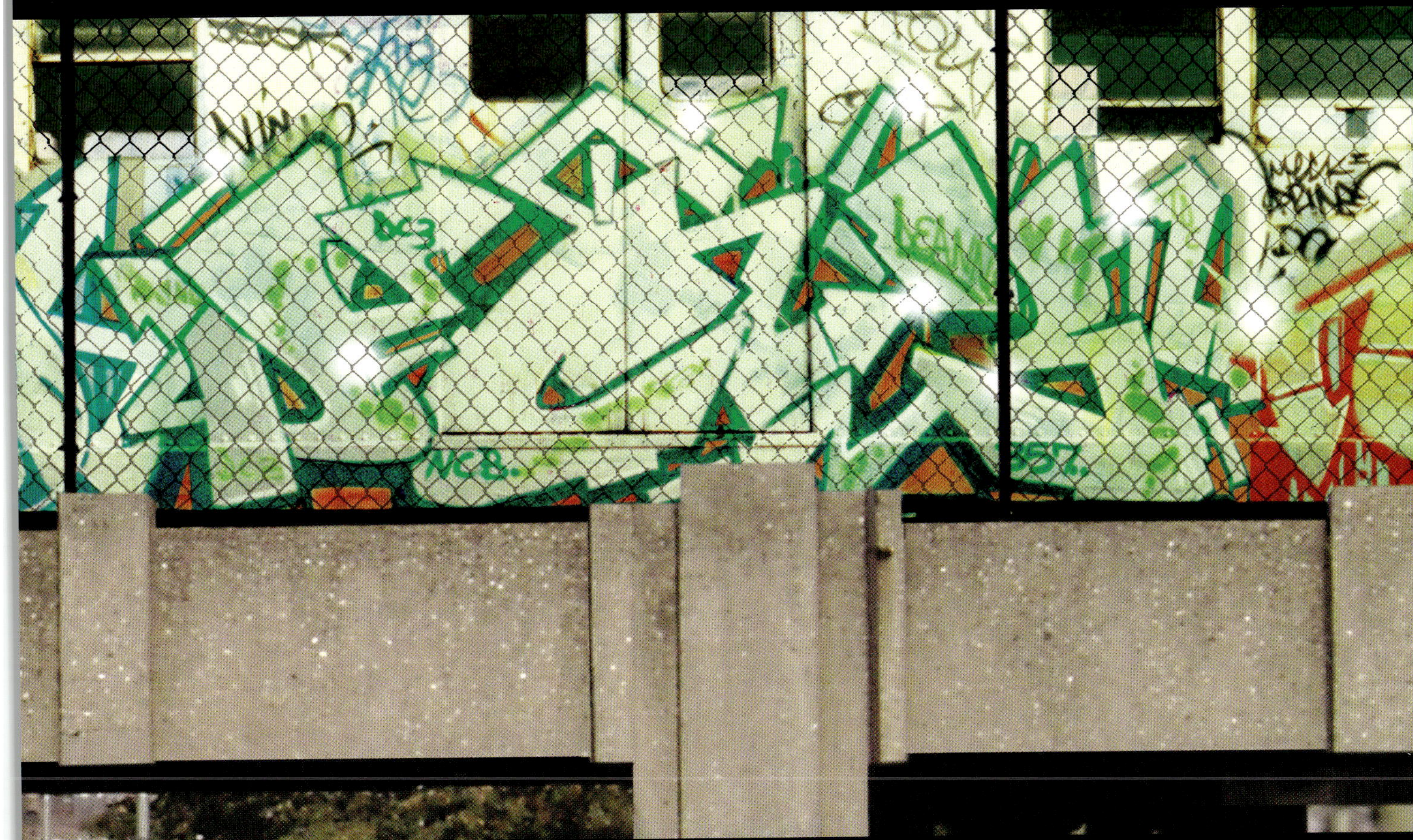

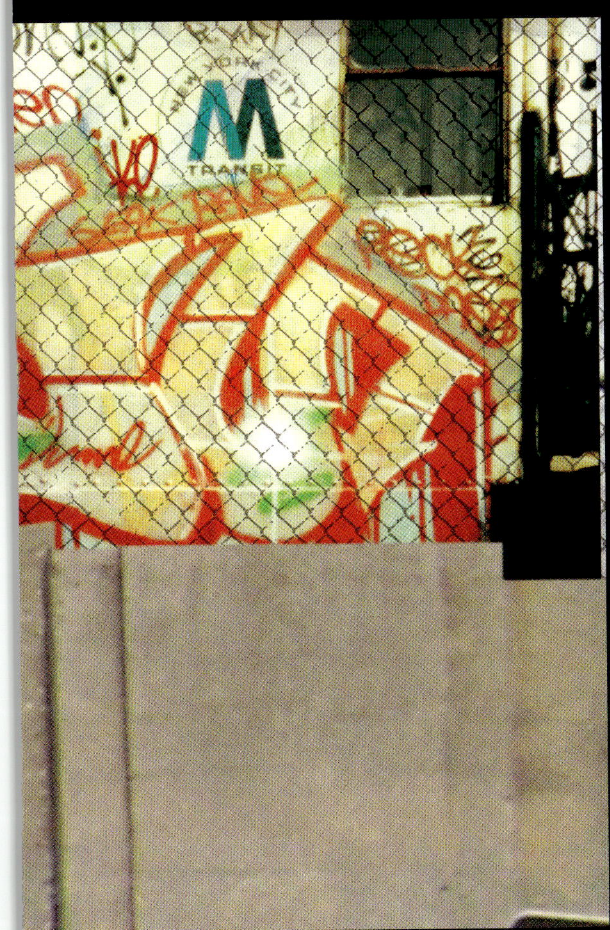

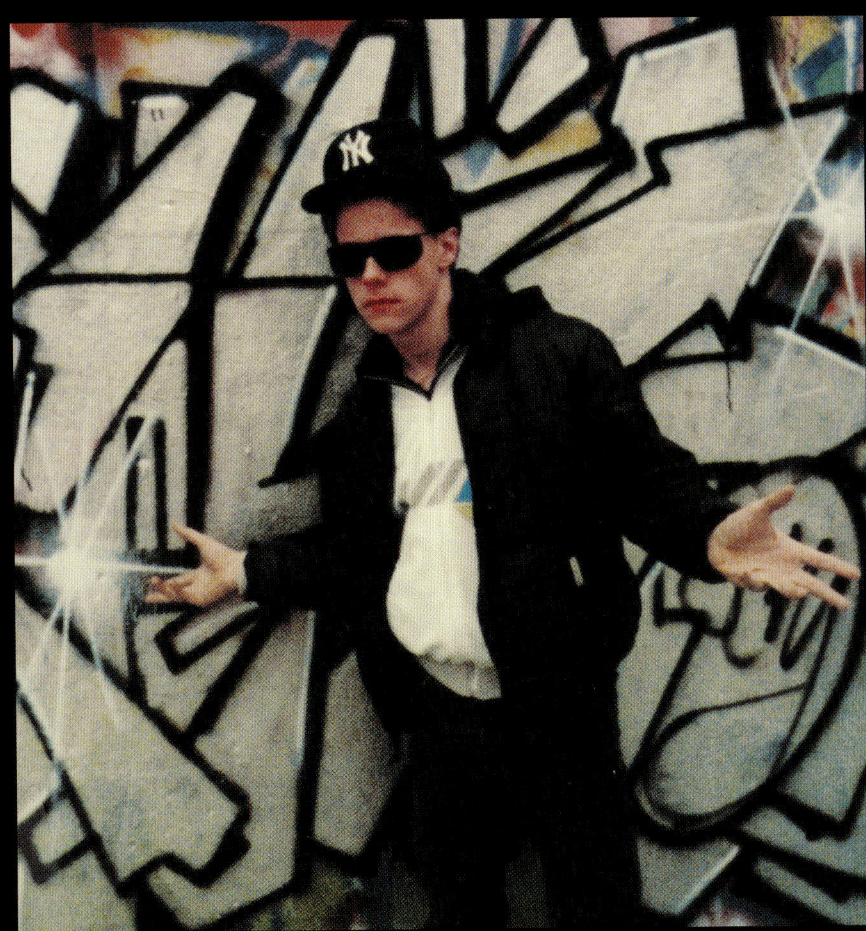

Early DC3 handball court, Mar. 1985.

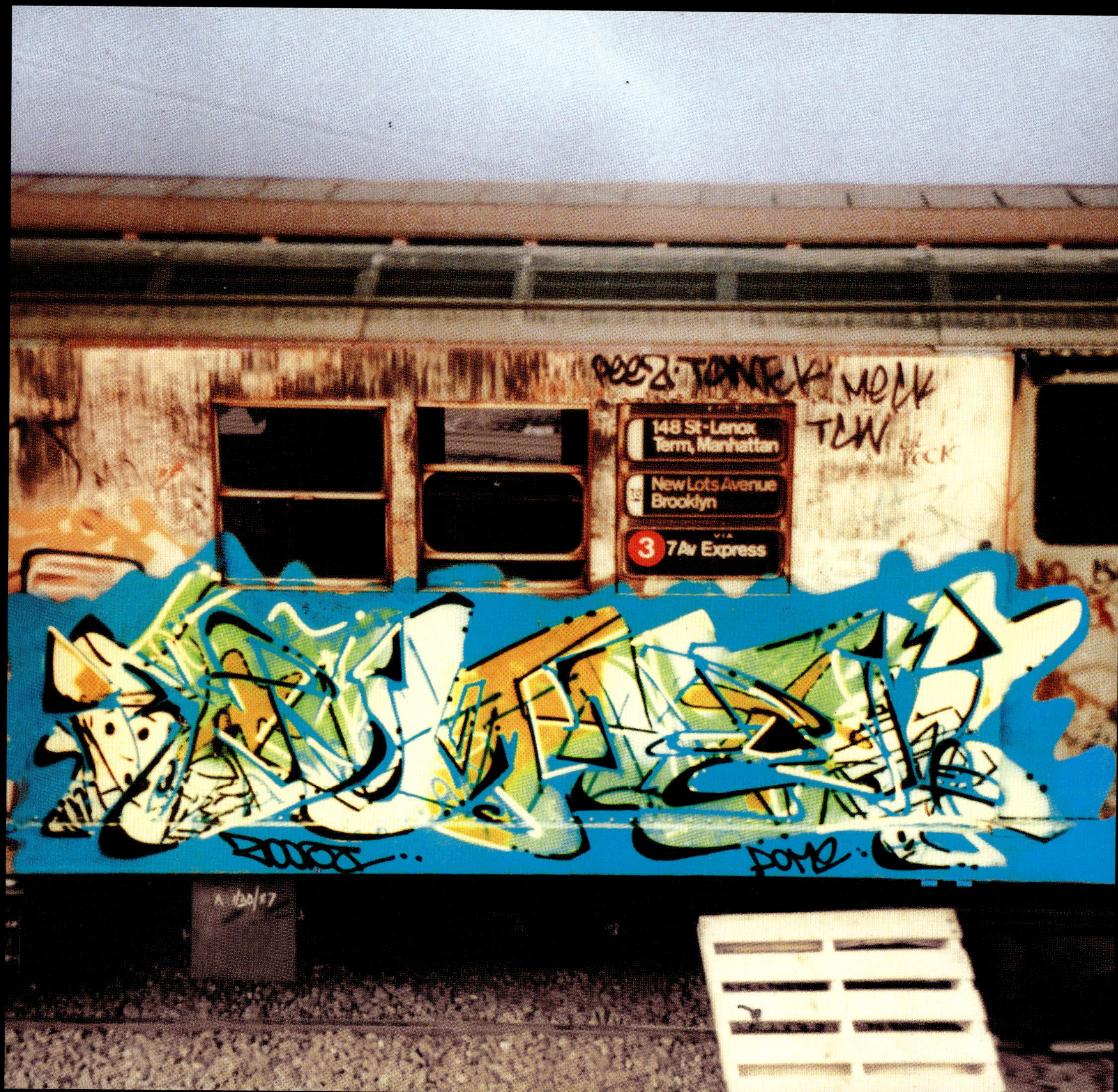

Dome, aka ZOOROC, 3 Train, Jul. 1988. Always trying out new styles.

Zoo, more so than DC3, and I was feeling Brooklyn. Zoo was originally from East New York and I worked at Funsa Tire and Custom Rim Shop on Atlantic and Pennsylvania Avenue. We was always scoping out New Lots yard on Elton street off of Linden Boulevard. We hit the yard a couple of times but mostly bombed it as there wasn't a lot of ways in or out, but depending on when you hit it once you were in, especially in the back, you had plenty of time usually. We got in by the command center over Linwood Park by climbing up 20 foot high fences onto the elevated tracks, but that was risky and you could get spotted. The best way into the Livonia Yard, believe it or not, was to get lucky or know the work bum's schedule and when the yard gate was up just walk the fuck in like you worked there. Funny shit!!!!!

New Lots after most of the bombed trains were out of service.

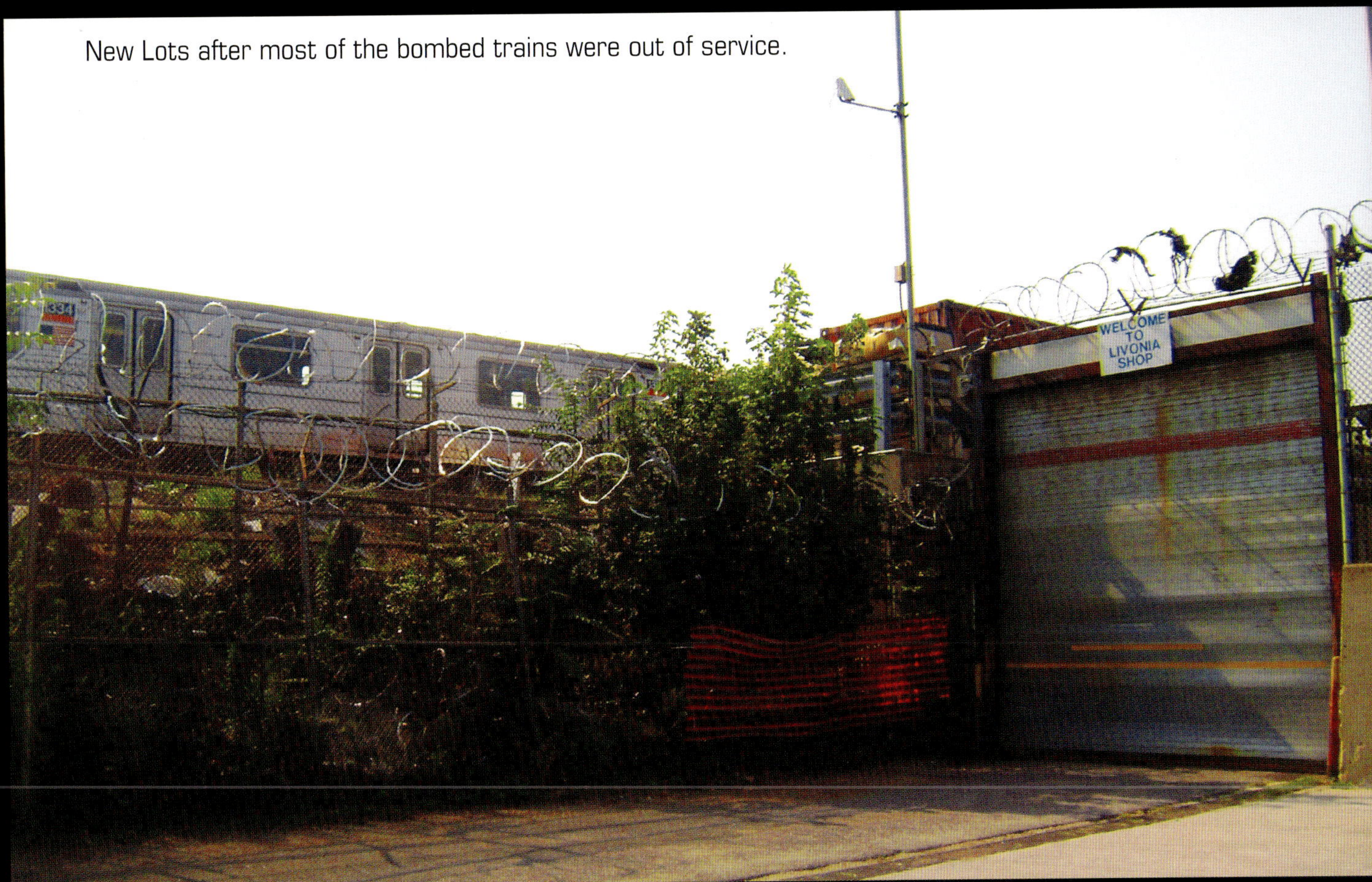

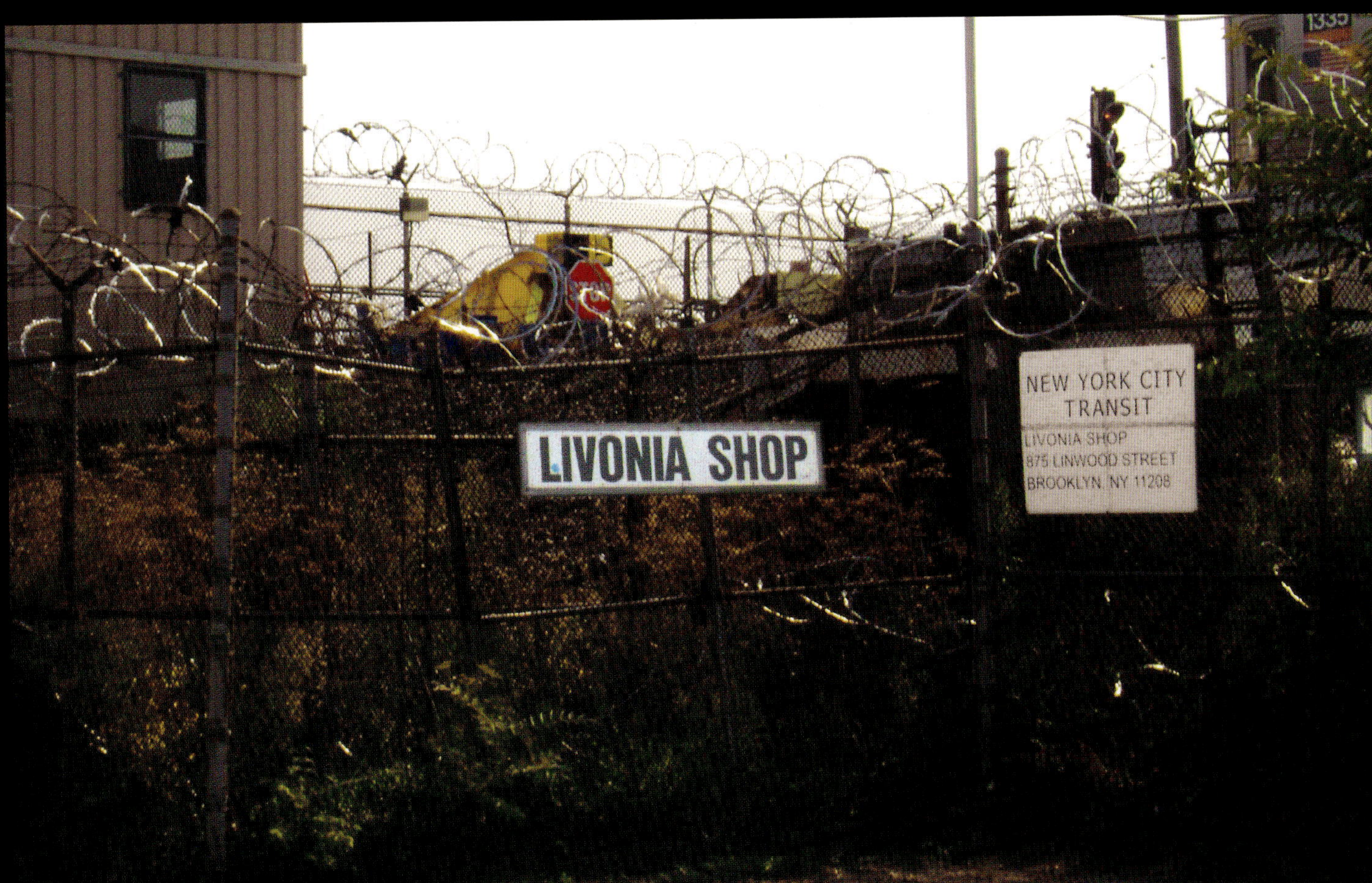

You wasn't getting in this way...

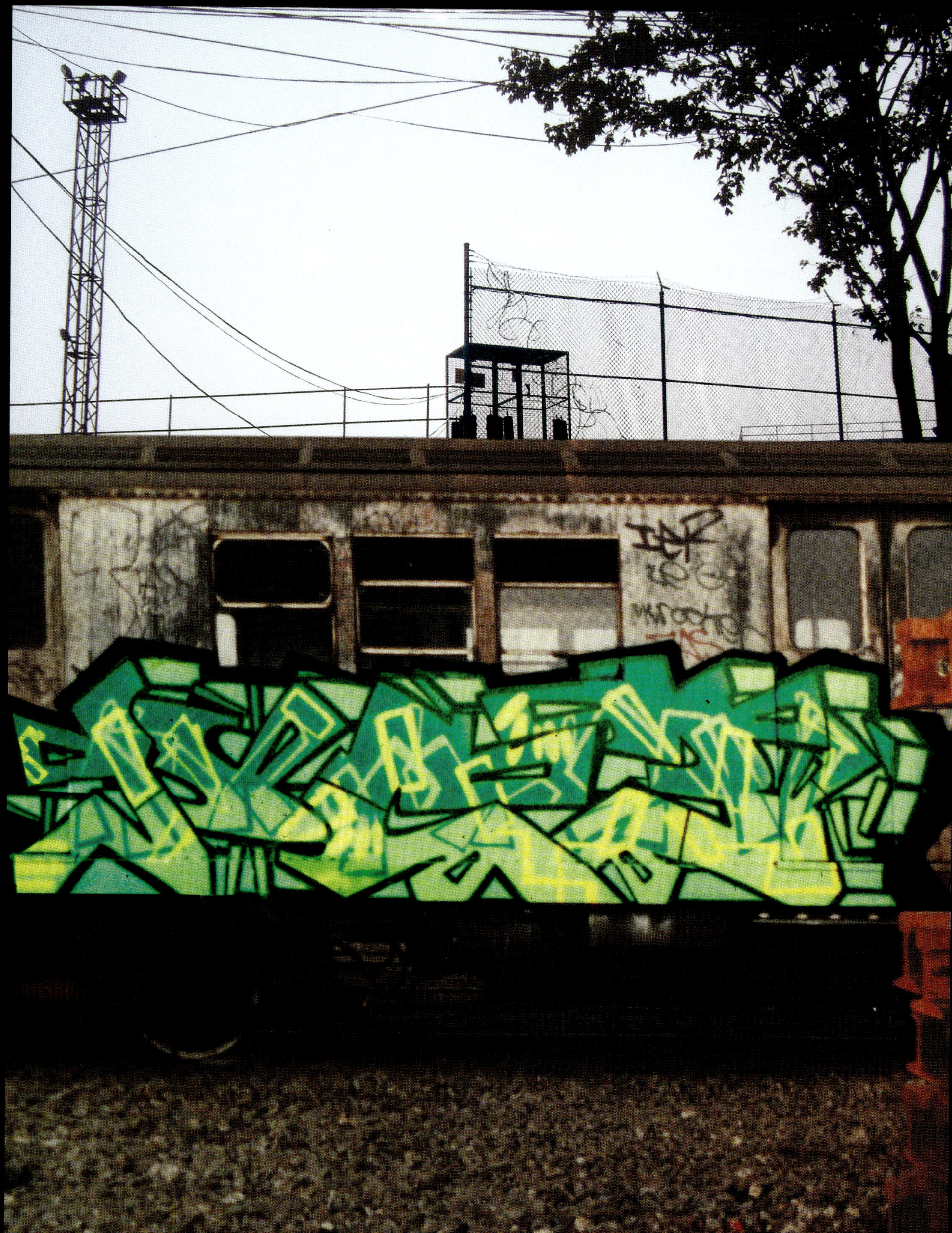

DC3 window-down 3 Train photographed in New Lots Yard, May 1988.

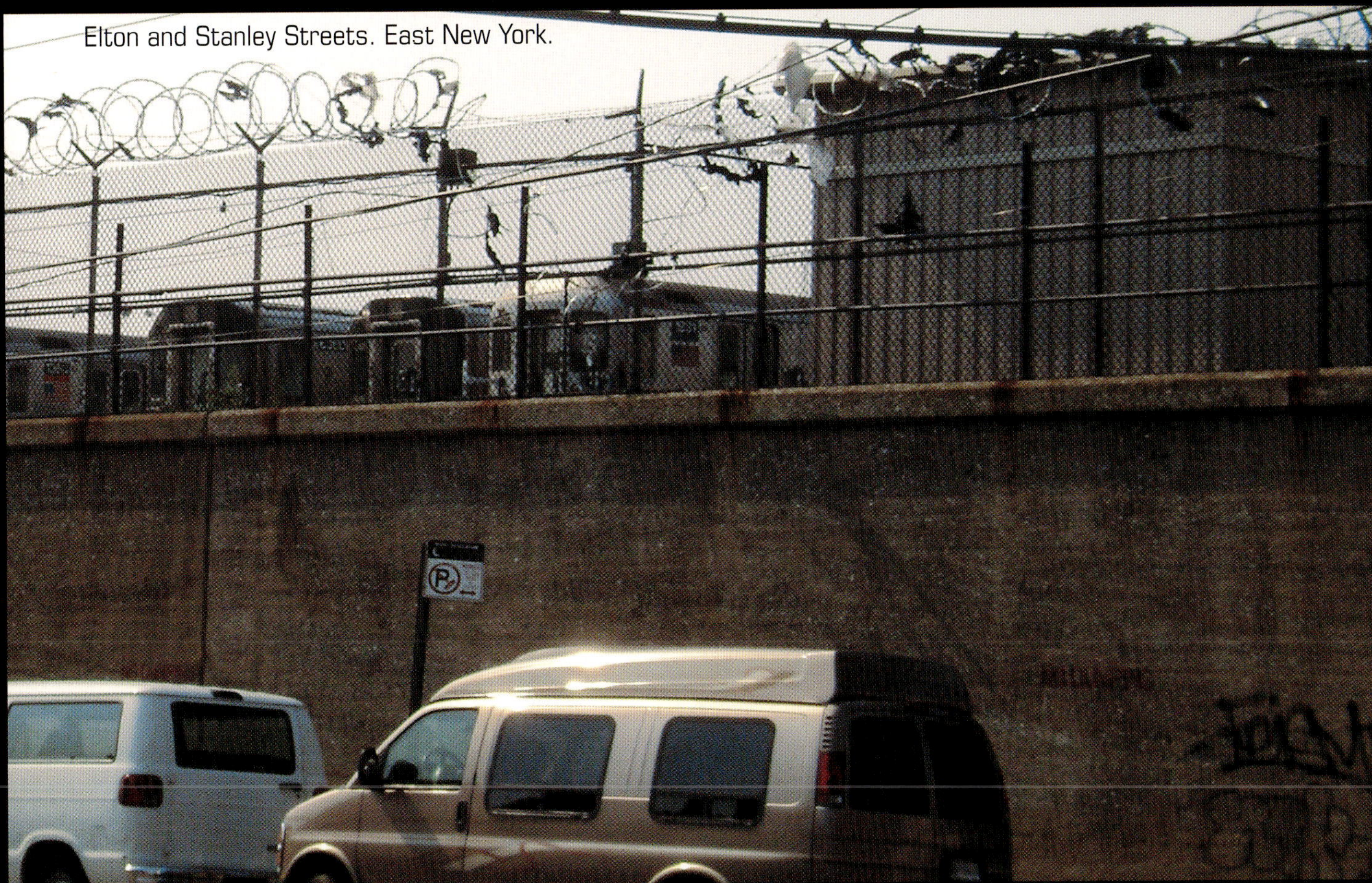
Elton and Stanley Streets. East New York.

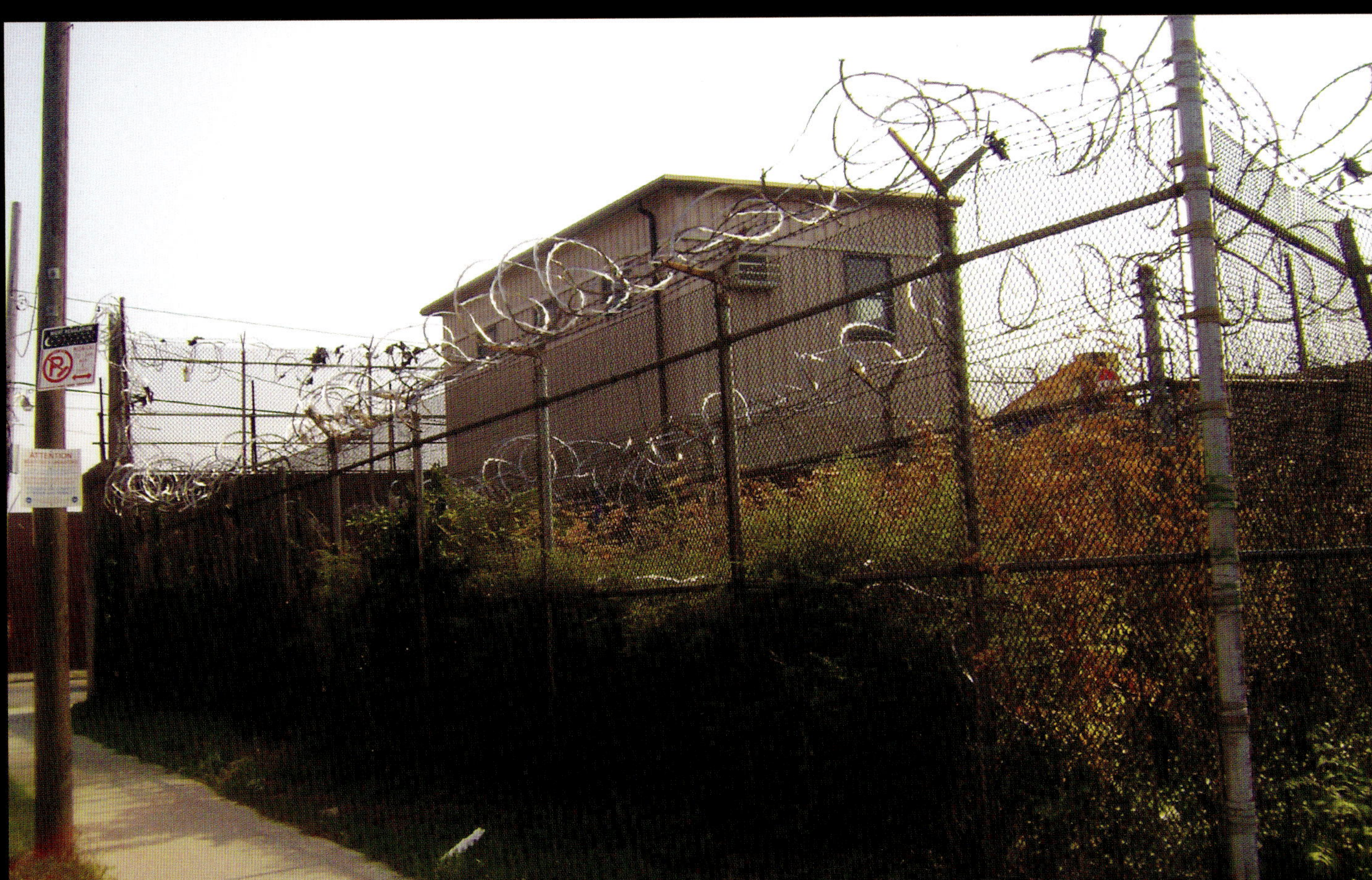

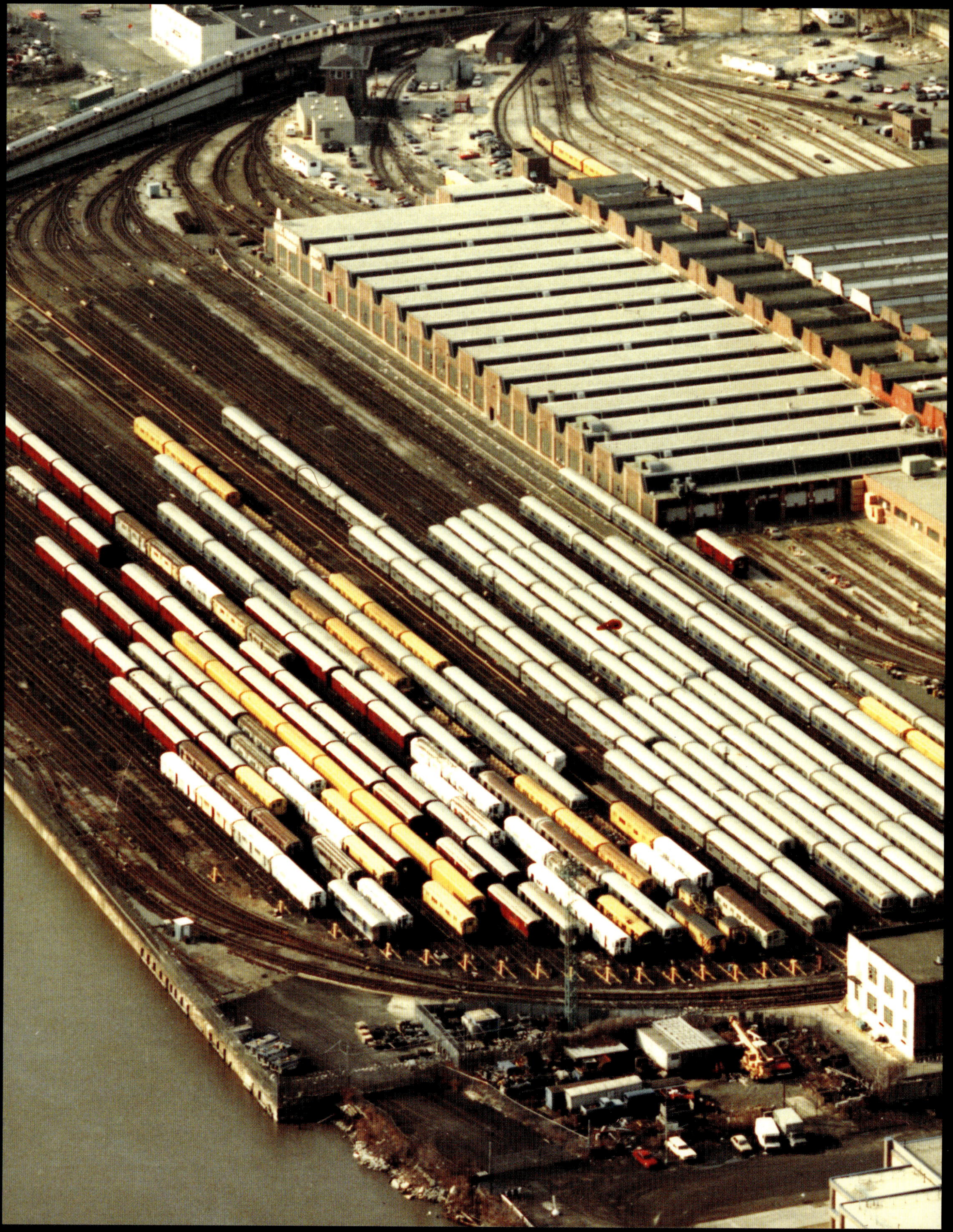

The Ghost Yard, MTA aerial view, 1990.

ROZ One, Fun Club Prez. Hells Kitchen

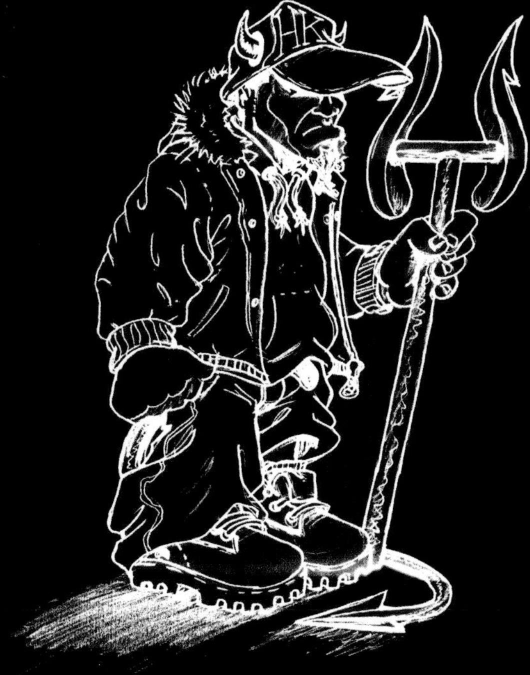

I started writing graffiti in 1975. I was a product of my environment, Hells Kitchen. If you met me you could describe me as a lil thug dirty kid. At the time I considered myself the only true writer from this Hells Kitchen, Midtown hood. My original first tag was Kool Cat for all of you that know me it still is what I also tag up. At the time I always loved tagging on walls, trucks, garbage trucks, mailboxes, park handball courts, and the hallways in high school. As I went to Wagner Jr. High School I met this kid who wrote (Surbo) and I would chill with him in class. He had real nice hand style when bombing with fat markers. In like 1978-1979 I saw a name (ROZ) in a school reading book and I liked the letters and I mastered them in tagging and piecing. So from there on people would call me ROZ, aka Kool Kat, because they seen I started getting up everywhere. I liked bombing Kool Kat but it was too long and ROZ was crazy easy to tag up being that it was only three letters.

Hells Kitchen was real wild back in the days and the 1 Train was right there for me to check out who was getting up on them, at 42nd Street and 50th Street. The first burner I had seen was by Revolt on the 1 line. This kid Rap2 would take me to the train station at 50th Street and Broadway to bench trains. For any writer with ambition, to see trains bombed and with pieces on them was a dream come thru and was a big influence. At the time I started checking out the R and N letter lines because they was right there in midtown also, they had mostly tags on them. After school I would go across town and check out the 4, 5, and 6 IND lines, they had a lot of burners on them and were getting bombed. 1979 was the year I started writing on trains myself. At the time it was the thing everyone was doing or wishing they could get down with. My original mentor was Mr. Mace. I worked hard to create my own style and have to this day kept it close to the original concepts. I also used to write, besides Kool Kat, a couple of other aliases. I wrote Hear, Kidnap 134, and Sizzle 144. The main lines that I hit was the 1s. Stan had put me down with the Spanish Five and that's when I did most of my damage insides. Then came the As, the Bs, the CCs, the Ds and mostly the 2s and 5s on the west side (All City). While I was in the 1 Tunnel I had seen Stan and Son 1 do the Donkey Kong train and had seen Tack FBA do the Shark TC5 train. My first partner was JAE. I wrote with everyone not just one dedicated partner because I always was hanging out at the Roxy meeting mad writers and knew crazy people just in general. I wrote with Jon One, Poke IBM, Woody, Juice TC5, and that was mostly it. As far as the crews that I pushed up, I repped NTA, TVS The Vamp Squad crew, TC5 The Cool 5, IBM Idolized by Millions, TP The Partners, TD The Destroyers, TC, CAC Cool Ass Criminals and the World Famous Fun Club. For all of you that don't know it stood for, "Fucking Up Niggas!!!!"

It was around 1980 and I was attending Printing High School on 49th Street and 10th Avenue. Fatback and Crook from The TMT crew took me to the 3 Yard uptown at 148th street and Lenox Terminal. That neighborhood was real ill and the yard is right next to the projects and you couldn't just be up there unless you was familiar. But they knew I was this crazy white boy and they asked me if I was down and I said hell's yeah. I bombed ROZ One that night doing crazy inside mop tags. Insides was what I was mostly know for on all of the lines I repped on and would catch all the "Headliners." Those were the flat long pieces over the windows which were perfect for tags. The headliners in the 1 Trains and insides in general at this point were destroyed so I would paint over them shits with a silver fat cap entirely throughout several cars and by the time I came back thru the paint would be dry. So now I could bomb them with tags with black mop ink like it was a clean canvas. Hey you did what you had to do to get noticed amongst stupid other writers. JAE was the one who first took me to the 1 Tunnel at 145th Street and Broadway. I was hitting that underground yard way before First Class crew and many others. Fun Club was the original FC and we had many affiliated members. Most were down with Fun Club before switching over to First Class, when I had slowed down painting in 1984 on the trains. I met many writers in the 1 Tunnel early on like Stan TSF, Son One, Swan3, Jon1, and Sep.

Mostly I bombed insides but did many burners on the outsides with writers like Sharp, Poke IBM. That shit was the life, we would come right from the Roxy or where ever we was at and be in there painting till the morning. Back then we was wilding, drinking and smoking dust, just not giving a fuck having a good time. There was crazy times we got raided out of there by uniformed police and always escaped whether up on the platform either side or directly up to the street via several escape hatches. The best raid story was when I was up in Gun Hill road in the Bronx on the 2s and 5s painting the white elephants. So a light was shined right in my face as I notice it was a work bum, I yelled out raid and starts to jet, meanwhile TC5 was there close to the platform painting and not to mention no names, but people were pushing each other and some people almost fell off the upper level to the platform below. The best writers of my time that I give props to is Mr Mace, Doze, Revolt, and Zephyr just to name a few. Respect to all those who came before me cause I was part of the new generation.

I stopped writing on trains in 1985-1986. I'm still active in art. I have my own clothing line called HELLS KITCHEN INC. I work with SHO and we collaborate on the design work on the Mac Pro for the best possible results. I sell hats, T-shirts, sweatshirts, headgear, wife beaters, etc. My store is located here in midtown on 48th Street and 9th Avenue @ Video Cafe come check us we got all sizes and the selection is crazy. I would like to give special thanks to SHO and everybody who was there with me then and now as we experienced the often illegal world of graffiti art together. Also, to those who I might have forgotten you're always in my heart & mind. Much respect to all those past and present...One love. I would like to say if it wasn't for this graff thing I wouldn't have the skills & talent to have created my own clothing line. Much love to all my Hells Kitchen people. Keep banging!!!!! The Freeze Rozzy train was done in the Ghost Yard after having been up two days in a row. Yeah that day was crazy!!!!!!!! On that night I bumped heads with Swan3 and Freeze at the 18th street subway station. They had come from the Fun House. I had come from the ROXY...that was my house. So we jumped on the 1 Train, to go to Swan3's house uptown in Manhattan at 225th Street. They have twelve bags of dust and Frosty Freeze says put it in the freezer. So we started to work out with Swan and his brother, he wrote Lan2. We all was busting it out, until Frosty try to bench 100 lbs, niggas was laughing cause he was having problems with it. Anyway, after that we went to play ball in the back of the pj's, they really didn't know I can play b-ball. Aight niggas sleep on me, I was busting they ass on their court. I think I had like twenty points and won the game after that we go back to Swan3's house, to take the twelve bags out the freezer. Man we got dusted, then we went to somebody's house who I think was this dude named Toolee. I know one thing, he look like a fucking cop...Ha Ha...Oh well. I would just say that was one funny looking white boy. He was chill and down with TAT cru. We was trying to get paint, so Swan3 says let's go to Cem TATs house. When we got there, the hallway was fucked up for real, about five steps was missing. Ha Ha. We was like hold up? Let's smoke some more dust. I think we smoked like two or four bags in the hallway. Now I'm really buggin out in this cat Cem's house, Freeze and I was like, is this dude Mexican or what? Then we went to the Ghost Yard. I said I'm doing a piece with Freeze and Swan3 did a piece with Cem. Cem hooked us up with paint and I did the Freeze Rozzy train from the dome with no outline. After we left later we copped some more dust and smoked a bag at 125th Street station and got stopped by a cop. We ran down stairs and the cop pulled out a gun as he pointed it at us and Cem started some Bruce Lee shit and said OHH AHHHHHH. Cem tried to kick the cop and the cop smacked him in the head and we broke out.

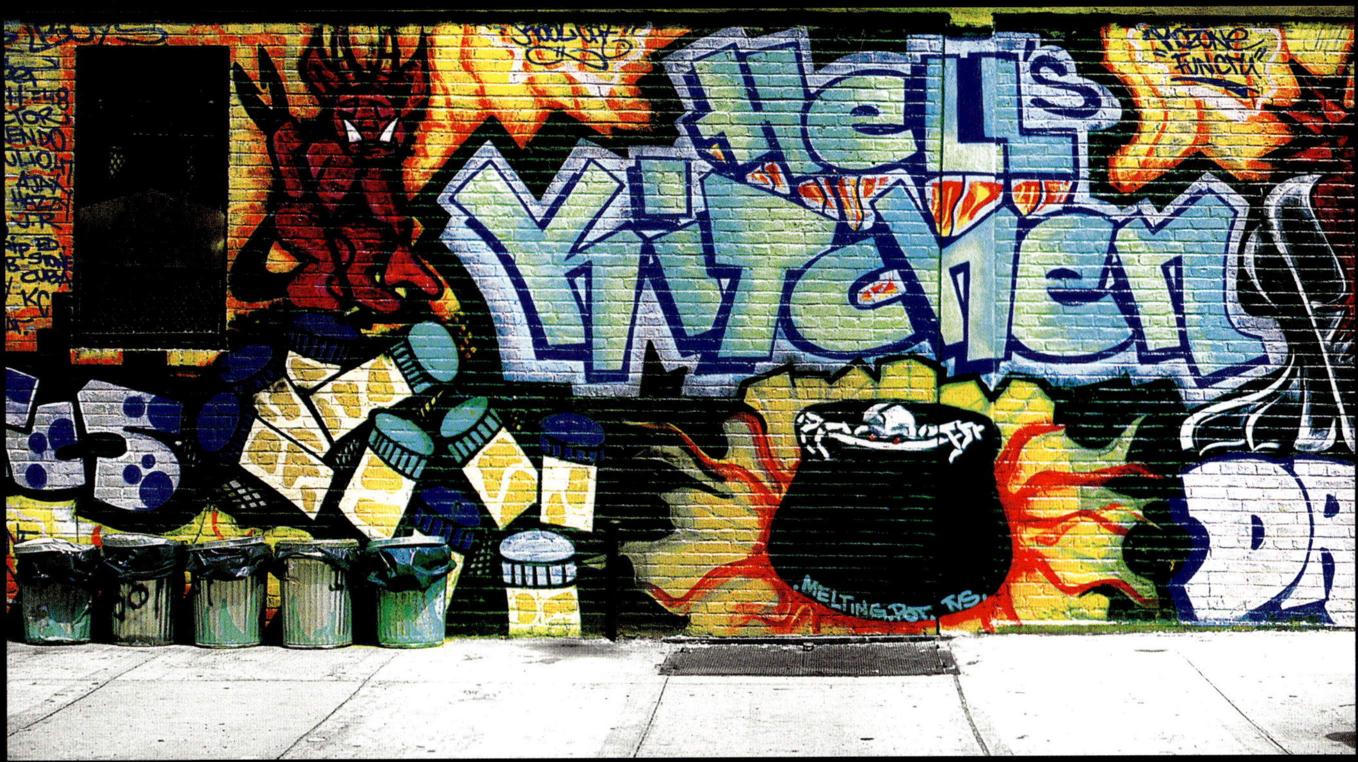

Hells Kitchen wall, "Melting Pot," by ROZ TC5 FUN CITY, 52nd and 10th Ave., Oct. 1984.

ROZ, KEV, and POKE IBM chilling at the ROXY Night Club after painting 1 Trains at 103rd Street, 1983.

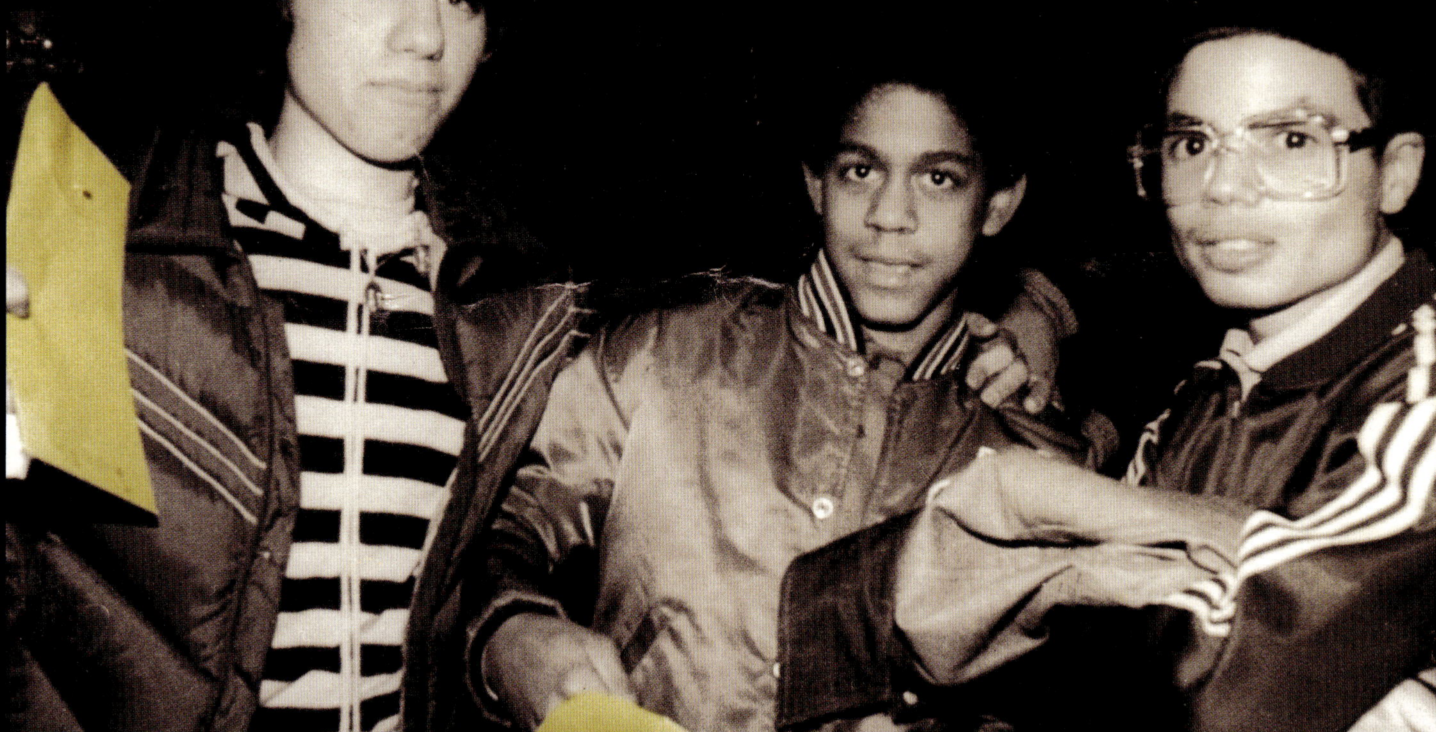

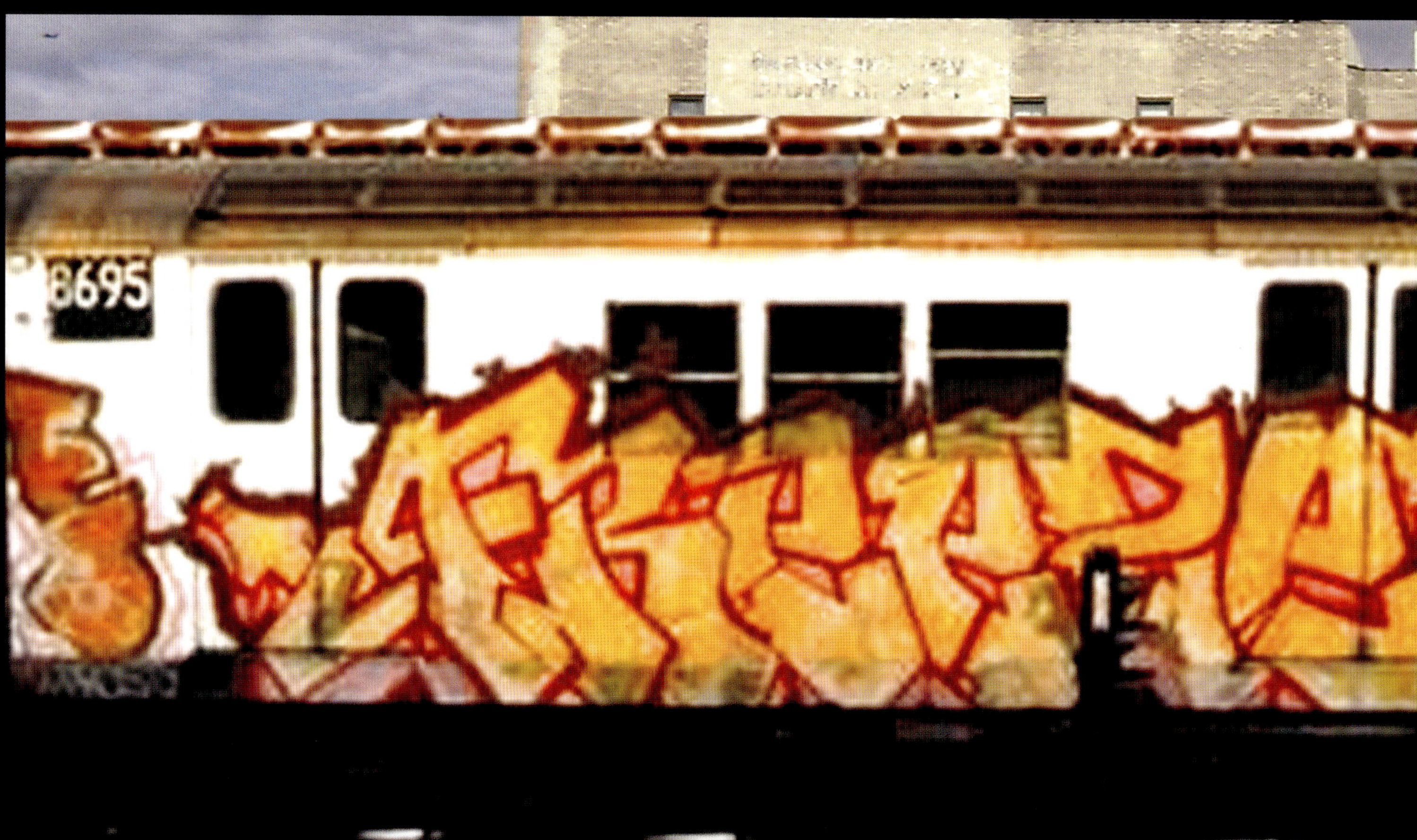

TC5 "FROSTY" FREEZE ROZZY, 2 Train rocked in the Ghost Yard, Jul. 1983.

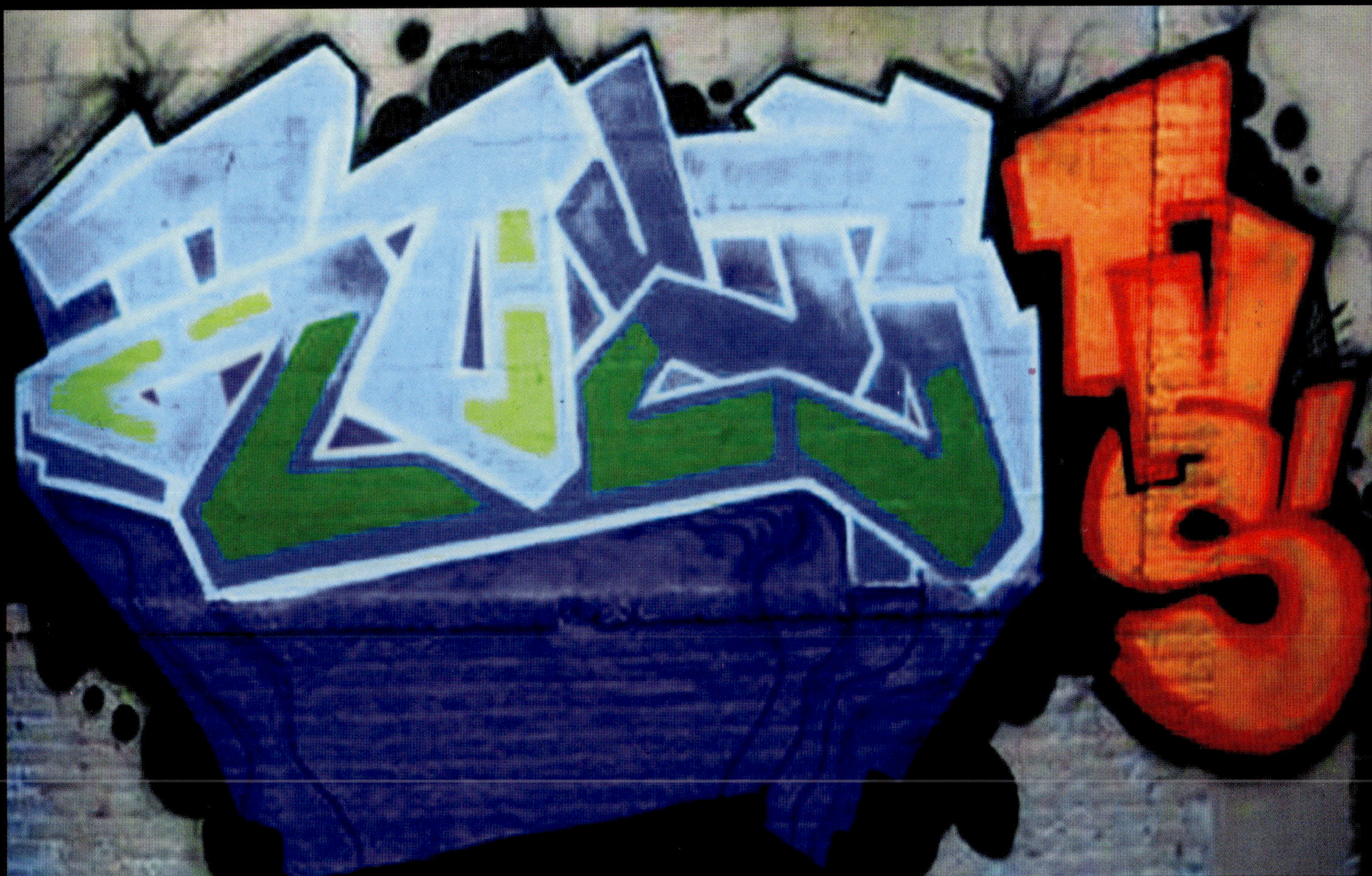

ROZ TVS "The Vamp Squad" In Jersey City with TATU X-Men.

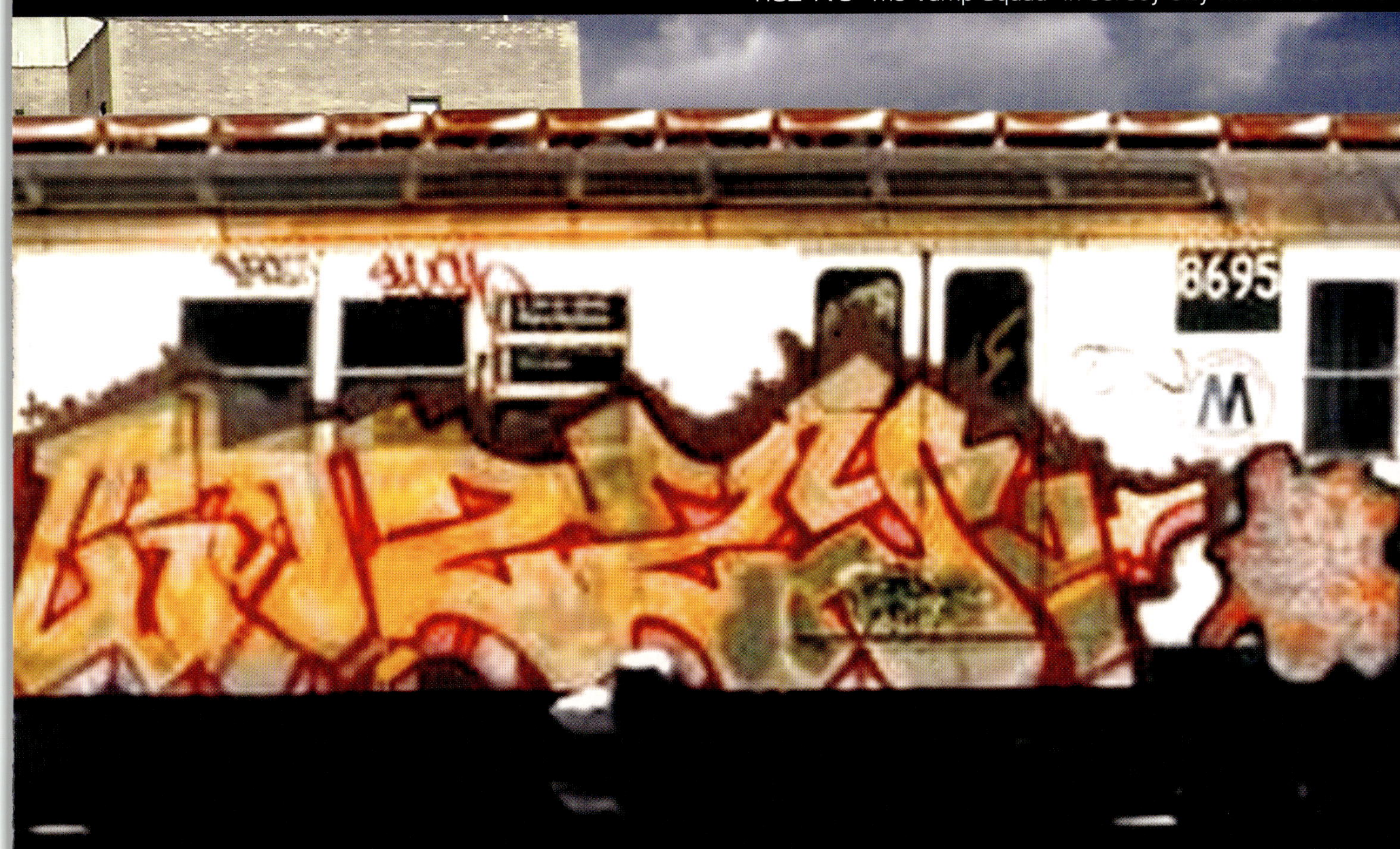

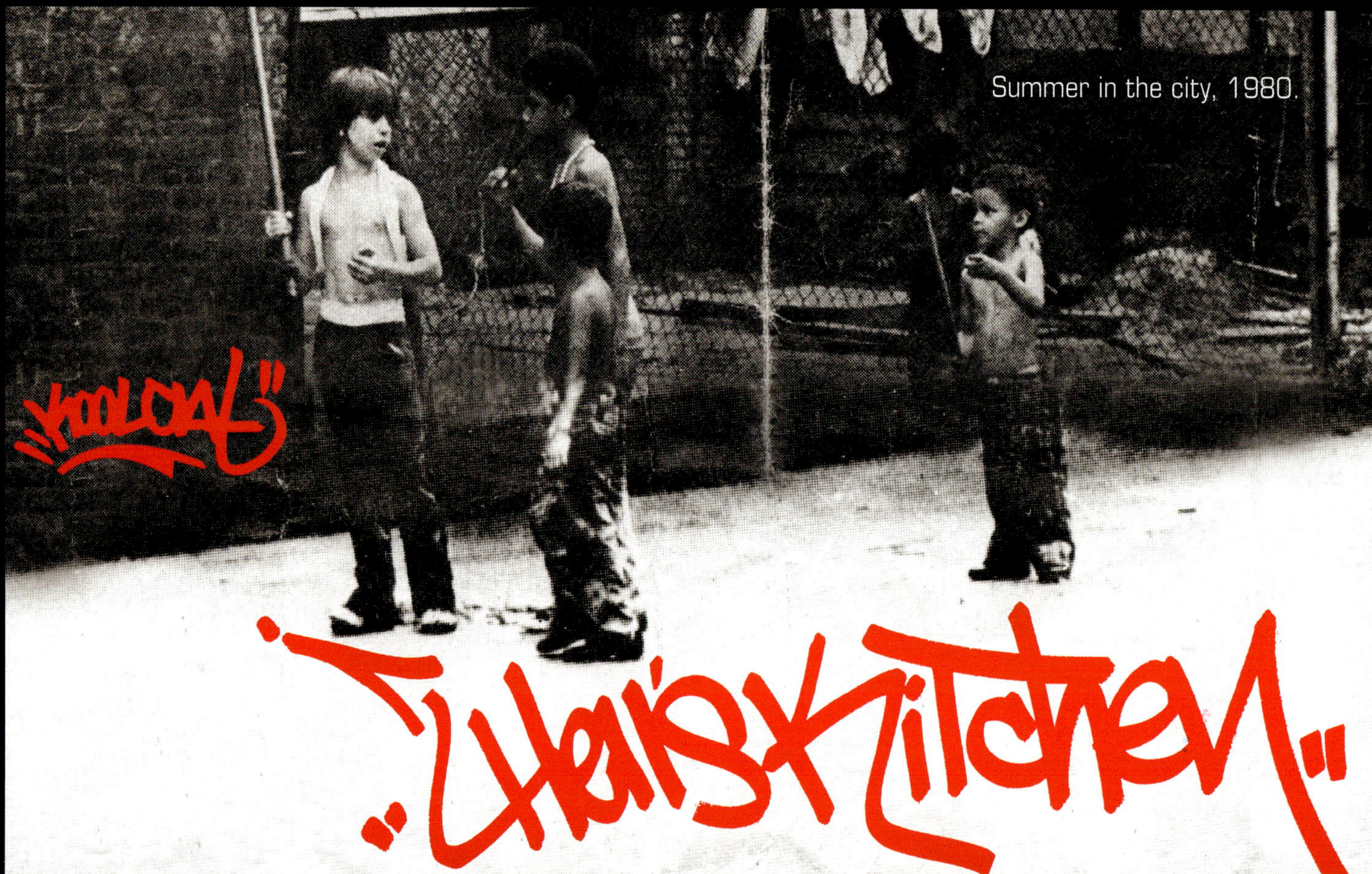

Summer in the city, 1980.

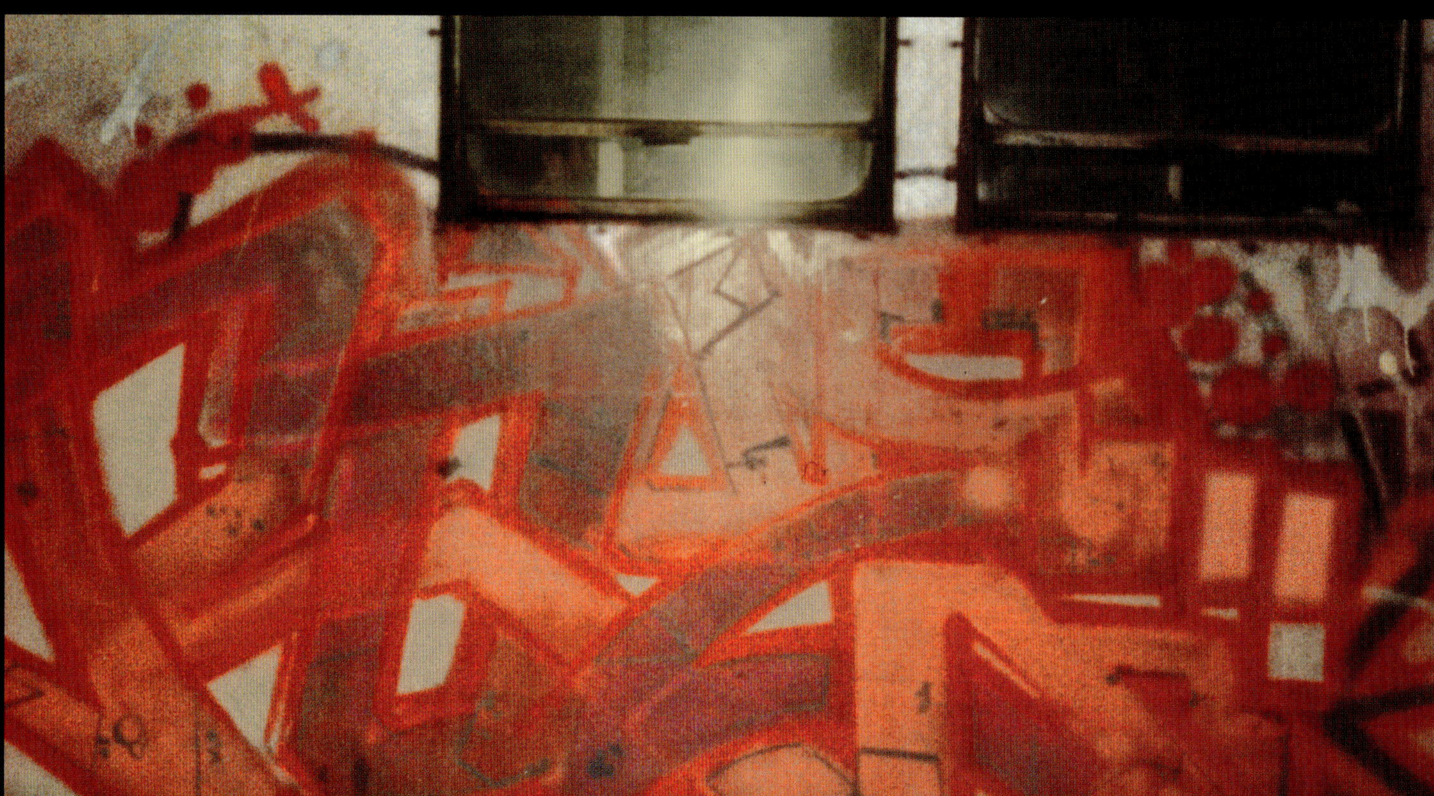

ROZ FUN CLUB, 1983.

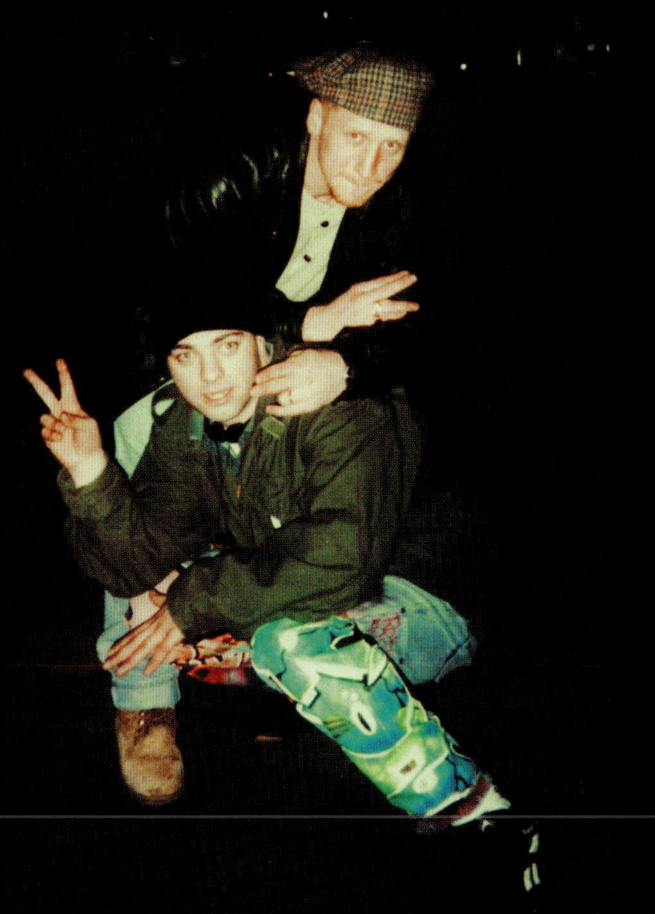

ROZ rocking graff pants with NEC One.

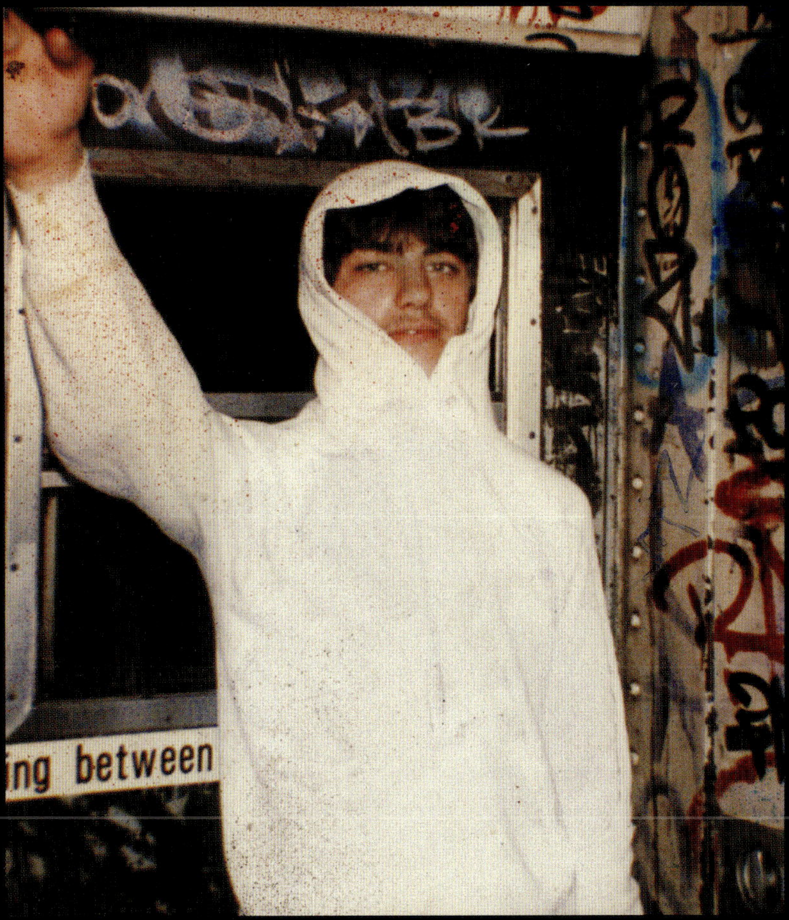

ROZ catching insides, 1 Train, Oct. 1984.

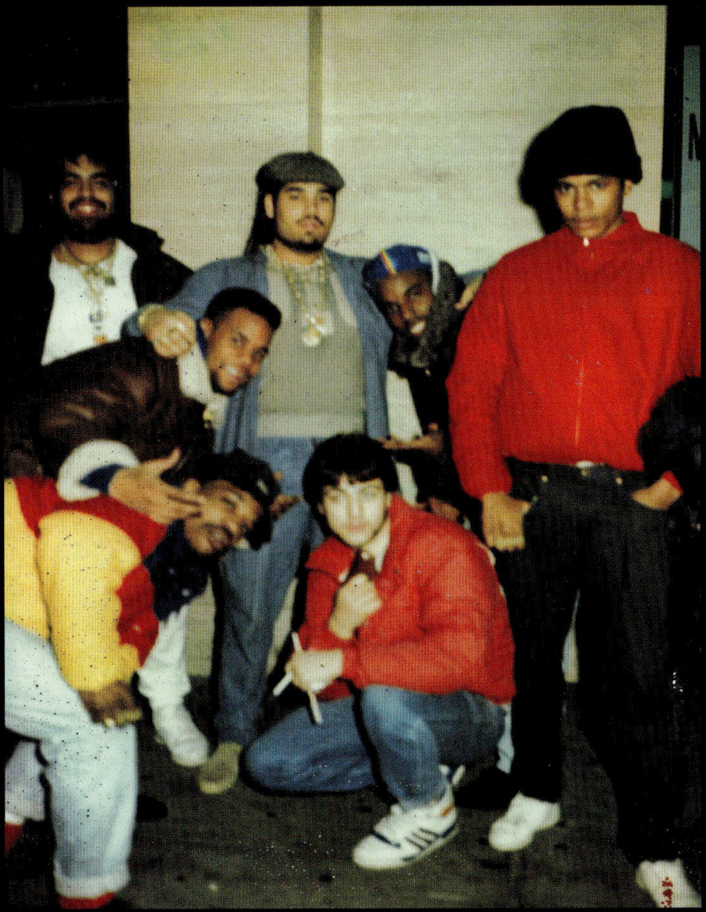

ROZ at Latin Quarters Night Club with fellow Hustlers.

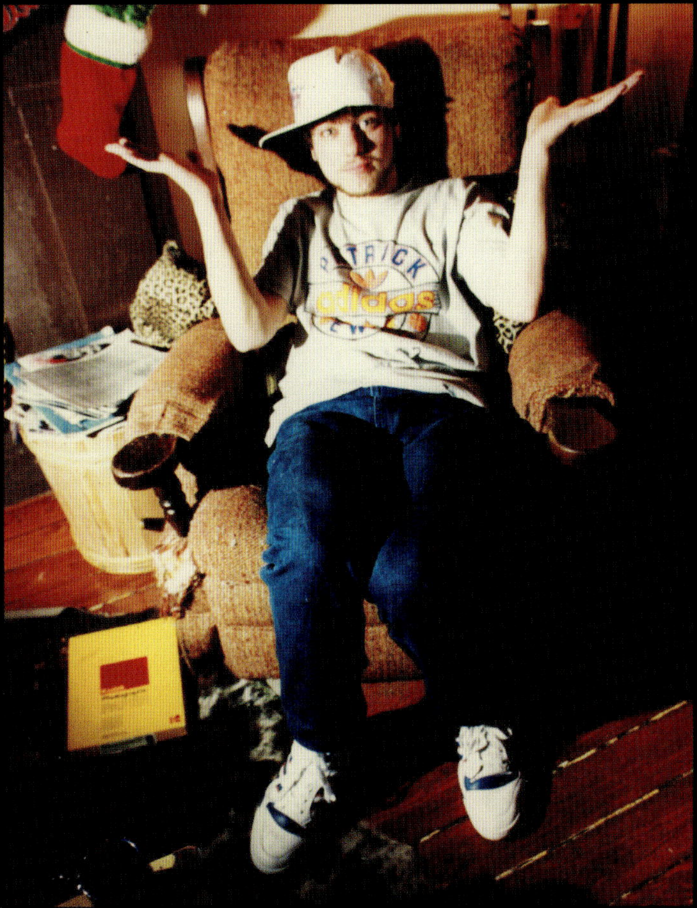

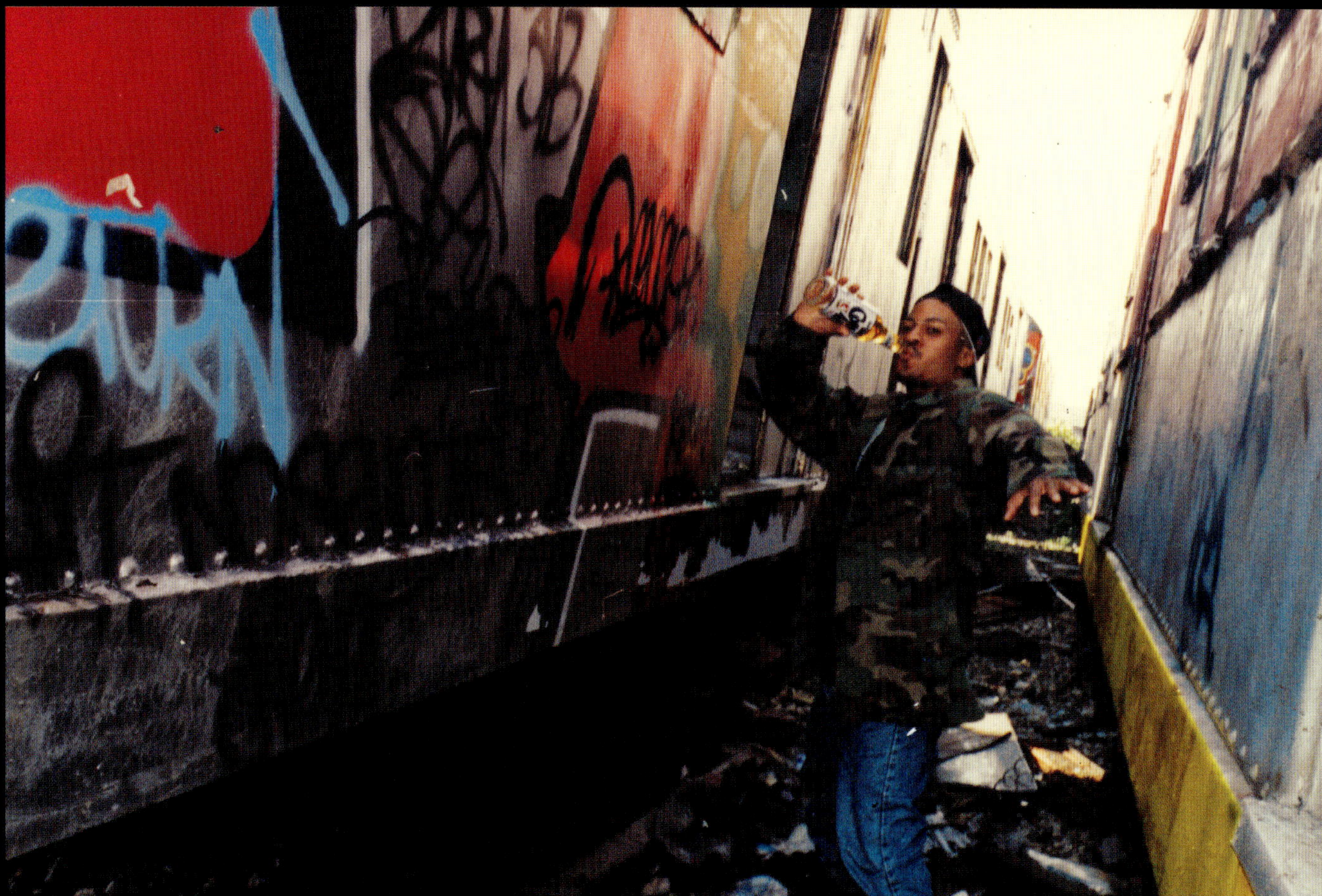

SHARE 37 drinking 40s in between lanes, Oct. 1995.

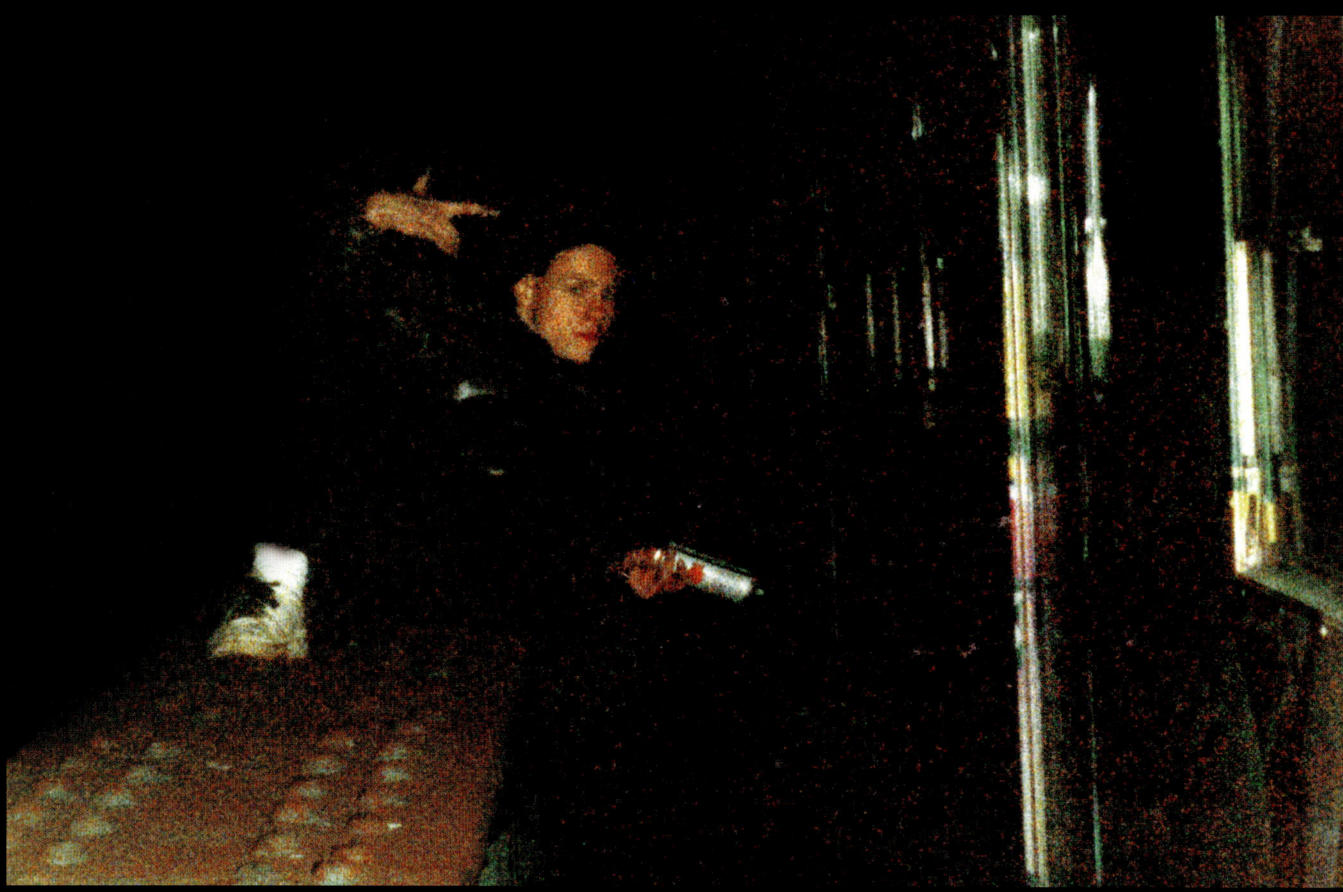

SHO next to ZOO, ONE2, and DC3 whole car, 1987.

ZOO and DC3 done in Kingston Ave., Brooklyn, Apr. 1988.

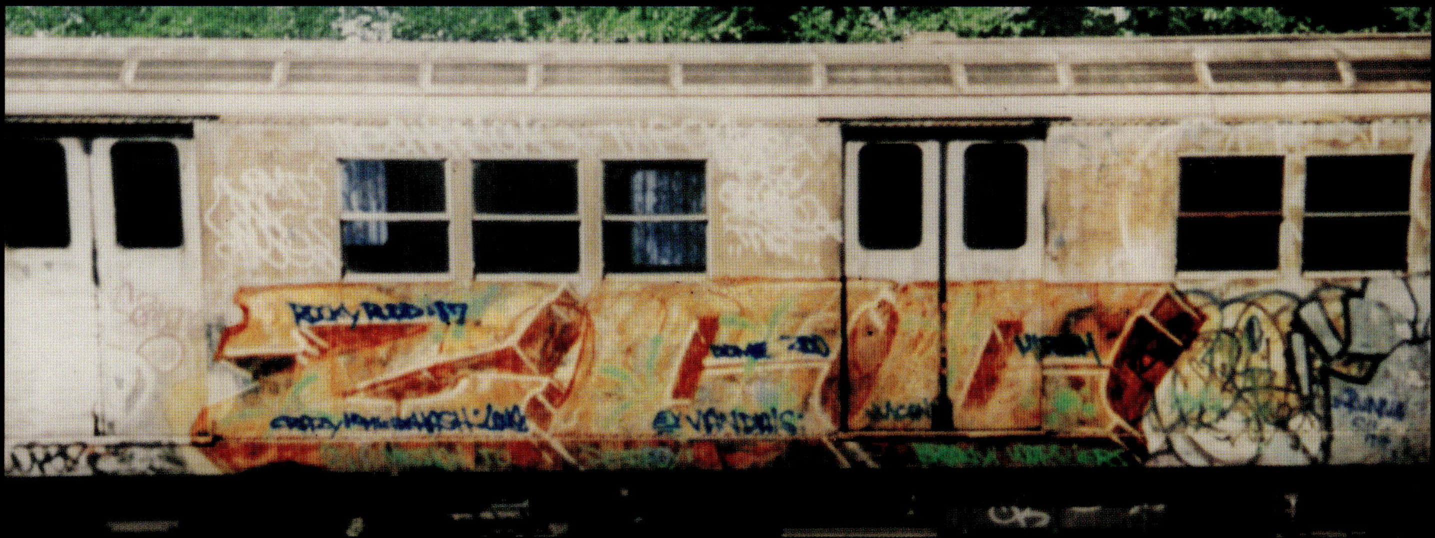

The MTA couldn't really buff the trains anymore, straight metal.

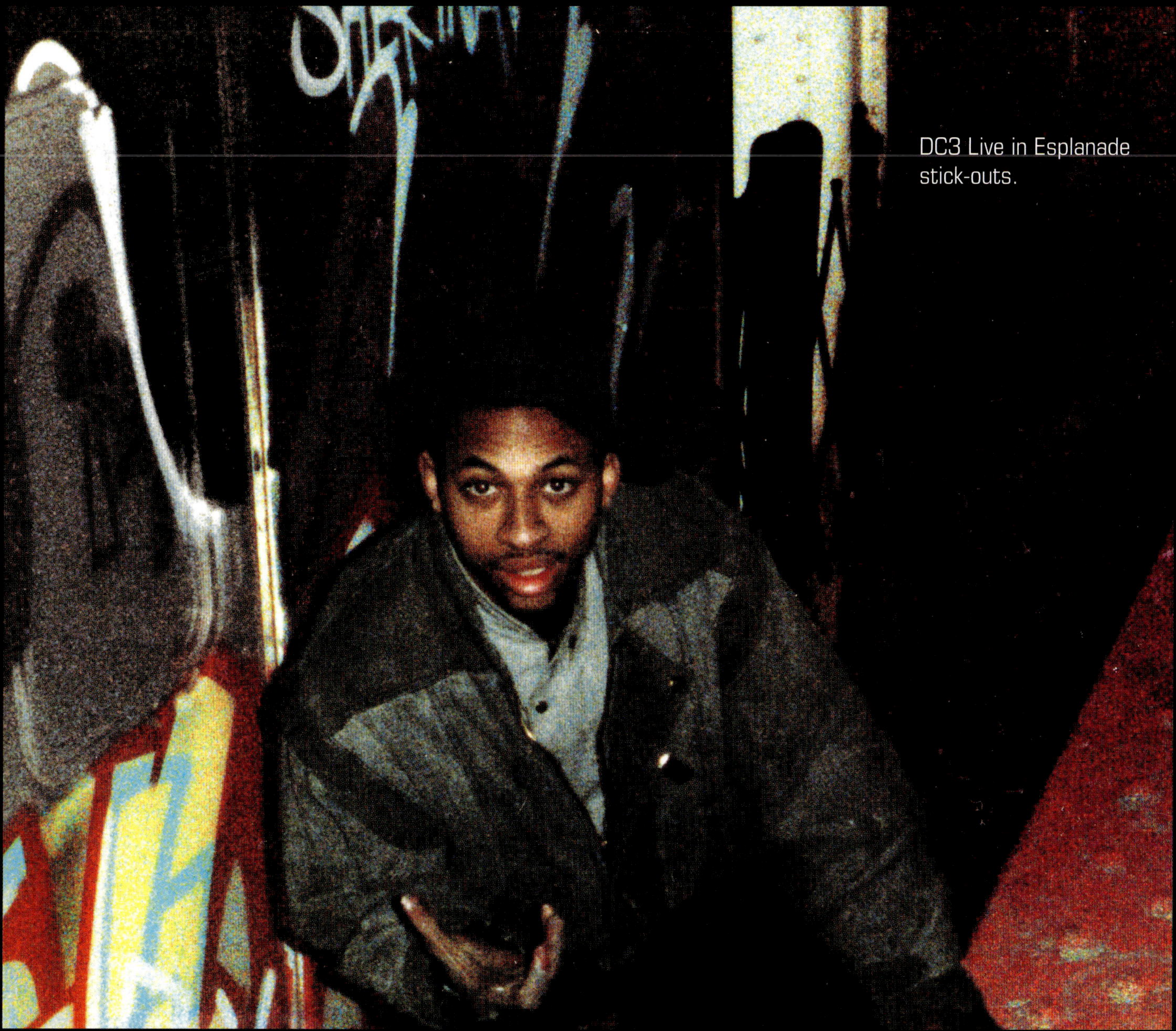

DC3 Live in Esplanade stick-outs.

Representing hard on his 20th birthday...

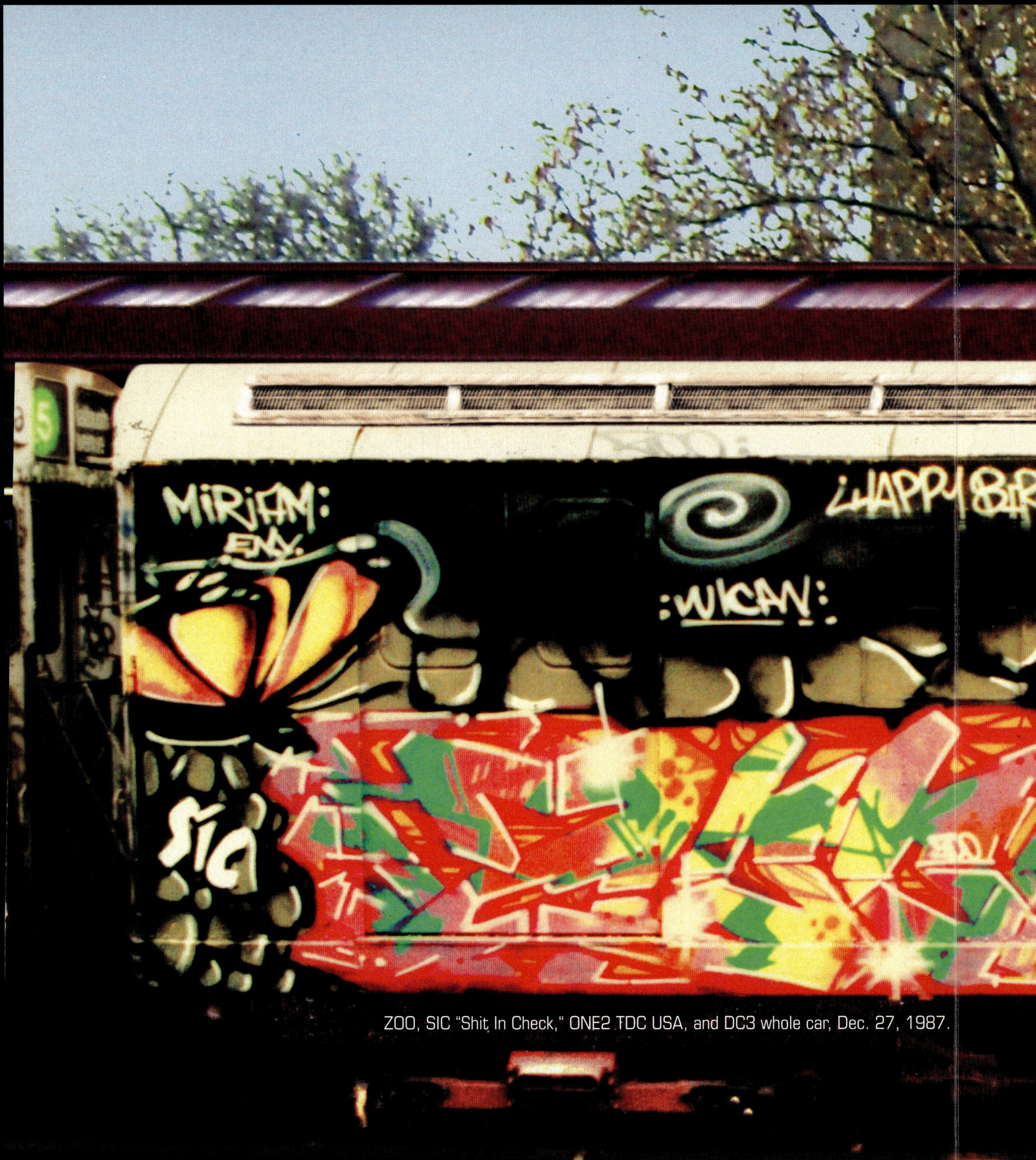

ZOO, SIC "Shit In Check," ONE2 TDC USA, and DC3 whole car, Dec. 27, 1987.

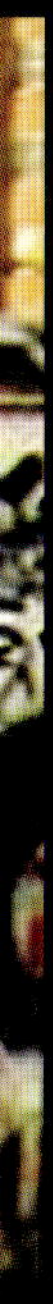

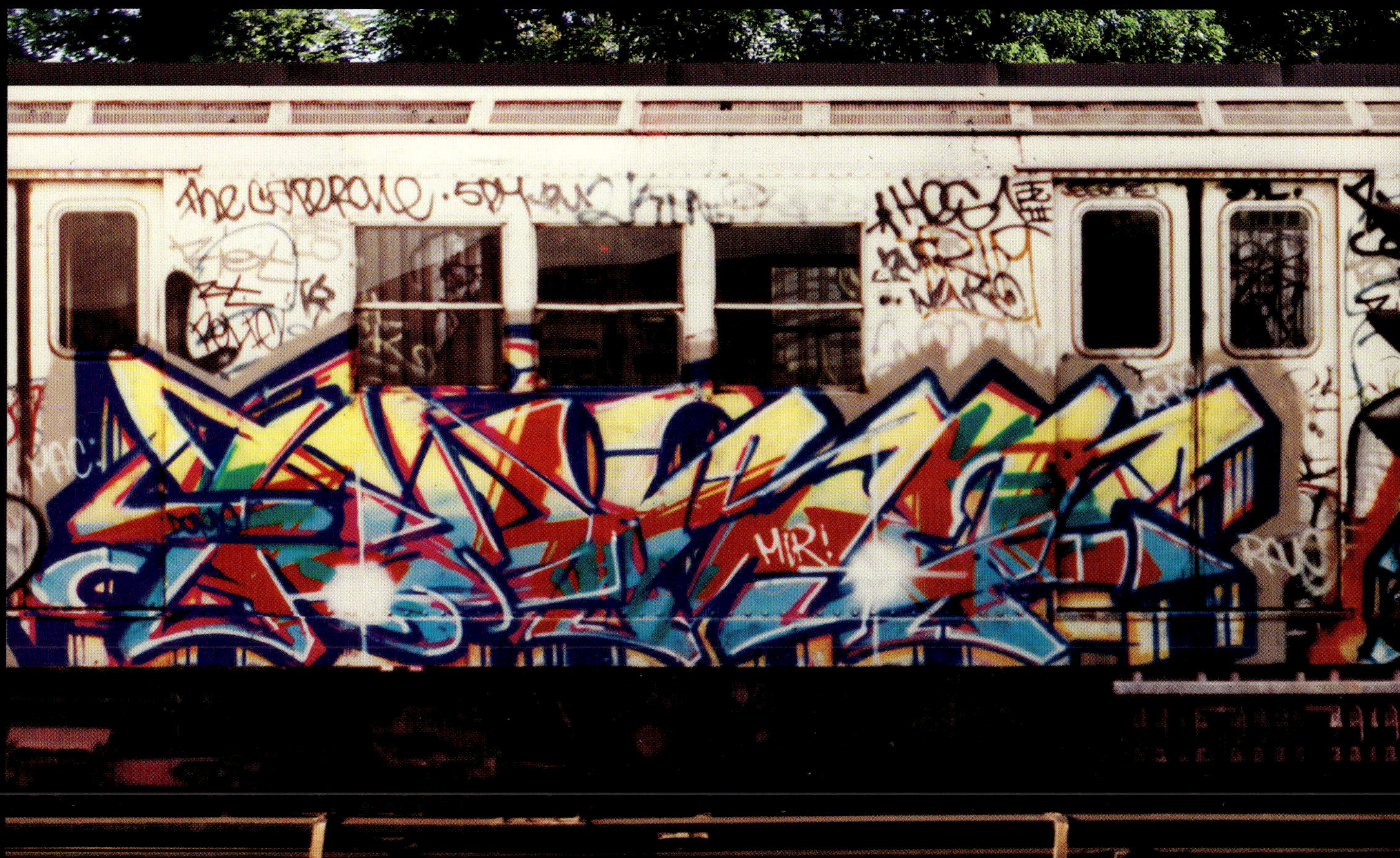

DOME "For Rave NCB and Mac KDM" with SUNE TCM, 5 train, Jan. 1987.

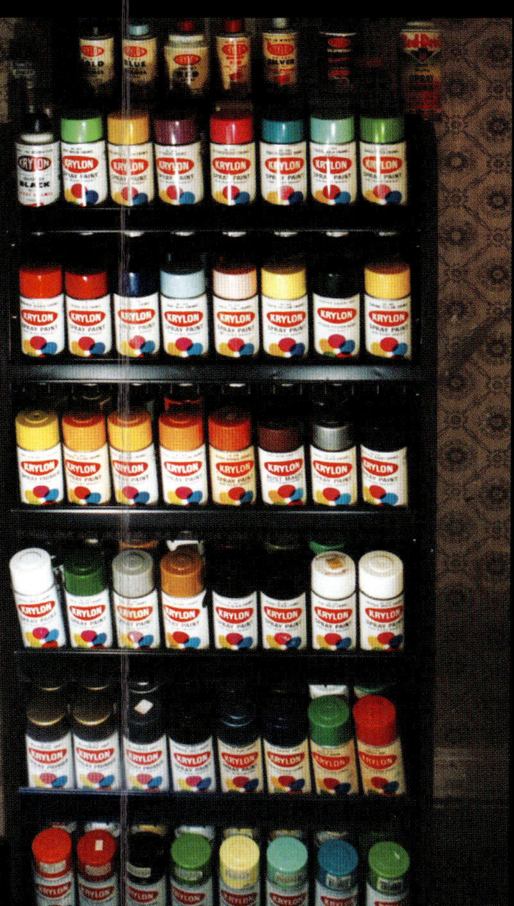

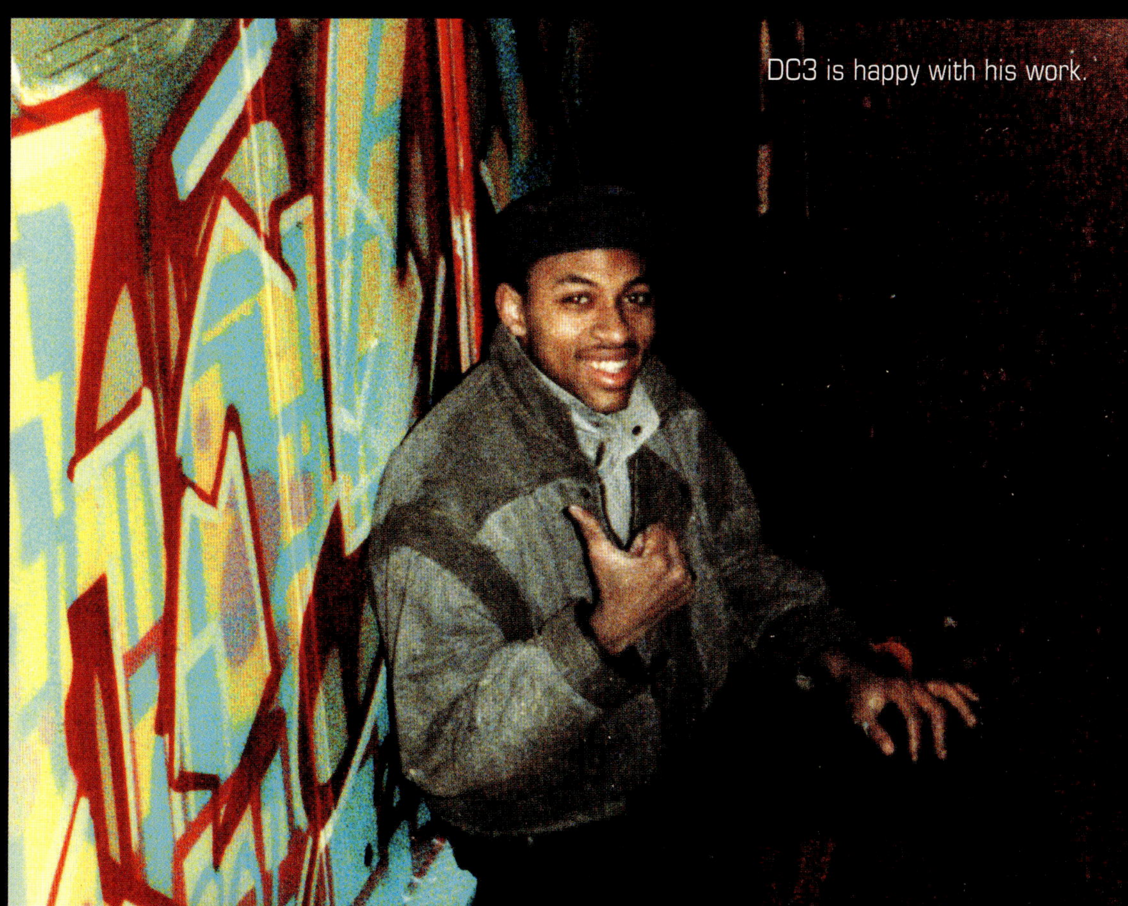

DC3 is happy with his work.

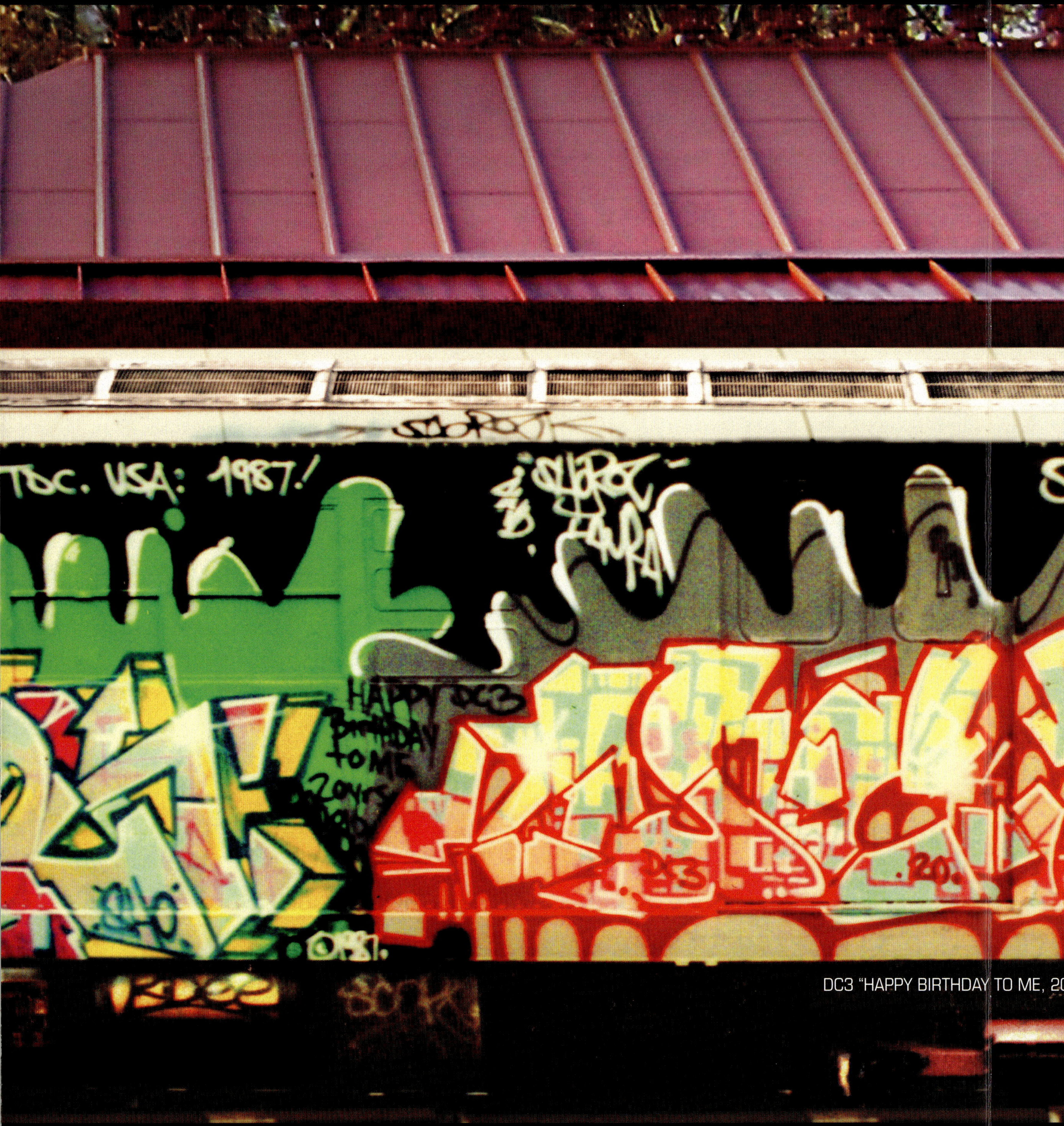

DC3 "HAPPY BIRTHDAY TO ME, 20

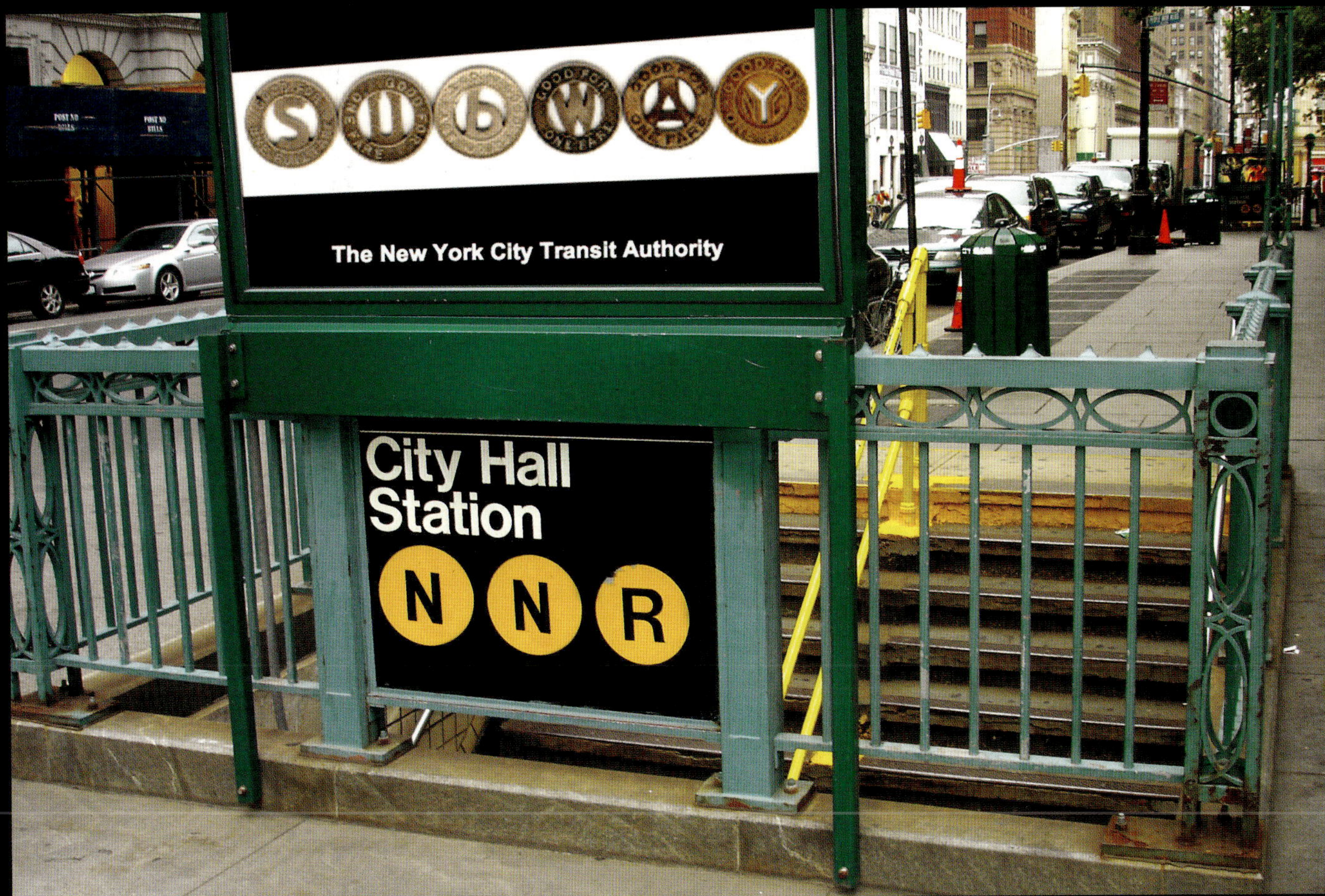

CHAPTER 7

City Hall, the J Yard, and the N Line. KOOL SPHERE Biography.

TDC was not playing when it came to bombing other lines. Niggas did not care, we was about hitting train lines period. I don't believe ever once we said we was The Top Graffiti Kings or All City!!! I always said fuck that!!!! You had to earn that shit and would only ever really be ever to claim that when mad other writers gave you that respect. We hit the N and R train a couple of times just to test the waters so to speak. After I saw Rakim and Eric B live at Union Square, we was coming uptown and a crew of at least twenty deep came thru our N train robbing and fucking everyone up, me and my boy Darrin jumped up on the seats and was like fuck y'all, we ain't the ones, yo. These kids robbed and assaulted at least eight people and bounced. I spit this because most people nowadays don't know shit about even riding trains in 1986. It was dangerous, especially at night, shit would jump off. We did several top-to-bottoms at City Hall on the N and R line. I was amazed that you would hop the turnstile and enter a protected stair case right down stairs to the lay ups and could get busy right there without even caring. Funny shit was that we didn't even bother to explore the lay up and did them right on the platform. I still cant believe we didn't get busted or raided, cause we was in plain sight. A lot of trains got hit here and in Astoria Station lay ups.

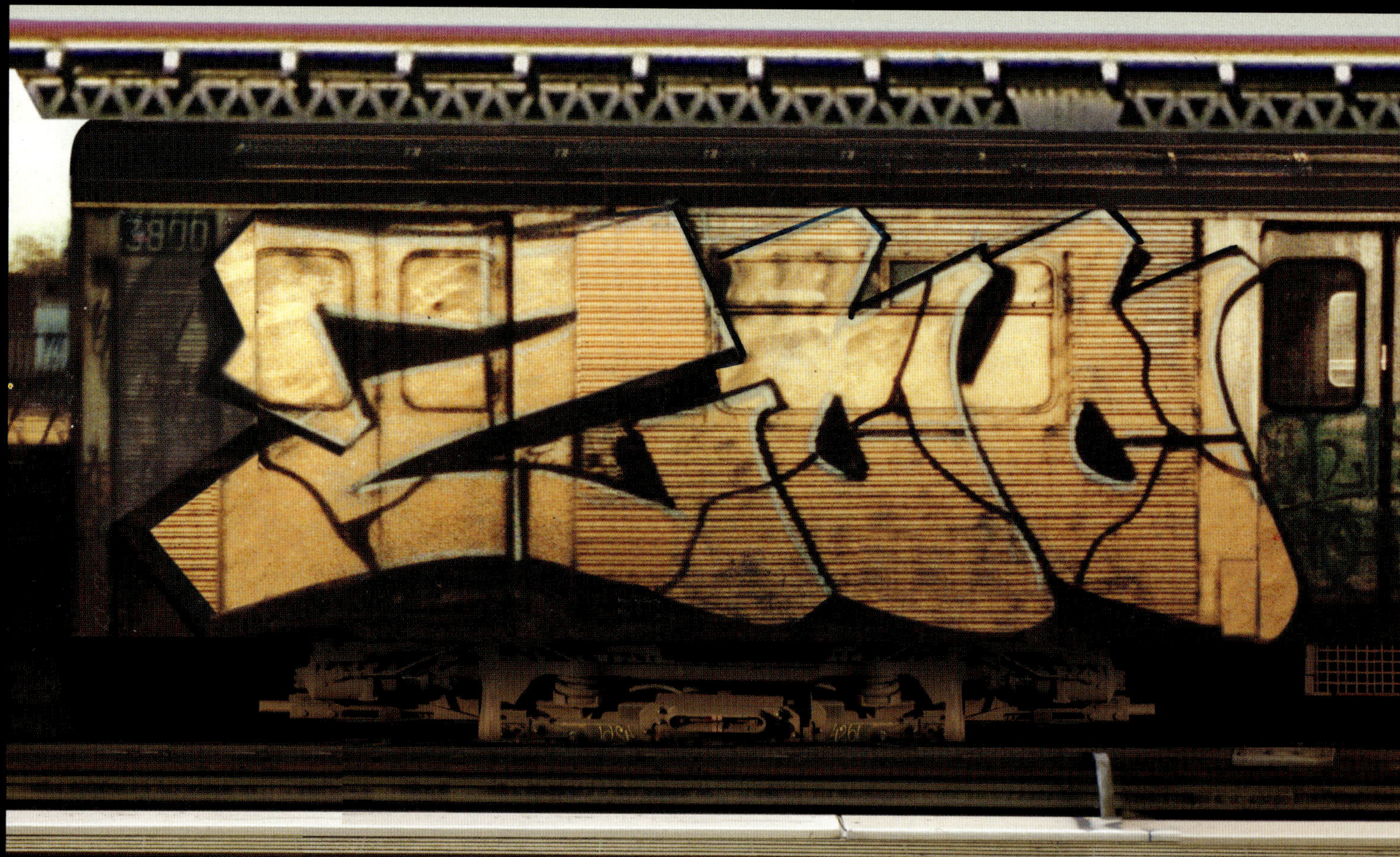

ZOO and USA DC3, top-to-bottoms bombed in City Hall, Aug. 1988.

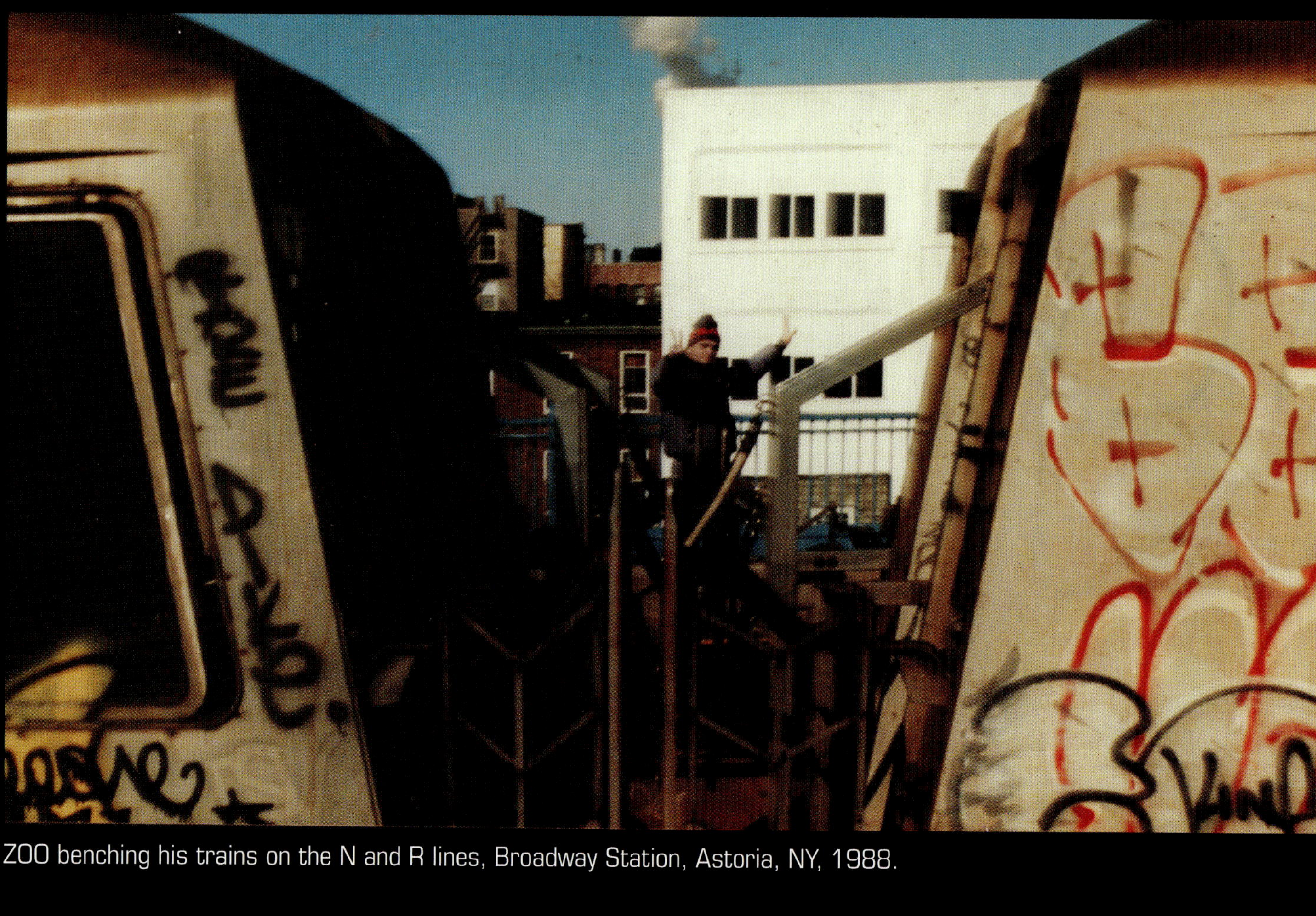

ZOO benching his trains on the N and R lines, Broadway Station, Astoria, NY, 1988.

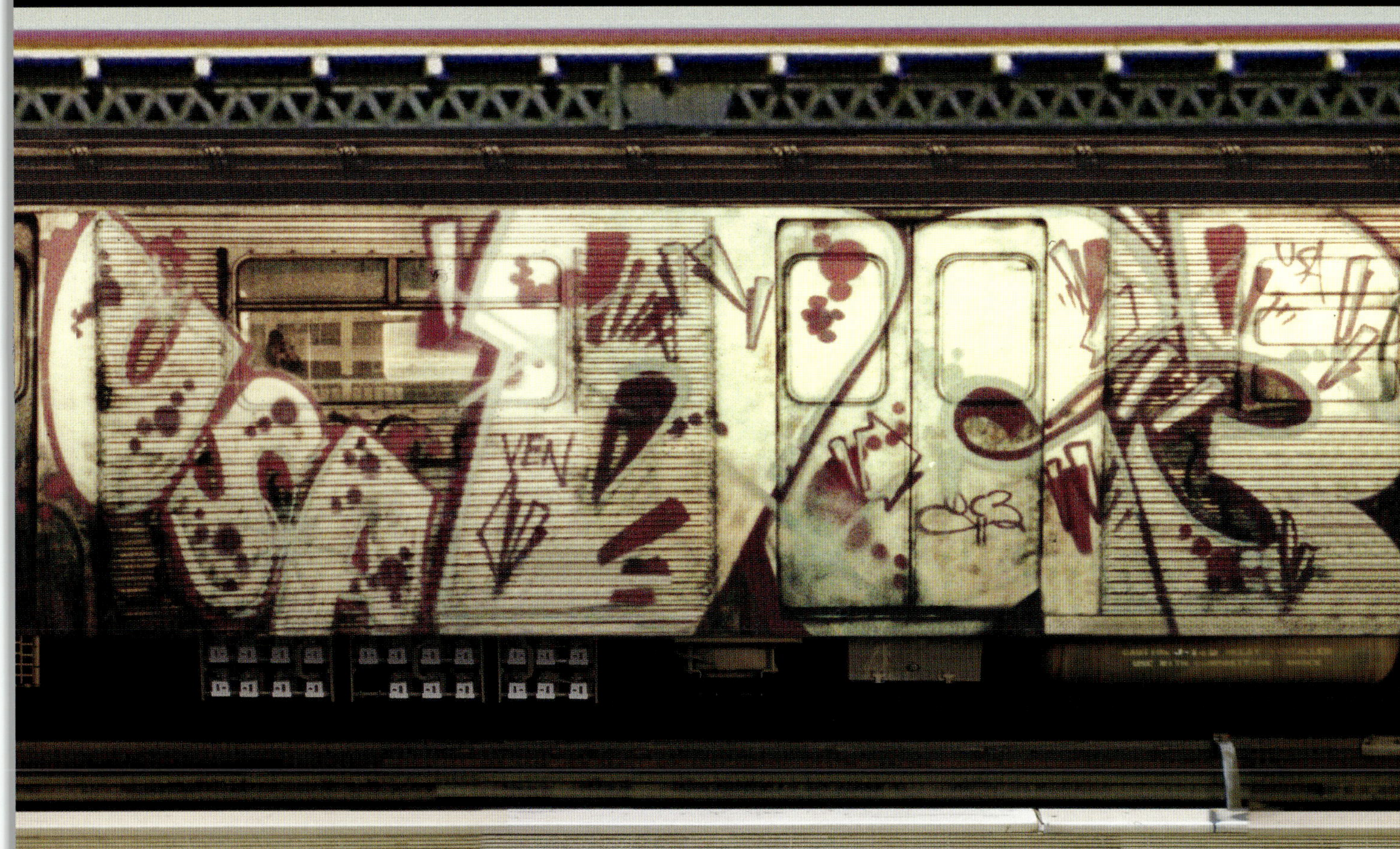

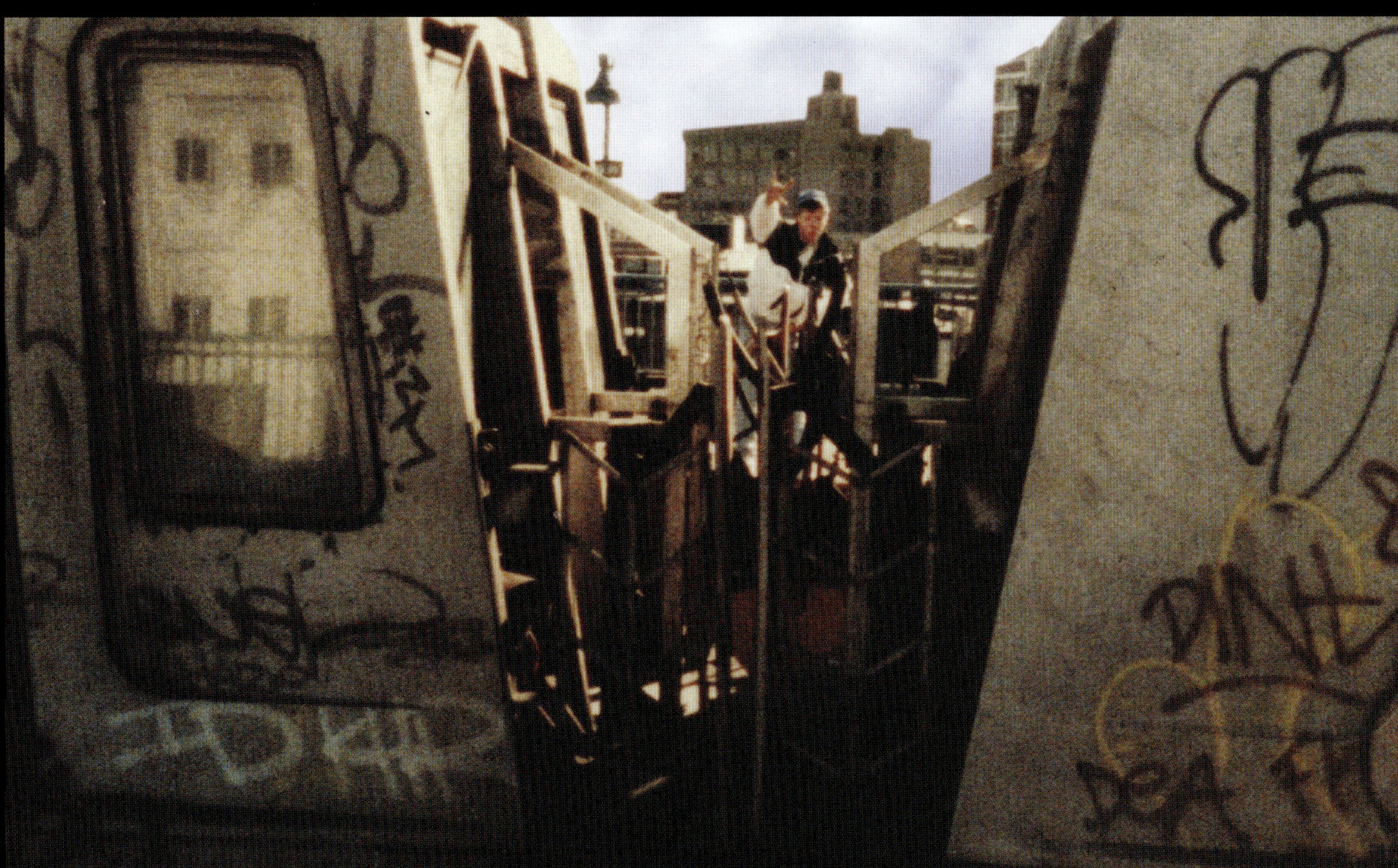

SHO catching flicks at 36th Street, Astoria, NY.

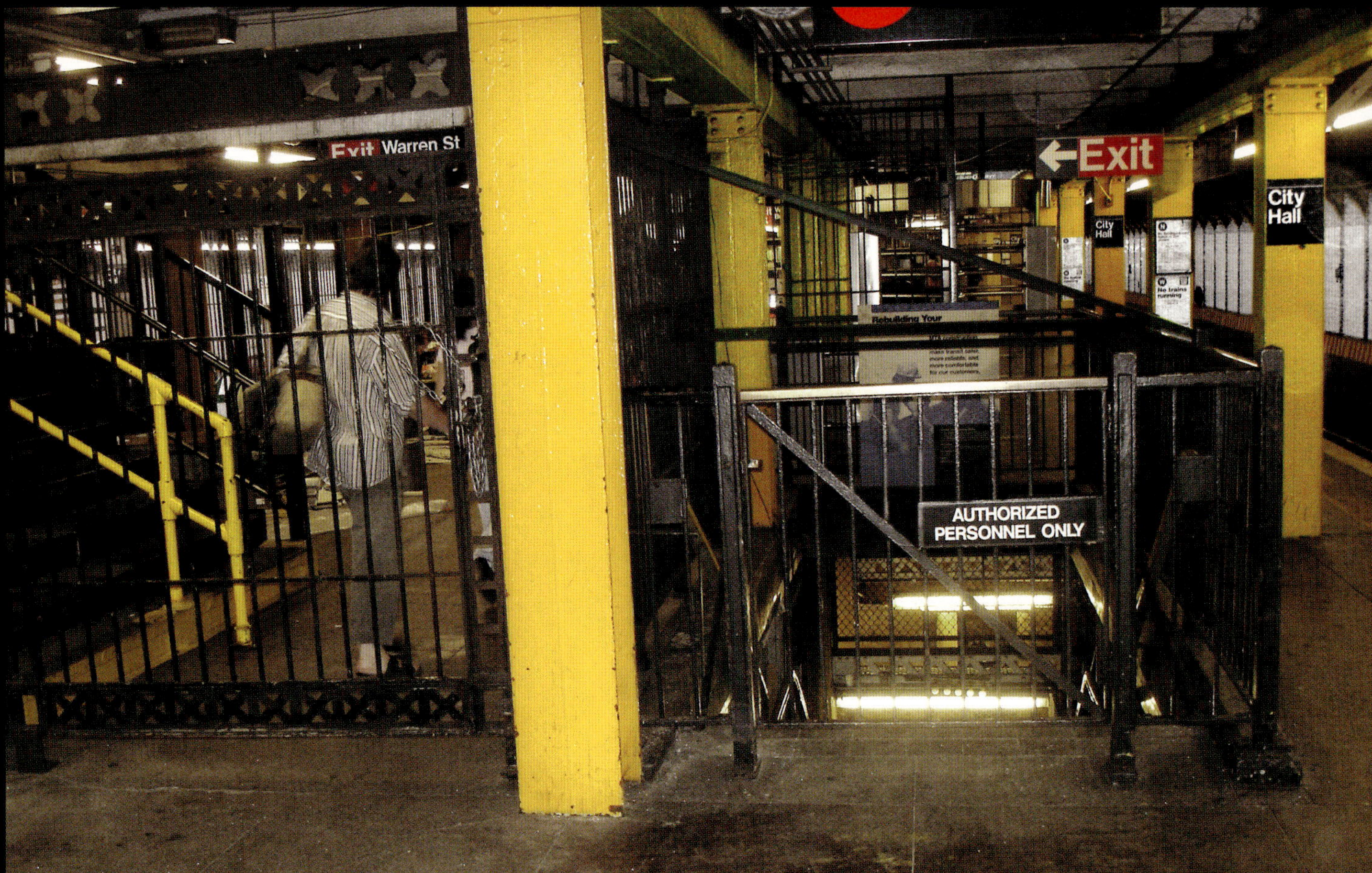

City Hall Station Underground, 4-track N and R Train lay ups, Oct. 1988.

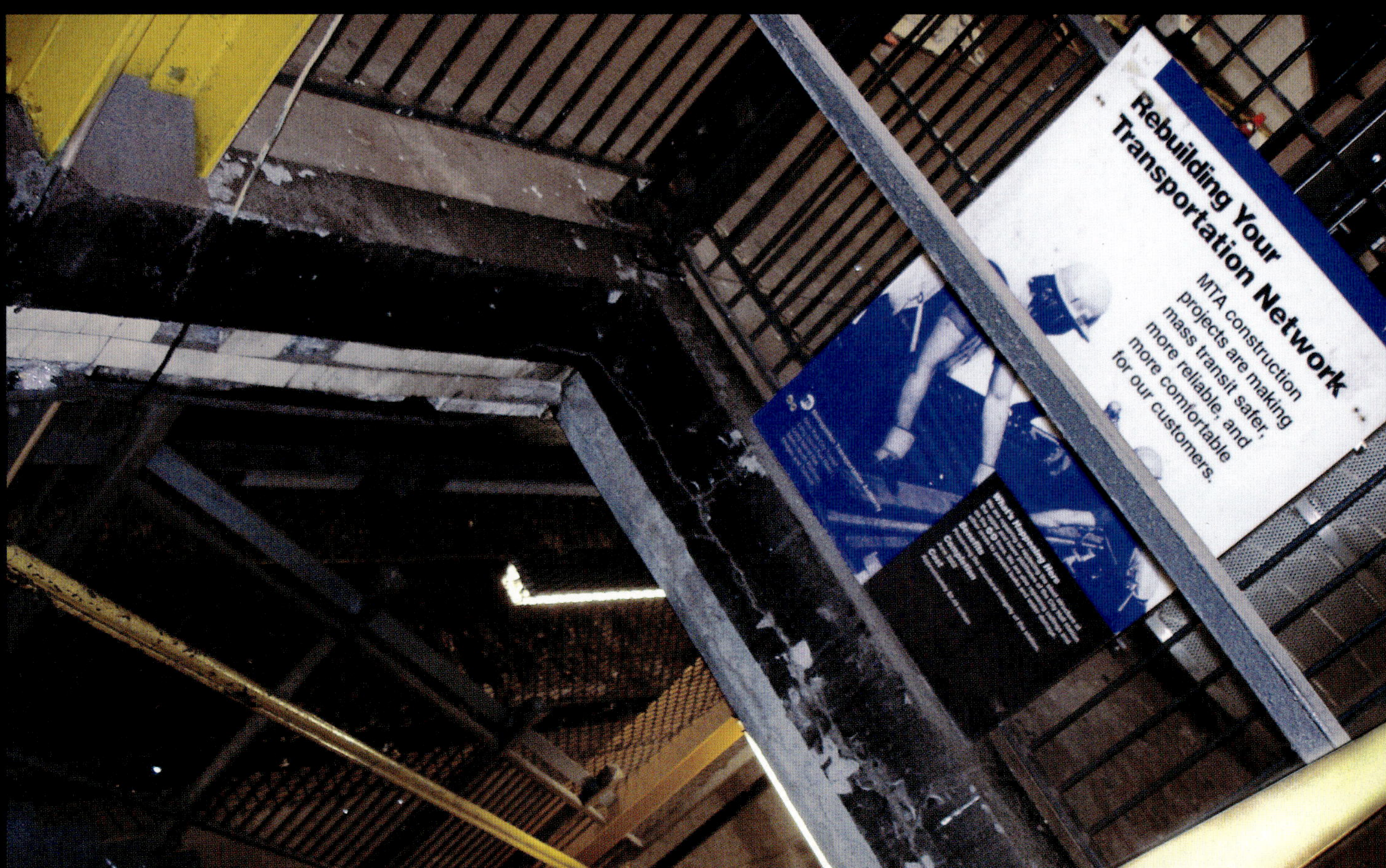

A daytime view from up above...

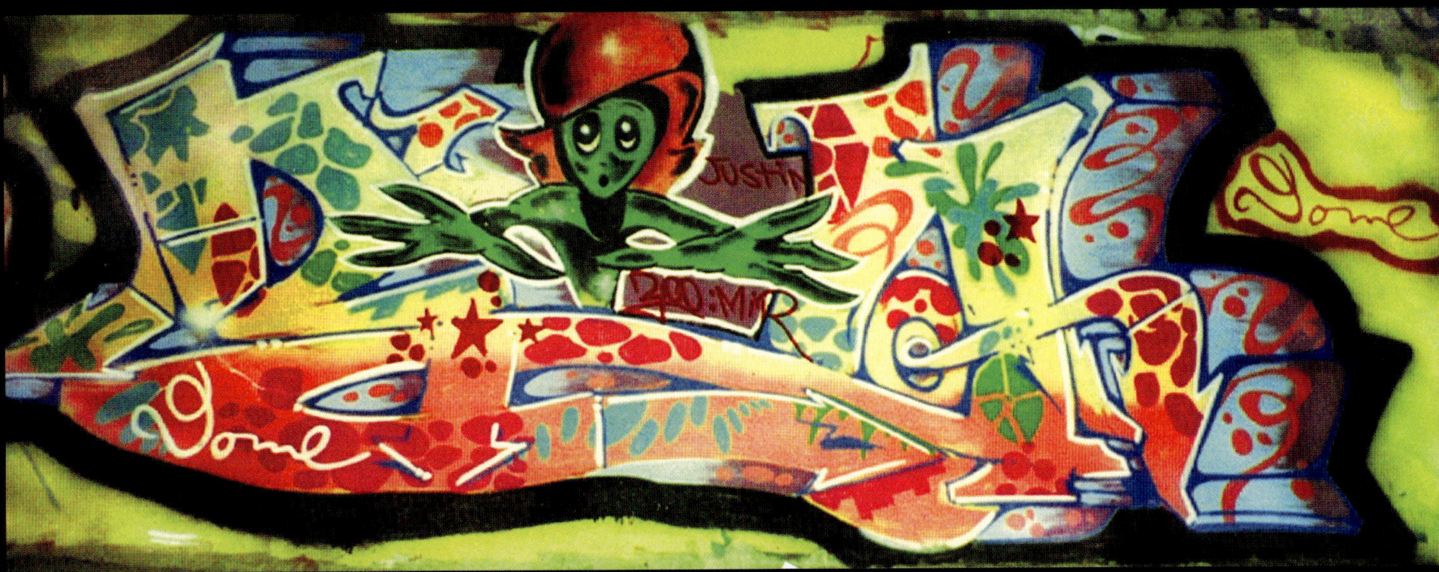

ZOO: MIR

Below is a ZOO burner in a writer's black book and above is the completed piece at Franklin K. Lane High School in Ridgewood Queens in 1992. As writers will tell you, that was a great spot to piece at for many years in the late 80s and all thru the 90s.

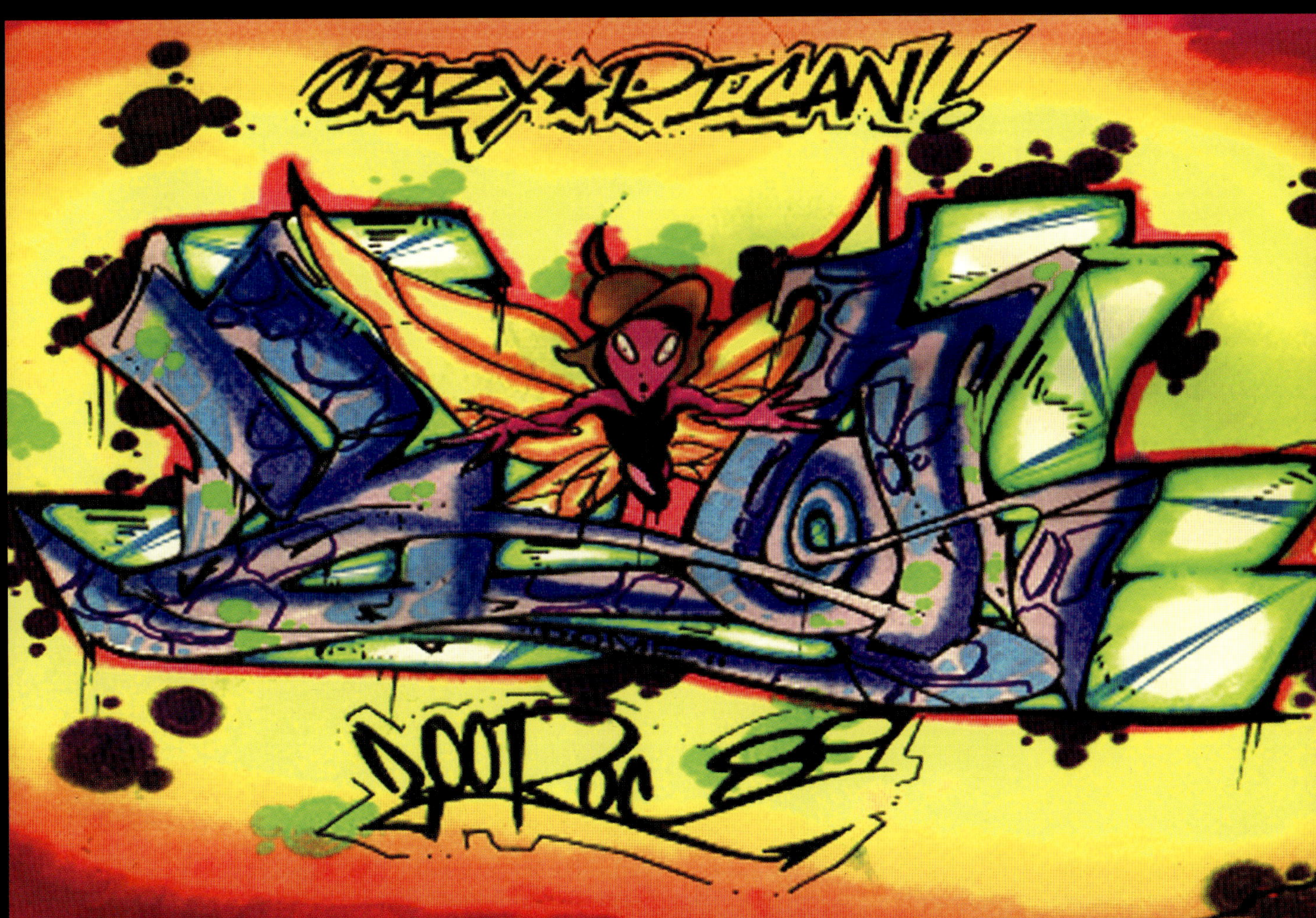

Crazy Rican, ZOO Black Book Burner in 1989.

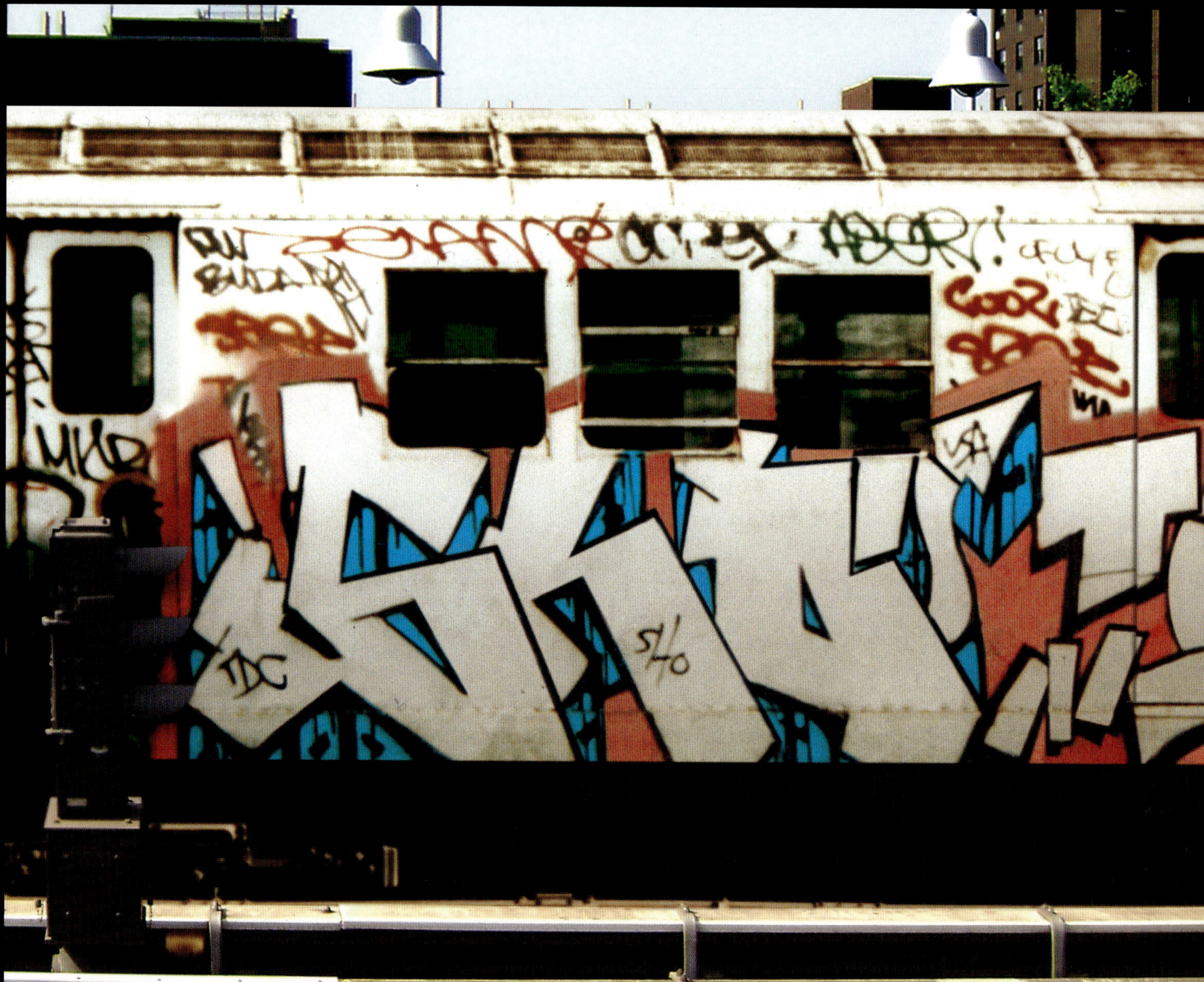

SHO, "NO SHORT CUTS," TDC and ZOO silver, Dec. 1986.

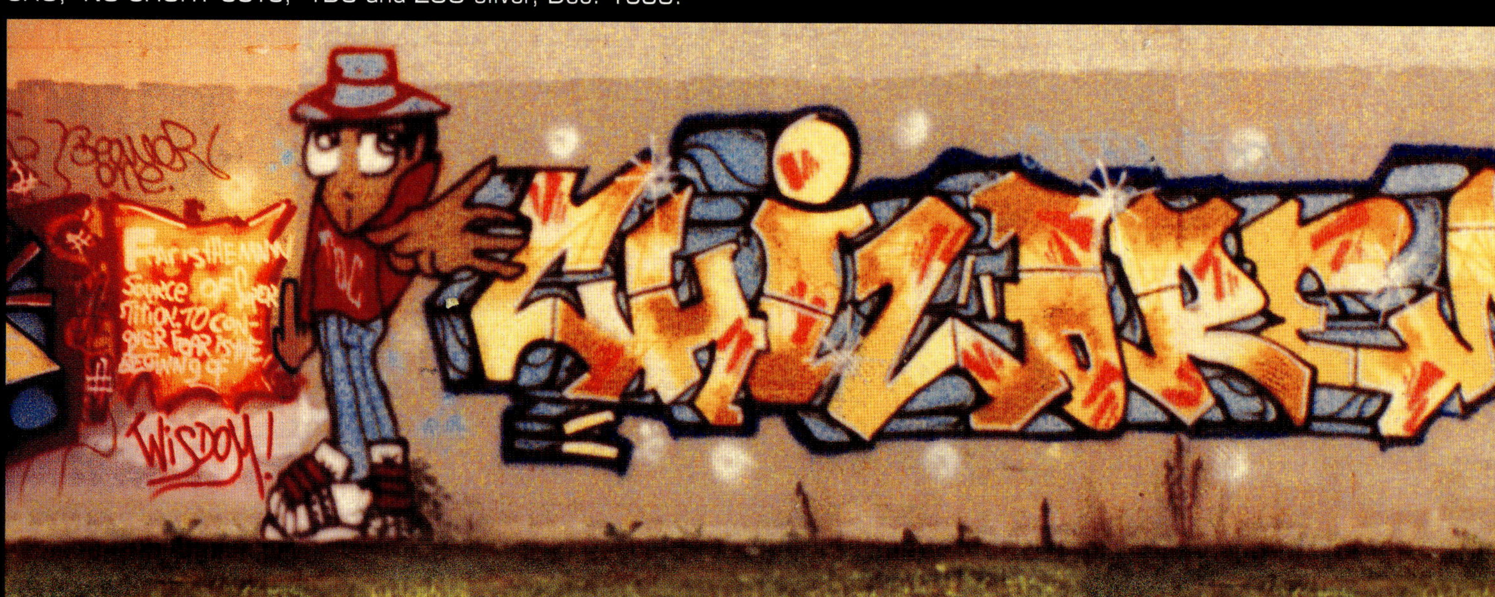

Children of Soul, "IN MEMORY OF JOHN MAYHAND," RIP 1967-1985, By DC3 and

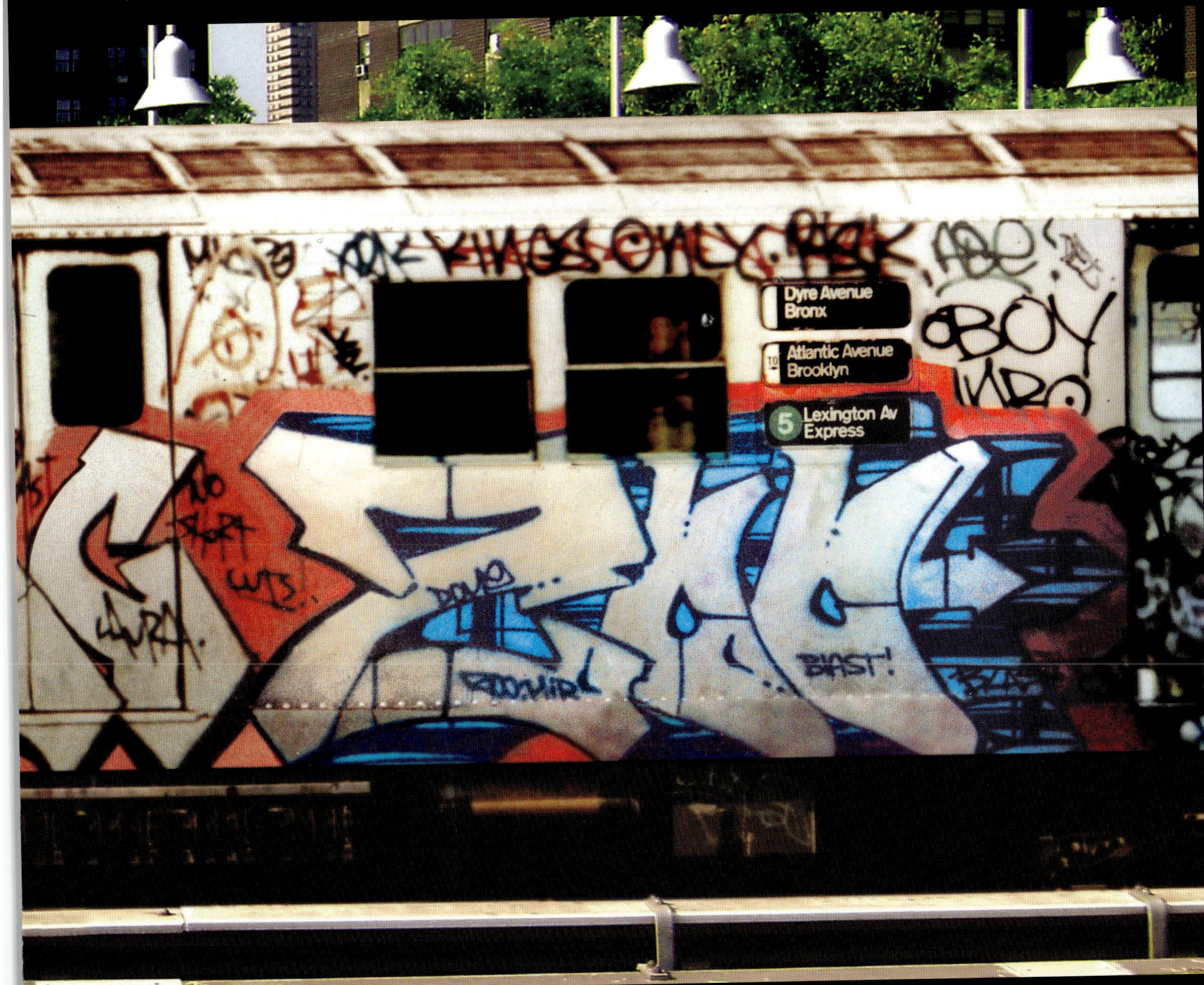

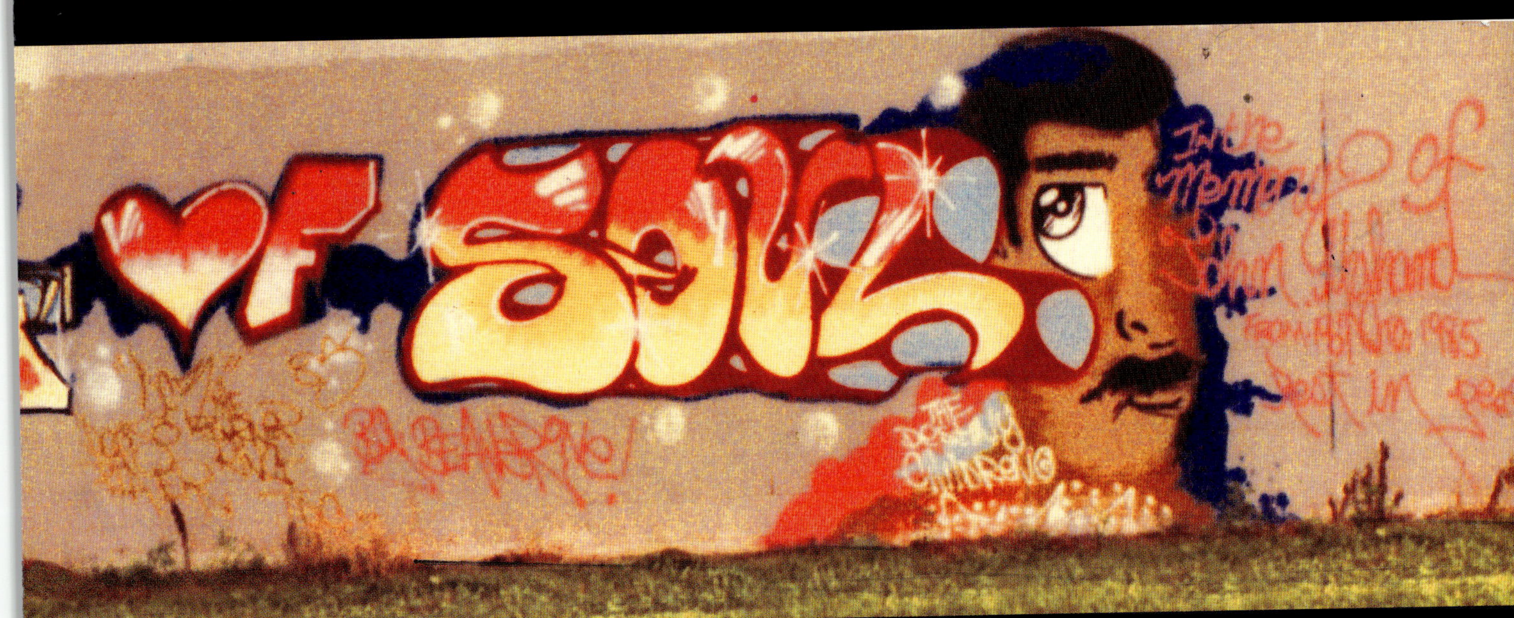

BEAVER One, The Destiny Children, Freeport, NY, Summer 1985.

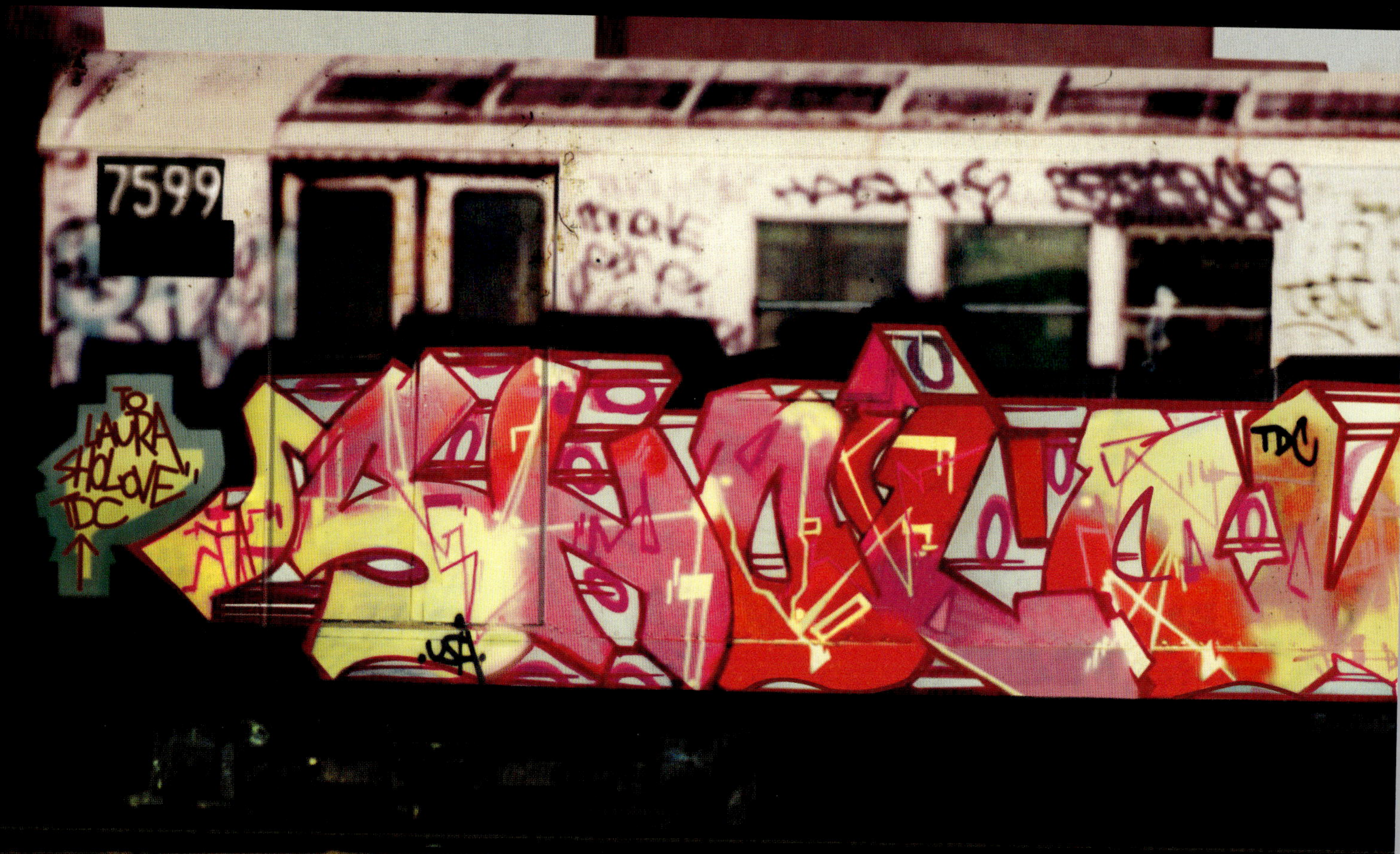

SHOLOVE and ZOO window-downs, Feb. 1987.

The SHOLOVE ZOO 5 Train was done in the Esplanade stick-outs in early February 1987. It was fucking freezing cold out this night and super dark out, but the train sets had all the lights on so it wasn't a problem to paint. We started at like 2 A.M. in the morning and was uneventful in the beginning and we hadn't see any other writers in the lay up. It was usually better to start this late because the work bums had already walked thru both sets and would sweep out the trains and reset all of the doors and put the electric subway engines into sleep/idle mode, this was done because subways are never turned off especially in the winter when the electronics could freeze. Shit got real ugly around 3 A.M. because all of a sudden we see other writer coming at us. Turns out it was Cap MPC and Gato RIS, who also pushed MPC. Problem was that Gato had crossed out a Dome top-to-bottom (see page 193). That train had been done in the 125th Street snow storm lay ups during the blizzard. He had just taking a tag on it and lined it out, but that shit was definitely beef, so Dome rolls up on him with a baseball bat and caught this nigga in between both third rails, meanwhile me and DC3 was watching Cap. I swear I thought Dome was gonna hit this cat in the head with the aluminum bat at which point he might of fallen to the ground and hit the third rail and fried. The shit was one of the illest stand offs of all time with these niggas yelling at each other and neither willing to back down, so I was like fuck this shit and just fucking squash the shit, which they ultimately did. After that Gato never went over Dome again and all of us went into the train later and smoked some dust and drank some OE with them. Peace.

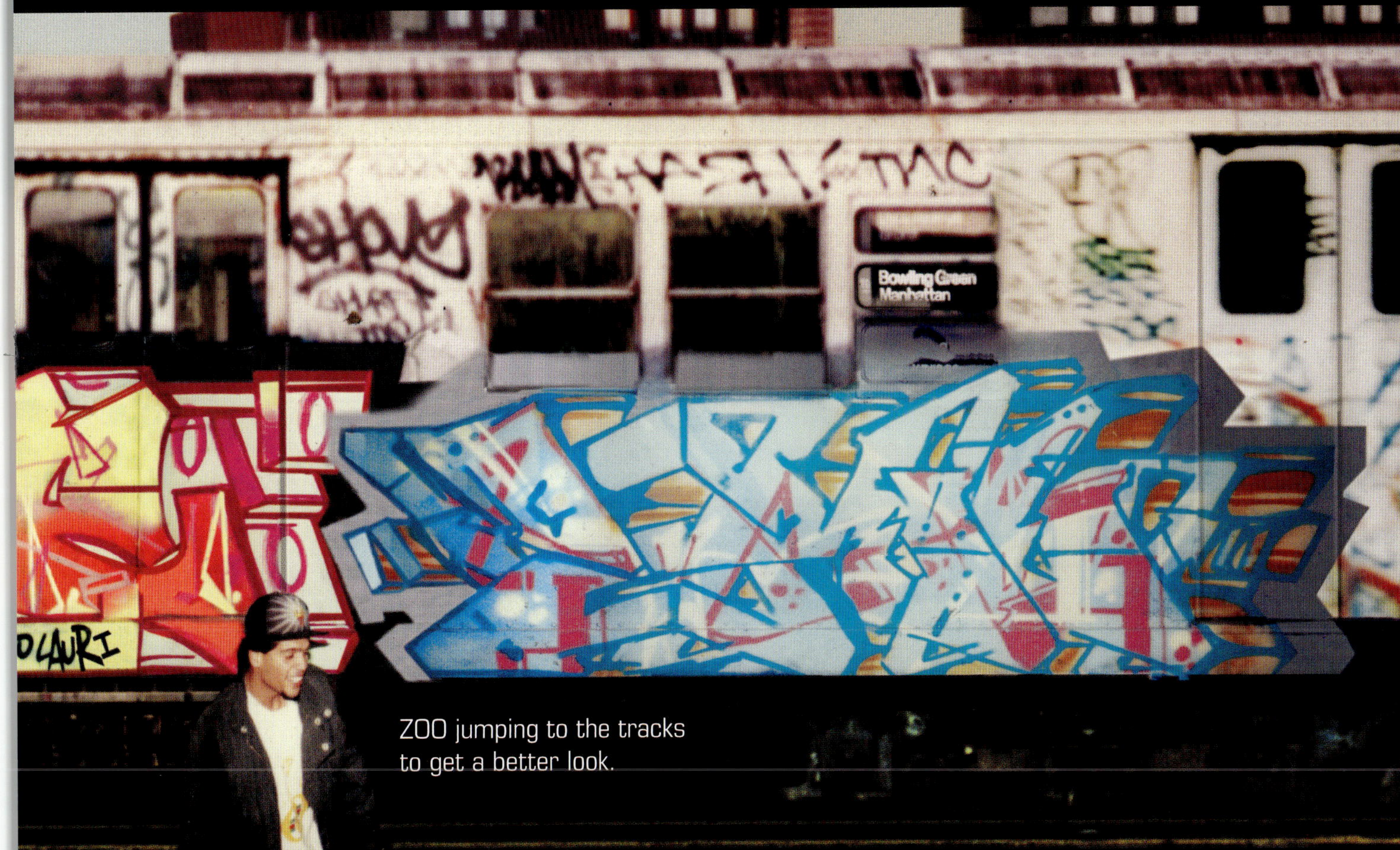

ZOO jumping to the tracks to get a better look.

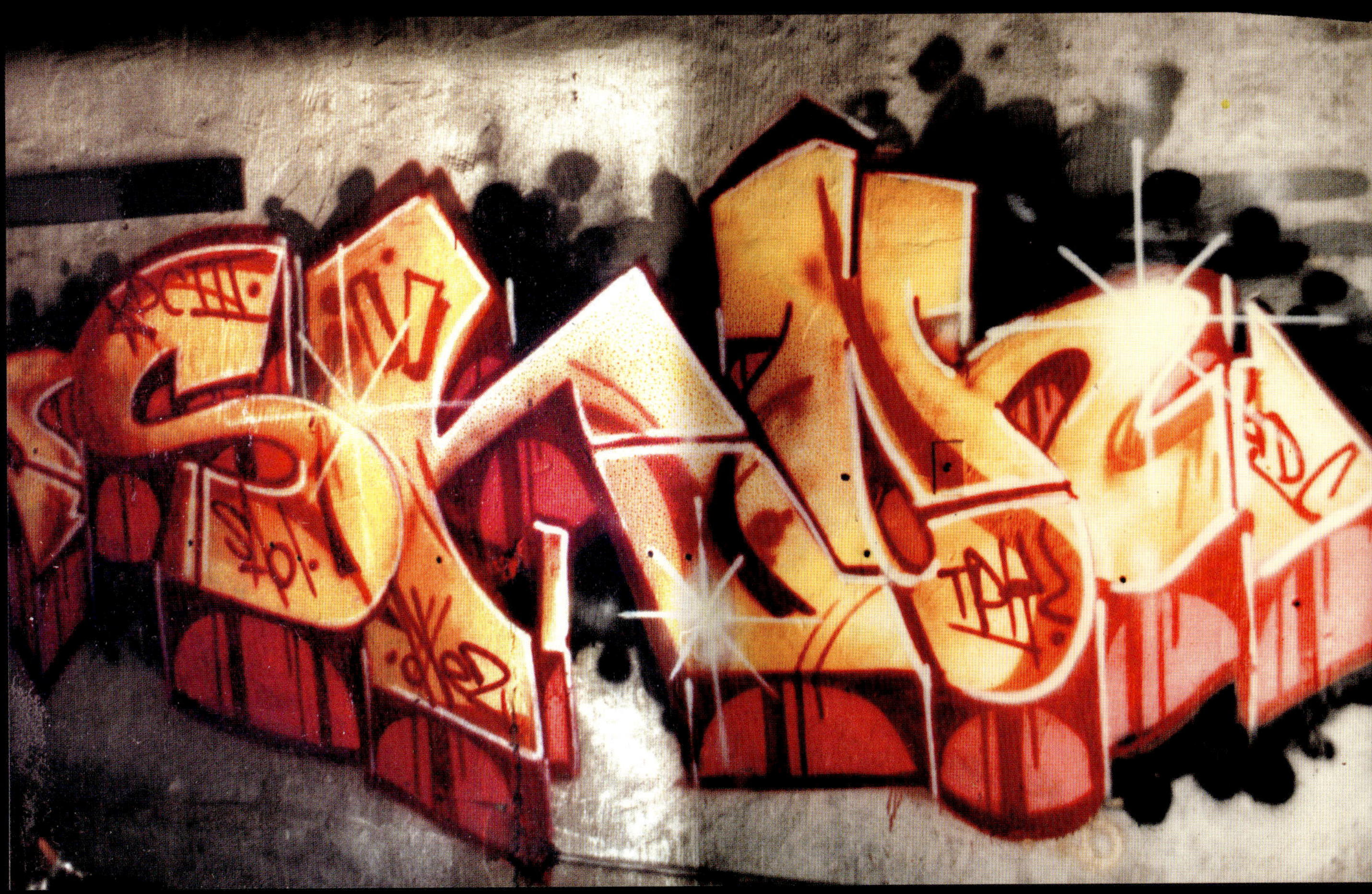

SHO TDC TPK, The Port Kings, Jun. 1985.

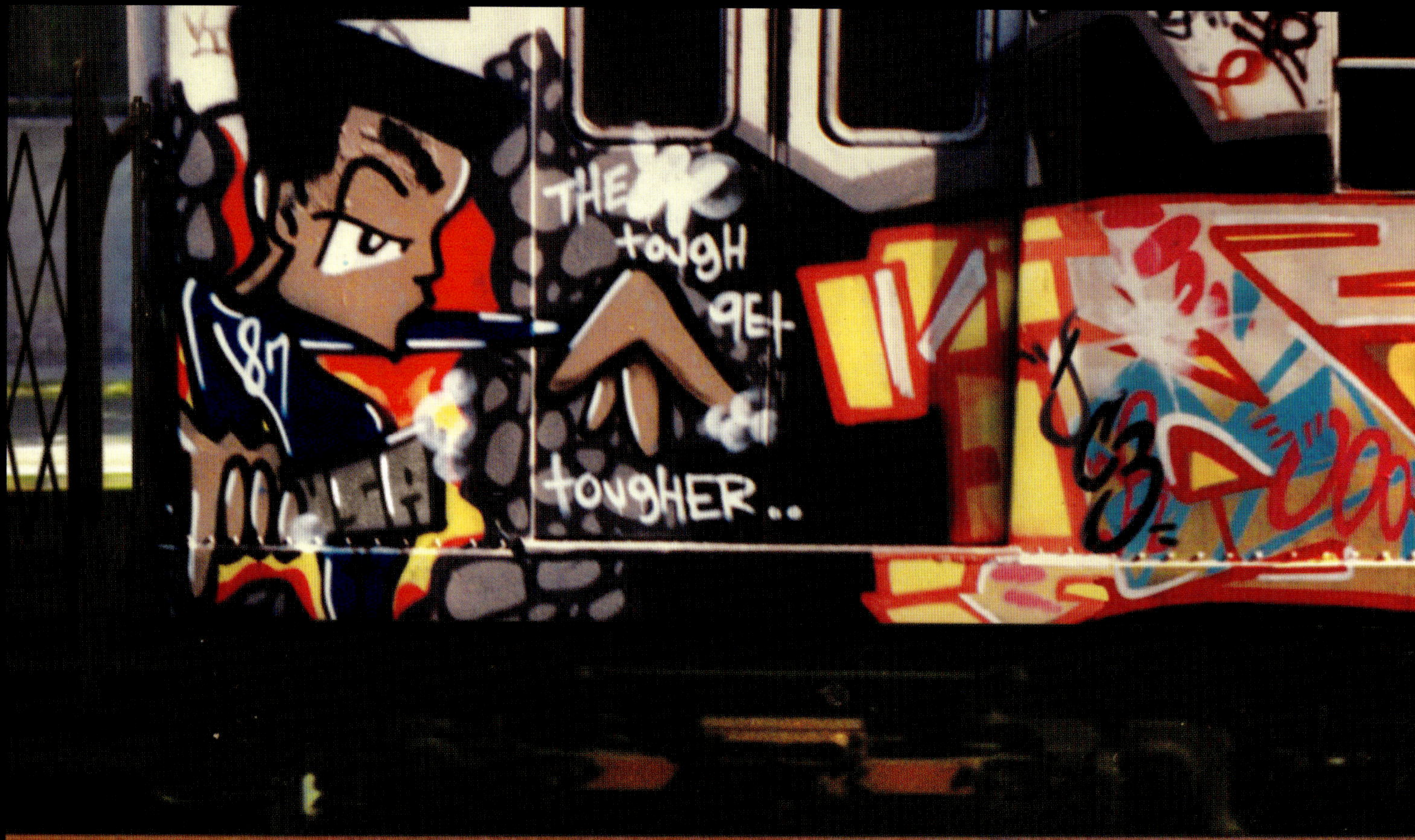

DC3, "THE TOUGH GET TOUGHER," USA, May 1987. Blazed at the Esplanade stick-outs.

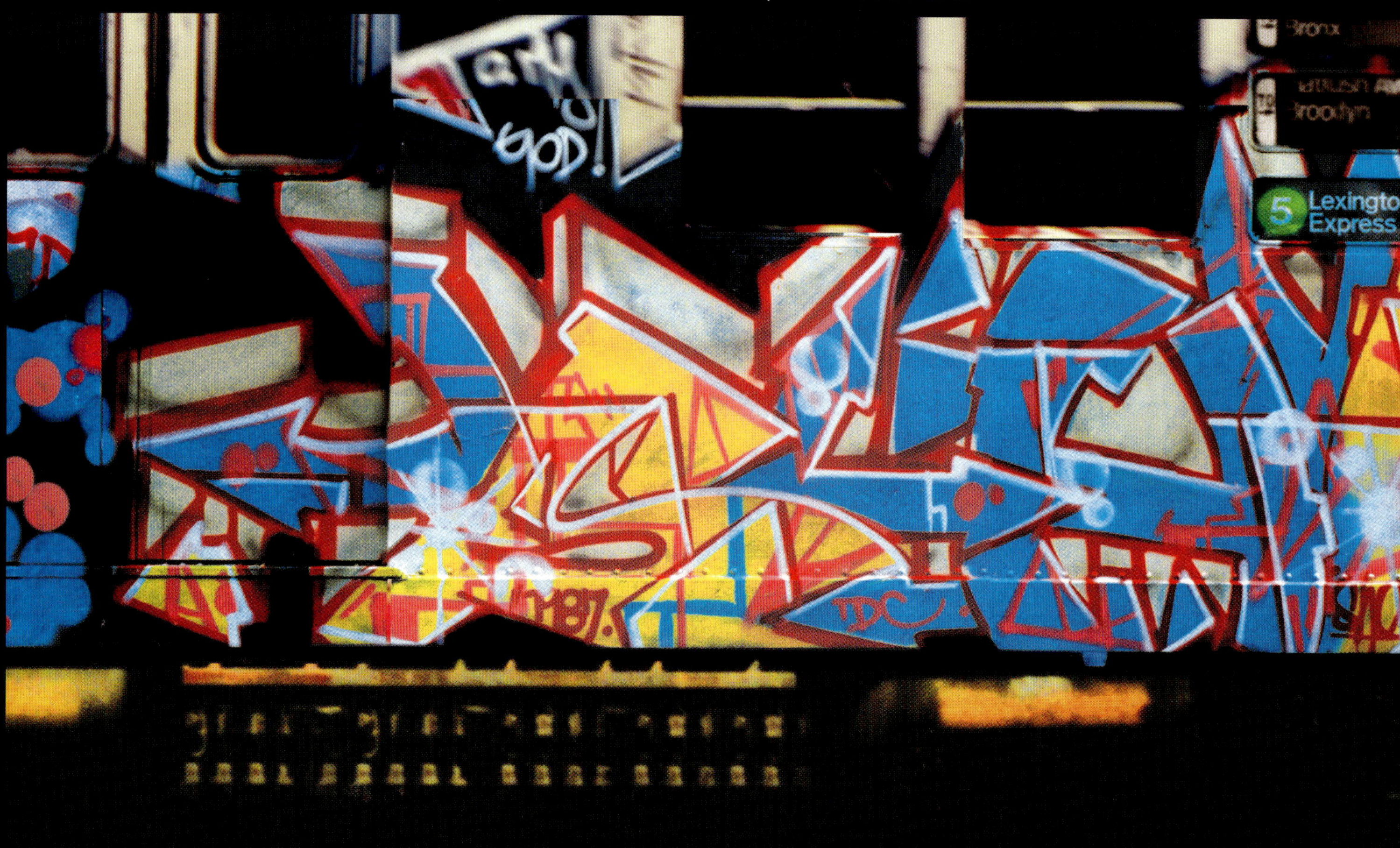

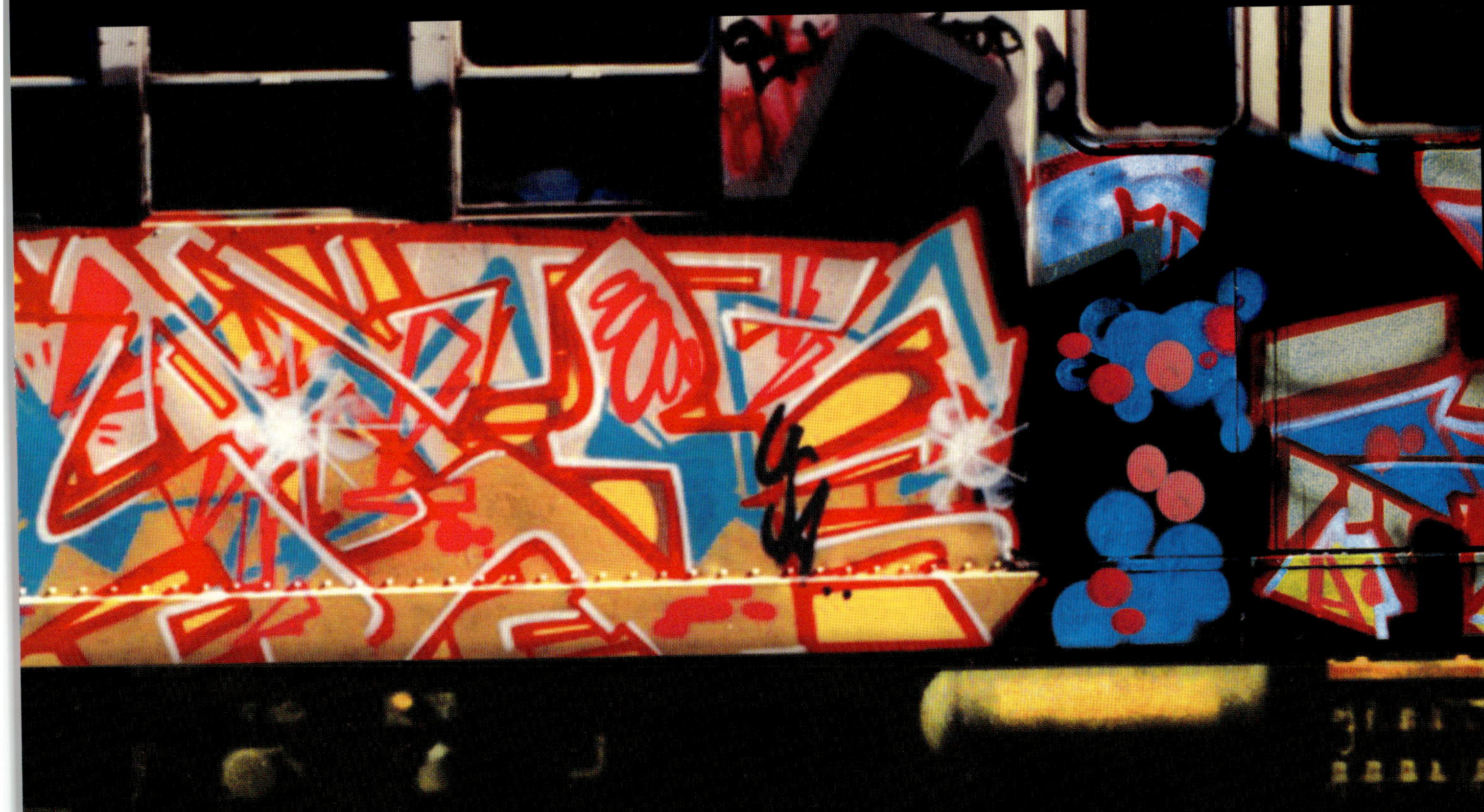

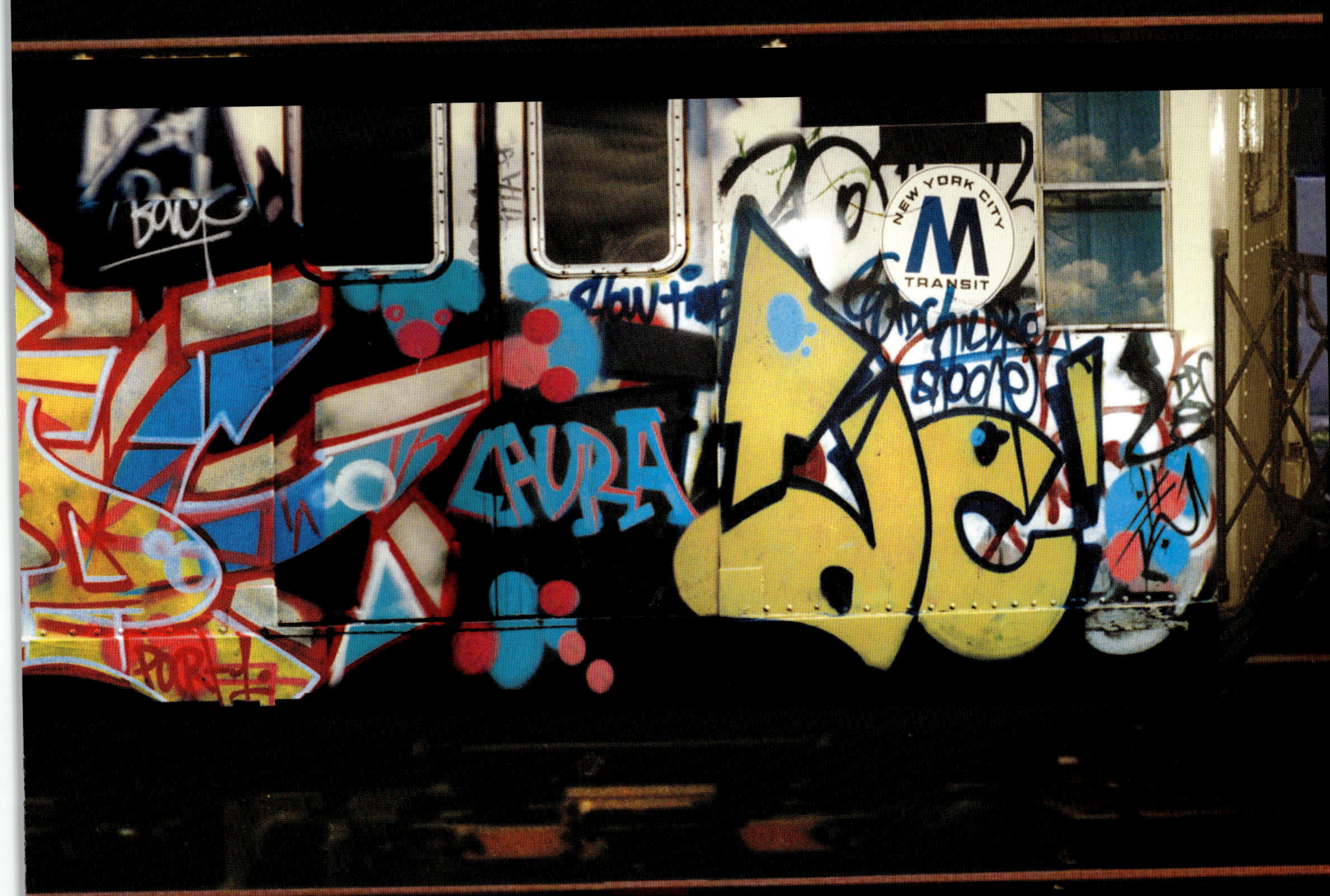

SHO TDC, "SHOW TIME," Part 1. For Laura.

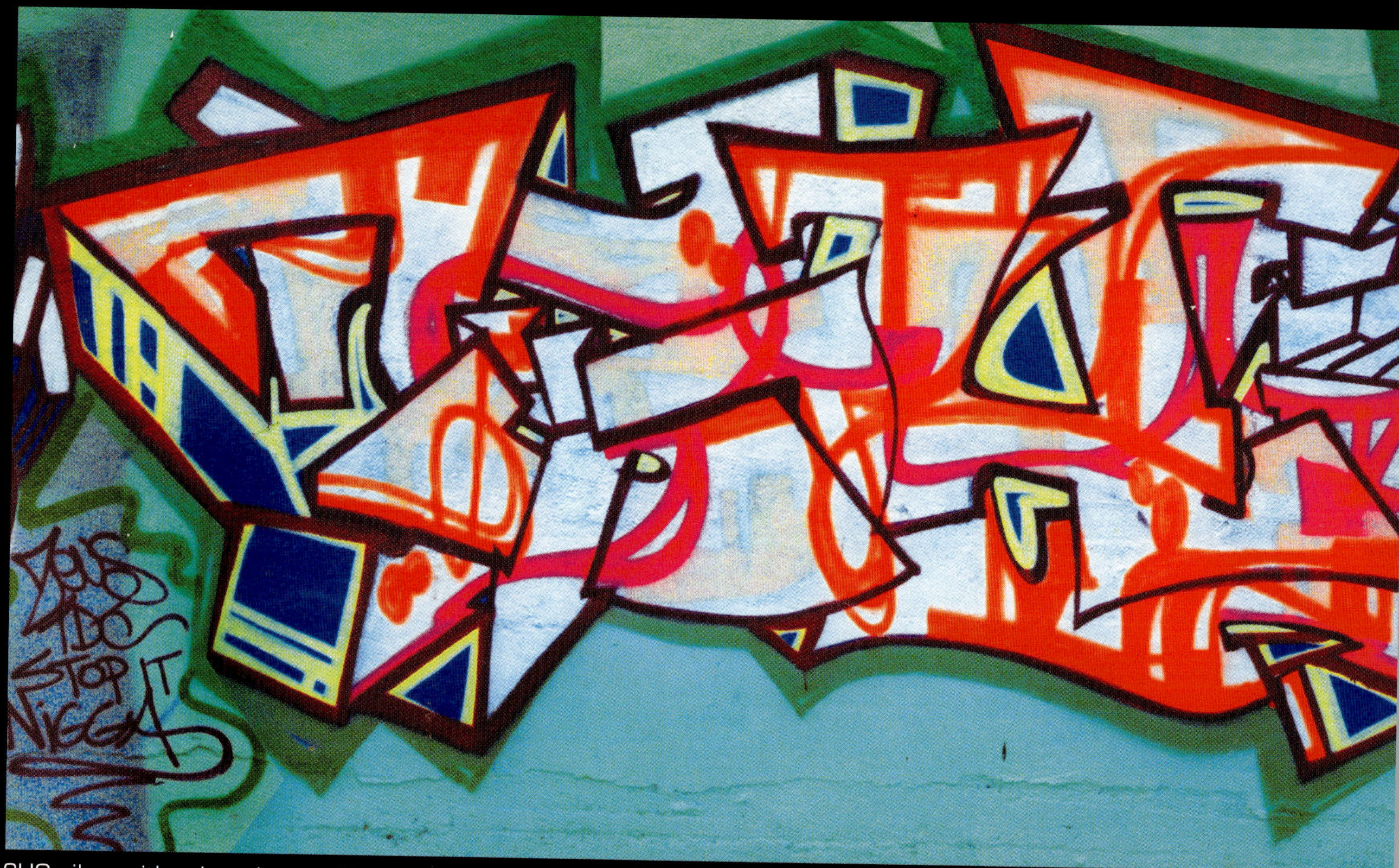

SHO silver with colors done at "Boys Field," Brooklyn, NY, Aug. 1995.

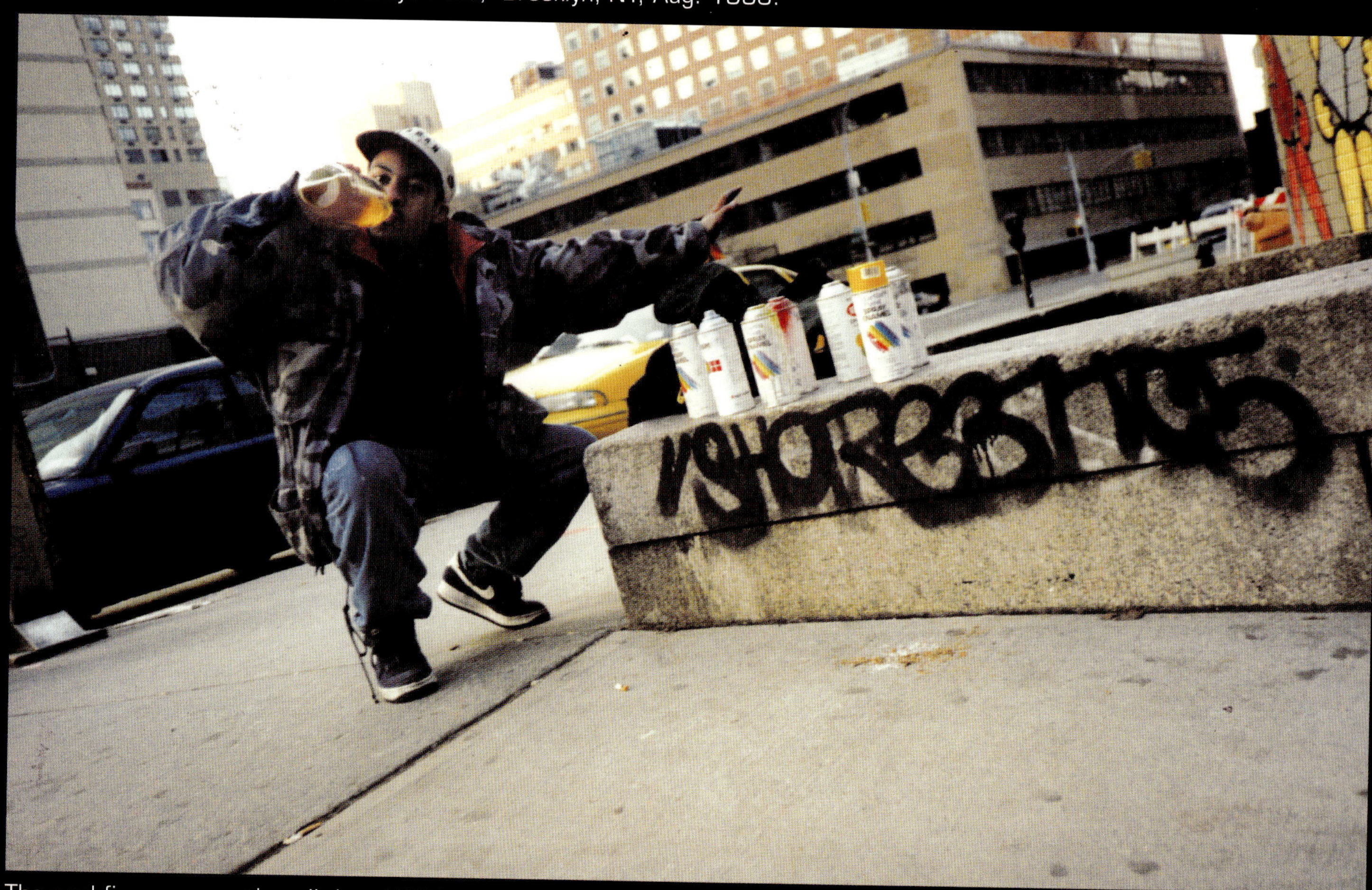

The cool five representing all day, 1995.

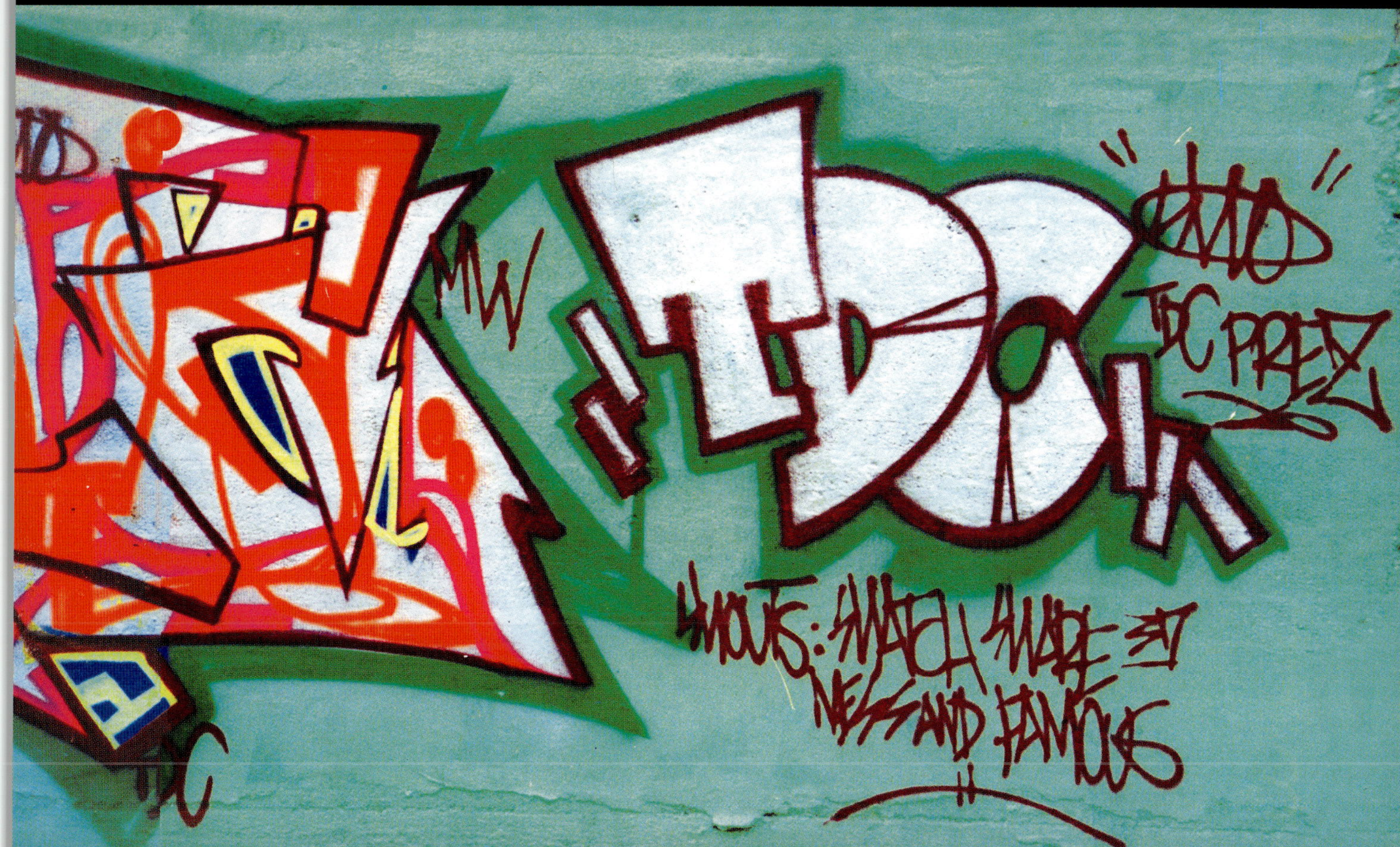

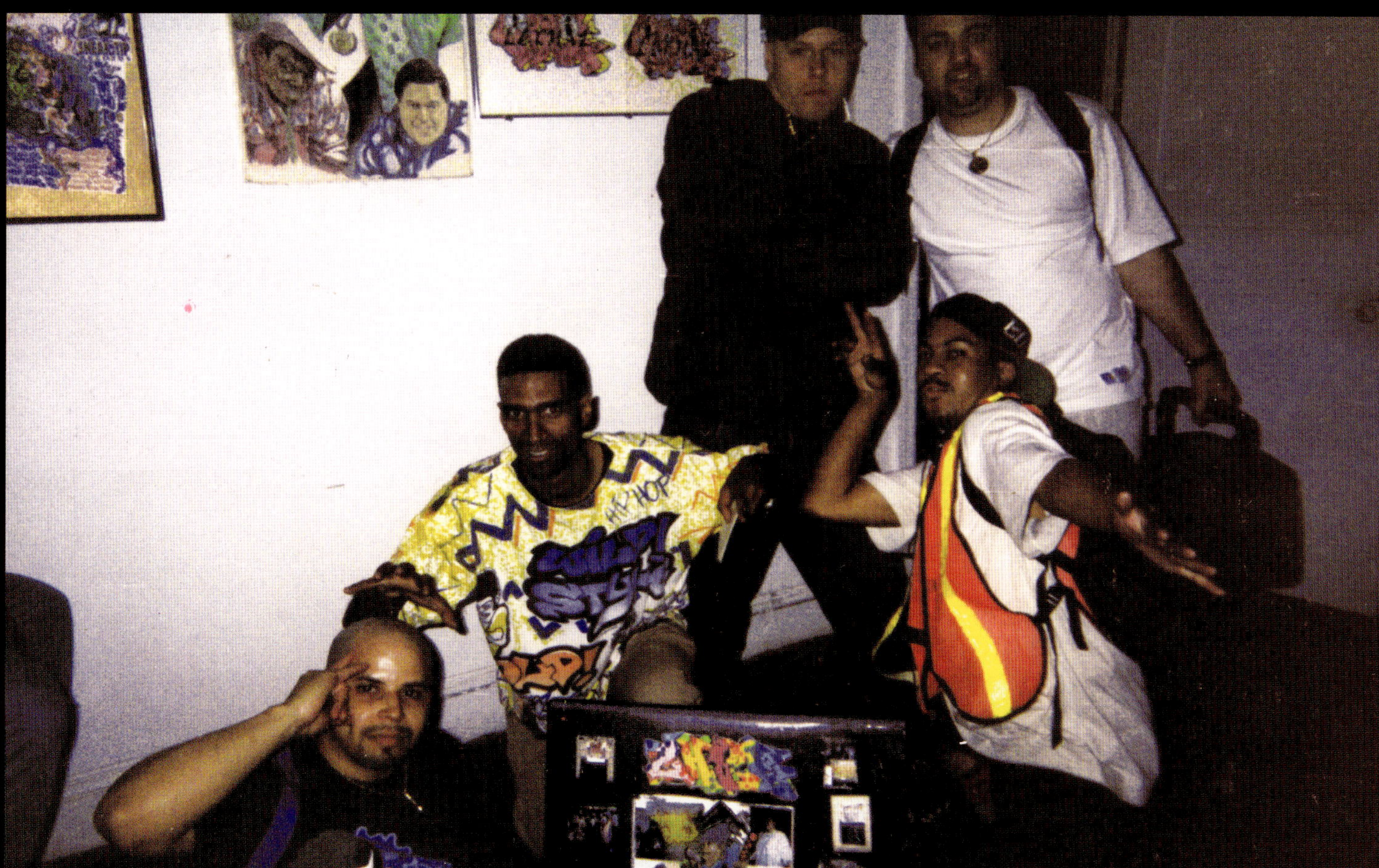

In memory of Frosty Freeze...

It was always an adventure doing graffiti. You get sucked into it and until you fall off or get locked up, you rep that shit if you had the nuts to do it. Many writers I know got busted many times, even with jail attached, and still came back, like DESA MTA and my man VE RIP...Shits real!!!! While benching these letter lines, which we had done just a couple of trains, I mean 50 or less when I say that by the way. ZooRoc and I had been coming from getting flicks from the N train in Astoria at Broadway Station and were driving back to Manhattan and got pulled over by the 114th Precinct blue and white. I said to the officer, "why you pull us over" and they pulled guns on us and had Zoo against the car and me with my face pressed against the hood with the cops elbow, definite uncalled for excessive force, turns out they said we matched the description of murder suspects just involved in a homicide in a queens laundromat. It was pouring rain and they had a witness drive by in a DT car to ID us. I was praying that they didn't say that's them. Cause they was wrong and knew it.

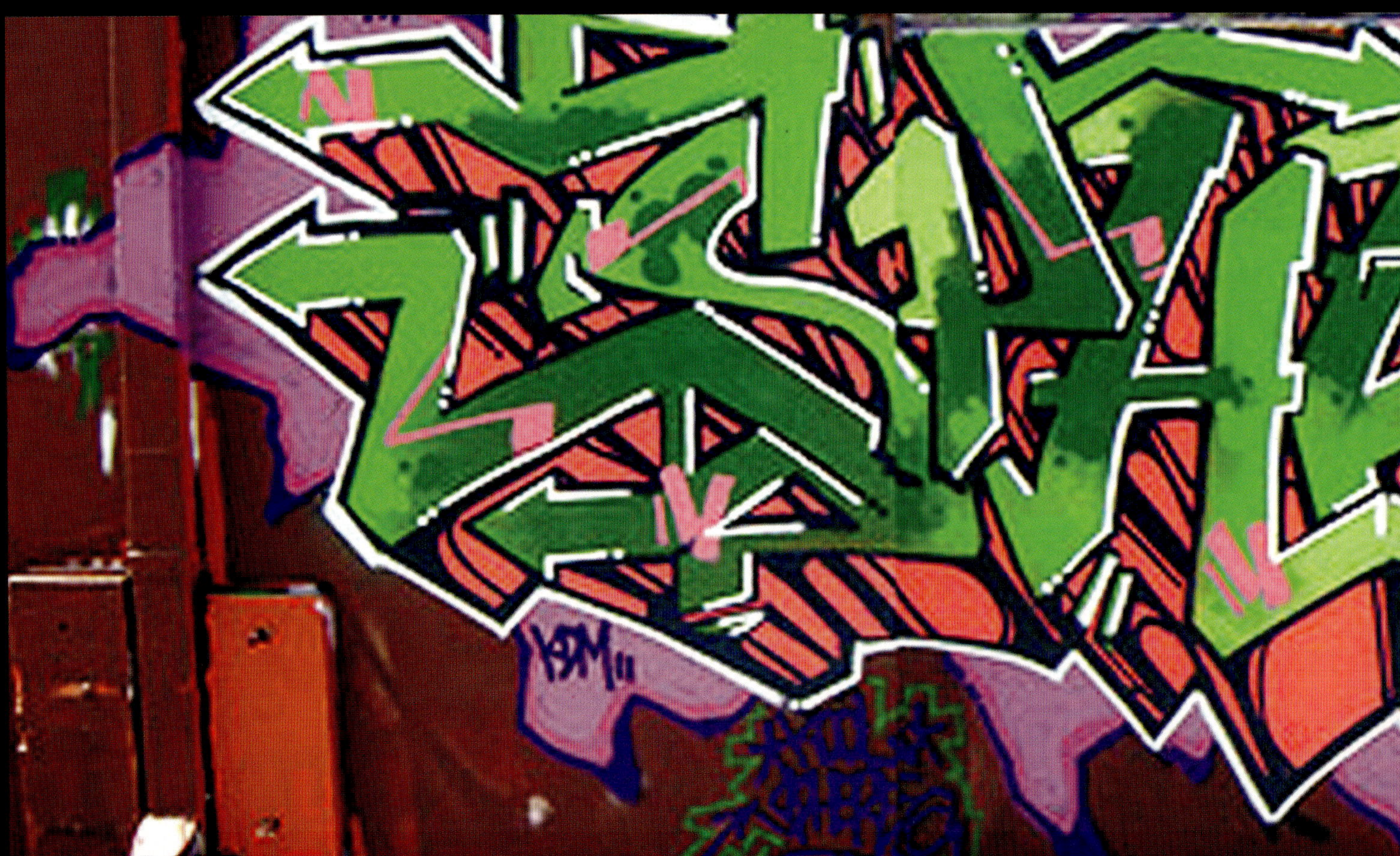

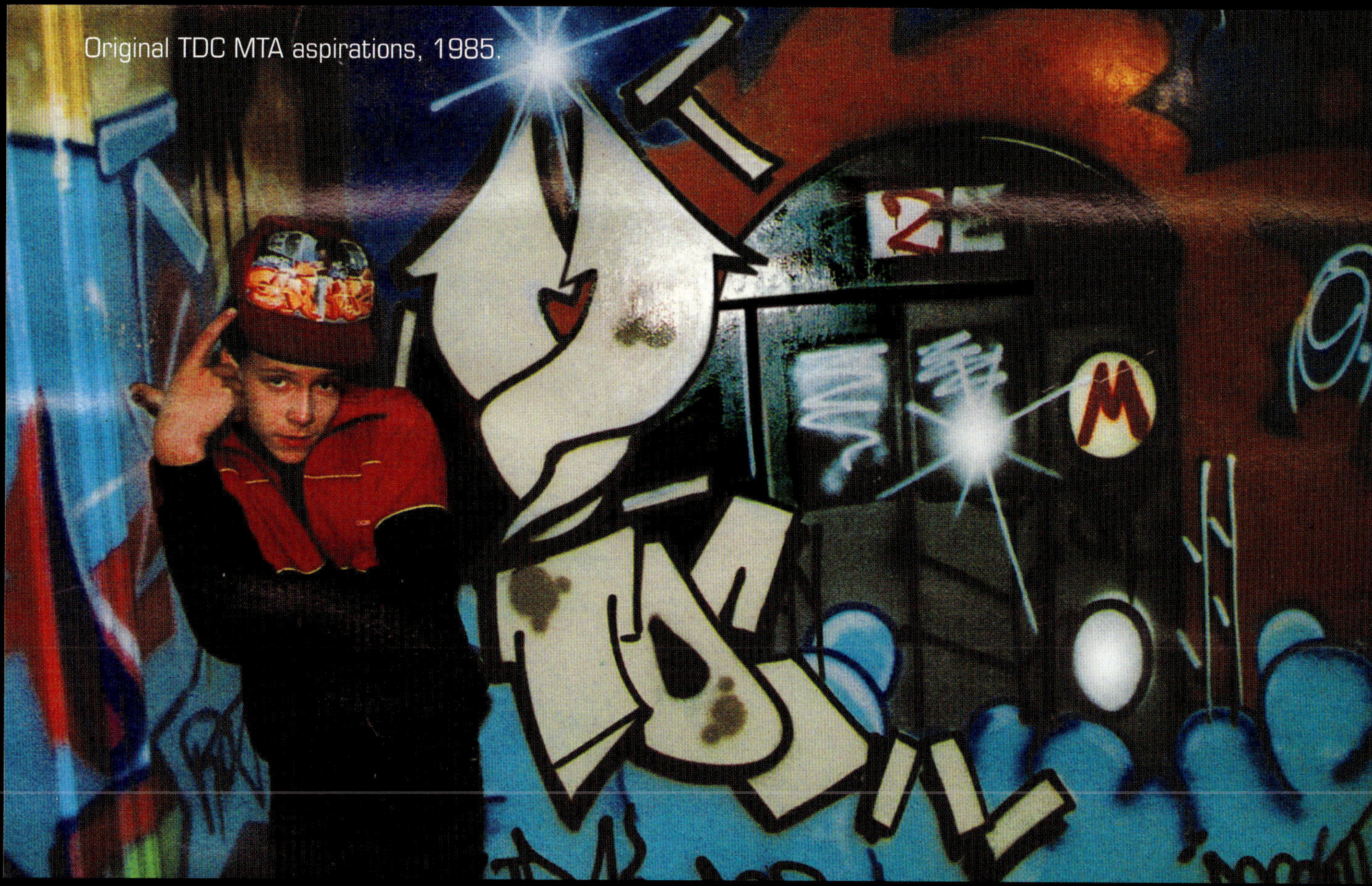

Original TDC MTA aspirations, 1985.

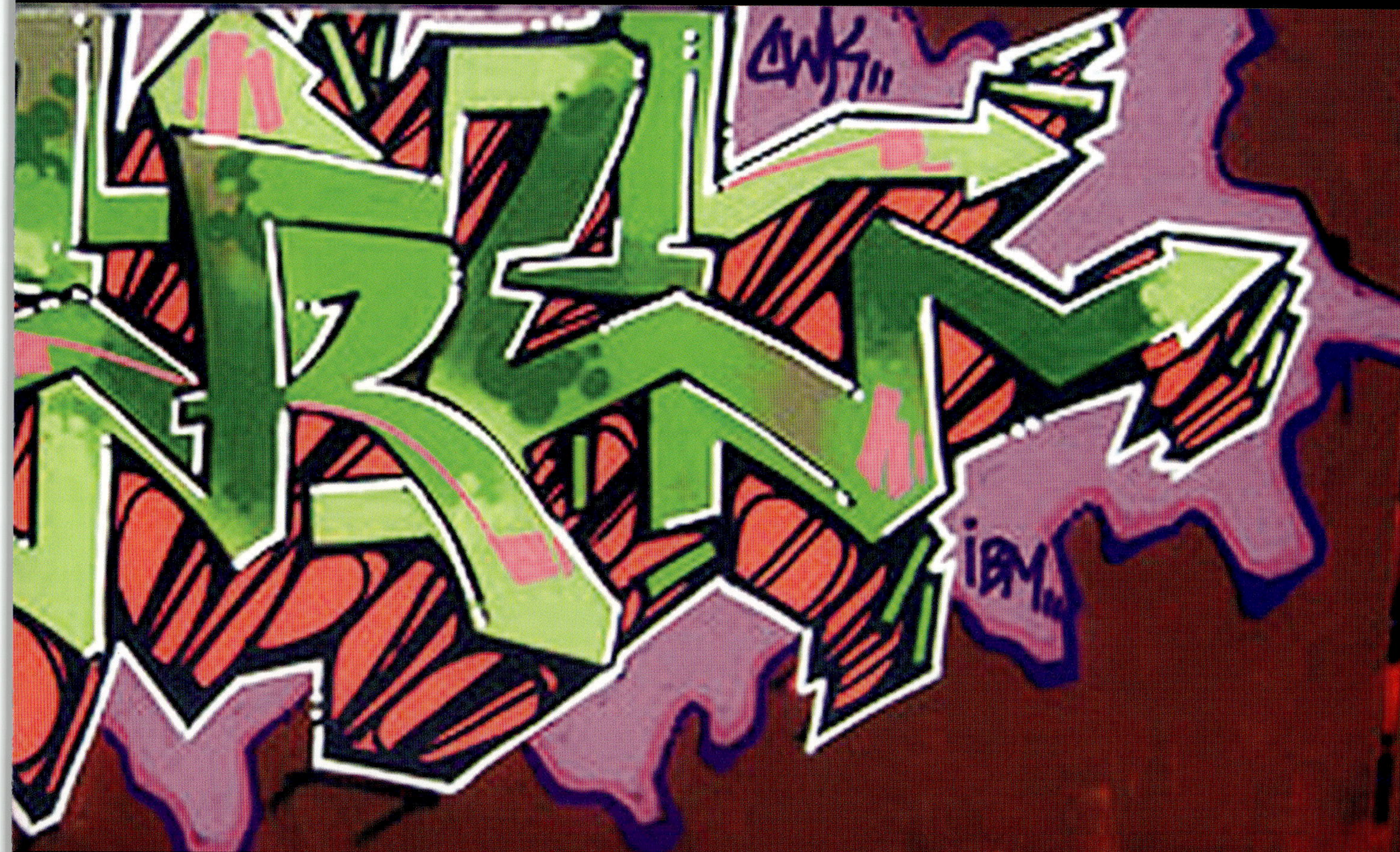

KOOL SPHERE, IBM, TDC, CWK, and KDM, Los Angeles CA.

"THE REAL," SHO TDC, Manhattan, NY, 1999.

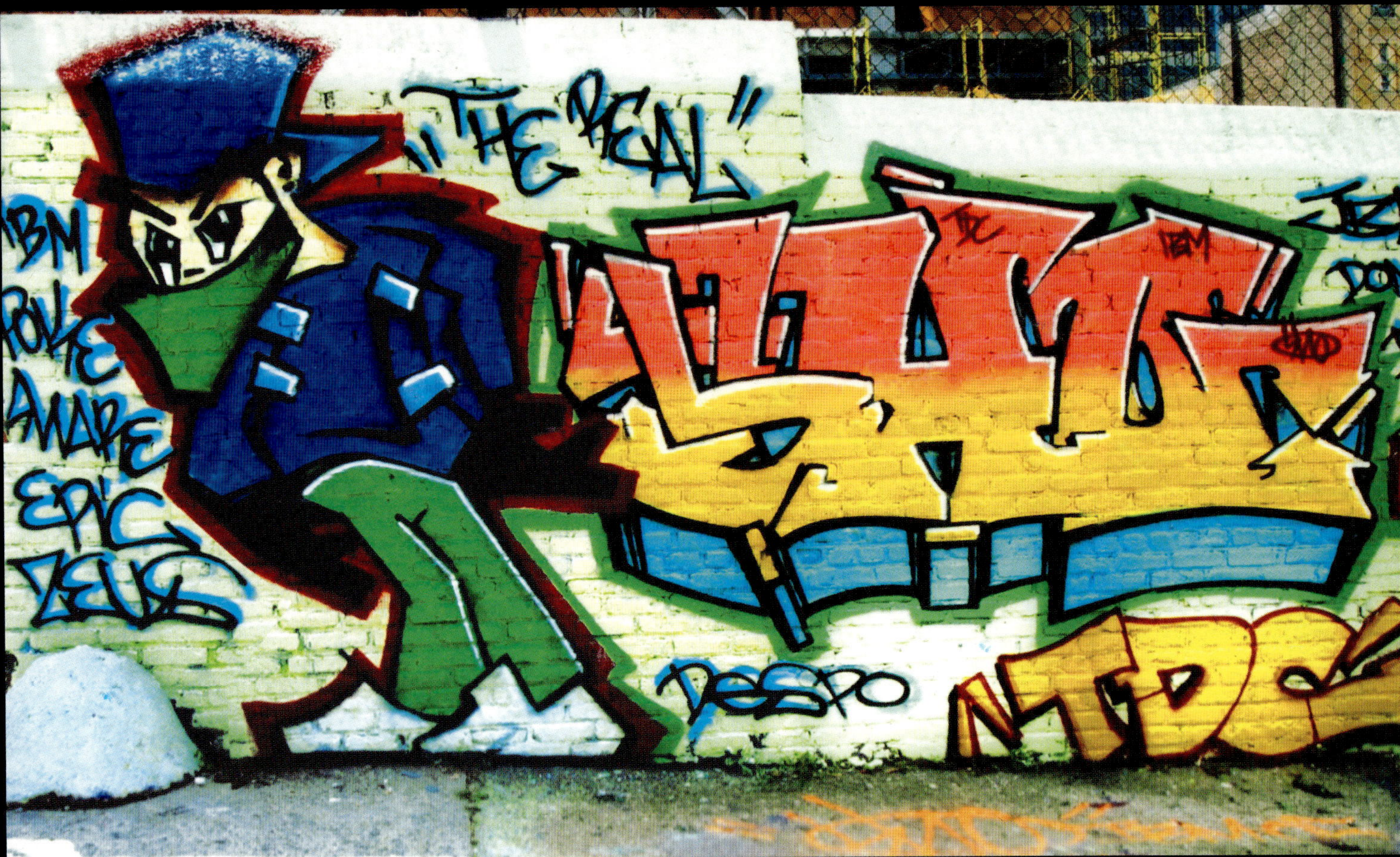

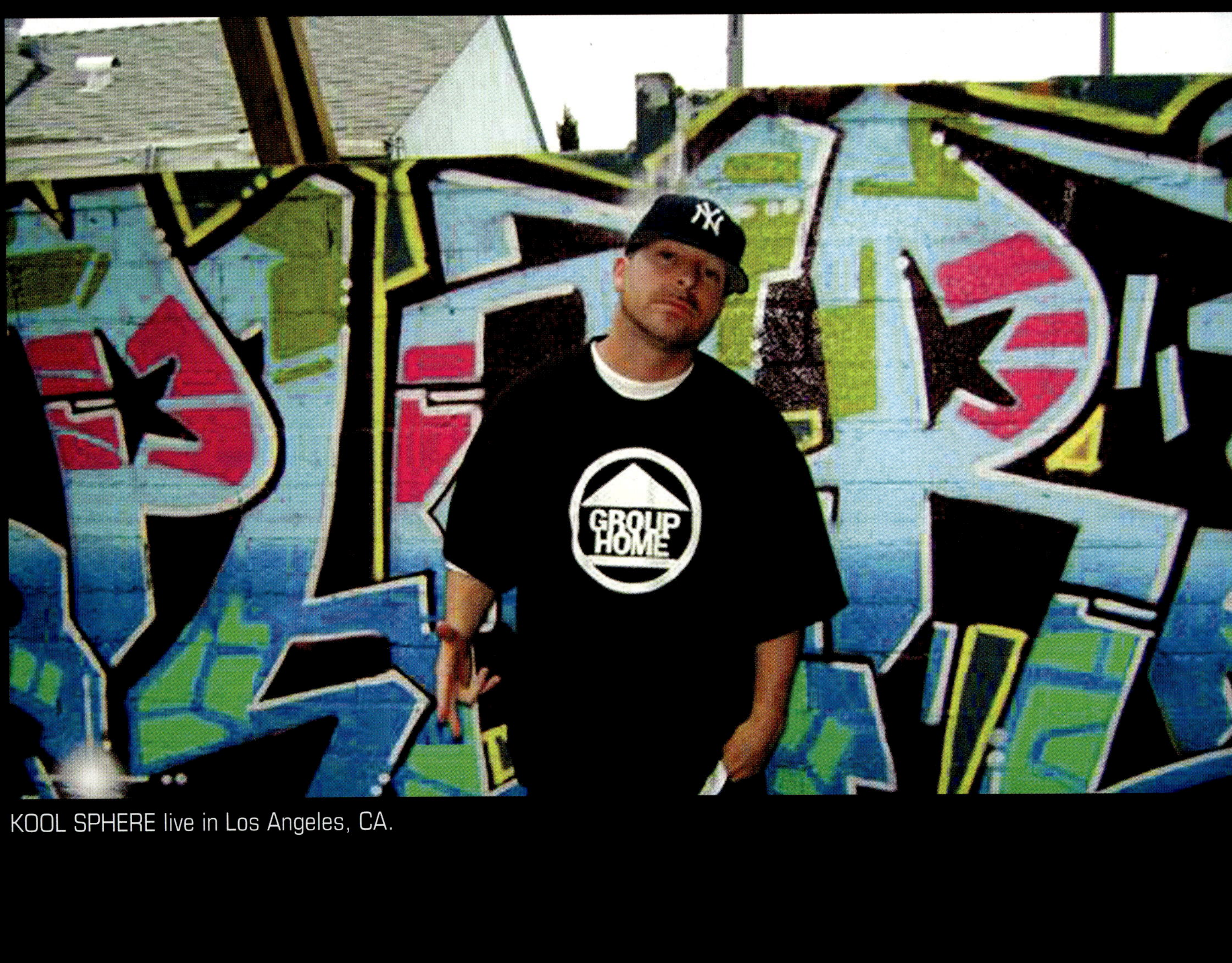

KOOL SPHERE live in Los Angeles, CA.

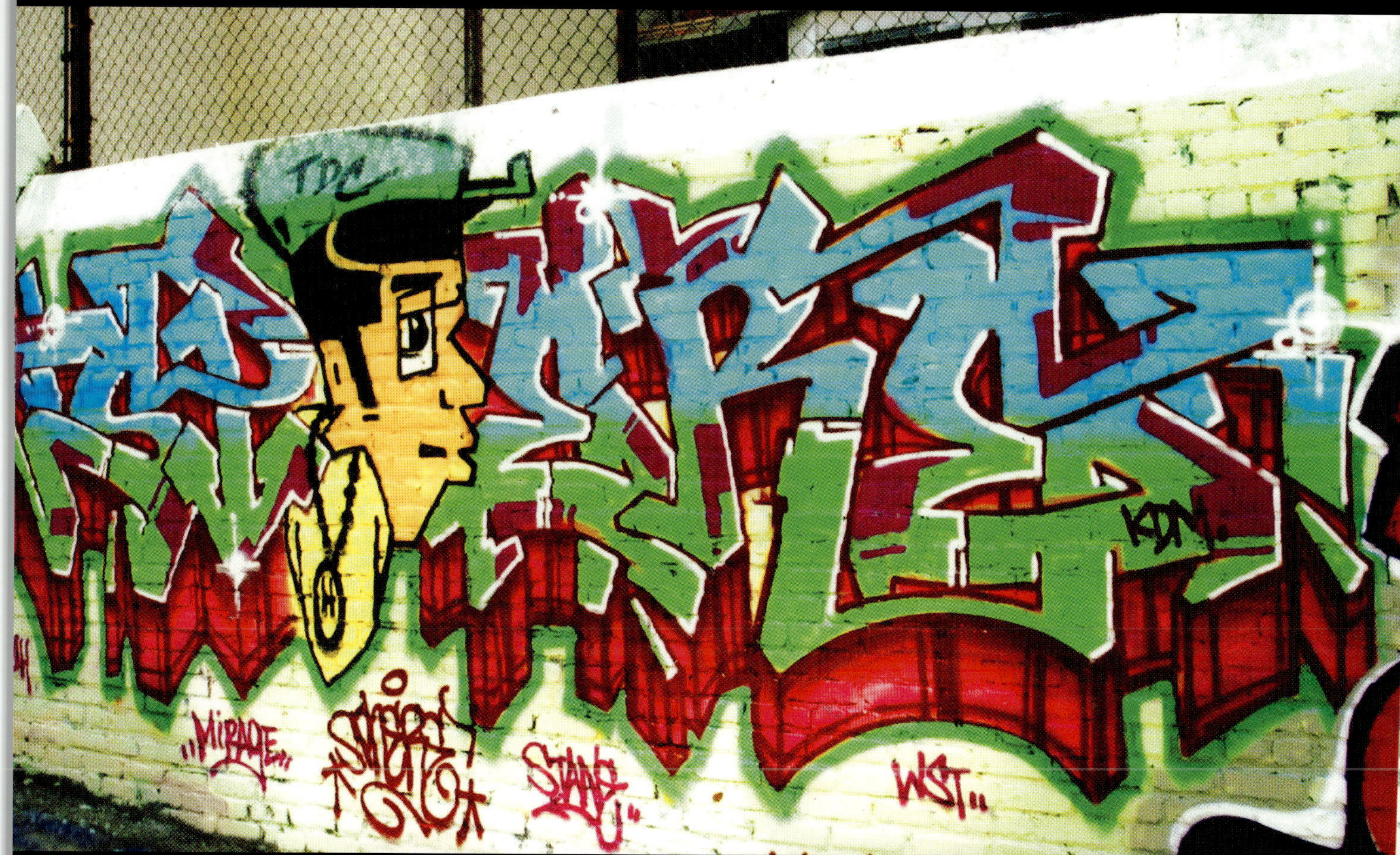

KOOL SPHERE WST, Manhattan, NY.

I started writing in 1983. Born in the Bronx, raised in Queens, NYC. First time I ever saw graffiti was back then, being carted around with my mom back and forth between the boroughs seeing Queens writers on the trains and highways like Kap TPA, Rec127, Sur 167, RIS Crew niggas. Ghost, Gato, Neo etc. and Saint TMRRIS...Sick from the Bronx, uptown piecers FBA especially...Kaze...Airborn...Spade127 and my personal mentor was Sketch CWK...(Craft Work Kingz). When I was a lil kidd... he would show me his pieces (back then him and Mirage R.I.P. were piecing the 2s, 5s, and then the 3 line). KDM was MAC, aka MIRAGE, original crew and that stood for KINGDOM. He was making major noise just about everywhere. Back then Sketch, Mirage, and Dome TDC took me to Hotel Amazon NYC to my first graffiti show. I was this lil shorty being introduced to established writers like Lee, Phase2, SHO, DC3 TDC, Gemini CWK, and ended the night watching a slide show of the featured writers and burnaz they recently had pulled off. Mad fresh styles.

-Kool Sphere, TDC, CWK, IBM, TMR, WST, KDM.

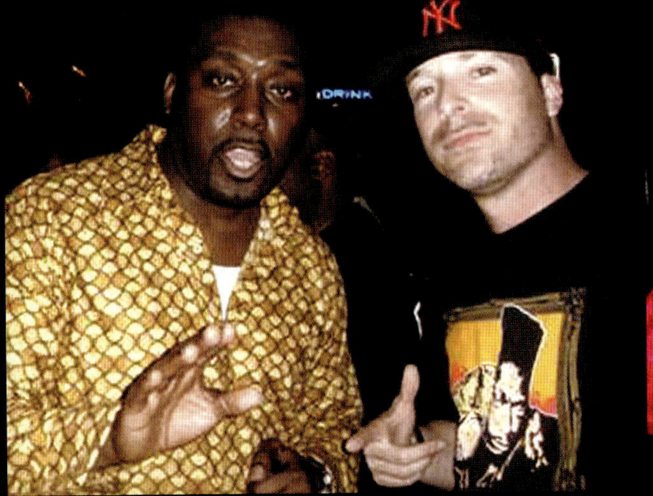

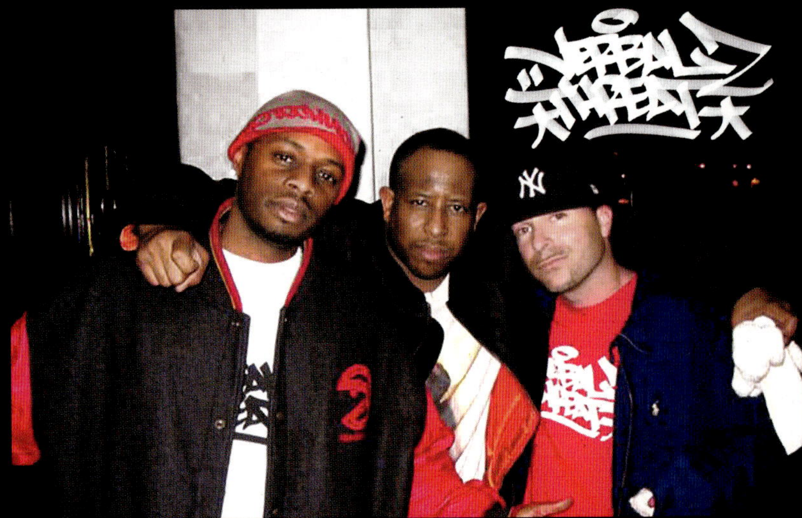

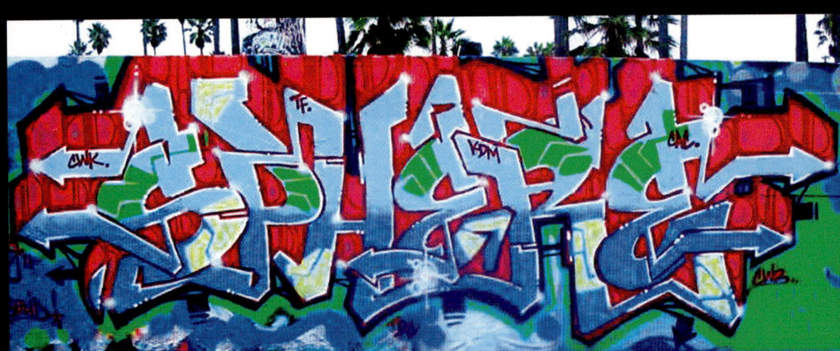

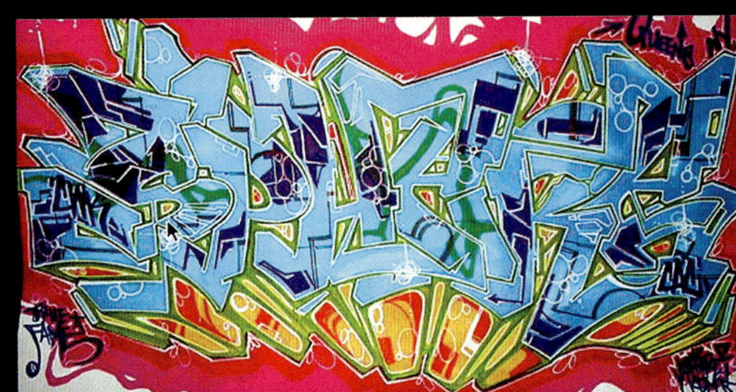

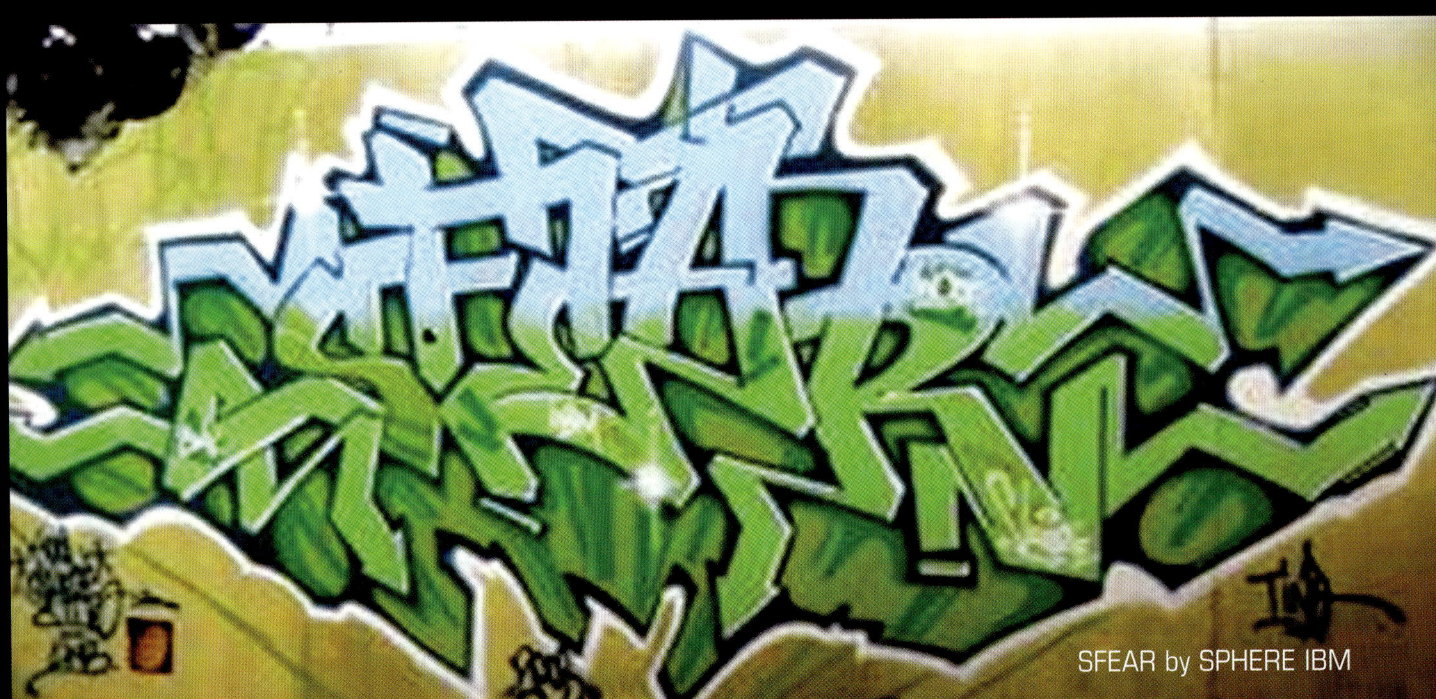

SFEAR by SPHERE IBM

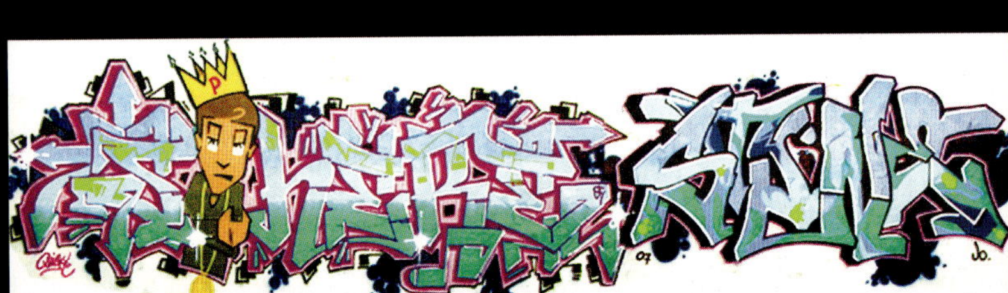

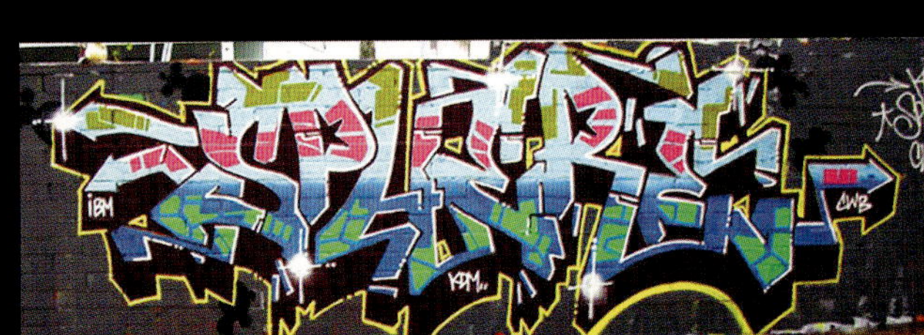

I believe the year was around 1988 in the fall. I was waiting in front of White Castle on Northern Blvd. in Queens to get scooped up for this graffiti show in Manhattan. The next thing I know I hear my name being called out from what sounds like a gigantic speaker. Yo, Sphere!!! Where you at?? All of a sudden a slick red Nissan 300 ZX screams around the corner and pulls up right in front of me. In the car was Sketch CWK, Mirage KDM, and Dome, aka Zoo, TDC. Turned out it was Mirage with some sort of megaphone yelling out the back passenger window. Sketch had his dime piece girlfriend at the time sitting shotgun, so I had to climb in the back cramped in between Mirage and Dome. We dropped her off with the quickness in Forest Hills and jetted to the city. We pull up and parked at this spot c alled Hotel Amazon in the Lower East Side. As we approached the front of the place I remember Sketch whispering into my ear, "They better let you in mother fucker!" I was mad young at the time and was hoping I didn't get sweated at the door. Sure enough, as everybody was going in the bouncer was like, "What's the deal with this kid?" Sketch quickly responded, "Come on money...let him in, he's just here to check out the graffiti."

★

As soon as we walked thru the door I hear this crazy reggae dance hall sounding beat coming from the DJ who just happened to be Phase2. The place was packed! Mad up writers were up in there, both street bombers and train piecers. Sketch was taking me around introducing me to writers all over the club. I quickly recognized Lee walk by and was buggin out that all these writers were all in the same spot chilling. We then went over to this section where there was chairs facing this wall with a projector displaying clips of pieces on trains. That was the first time I saw that whole car by Dome and SHO TDC that said "SLAVE TO STYLE." At that same moment, up walks SHO and DC3 TDC. Sketch introduced me to the crew and we lamped out looking at all the graff flicks for the rest of the night. From that moment TDC and CWK were connected and would burn together under their own crews. Shit was real enough that both crews already had crazy Dap and both had different styles and didn't push one crew in a real effort to morph styles or street credibility, it just wasn't necessary!!!!!

★

Soon after we broke out...on the way home Mirage started showing me these slides he was working on for this graff styled poster. It was a sick wild style that said "Grafeeti" it was spelled like that for the fact that he was doing his famous "feet" throw ups all over the city. It was definitely a special night to remember for me...and I thank Sketch to this day for being my mentor and showing me what time it was. Who would have thought twenty freaking years later I'd be meeting back up with Sketch during a Verbal Threat video and rocking a piece in Hells Kitchen with SHO and Roz TC5 on the same weekend.

-Sphere, TDC, CWK, WST

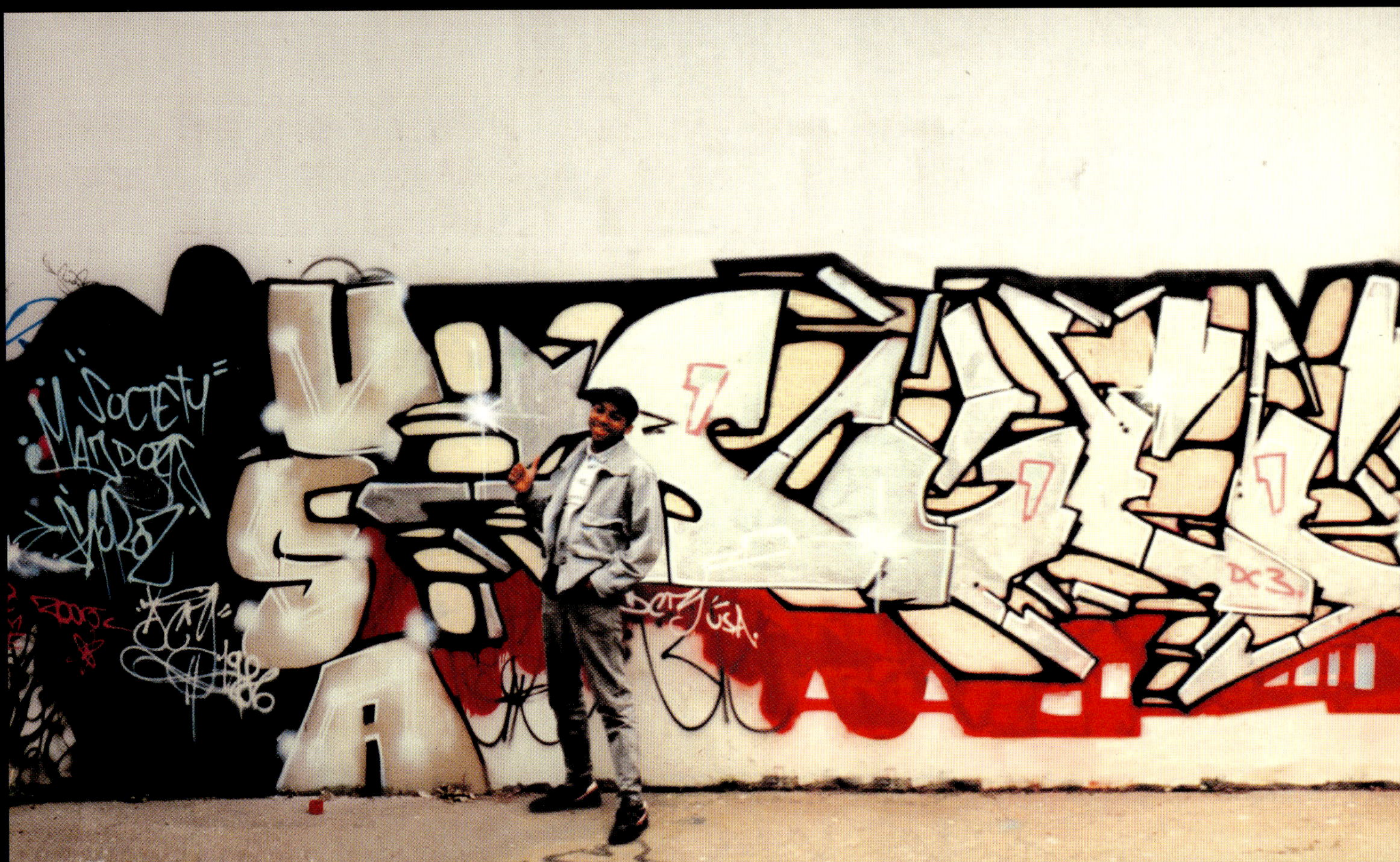

"SOCIETY MAD DOGS," by Unlimited Styled Artists, DCEETHREE.

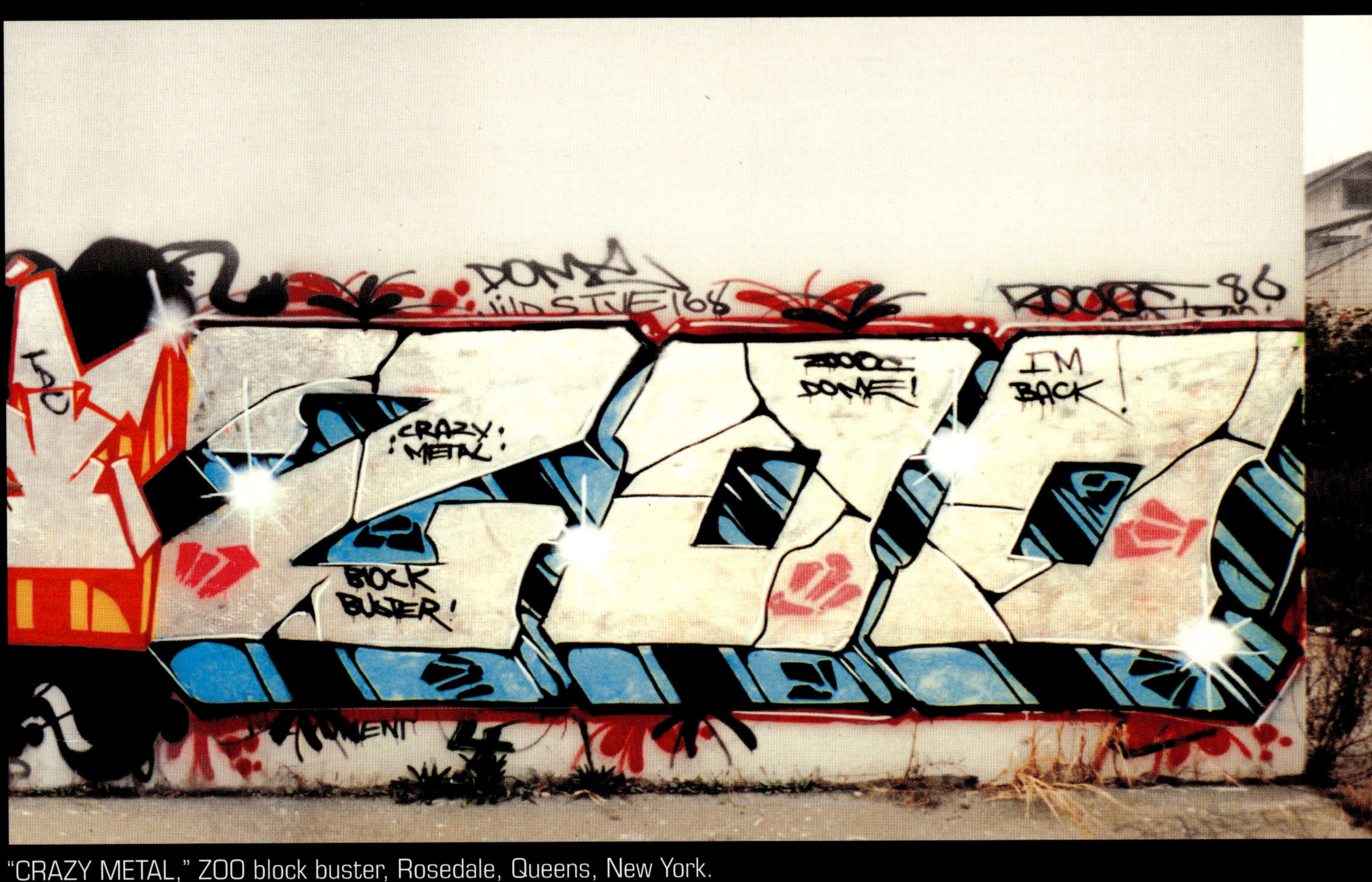

"CRAZY METAL," ZOO block buster, Rosedale, Queens, New York.

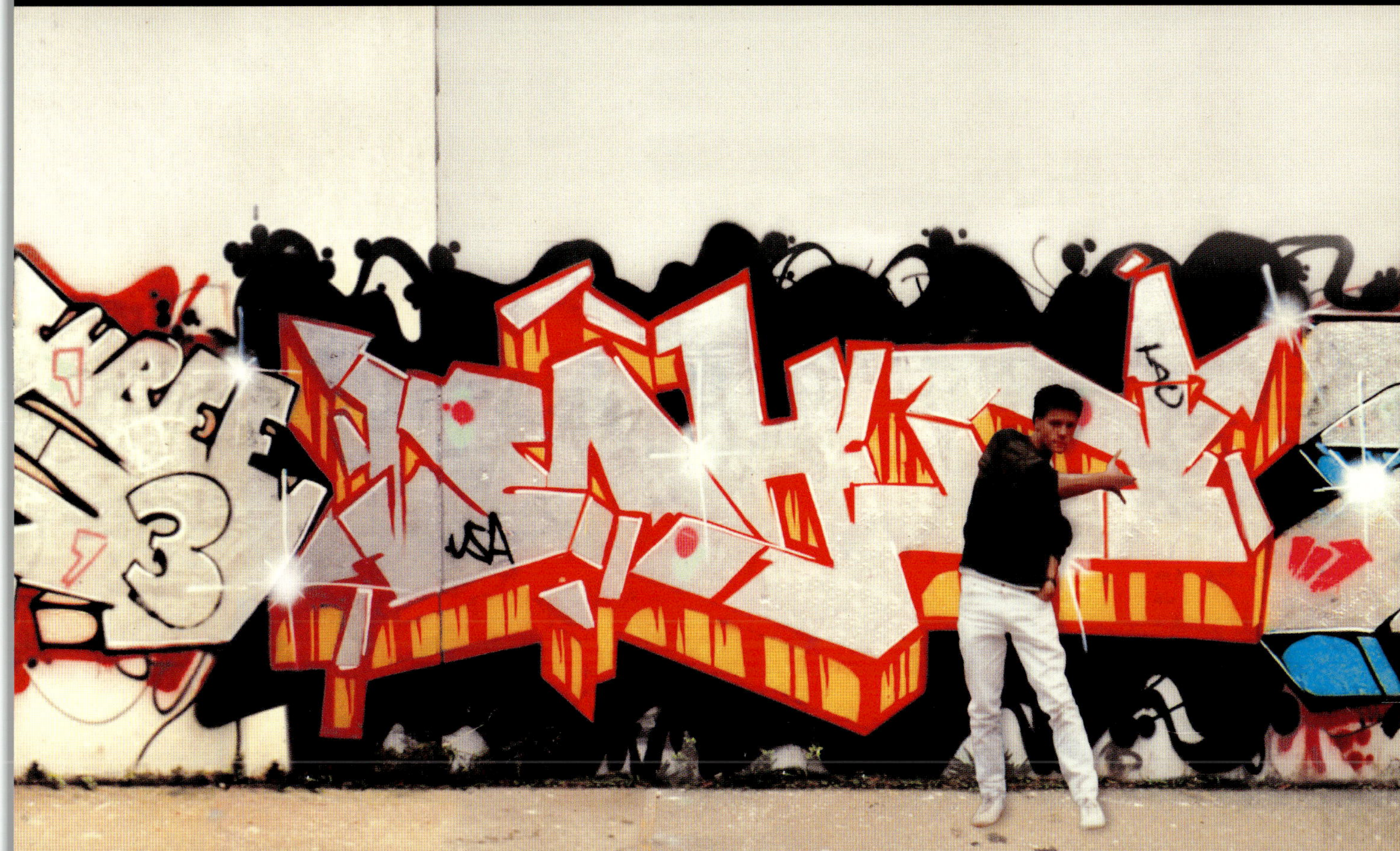

SHO USA TDC live on site at the Belt Parkway, Nov. 1986.

We called this wall "Society Mad Dogs"

This wall meant a lot to me because it's located on the Belt Parkway, right before it turns into the Southern State Parkway in LI. I first got turned onto graff back in the early 80s while driving to either my grandfathers house in Ozone Park from my fathers side or my grandfathers house in Ridgewood and Autumn Avenue in Brooklyn from my mothers side of the family. It was a prime spot being right in the park, right next to the parkway. You had maximum exposure all day long and the hot shit was it would stay up for a long time.

Back then if you got a month on a handball court in a dope spot you did real good. We hit this location a number of times and we rocked this at the end of 1986. We had already hit the 5 Train a couple of times and I remember that this wasn't our original mission. I recall that we had come from the Bronx lay ups and came up with snake eyes. A lot of time the lay ups were unpredictable and you'd get there to find unfavorable conditions or sometimes they wasn't there at all. We wasn't going home empty handed if we could help it. We did silver pieces with colors this night just to get up.

-SHO Unlimited Style Artists

The SHO "Slave To Style" DOME Train

We rocked this car at 131st Street and Jamaica Avenue lay up, right before it goes into the tunnel. Dome and I explored this tunnel after painting this train in June 1988 and went to another level down below via a hidden staircase. Low and behold, we found the JFK express silver trains layed up. We bombed those, too, a lil something just to add to our all-city status on trains. Never seen those and wasn't really looking. At the time the illest yard to hit was the East New York Yard on Bushwick Avenue, we had trains up in there, too. Back in the days, Risk FC told me he hit trains in the yard and got busted. There was always police actually patrolling in there and it was real easy to get caught because the Broadway Junction Yard is like a maximum security facility. The beauty of hitting the J Trains was that they, once in a while, switched over to the M Line and stayed there over in the Fresh Ponds Yard. That made us happy and that was where they filmed the opening scene of *Dreams Don't Die* in 1982.

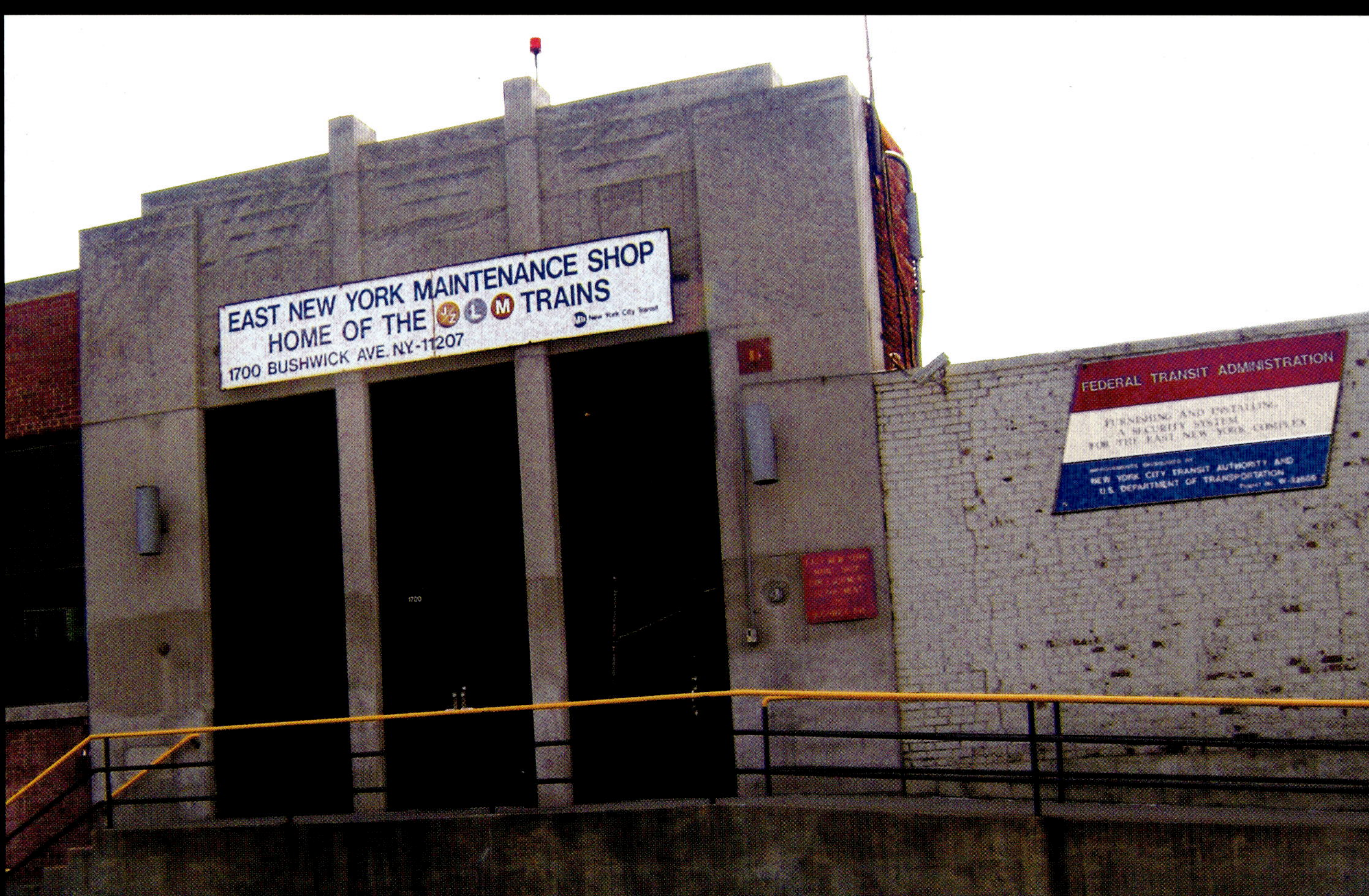

The J, L, M, and Z Yard on Bushwick Ave.

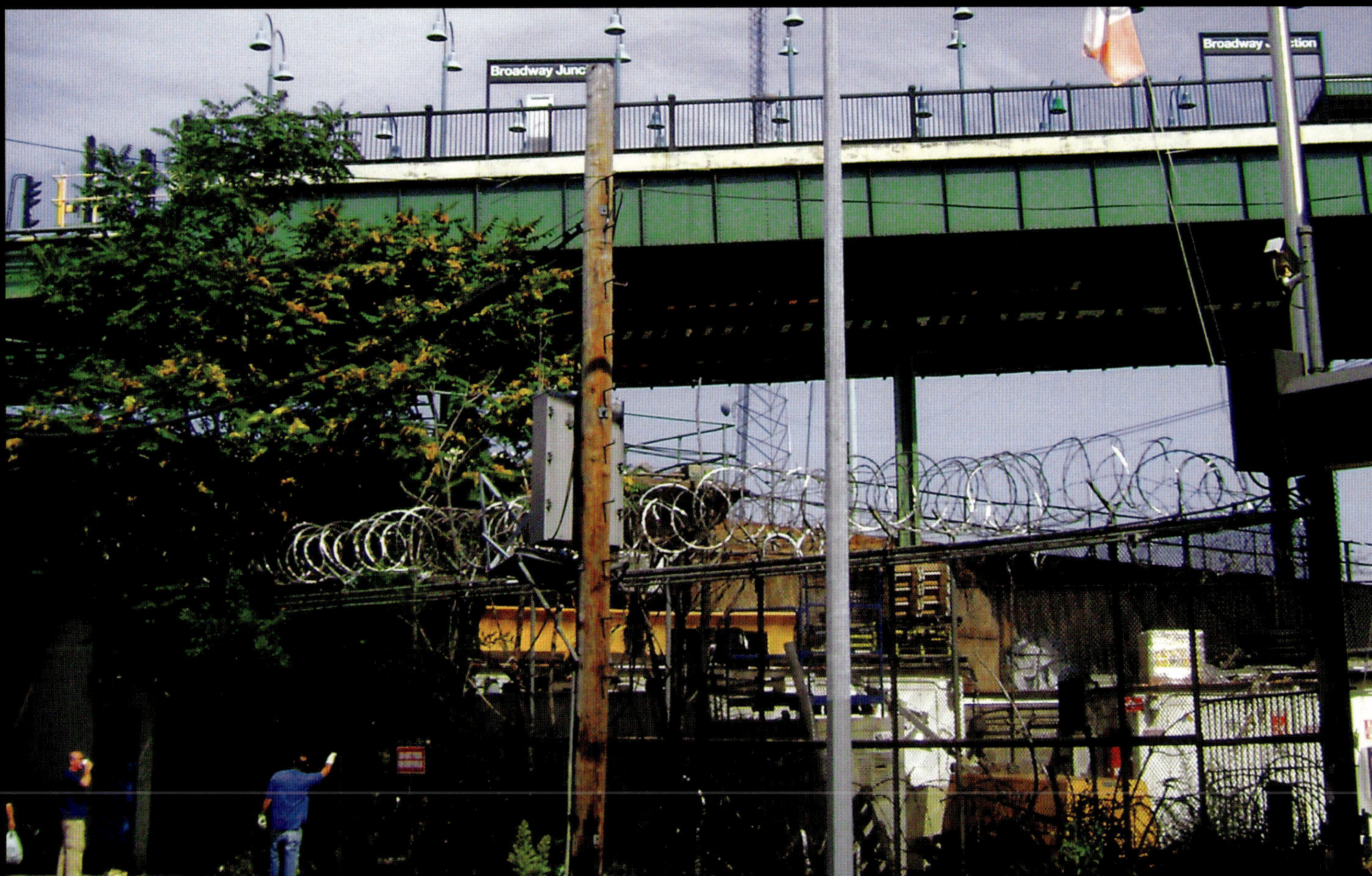

Broadway Junction.

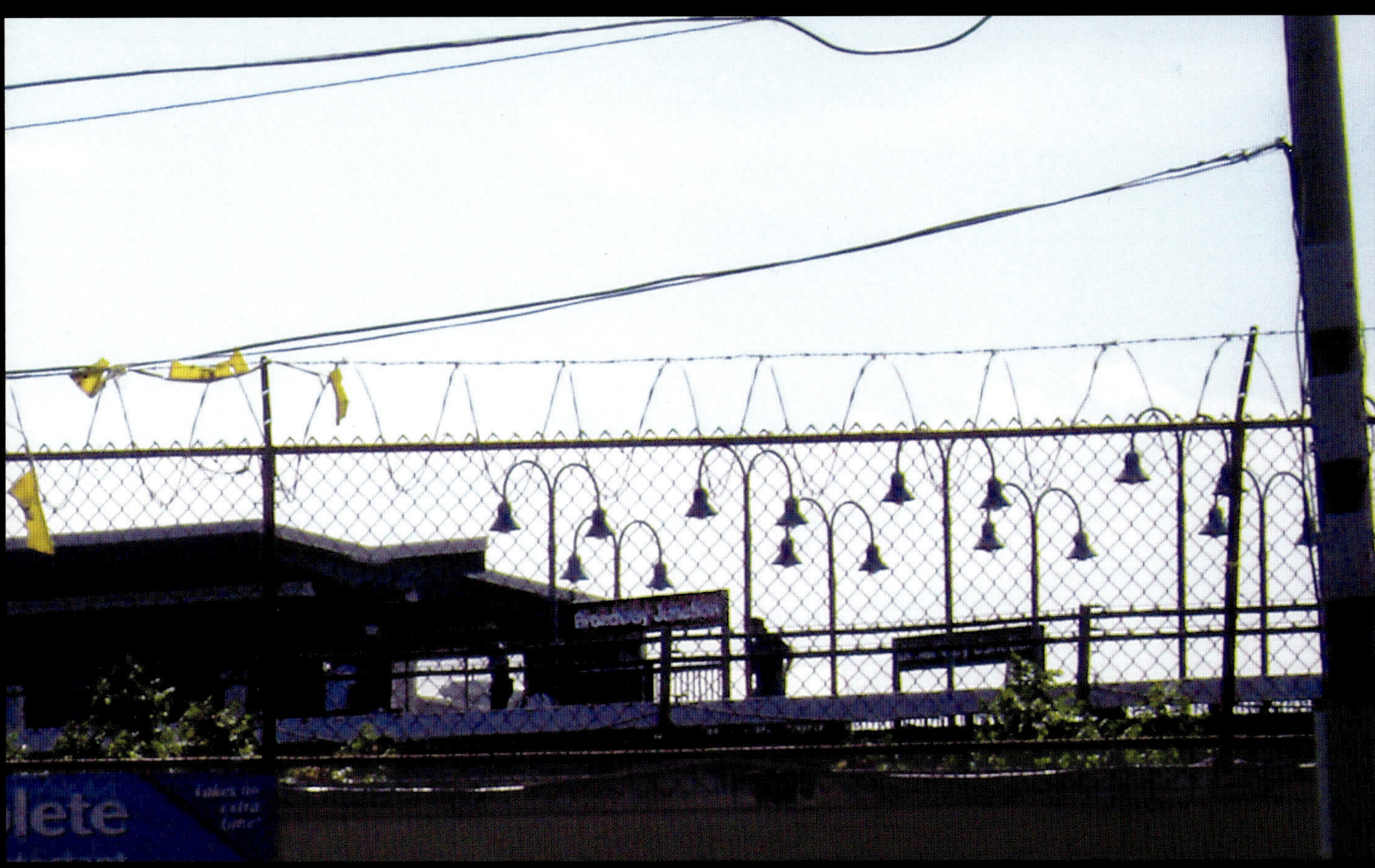

The back of the car wash was a way inside.

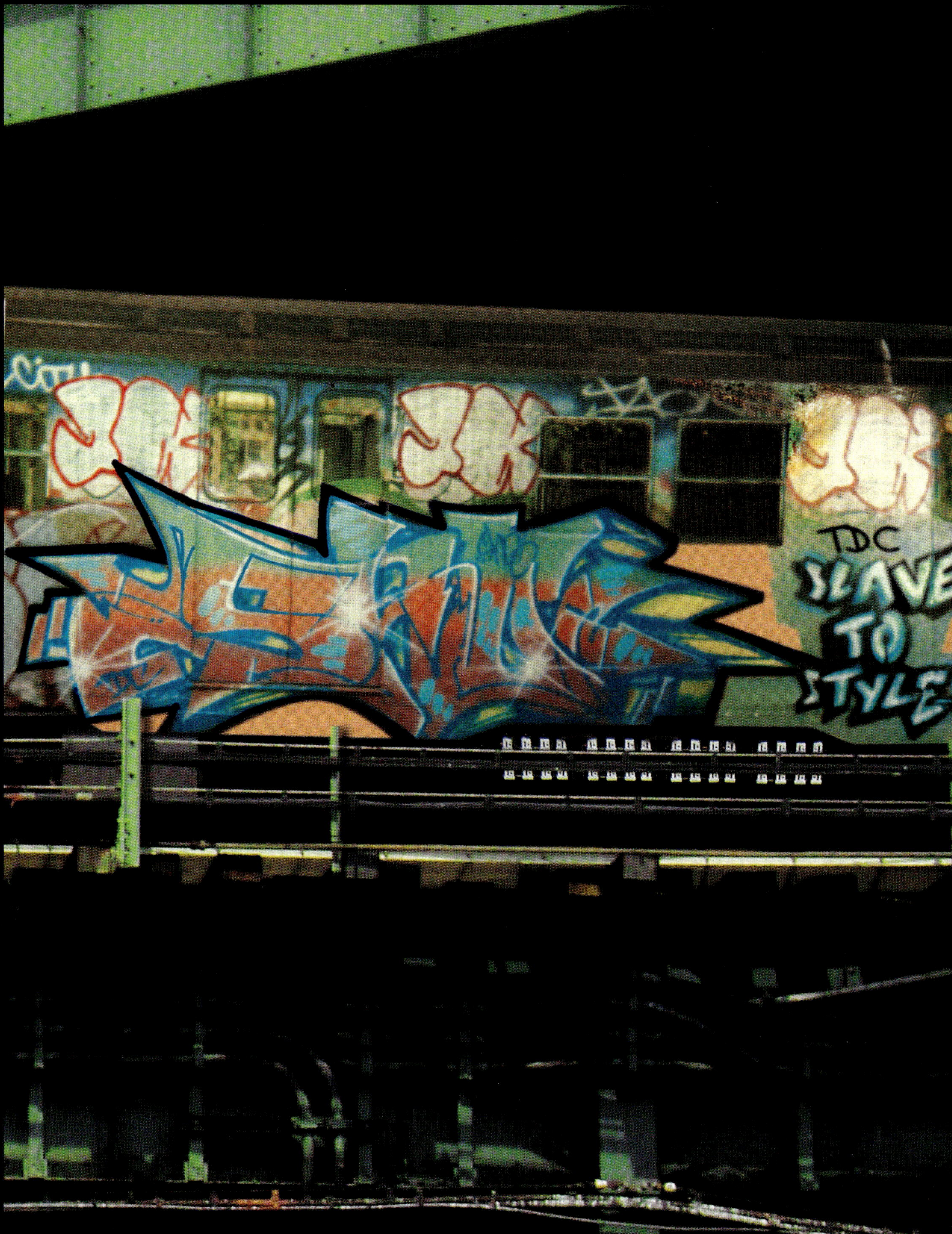

SHO, "SLAVE TO STYLE," DOME, J Train, Nov. 1988.

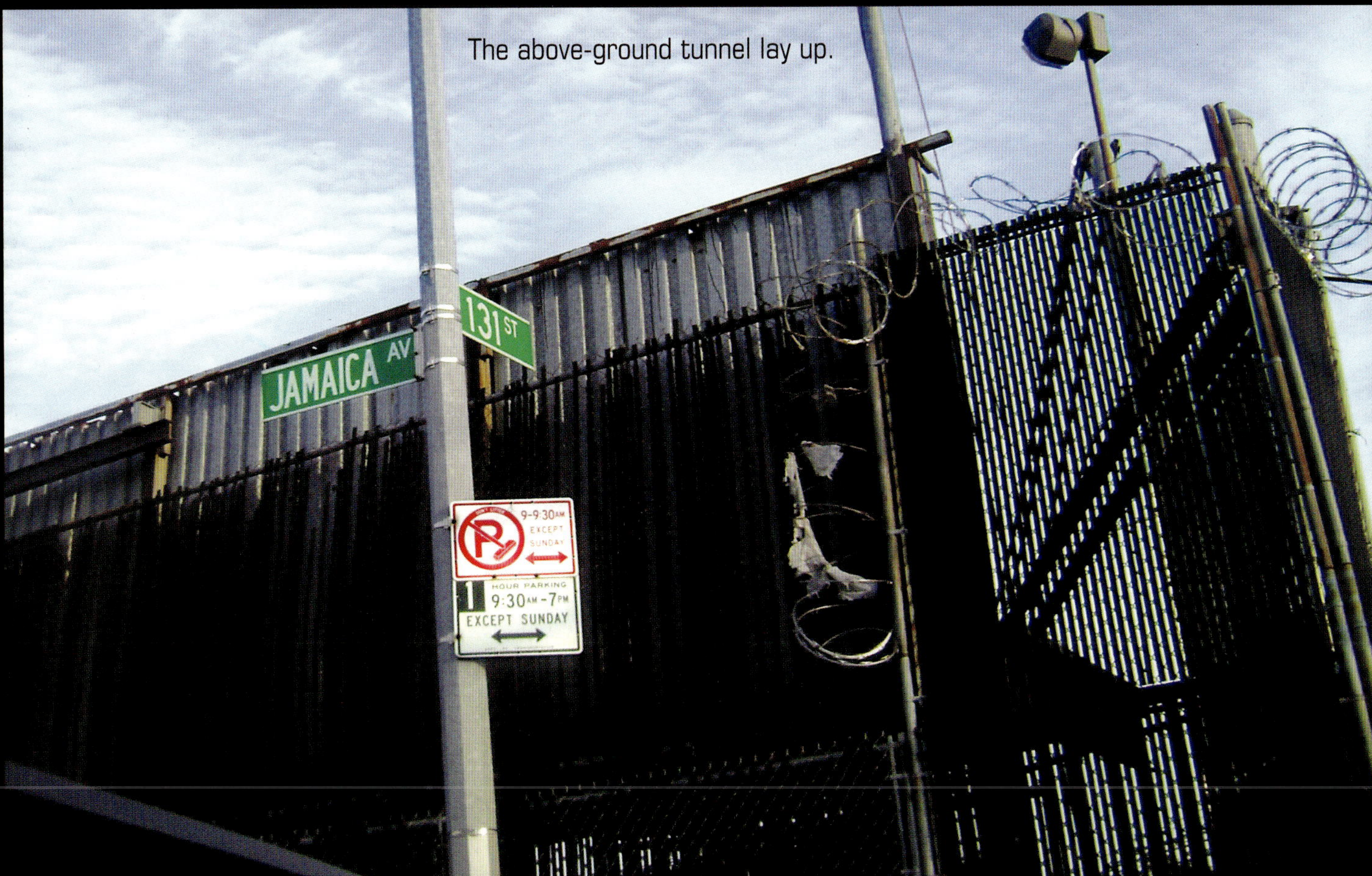

The above-ground tunnel lay up.

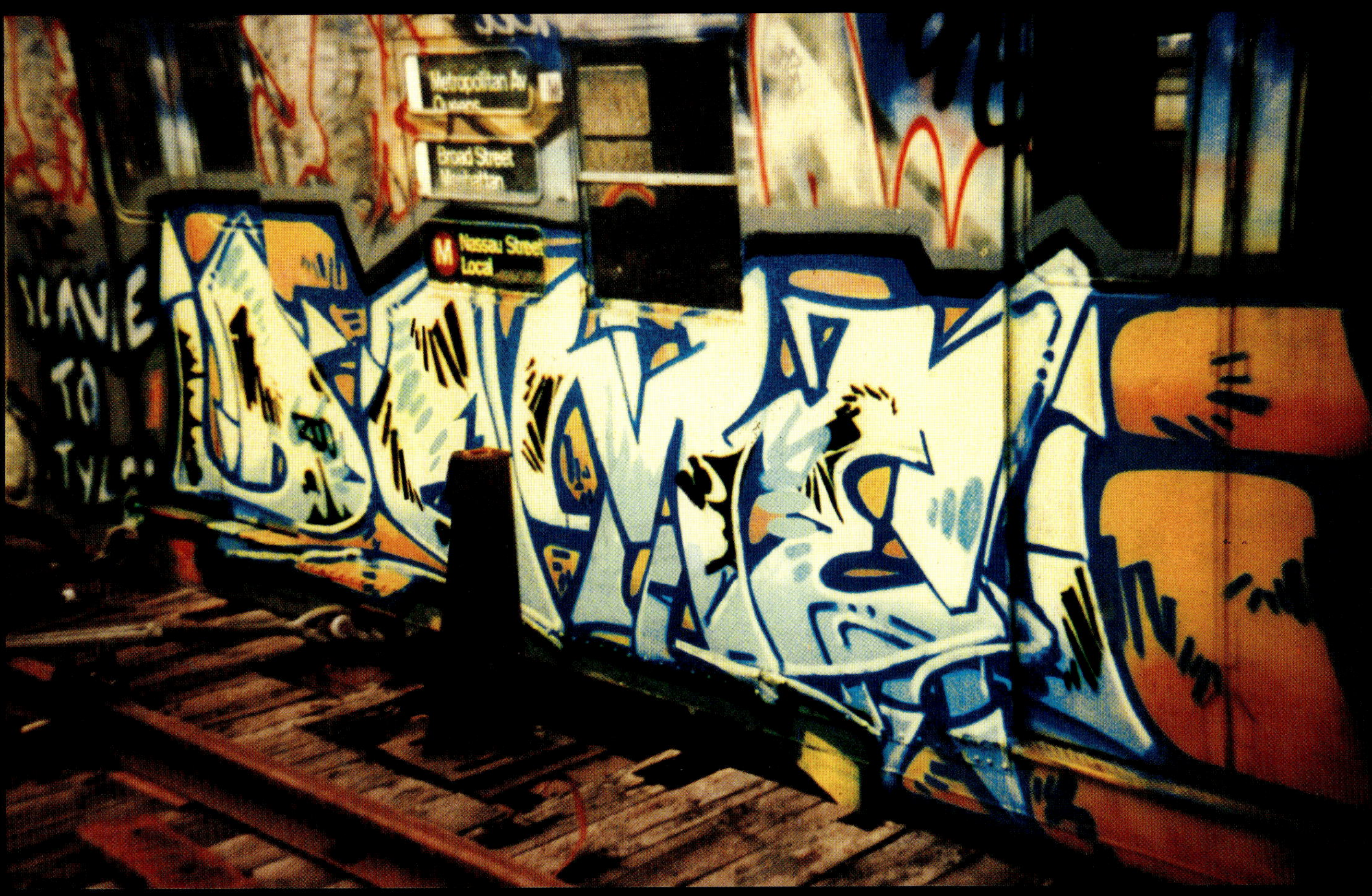

DOME months later after it had ran on the M Line.

DOME and SHO, "THE JUNGLE IS WILD AT NIGHT," J Train, done June 20, 1988.

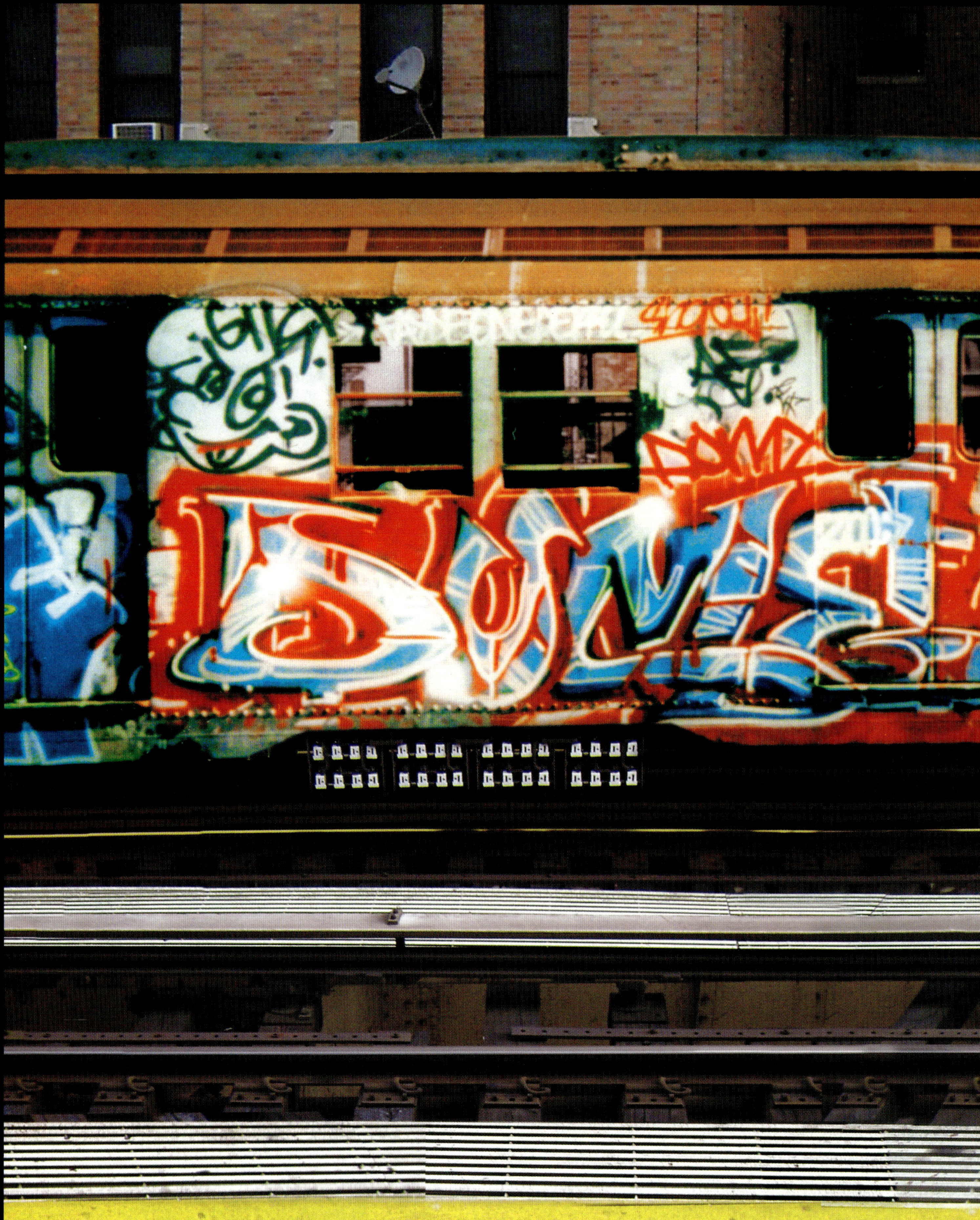

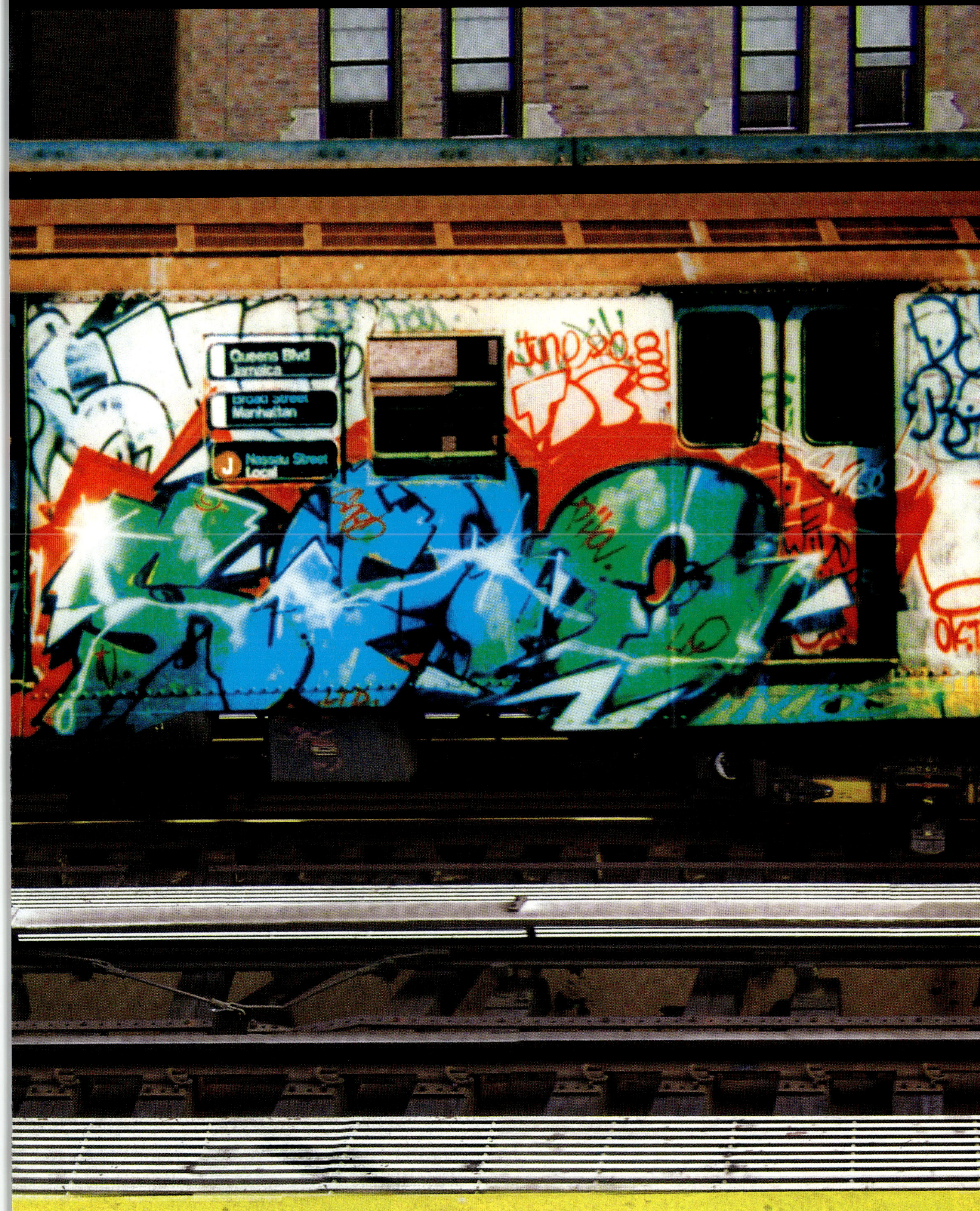

We rocked this in the J Train 121st St. Station lay up.

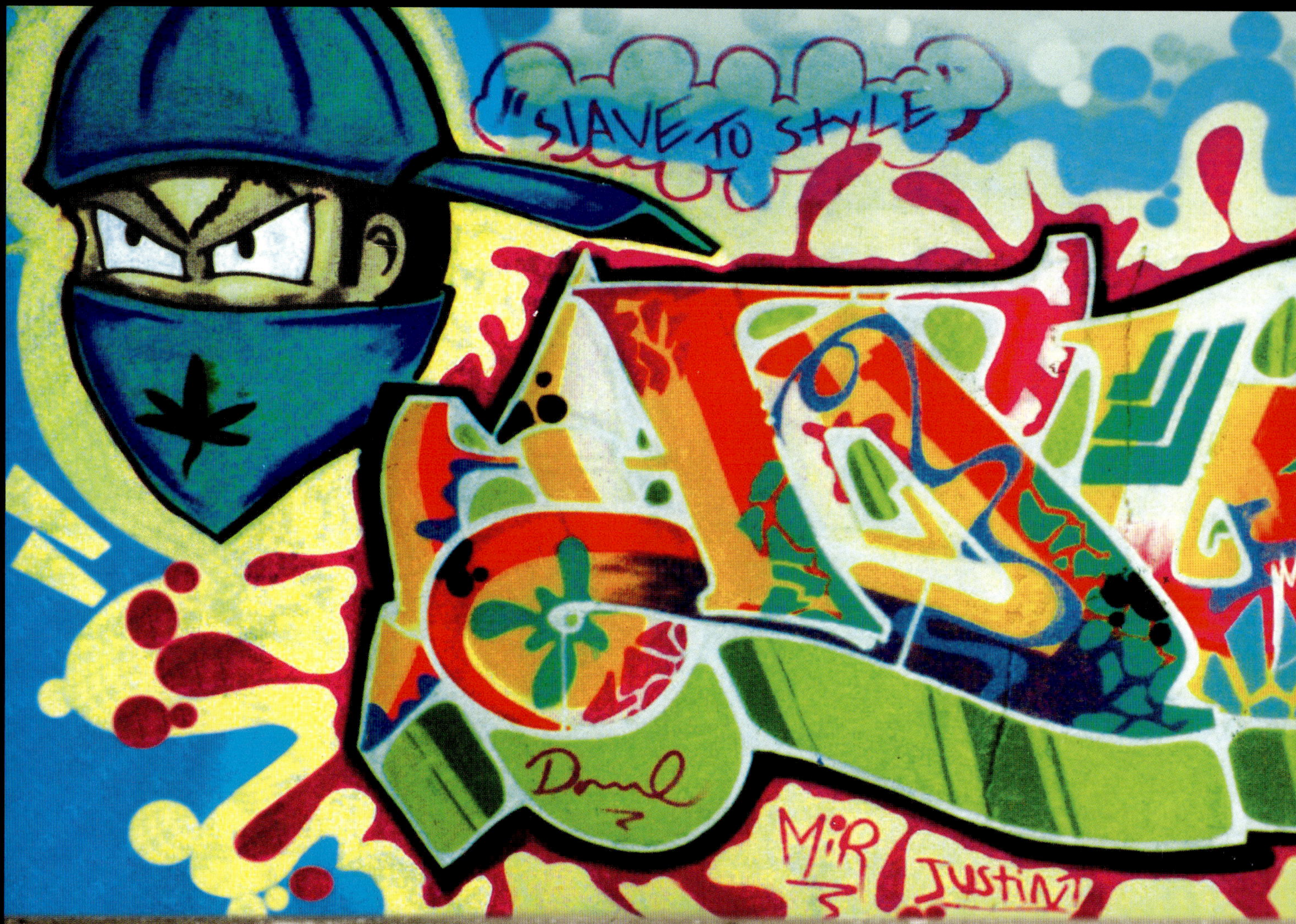

DOME done at Franklin K. Lane High School, Brooklyn, NY.

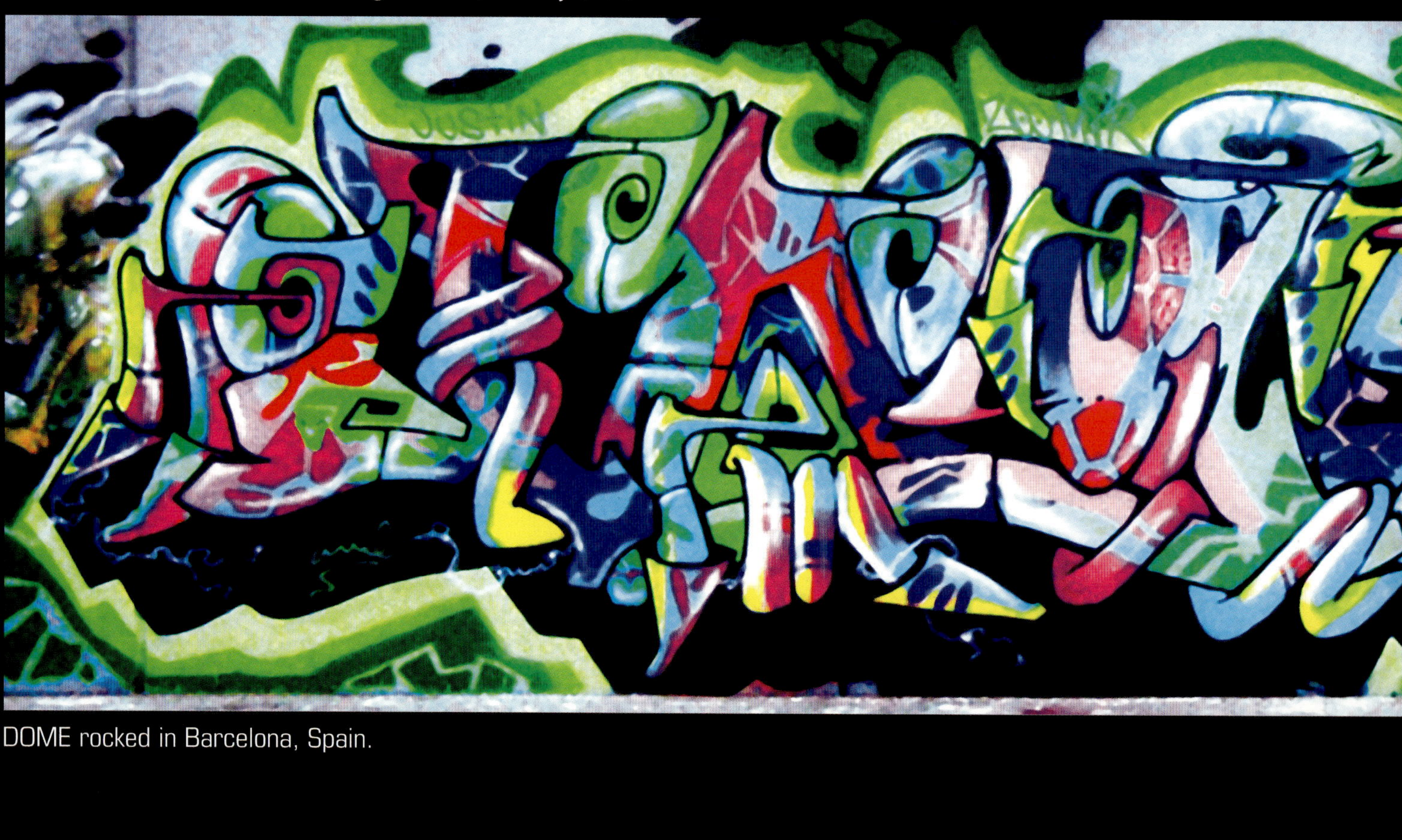
DOME rocked in Barcelona, Spain.

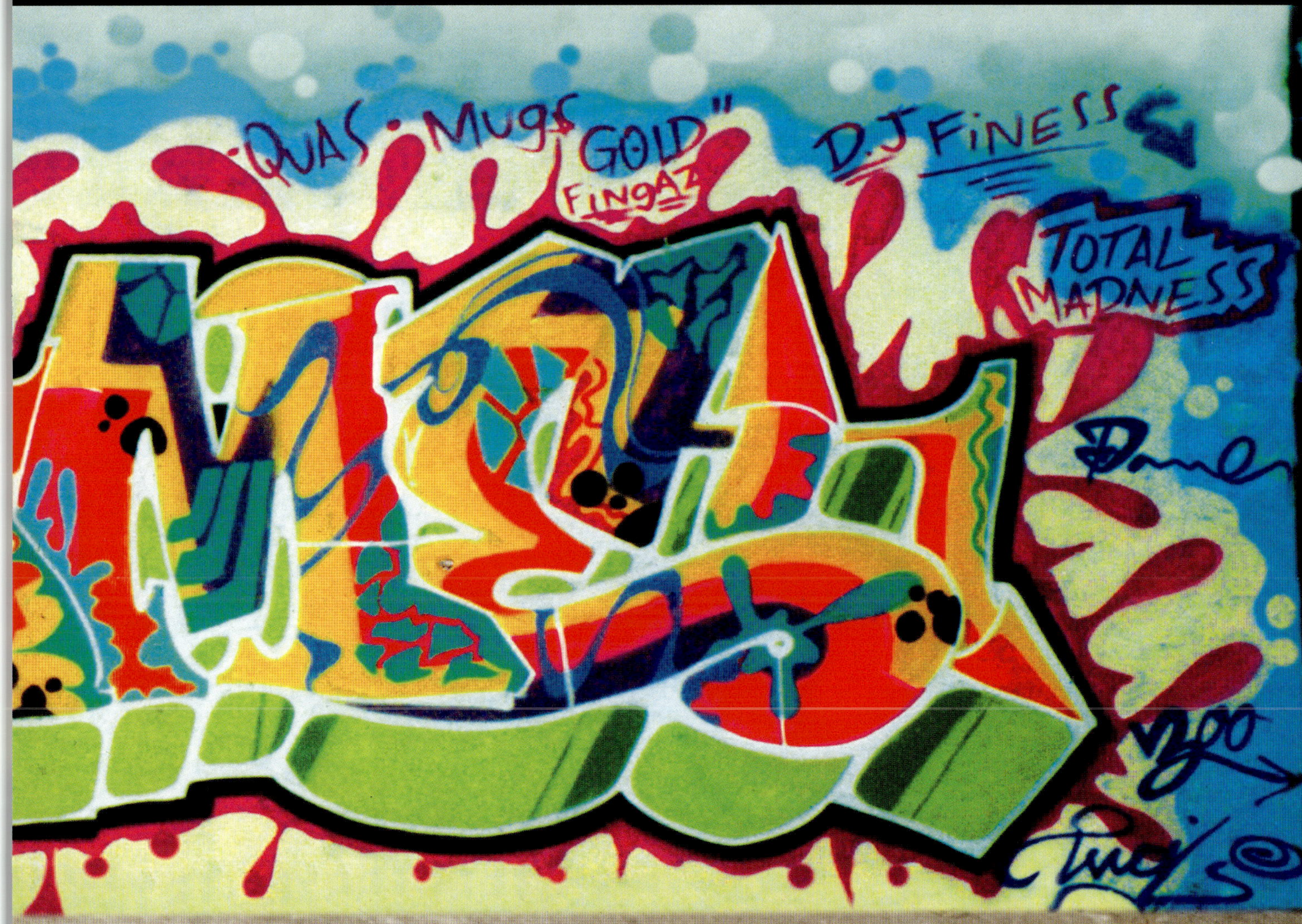

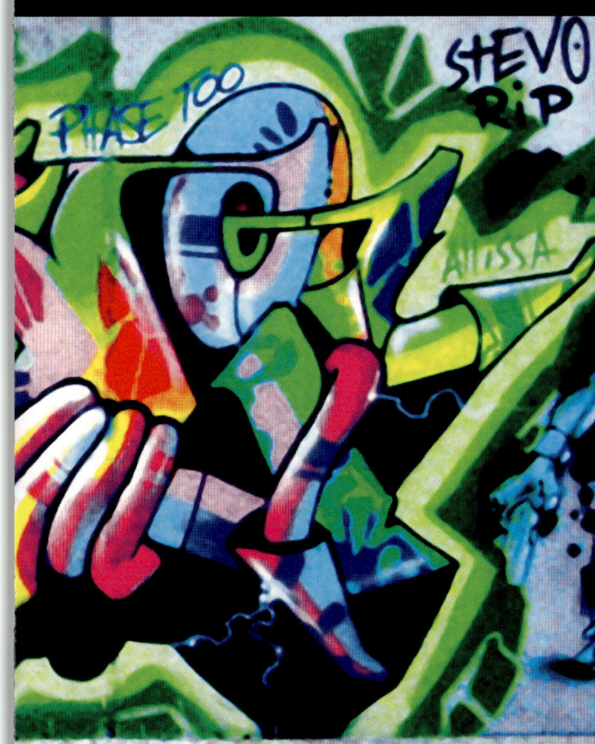

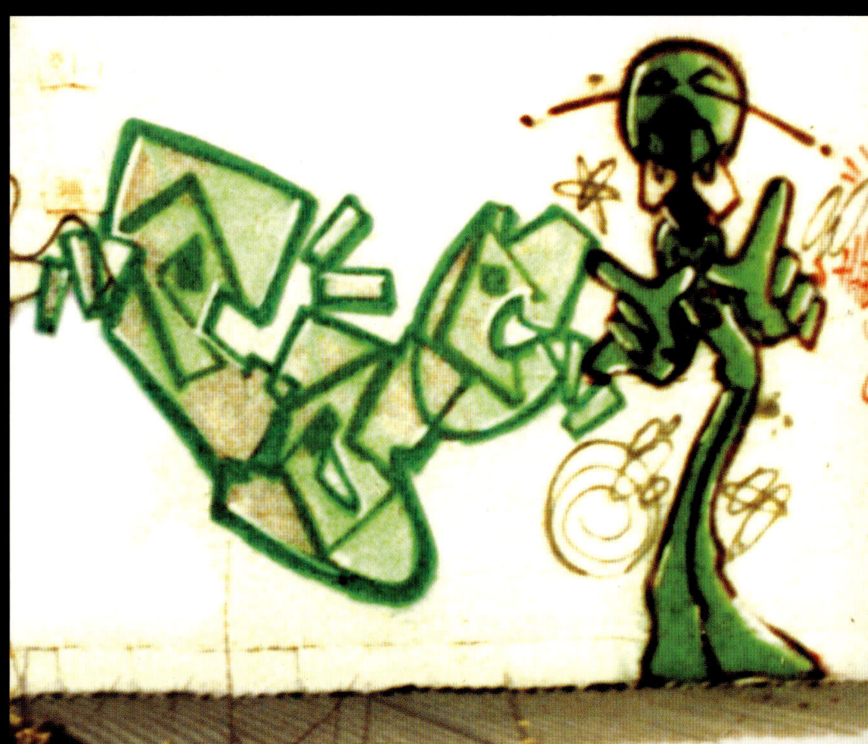

Early TDC Martian rooftop by DC3, Jun. 1985.

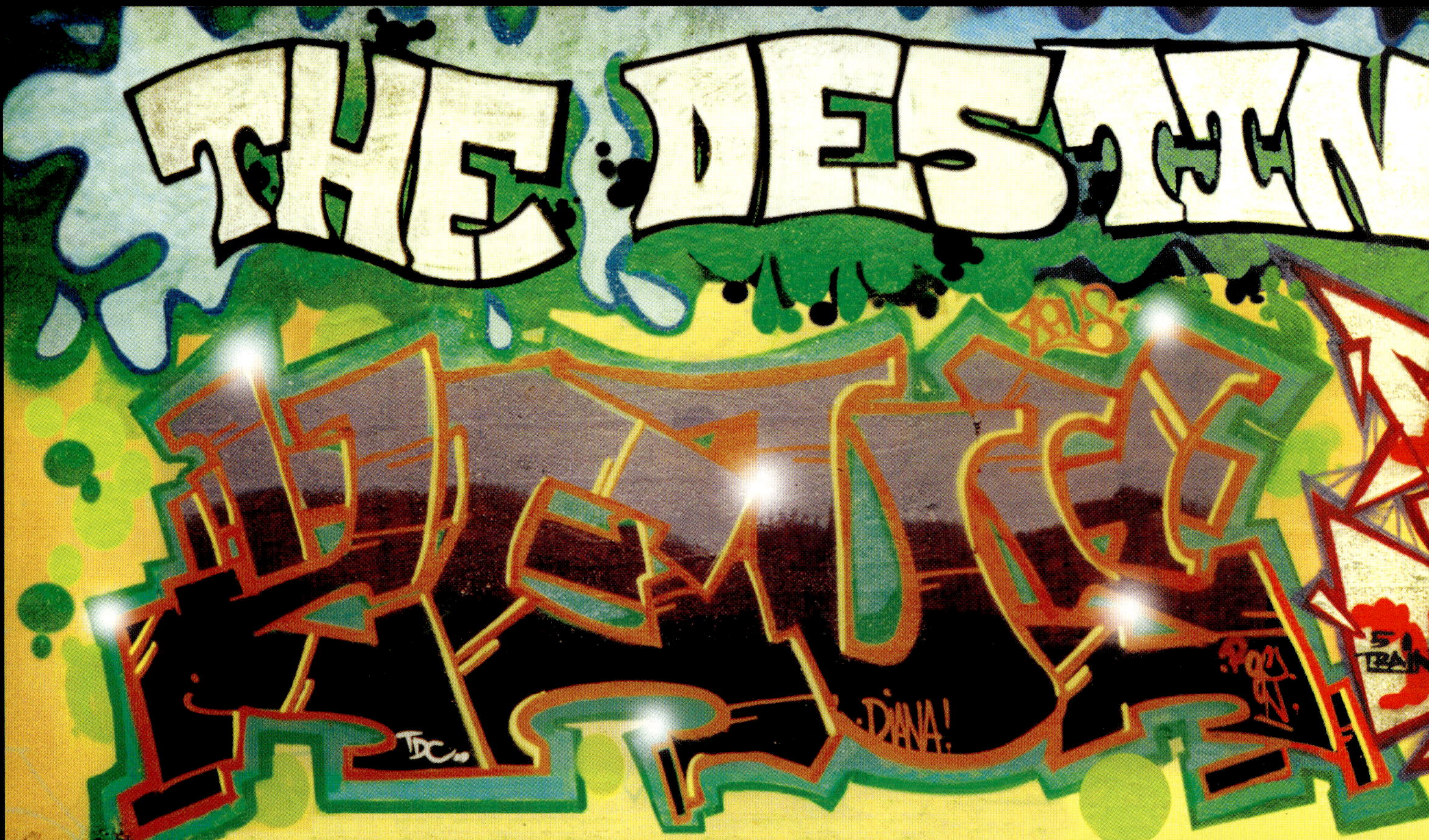

ZEUS and SHO, "THE DESTINY CHILDREN," production in "Boys Field." Brooklyn, NY, 1996.

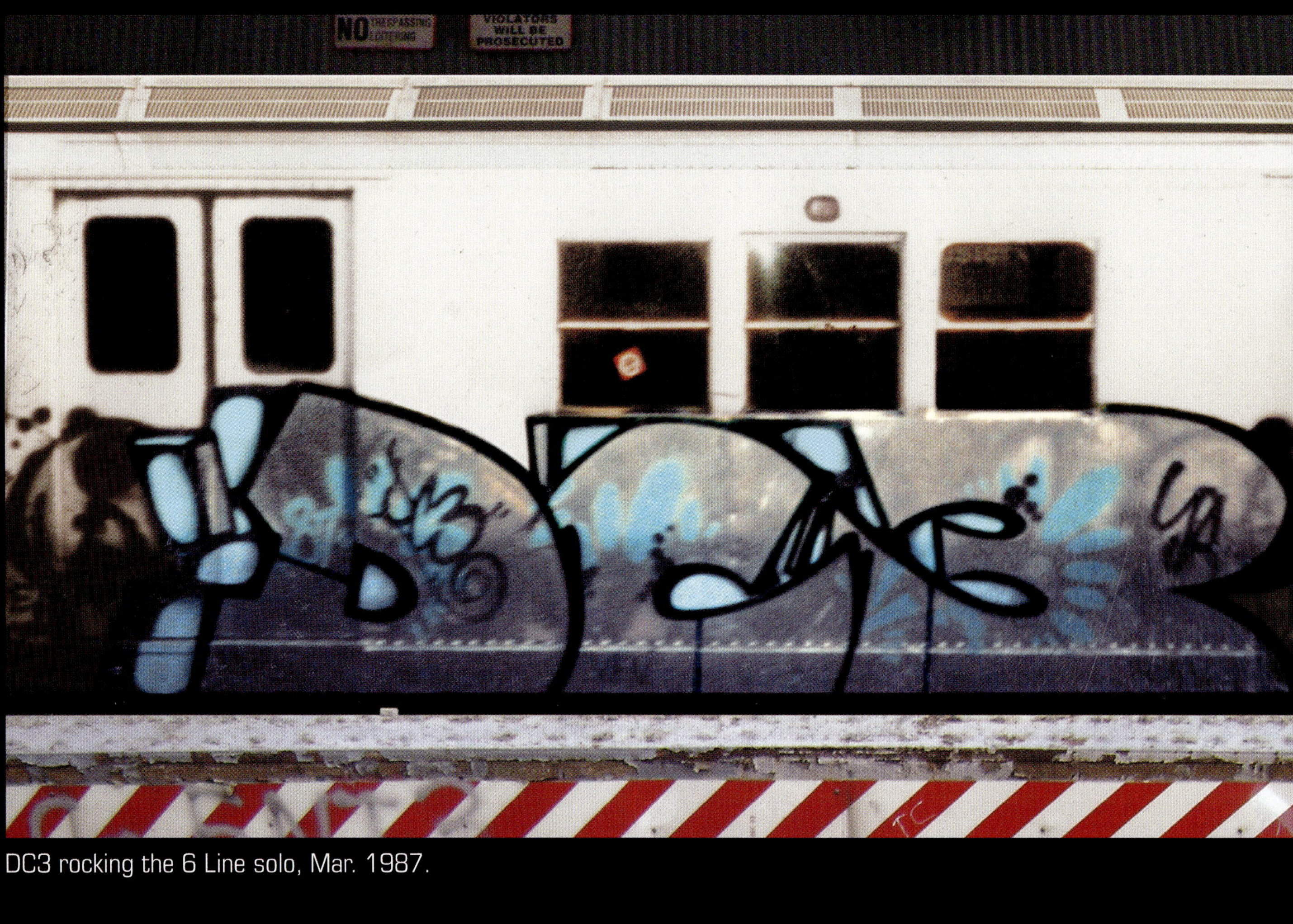

DC3 rocking the 6 Line solo, Mar. 1987.

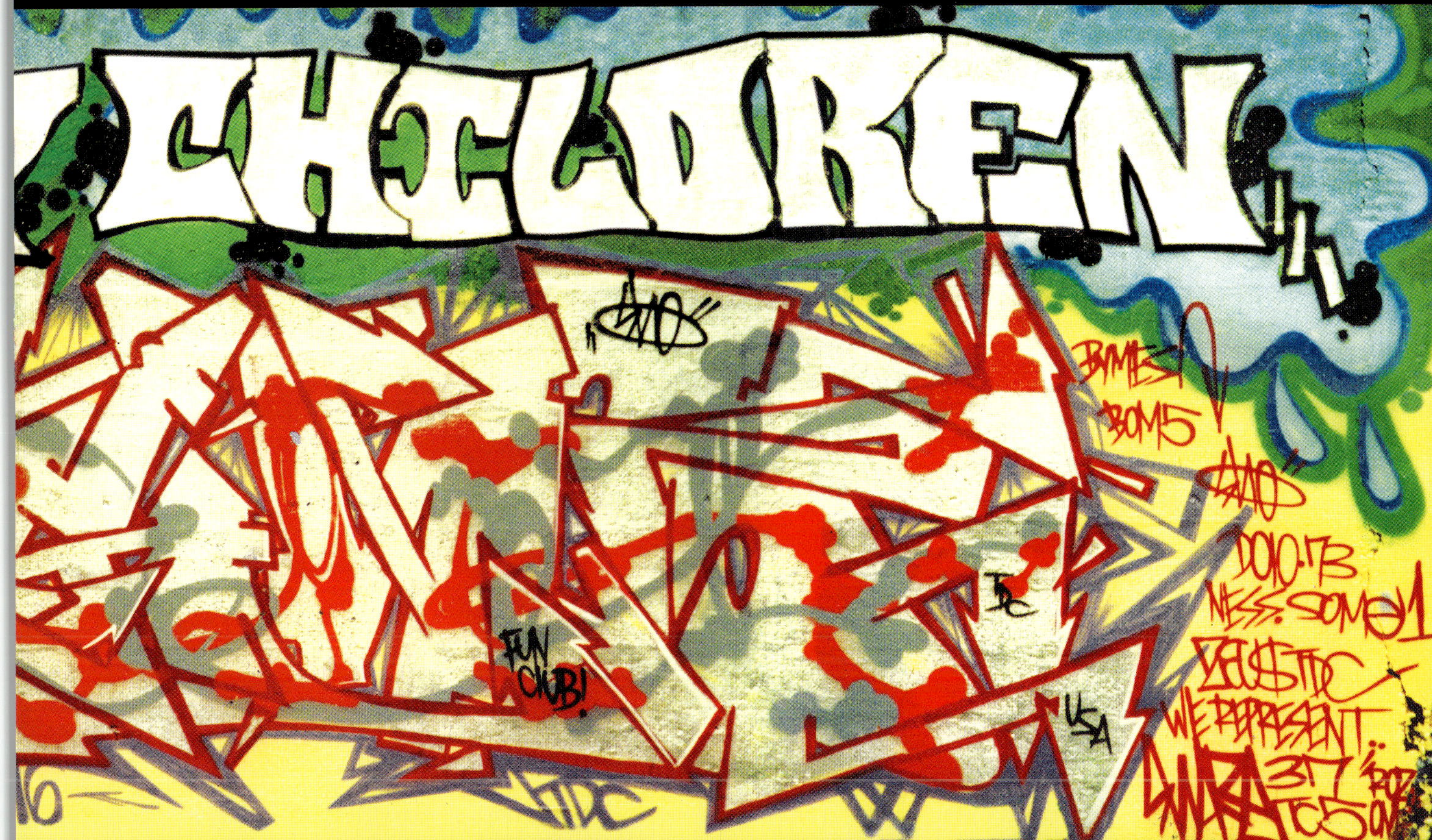

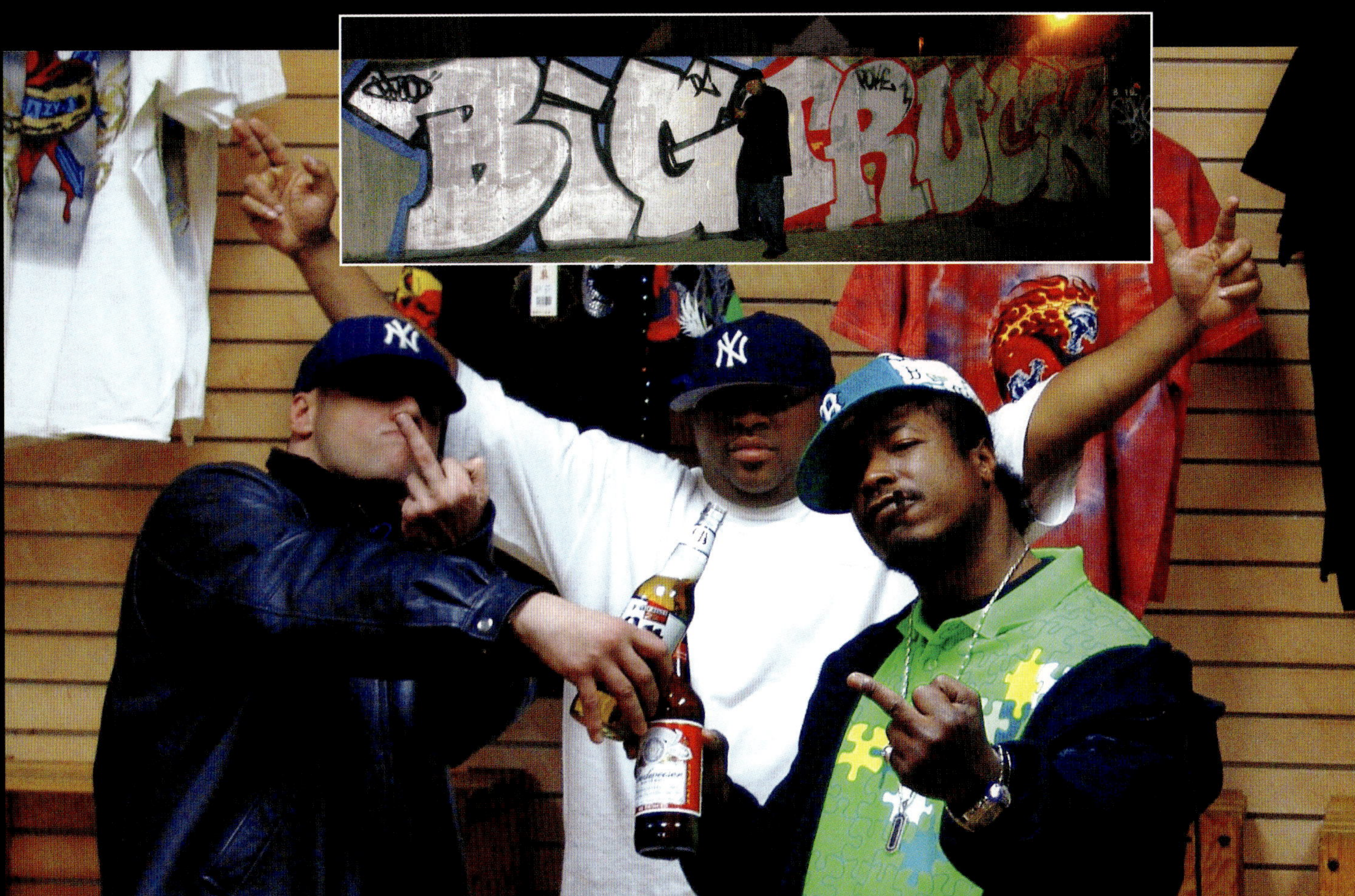

SHO, DC3, and Big Truck bigging up Uniondale.

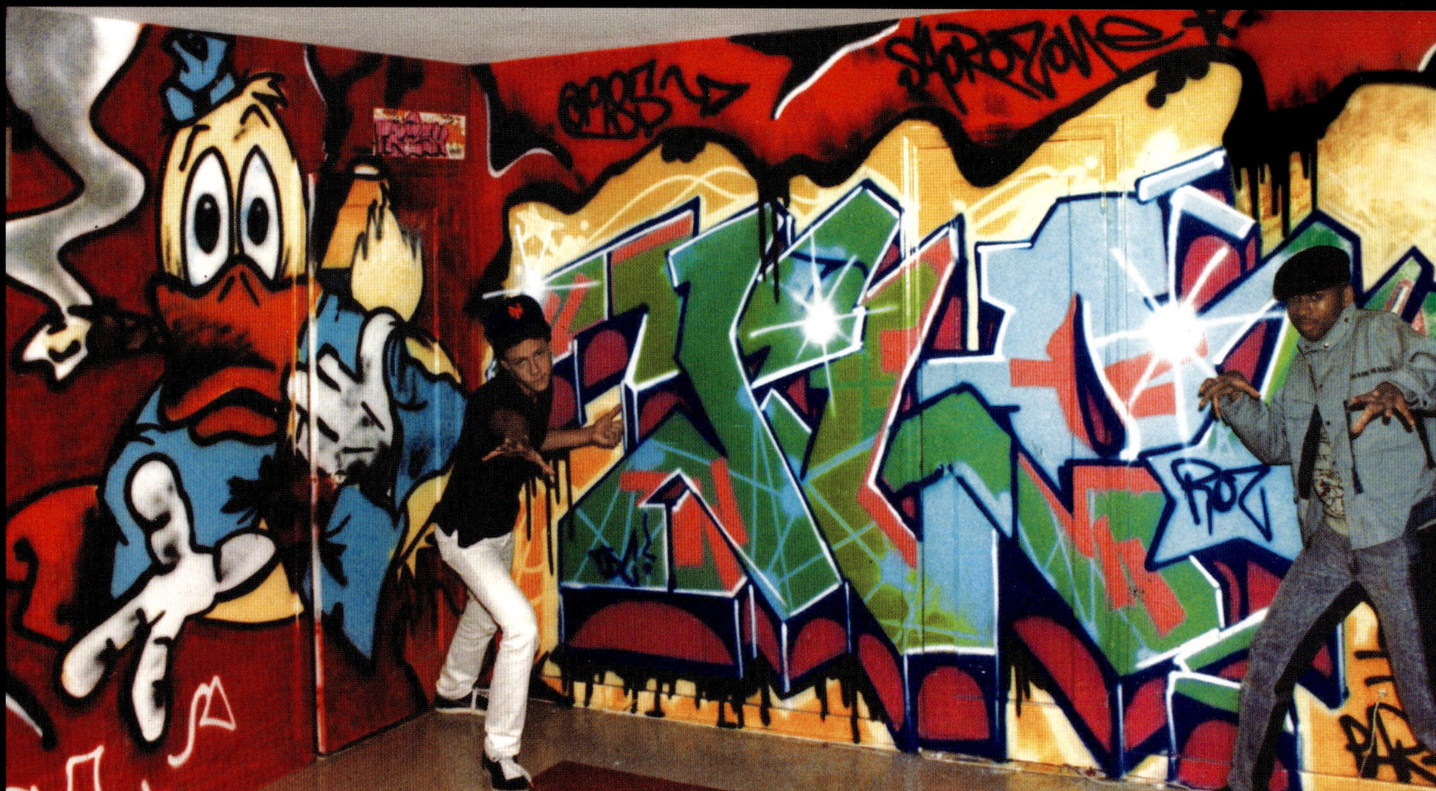

SHO and DC3 live in 1985.

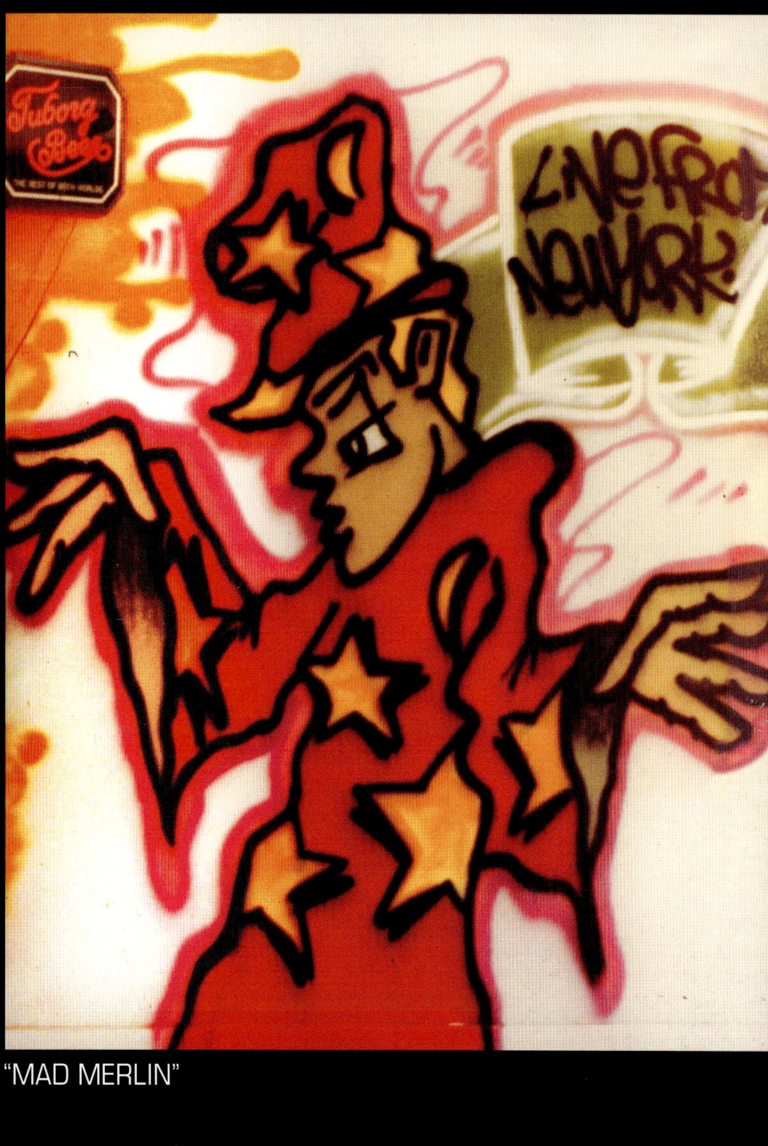

"MAD MERLIN"

One of the original things that inspired me was the movie *Dreams Don't Die* in 1982. I had watched this movie and had seen King 65, who also lived at home, bomb his entire bedroom with graffiti. Hey, why not? It was a great place to practice and me and DC3 did this wall back in September 12, 1985. Mom wasn't to happy if I recall, but we laugh about it to this day. *WildStyle* was also a dope flick. We had mad paint!! I grew up in Freeport and when we was coming up, it was early in the graff game for Long Island. We were the first writers in Long Island to really get busy and take it to the next level. We bombed, then did all the handball courts, and then really pretty quickly made the transition to running NYC subway trains and never looked back!!

-SHO TDC

SEE YOU IN THE LAND OF SURPRISES.

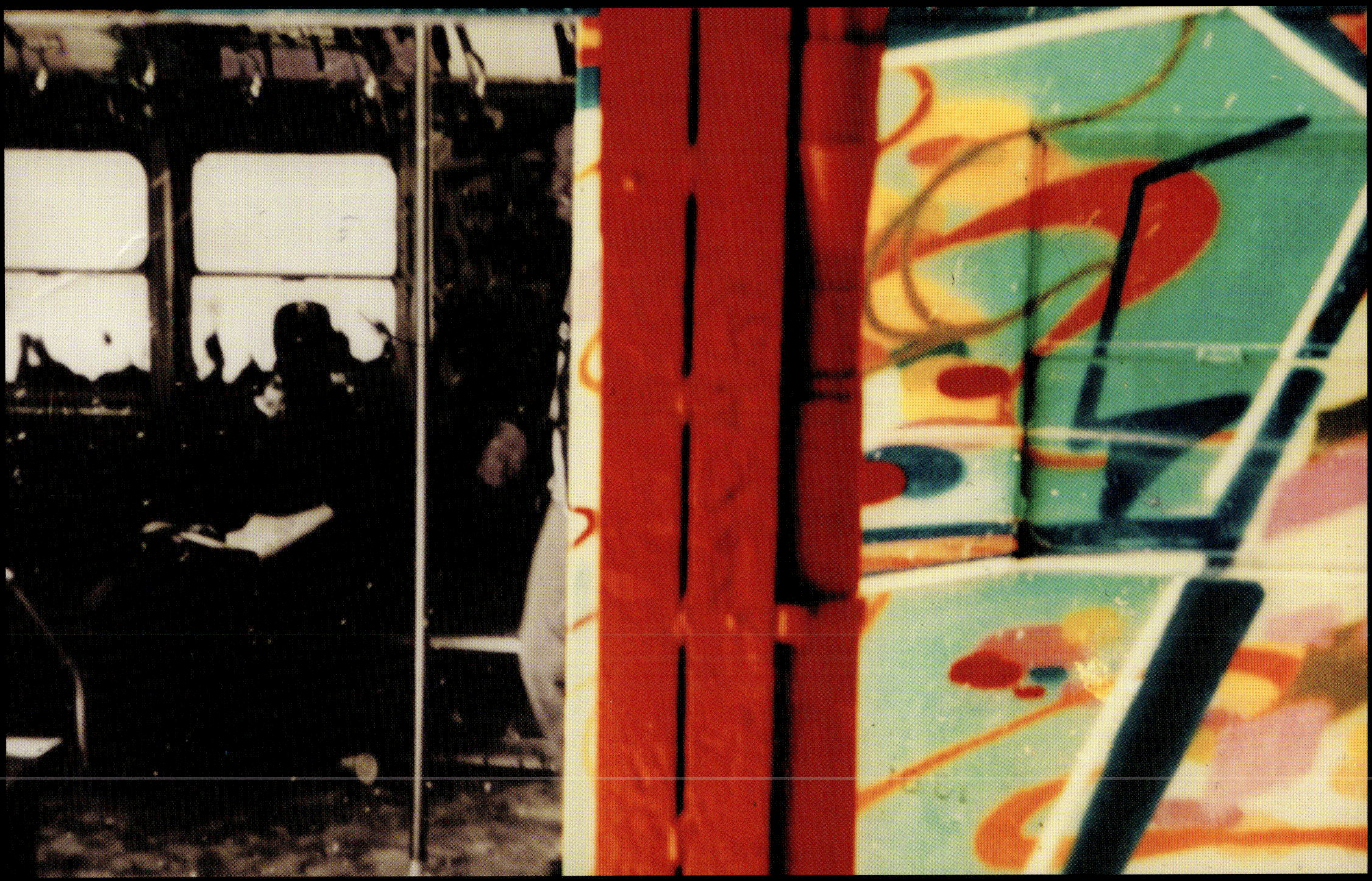

The DOME VULCAN, married, top-to-bottom trains were done in the 125th Street weekend tunnel lay up during the blizzard of 1987. These trains were a part of a disgusting amount of trains that would pull out that Monday morning. "The Juggernaut SHO" train was done the same weekend but not the same night and almost didn't happen, but Dome really came through for me. For whatever reason, I didn't go on Saturday, Dome and my man VULCAN EX Vandals went to represent. I was crazy hot to learn that these cats had wrecked shit and I missed out when Dome came to my crib. I was like, "what up!!!!!! Fuck this, lets go back." And he was always down for shit and did not take much convincing. Ha ha. This weekend was and still is fucking legendary. I brought like thirty cans and Dome helped me fill in my train and we got that shit done in like four hours. Mad writers got busy up in there. Wane FC, Dero TFA, Joey TDS, Jon 156, Kyle 156, Sent, Dome, DC3, and Poke IBM, just to name a few. Jon 156 said it best to Dome, with whom he knew and introduced me to, that this was the Super Bowl of graffiti with many top writers burning up the trains. There most have been at least fifty trains done over a three-day period, that shit was a dope week. We had already been having problems with jealous writers crossing our shit out, mostly anonymously, and we was at war with a couple of writers who you somehow would never bump into. So, as we go into the lay up via an escape hatch with Jon 156 on Lexington, Domes, who hadn't slept in two days and is drinking OE, snuffed Dero TFA for like no reason at all. Graff was all about painting and wanton violence. They later squashed that shit. Peace to Dero, aka Blue. Shit happens.

DOME, "A SLAVE TO STYLE" and VULCAN EX-VANDALS, married, top-to-bottoms, Mar. 1987.

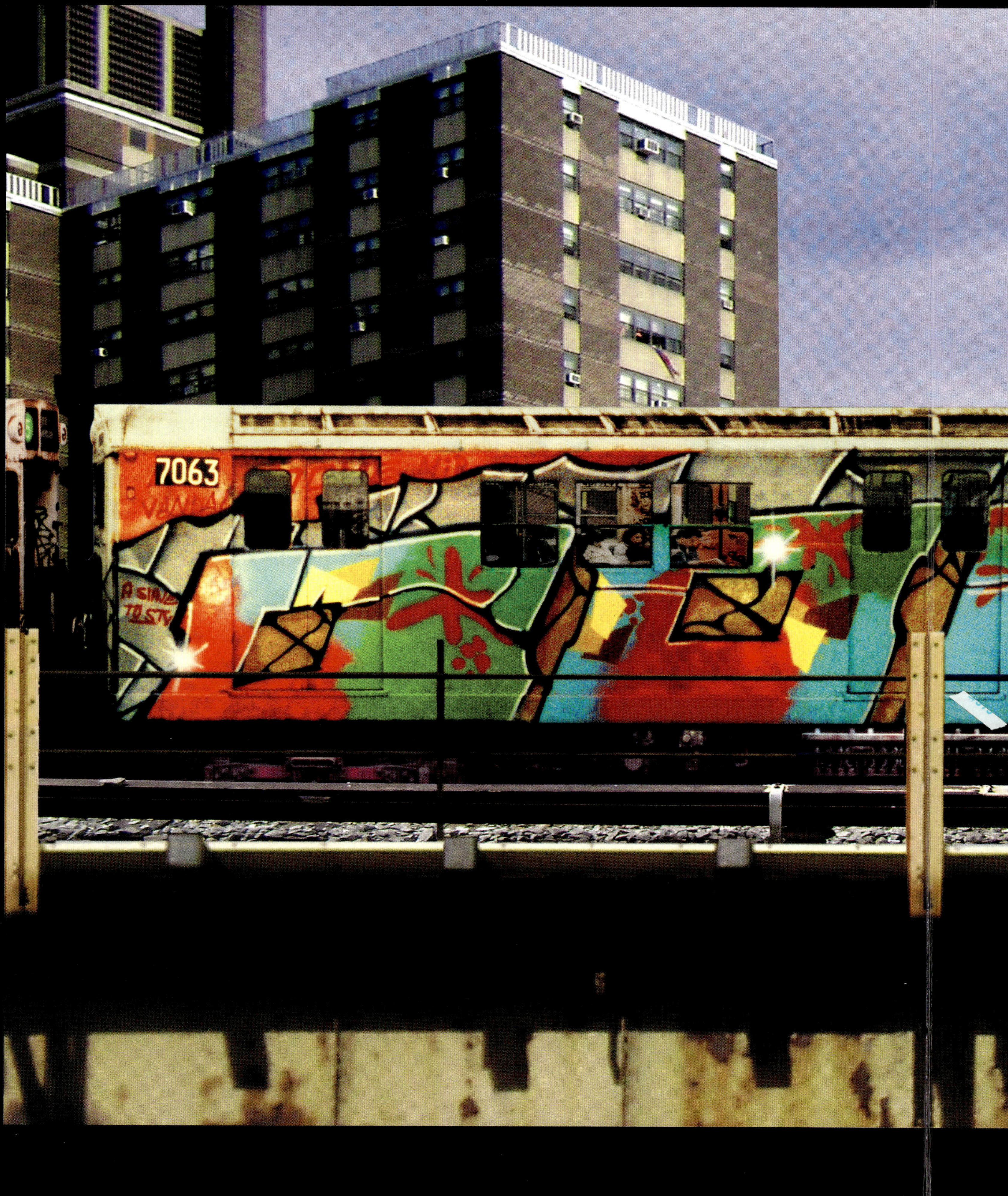

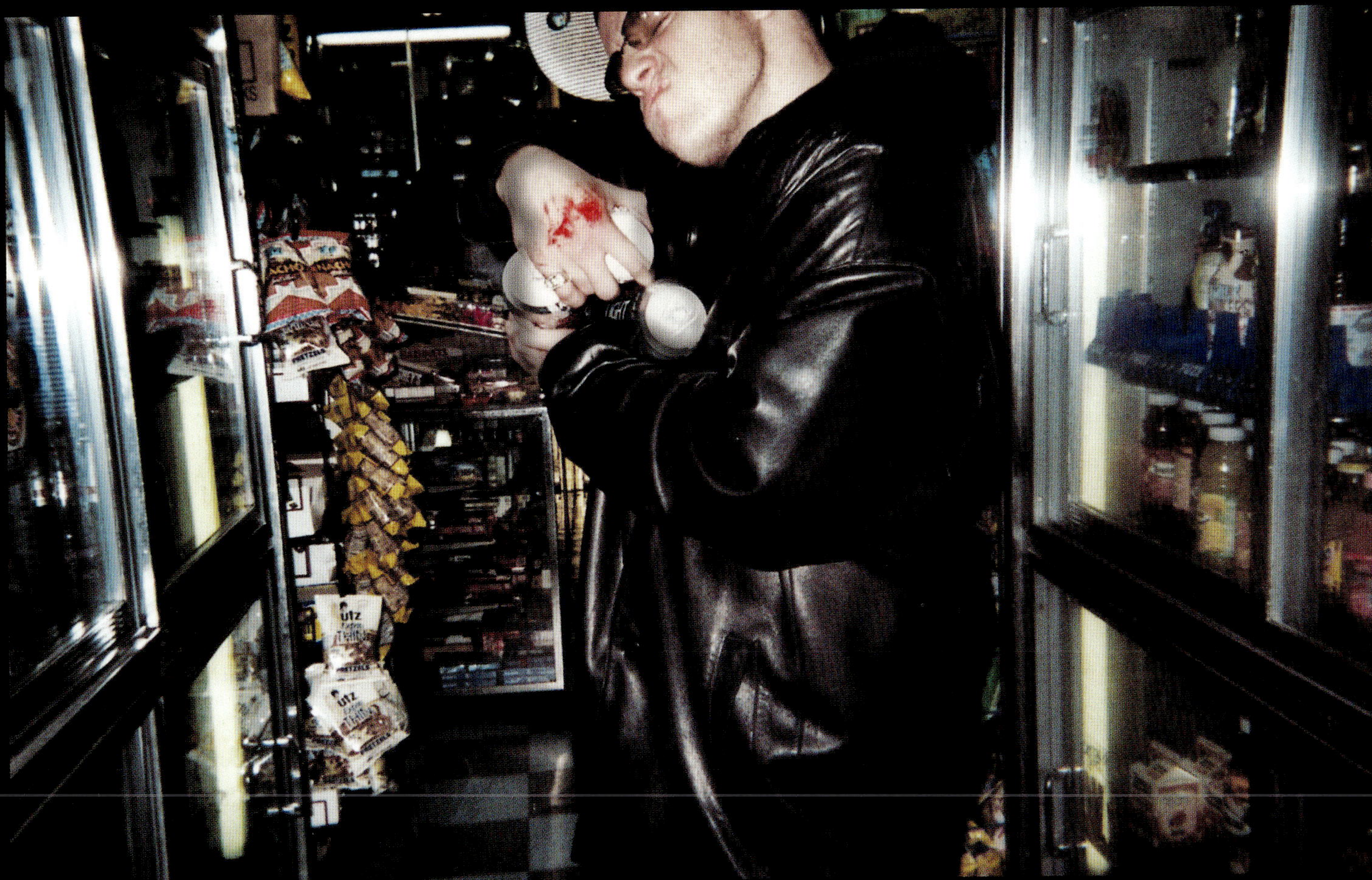

Bodega beef.

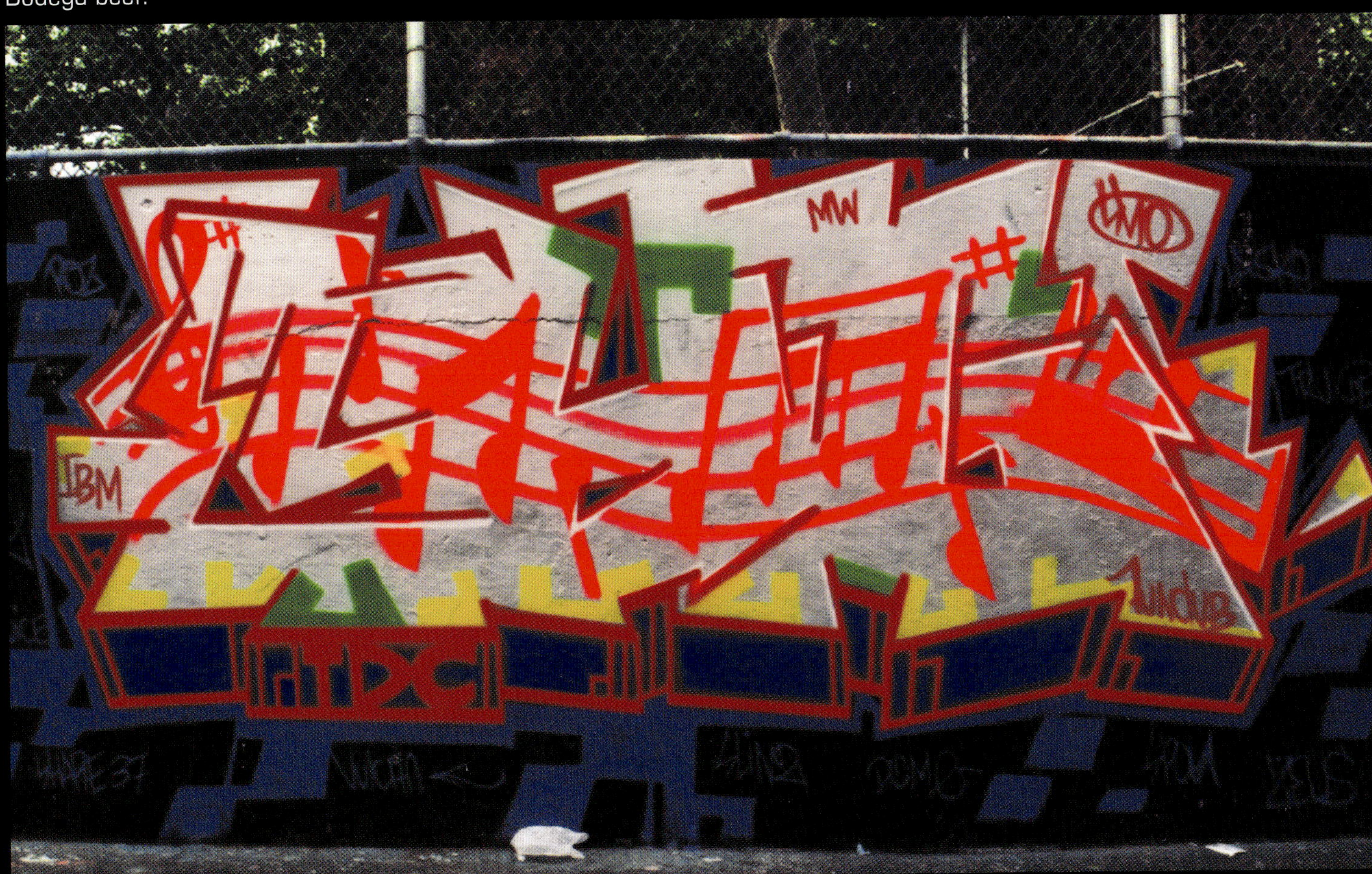

SHO TDC IBM "MOST WANTED," Hall of Fame, 2000.

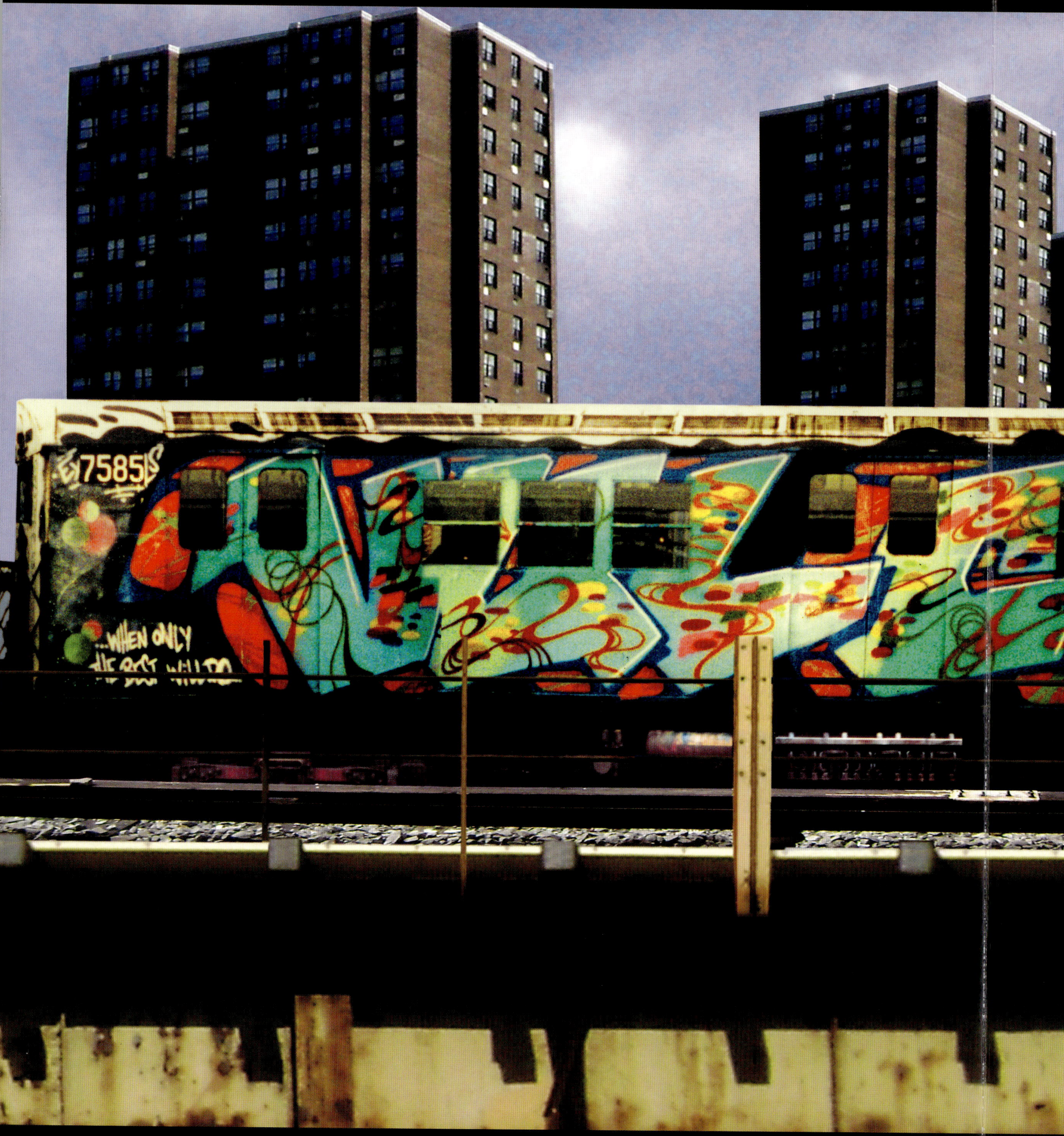
7585
...WHEN ONLY

CHAPTER 8

Hall of Fame Productions
The K Line, The B Line

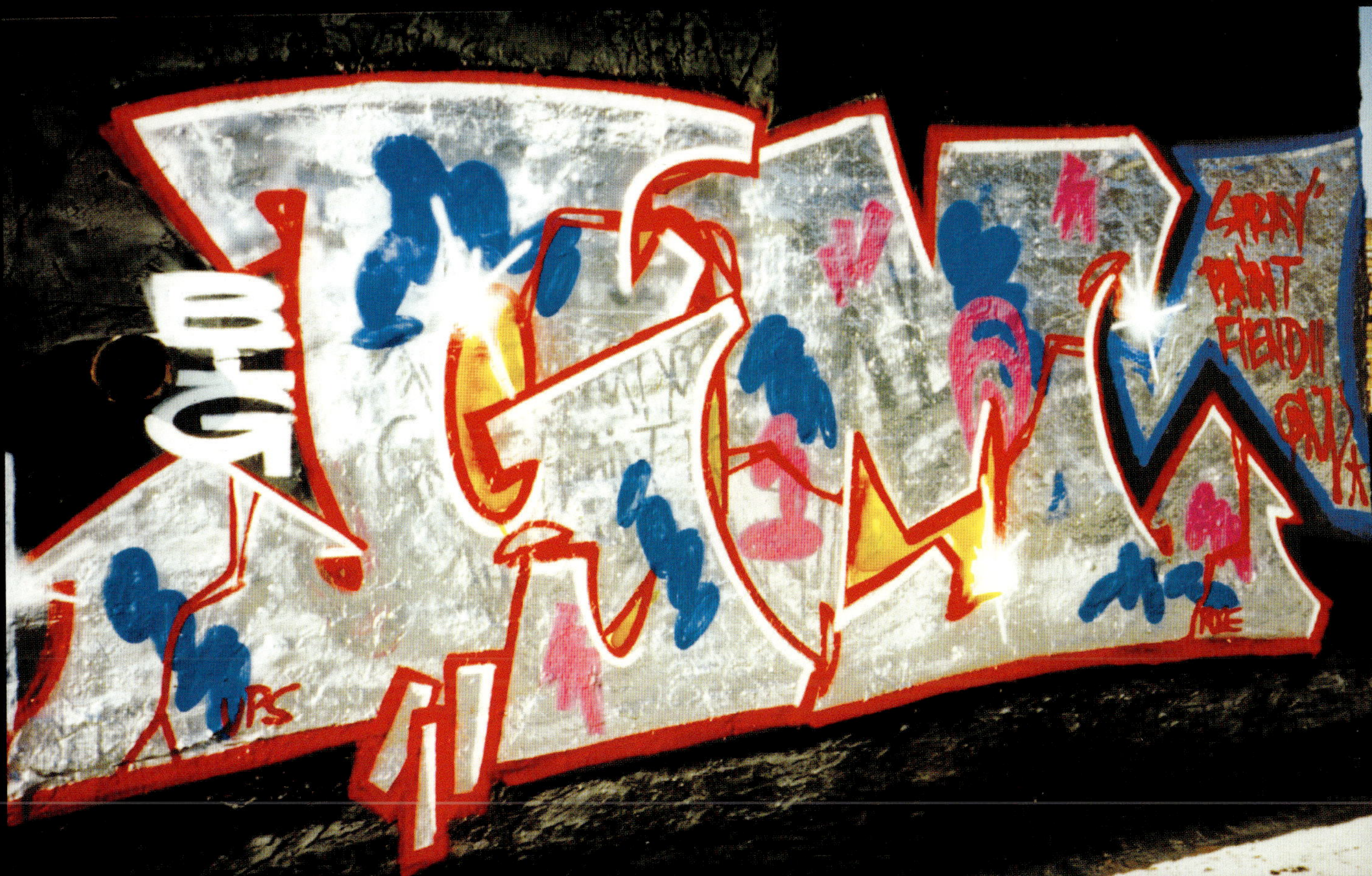

BIG GM Rooftop, "SPRAY PAINT FIEND," 1996.

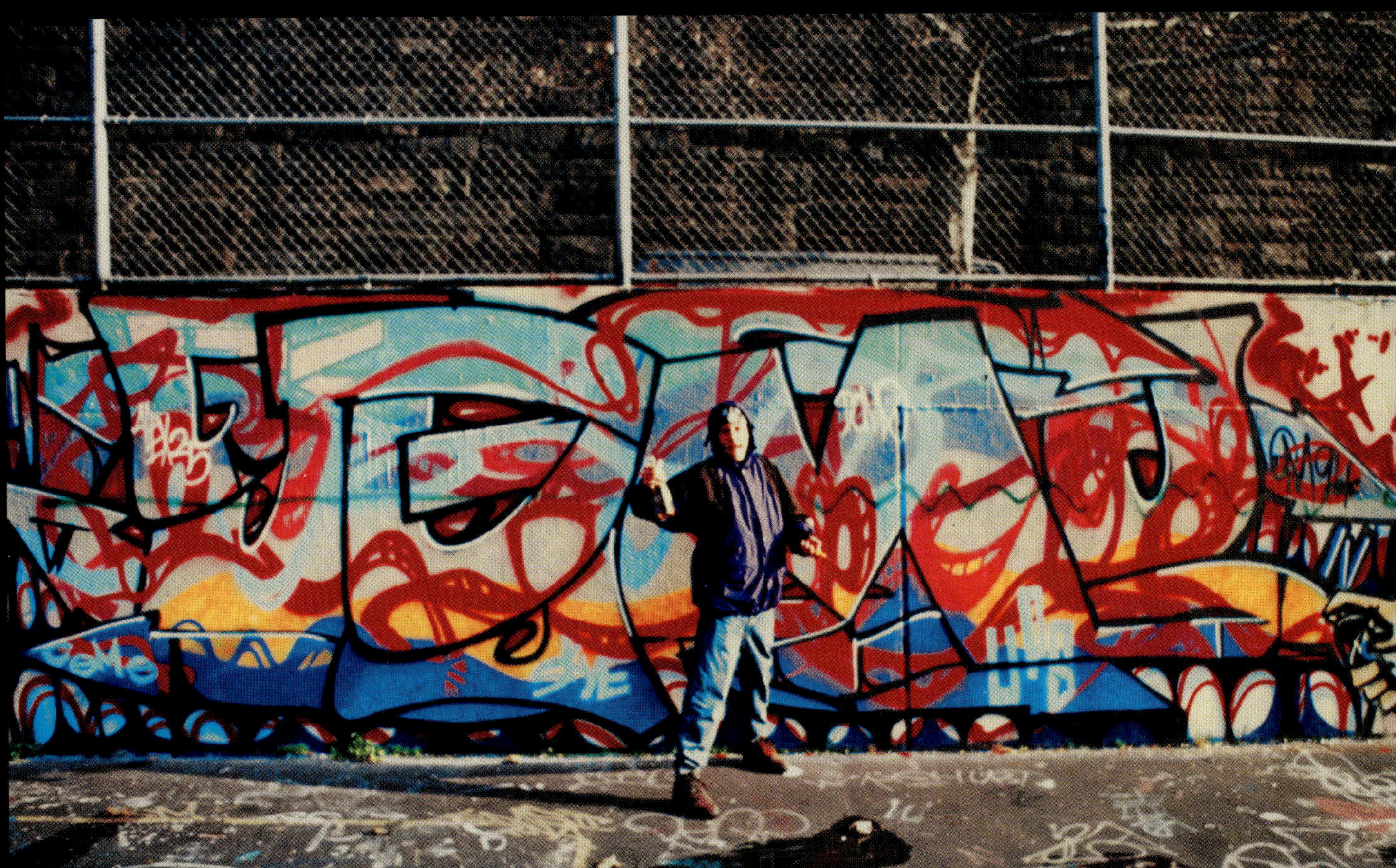

GM In the Hall of Fame, Oct. 1994.

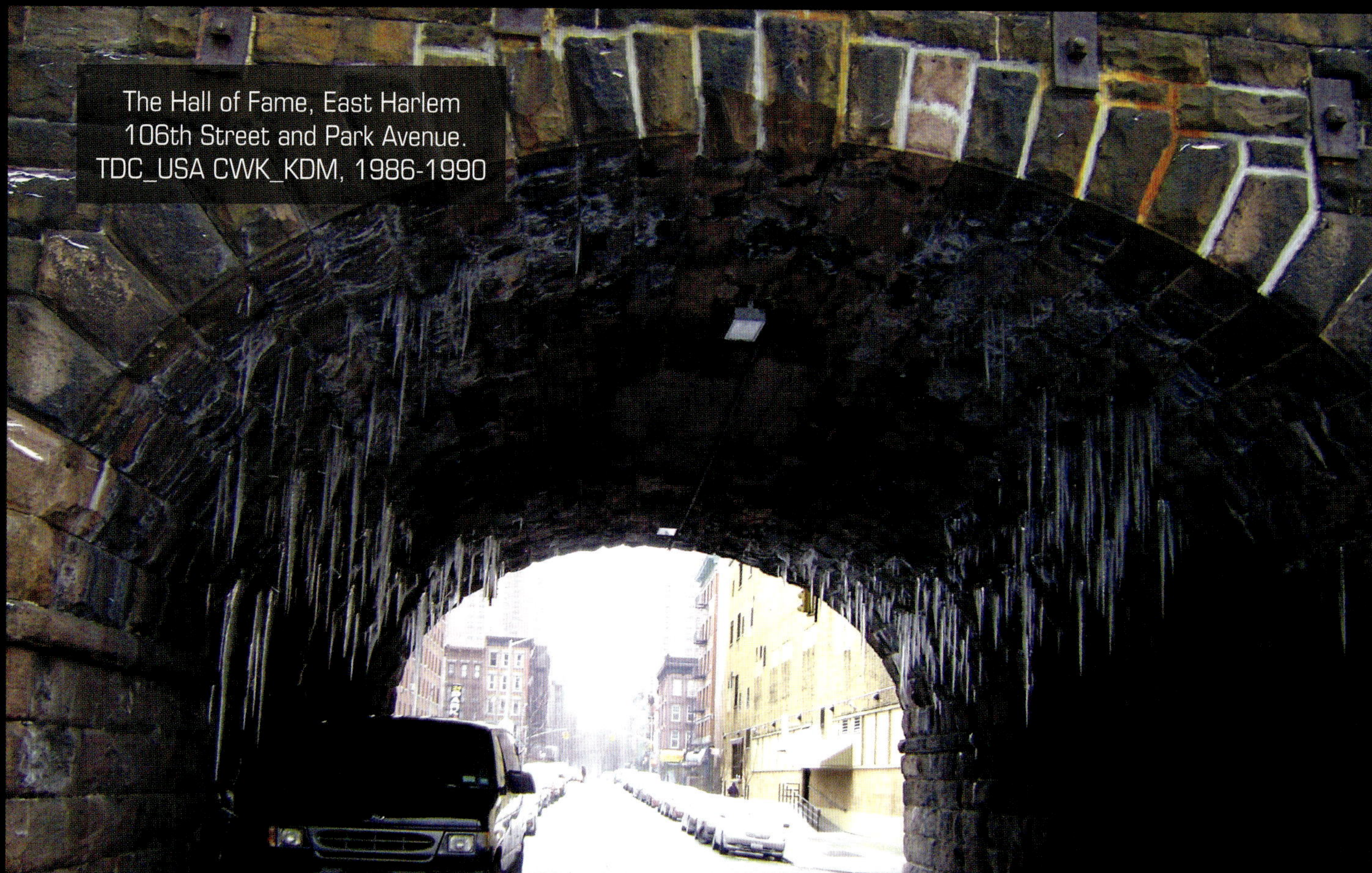

The Hall of Fame, East Harlem
106th Street and Park Avenue.
TDC_USA CWK_KDM, 1986-1990

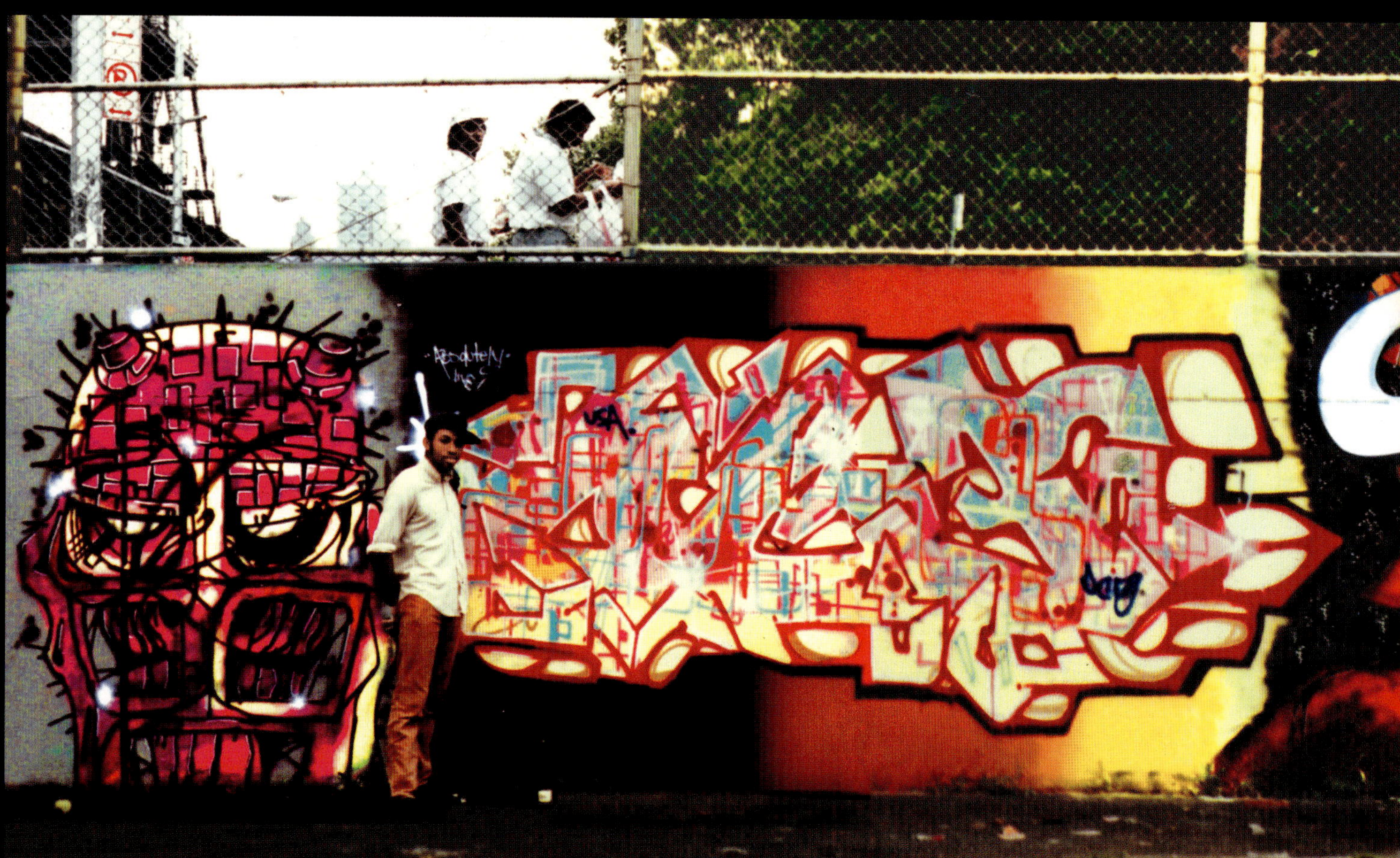

DC3, "ABSOLUTELY LIVE," 106th Street and Park, Hall of Fame.

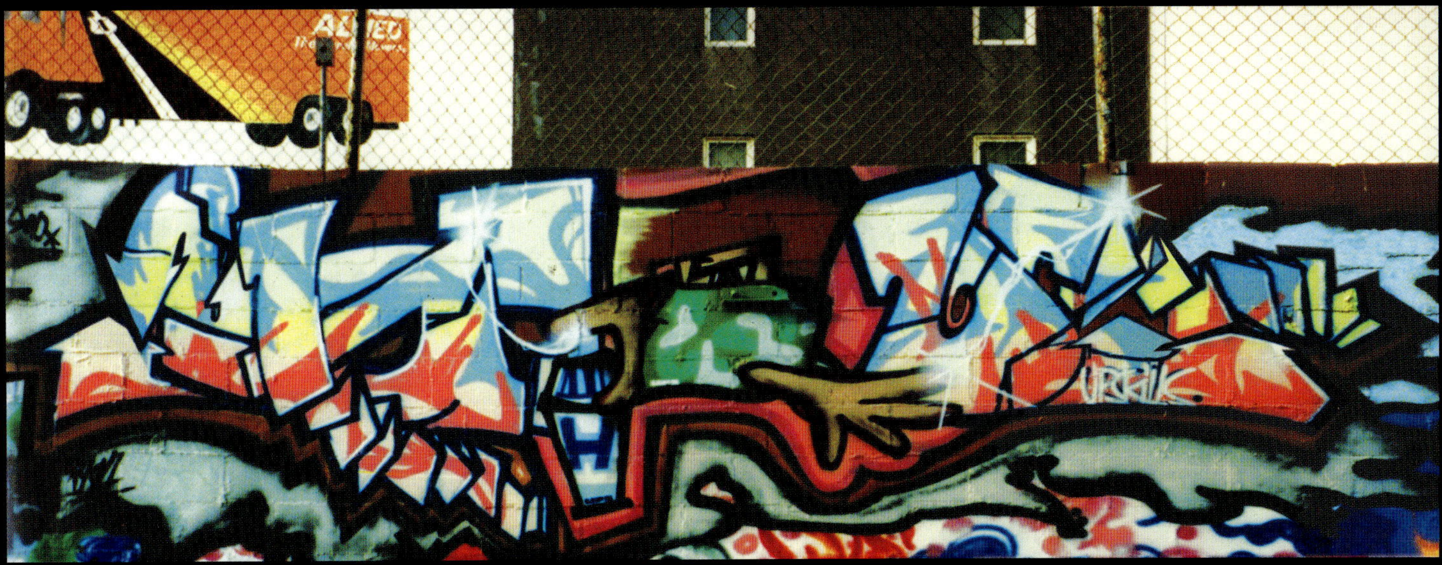

SHO, NY, 1994.

The wall above happened by accident in 1994, when I was in East Harlem on 3rd Avenue and 119th Street and bumped into Shame 125 and SAK MBT. They were doing a production with Zephyr and Boots. I was like "What's up? Let me get down," and they was with it. Good looking out. The below Hall of Fame wall was done early 1986 and the first one done by DC3 and SHO "ABSOLUTELY LIVE." One of many Hall of Fame productions to come from the crew. Harlem stand up!!

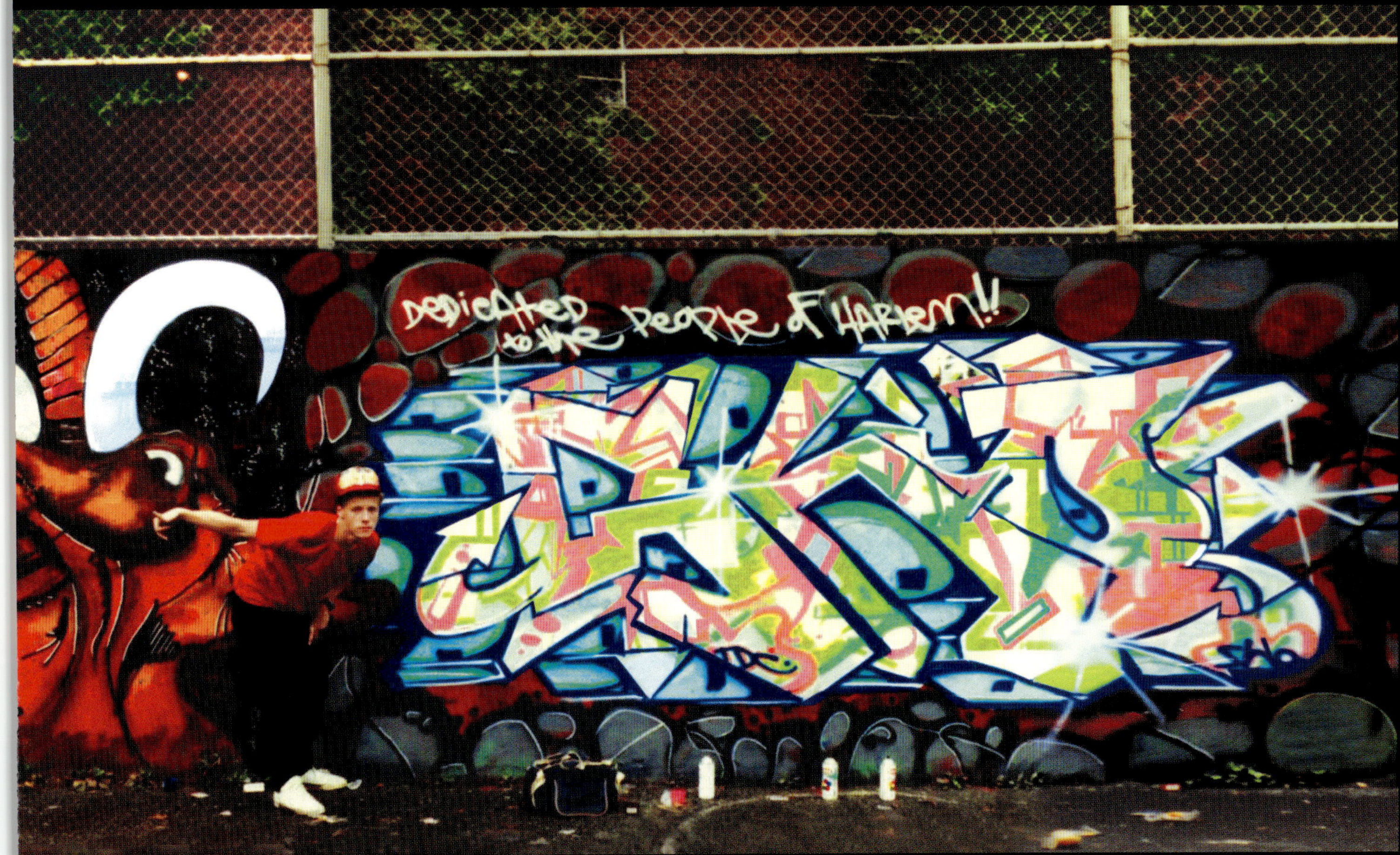

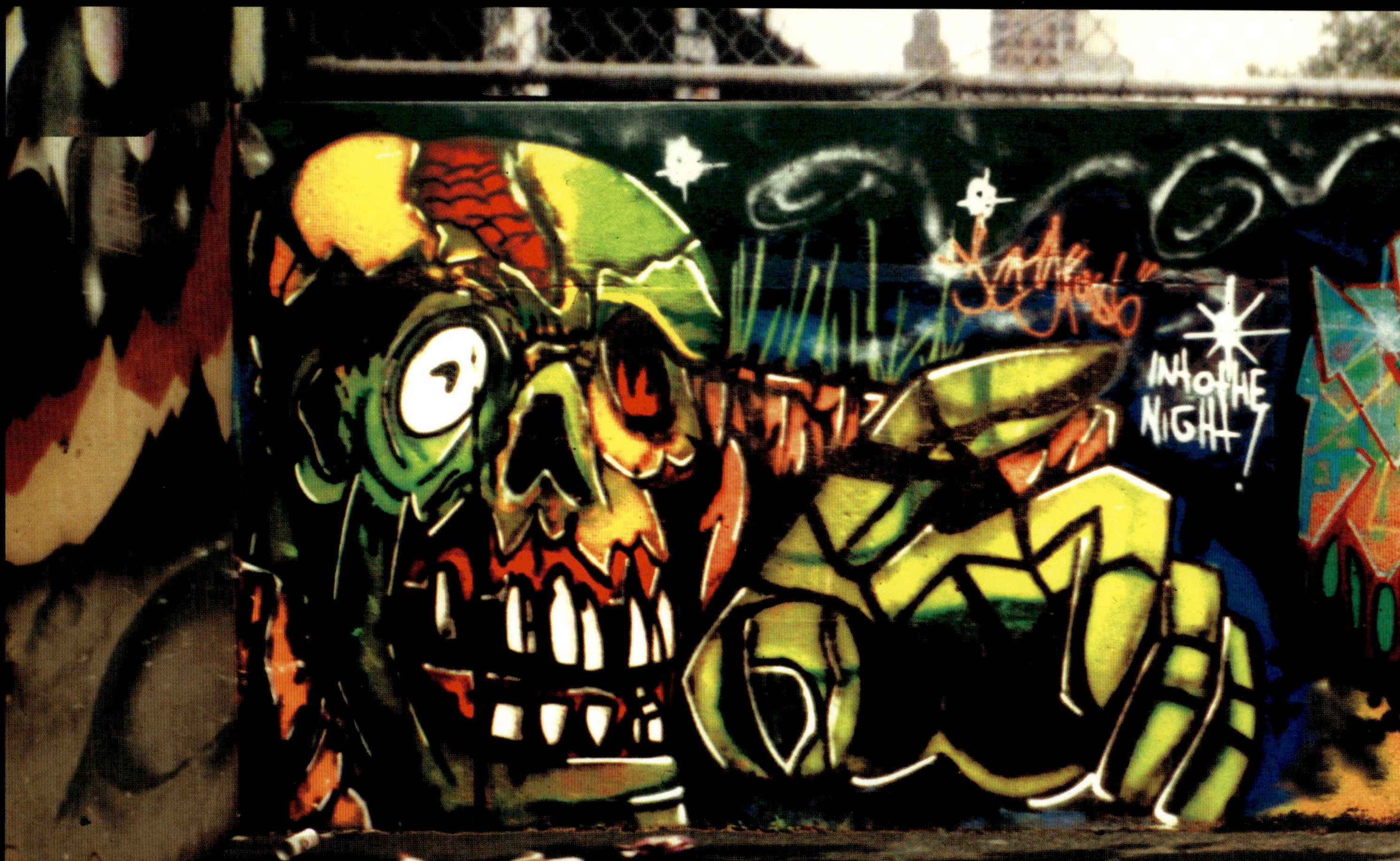

DC3, "INTO THE NIGHT," USA Hall of Fame, Part 2.

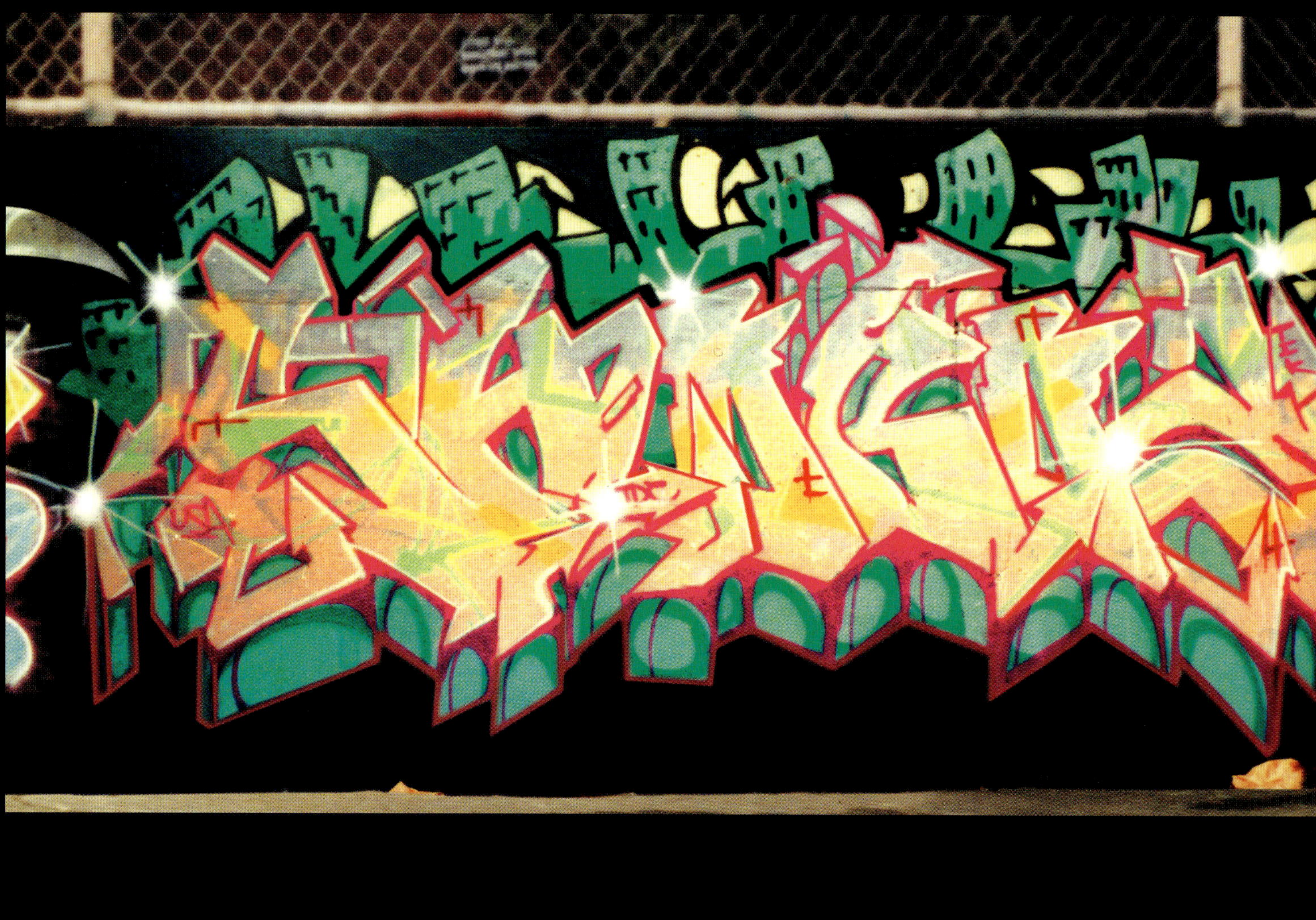

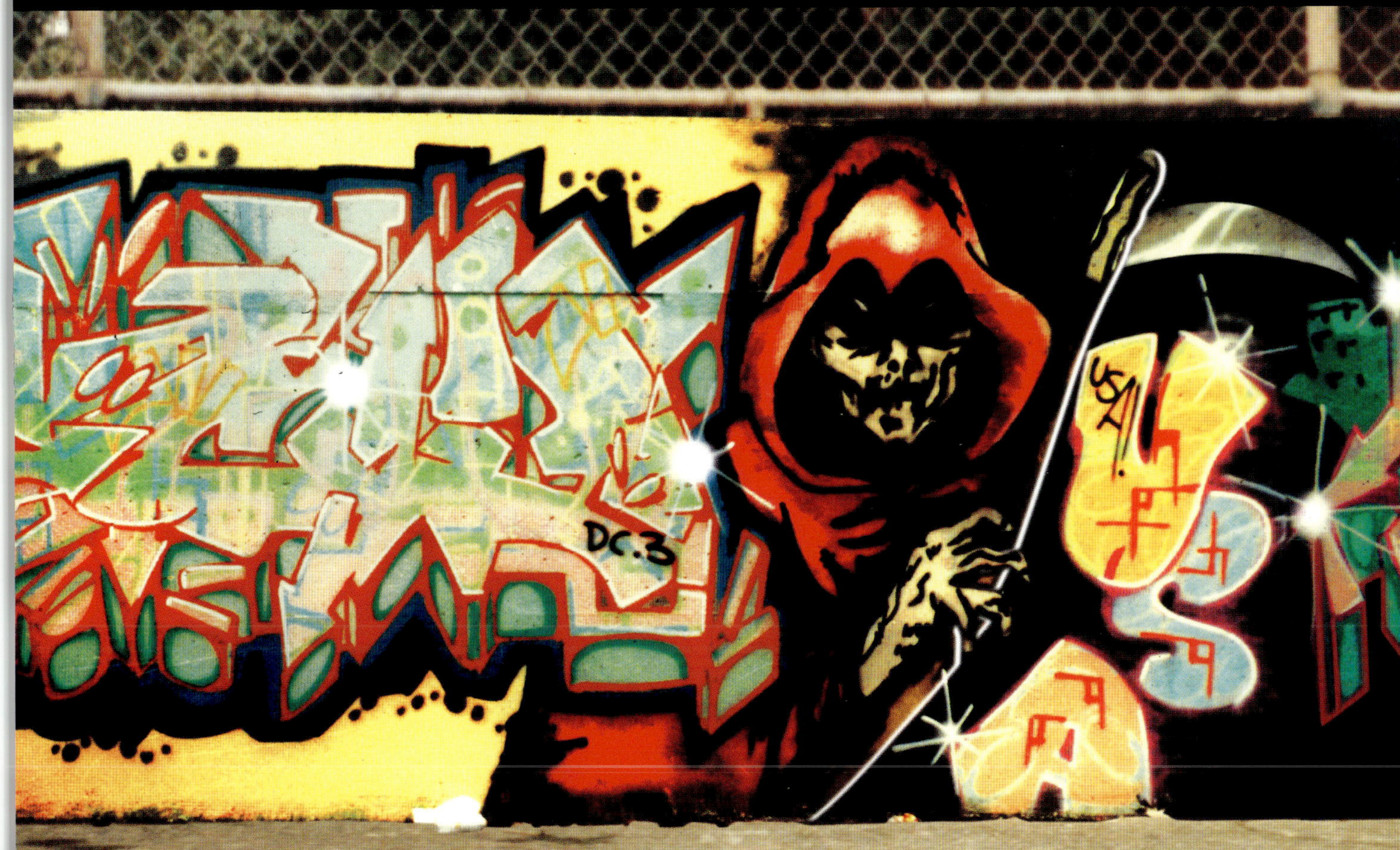

SHOROZ TDC, "THE DESTINY CHILDREN," Cerebus, Part 2, Harlem, Aug. 1986.

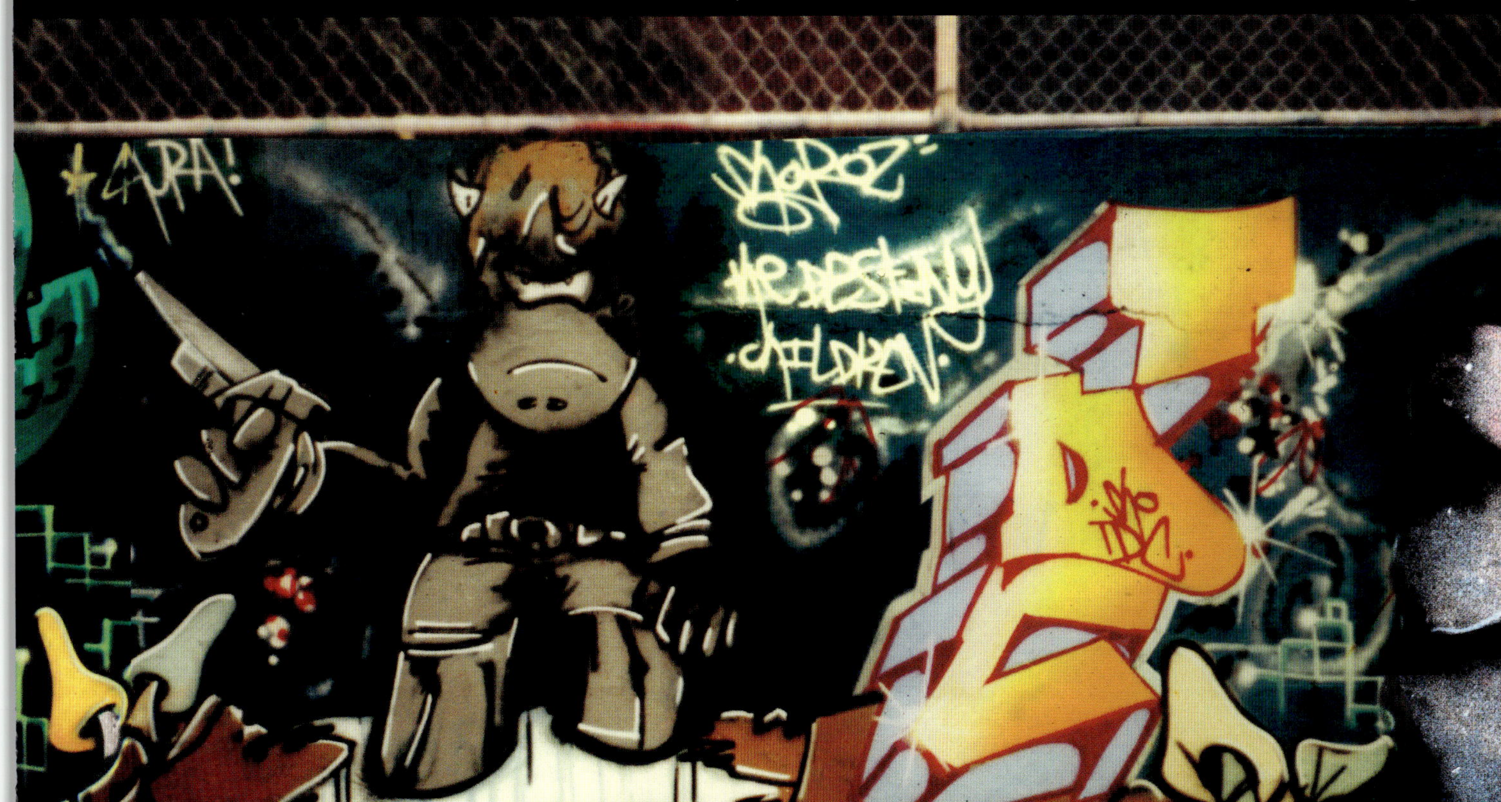

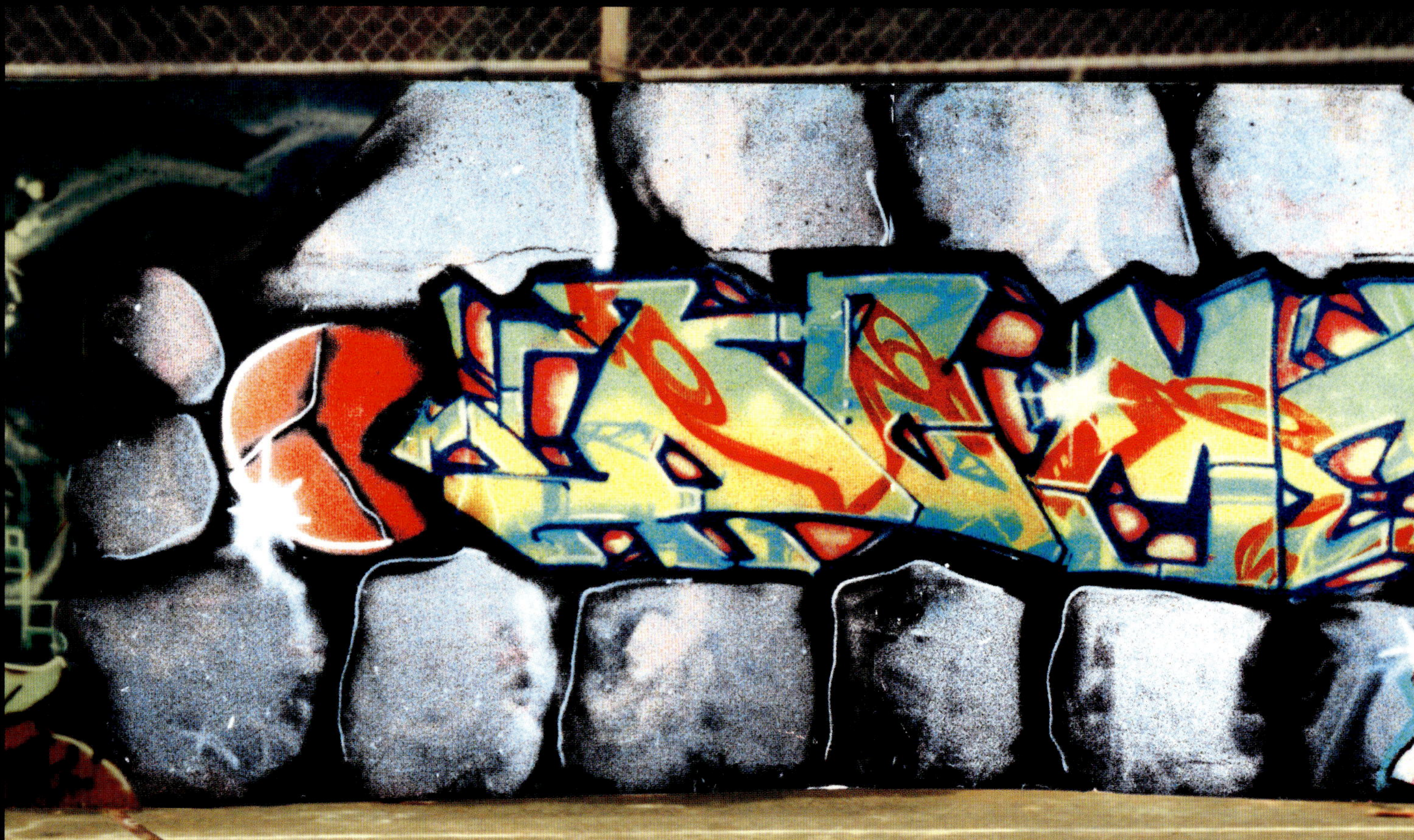

DOME, aka ZOO, loves Miriam, Harlem Hall of Fame, Jul. 1986.

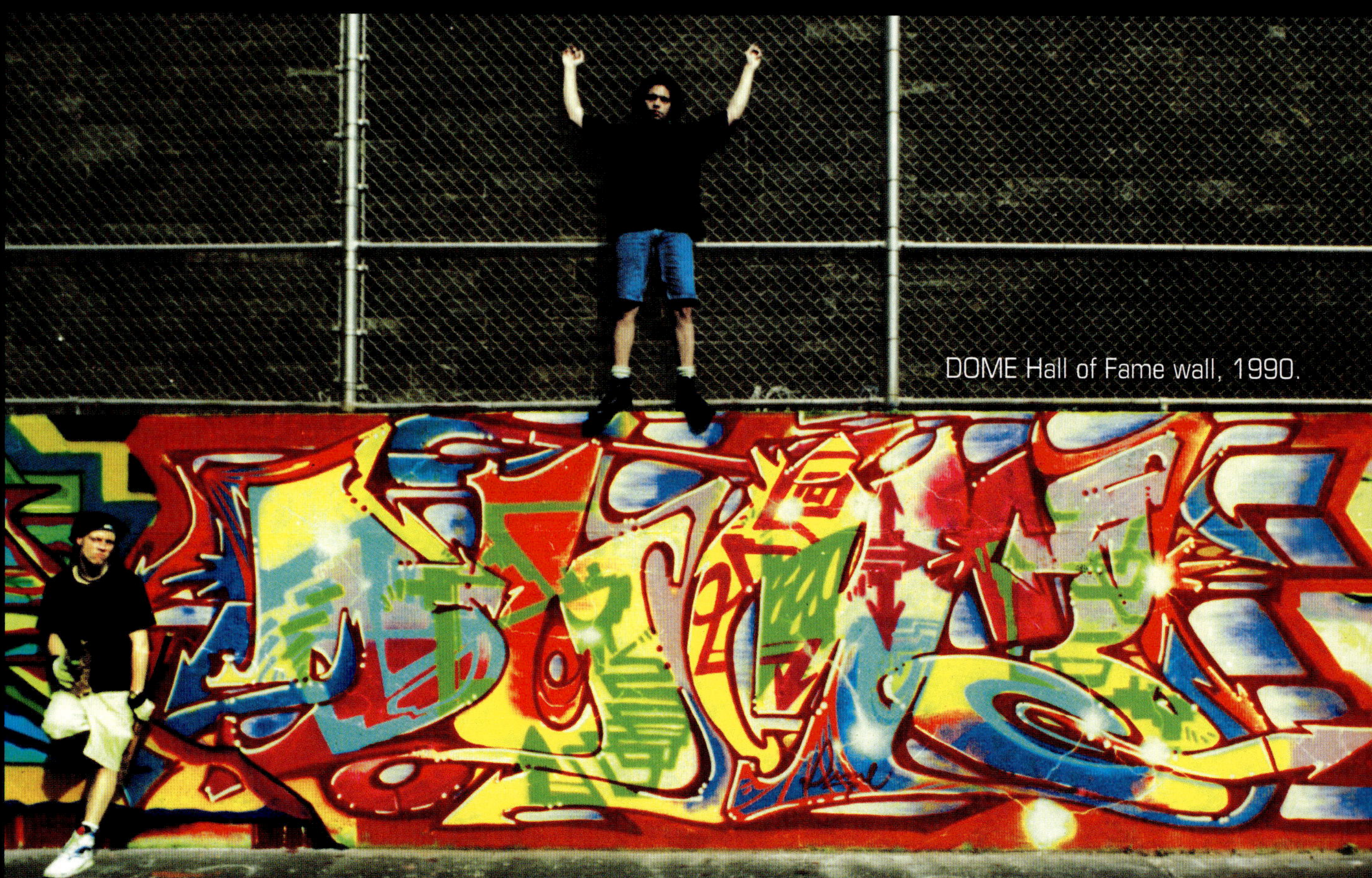

DOME Hall of Fame wall, 1990.

SHO and DOME repping.

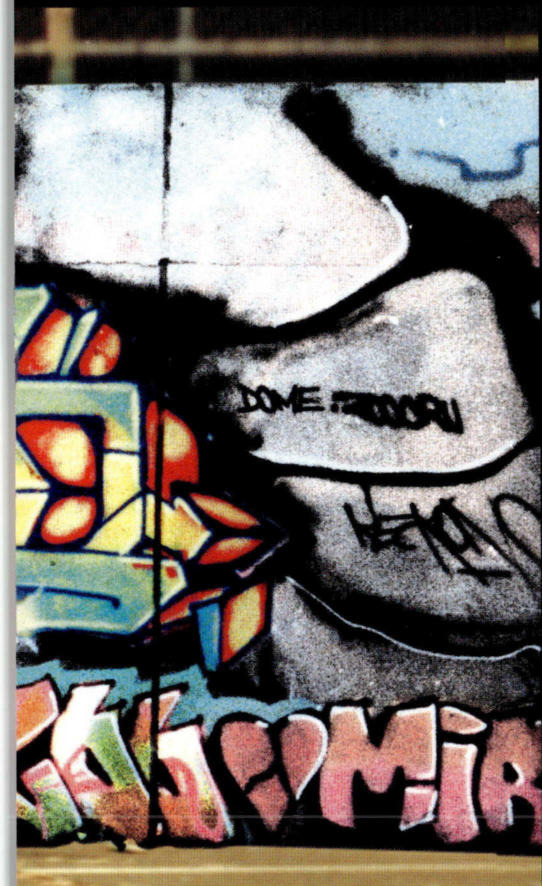

This was the second Hall of Fame production that TDC-USA had rocked together. Dome had did his spot the night before by himself. SHO and DC3 seen that and now wanted in on it. The Hall of Fame was status, and trust me, there was haters, y'all know who your bitch asses be. The Hall of Fame has always been a high turnover location. The first wall we did, didn't last long without hate and guess what? SHO and DC3 came back in broad daylight while school was on and fixed that shit. Everyone on the come-up dealt with lots of bull shit and drama from other writers and it really just became a war of "I'M HERE" and "FUCK YOU ALL...We will be back again & again & again!!!" These walls are very important to who we were as Team TDC. Always remember, however, running subway trains was the only thing that really mattered to us!!

-SHO

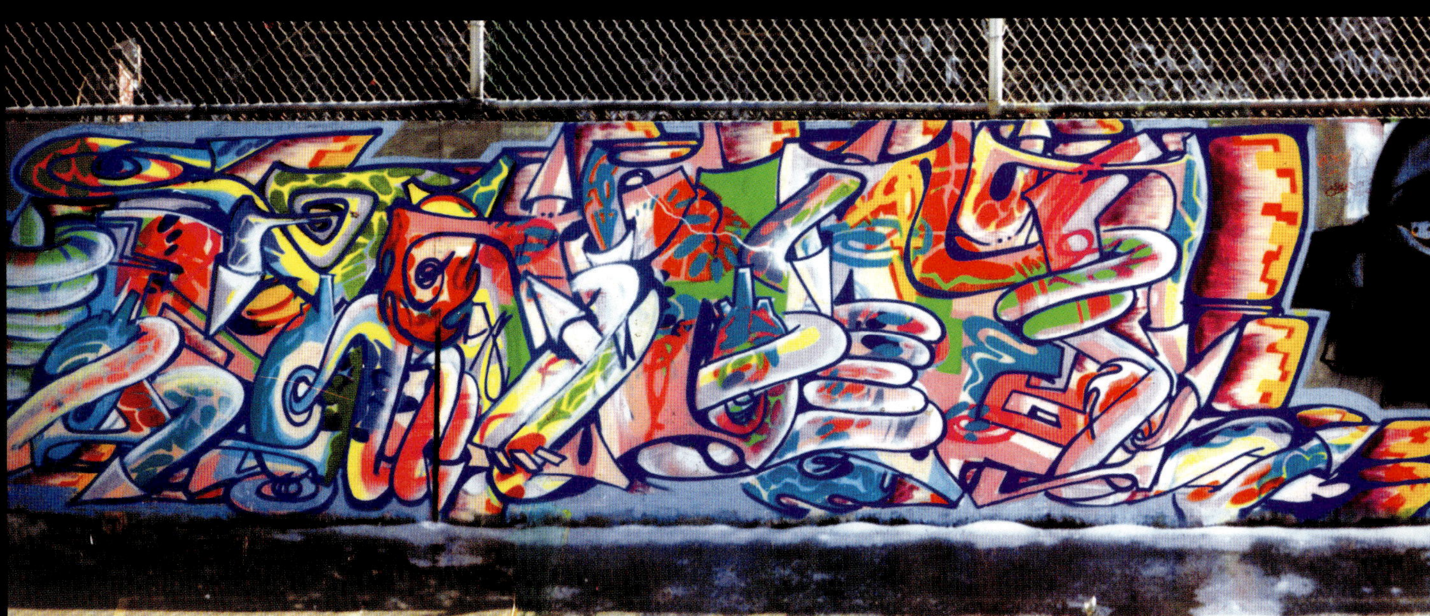

DOME Hall of Fame wall, 1989.

This spread is dedicated to my man Dome TDC. Getting wicked as usual!!!

Dome put in crazy work in the Hall of Fame and painted here many times with VULCAN Ex Vandals and PHASE2, one of the originators of graffiti. All of these walls were done from 1986-1989. Dome creatively developed one of the sickest, hardest to read wild styles for that era. When you push yourself to the limit and you're dope you can surprise even yourself.

The Graffiti Hall of Fame, Apr. 1987. MR. MIRAGE KDM TDC, "Dedicated to Michelle and SKETCH."

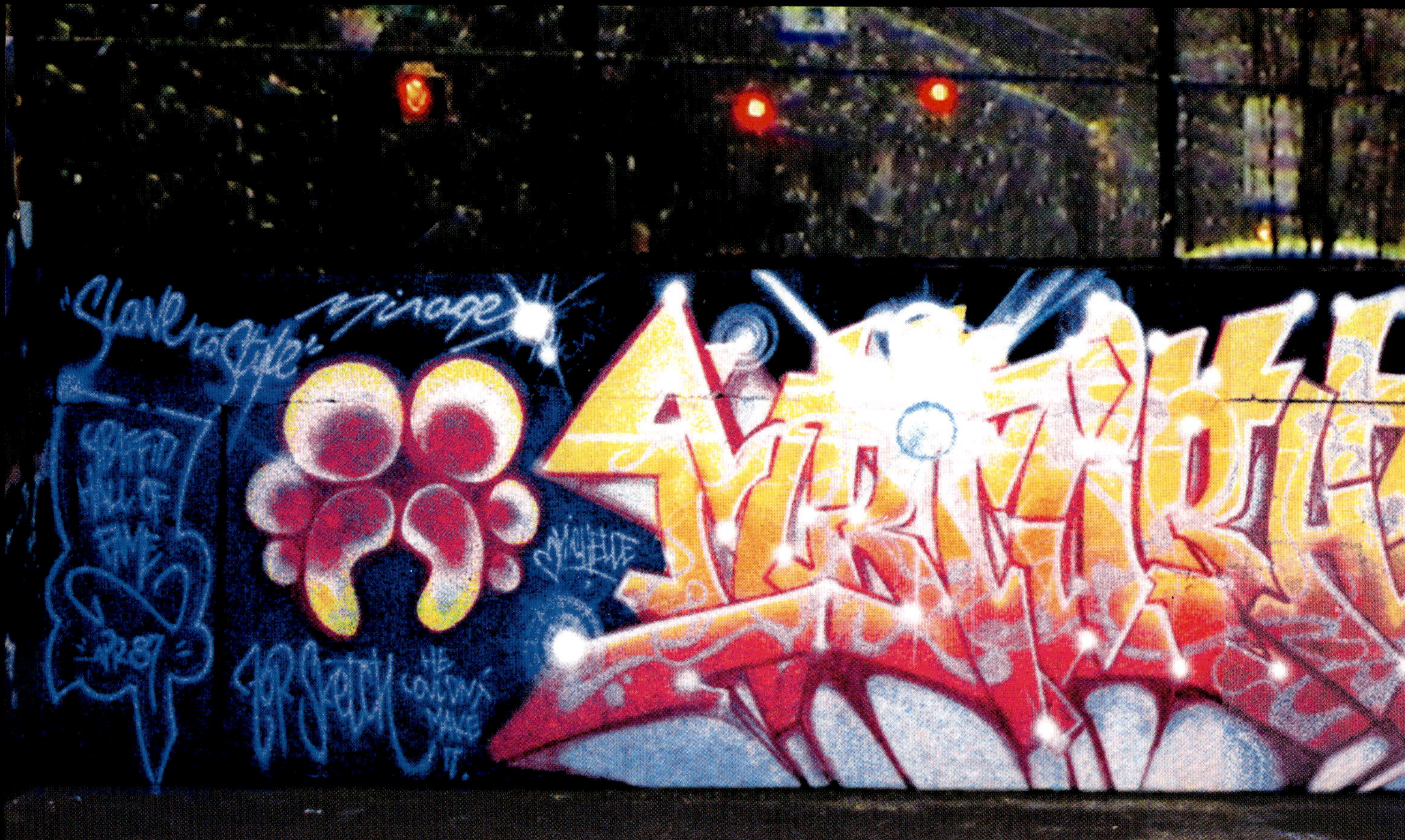

DC3 TDC USA, "CAUSING A STORM!!!"

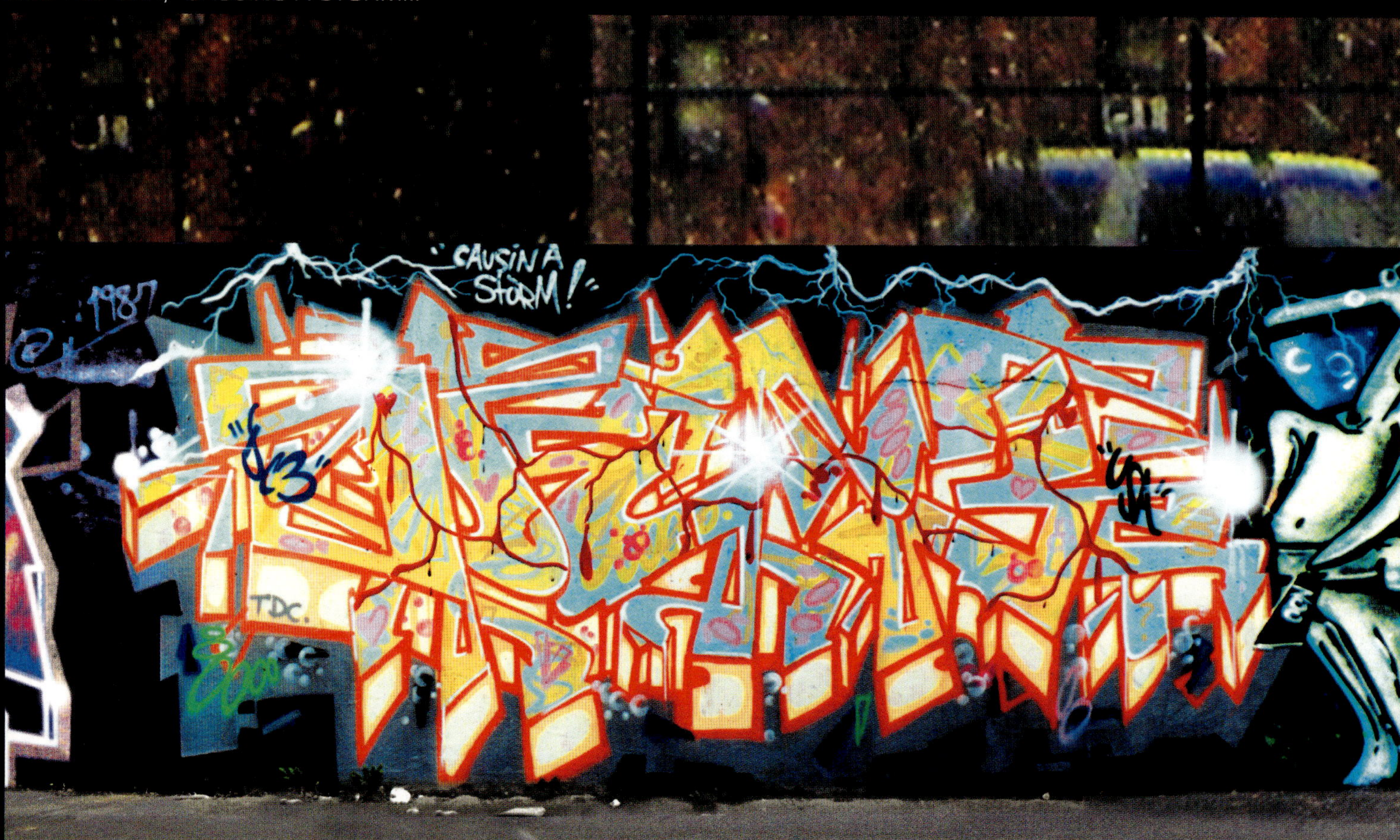

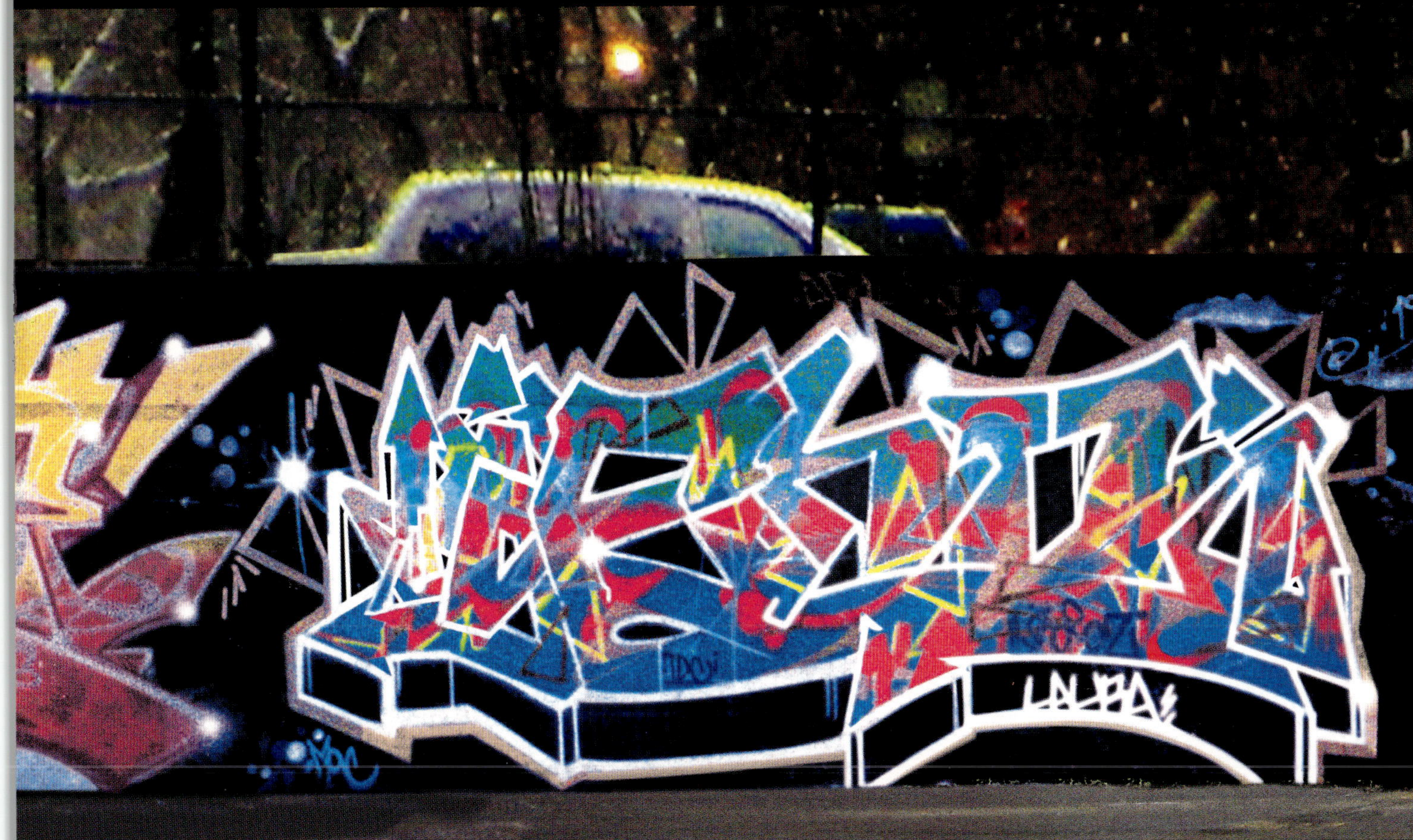

SHO TDC, for Laura.

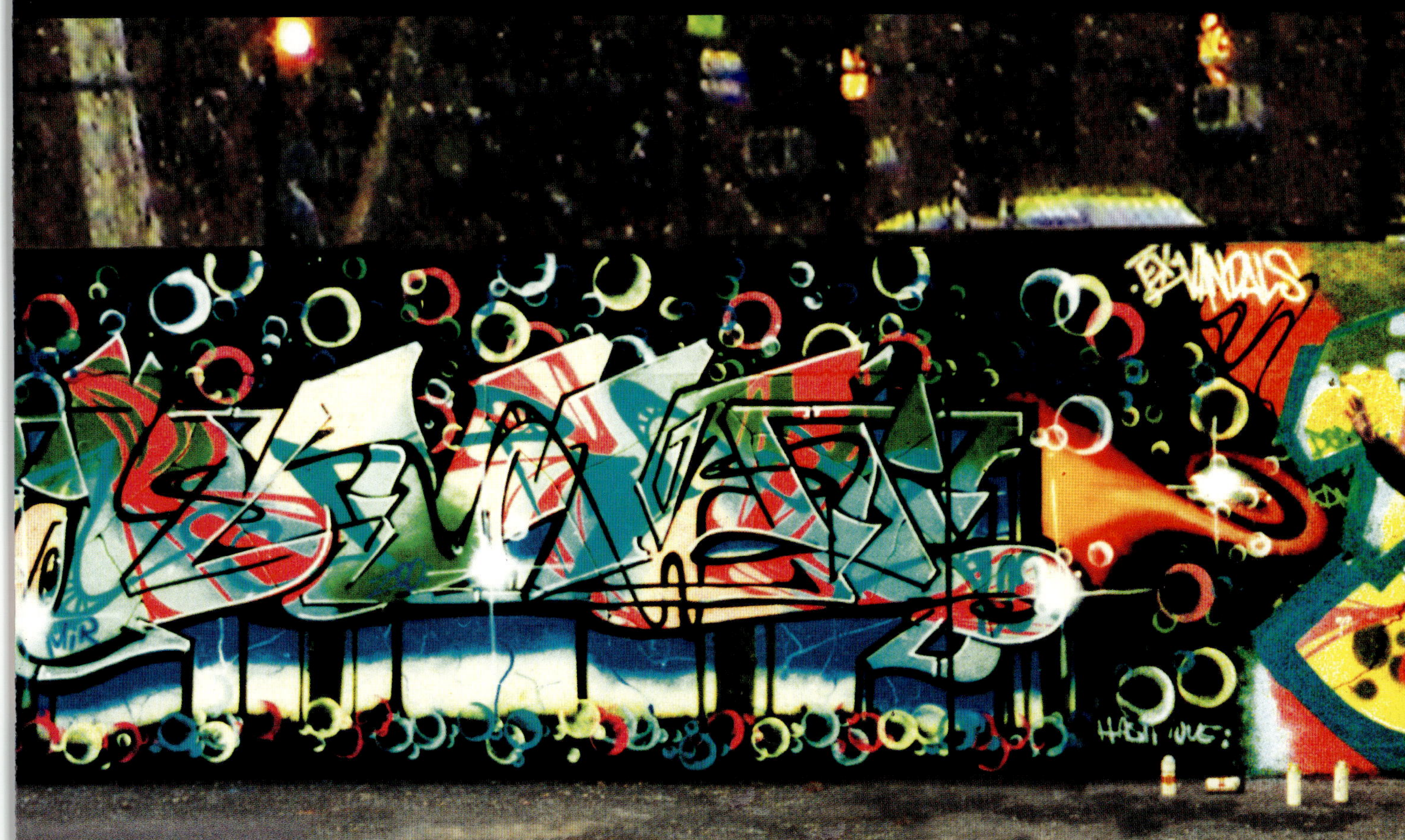

DOME EX-VANDALS, "NOW IS THE TIME TO ROCK SHIT."

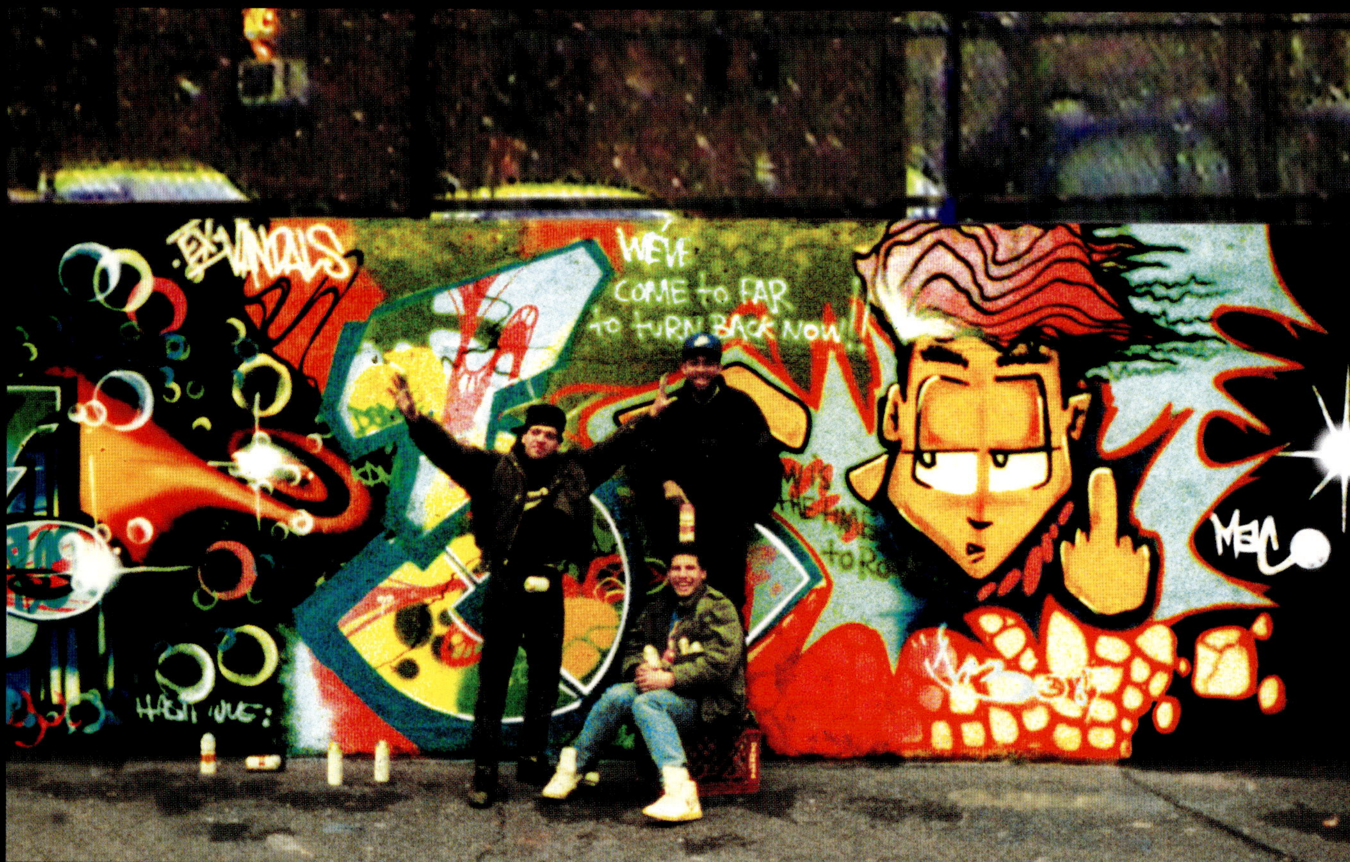

DOME, MIRAGE, aka MAC, and DC3 live at the Hall of Fame.

Mr. Mirage, SHO, Dome, and DC3.

The Hall of Fame, East Harlem @ 106th Street and Park Avenue.

This was a big production for us. We rocked this April 5, 1987, without permission; back then that wasn't an option. The Hall of Fame didn't operate like that, which I liked. If you had the balls to paint here and got over, as long as you had your props, your shit would stay up. I mean of course nothing lasts for ever and there always were haters. This was the only time Mirage, aka Mac, had painted here. We had now been hitting the subway trains for 1/2 a year and TDC/USA had hit Harlem several times before this production. Mirage had also started

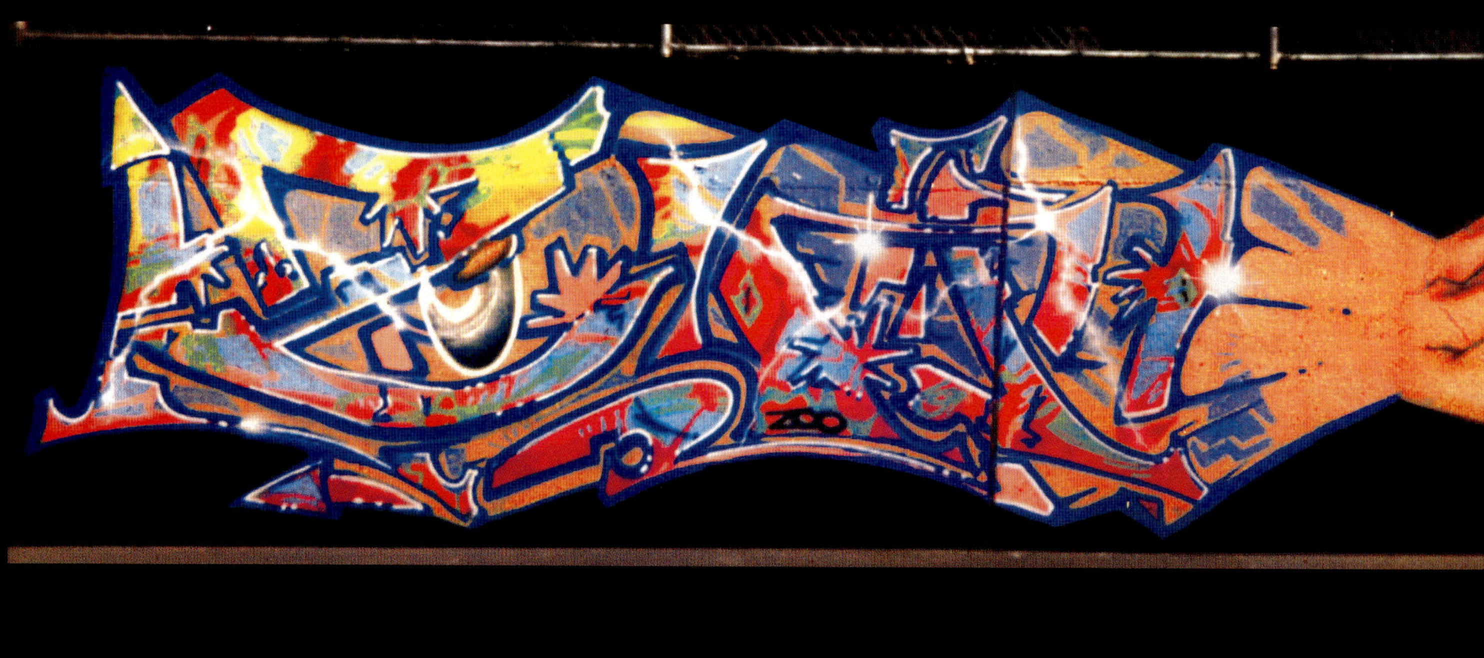

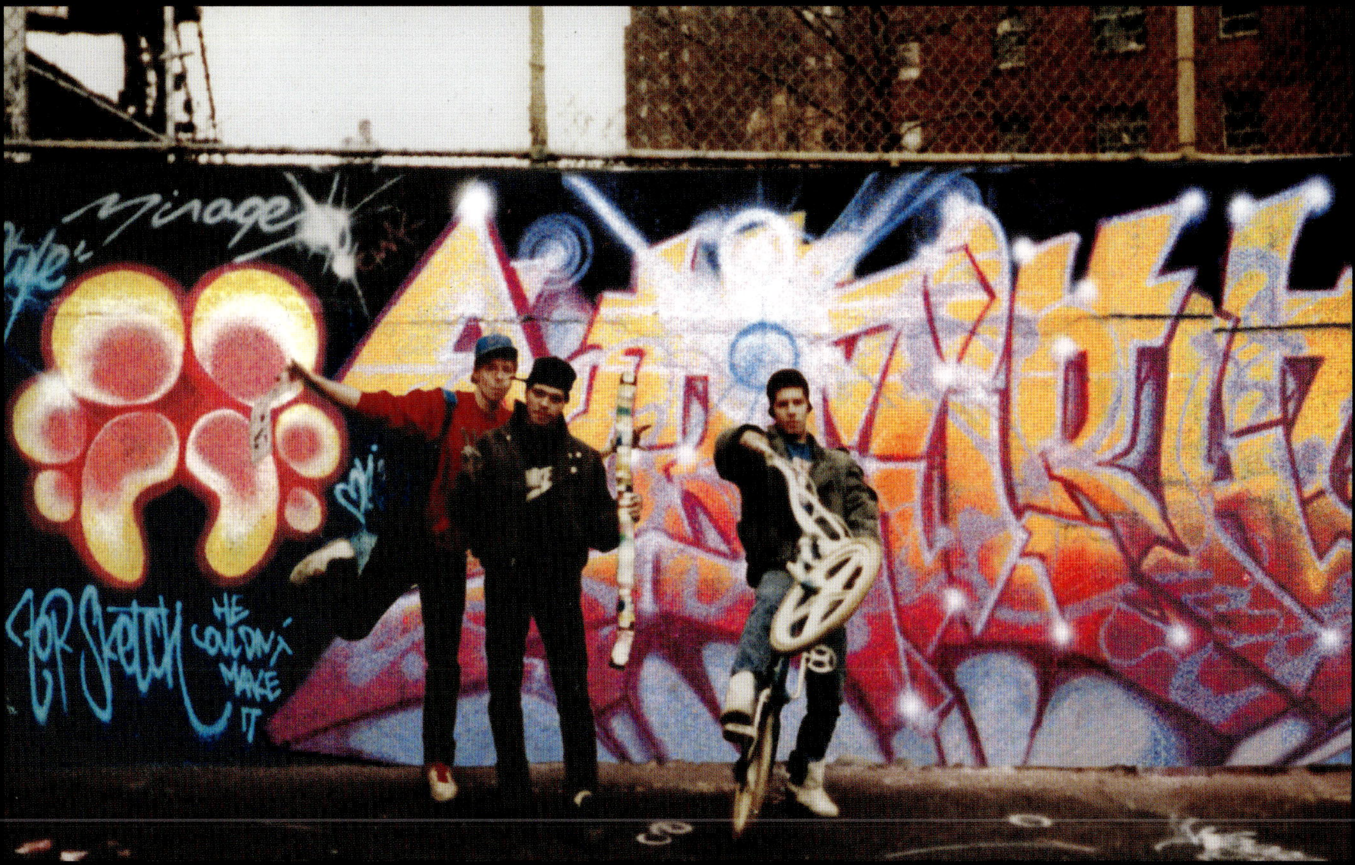

"WE'VE COME TO FAR TO TURN BACK NOW"

painting some trains with us as well as his original partner Sketch. Sketch was supposed to come this night, but for some reason couldn't. We used mad paint on this wall and it was all spray paint, not like how everybody's rolling their permission pieces with wall paint nowadays. This production lasted approximately three months.

★

ZOO SHO was the last piece we rocked together here in the of summer 1990.

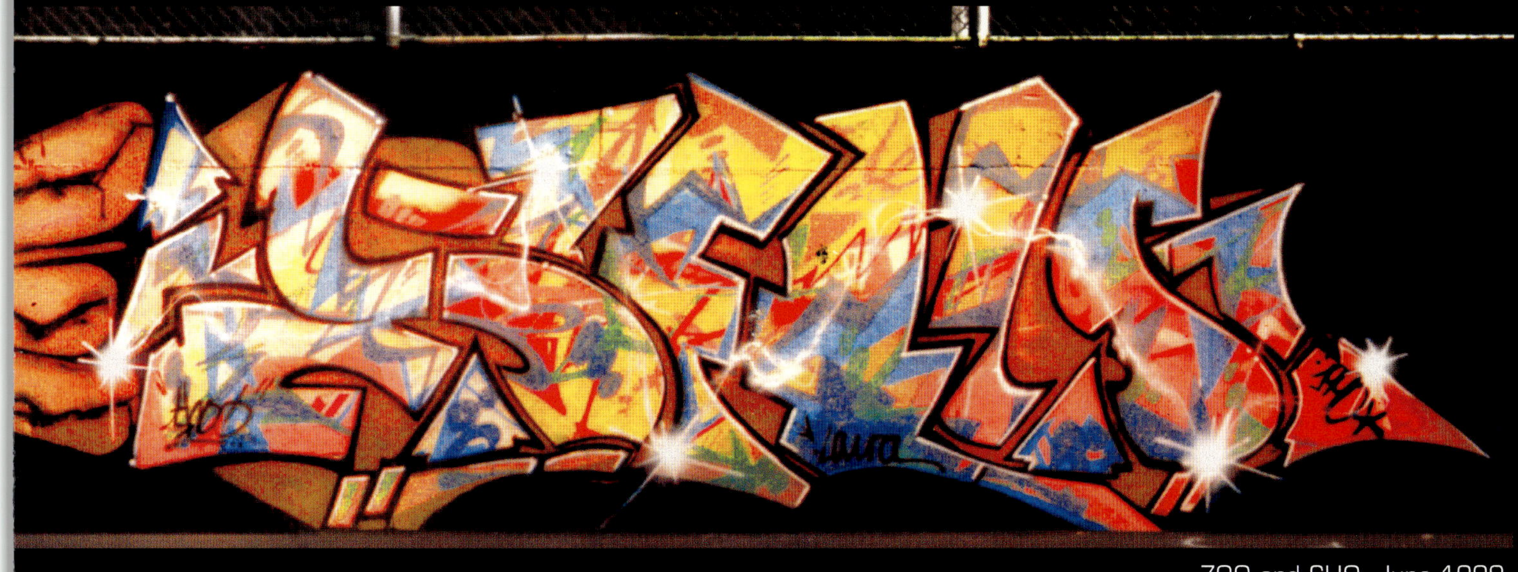

ZOO and SHO, June 1990.

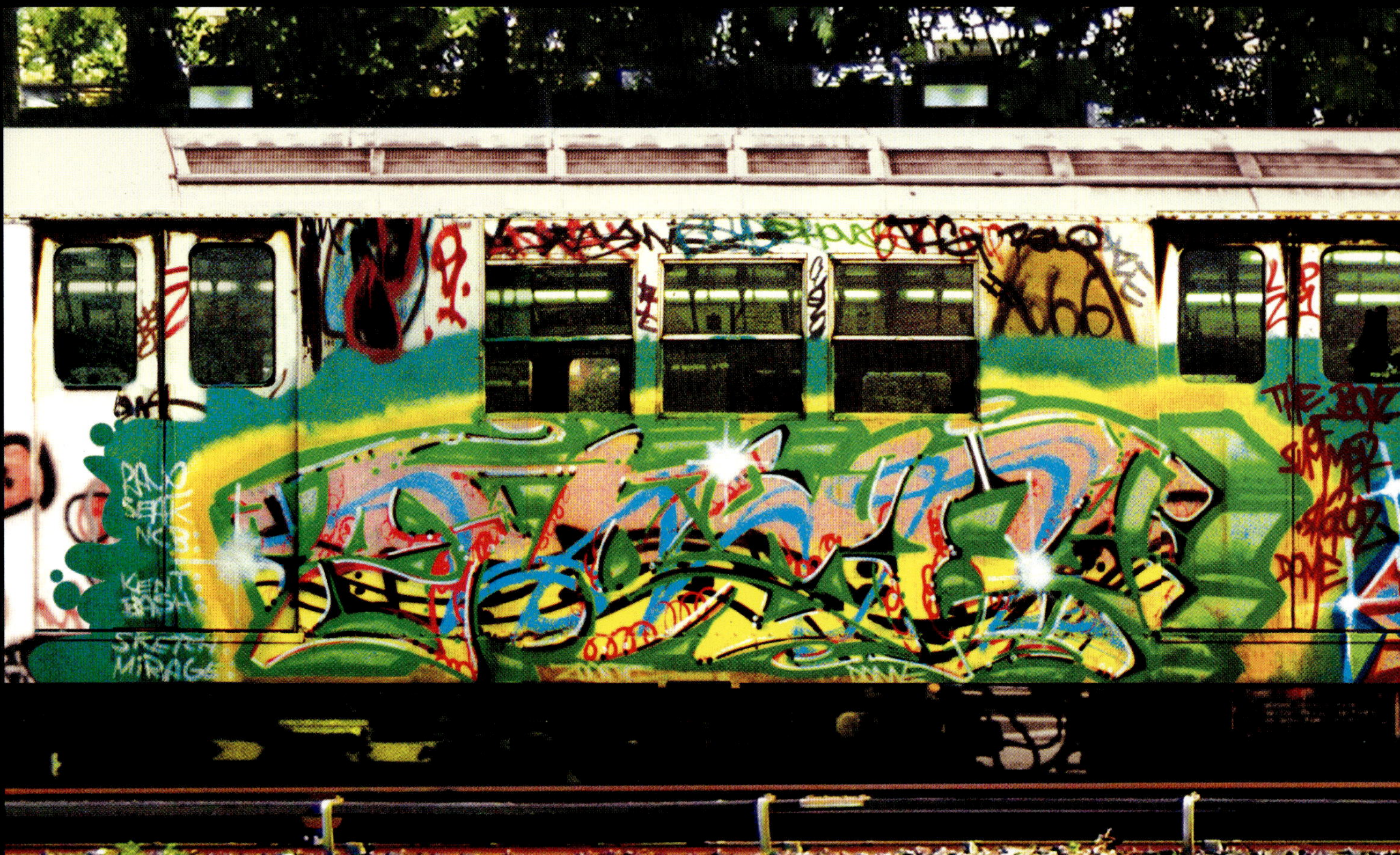

DOME and SHOROZ, "The Boys of Summer," 5 Train, Jul. 15, 1987.

The DOME SHOROZ was painted In mid-July 1987. This train was done at the end of the Esplanade stick-outs. I remember that we hadn't been hitting trains as much because it was summer and like 90 degrees all month, so you'd think we be at the beach or some shit. The summer really sucked for doing graffiti for a number of reasons. I mean sure it was great for doing walls I guess, but that definitely wasn't our focus. We liked cold weather because at night there would be way less people outside and especially police on the platforms. When it's summer every ones outside to all hours hanging outside. There are two main problems facing you in the summer, one was it's a lot harder to identify who might be potentially undercover transit police outside but also in the train yards and lay ups. You still had work bums doing their jobs in the train sets, but they seemed to stay much later—I guess because of the nice weather. It was always better to more or less know that the workers would come thru and do their jobs and leave and go back to the MTA buildings and station resource staging areas. Also, because of the nicer weather, transit police would absolutely chase and try to apprehend you even on the tracks and in the tunnels— this was a lot less likely when it was freezing cold out. The second problem is it's much harder to rack paint in the summer, but as you can see, we had plenty saved up from many racking sessions. We still had Esplanade on lock and even took my brother Dave with us. For this story I spoke to him and he said he still remembers it and was glad to experience it for himself. See you at the beach!!!!!

Painted in Morris Park, Bronx, NY, "Loving It."

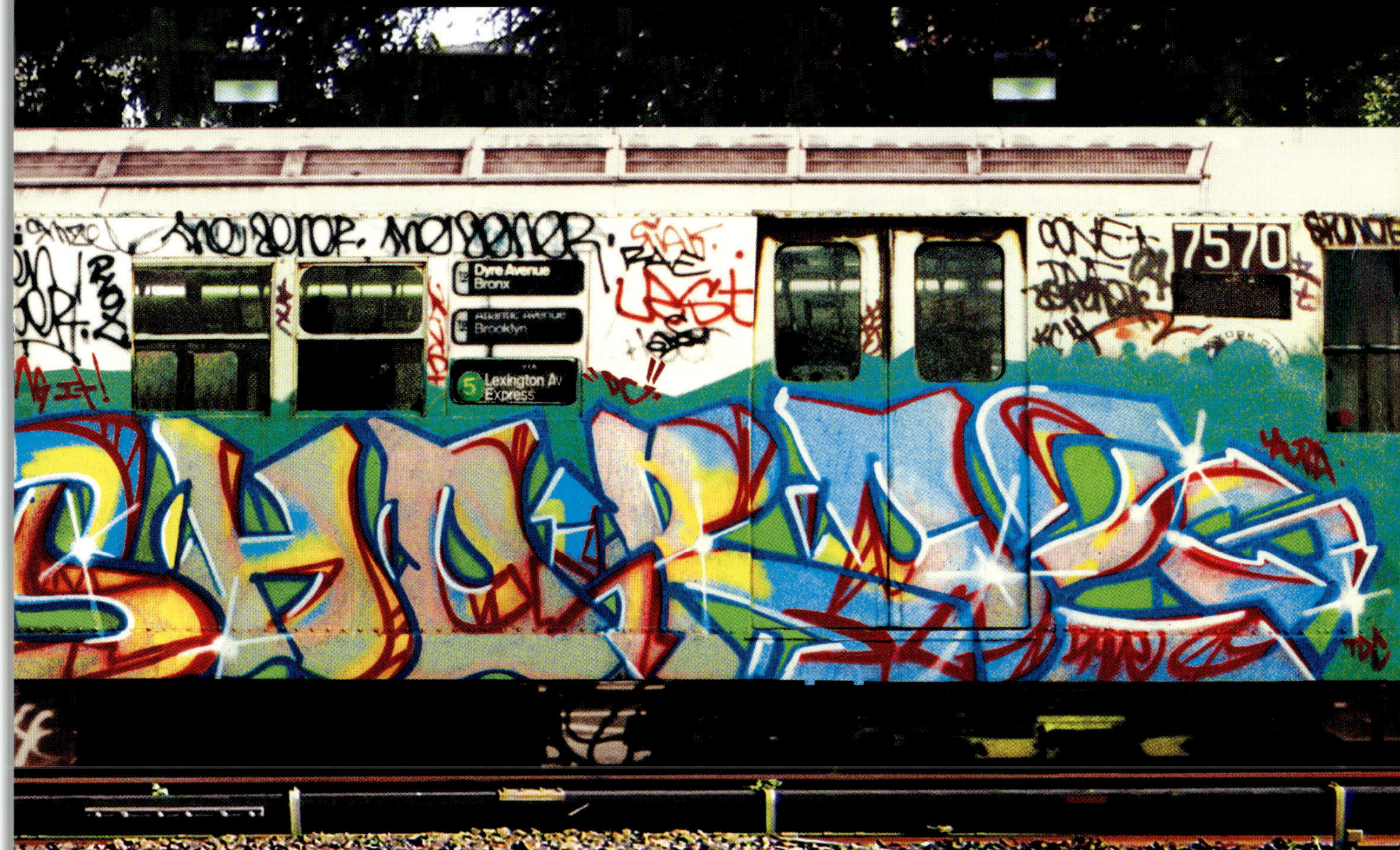

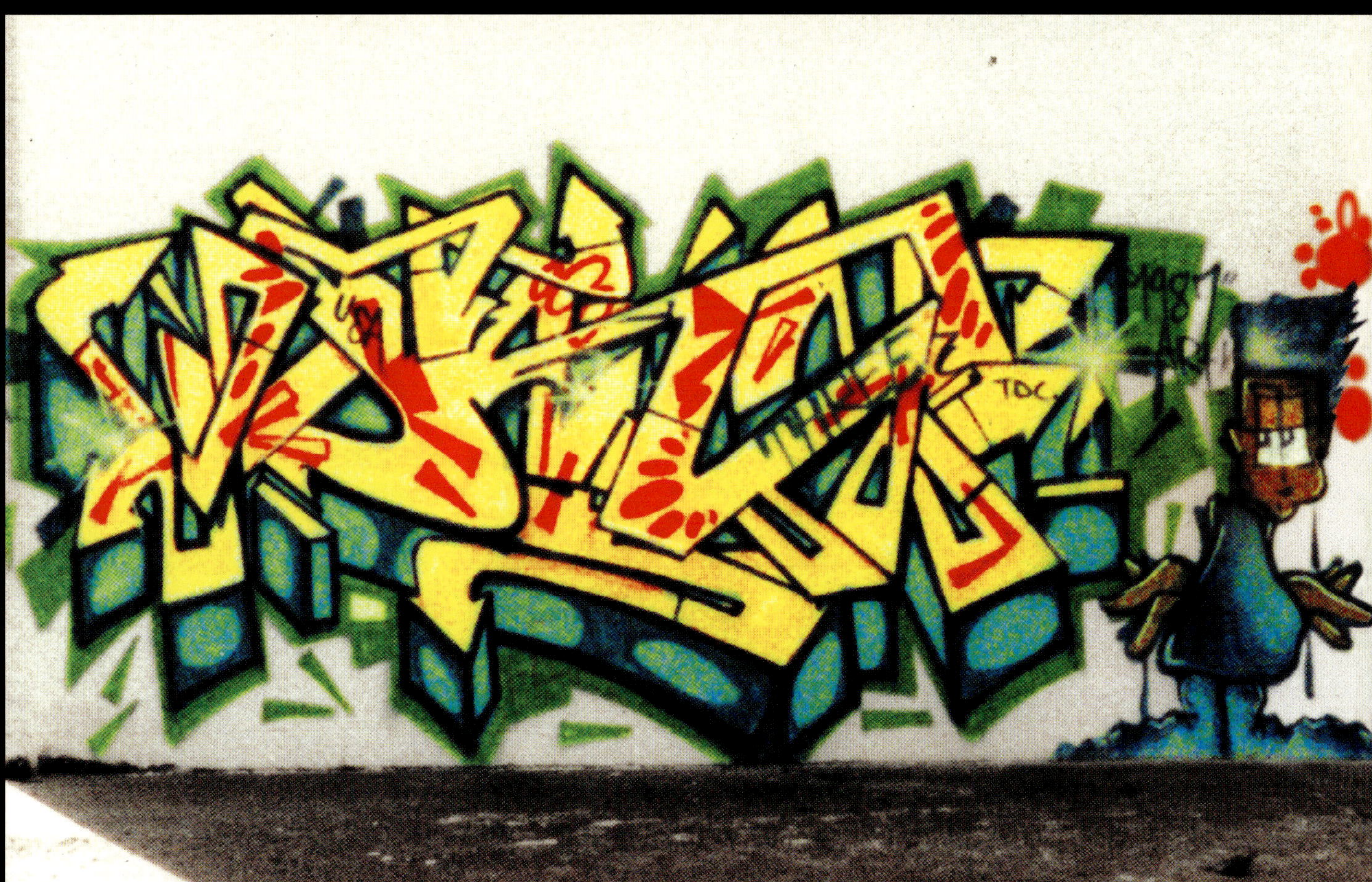

DC, "1987 ART," painted in Hempstead, NY, June 5, 1985.

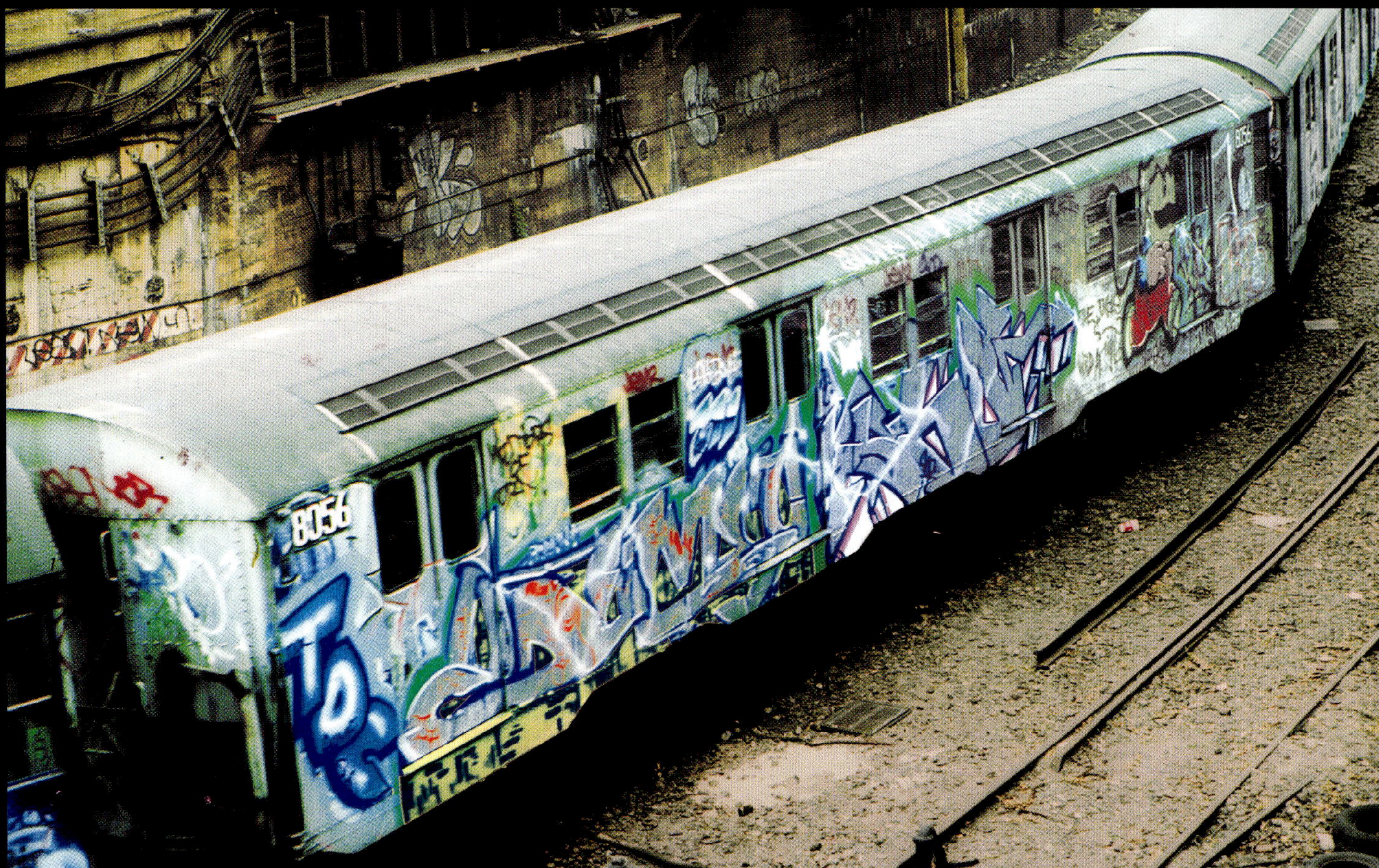

TDC DOME and SHO, "The Jungles Wild at Night," Part 2.

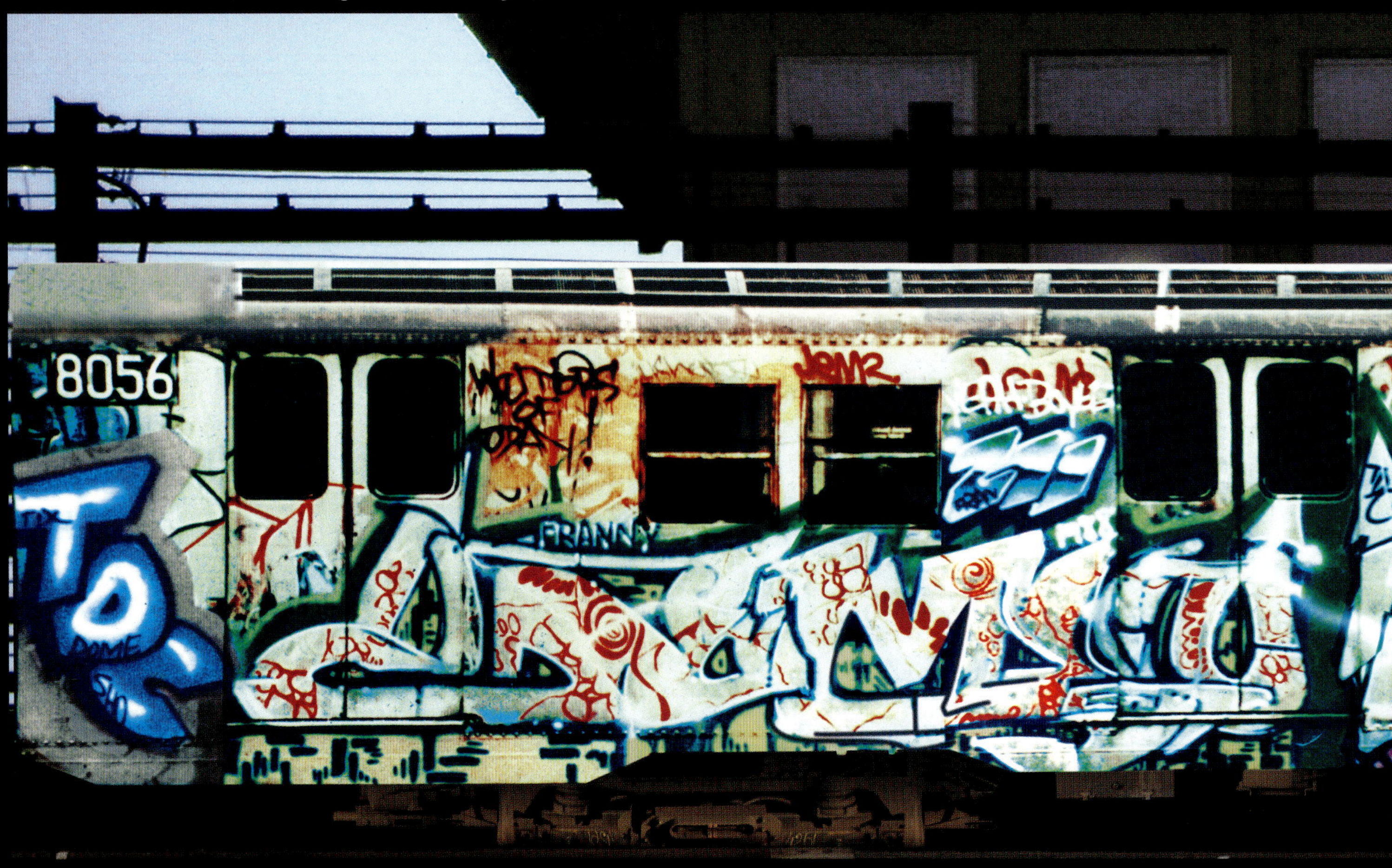

The B Train Underground Tunnels. This lay-up was sweet and was also called 57th Street Tishman. SHO and Dome hit this late in the graff game for the crew. We hit this car on April 6, 1988, and you'll see that at the end of the SHO piece. This train came to be known as the Mario Brothers Warriors of Today train. This was a double-lane tunnel lay-up that ran from the Columbus Circle subway station up Central Park West. We only had word of mouth information on where it was so we looked for that shit by walking north off the platform and the tracks separated into the lay-up. It wasn't that hard to find and we went all the way to the end of the trains in there so as to know how deep it ran and what was down there. We seen a couple of writers and paid them no mind. Dome and I started painting and was rocking for 1/2 hour on a ledge and all of a sudden here comes many writers beefing with bats like, "What you write?" So I pulled out the toast and Dome pointed it at them. Man, you ain't never seen drama end faster than that! Shit was cool after that shit.

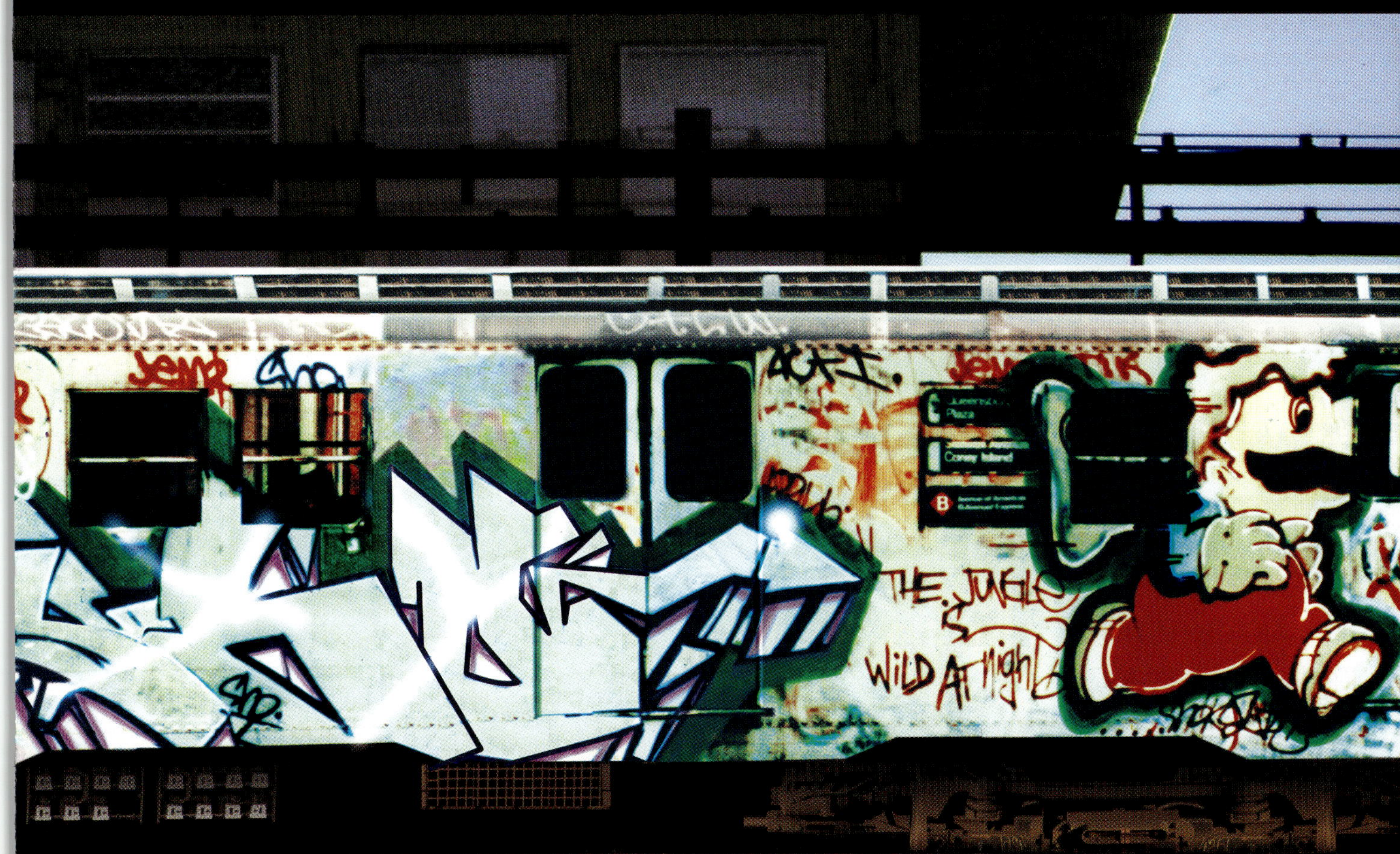

The MARIO BROTHERS B Train painted in 57th St. two-track underground tunnel lay up, Apr. 6, 1988.

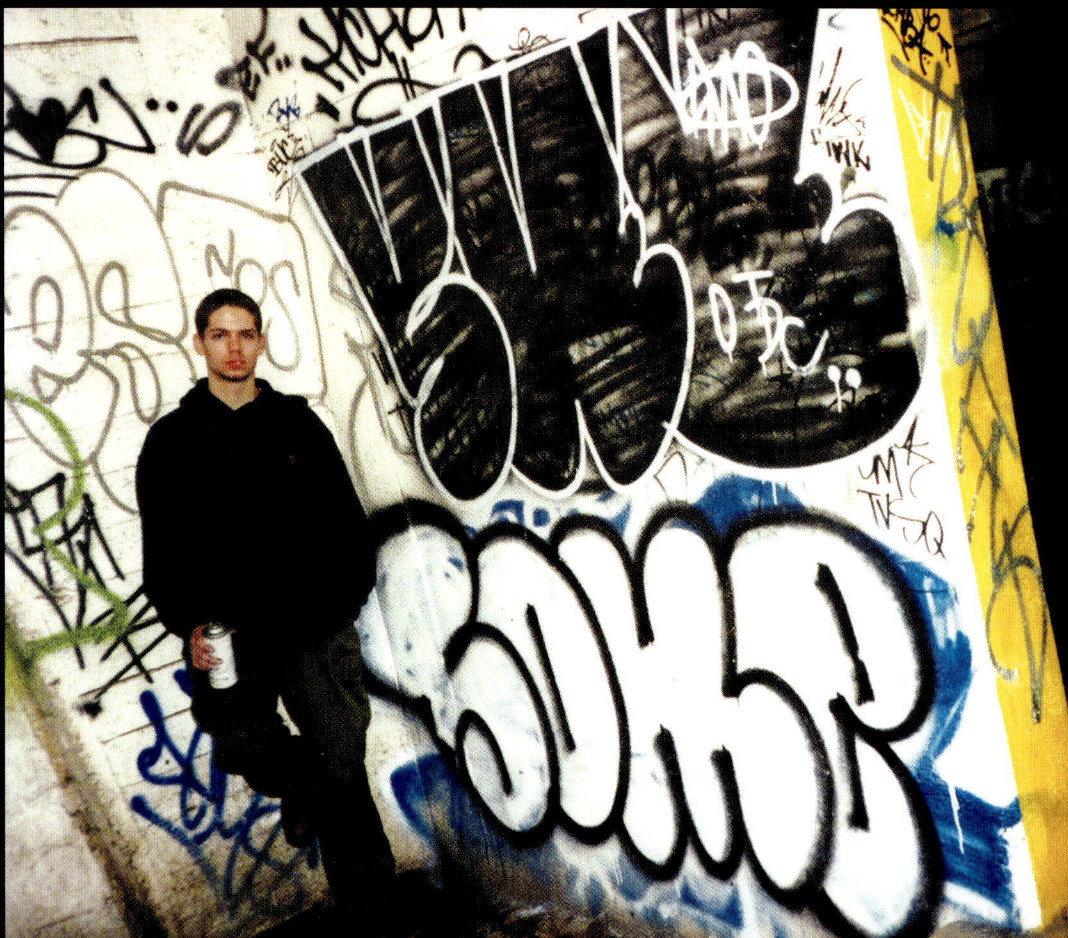

SOME AAB, 1995.
"In Memory of Shaun,"
aka BREY.
Chilling deep under
Manhattan in the
Freedom Tunnels.
Aug. 1994.

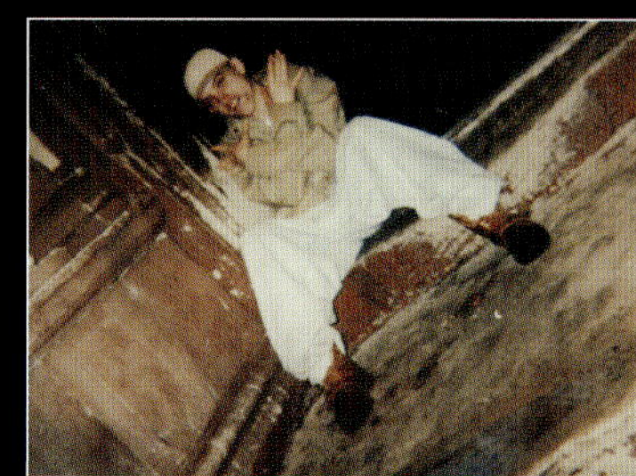

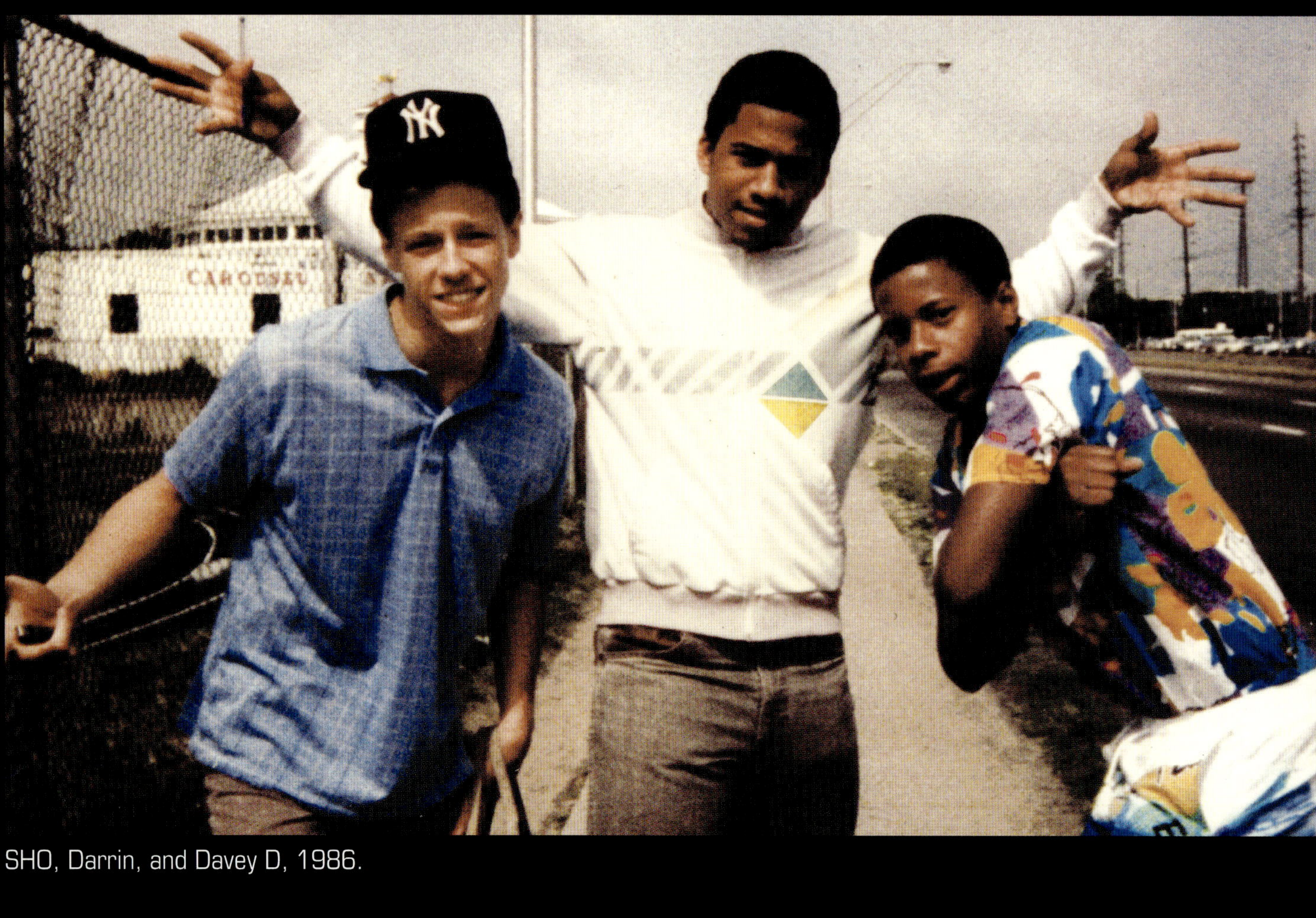

SHO, Darrin, and Davey D, 1986.

Sizzlened at Boys Field, Brooklyn, NY; Summer Time, July 15,1997.

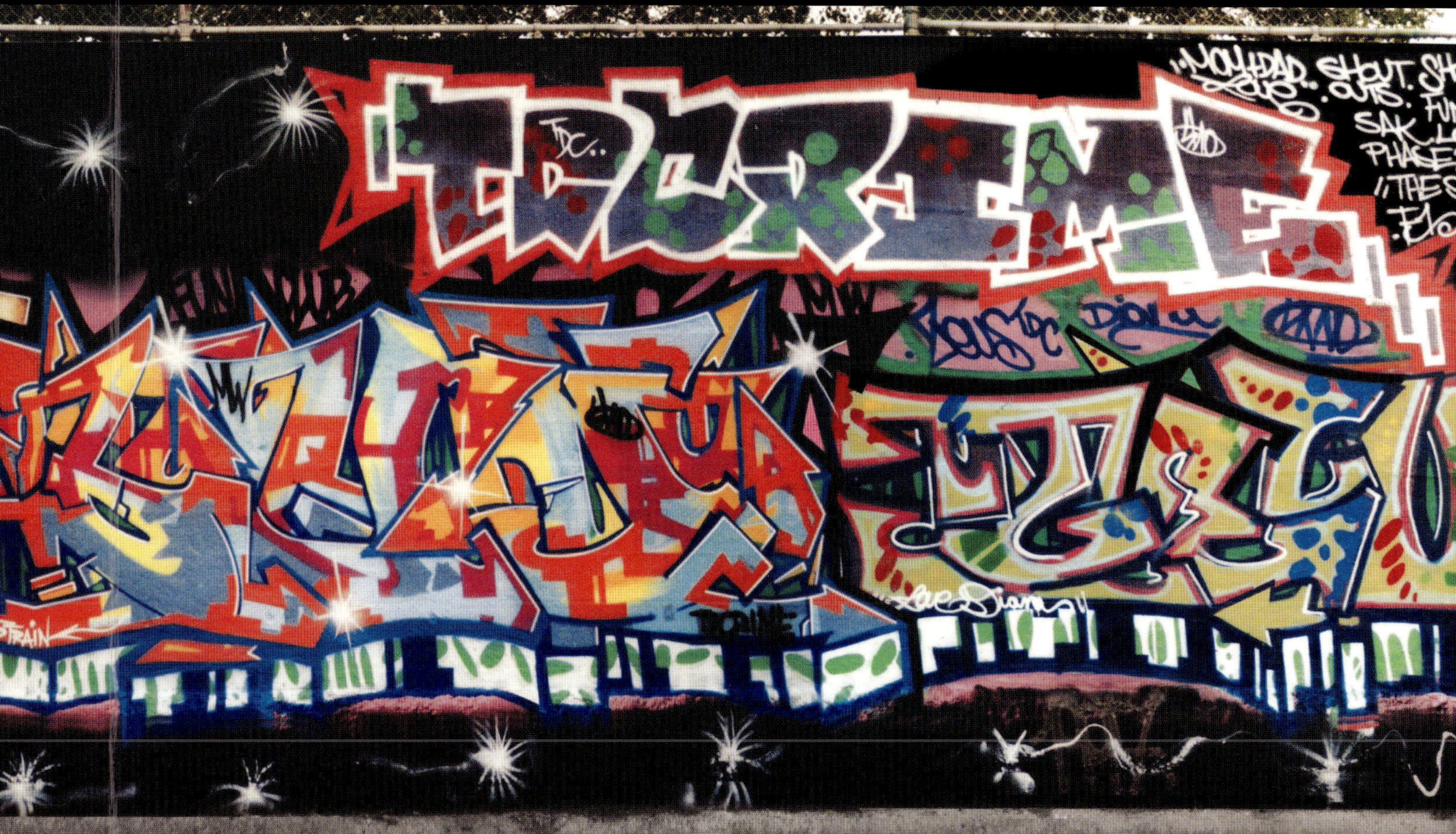

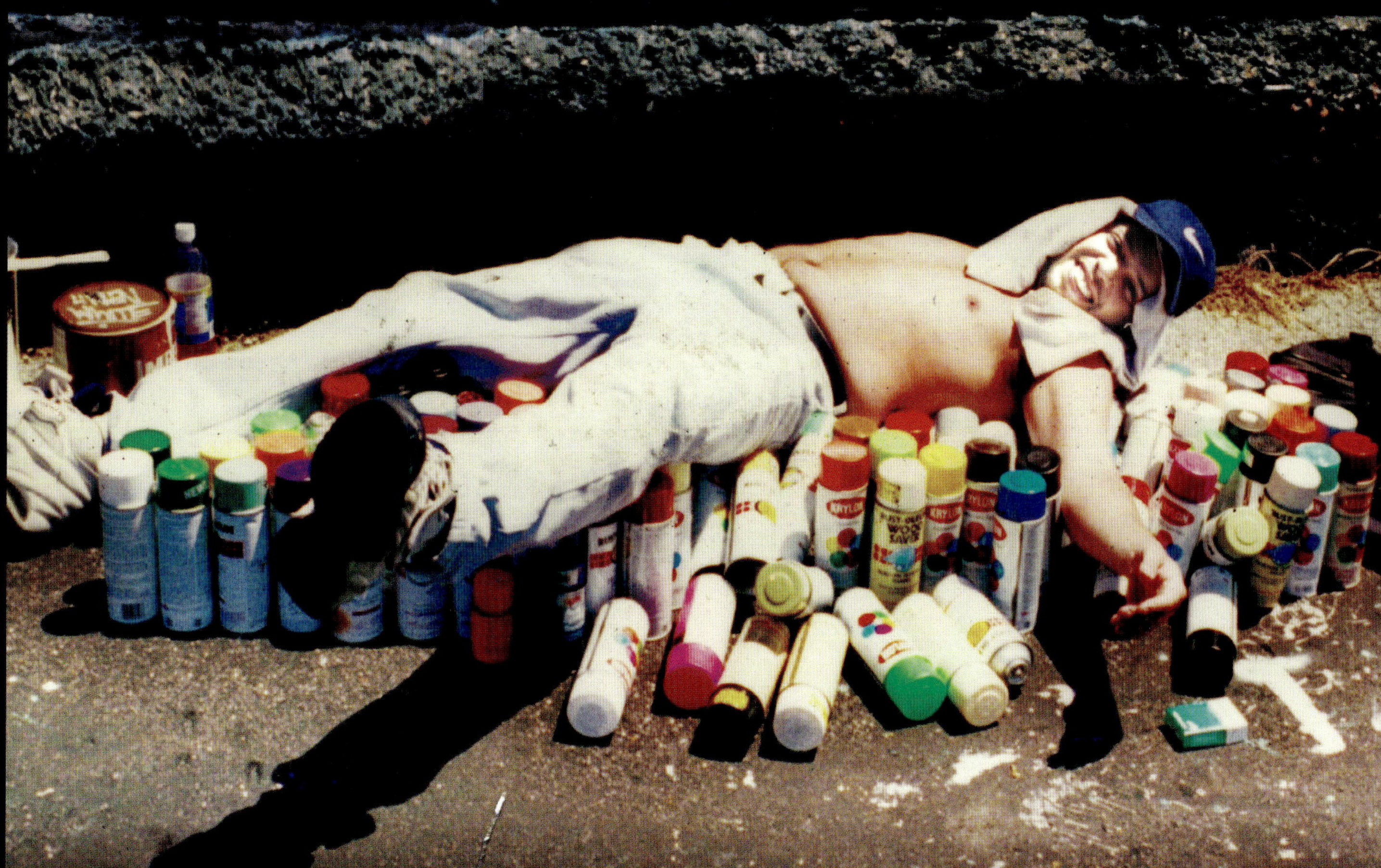

DOME taking a paint break....

ZOO top-to-bottom, two months later in the 180th St. Yard, Jan. 1988.

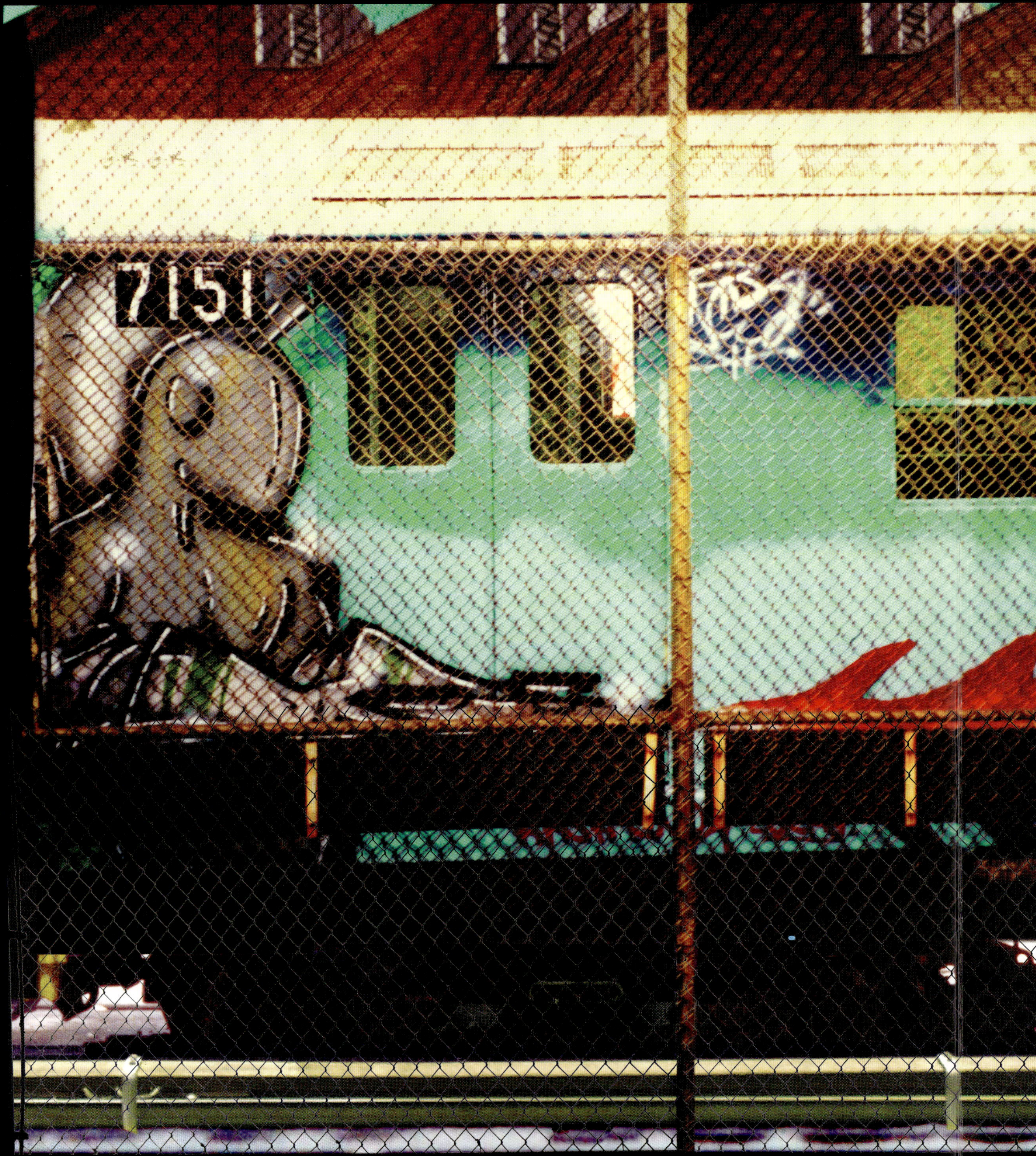

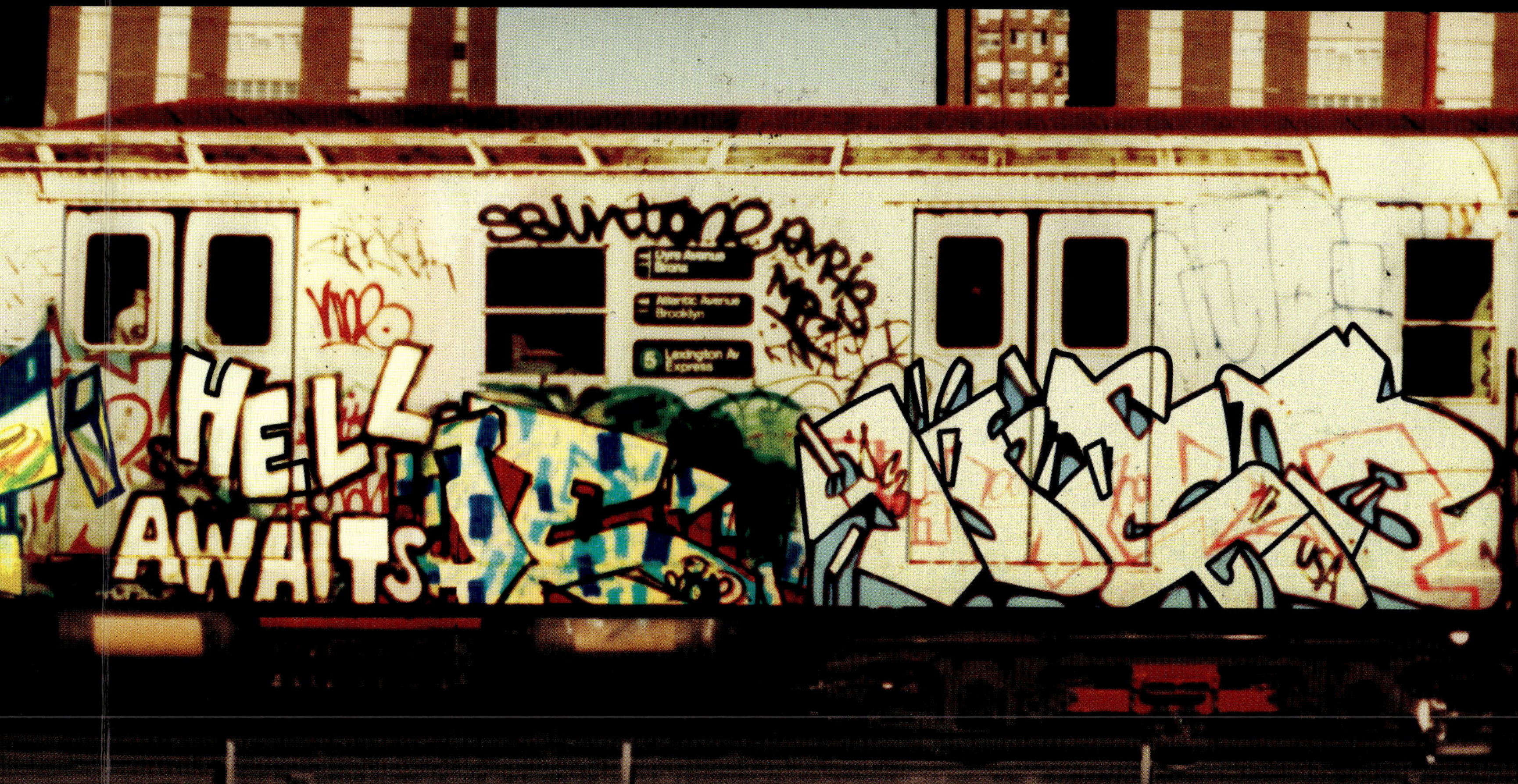

DERO gave us the paint and rocked a DERO KYLE whole car next to it with "A Sphynx."

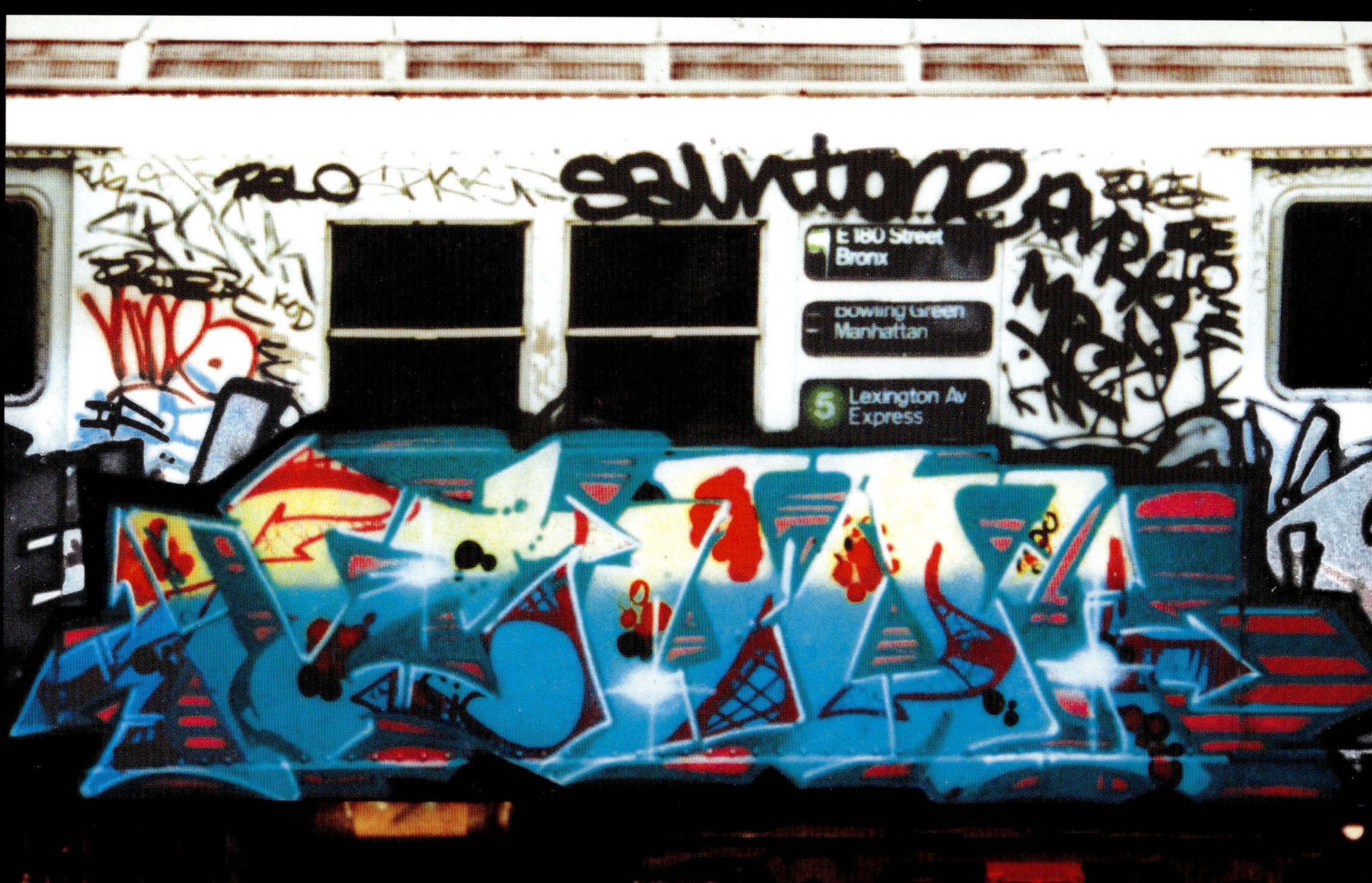

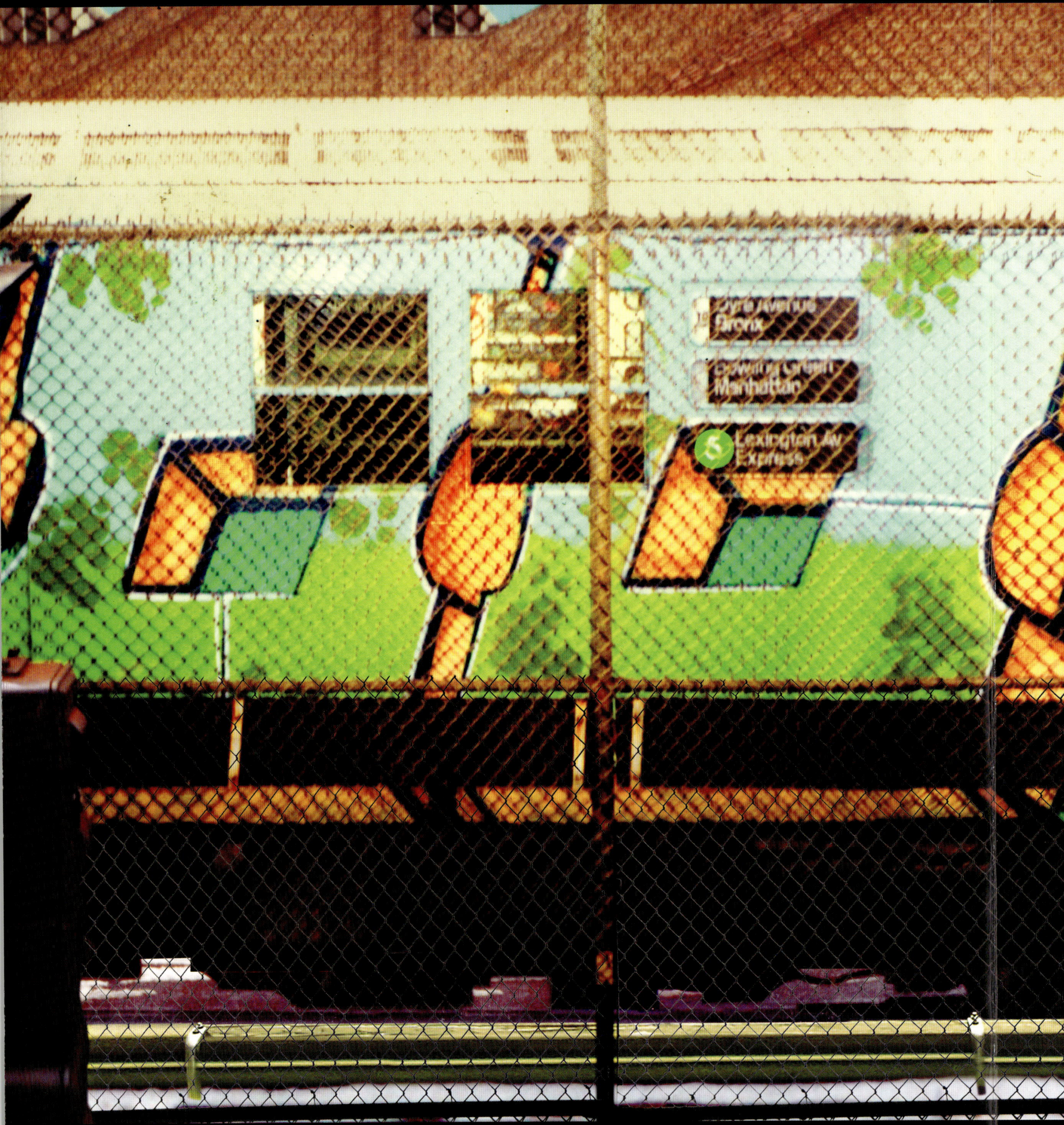
Bronx
Manhattan
5
Lexington Av
Express

CHAPTER 9

The K Line. The B Line. The C Line.

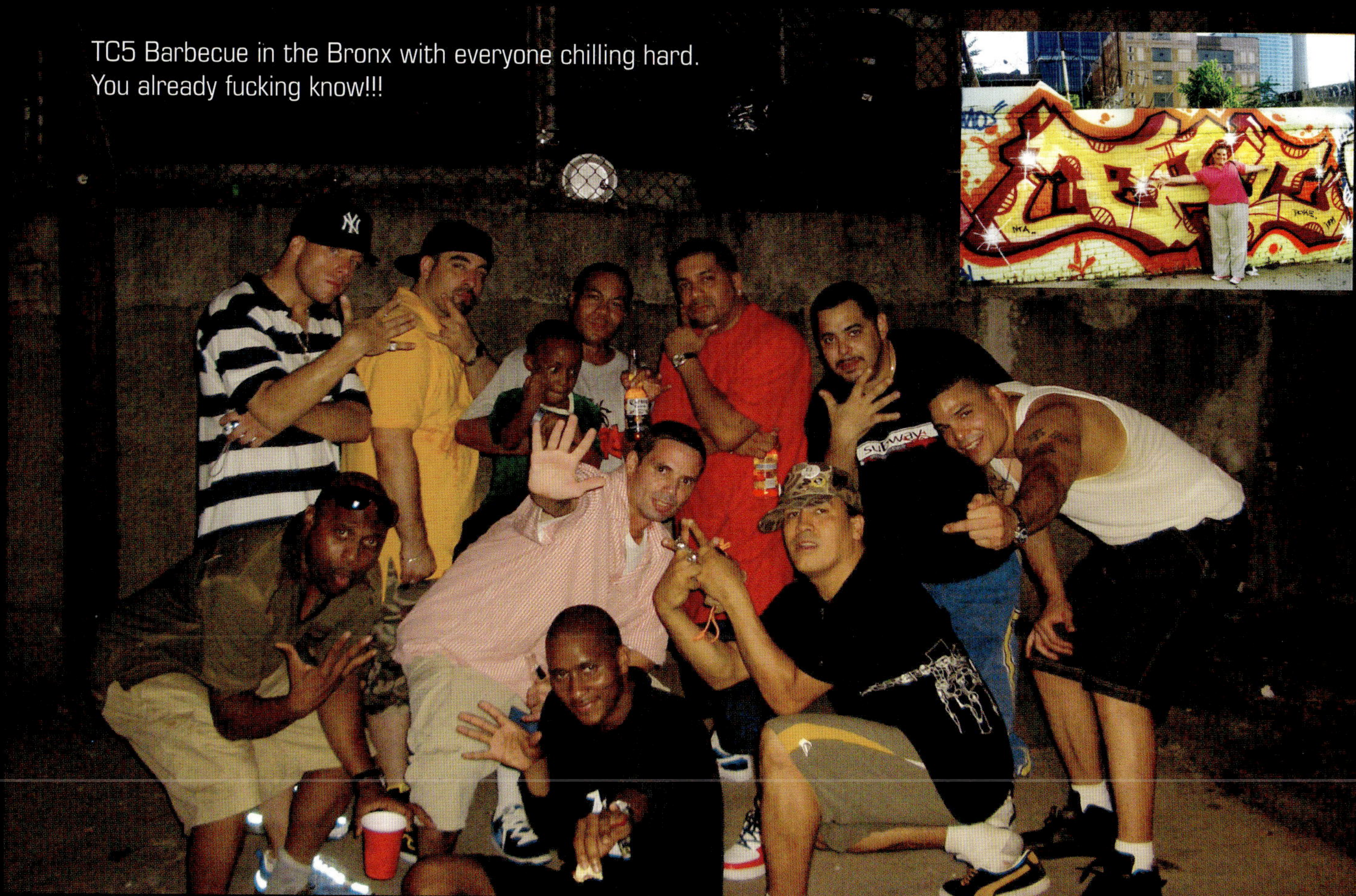

TC5 Barbecue in the Bronx with everyone chilling hard. You already fucking know!!!

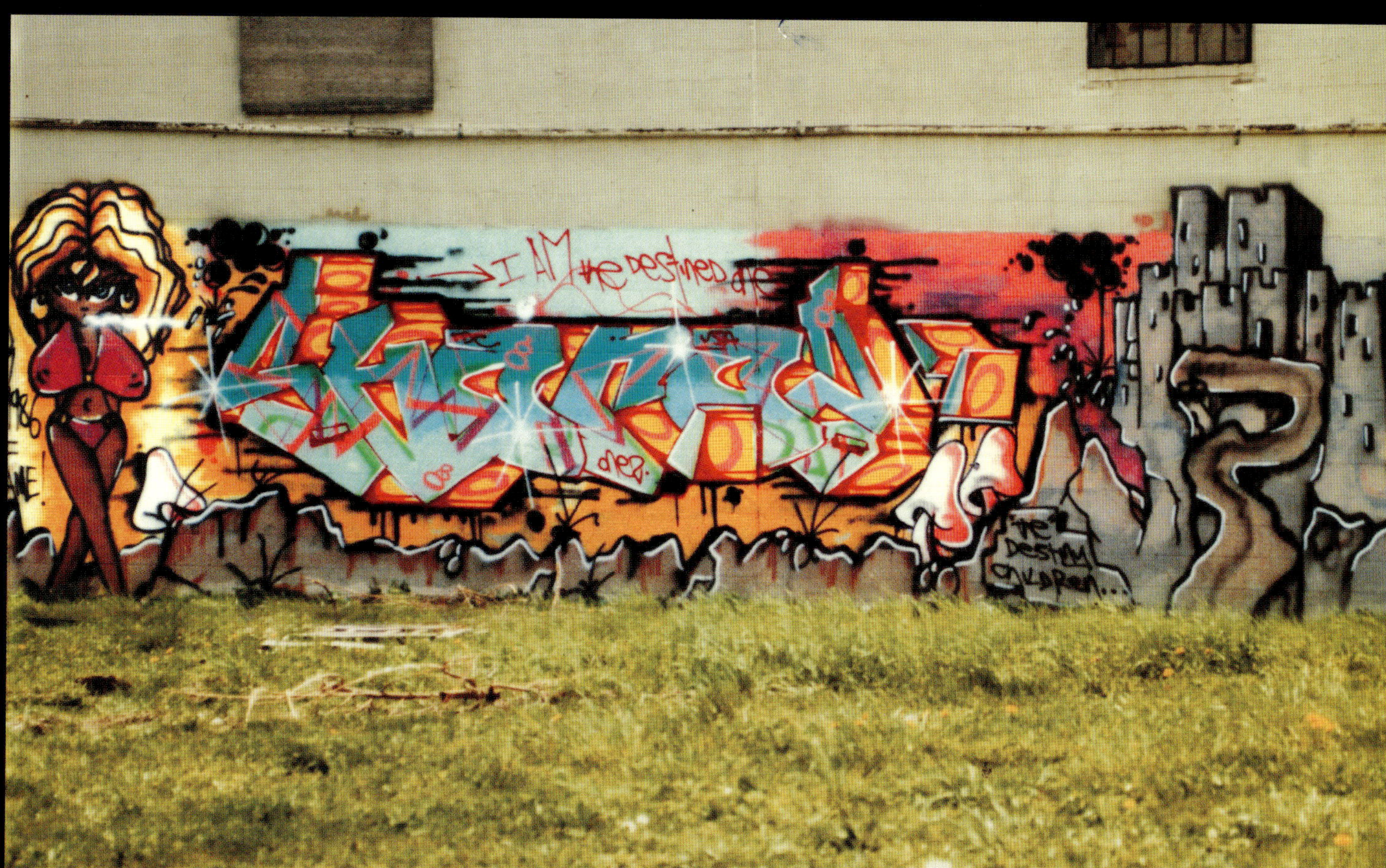

SHOROZ, "I AM THE DESTINED ONE," Freeport, Long Island, NY. 1986 Wall of Fame.

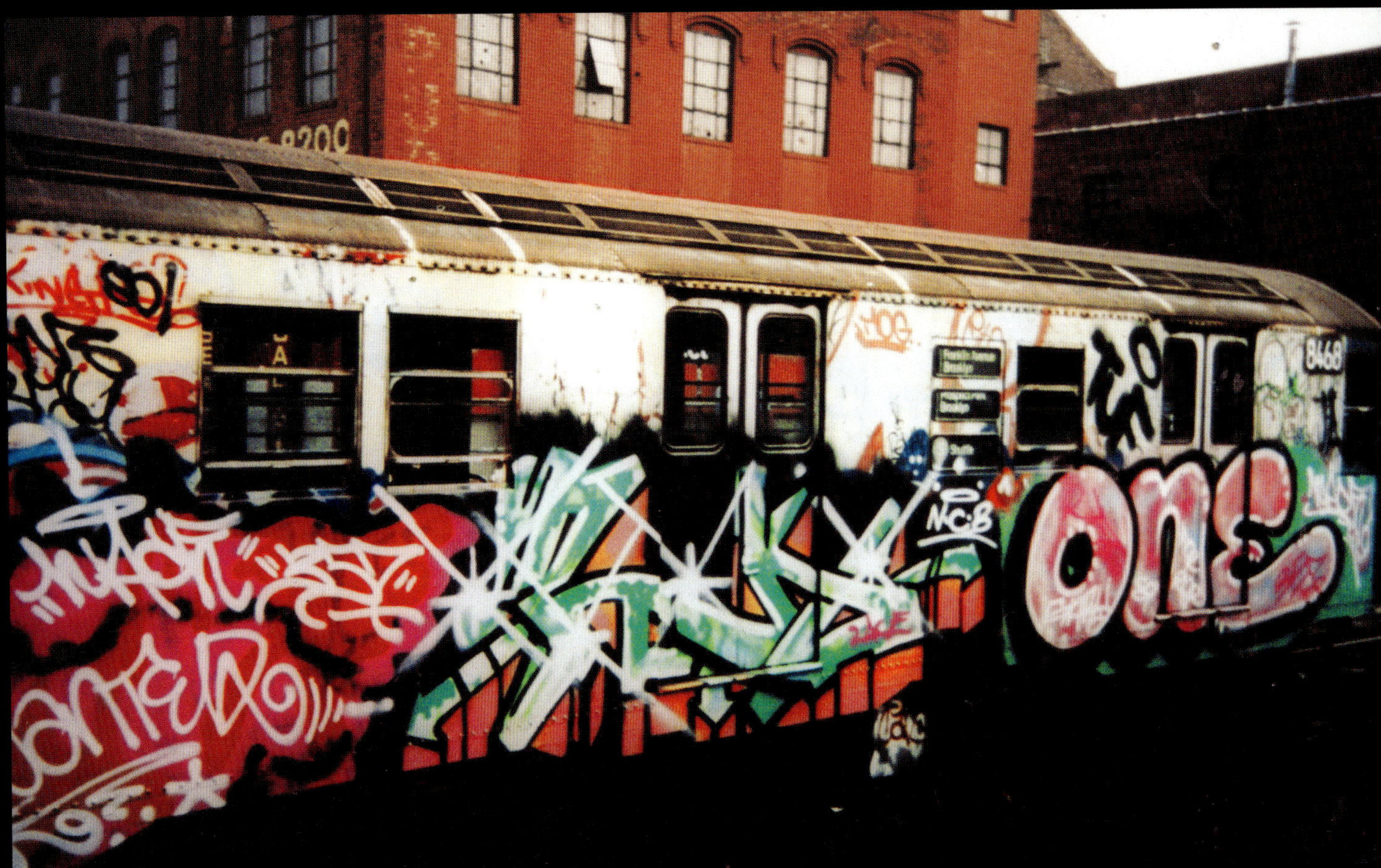

RD One and Lace 357, B Train, Sep. 1988.

It wasn't until as I was doing this historic, for the record book, account that I learned, thru my dogg Risk FC, who had rolled up on us that night. Turns out those writers were RD, JJ, Lace, KK, and other heads from 357 crew. So I wanted to let niggas in the graff game know just how real and fucking dangerous it was back then by including RD 357s account of what was what. Good looking out yo for your story people need to know the real deal.

-SHO TDCUSAMWANTED.

RD 357...I don't ever talk about who I beat down out of respect for them, so instead lets talk about me getting my ass kicked, it's more fun that way. I have honestly bled for the graff game more then most writers if not maybe even more then any other writers. Hell, I've been stabbed, sliced open, I've had my head beat open with sharp and blunt objects alike. I was stabbed by the Ball Busters in the left shoulder in the #1 Tunnel and Lace beat down Boozer once in 1983 at the Central Park band shell. I've even been shot in a lay up with a flair gun in the chest from three feet away, that shit set me on fire and broke three of my ribs. I think it was SHO, Dome, and DC3 that did it or maybe TMR, I really didn't catch their names. Shit was crazy, me, JJ, Lace, Caya, Sash, and Skate TC5 was there in the tunnel where we robbed everyone all the time for their paint.

As we approached, a group of writers who was on the cat walk between the train and the tunnel wall pulled out a gun—we didn't think they would pull the trigger, shit, I was like, "Cool I got a new gun," until Baaaam!!! I was set a blaze thinking I only had a few seconds of life in me and I grabbed the person in like a bare hug which put the fire out a bit and also set the shooter on fire as well. Then with my right hand I palmed his face sticking my fingers deep into his eye sockets like a bowling ball and thrusting the back of his skull threw a subway door window breaking the window. We all ran away in different directions thru stations and hatches that led up to the streets.

A few day later, after rolling around in pain, my mother took me to the hospital. I had three broken ribs and some other minor burns around my neck area...thank God for strong Army coats. Turns out it wasn't SHO, Dome, and DC3. Mistaken identity. 357 never had problem with TDC or vice versa. DC3 even pushed up 357 at one point and NCB. We never had crew problems I do remember y'all thinking we was TMR when we said 357. Y'all just went about ya bizz till y'all finished then y'all came over to our side to ask us not to cross ya shit out and we said we wouldn't and we didn't. I believe it got ragged possibly by Ghost and Ven, who we was warring with then anyway. All of a sudden, Bamm!, I'm on fire a week later on the same cat walk. I was thinking y'all laid in waiting for anyone after your shit got ragged and y'all popped off at any white boy y'all saw...lol lol lol. Who cares? I lived there and heads got cracked and we have let bygones be bygones. But for the record, we ain't fucked with y'all shit.

-RD 357, Who's the best!? Holla!

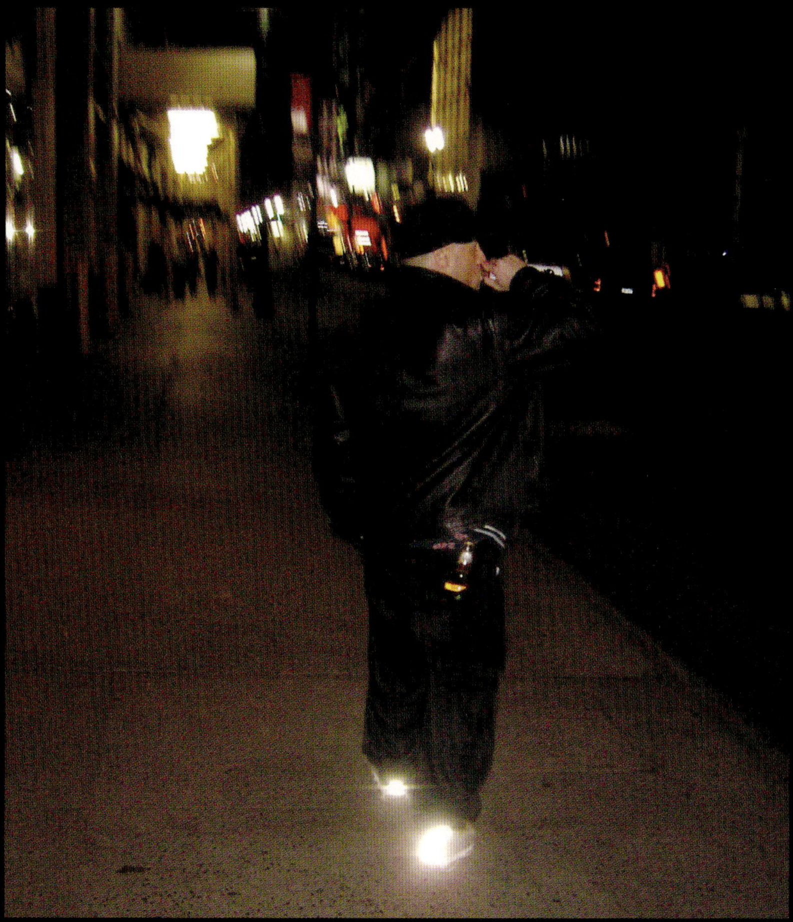

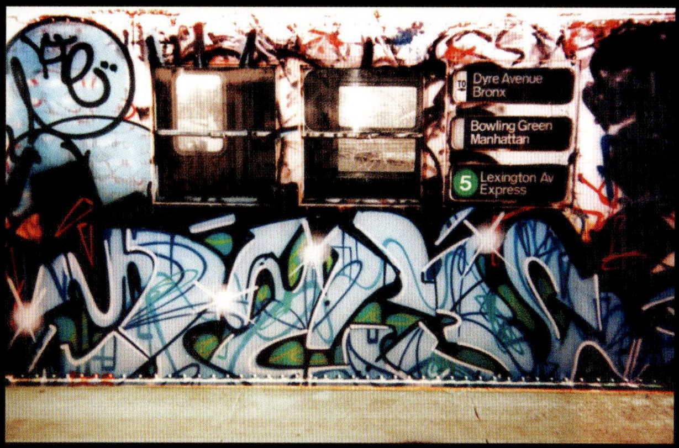

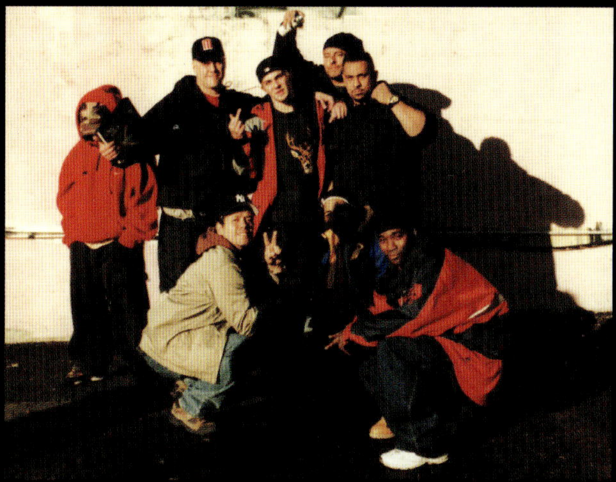

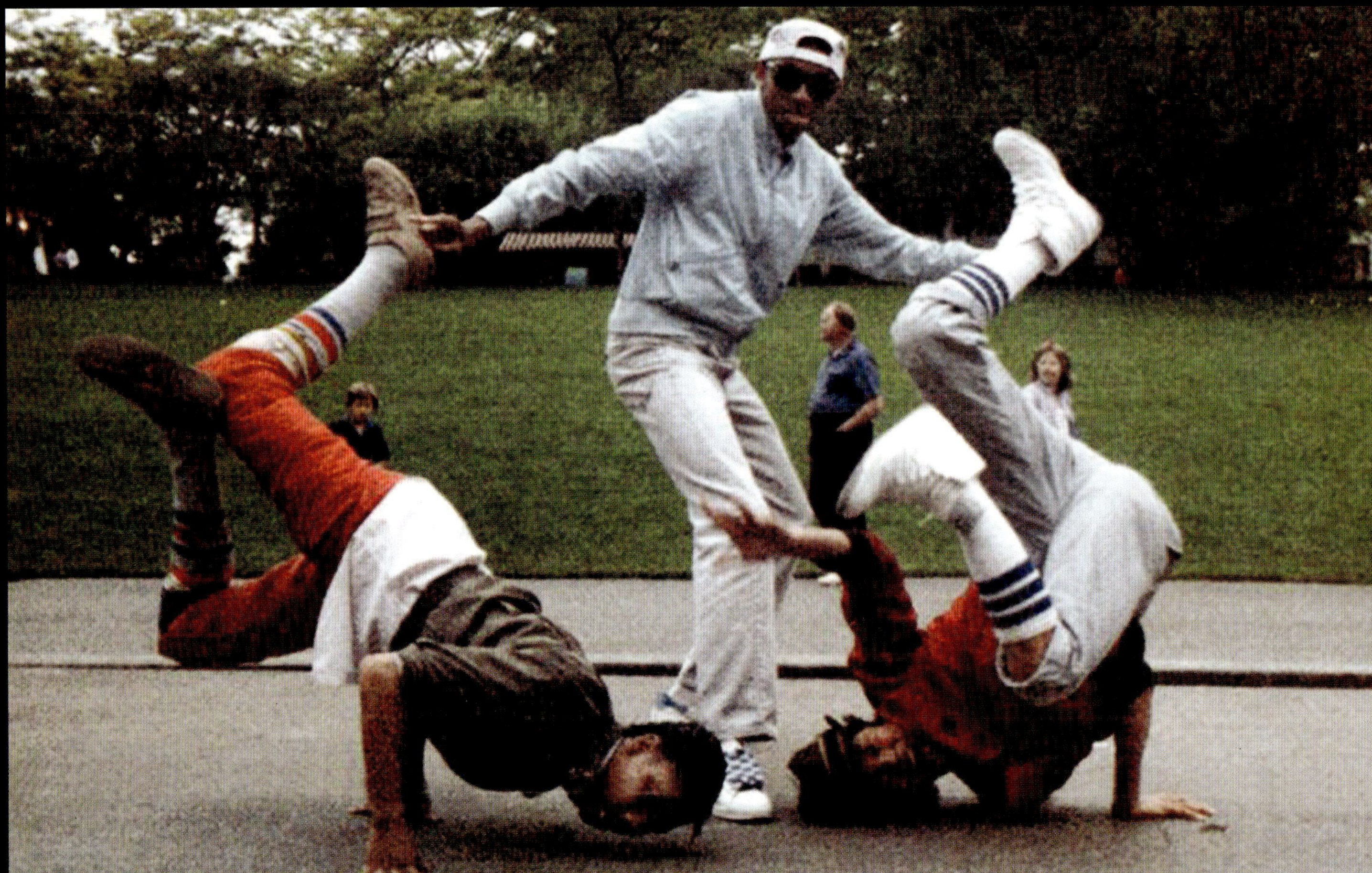

DC3 with Seattle breakdancers, 1984.

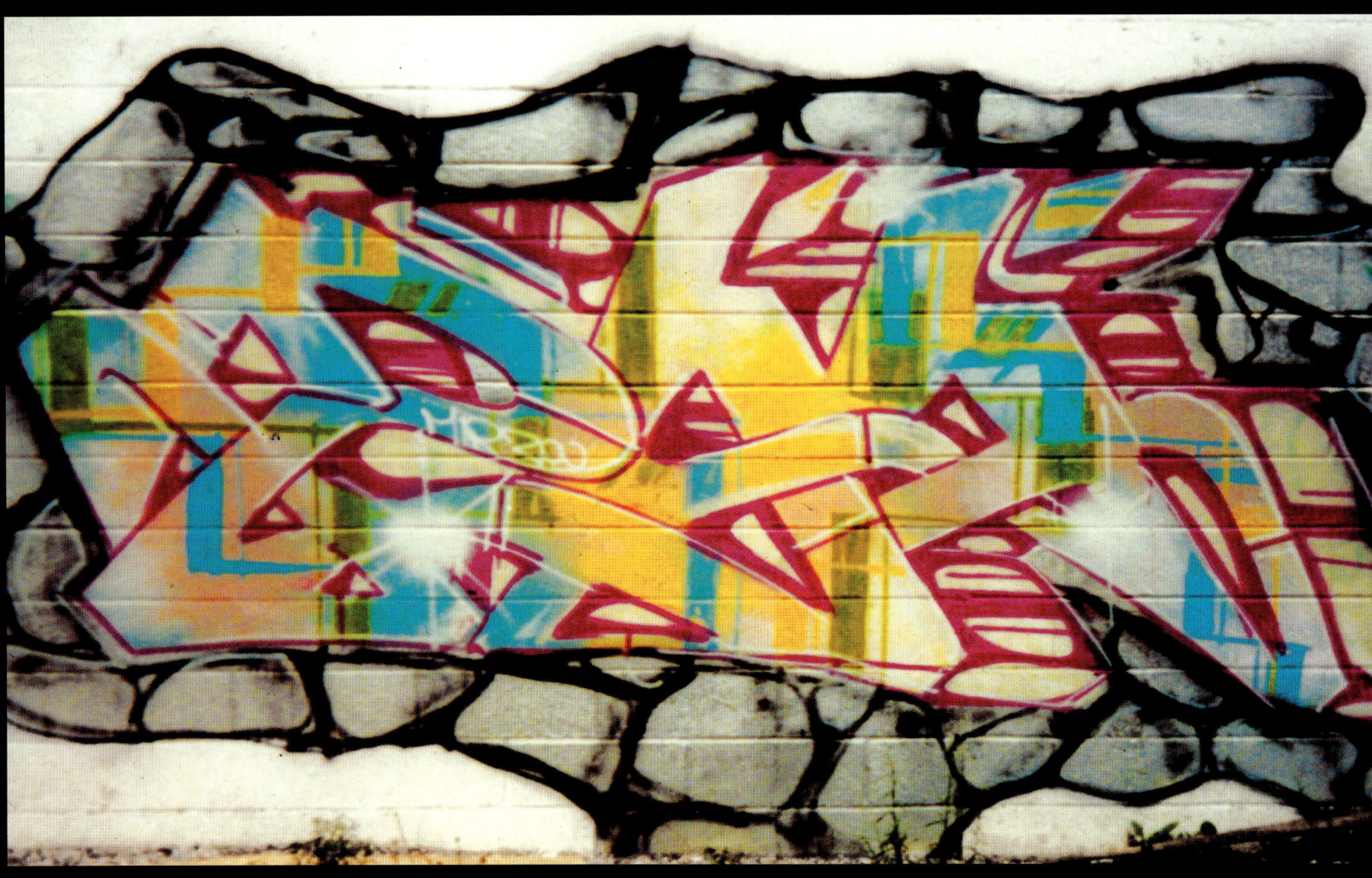

Early ZOO Burner in Hempstead, LI, 1985.

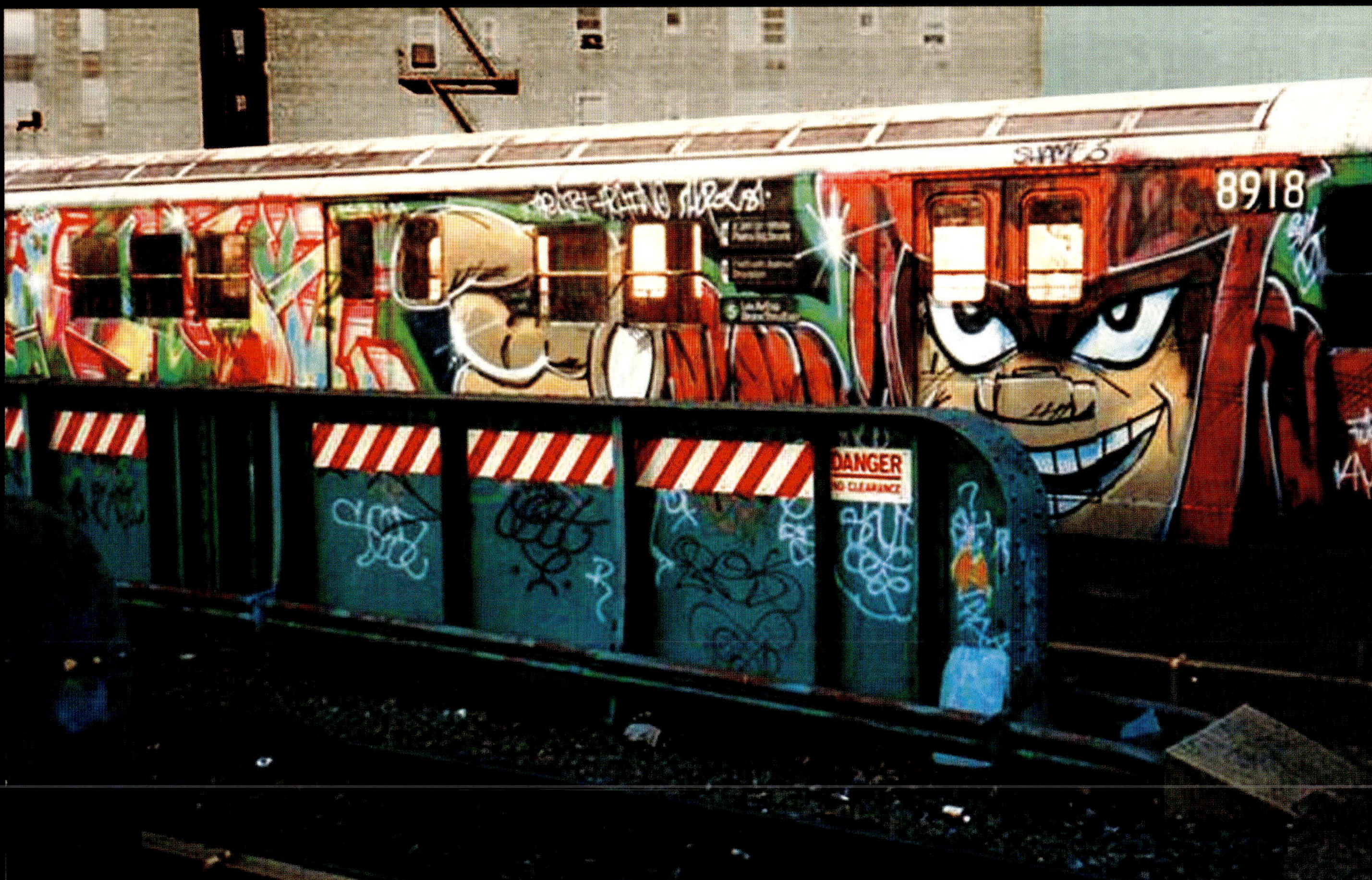

"The Juggernaut" car eight months later, touched up at Esplanade.

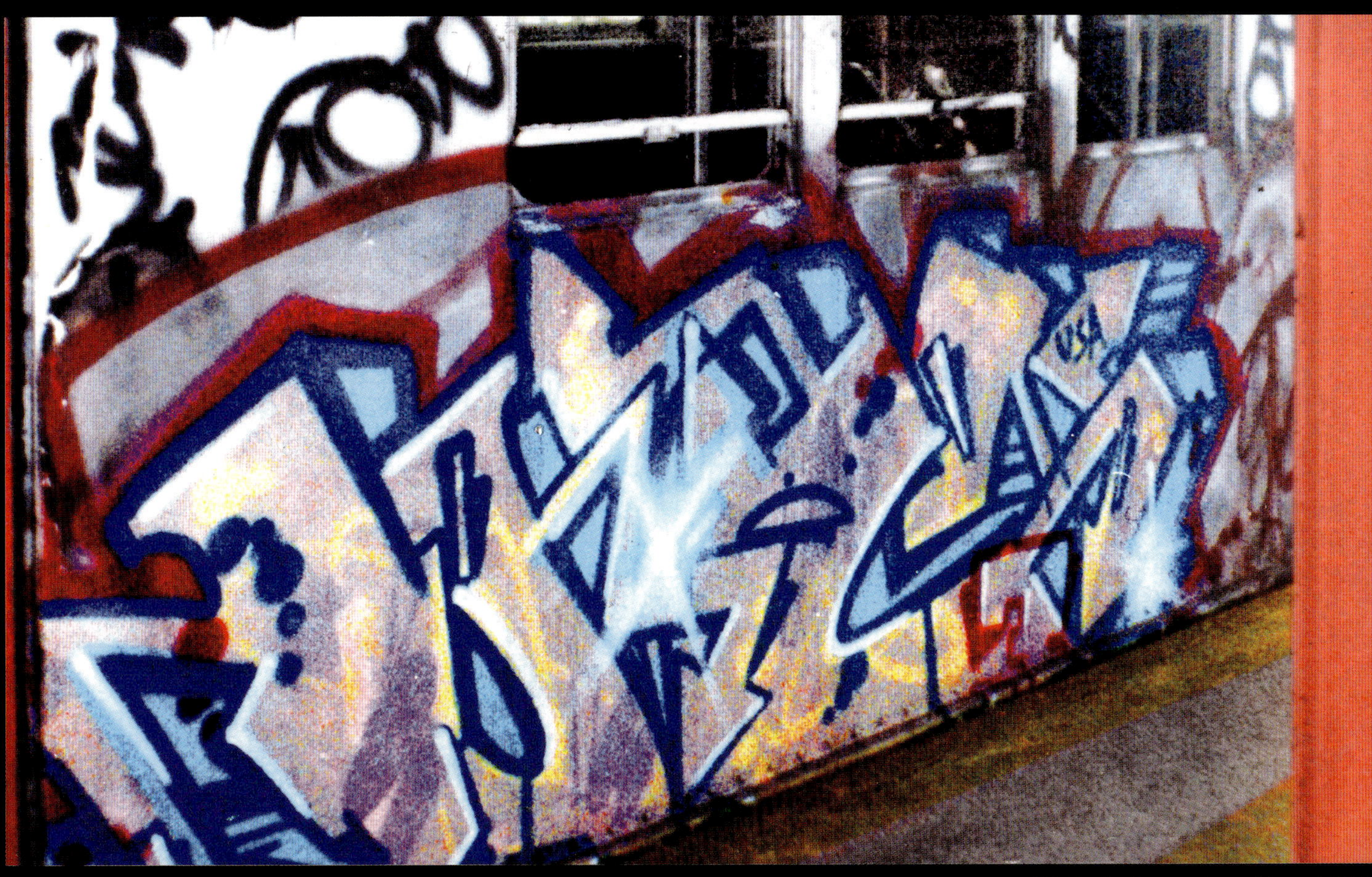

DC3 platform shot, Nov. 1986.

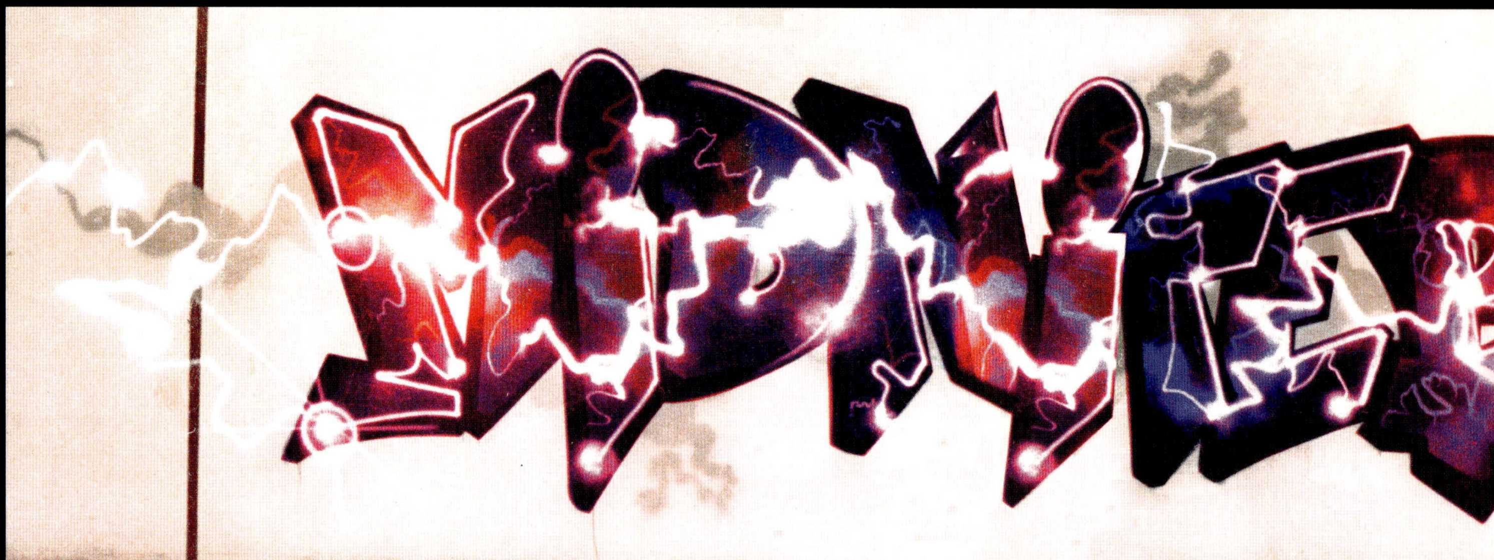

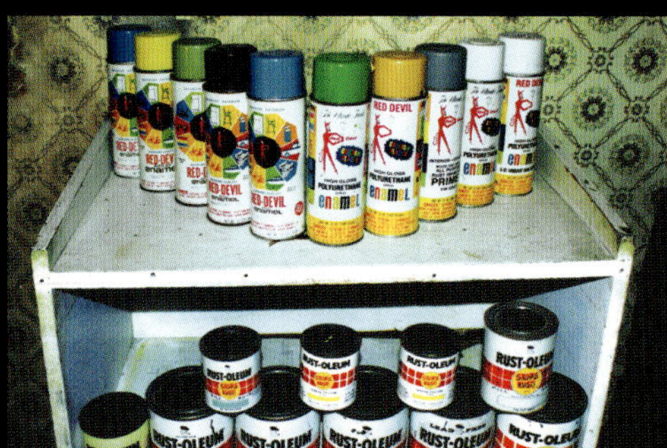

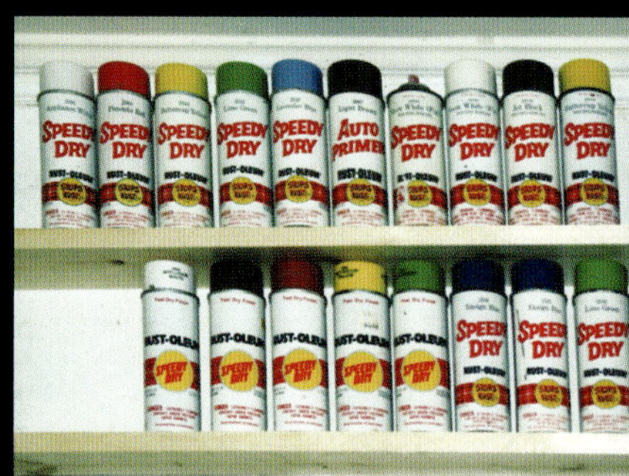

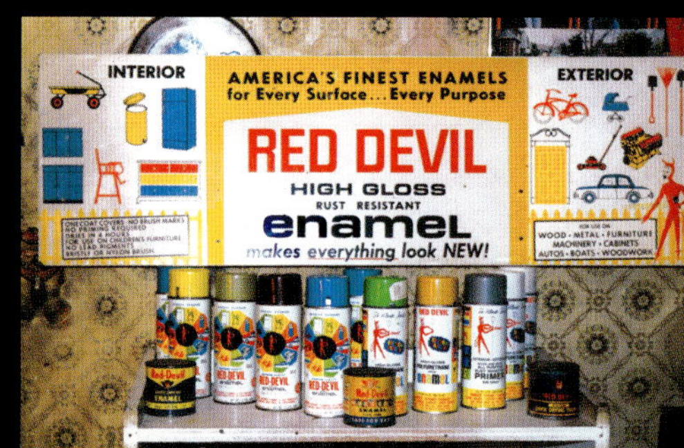

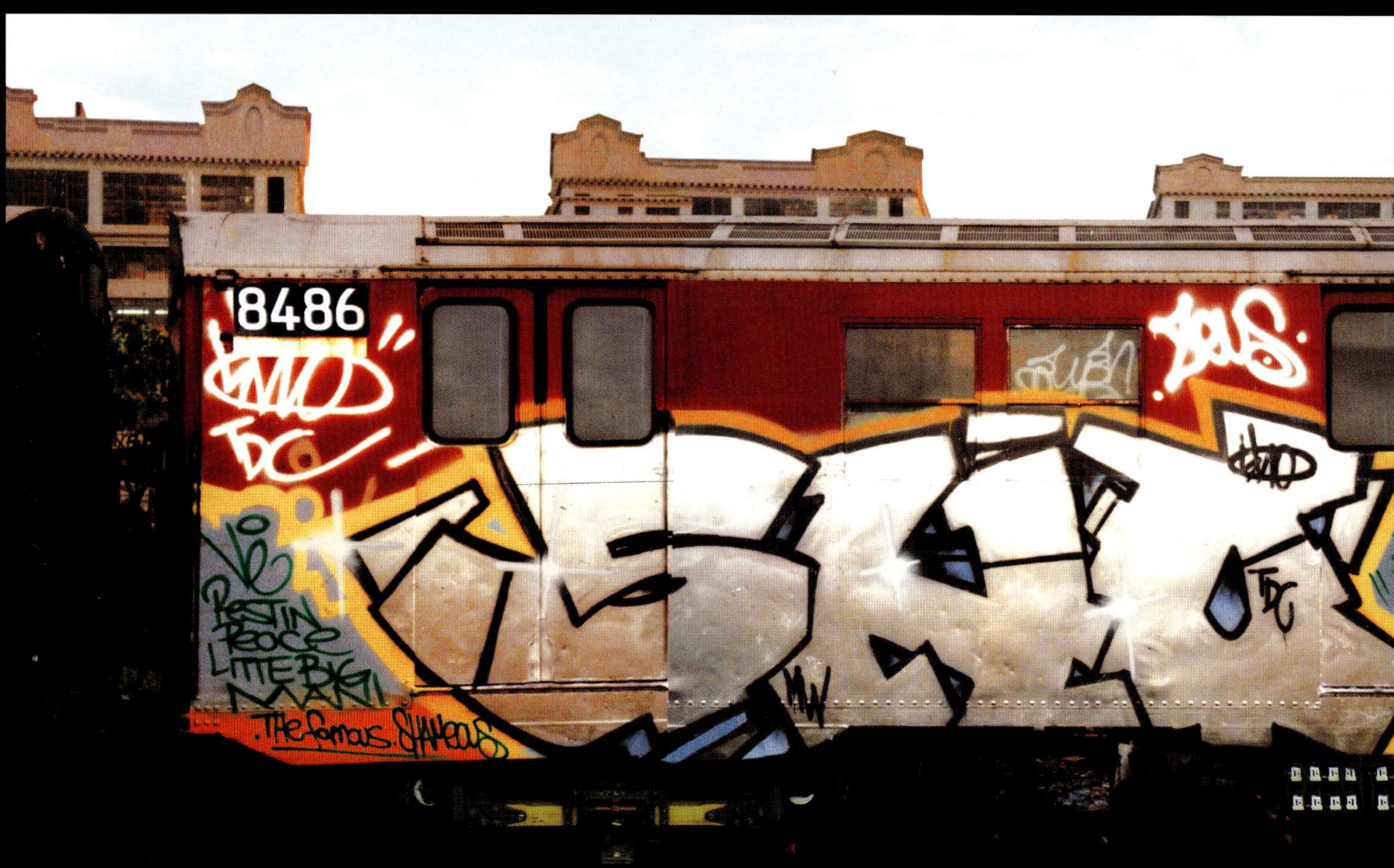

SHO TDC, "Most Wanted," and ZEUS, 7 Train "Dedicated to VE MTA" (RIP), Sep. 1995.

"MIDNIGHT BLUE," by MAC, "WHO'D Ya Think?"

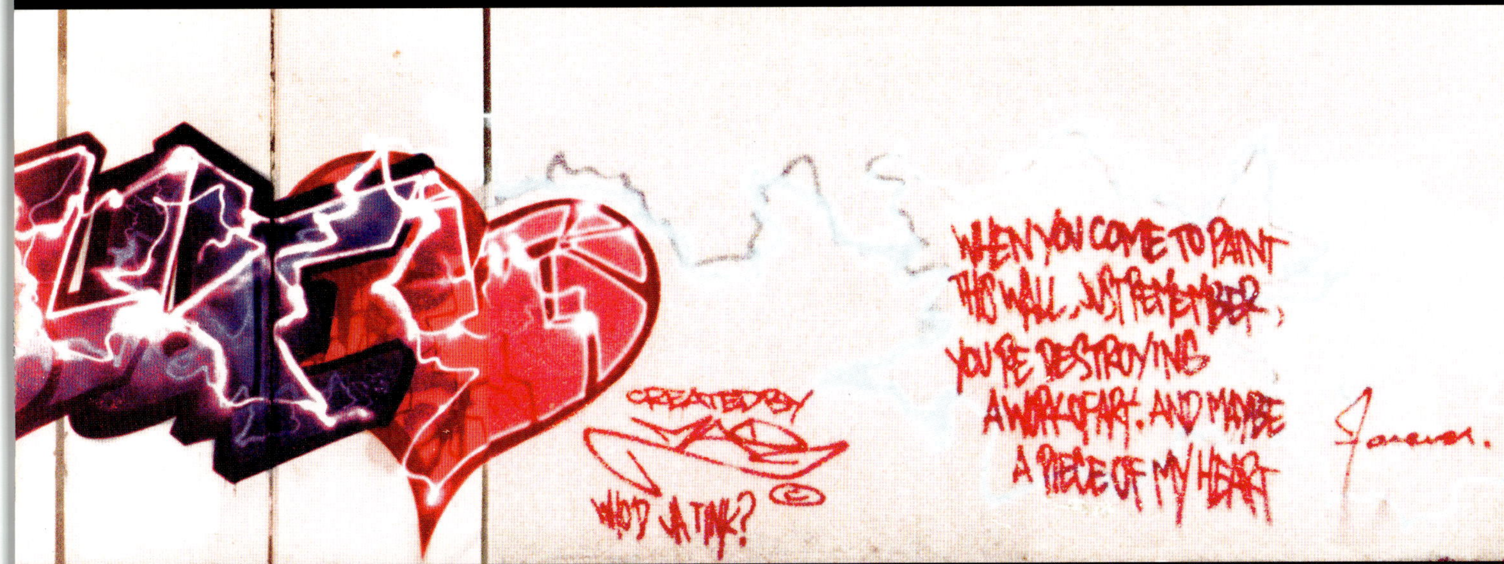

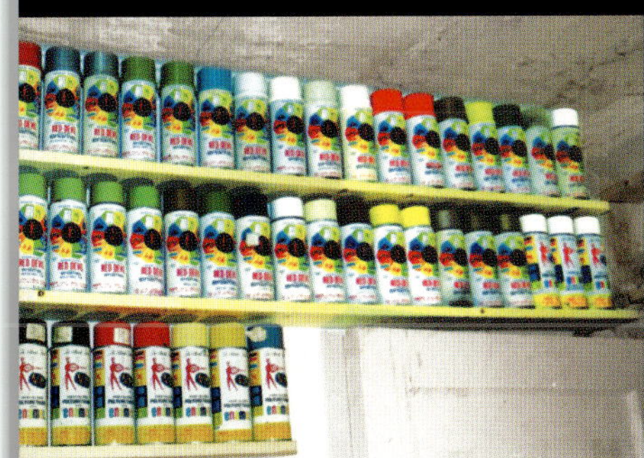

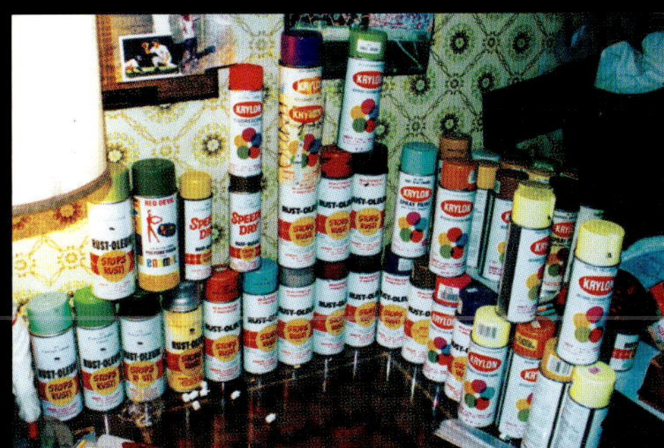

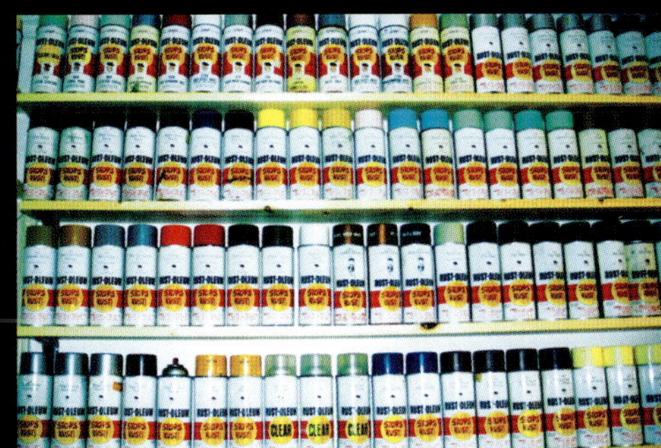

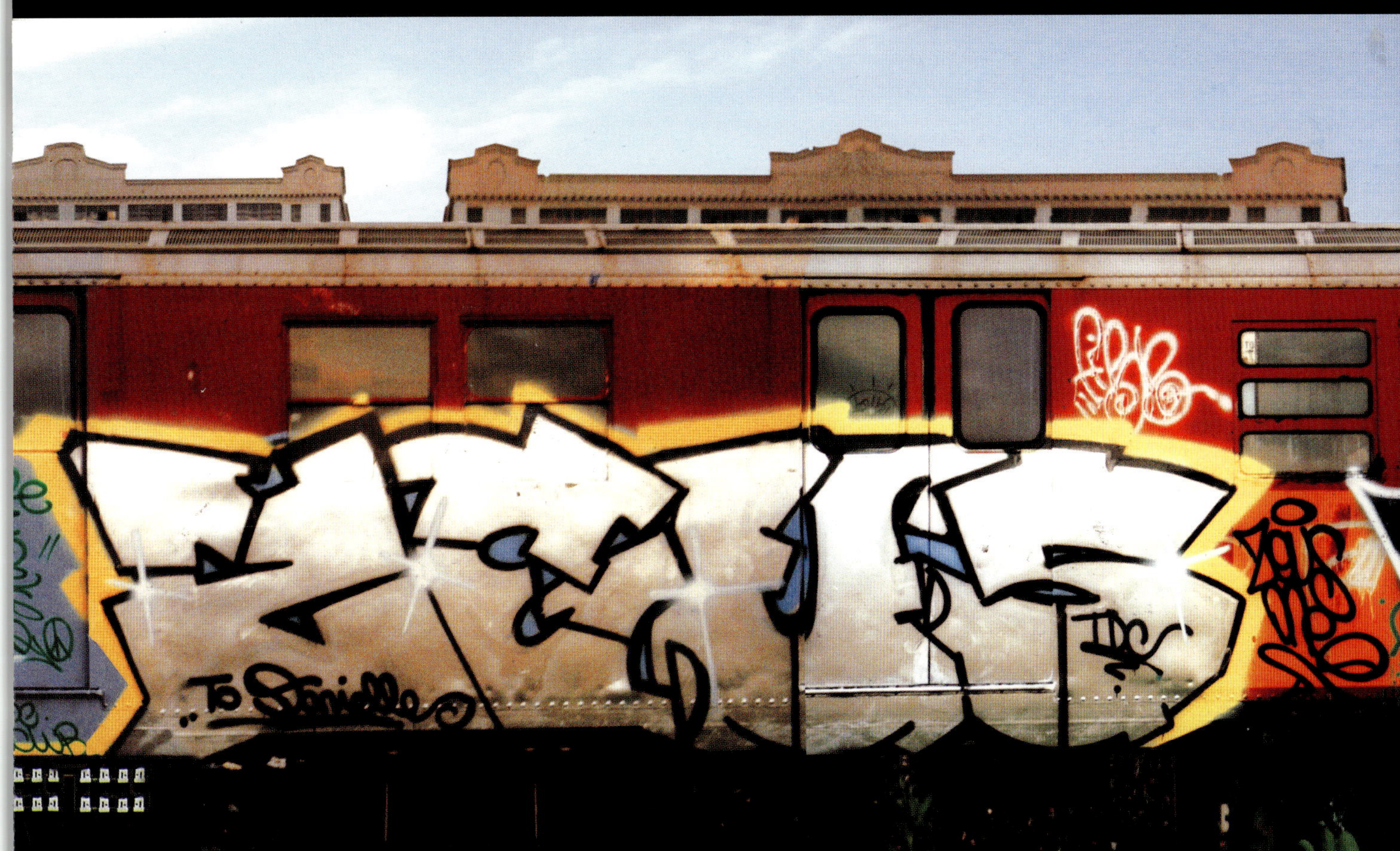

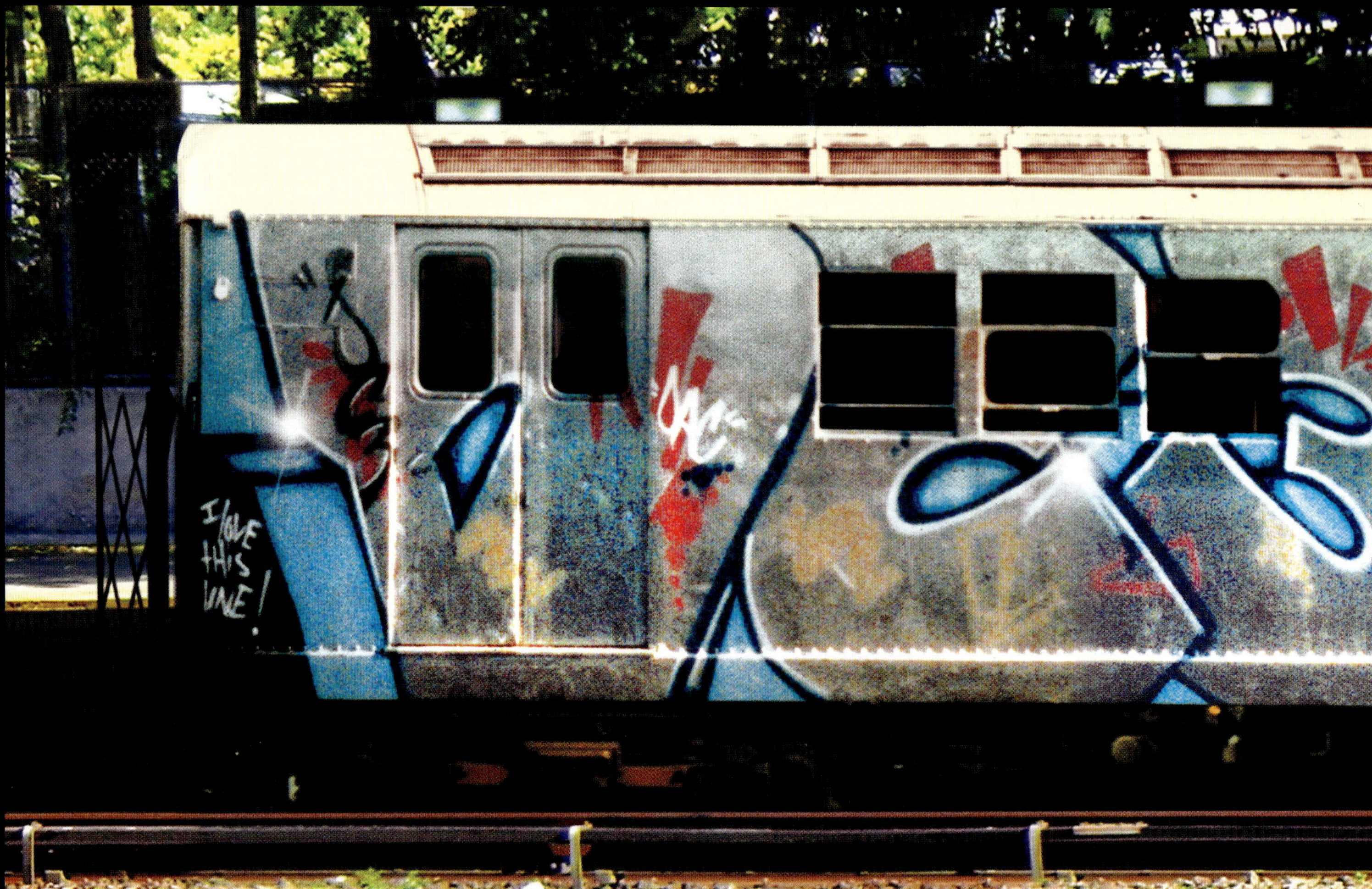

DC3 USA, "I LOVE THIS LINE," and ZOO, "HELL AWAITS FOR TOYS," photographed at Gun Hill Road, Aug. 1988.

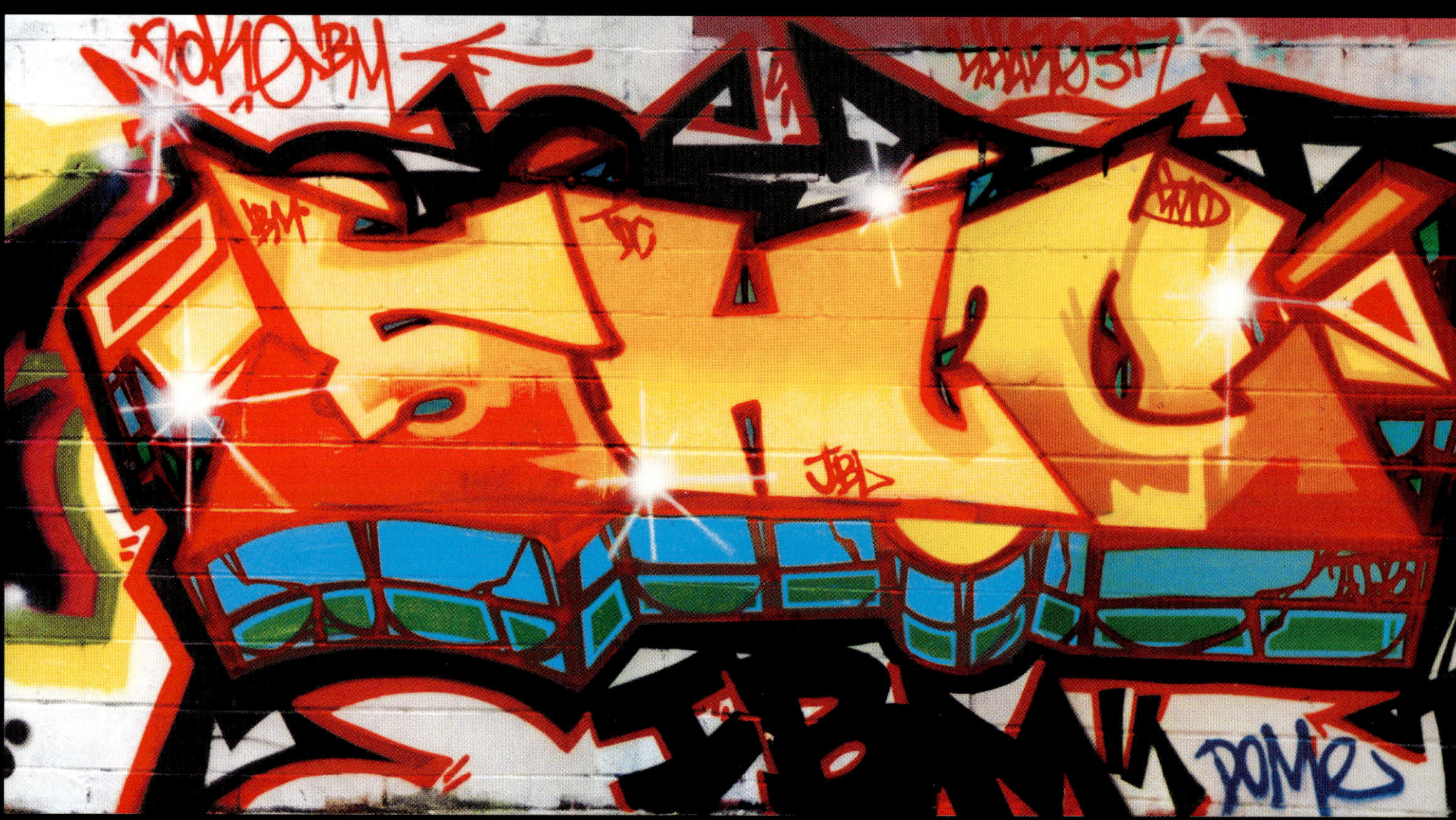

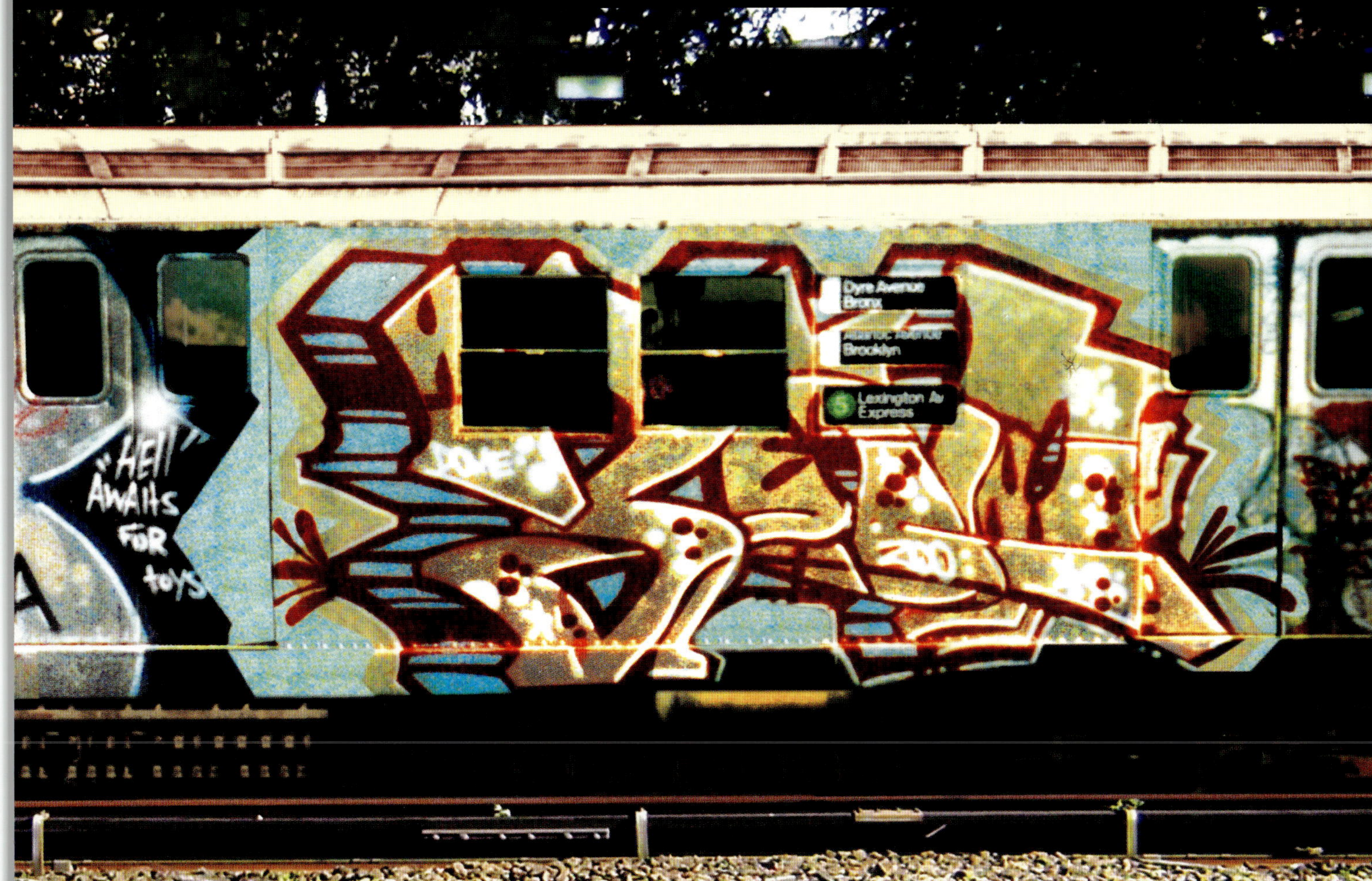

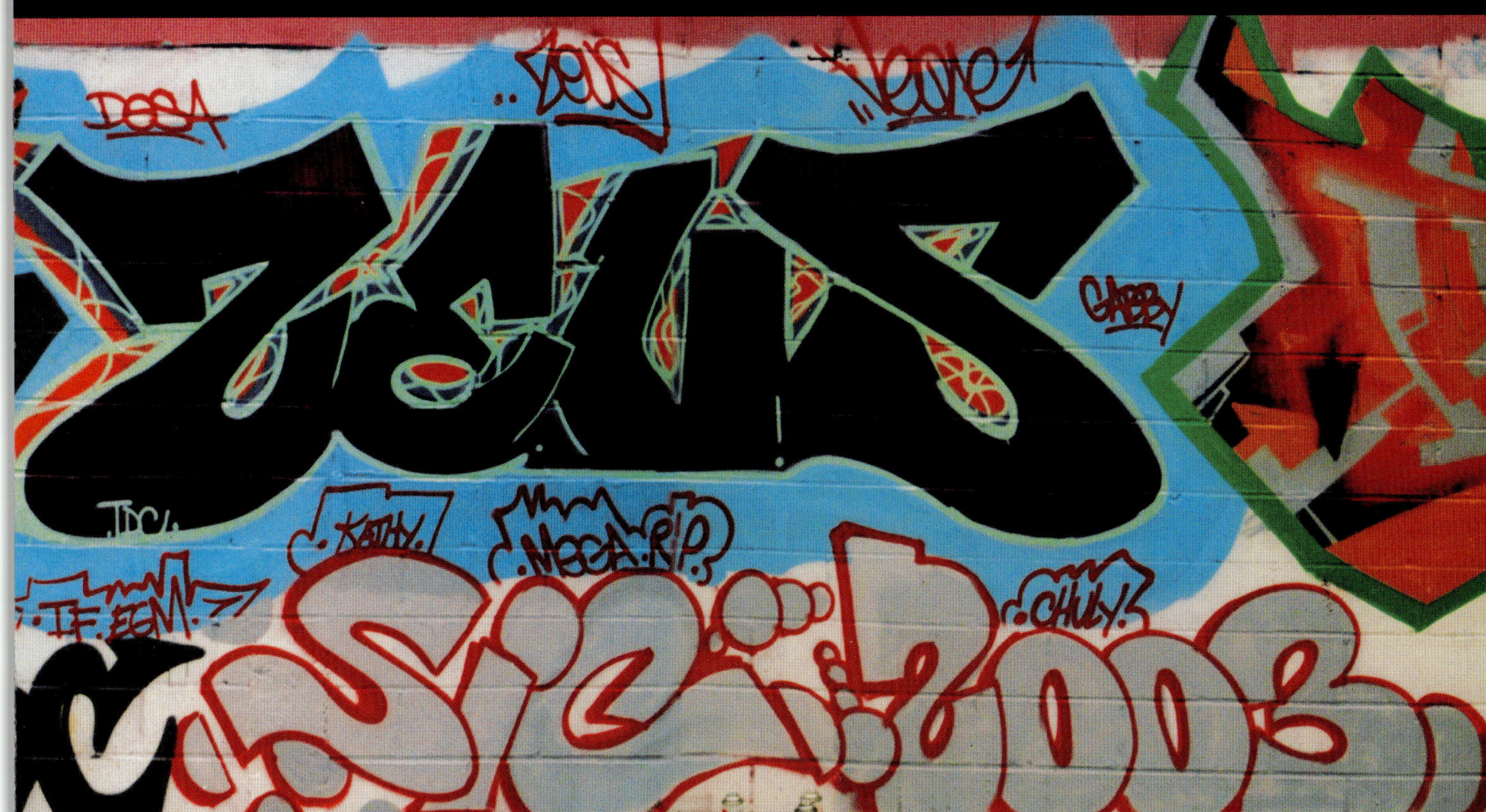

SHO, "IDOLIZED BY MILLIONS," and ZEUS TDC SIC ("Shit In Check Crew"), Evergreen St., Brooklyn, NY, 2003.

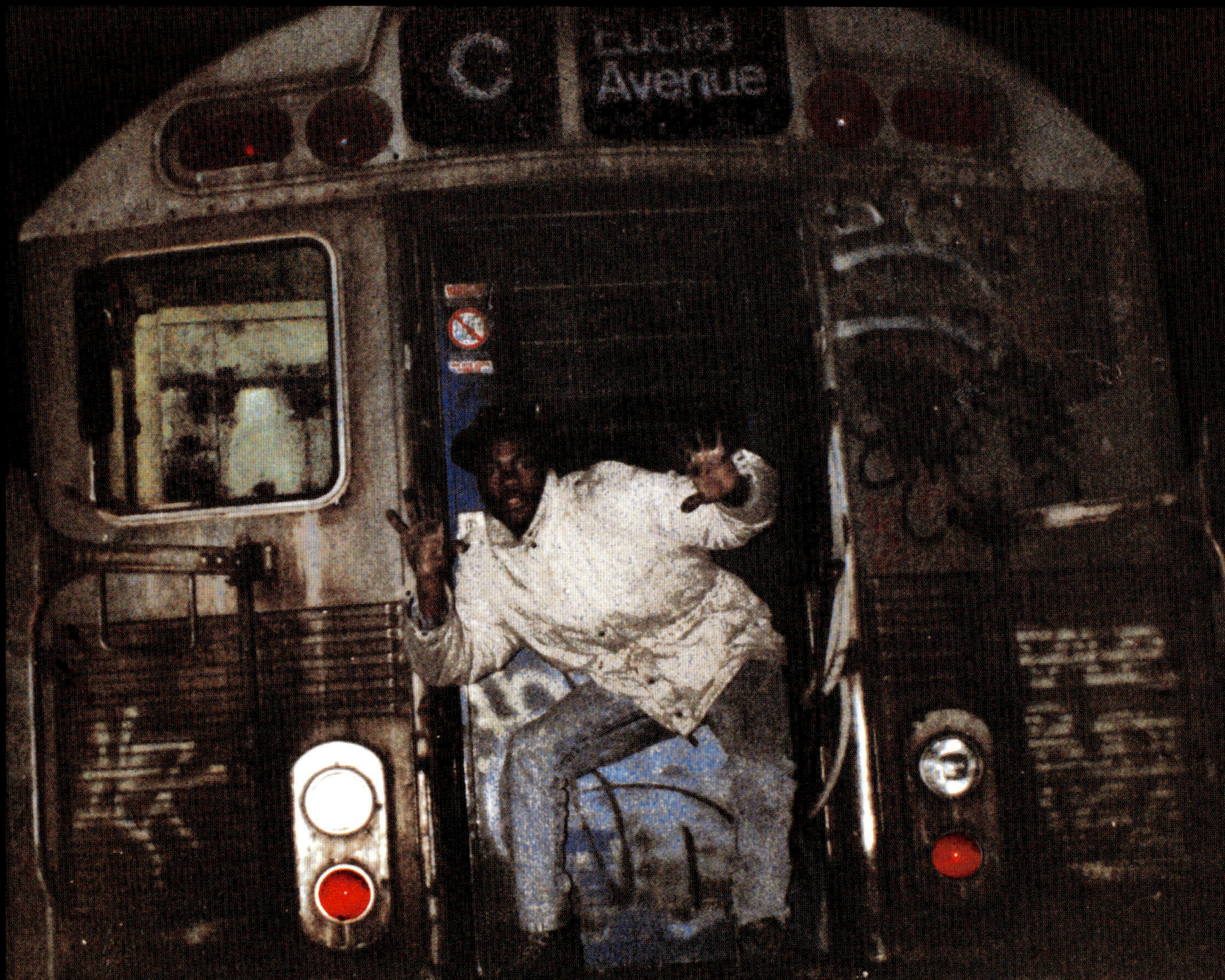

SHIM, C Train in Grant lay ups.

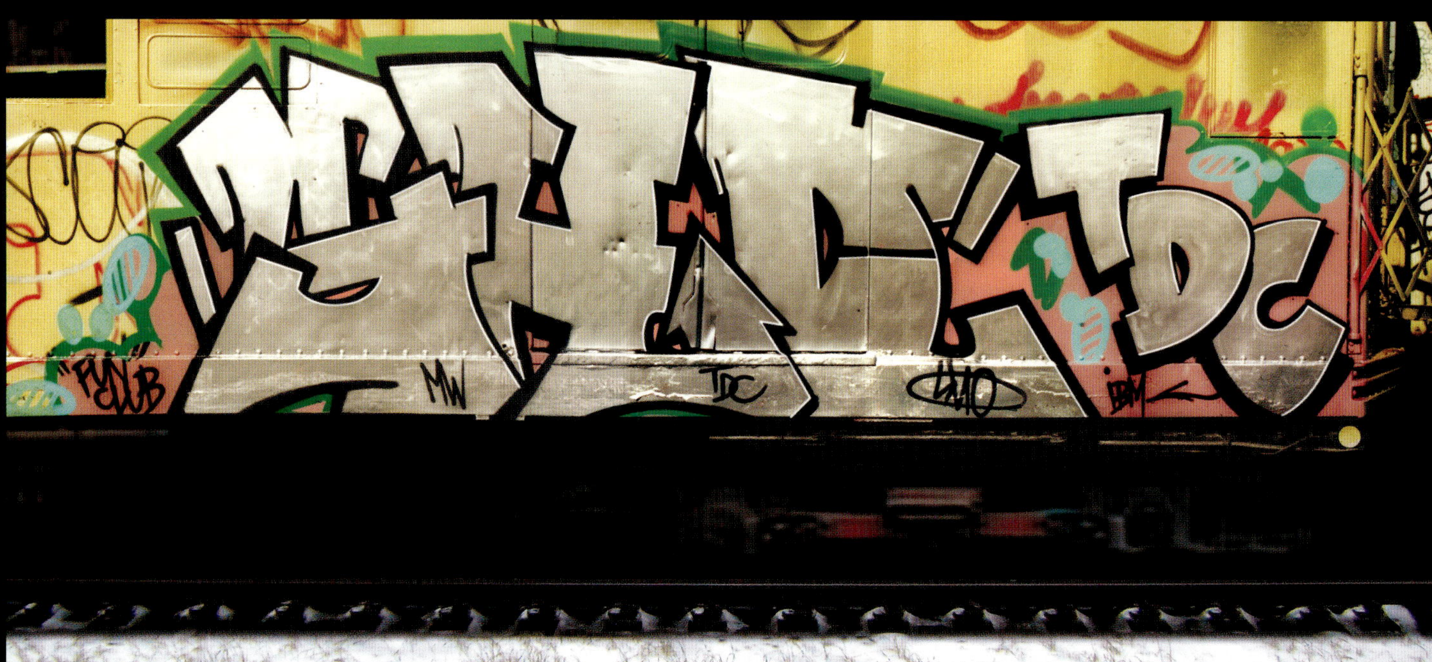

SHO TDC, "FUN CLUB," silver on a workbum train, Sep. 1995.

SHO and ZOO, AKA DOME, moved from the 5 Train along time ago. Whatever!!! We still loved the adventure of bombing running live trains and somewhat knew the end was near and to my recollection never actually discussed that shit, we rocked shit till the fucking end just for the fuck of it and always for fame...niggas know!!!!!!. On the previous page you got my boy Shim posing on a C Train in Grant Avenue subway train underground yard lay ups, which in case niggas didn't know, was two levels and led straight into the Pitkin Yard via a long tunnel. SHO took this picture on a quick daytime trip into Grant with Shim, who had never been there, just to see if I could catch a top-to-bottom, end-to-end on a C Train that Zoo and I had done a month earlier, it was now winter, January 1989. I benched that shit for like four days over a month fucking period just to catch that train most importantly, but also for two window-downs we did, one on an A Train and another on a C Flat, plus some bombing, mostly tags.

If you're a true graffiti aficionado, you'll see us up on an A Train door with a ZOOROC and a SHO tag when the doors close in Eddie Murphy's *Coming to America.* It happens when the doors close after Lisa McDowell turns down the Prince of Zumumbi's hand in marriage and his diamond ring. Right next to it on the next car was a Ai throw up. The reason I went back in was because shit was crazy, Zoo and I had stopped giving a fuck a long time ago but I always was in Brooklyn hanging out or getting smoke with Shim near City Line, so me and Shim climbed down the ladder into Grant lay up in broad daylight around 4 P.M. after smoking a fat blunt and I was getting desperate to try and see if that train was maybe still sitting up in there, it wasn't and I never ever fucking saw that shit so if you got it and you're a real writer and we ever meet holla at me, yo!!!

Dome and I hit Grant a number of times in which in the beginning we didn't know too much about the area at all but as always we would hear shit and go on a mission to find out for our God Dam selves. I liked Grant because earlier in this book I said that the first graffiti on trains I ever saw, benched, and took flicks of was at the A Train stop at 88th Street Boyd Hudson by my Aunts house in 1982, at which point I would just bounce from the crib and disappear for like an hour from holiday events where nobody would have any idea where I went. I liked what I saw from Sonic, IZ The Wiz, and Zone. IZ The Wiz blew my mind because he had most every train with fill-ins and stations, but some sets with like 50 plus throw ups some double deckers and I was like HOW THE FUCK ARE THESE KIDS GETTING AWAY WITH THIS!!!! I loved to see shit like that because being up is all about extreme fucking damage!!!!! The top-to-bottom, end-to-end on a C Train that Zoo and I had done a month earlier was crazy because we walked off the end of Grant platform down the ladder at 5 P.M. on a Saturday, barely even looking for cops and even jumped the turnstile with paint, several 40-ounce Balantines and Zepolies from City Line. We painted a C Flat on an edge of the lay up where, if you been in there, you know there's a sweet ledge. However, the lights on the whole set was off, so we went into the end conductor car and figured out how to turn on just that one cars interior lights. Now mind you there was very few A Trains in there yet.

I don't know how we didn't get raided to this day because at least five A trains set pulled in right next to us pulled in. We was 80% finished when at like 9 P.M. I believe Zoo noticed movement near by so we went to investigate who that was, really more because we wanted to catch niggas we had beef with, not to see if it was the transit police.

So we roll up two sets away and see this kid run away from the end of one A set and Zoo was like, "What The Fuck, Yo!!" Much to my surprise, and a real situation, five writers come back around that end with four thru the set or from somewhere behind us and even two from underneath the set. Some was writers but some were neighborhood drug dealers and they pulled several knives and guns on us thinking I was Ai. I told Zoo, who was from East New York, to speak some Puertica and he did fast because other wise we would have got caught the fuck out there. After that, shit was cool and they even chilled with us while we finished. Props to my man Dulie BBB and his peoples, some of who was holding shit down there in Brooklyn and Far Rockaway.

In May of 1986, trains identified with double letters lost their identity. Originally, the double letter represented IND nomenclature for local service; for example, the C was the Concourse Express; the CC represented the local. In 1968, when the Chrystie Street connection combined BMT and IND services, the definition between local double letters and express single letters became muddied. The Q train received variants of double letters—QT meant via tunnel, QB meant via bridge. Double letters were dropped and every line would be known by a single letter. An old letter was reintroduced—the K train, which until 1976 ran from Canarsie to 57th Street and 6th Avenue and would come back as the 8th Avenue local.

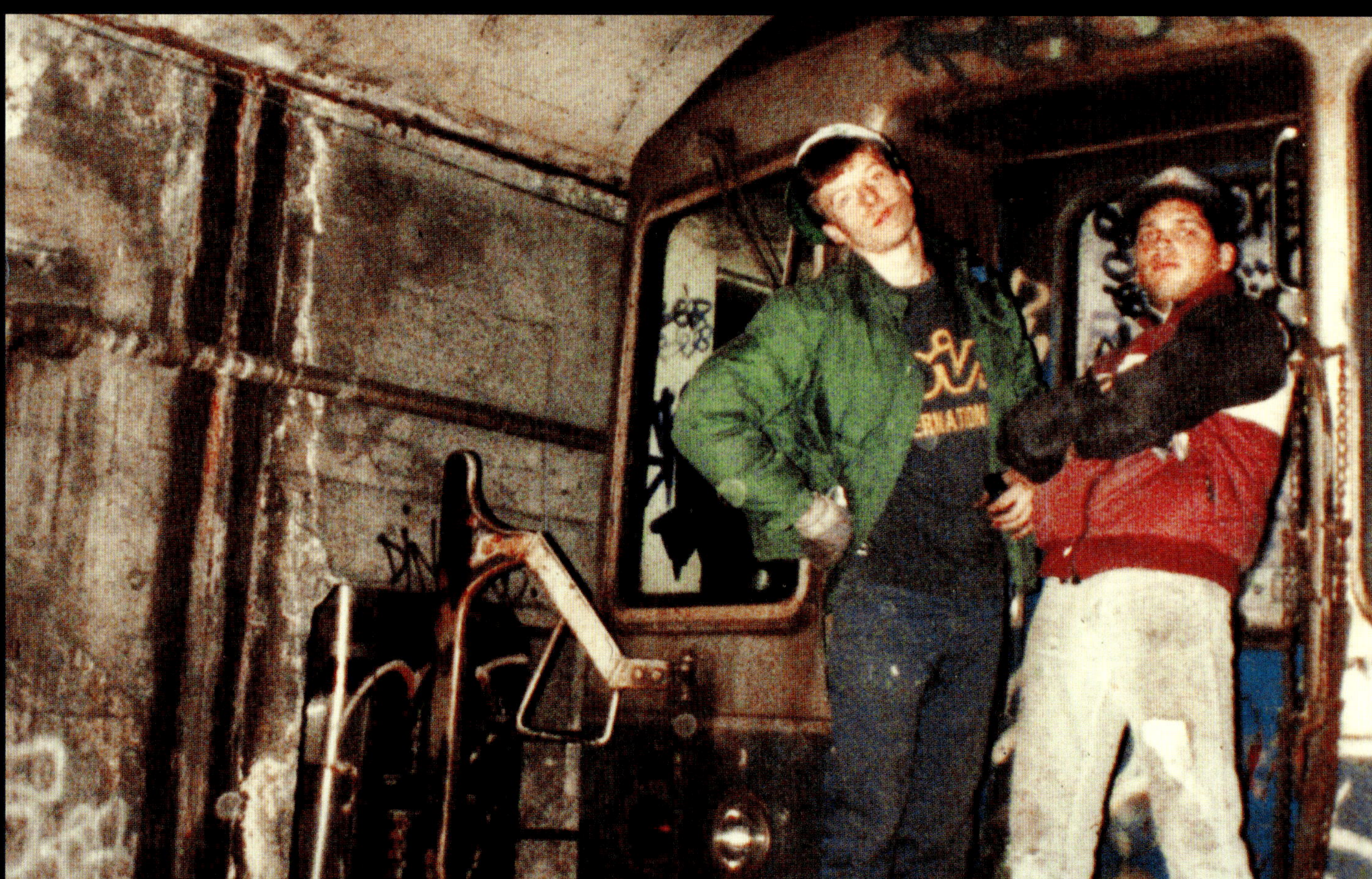

SHO and ZOO on a K Train in 175th St. underground yard.

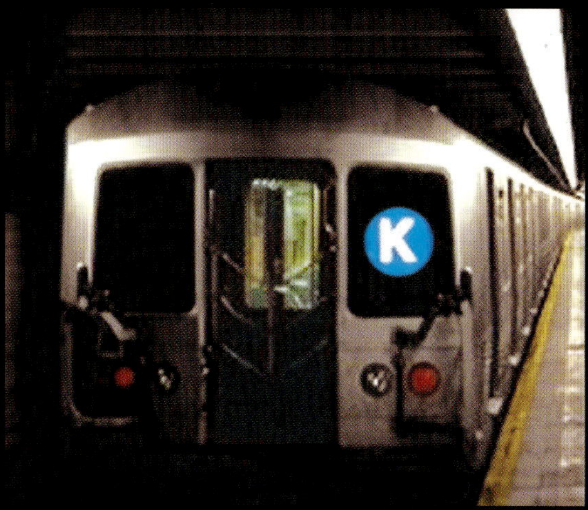

The K Train was another subway line that SHO, Zoo, and my boy LAC2 from Freeport hit. LAC2 was an original TDC member from LI and I knew him thru Raze. Raze was definitely there early on during the TDC come up and we had all hit numerous handball courts together with DC3. The K Train replaced the R-46 trains from "CC" service in 1980 after the move to single letter routes, the "K" replaced the "CC" but was short-lived itself. We hit these trains at 175th Street and Fort Washington Avenue. Shit was real because we had heard that FK and CAC was deep up in there. FK was this crew that ran with mad heads that bombed and was territorial. We went in thru a hatch a couple of blocks away and to our surprise nothing was there, so we waited and one by one they pulled in lanes at least twelve deep. We did fill-ins and marsh mop tags inside and out. 175th Street underground yard was a no-joke lay up with at least eighteen tracks. We had fourty's and it was a Saturday night. We went in late like after 2 A.M. and stayed there till almost 4:30 A.M. I benched the Ks like two times and just really didn't give a fuck enough about bombing to really even take flicks of it. But several cats I knew had said they seen us up. That was all that ever mattered to us, yo, was Fame B. We just bombed hard that night. Live flicks yo!!!

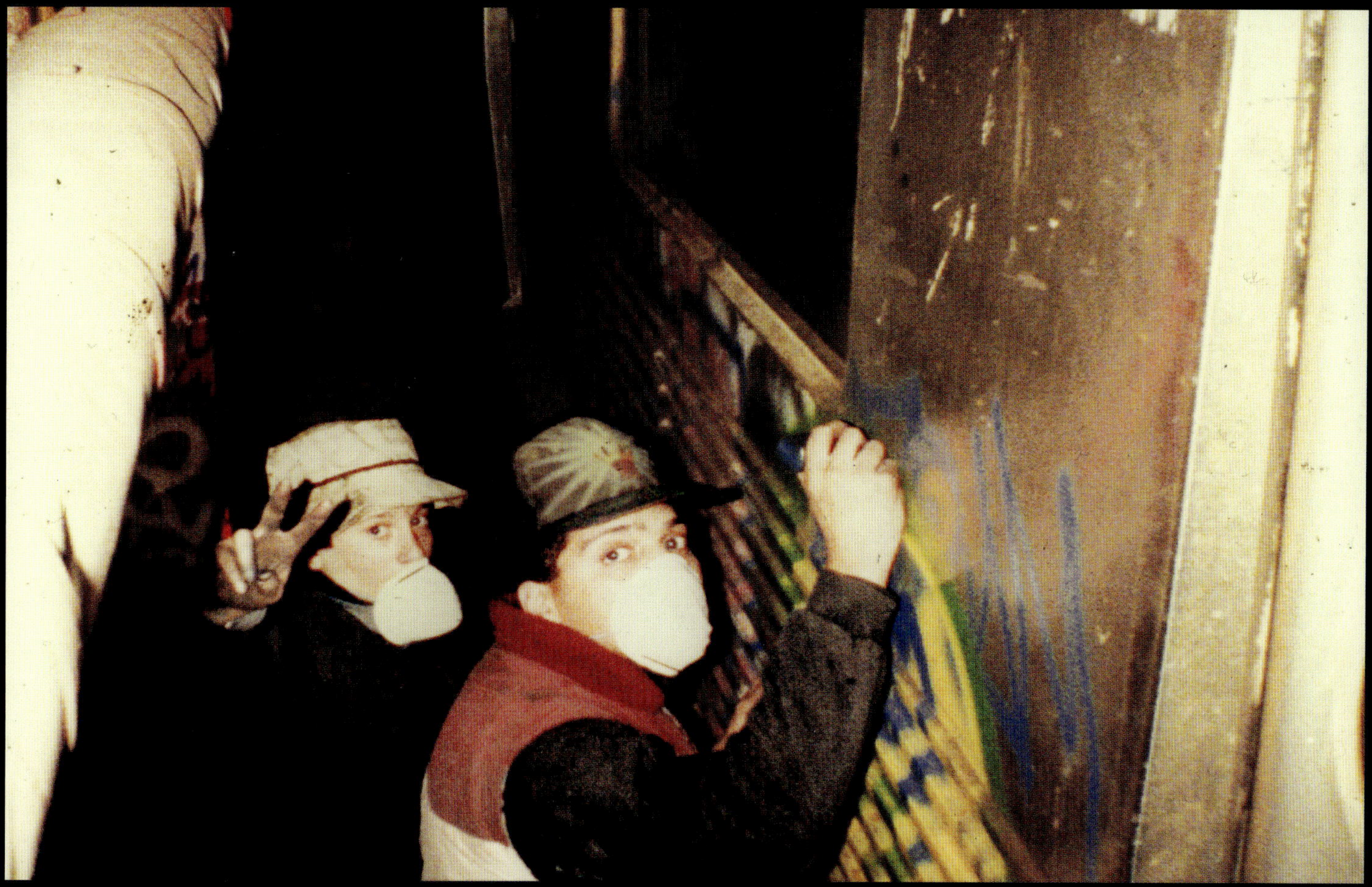

LAC2 and ZOO hitting the K Trains at 175th St. Yard, Mar. 1988.

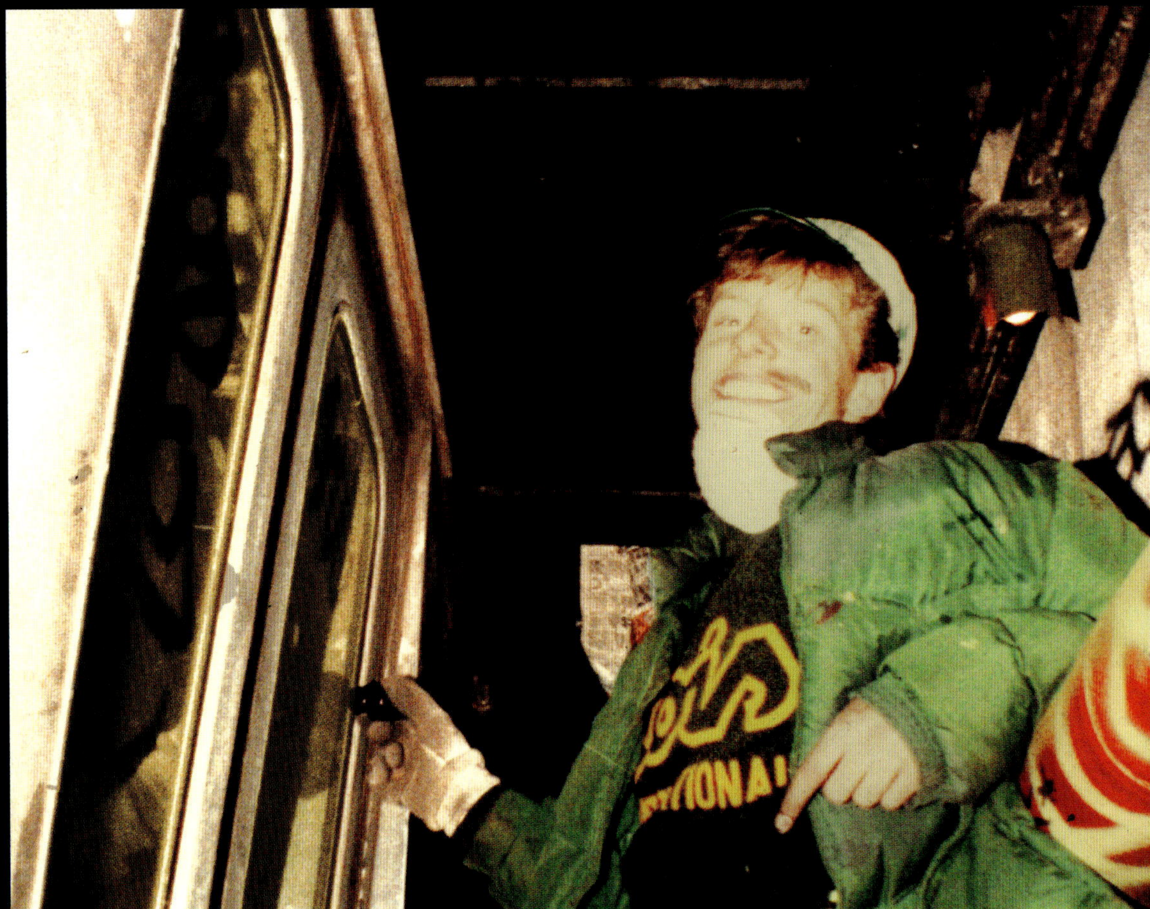

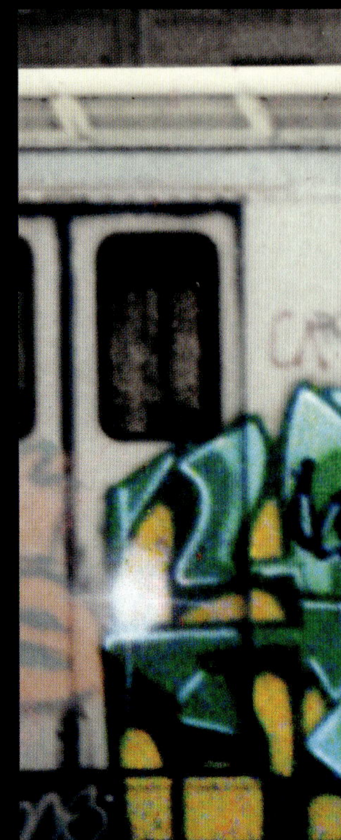

SHO mopping down a K Train, Mar. 1988.

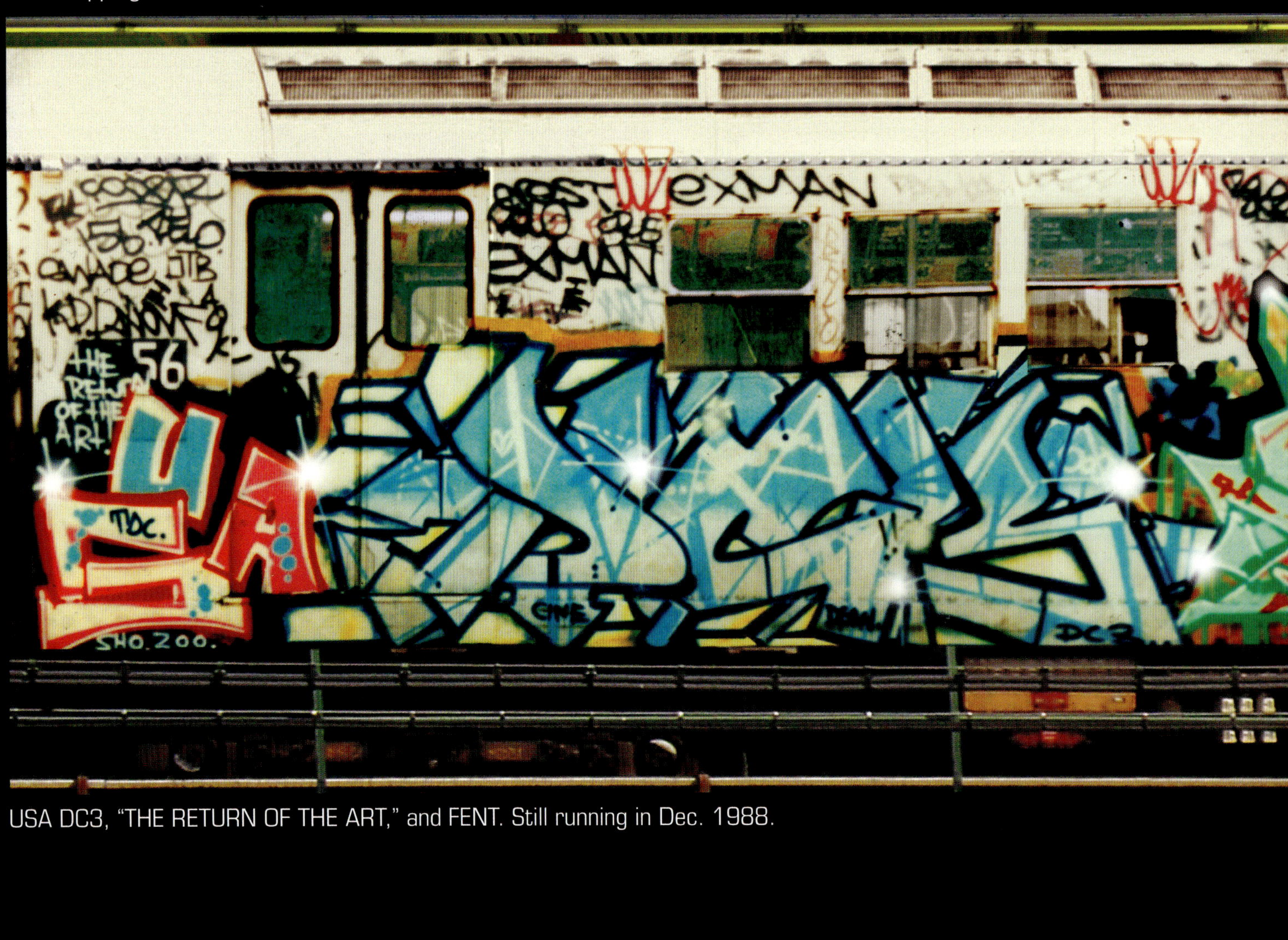

USA DC3, "THE RETURN OF THE ART," and FENT. Still running in Dec. 1988.

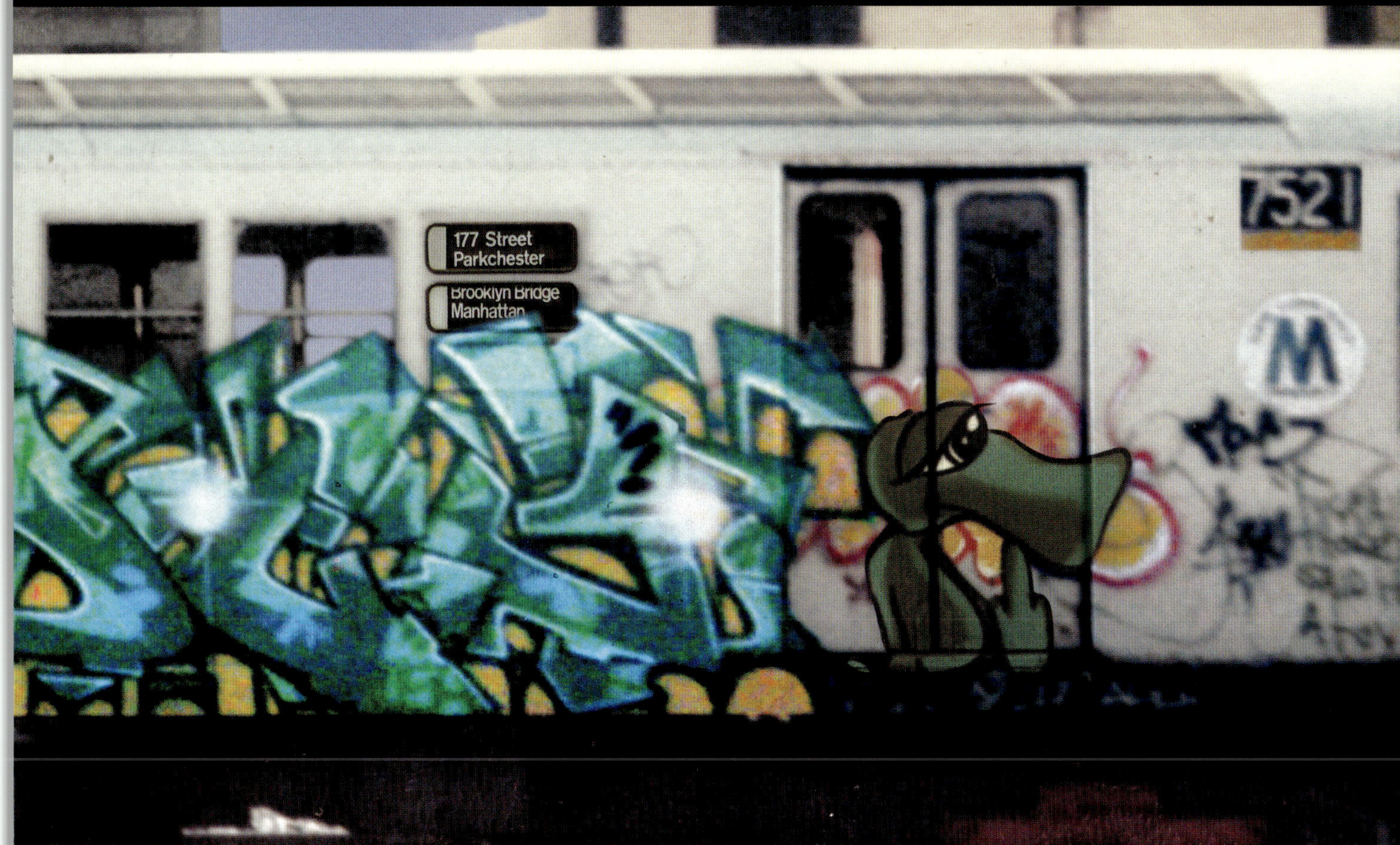

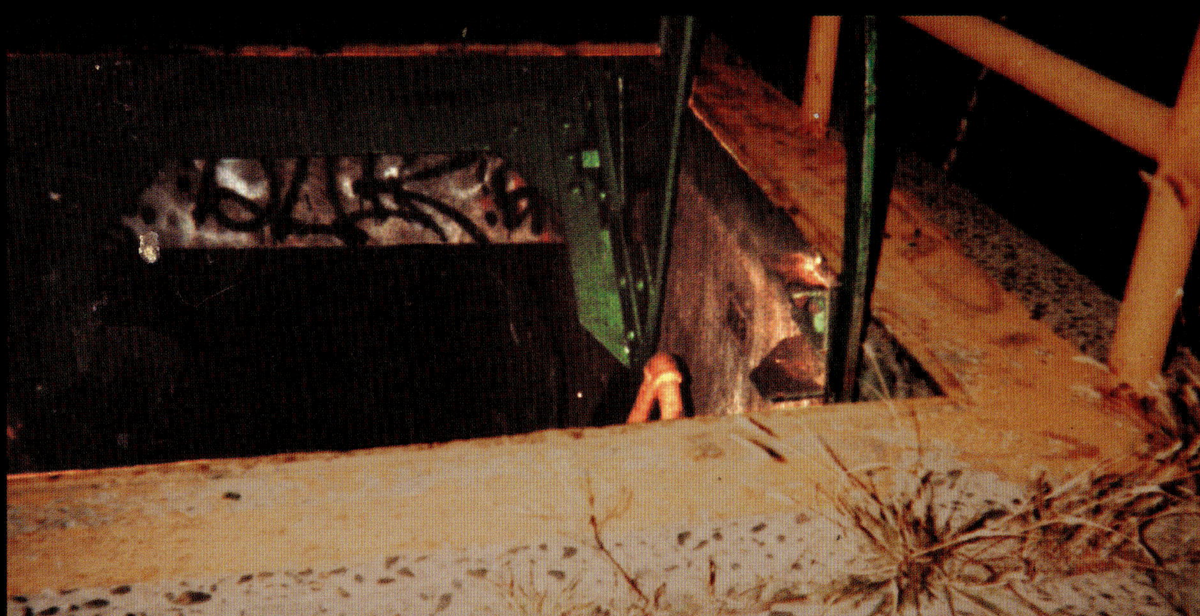

Hatches were one of our favorite ways into underground yards, tunnels, and lay ups. We always brought some tools with us so we could get them shits to pop open. Sometimes it was harder than others 'cause they'd be locked from inside. Once me and Dome found a special hatch key in a work bum staging area in 175th, boy that shit came in real handy. Then we killed all the lanes while dodging conductors.

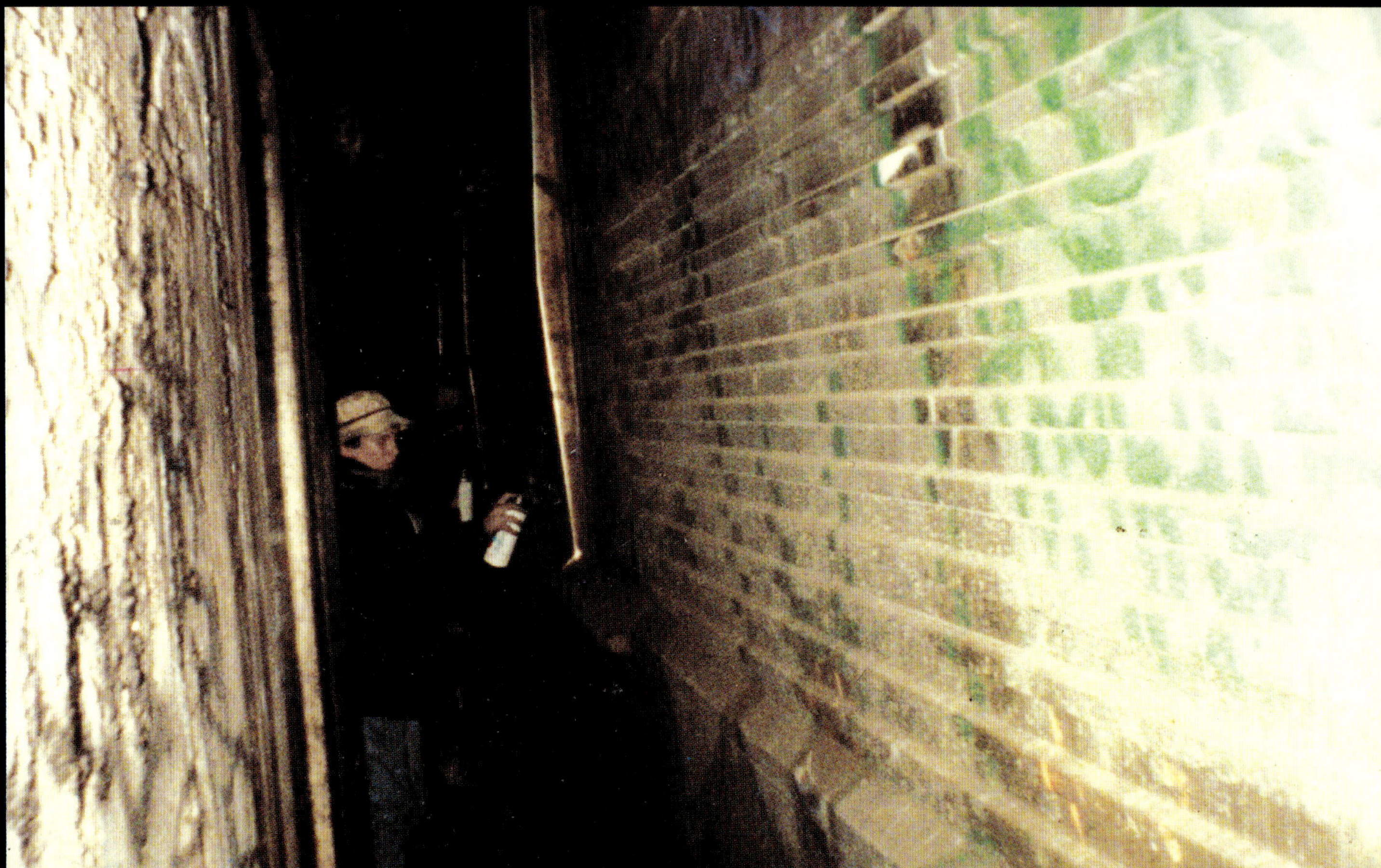

LAC2 TDC bombing a K Train.

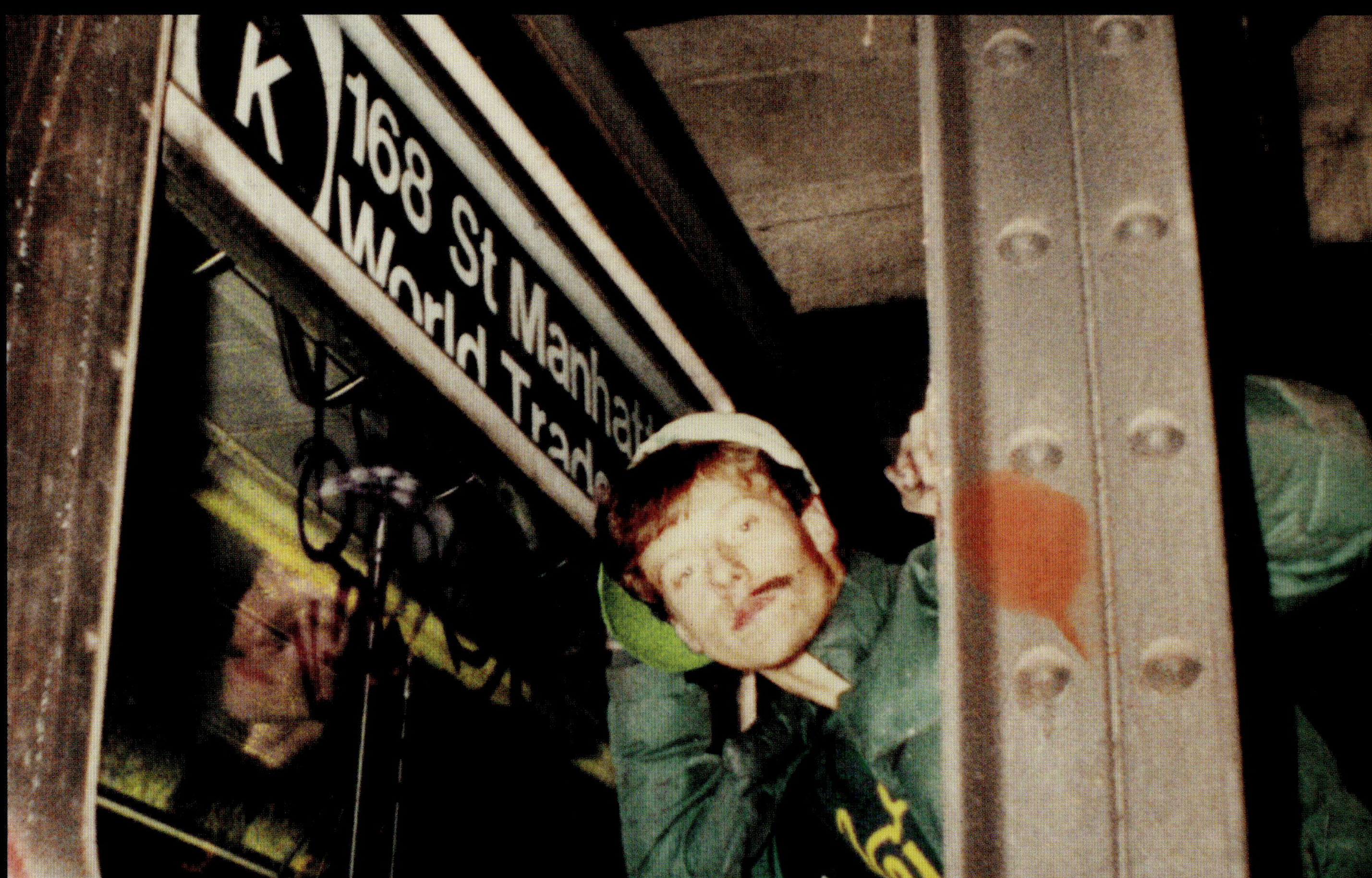

SHO bombing a K Train in Mar. 1988.

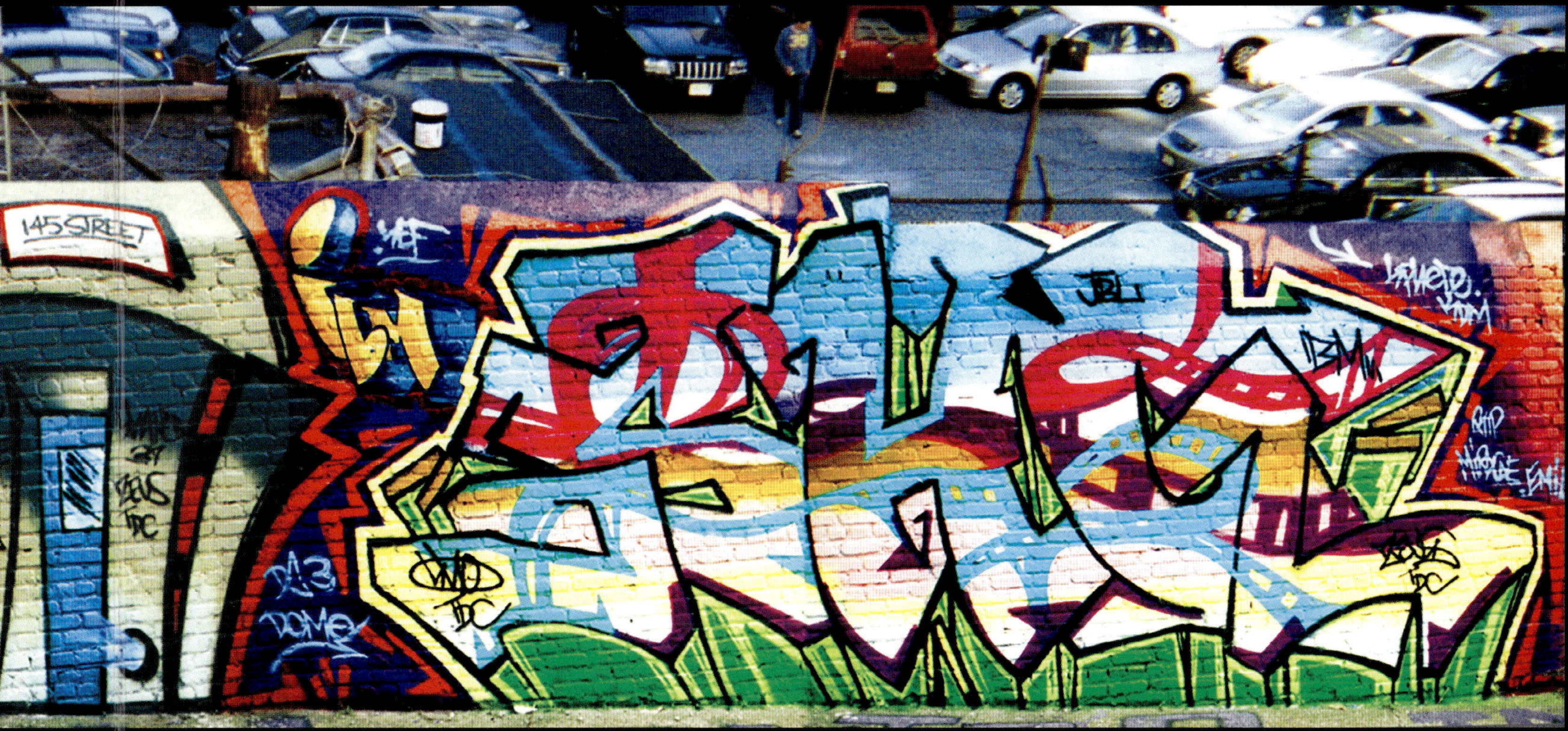

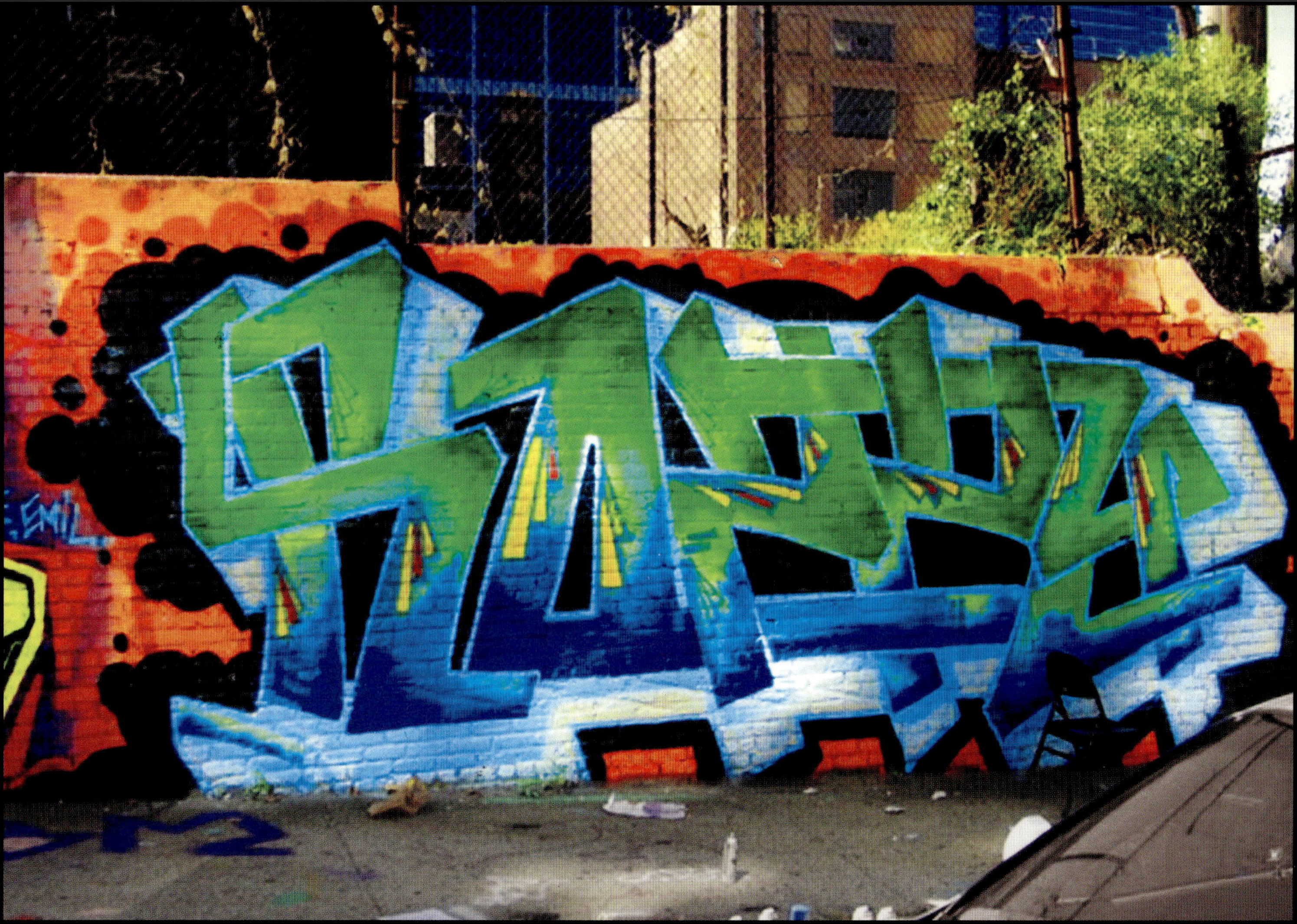

ROZZY gets busy, 66th St., NY.

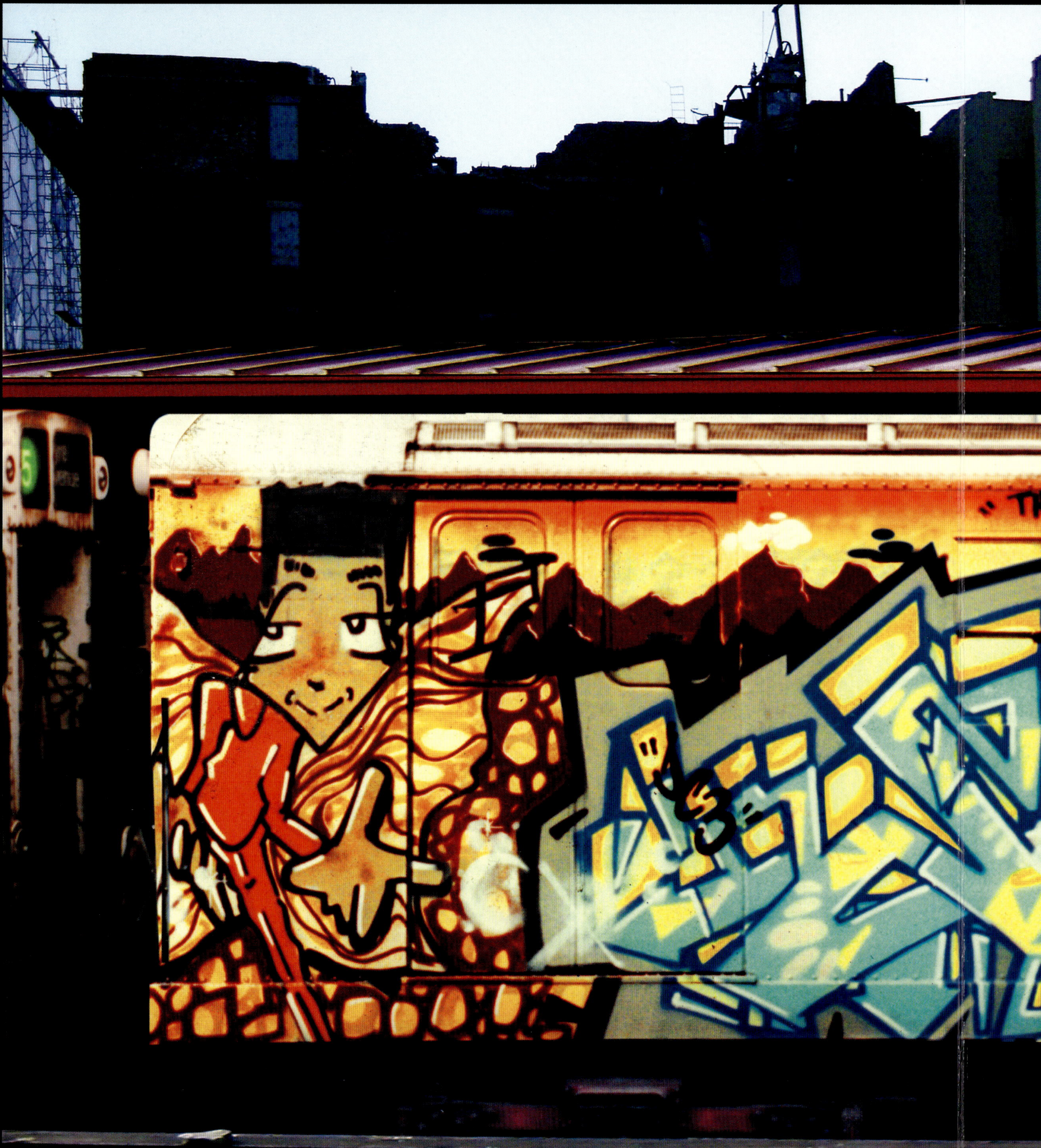

DC3 "THE NEW BEGINNING" KARL USA TCM, top-to-bottom, painted in Esplanade Tunnels, Dec. 1987.

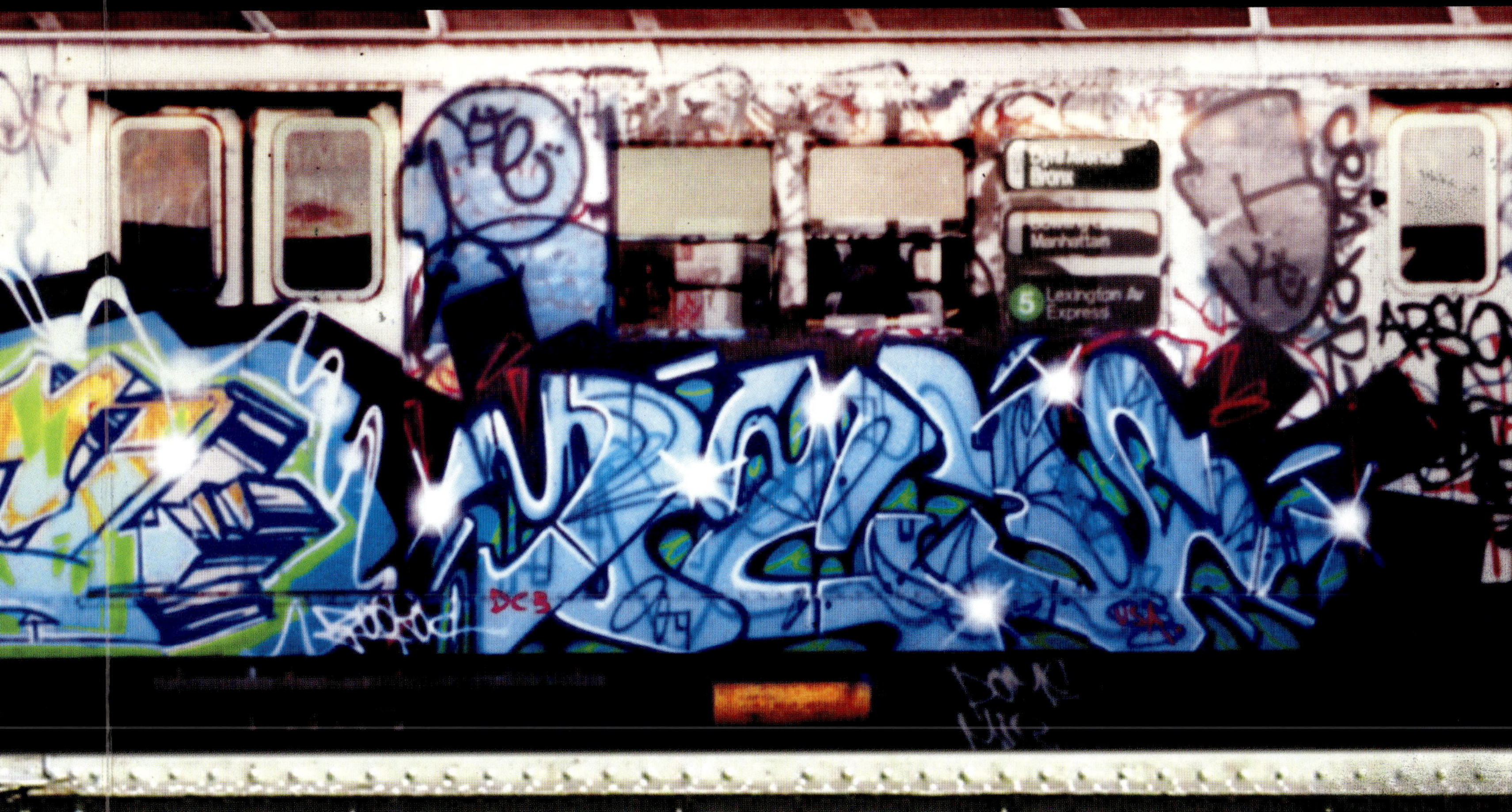

Below is a very early DC3 DOOJ wall rocking the Evil Donald Duck character that was also done in Freeport in 1985. DOOJ was an original TDC member who had a wicked tag style. I had met DOOJ in 1984 in a Freeport High school bathroom while getting ups. He only wrote for a couple of years and his crew was PIA, Partners In Art.

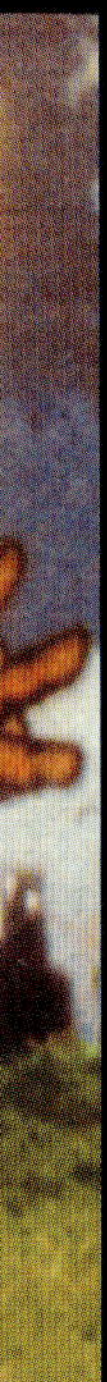

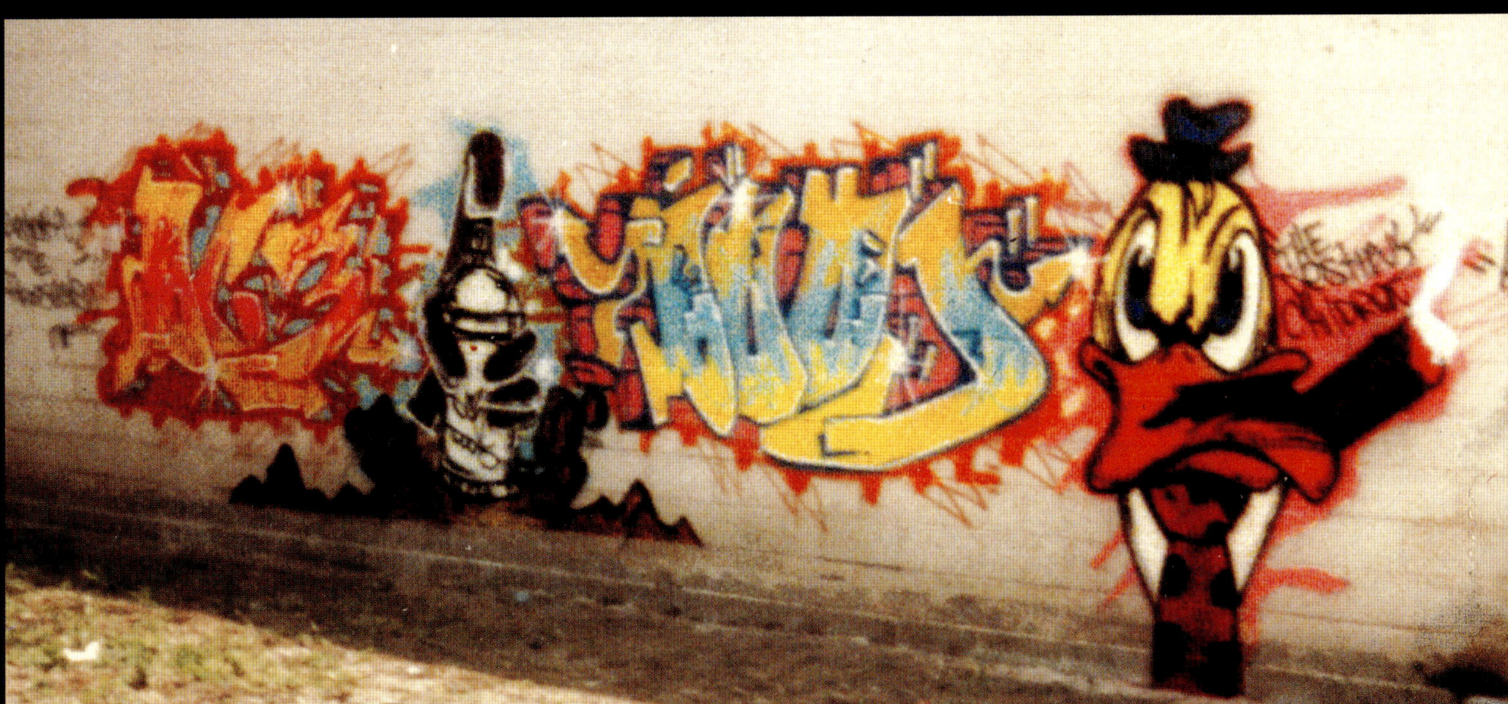

A DC3 and DOOJ "Evil Donald Duck" The Destiny Children production. Apr. 1985.

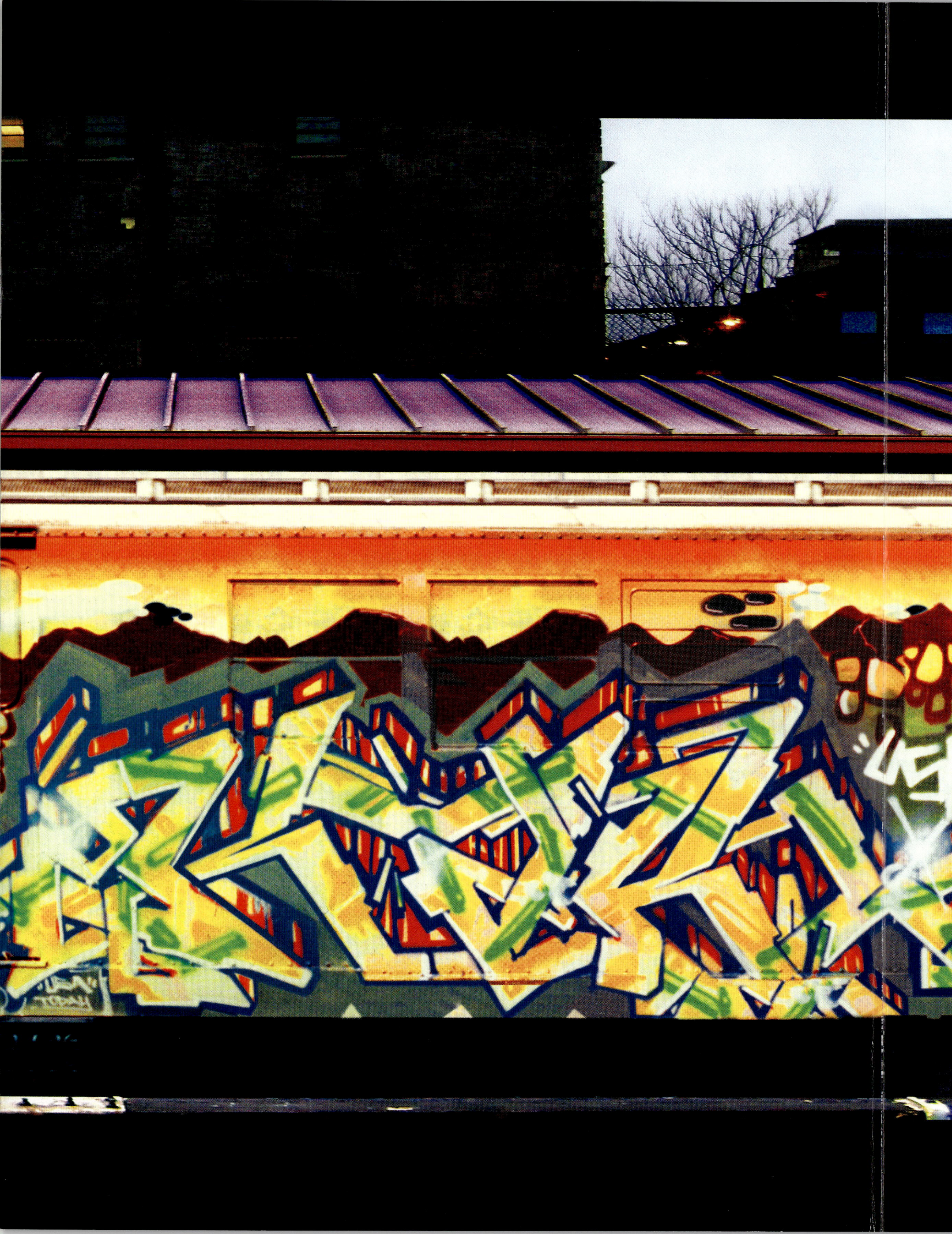

CHAPTER 10

Early Tractor Trailer Productions. Raid Stories

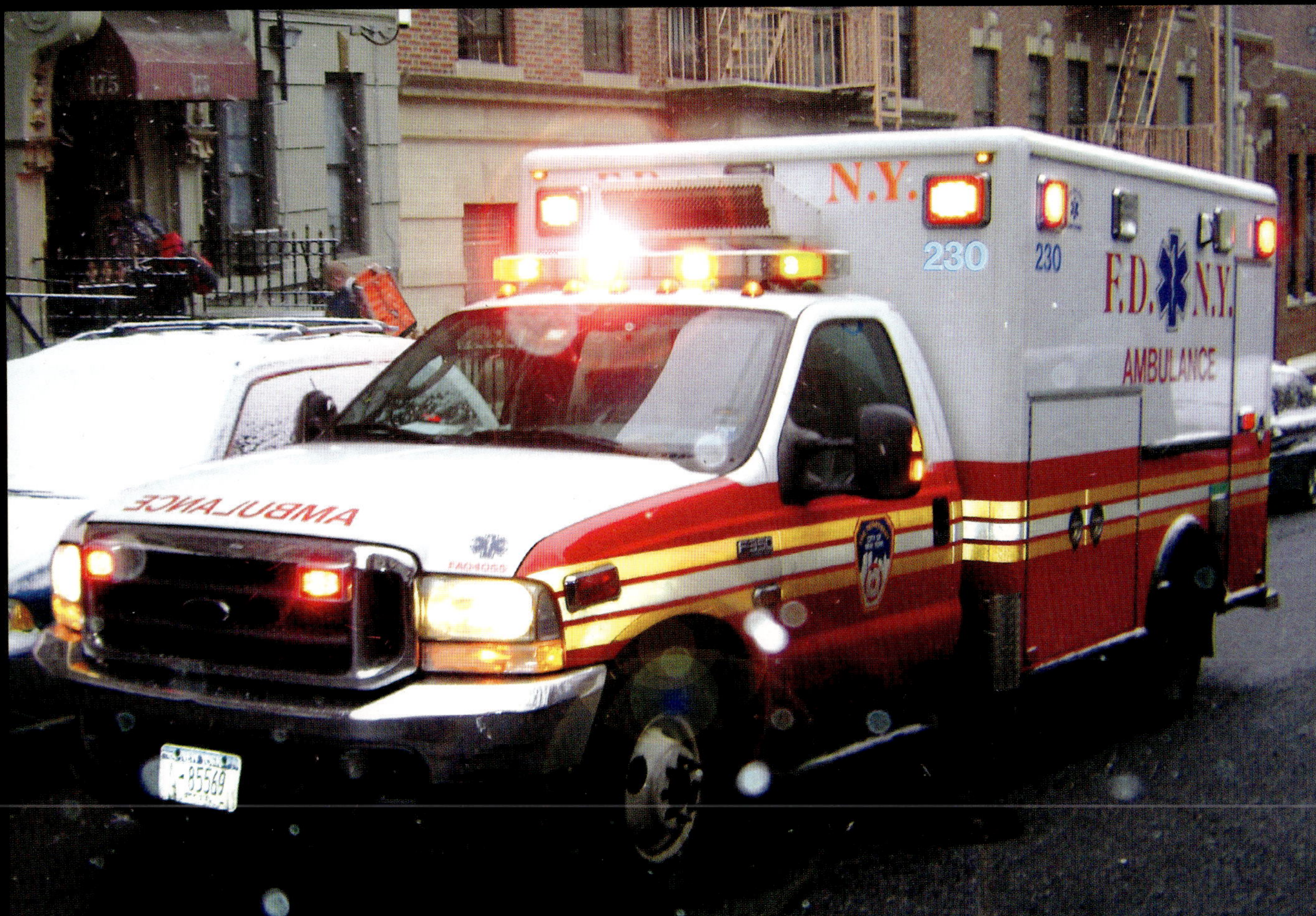

When the ambulances were lined up and the boys at the door, it wasn't for no reason and that's just the way the early nineties were. I used to live on 104th Street and Columbus. This was back in the real ill days when YTC, Young Talented Children, and PTC, which was called Purp, Purple Top crew, were running Manhattan Valley in the 24th Precinct. So you'd walk by 107th and Manhattan Avenue and there was always shooting and people getting fucked up.

I did not even live in Manhattan at the time we painted trains, so having come from that environment and seeing mad shit just made you get iller because as long as you broke right out after whatever just occurred chances are that you were all good! I spoke to some friends that were on the job and the police attitude was basically "You really just have to expect that to happen."

Then there was 2,250 murders citywide. I disagree but by and large now the city is a much better place than the early 90s when shit was Ra Ra. Big ups to JBL for getting away that night.

Like Master P said, "It ain't my fault." Long Live Club SHO!!!

DOME and DC3 "Non Stop Action," Dec. 1986.

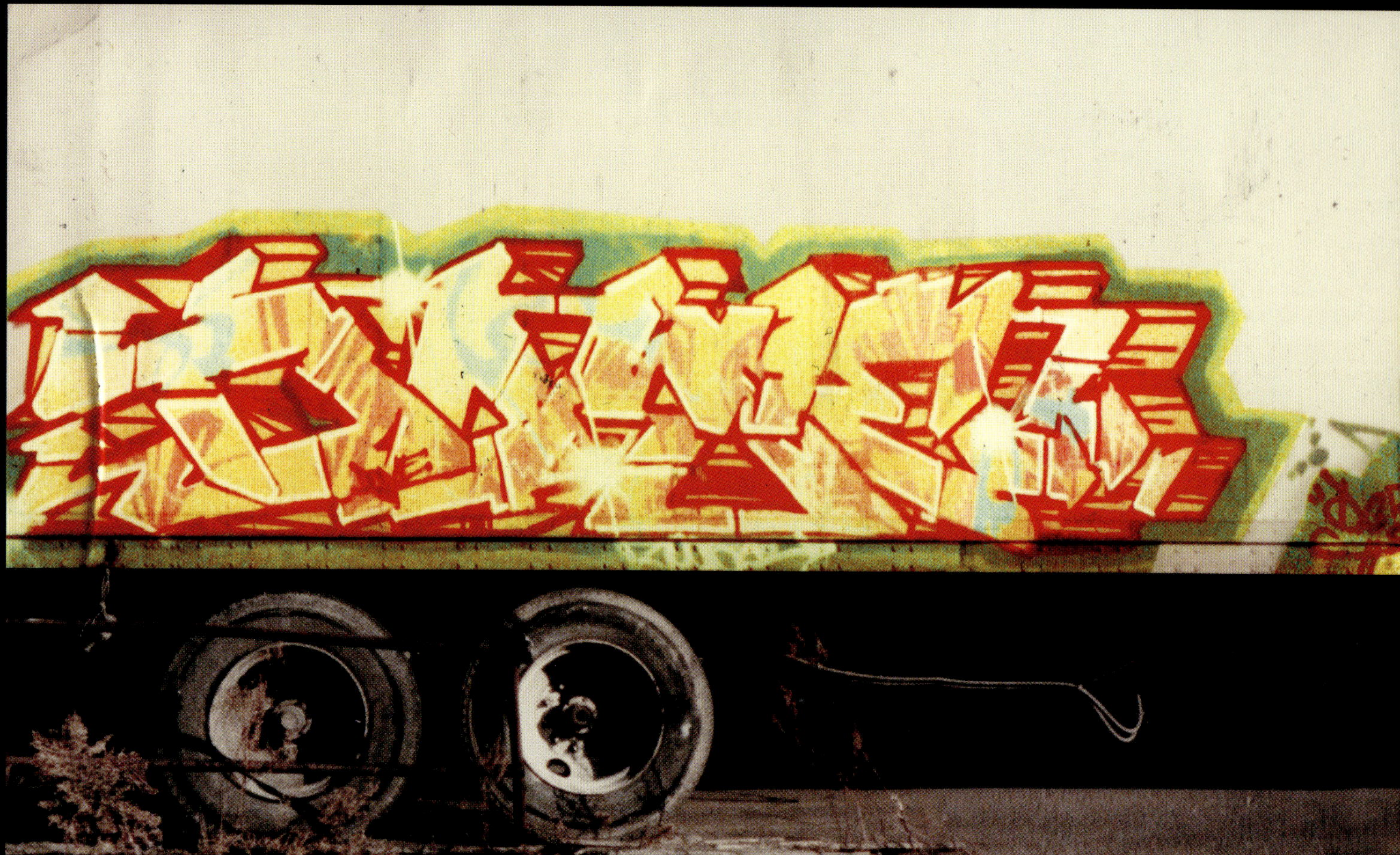

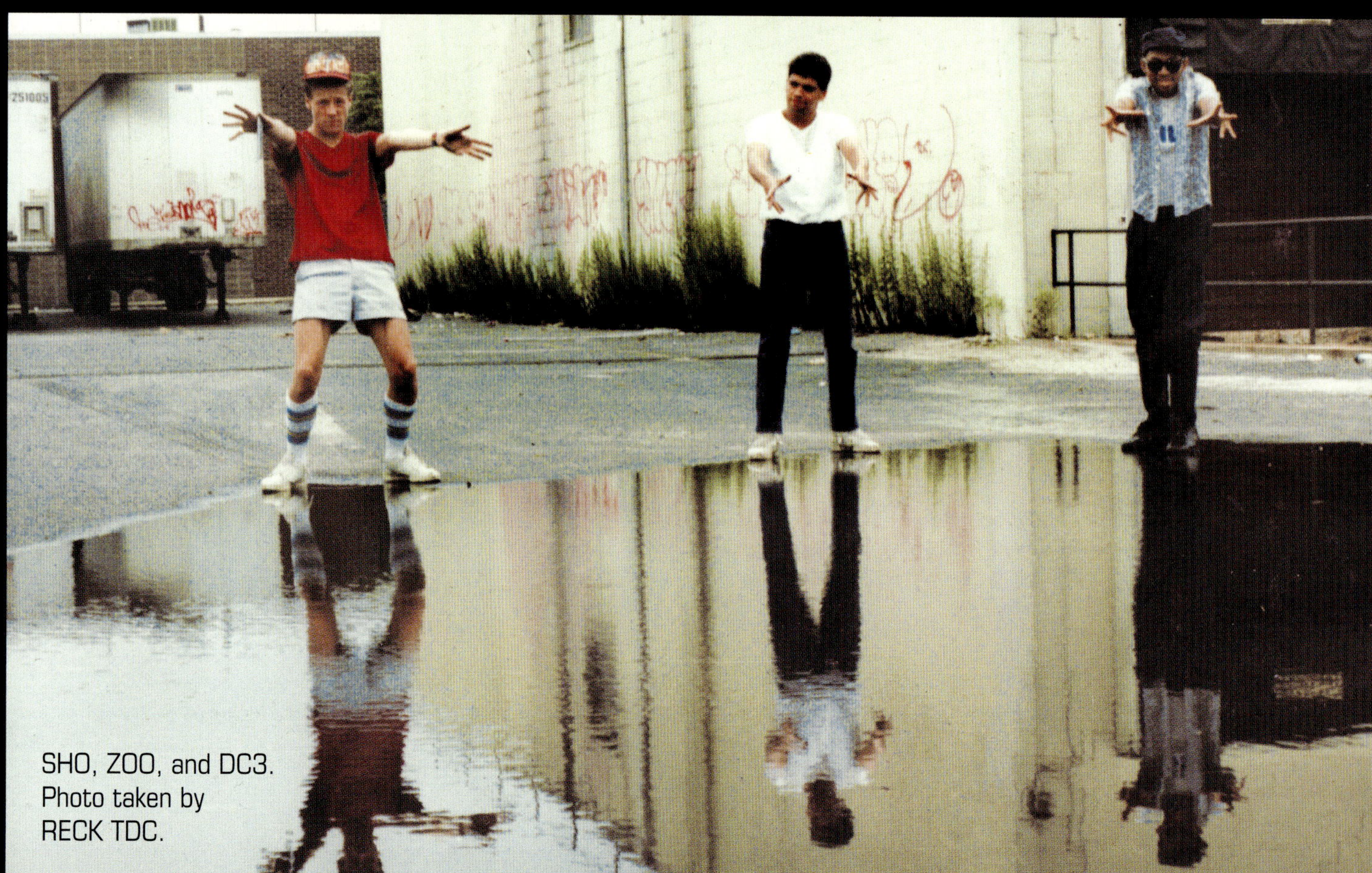

SHO, ZOO, and DC3. Photo taken by RECK TDC.

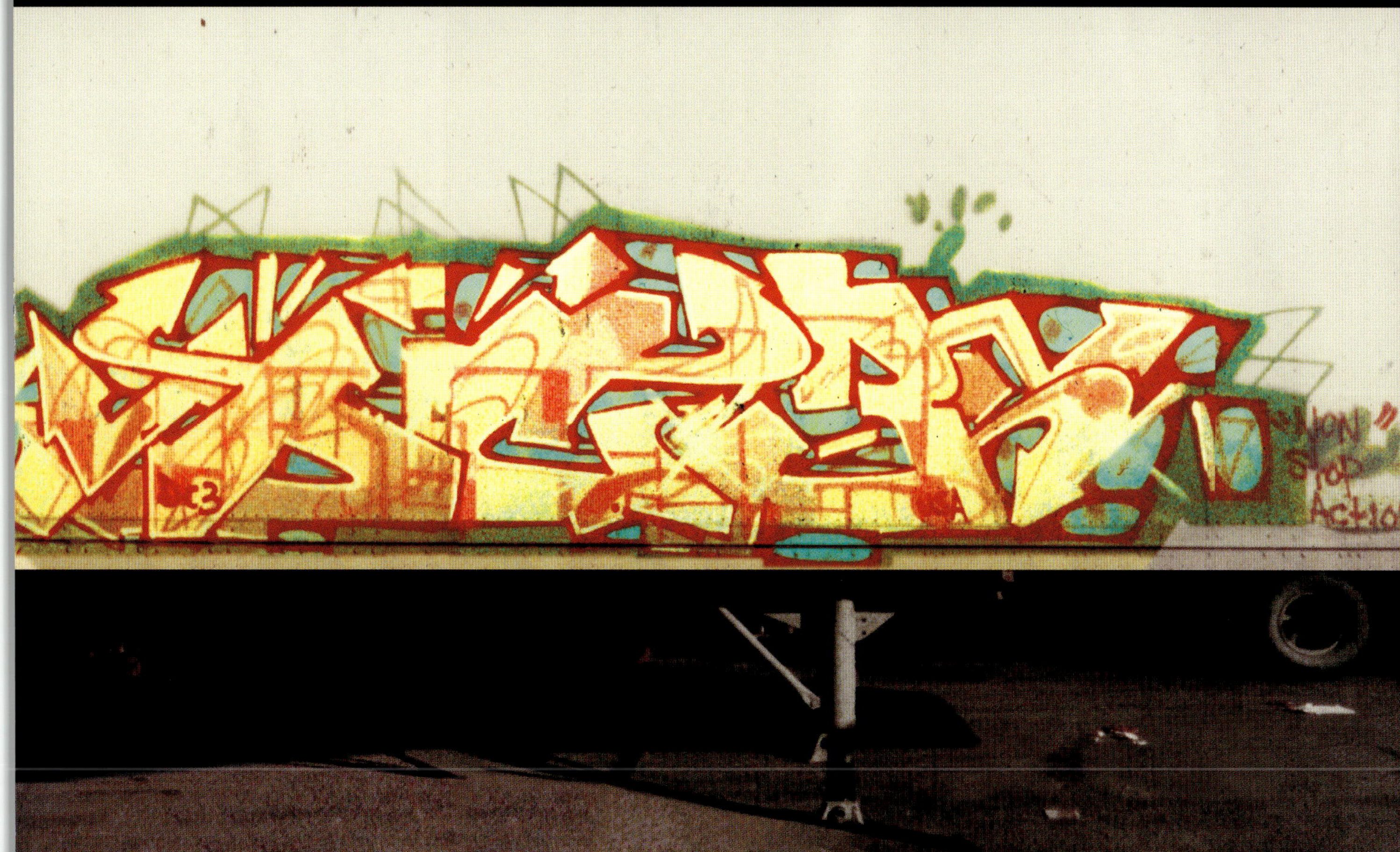

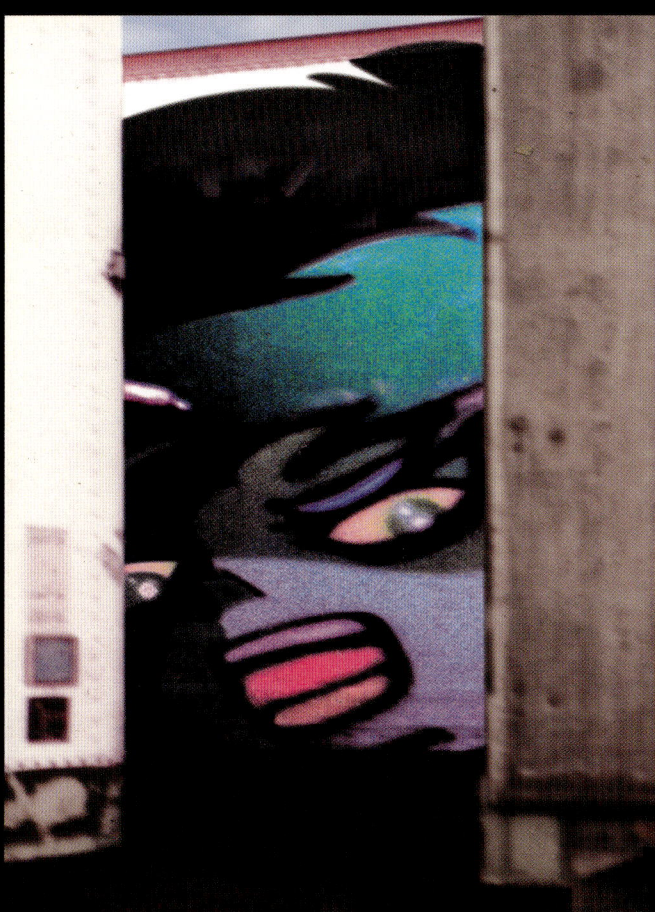

ZOO with top-to-bottom Martin, Feb. 1986.

Upon reflection, as you can clearly see, we had the Hempstead truck yard on lock. This picture was taken early on in 1986. Hitting moving targets became our favorite target i n the beginning. It would be rare, but when you did see one of your trucks pass by, it made it all worth it. Most importantly, as long as you had your pictures, it became immortalized in your portfolio. The main reason I did this book was to document shit from way early on in The Destiny Children/Unlimited Style Artists works. Throughout this production I've included as many tractor trailers as possible because all of them ran live on the street and that was what it was all about. We did at least 50 and don't have the ones in between the lanes that you couldn't take a flick of. I guess we shouldn't have done those, but someone seen thems.

-SHO

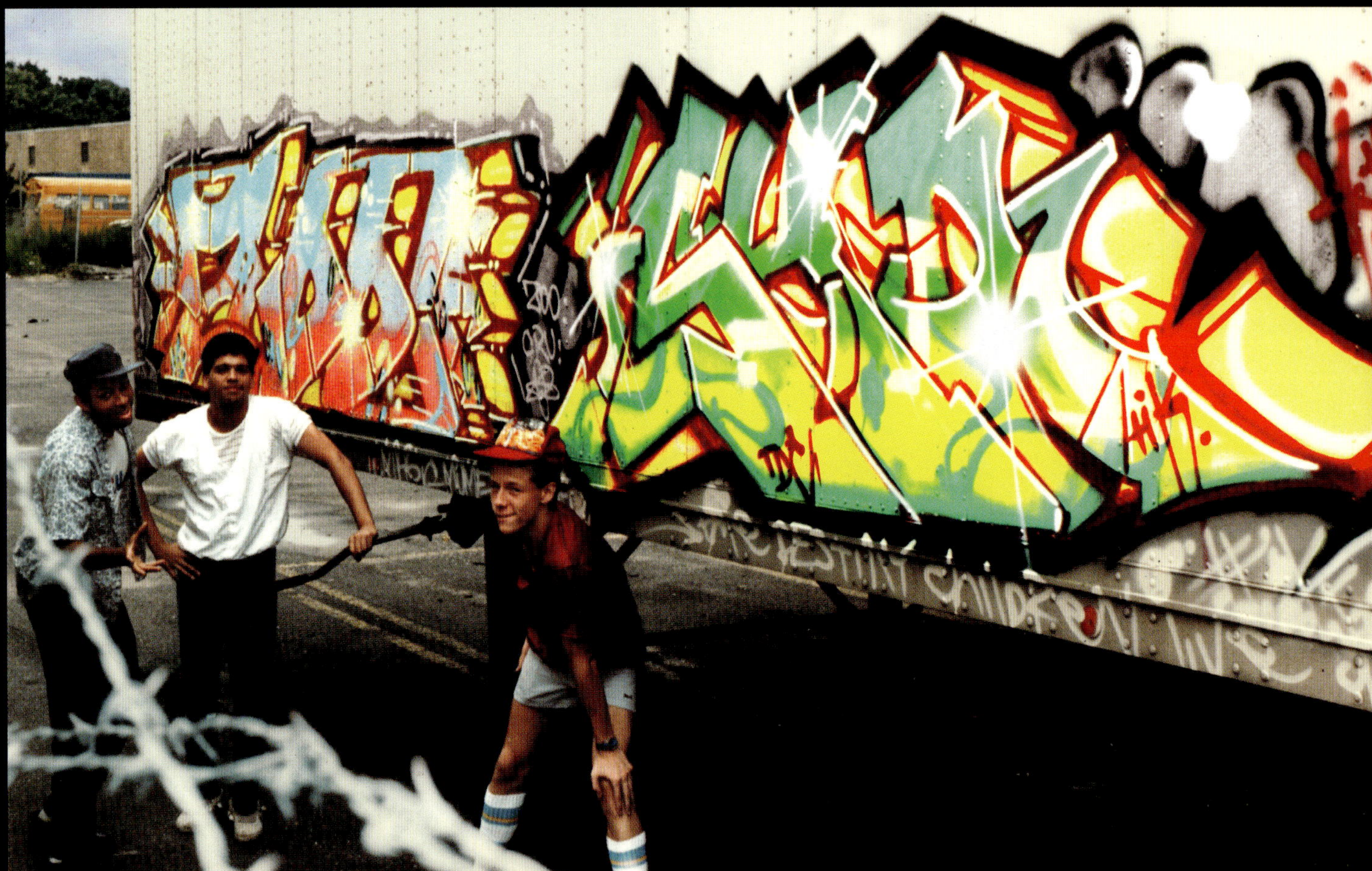

ZOO, SHO, and DC3's first tractor trailer burner.

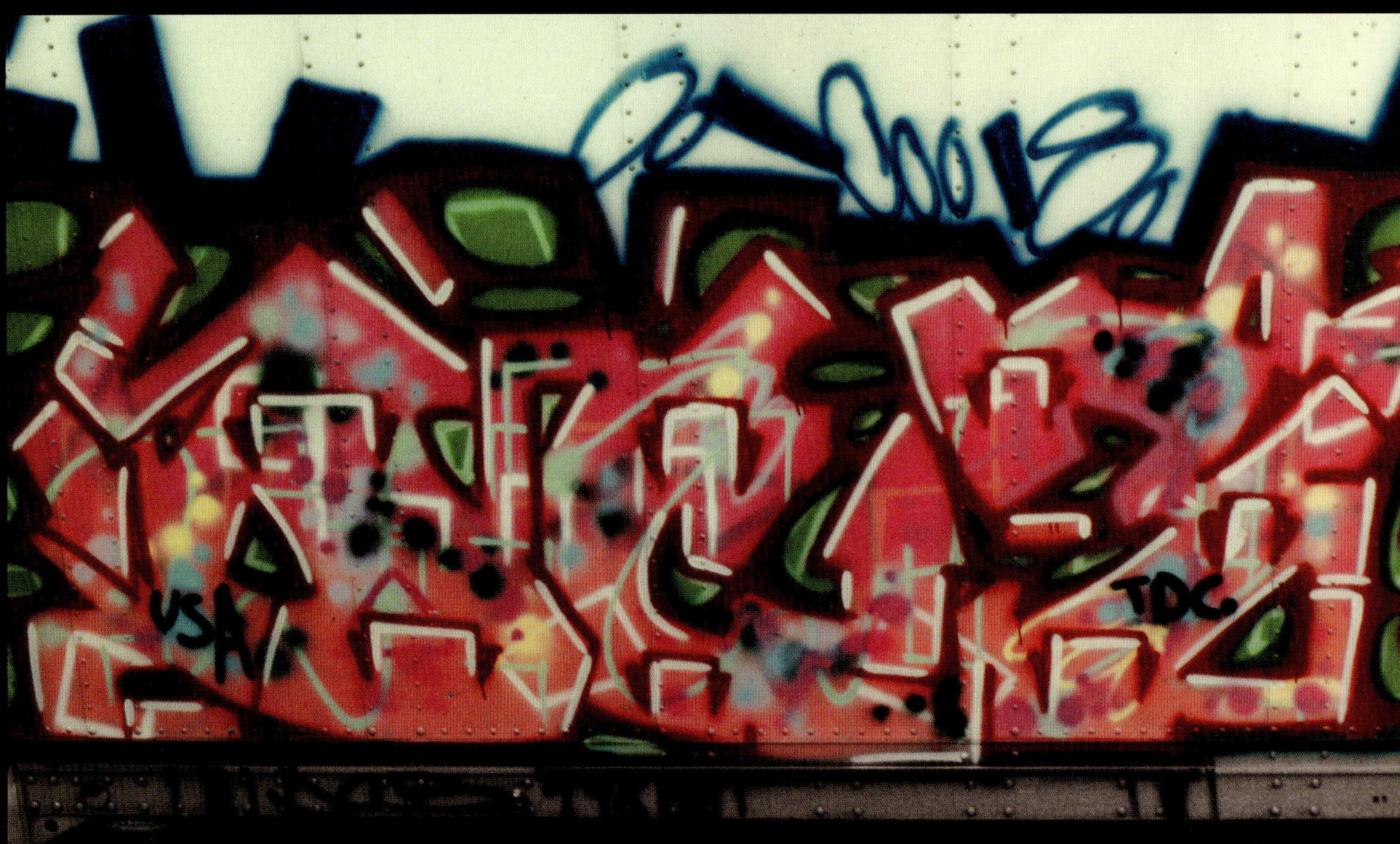

DC3, DOME "Wild Style," and RECK TDC, Jan. 1986.

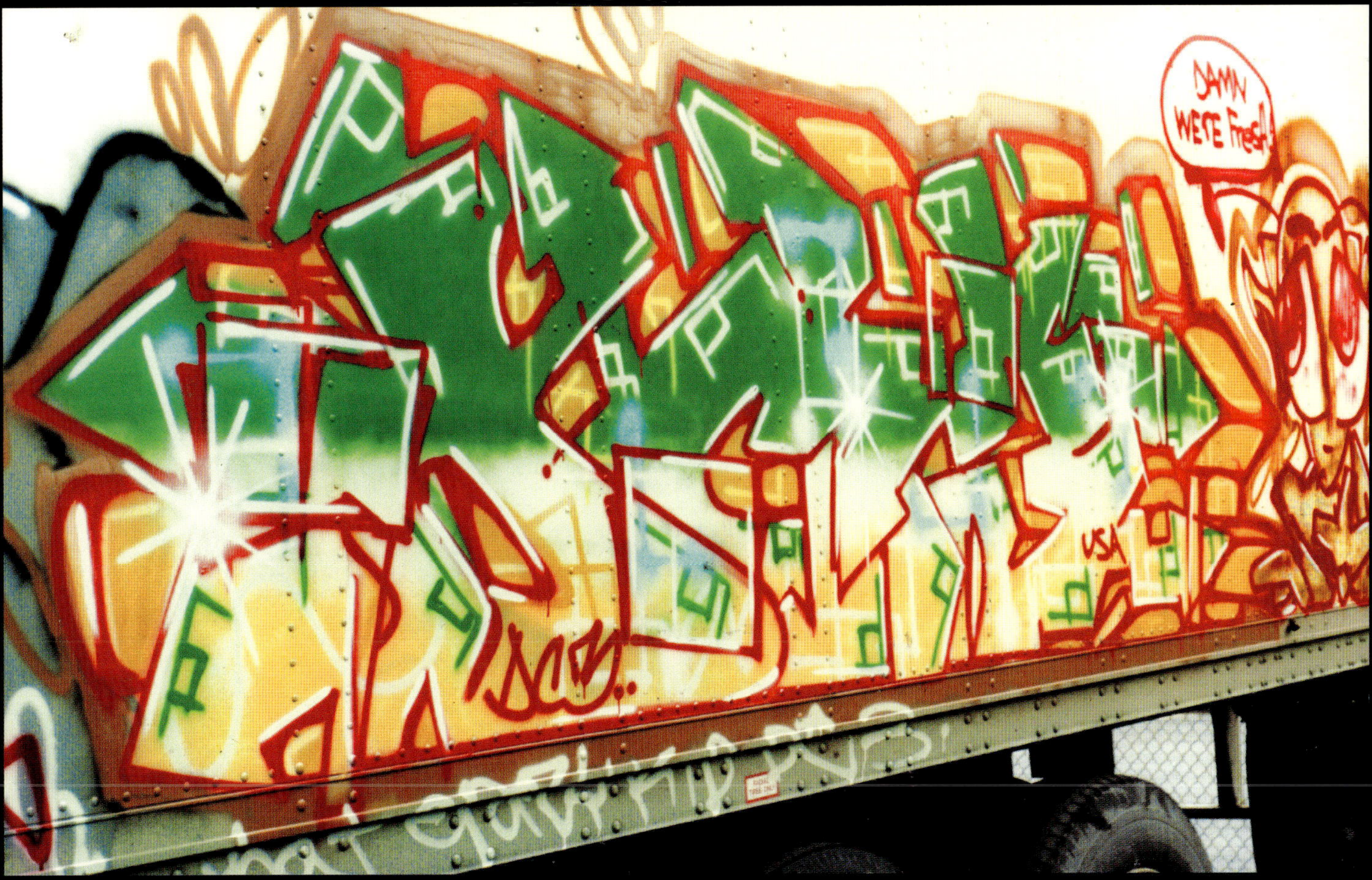

"DAMM WERE FRESH," Nov. 1985.

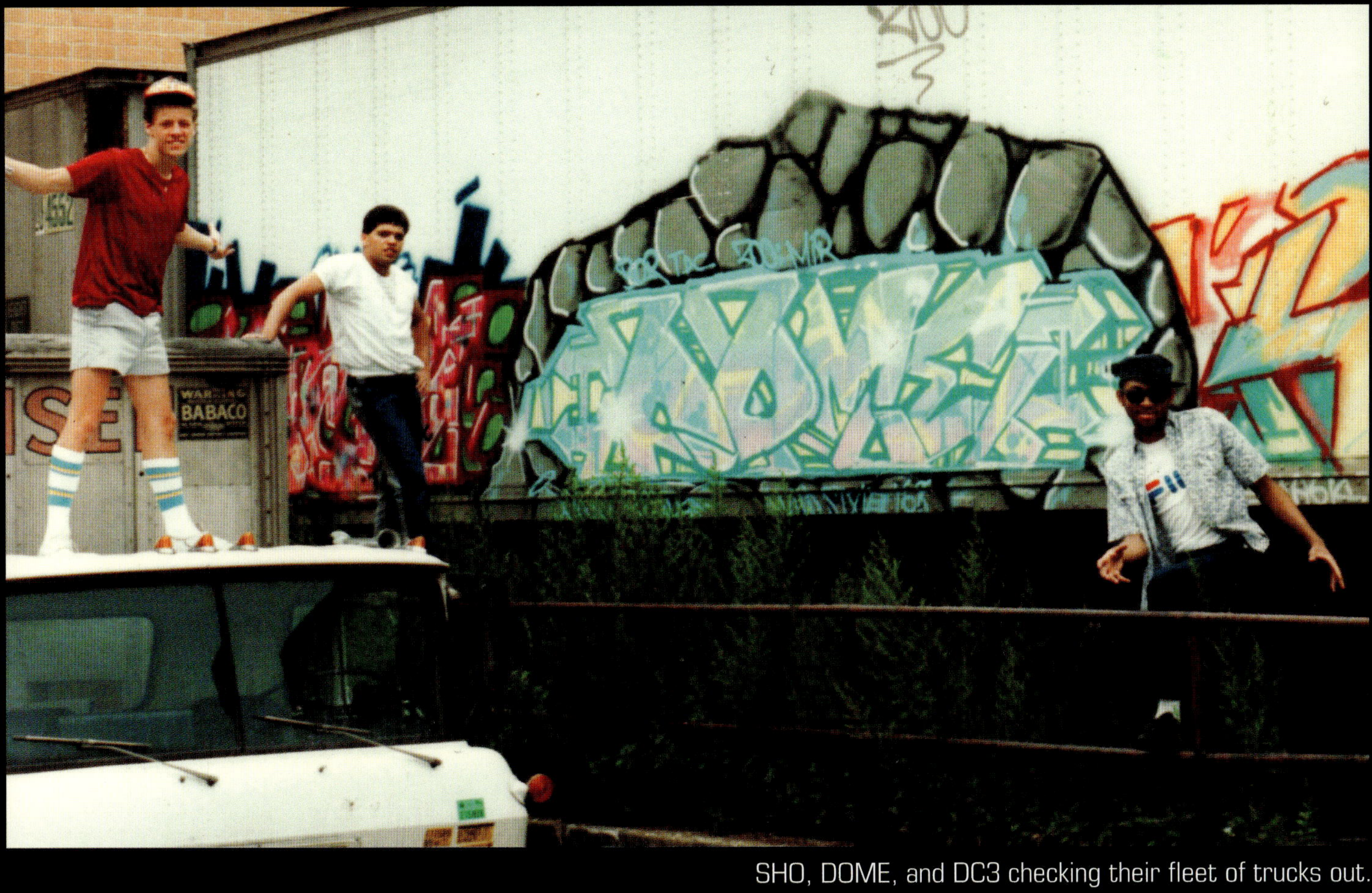

SHO, DOME, and DC3 checking their fleet of trucks out.

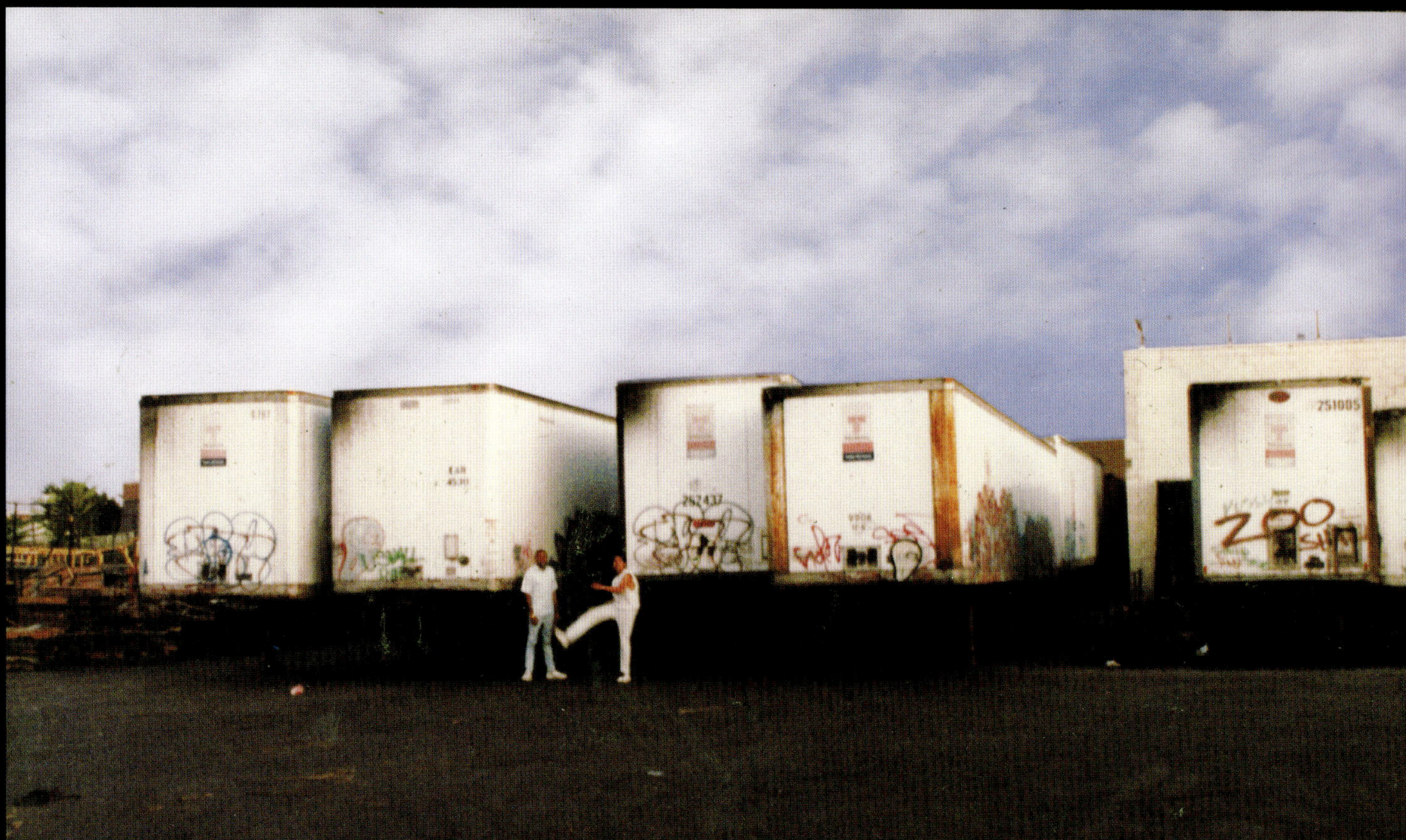

DC3 and ZOOROC patrolling their yard, making sure no toys had come through.

Man, life was good in the tractor trailer yard. When that shit was full it would be jammed packed with up to twenty-four full-sized trucks. Since it was mostly out of view from the surrounding streets you didn't have that much to worry about getting caught. Since this was 1985 it was rare that anybody would have security cameras like they do today. We're talking beepers had just came out technology wise. The thing I didn't understand or question is how they didn't catch on we was doing it in their home base? I guess maybe because we was smart and always took all the empty spray cans, caps, and empty 40s of beer with us.

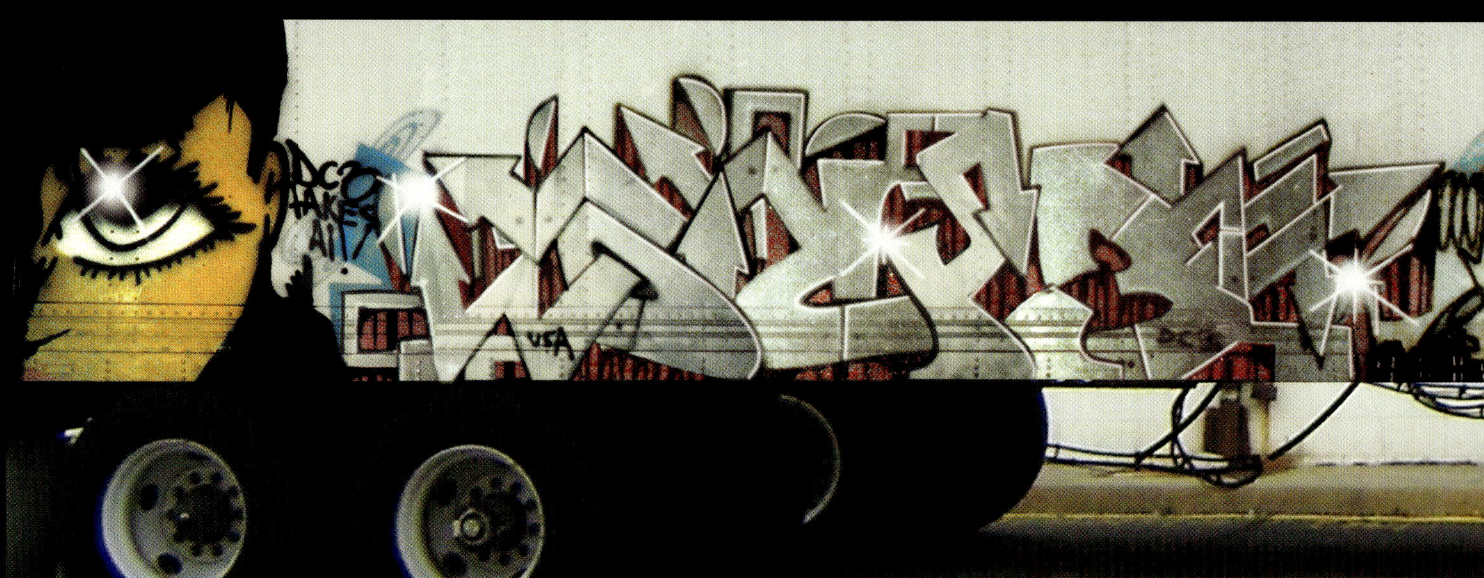

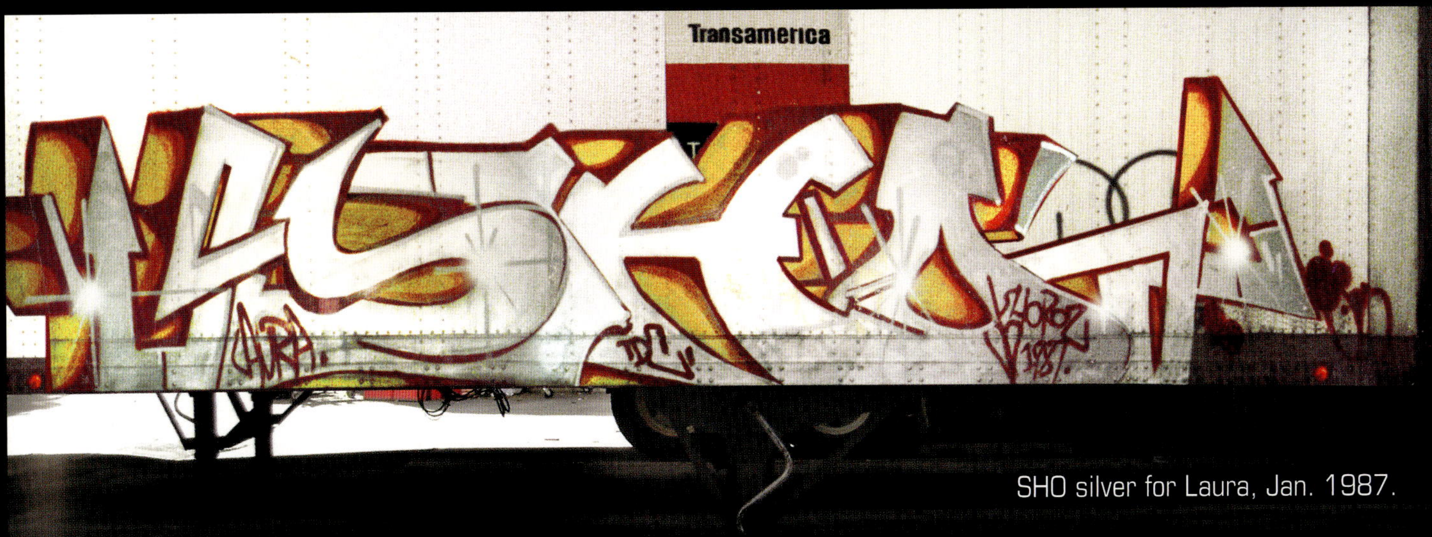

SHO silver for Laura, Jan. 1987.

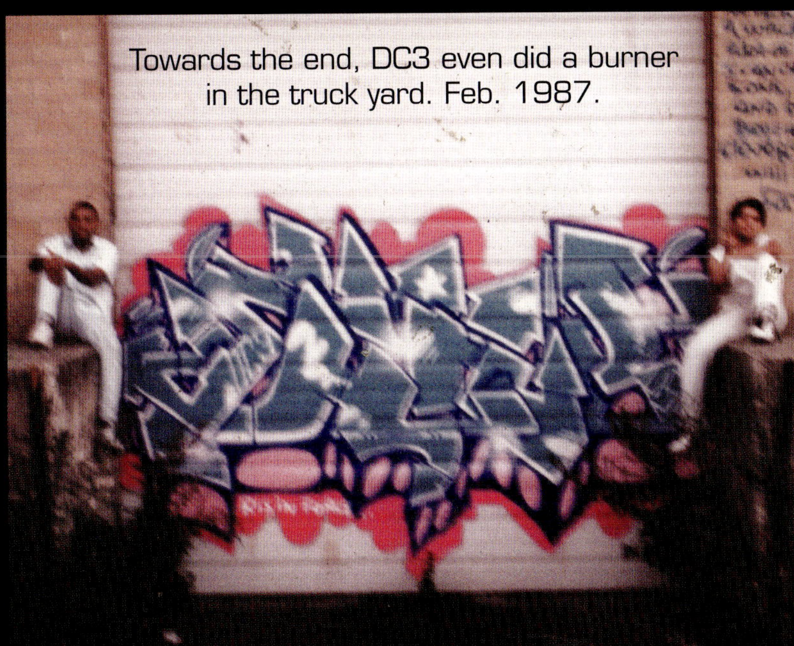

Towards the end, DC3 even did a burner in the truck yard. Feb. 1987.

That made shit really hot and we stopped hitting it up.

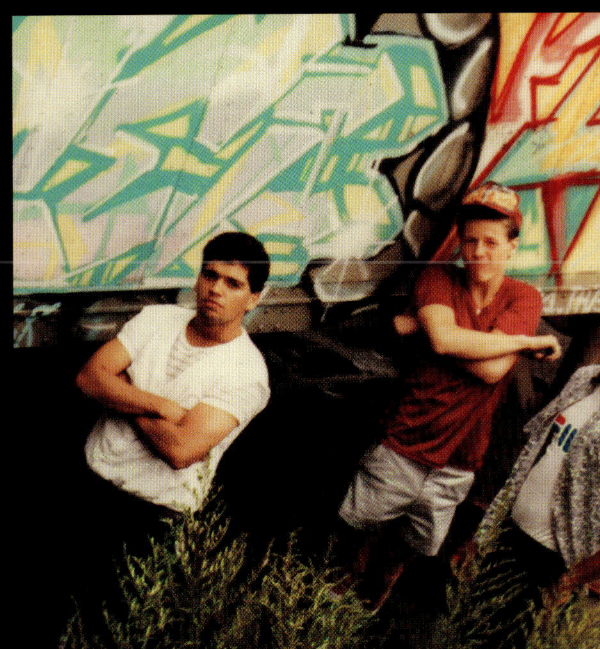

The Crew seeing what's good!!!

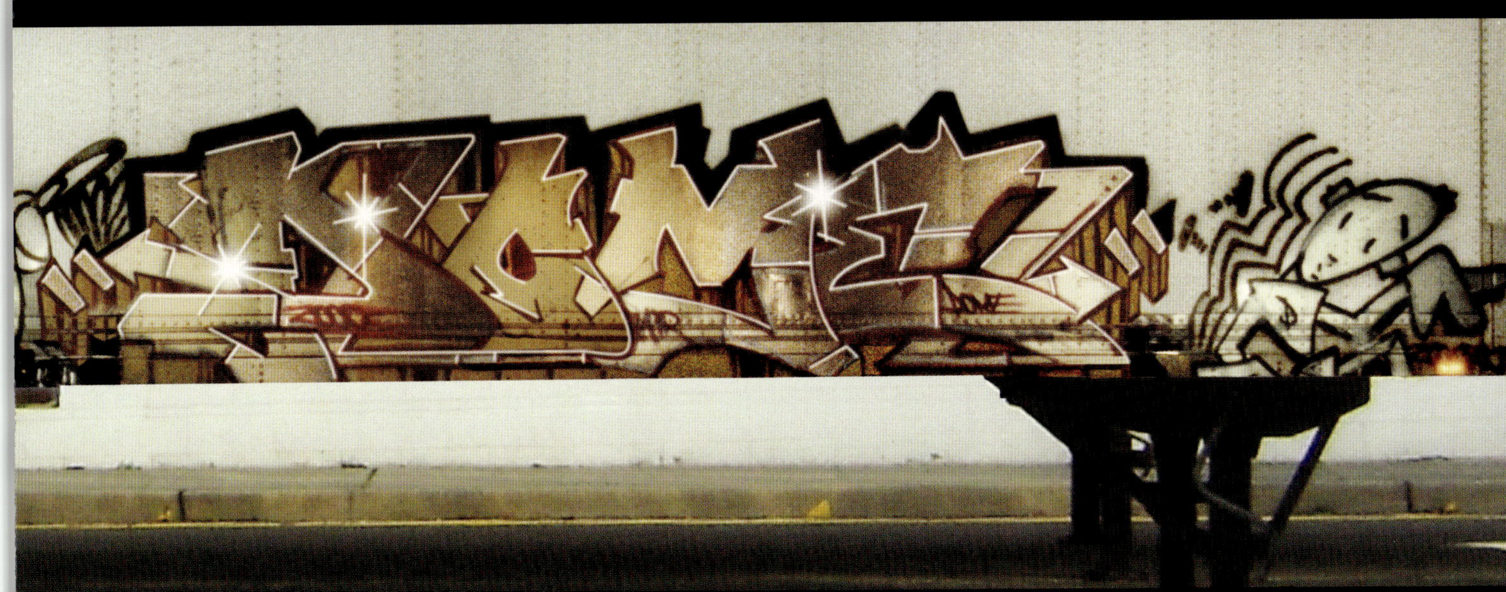

DC3, "TAKES ALL," and DOME, Oct. 1986.

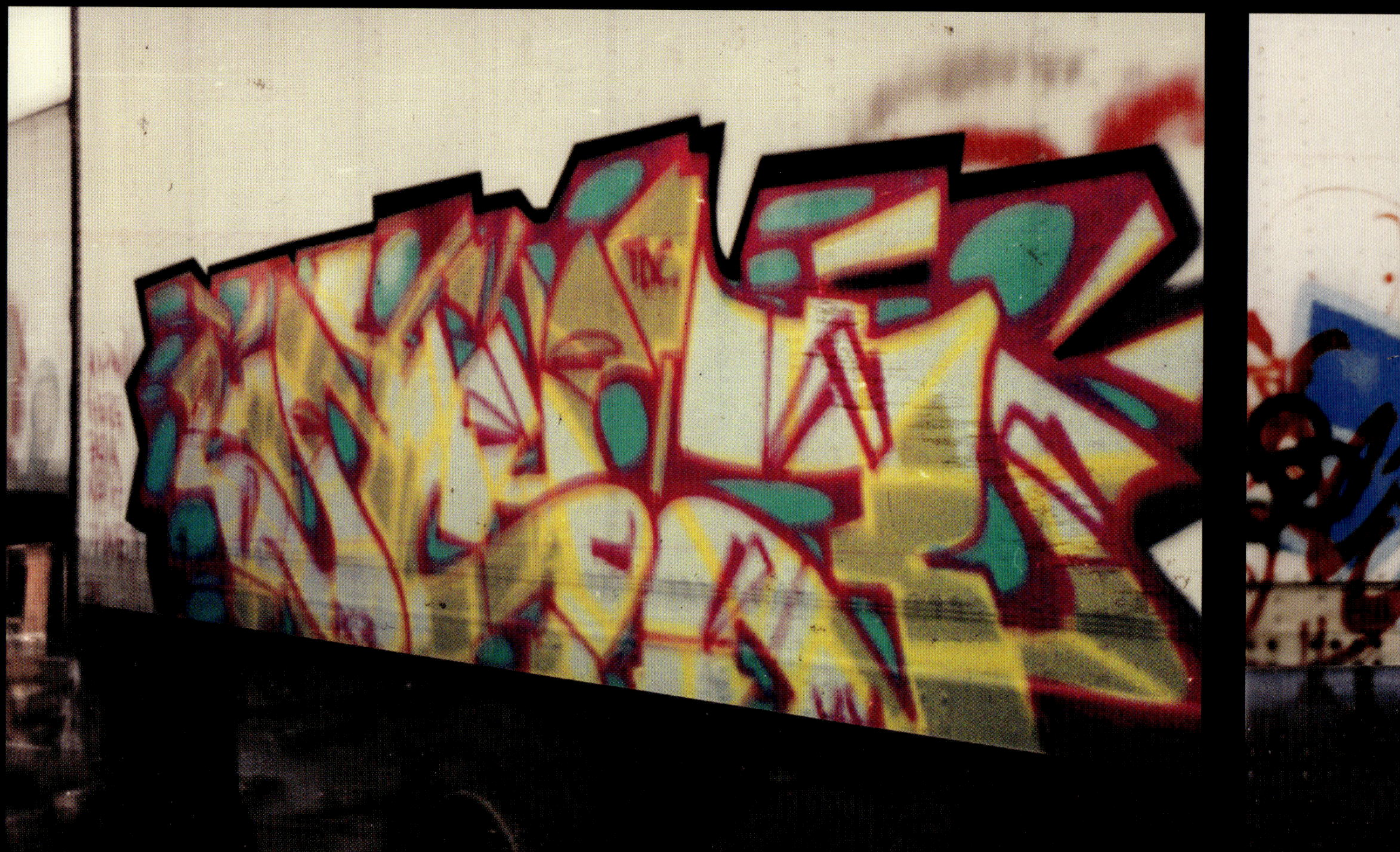

DC3 TDC solo truck, Sep. 1986.

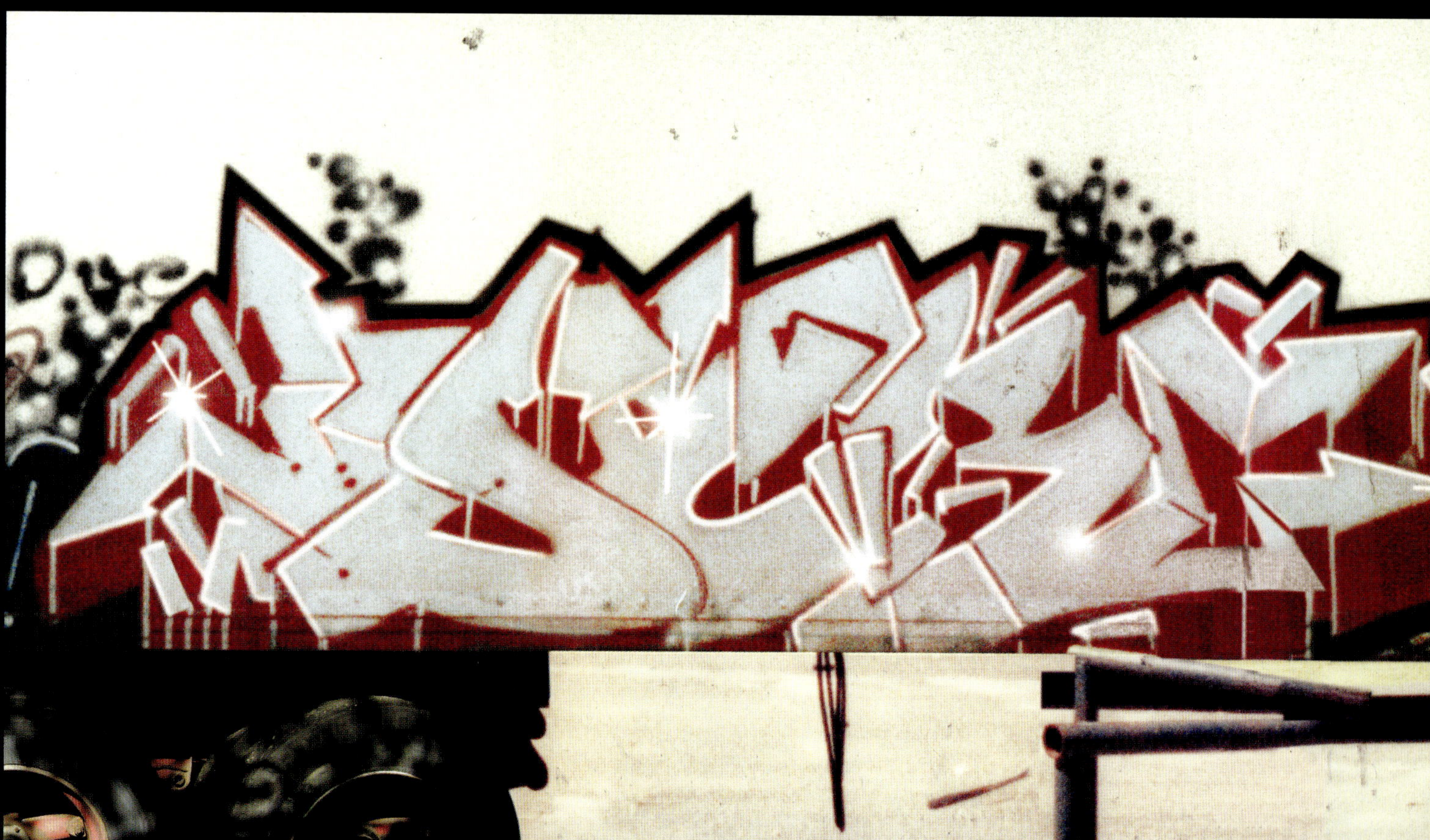

DC3 and ZOO silver pieces, Aug. 1986.

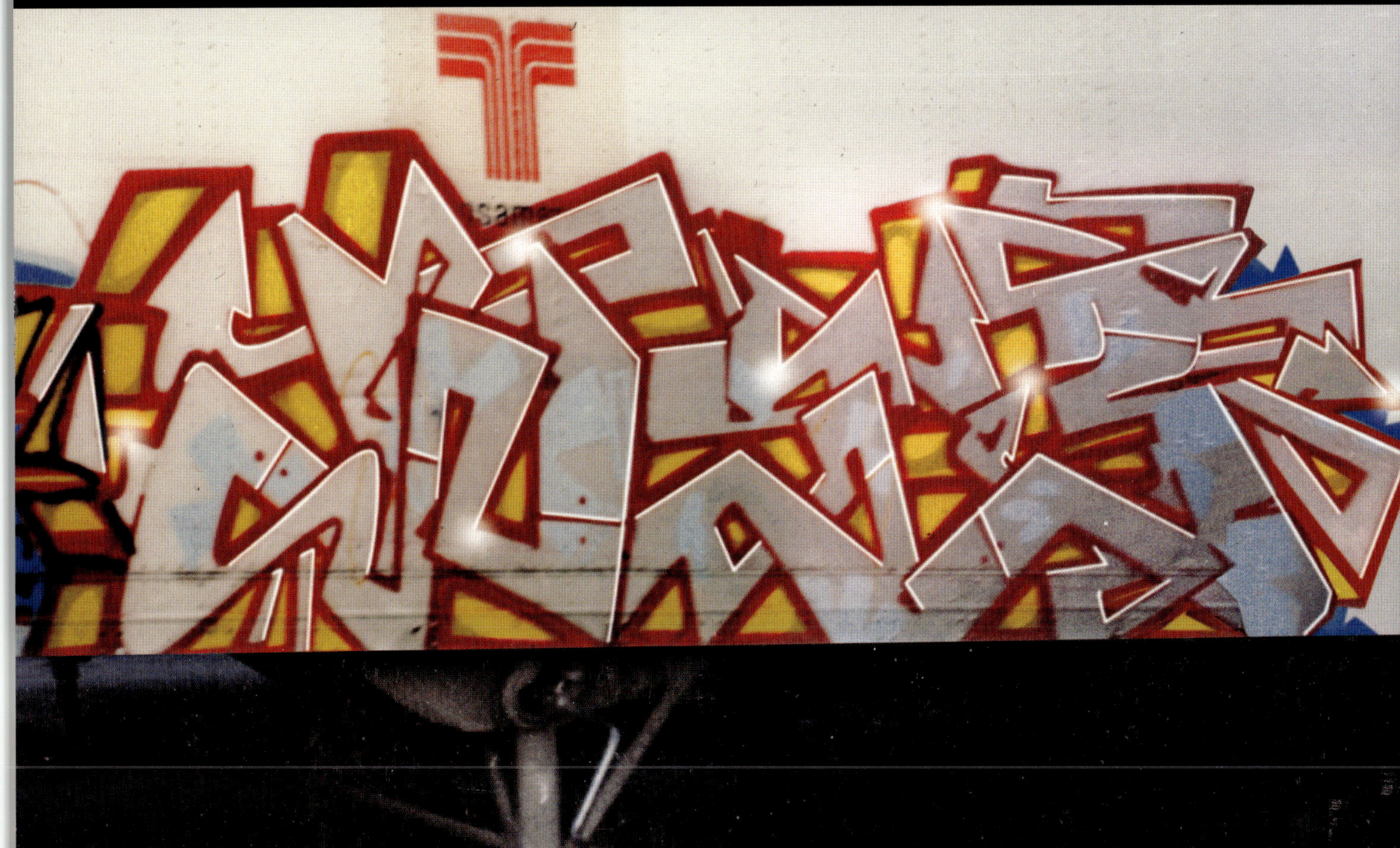

DC3 solo silver, wild style burner, Nov. 1986.

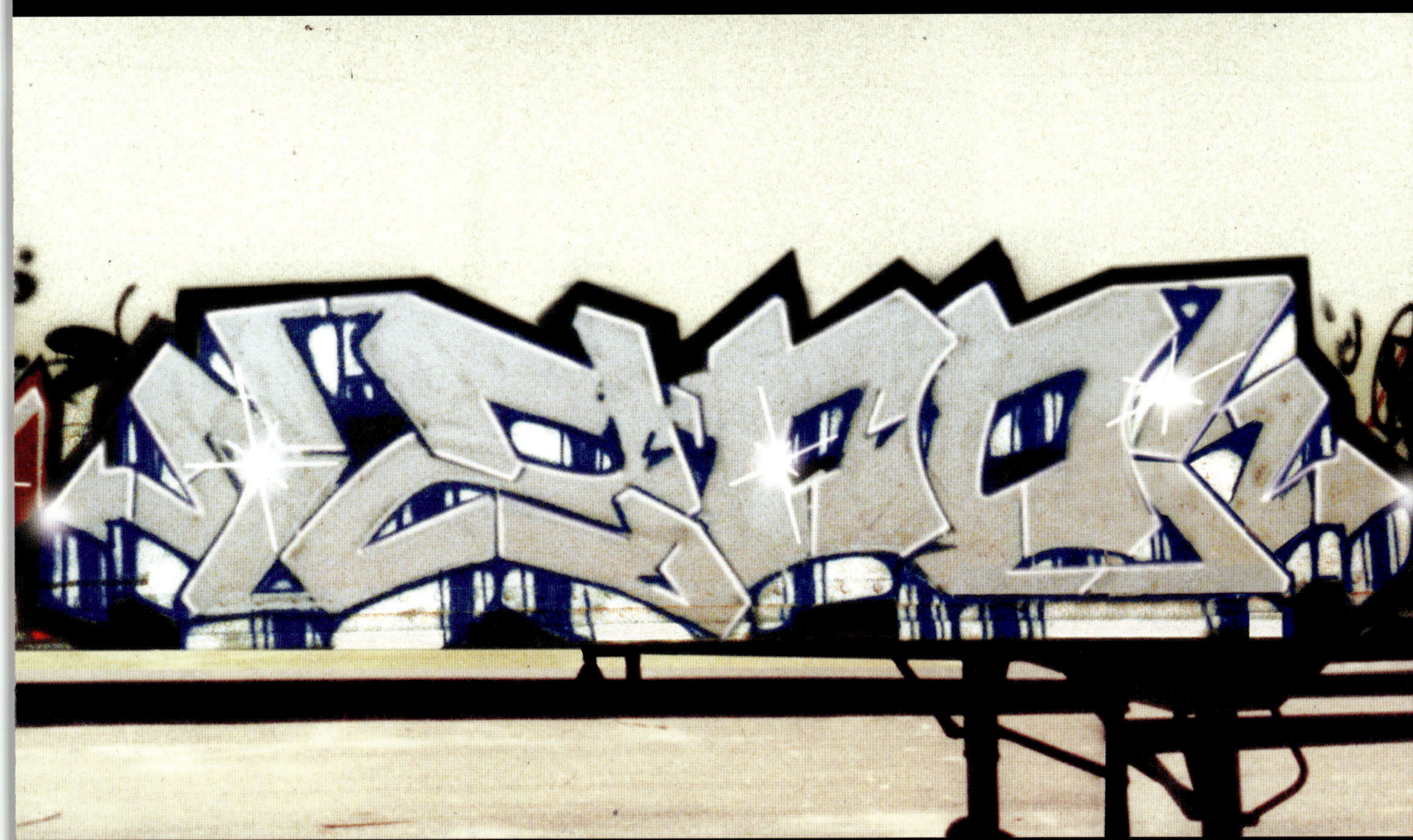

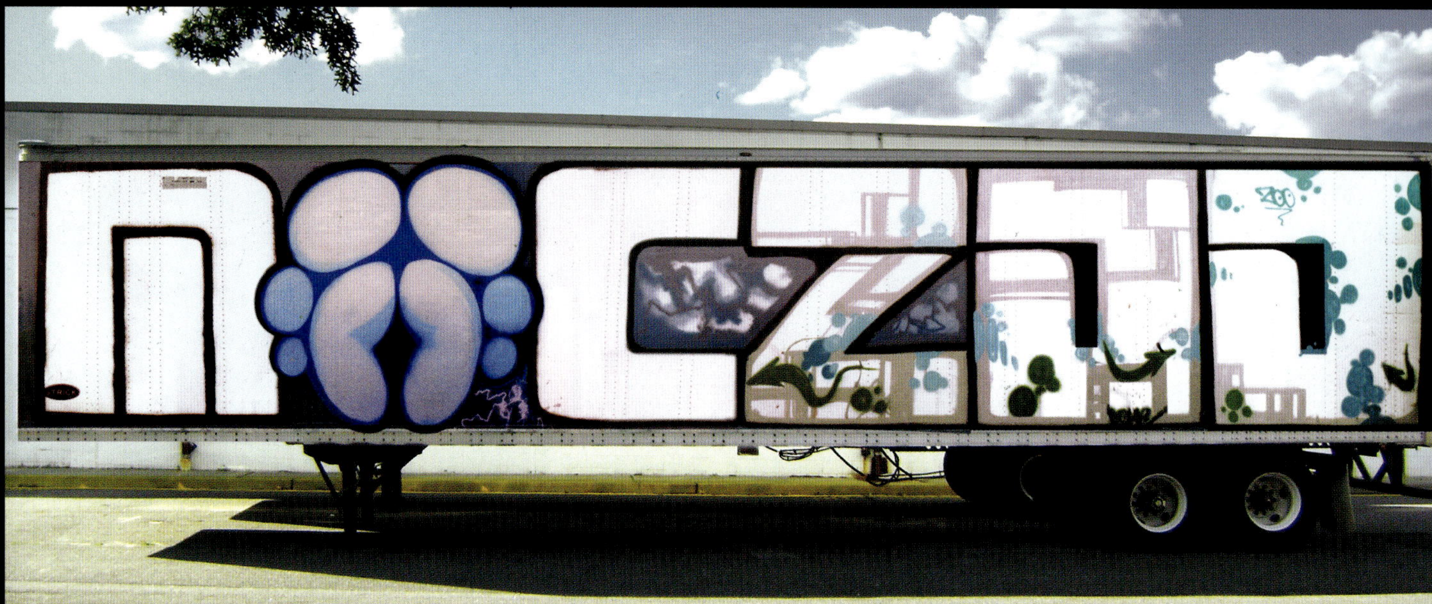

MAC and ZOO top-to-bottom truck, Aug. 1986.

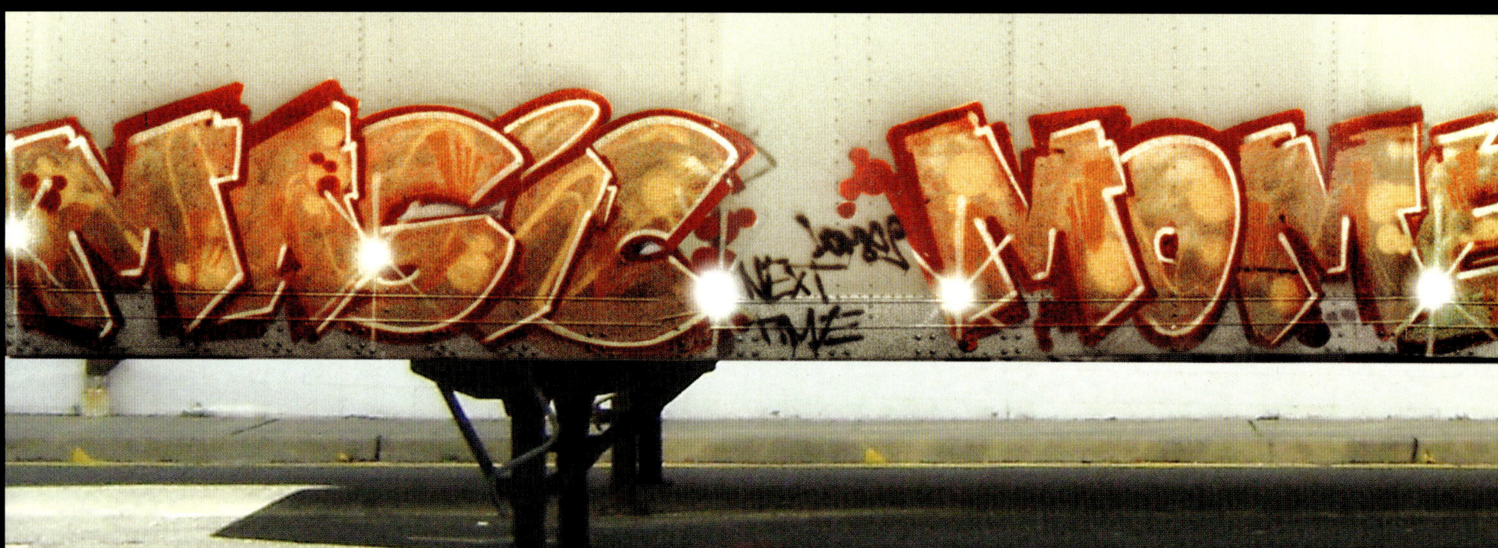

"MAGIC MOMENTS," by ZOO and DC3, Jun. 1986.

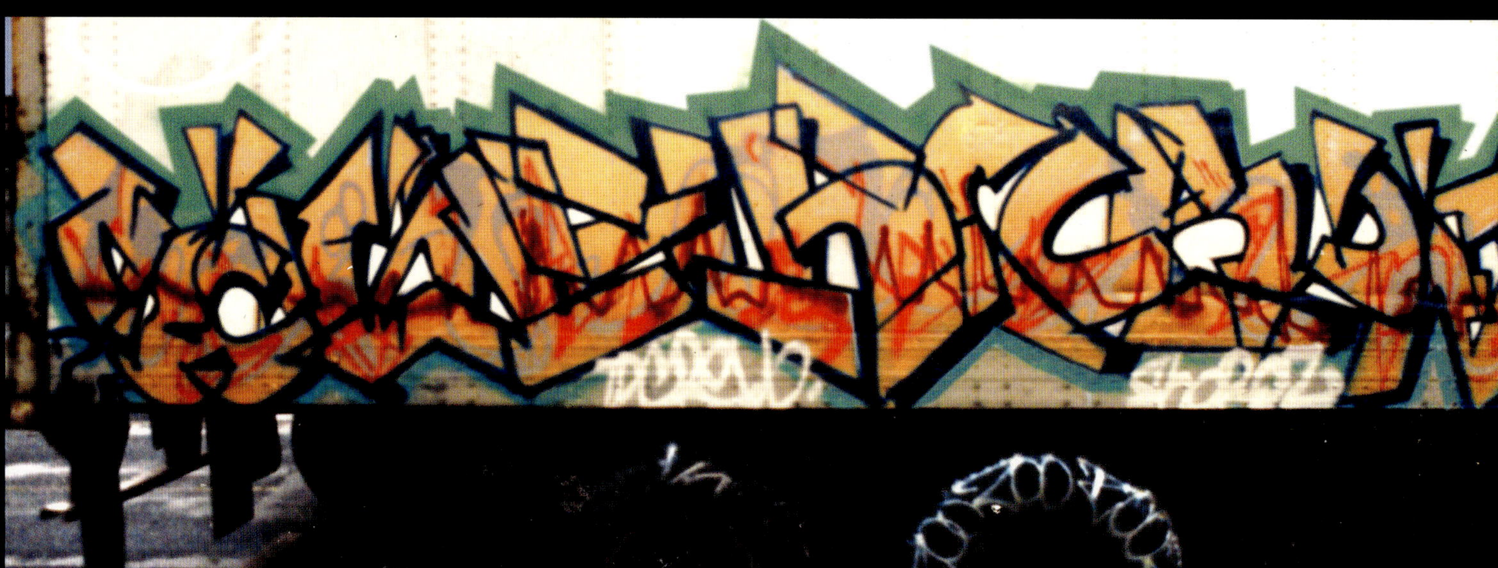

Painting tractor trailers was our come up to the subway trains. Mirage also originally wrote Mac and was getting a lot of fame for doing the feet. The feet was like doing a throw up but instead you became known by a symbol, he was one of the first. That was pretty original for back then. The truck yard was a weekend spot usually and sometimes you could hit that shit in broad daylight. You just had to be careful that you weren't seen going in. This was an industrial area and a lot of the surrounding businesses had armed private security who would call the cops. You could get trapped in there because it was surrounded by barbed wired fences, and on one side there was a Yellow Taxi repair center and depot with German Shepherds running around in the yard. Hell no, I wouldn't have tested them!!!!! We only hit these tractor trailers in 1985-1987 and it primed us to hit the subway lines. They were very similar to trains in size and length. Also, it takes a while to get used to painting on metal surfaces, you tend to get more drips. So here we learned spray paint control and how to space out 50- to 60-foot lengths for two or three writers.

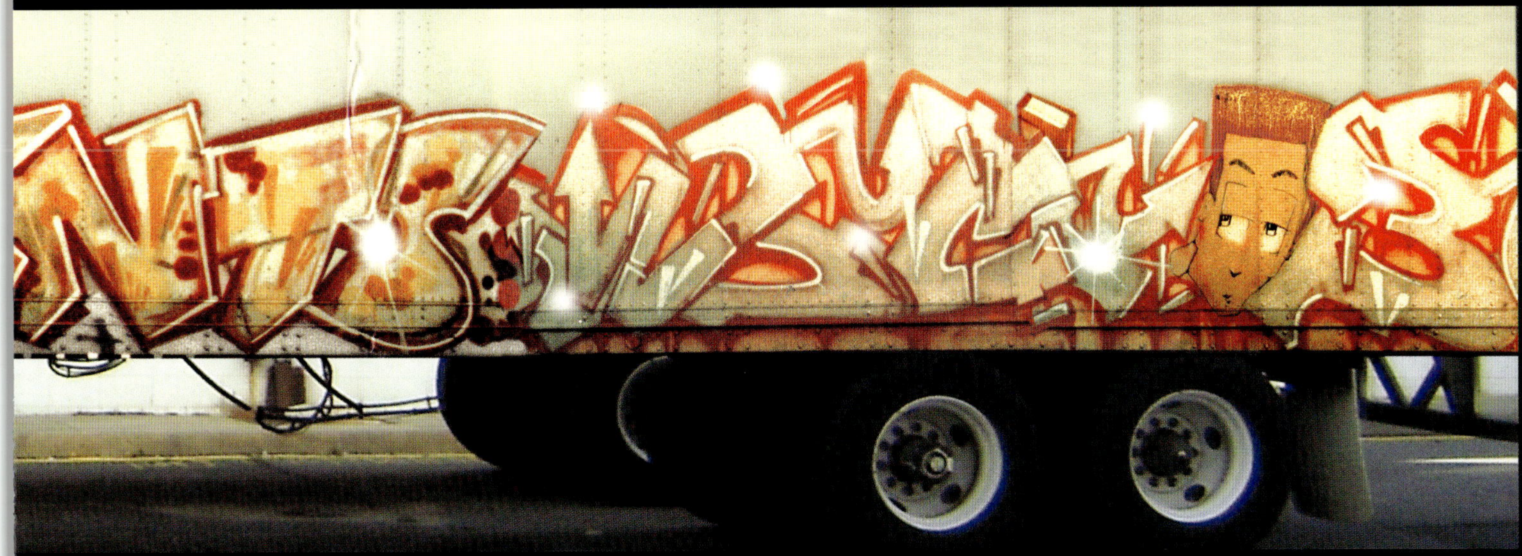

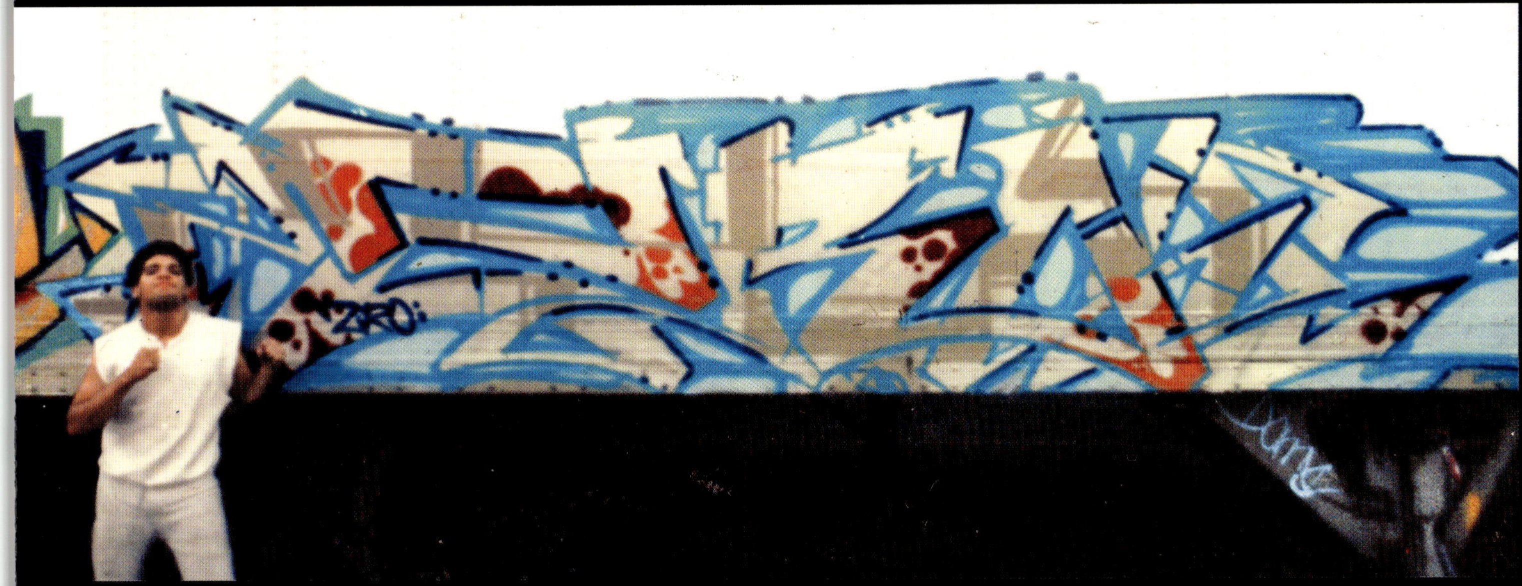

TDC SHO ONE and ZRO, by ZOO, Jul. 1986.

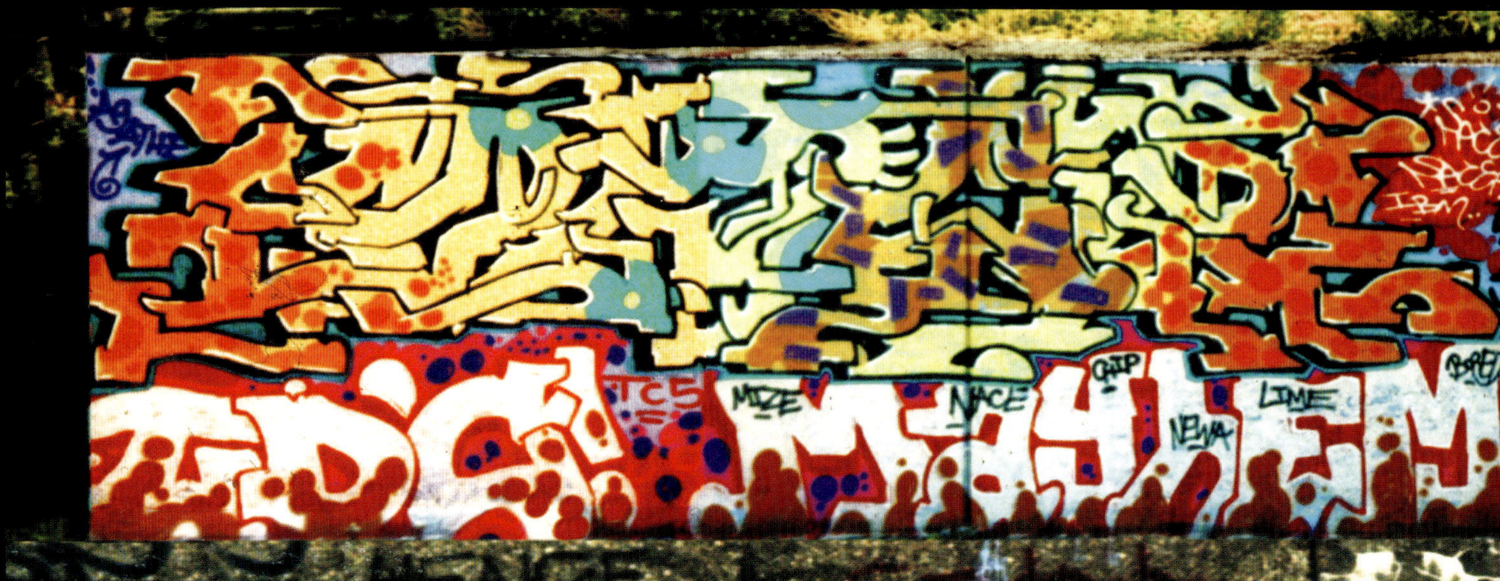

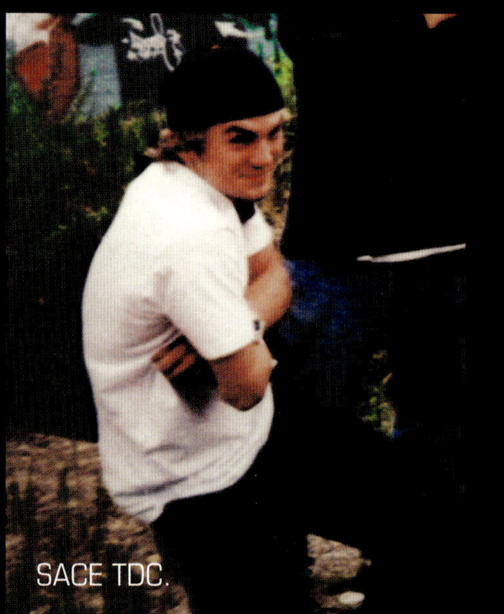

SACE TDC.

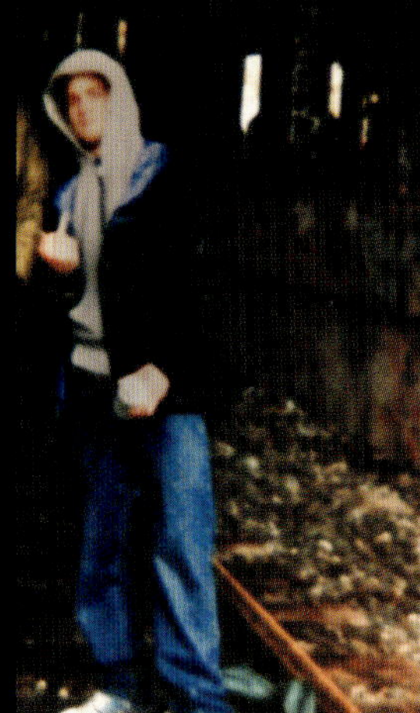

SACE in the Bronx, 1995.

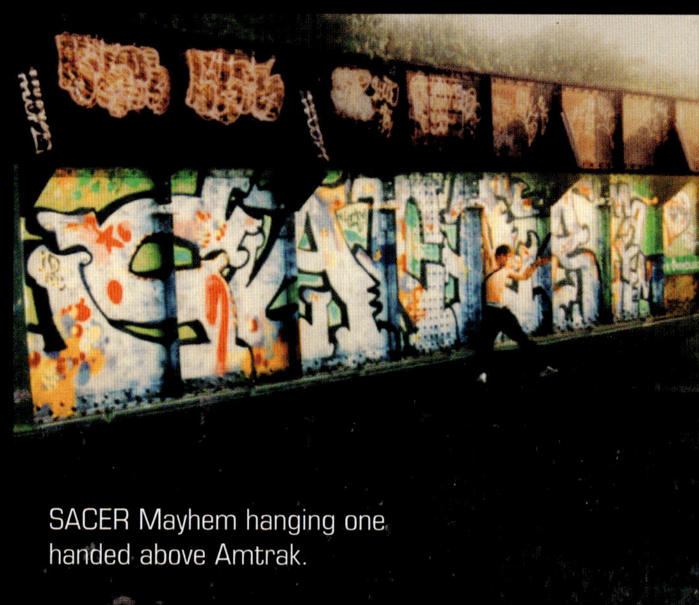

SACER Mayhem hanging one handed above Amtrak.

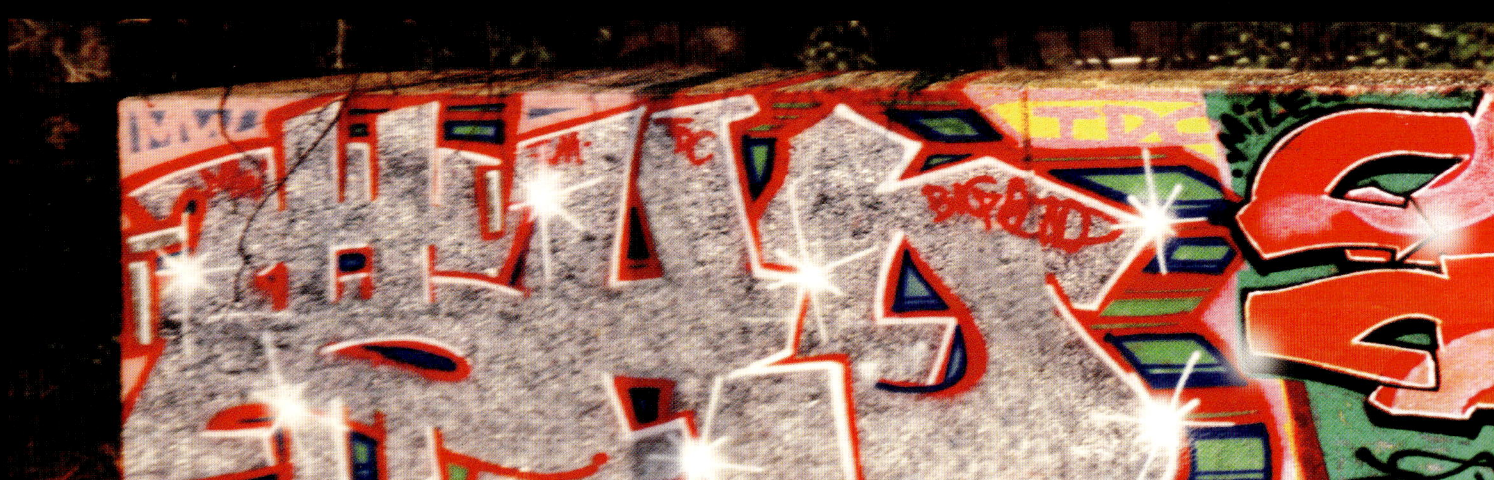

MW BIG SHO TDC AND SACER TDC, 1998.

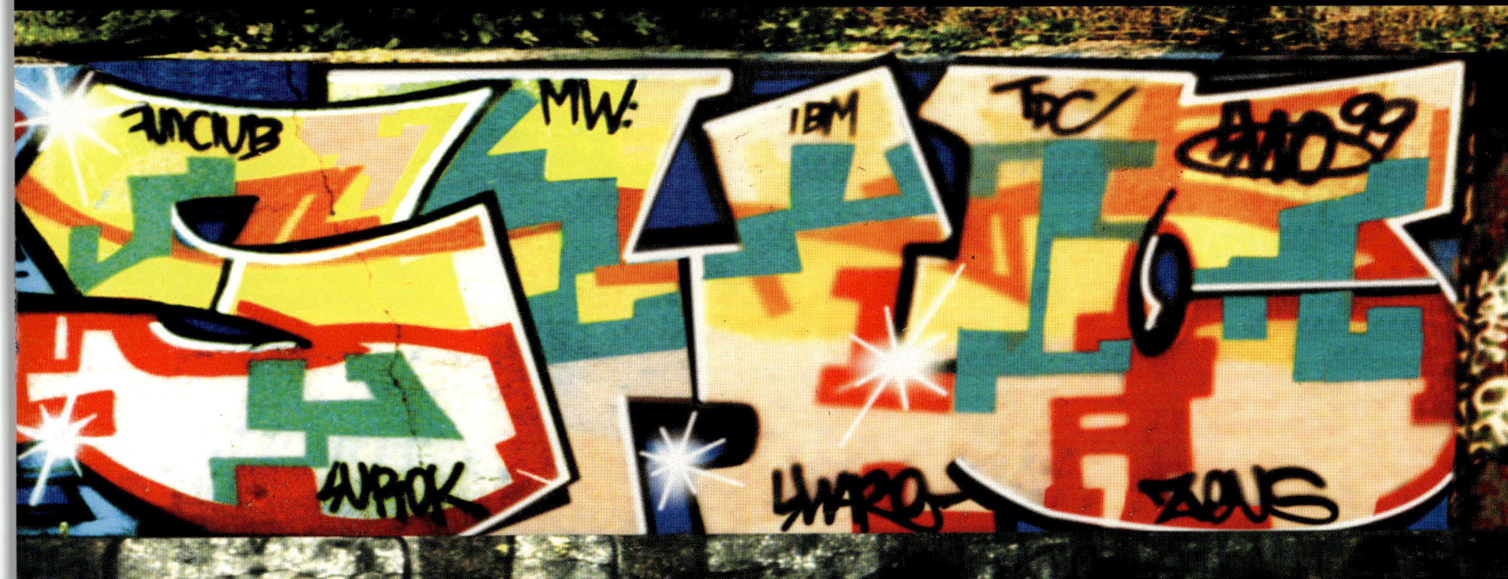

SACE TDC MAYHEM and SHO, 1999.

RIP Dash Snow, AKA SACE, TDC IBM TC5 IRAK

Unfortunately he died an early untimely death on July 13, 2009 of a Heroin overdose while at the Lafayette Hotel at the age of 27. He had been in rehab as recently as March of that year and had been staying off drugs. A major problem facing those trying to turn their life around, other than temptation, is that nowadays the "Ron" or "Baby Baby" has made a big come back and it's more potent than ever, more addictive, cheaper, and super easy to OD on, especially if your tolerance is way down. I painted with SACE in 1998 and 1999 and he was a cool kid with a lot of heart. I remember when Share 37 first brought him to Club SHO that he was down to paint whenever and where ever. He was mad young at the time, like 16 years old and was talking shit to me like you ain't so tough and that he would fight me. So I playfully fought him and he was losing but kept on saying hit me some more. He made a big impression on me that he had heart so I told him to push TDC. I last saw him downtown DJing at a bar club about four years ago and didn't recognize him at first. He will be missed!!!

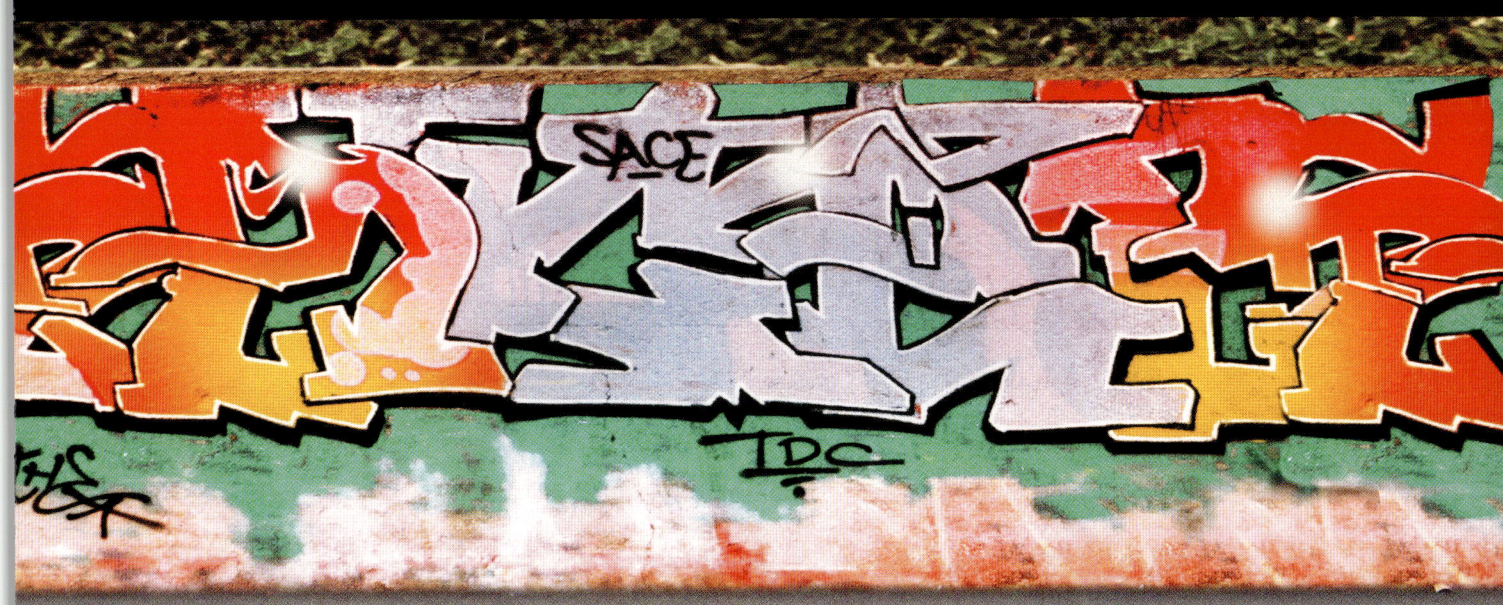

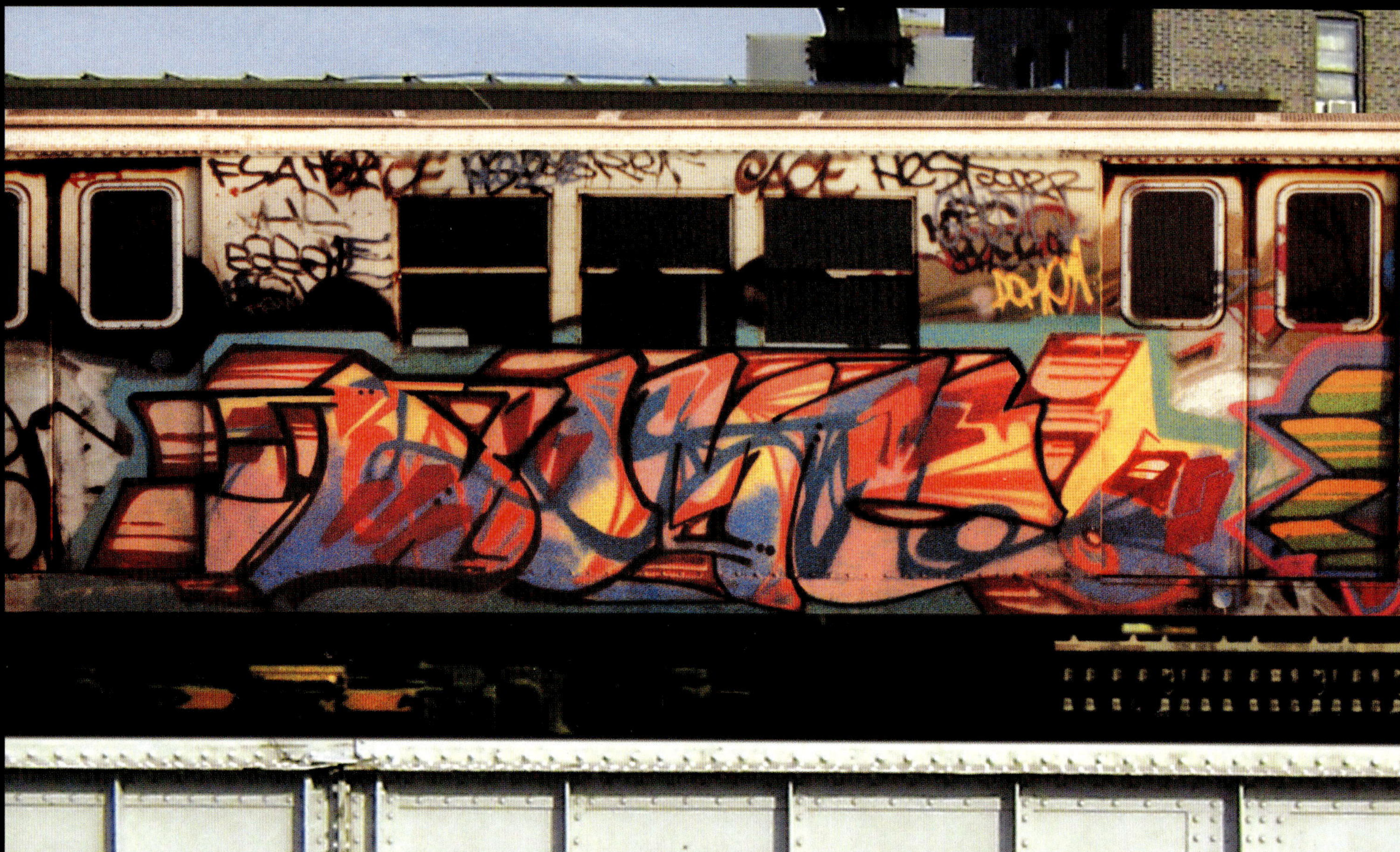

DOME and GOLDIE TAT, "For Geraldine," window-down 5 Train burner, Jan. 1987.

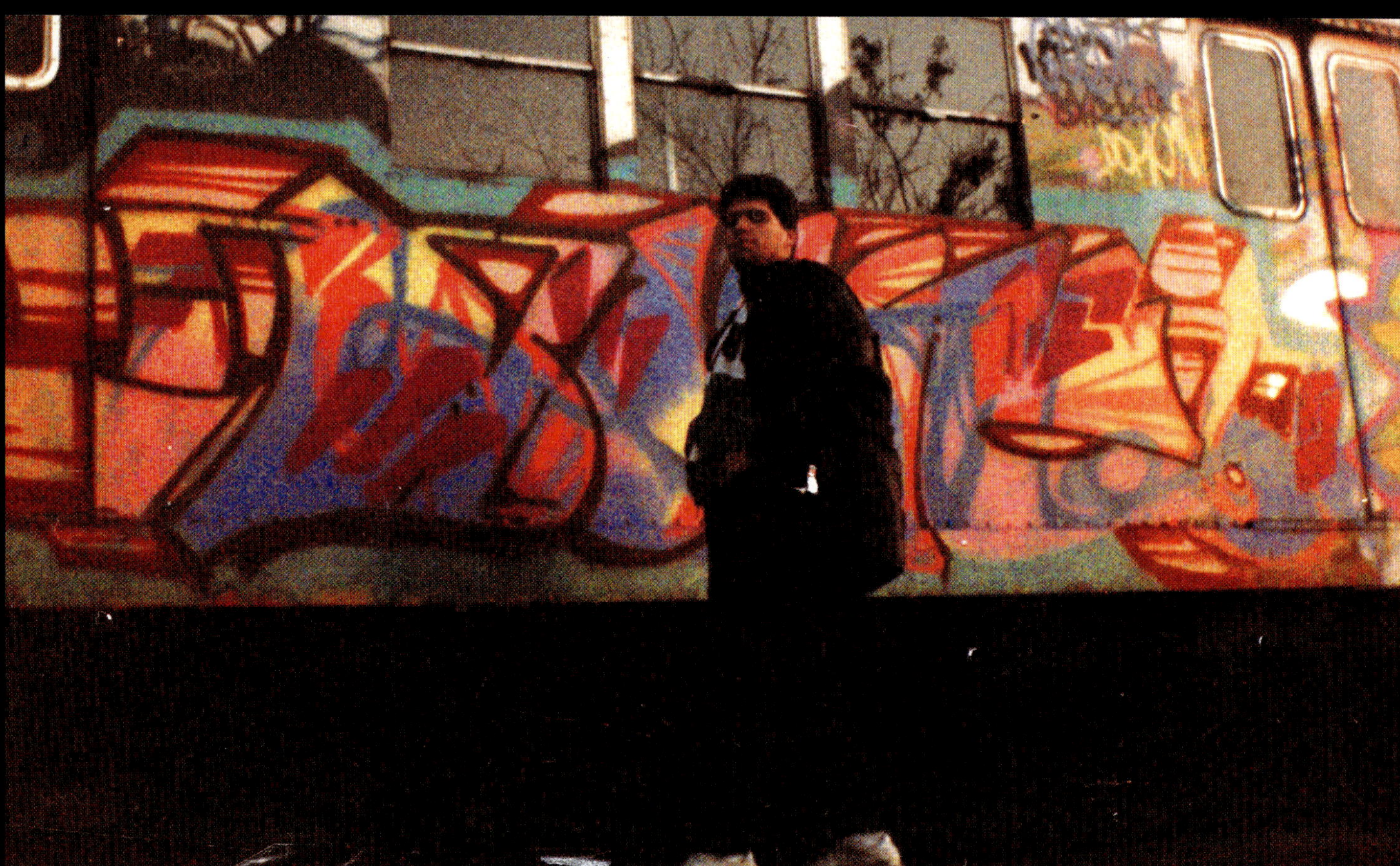

DOME on a mission to find his shit in Baychester lay ups on a Sunday at 4:10 P.M., 1987.

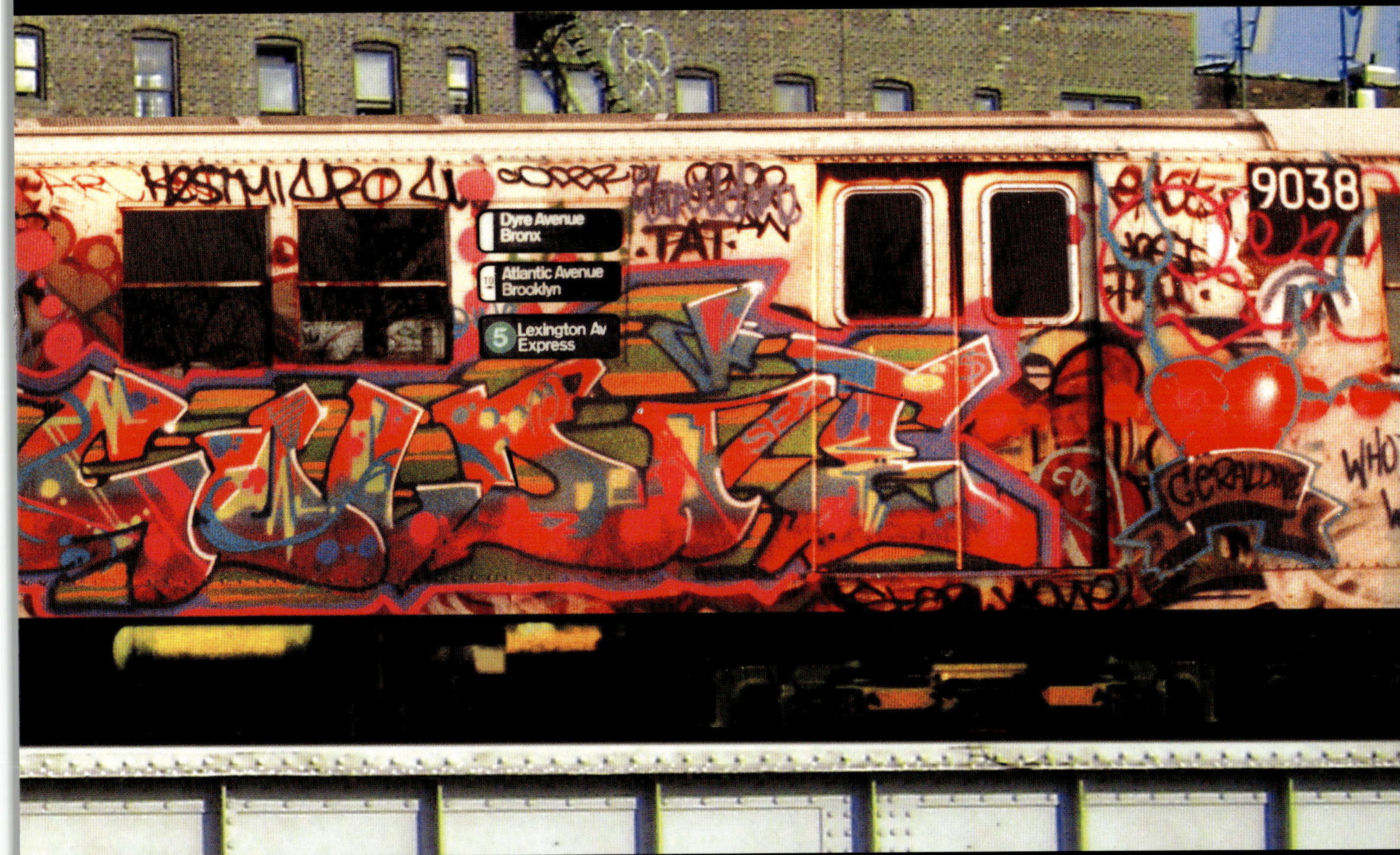

DOME GOLDIE TAT window-down burner. Illest Christmas raid story!!!!

This was a crazy weekend night during the winter blizzard of 1987 in the 116 Harlem Tunnels.
I was in from Europe and visiting NYC and was chilling with my man VULCAN TAT.
There had been a sick blizzard and snow storm and there was like a foot of snow on the ground
and still snowing when we went into the tunnels with VULCAN, Dome, SHO, and DC3 to paint some trains.
The Lexington Avenue line was the premier line to hit at the time. Man, the tunnels was rough this year.
Shit was dark and hectic but there was some light and you could see. Mad writers were there
and we bumped into Kaze FBA among others. There was a war going on between Dero, Wane, and Dome
and shit hit the fan, but it got sorted out for real.
You needed to have experienced writers to take you down into these tunnels, shit was no joke.
We were almost done at like 5 A.M. when we heard some noise in between cars and
turns out we were getting raided by transit police who pulled guns from all sides.
Everyone ran and they had grabbed Dome and SHO jumped over DC3 who was sitting.
As they went to grab DC3, Dome broke free and we jetted. Me and VULCAN was trapped in the tunnel
and some how escaped thru another level at 116th Street. I'll never forget that night.

-GOLDIE, Tough Ass Team

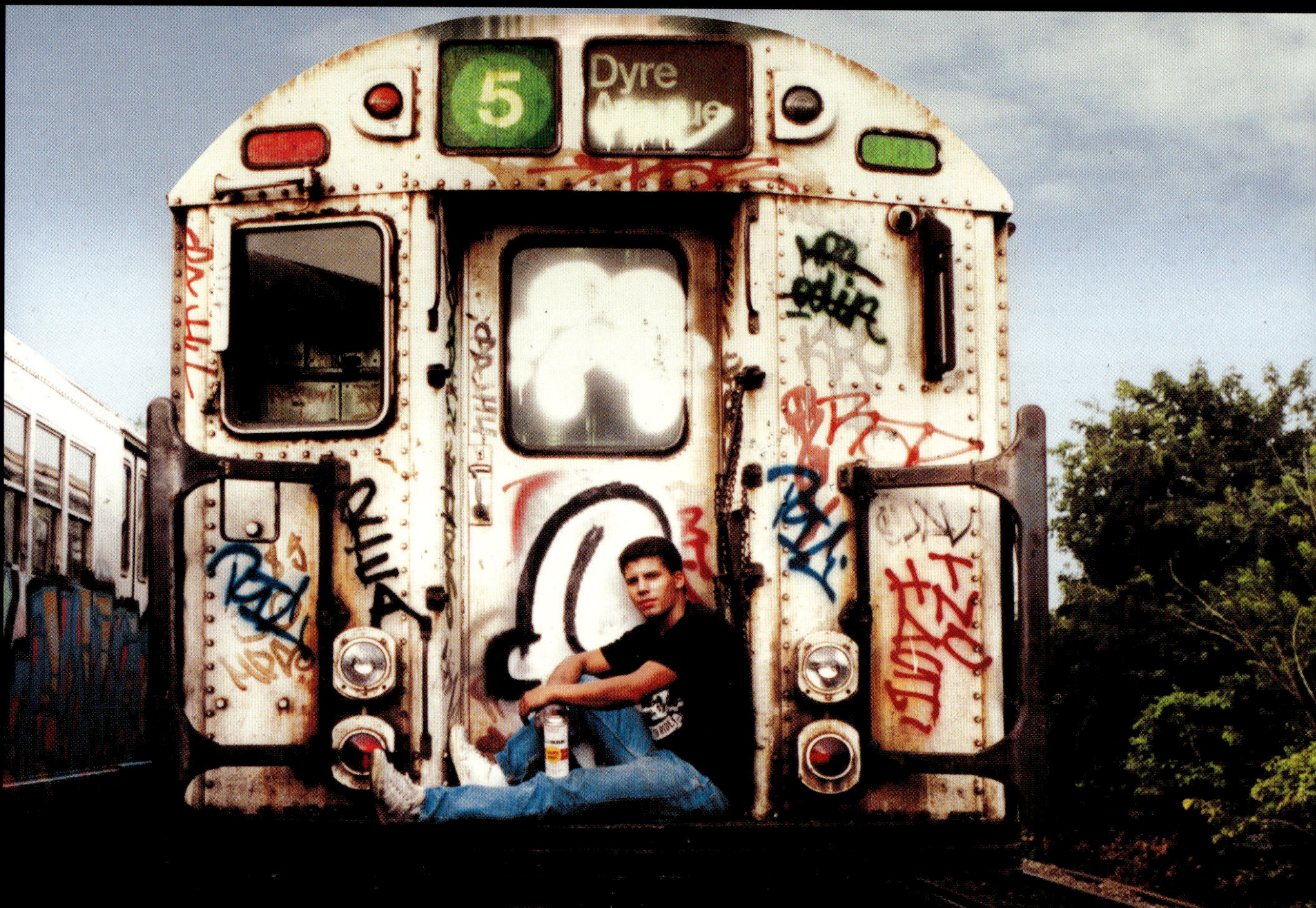

Mirage just rocked the MAC Concrete Jungle Car, May 1988, live In Baychester.

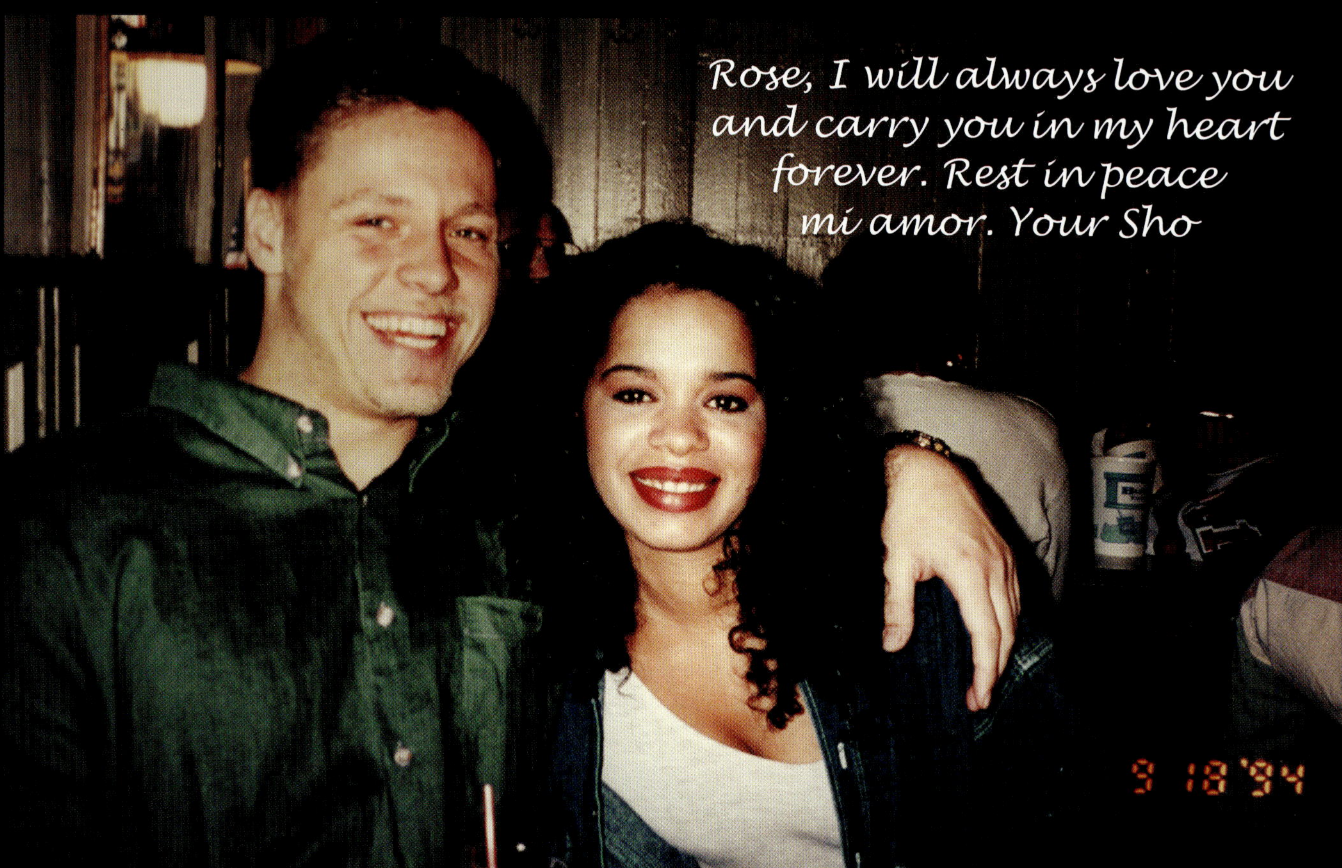

Hanging out at The Dive Bar.

7.

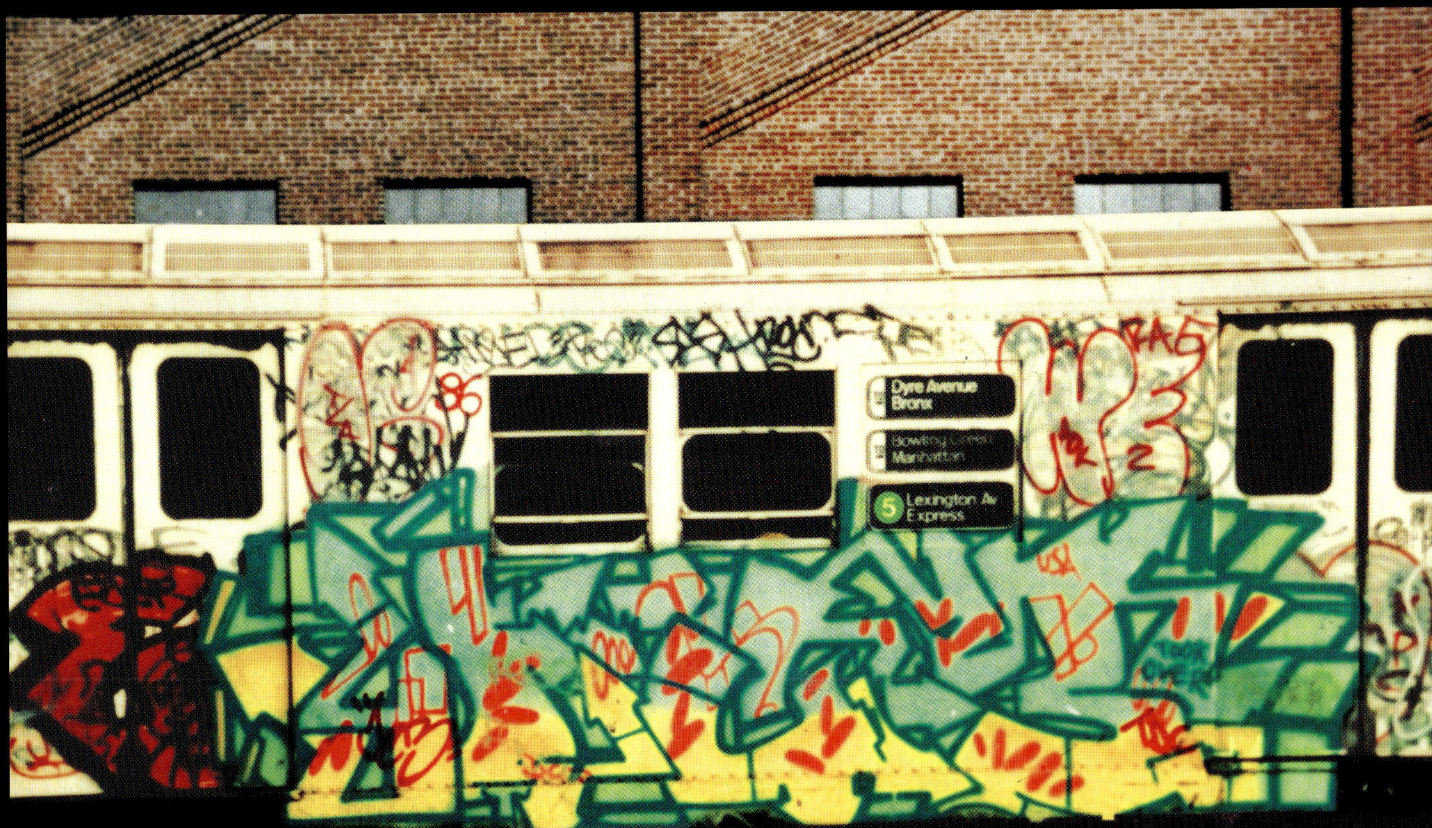

DC3 "TOOK OVER," window-down 5 Train, Jul. 1988.

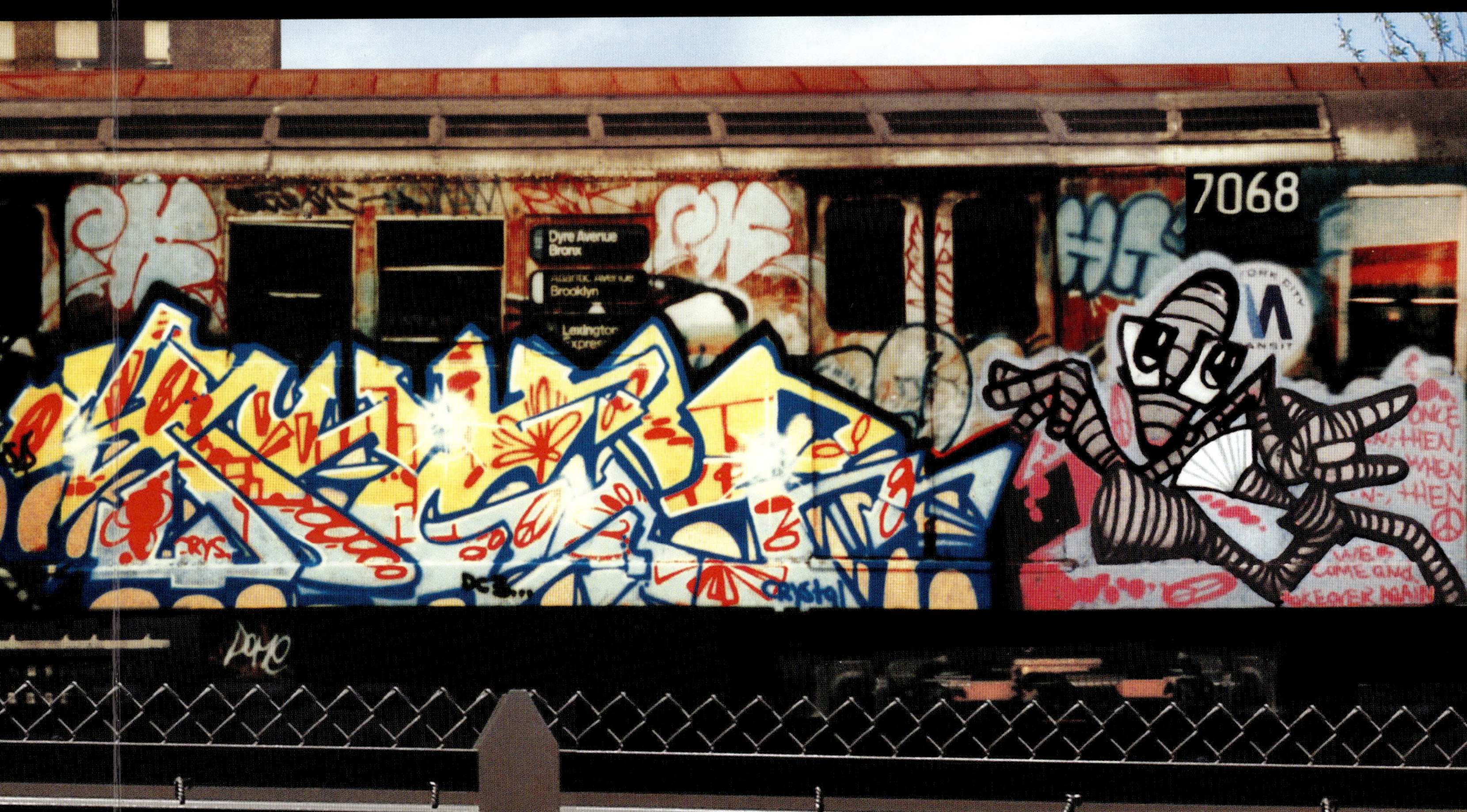

USA DOME "Metallic Robots" and DC3 USA "For Crystal" 5 Train, Aug. 1988.

USA TDC "KILLS" SHO and DC3 window-down burner rocked out in the open in Esplanade, Apr. 1988.

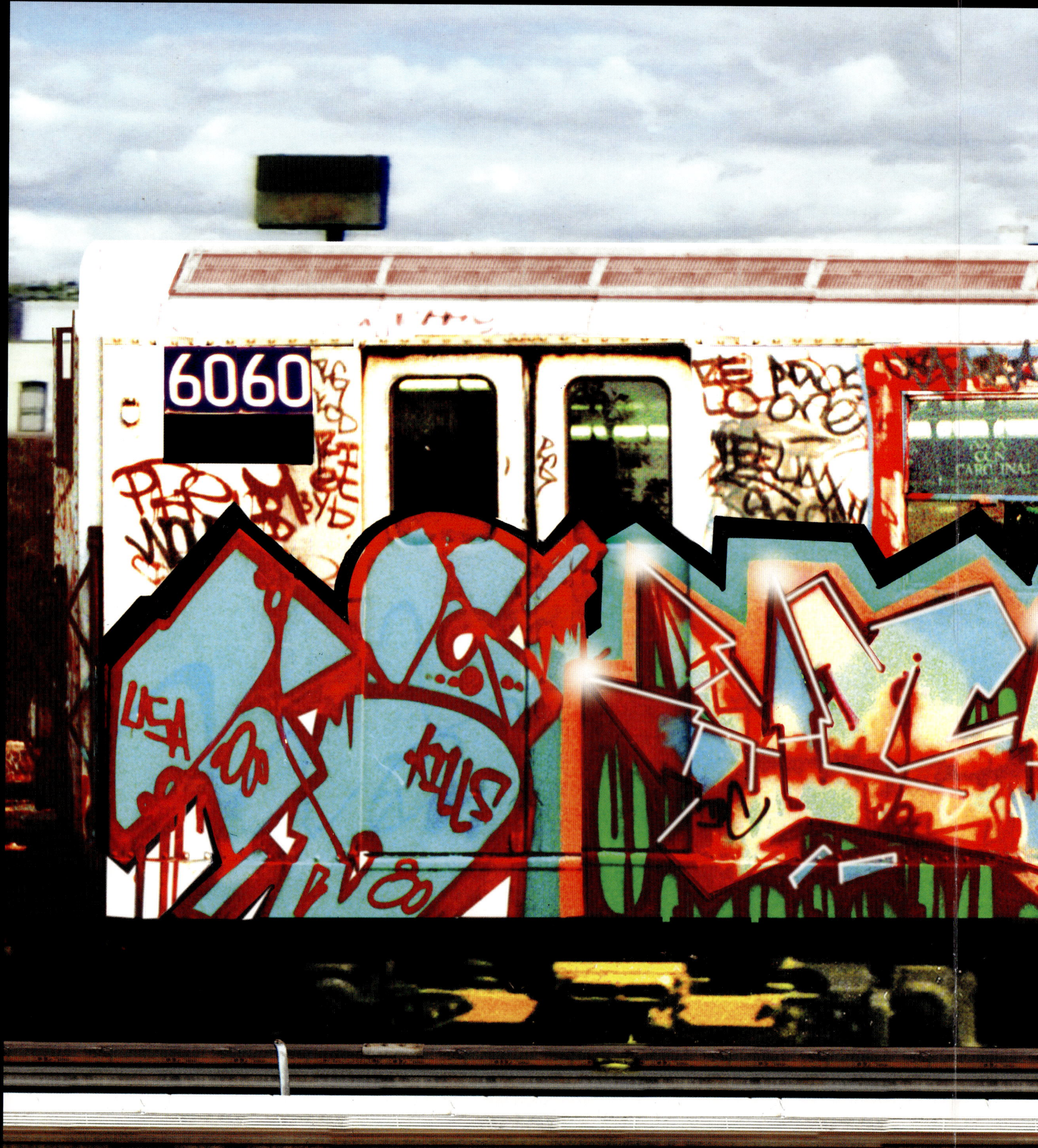

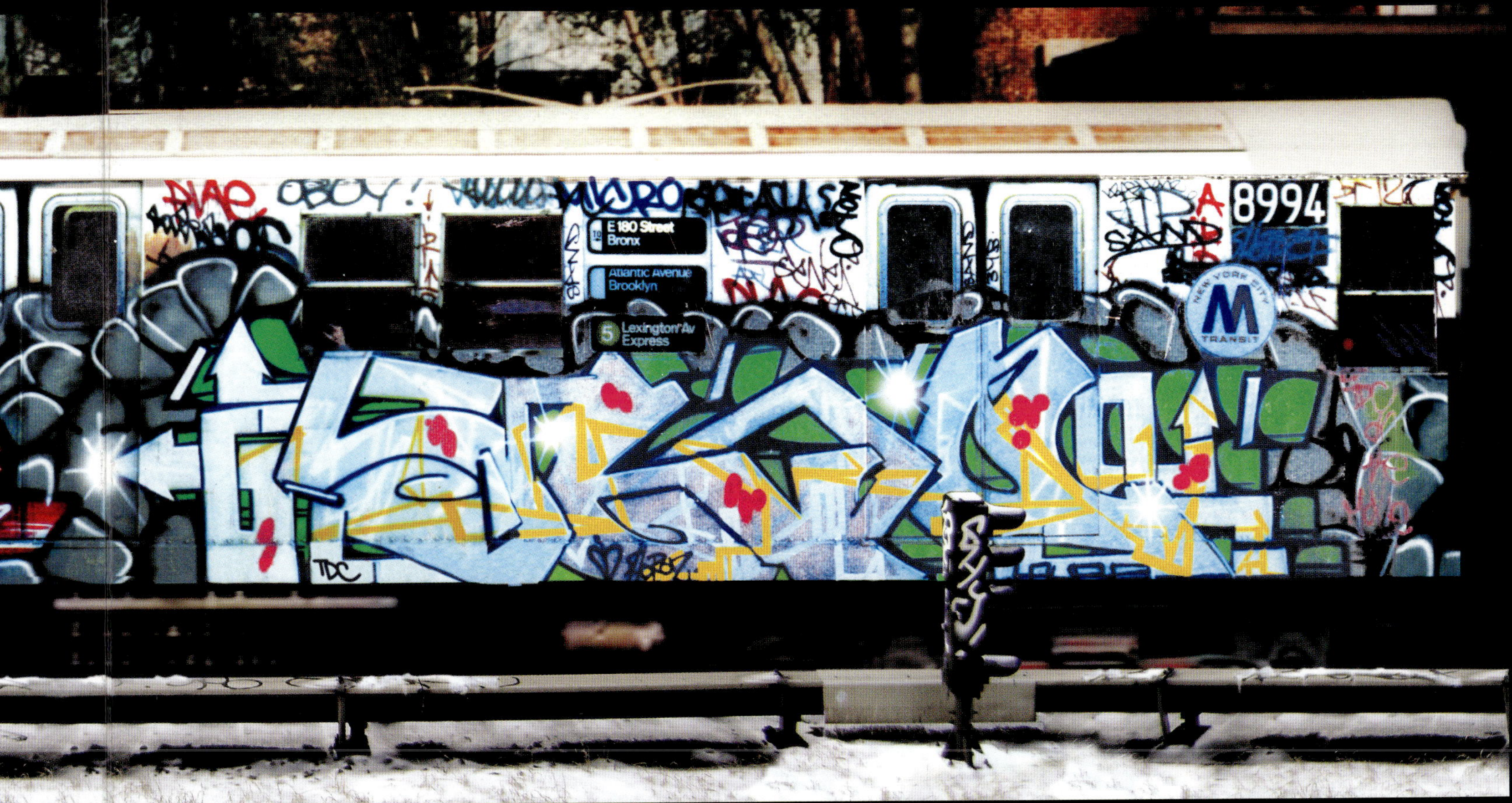

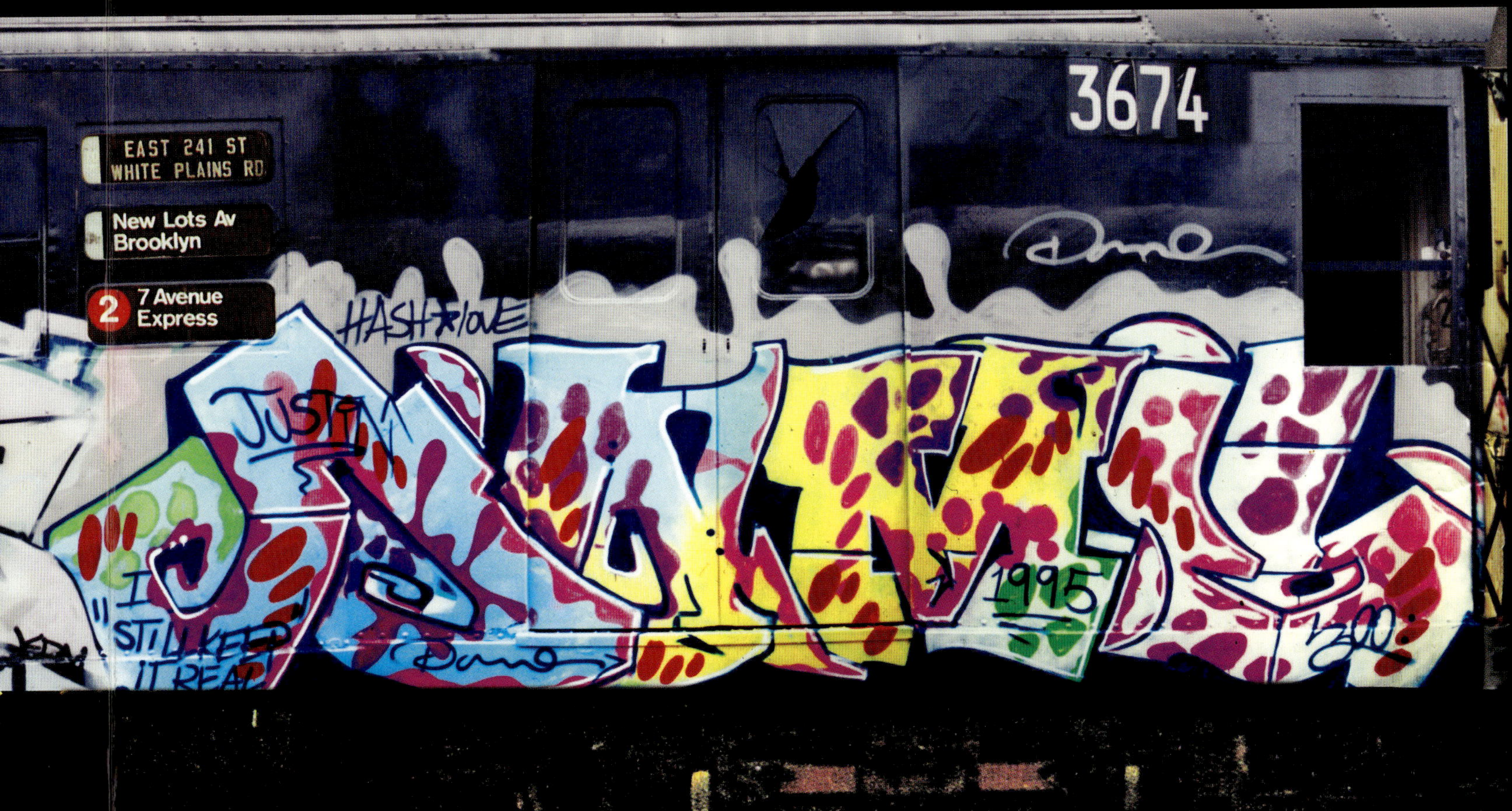

DOME "I STILL KEEP IT REAL" 2 Train.

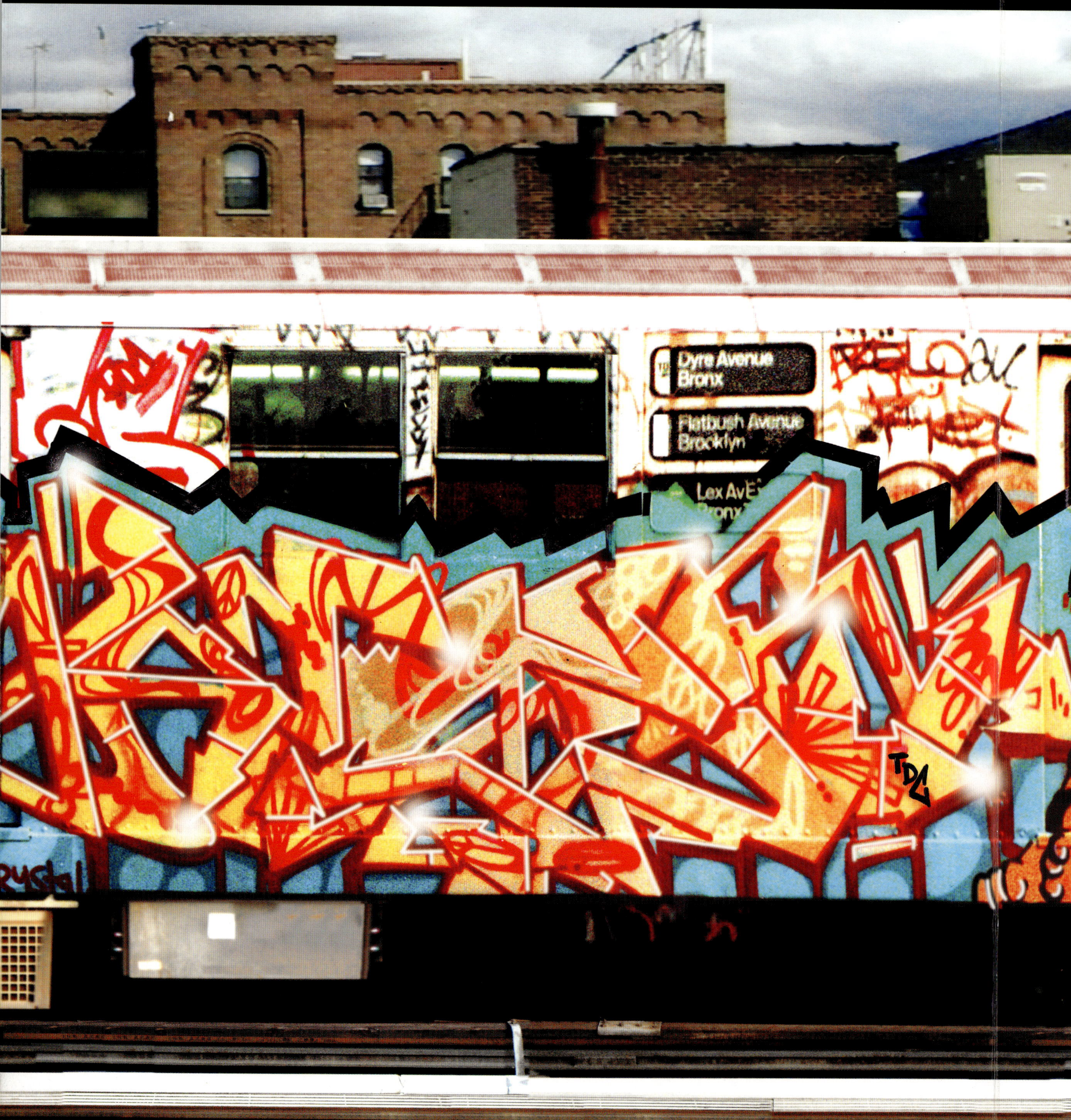

"ALL OF YOU SUCKERS ARE GOING TO HAVE TO LEARN THE HARD WAY THAT WE DON'T PLAY. UNDERSTAND!!!"

CHAPTER 11

Graffiti History and Anti-Graffiti News Coverage

Lets talk about remembering those who we need to pay respects to. First, my best friend Adib Akram who died in a tragic skateboard accident in 1982. My father consoled me while they were air lifting him and Matthew Gerich to the hospital. Mat made it but Adib didn't, devastating losses never leave you. RIP, Lil Kid, Chance, Thumper & Baby Sho. I dedicate this book to Marc Caranza, aka Mac, aka Mirage. I didn't learn of his tragic death until after his wake and upon learning of it Dome nearly destroyed the dashboard of my car. Near the conclusion of this book, tragedy took place on my block at 31st Avenue and 33rd Street, when on November 15, 2008, a drunk driver killed Panayito Demetrious and Betsey Valasquez RIP. There had been many severe car accidents here in the past. RIP to Emil Kaufmann, aka Big Right. Lastly I dedicate this book to Rose Echevarrria. RIP, my Angel and Love in Heaven, I miss you tremendously. I told you I would be there for you to the end and beyond.

-SHO TDC USA, 2010

"IM OUT"

PEACE

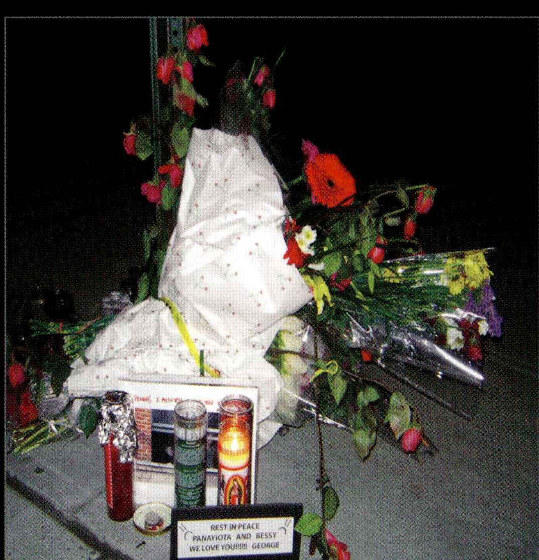

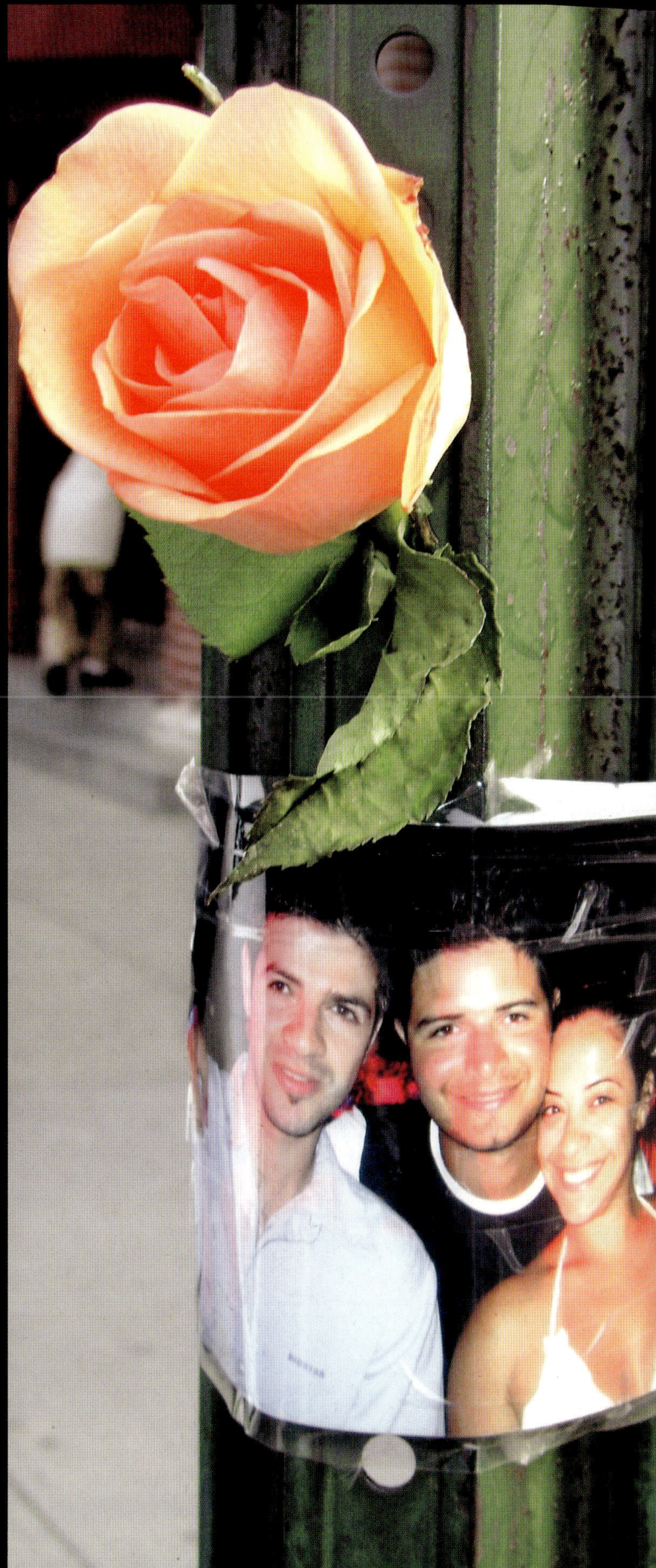

31st Ave., Astoria, New York, Nov. 16, 2008.

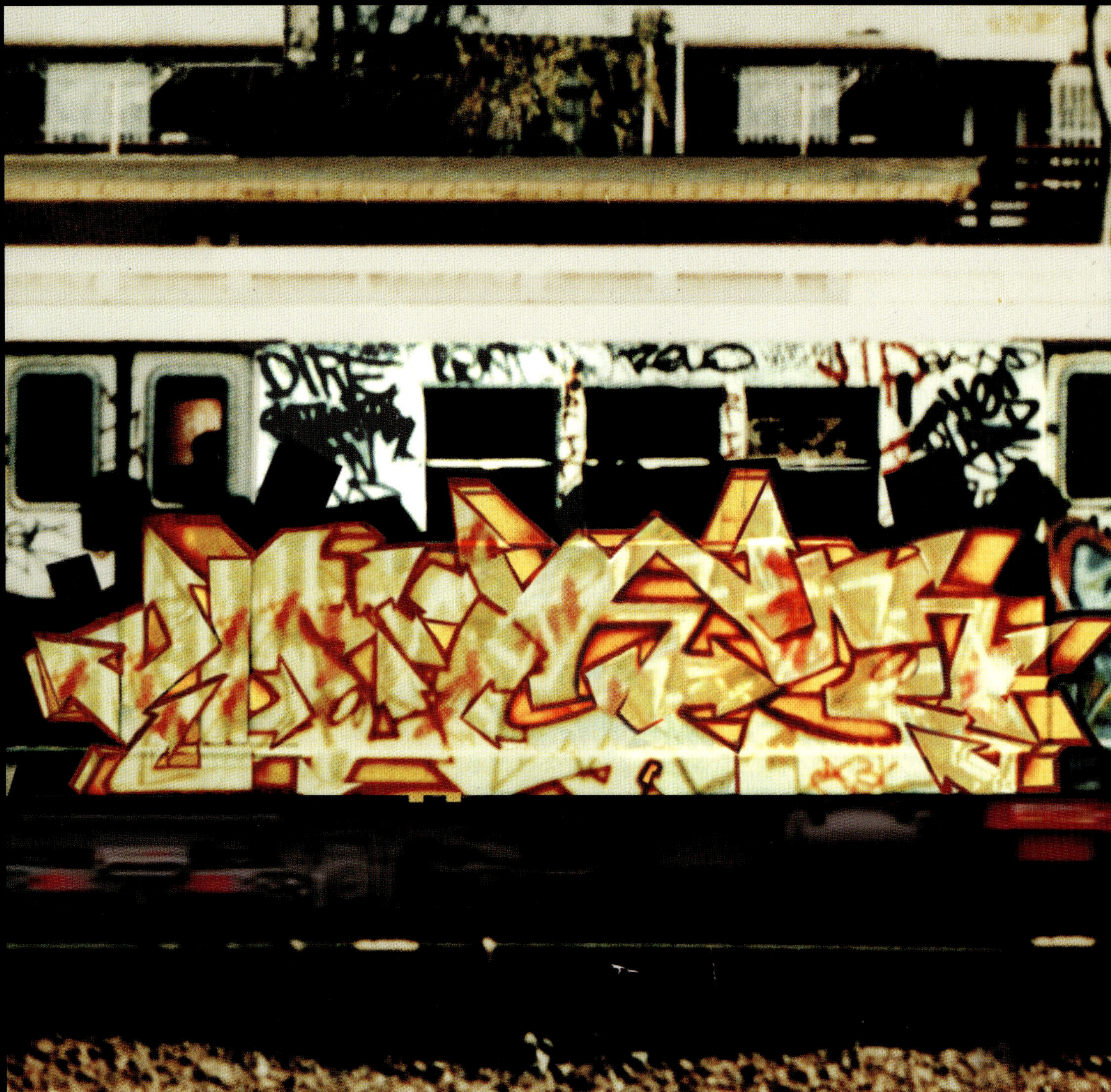

DC3 with FENT and DEON May, 1988. Photographed running in Baychester.

As far as Ven goes, in the beginning I knew of him thru DC3 and we chilled with him twice, once on the numbers and once just bombing the Q Line lay up over the Belt Parkway by the main Coney Island Yard.

Beef had started because him and his loser writer friends from the letters had trashed some of our cars for no reason other than jealousy. When I seen him outside of Henry Chaflant's studio walking down the street, I robbed him for his camera and he cried and none of his boys did anything about it at all.

-Dome

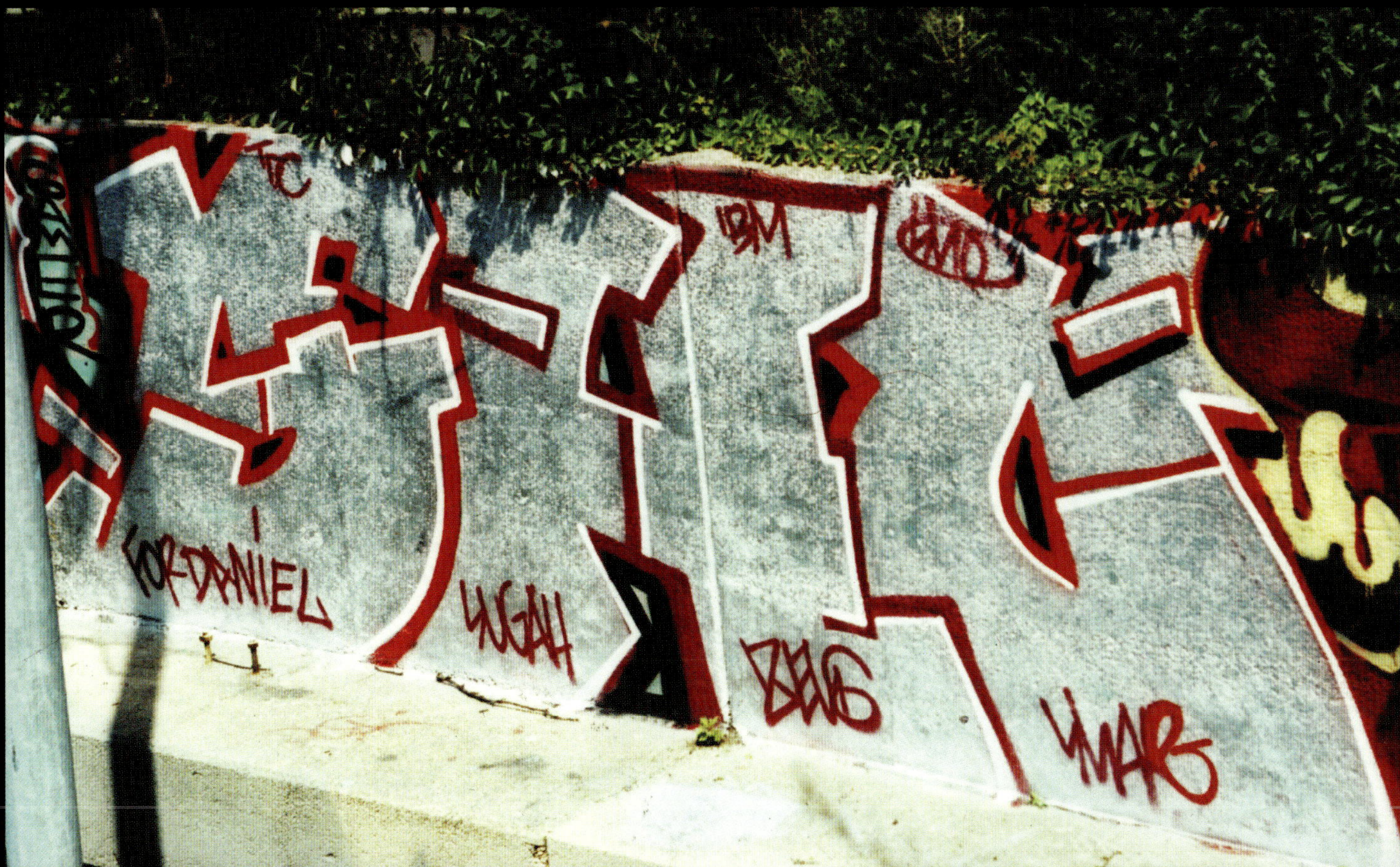

SHO silver for Daniel and Sugah. Manhattan, 1999.

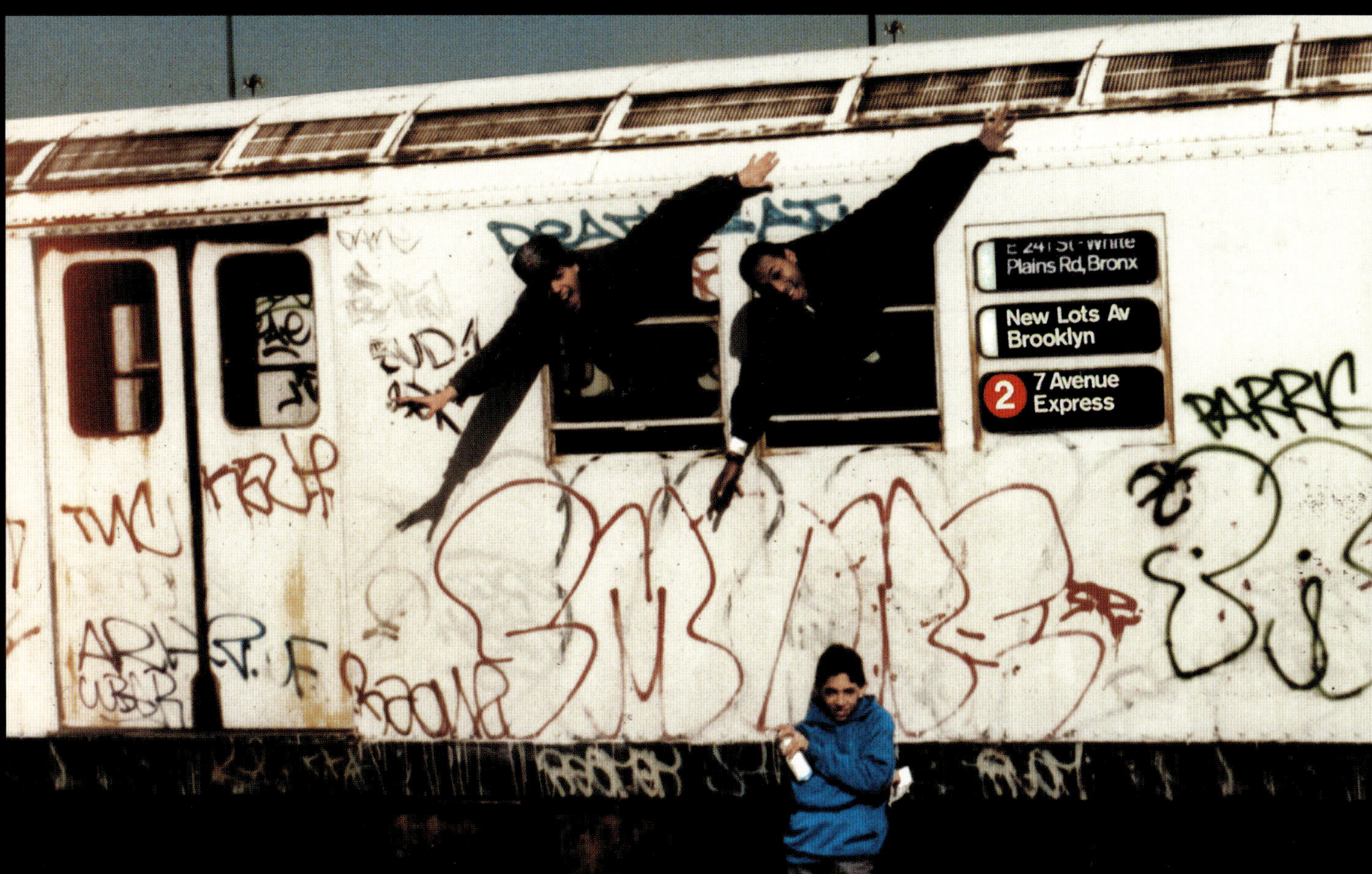

ZOO, DC3, and VEN, "We Fly High," 1988.

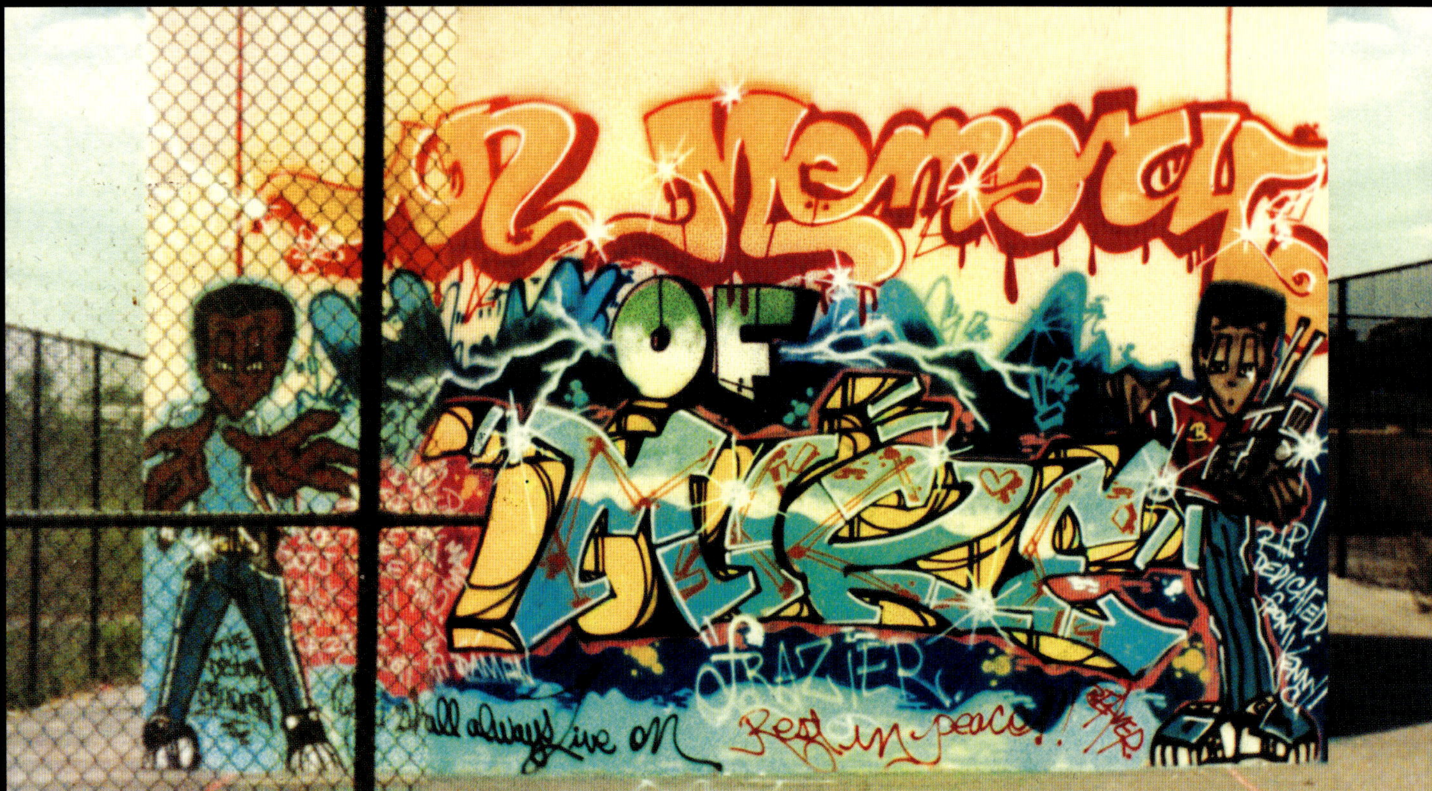

"IN MEMORY OF MIKE FRAZIER / You Shall Always Live On," tribute in Liberty Park, Freeport, NY, Apr. 1985. Mike, unfortunately, was gunned down by a sniper at a bar in North Freeport on Apr. 15, 1985. His brother Kenny C knew my man DC3 and DOOJ PIA and the rest is history. His killer was apprehended and jailed for life.

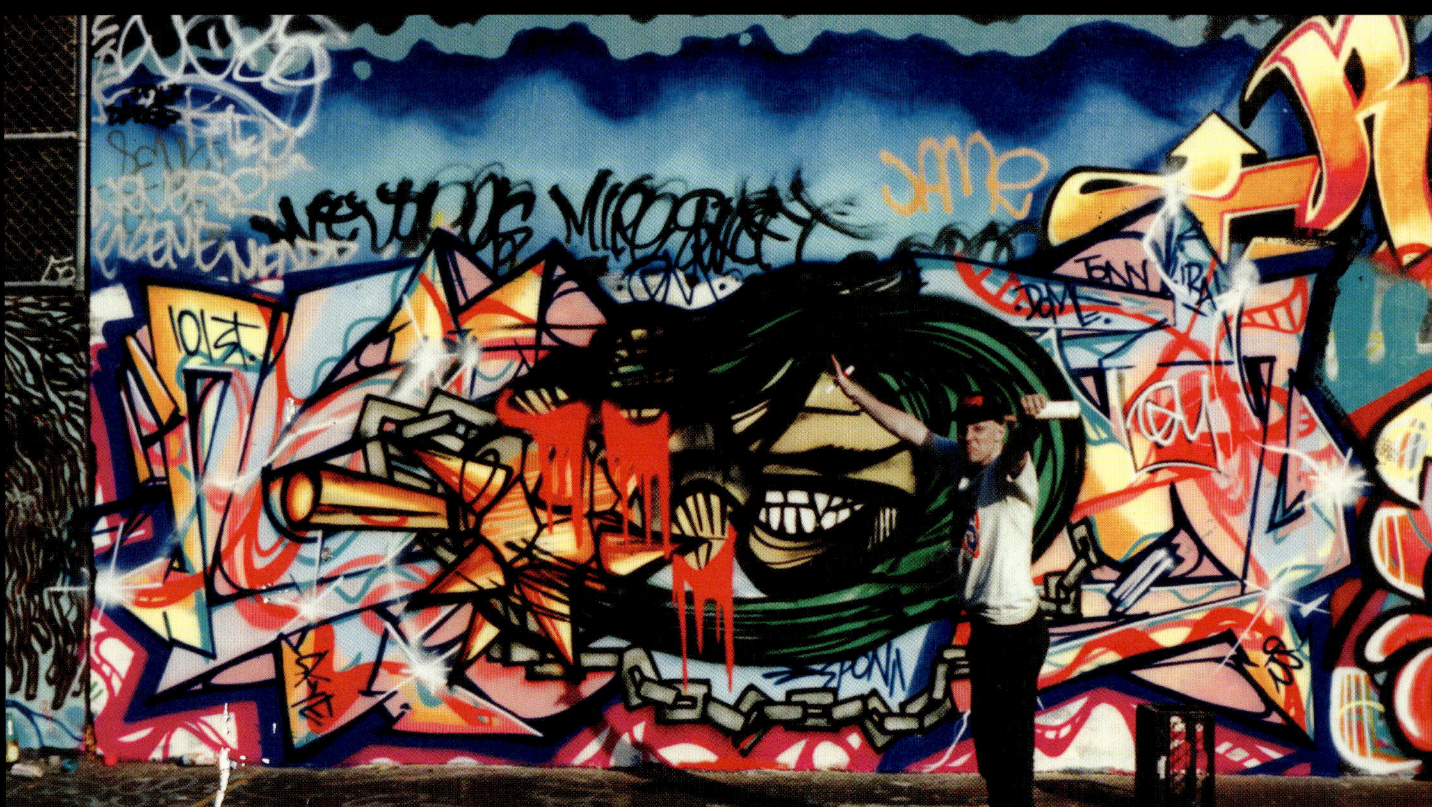

GM live, rocking the Hall of Fame, Manhattan, NY, Jun. 1993.

New York Newsday article.

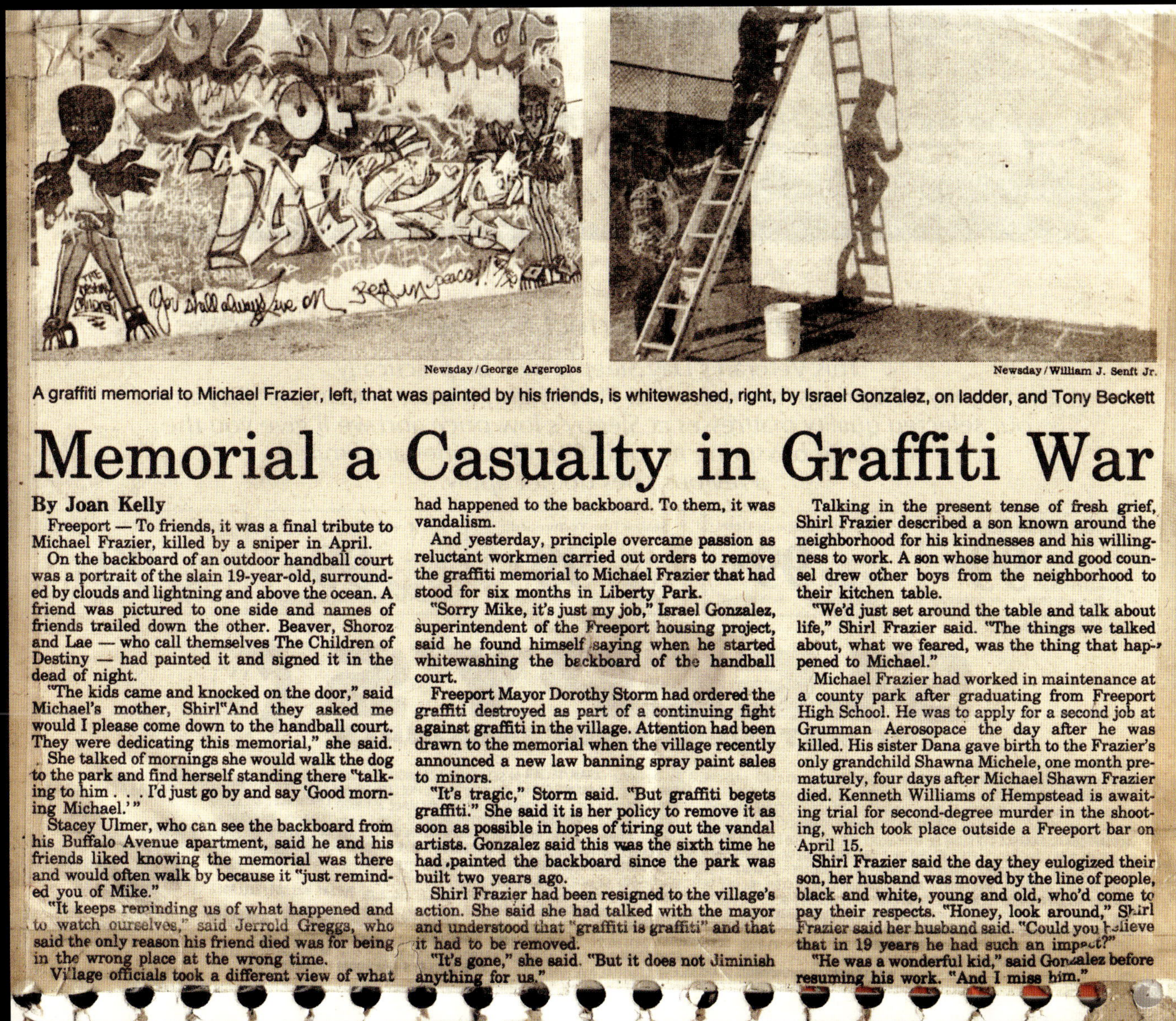

Newsday / George Argeroplos

Newsday / William J. Senft Jr.

A graffiti memorial to Michael Frazier, left, that was painted by his friends, is whitewashed, right, by Israel Gonzalez, on ladder, and Tony Beckett

Memorial a Casualty in Graffiti War

By Joan Kelly

Freeport — To friends, it was a final tribute to Michael Frazier, killed by a sniper in April.

On the backboard of an outdoor handball court was a portrait of the slain 19-year-old, surrounded by clouds and lightning and above the ocean. A friend was pictured to one side and names of friends trailed down the other. Beaver, Shoroz and Lae — who call themselves The Children of Destiny — had painted it and signed it in the dead of night.

"The kids came and knocked on the door," said Michael's mother, Shirl"And they asked me would I please come down to the handball court. They were dedicating this memorial," she said.

She talked of mornings she would walk the dog to the park and find herself standing there "talking to him . . . I'd just go by and say 'Good morning Michael.' "

Stacey Ulmer, who can see the backboard from his Buffalo Avenue apartment, said he and his friends liked knowing the memorial was there and would often walk by because it "just reminded you of Mike."

"It keeps reminding us of what happened and to watch ourselves," said Jerrold Greggs, who said the only reason his friend died was for being in the wrong place at the wrong time.

Village officials took a different view of what had happened to the backboard. To them, it was vandalism.

And yesterday, principle overcame passion as reluctant workmen carried out orders to remove the graffiti memorial to Michael Frazier that had stood for six months in Liberty Park.

"Sorry Mike, it's just my job," Israel Gonzalez, superintendent of the Freeport housing project, said he found himself saying when he started whitewashing the backboard of the handball court.

Freeport Mayor Dorothy Storm had ordered the graffiti destroyed as part of a continuing fight against graffiti in the village. Attention had been drawn to the memorial when the village recently announced a new law banning spray paint sales to minors.

"It's tragic," Storm said. "But graffiti begets graffiti." She said it is her policy to remove it as soon as possible in hopes of tiring out the vandal artists. Gonzalez said this was the sixth time he had painted the backboard since the park was built two years ago.

Shirl Frazier had been resigned to the village's action. She said she had talked with the mayor and understood that "graffiti is graffiti" and that it had to be removed.

"It's gone," she said. "But it does not diminish anything for us."

Talking in the present tense of fresh grief, Shirl Frazier described a son known around the neighborhood for his kindnesses and his willingness to work. A son whose humor and good counsel drew other boys from the neighborhood to their kitchen table.

"We'd just set around the table and talk about life," Shirl Frazier said. "The things we talked about, what we feared, was the thing that happened to Michael."

Michael Frazier had worked in maintenance at a county park after graduating from Freeport High School. He was to apply for a second job at Grumman Aerosopace the day after he was killed. His sister Dana gave birth to the Frazier's only grandchild Shawna Michele, one month prematurely, four days after Michael Shawn Frazier died. Kenneth Williams of Hempstead is awaiting trial for second-degree murder in the shooting, which took place outside a Freeport bar on April 15.

Shirl Frazier said the day they eulogized their son, her husband was moved by the line of people, black and white, young and old, who'd come to pay their respects. "Honey, look around," Shirl Frazier said her husband said. "Could you believe that in 19 years he had such an impact?"

"He was a wonderful kid," said Gonzalez before resuming his work. "And I miss him."

"Life Can Seem Like A Dream After The One You Love Is Gone"

"You Shall Always Live On"
done April 6, 1986, Part 2.
The authorities painted over the memorial for Mike and all of Buffalo Avenue, the projects, and people of Liberty Park reached out to us cause they was very mad. So we said fuck it and painted the entire hand ball court again, even though it was very hot and the boys was after us big time, we didn't care.
It was Hood appreciated.

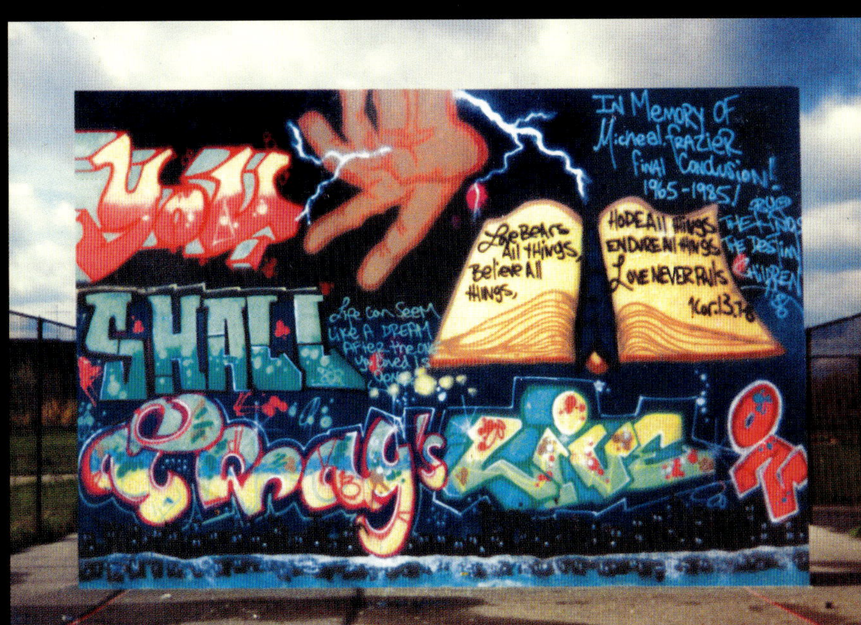

"YOU SHALL ALWAYS LIVE ON / Final Conclusion," in Memory of Mike, Part 2.

ROSE live at CENTRAL STATION in front of SHO IBM piece...

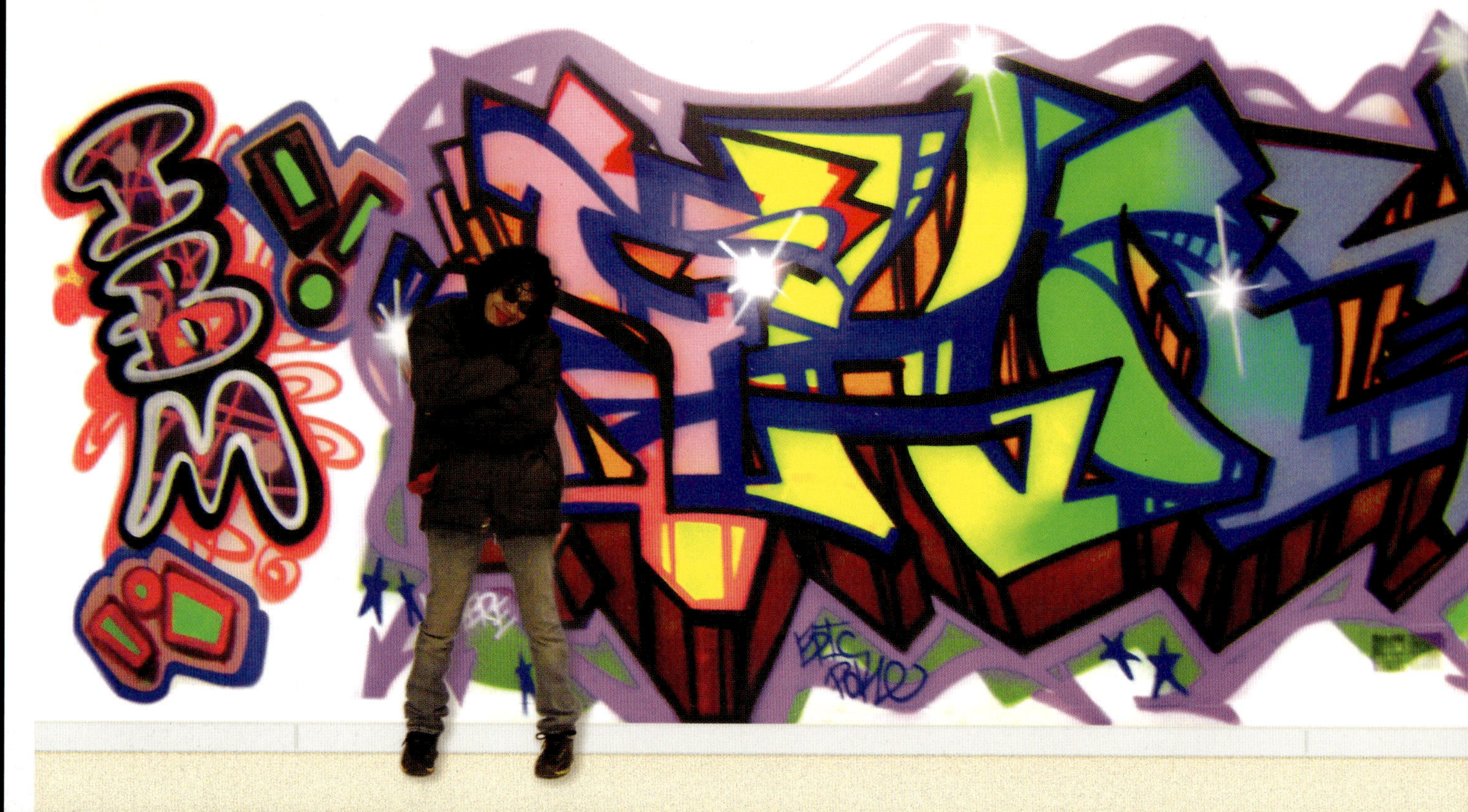

"This is Central Station."
"The Destiny Children / Idolized By Millions"
The Continuation.
Now we are legitimate business entrepreneurs like it was supposed to be all along.
SHO and DC3 once again, my friends!!!
It's the show that never ends. Central Station Standing Up, LI Standing Up repping for all LI.
This, for the record, is the first graffiti burner I did with DC3 since painting on trains, so this one was extra special. Plus, RIP, here is Rose repping for Manhattan all day and everyday for 101st Street, you heard? Rose, like most of the women I was with, didn't feel graffiti like I did, but was always, at the end of the day, down with it cause I was.
Thank you all, I was just being me.
-SHO

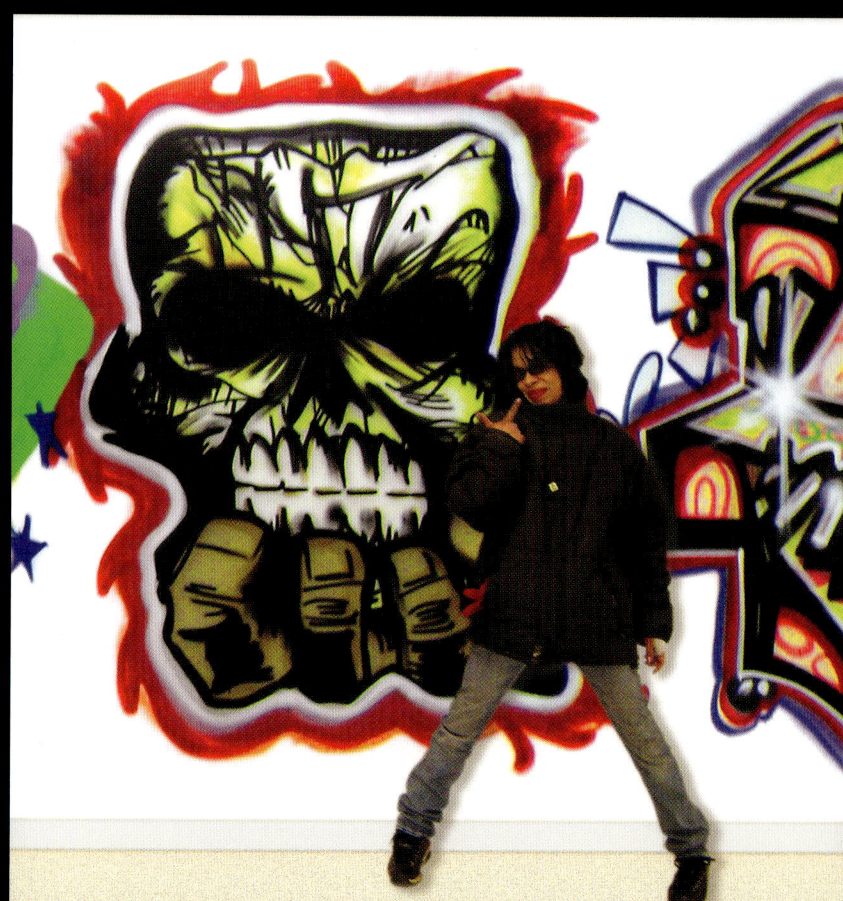

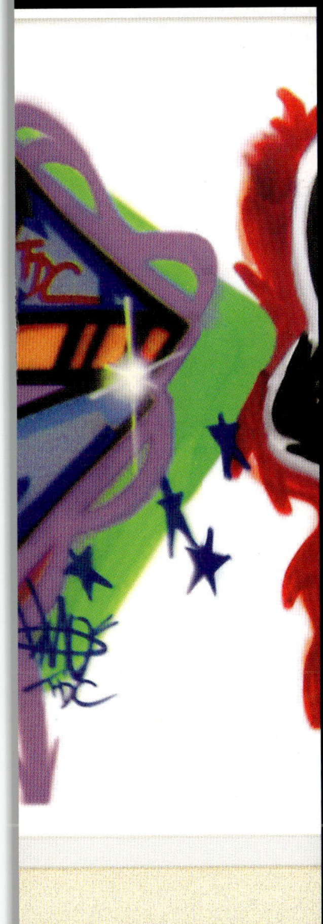

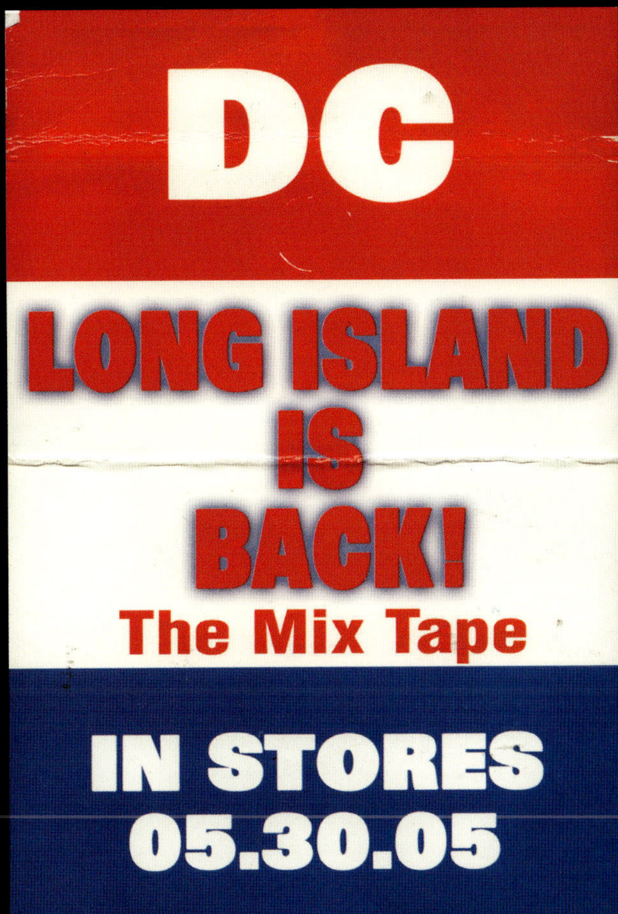

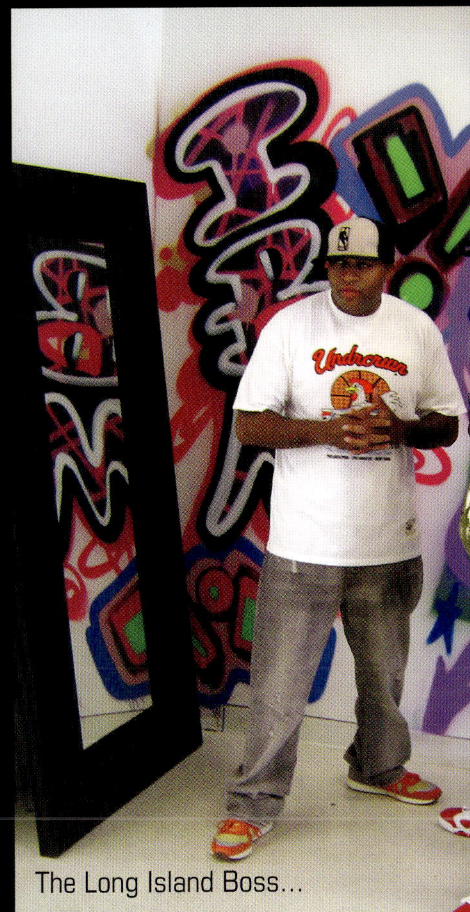
The Long Island Boss...

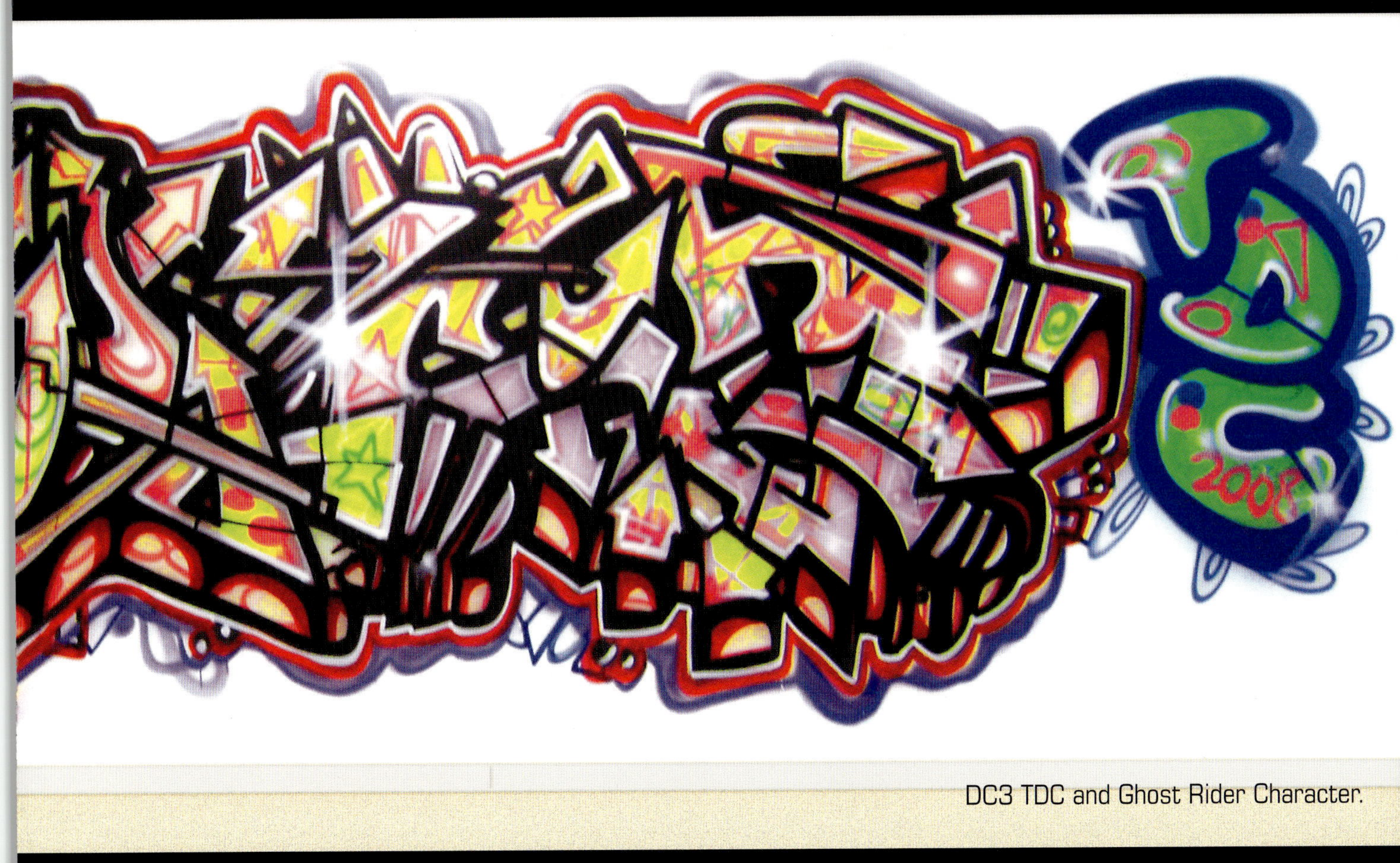
DC3 TDC and Ghost Rider Character.

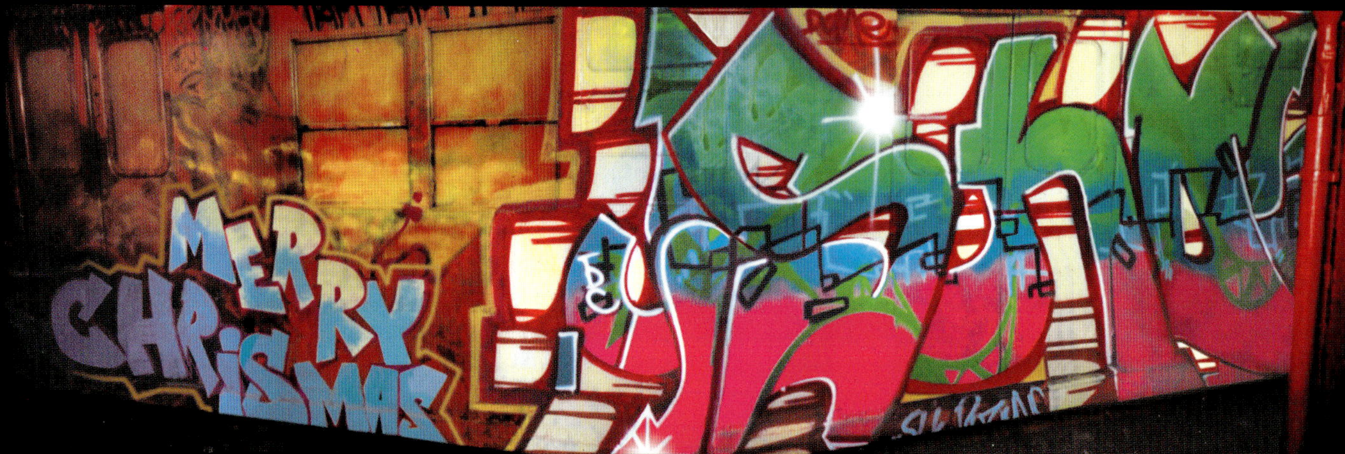

SHO Merry Christmas, Jan 1987.

I wanted to include this unfinished Merry Christmas train because of the raid story GOLDIE spit. I was rocking this train with DC3, and to this day never seen a flick of what he had done. Cops came at me to my right in between the cars and we was out. I ran down the catwalk until it ended and crashed into the wall and ran a couple of cars on the tracks with DC3 and then jumped up in between them straight down the middle of the tracks up to 103rd Street. Just as we left the station, mad cops came in a van and we hid in an abandoned building. We waited at the car and I couldn't believe it when I saw everyone got away.

-SHO

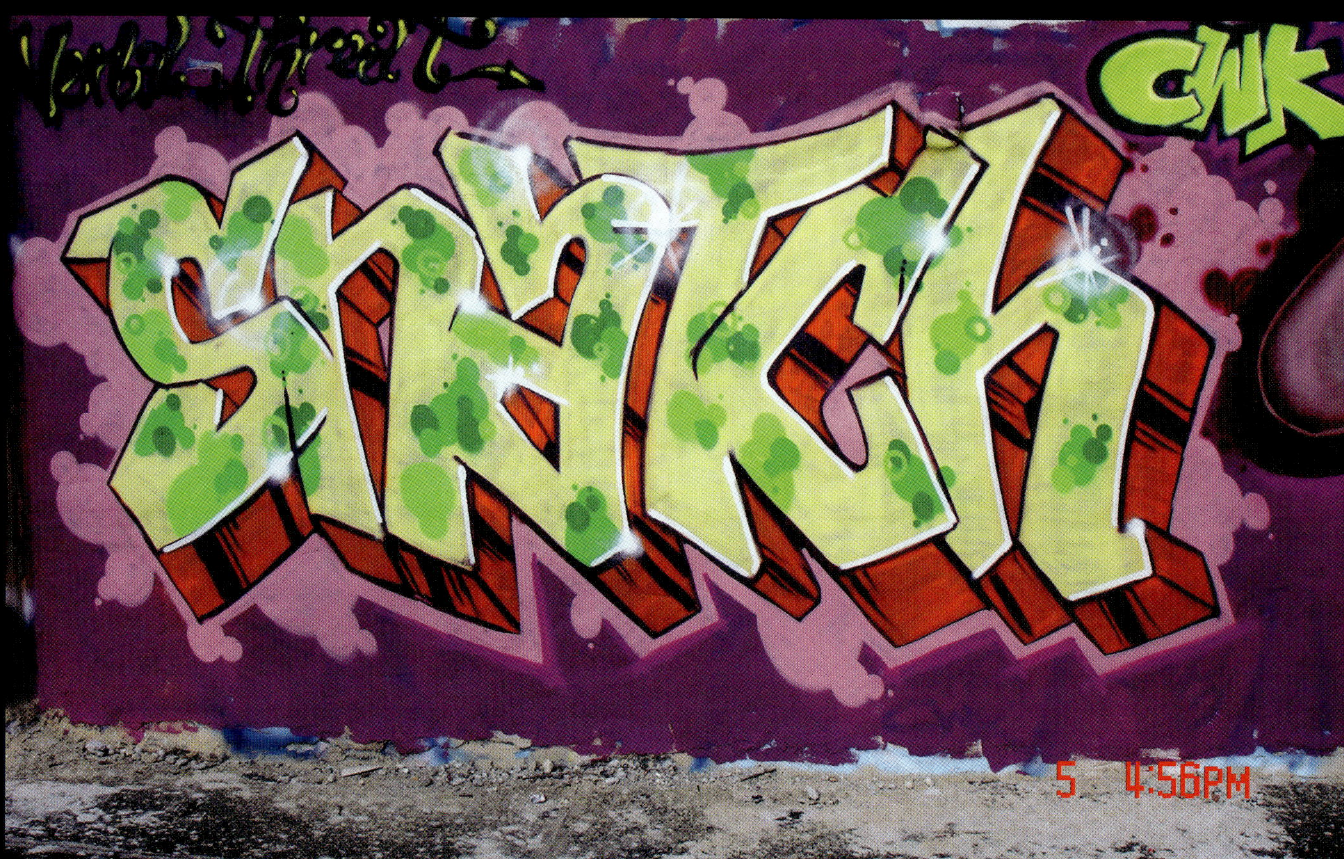

Verbal Threat Video Shoot. SNATCH CWK repping Brooklyn, NY, 2000.

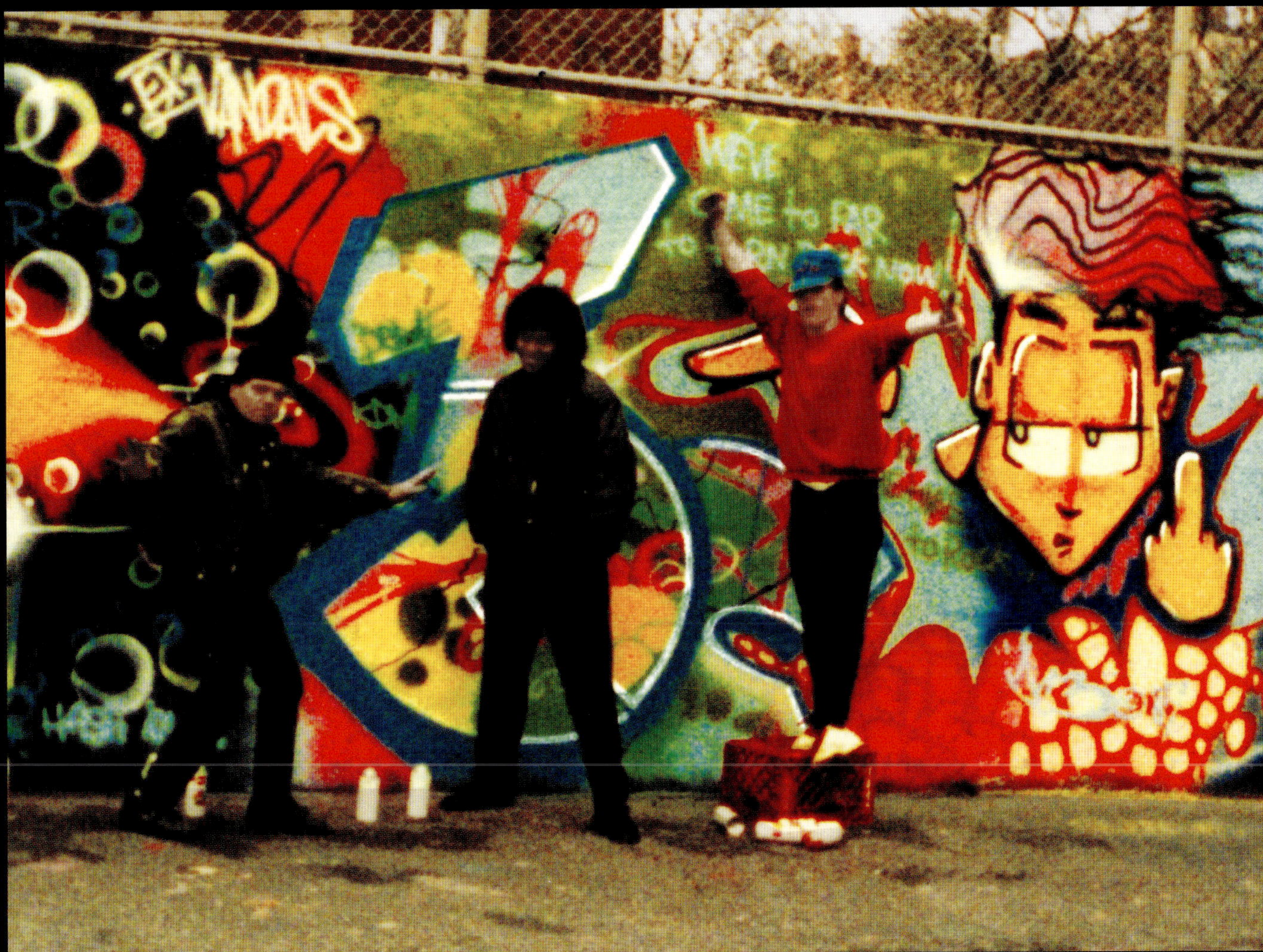

ZOOROC, VULCAN TAT EX-VANDALS, and SHO.

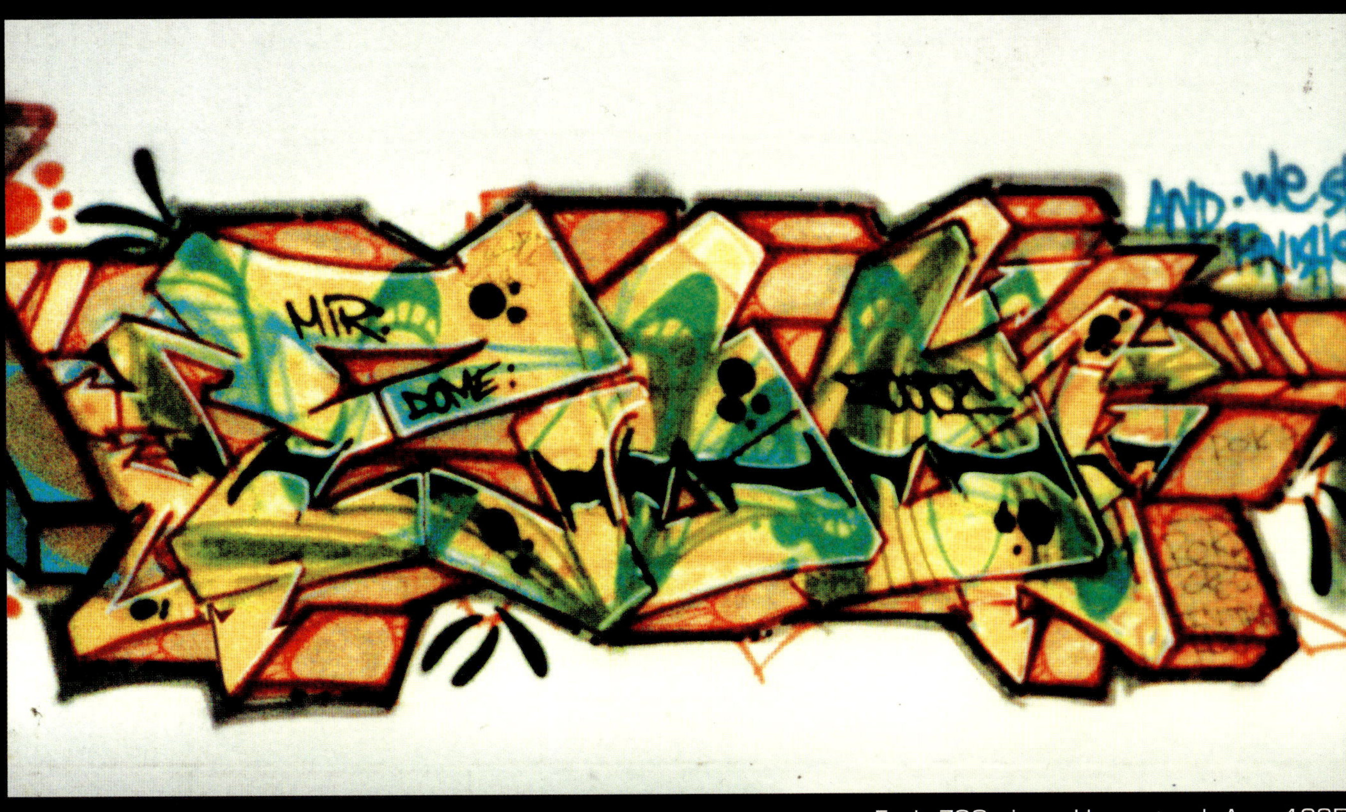

Early ZOO piece, Hempstead, Aug. 1985.

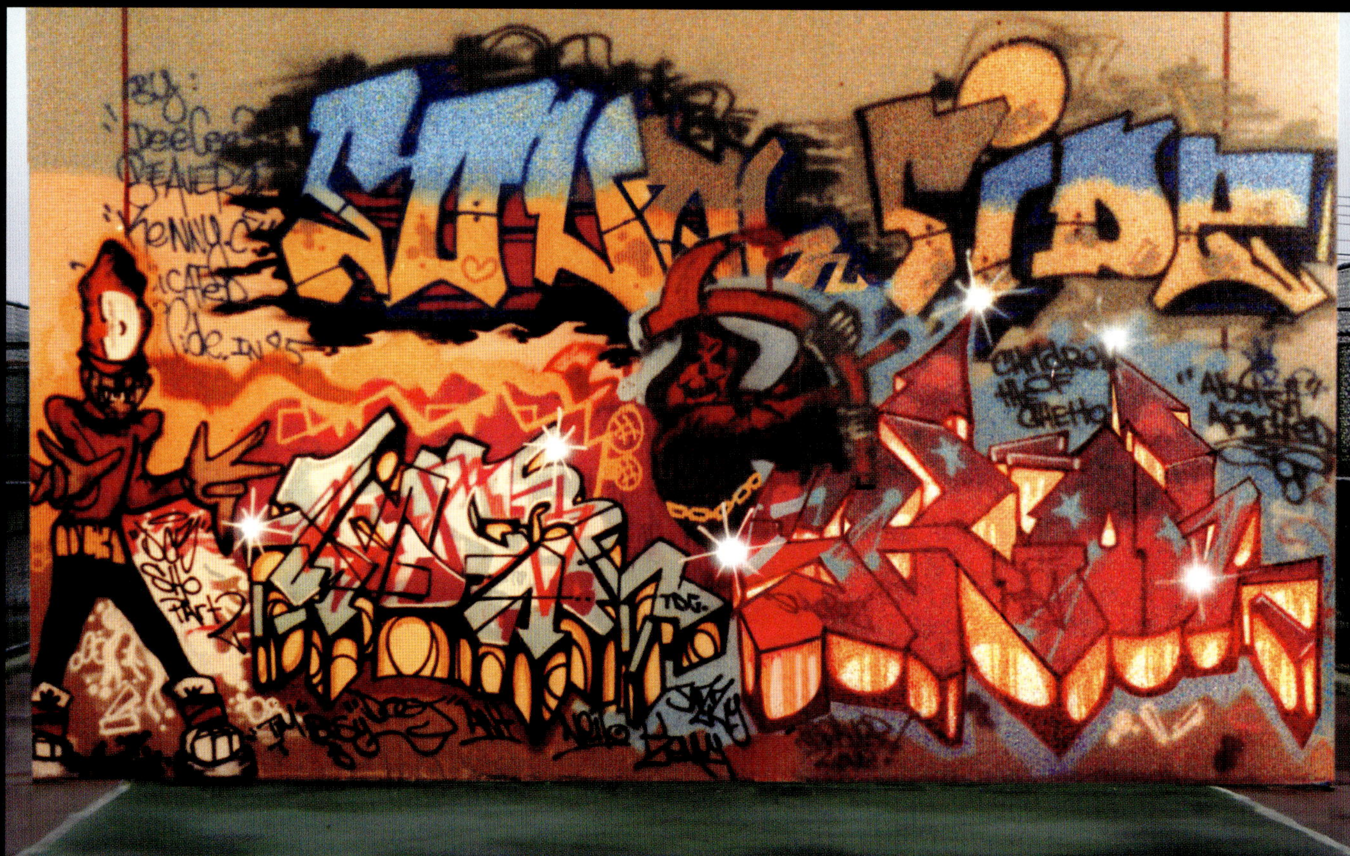

DC3, BEAVER, and SHO, "CHILDREN OF THE GHETTO," Part 2, South Side, Oct. 1985.

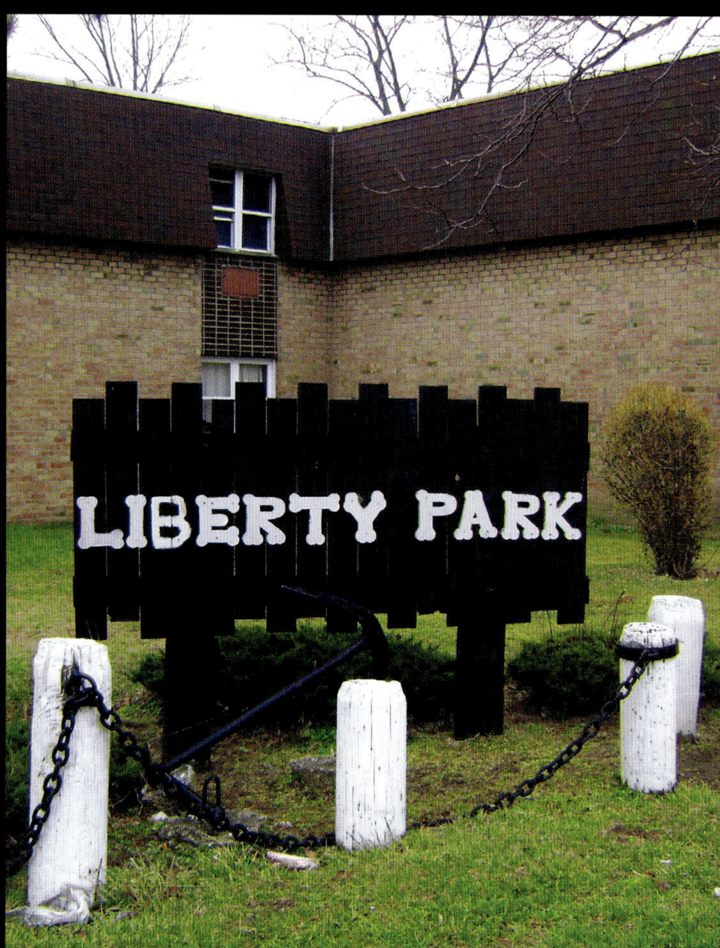

DC3 SHO "Grim Reaper Wall," Part 2

We rocked this wall early 1985 in Liberty Park in Freeport, the South Side had been done earlier by BEAVER one and DC3. Back then Liberty Park and the projects were mad wild with the crack come up and with it came a lot of guns and violence. I went back solo to touch up the SHO piece the next night by myself and had taken my brother's brand new 10 speed without him knowing. While painting here comes at least 20 heads coming from a project party. Two of them seen me and went to tell his boys. All of them tried to vamp me for the bike and my paint–they got some of the cans. I jetted on Buffalo Avenue and had the whole gang of 'em chasing me down Sunrise Highway. I got away luckily. Shit was much crazier then, fuck 'em!!!

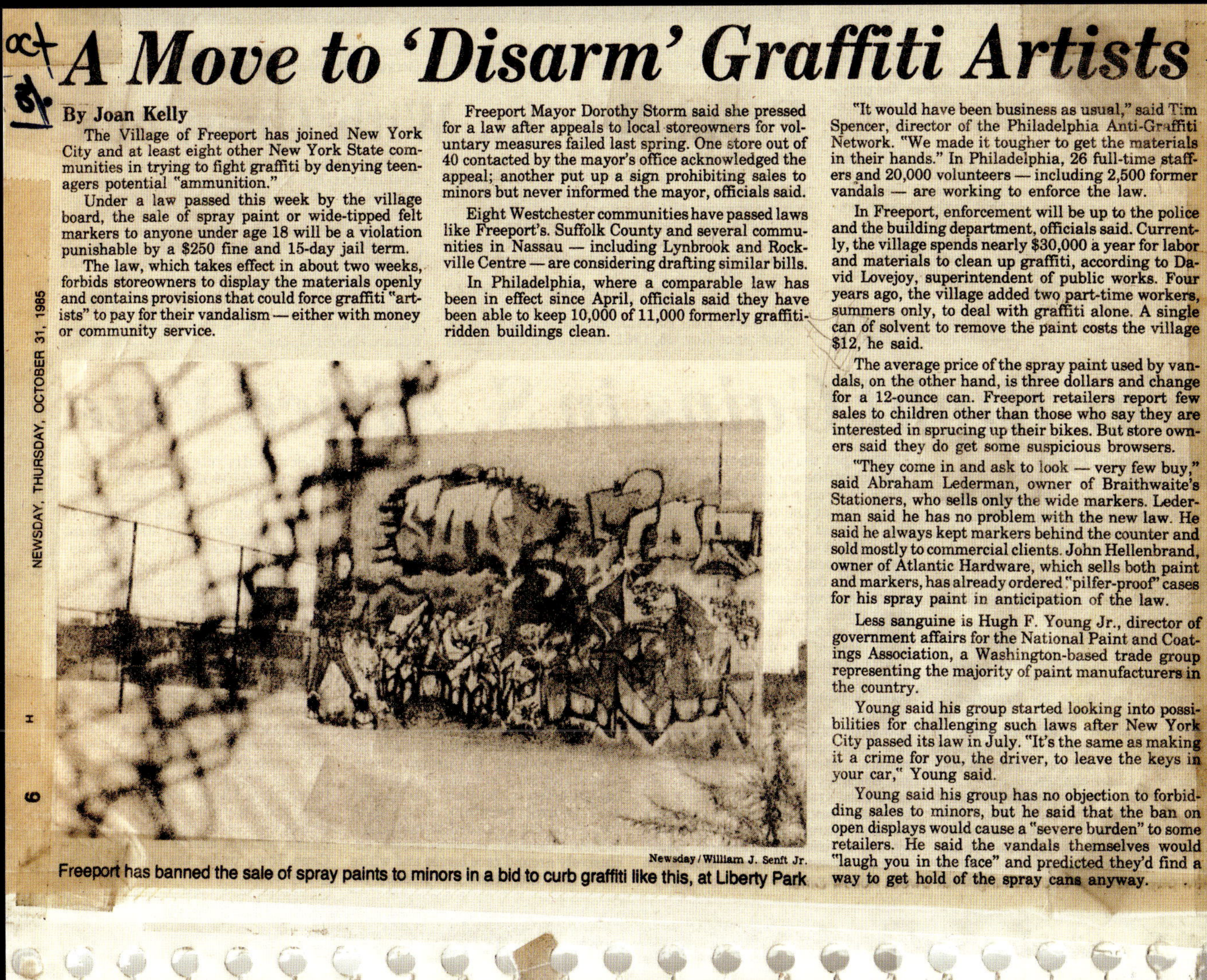

NEWSDAY, THURSDAY, OCTOBER 31, 1985 6 H

A Move to 'Disarm' Graffiti Artists

By Joan Kelly

The Village of Freeport has joined New York City and at least eight other New York State communities in trying to fight graffiti by denying teenagers potential "ammunition."

Under a law passed this week by the village board, the sale of spray paint or wide-tipped felt markers to anyone under age 18 will be a violation punishable by a $250 fine and 15-day jail term.

The law, which takes effect in about two weeks, forbids storeowners to display the materials openly and contains provisions that could force graffiti "artists" to pay for their vandalism — either with money or community service.

Freeport Mayor Dorothy Storm said she pressed for a law after appeals to local storeowners for voluntary measures failed last spring. One store out of 40 contacted by the mayor's office acknowledged the appeal; another put up a sign prohibiting sales to minors but never informed the mayor, officials said.

Eight Westchester communities have passed laws like Freeport's. Suffolk County and several communities in Nassau — including Lynbrook and Rockville Centre — are considering drafting similar bills.

In Philadelphia, where a comparable law has been in effect since April, officials said they have been able to keep 10,000 of 11,000 formerly graffiti-ridden buildings clean.

"It would have been business as usual," said Tim Spencer, director of the Philadelphia Anti-Graffiti Network. "We made it tougher to get the materials in their hands." In Philadelphia, 26 full-time staffers and 20,000 volunteers — including 2,500 former vandals — are working to enforce the law.

In Freeport, enforcement will be up to the police and the building department, officials said. Currently, the village spends nearly $30,000 a year for labor and materials to clean up graffiti, according to David Lovejoy, superintendent of public works. Four years ago, the village added two part-time workers, summers only, to deal with graffiti alone. A single can of solvent to remove the paint costs the village $12, he said.

The average price of the spray paint used by vandals, on the other hand, is three dollars and change for a 12-ounce can. Freeport retailers report few sales to children other than those who say they are interested in sprucing up their bikes. But store owners said they do get some suspicious browsers.

"They come in and ask to look — very few buy," said Abraham Lederman, owner of Braithwaite's Stationers, who sells only the wide markers. Lederman said he has no problem with the new law. He said he always kept markers behind the counter and sold mostly to commercial clients. John Hellenbrand, owner of Atlantic Hardware, which sells both paint and markers, has already ordered "pilfer-proof" cases for his spray paint in anticipation of the law.

Less sanguine is Hugh F. Young Jr., director of government affairs for the National Paint and Coatings Association, a Washington-based trade group representing the majority of paint manufacturers in the country.

Young said his group started looking into possibilities for challenging such laws after New York City passed its law in July. "It's the same as making it a crime for you, the driver, to leave the keys in your car," Young said.

Young said his group has no objection to forbidding sales to minors, but he said that the ban on open displays would cause a "severe burden" to some retailers. He said the vandals themselves would "laugh you in the face" and predicted they'd find a way to get hold of the spray cans anyway.

Newsday / William J. Senft Jr.

Freeport has banned the sale of spray paints to minors in a bid to curb graffiti like this, at Liberty Park

"A Move to 'Disarm' Graffiti Artists," *Long Island Newsday* article, Oct. 31, 1985,

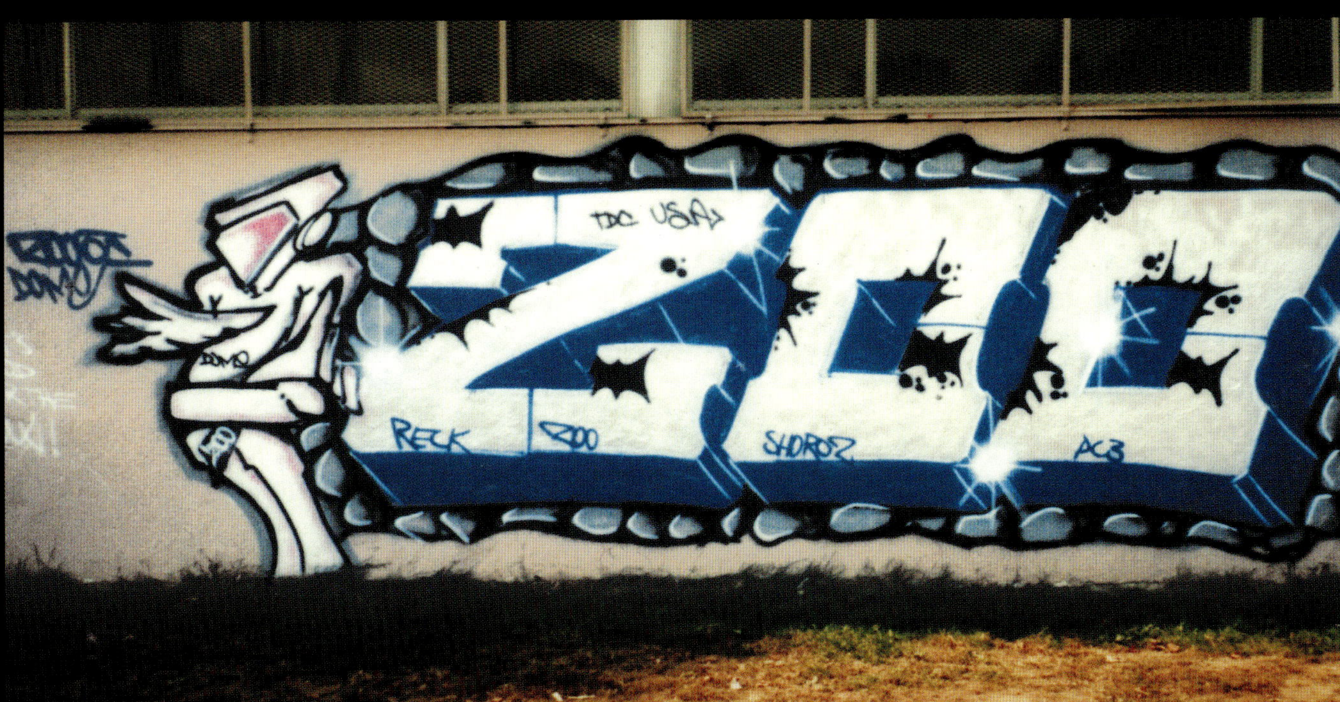

ZOO, "IT'S GOOD FOR THE SOUL," silver piece, Hempstead, LI, Jan. 1986.

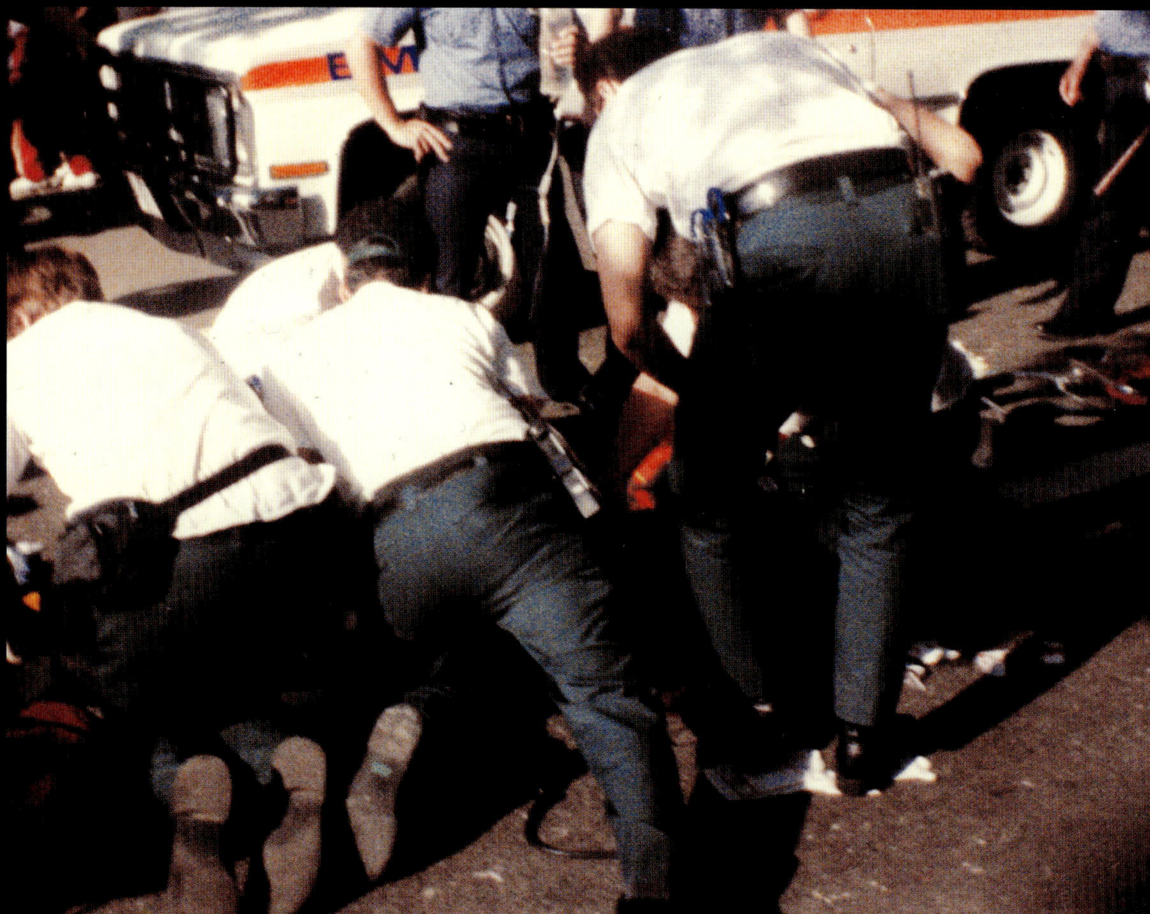

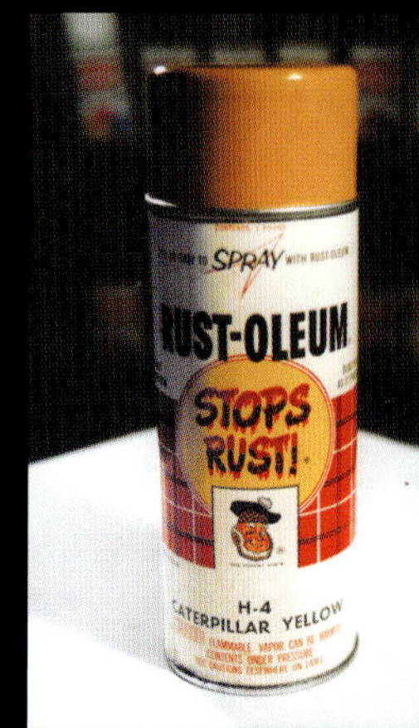

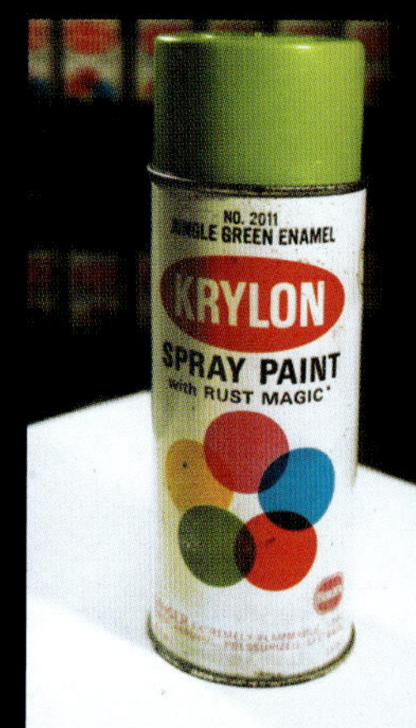

This guy got slashed in the neck with a box cutter at the Puerto Rican Day Parade.

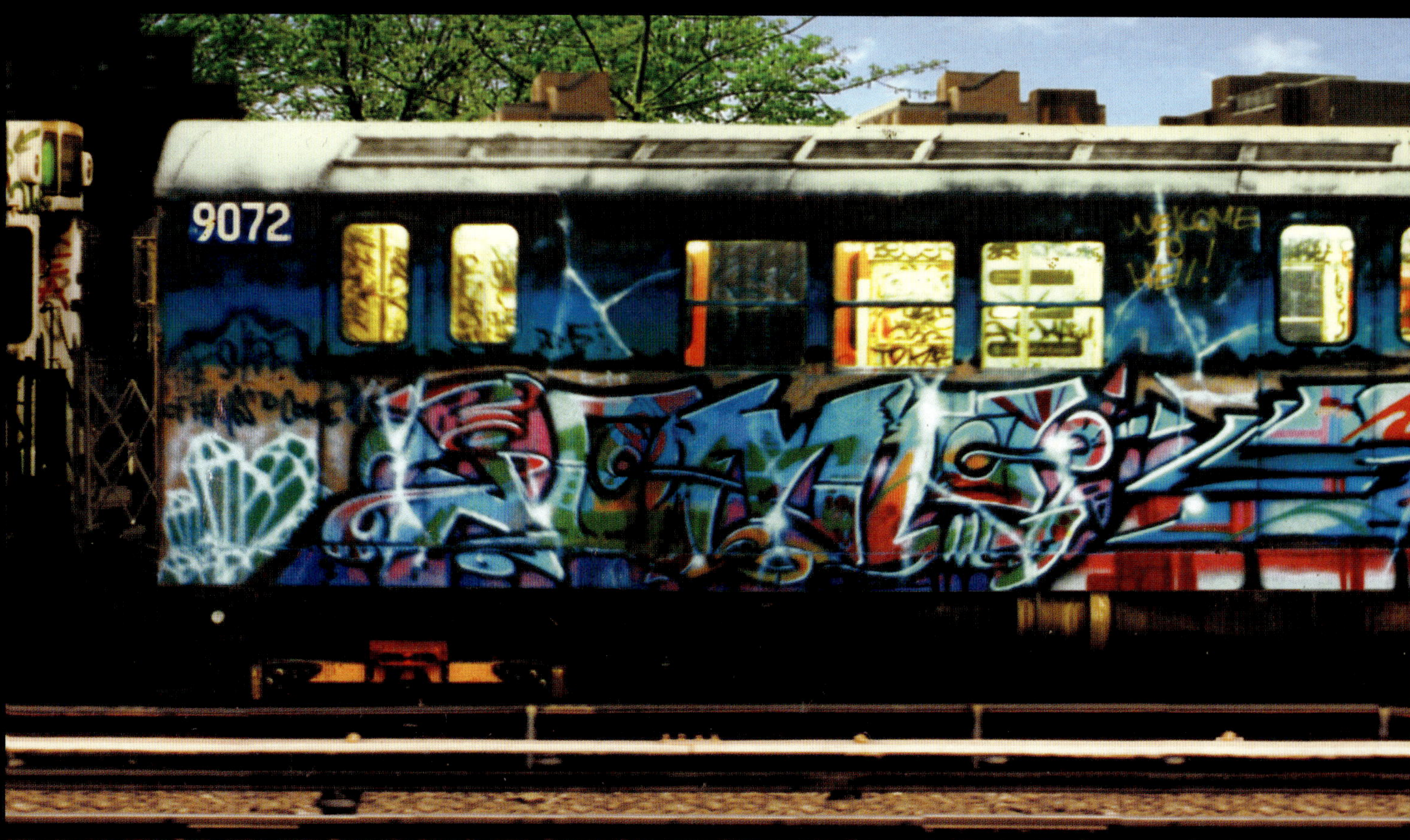

DOME, "WELCOME TO HELL," and VULCAN, "THE STYLE OF THINGS TO COME," 5 Train, Feb. 1988.

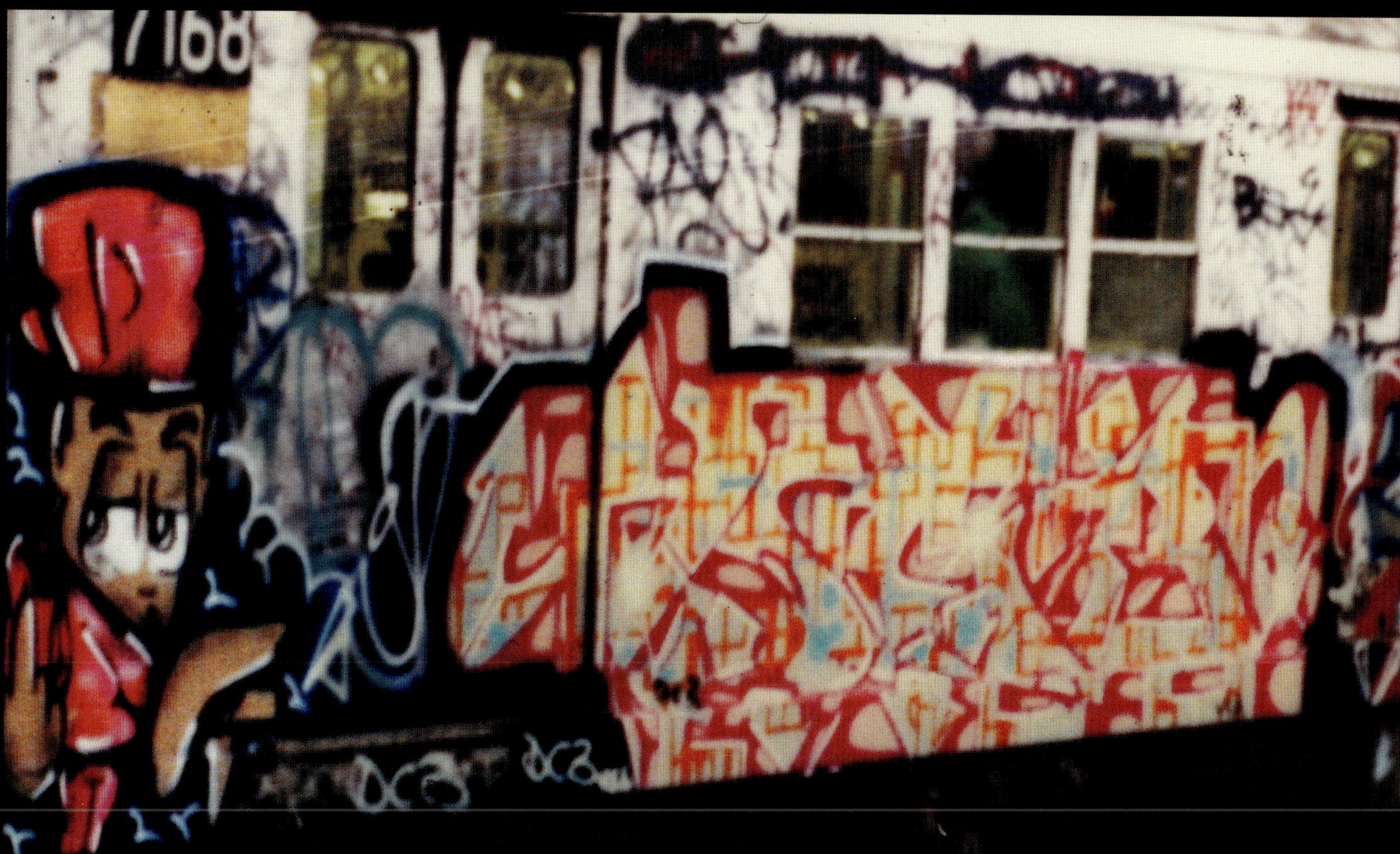

DC3 window-down, Jul. 1987. I dropped my 35mm camera from E. Tremont getting this flick. -SHO

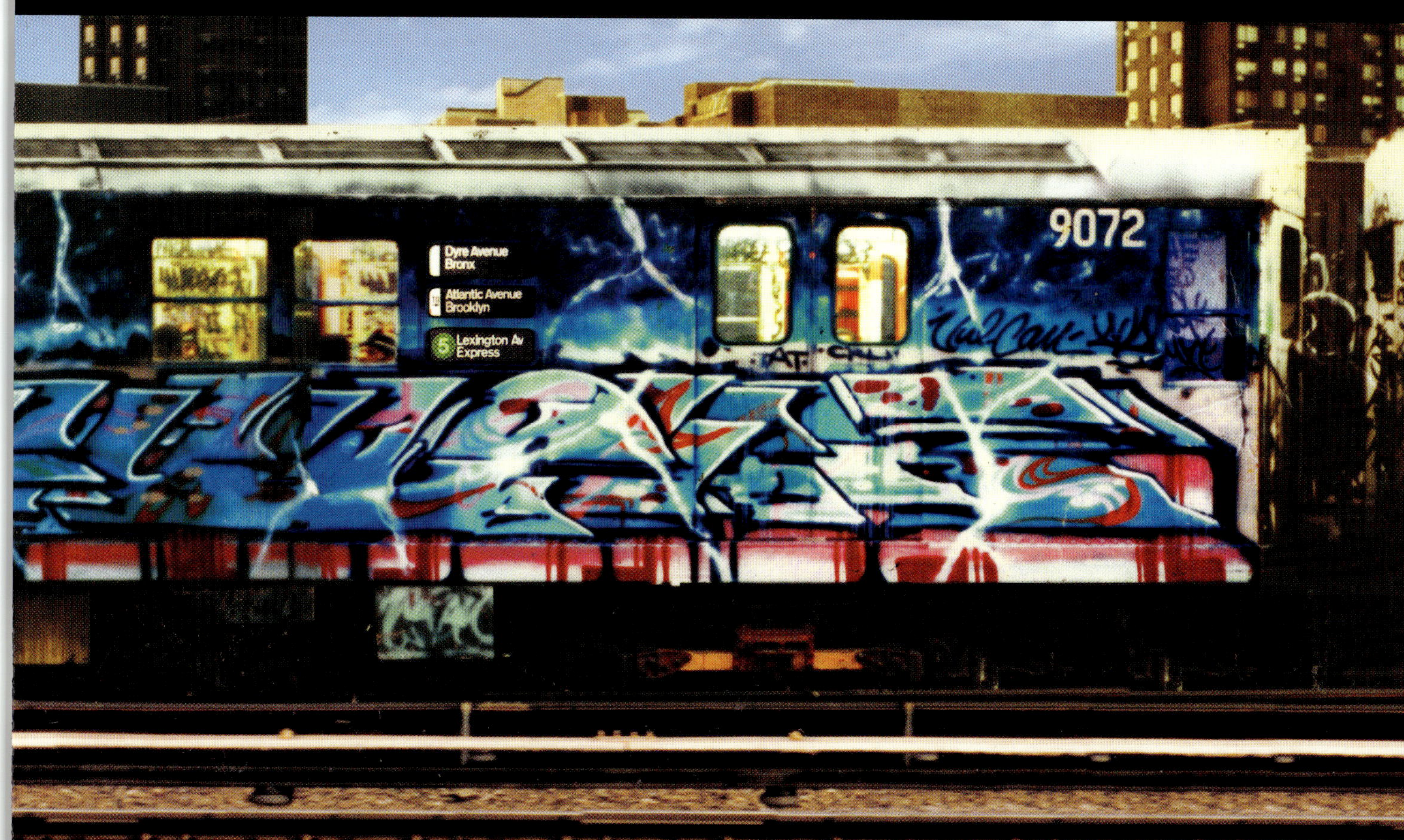

SHO and ZOOROC getting the cameo for the record books.

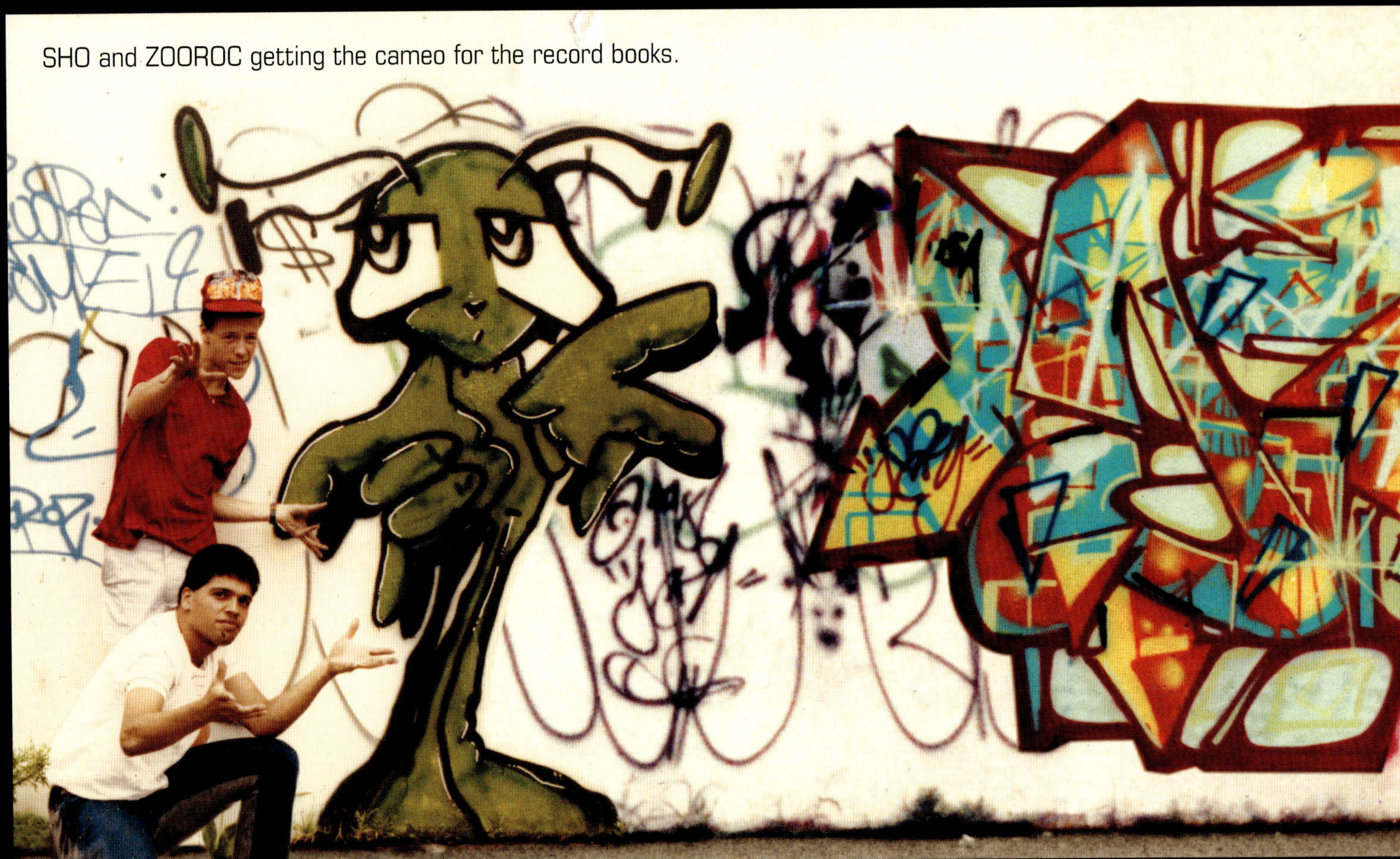

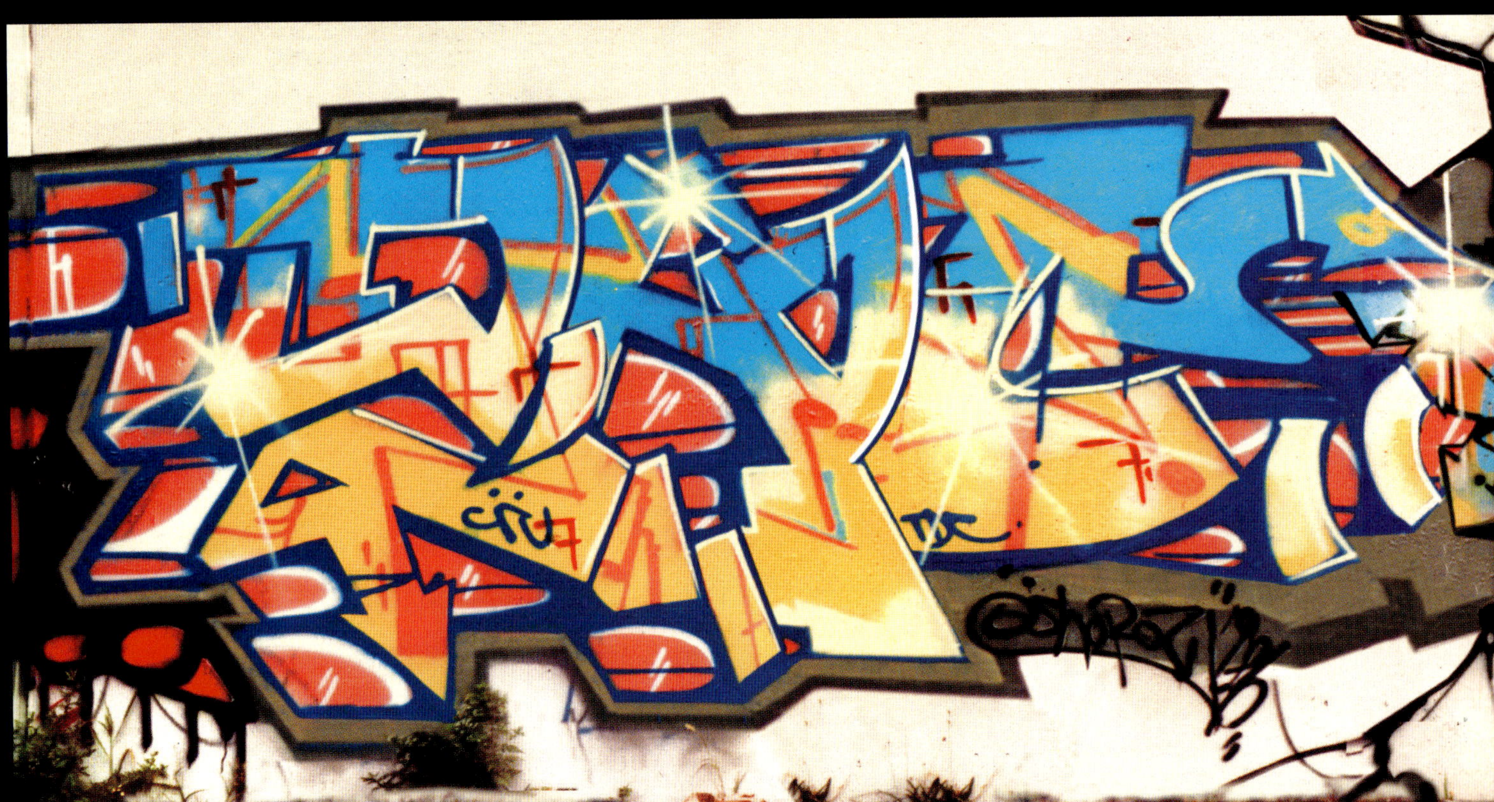

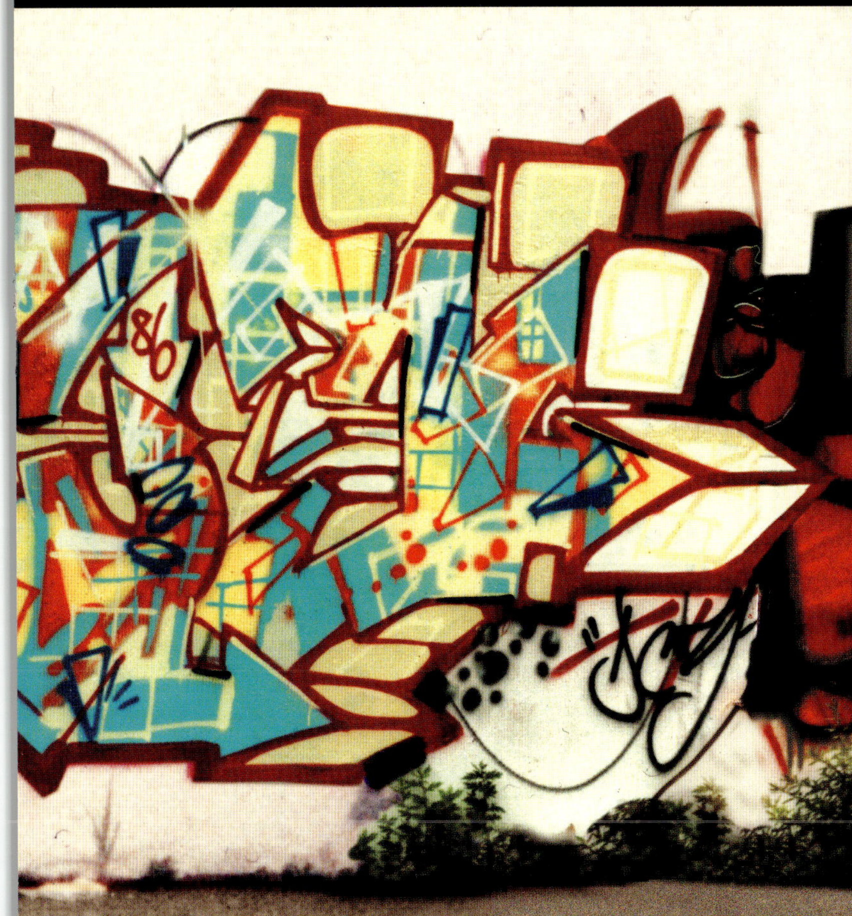

DC3, SHO, AND ZOO ZUCRU 1986 "THE MAGIC THE MOMENT," part 4.

This was rocked very early on on the double hand ball courts on the Belt Parkway. Many writers hit this wall up like Tron, Drip TC, Cer TPA, Doe, Cash, Zin, Lust, 2Nice and Sno, Den, Act, Ozone, and The Nassau Artists. I had rode my fucking ten speed like 11 miles all the way from Freeport to Belmont Racetrack to take flicks. So you know we was rocking the spot. I was working at Key Food part time in Baldwin and met Drip TC and his man, this 5 percenter who didn't even write graffiti. They were trying to lure me out of sight and beat me up and rob me like I was some average white boy. Not gonna happen, period!!

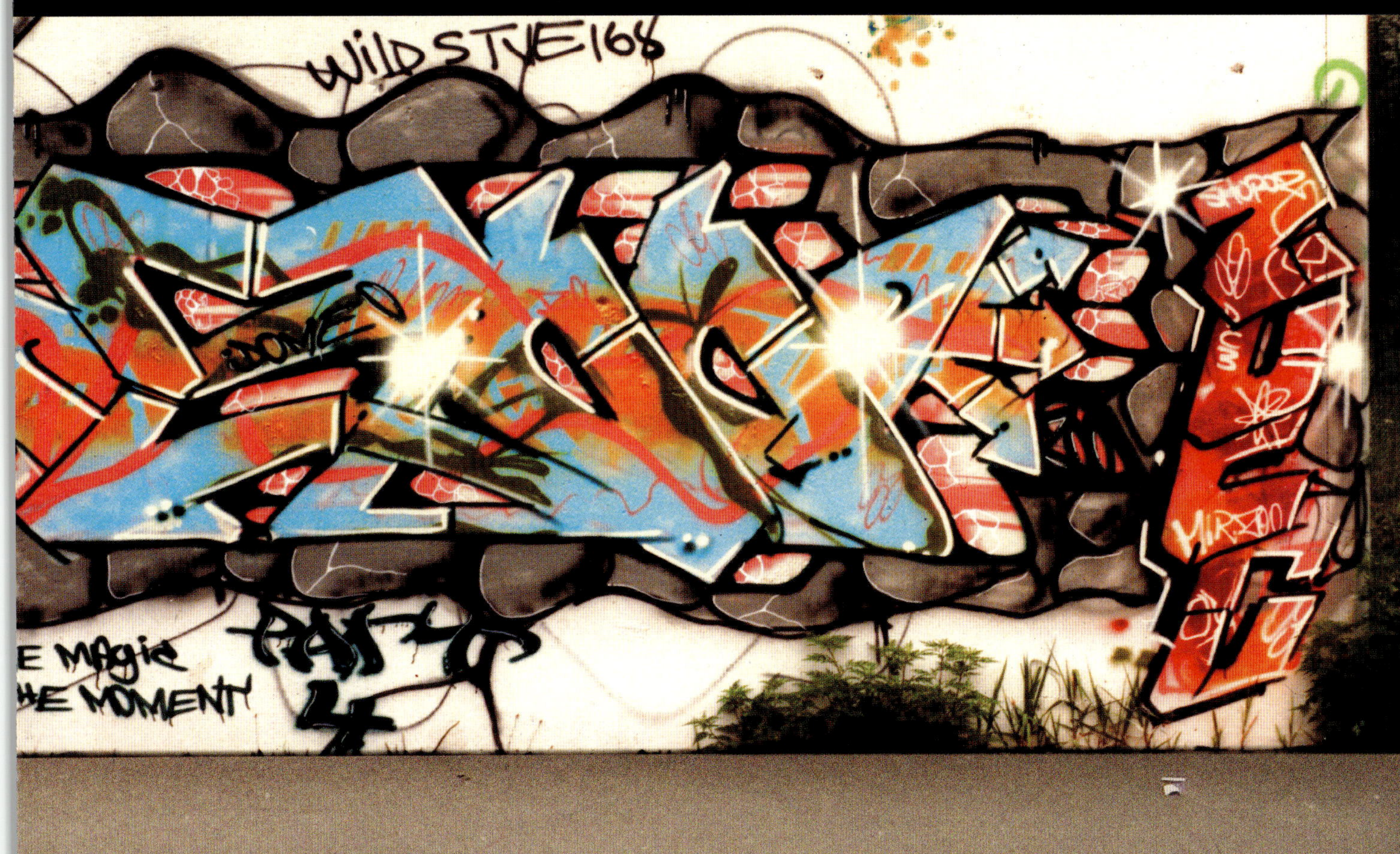

DC3 rocking a Martin, SHO and ZOO ZUCRU on the Belt Parkway, Jun. 1986.

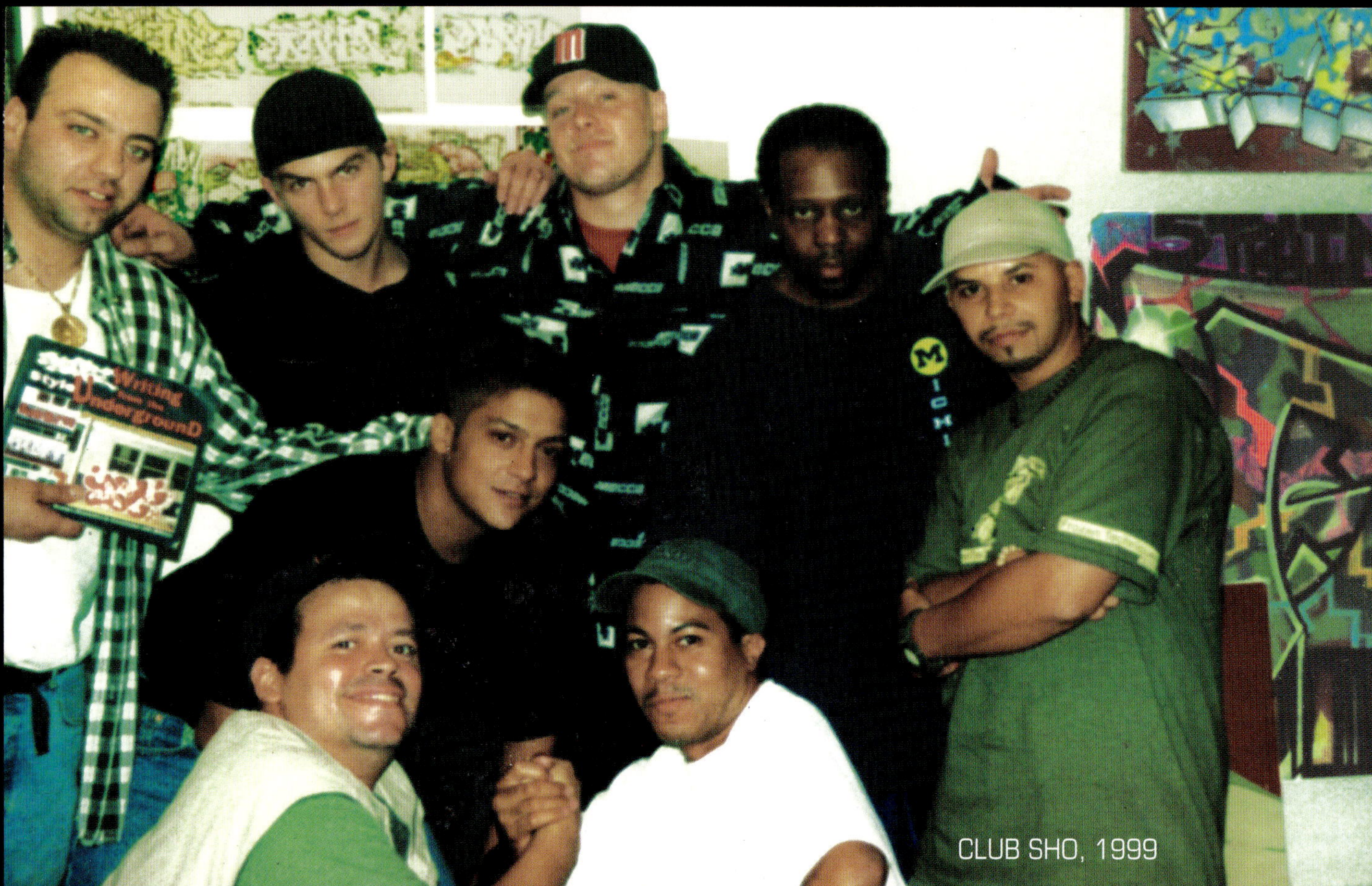

CLUB SHO, 1999

Ok, The ZOO SHO Back-To-Back Blockbuster Trains!!!!!

SHO'S grandfather Frank lived at Ridgewood and Autumn Avenue in Cypress Hill, Brooklyn NY, he always said he wanted to hit the J Train because it was an area of NY that was so bombed and because the J Yard was so gangster. These trains were done on the J Train in the middle of the summer in August 1989. The lay up was one SHO and Dome discovered by, as always, hunting them shits down ourselves after we learned of the lay up by word of mouth thru writers I had bumped into in Grant lay up while killing the A and C lines. Since we had the car, searching for spots was easy. The MTA had the J Trains layed up off the last stop at 121st Street in Jamaica Queens. The 2&5s were our babies, but they were all red trains by then and we were not done with writing on trains yet. We gained access thru the LIRR tracks that was parallel to it. As long as there's some flats running, we was hungry for them shits and was trying to go as All City as possible on trains thru the boroughs and we wanted to continue doing burners on trains. For the record we hit the 2, 3, 5, and 6 number lines and the A, B, C, J, K, L, M, N, Q, and R letter lines and the JFK express once. We went in the lay up with a plan to do big top-to-bottoms each and the challenge was there because the Js were bigger, with four doors, so we had our work cut out for the night. We went in past midnight and painted till the sun rose (YES!) it was a beautiful morning. After finishing we went to Franklin K. Lane High School and waited for our train to pull out the lay ups to take photos and the rest is history. That train ran till the end.

e
ing,
ou,
big
eam
rs,
it.

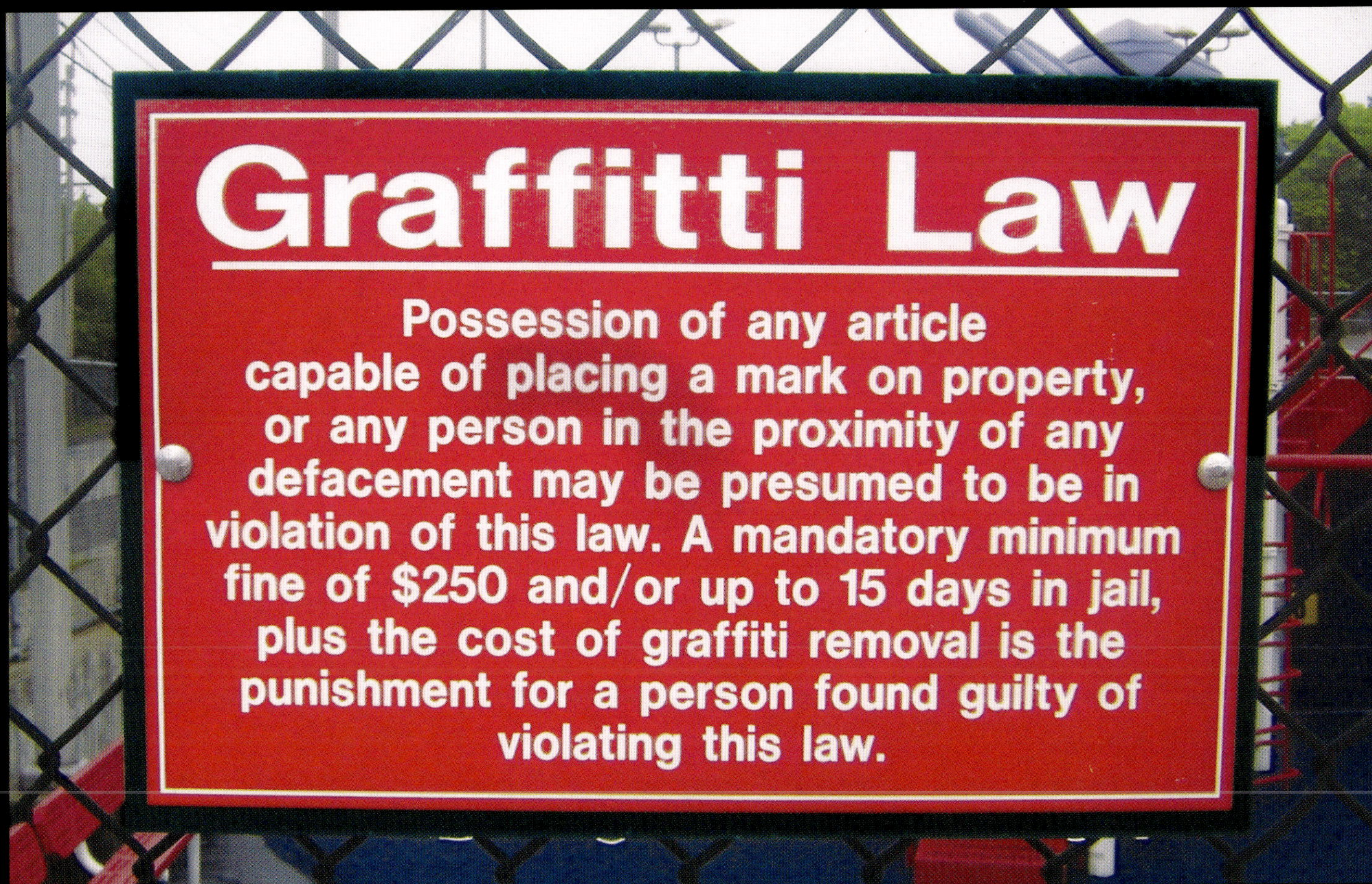

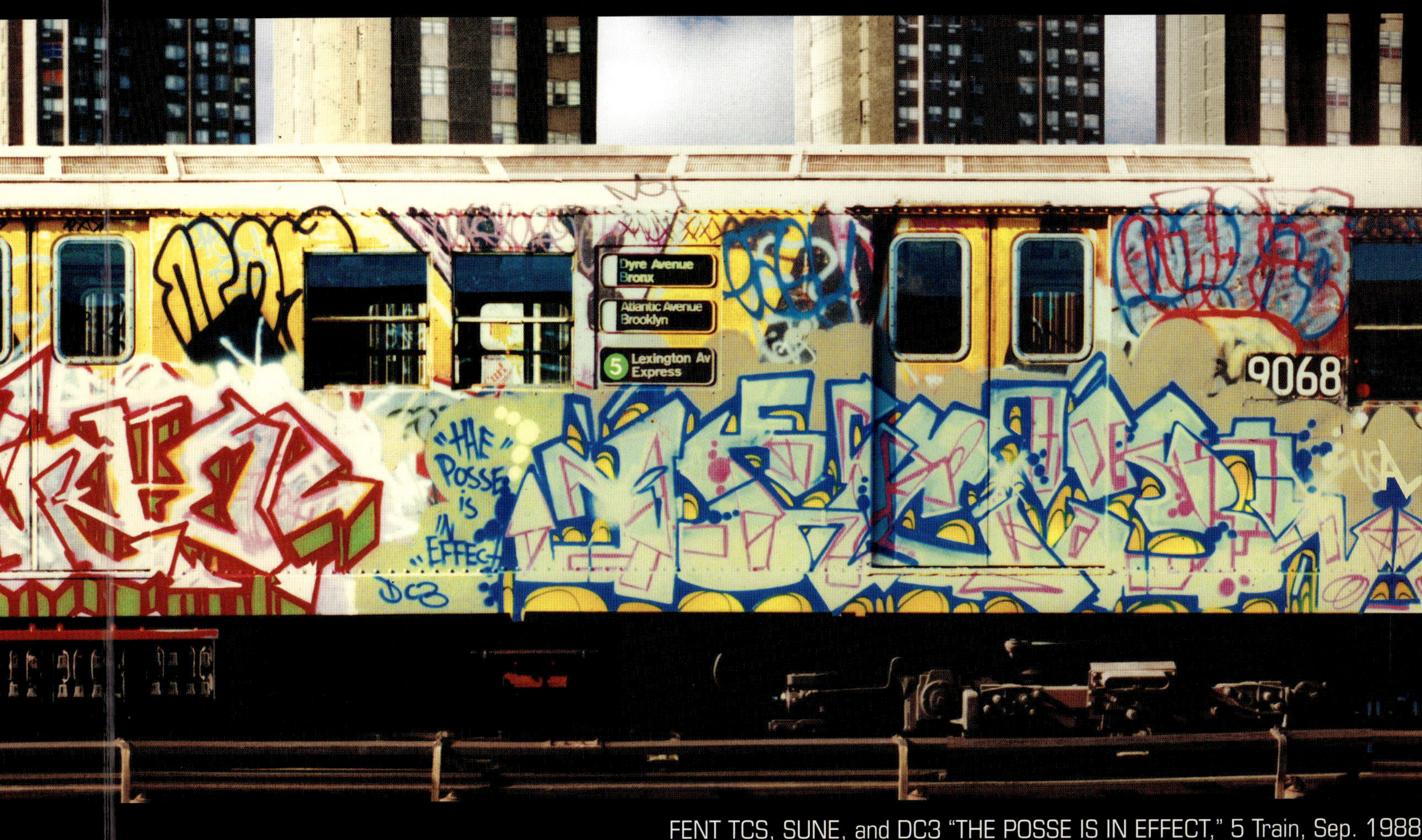

FENT TCS, SUNE, and DC3 "THE POSSE IS IN EFFECT," 5 Train, Sep. 1988.

ZOO "IT FEELS LIKE THE WEIGHT OF THE WORLD IS ON MY SHOULDERS," top-to-bottom J Train, Sep. 1988.

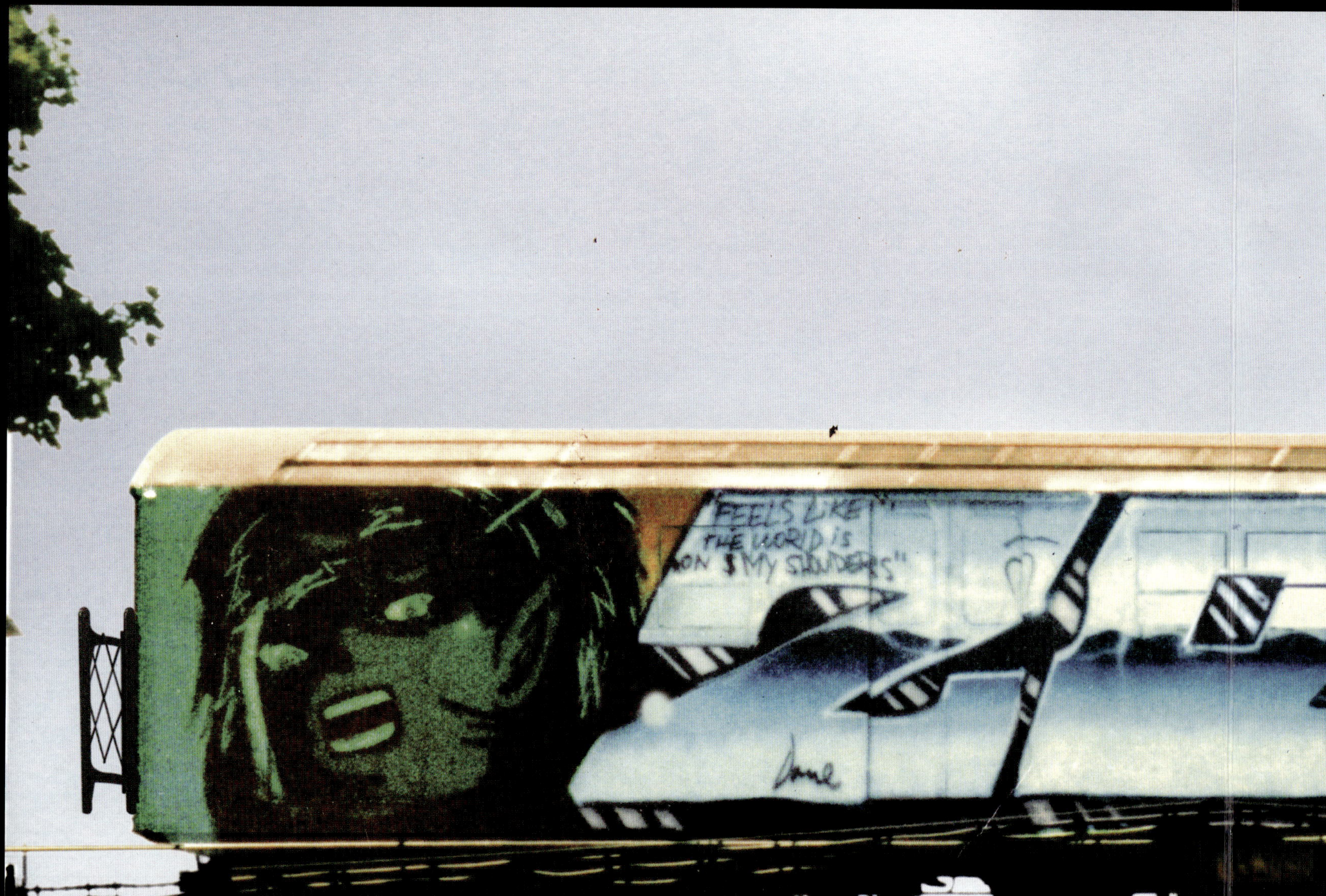

Photographed at Franklin K. Lane High School, 5:10 P.M.

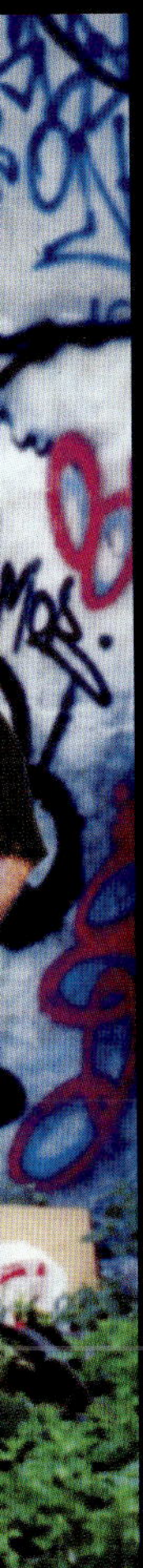

★

SHO and Rose at Canal Street

This was done August 27, 1994, right down the block from the graffiti store, which at the time was named Soho Zats, and now is named Subway Stop.
It was a prime location that I had rocked with my man at the time. Having some burners in Manhattan was necessary, as everyone fucking knows,
NYC was and always will be the birthplace of graffiti. As one of the five pillars of hip hop culture, it's right up there at the top. The five boroughs, literally, was where break dancing, graffiti, battling,
MC-ing, and rap music was created. If it wasn't for the Bronx mainly there wouldn't have been such an overwhelming subway bombing and piecing movement. We made our impact and presence felt on trains from 1986-1990 and that was that. History!!!!!

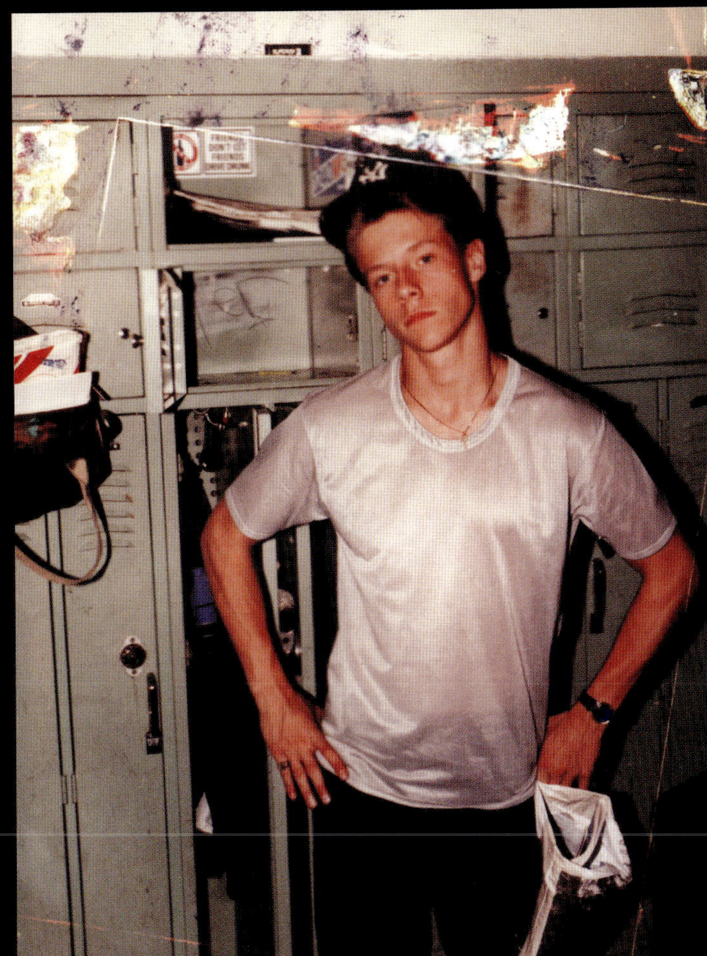

SHO TDC FHS.

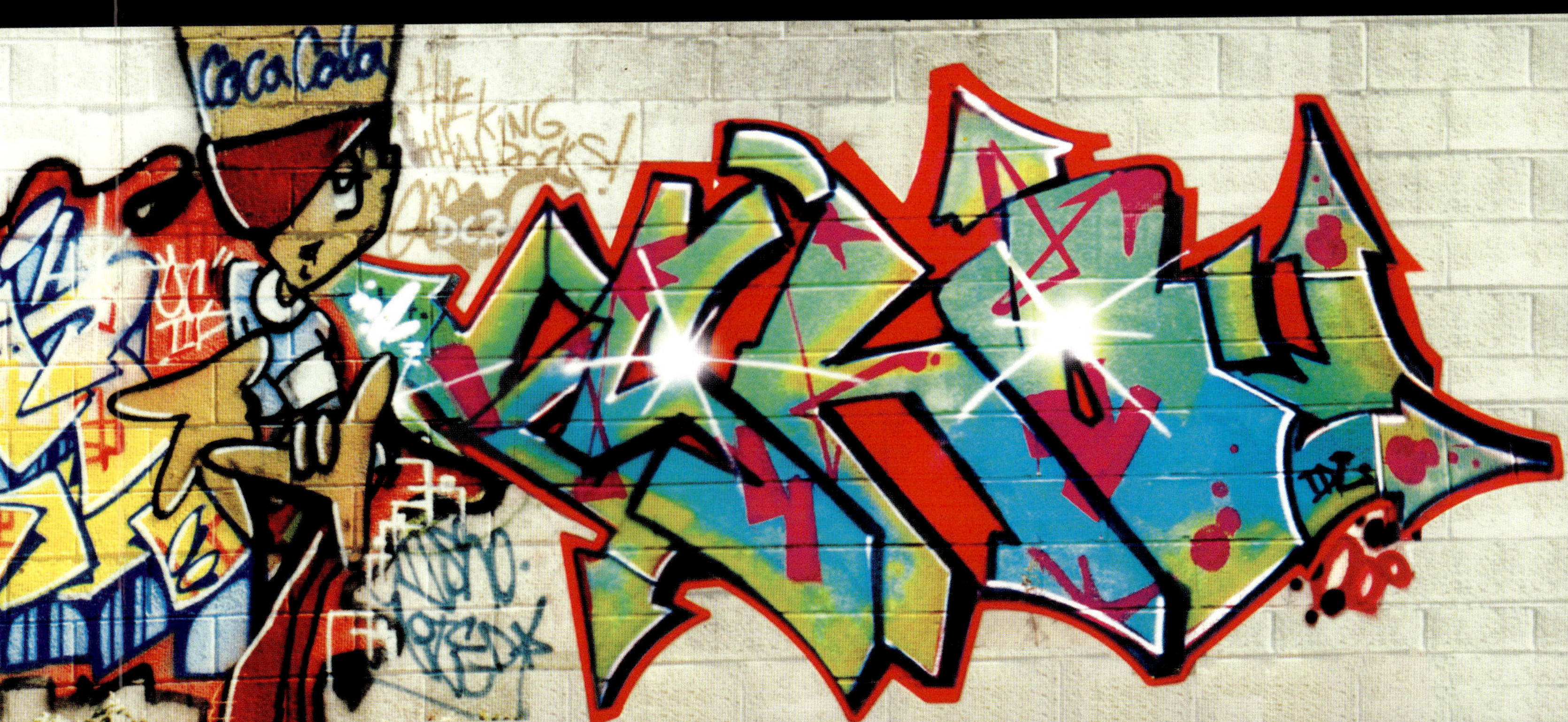

s time. It was right before we started to blaze the subways full time.

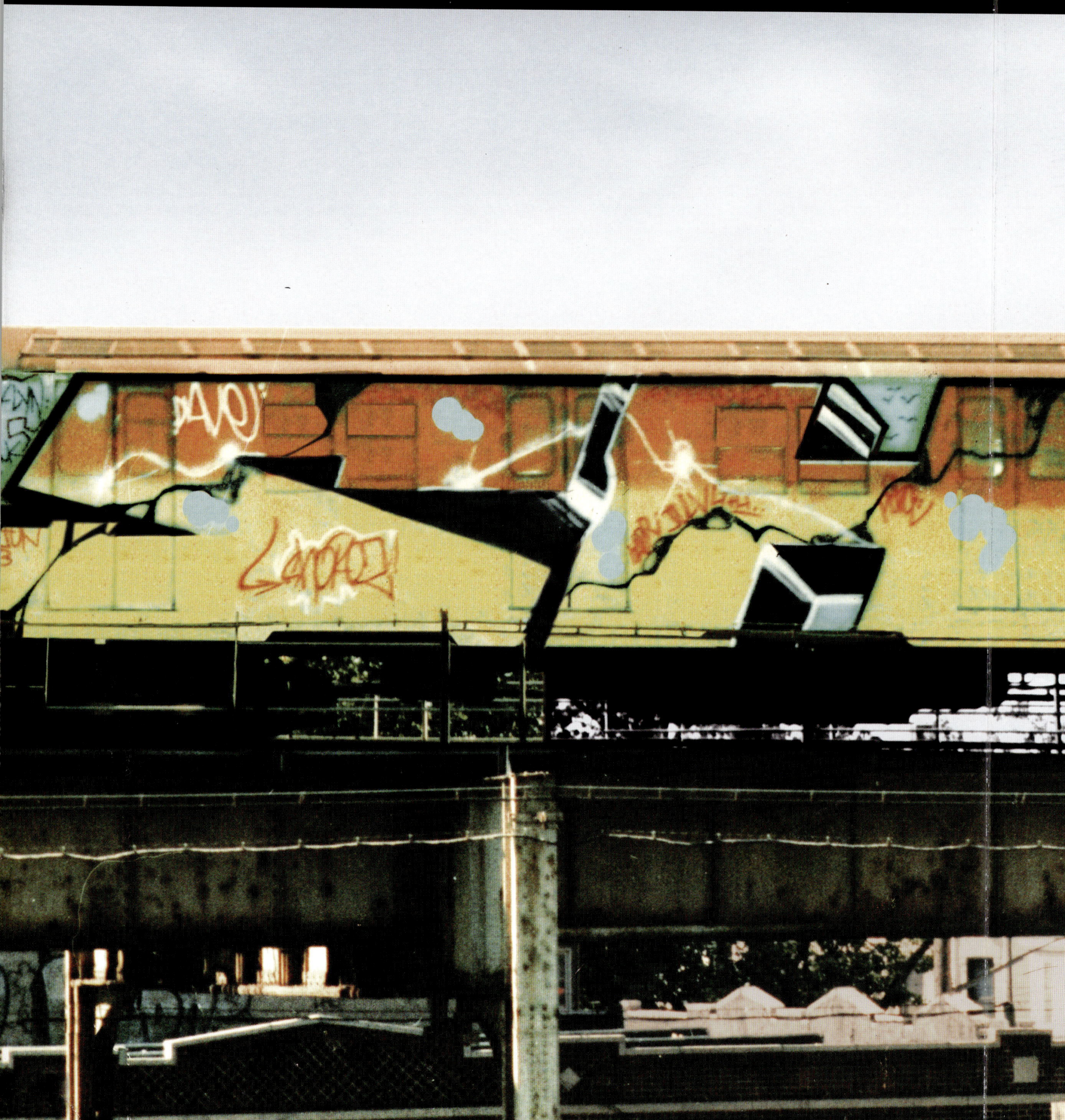

CHAPTER 12

Early Long Island Murals, IBM 1 trains, Window-down Burners Canvas Artwork and Special Thanks Appendix

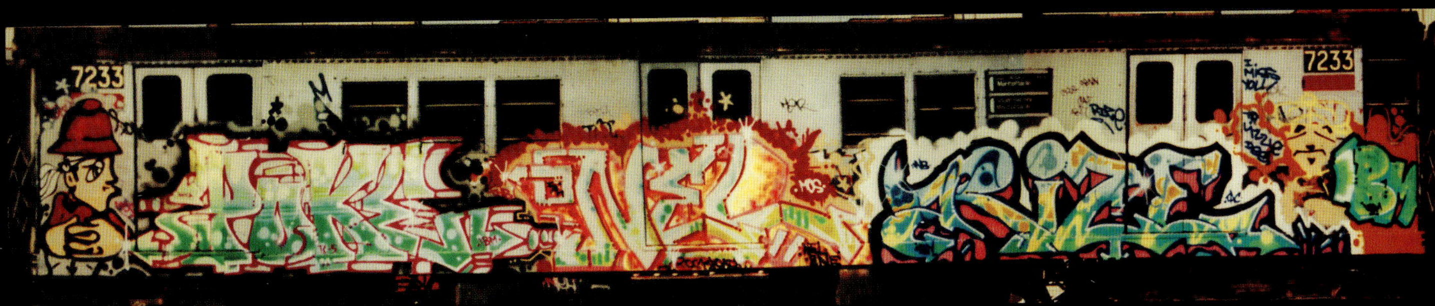

POKE, NEL, RIZE, IBM, MOS, 1 Train, 1984.

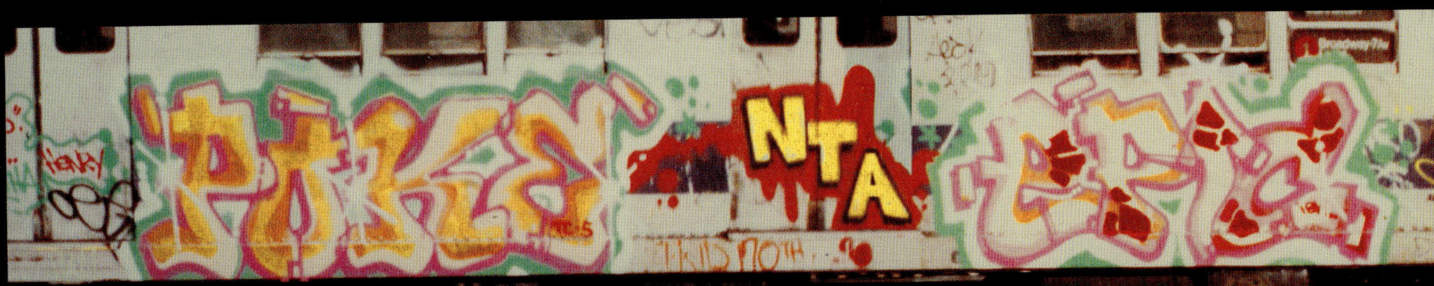

POKE, NTA, EPIC. No Toys Allowed, 1 Train, 1984.

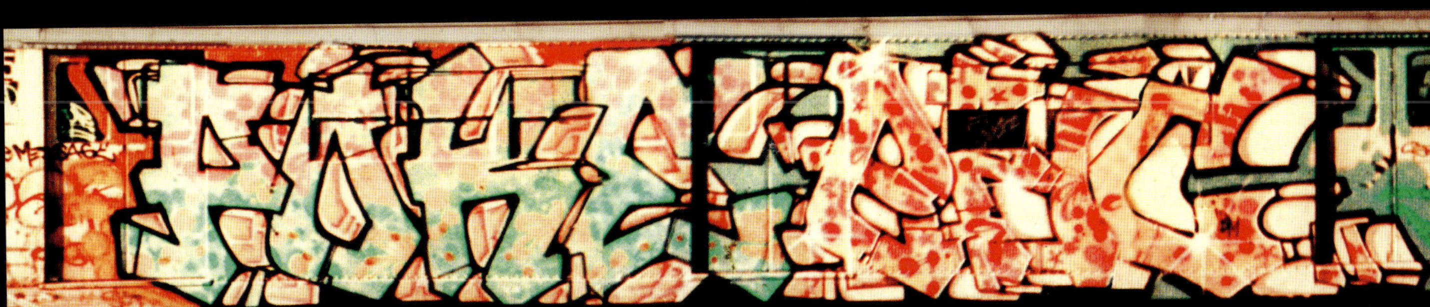

POKE EPIC, 5 Train, 1985.

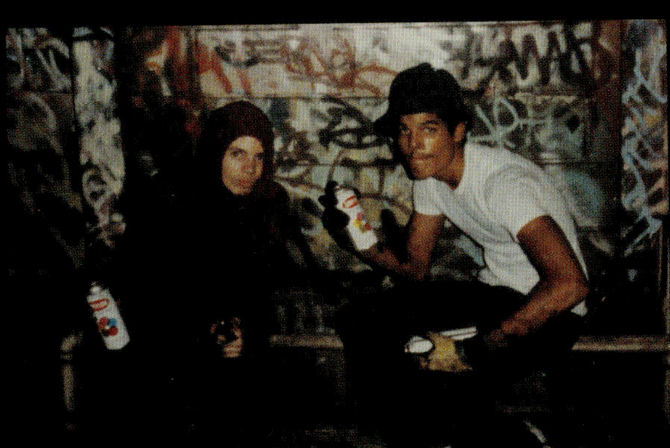

IBM, Idolized By Millions, You Heard?...

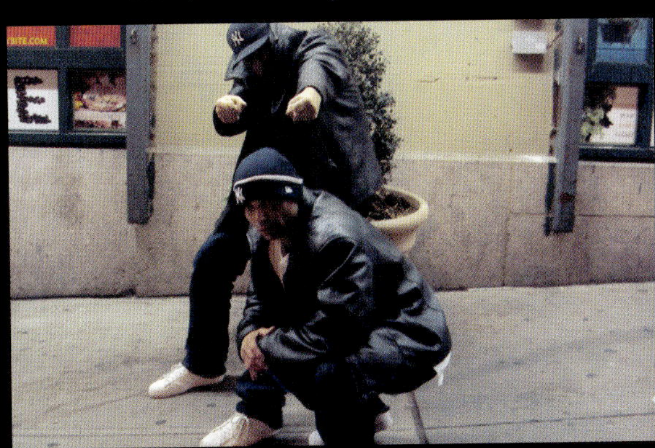

The POKE and EPIC top-to-bottom was done in Baychester. This was the first time we went and painted the line in the Bronx and we was still crushing the 1 Line on the regular. West invited us to go and we was cool with Michelob and Jase who said they had the spot on lock. We definitely wanted props on the 5s to rep for Manhattan. It was Spring 1985. Me, EPIC, West, and SKE hit that shit up late, we got started at 3 A.M. and didn't finish until late in the morning. We rocked three cars. West had a broken arm and it took longer cause we had to straddle the two lanes to paint top-to-bottom. Later we found out that we was being observed by the vandal squad task force. They had waited for us to finish but got impatient and had a conductor come and start to move the train so we would break out. We left and while at a nearby store buying shit, they came and raided the bodega and arrested all of us. Whatever B, they hit us with graffiti and weapons charges.

-POKE

DC3, "THE NOTORIOUS KING OF THE ART," Hempstead, "DEDICATED TO THE DREAM"

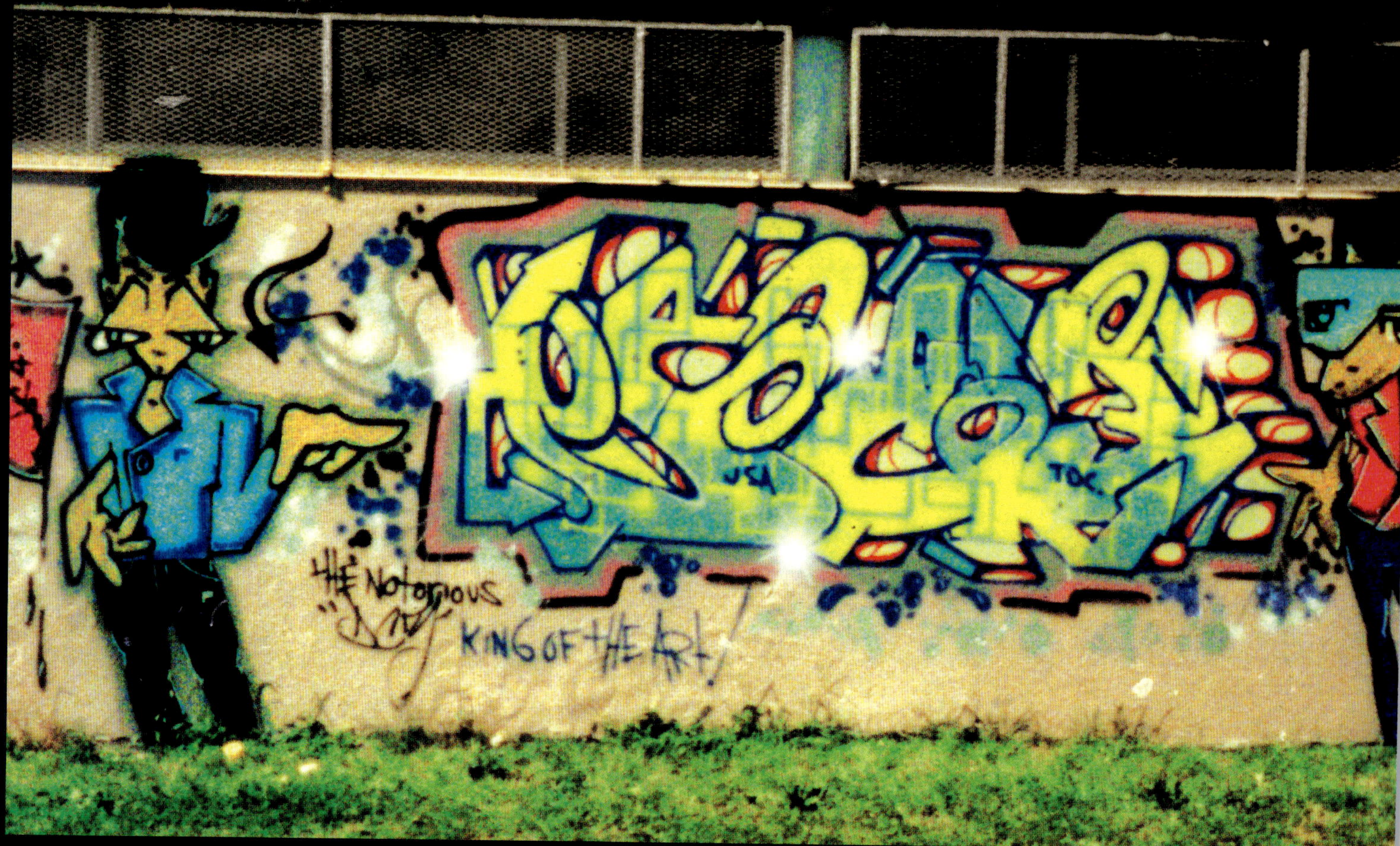

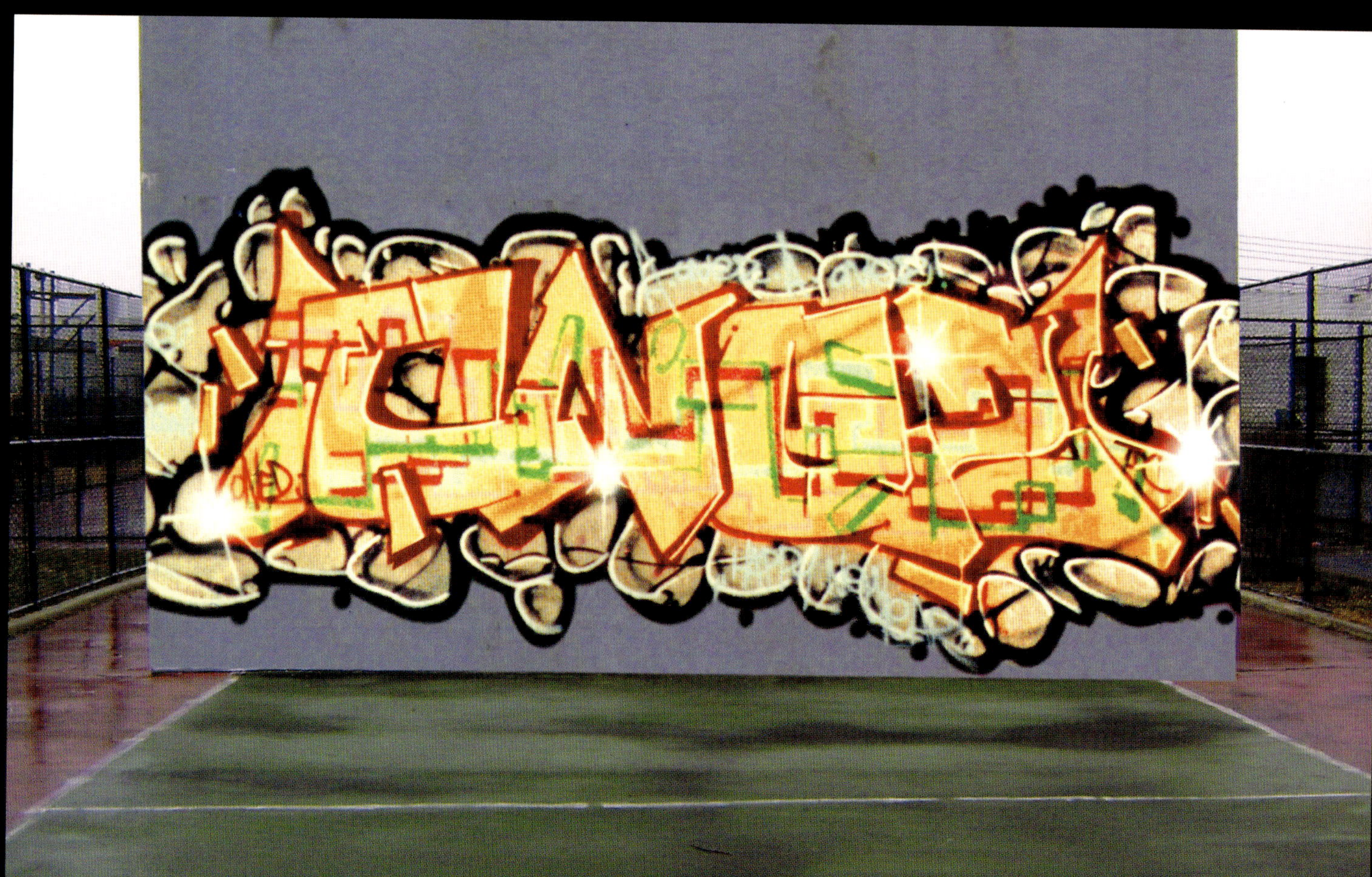

ONE2, "A ONE2 A ONE2," Happy New Year, 1986 Handball court. LI, stand the fuck up!!!

ZROC, "STOP THE MADNESS, STOP THE CRACK!!!!" Oct. 1986.

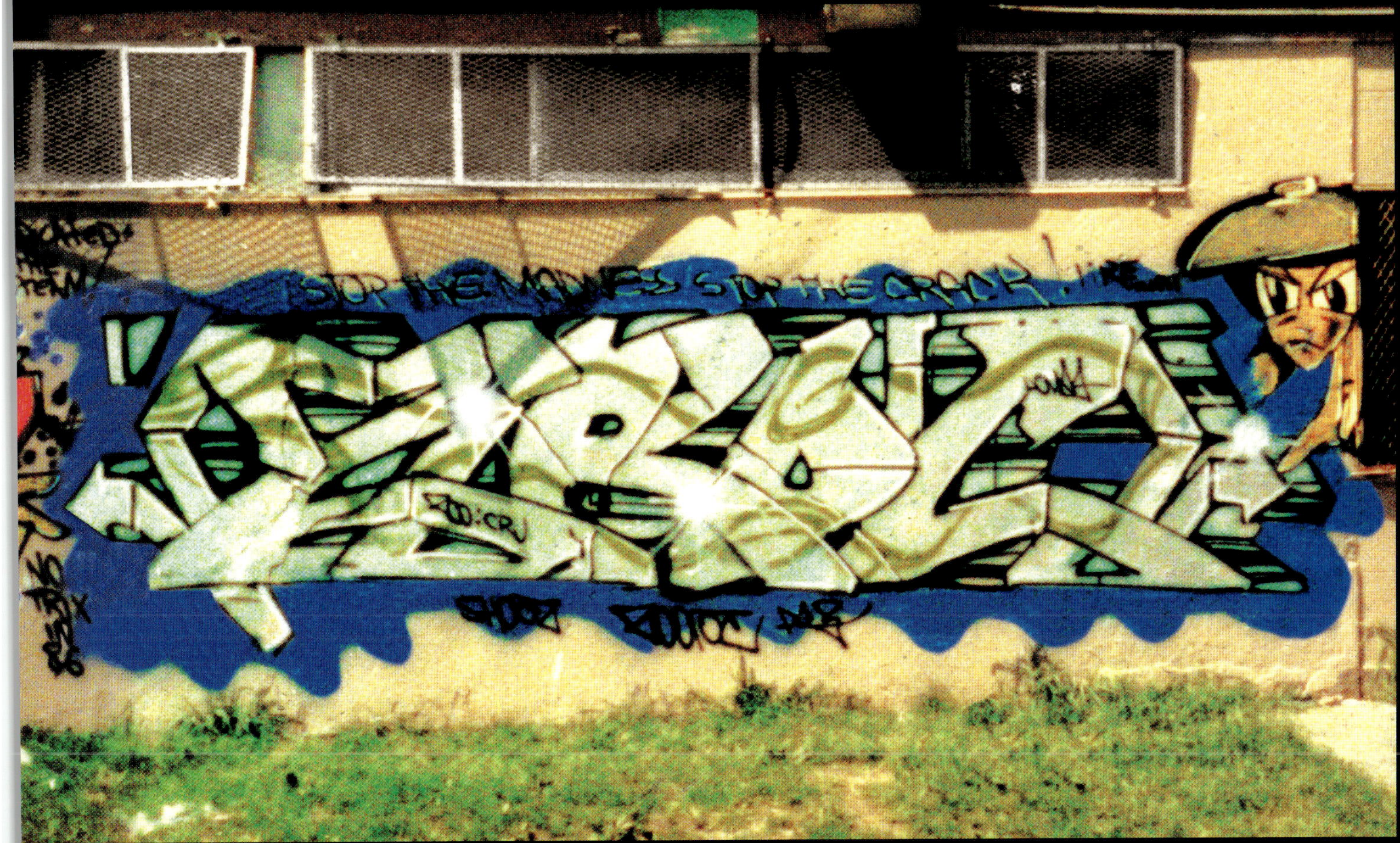

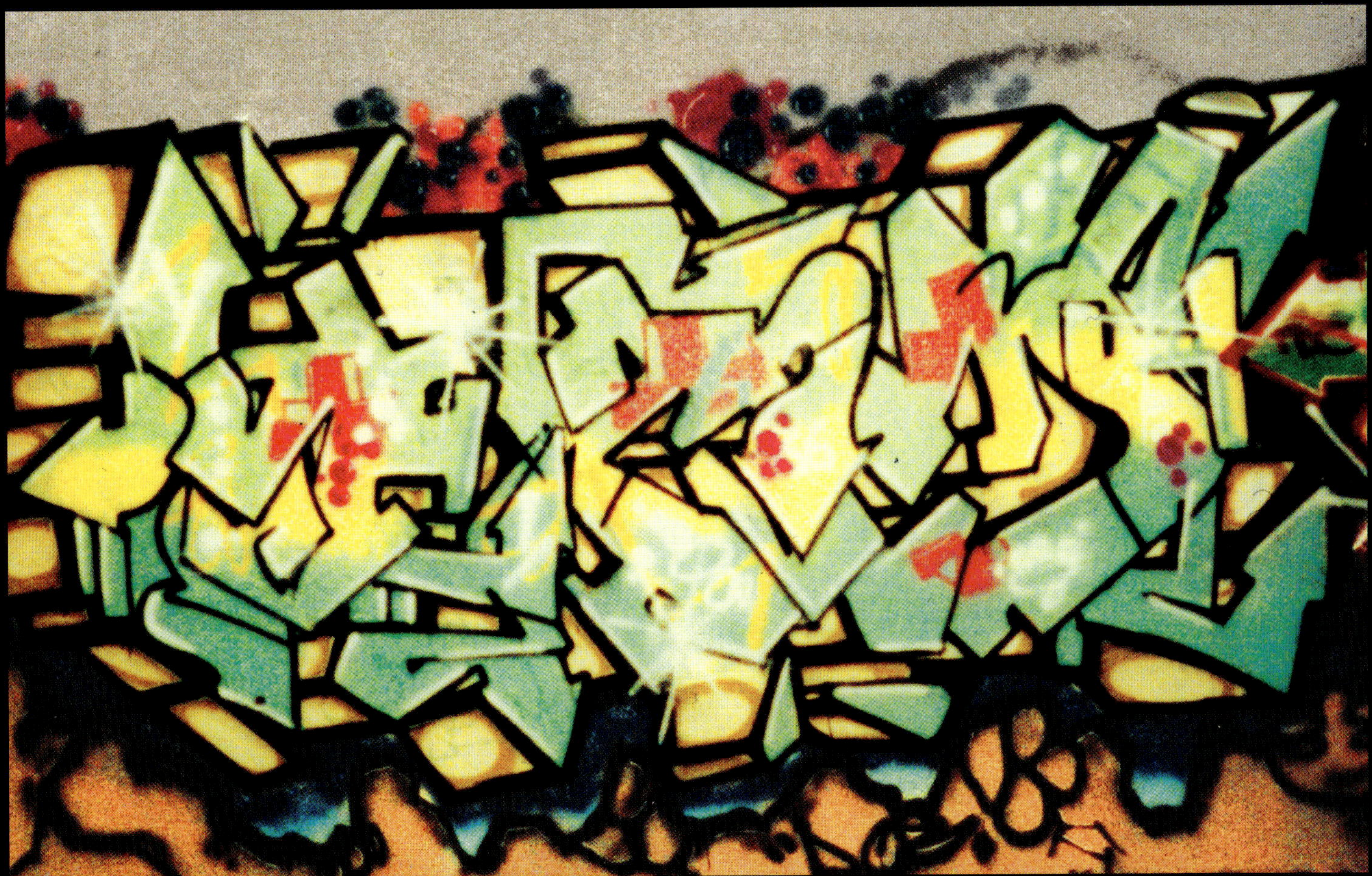

DC3 with SHO, Northwest Park, Freeport, May 1985.

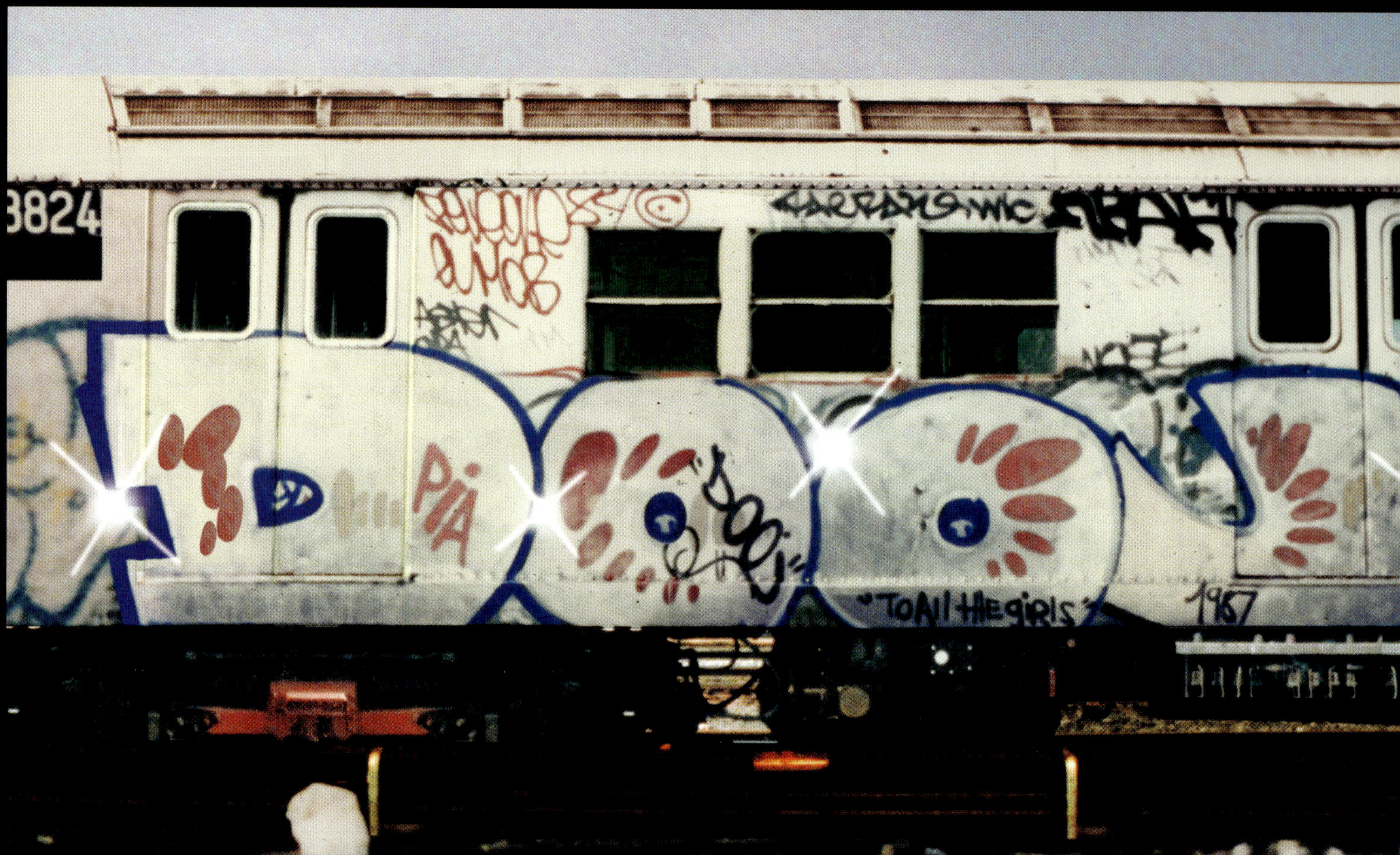

DOOJ Partners In Art Crew and DC3 USA, silver window-down 5 Train, Nov. 1987.

"Enter Our Realm Of Graffiti."

"The Destiny Children," October 5, 1986, DC3 and SHO at Lincoln Park. This TDC production was in Hempstead. DC3 and I were doing bigger and more elaborate handball courts at this time. This was a prime location because it was the front of the handball wall facing E. Graham Ave, so all car traffic seen it. Also it was always packed with local people playing basketball. Those courts are now known as The Eugene Henderson Courts of Hope.

-Sho TDCUSA

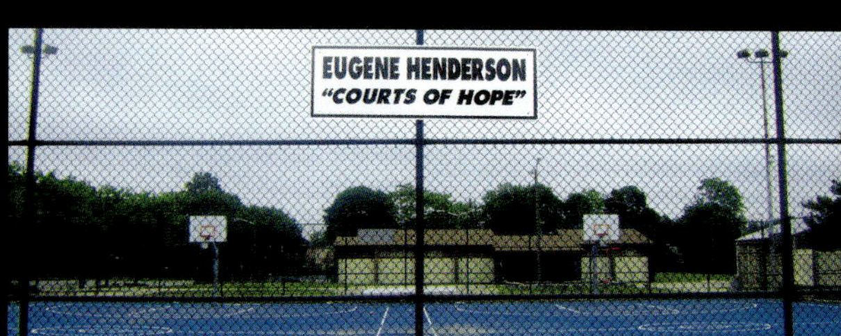

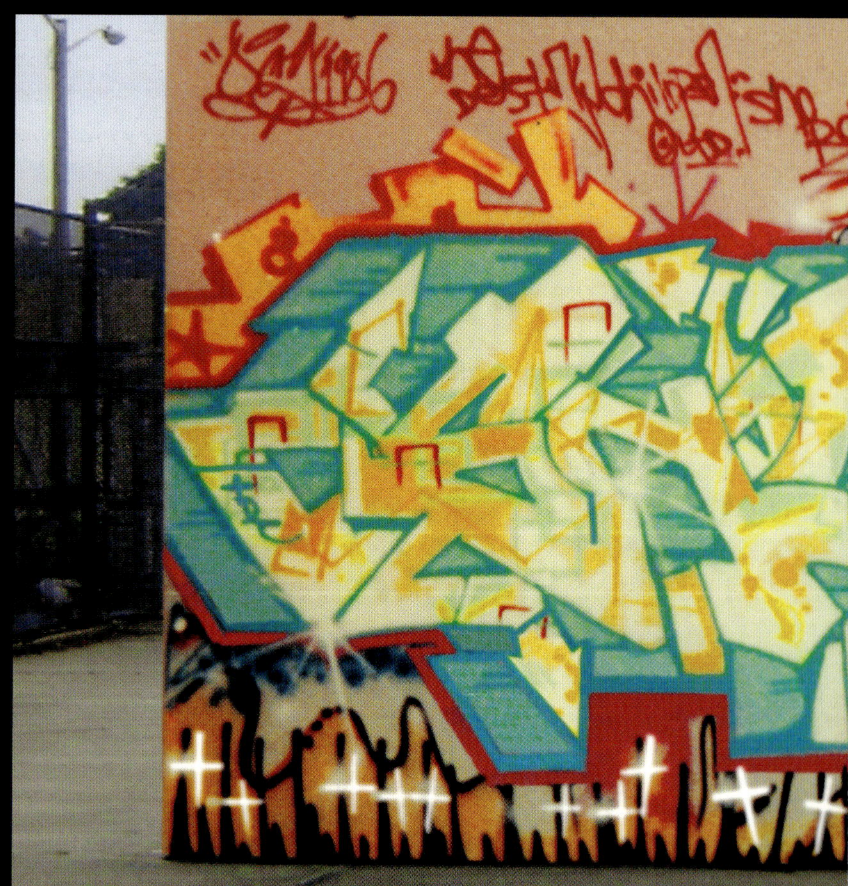

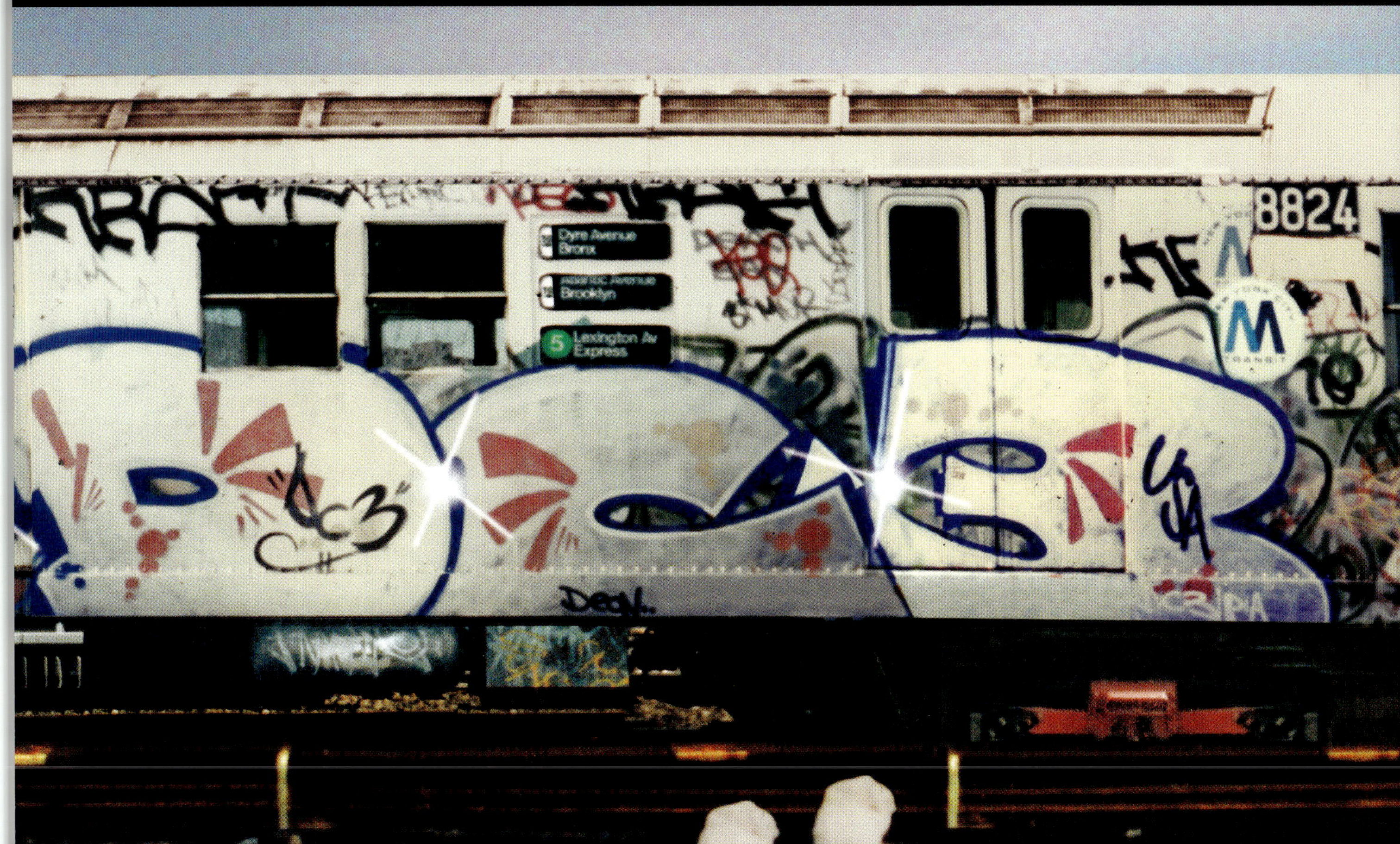

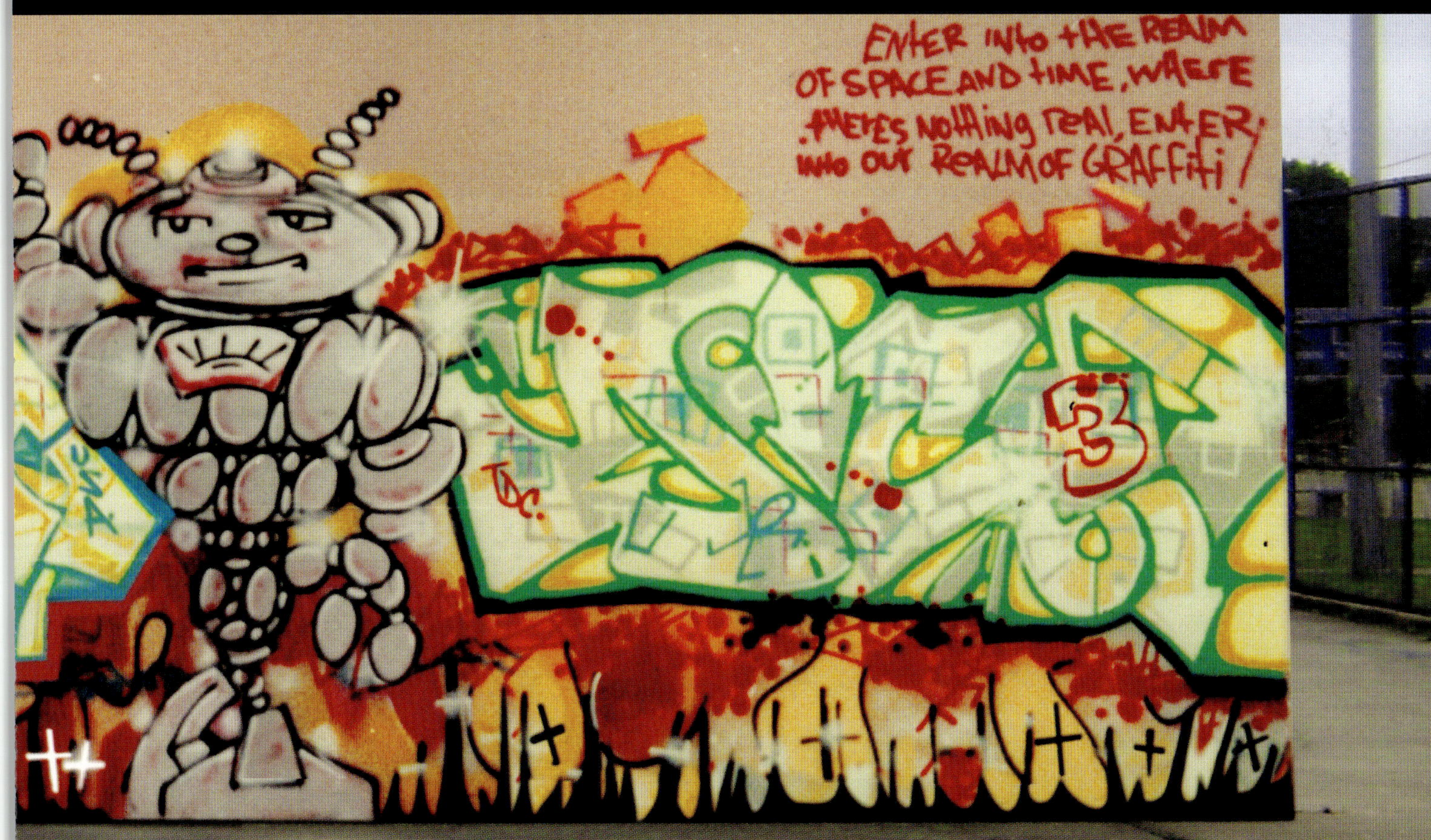

SHO and DC3, “Funky Robot Wall,” Lincoln Park, Hempstead, LI, Aug. 5,1986.

DC3 Production, Hempstead, NY, Jul. 1985.

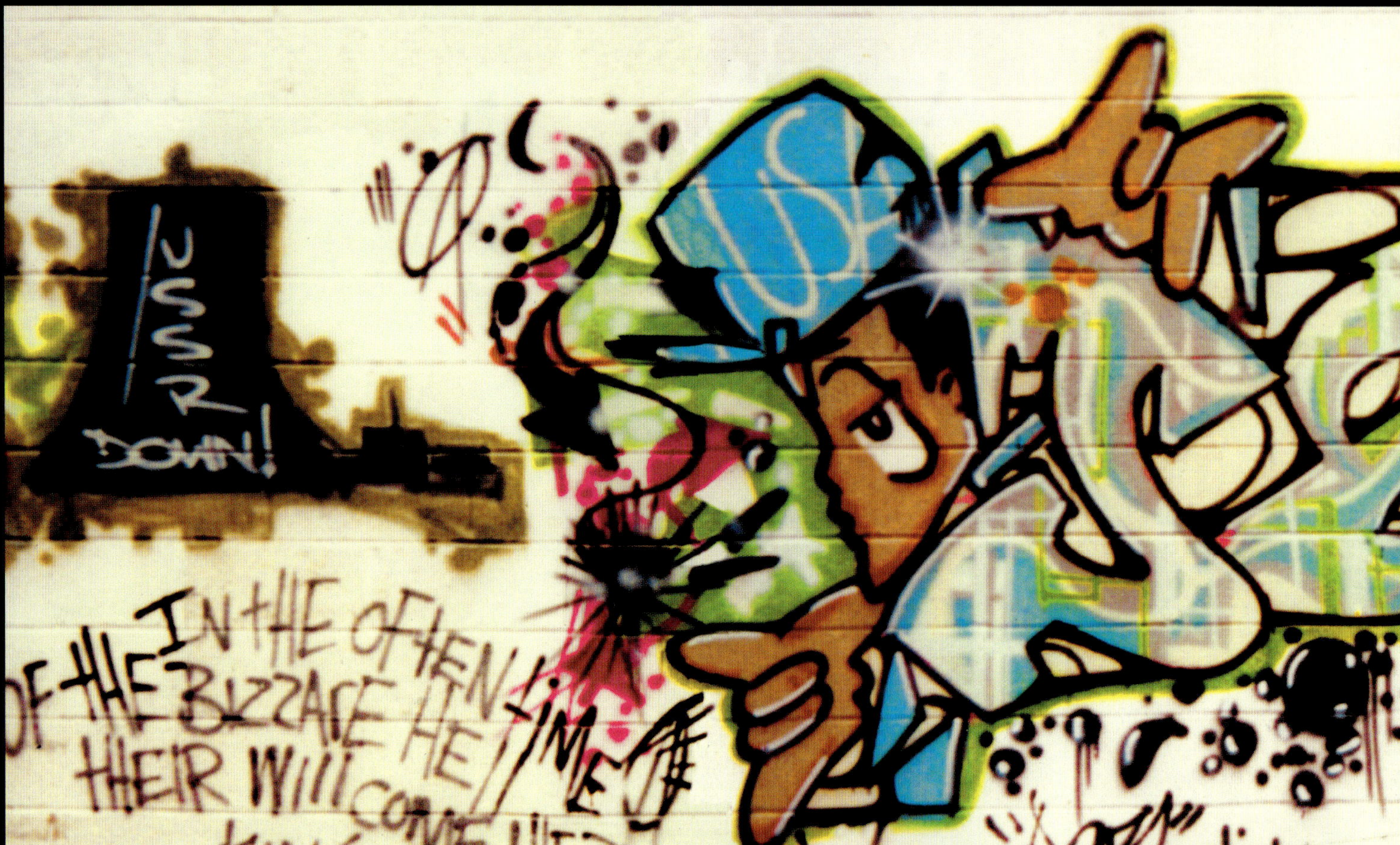

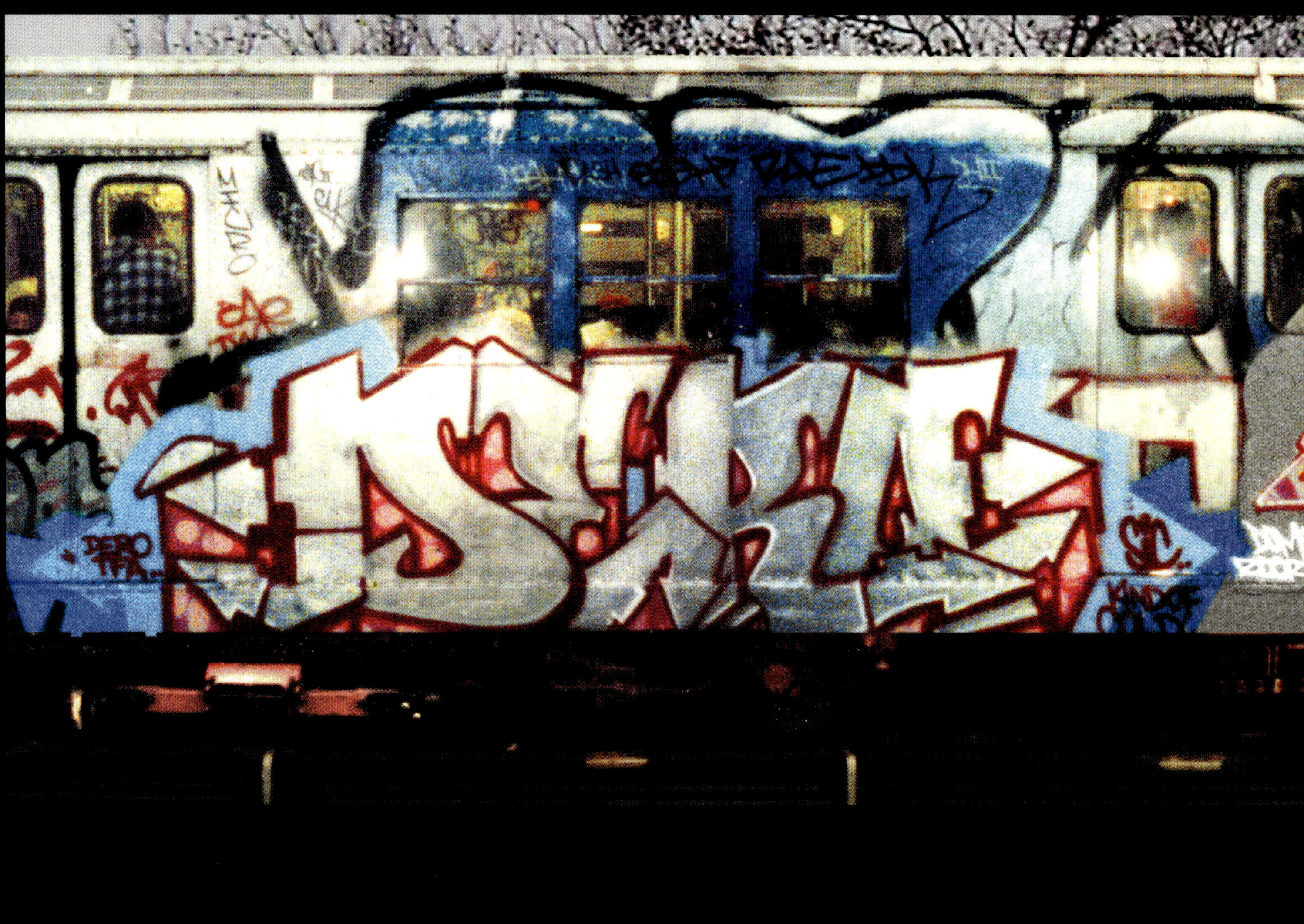

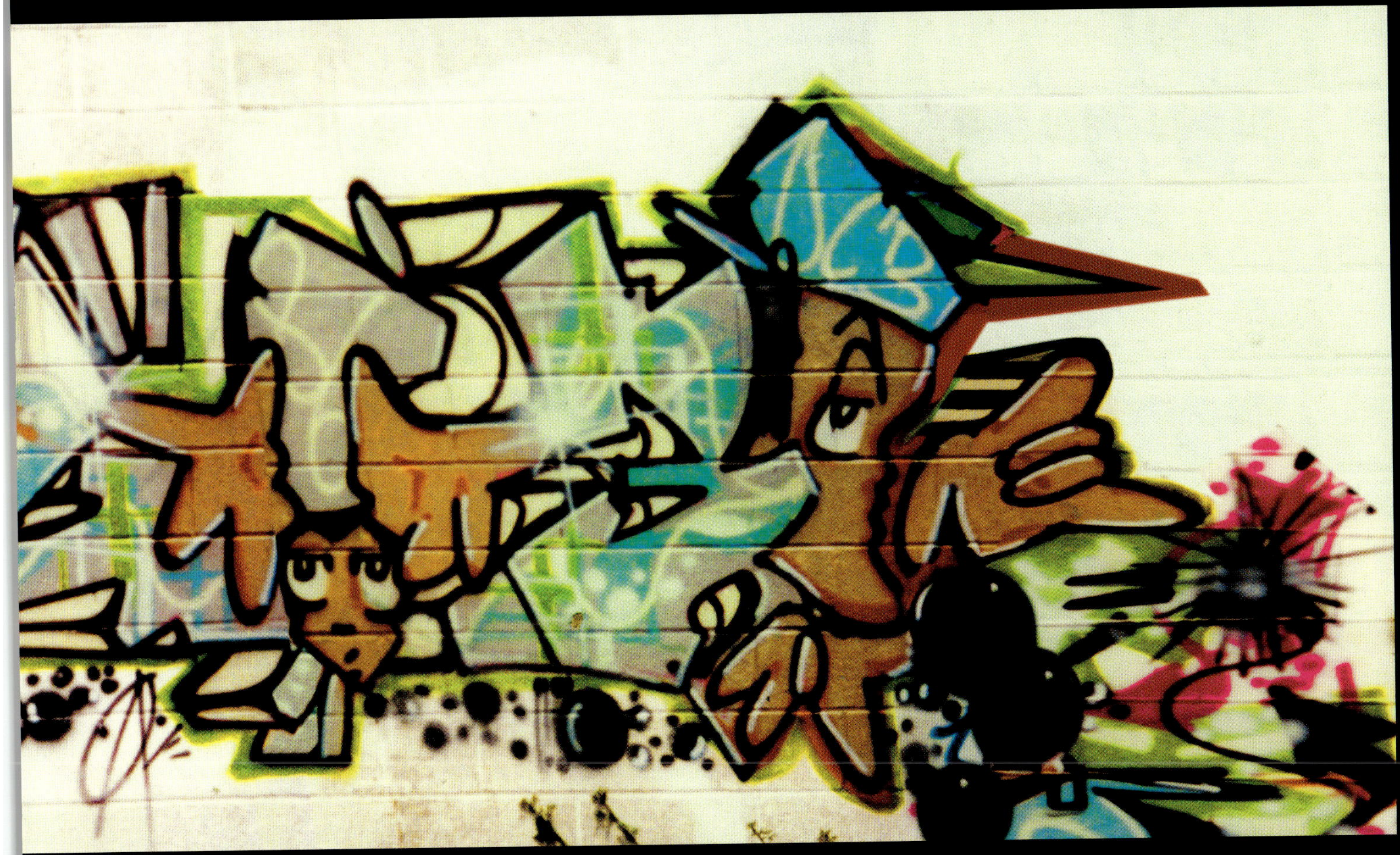

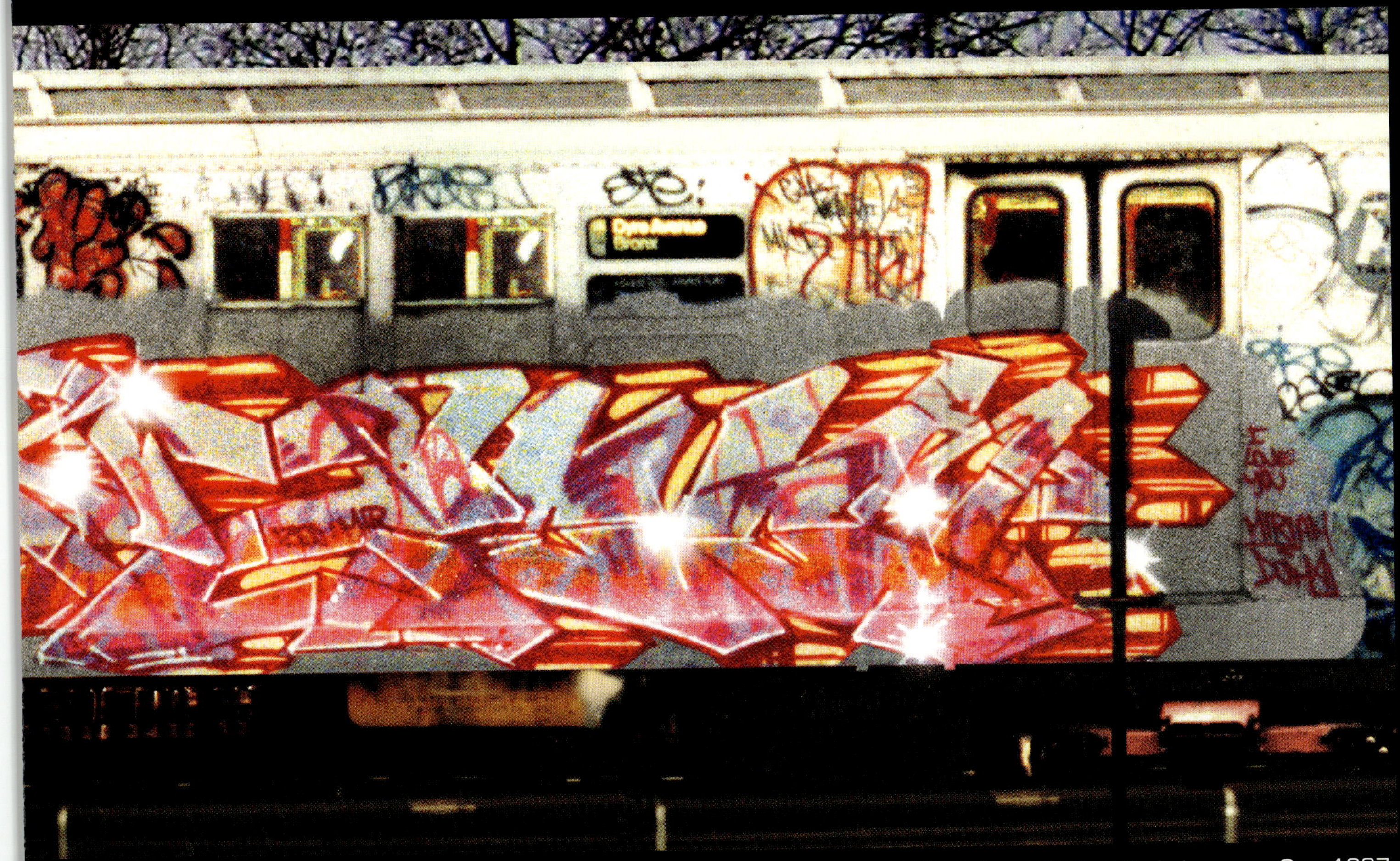

DERO TFA SIC, "KIND OF COLD," and ZOO, 5 Train burners, Oct. 1987.

SERT TCM, DC3 USA, and DOME, Jul. 1988.

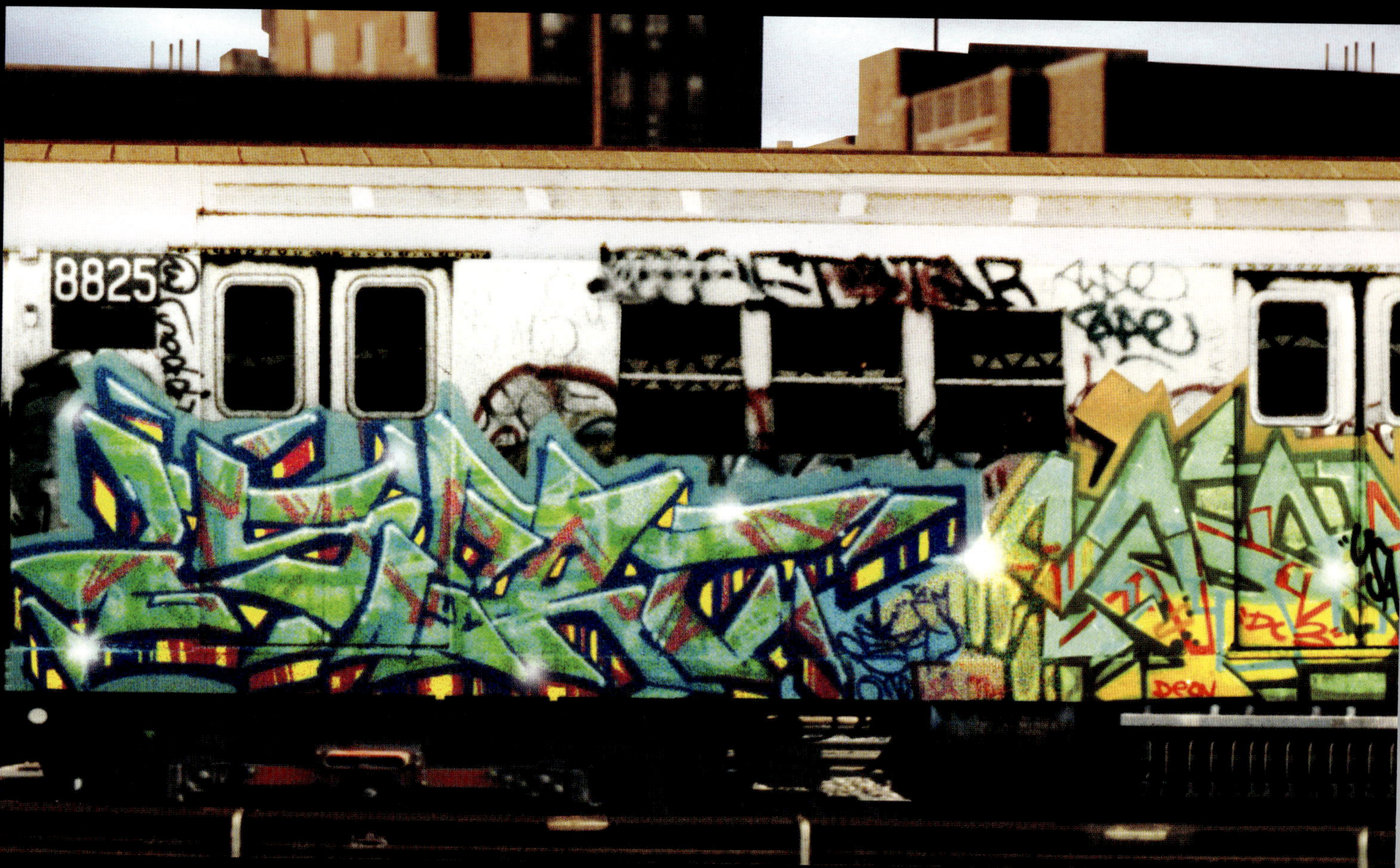

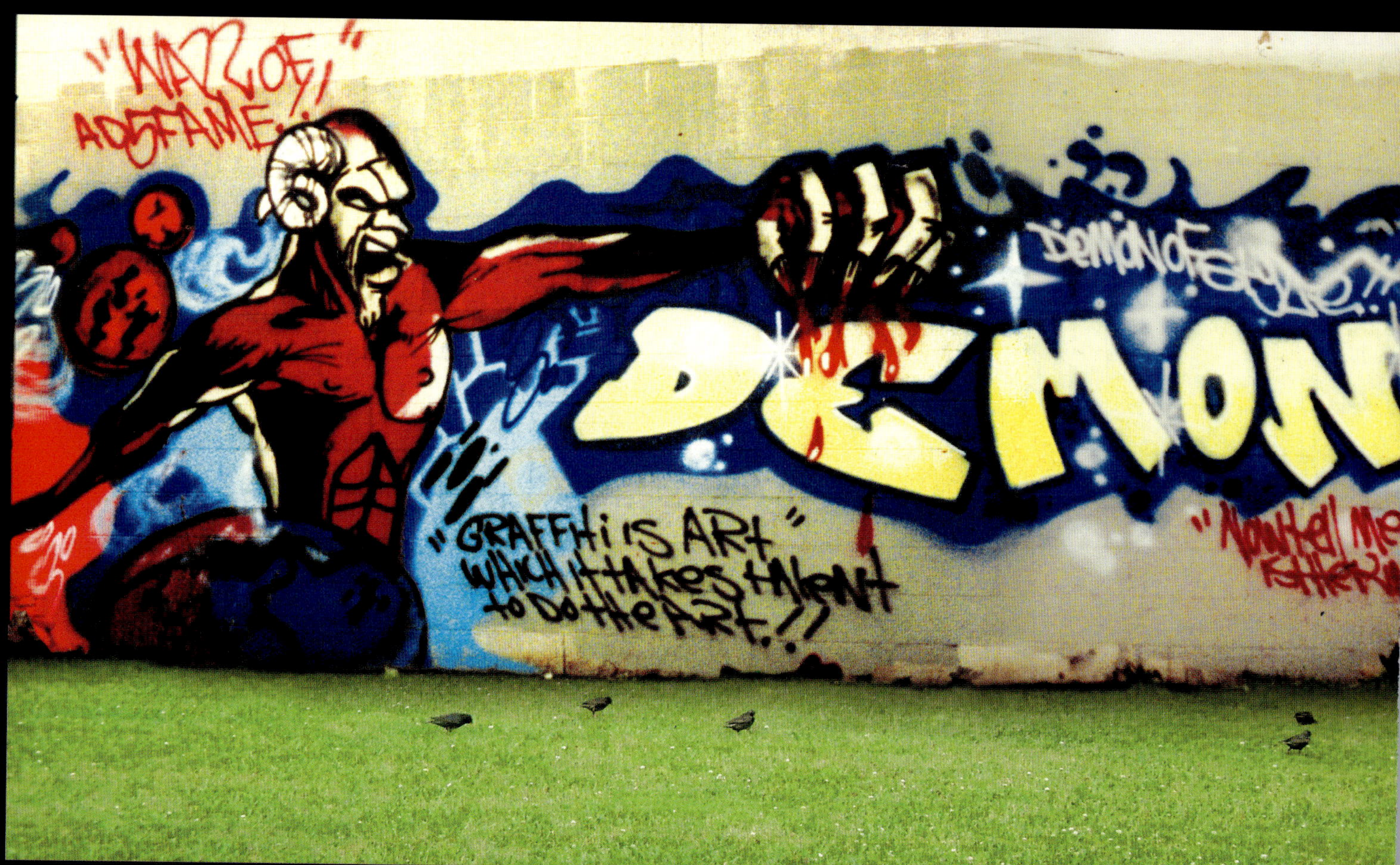

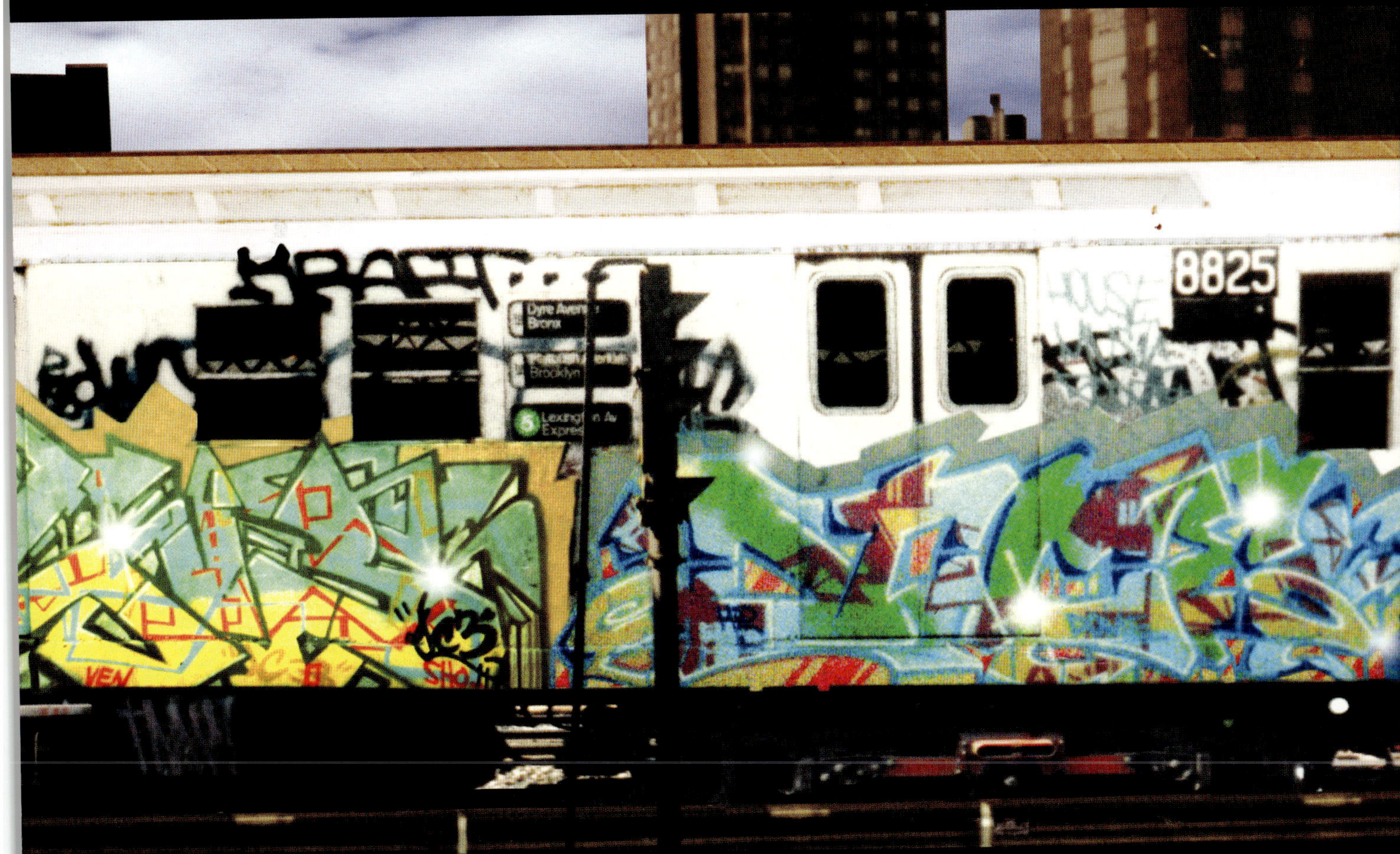

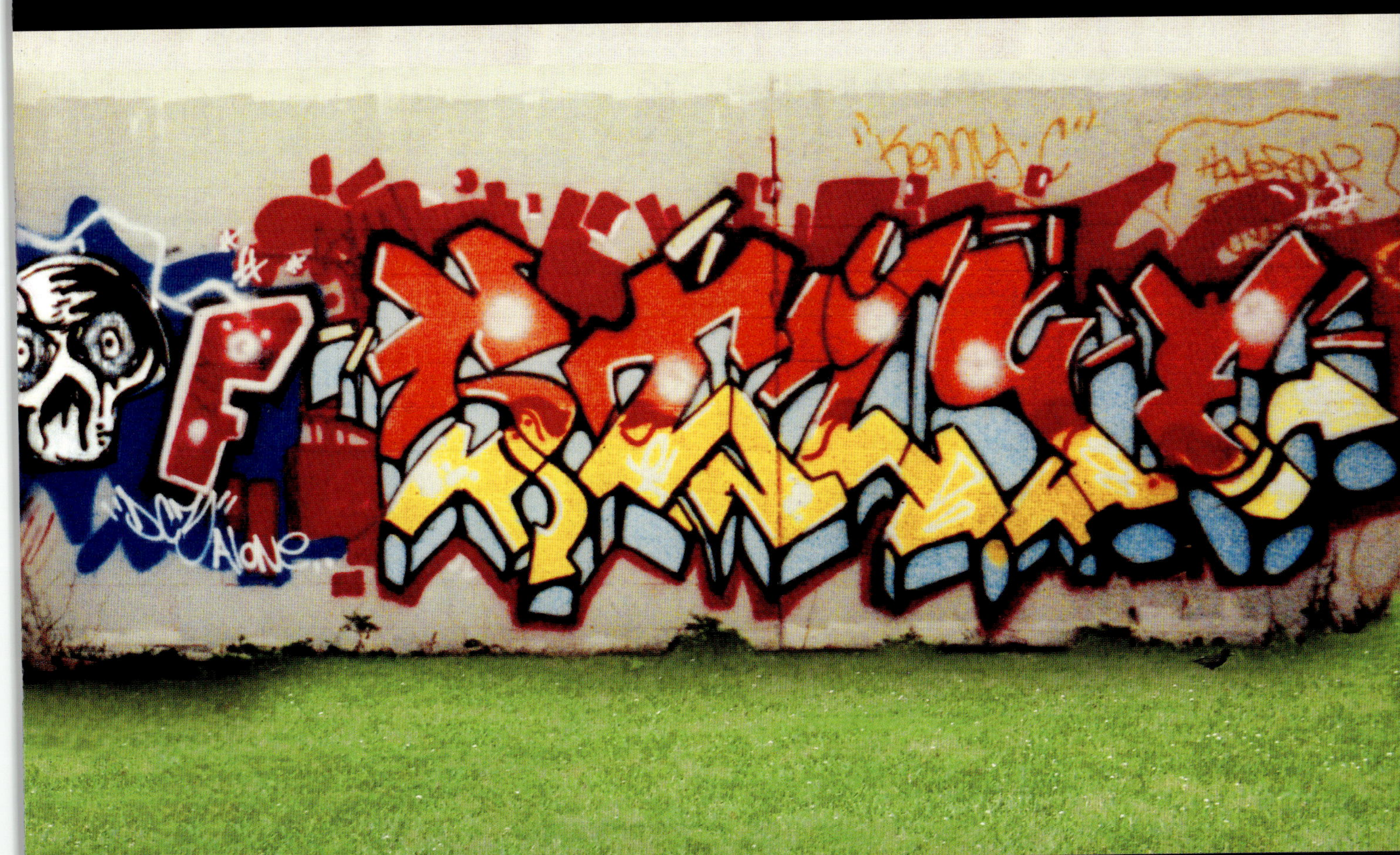

"DEMON OF STYLE," by DC3, "Wall Of AD5 Fame," North Freeport, LI, Mar. 1985.

DCEE3, "IN THE TIME OF FALLEN TOYS THERE IS A KING," mural at Liberty Park, Freeport, NY, May 1985.

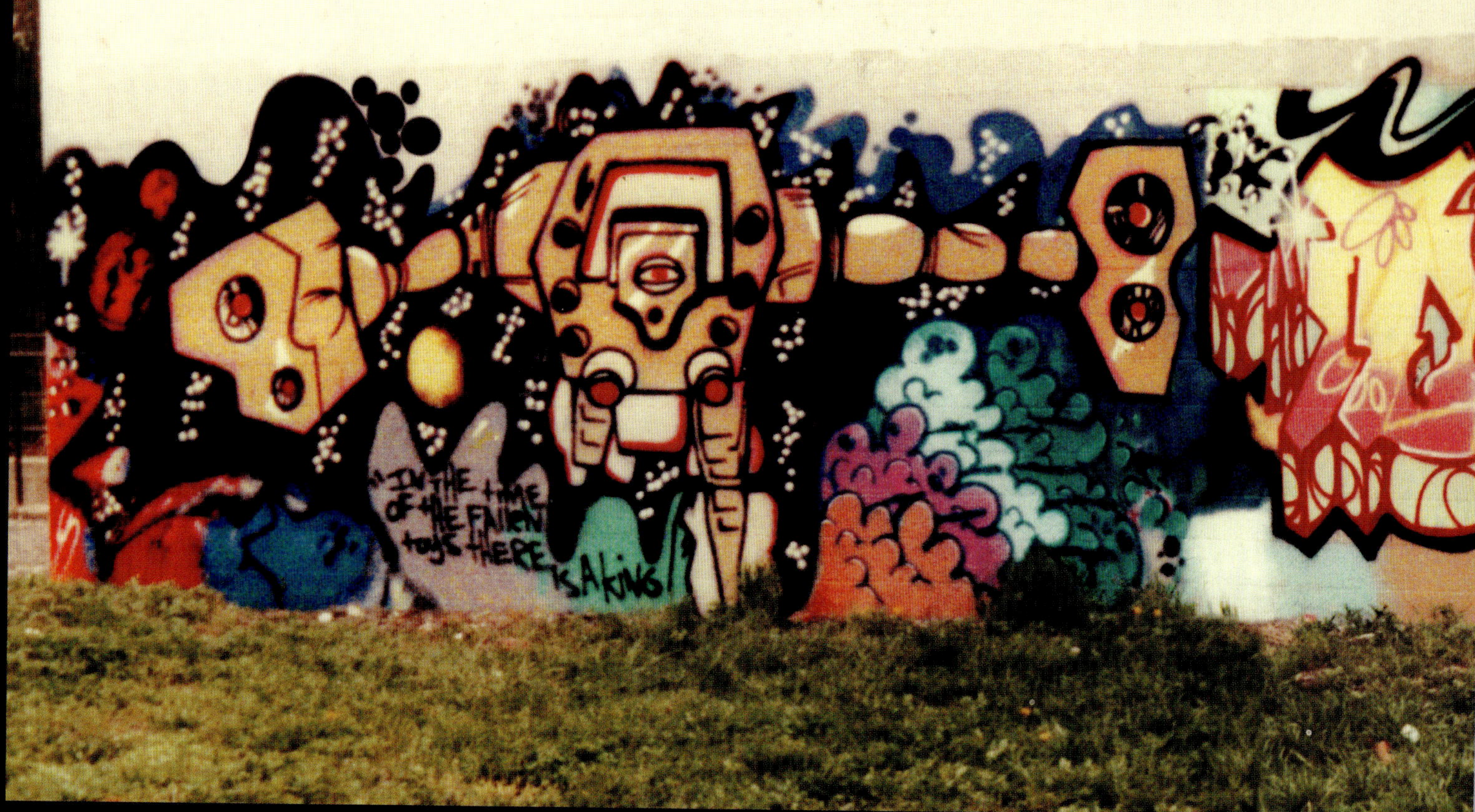

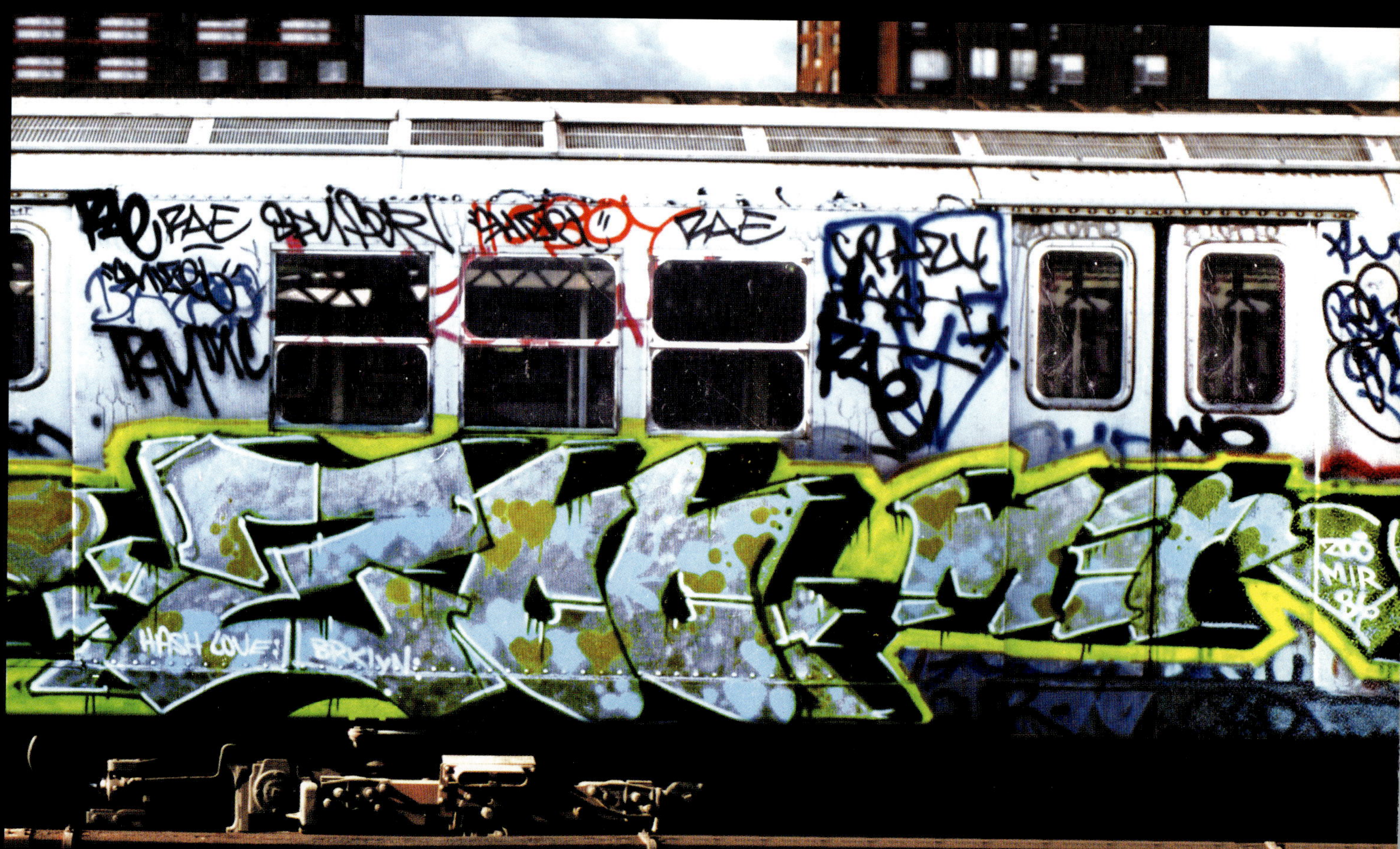

ZOO:MIR, 5 Train for HASH LOVE, Brooklyn, NY, Sep. 1986.

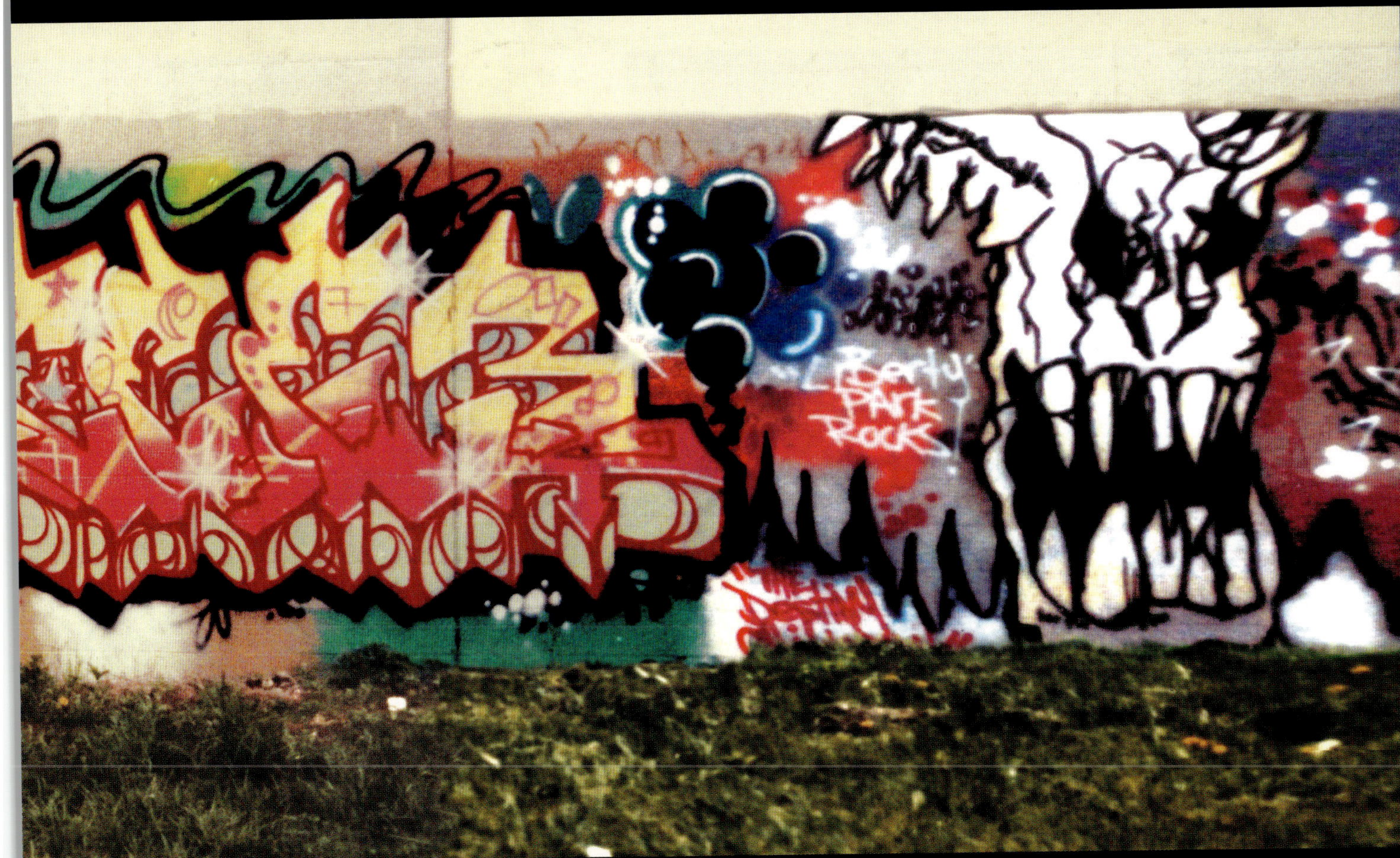

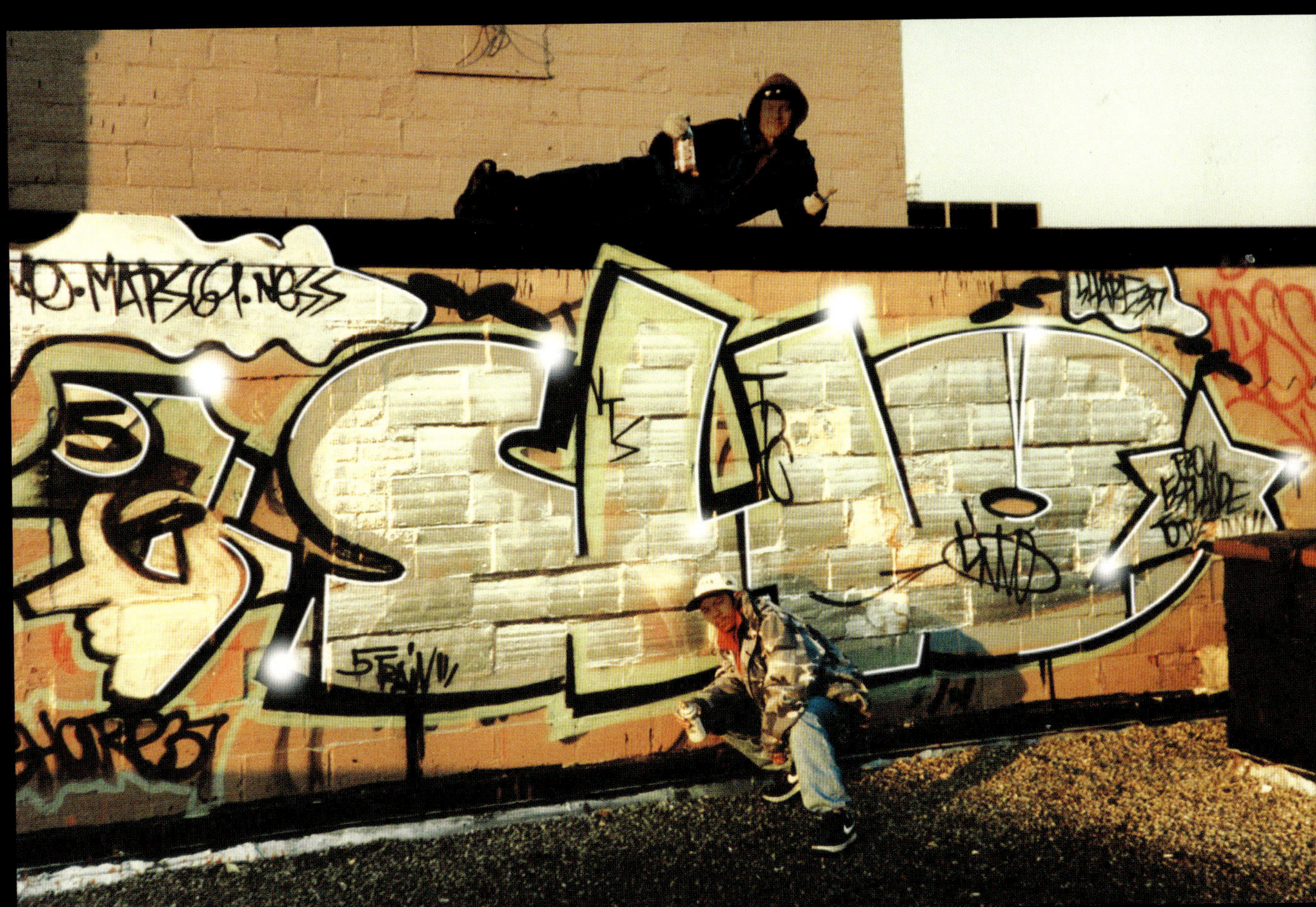

SHO on the Amsterdam Projects rooftop, Manhattan, NY, 1998.

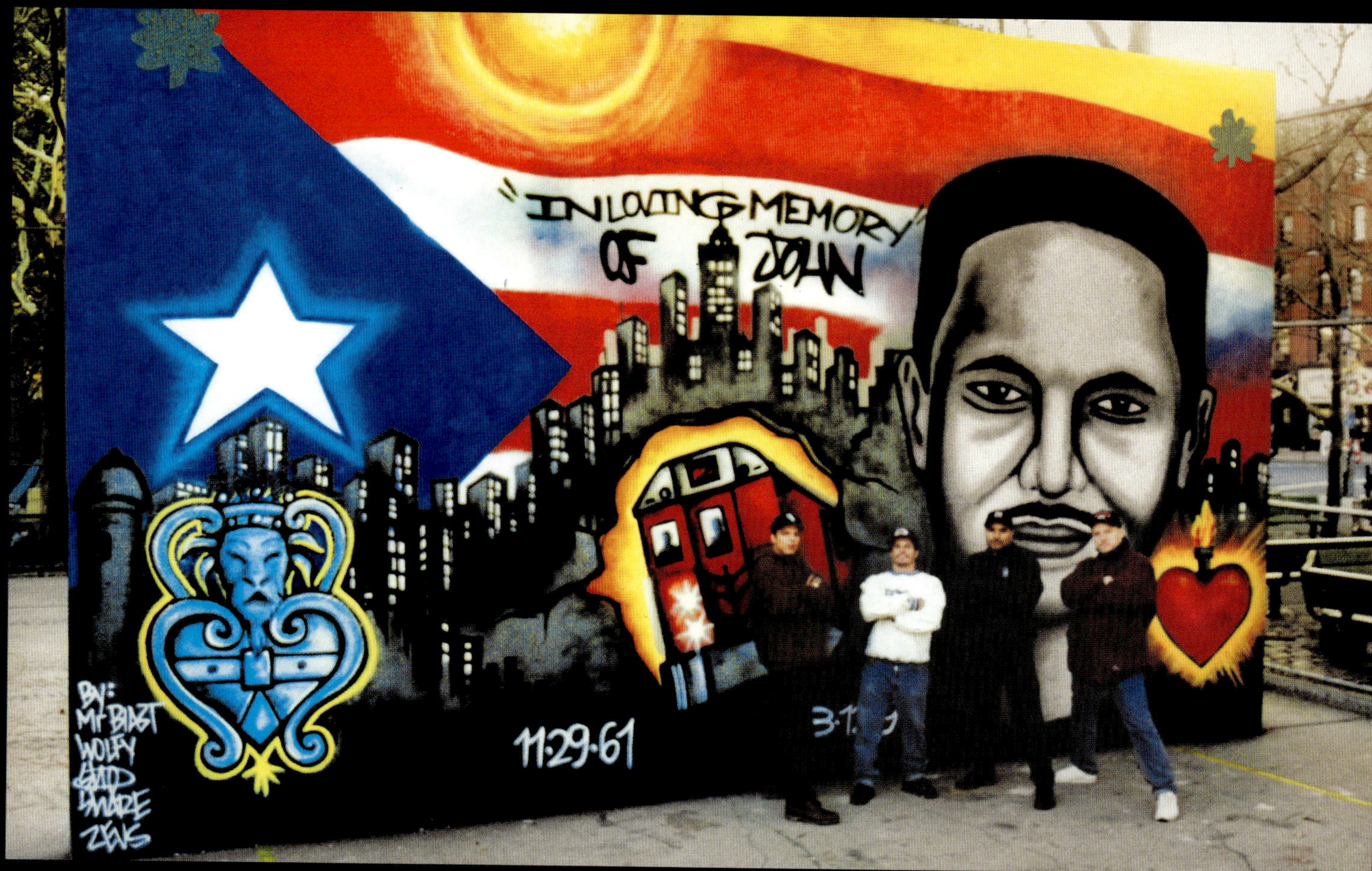

Rock Steady Park, Amsterdam Ave, Manhattan, NY.

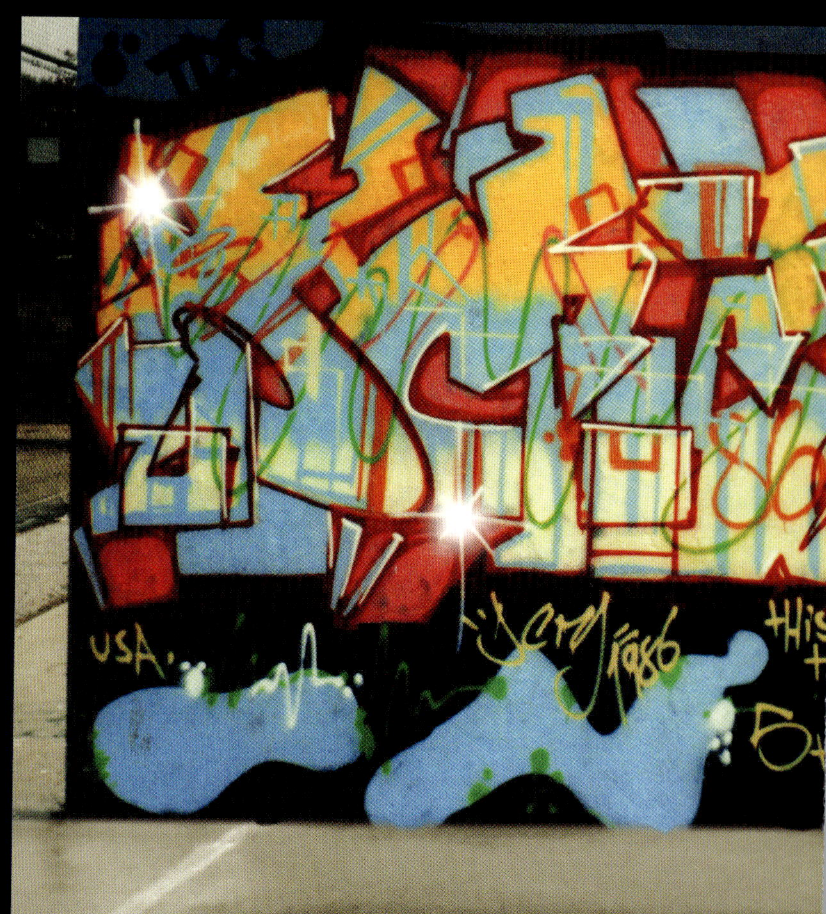

"THIS IS THE NEW STYLE"

"The Destiny Children" August 12, 1986, DC3 and SHO at North West Park.

This TDC production was done very early on, at the end of summer of 1986 in Freeport. Zoo had hit the 5 Train first with Kent and Bash from Bronx City Writers, BCR. I first got introduced to Zoo in this very park and he had brought flicks of a train he and DC3 had just rocked, as well as another previous burner on the subway. At this point I had yet to hit the trains but was dying to regardless of the risks involved. Some people smoked crack, but rocking burners was an addiction that, unless you were down, you wouldn't understand. I hit the 5s later that weekend.

-SHO TDCUSA

IN MEMORY OF JOHNNY. 11.29.1961 - 8.12.1990

I was living on 101st Street in Morningside Heights and I was walking by Rock Steady Park and seen a production in progress being led by Bill Blast and Wolfy. So I introduced myself and asked if they needed help. Bill had heard of me and said, "Yeah, no doubt." Wolfy and John are twin brothers and looked very much alike. The day he died was an awful, tragic day that should not even have happened. John was mistaken for being his brother by some people that had beef with Wolfy on the basketball courts. There were many people in the park at the time of the fatal encounter. Shit popped off and a fight ensued between John and an unknown assailant. Unfortunately, people don't fight fair in the streets and this individual struck him in the temple with brass knuckles. Wolfy heard of the incident and rushed to the park to defend his brother. Tragically there wasn't anything he could do to help him and his brother Johnny died in his arms. Life can really suck, but you have to be strong.

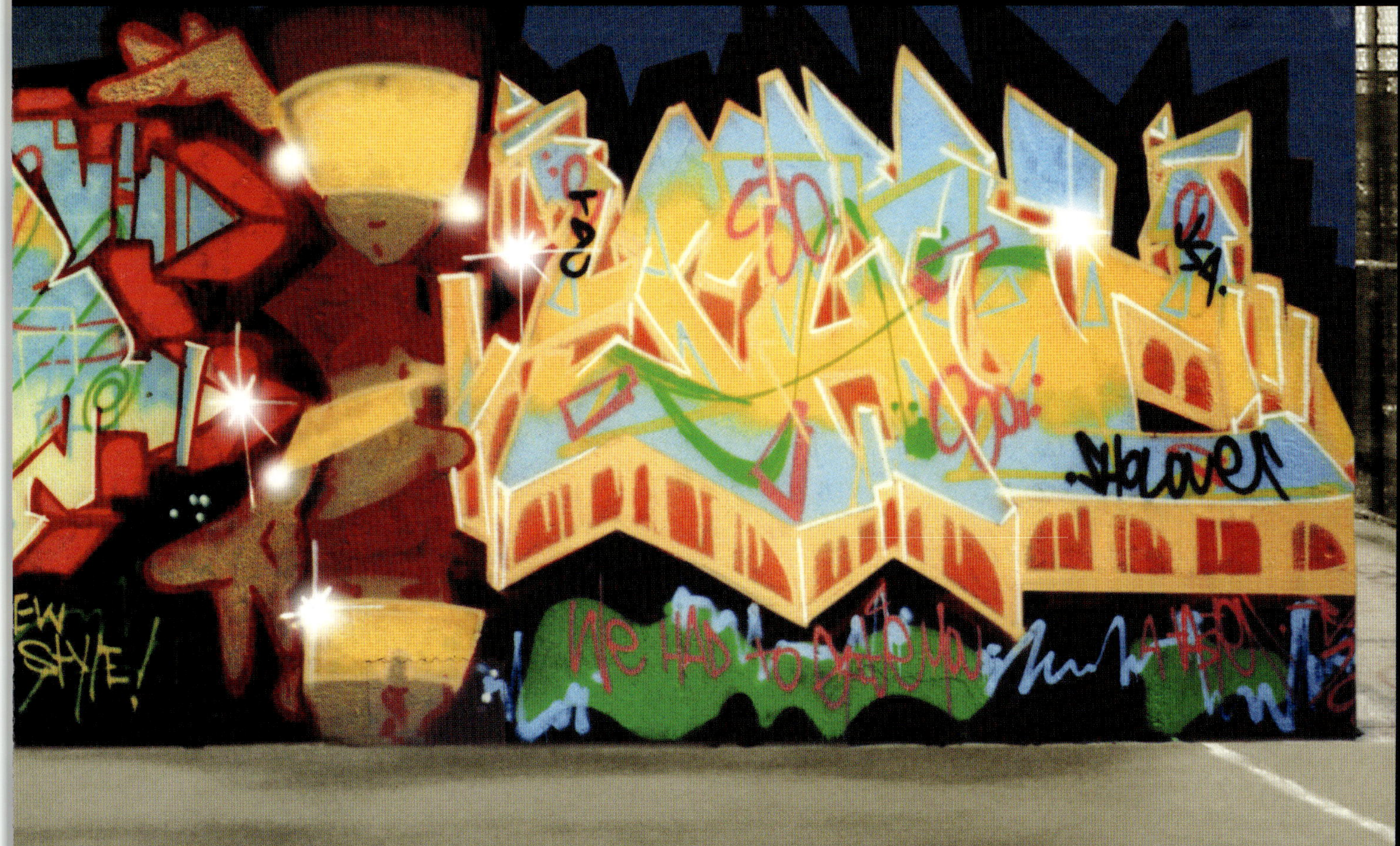

DC3 and SHO, "WE HAD TO GIVE YOU A TASTE," Freeport, NY, Aug. 12, 1986.

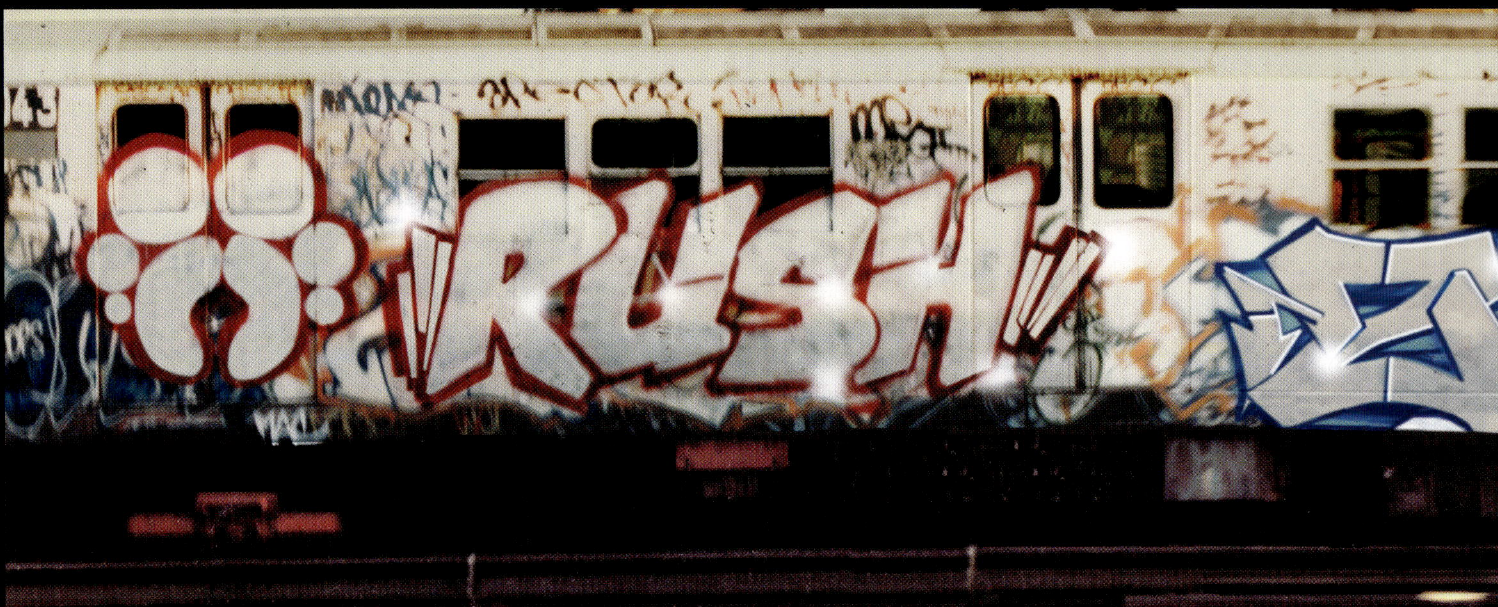

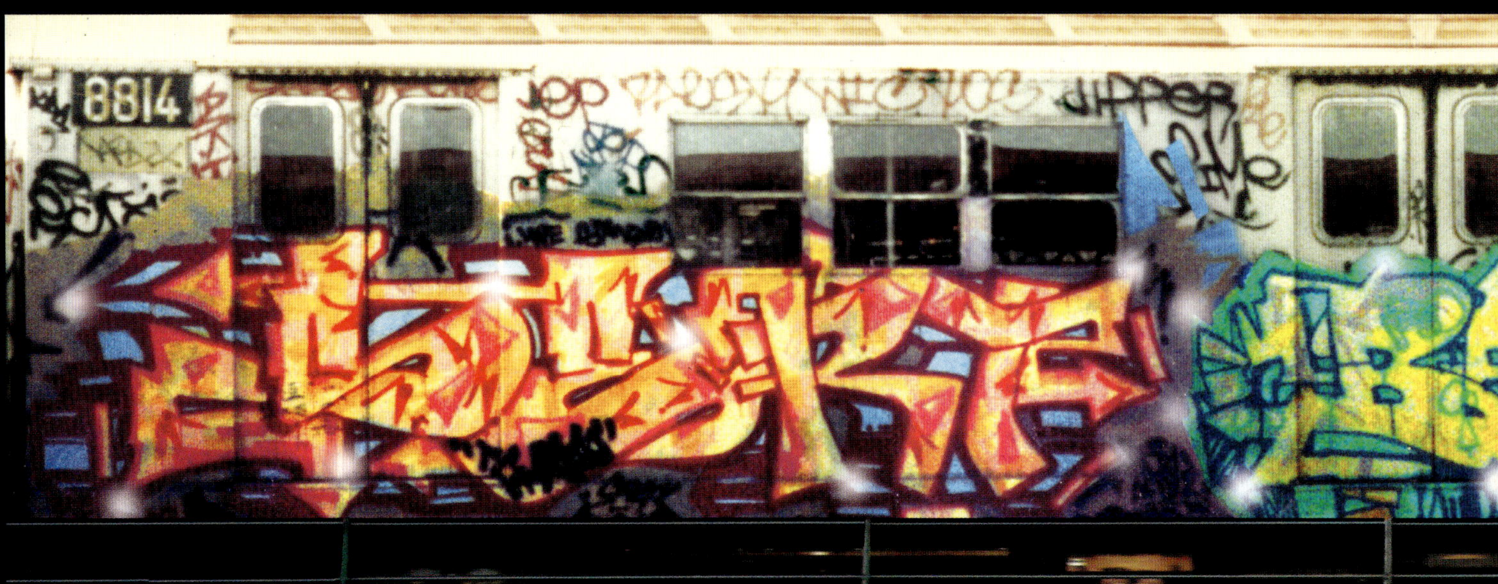

SERT TCM, BEAV, by BEAVER One, "NON STOP ACTION," and DC3, Sep. 1988.

TDC got introduced to TCM, The Crazy Mob, by DC3 early on in the winter of 1987. TCM was mainly Bronx writers Fent, Sune, Such, Deon, and Karl, the Prez, who also wrote Sert.

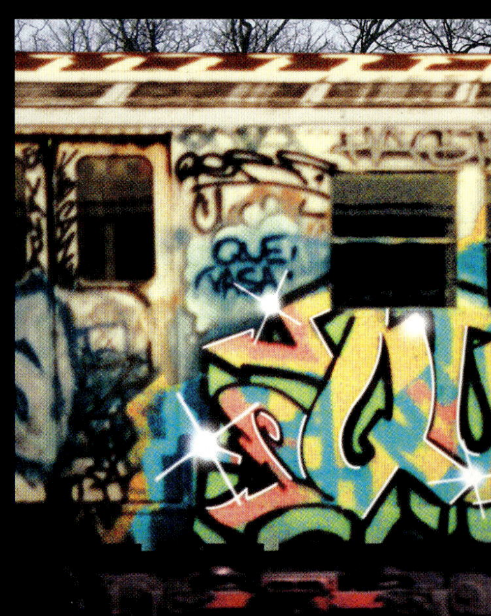

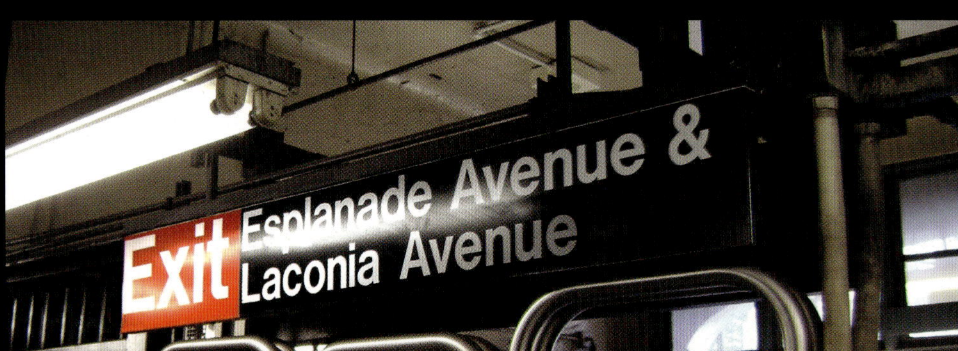

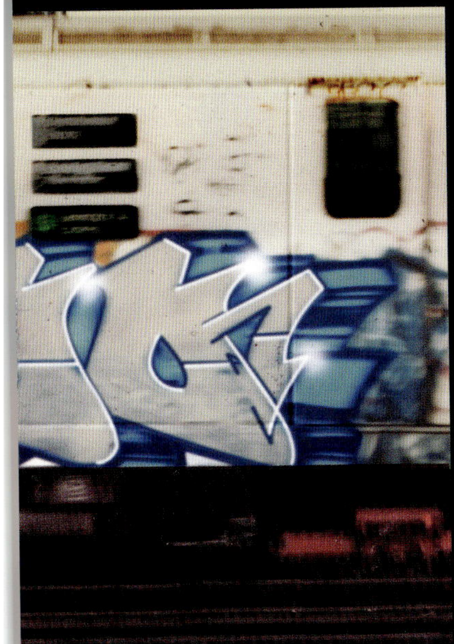

Mirage, Rush, and Zoo went out on a freezing cold night bombing Esplanade. This was one of those nights that was just about getting in and out while doing some damage. Anytime you could rock pieces when the work bums was real active was a good night. Rush was Mirage's boy from Queens and pushed up TMR and KDM. He drove the mission this trip and had come thru to Hempstead to pickup ZOOROC to paint. I didn't make it this trip but did hang out with Rush a couple of times, he was pretty crazy.

MIRAGE FEET, RUSH, and ZOO, Dec. 1987.

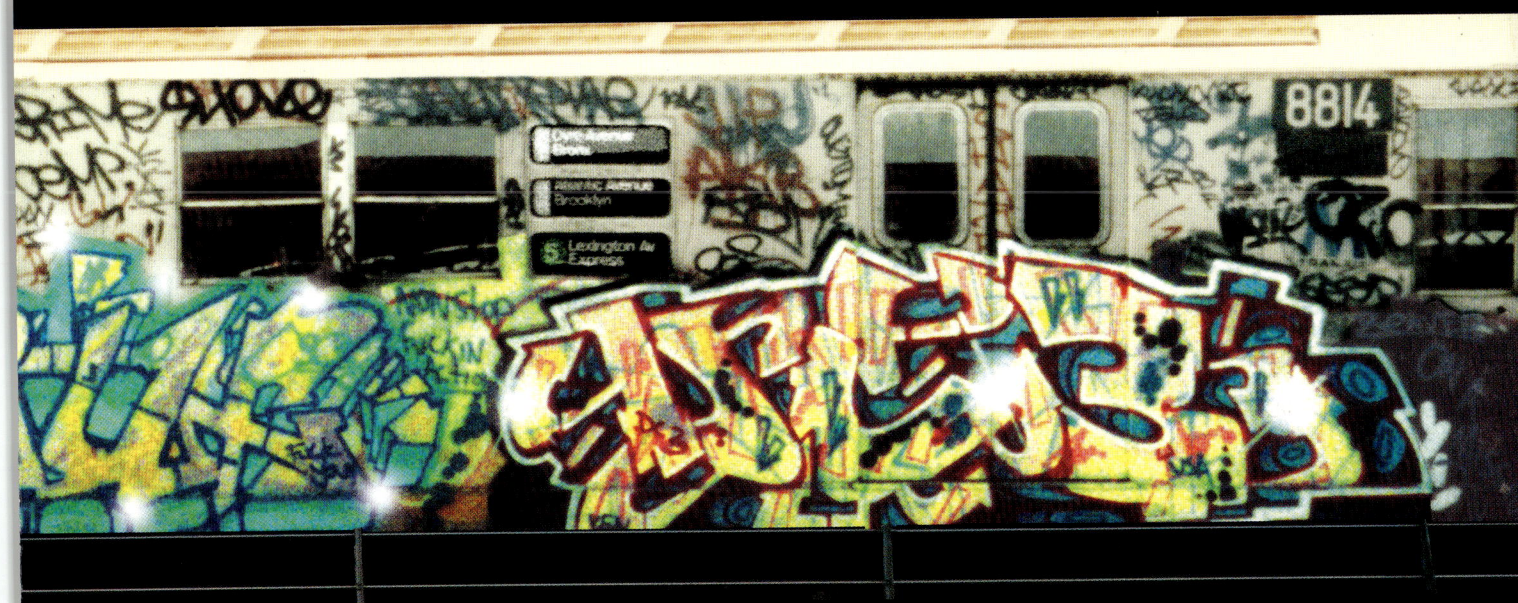

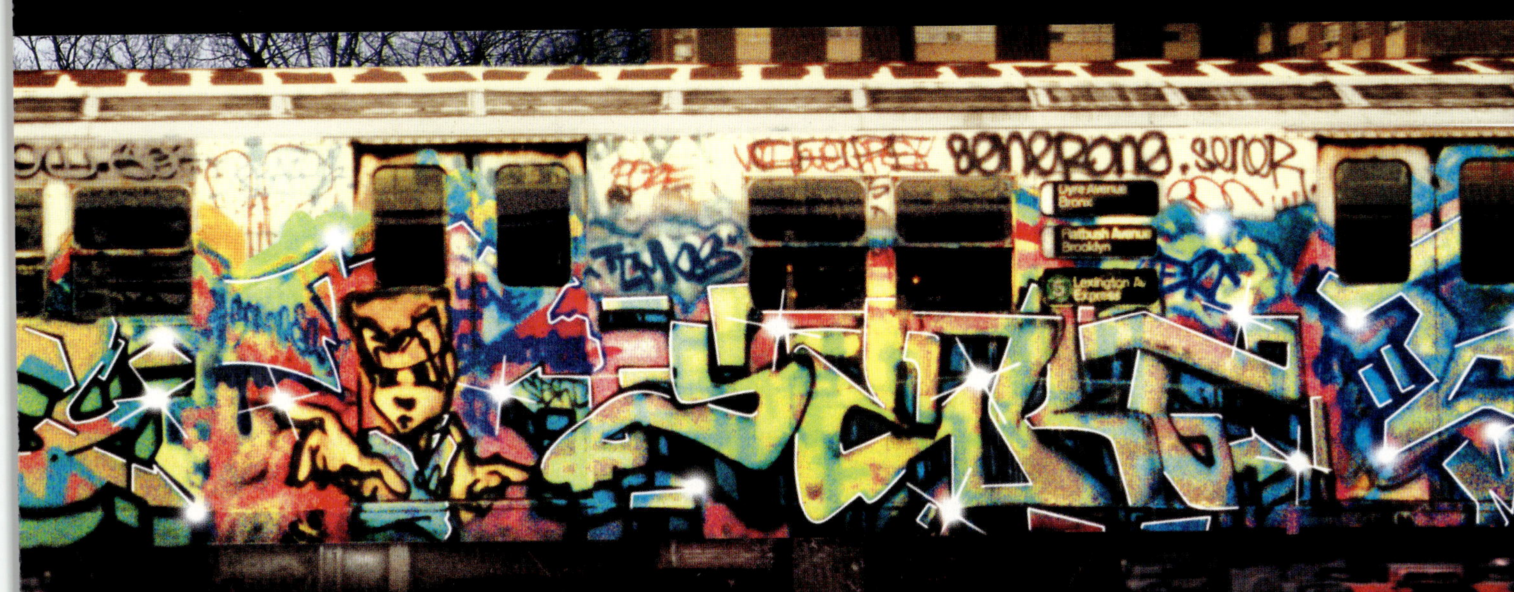

QUE PASA SERT, "THE CRAZY MOB," Dec. 1988.

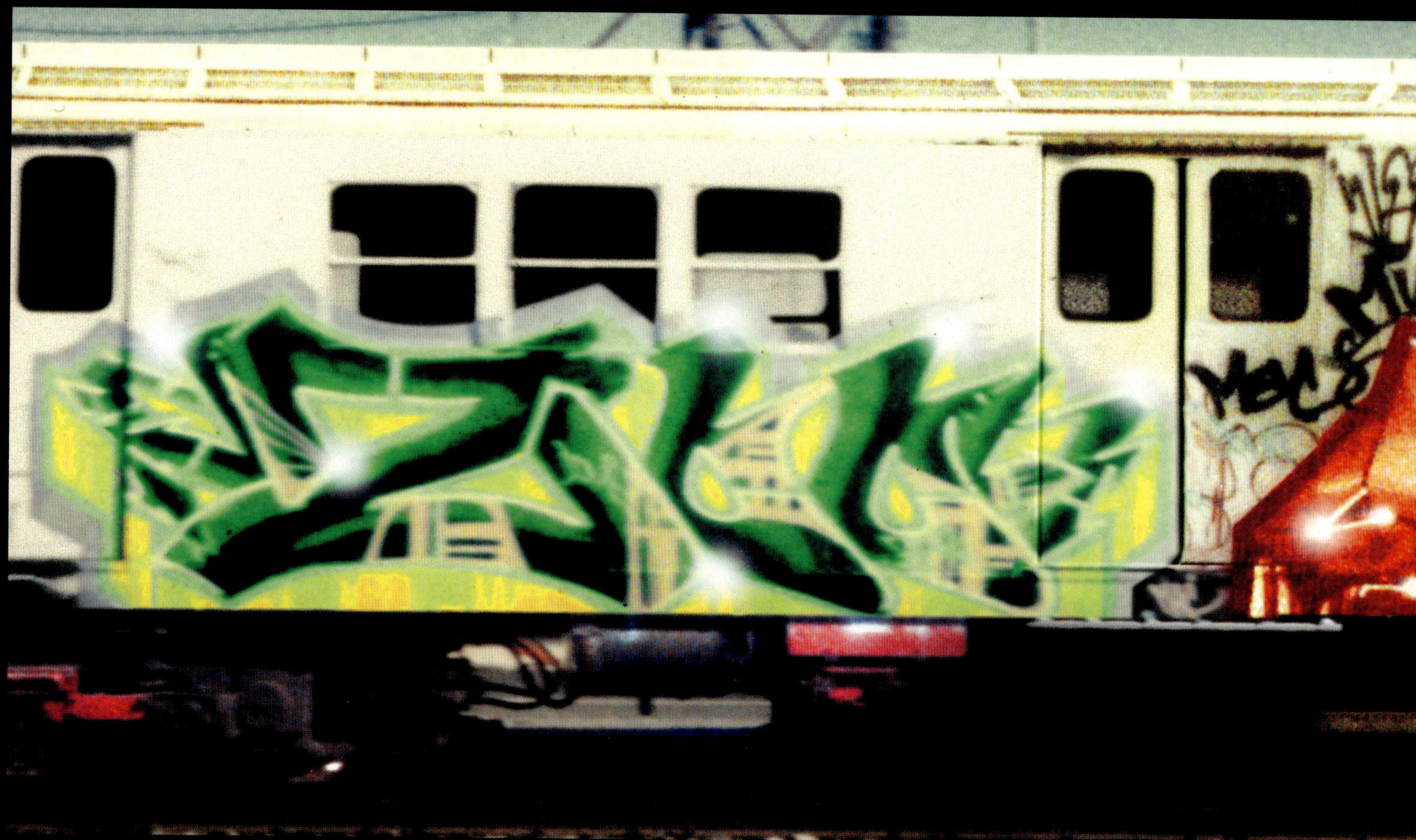

ZOO and MIRAGE, by MAC CWK, "LOVE STINKS," 6 Train, Sep. 1987.

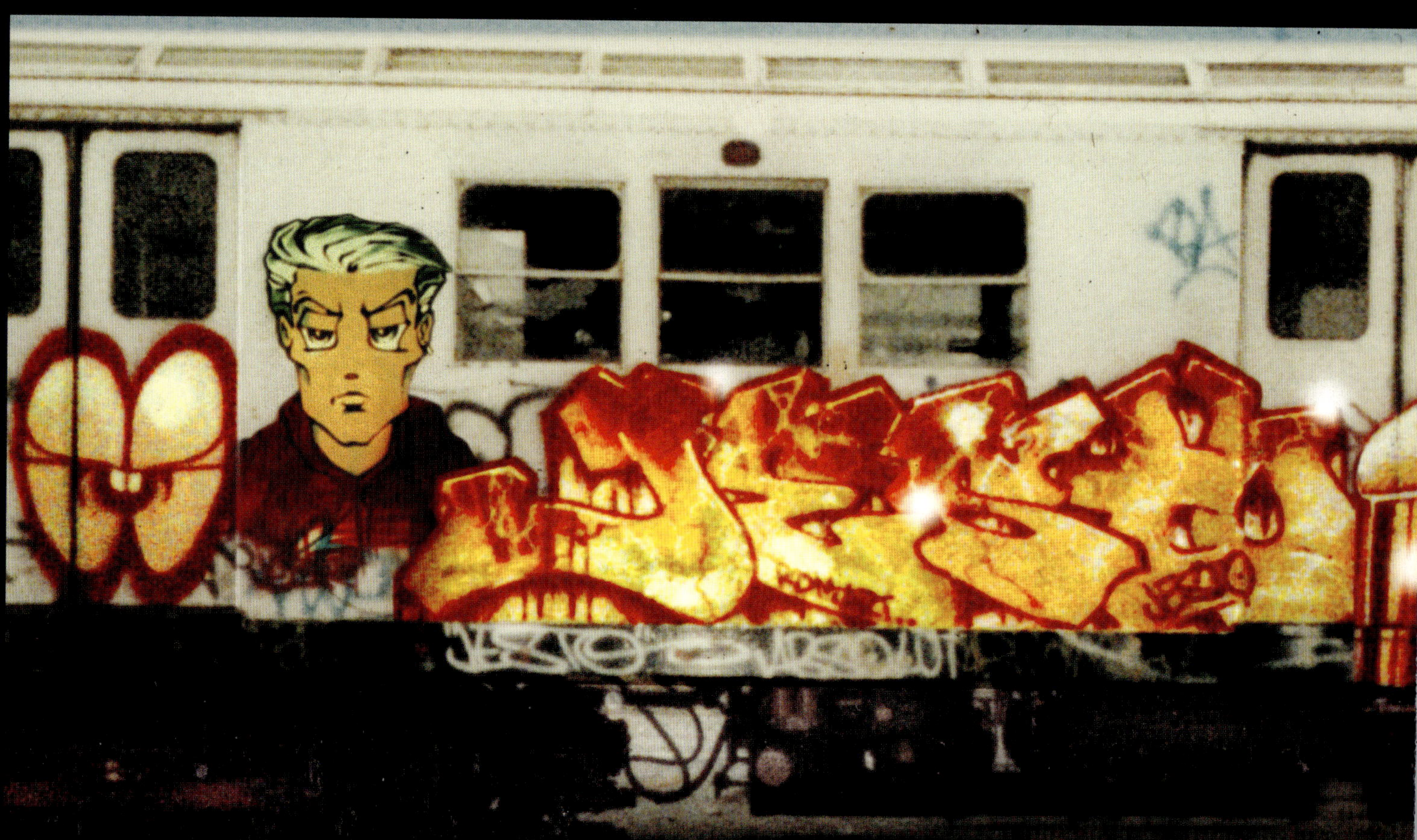

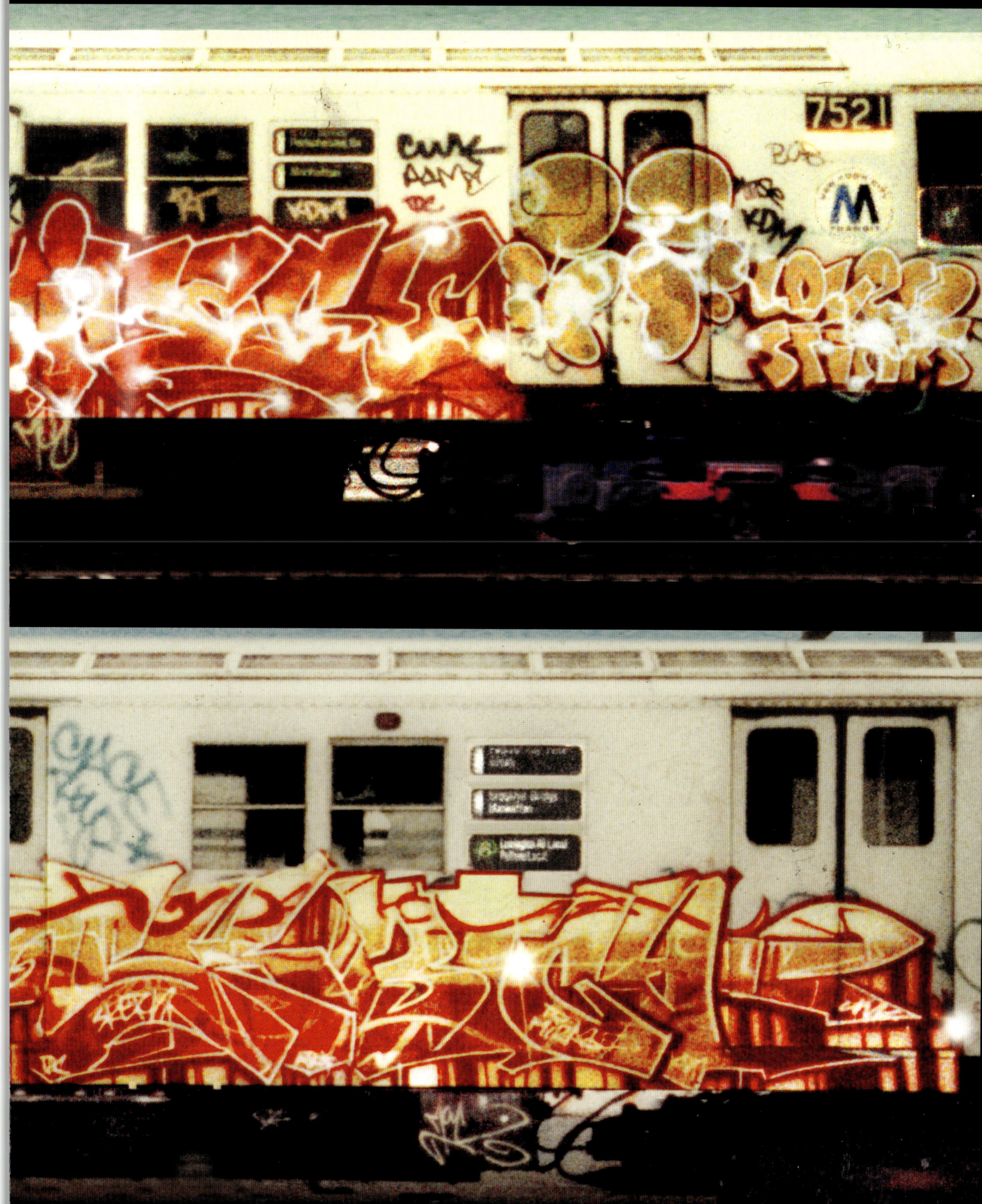

JESTO KDM and SKETCH CWK KDM, 6 Train, Sep. 1987.

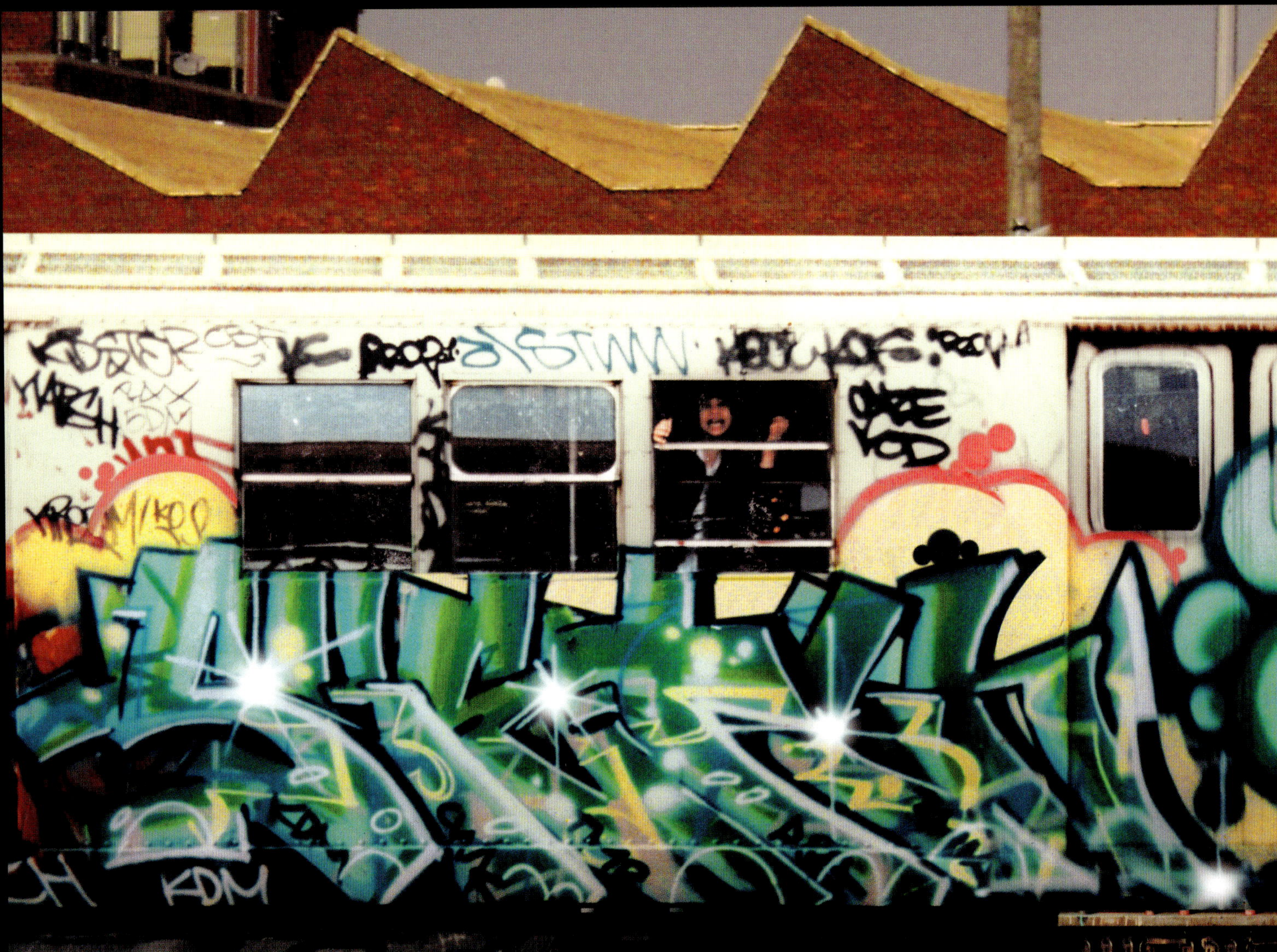

SKETCH, "CRAFTWORK KINGS," and MIRAGE, "KINGDOM," TMR SBK for Michelle, Nov. 1988.

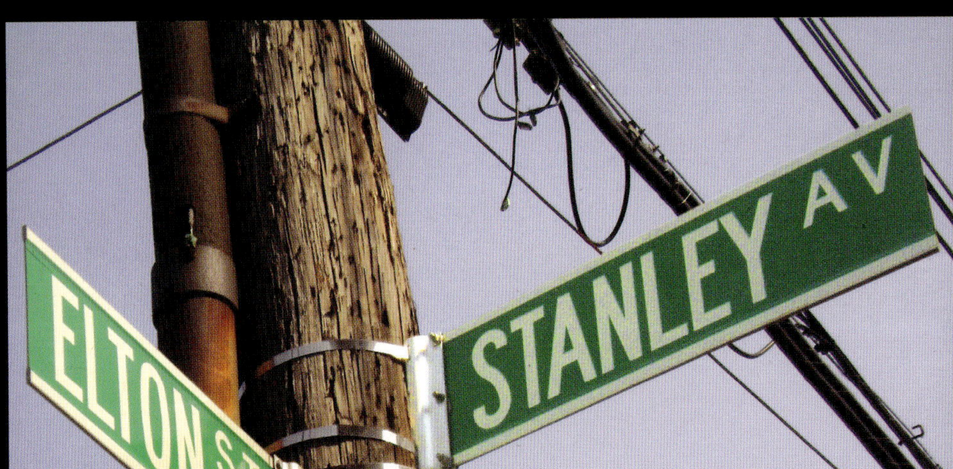

NEW LOTS, BK, NY.

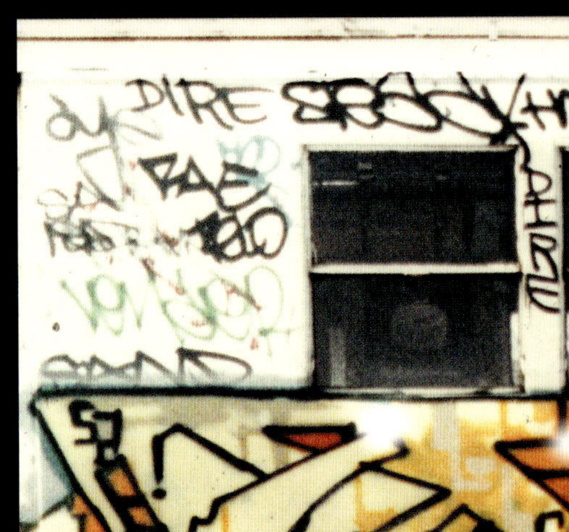

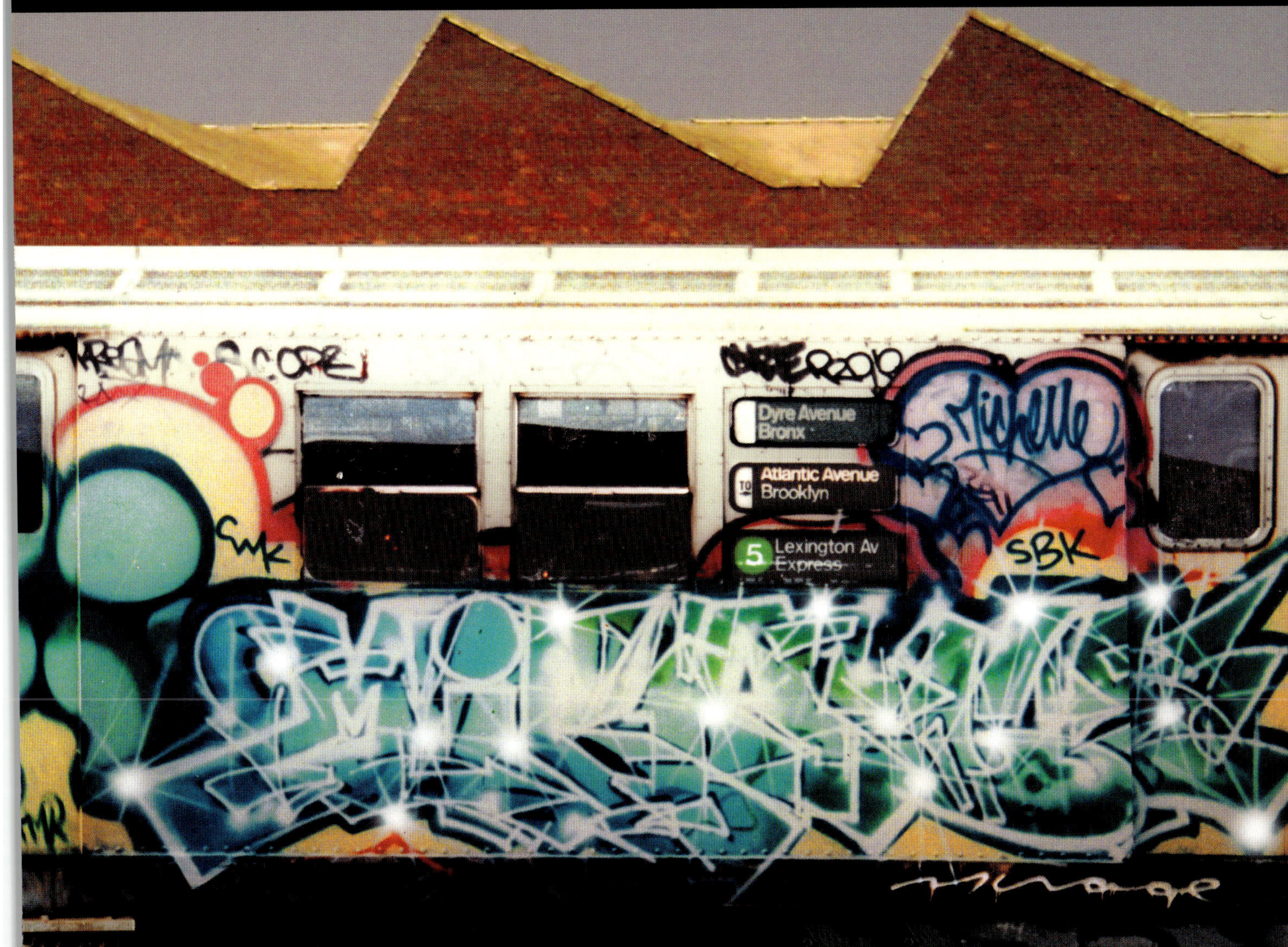

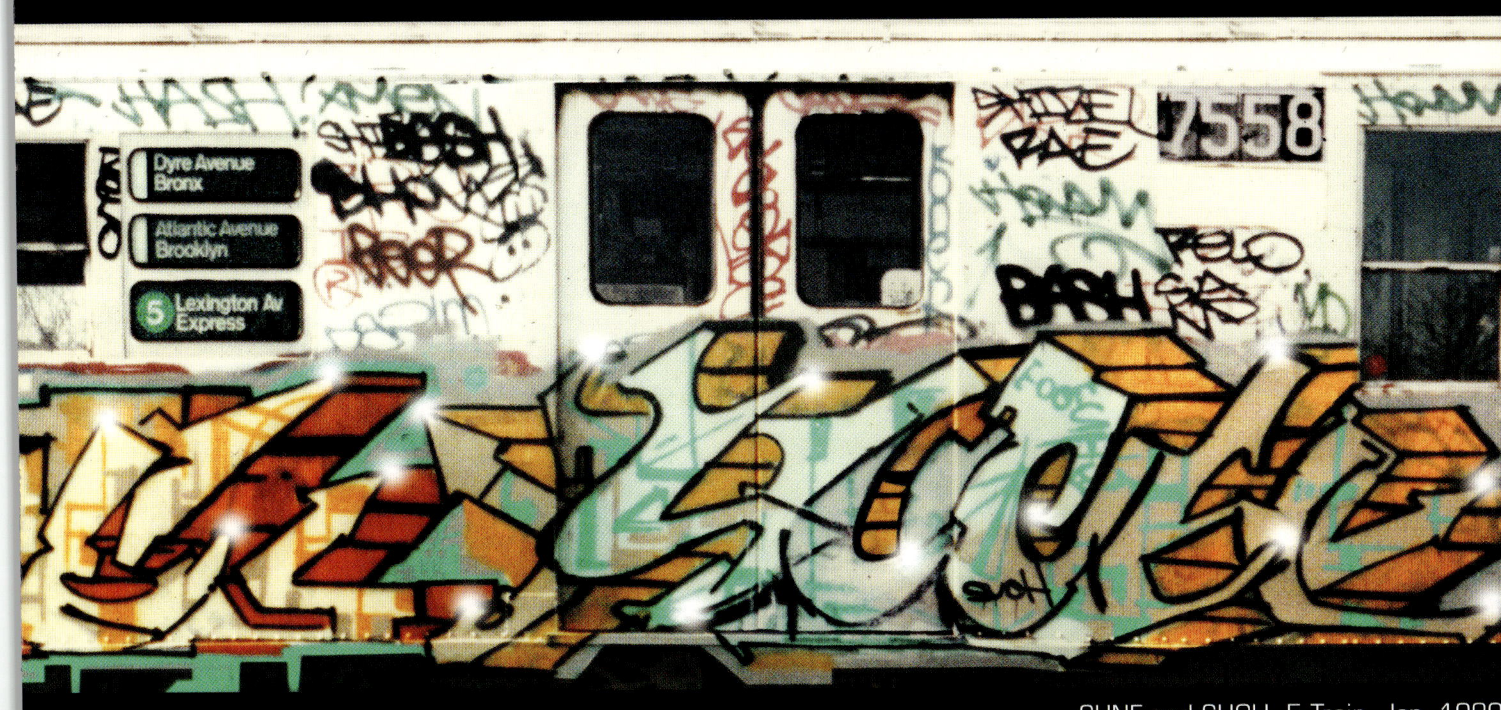

SUNE and SUCH, 5 Train, Jan. 1989.

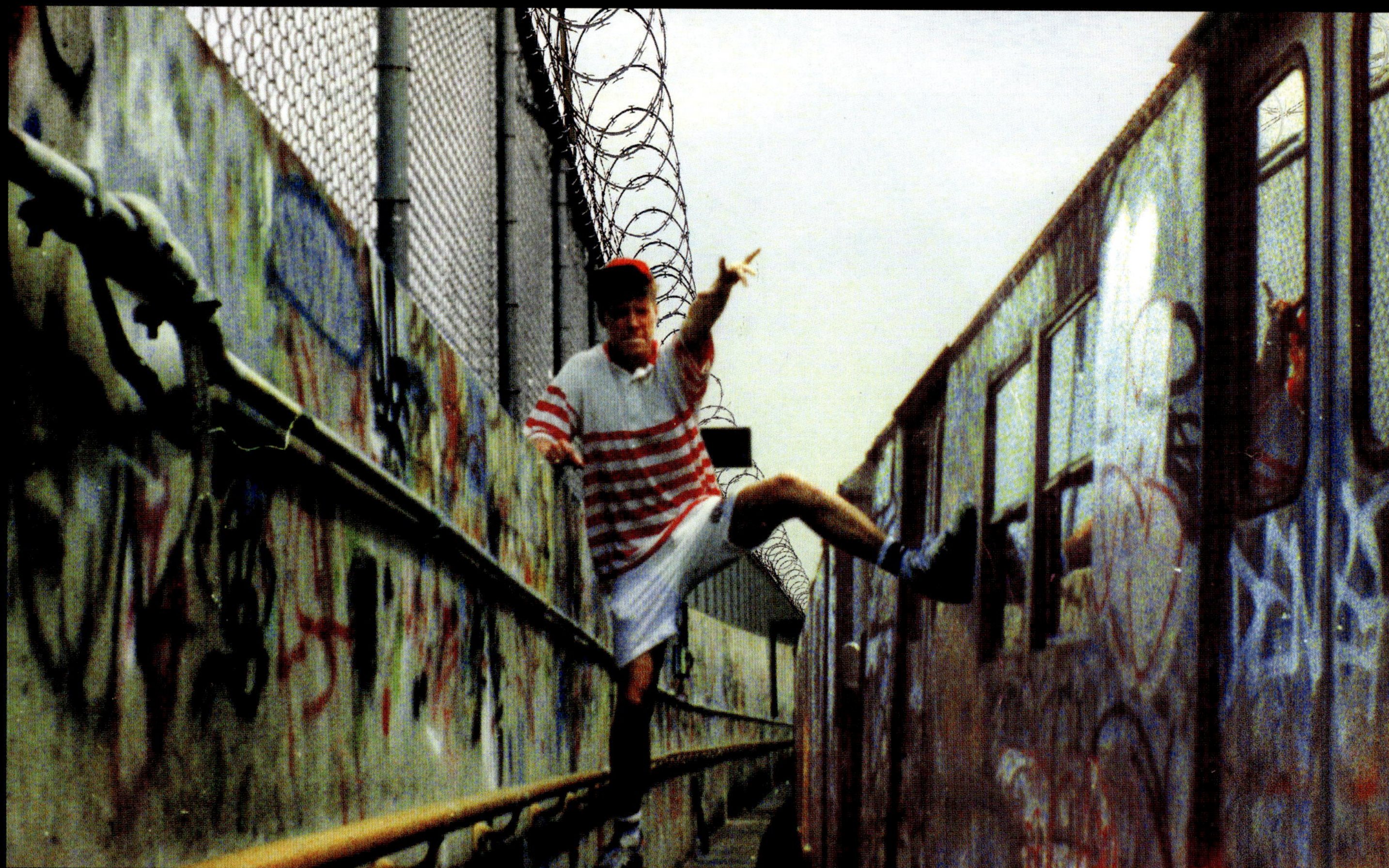

SHO bombing the J Train in broad daylight.

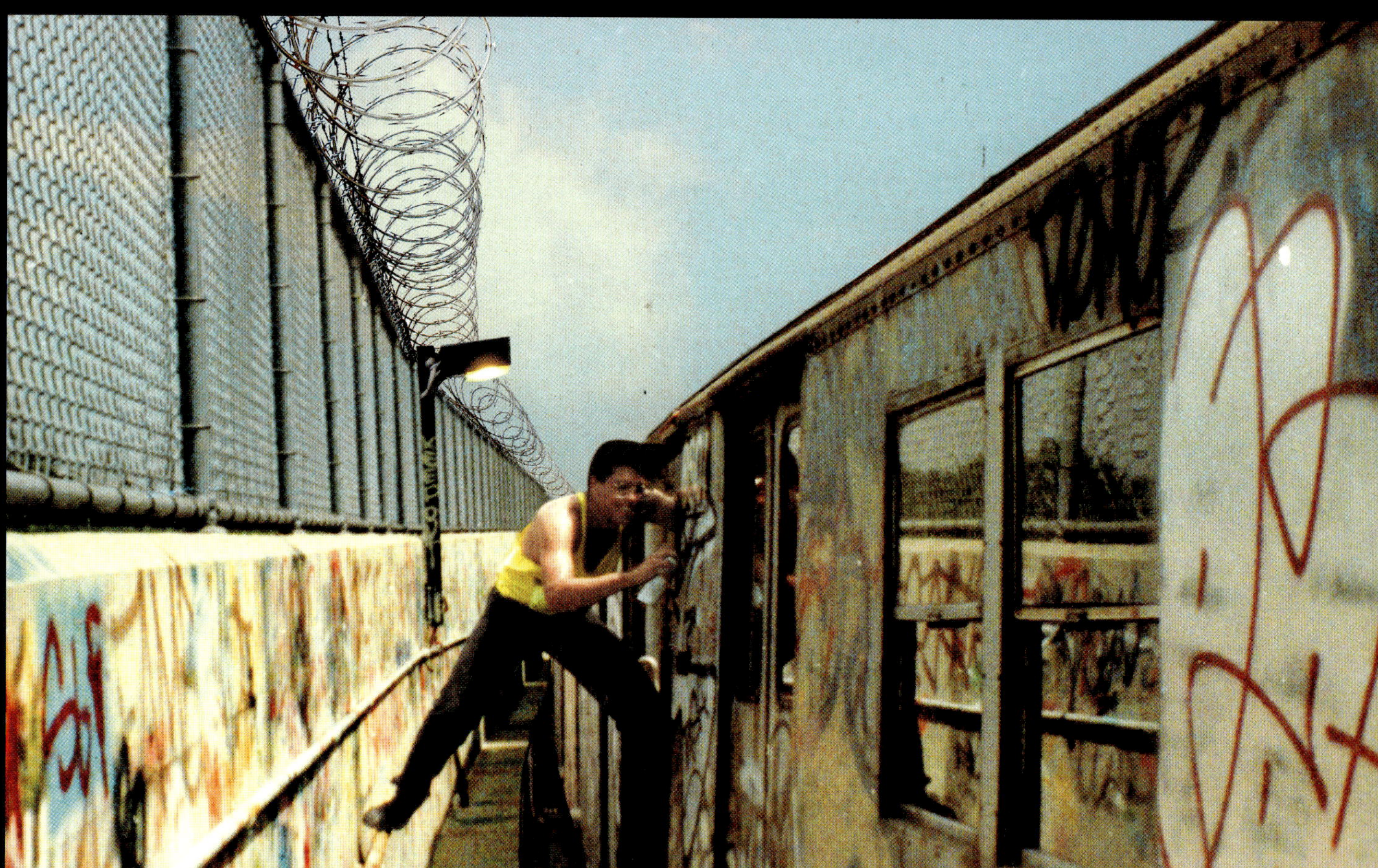

ZOO tagging up at 121st St., Sep. 1988.

BOM5 Most Wanted, 2009

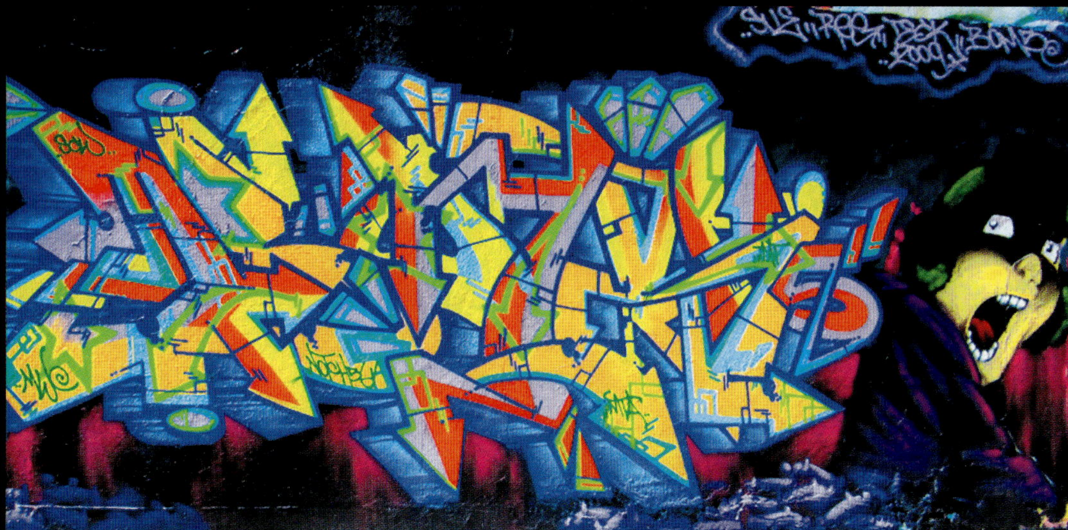

MECHANICAL WARFARE INC.

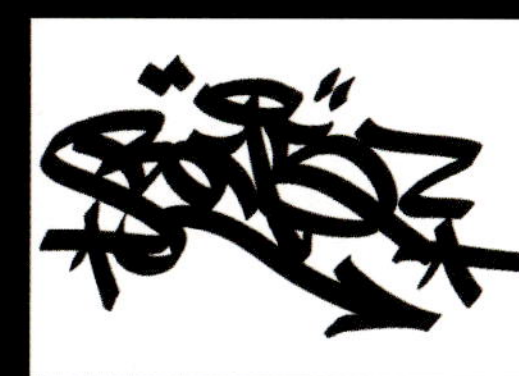

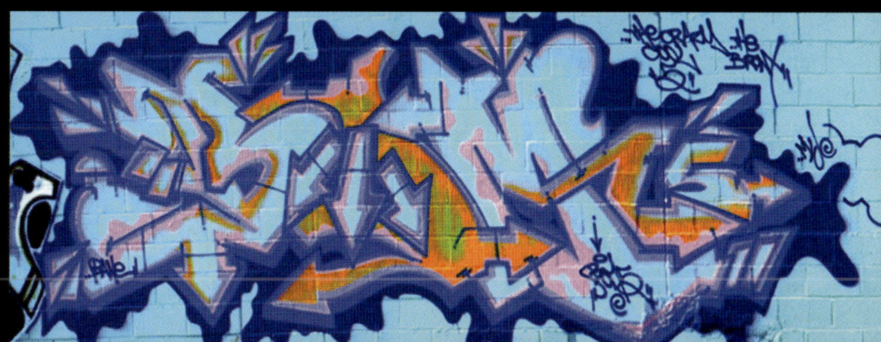

BOM5, 2 Train, 1979.

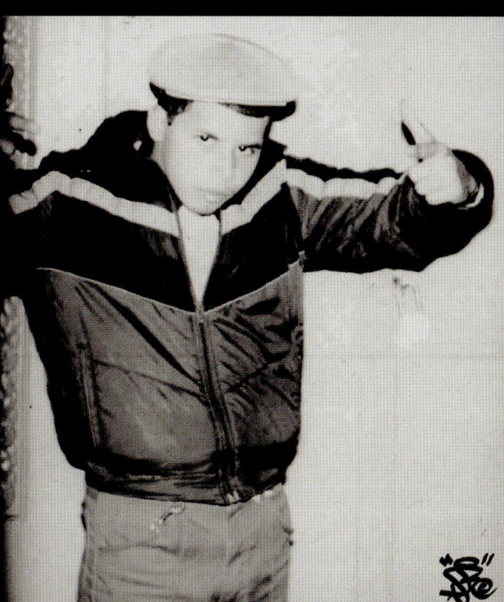

What up, y'all? My name is Bom5. Mad Writers inc. Est. 1978 from the bad ass Bronx...here to repp for my boy SHO1.TDC. My first memory about him and the crew was in 1986-87, when as a washed up old writer. I was heading to L.E.S. to meet my cousin Space, as I was waiting for the 2 or 5 Train on 180th Street Station...Bamm... there it was, a whole car, on the uptown platform with mad colors and was blazing with funky fresh hard block letters...I read it and it said SHO. Who the fuck was that? I never heard of him but I was like, damn...writers are still getting busy like that? I was shocked and amazed, and to tell you the truth, I was mad happy that writing was still alive, because over the years since I quit writing in 1980-81 I would just do some hits and piece once in awhile. Because I always had it in my blood, but after seeing this piece it made me want to come back. Funny, two years later, in 1989, I came back hard bugging out, like I never stopped! Much respect to my boy SHO and TDC! Shout outs to my crew...Mad Writers...Most Wanted...Mostly Weeded...Mad Walls...Makin' Ways...Mackin' Women...etc... Much love and respect to my brother Bane1. MW Vice Pres... my cousins and mentors...See2. Chinomalo. Rib1. Smily149. Billy167. Repel. I also was inspired by Phase2. StayHigh149. Elmarko174. Butch2. Riff170. Staff161. AJ and Blade.

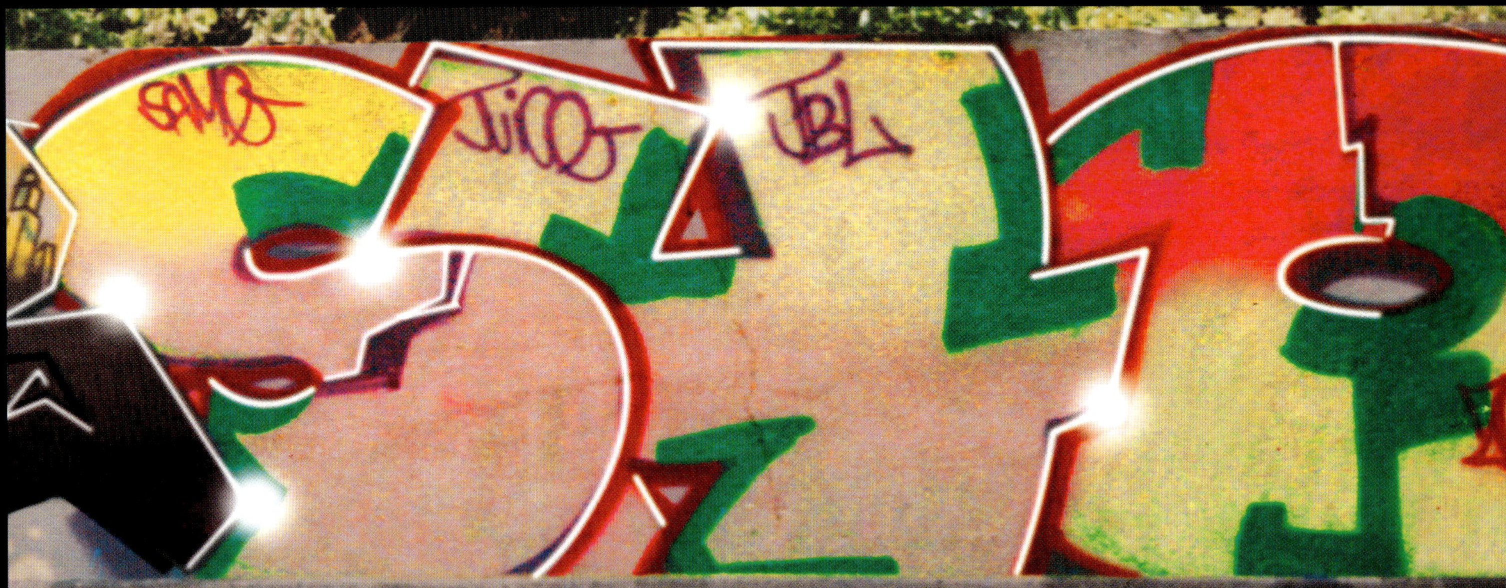

SHO TDC, Dec. 1999.

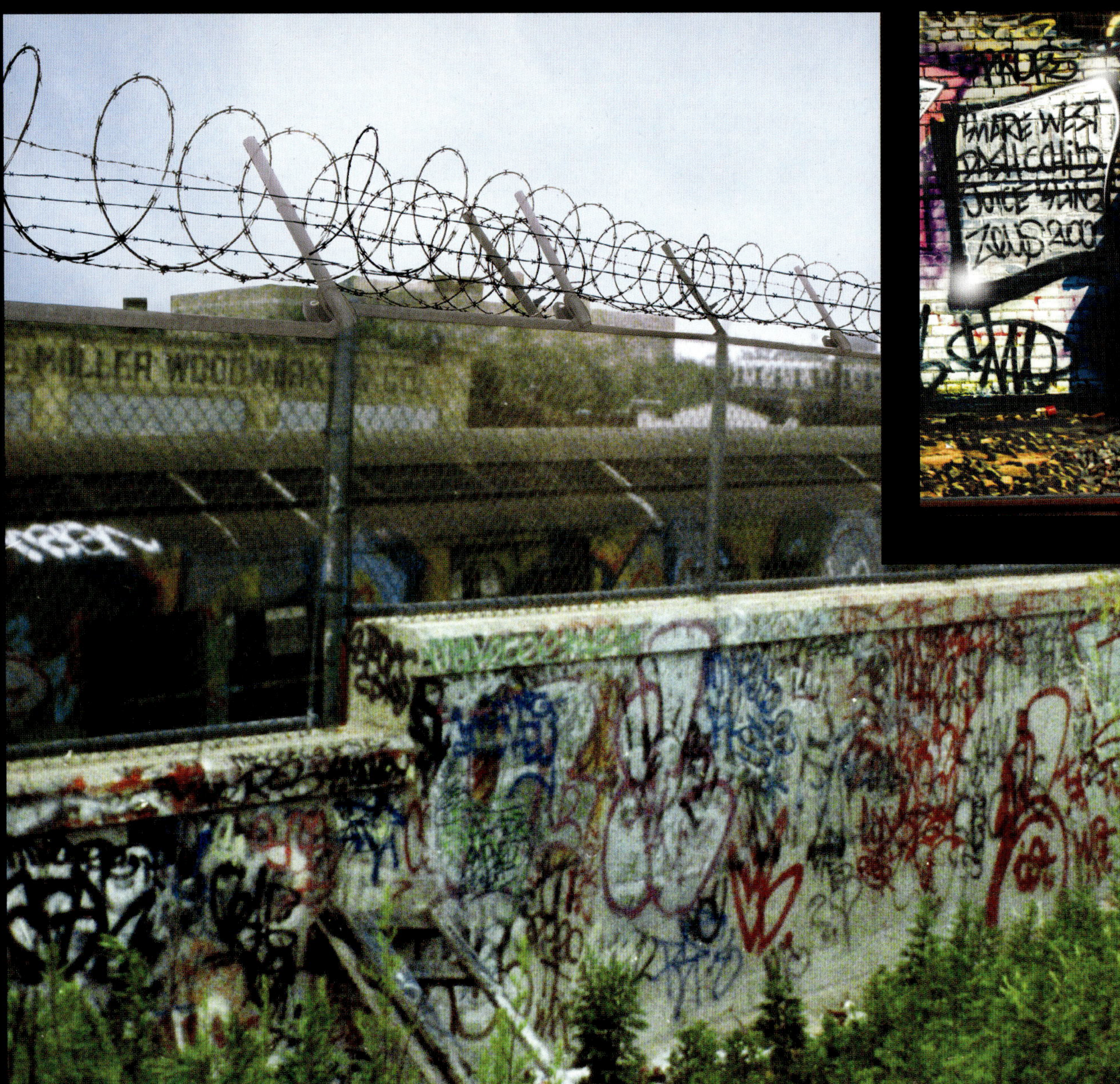

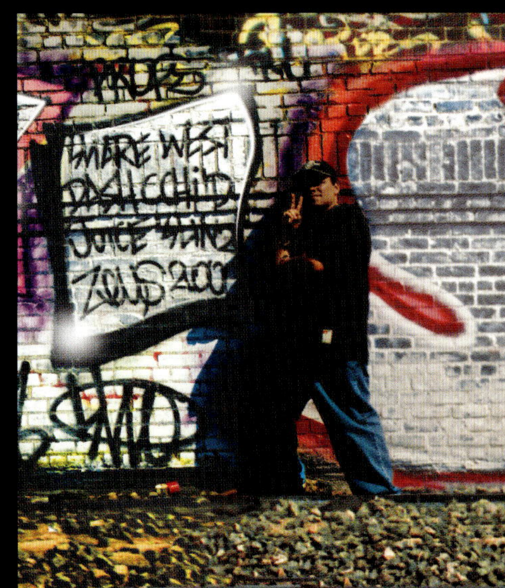

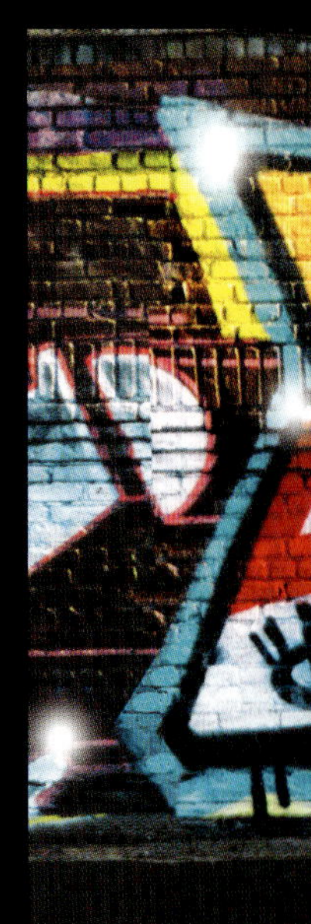

Outside view of the J Train lay up at 121st Street, Jamaica, New York, 1988.

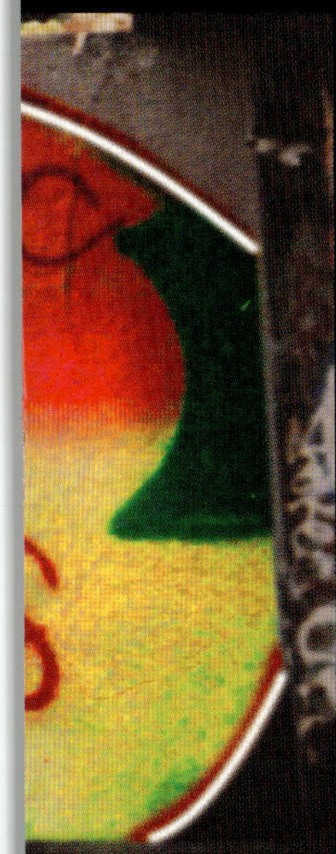

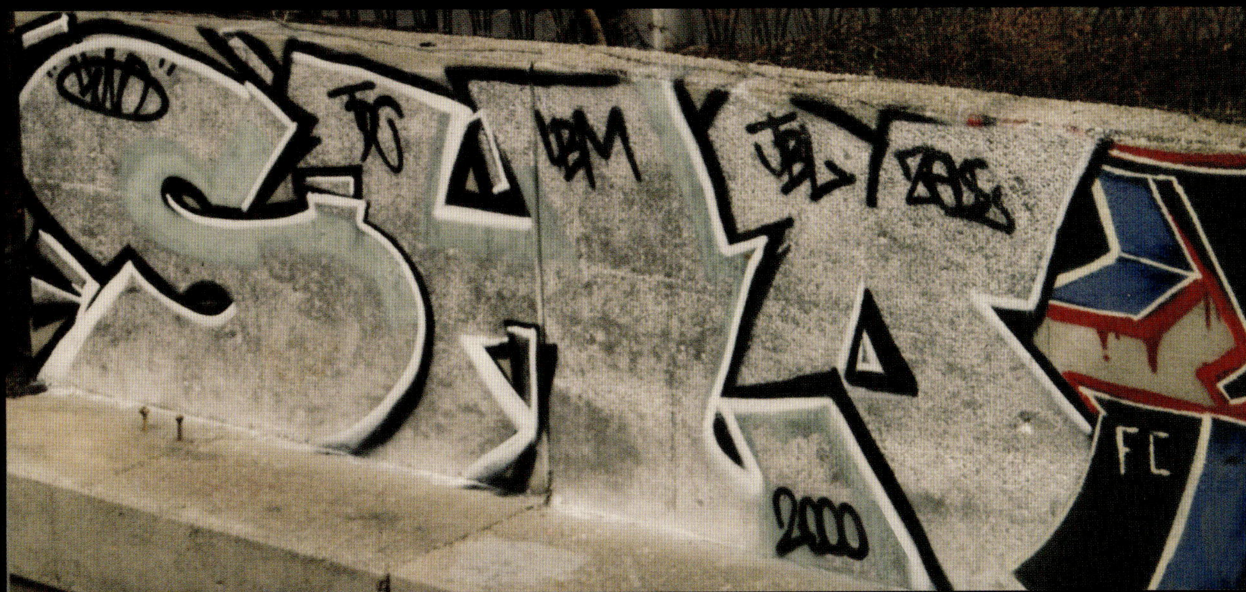

SHO TDC, Dec. 2000.

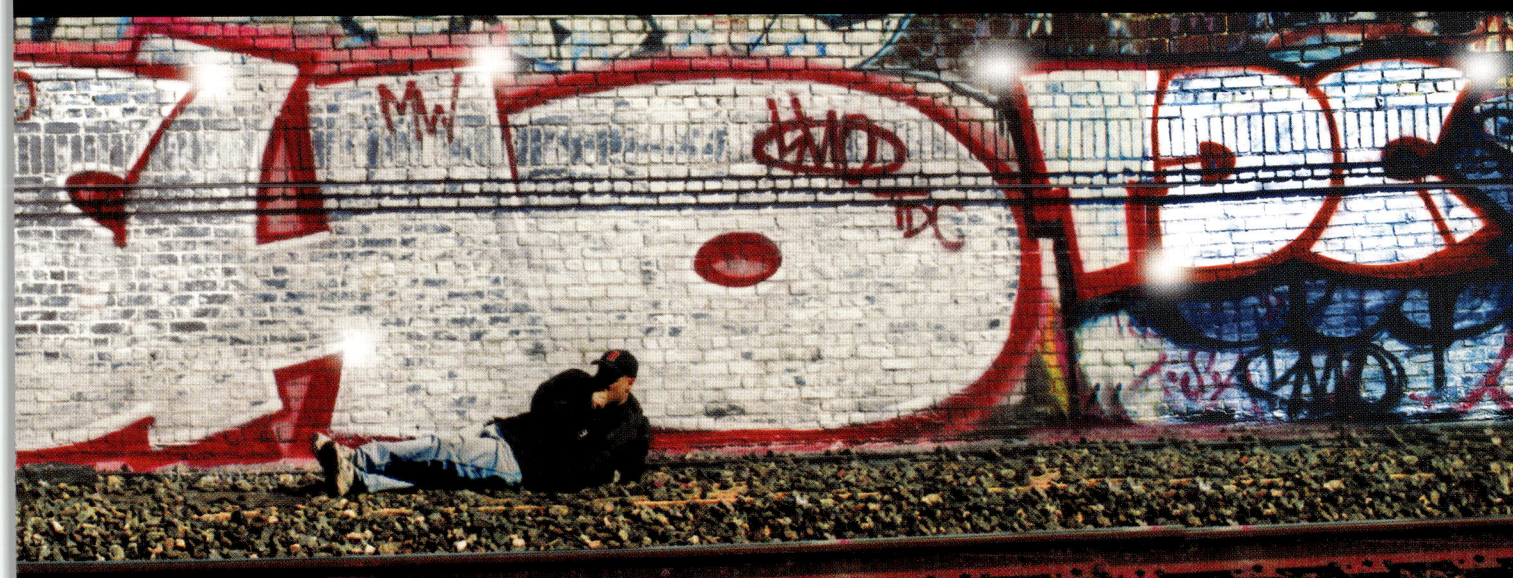

Manhattan, NY, 2000.

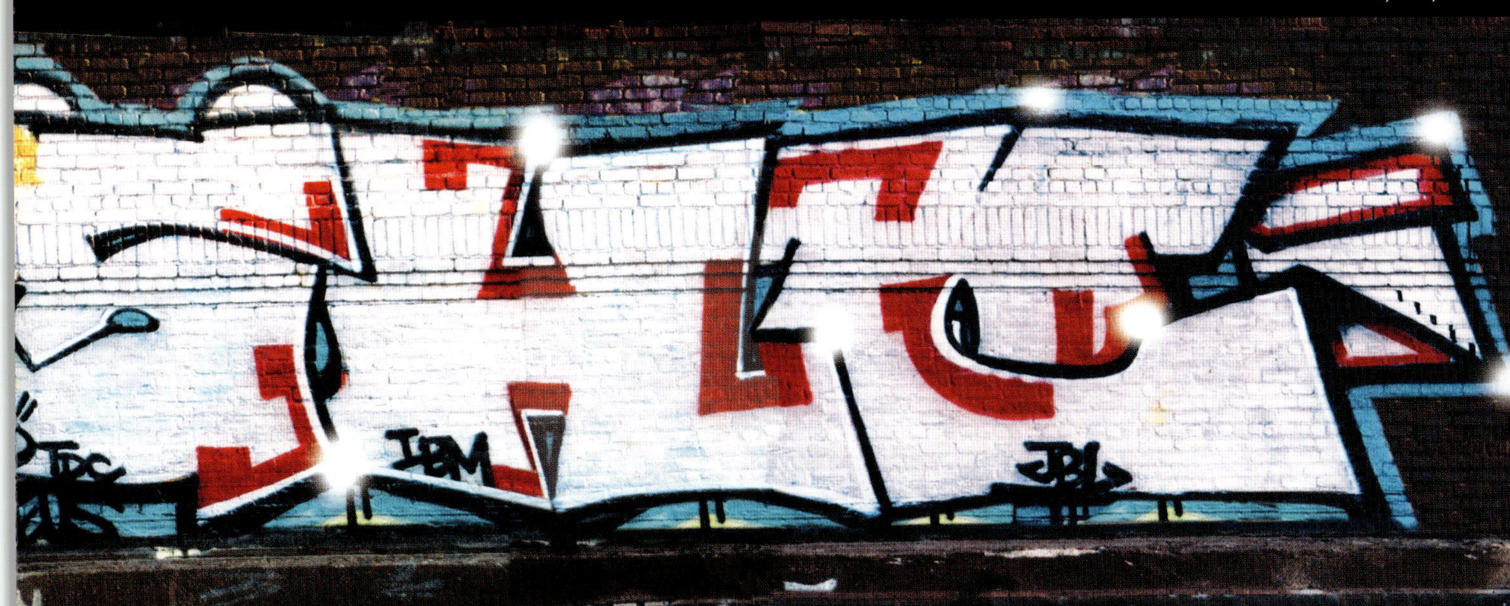

SHO TDC IBM for JBL and ZEUS, Manhattan, NY, 1999.

It was mid-summer in August 1997, SHO and I were extremely active at this point. I got a phone call from Desa MTA that they had put in fresh sets of 4-door red birds (bmts) in the 3rd Avenue Yard in Brooklyn. So SHO and I said let's rock out a whole car. I was down so I figured we would bust it out at night. SHO goes, "Meet me in Manhattan at 10 A.M." My reply was, "SHO are you buggin'?" SHO replies, "No Z let's go." In the mid 1990s the city was a different playing field as it is these days. I picked up SHO and two duffle bags of paint and it was on. If anybody knows the 3rd Avenue Yard during the day, it's a real industrial area, trucks everywhere, traffic cops, etc. We drop the duffle bags in the stash spot, parked the car, and in we went. We scoped it out for a minute and there was not a soul in site in the yard. We were busting out the outlines and rocking the car. About this time a really good friend of ours had just passed away (VE, aka James Conte), so we dedicated the car to him (pg. 230). I busted out a few fill-ins and a few insides. SHO was finishing up his piece. I told SHO, "I'm gonna grab the car, I'll meet you by the hole in the fence." I grabbed my bag and dipped. No problems, YET. As I pulled up by the hole I see an undercover Port Authority cop pulling up in his car on SHO. He had to run like 200 feet with his paint across a wide open parking lot. The Port Authority cop got out of his car but the gate was locked, I had noticed (don't ask me why I noticed that, it's just how my mind is), I yelled at SHO to be out. In a panic I opened my trunk and swung my passenger door open as SHO jumped in (at this time my heart was pumping like a 69 Charger 440 6 pack). Keep in mind it's like 3 P.M. on a weekday. By the time I got two blocks away there were sirens blaring everywhere. Under the Brooklyn Queens Expressway the DTs and Blue and Whites were everywhere like ants and were driving on the wrong side of the roadway to cut us off. We had only one objective, we were not getting bagged, by all means necessary. This went on for ten minutes and they definitely had a good description of us, it seemed to be endless. We got chased till 15th or 16th Avenue and 53rd or 54th Street. Then I got my chance, I saw a Johnny pump was open and pulled through it and pulled to the left. Four to five cop cars blew right passed us as we walked away from the car like we were gonna leave it if we had to. If you have ever had a chase like this you know the feeling of a mission accomplished. As soon as they turned the corner we was right behind them until we could get the hell out of there, which is exactly what we did. We was drinking 40-oz. Colt 45s all the way back to Manhattan. Me and SHO looked at each other in a sigh of relief and smirked. After that we went to Spinoni gardens for pizza. I dedicate this story to VE ONE: RIP (MTA Most Talked About), FTR (Fuck The Rest) Forever young...Xist RIP...BEZ RIP...EMIL RIP.

-ZEUS TDC

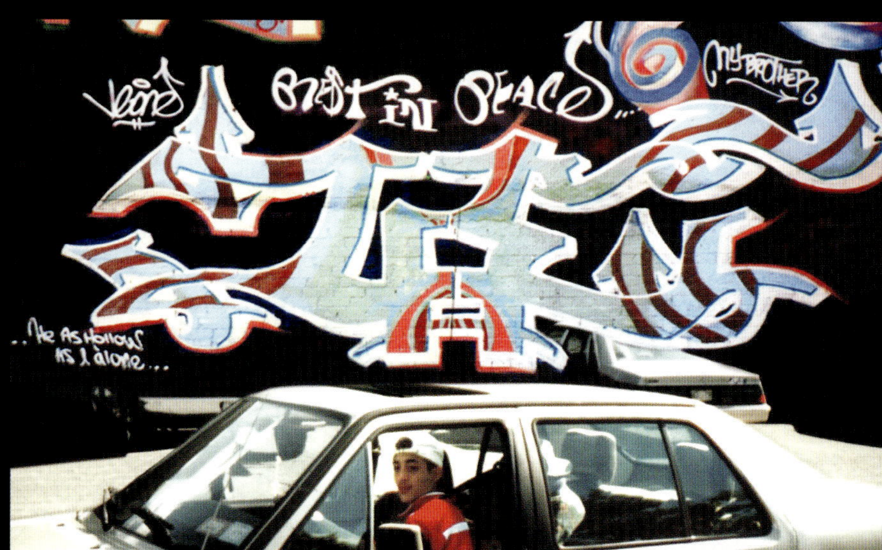

VE One RIP Tribute by Slash FTR MTA, 1998.

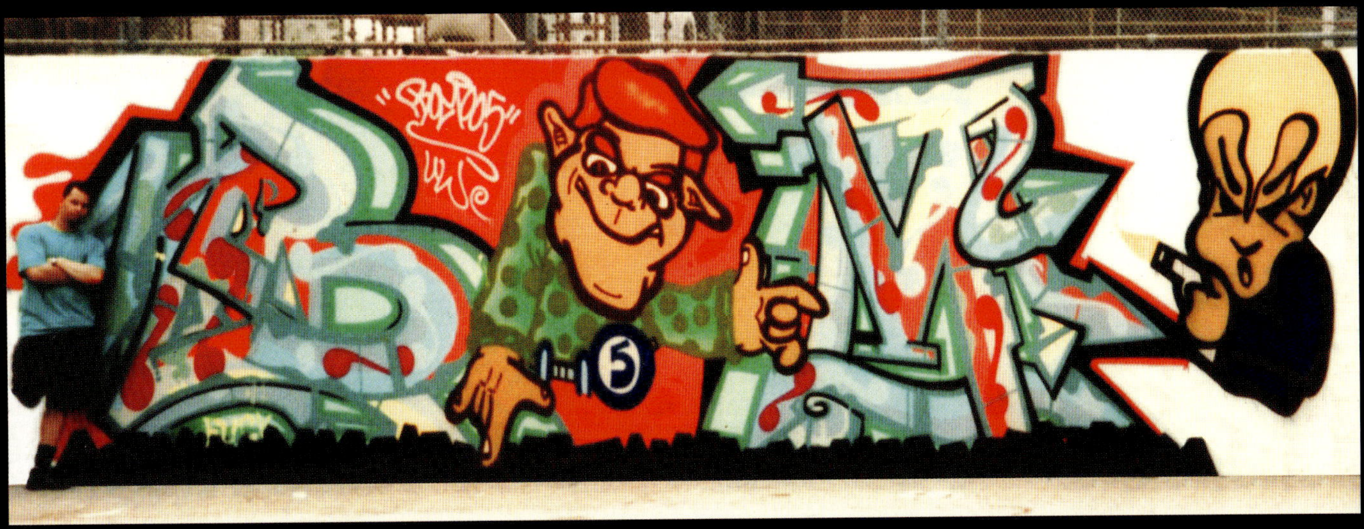

BOM 5 Most Wanted Prez.

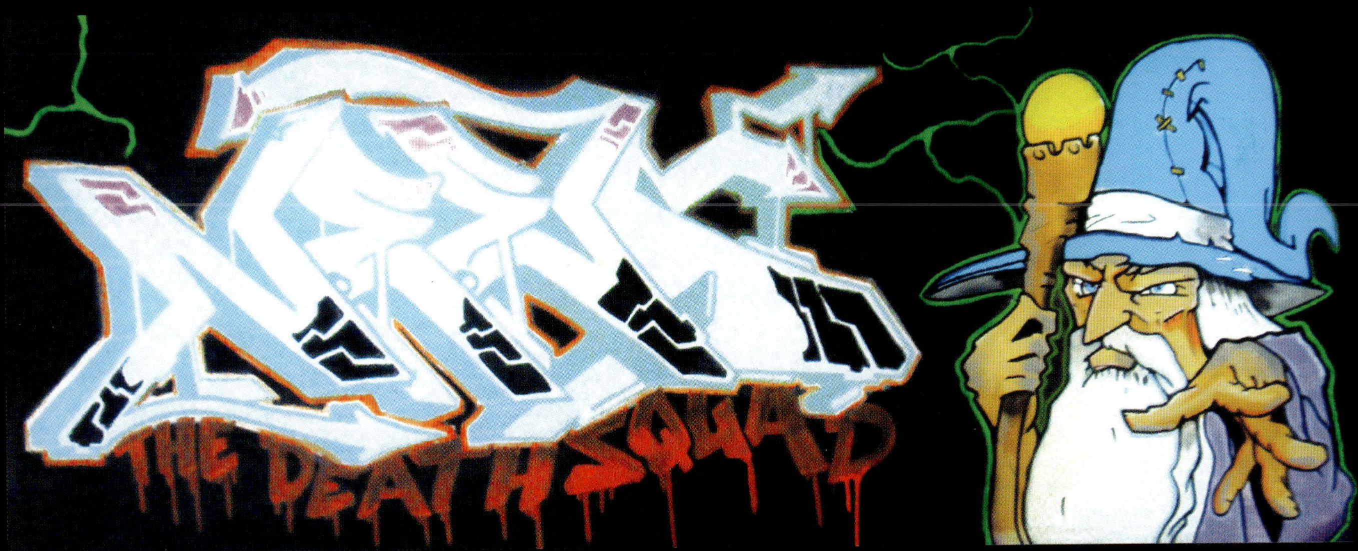

NEED TDS, "The Death Squad."

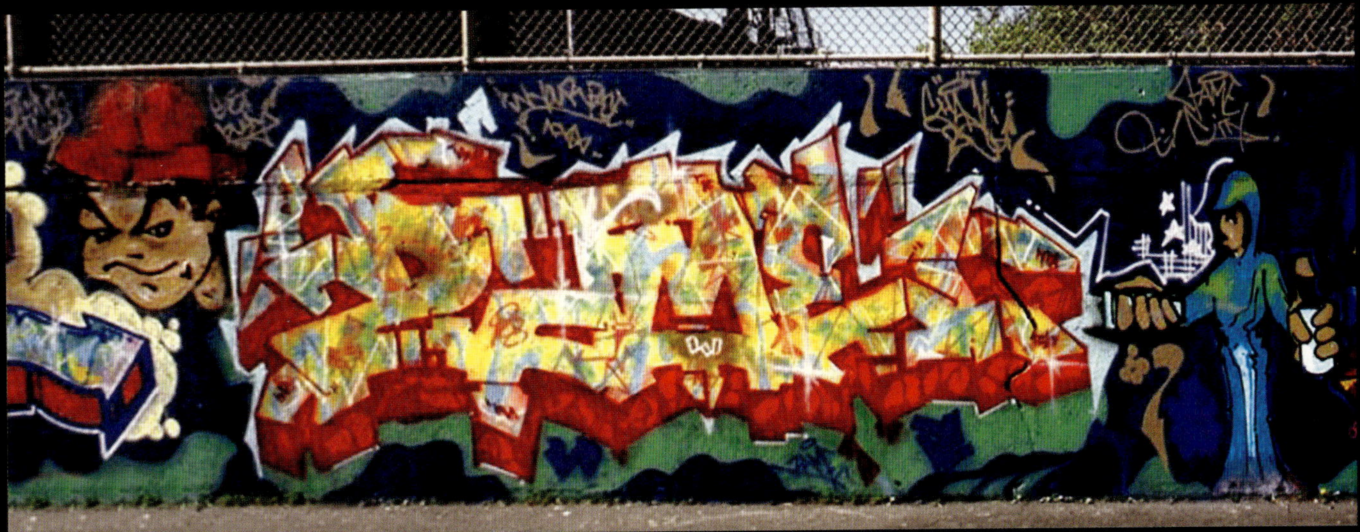

ZAME FC, Hall of Fame, 1986.

ROZIE ROZ rocking the Speed Racer character.

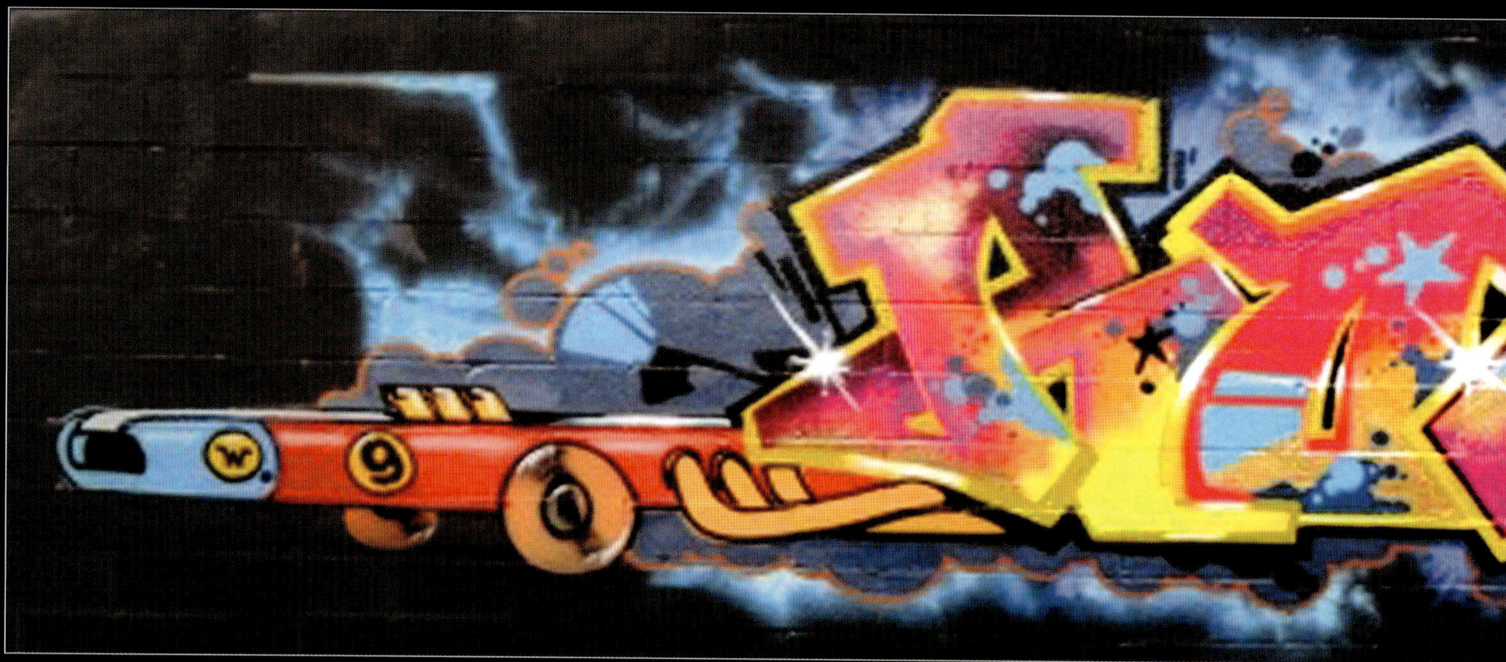

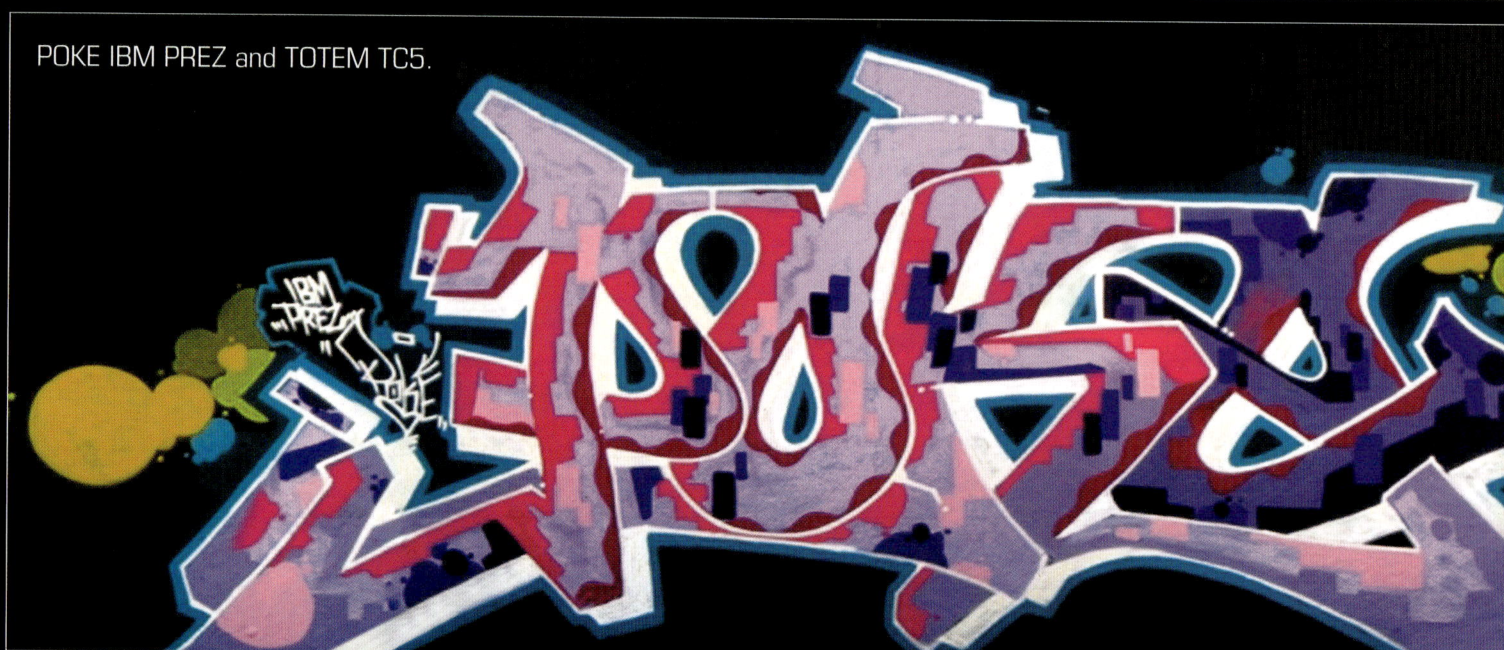

POKE IBM PREZ and TOTEM TC5.

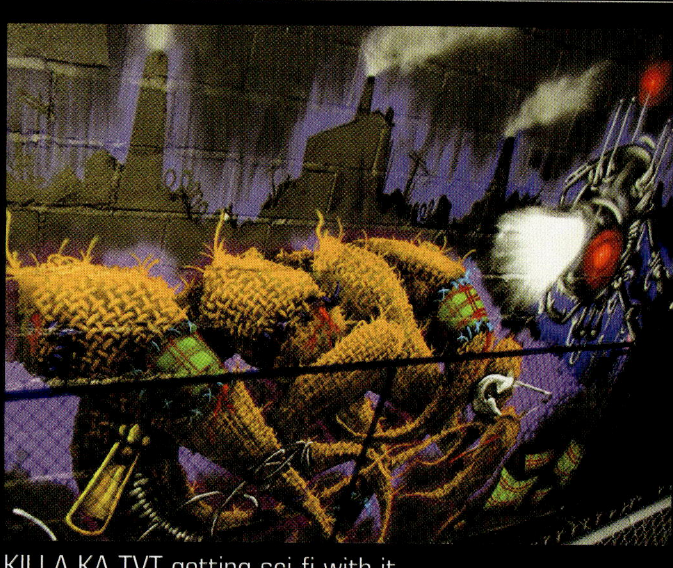

KILLA KA TVT getting sci-fi with it.

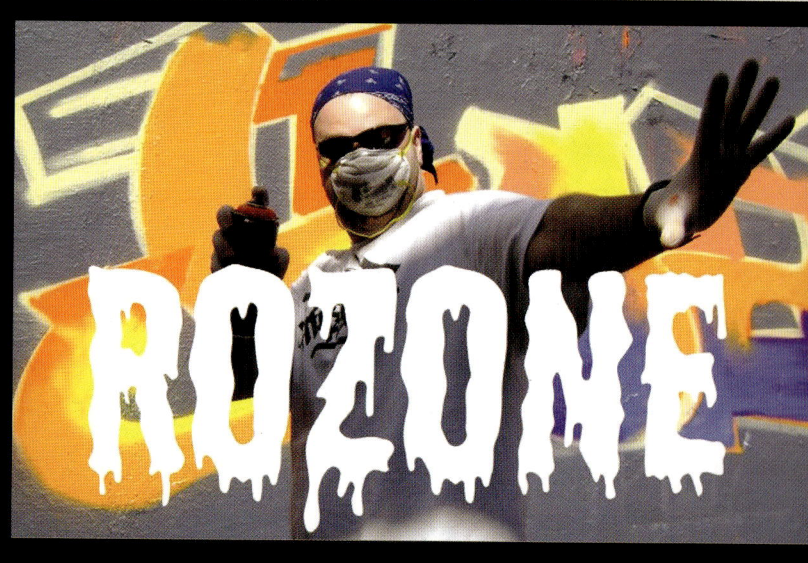

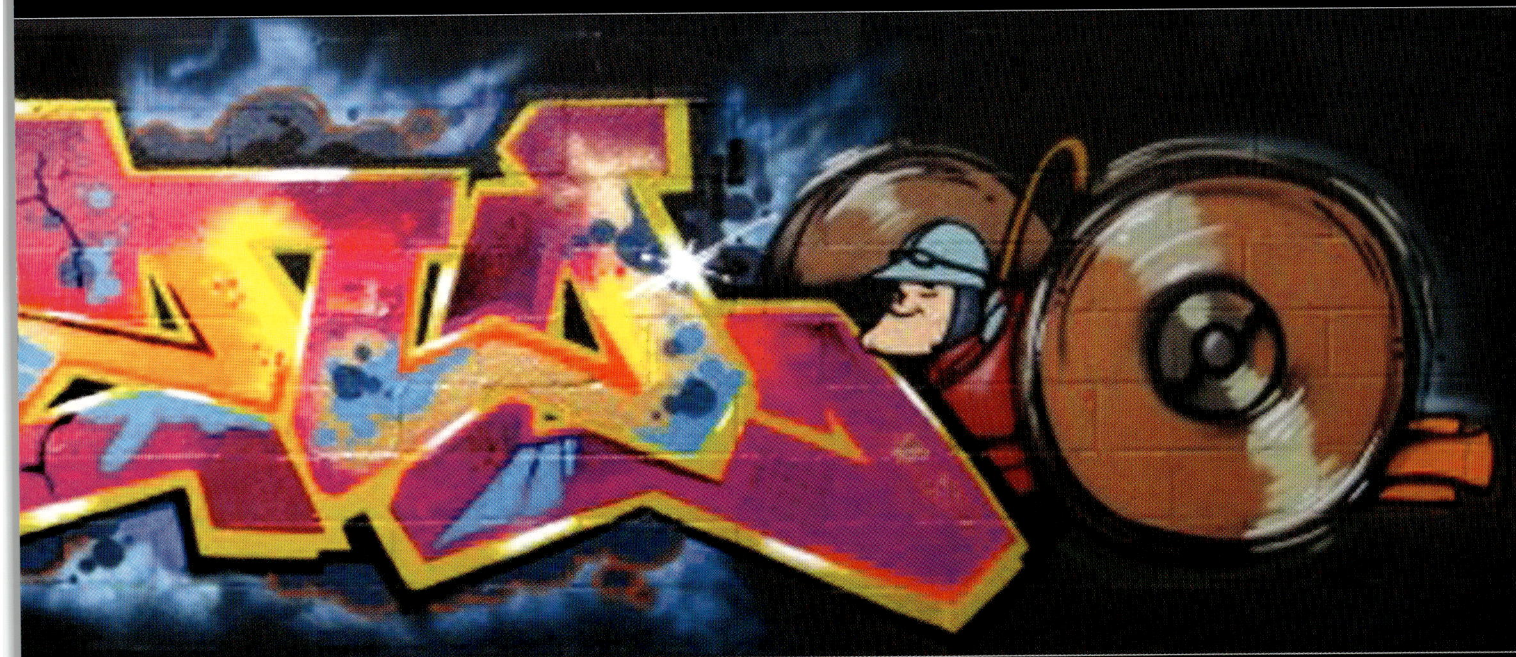

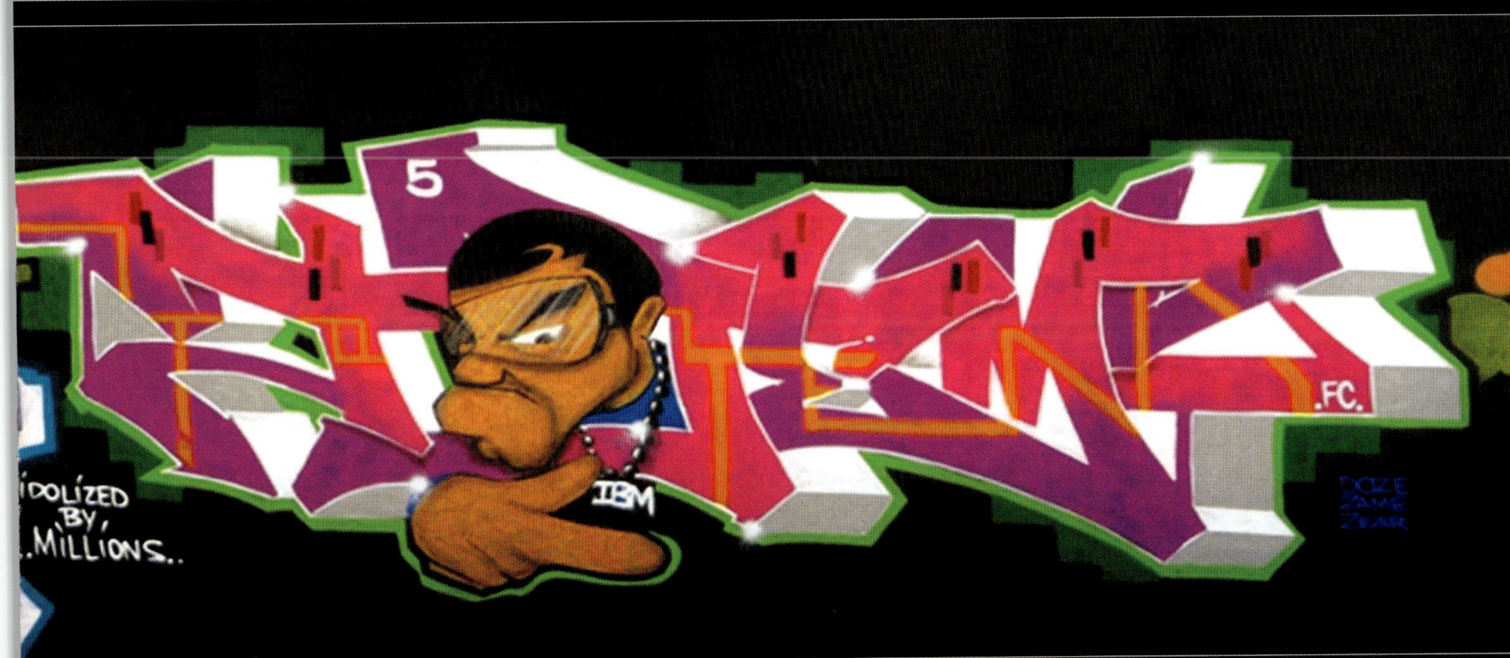

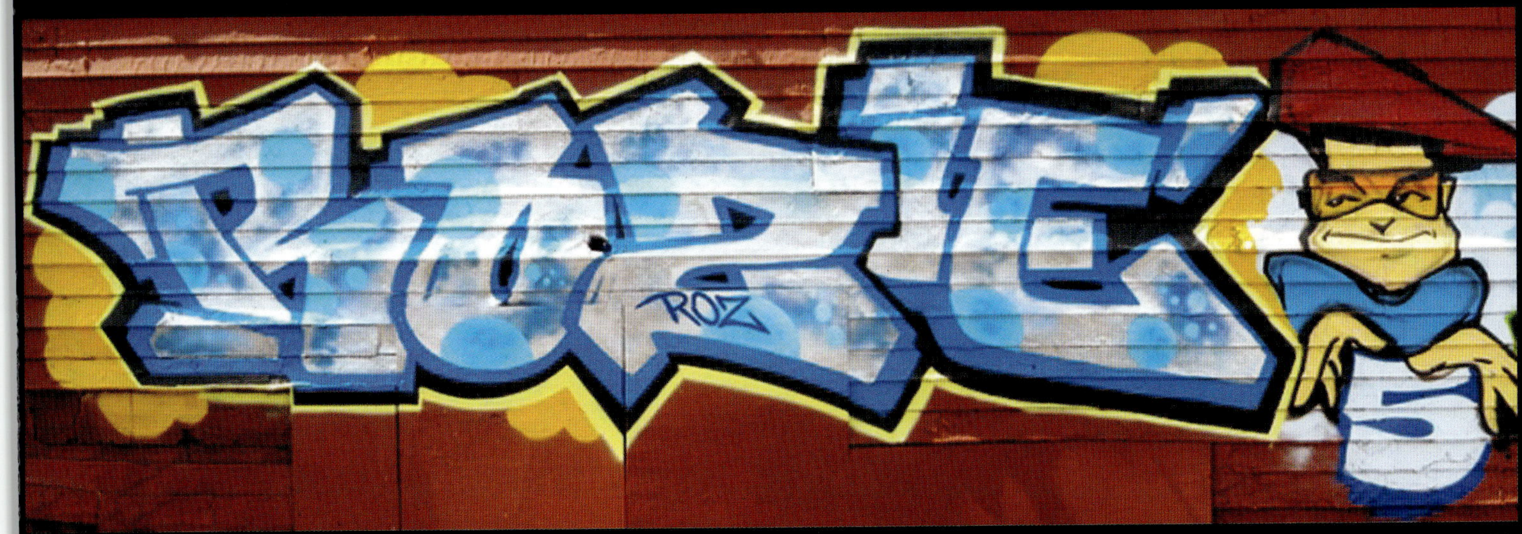

ROZ ONE TC5 FUN CLUB PREZ.

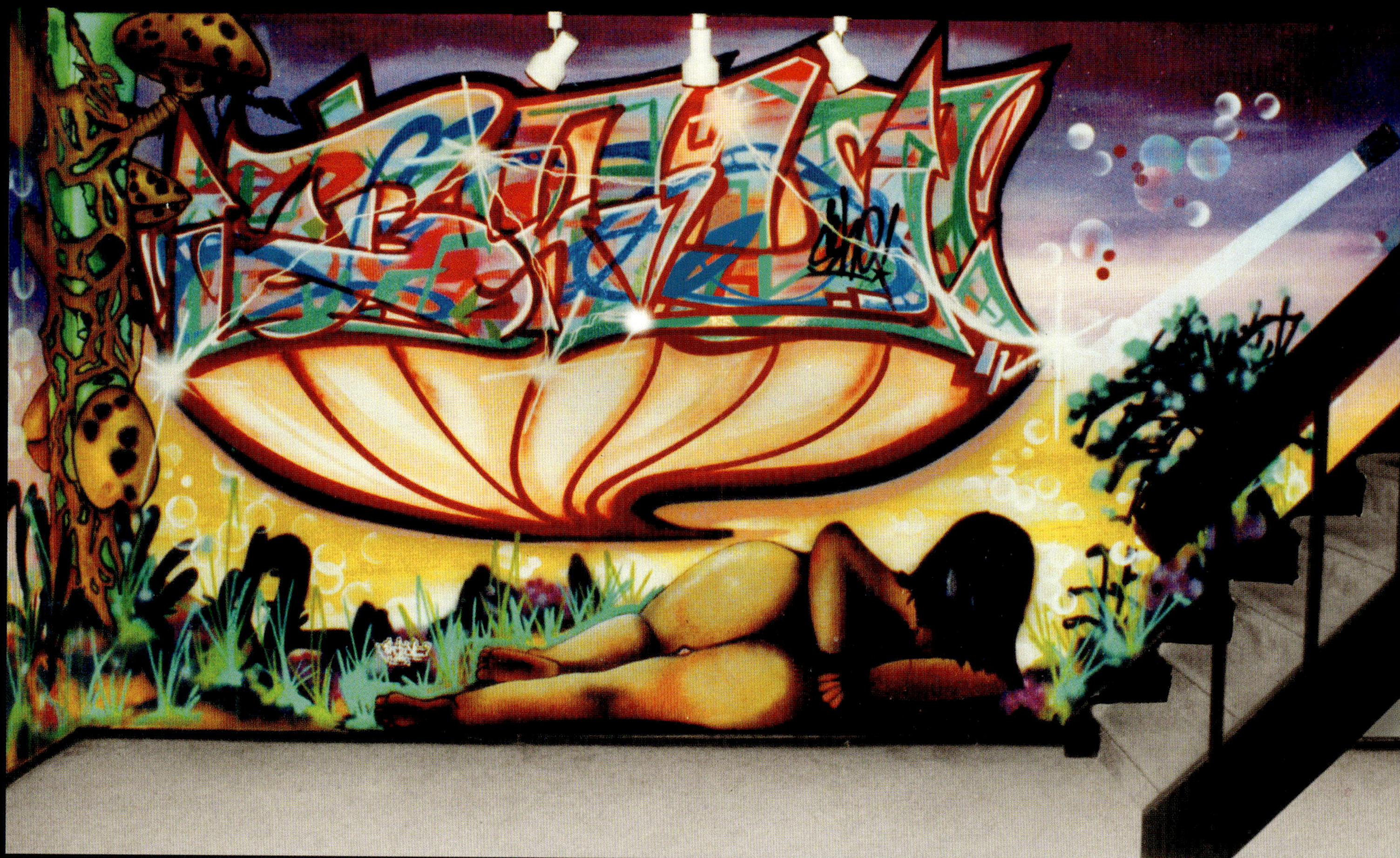

The SHO "Bitch in Bondage Wall," Part 2, Mulberry St.

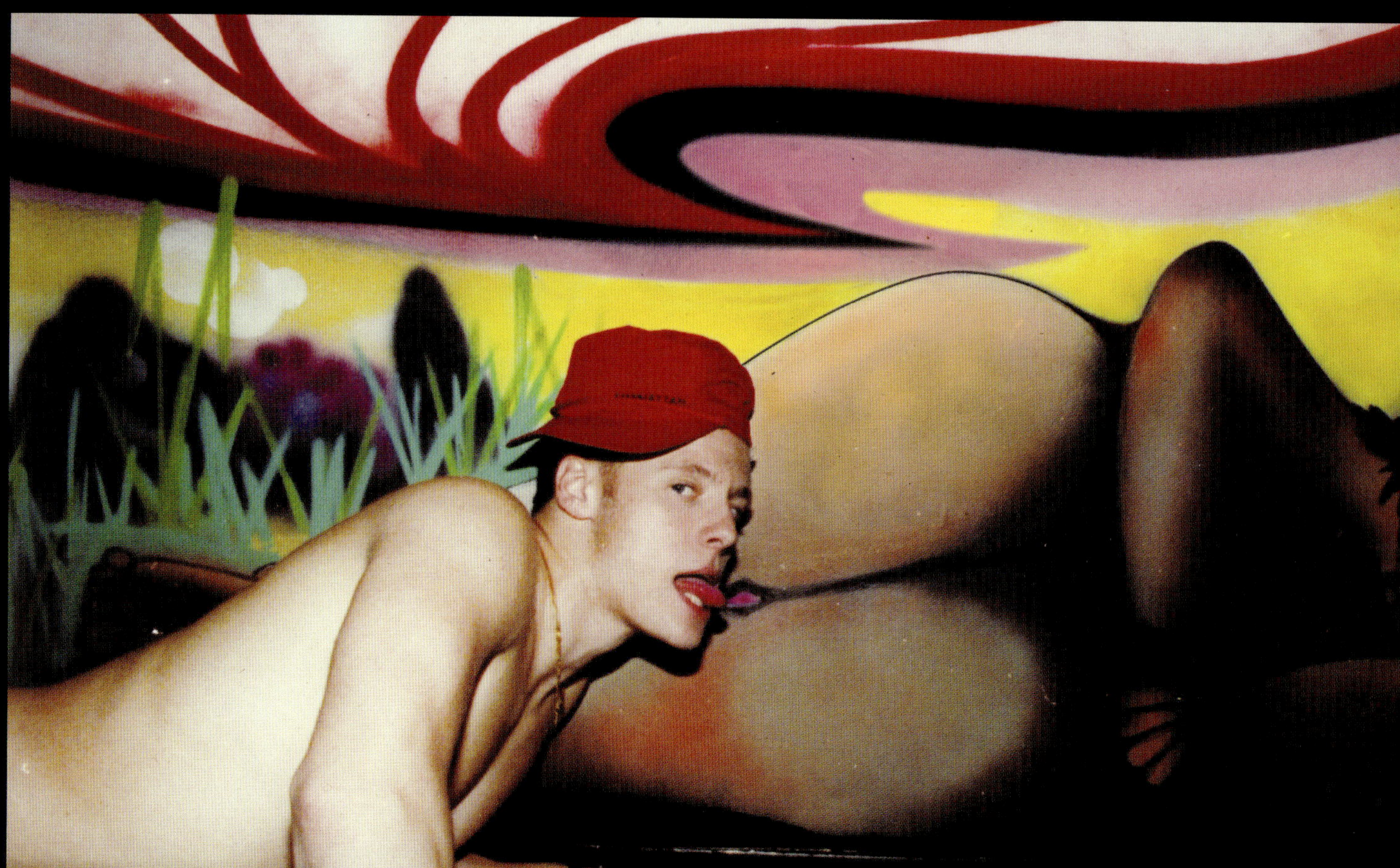

Mulberry St., fucking around, Sep. 1992.

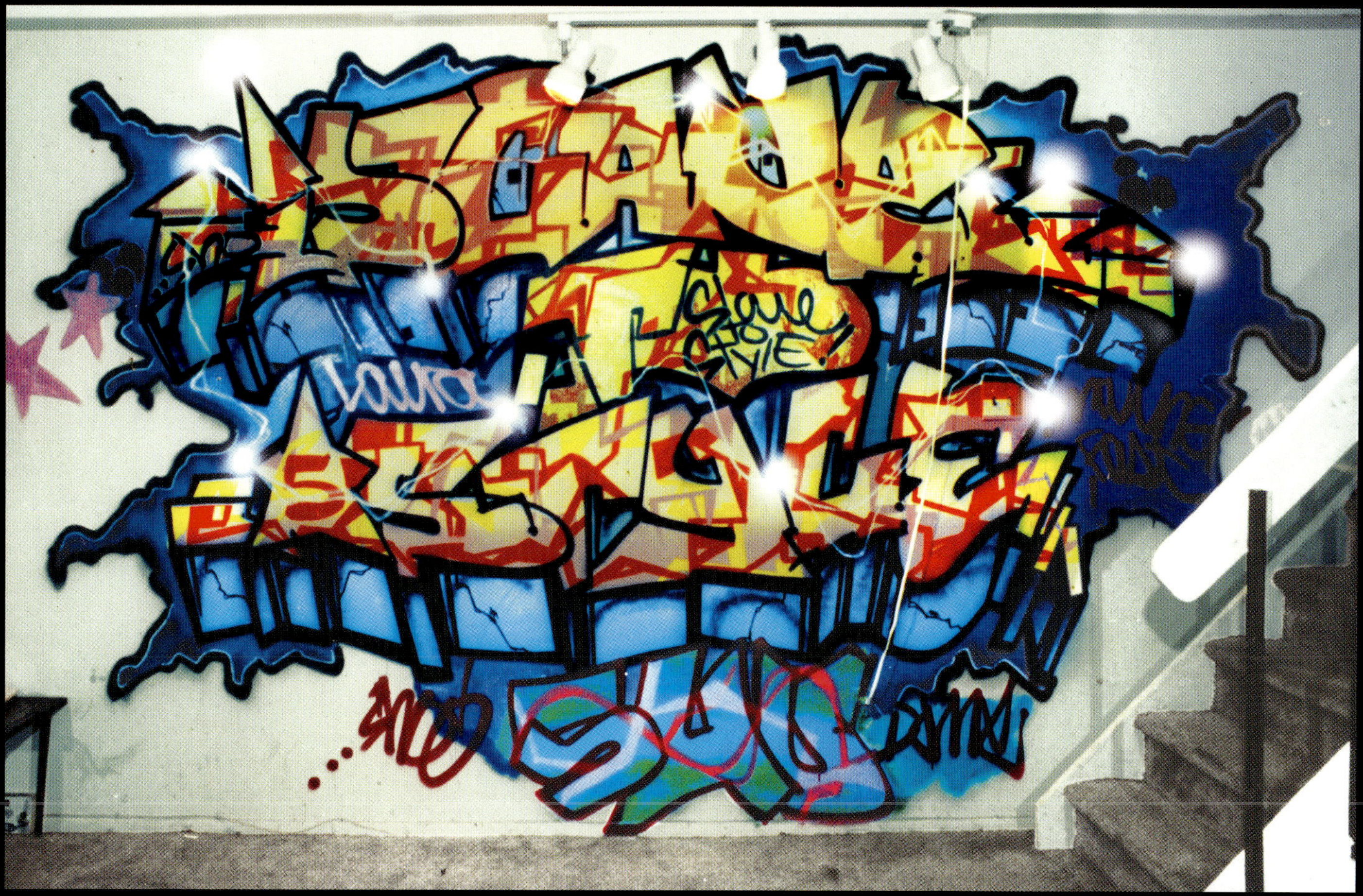

"SLAVE TO STYLE," Part 1, SHO Production, Mulberry St.,1991.

We did this one weekend on the low. "Freeport High School Variety Show Production," 1986. By SHO, DC3, and BEAVER TDC. Man we was crazy hot at the moment. They had said DC3 and ROE had bombed all these Long Island Railroad Trains at this North West Freeport lay up. Somehow DTS had everyone's info and called me up at home. We was at the show in the cut.

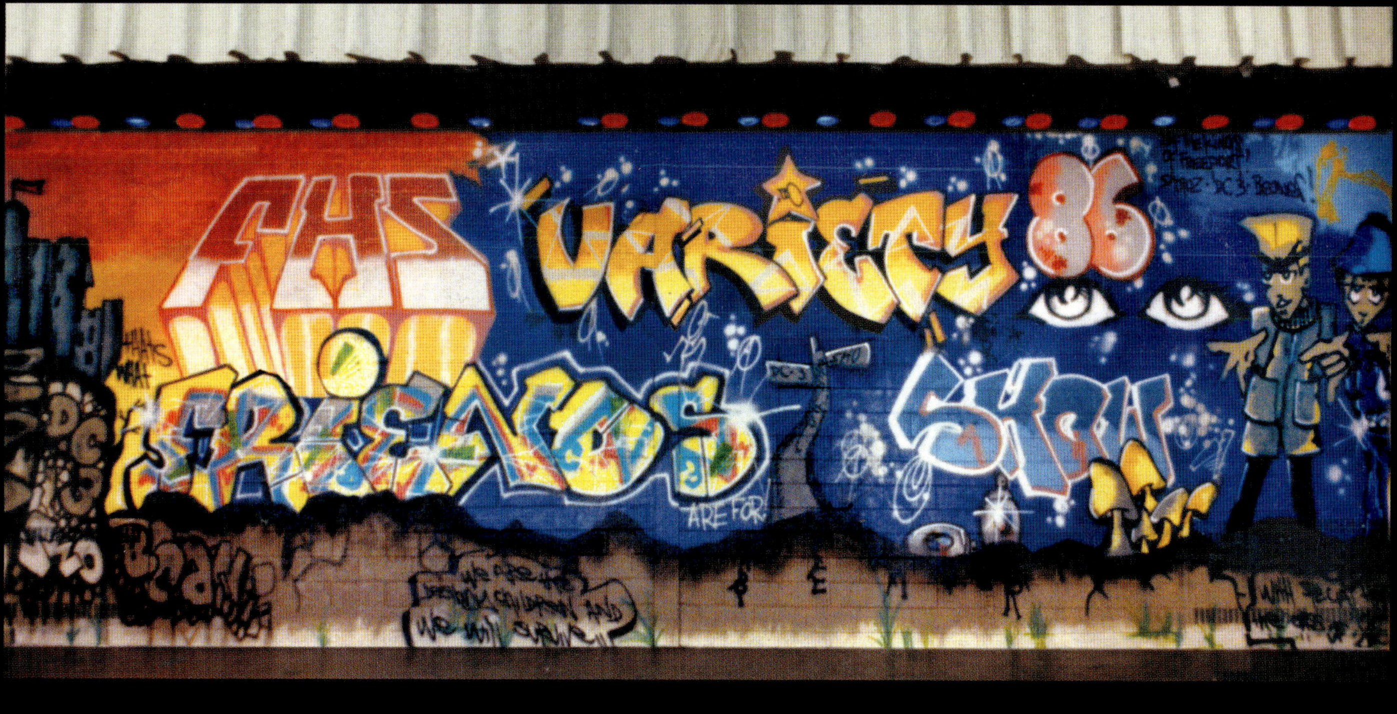

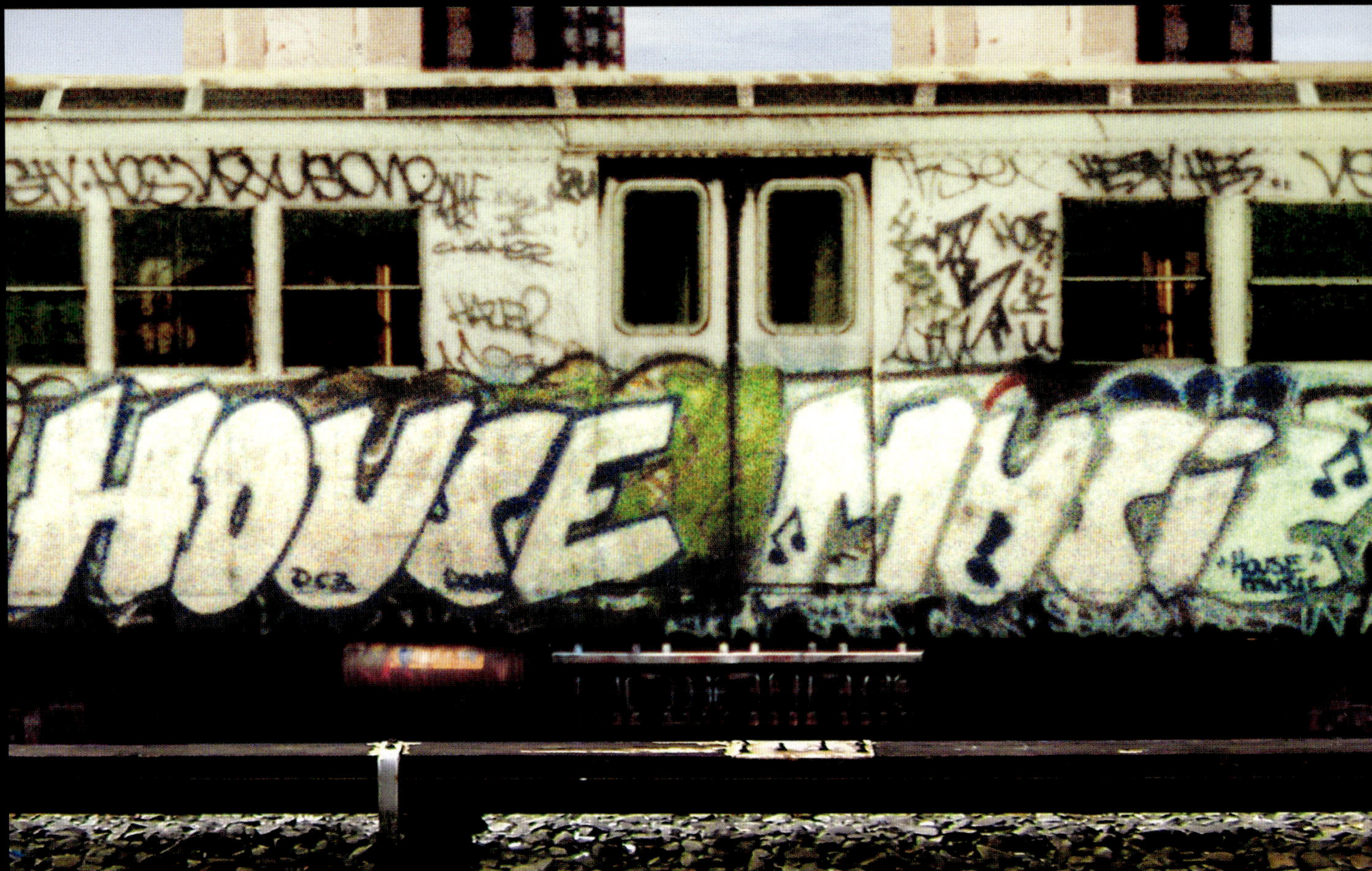

"House Music," 5 Train by DOME, Jan. 1989.

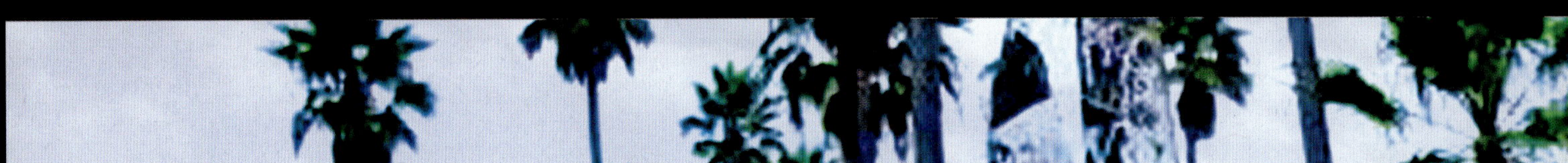

SPHERE IBM NOG and STANE burners In Los Angeles.

I give VULCAN props for this one. He came to the tunnels with letters cut out in foam and cemented them to the train. That shit must of fucked the work bums heads up. They were haters and ripped them off right away.

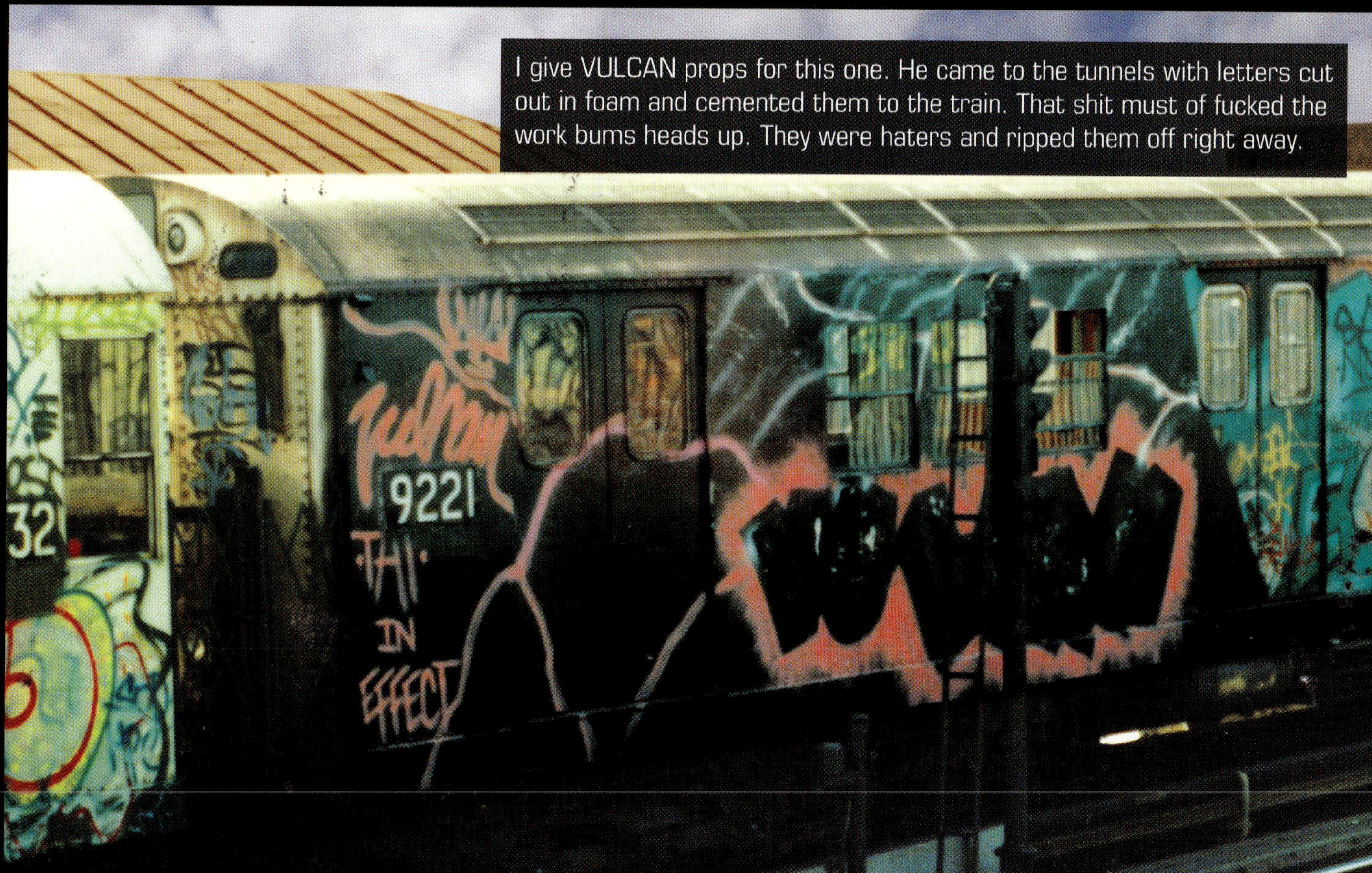

VULCAN, 5 Train, Feb. 1988. TATS CREW.

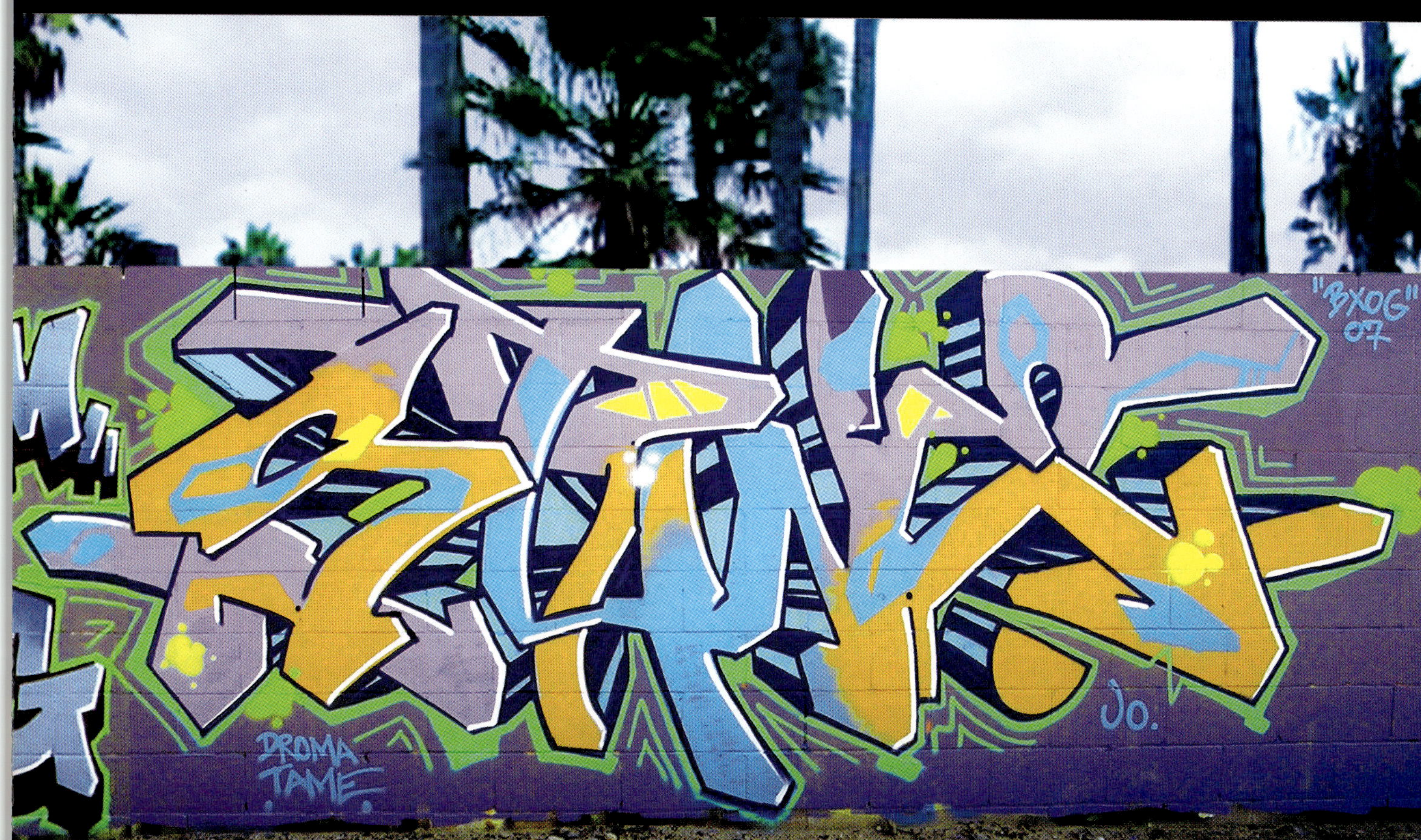

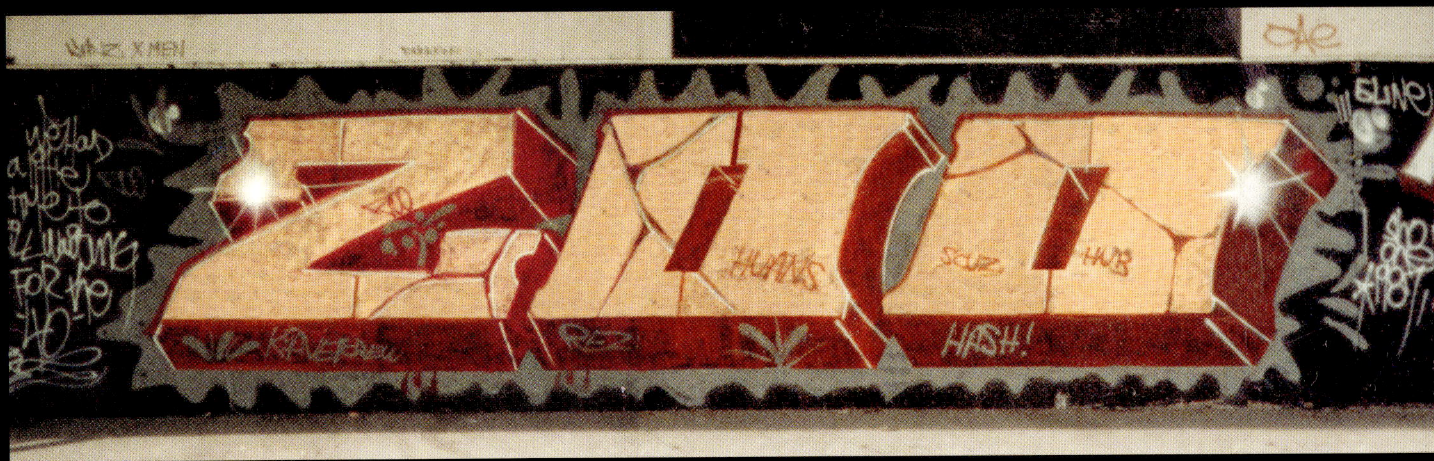

ZOO top-to-bottom gold piece rocked on Nassau Road in Hempstead, June 1987.
Zoo and I were chilling waiting for the N-40 bus to come and we had a little time to kill. So he hit this up.
This was just a super large throw up for us—drinking 40-oz. beers waiting for the 40 at 2 A.M.

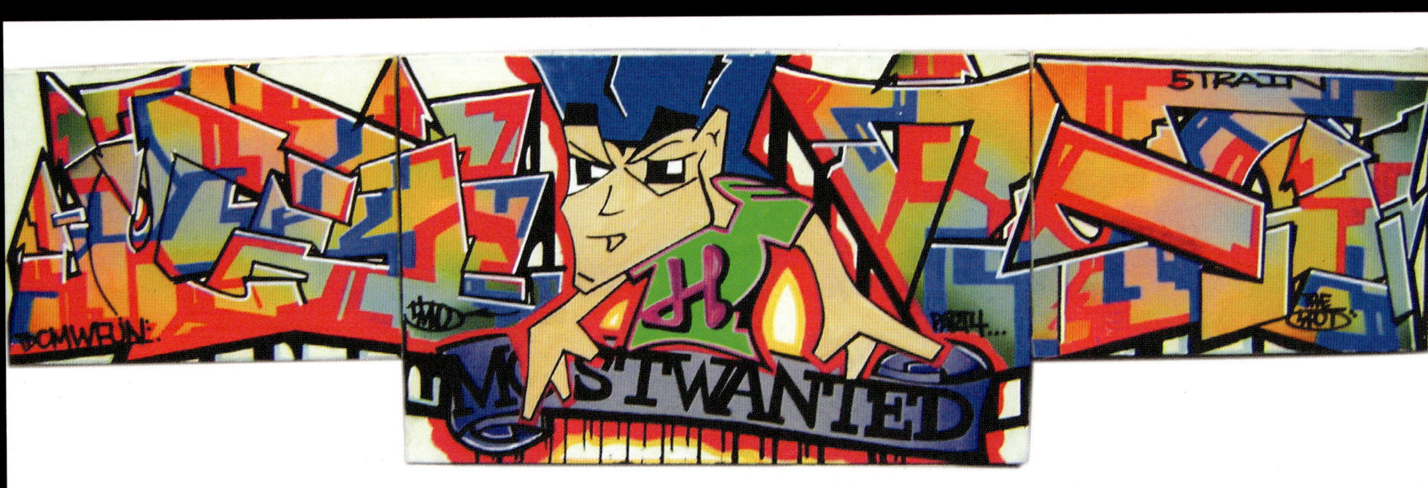

SHO, "MOST WANTED," rocked at The Spot Art Show. For BOM5.

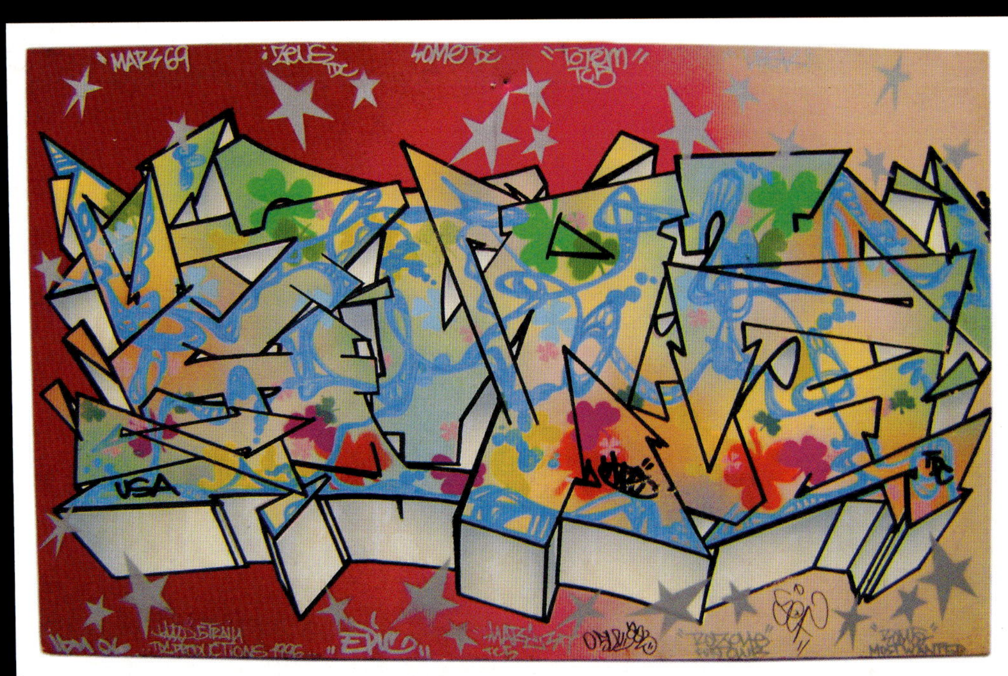

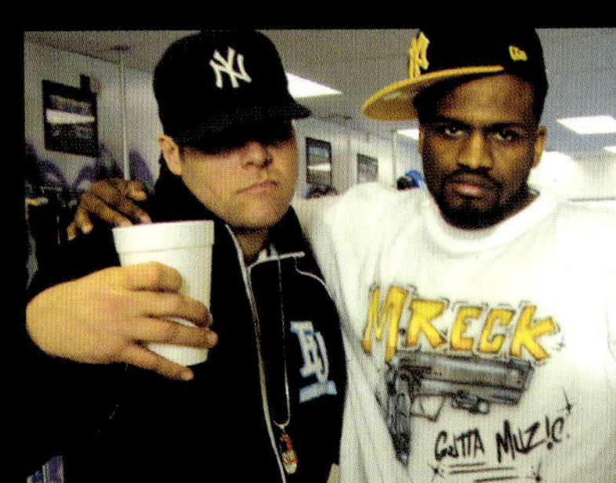

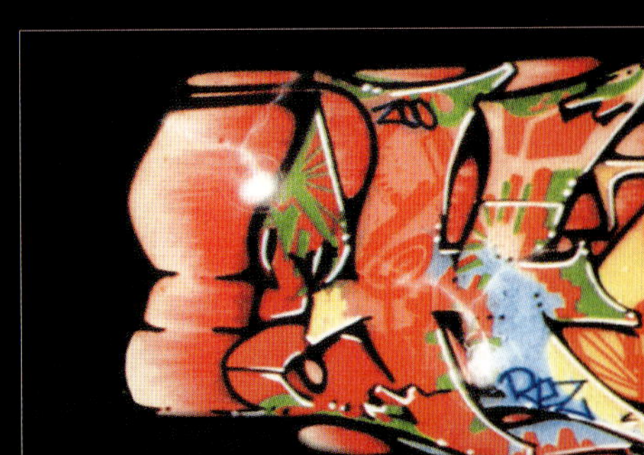

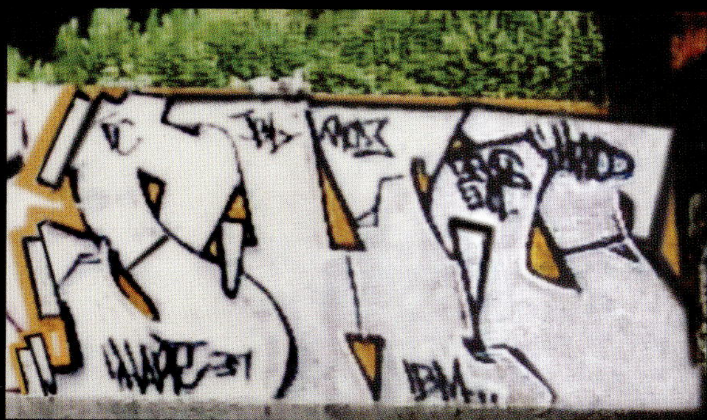

A quick silver, 1999.

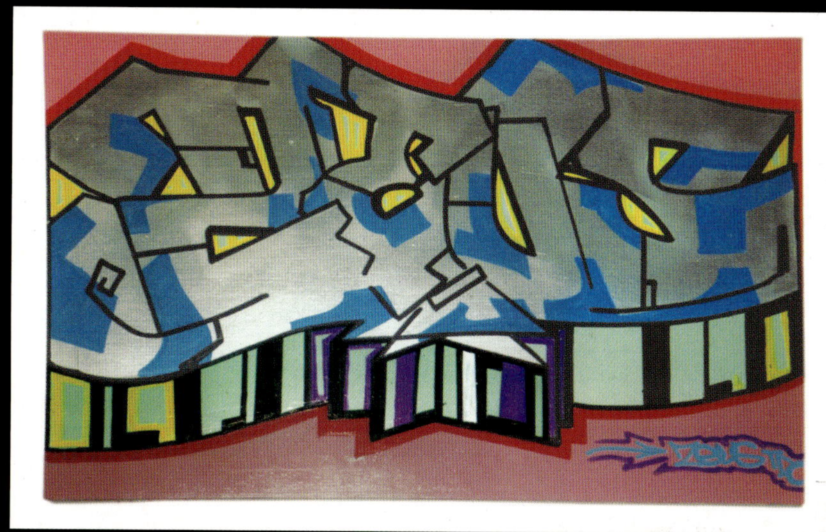

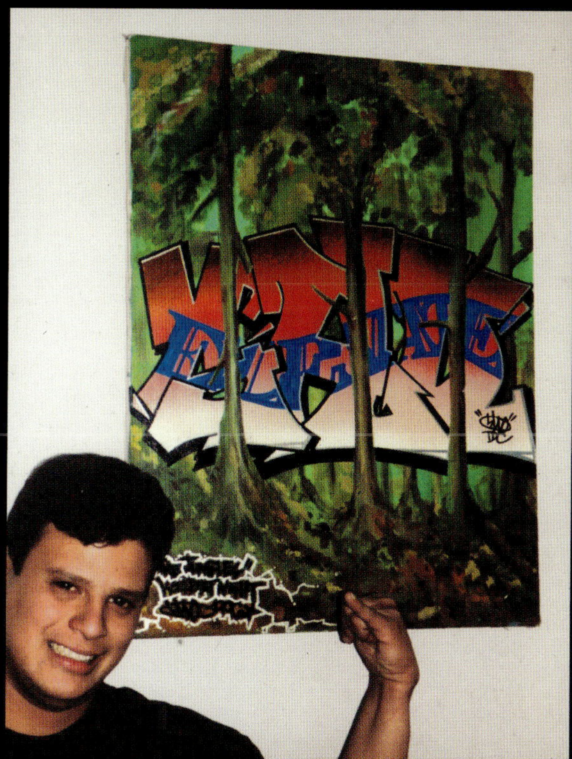

Roman live at "The Spot"

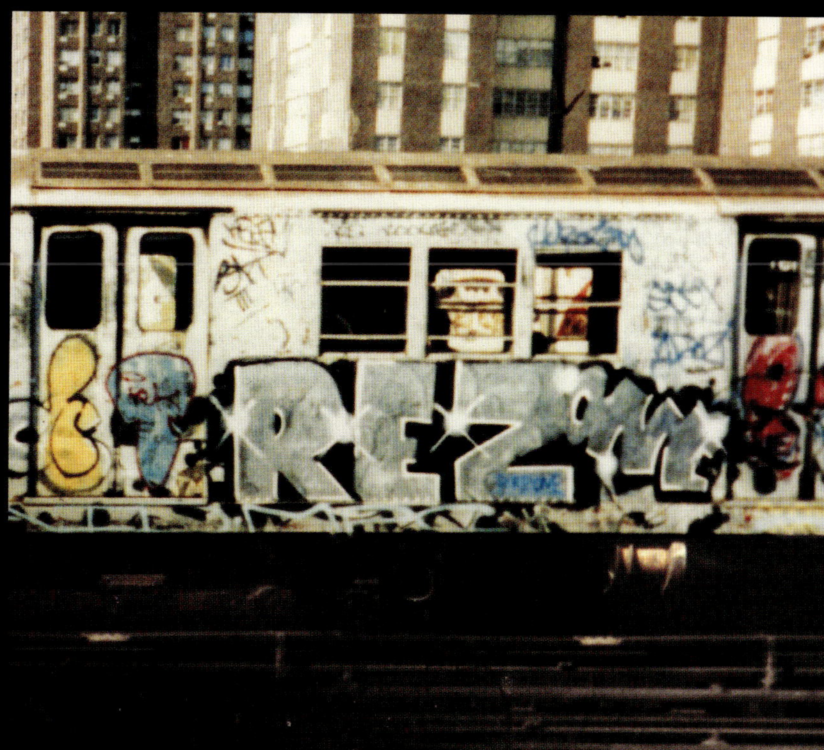

A silver quickie by ZOO for REZ One TDC, Dec. 1988.

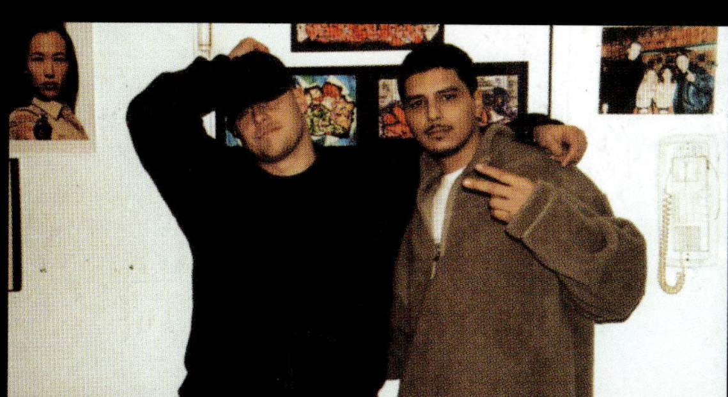

RIP Angel 106 Street

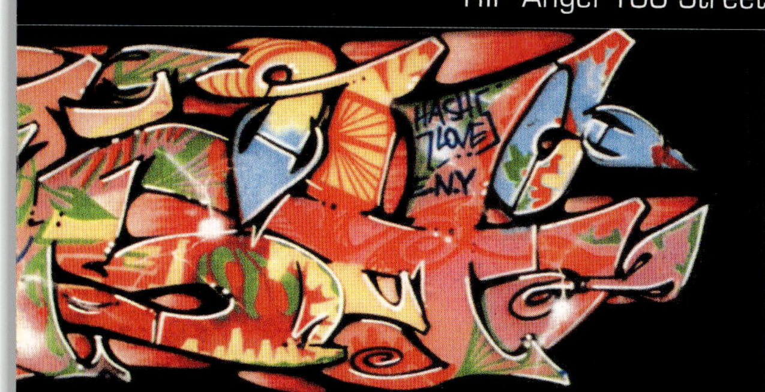

HASH by DOME 1987

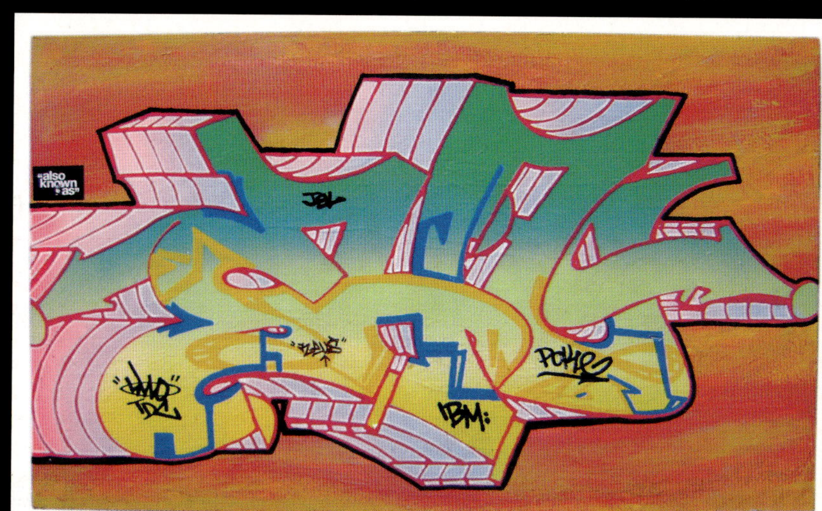

Also Known As Canvas rocked at Club SHO, 1993.

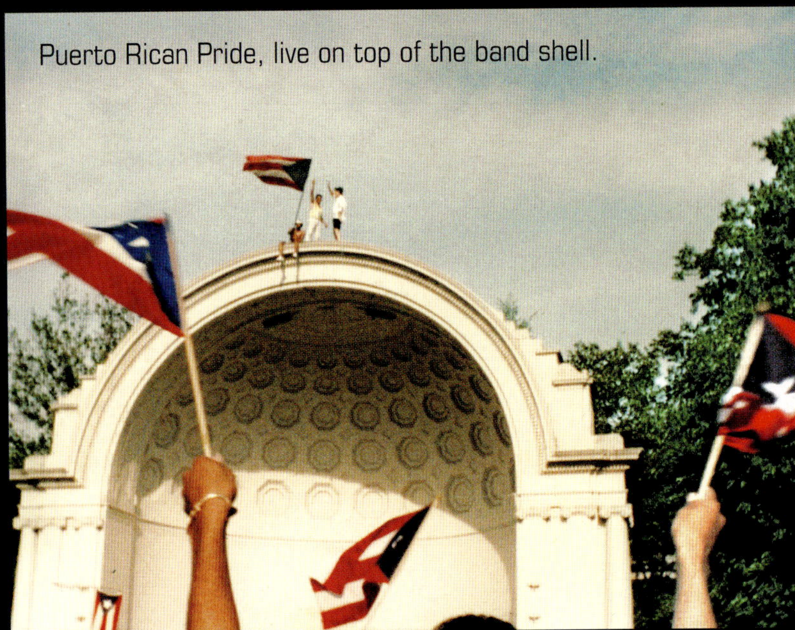

Puerto Rican Pride, live on top of the band shell.

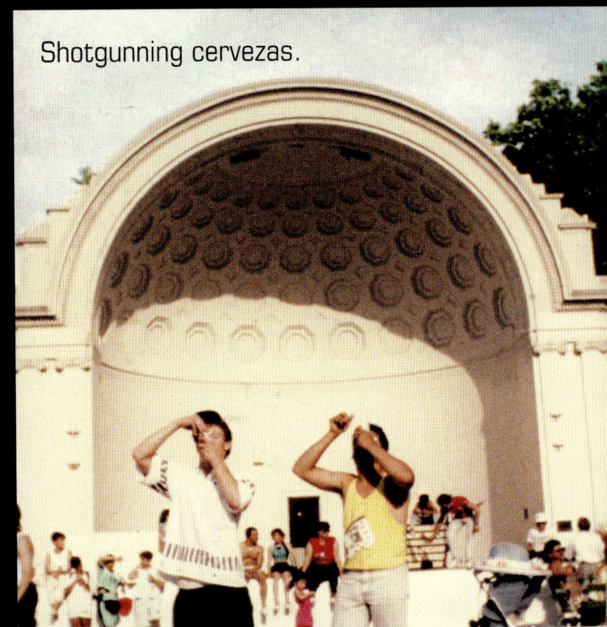

Shotgunning cervezas.

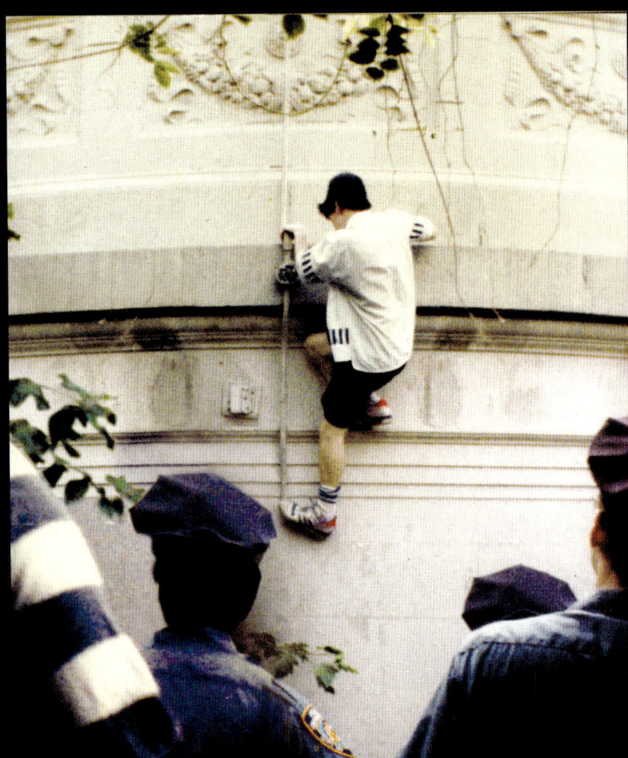

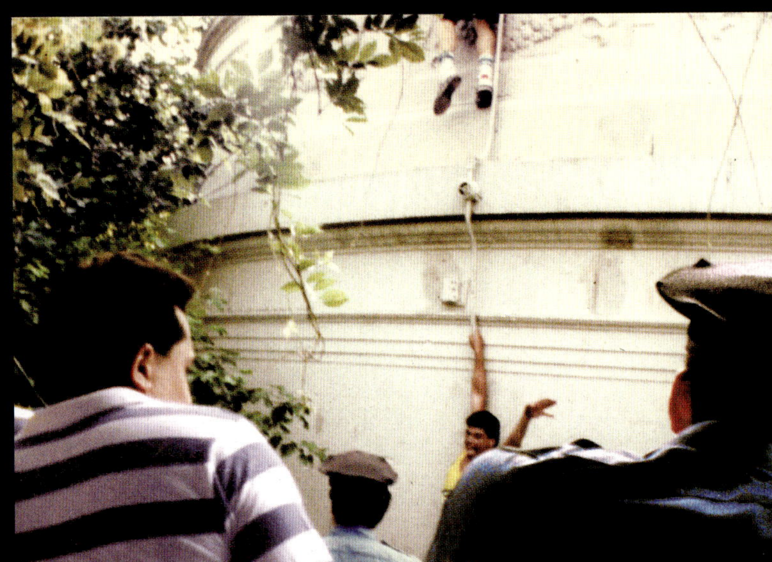

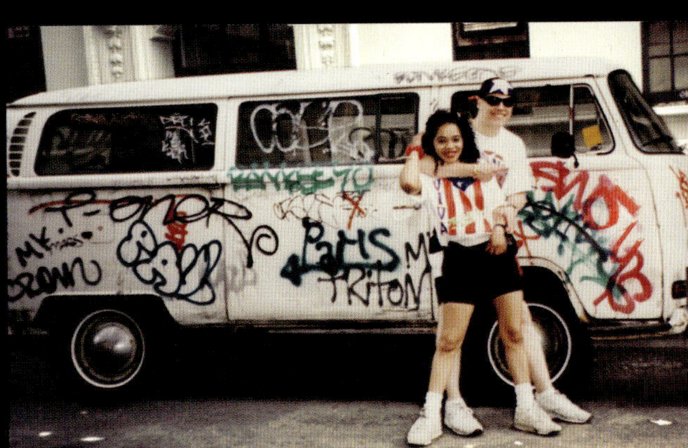

★

Here we have ZOOROC and SHO straight wilding at the Peurto Rican Parade in 1987. We had been drinking 40-oz. beers all day and Zoo was telling me every year somebody climbs to the top of the Central Park dome. So I was like, "Fuck it, lets see if we can do it." So we go around back and there's this guy all ready with the flag to go up. Yo, that shit was a crazy rush when the whole park went wild screaming. We didn't even get arrested, we dipped away as soon as they asked for ID and was hiding in and out thru the crowd, I got grabbed up by some plainclothes DTs but denied that shit saying you have to be crazy to do that. Ha Ha.

ZEUS TDC Rusto accessories and promo toys.

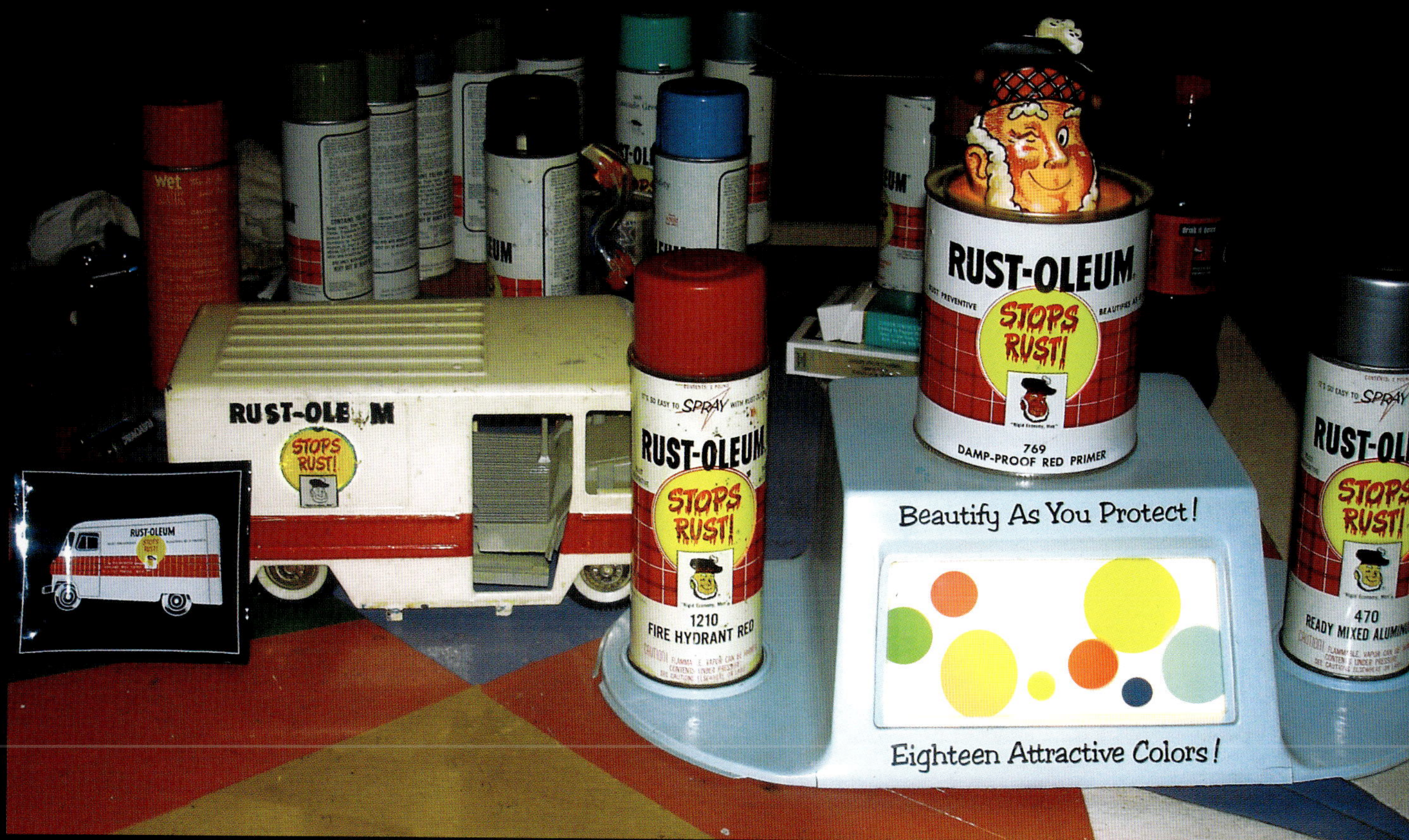

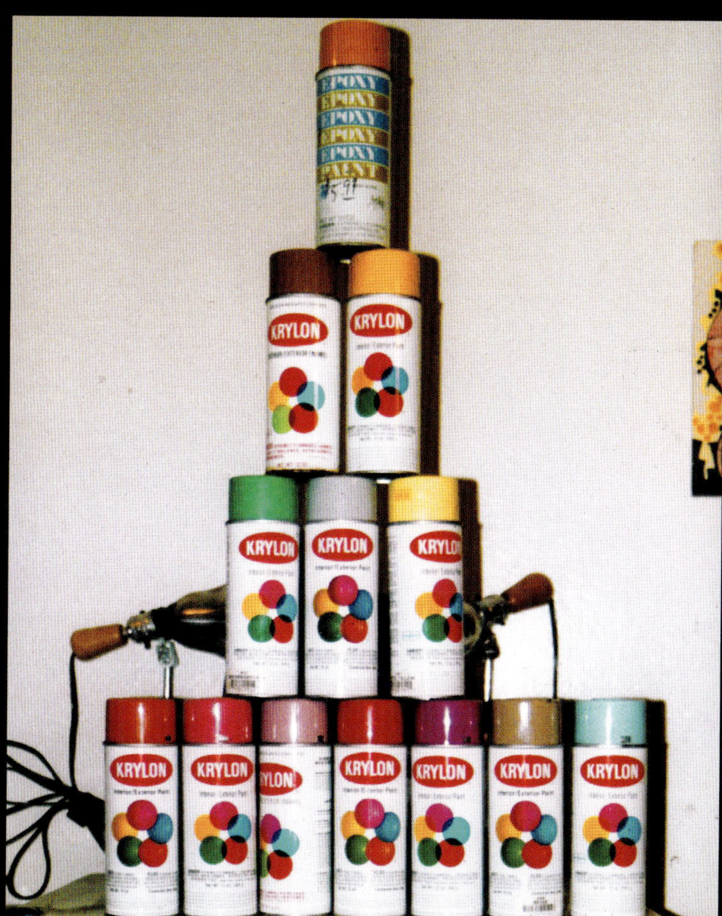

Krylon Pyramid.

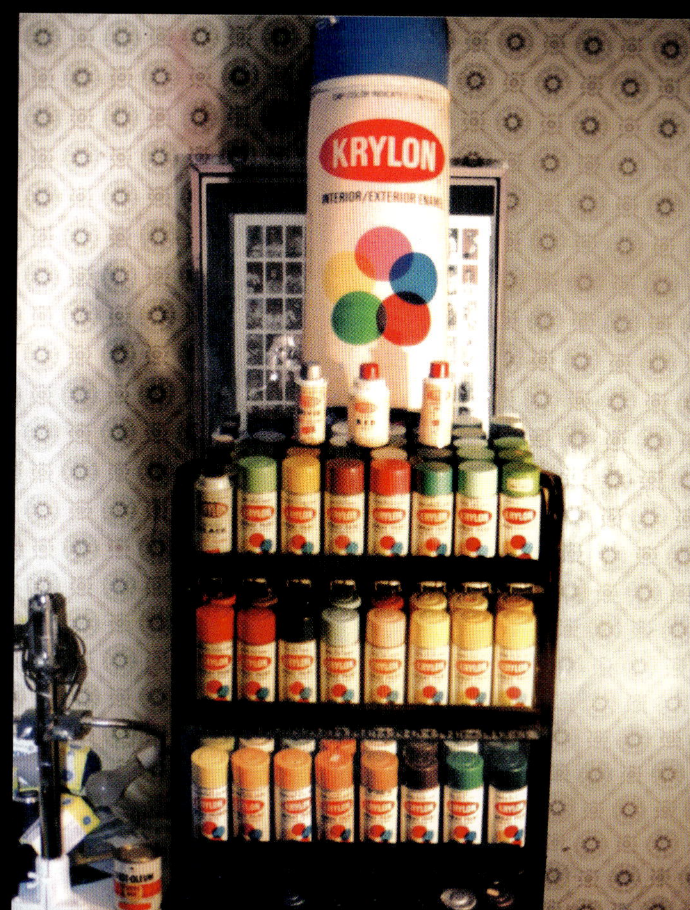

We racked the rack.

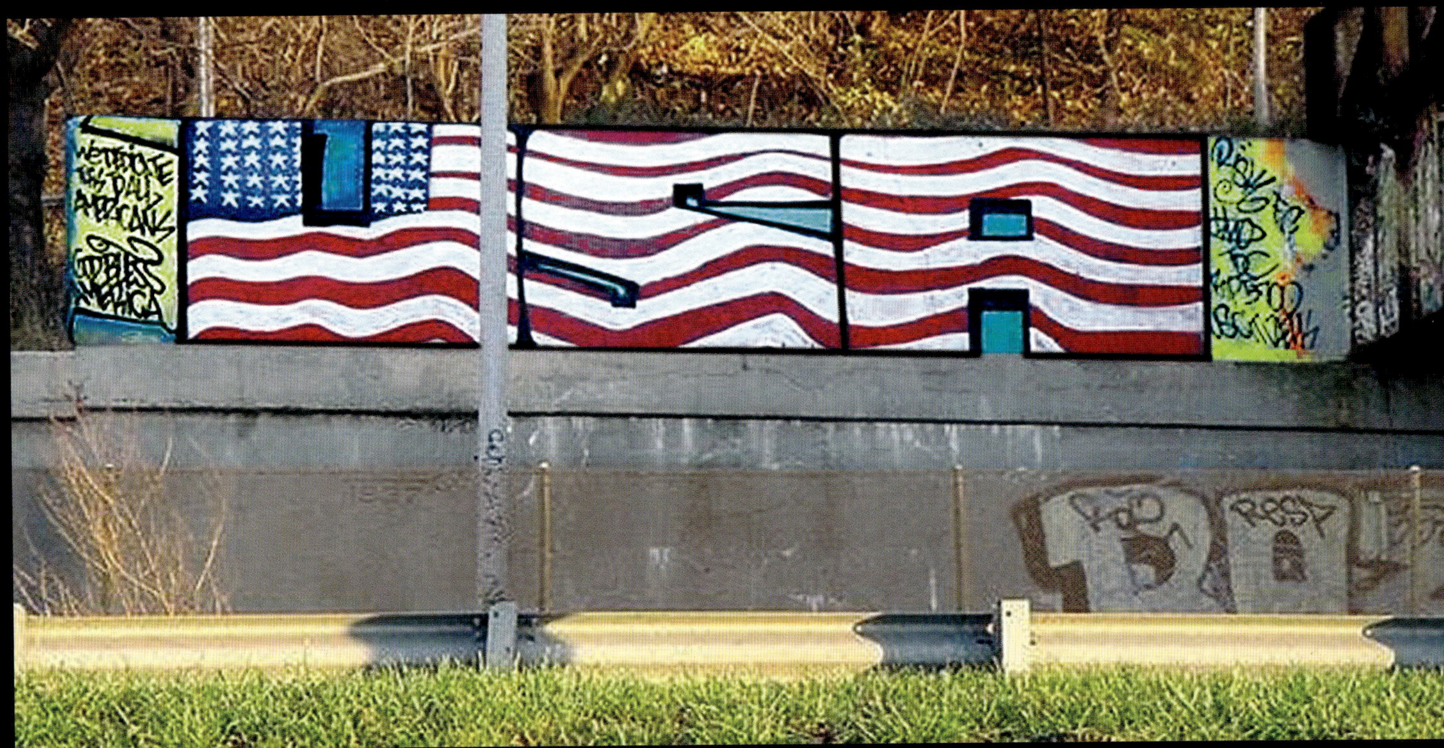

"The USA Ledge," dedicated to all Americans after the 911 attacks. To rep we did this wall September 2001 on the West Side Highway in memory of all the innocent people who died. It stayed up at least six months untouched, people gave it respect.

-SHO TDCUSA

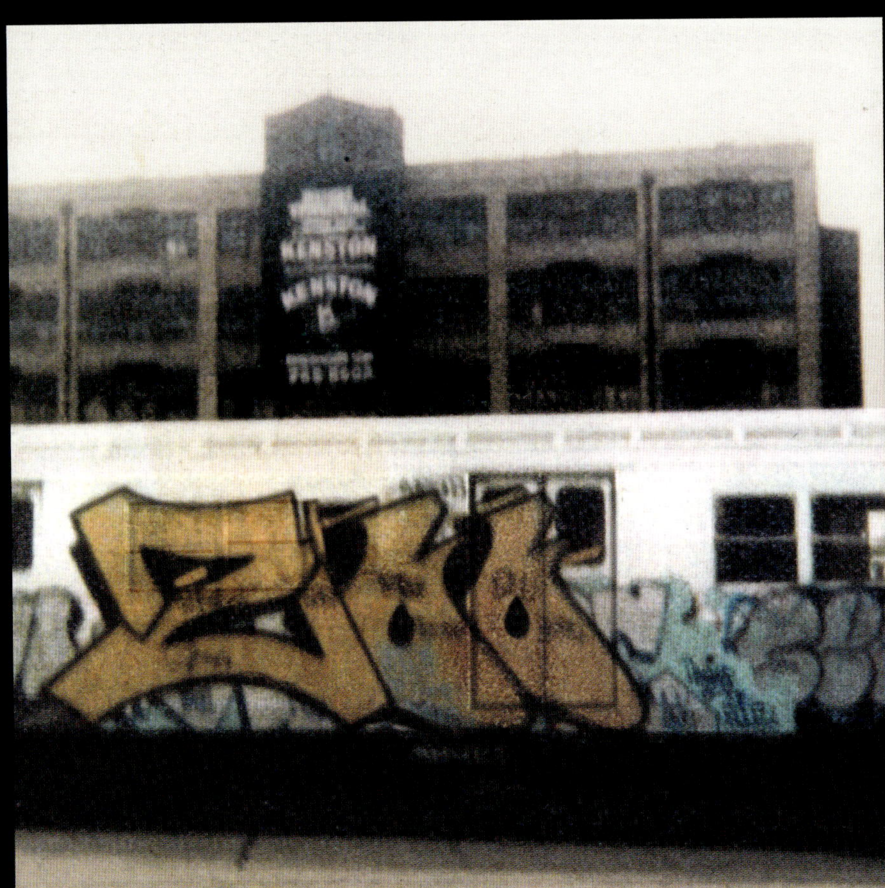

ZOO, 6 Train, Dec. 1987.

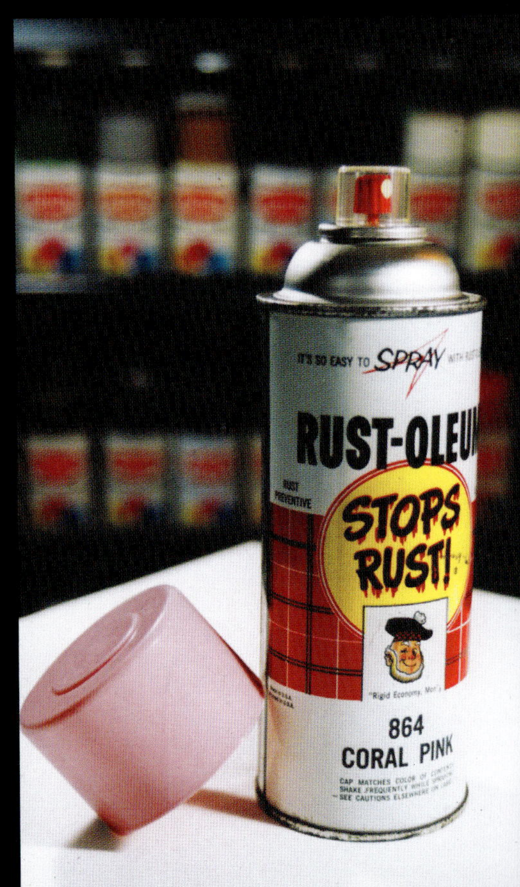

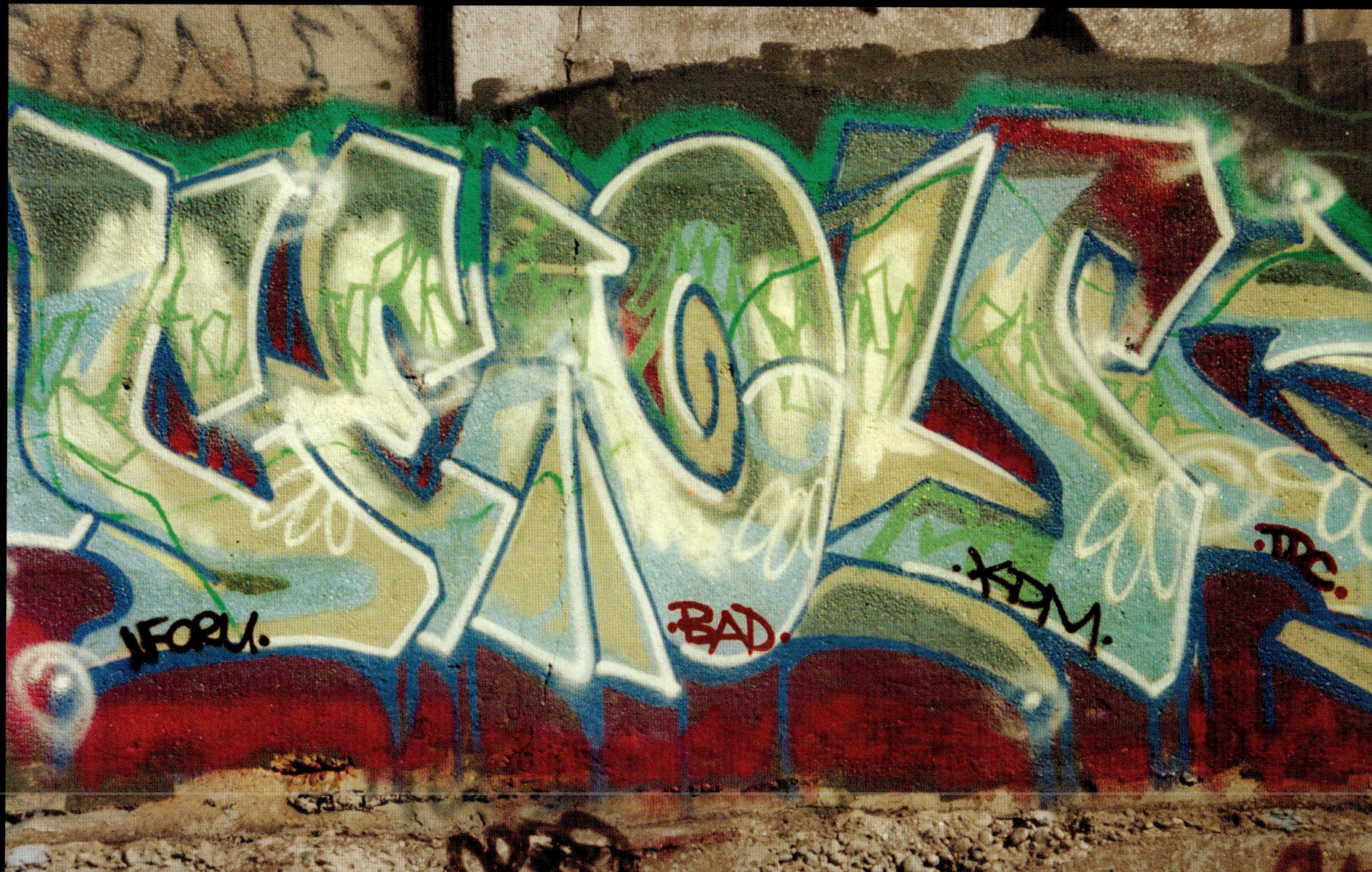

CEOS IF BAD KDM TDC, Boys Field, 1995.

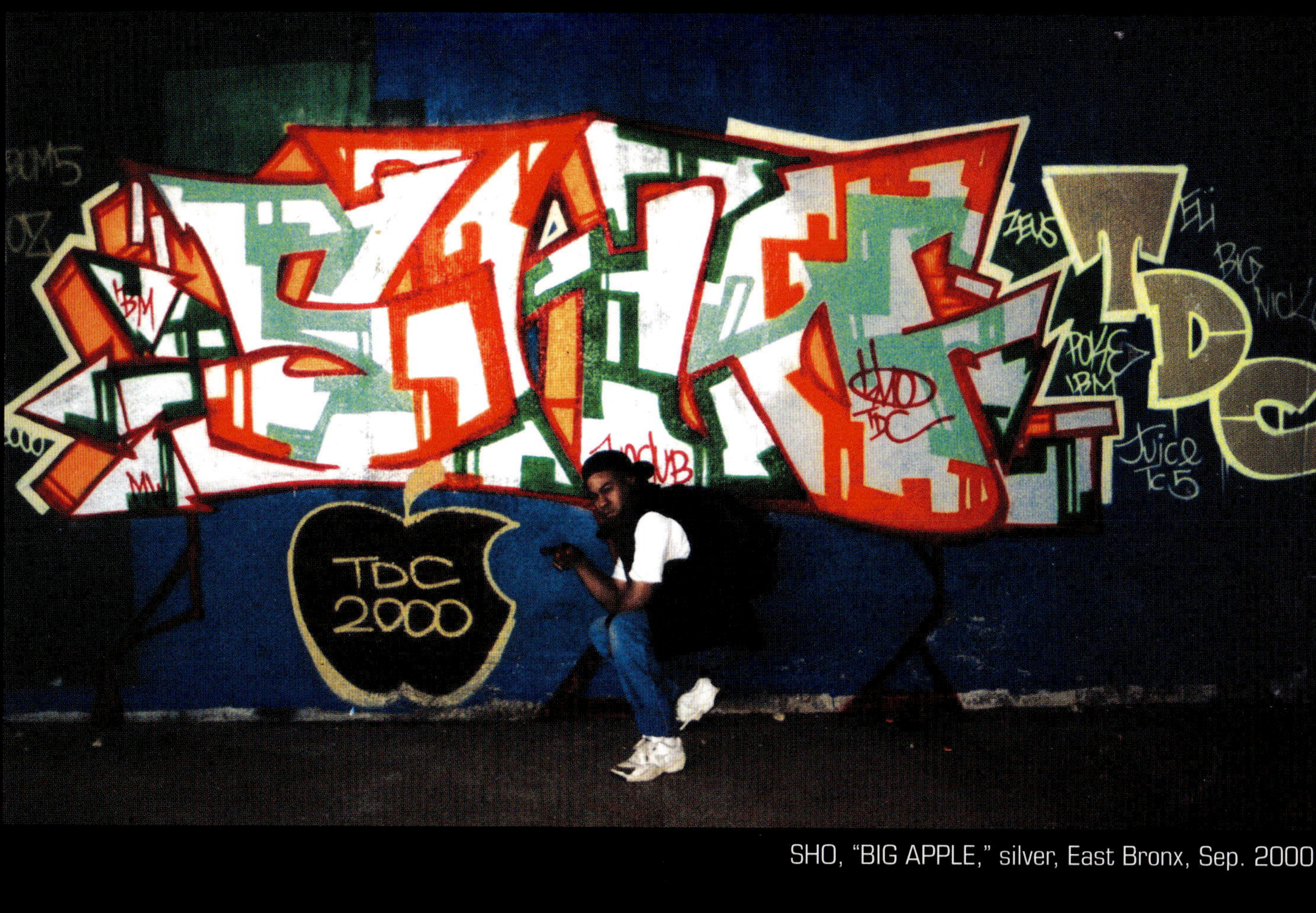

SHO, "BIG APPLE," silver, East Bronx, Sep. 2000.

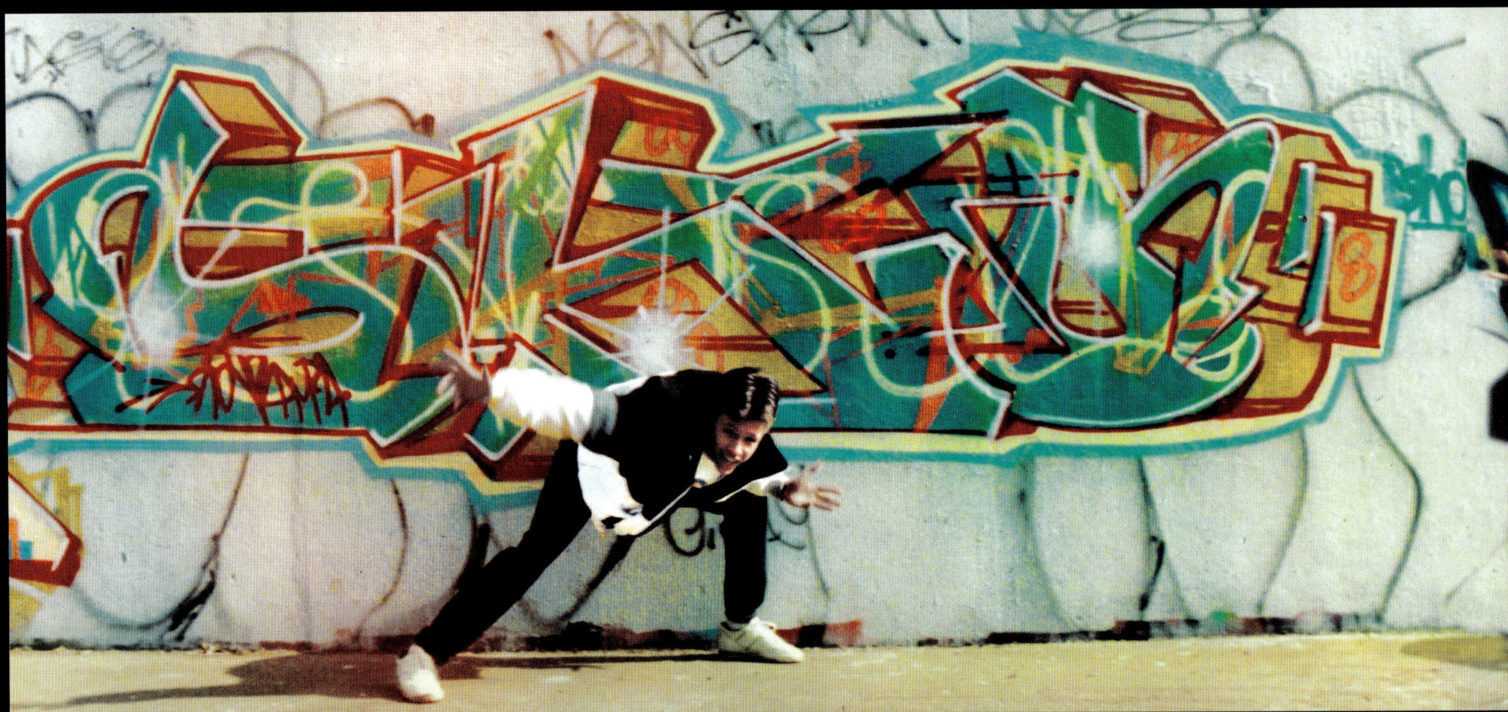

SHO and ZOO repping on the Belt Parkway, Feb. 1987.

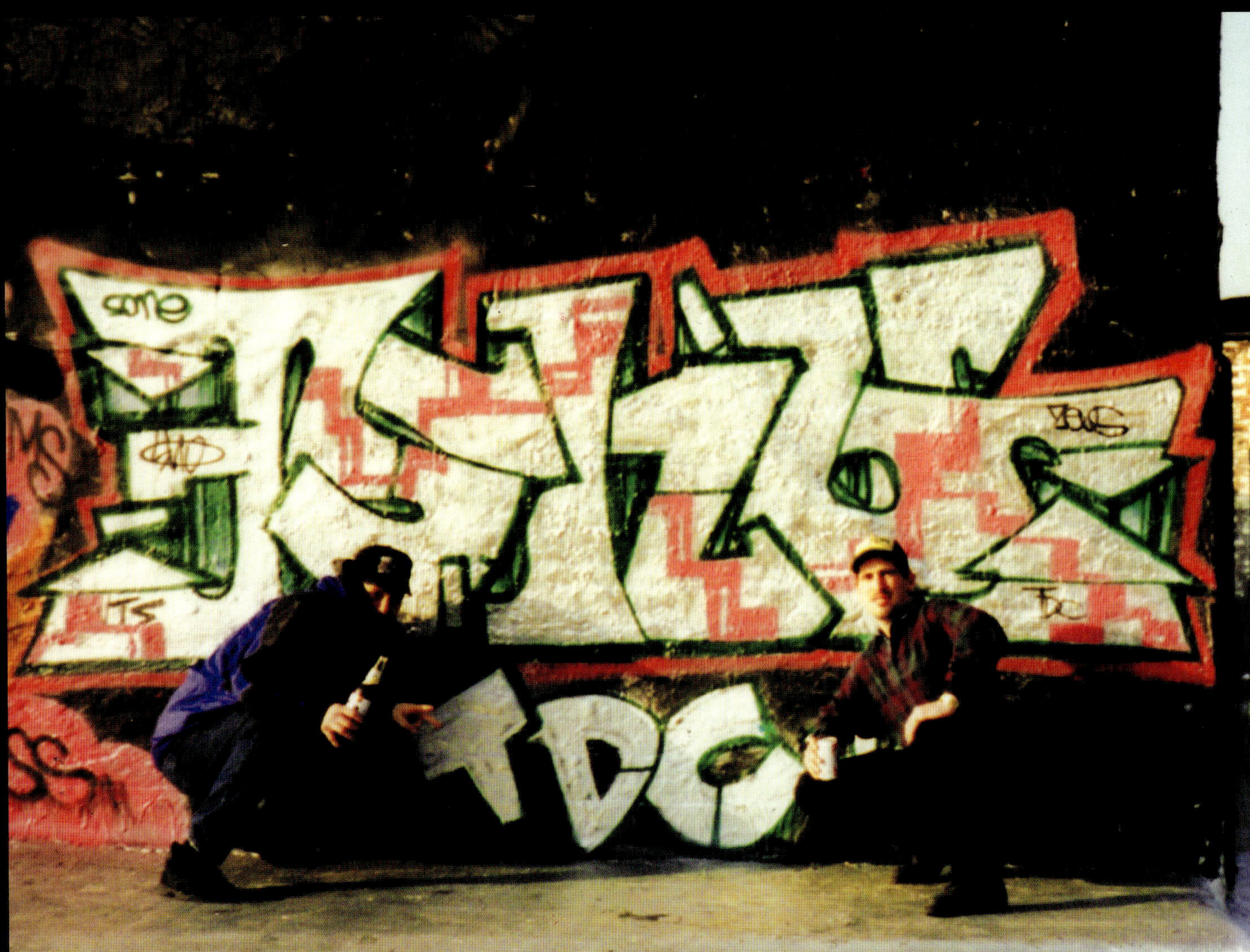

SHO TDC rooftop with 40 in hand, 1994.

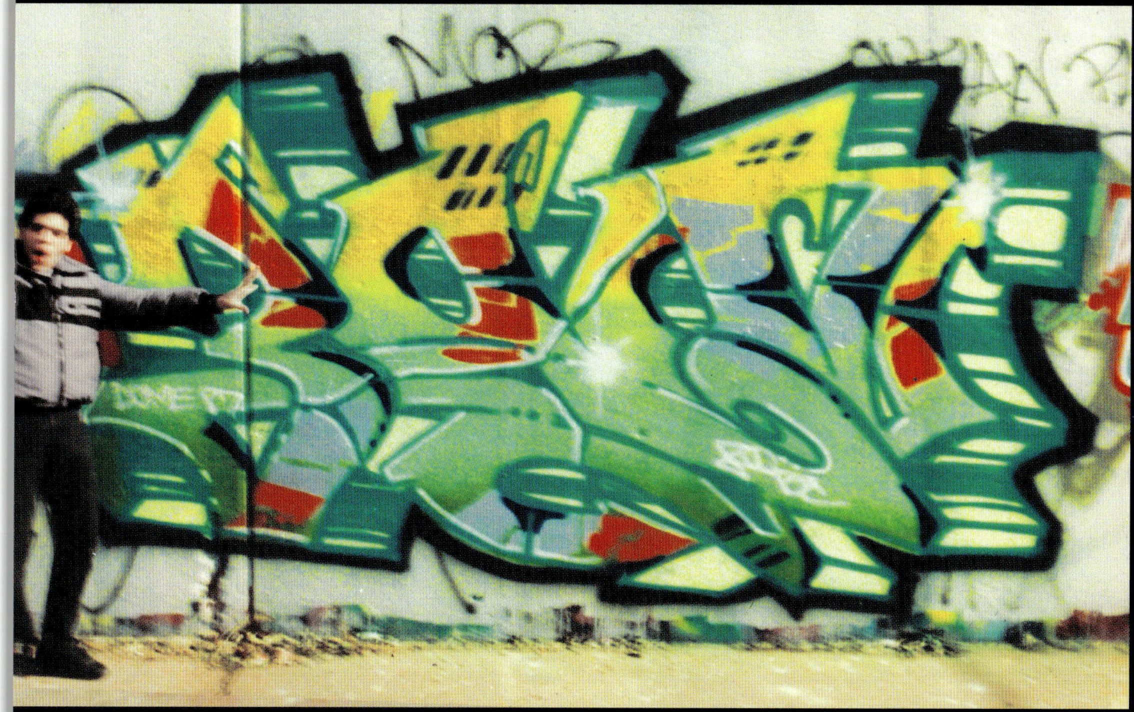

SHO AND ZOO 1987
This was also rocked very early on, at the double hand ball courts on the Belt Parkway. We was hungry to piece and didn't have any train missions planned. We would rack up hard before hitting the subway lines. Quick shit here, I don't even remember who painted with us that night.

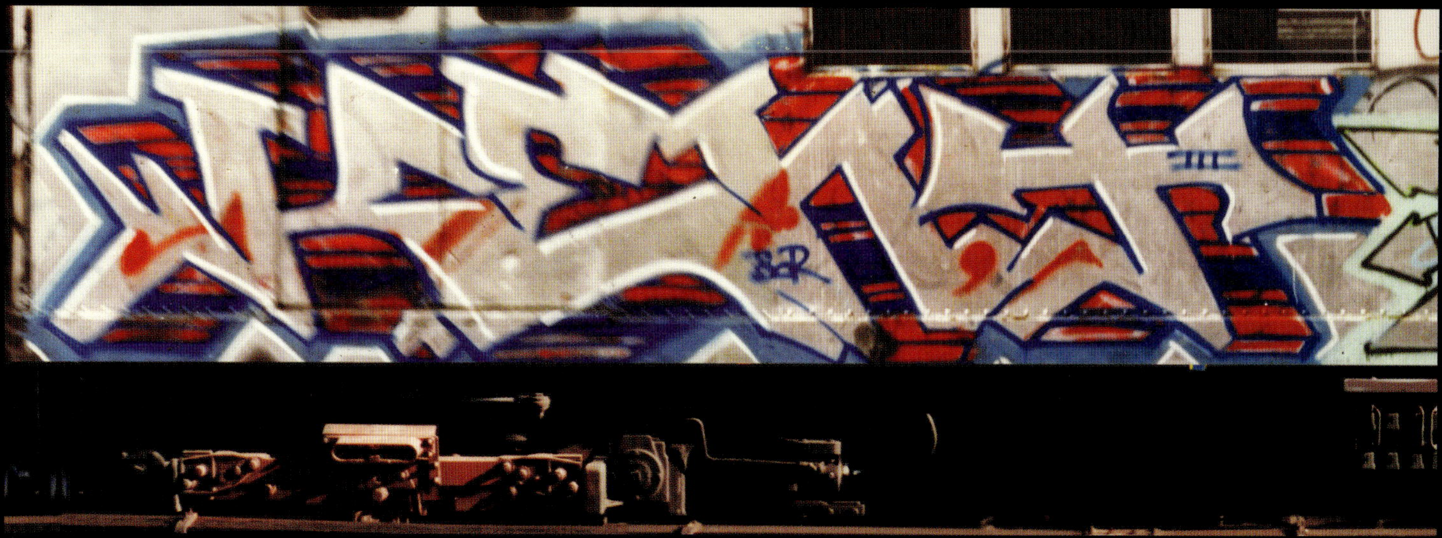

KENT3 BCR, FENT, "HELL AWAITS JEALOUS SUCKERS," and ZOO, 5 Train, Dec. 1986.

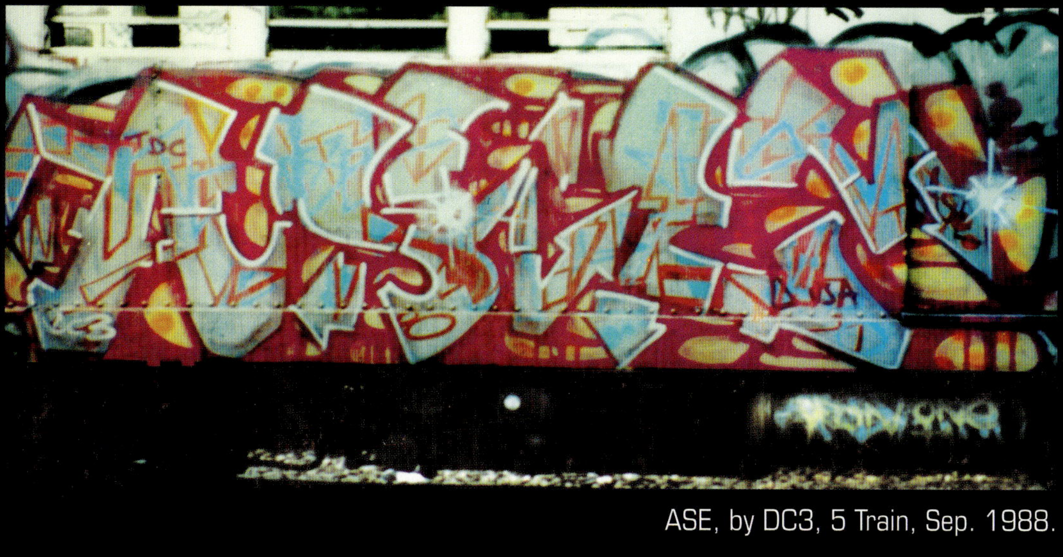

Ase by DC3 on a 5 Train mid-1988. A lot of people didn't know that DC3 also bombed pieces under aliases. I believe this was the only Ase piece he did. DC3 was fast and would be done and doing other burners with leftover paint.

ASE, by DC3, 5 Train, Sep. 1988.

DOME:MIR, COD, and RECK TDC, 5 Train wild style, Aug. 1987.

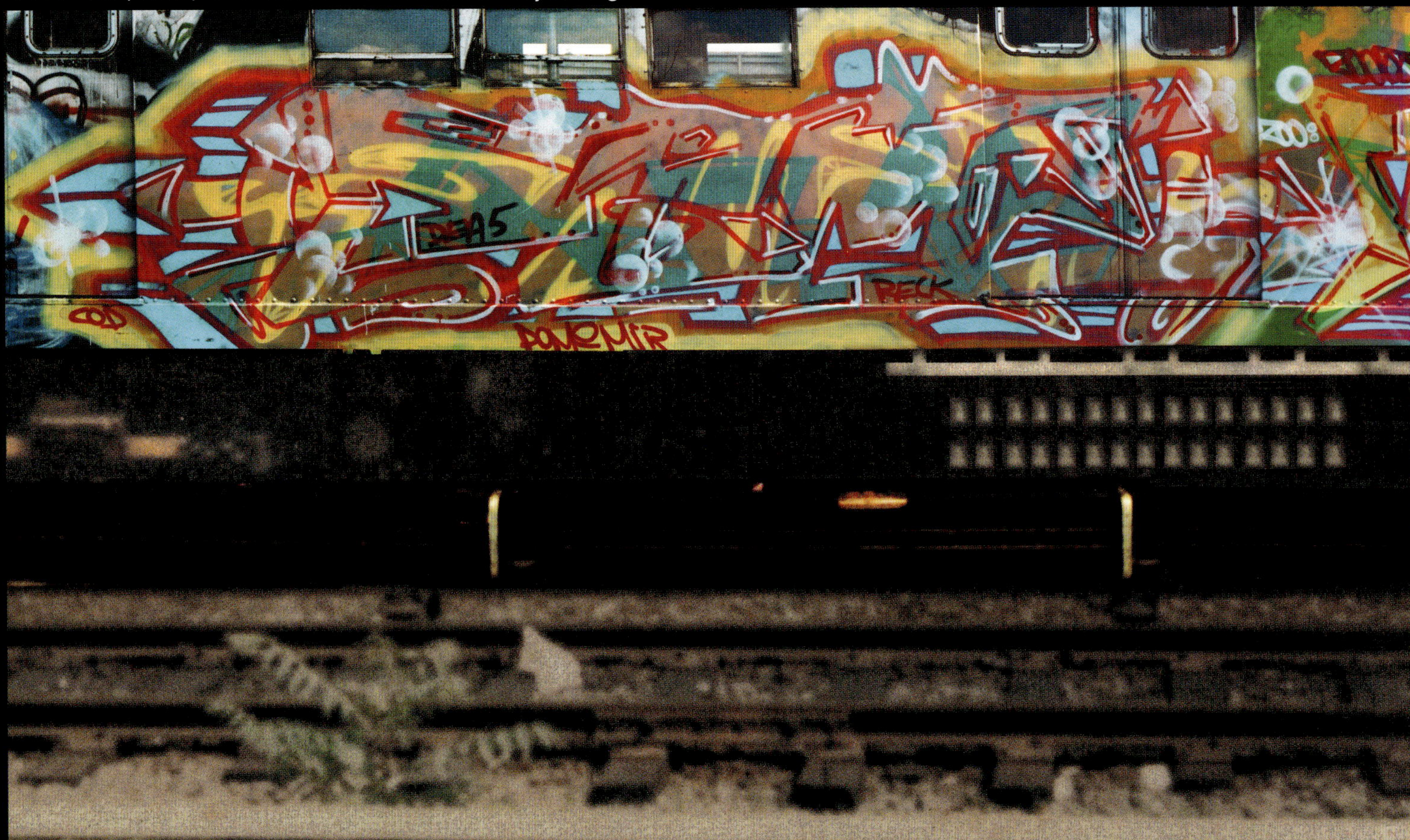

"Love is the Key to End All Wars,"
"The Destiny Children," August 15, 1985.
DC3 and SHO at Hemp Street Park. This TDC production was done very early on in the summer of 1985. DC3 lived down the block in Hempstead and we had been rocking Freeport hard and started piecing here and in Roosevelt. At this point we didn't know ZOOROC. I had seen him up crazy bombing on the N-4 and N-6 busses and at the bus terminal. Turns out he lived in the 'Stead also and had been checking out our shit and was feeling it, but had no idea who we was. It wasn't until his boy fat Stevo from the Dairy Barn had him meet DC3 that we all joined forces and made Graff history.

-The Port Kings

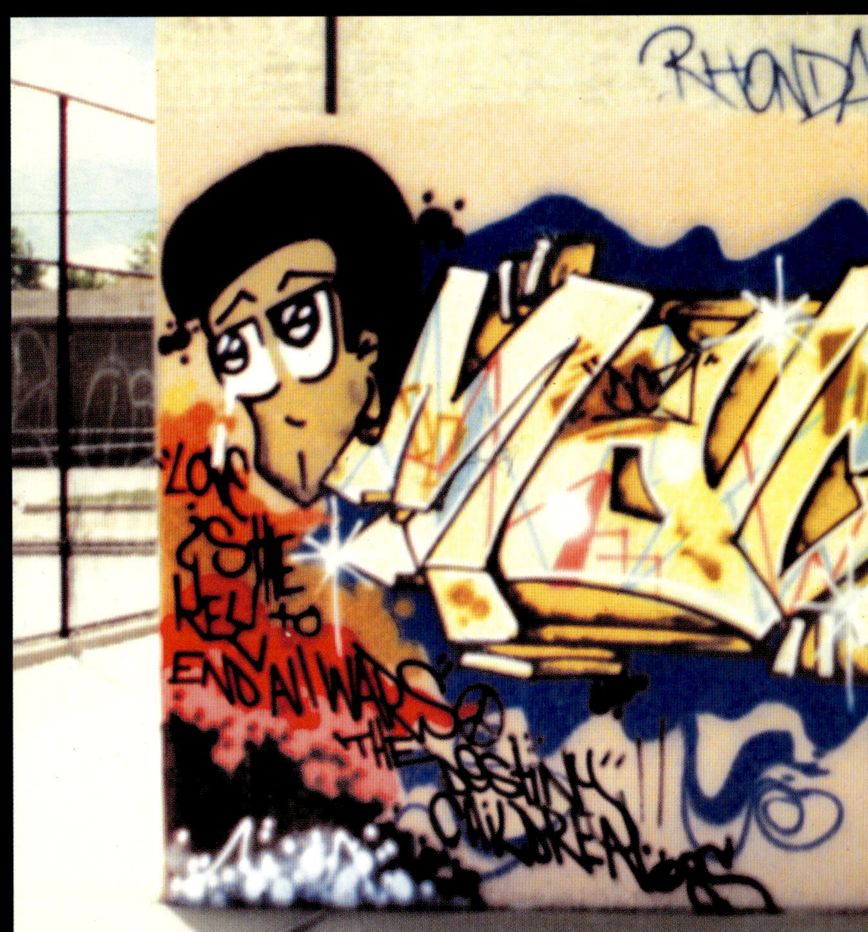

DC3, "LOVE IS THE KEY TO END ALL WARS," and

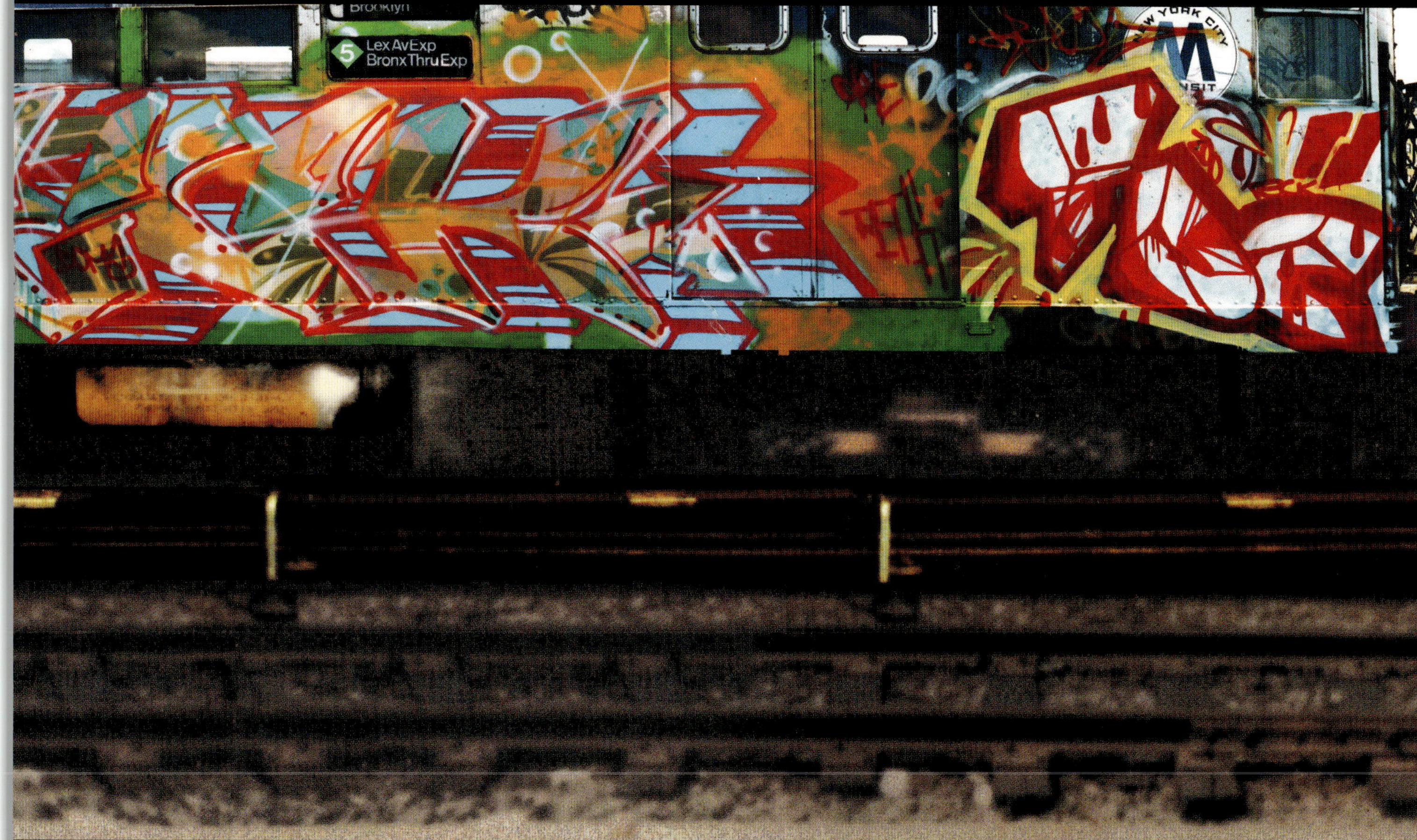

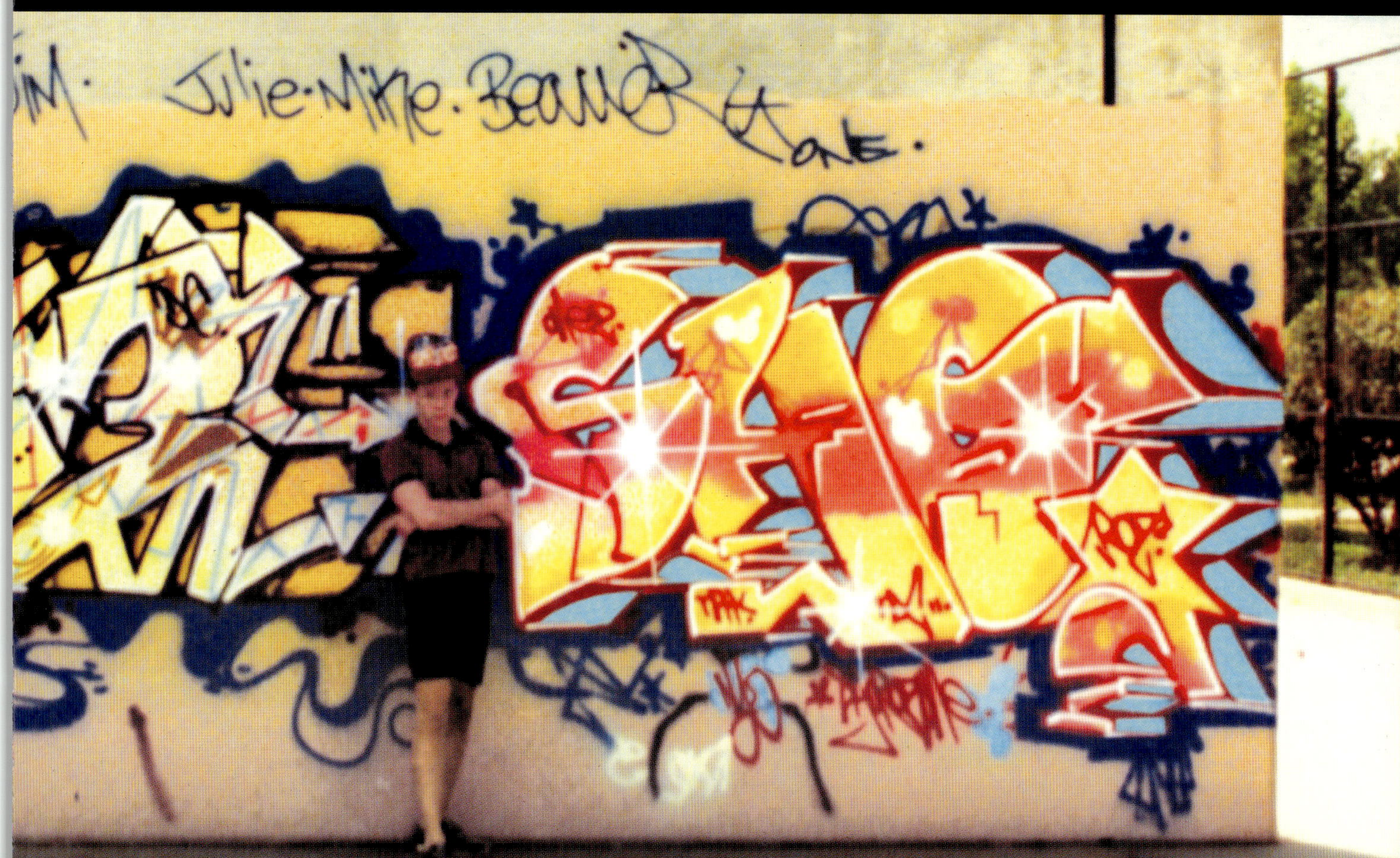

SHO, "NEW YORK'S OWN," Lincoln Park, Hempstead, NY, Aug. 1985.

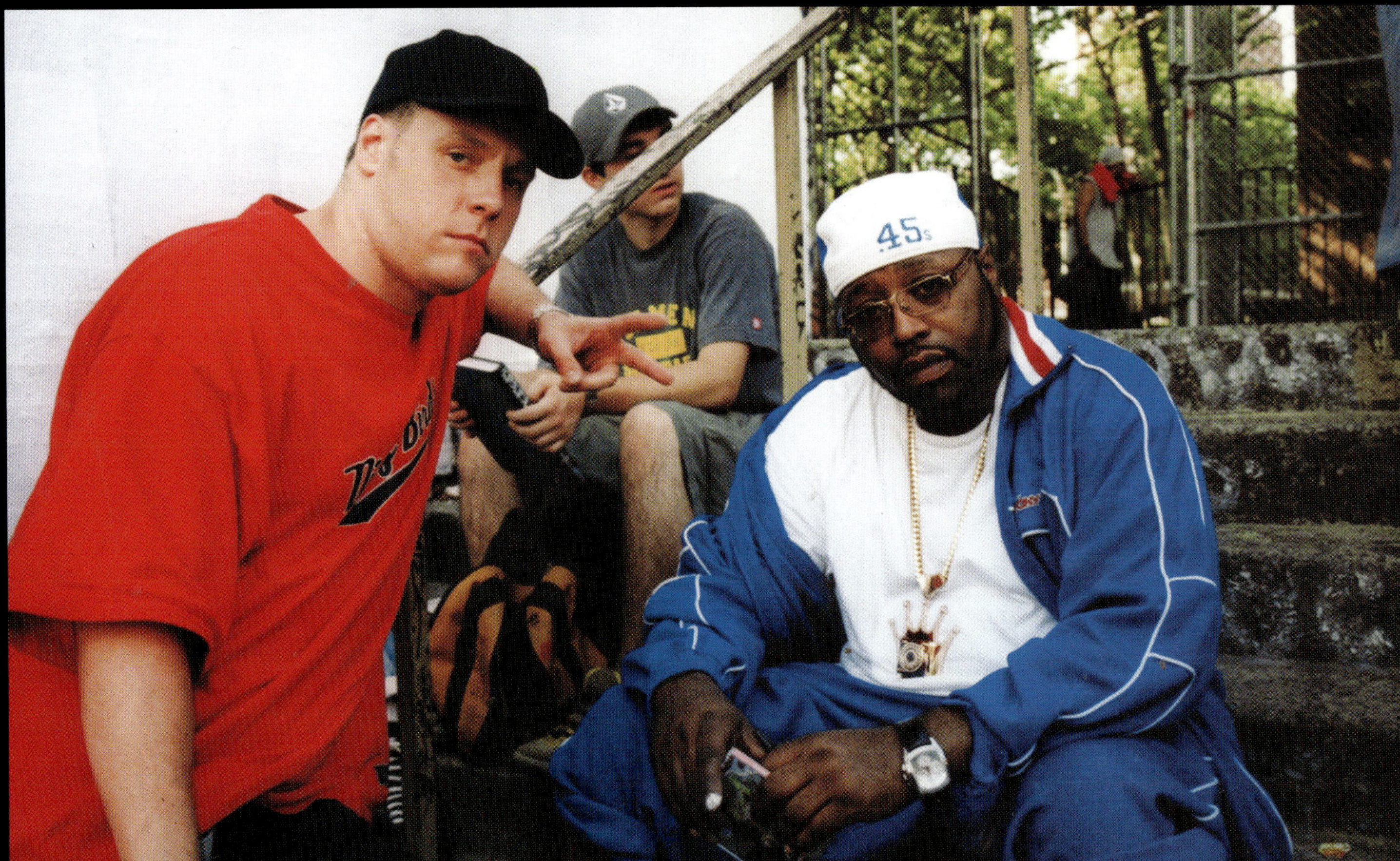

DEZ TFA, aka Kay Slay, at the Hall of Fame.

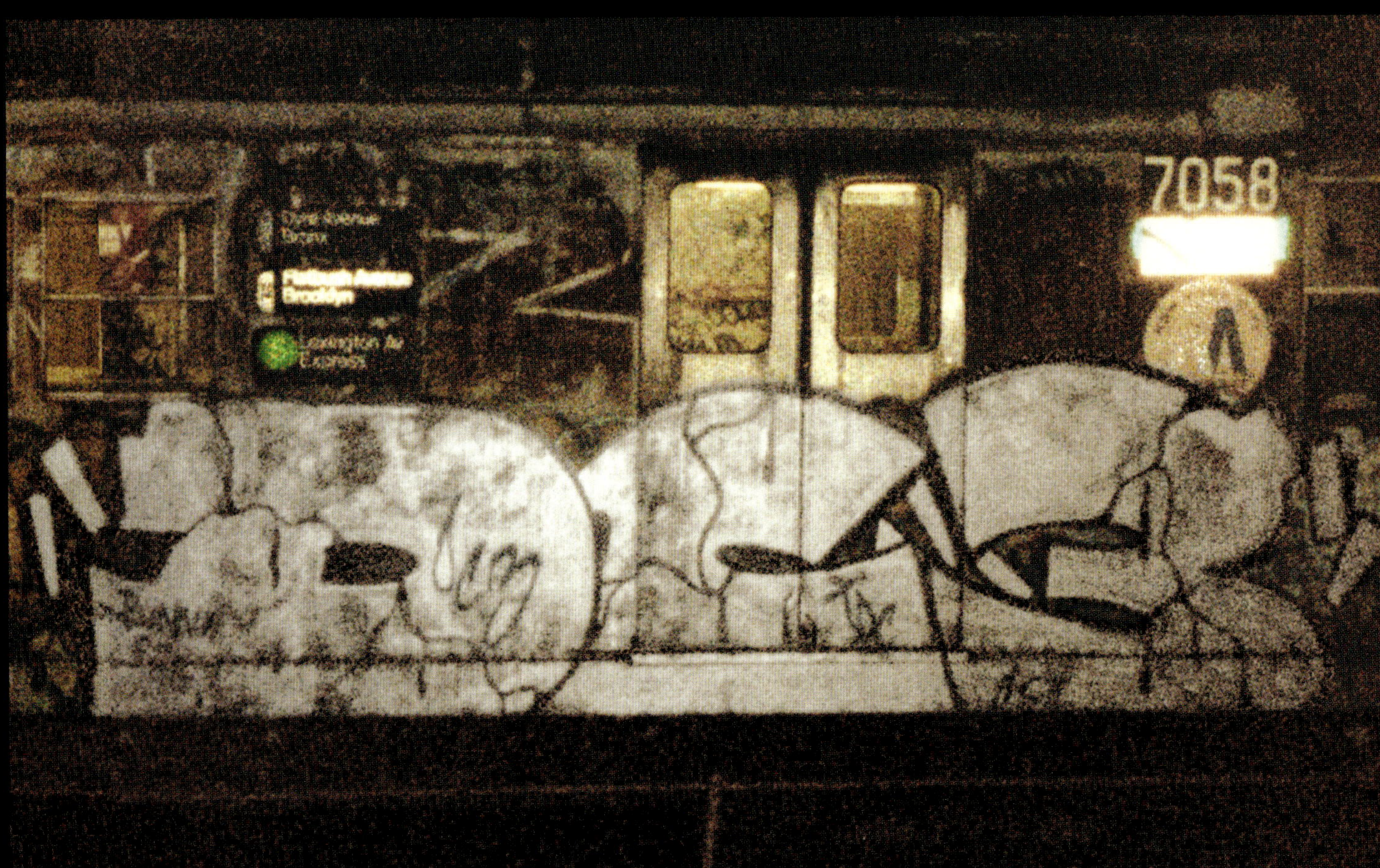

DC3, 5 Train silver, still running Jun. 1989.

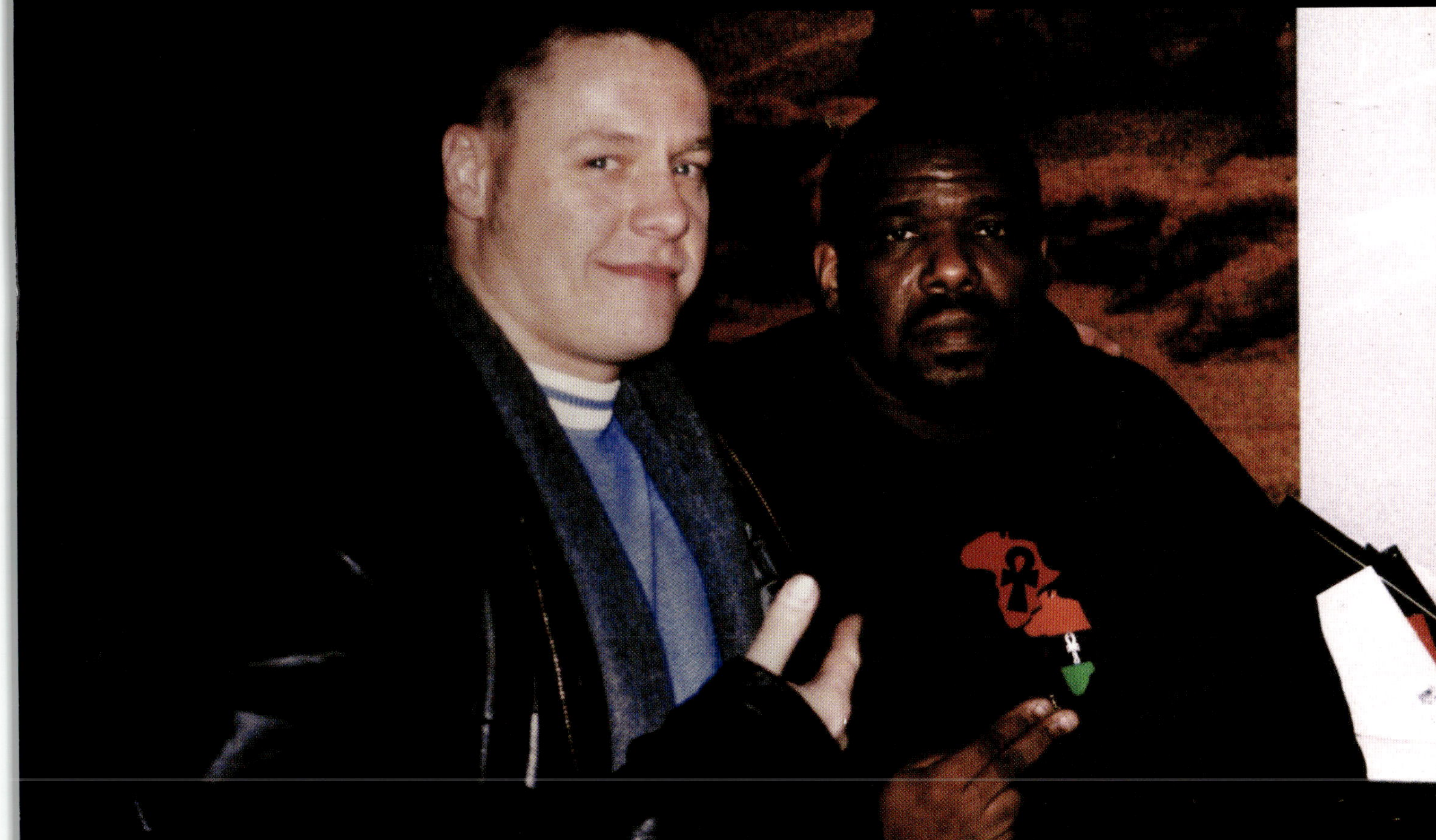

Afrika Bambaataa Zulu Nation.

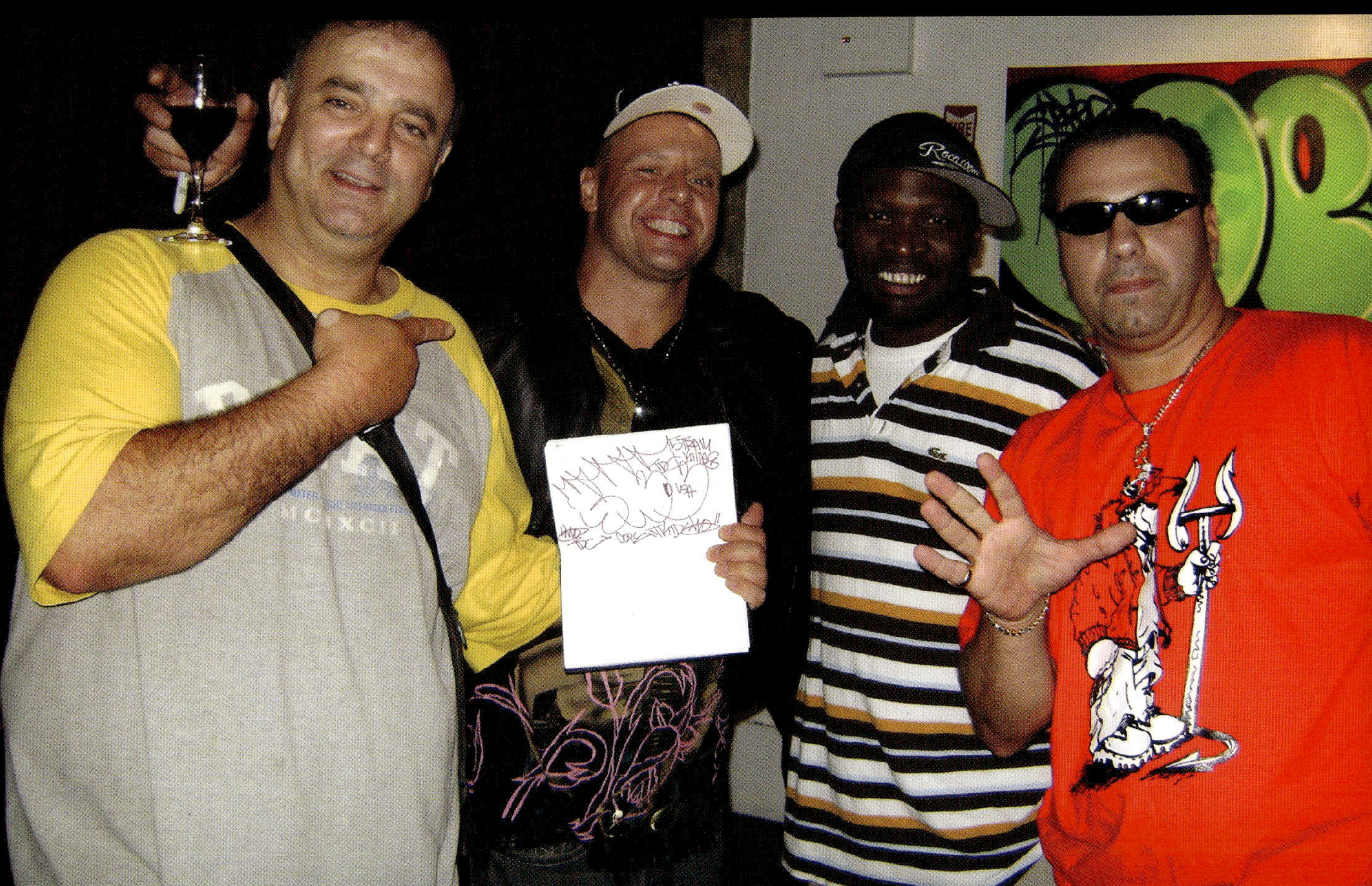

Chilling with OTB Crew originals at Mansion M2.

"ESPLANADE ADDICTION"

Yo, in October 2008, I took ROSE
to the stick-outs and walked thru the tunnels
to Pelham Parkway, in broad daylight, to reminisce.
Little did I know I'd be reminiscing about that so soon.

"Live Life to The Fullest
and Always put it
ALL ON THE LINE."
-SHOROSE

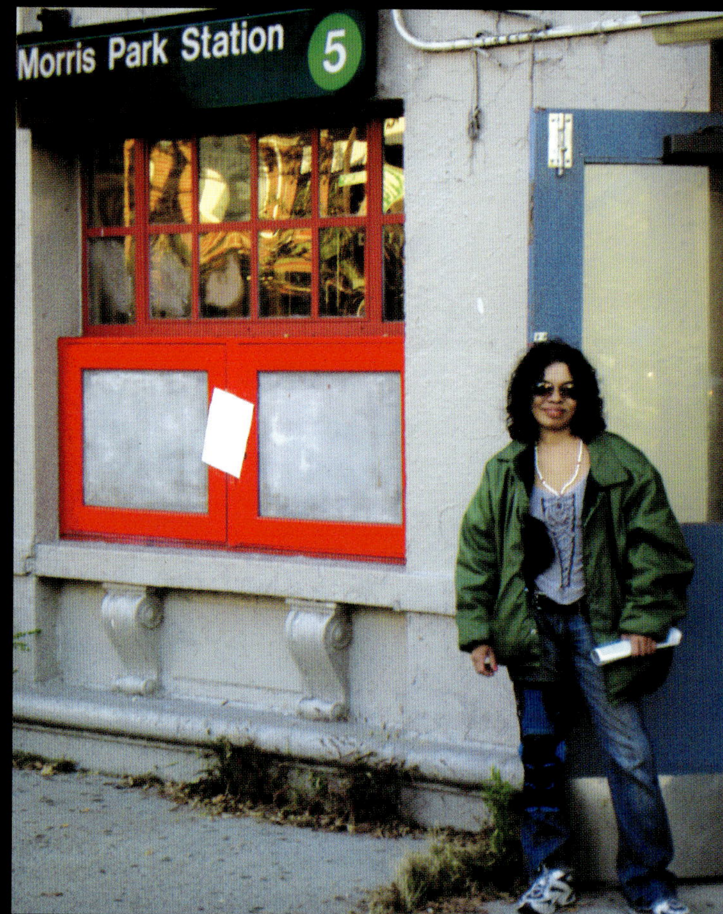

For y'all that know me, or thinks you do: "I do not give a flying fuck." No props to the TDC haters. Bottom line is, everything in this book is Old School. My intentions are good. I wanted to tell and document a period of time that was sacred to me. Very rarely has there been a graffiti crew book that is so all-inclusive that it includes the real associates. Representing those writers artwork was important because here they get their shine whereas they might not have otherwise. Most writers are fame hungry and very selfish and would not do this. I know most of the people in this book personally and felt it will make this production a real standout. Please know and respect that all I ever wanted to do was be a part of GRAFF HISTORY. New York City, where it all started, the Mecca, The Birthplace. We did it!! Hope you enjoyed the ride as much as we did. Peace Out, Yo...
-SHO TDCMWUSAIBM2012

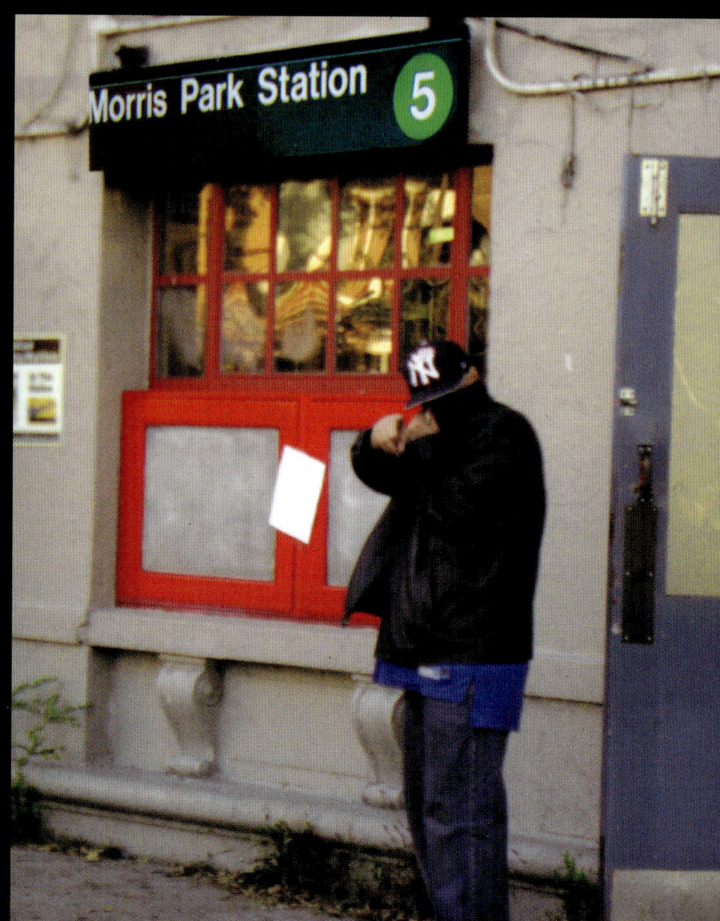

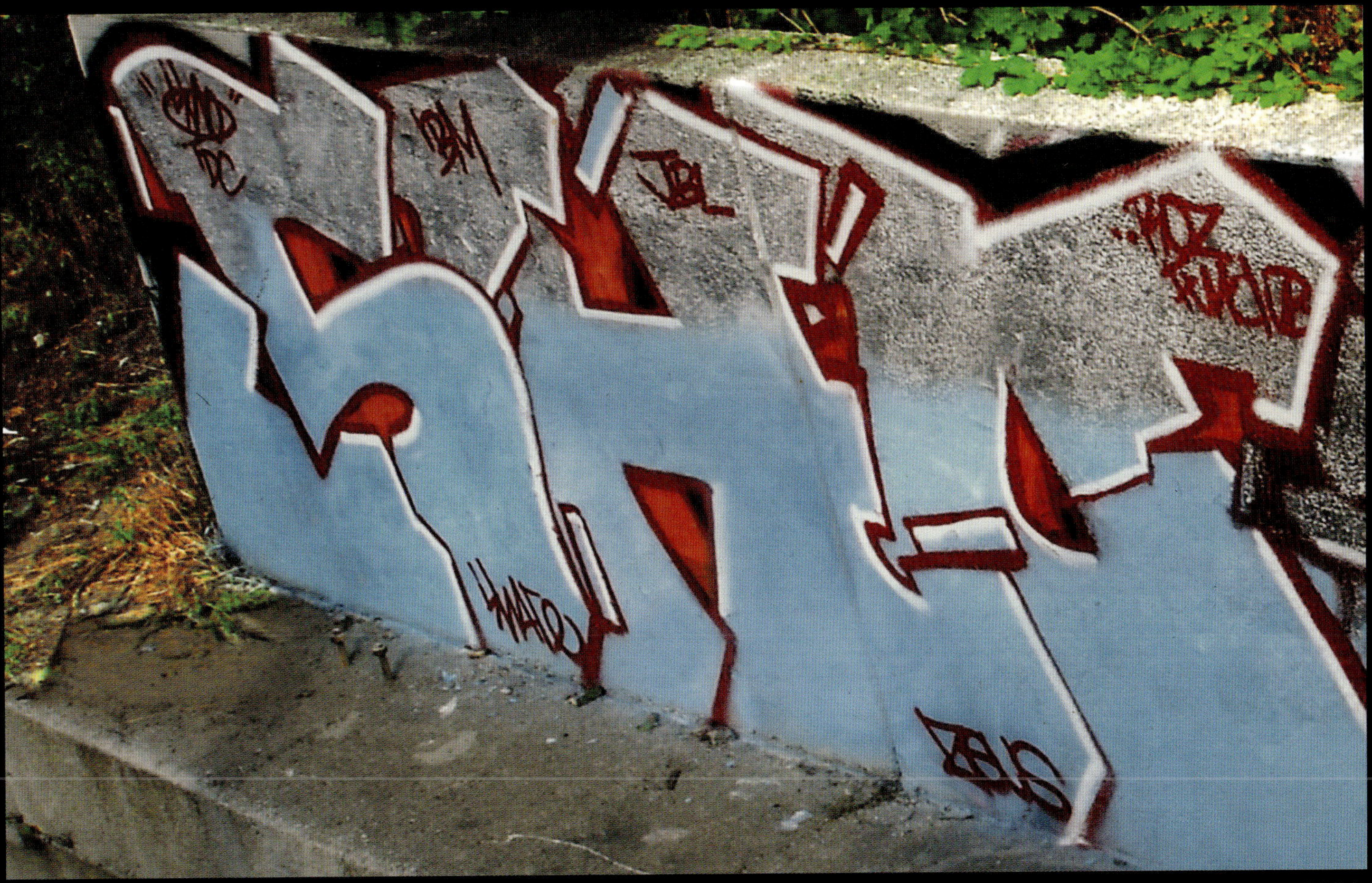

SHO, again and again and again!!! 2001.

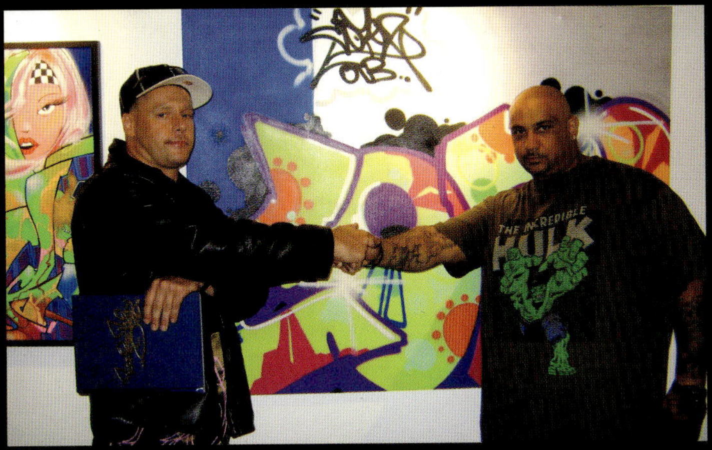

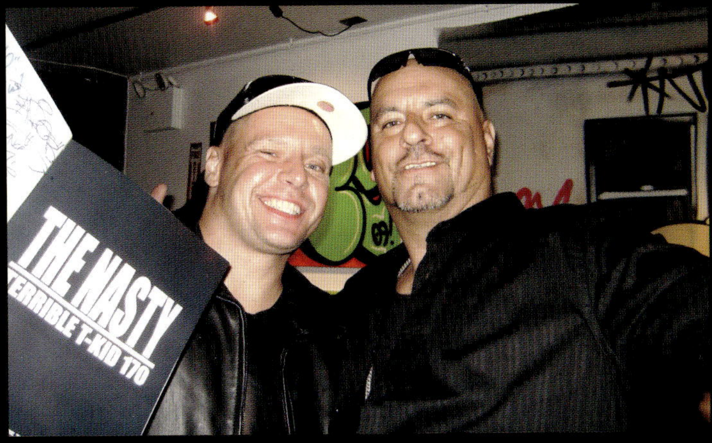

"At the End of the Day"

I had to spit this to tell the whole story.
From the start of my graff career to the end
there was always graff beefs and wars.
TDC had major beef on the 5 Train and that continued
after because I couldn't let it go. I laugh at toys like Rob and
PJ, who in an issue of *Urban Ink* say they was Morris Park
legends; that's not true, they were haters that was doing
weak fill-ins over you and never stepped to us in Esplanade.
I had extended street beefs with Rad 501 who I pounded
out in a supermarket and some biter pussy toy fake "sho"
whose shit I stomped out, What! The illest graff war I
had was with COPE2. The shit lasted nine months on the
streets in 1994, long after the trains was gone.
Copes been a friend for years now
"REAL RECOGNIZES REAL."

-SHO

Special Thanks Appendix

★

People to thank for recognizing us early on in the Graff come up.

1. *Stress* Magazine / Ket_Issue #8, 1993
Stress Magazine, Issue #25, Hall Of Fame Issue, 2000
Stress Magazine, Issue #21, Capone and Noreaga, 1999

2. James Top and Ket / *Strictly Kings or Better* video, 2006.

3. IGT *International Graffiti Times* / Dave Schmidlap / Phase2, 1984
Volumes #4, #9, #10, 1985-1986
Critical Beat Down, Volume #13, 1987

4. *Broken Windows: Graffiti NYC*, for Share 37, 2002

5. *Taking the Train: How Graffiti Became an Urban Crisis in New York City*, 2001

6. Hip Hop Honors / Nic One, Blondie, and Fab 5 Freddy featuring the "Juggernaut Train," 2004

7. *Style: Writings from The Underground (R)evolutions of Aerosol Linguistics*, 1997

8. *Beat Down* Magazine, Volume #3, Raekwon & Ghost Face Killer Issue, 1995

9. *Skills* Magazine, Volume #5, 1994
Skills Magazine, Volume #7, 1995

10. *On The Go* Magazine, Volume #9, Method Man Issue, 1995
On The Go Magazine, Volume #11, Fat Joe Issue, 1996

11. The Spot Graffiti Show @ Taller Latino Americano, 104th St. and Broadway, 1996
The Spot Graffiti Show @ Amsterdam Projects Community Center, 1997
The Spot Graffiti Show @ 113th St. and Broadway, 1997
The Spot Graffiti Show @ Amsterdam Projects Community Center, New Years Jump Off, 1998
Bom 5, SHO TDC, Roz Fun Club, Share 37, Double AB, Snatch CWK, Nacho, and Lethal

12. *Flashbacks,* Issue #7, 1994

13. *Crazy Kings* Magazine, Issue #1, 1993

14. *Undercover* Magazine "Painted In Prison," Issue #5, Spring, 1995

15. *Mass Appeal* Magazine, Manhattan Edition #14, 1994

16. *Also Known As*, Volume #1 book launch, 12oz Prophet
"Cans of Distinction Display," Zeus Roc TDC, 2005

17. *Elementary* Magazine, Lethal, November 15, 1994.

Other Schiffer Books on Related Subjects:

From the Platform, 978-0-7643-3723-9, $34.99
Fresh Paint: NYC, 978-0-7643-3495-5, $34.99
Truck Art: A Decade of Graffiti, 978-0-7643-3493-1, $29.99

Project created, conceived, and produced by SHO, including image and graphic desktop work.
Some text by featured artists and accredited to ZOO, DC3, ROZ, POKE, SPHERE, BOM5, LAE, and ZEUS. Thanks for the recollections you sent me. Photos from SHO's collection. Original photography from many TDC members and affiliates. Some jpegs from Mr. Clean, Swift, and DC3.

Thanks to all the people who supported me in this epic effort. You know who you are and I really appreciate it.
Much respect!! We made history.

Works roughly in chronological order, it was a long time ago. Photo credits go to my team members and associates who were down for action and in the right place at the right time in the final three years of The Running Bombed Subway Train Era from 1985-1989 and Circa NYC thereafter: DC3; ZOO, aka DOME; MERLIN; DOOJ; BEAVER; ZEUS; RECK; SACER (RIP); SOME; LAC2; MAZE; SHIM; ONE2; RAZE; LAURA; MIRAGE, aka MAC KDM; SKETCH CWK; KOOL SPHERE; RUSH; JESTO; CEOS TDC; CRAZE; SWIFT; ROE1; SNATCH CWK; KARL TCM; SERT; DEON; FENT; SUNE TCM; KENT3; BASH BCR; ROZ FUN CLUB; SHARE 37; BAN2; VULCAN; SPON GNR; GOLDIE TAT; SLIN2; DERO TFA; BLUE; HIMS; WANE; BILL BLAST; WOLFY; JUICE TC5; RD 357; COPE2; TKID; Afrika Bambaataa; BOM5; FROSTY FREEZE; NEC; TACK; DOZE; MAGOO; KEV; SUCH & LAE TDC; POKE; EPIC; RIZE; NEL; SOON; BOM5; DAD 1; 2KOOL; ME2; REZ; HENRY ARIAS (RIP); VE (RIP); DESA MTA; SAME TDC: NEVA, DIOS, CE UK, NEED, KA, and DEZ TFA; TOTEM TC5; ZAME FC; and SLASH FTR.

Photo cameo credits go to Bom5; Riff; Juice TC5; Dez, aka Kay Slay; Frosty Freeze; Brey (RIP); Afrika Bambaataa; Uncle Ralph McDaniels; Rose (RIP); Tyke; Rea; Laura; Darrin; Poke; Epic; Share37; Kev One; Nec One; Davey D; Big Daddy Kane; Primo; Verbal Threat; Repond; Big Truck; Cope2; Tkid; Some; Slin 2; Dash FBA; Tack; Serve FBA; Maggoo; Wave; Totem TC5; Doze Green; Ven; Wolfy; Wane FC; Angel (RIP); Roman; Ban2; Big Truck; VE (RIP); and LAC2, aka Gino Green.

Shout OUTS: All of LI, PORT KNOXXS, Hempstead, Roosevelt, Uniondale, ENJ, SHA, DRAMA, G-LIGHT, BOSS LADYS, LADY J, KILLA B, BUSTA RHYMES, DBL CREW, M-RECK, K-TONE, MOOK DIAMONDS, CHRIS LIGHTY, THE SMITHS, RJ REED, BIGGA DON, RAH BELL, DESA MTA, FETUS, CANDYMAN, POLO TAGALUCHI, TATS CREW, and anyone else I forgot up in here.

Library of Congress Control Number: 2011933868

Type set in Abadi MT Condensed/Abadi MT Condensed Extra Bold/ Eurostyle LT Std

ISBN: 978-0-7643-3720-8
Printed in China

Schiffer Books are available at special discounts for bulk purchases for sales promotions or premiums. Special editions, including personalized covers, corporate imprints, and excerpts can be created in large quantities for special needs. For more information contact the publisher:

Published by Schiffer Publishing Ltd.
4880 Lower Valley Road
Atglen, PA 19310
Phone: (610) 593-1777; Fax: (610) 593-2002
E-mail: Info@schifferbooks.com

For the largest selection of fine reference books on this and related subjects, please visit our website at **www.schifferbooks.com**

We are always looking for people to write books on new and related subjects. If you have an idea for a book, please contact us at proposals@schifferbooks.com

This book may be purchased from the publisher.
Include $5.00 for shipping.
Please try your bookstore first.
You may write for a free catalog.

In Europe, Schiffer books are distributed by
Bushwood Books
6 Marksbury Ave.
Kew Gardens
Surrey TW9 4JF England
Phone: 44 (0) 20 8392 8585; Fax: 44 (0) 20 8392 9876
E-mail: info@bushwoodbooks.co.uk
Website: www.bushwoodbooks.co.uk

★

TDCUSA 2010

★

THE END

★

Hopeyouenjoyedtheride.com

New York Criminal Statute of Limitations Laws

More Information on Criminal Statute of Limitations

Code Section	Crim. Proc. §30.10
Felonies	Murder, Class A felony: none; others: 5 yrs.; violation of collection, treatment, disposal of refuse and solid waste: 4 yrs.; breach of fiduciary duty: within 1 yr. of discovery of offense; official misconduct: 5 yrs. of offense
Misdemeanors	2 yrs.; petty offenses: 1 yr.; tax law misdemeanor: 3 yrs. (NY City adm. code)
Acts During Which Statute Does Not Run	Absent state or whereabouts unknown: up to 5 yrs.